England

a photo essay

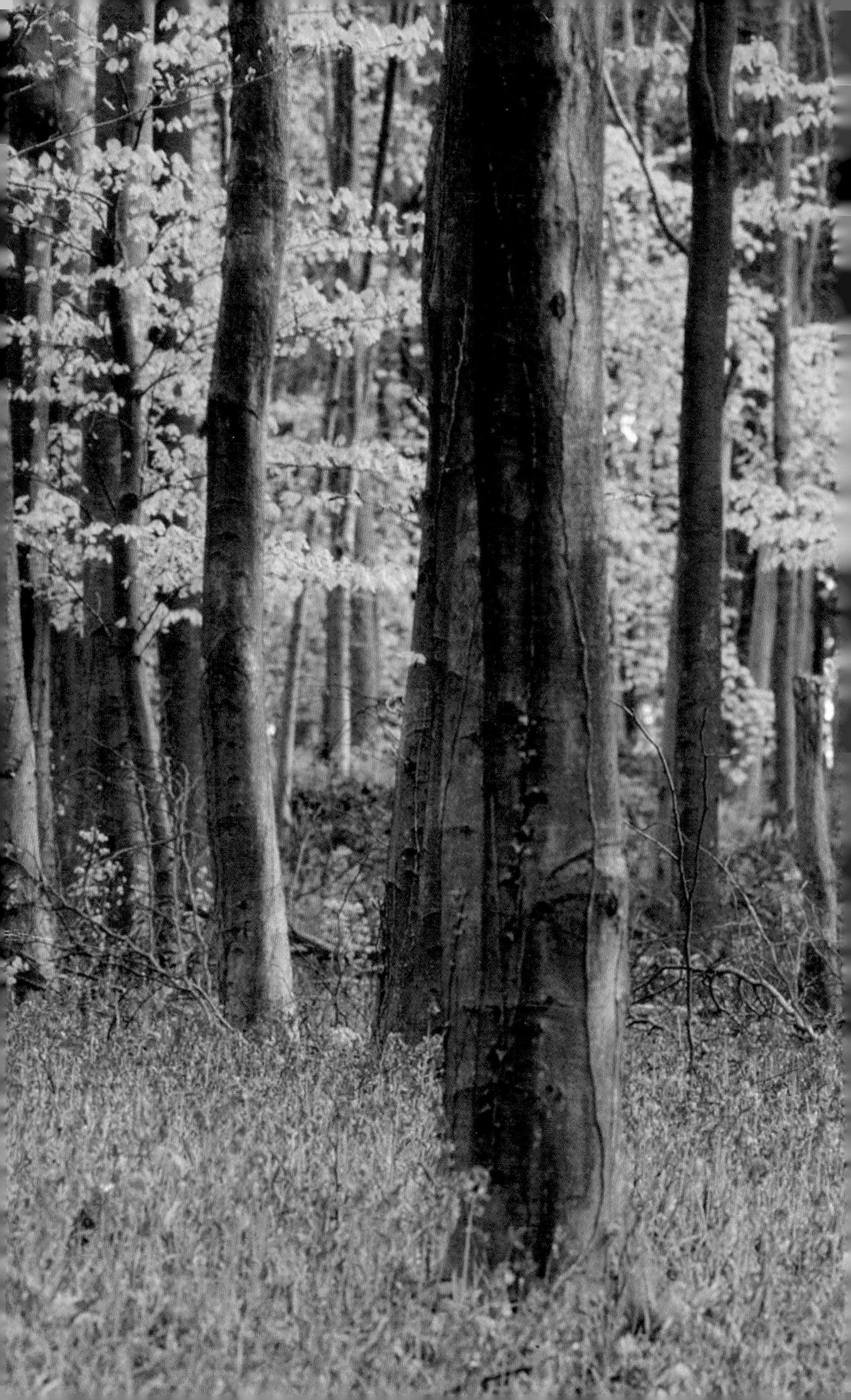

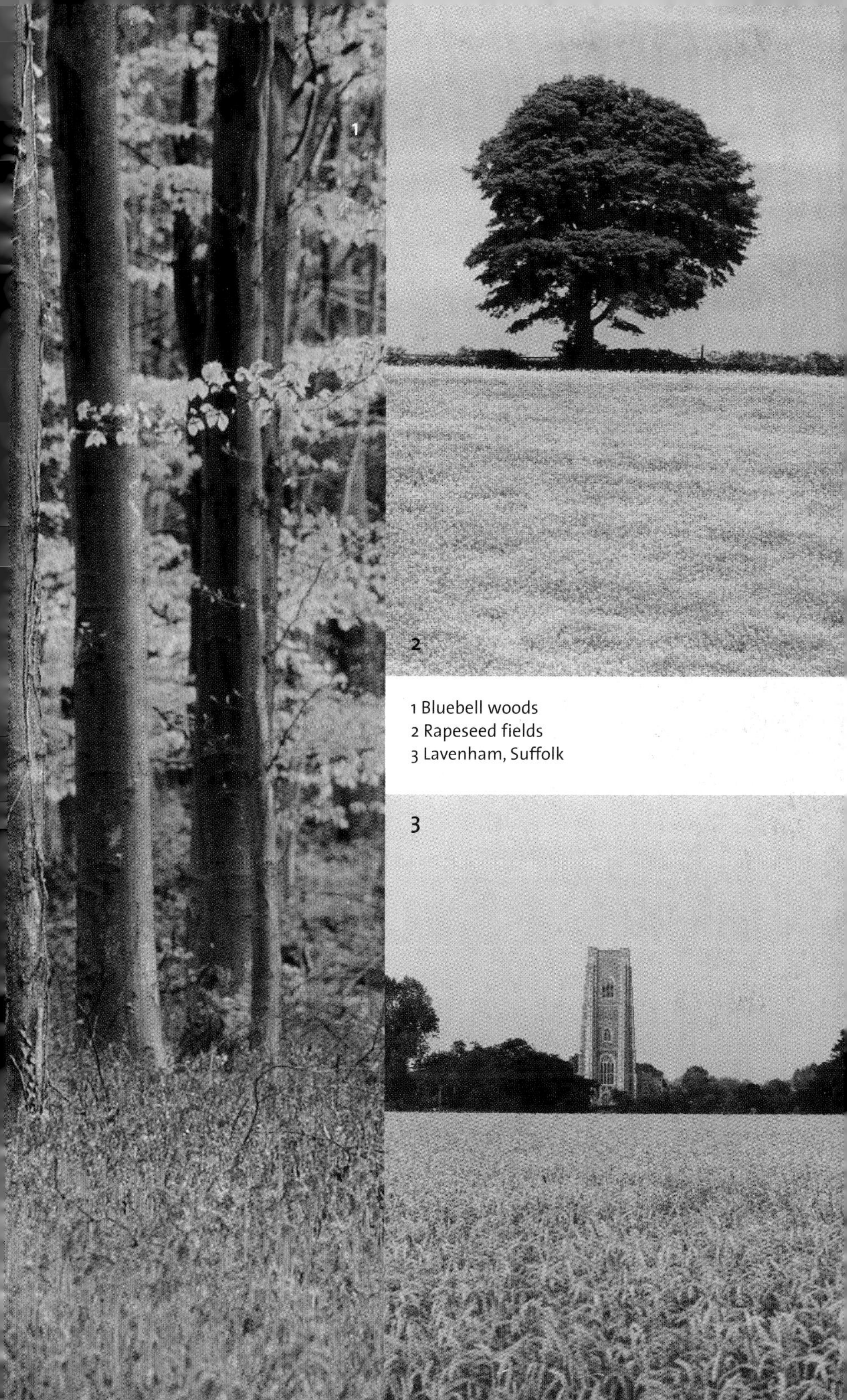

1 Bluebell woods
2 Rapeseed fields
3 Lavenham, Suffolk

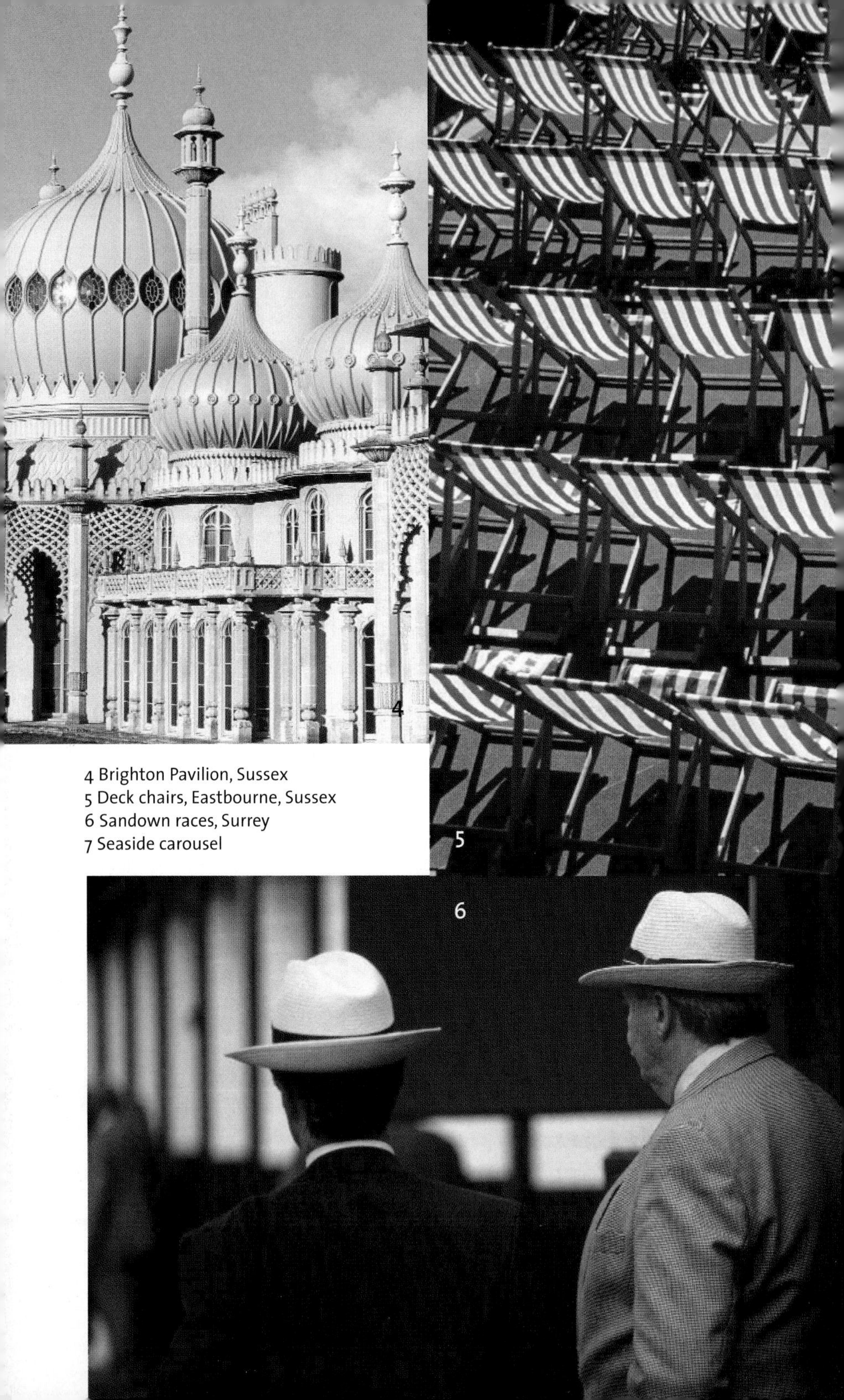

4 Brighton Pavilion, Sussex
5 Deck chairs, Eastbourne, Sussex
6 Sandown races, Surrey
7 Seaside carousel

7

8
9

8 Fishermen's sheds on the Stade, Hastings, Sussex
9 Seven Sisters, Sussex
10 Kynance Cove, Cornwall

11
12
14

11 and 12 Half-timbered houses, Lavenham, Suffolk
13 Black-and-white house, Chester, Cheshire
14 Painted cottages, Essex
15 Pastel houses, Salcombe, Devon

16

16 Sidmouth, Devon
17 Beachy Head, Kent
18 Botallack, Cornwall

17
18

19

20

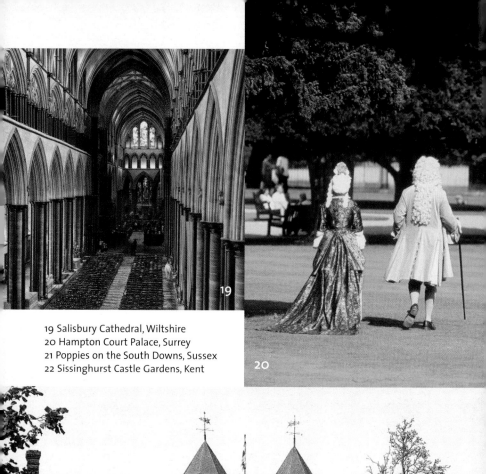

19 Salisbury Cathedral, Wiltshire
20 Hampton Court Palace, Surrey
21 Poppies on the South Downs, Sussex
22 Sissinghurst Castle Gardens, Kent

22

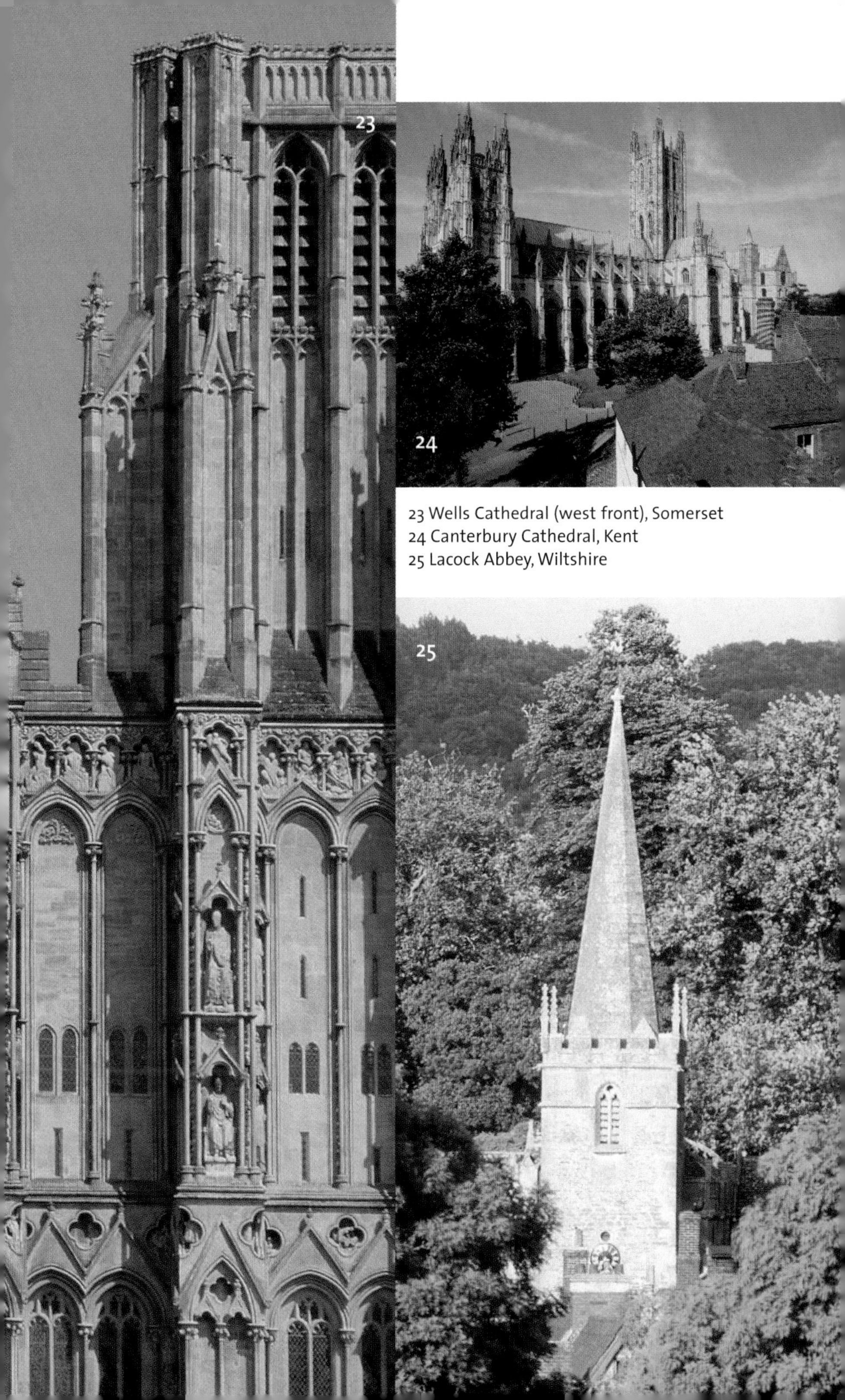

23 Wells Cathedral (west front), Somerset
24 Canterbury Cathedral, Kent
25 Lacock Abbey, Wiltshire

26

27

26 Devon mists
27 Shropshire landscape
28 Full moon over Salisbury Plain, Wiltshire

29 Ullswater, Lake District, Cumbria
30 The Cobb, Lyme Regis, Dorset
31 The Devil's Dyke, Surrey

30

31

32

32 Brighton Pier, Sussex
33 and 34 Blackpool, Lancashire

BRIGHTON PIER
FREE ADMISSION & DECK CHAIRS FREE
33
34

35

36

35 Bluebell Railway, Sussex
36 Buckler's Hard, Hampshire
37 Ironbridge Gorge, Shropshire

38
39
JONES
BARKER
FREE
E-ST
BANK S
CROS
RE
S
BRAMHAL
LA
40

38 Cranbrook, Kent
39 A scrapyard, Morecambe, Lancashire
40 Arlington, Gloucestershire

41 Jodrell Bank, Cheshire
42 Statue of Winston Churchill, Westerham, Kent
43 Manchester

44 Shrewsbury, Shropshire
45 Norfolk Broads, Norfolk
46 Flatford Mill, Dedham Vale, Essex

45
46

47 Yorkshire Dales, Yorkshire

48 Viking graves, Old Heysham, Lancashire
49 Wheat fields, Devon

Guy Macdonald

ENGLAND

'a pebbly subcontinent of migrating sea birds, shingle-loving plant life, lighthouses, nuclear power stations, night fishermen and film students'

CADOGANguides

Contents

Acknowledgements

Guy Macdonald would like to thank: mum, dad, Hayley and Simon for keeping me in health and happiness over the last four years, and all my friends and friends-of-friends around England, for letting me into your lovely homes for a night or four, offering local knowledge and encouragement at meal times, and home comforts when necessary. Thanks also to my trusty Peugeot 309, which has been thumped and bumped around the country, preyed on by window-smashers and battered by long winters out of doors – yet has remained loyal and dependable. And finally thank you, Anita, for your saintly patience throughout.

About the Authors

Guy Macdonald, Man of Kent, or possibly Kentish Man, quite suddenly fell in love with England while working in Munich, Germany, after graduating from Leeds University. Until then it had been a relationship of convenience and everything beyond Bedfordshire a vast unknown. This book was undertaken as a personal quest, a Grand Tour over the garden wall. Guy now lives in an absurd bliss of thatch and garden herbs in Kent.

Nick Inman, contributor of the Yorkshire and Northumbria chapters, is a travel writer who specializes in France and Spain but jumped at the chance to apply his skills to his native north of England.

Cadogan Guides
Highlands House, 165 The Broadway, Wimbledon, London SW19 1NE
info@cadoganguides.co.uk
www.cadoganguides.com

The Globe Pequot Press
246 Goose Lane, PO Box 480, Guilford, Connecticut 06437–0480

Cover and photo essay design by Sarah Rianhard-Gardner
Book design by Andrew Barker
Photography © John Miller
Maps © Cadogan Guides, drawn by Map Creation Ltd
Managing Editor: Christine Stroyan, with thanks to Antonia Cunningham
Editor: Georgina Palffy
Map editor: Linda McQueen, with thanks to Jocolyn Waterfall
Layout: Sarah Rianhard-Gardner
Proofreading: Patricia Briggs
Indexing: Isobel McLean
Production: Navigator Guides Ltd

Printed in Italy by Legoprint
A catalogue record for this book is available from the British Library
ISBN 1-86011-116-5

This product includes mapping data licensed from Ordnance Survey® with the permission of the Controller of Her Majesty's Stationery Office.

Please help us to keep this guide up to date. We have done our best to ensure that the information in this guide is correct at the time of going to press. But places and facilities are constantly changing, and standards and prices in hotels and restaurants fluctuate. We would be delighted to receive any comments concerning existing entries or omissions. Authors of the best letters will receive a Cadogan Guide of their choice.

Introduction

01

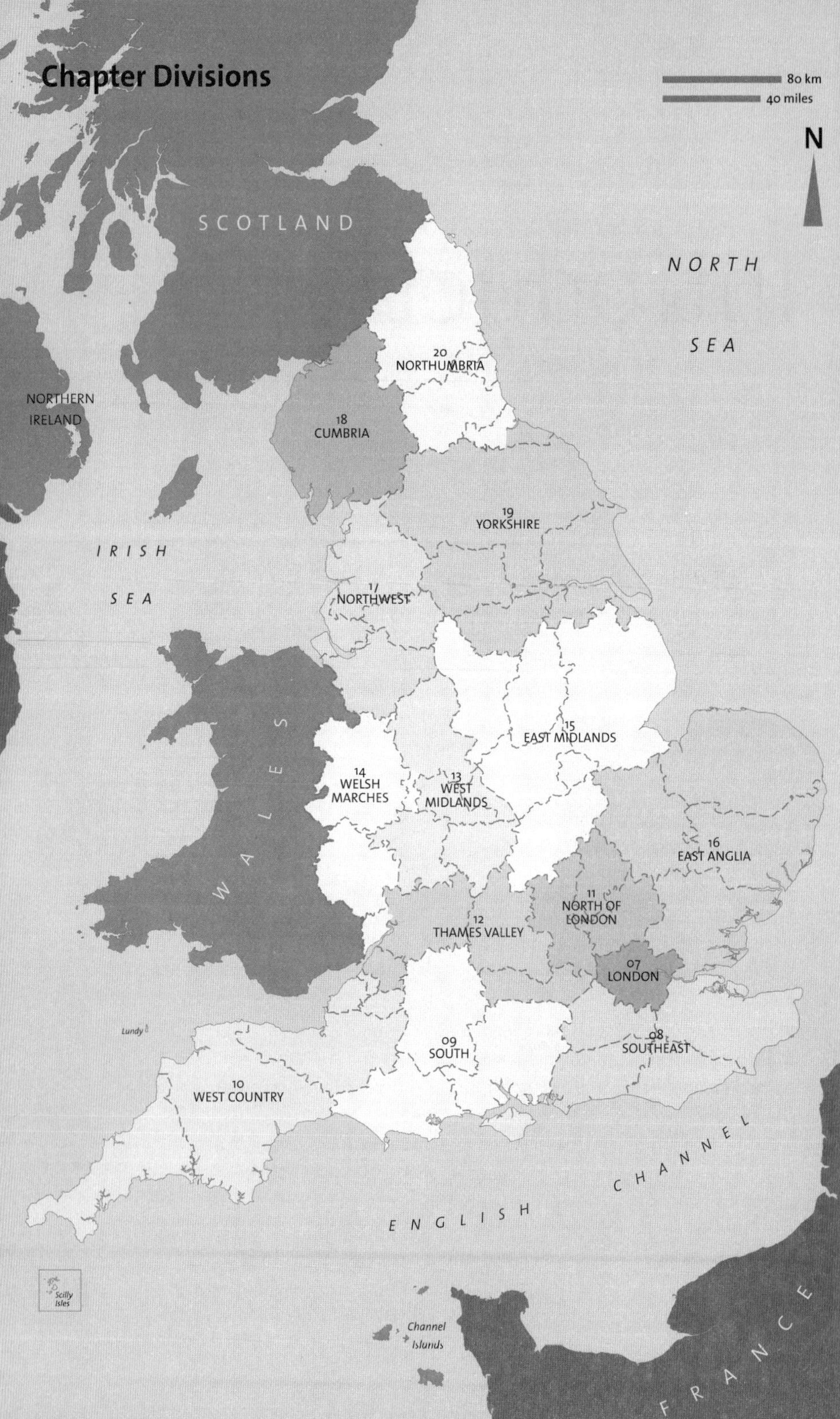
Chapter Divisions
80 km
40 miles
N
SCOTLAND
NORTH
SEA
NORTHERN
IRELAND
20
NORTHUMBRIA
18
CUMBRIA
19
YORKSHIRE
IRISH
SEA
17
NORTHWEST
WALES
15
EAST MIDLANDS
14
WELSH
MARCHES
13
WEST
MIDLANDS
16
EAST ANGLIA
11
NORTH OF
LONDON
12
THAMES VALLEY
07
LONDON
Lundy
09
SOUTH
08
SOUTHEAST
10
WEST COUNTRY
ENGLISH
CHANNEL
Scilly
Isles
Channel
Islands
FRANCE

The magic starts with the astonishing difference between the geographical size of England and her real size. She is just pretending to be so small. Once you have made her acquaintance, letting her see that you find her attractive, then you discover there is more and more of her.

J.B. Priestley

England is the southern part of Great Britain, an offshore European island between the Atlantic Ocean and the North Sea. On the map it resembles the body of a running pig whose head is Wales. It is only 425 miles long and 225 miles wide at the fattest point of its girth, and it tilts down from the high Atlantic cliffs and western uplands to the ragged, waterlogged fringes of the eastern shore. It has 36 counties, 12 cities, 12 ports, 10 spa resorts and seven national parks. Its 49 million inhabitants wave the flag of a patron saint called George (despite St George's debunking by the Vatican – not the first time this country has deviated from the papal prescription).

Such a crowded and well-mapped country as England has no secret corners or wild and uncharted tracts left to explore, and if guidebooks (including this one) occasionally use the word 'remote', it is more to describe the feeling of the place than a genuine isolation. 'There were no blank spaces on the map of Great Britain,' wrote Paul Theroux in *The Kingdom by the Sea*, 'the best-known, most fastidiously mapped and most widely trampled piece of geography on earth.' Theroux, like J.B. Priestley before him, noticed England's habit of seeming small while managing to cram whole worlds of deep and distinct fascination into its borders. From the ground, the Lincolnshire Fens seem 'vast', the Cumbrian fells seem like 'mountains', Dartmoor seems like a 'wilderness', and Dungeness seems like 'the world's end'. It is England's greatest trick.

Travelling can be a lonely occupation anywhere, but you are always in good company in England, one of the most companionable corners of the world, with a noble tradition of travel and exploration. The great travellers of England like Daniel Defoe, William Cobbett, Henry James, Priestley and Theroux ('It was so easy to speed through the country, I would have to make strict rules in order to slow myself down') were all on missions, whether they stuck to them or not, to find out the state of the country at the time. This is not the most rewarding way of travelling England any more. The old outdoors country of farming and heavy industry, robust fishing harbours and trading ports has been replaced by another tamer, quieter, indoors country of bankers, IT managers, lawyers, dentists and 'heritage' operatives. In these terms, England is a cleaner, better-off, better-run, yet somewhat emasculated shadow of its old self.

The next budding Defoe has a job on his hands, since the wheels that turn 21st-century England do so behind closed doors, without spectacle. Travelling England today is about time travel, warming up chilly textbook history by tracking down the prime movers and shakers of old to their homes, workplaces and beloved, ever-beautiful countryside, magnified through the lens of personality into a Wordsworth poem, Turner landscape, Dickens set piece, Brontë tragedy, Elgar concerto, or geological and archaeological shrine. It is one of the most exciting

elements of English travel that no matter where you go there is always some larger-than-life local boy or girl whose universally regarded works and reputation were shaped by the landscape around them. It might be William Shakespeare, Winston Churchill, John Bunyan, Samuel Taylor Coleridge, Rudyard Kipling, Richard Murchison, Virginia Woolf or Barbara Hepworth...the list goes on and on and on.

If you allow it to be, if you travel like you are gathering material for your next crime thriller or romantic historical novel, England is a thousand times more interesting than this guidebook, or any book, portrays. And what will become of this small and vulnerable country? The doom-and-gloom mongers need to apply a little generosity of spirit. England must always tell a story of evolutionary change as the old country adapts to modern usage: a bruising here and an improving touch there; a cunning readjustment here and a right mess there. The natives sometimes seem to have written England off already, tracing back the rot to the 1930s, or thereabouts. But there is no such thing as a long, slow slide, only a lack of care, and there are legions of people around the country who care intensely about England, its countryside, its urban life, its ghosts – as any traveller of England must know. You meet them everywhere, tending private collections, rambling around country lanes, restoring old boats, pottering in gardens, stewarding country houses, staffing dusty old museums. From the shire to the misty mountains and back again, England is a treasure trove whose riches are part of world culture (that's not just Shakespeare, steam engines and the Beatles, but Winnie the Pooh and Harry Potter). If ever a country were capable of inspiring deep, affectionate fascination, it is this one.

Guide to the Guide

London: The capital goes through drastic mood swings: grey, worthy and dull one minute, hip and happening the next. Its most recent swing has been up; London has come roaring back to life again. Suddenly, everything seems possible and Londoners are embracing the changes with barely a whiff of scepticism. Be warned, however: it may be the most exciting city in Europe, but it is not the most beautiful, nor the easiest to get around.

The Southeast: You are never far from a busy main road in this crowded vale and ridge countryside, which comes under huge and mounting urban pressure. Nevertheless Kipling's beloved 'Weald and Downs countree' holds some of the greatest charms in the whole of England, including the Cinque Ports, cathedral towns, bracing ridge walks, medieval castles, country houses and seaside.

The South: Hardy's 'partly real, partly dream country' of Wessex, too close to London for total comfort, still beats to the drums of Alfred the Great and the strange pulse of life on the late-Stone Age–early-Bronze Age plain. Stick to the chalklands and you won't go wrong.

The West Country: this tapering peninsular knows how to tell a great story, of kidnapping, outlaws, ferocious ghostly beasts of the moor, Arthurian legend, Cornish smuggling, and wandering 18th-century Romantic poets. A place of considerable former greatness, as soon as you fix the modern region in your sights, there it goes again, slipping backwards in time another few notches.

North of London: The unassuming counties of Bedfordshire, Hertfordshire and Buckinghamshire offer intriguing pleasures including the homes of the Rothschild banking tribe and Disraeli, and the prime minister's country residence at Chequers; the life and times of John Bunyan; and the quiet drama of secret Second World War airfields. Head for St Albans or the Chilterns towns of Wendover and Tring.

Thames Valley and Cotswolds: Let the River Thames be your guide for this chapter. It rolls off the Cotswolds, a gentle limestone upland whose mellowed stone villages were the inspiration for the Arts and Crafts movement, many of whose practitioners settled here. It glides past the bustling riverside towns of Henley and Marlow, whose top oarsmen have projected these broad middle reaches into sporting legend, skirting royal Windsor on its way into the suburbs of London, where it washes the walls of another royal palace and thereafter transforms even the dullest London boroughs into somewhere to be.

West Midlands: Partly the quintessential English countryside of Shakespeare and Elgar – wholesome country boys if ever there were – and partly sprawling conurbation, around the cities of Birmingham and Stoke-on-Trent. Town and country, nevertheless, have their own distinct and special interest, nuzzling the Malvern Hills to the west, beyond which lie the open-country delights of the Welsh Marches.

The Welsh Marches: A Tolkienesque landscape of fast-flowing rivers, dense forest, green plains dotted with distinctive hills and the ever-present shadow of the Welsh mountains on your peripheral vision. These fiercely contested borderlands revolved around the Marcher castles of powerful Norman earls at Chester, Shrewsbury, Hereford, Ludlow and Chepstow. The hilltops in between supported a lesser range of fortifications. Look out for traces of Roger de Montgomery, Owen Glendower, Edward of March and the Llywellyns, princes of Wales.

East Midlands: Disparate landscapes form the East Midlands, from the Lincolnshire Fens via Sherwood Forest to Derbyshire's Peak District. Surrounded by post-industrial cities, Britain's first national park offers a sizeable chunk of England's population immediate access into sublime rough countryside.

East Anglia: A haunting region whose reed-fringed marshes, lazy rivers and shingle coasts are backed by broad marine vistas. It possesses the shimmering, liminal quality of a ghost story by M.R. James or a landscape painting by Constable. Avoid most of Essex, and head into Suffolk and Norfolk, whose churches, disappearing shoreline and old wool towns are a joy.

The Northwest: Manchester and Liverpool form a nexus of heavyweight metropolitan attractions amid a web of motorways and canals. Lancashire's mill valleys repel rather than attract the casual tourist, who nevertheless can look down on them like a modern-day George Fox from the flanking hilltops. Follow the trail of the Pendle witches from Pendle Hill over Bowland Forest to Lancaster Prison, a massive, eerie castle dominating the town.

Itineraries

Kipling's 'Weald and Downs Countree'

1–2 **London** (Bloomsbury, to meet the literary group, and Cheyne Walk, to make the acquaintance of Henry James).

3 **Knole House** (Vita Sackville-West's birthplace).

4 **Lewes** (Thomas Paine, dinosaur-hunter Gideon Mantel and Simon de Montfort).

5 **Monk's House**, Rodmell, **Charleston Farmhouse** (the downland homes of Virginia Woolf and her sister Vanessa Bell) and **Berwick church** (decorated by Vanessa Bell, Duncan Grant and Quentin Bell).

6 **Brighton** (Rudyard Kipling lived in neighbouring Rottingdean).

7 Gardens of the **Forest Ridge** (pioneering, exotic Edwardian gardens).

8 Head over the **High Weald** via **Batemans** (where Kipling wrote *Puck of Pook's Hill*).

9 **Great Dixter** (Christopher Lloyd's famous garden) and **Sissinghurst** (created by Vita-Sackville West and Harold Nicholson).

10 **Rye** (Lamb House, where Henry James lived for a while, writing in the garden summer house).

East Kent: Conquest and Invasion

1–3 **London** (Tower of London, built by William the Conqueror; City of London, the square mile of Roman *Londinium*; London Bridge, on the site of the old Roman bridge).

4 **Canterbury** (inhabited by Roman soldiers and Saxon kings, and evangelized by St Augustine; cathedral and Roman remains in museum).

5 **Richborough Castle** (Roman fortress) and the **Isle of Thanet** (the point of arrival of two Roman invading fleets, the first Saxon warriors under Hengest and Horsa and the Roman missionary St Augustine).

6 Tudor castles of **Deal** and **Walmer** (built to stop Catholic European invaders).

7 **Dover Castle** (the 'key of England', with its Roman lighthouse and Second World War military tunnels; headquarters of the Romano-British fleet, and later a Roman garrison. Destroyed by the Normans and attacked by the French and Germans).

Sons of England: Shakespeare, Dickens and Elgar

1–3 **London** (Shakespeare's Globe Theatre; guided Dickens walk of the Embankment and Covent Garden). Day trip to **Rochester**, the town of Dickens' childhood affections, visited by the Pickwick Club, and full of Dickensian associations.

4–5 **Stratford-upon-Avon** (birthplace, home and burial place of Shakespeare) via **Warwick Castle** (base of Richard Neville 'the kingmaker' during the Wars of the Roses, one of Shakespeare's favourite subjects).

6 **Great Malvern** via **Vale of Evesham** (where Elgar cycled and composed).

7 Elgar's birthplace at **Lower Broadheath**, and **Worcester Cathedral**, where he performed many times. Elgar's grave in **Little Malvern**, and the beautiful Malvern walks and views that inspired his music.

Potted Suffolk: Artists and Churches

1–3 **London** (Constable and Gainsborough in the National Gallery and Tate Britain).

4 **Flatford Mill** in Dedham Vale, home of Constable and setting for the *Hay Wain*.

5–6 Magnificent wool churches (altar paintings by Constable in **Nayland** church). **Kentwell Hall** in Long Melford (Tudor mansion of the Cloptons, who paid for the church). Gainsborough's home in **Sudbury** (now a gallery of his work).

7 The churches of **Lavenham**, **Ufford**, **Grundisburgh** and **Boulge** are all must-sees.

8 Christchurch Mansion in **Ipswich** (for more Constable and Gainsborough, and Suffolk artists including Frederick George Cotman and Thomas Churchyard).

9 **Aldeburgh** (seaside town with Benjamin Britten connections).

10 **Framlingham** (church and castle).

11 **Bury St Edmunds** (ruined abbey, cathedral and museum).

Alfred the Great's Wessex

1–2 King of Wessex, Alfred the Great, defended **London** against the Danes.

3 **Oxford** for the Alfred Jewel in the **Ashmolean Museum**.

4 **Wantage**, birthplace of Alfred. Walk up **White Horse Hill** onto the Berkshire Downs, where KingAlfred fought one of fiercest battles against Danes.

5 **Winchester**, heart of Alfred's Wessex, and home of Alfred memorial. Cathedral stands on the site of three Saxon minsters, one founded by Alfred's queen, another by his son; Alfred was buried in the old minster, although his grave is long gone.

6 **Wareham** on Poole Bay in Dorset (charming old Saxon town with almost complete set of Saxon earth walls). **Wimborne Minster** (founded by Saxon kings and burial place of Alfred's brother, King Æthelred).

7 **Shaftesbury**, where Alfred founded a nunnery and installed his daughter as abbess. **Sherborne** cathedral was founded by Saxon bishop Adhelm in 705, succeeded by Asser, Alfred's biographer. Two of Alfred's brothers were buried at Sherborne Abbey.

8 **Athelney** on the Somerset Levels, where Alfred mustered army to fight the Danes and commemorated his victory by founding monastery on the hill.

9 **Glastonbury**, **Wells Cathedral**.

Arts and Crafts in the Cotswolds

1–3 **London** (Liberty on Regent Street, William Morris's Red House and his old factory in Colliers Wood; the Art Nouveau collections at the V&A).

4–5 **Oxford** (where Morris, Rossetti and Burne-Jones formed the Pre-Raphaelite Brotherhood, and decorated university buildings including Exeter College chapel).

6 **Kelmscott Manor**, near Lechlade on Thames (Morris's country home, now full of Morris furniture). Village of **Bibury** (which Morris called 'the most beautiful village in England') and **Burford** (where Morris castigated the vicar for his restoration).

7 **Broadway Tower** (home of Carmel Price, a friend of the Pre-Raphaelites, who often came to stay). **Broadway** was also home of furniture maker Gordon Russell.

8 **Winchcombe pottery** where Michael Cardew and Ray Finch set up a pottery.

9 Chipping Campden (the Guild of Handicraft, a social experiment set up in 1902 by Robert Ashby) and Hidcote Garden, the Arts and Crafts gardens of Lawrence Johnson.

Highlights of the Northwest

1–3 Manchester (lively, booming metropolis, now home of Lowry Museum and Imperial War Museum North on Salford Quays, and endless bars and cafés).

4–5 Liverpool (Pierhead, Walker Art Gallery, Albert Docks and Beatles tour).

6–7 Fortress town of **Lancaster**, Art Deco **Morecambe** and **Forest of Bowland**.

8 Lake District. Start with a boat trip on Lake Windermere.

9 Grasmere, **Rydal Mount** and **Dove Cottage** (Wordsworth homes).

10 Coniston (Ruskin connections) and **Brantwood** (Ruskin home) on Coniston Water. Climb the **Old Man**.

11 Keswick, **Derwent Water** and **Borrowdale**, then the fells behind Seathwaite.

12 Carlisle (border fortress town in Hadrian's Wall country).

13 Hadrian's Wall (the northern extent of Roman civilization).

Welsh Marches

1–2 Birmingham (city centre of Joseph Chamberlain, the Jewellery Quarter and swanky Eastside development; Walsall New Art Gallery).

3 Shrewsbury (Marcher frontier castle).

4 Battlefield church (built to commemorate Prince Hal and Hotspur's bravery in Wars of Roses battle). Remains of **Wroxeter** Roman city (once a military garrison on Celtic border), and the Wrekin (a Celtic fortress).

5 Church Stretton (walks on Long Mynd, site of more Celtic hill forts) and fortress town of Ludlow, stronghold of earls of March (ruins of Wigmore Castle in ruins on hills behind the town).

6 Mortimer's Trail (Croft Castle, Wigmore Castle and Kington).

7 Black-and-white villages of **Pembridge** and **Eardisland**. Twelfth-century Hereford School of sculpture at **Shobdon** and **Leominster**.

8 Book town of **Hay-on-Wye** and rugged **Black Mountains**.

9 Golden Valley, **Abbey Dore** and **Kilpeck** church (more Hereford School sculpture).

10 Hereford, whose cathedral contains *Mappa Mundi* and chained library.

11 Follow the River Wye to **Ross-on-Wye**, Goodrich Castle and Symonds Yat.

Highlights of Southern England

1–3 London (a whistlestop tour).

4–5 Stratford-upon-Avon via **Oxford**.

6 Cotswolds, stopping at **Stow-on-the-Wold** and **Cirencester**.

7 Jane Austen's Regency **Bath**.

8 Glastonbury, **Cheddar Gorge** and **Wells**.

9 Stonehenge and **Salisbury**.

10 Seaside town of **Brighton**.

English Counties
80 km
40 miles
N
SCOTLAND
NORTH SEA
NORTHERN IRELAND
IRISH SEA
WALES
NORTHUMBERLAND
TYNE & WEAR
DURHAM
CLEVELAND
CUMBRIA
NORTH YORKSHIRE
E. RIDING OF YORKSHIRE
LANCASHIRE
W. YORKS.
N. LINCS
N.E. LINCS
GREATER MANCHESTER
MERSEYSIDE
S. YORKS.
CHESHIRE
DERBYSHIRE
NOTTINGHAMSHIRE
LINCOLNSHIRE
STAFFORDSHIRE
SHROPSHIRE
LEICESTERSHIRE
RUTLAND
NORFOLK
NORTHAMPTONSHIRE
CAMBRIDGESHIRE
SUFFOLK
WORCESTERSHIRE
WARWICKSHIRE
HEREFORDSHIRE
BEDS.
BUCKINGHAMSHIRE
HERTFORDSHIRE
ESSEX
GLOUCESTERSHIRE
OXFORDSHIRE
S. GLOS.
N.W. SOM.
BATH & N.E.SOM.
LONDON
BERKSHIRE
WILTSHIRE
SURREY
KENT
Lundy
SOMERSET
HAMPSHIRE
W. SUSSEX
E. SUSSEX
DORSET
DEVON
ISLE OF WIGHT
CORNWALL
ENGLISH CHANNEL
Scilly Isles
Channel Islands
FRANCE

England's Top 60 Attractions

1 **Rye** Smugglers' inns and Henry James' haunts on the edge of Romney Marsh.
2 **Charleston Farmhouse** Treasure house of the Bloomsbury Group.
3 **Dover Castle** Bracing symbolism and Second World War tunnels.
4 **Broadstairs beach** English seaside with Dickensian knobs on.
5 **Richborough Roman Fort** Great wafts of Rome.
6 **The Wakes, Selborne** An oasis of birdsong and green at naturalist Gilbert White's.
7 **Lyme Regis** Fossil hunting and Meryl Streep as *The French Lieutenant's Woman*.
8 **Avebury** Endless antiquarian antics.
9 **The Undercliff, Isle of Wight** Crab sandwiches and sea views.
10 **Cloud's Hill** Surely Lawrence of Arabia will return at any moment?
11 The **Great Western train** from London Paddington to Penzance and a helicopter to the Scilly Isles English travel at its most exciting.
12 **Bath** Neoclassical fireworks on a Roman hypocaust.
13 **Wells Cathedral** Sculpture, singing holes, fruit stealers and the Vicar's Choral.
14 **Cheddar Gorge** Magnificent English scenery.
15 **Dartmouth Harbour** Heavenly in the sun.
16 **Hartland Quay** Far-flung, wave-battered promontory.
17 **Stowe Garden** Set the standard for the heroic 18th-century garden.
18 **Bletchley Park** Second World War intrigue.
19 **Shaw's Corner** Bernard Shaw's rural bolt-hole.
20 **Tring Museum** Classic Victorian museum of natural history.
21 **Oxford** Unbeatable university buildings and the Pitt Rivers Museum.
22 **Blenheim Palace** A soldier's palace with Winston Churchill connections.
23 **Uffington Monuments** Prehistory, myth and great views of Thames Valley.
24 **Chipping Campden** Perfect Arts and Crafts town.
25 **Hidcote Gardens** The most influential garden of the century.
26 **Great Malvern** Elgar, hill walks and the water cure.
27 **Stratford-upon-Avon** Shakespeare bonanza.
28 **St Mary's Church, Warwick** Beauchamp tombs.
29 **Witley Court** The pleasure palace of a factory owner.
30 **Wroxeter Roman City** Ruined Roman *civitas* under the Wrekin.
31 **Ludlow** Classy country town of the Earls of March, with Michelin-starred chefs.
32 **Kilpeck Church** Stone carvings from the sublime to the downright rude.
33 **Caer Caradoc** The great outdoors (up a hill).
34 **Kinder Scout** The ascent from Edale.
35 **Stamford** Delightful stone town of many churches.

36 Woolsthorpe Manor Revolutionary science and rural charm.

37 Bosworth Battlefield Final dust-up of the Wars of the Roses.

38 Chester The medieval Rows and cathedral wood-carvings.

39 Liverpool's Docks Magnificent port buildings and Victorian docks.

40 Manchester's Salford Quays Regeneration with style.

41 Lancaster Castle Shakespeare in the court and dungeon.

42 The Lake District Coniston for its Ruskin connections and Old Man walks; the gentle Wordsworthian walk from Grasmere to Easedale Tarn; the nail-biting mountain drama of Helvellyn; Seathwaite Farm, overnighting at the foot of Scafell.

43 Ufford Church Breathtaking font.

44 Southwold Unbeatable seaside town.

45 Grimes Graves Stone Age flint mines.

46 Cambridge The other unbeatable university town, with tea at Grantchester.

47 London's South Bank The once unfashionable side of the River Thames, now a buzz of activity as Londoners troop to the Tate Modern, Shakespeare's Globe and the Millennium Wheel.

48 The British Museum A treasure trove of ancient art.

49 Durham Cathedral The Norman splendour of the cathedral, alongside the castle home of Durham's prince bishops.

50 Beamish Open Air Museum England's industrial heritage resuscitated.

51 Bowes Museum An eclectic collection whose highpoint is a swan automaton.

52 Hadrian's Wall Far and away England's longest Roman monument, built to mark the extreme of Roman civilization. The best-preserved section of the wall is between Once Brewed and Housesteads, with cliff-top views over the moors.

53 Newcastle Gateshead Once two separate, rival towns on either side of the Tyne, now joined at the hip and rebranded as hip art capital of the northeast.

54 Lindisfarne and the Farne Islands The home of England's earliest Christians, who illuminated the Lindisfarne Gospels, as well as a modern-day sea-bird sanctuary.

55 The Yorkshire Dales The pride of Yorkshire's countryside, a part of the Pennine chain in which hills and valleys form a pleasing harmony of forms and vistas.

56 York The great Gothic towers of the Minster, encircling medieval walls and traces of Romans and Vikings.

57 Fountains Abbey The largest monastic ruin in the country.

58 Whitby A Yorkshire seaside resort which brashness with the sort of history and tradition that most towns would kill for.

59 Magna The Cinderella of steelworks, all dressed up for a technophile ball.

60 National Museum of Photography, Film and Television, Bradford Five stories of cinematic action.

Cumbria and the Lake District: England's own mini-Alps are only the most conspicuous rural attraction in a county full of them. Kendal, Windermere, Grasmere, Coniston and Keswick are popular bases for the lake and fell country of the Romantic poets, walker Alfred Wainwright, and *Peter Rabbit* author Beatrix Potter. Next on your list must be the borderlands around Carlisle, powerfully delineated by Hadrian's Wall.

Yorkshire: Yorkshire is more than just a county: it's a spiritual homeland. It is also England's biggest county, stretching from the endless grey industrial conurbations of South and West Yorkshire to the empty open spaces of the Dales, Wolds, North York Moors and Pennines. And then there's the walled city of York with its immense cathedral, where layers of history seem to have been painted thickly over each other.

Northumbria: The Romans saw this region as the end of the civilized world, but by the 7th century it was undergoing a religious and cultural flowering, based on the holy island of Lindisfarne. The Normans installed prince bishops in Durham to maintain this civilization. Now even the industrial remains of the 19th century are heritage.

History

02

The Year Dot Until AD 410: After a Frosty Start, Britain Becomes an Island, and Is Conquered by the Romans

Settlement in northern Europe was retarded by a series of Ice Ages, which started about a million years ago and turned everything north of Derbyshire into a block of ice. The first arrival was **Creswell Man**, a well-tooled late Mesolithic hunter who commemorated his sojourn in the Midlands by scratching a horse onto a piece of bone. At that time, the British Isles were part of the Continental mainland; they were not shorn off until the end of the last Ice Age, around 5500 BC, when the woollier, toothier mammals became extinct, and the islands began to assume their distinctly non-European character.

The agricultural revolution of the **Neolithic period** (4000–1800 BC) came from the Near East, reaching the south coast of a densely forested Britain around 4000 BC, and spreading northwards along the upland ridges that were prehistoric highways. The taming of the land brought religion, flint mining and standing stones – particularly well represented on the southern chalklands and the southwestern moors.

The increasing emphasis on owning land and possessions in the **Bronze Age** (1800–600 BC), and the arrival of warrior-sophisticates from the Continent with improved weapons and craftsmanship, led to the formation of social hierarchies. The highest-ranking chiefs were buried in round mounds. The south found itself at the centre of a civilization in touch with the latest Continental fashions in pottery, metalwork and henges.

Stone monuments were abandoned in the **Iron Age** (750 BC–AD 43), a period which saw the consolidation of tribal kingdoms around the hill forts of the Celts. The vibrant Celtic culture had its roots in central Europe, but British **Celts** had their own language and identity. They produced exquisite metal rings and brooches, gave birth to story tellers, exported tin and imported Mediterranean wine.

The name 'Britain' is thought to have Celtic origins, relayed through Greek and Roman translations. Descriptions of the Celtic world were left to **Romans** like **Julius Caesar**, pro-consul of Gaul, who made two fleeting invasions of 'Britannia' in 55 BC and 54 BC, had trouble with the unpredictable channel tides and hurried back to Rome declaring a conquest. Caesar got his glory, but the constant threat of a Celtic rebellion in Gaul made Rome very uncomfortable. In AD 43, under **Aulus Plautius**, four Roman legions and their auxiliaries – about 40,000 men in all – marched north from the invasion beaches of southeast *Britannia* and smashed the stronghold of *Camulodunum* (Colchester), controlled by the most powerful Celtic tribe, the Catuvellauni. But the defeat of all the Celtic tribes took another 40 years. Some rolled over and reaped the rewards of the imperial free-trade network; as semi-independent 'client kingdoms' of Rome their kinglings were installed in palaces such as Fishbourne near Chichester. Others were pummelled into submission by Roman *ballista* bolts. The Romans exploited rivalries among disunited tribes. The queen of the Brigantes eventually betrayed **Caractacus**, heroic leader of the Celtic resistance. **Boudicca**, Celtic queen of the Iceni, welcomed Rome but was stung into rebellion when she and her daughters were brutalized by Roman soldiers after her husband's death. When her revolt was crushed, Boudicca poisoned herself. Three Roman legions stayed to prevent uprisings.

The heartland of Roman *Britannia* roughly corresponds to England. Here towns like *Camulodunum* were built on the site of old tribal centres, surrounded by sumptuous rural villas with mosaic-tiled floors. *Londinium* (London) was at the hub of a network of Roman roads.

In AD 122, when **Emperor Hadrian** ordered the building of a wall 80 miles long to secure the northern frontier, he doubtless assumed that the northern barbarians would one day surrender. But Rome had overstretched itself on all fronts: imperial supplies and military aid to *Britannia* dried up; in AD 410 the legions marched off. The collapse of the Western Roman Empire triggered the biggest popular migration in history, out of which modern Europe emerged.

AD 410–793: The Rudderless Roman Province Gets Caught Up in the Age of Germanic Migration, and Explodes into Tiny Fragments

The Roman way – trade, town life and Christianity – did not, however, come to a crashing halt. Coastal attacks by raiding parties from northern Europe had long been a fact of life and the political vacuum left by the Romans seemed like a matter for the kinglings to sort out among themselves. But in AD 449 the British overlord, or Vortigern, invited a gang of **Germanic toughs**, led by the notorious Continental outlaw **Hengest**, to get shot of pesky northern Celtic raiders. He did not anticipate that his mercenaries would want to stay. They did, chasing the Romano-Brits out of *Cantium*, which became Germanic, pagan Kent. At the same time another group of Continental drifters – the **Saxons** – settled on the south coast, and yet another – the **Angles** – along the east coast. The immigrants pressed inland up the rivers, and the former Roman province exploded into enclaves of Celts and Germanic migrants, including **Frisians, Geats, Jutes and Danes**, who proceeded to fight each other. Although there was no unified Celtic defence of the island, a Romano-British warlord, identified with the legendary **King Arthur**, stemmed the tide of Germanic incomers between 490 and 499. But it didn't last: in a few years the 500-year-old Romano-Celtic character of the province was destroyed by the newcomers. The population of 3 million either died fighting or fled into *Dumnonia* (Devon), *Cambria* (Wales) or overseas (Brittany). To the Britons, the Germanics seemed outlandish with their moustaches and combed hair; they allowed the old Roman towns to crumble, preferring to live in their own muddy villages. If one Germanic kingling stole the advantage over the others he proclaimed himself Bretwalda – overlord of Britannia.

When the Roman Christian missionary **St Augustine** landed in Kent in 597, the province was occupied by seven Germanic kingdoms – **Kent, Essex, Wessex, Mercia, Northumbria, Sussex and East Anglia** – while the Celts were established in *Cambria* and *Kerno* (Cornwall). The King of Kent renounced Thor and embraced Christianity, a canny political move to gain the moral high-ground. In the Celtic regions Christianity was doing the rounds too, making an impression on powerful Northumbria. Celtic Christianity eschewed the grandiose hierarchies of the Roman church, revolving instead around monasteries like the one at Lindisfarne, founded by the Irish monk St Aidan. At the **Synod of Whitby** in 664 the two forms of Christianity went head to head; the Roman version won, cementing the Germanic kingdoms into a relationship with Rome. The late 8th-century **King Offa of Mercia** (now the dominant kingdom), styled himself *Rex Anglorum*, King of the English, reflecting the origins of his tribe in Angeln, and England was conceived.

793–1066: The Vikings Inadvertently Hasten the Birth of England

The monasteries had flowered into the guardians of culture. Monks illuminated biblical manuscripts in Latin, such as the Lindisfarne Gospels, and collated the first histories of the English people. These unguarded monkish treasure houses were obvious targets for the **Vikings**, pagan Germanics from Scandinavia who prayed to hammer-wielding gods and wanted to die in battle so that they could enter Valhalla in the afterlife. They threw in rape, pillage and slaughter for good measure. The Christianized Germanic kingdoms were too busy fighting each other to resist. The Norwegian Vikings terrorized Lindisfarne in 793, picked off the remote west-coast islands and established a colony in Ireland, from where they continued to raid Britain. The Danish Vikings were an even greater menace, sailing south from Denmark with large armies, fighting Charlemagne on the Continent and heading for the coast of Kent. In 839 they allied with the Cornish against dominant **Egbert of Wessex**, who resisted hard, so they sailed up the Thames and Wash and overran Northumbria in 854, and East Anglia and Mercia in 870. Only Wessex stood between the Danes and conquest in 871 when **Alfred**, grandson of Egbert, became king of Wessex. King Alfred held out against three Danish invasions, employing all the tricks in the embattled warlord's book – fighting, paying tribute, giving and taking hostages and exhorting oaths of allegiance. He famously fled into the Somerset marshes after a surprise winter raid of his royal stronghold at Chippenham in 878, and for four months the Danes were the masters of everything between Scotland and Cornwall. But Alfred regrouped at Athelney, burned some cakes while planning his counter-attack, and defeated the Danes on Salisbury Plain in May 878 – earning himself the epithet 'Great'. The **Treaty of Wedmore**, between Alfred and Guthrun the Dane, established the new *Britannia*. The Danes controlled everything east of the Danelaw line – Northumbria, eastern Mercia and East Anglia. They farmed, built villages and spoke Old Norse, making the Danelaw England's most productive region. Alfred became *de facto* overlord of everywhere else except Cornwall, adopting the title King of the English. Wessex became an all-conquering imperial force and Alfred's successors defeated the Danes and Cornish in the 10th century. The title of King of England assumed by **King Edgar** in 959 was no longer aspirational: the English, Danes and Britons lived under one rule. However, the right of the House of Wessex to rule was still under fire from Scandinavia. In 1003 **King Æthelred the Unready** was driven into exile in Normandy by King Sveyn Forkbeard of Denmark. But when Forkbeard's son **Cnut** took over in 1014 he converted to Christianity and married a Wessex princess. When Cnut's heirs ran out, Æthelred's son, **Edward the Confessor**, was invited back to reclaim the English crown. Edward preferred reading the Scriptures to 'leading from the front' and brought with him a ruling class of Normans, the vanguard of the Norman Conquest. The disgruntled Anglo-Danish aristocracy was headed by Harold Godwinson, who assumed the reins of power while Edward busied himself with the

The Age of Beowulf

The Germanic settlers of the so-called Dark Ages did not inhabit a cultural void, although it was a bad time for the native Romano-Celts. The darkness of the age was chiefly from the perspective of historians deprived of illuminating contemporary commentary after the Romans and conscious of a backwards step into a barbarous, heathen time. However archaeology has thrown up Germanic treasures showing the value placed on craftsmanship and beautiful things: the royal ship burial at Sutton Hoo in Suffolk has yielded some of the richest finds, including a warrior's helmet detailed with gilt-bronze eyebrows and a moustache, the most powerful image of the Age of Migration. The stories that were told concentrated on the heroic deeds of great warriors seeking out new lands or the sad passing of earlier, better times. Both heroic and elegiac traditions were capable of expressing a well of loss, longing and fear. The epic story of the 5th century warrior Beowulf was written down after centuries of telling. In it, the 10th-century poet describes the Germanic tradition of story-telling: 'And sometimes a proud old solider who had heard songs of the ancient heroes and could sing them all through...would weave a net of words for Beowulf's victory, tying the knot of his verses smoothly, swiftly, into place with a poet's quick skill, singing his new song aloud while he shaped it.'

The cultural flowering of the Germanic period occurred after Christian conversions in the monasteries, where churchmen like Caedman, Theodore, Adhelm and Bede composed songs, illuminated manuscripts, compiled histories and set up schools which were the centres of excellence of the time. By destroying the monasteries, the Vikings aborted the emerging culture. King Alfred earned his suffix 'Great' not just for defeating the Vikings but for putting the would-be national culture back on track. He commissioned art and books (not in Latin, but Old English) including a translation of Bede's *Ecclesiastical History of the English People* and his own biography, recruiting the greatest churchmen of the day from abroad to do it.

building of his new Benedictine abbey at Westminster, crowning himself **Harold II** when Edward died, despite rival claims from Denmark, Norway and the Duke of Normandy. In the epic climax, it is easy to sympathise with Harold II, the defending English champion, as he marched north to Yorkshire and crushed the Viking army under Harold Hardrada, then 250 miles back down south to meet William the Bastard of Normandy 18 days later in the wooded countryside of the Sussex Weald. The **Battle of Hastings** was a clash of military cultures – chain-mail-clad knights on horses against Harold's foot soldiers with double-headed hand-axes – but the odds were pretty even. The Norman knights gained the upper hand by feigning a cavalry charge, drawing Harold's men into the open and breaking the Saxon lines. Harold famously died on the battlefield with an arrow in his eye. William, now the Conqueror, had himself crowned in Westminster Abbey.

1066–1154: William the Conqueror Annexes England

William I took several years to secure his conquest, dispossessing the Anglo-Danish aristocracy and parcelling out land to family and friends. In the 20 years of William's reign, England gained a tier of Francophone Norman aristocrats under 'Guillaume'. Norman castles and cathedrals sprung up around the country in Conqueror style. In 1085 William decided to value his kingdom. The resulting Domesday Book (1085–6) listed everything of material value and who owned it. Power was land, leased from the king and sub-leased in a feudal chain that tied everybody into a network of personal and territorial relationships. As Duke of Normandy, William was the feudal subject of the King of France, and for a long time the Norman Kings of England were called upon to serve as feudal vassals to their king. After William I died in 1087 a feudal Pandora's Box was opened. Ill-advised by his bishops, William split his empire between his sons: his eldest son, Robert, got Normandy (the top prize); his second son, William Rufus, got England and became William II; Henry, the youngest, got lots of cash. Inevitably the sons fell out: Robert invaded England; Rufus was mysteriously killed while hunting in the New Forest; Henry grabbed the crown, invaded Normandy, imprisoned Robert for life and got the Duchy too – reuniting the realm and crowning himself Henry I. He restored some order by marrying the great-granddaughter of Æthelred the Unready. But when he died heirless in 1135 his daughter Matilda and nephew Stephen both claimed the succession. Matilda was married to Geoffrey Plantagenet, heir of Anjou; France and the Anglo-Norman barons opposed Plantagenet rule. Stephen came from Blois and was backed by the King of France and his brother, the powerful Bishop of Winchester. England and Normandy plunged into 'the Anarchy' of civil war; every man and his dog entered the fray. Stephen got the kingdom, but ceded it to Matilda's son, Henry Plantagenet, on his death in 1154 – to a sigh of relief in England, but consternation on the other side of the Channel.

1154–1216: England is Rolled into the Angevin Empire

Early-medieval France was made up of many nations, including Normandy and Anjou, loosely federated under the King of France. The counts of Anjou wore a sprig of broom, or Plantagenet, on their helmets. When Henry Plantagenet was crowned Henry II in Westminster Abbey in 1154, he became head of a territory stretching from the Welsh and Scottish borders to Jerusalem, one that made him more powerful than his feudal boss, the King of France, to whom he had sworn allegiance but spent his reign fighting. Henry is remembered in England for re-establishing the rule of law and killing the Archbishop of Canterbury – both to the same end: imposing the authority of the absentee king. The Church posed the biggest challenge to his power, as clergymen were accountable to the pope, who could excommunicate whole countries. The power of the Church in England rested on the personality of the Archbishop, who was either the king's or the pope's man – so Henry gave his old chancellor **Thomas à Becket**, a worldly man and a good friend, the job. Henry thought he could rely on Thomas to back his reforming secular agenda, but Thomas took the job seriously, surprising even his bishops. The exasperated king in Bayeux uttered the much-quoted line: 'Who will rid me of this low-born cleric?' (or something similar in French). Four French knights took up the commission, slicing off the Archbishop's head in Canterbury Cathedral on 29 December 1170. Meanwhile back in France, Henry's estranged wife Eleanor of Aquitaine was turning Henry's sons against him and provoking the King of France. Henry died broken-hearted in France in 1189. His eldest son became Richard I; his mother's son, a romantic rather than pragmatist, he preferred jousting and crusading to running the country. He spent less than six months of his 10-year reign in England and is buried next to his father in Anjou. But to the English he is still **Richard Lionheart** (Coeur de Lion), while his brother, who ruled in his absence, bore the brunt of England's falling-out with the Plantagenets and will always be known as **Bad King John**. The English barons, fed up with fruitless battles in France, forced John to sign the Magna Carta at Runnymede near Windsor in June 1215. Not really the birth of democracy, Magna Carta did signal an end to the tyranny of kings. King John stuck to it for three months, then renewed his pursuit of the treacherous barons until his death in October 1216. He lost Normandy too, putting the English Channel back in business as one of the world's biggest moats.

1216–1399: After a String of Defeats by the King of France, the Plantagenets Go After His Crown

Though the Angevin empire of the Plantagenets had disintegrated, John's nine-year-old son Henry III was still one of them, with vast lands in southern Europe. The Plantagenets were not English and were only really happy galloping around waging Continental wars; they were Plantagenets first, kings of England second. In a bid to get the King's attention, the 1258 Provisions of Oxford aimed to succeed where Magna Carta had failed. The Provisions included plans for regular 'parliaments' with the magnates of the realm. Heading the barons was Simon de Montfort, an unlikely champion of English democracy – a French aristocrat who had inherited the earldom of Leicester and a castle at Kenilworth. The crisis had two flashpoints. At the Battle of Lewes in 1263, de Montfort scored a coup by capturing both Henry III and Prince Edward. The Battle of Evesham in 1265 saw a reverse, with de Montfort's death and mutilation at the hands of a vengeful Prince Edward.

Edward I became king in 1272. He was the archetypal Plantagenet, a politically ruthless warlord who fought on the Continent for two years and for whom England was an offshoot of crusading Europe. The Plantagenet religious zealotry seems alien, but Edward's expulsion of the Jews from England in 1290 came after pogroms in London and York. Turning his attention away from France, Edward conquered Wales and brought Scotland to its knees. But Scotland rallied under William Braveheart Wallace and Robert the Bruce, and Edward was killed in a campaign near Carlisle.

Edward's successor was the feckless **Edward II**, who lost Scotland in 1314 and came to a gruesome end in 1327 at the hands of his wife, Isabella, her lover, Roger Mortimer, and a red hot poker. But the effeminate Edward II did produce an heir, **Edward III**, who was a towering hunk of a man. To each of his five strapping sons he gave a newly-created English duchy, including the duchies of Cornwall, Lancaster and York. (It was the descendants of Lancaster and York who would stir up the Wars of the Roses in the next century.) Edward also encouraged the English wool trade with the Low Countries, creating a new breed of wool tycoons (who built the grand churches of the Cotswolds and East Anglia). England was moving away from France and, as if to make the point that Plantagenet England was no longer a feudal dependency of the

The Age of Chaucer

In architecture, art, costume, music and literature, the Middle Ages offers an endless stock of characters: mail-clad knights, mysterious hooded monks, crusaders, squires, troubadours, warty peasants and lonely princesses in hilltop castles. The Normans preferred their home-grown culture to that of the conquered English; and they especially liked hearing the old French romances set either in the court of Charlemagne or – oddly – the glittering halls of King Arthur of Britain and his Round Table of knights. Three centuries after the Norman Conquest a national culture powerfully reasserted itself. The uniquely English Perpendicular Gothic style of church architecture, characterized by strong vertical lines, contrasted with the flowing extravagances of Continental styles. Likewise, the French stories of chivalry and courtly love were now retold in English dialects grafted onto native traditions of story telling. In the story of *Sir Gawain and the Green Knight*, the folkish figure of a woodland giant barges into the chivalrous world of King Arthur's Hall during the Christmas festivities and picks a fight with Sir Gawain. The resulting knightly quest follows the natural cycle of the year to the following Christmas. Sir Gawain is a chance survival of an oral tradition of muscular, alliterative poetry ('Thay boghen bi bonkkes ther boghes ar bare, Thay clombed bi clyffes ther clenges the colde'), told and retold over centuries. In the 14th century two named authors produced original pieces of literature: the long alliterative allegory *Piers Plowman* was written by William Langland, an obscure church cleric from the Midlands; Geoffrey Chaucer, on the other hand, was a sophisticated, multilingual public servant at the courts of Edward III and Richard II. His unfinished narrative poem *The Canterbury Tales* has set the standard for English literature. Although there was nothing new in the idea of a story about a story-telling competition between a group of people, Chaucer takes giant strides forward with his closely-observed characterization and dialogue, and the way that the tales and characters interact with gentle irony: when the Friar tells a story about a criminal Summoner who is carted off to hell by the devil we know that the Summoner in the party will get revenge in his tale later on.

Kingdom of France, Edward announced a claim to the French throne in 1340 – dragging the two countries into 118 years of war, more commonly known as the **Hundred Years War**. The creation of a national enemy helped to form the English national character : imperial, defiant, embattled and wary of all things French. Englishness was in fashion in the 14th century. Chaucer and Langland made English, not Latin or French, their literary language, and English became the language of the Anglicized aristocracy. But the victorious battles of Edward III and his dazzling son **Edward the Black Prince** at Crécy and Poitiers in 1356 made impossible tax demands on the English people, on top of bad harvests. As if that were not enough, the **Black Death** arrived from Europe in 1348, killing almost half the population of Britain. The misery found an outlet in a series of Peasants' Revolts. The biggest, led by Wat Tyler in 1380, was put down by the precocious boy-king **Richard II**. He was son of the Black Prince, who had died prematurely of dysentery. Delusional, Richard II alienated a generation of English barons with his pretensions of divinity. One of the barons was Henry Bolingbroke, the second Duke of Lancaster, who killed the king, led the public mourning and then, with great show of reluctance, crowned himself **Henry IV**.

1399–1485: The Lancastrian Kings Do Well in France, but Are Defeated on Home Ground by the Yorkists

Bolingbroke was a Lincolnshire boy who had defeated the last of the Plantaganets and the King of England, over the Duchy of Lancaster. Henry was himself a usurper and his 14-year reign was blighted by pretenders. But the King bonded with his Kingdom. In the short reign of his son, **Henry V**, the bond became a love affair. The King was England's champion, speaking English, beating the French and making good Edward III's claims to the French throne. The Anglo-French empire couldn't last; within 40 years of Henry V's victory at Agincourt in 1415, the French had won it all back. Turfed off the Continent, England launched into the most English of royal squabbles, the **Wars of the Roses**. The opponents were the dukes of Lancaster and the dukes of York, fighting under the red and the white rose, and the issue was the usurping of Richard II by the Lancastrian Bolingbroke in 1377. Lancastrian **Henry VI**, son of Henry V, failed to put a lid on it. The barons fell in behind either Henry or the Yorkist pretender, Edward of March. After countless bloody battles, with heroes and villains immortalized by Shakespeare (Queen Margaret, Richard Neville and Owen Tudor), a golden-haired knight called Edward emerged with the crown in 1461.

The 22-year reign of **Edward IV** lacked drama, but cathedrals were rebuilt in Perpendicular style and England's ports traded wool, salt, grain, coal, herring and hides. However the Wars of the Roses were not quite over: just before Edward IV died, suddenly, in 1483, he nominated his dependable brother Richard of Gloucester as protector of his two young sons, the heirs to the Crown. In no time Richard had swapped his personality for another one, murdered the princes and all opponents, and crowned himself **Richard III**. Shakespeare gave him a hunchback and a crooked smile, and his reputation was finally buried at the Battle of Bosworth in 1485. The King was killed by Henry Tudor – half-brother of Henry VI – who picked the crown out of a thorn bush, and pronounced himself **Henry VII** on the battlefield. Just to be sure of the crown, Henry married Elizabeth of York, reconciling the houses of York and Lancaster and opening a new chapter in English history.

1485–1603: The Tudors Convince the English of the Benefits of Being Different

The England inherited by Henry VII was still immature, its formative years misspent in Continental wars and civil war. Henry himself had been brought up in France, son of Queen Katherine of France and the Duke of Pembroke, a Welshman called Owen Tudor. Henry played up his Welsh credentials, named his eldest son Arthur after the legendary Celtic warrior-king, and married off his daughter Margaret to the Scottish king, James Stuart, in preparation for union. Tudor England was reborn in the Celtic peripheries: Cornwall was pummelled into a brooding silence, from which it has never recovered, and Wales was annexed in the creation of the new Kingdom of England

The Age of Shakespeare

'I anticipate the approach of a golden age,' wrote Erasmus of Rotterdam, who frequently visited England between 1499 and 1514. 'I am led to a confident hope that not only morality and Christian piety, but also a genuine and purer literature may come to renewed life or greater splendor.'

The Renaissance meant the rebirth of those artistic energies that carried the ancient Greek and Roman civilizations to such heights, and in England is associated with the reign of Elizatheth I. It began in Italy in the 14th and 15th centuries and spread through France and Germany to England, which was embroiled in the Wars of the Roses and too busy slipping into anarchy to notice the end of the Middle Ages. For a while Henry VIII styled himself a Renaissance king and professed an interest in humanism, but the Reformation broke up the charmed circle around his trophy humanist, Sir Thomas More, whom he beheaded. By the reign of Elizabeth I, bright young courtiers were emerging from their Protestant humanist education at Oxford and Cambridge eager to impress their Queen. None more so than Sir Philip Sidney and Edmund Spenser who perfected the English sonnet, modelling it on the sonnet cycles of Petrarch and other Italian and French Renaissance poets. Meanwhile, the plays of Christopher Marlow, Ben Jonson and William Shakespeare were igniting the Elizabethan stage. Before then, the only truly national drama was the Mystery cycle, a ritual re-enactment of the Bible story from the Creation to the Last Judgement performed by the trade guilds every June on the back of hay wagons. In the first purpose-built theatres, including the Globe on the south bank of the Thames, raucous, appreciative crowds from the whole of English society were hungry for full, rounded entertainment. What they got was a never-to-be-repeated Golden Age.

and Wales in 1537. The Royal Navy, and a feeling of superiority to the rest of Europe – at the heart of the English character – emerged in the Tudor period.

In 1509 **Henry VIII** succeeded his father, adding vigour to the Tudor enterprise. According to the myth, strapping six-foot-tall Henry dragged England into the modern world. Out went the medieval world, idolatrous Roman Catholicism, vice-ridden monasteries and the Celtic fringes; in came the reforms of English Protestantism and Renaissance thought, against a backdrop of banqueting peasants dancing around maypoles. Except that is not what happened. In reality, Henry, a good Roman Catholic, triggered the Reformation in order to get a divorce from Catherine of Aragon, who had failed to give him a son and heir. Archbishop Thomas Cranmer provided theological justification for the break with Rome in 1534. The Dissolution of the monasteries was the inevitable result of the Reformation. A thousand years of Roman Catholic history were replaced by patriotism: Henry had offended the whole Roman Church, and the pope had only to say the word to launch a European Catholic invasion of England. To be openly Catholic became treasonable. Meanwhile Henry ploughed through another five wives – Anne Boleyn, Jane Seymour, Anne of Cleves, Catherine Howard and Catherine Parr – dispatching two of them by hanging.

The death of Henry VIII in 1547 – corpulent, cantankerous and festering in his bed – put the young **Edward VI**, son of Jane Seymour, on the throne. Over the next six years the Reformation gathered steam: out went religious guilds and colourful church paintings, and in came the Book of Common Prayer and municipal grammar schools. On Edward's deathbed, aged 15, plans were made to keep his Catholic half-sister Mary, daughter of Catherine of Aragon, off the throne. The puppet queen, Lady Jane Grey, was executed after nine days. Crowned on 19 July 1553, Mary I set about reversing 20 years of Protestantism. Back came Papal supremacy, and onto the bonfire went the Reformation's champions, including Cranmer. To secure a Catholic future for England, Bloody Mary married Philip II of Spain, but failed to produce a son. In 1558 Henry VIII's daughter by Anne Boleyn became Queen of England.

Protestant **Elizabeth I** styled herself the Virgin Queen: rather than marry a Catholic European prince, or create factions by marrying an English nobleman, Elizabeth wedded her country. The strategy worked well: the sexually frustrated Elizabethan court had its Golden Age. Desperate-to-impress courtiers such as Walter Raleigh, Robert Dudley and Philip Sydney competed for their Queen's affections with sonnets and country houses. Meanwhile, Spain had backed Catholic Mary Queen of Scots as English queen, while English pirates such as Sir Francis Drake were constantly harassing Spanish ships. Spain bridled at the arrogance of Protestant England. The execution of Mary provoked Spain to launch an invasion of England in 1588. The naval defeat of the Armada was a disaster for the Spanish and cemented the English nation in its Protestant, isolationist, anti-European destiny, behind the resplendent figure of victorious Queen Elizabeth I.

1603–1714: In Which the Stuarts Are Twice Sent Packing

On Elizabeth's death in 1603, the English Crown passed to James VI of Scotland, who became **James I** of England and Ireland – three separate Crowns on one head. James was a Stuart, the son of Mary Queen of Scots. Raised among Protestant Scottish nobles, he was no Bloody Mary. The Reformation had created an embittered, oppressed Catholic minority and Ireland had become more Catholic than ever. Bookish, diffident King James favoured constitutional union of his kingdoms, but failed to deal with the Catholics. On 5 November 1605 a group of Catholics tried to blow him up at the opening of parliament. The Gunpowder Plot, foiled at the last moment, gave the anti-Catholics the justification they had been lacking. Religious intolerance set in; both Catholics and Puritans were suppressed. This was the atmosphere in which the Pilgrim Fathers set sail for the New World in the Mayflower.

Where James had failed, his son **Charles I**, crowned in 1625, made things much worse. When parliament complained, he closed it. He caused riots in Scotland by trying to impose Anglicanism. Ireland was already poised in rebellion. Charles I was insensitive to it all. In 1639 the Anglo-Scottish War kicked off, followed in 1641 by the Ulster Uprising, and then in 1642 the King declared war on Parliament and England shattered into pieces in the Civil War. The Parliamentarians nicknamed the Royalists 'Cavaliers', implying they were all closet Spaniards and Catholics. The Royalists called the Parliamentarians 'Roundheads', implying they were all radical Puritans. The King had support in the counties among the landed aristocrats, while Parliament controlled most of the towns and ports. The war lasted four years. The final battles of

The Age of Reason: Swift, Johnson and Pope

Samuel Pepys, Secretary of the Admiralty and secret diarist, describes the splendid coronation of Charles II on 23 April 1661 in Westminster Abbey. His six-volume diary, decoded in 1825, provides a keyhole glimpse of London in the 1660s through the eyes of one of its most senior public figures as well as open personal accounts of family life. England after the Restoration was a place of civilized manners and scientific rationality between the darker excesses of the British Civil War and the Industrial Revolution. Much of the credit goes to the Oxford philosopher John Locke's *Essay Concerning Human Understanding*, which proposed a scientific account of our mental processes, and the Cambridge mathematician and astronomer Isaac Newton, whose system of natural laws seemed capable of explaining almost everything. 'God said, 'Let Newton be!' And all was light,' wrote the poet Alexander Pope, whose biting and witty moral analysis typified the intellectual brilliance of the period, by turns called the Age of Pope, the Augustan Age or Neo-classical Age. Poets stayed clear of personal feelings, sticking to public themes of society and human behaviour. The greatest painters of the age, Reynolds and Gainsborough, preferred portraits and familiar landscapes to over-stretching the imagination, although Hogarth added a pinch of satire. Wit was the ultimate requirement of Restoration theatre too, which was written for the diversion of the fashion-conscious nobility. This was the age of polished critical analysis and comment in the coffee houses, newspapers and 'familiar essays' of two new periodicals, *The Tatler* (1709) and *The Spectator* (1711), whose journalistic persona was a mild, affable, clubbable sort of chap observing other people's social pretensions and offering advice on how to correct them. The great men of the age were the literary critic and dictionary author Samuel Johnson, the biographer James Boswell and the historian Edward Gibbon: men devoted to real life. In 1719 Daniel Defoe, a London merchant's son and political essayist, published *The Life and Strange Surprising Adventurers of Robinson Crusoe*, and accidentally invented the novel. Fiction being seen as rather low-brow, he followed it up with several more novels claiming to be autobiographies of flawed individuals who can only achieve moral redemption by honestly writing it all down. Jonathon Swift's satirical novel *Gulliver's Travels* (1726) is a scathing attack of English society wrapped up as charming prose fiction. Popean Man – moral, good-natured, but misguided – is rejected in favour of Swiftian Man, a filthy brute capable of untold stupidity.

Marston Moor and Naseby saw the Royalist army wiped out by the New Model Army, a highly-disciplined fighting machine. It had been trained by Oliver Cromwell, a powerful military commander and Puritan zealot, who decided to execute the King. Before the axe fell, on 30 January 1649, Charles I said he believed in freedom, but kings were accountable only to God. Not any more. The House of Lords and the Anglican Church fell too, briefly. As Lord Protector, Cromwell dismissed Parliament more frequently than Charles had. The alternative to the monarchy was Cromwell, but he was the enemy of fun, so when he died in 1658 the monarchy was restored.

Charles II came back to England in triumph in 1660, billed Parliament for his expenses in exile and got down to the frivolous stuff – but his mood was not echoed by the people. Catholics were barred from public office and Nonconformity was illegal. Religion and politics had grown inseparable and the first political parties – the Whigs and the Tories – emerged around the succession of Charles's brother, **James II**, seen to be pro-Catholic. The Whigs wanted to block the Stuart succession, while the Tories backed it. Behind that issue was the balance of power between parliament and the king. The debate marked a step towards parliamentary democracy.

In 1685 James Stuart became James VII of Scotland, James II of England and of Ireland. Catholic in private, Anglican in public, his reign was bound to come unstuck. In the Coronation year, James's nephew, the Duke of Monmouth, went after the Crown. It was a popular but hopeless rebellion and James responded with disproportionate brutality. The honeymoon of the Restoration was over. Both Whigs and Tories hoped that James would die soon and heirless, so that his Protestant daughter Mary might become queen. But instead he had a son, James Francis Edward, so the Whigs and Tories took pre-emptive action: they invited Mary's husband – hunchbacked, arrogant Willem van Oranje – to invade England. **William of Orange** was Protestant Stadholder of Holland. While Parliament hoped he would leave it to run the country, he was keen to get resources for his unending wars against France. In November 1688, after the so-called Glorious Revolution, the English throne was handed to the Dutchman. Scotland accepted William. Ireland resisted. England was back in the Continental wars.

In 1702 William's sister **Anne** became queen and England entered another decade of Continental wars to stop France getting Spain and its colonies. It was also feared that France, which had recognized the son of exiled James II as James III of England and James VIII of Scotland, might enforce the Stuart succession. The long war excited little public interest until John Churchill, Duke of Marlborough, started winning battles. England got a new national hero; Marlborough got Blenheim Palace in Oxfordshire. The French threat had frightened Parliament into blocking the hereditary right of the Stuarts, by the Act of Settlement (1701) through the Protestant line, in favour of the Hanovers – minor northern European royalty who couldn't speak a word of English. Parliament's idea was that it could govern without royal interference. To eliminate the threat of Stuart succession in Scotland, the monumental Act of Union (1707) united England and Scotland as the Kingdom of Great Britain – with one monarch, one parliament, one army and one empire. The new British Empire had just won a collection of former Spanish colonies after the war. A surge of imperial pride led Britain to believe that it had inherited the mantle of classical Greece and Rome.

1714–1830: A Remarkable Age for Parliament

Crowned in 1714, German-speaking **George I** spent half the year in Hanover. It was six months too little for the British Parliament. The running of the country was left to dominant Whig politician Robert Walpole, prime minister in all but name. For two decades this Norfolk squire's political mastery and handling of the economy put him in charge. With George's patronage, Walpole placed his cronies in key positions and blighted the careers of Tory opponents by branding them Jacobite or Catholic sympathizers. The accession of **George II** in 1727 made little impression on the Whig political

The Romantic Movement: 'Strange Fits of Passion'

William Blake's *Songs of Innocence* about the corrupting influence of politics and society was published in 1789, the year that the French Revolution caused English people to dream of (or fear) the end of the complacent old world and the appearance of something better (or worse) in its place. The idealistic 19-year-old Wordsworth raced off to France where he thought he saw 'human nature seeming born again'. Disillusionment was bound to follow, and it did. The Romantic Age starts in 1798, the year in which Wordsworth and Coleridge published *Lyrical Ballads*, and runs parallel to the early decades of the Industrial Revolution up to the Reform Bill of 1832. In the literature of Wordsworth and Coleridge, the rights of the imagination, emotion, human dignity and individualism were asserted above the universal man of the last century and the mechanized factory worker of this one. The second generation of Romantic poets were Lord Byron (1788–1824), Percy Bysshe Shelley (1792–1822) and John Keats (1795–1821), who lived fast and died young like proto-rock and rollers; their precocious talent and radicalism counterpoising the conservatism of the aging Wordsworth and Coleridge. To some extent the period best expressed itself in Mary Shelley's Gothic novel *Frankenstein* (1818), which handled big Romantic themes of corrupted innocence and unguided scientific progress against a background of snowy wastes and Alpine mountains, in an atmosphere of mounting panic. In this context the novels of Jane Austen (1775–1817) with their needle-sharp irony and close social observation seem to belong to the ordered universe of the Age of Pope; when she touches on Romantic feeling it is to gently mock it.

machine, oiled by Walpole. After centuries of conflict, the 18th century saw itself as a reasonable age of coffee shops, daily newspapers and good-humoured materialism. Peace and prosperity at home did not mean that the days of warmongering were over. Now the major European powers – Britain, France, Spain and Prussia – had empires, so the battlefield had spread across the world. From 1739 until 1815 Britain waged war constantly against shifting European alliances that always seemed to include the old enemy, France. Walpole resigned in 1742, under attack from a new generation of Whigs led by William Pitt the Elder, with his principled, outspoken brand of politics. While George wanted to defend Hanover at the head of an army, and Walpole wanted the navy to secure British interests in North America, Pitt had the backing of the House of Commons, something 18th-century British kings could no longer ignore. In 1756, George II reluctantly invited Pitt to form a government for another round of wars. The Seven Years War (1756–63), fought at opposite ends of the earth by Robert Clive and General James Wolfe, brought major colonial gains for Britain (including India and Canada), most of them at the expense of the French. 'Rule Britannia' was sung around the country, exhorting Britain to continue its global expansion. The confident mood was reflected in the Palladian architecture of Bath and London, and the landscaped gardens of Stowe. The colonial wealth turned London into the financial centre of Europe. But Britain was generating its own wealth too. Daniel Defoe's round-Britain travelogue in the early part of the century reported the beginnings of the Industrial Revolution – toll roads, canals, cotton factories, manufacturing towns and booming ports. Traders, industrialists and entrepreneurs were becoming the new gentry, and were starting to demand a stake in power. Reforms were needed. The Hanoverian kings barely travelled beyond the cloistered walls of Windsor Great Park, and certainly never got as far as Scotland, Ireland or Wales. This was fine until **George III** came along in 1760, putting his own men into government and ignoring the burning issues of the day – slavery, Ireland, and the vote. After the humiliation of the anti-colonial wars in America, he finally asked William Pitt the Younger to form a government in 1783, aged only 24.

At the outbreak of the French Revolution in 1789, the great war-leader's son had failed on the key issues of social reform, and the King was ill and mad. A jittery British Government clamped down on radicalism and republicanism, causing many people – including Thomas Paine, author of *The Rights of Man* – to flee the country. Fear that revolution might spread to the British Isles via Ireland prompted the Act of Union between Great Britain and Ireland to be rushed through both parliaments in 1800. The name of the new British state was to be the United Kingdom of Great Britain and Ireland. Representatives from England, Wales, Scotland and Ireland would now all sit together at Westminster. Confronted with its traditional enemy, embodied in Napoleon Bonaparte, Britain awoke from its revolutionary dreams and followed the heroic military exploits of Horatio Nelson in the Mediterranean, and Sir Arthur Wellesley, Duke of Wellington, in Portugal, Spain and France. In June 1815, Napoleon was defeated and exiled to the island of St Helena. Britain was now the dominant European power, with the best navy and greatest empire. The names of Waterloo and Trafalgar, the battlegrounds of Napoleon's defeat, were on everyone's lips. But the post-war economy slumped, as discharged soldiers returned home sick and injured and with no prospect of finding work.

The 19th century was already awash with radical pamphlets and public meetings calling for an extension of the vote, representation in Parliament for the northern industrial towns, free trade and improved social welfare. In 1820, the year after hundreds of protesters had been trampled by troops at St Peter's Fields in Manchester, **George IV** succeeded to the throne. Long past his raffish Regency days, the 49-year-old king was alcoholic, gluttonous and gouty. His death in 1830, bedridden and obese, brought the Georgian period to its close.

1830–1901: Empire and Revolution

1830 was a good year: the mild-mannered **William IV** inherited his father's throne and the Whigs took office, championing liberty. The Whigs began an era of major reform. The industrial towns gained representation in Parliament and slavery was finally abolished. Social conditions were not so good: welfare was tied to inhumane workhouses and factory workers toiled under wretched conditions. In 1834, the year that Darwin set sail in the *Beagle*, six farm workers from Tolpuddle in Dorset, who had tried to form a trade union, were deported to Australia – and became martyrs.

On 20 June 1837, William's niece **Victoria**, aged only 18, became Queen of Great Britain and Ireland. German was her first language and her family was German, as was her husband, Albrecht von Sachsen-Coburg und Gotha. Nevertheless, the short,

The Victorian Age: 'Awake, ye noble workers, warriors in the one true war'

The dark divisions and conflicts of the Victorian Age were best dealt with in prose writing, while the poet laureate Alfred, Lord Tennyson (1809–92) either trumpeted the great imperial and state occasions or longed for an Arthurian past. One of the most authoritative Victorian social critics was Thomas Carlyle (1795–1881), who was greatly influenced by the Romantic notion of human dignity and individualism which he felt had been lost in the Industrial Revolution. He saw himself as a prophet of the spiritual order of things, the joists of which were hard work, sensible autocratic government, and white, male supremacy. His idealization of the 'noble spirit of the Middle Ages' was directly influenced John Ruskin (1819–1900), an art critic and social reformer who thought society could only be delivered from the perils of unfettered materialism and machine-led industry by returning to the medieval-style craft guilds. In 1843, seven young men including Dante Gabriel Rosetti, John Everett Millias and William Holman Hunt founded the Pre-Raphaelite Brotherhood. Their aim was to practice an art that would be a Ruskinian protest against the materialistic spirit of the age. Wearing his art critic's hat, Ruskin, in turn, became the PRB's greatest fan and a friend to Holman Hunt and Millais. Unlike the Romantic novels of Walter Scott, whom Ruskin and Millais both adored, the natural setting of the Victorian novel was the present. These novels were long and episodic because they were published in installments in magazines. Charles Dickens (1812–70), the most prolific of the Victorian novelists condensed every kind of contemporary evil, ugliness and social injustice into a heightened parallel world more vivid and real to us than the real one.

stout, plain-faced Queen became the embodiment of 19th-century Britain. During her reign, the country changed beyond recognition. The centre of wealth and population shifted from the southeast to the coalfields of northern England and Scotland. Coal fuelled the iron furnaces and steam engines of the Industrial Revolution and the factory took over from the farm as the biggest employer. Villages grew into towns, and towns into cities, without planning or sanitation. The phrase 'Two Nations' was coined to describe the gulf between middle-class factory owners and the disenfranchised and underpaid men, women and children who laboured in them. Out of Manchester emerged the two defining political movements of the era: the Chartists demanded the extension of the franchise and annual parliaments; the Anti-Corn Law League demanded a repeal of the Corn Laws, which had been designed to protect the interests of landowners by blocking cheap imports of corn but had inflated the price of bread for ordinary people. By 1851, the booming industrial cities had been linked by 5,000 of miles of railways, with London at the hub of it all. Millions of people came by train from all over Britain to see the Great Exhibition that year, held in London's Hyde Park. The money raised went into the building of the Victoria and Albert Museum and the Natural History Museum. This was the great museum age. The new sciences of archaeology, anthropology, geology and biology had attracted gentlemen of means, who pursued them across the Empire; the private collections of these Victorian amateur scientists ended up in small provincial museums. Wars rumbled on in India, New Zealand, China, Afghanistan, Crimea and Africa – none of them glorious and some quite shameful. At home, under the leadership of Gladstone, for the Liberals, and Disraeli, for the Conservatives, modern politics took its shape in two opposing parties. Gladstone reformed the army, civil service, education and the Church. Disraeli feathered the imperial nest, and made Victoria Empress of India. At the end of the century, the new Labour Party, representing the trade unions, joined the fray in the House of Commons. In 1901 Queen Victoria died at Osborne House on the Isle of Wight. She had reigned for 64 years, through 10 prime ministers. Most of the eminent Victorians had predeceased her, including Tennyson, Ruskin, Gladstone, Dickens and Brunel. Victorian Britain had commanded a great empire, but the world was changing. The new nations of Europe (including Germany and Italy) and America had industrialized, and they were looking to get hold of a piece of Empire too.

1901–45: Two More European Wars, and Another Churchill Rides to the Rescue

England entered the 20th century as the dominant member of the United Kingdom of Great Britain and Ireland, whose vast empire included Canada, Australia, India and large parts of Africa. The political scene was dominated by the Liberal, Conservative and Labour parties; the main issues were social reform – the minimum wage, pensions, slum clearance – and Home Rule for Ireland. Victoria was the last monarch to intervene in the running of the country. King **Edward VII** behaved like the perfect constitutional monarch: keeping up the pomp and ceremony of regal appearances and travelling the world on public relations exercises. The drivers of change over the next four decades were prime ministers – Asquith, Lloyd George, MacDonald, Baldwin, Chamberlain and Winston Churchill – and political groups like the Suffragettes, who campaigned for votes for women. The **First World War** (1914–18) was the last in the centuries-old European tradition of imperial warmongering, but the powers had industrialized and the armies were composed largely of imperial conscripts. Britain sent five million soldiers to war – a fifth of the male population – plus another four million from its empire. Most of the battles took place in the trenches of northern France, where tanks, aeroplanes, poison gas, artillery and machine guns added a dimension of horror to warfare, and killed tens of millions. Britain and its Empire lost a million men – considerably fewer than Germany, Russia, Austro-Hungary and France. King George V changed his family name from Sachsen-Coburg und Gotha to the House of Windsor mid-war. Post-war, women at last got the vote. However, after some initial jazz-fuelled euphoria, the 1920s and '30s brought economic depression and mass emigration to the New World.

First World War Poetry

'If I should die think only this of me;/ That there is some corner of a foreign field/ That is for ever England.' These were the noble, patriotic sentiments of Rupert Brooke (1887–1915), who died on active service *en route* to the Dardanelles without experiencing for himself the killing fields of the northern Europe. Other poets like Siegfried Sassoon (1886–1967) and Wilfred Owen (1893–1915) did, and exposed 'The old Lie:/ *Dulce et decorum est/ Pro patria mori*' with vivid descriptions of carnage and misery.

Britain found itself back at war in 1939, against Hitler's Germany, in the **Second World War** (1939–45). In May 1940 Winston Churchill replaced Chamberlain as prime minster, a few weeks before the French surrendered and Italy allied itself to Germany. The RAF saw off the invading Luftwaffe during the Battle of Britain in the skies over Kent and Sussex. 'Never in the field of human conflict has so much been owed by so many to so few,' said Churchill of the air force men. His decisive leadership was the foundation of Allied victory. The night-time air raids of the Blitz brought the war to the civilian populations of Coventry, Portsmouth, Liverpool and London (manufacturing cities and ports), but soon the historic cities were being targeted too in the war on morale. The spirit of defiance and solidarity brought out the best of the English national character. The D-Day landings in June 1944 marked the beginning of the end of the war: 4,000 ships of all shapes and sizes crossed the Channel to Normandy carrying Allied soldiers and supplies for the final push on Berlin. France was liberated shortly afterwards and Germany finally surrendered in May 1945.

1945 to the Present: From Stiff Upper Lip to Multicultural Society

The priority of the post-war Labour Government that replaced Churchill was the reconstruction of bomb-flattened cities and the welfare of ordinary working people. The redistribution of health and wealth financially crippled the old aristocracy, who were made to fund it. Death duties meant the aristocracy could no longer afford to live in their ancestral homes: around 500 country houses were demolished after 1945, and twice as many again sold off as schools, hospitals and hotels.

Post-war administrations also began the politically necessary but messy process of dissolving the British Empire: 'Scuttle is the only word that can be applied,' said Churchill. Ireland became a Republic in 1949, the same year that the Soviet Union became a nuclear power and NATO was founded to oppose Stalinist imperialism. The Cold War provided the plot for some excellent films (*The Spy Who Came in From the Cold*) and brought the world to the brink of nuclear war in 1962. In retrospect, the 1950s seem an innocent decade in England – of buoyant nationalized industries, early TV broadcasts aimed to educate as well as entertain, the breezy welcome of the first West Indian immigrants, and rock around the clock.

The young people of the 1960s had no personal memories of the Second World War, and were free from conscription. But they had been exposed to the subversive hip-wiggling of Elvis Presley. In such a climate, Enoch Powell, a member of Edward Heath's Conservative shadow cabinet, made his inflammatory 'Rivers of Blood' speech, warning of the consequences of immigration in rabble-rousing biblical language. He was sacked, but Britain was changing.

In 1970 Edward Heath became the new Conservative prime minister, beginning a decade of industrial disputes between the State and workers' unions (especially the miners), which demanded more money for their members in a Britain that was less and less industrially viable. After centuries of mistrust of all things Continental, on 1 January 1973 Britain joined what is now the European Union. Few people actually took this in at the time, they were too busy being cold and annoyed by the three-day working week and black-outs.

Harold Wilson's Labour Government replaced the Conservatives in 1974 and immediately dished out pay rises but failed to revive the economy or stop the striking. The dockers, dustmen, railwaymen, hospital wardens, lorry drivers and coalminers were all at it. Margaret Thatcher will always be loved by history, if not by her people; she enters the narrative just when a strong personality is needed, becoming the first female prime minister, at the head of a Conservative Government, in 1979. She lowered taxes, encouraged home-ownership, sold off the nationalized industries, stood up to the National Miners Union during the year-long strike of 1984–5, stood up to the IRA after it bombed the Brighton hotel in which she was staying during the annual Party Conference in 1984, and won back the Falkland Islands from Argentina against the odds in 1982. She put her name to a new brand of politics and economics that became synonymous with the 1980s: Thatcherism (aka monetarism). Historians love the effrontery, handbags, haircuts and shrill piping voice of the Iron Lady, but she has many detractors too. She encouraged a form of philistinism in which everything, including the cultural life of the country, was reduced to the level of the market place.

BritPop

In 1995, Blur and Oasis brought out singles on the same day (Country House versus Roll With It) and the Nine o'Clock News carried the story with reference to the chart wars between the Beatles and Rolling Stones. Other British bands including Pulp, Suede, Supergrass, Portishead, Massive Attack and Radiohead added to the sense of excitement surrounding the British pop industry. Like in the 1960s, the creatives – pop stars, fashion designers, shock artists, supermodels and style editors – all seemed to be attending the same parties and sharing taxis. Whether or not it is true, or the result of premature TV retrospectives, those British icons the Union Jack flag, John Lennon spectacles and the British Bulldog were the badges of Britpop, and the Royal Academy's Sensation exhibition, *Loaded* magazine, Danny Boyle's *Trainspotting* (with its Britpop soundtrack) now seem part of the same British creative resurgence. *Vanity Fair* did a 'Cool Britannia' issue featuring Oasis frontman Leam Gallagher under a Union Jack bedcover with his then wife, Patsy Kensit, on the front cover. There was a distinctly British feel about Blur's 1994 Park Life album, and Damon Albarn's jaunty Cockney persona in many of the tracks; likewise Oasis seemed to express a powerful northern rock and roll with more in common with the Beatles than Nirvana or the American superbands. Jarvis Cocker, the lead singer of Pulp, seemed the incarnation of Britpop with his wiry, intelligent championing of working-class culture in Different Class, and dropping his trousers during Michael Jackson's set at the Brit Awards – the ultimate Britpop coup. Although most of the action of Cool Britannia took place under John Major's Conservative government, Britpop seemed to be promising something new so New Labour could legitimately associate itself with it. Oasis' Some Might Say ('we will find a brighter day') captured the spirit of pre-1997 election hope for a generation that had grown up under 18 years of Tory government. Quickly after Labour victory Oasis, self-confessed former petty thieves, were publicly invited to Number 10 Downing Street as members of the new Establishment.

She is perhaps best remembered for saying that there is no such thing as society. On 28 November 1990 Thatcher left government in tears, forced out not by the country but by her own Cabinet, who were fed up with her presidential way of running things and her antipathy towards Europe. Her ash-faced successor John Major made a decent fist of the premiership, backing the Americans in the first Gulf War of 1991 and daring to initiate talks with Sinn Fein, seen as the political wing of the IRA. But he was not a charismatic leader, and the country had had enough of a Conservative Party by now steeped in sleaze and permanently divided over Europe.

In May 1997 Tony Blair's 'New' Labour Party formed a Government, and a nation in big need of a change rejoiced. However New Labour's election-winning disavowal of Clause 4 of the party's constitution, which committed it to public ownership of the major industries, signalled an effective end of party politics. The Labour and the Conservative parties have become virtually indistinguishable; despite Blair's talk of the 'Third Way', both parties are committed to out and out free-market capitalism. The only divisive issue left is Europe, which still provokes ardent nationalism among the tabloid-reading Brits. The single European currency was launched in 2002 while Britain still dithered.

Blair's Government has completed the breakaway of the Celtic nations from England that started with the creation of the Republic of Eire in 1949; Scotland got its parliament and Wales an assembly in 1999, and the principle of a Northern Ireland assembly has been agreed.

All the defining aspects of the traditional British and English identity have taken a battering in the last fifty years – the Church of England, the Royal Navy, the British Empire, the British Parliament, the British monarchy, the 'green and pleasant land', and the Anglo-Saxon monopoly on Britishness. Not all of this has been bad, but the small corner of Europe's main island group that is England is still searching for a new, 21st-century identity.

Beyond the Rolling English Road

03

Beyond the Rolling English Road

Attitudes to English roads are as various as the roads themselves, ranging from deep affection for the 'rolling English road' of G.K. Chesterton's poem to suspicion of bypasses, grudging respect for motorways, gruesome fascination for grungy A-roads leading into big cities (where people actually *live*), and horror of all new roads, which are just another measly cup to catch the flowing water. The polarities are sharply focused in the attitudes of England's two greatest travellers, William Cobbett, who refused to travel on the new toll roads for what they symbolized (the encroachment of urban values on the countryside), and Daniel Defoe, to whom roads were the vibrant arteries of trade connecting and nourishing the nation's great towns and cities. Most of us feel a bit of both, but as the car's domination of English life goes unchallenged, we are bound to turn into a nation of Cobbetts. Nor is the positive symbolism of roads helped by the network's prosaic letter-number coding of A-roads, B-roads and M-roads. Whatever happened to the Great North Road? Buried under the A1, that's what. The great historic route ways all have names with which to conjure: Icknield Way, Ermine Street, Watling Street, The Ridgeway, Fosse Way, The Salter's Way. What stories English roads might tell, if they were only allowed, of kings, poets, painters, armies, highwaymen, Romans; of heroic advances and doomed retreats, poignant journeys and comic escapades.

You can feel the thrill of historic roads at the most unlikely spots, like Dunstable, a middling-ugly town north of London, built to safeguard the crossroads of prehistoric Icknield Way – one of the country's oldest 'green' roads – and Roman Watling Street, running from the Kent coast to north Wales. An Eleanor Cross once stood here, one of 12 erected by the grief-stricken Edward I at each stop of the funeral procession of his queen from Lincoln to London: you can follow this romantic route, down Ermine Street, the Roman highway between the two towns, followed closely by the B6403 and A1 to Stamford and striking southwest to Watling Street (the modern A5 and A2).

The Romans, whom we all admire, built 10,000 miles of roads in *Britannia* in the first century of occupation, about a mile every four days, between forts, posting stations, towns and tribal capitals. London was the hub from which main roads branched out across the country (apart from the Fosse Way from Lincoln to Exeter). You can still follow the line of Roman roads, and find preserved Roman paving on Blackstone Edge in Greater Manchester, complete with a groove running down the middle supposed to have been for a brake-pole to steady carts down the steep descent.

William Cowper's comic poem 'John Gilpin' recounts the thunderous, breakneck ride of the eponymous hero up the A10, from London to Ware and back, his hat and wig blown off, bursting through turnpike gates on his madcap horse. On the subject of poets, the A5 could be named after John Clare's immortal, penniless escape on foot to Northampton from his sanatorium in Epping Forest.

Toll roads in England are not a thing of the past. A new road around the congested northeast side of Birmingham demands payment at either end, and is perhaps a sign of the future of British motorways. If it lessens congestion, then it is worth it. Travelling on motorways ought to be a pleasant experience, opening up classic rural views on both sides. The M6 north of Preston is the most scenic motorway of all. Heading west on the M4 out of London into the early evening sunset is uplifting, and the M11's views of the East Anglian wheat fields do a good job of calming the brain. Even the notorious M25 London orbital motorway is surprisingly scenic between Reigate and the M26 turn-off – horses graze amid dreamy Weald and downland countryside. It is hard to feel affection for these highways, but after 20 or 30 years they are at last beginning to settle into the landscape, with mature trees and yellow-flowering gorse bushes healing the scars and muffling the noise of the traffic.

If you have patience, use the old A-roads (which used to be known by their end destination, the Portsmouth Road for example), retracing the lines of the old country of Jane Austen and Charles Dickens, with its coaching towns and posting inns. The chances are, however, that sooner or later you will want to roar off to the nearest motorway slip road to escape the infuriating frequency of roundabouts. England has an unholy marriage bond with roundabouts. In Milton Keynes, the roundabout capital of the world, they are sponsored by local businesses and have individual names, like John James Electricals or Wilkins' Office Supplies – surprising in a country that prides itself on conjuring images of Arcadia in suburban settings, where many a residential road is called Buttercup Close, Badger Crescent or Sunrise Cul-de-Sac.

The English Country House and Garden

The story of the English country house and garden might start in the 14th century, with wealthy city lawyer John Bell retiring to the countryside to found a dynasty. As county sheriff, he builds a small moated manor house using local stone and forest timber, encasing the interiors with oak panelling, and eats fish, pigeon and vegetables from the garden. After vacillating during the Wars of the Roses, his grandson, also John Bell, finds himself on the right side at Bosworth and is rewarded with an earldom. He promptly marries a wealthy heiress, changing his name to Dubell to make himself sound nobler. The 2nd Earl renounces Roman Catholicism at the Reformation, becomes general Tudor Machiavellian for Henry VIII, acquiring the abbey lands he has helped to dissolve. His son Sir Philip Dubell, 3rd Earl, dabbles in the Italian sonnet, extolling the beauty and bounty of Elizabeth I. He nearly bankrupts himself adding rangy quadrangles to his house, and improving the skyline with domes and minarets. He is proud to say that his house has more glass windows than any other in England, and entertains the wild notion of marrying the Queen. Ben Jonson is a personal friend and writes a poem celebrating Dubell's patronage of the arts and pleasant garden. The 5th Earl marries a Cavendish heiress, and they go on a European shopping spree, while Louis Laguerre and Grinling Gibbons redesign the interiors, returning with Italian paintings, French furniture and Dutch tapestries. The 6th Earl leads a successful minor assault on a small Belgian village during a gloomy spell of the Spanish Wars of Succession, and is rewarded with a Roman-style portico by John Vanbrugh, who tries to talk him into recreating the battle plan in trees. His wife doesn't like the martial tone, and throws Vanbrugh off the estate, hiring the up-and-coming Lancelot 'Capability' Brown to soften the parklands in the new Romantic style. The 7th Earl is a minor political figure with no social graces but is passionate about art and taxidermy, amassing a huge collection of stuffed animals and putting up Turner for a whole summer. He dies bankrupt and heirless, and the house goes to a cousin called Dundy, who adopts the name Dubell. He knocks down the wings, and sells most of the art collection to pay off debts. His son resurrects the family fortunes by exploiting the mineral wealth of estate lands in the north. He buys a baronetcy, and hires Wyatville to turn the house into the castle that he imagines his 14th-century ancestor to have inhabited, filling the great hall with suits of armour. He befriends artists and poets and marries a famous society beauty who hosts garden parties on the terrace. Gertrude Jekyll creates a herbaceous garden where medieval vegetables once grew. The house becomes the headquarters of a covert military communications centre in the Second World War, broadcasting black propaganda into Nazi Germany and Occupied France. By the end of the war the roof is leaking and the Laguerre ceilings are mouldy. In lieu of the new death tax, Lord Dundy-Dubell, now an aging widower, gives the whole sorry estate to the National Trust.

Thousands of country houses were demolished in the late 20th century, others have been converted into grand hotels and country clubs, yet it still seems that you are never more than 10 minutes away from an English country house in delightful gardens or parkland; to the tourist, at least, these are the still points around which the country whirls. Reassuring as churches with their great halls and pleached alleys, they send you out into the 21st century solid and grounded. The first named English architect was Robert Smythson, the prolific genius behind the Renaissance palaces of Longleat, Hardwick Hall and Wollaton. This was the first great age of the English stately home, producing the testosterone-fuelled Burghley House for Sir William Cecil to please the Queen, and Hatfield House, the Jacobean corporate headquarters of the Salisbury family firm. If this was the preening, self-glorifying, look-at-me period of English culture, by the 18th century architectural manners were as refined as the social niceties in Tunbridge Wells. Chatsworth, Blenheim and Castle Howard were statements of a supremely confident aristocracy, enjoying the upper hand over the monarchy after the Glorious Revolution of 1688. The architect of the day, John Vanbrugh, was a soldier turned architect, who worked with a heroic military vision, sweeping away villages as though he were on campaign, damming rivers and erecting bridges to create the perfect setting for his architectural masterpieces. The poet Alexander Pope turned the garden into the canvas on which a classical idealization of nature might be painted with the consummate art of a Claude Lorraine. 'All gardening is landscape painting,' he wrote, 'the eye is generally the properest judge...you may distance things by darkening them, and by narrowing the plantation more and more towards the end, in the same manner as they do in painting.' Pope's friend William Kent was the first practitioner of the painterly approach to landscape design, at Holkham Hall and Stowe. In the garden of Stourhead, created by Henry Hall in the 1740s, the enhanced naturalistic landscape achieved perfection, embroidered with classical temples and rustic grottos. From 1750, Capability Brown dismantled the boundaries between garden and surrounding countryside, landscaping whole estates by planting trees in picturesque clumps, raising hills and digging serpentine lakes. How ordered, well-off and stable England must have seemed. Humphrey Repton continued the tradition at Attingham, Hatton Park and Antony, sketching planting schemes in his famous little red books.

Back came the formal Italian garden in the Victorian era. The leading figure was Harold Peto, who laid out gardens at Buscot, Heale and Iford in an architectural rather than painterly style, with paved terraces and long vistas, fountains and statuary. Meanwhile Japanese gardens, rock gardens and heath gardens were the rage among the new breed of wealthy middle-class amateur gardeners, whose glasshouses were the receiving houses for exotic shrubs, notably rhododendrons, camellias and magnolias, brought back from all corners of the world by plant hunters like Ernest 'Chinese' Wilson, Robert Fortune and George Forrest.

Edwin Lutyens worked in Harold Peto's practice, and earned a reputation for building in the Arts and Crafts style of William Webb, incorporating a range of local building materials and styles to give an impression of organic growth over centuries. His countless collaborations with Gertrude Jekyll, the fairy godmother of 20th-century Arts and Crafts gardening, involved the synthesis of house and garden. Together they dominated Edwardian gardening. 'Show me your spaces,' she said, 'and I will tell you what plants to get for them.' The greatest gardens of the 20th century, elaborating the main traditions of English gardening, are Hidcote, created by amateur American expat Major Lawrence Waterbury Johnston, Sissinghurst, coaxed out of weeds by Vita Sackville-West and Harold Nicolson; and Great Dixter, the gardens of contemporary gardening guru Christopher Lloyd.

Many of the historic houses and gardens open to the public are owned and managed by either the National Trust or English Heritage. Both of these publish their own books of sights with opening hours and times, and issue their own membership cards. If you plan to visit more than a couple of their properties it is well worth acquiring a membership pass. Most country properties are open for a summer season from around Easter until the end of October, while some remain open for more limited hours the rest of the year. Opening periods as listed in this book are inclusive (open April–Oct includes the months of April and October).

The English Season

The English Season is a series of social events rooted in tradition, some dating back hundreds of years. The themes range from competitive sport, garden design, farming and classical music to royal pageantry, but all of them share an element of dressing up, good food and drink. Confusingly, the season runs throughout the whole year, although summer has the greatest concentration of events.

Some events have been encouraged by royal patronage, horse-racing in particular. Charles I established regular race meetings at Newmarket, since when all monarchs have had horse-racing connections, including Queen Elizabeth II, who has her horses trained there. The Epsom Derby was first run in 1780 as a sideshow for the idle rich

Calendar of the Season

March

National Hunt Festival: The highlight of the jump-racing season with around 20 horse races featuring the Champion Hurdle and Cheltenham Gold Cup; **t** (01242) 513 014, *www.cheltenham.co.uk*

April

Harrogate Spring Flower Show: The biggest spring flower show in the UK.

May

Chelsea Flower Show: At the Chelsea Royal Hospital. Complete gardens designed by top designers compete for coveted RHS medals; **t** (020) 7649 1885.

Brighton Festival: One of the biggest arts festivals; music, theatre, comedy and fringe events in venues all over town; **t** (01273) 700 747, *www.brighton-festival.org.uk*

Bath Music Festival: One of the older festivals (well past its 50th birthday); mainly classical music, with jazz, contemporary and world music days. Opens with a free concert in Victoria Park and fireworks; **t** (01225) 463 362, *www.bathmusicfest.org.uk*

Glyndebourne Summer Season: Six opera productions at purpose-built theatre in beautiful Sussex gardens; audiences in evening dress picnic in the long interval; **t** (01273) 815 000, *www.glyndebourne.com*

June

Trooping the Colour: Performed on second Saturday by the Household Division to celebrate the Queen's official birthday. She leaves Buckingham Palace at 10.40am and proceeds along the Mall with an escort of Life Guards and regiments of the Household Cavalry, inspects the parade at Horse Guards at 11am and watches the regiments march past to familiar tunes; **t** (020) 7414 2353.

Royal Cornwall Show: Three-day countryside festival in early June; livestock and flower shows, horse-jumping, hot-air balloons and music. Royal Cornwall Showground, Wadebridge, *www.royalcornwall.co.uk*

Royal Ascot: Mix of racing, hats and royal pomp. Ascot Racecourse, Ascot, Berkshire, **t** (01344) 622 211.

Goodwood Festival of Speed: Three-day event with classic racing cars driven by legends of motor racing; **t** (01243) 755 000, *www.goodwood.co.uk*

Salisbury Festival: Performing arts festival; two weeks, late May to early June, in the cathedral, Playhouse, City Hall and Guildhall; **t** (01722) 332 977, *www.salisburyfestival.co.uk*

Aldeburgh Festival of Music and Arts: Two weeks in June in Aldeburgh church and Jubilee Hall, the purpose-built concert hall at Snape, Blythburgh and Orford churches. It was started by Benjamin Britten in 1948, and now attracts international celebrities as well as newcomers. Book well in advance for concerts, hotels and restaurants; **t** (01728) 687 110, *enquiries@aldeburgh.co.uk*

Cambridge May Bumps: College rowing teams of eight line up in boats down the River Cam, and at the starter's gun try to 'bump' the boat in front; **t** (01223) 467 304.

Hay Literary Festival: Ten days over Whitsun; attracts around 50,000 visitors to hear well-known writers talk and debate; **t** (01497) 821 299, *www.hayfestival.co.uk*

Glastonbury Music Festival: Largest green-field music festival in the world, takes place behind an 8½-mile perimeter fence, with dance, new bands, theatre, circus, cabaret, jazz, world and acoustic music, 'sacred space' and food stalls. **t** (01159) 129 129, *www.glastonburyfestivals.co.uk*

Broadstairs Dickens Festival: Nine days in mid-June, with drama at the Pavilion, Victorian music hall and talks in the Dickens House Museum and Royal Albion Hotel; **t** (01843) 861 827, *www.dickensweekbroadstairs.co.uk*

Ludlow Festival: Three weeks of Shakespeare in the castle; talks and concerts in church and Assembly Room; **t** (01584) 872 150, *www.ludlowfestival.co.uk*. A fringe **Jazz Festival** takes place over one weekend in the courtyard of the Bull Hotel, **t** (01584) 873 611.

Wimbledon: The Lawn Tennis Championships are the focus of the grass court season; Lawn Tennis Association, **t** (020) 7381 7000; *www.wimbledon.org*

July

Hampton Court Flower Show: One of the largest of its kind; **t** 0870 906 3791, *www.rhs.org.uk/hamptoncourt/*

The Royal Show: The biggest agricultural show, attracting royalty, with horse-jumping, a flower show, stalls selling the latest farm machinery and a smart social side; Stoneleigh Park, Warwickshire, **t** (02476) 696 969, *www.royalshow.org.uk*

Great Yorkshire Show: Three-day countryside show on 450-acre site at edge of Harrogate; features dancing diggers display team, sheep-dog trials, show-jumping, livestock and flower shows, and horse-shoeing; Great Yorkshire Showground, **t** (01423) 541 000, *www.yorkshireshow.org*

Chichester Festivities: Exhibitions and shows including jazz and candle-lit concerts in the cathedral and chamber music in the ballroom at Goodwood House; **t** (01243) 785 718.

The British Grand Prix: Britain's top event in Formula One motor-racing, held on the second Sunday of month at Silverstone, Northamptonshire; **t** (01327) 850 124, *www.silverstone-circuit.com*

Buxton Opera Festival: Five operas, and recitals and concerts; **Literary Festival** too; **t** (01298) 70395, *www.buxtonfestival.co.uk*. Followed by **Gilbert and Sullivan Festival**, late July to mid-Aug; **t** (01422) 323 252.

BBC Proms: Popular series of concerts at the Royal Albert Hall, London; **t** (020) 7589 8212, *www.royalalberthall.com*

Harrogate Festival: Arts festival: classical music, open-air theatre, jazz, world music, dance, comedy and walks; Harrogate International Centre, **t** (01423) 537 230, *www.harrogate-festival.org.uk*

Glorious Goodwood: Five-day horse-racing meeting on the country estate of the Duke of Richmond, Lennox and Gordon at the end of July on one of the most scenic tracks in the country. The Racecourse, Chichester, West Sussex, **t** (01243) 755 022.

Henley Royal Regatta: Held over five days at the end of June every year since 1839. There are 19 events including eights, coxed fours and single sculls, with two boats racing in each heat of knock-out draws. There may be up to 100 races a day on the 1 mile 550 yards straight course; Regatta Headquarters, Henley-on-Thames, **t** (01491) 572 153.

Ways With Words: Ten-day literature festival at Dartington Hall; 200 speakers and more than 100 events. Strong on non-fiction, with psychology, philosophy and science days; **t** (01803) 867 373, *www.wayswithwords.co.uk*

The Dartington International Summer School and Music Festival: Follows straight on from the literature festival; at least three high-calibre professional concerts every evening (classical, jazz and rock) for which you need to book well ahead; **t** (01803) 847 080, *www.dartingtonsummerschool.co.uk*

Frinton Summer Repertory Season: Founded in 1940, this is the last bastion of summer repertory theatre; Frinton Summer Theatre, Fourth Avenue, **t** (01255) 674 443.

August

Cambridge Summer Shakespeare Festival: Six open-air productions in college quads and gardens; **t** (01223) 511 139, *www.cambridge shakespeare.com*

The Three Choirs Festival: Oldest music festival in Europe (250 years). Rotates between Worcester, Gloucester and Hereford. Barbershop, brass and jazz as well as the festival chorus and orchestra. Elgar headlined in the 1920s and '30s; *www.3choirs.org*

Snape Proms: August in the Snape Maltings Concert Hall; features light classical, folk, jazz and cabaret; **t** (01728) 687 110, *enquiries@aldeburgh.co.uk*

Cowes Week: International sailing event on the Isle of Wight; the Duke of Edinburgh and Princess Royal have both competed; **t** (01983) 295 744; *www.cowesweek2.co.uk*

September

Burghley Horse Trials: Three-day event over first weekend in Sept with dressage, cross-country and show-jumping; **t** (01780) 752 131.

October

The Britten Festival: Last weekend in Oct; music by Benjamin Britten and a guest composer in Snape Maltings Concert Hall; **t** (01728) 687 110, *enquiries@aldeburgh.co.uk*

Canterbury Festival: Two weeks in mid-Oct; opera, drama, exhibitions, comedy, talks and concerts; **t** (01227) 452 853, *www.canterbury festival.co.uk*

Cheltenham Festival of Literature: Mid-Oct for 10 days; well-established over 50 years and attracts literary speakers with international reputations; **t** (01242) 227 979.

spa-goers, and was named after the 12th Earl of Derby, who had a house nearby. Queen Anne began racing at Ascot in 1711, and the incumbent Queen holds a week-long house party at Windsor Castle, driving across the Great Park through the Golden Gates onto the course every day. Polo was originally a cavalry sport, and might have died out in the 20th century had Prince Charles not taken it up so enthusiastically. The ceremony of Trooping the Colour, celebrating the Queen's official birthday, grew out of army rituals around the regimental flag, the rallying point on the battlefield.

The focus of the summer season was traditionally the coming-out of the 18-year-old daughters of the aristocracy. They were first presented at Court, and then free to attend all the balls and dances on offer and perhaps catch a Mr Darcy with their unspoiled charms and ingenuous graces. To the relief of all parties, the present Queen stopped the custom of meeting debutantes in the late 1950s, since when the social season has lost some of its stiff upper-class connotations. Nevertheless, complex who-you-know booking procedures, exclusive stands and enclosures, strict dress-codes, and the alluring presence of royalty appear as class-related obstacles to the uninitiated. The Epsom Derby, Royal Ascot and Henley Royal Regatta all have unswervingly strict (and absurdly dated) codes: morning suits and top hats for men, elegant day suits and hats for women. A letter is the correct form of application for a ticket to Ascot's Royal Enclosure, according to the authoritative *Debrett's Guide to the Season* by Lady Celestria Noel, in which the wording must be in the third person: Mr Andrew Vaughan-Payne presents his compliments to Her Majesty's Representative and wishes to apply...

For all that, the social element most at home in the modern season is to be found getting tipsy with clients in the corporate hospitality tents. Corporate Man merely has to turn up with a laminated company badge fixed to his lapel (for which the corporation has paid its dues in sponsorship) to avoid the rigmarole of advance booking that the rest of us must go through. While undoubtedly changing the tone of some traditional events, corporate hospitality has been the saviour of the season, showering the sedate, male-dominated world of rowing, flat-racing and tennis with the colourful smelling salts of PR-led celebrity glitz.

Book-ending the London season are the Chelsea Flower Show in May and Cowes Week (sailing) in August, both of which claim firm royal support. Chelsea is quintessential in so many ways, several hundred years old and determinedly summery in a month prone to wintery blasts. It starts with a private royal preview, followed by Royal Horticultural Society members days, followed by a public free-for-all.

May is also the start of the polo season, and the summer seasons of opera and picnicking at Glyndebourne and outdoor Shakespeare in Regent's Park. June is the busiest month of all, with classical music at Aldeburgh, contemporary music at Glastonbury, the start of the Royal Academy's Summer Exhibition of contemporary art (founded in 1769), and the Goodwood Festival of Speed (an upstart, founded in 1993). It is also the month of the Wimbledon tennis championships (still at the mercy of the weather, although it is now midsummer). A mainstay of the season, founded in 1877, it offers a delightful strawberries-and-cream version of tennis. Meanwhile star-studded arts festivals have popped up left, right and centre around the country, with an international flavour, while village cricket and its offshoot, country-house cricket, represent the gentler, local side of the summer season, redolent of tea and cucumber sandwiches and frothy pints of real ale.

After the summer season, National Hunt Racing picks up the slack. It is known as the winter game, having grown out of rough and tough fox and stag hunting, and is not as fashion-conscious as flat-racing. The high-point of this season is the Cheltenham Festival in March, the Ascot of jump-racing.

The backbone of English social life, the season offers a uniquely English cultural experience: picnicking in evening dress, travelling by train in full morning suit, jostling with crowds in an oversized hat, or being sophisticated and highbrow in a tent.

The Phoenix Effect of Galleries and Museums

You can't help noticing the number of snazzy new multi-million-pound museums and art galleries that have appeared around England in the last 10 years, particularly around the millennium. Salford's Lowry Centre and Imperial War Museum North, Manchester's Urbis, St Austell's Eden Project, London's Tate Modern, Birmingham's ThinkTank, Walsall's New Gallery, Leicester's National Space Centre and Rotherham's Earth Centre are just some. All this investment is linked to the regeneration of run-down, usually post-industrial, areas. In 1996 the Millennium Commission was set up specifically to channel profits made by the National Lottery into building new cultural attractions, spurring regional councils and enterprising individuals to think big. But the location of cultural institutions at the heart of urban regeneration is not new.

Manchester started it all in the 1980s, converting the old warehouses and railway buildings of Castlefields into a high-powered science and technology museum, its quayside flanked by cafés and bars. Its success spurred other industrial towns to think of urban regeneration in cultural and social terms. The Lowry Centre is the headline-grabbing showpiece of the wholesale renewal of Salford Quays. Manchester was ironically helped along its way by IRA terrorism. When the architectural writer Charles Jennings went to Manchester in 1995 to challenge his preconceptions, he found an 'economically troubled, beaten up, chilly, belligerently ugly city'. The very next year a bomb blew up the commercial hub, triggering a total transformation of the city centre with public squares and the new-fangled Urbis Museum, which celebrates city life around the world. Birmingham began its renaissance in the 1990s by declaring to the world that it was now an international conference centre. Liverpool's Albert Docks, built in 1860, faced demolition but were put to new cultural uses instead. Among new dockside attractions is Tate Liverpool, the first of the new high-powered provincial art galleries, opened in 1988. Tate St Ives opened in 1993, and has been the engine of the sleepy seaside town's revival. Coventry is revisiting the symbolism of the phoenix, at the heart of the post-war reconstruction of the city: the Phoenix Initiative is turning a dreary hillside into a series of café-fringed piazzas, with a Transport Museum dedicated to the city's history of car manufacturing.

There are three keys to the success of these new ventures: the core collection (the St Ives School at Tate St Ives, L.S. Lowry at the Lowry Centre, the Garman-Ryan collection at the Walsall New Gallery); the association with its setting (a new spa building for Bath, a Space Centre for Leicester University's department of physics and astronomy,a Rowing Museum for Henley, while the former industrial powerhouses of Manchester and Birmingham get museums of science and technology); and the building itself, ideally built by a celebrated architect like Richard Rogers, Nicholas Grimshaw or Norman Forster. Not all have succeeded: the Millennium Dome was all show and no substance, while Sheffield's Museum of Pop was not much show either.

Alongside nationally important art galleries in unsuspecting backwaters, public art commissions have brought sparks of magic to forgotten corners of the country. Birmingham city council has commissioned a statue representing the town emerging from its industrial past as a centre-piece for Centenary Square. Antony Gormley's Angel of the North, towering above the A1 outside Gateshead, has become part of the regional identity of the Northeast, a true modern-day icon. Meanwhile the plinths in Trafalgar Square, at the heart of London, are again without sculptures.

Food and Drink

04

While the rest of the world thinks England is the land of bland, stodgy food like gravy-doused meat-and-two-veg, Yorkshire pudding, pies, fish and chips, steamed suet puddings, and sickly confectionery like Bakewell tarts and Sally Lunn buns, all masquerading as a national cuisine, mercifully this is not the whole picture. The Norman Conquest had a culinary dimension, introducing pungent foreign herbs and spices into the plain Anglo-Saxon cookbook. Richard II's court, famous for its gourmet tastes, ate food dyed gold with saffron and elaborate sculpted marzipan. A rare Tudor cookbook gives a glimpse into the cooking of that era. Starting with some general advice on meat conservation ('mallard is good after a frost' and 'goose is worse in the midsummer month and best in stubble time' while 'goat is always good'), the wife of the master of Corpus Christi college offers mouth-watering recipes for fish or meat soup, dressed crab, meat pies, fish sauce, roast venison and fruit tarts. Fish is cooked with butter, salt, pepper and parsley, and sachets of rosemary and thyme, or fried in parsley butter; meat, spiced with cinnamon and sugar, is charcoal-roasted; mutton pies are packed with prunes, raisins and dates. So where did it go wrong?

Modern English Food

England 'once had a fine food culture, mislaid it out of carelessness, and then realized to its horror that the rest of the world regarded its eating habits with contempt', writes food critic Paul Richardson in *Cornucopia: A Gastronomic Tour of Britain*. Although there is evidence of an enduring English regard for fried breakfasts and vegetables boiled to a pulp, the menus of England's proliferating restaurants, café-bars and gastro pubs are now filled with fresh, home-made, organic, locally sourced and seasonal produce, and a wide choice of dishes. Food is now fashionable, alongside other elements of modern style like architecture, music, design and art.

The new style of English cooking takes good old comfort food, like pork sausages, roast lamb and fried fish, and throws in the pilferings of Mediterranean holidays, spicy immigrant foods and colonial exotica. Lunch in any English provincial town today might start with salad Niçoise, chickpea burgers or salsa-dipped potato wedges and go on to pan-seared eye fillet, game casserole or fish with piquant Oriental seasonings, served with grilled vegetables or rocket salad topped with shaved Parmesan. This so-called modern English style is in itself no guarantee of quality: it can scale the heights or plumb the depths, offering mediocre dishes that are fast becoming contemporary clichés (pork and leek sausages with mustard mash, or Thai fishcakes), or new and exciting combinations of familiar and unfamiliar ingredients.

Unless otherwise indicated, restaurants in this book are usually open daily for lunch, from around 12 until roughly 2.30, and again for dinner from 6ish until 10.30 or so. Café-bars may be open all day and late into the evening, whereas cafés and tea shops tend to close at 5pm. Many restaurants stay open all day at weekends too. For pubs, *see* below.

Eating Out

Café-Bars

The main purveyor of modern English food is the café-bar, a newish concept in eating, drinking and lounging that grew out of Manchester clubbers' need for somewhere to hang out before and after clubs; they provided the natural context, with cool décor, chill-out music and art on the walls; eating was made compulsory by the licensing laws.

The café scene has exploded in England, which astoundingly now has more cafés than anywhere else in Europe after Portugal, although France and Italy drink more coffee per head (8lbs 13oz a year compared to 5lbs 8oz in Britain). In Continental Europe, however, café culture is more laid back: sipping, talking, relaxing all come from the same impulse to savour the moment, alone or with friends. As the English self-consciously get their minds and mouths around the cappuccino, mocha, espresso, macchiato, frappé, latte and even chai latte, they have more in common with Americans than with their European counterparts; empowered by the number of choices on offer, but not yet raising coffee-drinking to the level of culture.

Country House Hotels and Gastro Pubs

The 'meat and two veg' soul of traditional English cooking – roasts, stews, pies, puddings, fruit and cheese – resides in the country-house hotel restaurant and gastro pub. In the hotels, delicious meals of roast pheasant, rack of lamb, rabbit stew, venison, game and grilled trout come with herb dumplings, red cabbage and parsley butter. They will usually be followed by divinely filling puddings.

Gastro pubs, on the other hand, are the French bistros of British catering: once gloomy old boozers turned friendly, no-smoking, reasonably priced family restaurants with bars. While the licensing laws are a national embarrassment, the food is better than ever, with revamped pub-grub favourites like Cumberland sausages and herb mash, beer-battered Whitby cod, thick-cut chips and mushy peas and steak and kidney ale pie regularly chalked up on the blackboard.

Fish and Chips

Every English town has its fish and chips shop; according to surveys, fish and chips are England's most popular food – and it's still a great fall-back when the round of chorizo ploughman's and ricotta tarts with raspberry coulis starts to get you down. Despite depleted stocks worldwide, customers routinely demand cod, not because of the flavour, which is indistinguishable from haddock or coley when deep fried and drowned in salt, vinegar and ketchup, but because 'cod and chips' rolls off the tongue so nicely. The fish supper, redolent of island living, is undoubtedly the national dish.

Indian, Chinese, Thai and Exotic Cuisines

The main opposition in provincial towns is the Indian restaurant. The preferred dish is chicken tikka masala, a combination dreamed up for the beer-swilling English

The English Shopping Basket

England has the goods in abundance, despite a decline in British agriculture and overfishing of the seas since the Second World War: green pastures; hedgerows full of blackberries, elderberries and crab apples; fruitful orchards; fungi-filled woods; and a world of rivers and seas.

Many English county names have food connotations (now protected by the European Union), among them Cheshire (cheese), Yorkshire (puddings), Lancashire (cured ham and cheese), Staffordshire (oatcakes), Cumberland (sausage), Kent (fruit and vegetables) and Cornwall (pasties and clotted cream). You can narrow the focus to Cromer crab, Aylesford watercress and Whitstable oysters. The most popular cheese in the world comes from the small town of Cheddar at the foot of the Mendip Hills in Somerset; Stilton takes its name from a village near Peterborough in Cambridgeshire.

Cheese is a growth industry in England. Of the 70 cheeses on display in a Kent branch of the upmarket supermarket Waitrose, 20 are produced in the UK and Ireland, including Cornish Yarg matured in an edible wrap of nettle leaves, and six are produced locally, including the tangy Sussex Yeoman and Ashdown Foresters.

hordes; in fact these restaurants are suspiciously devoid of Anglo-Indian families, who presumably don't recognize the brightly coloured oily slop served up as Indian food. The best immigrant food is found in the suburbs and Chinatowns of cities like London, Manchester, Birmingham and Leicester, where the incoming populations have transformed the grey, rainy English streets into something more fragrant. In line with the modern English revival, however, you will find some excellent modern Indian restaurants serving really fresh, unusual dishes. You may also be surprised to find pubs everywhere serving Thai green curry – sometimes excellent. In the metropolitan centres you may also find Japanese sushi and noodle bars, and cuisines ranging from Sudanese to Indonesian.

Pizza and Pasta

Cropping up everywhere are pizza and pasta chain restaurants: Pizza Express, Zizzi, Bella Pasta, Ask, Pizza Piazza. Although their dishes tend to be bland substitutes for the real thing, the benefits of relatively healthy, inexpensive food, served in a cheerful setting, are hard to resist. Not having to deal with the awkward intimacies shared by staff and diners in traditional low-lit provincial restaurants might be seen as another selling point. Other chains that are palatable and affordable, if not sizzling with originality, include Café Rouge, Café Flo and Browns – all pseudo-French-style bistros.

Roadside Dining

The Little Chef is still the king of roadside dining, the cheap, plastic décor in close harmony with the saccharine offerings on the laminated menu. The motorway service station offers lamentable self-serve grills, fried breakfasts and plastic-tasting sandwiches as the only alternative to fast food – and at a price.

In summer, all around the country, roadside stalls appear selling fruit and vegetables to passers-by and cardboard signs encourage you to pick your own (PYO) strawberries. Four hundred and seventy five farmers' markets have sprung up around the country since the first (Bath, 1997), where you can buy meat, vegetables, fruit, eggs, honey, pickles, jam, bread, cakes and cheese directly from the farmer with old-fashioned guarantees of quality and no middlemen upping the prices (sometimes the stallholders do instead).

Leading the march against the homogenization of food represented by supermarkets is a posse of TV chefs who preach the benefits of using seasonal local produce while knocking the dirt off potatoes and thrusting their noses into herbs. The whole-food movement of the last 40 years has found fresh momentum in the organic revolution. Many supermarkets boast well-stocked organic sections and have meat, fish and cheese counters resembling local shops. But the tantalizing image of gastro England is largely a product of the countryside not the towns and cities, which are bereft of decent food markets and losing interest in traditional grocers, butchers and fishmongers. According to Paul Richardson in *Cornucopia*, 50,000 British grocers shut up shop between 1986 and 1996, while the number of supermarkets trebled.

Tea Shops

The much-loved institution of the English tea shop, often styled Ye Olde Tea Shoppe, is to be found all over the country. At the top end are famous tea shops like Bettys of York and Sally Lunn's of Bath, where frilly-shirted and bonneted waitresses entice customers with well-garnished sandwiches, jammy pikelets, sweet and savoury tarts, scones and the joys of the English cream tea (scones with jam and clotted cream).

Otherwise your basic English caff serves all-day greasy breakfasts and lunches of meat, potatoes and gravy, washed down with the obligatory strong, milky 'cuppa tea'.

Food in England, like so many things, is a class thing. Gastronomy tends to have strong links with other forms of middle-class culture: the music festival has turned the small fishing town of Aldeburgh into a hive of good restaurants, TV chef Rick Stein has turned Padstow into a huge middle-class tourist destination and the well-heeled Shropshire town of Ludlow has a French-style food market and three Michelin-starred restaurants. But until good cooking has fully permeated English society, it is safe to say that what you eat in England may still be a bit hit and miss: not every roadside café or country pub will serve you gastronomic delights, although these are to be had, for a price, at superior establishments.

Pubs

The traditional English pub, a great national institution, comes in many shapes and sizes. There are those that have been refurbished for families, with patterned carpets, highly polished woodwork, soft lighting and piped mood music. There are the unreconstructed old boozers that subsist on a gang of aging locals and will have to close (or go gastro) when they die. Either of these two might offer Sky Sports to raucous single-sex audiences in the evenings. There are pubs that have chucked out the musty old carpets and dark brewery furniture in favour of rustic décor, hiring top-notch chefs, stocking carefully chosen wines and beers, and banning mobile phones to complete the back-to-basics ambience. And there are pubs of varying quality that trade on the character of the building, which may be Art Nouveau (stained glass and carved woodwork), Tudor (heavy timbers and inglenooks), converted High Street banks, opera houses or even a gents' public toilet.

Once upon a time virtually every town had its own brewery, pumping out a nourishing aroma on brew days and giving the town a distinctive, recognizable taste in its range of beers. Not many are left, although a few are still going strong, like Shepherd Neame in Faversham, Adnams in Southwold, Bass in Burton-upon-Trent and Green King in Bury St Edmunds. It is a great shame that the market is dominated by four big national brewing companies, Bass, Carlsberg, Tetleys, Scottish Courage and Whitbreads, who also control most of the pubs. A promising new development is the number of pubs that brew their own beer, almost always cheaper, and more interesting, than brewery beers. As for cider and perry (made with pears), there is nothing more refreshing to drink sitting outside on a sunny afternoon, particularly in Herefordshire where most of them are made. In drinking local beers, ciders and perries, in preference to imported lagers, you are also supporting a raft of ailing industries, including hop-growers, barley producers, and breweries. Many metropolitan pubs now also keep some reasonable bottles of wine behind the bar and mix decent cocktails, but in country pubs you're best off sticking to beer.

For many years, English pubs were forced by law to close in the afternoons (a measure introduced to enforce the work ethic). They are still obliged to throw out their customers at 11pm (you'll hear the bar staff shouting out for last orders a little before 11, then, increasingly desperate, urging drinkers to 'drink up please' or, in the words adopted by T.S. Eliot in *The Wasteland*, 'hurry up please, it's time'. Despite a recent liberalization of the licensing laws, many pubs stick to the old custom of closing between 3pm and 6pm, especially in rural areas. You may also get a rude response if you ask for something to eat after 2pm.

Travel

05

Getting There

By Air from the USA and Canada

Most transatlantic flights to England land at **London Heathrow** or **London Gatwick**; a few fly to **Birmingham** or **Manchester**. The main carriers listed below fly direct to England. The journey time from the east coast of America is 6–7 hours; from Los Angeles or Vancouver 10 hours (excluding stop-offs).

Ticket prices vary madly: the round trip from **New York** costs around $650–700 in peak season, but can rise to as much as $1,800, and drops to as low as $430 in February. From **Los Angeles**, the round trip costs around $1,000 in peak season, dropping to around $600 in February. From **Vancouver**, round-trip peak-season fares cost around $1,500; in February $805. The season of travel and how far in advance you book are the main factors determining the price of a flight. No single airline works out consistently cheaper than the rest, and no single internet agent always comes in at rock-bottom prices. Comparison shopping is the only thing for it: get yourself a good travel agent, who will look at the complete fare picture and suggest cost-saving strategies like switching airports and departure/arrival dates. It is then worth seeing if you can find something cheaper online, without going goggle-eyed with confusion.

Discount Fares

If you are a full-time **student** and have an International Student Identity Card (ISIC) you can get often substantial discounts on standard flight rates and on buses and trains around Europe (and small discounts getting into cultural attractions). If you are under 26, you can get a **youth** card (IYTC) for similar discounts. Both cards are provided on both sides of the Atlantic by the agencies specializing in student/youth travel below. The **longer-in-the-tooth** should enquire here for travel deals too.

STA Travel: In the USA, 7890 South Hardy, Tempe, Arizona 85284, **t** 1 800 777 0112, *www.statravel.com*. Around 90 branches in major cities like San Francisco, Los Angeles and New York, and the main university towns. In the UK, Priory House, 6 Wright's Lane, London W8 6TA, **t** 0870 1606 070, *www.statravel.com*. Branches in all the main university towns and campuses in the UK, including several in London.

Travel Cuts: 187 College St, Toronto, Ontario, M5T 1P7, Canada, **t** (416) 979 2406, *www.travelcuts.com*. Owned by Canada's national student organization, the Canadian Federation of Students; branches all over the country.

By Air from the UK and Ireland

The main domestic carriers and low-cost airlines, BA, bmi, bmibaby, flybe and Easyjet, operate services connecting the major UK cities, the Irish Republic and the Channel Islands. The Irish national airline, Aer Lingus flies to Bristol, Leeds, London and Manchester. Budget carrier Ryanair offers a cheaper alternative for flights from Dublin to Birmingham, Leeds, Liverpool, Manchester and Luton.

Again, prices fluctuate wildly. An economy return from Dublin to London can cost you anywhere from £70 to £300. A return flight between Belfast and London might be as low as £20. For cheap fares, fly off-peak and book early online rather than through a call centre. The no-frills, low-cost carriers such as flybe, Easyjet, Ryanair and bmibaby fly point-to-point at very low prices. Their best deals are online, with small discounts on standard fares, and frequent promotions if you book early. However low-cost airlines do not guarantee departure and arrival times, and some of them really are no-frills: Ryanair has no customer services at all, to the extent that if you have any problems at all with your flight (including flight cancellations or lost baggage) all you can do is fax the airline headquarters in Dublin, with little chance of a response.

Internet Travel

It can be cheaper to book on the internet, but travel agents are often able to undercut online companies – and know the ropes, saving you headaches. You can, however, make

Airlines

From the USA and Canada

American Airlines: USA **t** 1 800 433 7300, UK **t** 0845 778 9789, *www.aa.com*. Flies to London and Manchester from Boston, Chicago, Dallas, Denver, Los Angeles, Miami, New York and San Francisco.

British Airways: USA **t** 1 800 247 9297, UK **t** 0845 779 9977, *www.britishairways.com*. UK's largest scheduled airline, flies from most major US and Canadian cities to London and Manchester.

Continental Airlines: USA **t** 1 800 231 0856, UK **t** 0800 776 464, *www.continentalairlines.com*. Flies to London, Manchester and Birmingham from Atlanta, Boston, Denver, Houston, Miami, New York, San Francisco, Washington DC and Newark.

Delta Airlines: USA **t** 1 800 241 4141, UK **t** 0800 414 767, *www.delta.com*. Flies to London and Manchester from Atlanta, Cincinnati and NY.

United Airlines: USA **t** 1 800 538 2929, UK **t** 0845 844 4777, *www.ual.com*. Flies to London from Atlanta, Chicago, Denver, Las Vegas, Los Angeles, NY, Orlando, Phoenix, San Diego, Seattle and Washington DC.

US Airways: USA **t** 1 800 622 1015, *www.usairways.com*. Flies to London Gatwick and Manchester from Charlotte, Philadelphia, Pittsburgh, Boston and NY.

Northwest Airlines: USA **t** 1 800 447 4747, UK **t** 0870 507 4074, *www.nwa.com*. Flies direct to London Gatwick from Minneapolis and Detroit. Northwest is in partnership with Dutch airline KLM, giving you the option of flying via Amsterdam, or Paris since KLM merged with Air France.

Virgin Atlantic Airways: US **t** 1 800 862 8621, UK **t** (01293) 747 747; *www.virgin-atlantic.com*. Flies to London from Boston, Chicago, Las Vegas, Los Angeles, Miami, NY, Orlando, San Francisco and Washington DC.

Bmi: USA **t** 1 800 788 0555, UK **t** 0870 607 0222, *www.flybmi.com*. Daily services into Manchester from Chicago and Washington DC and from other cities in conjunction with United Airlines. Bmi also flies into London Heathrow from Calgary, Montreal, Ottawa, St John's, Toronto and Vancouver.

Air Canada: USA and Canada **t** 1 888 247 2262, UK **t** 08705 247 226, *www.aircanada.ca*. Flies into London Heathrow and Manchester from Toronto, Montreal, Vancouver, Ottowa, Halifax and Calgary. Flight-code-sharing through-tickets are booked on bmi flights from Heathrow or Manchester to other UK destinations.

From the UK and Ireland

Aer Lingus: Ireland **t** 0818 365 000, UK **t** 0845 084 4444, *www.aerlingus.com*. Flies to London from Dublin, Shannon and Cork. High season (August) flights from Dublin to London, range from €121 to €230.

Bmi: UK **t** 0870 607 0555, *www.flybmi.com*. Flies out of Manchester, Leeds, Bradford and Teesside to London Heathrow, Glasgow, Belfast, Aberdeen and Edinburgh as well as the Channel Islands and mainland Europe. Formerly British Midlands.

British Airways: UK **t** 0870 850 9850, *www.britishairways.com*. Frequent flights around the UK, and to the Channel Islands and the Republic of Ireland.

Scot Airways: Scotland **t** 0870 606 0707, *www.scotairways.com*. Flies from Edinburgh and Dundee to London City Airport.

Flybe: UK **t** 08705 676 676, *www.flybe.com*. Based at Exeter International Airport, from where most of its flights to European cities begin; also flies Belfast to London, Channel Islands to London and between the major UK cities. Formerly British European.

Easyjet: UK **t** 0870 600 0000, *www.easyjet.com*. Flies out of London Gatwick, Stansted, Bristol, East Midlands, Liverpool and Newcastle to destinations in Europe. Flights from Aberdeen, Glasgow, Belfast, Edinburgh and Inverness into Bristol and London Luton. Recently merged with British Airways' low-cost airline GO.

Ryanair: Republic of Ireland **t** 0818 303 030, UK **t** 0871 246 0000, *www.ryanair.com*. Dublin to London (Stansted, Gatwick and Luton), Birmingham, Bournemouth, Bristol, Leeds, Liverpoool, Manchester. Shannon, Cork, Derry, Kerry and Knock to London Stansted. No frills, no customer service.

Bmibaby: UK **t** 0870 264 2229, *www.bmibaby.com*. Bmi's baby flies into East Midlands from Belfast, Glasgow and Edinburgh; and into Manchester and Teesside from Belfast.

Internet Travel Agencies

USA and Canada

www.orbitz.com
www.travelocity.com
www.expedia.com
www.flights.com
www.air-fare.com

UK and Ireland

www.cheapflights.com
www.trailfinders.com
www.ebookers.com
www.expedia.co.uk
www.lastminute.com
www.thomascook.co.uk
www.airtickets.co.uk

savings on the price of processing a paper ticket and may be lucky with last-minute offers and cheap deals. Having booked your flight, with a credit card, you will be emailed the confirmed details of your flight and a booking reference number. Your passport (or photo-ID for domestic flights) is then all that is required to check in.

Getting to and from UK Airports

There are trains and buses to and from all the international airports; otherwise you can spend a fortune on a taxi for the privilege of sitting in a traffic jam for hours.

London Heathrow is about 15 miles from central London. The Heathrow Express to London Paddington takes 15 minutes, with trains departing every 15 minutes for around £20. It is slower (about an hour) on the London Underground, but costs less (£4). Heathrow is at the western end of the Piccadilly Line, which serves London King's Cross and Euston mainline stations. Rail Air buses go from terminals 1, 2 and 3 to Reading, where you can pick up trains westbound, avoiding London.

London Gatwick is 27 miles south of London with its own railway station. The Gatwick Express serves London Victoria, and takes about 30 minutes (£21.50 return), or you can do the same journey slightly more slowly on South Central trains (£16.40). Thameslink trains serve London King's Cross Thameslink Station, about 200 yards from King's Cross mainline station. There are direct rail services to Reading too, from where you can pick up westbound trains. Southbound trains take you straight to the seaside towns of Brighton, Eastbourne and Hastings.

From **London Stansted** trains go direct to London Liverpool Street Station in 42 minutes. Other trains head cross-country through Cambridge and Peterborough (connections to York and Edinburgh) to Birmingham, Manchester and Liverpool (3 hours 25 mins).

London Luton is the hardest airport to reach other than by car. You can catch a Thameslink train to it from London King's Cross, or a coach from London Victoria.

Birmingham International Airport has its own station on the main London to Birmingham route: 1 hour 20 minutes to London Euston or 10 minutes to Birmingham New Street in the city centre.

Manchester Airport is served by quick and frequent train services to Manchester Piccadilly station in the city centre. There are direct services to Leeds, York, Blackpool, Windermere and Liverpool; if you are heading south to London (2 hours 40 mins), change at either Manchester Piccadilly or Wilmslow.

By Train

If you are travelling to England from mainland Europe, the Eurostar trains run from Paris, Lille, Brussels and (less frequently) Avignon through the Channel Tunnel to Ashford International and London Waterloo International station, next to mainline Waterloo station. Since the high-speed rail link between London and the Channel Tunnel opened in September 2003, the Paris to London journey time has been reduced to 2 hours and 40 minutes.

Eurostar: UK **t** 08705 186 186, France **t** 0892 353 539; Belgium **t** 025 282 828, *www.eurostar.com*.

By Boat

The main ports for ferry services to mainland Europe are Dover (Calais), Newhaven (Dieppe), Portsmouth (Bilbao, Cherbourg,

Ferry Operators

Hoverspeed: t 0870 240 8070, *www.hoverspeed.co.uk*. Fast, frequent services between Calais and Dover, Dieppe and Newhaven.

Sea France: t 08705 711 711, *www.seafrance.com*. Ferry services between Calais and Dover.

Brittany Ferries: UK t 08703 665 333, France t 0825 828 828, Spain t 942 360 611, *www.brittanyferries.com*. From France and Spain to Plymouth, Portsmouth and Poole.

P&O Ferries: UK t 08705 980 980, *www.poferries.com*. Regular North Sea and Channel crossings from France, Spain, Belgium and Holland into Dover, Portsmouth and Hull, including night crossings from Zeebrügge and Rotterdam.

Irish Ferries: t 08705 171 717, *www.irishferries.com*. Dublin to Holyhead, from where you can catch a direct train into London Euston.

Stena Line: t (02890) 747 747, *www.stenaline.com*. Ferry services to Fishguard, from where you can catch the train to London Paddington, changing at Bridgend or Neath in South Wales; and Dublin to Holyhead where you can catch a direct train into London Euston.

Condor Ferries: t 0845 345 2000, *www.condorferries.co.uk*. Ferries from the Channel Islands and Britanny to Portsmouth, Weymouth and Poole.

Cunard Line: In the USA, 6100 Blue Lagoon Drive, Miami, Florida, t (305) 463 3000 or t 1 800 CUNARD, *www.cunard.co.uk*. From April 2004 the new *Queen Mary II* will be taking over the transatlantic voyage from the *QEII*. She will make one or two voyages a month between April and October from New York to Southampton. The voyage takes six days, and Cunard can either book you on a cruise back, or offer a return flight.

Caen), Plymouth (Santander), Hull (Zeebrügge) and Newcastle (Amsterdam). Ferries from the Channel Islands come into Poole, Weymouth and Portsmouth. From Ireland you can come into Fishguard or Holyhead in Wales, and link up with a rail service to London from the landing dock, or into Swansea. Book direct with the ferry company (*see* below), or look for deals on *www.ferry.co.uk* or *www.ferrybooker.com*.

Entry Formalities

Passports and Visas

Britain decided not to join the eight European countries practicing an open-border policy (the Schengen Group) so citizens of the EU need passports or identity cards, but not a visa. They can still expect to breeze through Immigration in a separate queue. Citizens of the USA, Canada, Australia and NZ must have a valid passport, don't need visas, and can expect slightly longer queues at Immigration. Other nationals may need visas; check with your nearest travel agent or British embassy.

Customs

Coming into the UK from another EU country, you won't have to pay tax or duty on any quantity of tobacco or alcohol that you can convince Customs is for your own consumption. If they think you are going to sell it they will confiscate it, often along with your car at ferry ports. The guidelines are: 3,200 cigarettes, 200 cigars, 110 litres of beer, 90 litres of wine, 10 litres of spirits and 20 litres of fortified wine such as port or sherry. The restrictions are tighter if you are arriving from outside the EU: 200 cigarettes or 100 cigarillos or 50 cigars, 2 litres of still table wine, 1 litre of spirits or strong liqueurs or 2 litres of fortified wine, 66cc/ml of perfume, and £145 worth of other goods including gifts and souvenirs.

Returning from the UK, residents of the USA must declare everything that they did not take with them, including gifts, purchases and duty-free items bought on the plane or boat. You can bring home $800 of merchandise without having to pay duties, including alcohol and tobacco allowances. Antiques more than 100 years old and fine art are duty free. Canadian citizens need to keep tabs on how long they have been away. If it has been longer than a week they can take home CAN$750 worth of goods without paying any duties, including alcohol and tobacco allowances (200 cigarettes, 50 cigars, 200 tobacco sticks, 200 grams of manufactured tobacco, 1.5 litres of wine, 1.14 litres of liquor or 24 355ml cans/bottles of beer). There may be a minimum duty to pay on tobacco products

Customs Information
Canada: t 1 800 461 9999, *www.ccra-adric.gc.ca*
USA: t (202) 927 6724, *www.customs.ustreas.gov*
UK: t 0845 010 9000, *www.hmce.gov.uk*

unless they are Canadian-made and marked CANADA DUTY PAID.

VAT Refunds

Value Added Tax (VAT) is included in the selling price of everything you buy in the UK. You can claim this back if you are travelling from outside the European Community (Austria, Belgium, Denmark, Finland, France, Germany, Republic of Ireland, Italy, Luxembourg, The Netherlands, Portugal, Spain, Sweden, Hungary, the Czech Republic, Poland or UK and the Isle of Mann) and leave the UK within 3 months of your purchase. You need to complete a tax refund document from the retailer and present it to Customs at the air/ferry port on your departure. Do it before checking in your suitcases, because you need all the goods and receipts for inspection.

Getting Around

By Air

BA flies between London and Birmingham, Manchester, Newcastle, Bristol, Southampton, Plymouth and Newquay, but you won't find many flights between England's regional airports. Bmi flies between London Heathrow and Manchester, Leeds, Bradford and Teesside. Easyjet has services between London Stansted and Newcastle, and Bristol and Newcastle. Ryanair does a short-hop flight from London to Newquay, but you are better off catching the train, which is far less trouble and gets you right into the town centre.

By Train

Privatization in 1996 split up the railway network (formerly British Rail) into pieces, and those pieces are still being re-jigged. A non-profit making company, Network Rail now controls the track, stations and signals, having taken over from RailTrack, a private company which failed to invest in the groaning old infrastructure while its 'fat cat' company heads did very nicely. Another 24 private companies – First Great Western, First Great Eastern, Great North Eastern, Virgin, Anglia, Central, South Central and so on – operate the trains, overseen by a watchdog, the Strategic Rail Authority, which also hands out franchises. The train companies, partly subsidized by the tax-payer, pay Network Rail to use the track. In other words, both public and private money is circulating around the main and branch lines of the British rail network.

Fast, intercity trains run on the major routes – for example, the main north-south arteries, the West Coast Main Line and East Coast Main Line. The Southeast is the most overtaxed part of the network, and the train operating companies South Central, Thames Link, South West Trains and Connex South East have come under the heaviest public criticism. But arriving by car in some cities can be such a nightmare you are well advised to take the train. The scenery out of the window on some lines is a bonus, for example the journey into Bath gives a superb first glimpse of the town, and the First Great Western line from London Paddington to Penzance is a long scenic tour.

It is best to travel off-peak, both to get a seat and for the prices. You can buy through-tickets to travel with different train companies. Prices are universally high, but there are ways of reducing the expense. For longer journeys you can often buy a cheaper **Advanced Purchase Ticket**. These are sold in limited numbers for a specific scheduled train, which means that they go like hot cakes. Individual companies have different deals. For example, First trains (Great Eastern, Great Western, North Western) call advanced purchase tickets APEX, and they must be booked at least a week in advance.

There are numerous **Rover** tickets available at railway stations for unlimited travel between certain times and places. Every region has its own version. In the Northeast, you can buy a 7-day pass for £73 which lets you travel by Arriva, Virgin, First North Western, Great North Eastern and Midlands Main Line. The FlexiRover lets you travel any 3 days out of 7 for about £50. The Cornish Rover lets you travel 8 days in 15 for £40.50. The Cotswolds

Narrow-gauge and Steam Trains

Bluebell Railway: **t** (01825) 722 370, *www.bluebell-railway.co.uk*. The UK's first preserved standard-gauge passenger railway on a section of the Lewes to East Grinstead line of the old London to Brighton and South Coast Railway

Romney, Hythe and Dymchurch Railway: New Romney Station, New Romney, Kent, **t** (01797) 362 353. Miniature railway purpose-built in 1927; travels 13.5 miles from Hythe to Dungeness.

Ravenglass to Eskdale Railway: **t** (01229) 717 171, *www.ravenglass-railway.co.uk*. World's oldest narrow-gauge railway, dating back to 1875 when iron ore was transported from Eskdale to the coast at Ravenglass; it now takes walkers into Lake District fell country.

The Watercress Line: The Railway Station, Alresford, Hampshire, **t** (01962) 733 810, *www.watercressline.co.uk*. Ten miles between Alresford and Alton, where you can link up with mainline trains to and from London. The line used to be used for transporting watercress from the nearby beds up to the London markets.

Bure Valley Railway: Aylsham Station, Norwich Road, Aylsham Norfolk, **t** (01263) 733 858. Narrow-gauge steam railway from Aylsham to Wroxham on the Norfolk Broads.

Gloucestershire–Warwickshire Railway: Toddington, **t** (01242) 621 405. Through Cotswolds on old section of Great Western Railway's mainline from Birmingham to Cheltenham, built in 1902–7; 20-mile round trip from Toddington Station lasting just over 1 hour 30 mins through Winchcombe to Cheltenham Race Course Station.

North Norfolk Railway (The Poppy Line): **t** (01263) 820 800, *www.nnr.co.uk*. A 10.5-mile round trip by steam train through delightful coastal scenery and poppy fields from Sheringham to Georgian town of Holt.

North Yorkshire Moors Railway: **t** (01751) 472 508, *www.northyorkshiremoorsrailway.com*. Eighteen miles of steam railway from Pickering to Grosmont through North York Moors; appears in *Heartbeat* and *Harry Potter and The Philosopher's Stone*.

Lakeside and Haverthwaite Railway: Haverthwaite Station, near Ulverston, Cumbria, **t** (01539) 531 594. Built as a branch line of Furness Railway in 1869 to establish a tourist link with lake steamers on Windermere. Steam trains ply the 31-mile section from Haverthwaite through Newby Bridge to the terminus at Lakeside.

Kent & East Sussex Railway: Tenterden Town Station, Tenterden, Kent, **t** (01580) 765 155, *www.kesr.org.uk*. Steam trains from Tenterden to Bodiam on the old Rother Valley Railway, about 10 miles.

Rover gives you 3 days in 7 for £25.50. The Hadrian's Wall Rover gives you 2 days in 3 for £12.50, and the Freedom of Settle Rover gives you 3 days for £35 on the famous Leeds to Carlisle route with all its viaducts and moorland scenery.

BritRail passes (*www.britrail.net*) are on offer to overseas visitors. They can be a money saver if you plan to travel a lot by train, with flexi-passes, consecutive-day passes, and passes for special days out from London.

National Rail Enquiries: **t** 08457 484950, *www.nationalrail.co.uk*. Train times and prices for all the different companies.

Traveline: **t** 08706 082608. Information on how to get from A to B on train, bus, coach and ferry. This new national public transport enquiry service brings together the routes and times of all public transport services .

By Bus

If you are keen to explore the backwaters of England at a snail's pace, you will enjoy riding the buses. It is a soporific experience, in the course of which you may forget where you're trying to go. Single-decker, double-decker and mini-buses are operated by countless different companies around the country, with services very infrequent outside towns. However, the buses penetrate places not reached by the railway or anybody without a car. In the National Parks, walkers are actively encouraged to dump their cars and use the buses.

The UK's long-distance routes are operated by **National Express** coaches, including services to and from the major airports and most larger towns. The major terminals are London Victoria, Gatwick Airport, Bristol, Manchester,

Leeds and Birmingham. Coach travel is much cheaper than the trains, and if you are a student, aged 16–25, or over 50 years old, you get savings on many journeys.

National Express: **t** 08705 808080, *www.gobycoach.com*

Traveline: **t** 0870 6082608.

By Car

Car is really the best way of getting into the English countryside, although not for visiting towns and cities. Hellish ring roads, awkward one-way systems, expensive car parks or scarce parking spaces and financially crippling fines for illegal parking are enough to put you off taking you car into town centres and persuade you to use **Park and Ride** services. These enable you to park cheaply out of town and catch a shuttle bus into the centre.

If you are travelling from any of the main English-speaking countries you will not need an **international licence** to drive in the UK, provided you can cope with manual-drive cars, and working the gears with your left hand. You will be driving on the left-hand side of the road in the UK, a custom that goes back to the old days when travellers held the reins of their horse in their right hand and walked beside on the left edge of the road.

Get valid **insurance** before you leave if you're bringing your own car and remember that seatbelts are compulsory, front and back. **Speed limits** are in miles per hour: 30mph in built-up areas; 60mph on main roads; 70mph on motorways. If you are stopped by the police, you can be asked to show your driving papers at a police station within 5 days. Familiarize yourself with the British Highway Code (available in newsagents) and take note of the strict drink-drive laws.

Car Rental Companies

Avis: **t** 0870 6060100. Lots of branches, including airports.

Hertz: **t** 08708 448844. Branches, including airports.

Alamo: **t** 0870 4004580. Branches, including airports.

Thrifty: **t** (01494) 751 500. Branches, including major airports except Stansted.

To **hire a car** in the UK you must be over 21 (or sometimes 23 or even 25) and have at least one years' driving experience; a valid credit card is often required too. It is best to pre-book for cheaper deals and to guarantee a car. The big car-hire firms have branches in the major airports. Basic hire cost usually includes unlimited mileage and insurance (with an excess of up to £600 on any loss or damage). Prices vary, but as a guideline for a week's car rental the main companies ask around £150 if you book early. This price goes down if you use a small, local firm, but aftercare (breakdown service, replacement car) may be less reliable if you travel out of the local area.

By Bike

Arm yourself with an Ordnace Survey (OS) map and a puncture repair kit and head out into the country's network of bridlepaths, disused railway lines, forest tracks, country lanes and towpaths. Once out of the vacuum-pack of your car, you start to notice the small things, and soon you'll feel sorry for anyone travelling over 30 miles per hour. The **National Cycle Network** is the flagship project of Sustrans (a charity that promotes sustainable transport) and provides 7,000 miles of cycle routes in the UK, which should be extended to 10,000 miles by 2005. About one-third of it is on paths free from motor traffic. Route maps are available from tourist information centres and cycle-hire shops. Some of the National Trails are suitable for bikes, including the Ridgeway and South Downs Way.

For **cycle hire**, see individual areas.

Sustrans Head Office: 35 King Street, Bristol BS1 4DZ, **t** (0117) 929 0888, *www.sustrans.org.uk*. Route maps, mileage and so on.

On Foot

The network of long-distance footpaths across England includes National Trails (routes selected by the Countryside Agency for the best walking) and routes developed by local authorities or individuals, like Wainwright's Coast-to-Coast Walk. They range from 10 to 600 miles. The **Long Distance Walkers'**

Special-interest Holidays

National Trust Holidays, 136–40 London Road, Leicester LE2 1EN, **t** 0870 010 6238. Page and Moy organize one themed tour for the National Trust called Great Houses and Gardens of England.

The Great Events Group, P.O. Box 120, Hereford HR4 8YB, **t** (01432) 830 083, *www.thegreateventsgroup.com*. Any number of Great Escapes including fast driving in Rockingham, Northamptonshire; shoe-making in London; steam-train driving on the Aylsham–Wroxham railway and hot-air ballooning.

Fishing Breaks, Islington, London, **t** (020) 7359 8818, *www.fishingbreaks.co.uk*. Fishing beats on rivers all over southern England for trout- and fly-fishing.

www.free-living.com. Complete listings of tour companies offering bird-watching holidays: click England, and a calendar of birding holidays with different companies appears.

HF Holidays, Imperial House, Edgware Road, London NW9 5AL, **t** (020) 8905 9558, *www.hfholidays.co.uk*. Range of guided walking and cycling holidays in classic countryside including Cotswolds, Lake District, Dartmoor, Yorkshire Dales and Exmoor. From your country-house hotel, you go off every day on a choice of walks. Special-interest holidays include Elgar, country dancing, fossil-hunting and fungi gathering.

Sherpa Expeditions, 131/a Heston Road, Hounslow TW5 ORF, **t** (020) 8577 2717, *www.sherpaexpeditions.com*. Self-guided bike rides in the Cotswolds, walks around the coastline of Britain, and inn-to-inn walks in the Lake District.

Naturetrek, Cheriton Mill, Cheriton, Alresford, Hampshire SO24 ONG, **t** (01962) 733 051, *www.naturetrek.co.uk*. Bird-watching and botanical holidays in Norfolk, the New Forest, Isles of Scilly and south coast.

PGL Activity Holidays, Alton Court, Penyard Lane, Ross-on-Wye, Herefordshire HR9 5GL, **t** 0870 050 7507, *www.pgl.co.uk*. While you are off travelling, check children into 3- or 7-night activity holidays in centres in Devon, Shropshire, Herefordshire and Surrey with golf, kayaking, circus skills, football and mountain biking on the agenda.

Cumbria Discoveries, Mickle Bower, Temple Sowerby, Penrith, Cumbria CA10 1RZ, **t** (01768) 362 201, *www.cumbria.com/cumbrian*. Driver-guided and walking tours in Cumbria, some of which draw on expertise of Blue Badge Guides.

Golf Vacations Ltd, First Floor, 39 Castle Street, Carlisle CA3 8SY, **t** (01228) 527 136, *www.golfvacationsuk.com* (**t** 1 888 209 4094 in USA and Canada). Self-drive or escorted golf packages around the UK, including the Royal Lytham St Anne's, Royal Liverpool and Royal Birkdale (as well as guaranteed tee-off times on the Old Course at St Andrews).

Dedham Hall, Brook Street, Dedham, **t** (01206) 323 027, *www.dedhamhall.demon.co.uk*. Painting holidays in beautiful country house in heart of Constable country, beside River Stour. Courses in watercolour, drawing, oils and Chinese brush painting, pastel, landscape painting and botanical drawing. Complex includes excellent restaurant.

Northumbria Horse Holidays, East Castle Stanley, Co Durham DH9 8PH, **t** (01207) 230 555, *www.dalehotel.freeserve.co.uk*. Seven-day trail riding, 5-day instructional, or long weekends horse riding at the Dale Hotel in Allendale, Northumbria.

Aldeburgh Cookery School, 84 High Street, Aldeburgh, Suffolk IP15 5AB, **t** (01728) 454 039, *www.aldeburghcookeryschool.com*. Long weekend courses include plenty of eating and drinking and some out-and-about time in pretty East Anglian seaside town of Aldeburgh.

The National Surfing Centre, Fistral Beach, Newquay, Cornwall, **t** (01673) 850 737, *www.nationalsurfingcentre.co.uk*. Professional coaches run surf courses for beginners and improvers, as well as workshops for longboarders, shortboarders and bodyboarders, and women only. *Easter–Nov*.

The Devonshire Arms, Bolton Abbey near Skipton, North Yorkshire, **t** (01756) 718 111, *www.devonshirehotels.co.uk*. Packages including fly-fishing for brown trout on River Wharfe.

Ston Easton Park Hotel, near Bath, Somerset, **t** (01761) 241 631, *www.stoneaston.co.uk*. Two-night stay between April and September includes tour of Victorian vegetable, flower and herb gardens and talk byhead gardener.

National Trails

Each trail has its own office. For general information and details of specific trail offices contact the **Countryside Agency**, **t** (01242) 521 381, *www.countryside.gov.uk/nationaltrails* or *www.nationaltrail.co.uk*. The *National Trails Guide* is published by Aurum Press.

Pennine Way (269 miles)
Hadrian's Wall Path (84 miles)
Cleveland Way (110 miles)
Wolds Way (79 miles)
Norfolk Coast Path (93 miles)
Offa's Dyke (168 miles)
Cotswold Way (100 miles)
Thames Path (180 miles)
Ridgeway (85 miles)
North Downs Way (153 miles)
South Downs Way (106 miles)
Southwest Coastal Path (600 miles)

Association (LDWA) produces a handbook (*LDWA Handbook*) featuring information on more than 500 of them. Some follow ancient or prehistoric trackways, such as the Ridgeway (85 miles) through the Berkshire Downs, and the Peddars Way, which incorporates a Roman Road through Breckland.

Coastal paths are some of the most satisfying to walk, but almost all paths follow landscape features, whether rivers, coastlines or ridgeways, or are in designated areas of outstanding natural beauty (AONBs).

The longest national trail, the Pennine Way (269 miles) takes 16 days on average, climbs 2,500 feet at Cross Fell and traverses the backbone of England through three national parks. Some of the trails link up, for example the Peddars Way and Norfolk Coast Path meet the Weavers Way and Angles Way to form a circuit of eastern Norfolk.

By Boat

There are more than 2,000 miles of canals, rivers and man-made waterways, built more than 200 years ago, to explore on narrow boats. Years of dereliction have been reversed by canal enthusiasts and charities devoted to getting the network up and running, with pristine lock gates, navigable tunnels and restored aqueducts. The main canal system stretches from the south of England to Ripon in the northeast and Wales in the west. The maximum speed on the canals is 4mph, roughly walking pace. This means you can cover about 20 miles a day maximum. Narrow boats are usually available to hire from March to late October. Prices are highest and queues for locks longest during the school summer holidays, mid-July to early September.

Canal Holidays

www.canaljunction.com lists all the hire companies, and gives information on canals and routes.

Leeds & Liverpool Canal: Pennine Cruisers, The Boat Shop, 19 Coach Street, Skipton, North Yorkshire, **t** (01756) 795 478.

Shropshire Union Canal: Chas Hardern Boats, Beeston Castle, Whard, Beeston, Tarporley, Cheshire, **t** (01829) 732 595.

Kennet & Avon Canal: Foxhangers Canal Holidays, Lower Foxhangers Farm, Devizes, Wiltshire, **t** (01380) 828 795.

Grand Union Canal and River Great Ouse: Nationwide Narrowboats, 86 Wingfield Road, Tebworth, Bedfordshire, **t** (01525) 874 335.

Oxford Canal and River Thames: College Cruisers, Combe Road Wharf, Oxford, **t** (01865) 554 343.

Practical A–Z

06

Art and Antiques

The ultimate souvenir of an English trip might be the *Conker-nosed Member for Little Snoozing-on-the-Wold and Winsome Beauty* by Gainsborough, or a Chippendale chair. Here's how to impress friends and horrify creditors.

Art

You could start your search for affordable contemporary English art on the internet: try *countereditions.com, eyestorm.com or britart.co.uk*. London remains the centre of the British art world. The traditional heart of the art gallery scene is **Cork Street and Soho** (W1), but the real action is now in **Brick Lane, Old Street, Hoxton and Whitechapel** (E1). Go to *newexhibitions.com* for a list of commercial galleries, with maps and exhibition details; the leaflet *Galleries* (published bi-monthly) contains the same information, and can be picked up free from listed galleries. Despite the hype about YBAs (Young British Artists), it's not all pickled cows (Damien Hirst) or unmade beds (Tracy Emin). If you're after Old Masters contact the **Society of London Art Dealers** (SLAD), 91 Jermyn Street, London SW1Y 6JB, **t** (020) 7930 6137. Not only serious collectors haunt Christies and Sotheby's auction houses, but the steep catalogue fee separates buyers from voyeurs. Outside London, many larger cities (Manchester, Liverpool) have thriving contemporary art scenes. St Ives is noted for its profusion of galleries, and many small towns boast a gallery selling high-quality art, often inspired by the local area.

Antiques Fairs

March

BADA Antiques and Fine Art Fair, Duke of York's Headquarters, Chelsea, London, *www.bada-antiques-fair.co.uk*

Olympia Spring Antiques and Fine Art Fair, Olympia Exhibition Centre, Hammersmith, London, *www.olympia-antiques.com*

June

The Grosvenor House Antiques and Fine Art Fair, Grosvenor House, Park Lane, London, *www.grosvenor-antiquesfair.co.uk*

Olympia Summer Antiques and Fine Art Fair, as spring fair, above.

September

Chelsea Antiques Fair, Chelsea Old Town Hall, Kings Road, London *www.penman-fairs.co.uk*

The Harrogate Antique Fair, Harrogate International Centre, Harrogate, Yorkshire, *www.harrogateantiquefair.com*

October

The Thames Valley Antique Dealers Association Autumn Fair, Radley College, Oxfordshire, *www.tvada.co.uk*

LAPADA Fair, Commonwealth Institute, Kensington, London, *www.lapadafair.co.uk*

Chester Antiques and Fine Art Show, County Grandstand, Chester Racecourse, Cheshire, *www.penman-fairs.co.uk*

Antiques

The rule of thumb for an 'antique' is that it must be at least 100 years old; moth-eaten teddy bears and prototype computers fall into the dimly related category of 'collectables'. The good news is that antique dealers cluster together; famous centres include London's Portobello Road, Petworth in Sussex, Woburn in Bedfordshire, the Cotswolds, Bath and Bradford on Avon, Long Melford in Suffolk and Harrogate in Yorkshire. Each antiques-rich area has its own association of dealers who put on exhibitions together. Many are also members of two national antique dealers' associations, based in London: **The Association of Art and Antique Dealers** (LAPADA), 535 King's Road, London SW10 OSZ, **t** (020) 7823 3511, *www.lapada.co.uk*; and **British Antiques Dealers Association** (BADA), 20 Rutland Gate, London SW7 1BD, **t** (020) 7589 4128, *www.bada.org* – which give you assurance that you are not taking home a white elephant. The buyers' bible is *The Guide to the Antique Shops of Great Britain*, published annually by **Antique Collectors' Club**, **t** (01394) 385 501, *www.antique-acc.com*; it also lists auctioneers, trade associations and shipping agents; *www.antiquesandfineart.com* has an inventory of dealers according to specialism and area. A fun way to hunt is at antiques fairs, which spare you the legwork by bringing traders together under one roof.

Children

When you've exhausted beaches, walks and ruined castles, you'll be relieved to find that England's cultural attractions are peppered with interactive exhibits for children. Children pay less almost everywhere, and you can often get family deals – but bring proof of age if your teenagers are tall or hairy. Hotels, pubs and restaurants have always been the sticking point, but things are improving. The shift from smoky, man's boozer to smokeless, family pub-restaurant is near complete; segregation of bars and dining rooms ensures that the innocence of under 15s is preserved and the law upheld. The Whitbread and Harvester chains trade on child-friendliness, with children's menus and play areas. However some traditional pubs still take pride in excluding anyone who can't down a pint. Convivial family eating is not as customary in England as it is in Italy, Spain or Greece; for every restaurant that openly welcomes children with high chairs and smiles there will be another that barely tolerates the noise and mess, with pursed lips. Seaside resorts are the most accommodating, but few English hotels yet provide cots, extra beds or bottle-warming facilities.

Countryside Code

Guard against risk of fire.
Fasten all gates.
Keep dogs under close control.
Keep to public footpaths across farmland, using gates and stiles to cross fences, hedges and walls.
Leave livestock, crops and machinery alone.
Take your litter home.
Don't remove any wildlife, plants and trees.
Don't make unnecessary noise.
Don't leave valuables in your car.
Don't take souvenirs of ancient monuments.

Disabled Travellers

Travellers with disabilities are well catered for nowadays, but difficulties do still arise because of the age of the infrastructure, including hotels, attractions and transport. For help and advice contact **RADAR**, a mine of information. It publishes an annual guide, *Holidays in Britain & Ireland – A Guide for Disabled People*, with advice on transport and accommodation; much of the information is also online. As a rule, they advise newer, purpose-built hotels that have had to comply with modern building regulations regarding accessibility, which often means staying in blandly reliable chains like Travelodge, Travel Inn, Formula One, Ibis or Holiday Inn.
The Tourist Board's official accommodation guide also provides a list of places to stay geared towards disabled people.

Organizations for Disabled Travellers

RADAR (Royal Association for Disability and Rehabilitation), 12 City Forum, 250 City Road, London EC1V 8AF, **t** (020) 7250 3222, *www.radar.org.uk*

Holiday Care, **t** 0845 1249971, *www.holiday-care.org.uk*. Advice on accommodation and transport. Works with the tourist boards.

Tripscope, **t** 08457 585641, *www.tripscope.org.uk*. Information and advice on transport for disabled and elderly people.

Disabled Living Foundation, **t** (020) 7289 6111. Information on disability equipment.

Good Access Guide, Avionics House, Naas Lane, Quedgeley, Gloucester, **t** 0870 2416129, *www.goodaccessguide.co.uk*. Information on leisure, lifestyle and holidays in the UK.

Wheelchair Travel, 1 Johnston Green, Guildford, Surrey GU2 6XS, **t** (01483) 233 640. Hires self-drive adapted cars and can also arrange guides and drivers.

SATH (Society for Accessible Travel and Hospitality), 347 Fifth Ave, Suite 610, New York, NY 10016, **t** (212) 447 7284. Access information and resources before you set off.

National Trust 'Access for All' Department, P.O. Box 39, Bromley, Kent BR1 3XL, **t** (020) 7222 9251, *www.nationaltrust.org*

English Heritage Customer Services, P.O. Box 570, Swindon, SN2 2UR, **t** 0870 3331181, *customers@english-heritage.org.uk*

Websites for Disabled Travellers

www.disabledholidaydirectory.co.uk for self-catering properties and hotels.

www.abletogo.com for hotels, motels, guest-houses, self-catering and caravans.

www.motability.co.uk for a range of schemes for disabled people to contract hire cars.

Trains and planes are supposed to provide practical help for wheelchair users or anyone who needs help getting on and off. Phone the airline or train operating company in advance to find out exactly what help you can get, and book it. Ryanair is the only airline to charge for wheelchair use – part of its zero-frills service. If you are travelling by train, you may have to get between London stations, which you can do by bus (no. 205 runs from Paddington to Whitechapel, stopping at Marylebone, Euston and King's Cross; no. 705 runs from Liverpool Street to Paddington via Waterloo), which is not ideal, or expensive taxi. Phone **London Travel Information**, **t** (020) 7222 1234, for advice. Coach travel is virtually impossible for wheelchair users.

The **National Trust** publishes an annual booklet, *Information for Visitors with Disabilities*, with details of accessibility. **English Heritage** produces a similar *Access Guide*. Phone private attractions for details.

Disease

In 2001 Foot and Mouth disease decimated herds of sheep and cows, bankrupting farmers and devastating the tourist industry. As foot-paths closed, national parks, including the Lake District and Dartmoor, became bereft of visitors. Britain was officially declared free of Foot and Mouth on 15 January 2002.

Eating Out

For general information on food, drink and English eating habits, *see* pp.43–8.

In this book, prices quoted for a meal are for two courses (a main course and either a starter or dessert) not including drinks. We have divided prices into categories (*see* below). Many restaurants offer good-value set menus, especially at lunchtime. Always ask. Most restaurants open for lunch and dinner. Some stay open all day, especially at weekends.

Restaurant Price Categories

very expensive cost no object
expensive £30–50
moderate £15–30
cheap under £15

Electricity

The current is 250 volts AC, so you need a converter for US appliances. Wall sockets take uniquely British three-pin (square) fused plugs, so you will need a plug adaptor too. You can pick them up quite cheaply at airports, department stores and some chemists.

Embassies and Consulates

Australian High Commission, Australia House, Strand, London WC2B 4LA, **t** (020) 7379 4334, *www.australia.org.uk*

Canadian High Commission, 1 Grosvenor Square, London W1K 4AA, **t** (020) 7258 6600, *www.canada.org.uk*

Republic of Ireland Embassy, 17 Grosvenor Place, London SW1X 7HR, **t** (020) 7245 9033.

New Zealand High Commission, New Zealand House, Haymarket, London SW1Y 4TQ, **t** (020) 7930 8422, *www.nzembassy.com*

US Embassy, 24 Grosvenor Square, London W1A 1AE, **t** (020) 7499 9000, *www.usembassy.org.uk*

Emergencies

The UK emergency telephone number is 999; an emergency operator will put you through to police, fire, ambulance, coastguard, mountain rescue or cave rescue (the last two via the police). The European emergency number, 112, works in the UK too. Carry a mobile phone on long walks.

For **vehicle breakdowns**, check with your car-hire firm if the roadside recovery policy is with the AA, **t** 0870 5448866, or RAC, **t** 0870 5722722. Call the rental company if you are going to need a new car.

Health and Insurance

If you injure yourself, you will be seen for free in a hospital Accident and Emergency department, but prepare for a long wait. If it's not urgent, ask at your hotel to find a doctor. European nationals are eligible for free medical treatment if they bring an E111 form, and Australians and New Zealanders may also benefit from reciprocal arrangements. To find out more about what you may be entitled to, go to *www.doh.gov.uk/overseasvisitors*.

Anyone else is advised to take out travel insurance, or check if you are covered by your credit card or home policy. All travellers will still need cover for baggage loss, cancellations and so on. Keep two copies of your policy in separate places, lest your luggage disappears, and hang on to any receipts.

IAMAT (International Association for Medical Assistance to Travellers), 417 Center Street, Lewiston, NY 14092, **t** (716) 754 4883. Can advise on health risks around world.

Maps

Ordnance Survey has been producing small-scale, accurate maps of Britain since the Napoleonic Wars, when it was necessary to know the south coast like the back of an Englishman's hand to defend it from invasion. The defence ministry published the first map of Kent in 1801, closely followed by another of Essex. Now Ordnance Survey publishes high-quality leisure maps. The *Explorer 1:25,000* series (4cm to 1km or 2.5 inches to 1 mile) is the most detailed for walkers, off-road cyclists and horse riders. It shows places of interest, rights of way and camping sites. The Landranger 1:50,000 series is still small-scale but not detailed enough to entirely depend upon for orienteering, say in a Dartmoor mist. An excellent source of maps is **Stanfords**, 12–14 Long Acre, London, WC2 9LP, **t** (020) 7836 1321. Otherwise you can pick masp up locally.

Media

Newspapers

British newspapers have a mixed reputation, for quality journalism and sensationalism. They fall into two categories, broadsheets and tabloids, describing their format but also indicative of the type of journalism – the former are regarded as serious, the latter as trashy, although the boundaries may sometimes be blurred. The best-known broadsheet is the *Times*, also known as The Thunderer, once the British Establishment's paper of record. It still aims to be politically neutral and is highly regarded for the quality of its editorial and columnists, but many would contend that it went downhill when Rupert Murdoch took it over, relieving the editor of much of his independence. The *Independent* stepped into the breach, with mixed success. The left-leaning *Guardian*, favoured by young metropolitans, is known for its coverage of the arts. The right-leaning *Telegraph* has an excellent sports section. The middle-brow *Daily Mail* and *Daily Express* offer a mixture of serious journalism, right-wing opinion columns, and a variety of showbiz and gossip stories. The red-top tabloids – the *Sun*, *Mirror* and *Daily Star* – are known for their celebrity content and gung-ho nationalism; foreigners may be shocked by the *Sun*'s page 3 girls. These papers sell in vast numbers and are surprisingly influential. Local papers are often high quality and especially good for local listings and events. Some to look out for include the *Manchester Guardian*, the *Birmingham Post* and the *Liverpool Echo*.

Distinctly British political magazines include the *Spectator* (right of centre) and the *New Statesman* (left of centre), which offer in-depth analysis and columnists. The *Week* (mainly subscriptions) provides an excellent roundup of the press each week. Alternatively, *Private Eye* provides a fortnightly satirical view of Britain, from parliament and local government to the arts and media; it often unearths the worst cases of corruption and hypocrisy.

TV and Radio

Although satellite and cable have proliferated over the last few years, most households still rely on terrestrial networks for their entertainment. The two public service channels, **BBC1** and **BBC2** also have a remit to educate and inform, although you wouldn't always know it. **ITV** is lowest-common-denominator broadcasting, while **Channel 4** is meant to cater especially for ethnic and other minorities – which bizarrely translates into lots of shows involving sex. No one knew what to do with **Channel 5**, and not many people watch it either. BBC1 has **news programmes** at 1pm and 6pm (undemanding for families), and a more substantial news at 10pm. ITV news at 6.30 and 10.30 is largely infotainment. The best news is on Channel 4 at 7pm; lasting an hour, it provides some analysis and context.

Newsnight at 10.30pm on BBC2 often stirs up controversy, with presenter Jeremy Paxman needling top politicians.

The BBC dominates the airwaves too: **Radio 1** is pop, **Radio 2** adult easy listening, **Radio 3** classical and **Radio 4** the favoured talk radio of the chattering classes. Radio 4's morning news programme, *Today* (6–9am), sets the national news agenda, although the constant interruption of guests by the presenters is legendary.

Money and Banks

Currency

While the rest of Europe is now happily bartering the euro, British euro-phobia means that currency still comes in pounds (sterling) and pence, with a hundred pennies to one pound, 2, 5, 10, 20 and 50 pence pieces, and £1 and £2 coins. A pint of milk will cost you about 70p, a pint of beer about £2.50, an off-peak return train ticket from London to York about £65, a filled sandwich from £2 to £5, a desk-top computer roughly £1,000, and an average three-bedroom house in the Southeast around £190,000. At the time of writing one dollar will buy you 61p and one euro will buy you 69p; put the other way around, one pound is worth 1.58 dollars and 1.38 euros, but of course foreign exchange rates fluctuate wildly. Shop around for the best rates in banks and bureaux de change: the worst rates tends to be hotels, followed by bureaux de change in tourist areas, at airports and ferry terminals. Banks usually offer a slightly better rate. Always check the commission fee.

Cash and Credit Cards

If you are travelling from abroad, bring enough cash to get you to your first stop. Travellers' cheques remain the most secure means of carrying money around, but these days you can use credit and debit cards just about anywhere.

ATM machines abound in airports, towns and cities, allowing you to draw out money in local currency with your card. Some cards exact a fee for the currency conversion. Visa and MasterCard/Access are widely accepted in hotels, restaurants and shops; American Express and Diners Club slightly less so. If the Sirrus or Maestro logo appears both on your card and the ATM machine, you can make international transactions from your home account. If you lose your credit card, a new one can be issued, but never quickly enough.

Travellers' Cheques

Travellers' cheques, on the other hand, can be replaced within 24 hours if they are lost or stolen, providing you keep a separate record of the cheque numbers. The main brands of cheques (American Express, Visa and Thomas Cook) are accepted by banks and bureaux de changes, but not usually in shops.

American Express Foreign Exchange Bureau, 30–31 Haymarket, London W1, **t** (020) 7484 9610. *Open Mon–Sat 9–6, Sun 10–5*. Also 7 Wilton Road, Victoria, London SW1, **t** (020) 7630 6365; Whiteley's Shopping Centre, Queensway, London W2, **t** (020) 7221 7190.

Thomas Cook, 1 Marble Arch, London W1, **t** (020) 7530 7100. Thomas Cook travellers' cheques can be exchanged at Thomas Cook branches anywhere commission-free.

Banks

Opening hours are usually Mon–Fri 9–4.30, although larger banks may stay open until 5pm and small-town banks may close at 3pm. Some banks open on Saturday mornings, but usually just to sell you a mortgage.

Tipping

If there is a relaxed etiquette for tipping in England, English people have yet to master it. You would usually tip about 10–15 percent of the price of the meal in a restaurant where there is table service and your waiter or waitress has been attentive. Taxi drivers, porters, hairdressers and tour guides might expect a little something, but don't feel obliged unless they are particularly deserving.

Packing

Don't forget that the English weather is changeable, even in summer. Your best bet is to pack lots of layers, which can be peeled off should there be a heatwave or piled on when temperatures plummet. Bring a couple of jerseys even in summer. Jeans-weight trousers or skirts should do you all year, but you might want to pack shorts and T-shirts or a light dress in summer. A waterproof jacket is a year-round necessity; in winter you'll need a coat. Always pack at least two pairs of shoes, and make sure one is good for walking. You'll only need smart clothes if you plan to stay in very grand hotels and eat in the classiest of restaurants (even then smart casual would do), or to attend a posh event such as Glyndebourne or Ascot. Launderettes are everywhere, and the more upmarket hotels have their own laundry services, so it's easy to get cleaned up.

The only accessory worth packing is a pair of **binoculars**. They come in handy not only for spotting wildlife, but also for admiring high ornate roof bosses and winged angels in churches and for reading road signs that you have passed in the car, saving you the trouble of reversing or getting out on a busy road.

Pets

You can bring a dog or cat into Britain from the USA, Canada and some European countries under the **Pet Travel Scheme** (PETS) without quarantine on certain approved airlines, sea and rail crossings providing they have been micro-chipped and vaccinated, and had a blood test at least six months before travelling. For more information contact the **Pet Travel Scheme Helpline**, Department for Environment, Food and Rural Affairs, Area 201, 1/a Page Street, London SW1P 4PQ, **t** 0870 241 1710, *www.defra.gov.uk*. Ask your airline about the specifics of pet transport. The majority of hotels don't welcome pets, but farmhouse B&Bs may accommodate well-behaved dogs, who are also allowed in most pubs.

Post Offices

The short-lived rebranding of the Royal Mail as Consignia appeared to herald the beginning of the end for a much-loved and once famously efficient national institution. These days, it's a pleasant surprise if a first-class letter arrives the next day (once this was the norm, and if it didn't come with the first post before breakfast it would be delivered later in the day); post offices are shabby and there are often queues. However the service battles on in the face of competition from email and courier companies. Main post offices provide a dizzying array of services on top of letter and parcel post, including currency exchange; sub-post offices often sit at the back of a corner shop. A first-class stamp currently costs 28p and is allowed six days travel time before it's given up for lost. A second-class stamp costs 20p and delivery takes three to 10 working days. Special Delivery guarantees next-working-day delivery, but someone has to be in to sign for the parcel or it gets dumped at a depot miles away. Recorded delivery can take any number of days, as long as it's signed for. Delivery of letters or parcels to the USA, Canada, Australia or New Zealand by air mail takes about 5 days. You can get mail sent Poste Restante to any post office in the UK and pick it up with some form of identity.

Post offices are open Mon–Fri 9–5.30, Sat 9–12.30. Sub-post offices often close on Wed at 1pm. For information about services call **t** 0845 7223344 or go to *www.royalmail,com.*

Public Holidays

January: New Year's Day (1st)
March/April: Good Friday and Easter Monday
May: May Day (1st Mon); Spring Holiday (last Mon)
August: Late Summer Bank Holiday (last Mon)
December: Christmas Day (25th) and Boxing Day (26th)

Shopping

Once upon a time rural crafts relied on locally available raw materials: Devon, the Midlands and Poole were known for pottery; the Somerset Levels for basket-making; the Weald of Kent and Sussex for trug-making and so on. The demise of many traditional crafts with the Industrial Revolution was remedied by the middle-class artisans of the Arts and Crafts movement; these days every rural area supports a mixture of craftspeople, especially the West Country. Two books might help in a quest for crafts: *Craftworkers Year Book*, Write Angle Press, 16 Holm Oak Drive, Madeley, Crewe CW3 9HR, **t** (01782) 750 986, for a diary of craft fairs; or *Craft Galleries Guide*, BCF Books, *www.bcfbooks.co.uk*.

For details of craft guilds and contemporary makers, contact **The Craft Council Resource Centre**, 44/a Pentonville Road, Islington,

London N1 9BY, **t** (020) 7806 2501, *www.craftscouncil.org.uk*, or **The Rural Crafts Association**, Heights Cottages, Brook Road, Wormley, Surrey GU8 5UA, **t** (01428) 682 292.

For **glass**, try Dartington Crystal in Torrington, North Devon, or the Barbican Glass Centre in Plymouth. Dudley, in the West Midlands, still boasts its Crystal Mile. The National Glass Centre in Sunderland has a shop too. In the Lake District you will find Adrian Sankey's hand-blown glass in Ambleside, and the Lakes Glass Centre in Ulverston

The Stoke-on-Trent **porcelain** manufacturers (Wedgwood, Spode and Royal Dalton) all have shops selling their wares, as does Royal Worcester. Small potteries, like Winchcombe in the Cotswolds, Muchelney in Somerset, and David Leach's pottery in Bovey Tracy welcome visitors, as do the craft potters of North Devon.

The historic centre for **jewellery** retail is Birmingham's Jewellery Quarter. The rare Blue John stone still supports a small trinket trade in Castleton in the Peak District, while Whitby in Yorkshire is still the centre for jet jewellery.

Basket-making still goes on in the Somerset Levels around Bridgwater, where the withy or willow beds provide the raw material. The **Willows and Wetland Visitor Centre** in Stoke St Gregory, **t** (01823) 490 249, sells wicker baskets and furniture.

Opening Hours

Most shops are open Mon–Sat 9.30–5.30 and Sun 11–4. Many city supermarkets stay open until 8pm or later (some are open 24 hours), although Sunday opening is restricted by law to six hours (generally 10–4). Petrol stations remain open long hours (often all night except in rural areas), and also sell necessities such as milk and toiletries. London has late opening on Thursday eves (until 8pm).

Sports

To participate in any sports or outdoor activities in England contact **Sport England**, **t** (020) 8778 8600, *www.sportengland.org*, who will put you in touch with the relevant body: the **British Canoe Union** (*www.bcu.org.uk*), **British Mountaineering Council** (*www.thebmc.co.uk*), **British Horse Society** (*www.bhs.org.uk*) and **Royal Yachting Association** (*www.rya.org.uk*) are a few. Other information sources for outdoor activities include the **British Activity Holiday Association, t** (01932) 252 994, *www.baha.org.uk*, the **Association of National Parks**, *www.anpa.gov.uk*, **Forestry Commission**, **t** (0131) 314 6100, *www.forestry.gov.uk* and **RSPB, t** (01767) 681 577, *www.rspb.org.uk*.

If you prefer to watch, read on. For the big annual sporting jamborees, *see* also 'The English Season', pp.37–41.

Cricket

The sound of leather on willow on a village green is traditional England at its most dreamy. It might well be a highlight of your trip to go and see a **county game** (just turn up), or better still one of the **Test matches**. The five-day Tests take place at The Oval or Lords in London, Edgbaston in Birmingham, Trent Bridge in Nottinghamshire, Headingley in Leeds, Old Trafford in Manchester or Chester-le-Street in County Durham (tickets in advance from the grounds). Contact the **England Cricket Board, t** (020) 7432 1200, *www.ecb.co.uk*, for more information.

Football

Otherwise known as soccer, this is England's most popular sport. It's played in the autumn, winter and spring months, with a brief respite in summer. The rules are simple (once you've mastered the offside rule) leaving spectators free to concentrate on the celebrity players, who change clubs for millions of pounds and have lifestyles to show it. **Premiership** games are where you get to see the stars, but tickets are expensive. In London, the best-known clubs are Arsenal and Chelsea, while outside the capital Manchester United, Liverpool, Everton and Newcastle United are currently top of the league. If you're more interested in the game than the stars, the **First and Second Division matches** are great entertainment on a Saturday afternoon, and there are mid-week matches too. Go to *www.premierleague.com* or *www.football-league.co.uk* for information, or contact clubs directly.

Golf

In 1608 golf came down from Scotland to England, where the mild weather and landscapes are ideally suited to the game. There are hundreds of golf courses, with strict dress codes and exclusive membership policies. Few of the best courses, and none of the most prestigious, allow buggies (carts), and caddies are rarely on offer. Course fees vary for visitors and there may be a maximum handicap allowed, so check with the club.

There are three main centres of golfing excellence in England: the Lancashire coast, the Home Counties west of London, and the south coast. Then there is The Belfry in the West Midlands, a Ryder Cup venue.

Lancashire's top seaside links courses boast **Royal Lytham St Anne's**, one of the oldest in the British Isles; **Royal Birkdale**, with its flat fairways and devilish sand dunes; the Championship course at **Formby**; and **Hillside**, with its natural hazards and strong winds. The south coast links courses have challenged the world's finest golfers: **Royal St George's** is the best known, having hosted the Open 12 times. Park and heathland courses west of London include **Sunningdale**, the snootiest in England; the Championship courses of **Walton Heath** and **Wentworth**; and **Stoke Poges**, which features in two James Bond films, *Tomorrow Never Dies* and *Goldfinger*.

Hockey

The national hockey league has three divisions, Premier, Division One and Division Two. The big club sides are Cannock, Reading, Canterbury, Chelmsford, Southgate and Loughborough. Sadly, the national hockey stadium at Milton Keynes has been taken over by Wimbledon FC, leaving the game homeless.

Horse-racing

Founded in 1711 by Queen Anne, **Ascot** is Britain's most famous racecourse. **Ascot Racecourse**, Ascot, Berkshire, **t** (01344) 622 211.

Newmarket is the headquarters of British racing. There are two courses: the **Rowley Mile** features Sagitta 1000 and 200 Guineas in early May and Champions' Day in October. The **July Course** hosts six summer evening fixtures followed by entertainments. The Racecourse, Westfield House, The Links, Newmarket, Suffolk, **t** (01638) 663 482.

The three-day May meeting and Sunday fixtures in August attract huge crowds to the old race course at **Chester**. You can even watch from the Roman Walls. The Racecourse, Chester, Cheshire, **t** (01244) 304 600.

Cheltenham is the home of national hunt racing; the highlight is the three-day national hunt festival in March with 10 Championship events including the Cheltenham Gold Cup and Champion Hurdle. The Racecourse, Prestbury Park, Cheltenham, Gloucestershire, **t** (01242) 513 014, *www.cheltenham.co.uk*.

The **Epsom Derby** on Epsom Downs is one of the best-known flat races in the world. There are also four evening fixtures followed by music. The Racecourse, Epsom Downs, Epsom, Surrey, **t** (01372) 726 311.

Polo

The polo season takes place from May to September with the High Goal season in June and July. The rules of polo are even more complex than those of cricket. The sides have four players, who each have handicaps from minus two to a perfect 10. Polo games are ranked High, Medium or Low Goal, referring to the combined handicap of the team. A High Goal game lasts six chukkas, Medium Goal five chukkas and Low Goal four chukkas: a 'chukka' is 7 minutes, at the end of which players have a 3-minute interval to change horses. Teams change ends after every goal, and there is a short half-time for the crowds to rush on and tread in the divets. There are five main (High Goal) contests in the polo calendar: the **Prince of Wales Trophy** at the Royal County of Berkshire Polo Club, the **Queen's Cup** at Guard's Polo Club in Windsor Great Park, the **Warwickshire Cup** at the Cirencester Park Polo Club, and the **Cowdray Park Gold Cup British Open Championship** at the Cowdray Park Polo Club in Midhurst. The **Coronation Cup** is a one-off international match at Cowdray on the fourth Sunday of July. For tickets contact the clubs, for information the **Hurlingham Polo Association**, **t** (01367) 242 828.

Rowing

The best-known event in the rowing calendar is the **Boat Race** between Oxford and Cambridge universities, which takes place the Saturday before Easter on the River Thames. The 149th meeting in 2003 was won by the Dark Blue Oxford crew, who edged in by a foot. The best viewpoints for the 4-mile course from Putney Bridge to Chiswick Bridge are: Putney Bridge, Putney Embankment and Bishops Park (for the start); Hammersmith and Barnes (mid-course); Dukes Meadows and Chiswick Bridge (for the finish). Riverside pubs get very jolly (and packed) on the day. Go to *www.theboatrace.com* for more details.

The first varsity boat race took place in 1829 at Henley-on-Thames in Oxfordshire, now the venue for the annual Henley Royal Regatta (*see* p.39).

Rugby League

The question of pay for players missing work for matches split the RFU in 1895. The new Northern Rugby Football Union – until recently the sole professional union – also abolished line-outs, rucks and malls and reduced teams from 15 to 13 to make the game faster and more exciting to spectators. In 1922 the NRFU changed its name to the **Rugby Football League**, although at the top level it is still played only in the north of England, with the exception of the London Broncos. There are 12 clubs in the **Super League**, including St Helens, Bradford Bulls, Wigan Warriors, Leeds Rhinos, Widnes, Halifax and Hull. Games take place between February and October, climaxing with the Grand Final at Old Trafford on 18 October. The **PowerGen Challenge Cup** is the knock-out competition. Main international tournaments are the **Ashes** between Great Britain and Australia in November, and the **Tri Nations** between Australia, New Zealand and Great Britain in autumn. For international and league games call **t** 0870 9901313, or the RFL, **t** (0113) 232 9222, *www.rfl.uk.com*.

Rugby Union

Rugby Football in England is associated with grammar schools and public schools, which encourage fiercely competitive rivalry. Twickenham is the home of national rugby union, including the **Six Nations** tournament and the **Middlesex Sevens,** played in August and accompanied by a mass orgy of picnics in the car park. The **Premier League** has about 12 big teams including Harlequins, London Irish, Leicester, Wasps, Gloucester and Bath, whose matches are titanic clashes in the mud and rain with tribal followings. Go to the Rugby Football Union website for tickets, *www.rfu.com*. Tickets for international fixtures are largely distributed through the RFU's member clubs, otherwise try Twickenham's ticket line, **t** 0870 902 0000, or *www.ticketmaster.co.uk*.

Surfing

The **British Surfing Association, t** (01637) 876 474, *www.bsa.org.uk*, produces a calendar of events for the year. The major dates are the **Newquay Open** in late May, **South Coast Challenge** in Challaborough, South Devon in late October, the **North East Open** in Cayton in Yorkshire in early November and the **North Devon Open** in Croyde, North Devon, in early November. If you want to ride the waves yourself, *www.britsurf.org* has links to surfing organizations and clubs, and details of surf schools, boards, shops and wetsuits.

Tennis

The hub of the grass court season (late May to July) is England, climaxing at the **Lawn Tennis Championships** at **Wimbledon**, one of four international Grand Slam tournaments (along with the French Open, US Open and Australian Open). Two outdoor grass court tournaments lead up to Wimbledon: the men's **Stella Artois Championship** at Queen's Club London takes place two weeks before the start of Wimbledon, *www.stellaartoistennis.com*. A women's grass court tournament is held at Eastbourne at the same time. The **Samsung Open** takes place in Nottingham the week before Wimbledon, at the City of Nottingham Tennis Centre, University Boulevard, Nottingham, **t** (0115) 915 0000. Founded in 1877, Wimbledon is a classic English event, often disrupted by rain. It starts six weeks before the first Monday in August and lasts a fortnight. Tickets are sold through tennis clubs and schools affiliated to the Lawn Tennis Association, by public ballot, or by queueing on the day. To apply for tickets send an SAE to The All England Lawn Tennis & Croquet Club, P.O. Box 98, Wimbledon, London SW19 5AE (overseas applicants should send a self-addressed envelope with an International Reply Coupon instead of a stamp) by the end of the year before. Successful applicants will be informed by February. You can still buy tickets on the day, but you will have to queue. For details go to *www.wimbledon.org*, or call **AELTC, t** (020) 8971 2473 or the **Lawn Tennis Association, t** (020) 7381 7000.

Telephone and Internet

England has embraced the internet despite the reluctance of phone companies to provide cheap, fast access; it's a great place to research flights, train timetables, hotels, self-catering accommodation and special events.

You will find an internet café in most towns, or you may be able to log on at public libraries. Some hotels have internet facilities too.

Now that mobile phones are ubiquitous, payphones are being phased out; if you have a mobile, see if you can replace your SIM card with a local pay-as-you-go card for your stay (or pay extortionate international call charges). Payphone calls cost a minimum of 20p for local calls, more for long-distance and international calls; phone cards can be bought from any newsagent for £5 or £10. If you plan to make lots of calls home or abroad, it's worth getting a Onetel phone card for cheap rates; go to *www.onetel.com* for detail. Calls from hotel phones are always expensive.

Directory enquiries: 118500 (British Telecom) 118118, 118888 or 118000.

International directory enquiries: 118505 (British Telecom).

Operator: 100.

Emergency services: 999 or 112

Time

Greenwich Mean Time (GMT) is the local time of the prime meridian or zero degrees longitude, which passes through Greenwich in London. It remains constant; from it standard times around the globe are measured. British Summer Time runs from the end of March to the end of October; clocks are put forward one hour ahead of GMT to make the most of daylight hours. It wasn't so long ago that England was carved into time zones. The clock of Tom Tower in Christchurch College is still 5 minutes behind GMT, marking Oxford Time.

Tourist Information

Since 1 April 2003, England has a new tourist information service: **VisitBritain**. Contact the **Britain and London Visitor Centre**, 1 Regent Street, **t** (020) 8846 9000, *www.visitbritain.com*, or one of the 560 tourist information centres in English cities, towns and villages. They can give good up-to-date information on places to visit, events, where to stay and eat, and local transport. They also sell maps, guides and entertainment tickets, and can book your accommodation on arrival or in advance. Frustratingly, assistants are sworn to impartiality; only a few are prepared to break the rules and tell you their favourite restaurant or beach. National Park information centres can give specific advice on walking in the parks.

Tourist Information Centres Abroad

Australia: British Tourist Authority, Level 2, 15 Blue Street, North Sydney, NSW 2060, **t** (01300) 858 589, *www.visitbritain.com.au*

Canada: British Tourist Authority, 5915 Airport Road, Suite 120, Mississauga, Ontario L4V 1T1, **t** 1 888 VISIT UK, *www.visitbritain.com/ca*

USA: British Tourist Authority, 551 Fifth Avenue, Suite 701, New York, NY 10176-0799, **t** 1 800 462 2748, *www.visitbritain.com/usa*; 625 North Michigan Avenue, Suite 1001, Chicago IL 606111, **t** 1 800 462 2748.

Weather and Climate

On the one hand, Britain's latitude is Arctic, and on the other the island is warmed by the Gulf Stream that carries warm water from the Gulf of Mexico across the Atlantic. Where these extremes collide you get the endlessly changeable British weather, the natural enemy of barbecues and music festivals. Unpack your kite and the wind will drop; plant your tomatoes and it won't rain for a month; put on your swimming togs and a cloud goes over the sun. And just when you are getting used to the drizzle, along comes a hurricane, flood or heatwave. Such severe weather is seen by the natives as evidence of cosmic displeasure, a tradition that goes back to the time of Bede, who announced the arrival of the Vikings with a worsening of the weather.

It's no surprise, then, that the weather is the Englishman's favourite conversational gambit; it's an apparently neutral topic that opens up limitless conversational possibilities, a perfect marriage of national and natural temperaments. In general, the south coast is the sunniest part of England and the mountains of the west and north the dullest. The Lake District is wettest, followed by the Pennines and the West Country; East Anglia, the Midlands and eastern England are driest. The north coasts of Devon and Cornwall are windiest, but wind speeds increase with height so the strongest winds are on top of the Lakeland fells. The average temperature is 8.5 to 11 degrees Celsius, with the highest temperatures on the Cornish coast (where palm trees grow). July is the warmest month, and it may snow between December and March on the uplands.

Where to Stay

Confine yourself to the mustier guesthouses lining every A-road, and England seems a sad place. Seek out the abundance of charming places to stay and England warms up. On offer are a variety of places to stay, from medieval pilgrim inns and hospices to rustic cottages buried in wisteria, white-painted Victorian seafront hotels, elegant 18th-century merchants' houses, assorted barns, windmills, chapels, lighthouses and castles, country pubs and farmhouses, family homes full of clutter and home-cooking smells, and a mass of bay-windowed townhouses.

Of those approved by the Tourist Board, standards range from functional – 'here's your key, breakfast's at 8' – to gorgeous and/or luxurious. The board, in common with the AA and RAC, uses a 1–5 rating scheme: stars for hotels and diamonds for guesthouses, inns, farmhouses and bed and breakfasts. They slap gold and silver awards on anywhere outstanding. Small 5-diamond guesthouses do not offer the same service as 5-star hotel – don't expect liveried flunkies and 24-hour room service in your B&B. The rating system works well for hotels, hostels, camping and caravan sites, but less well for guesthouses and B&Bs because it rewards facilities to the detriment of the charm that makes guests feel lucky. This partly explains the number of L-shaped bedrooms with the obligatory bathroom squeezed into the corners. Not all properties put themselves up for inspection.

At the beginning of each section of this book there is a list of recommended places to stay. All of them have something special, whether it is a warm welcome, architecture, the character of the rooms, the garden or proximity to the main tourist attraction – or all of the above. The worst of the anonymous chain hotels, creepy roadside motels and jaded B&Bs have been avoided, but not every place is brimming with delightful places to stay. In some instances the rum old establishments of the town have been avoided and a crop of lovely B&Bs, inns and farmhouses found in the surrounding countryside. In all cases, you will be spared the desire to high-tail it back to the car or train station on first stepping through the front door. 'Friendly' is the first pre-requisite for this book.

Booking

There are large numbers of contract workers, sales people, visiting relatives, stand-up comedians and guide-book writers booking rooms all around the country at all times of year. Always book in advance to avoid trouble or disappointment. It is a depressing business working your way down a dwindling list of phone numbers from the train or car and finding that each one in turn is full. If you exhaust the lists in this book, contact the tourist information centres, who will give you another clutch of phone numbers and often make a reservation for you for a small fee. If all else fails, it is not bad manners to ask B&Bs for recommendations; you will soon find yourself being passed from one helpful voice to another, all demanding you call back if you don't have any luck; eventually you always do.

Prices

Prices in this book have been divided into five categories, from cheap to luxury (*see* box). The prices quoted are for a full-price double room with bath, where there is one. Hotels, as a rule, are overpriced in England; what you pay is often only distantly related to the quality of service you get in return. However many hotels do deals out of season, midweek or at

Hotel Price Categories

luxury over £180
very expensive £135–£180
expensive £90–£135
moderate £45–£90
cheap under £45

weekends, if you stay for more than one night or if dinner is included. Don't be put off by the rack rate; try subtle negotiation.

Hotels

The luxury hotels are fabulous properties including country houses, castles and swanky city-centre hotels with beautifully furnished public rooms and bedrooms with character. Some are set in gorgeous gardens; all have leisure facilities. The dining is superb and the service all you could wish for.

As for the expensive hotels, in most cases you will be won over by elegant rooms, high-quality food and attractive furnishings. Not always, though. To stay in the centre of town, you may be forced to pay these prices.

The moderate places include delightful properties with an eye for home comforts and charm, from Victorian townhouses, Georgian rectories and old stone farmhouses to quaint seaside B&Bs. Remarkably few places fall into the cheap category, generally the smaller B&Bs in remote areas. The prices reflect a down-to-earth quality in their proprietors.

Accommodation Guides

VisitBritain publishes a range of brochures, mostly free, available from tourist information centres to help you find somewhere to stay. They include: *Hotels, Guesthouses, Inns and B&Bs*; *Self-catering Holiday Homes*; *Stay on a Farm*; and *Camping and Caravanning* (which costs a few pounds). It also produces a list of castles that do B&B or self-catering.

B&Bs, Guesthouses, Farms and Inns

At the top end, where you might find a rambling country house with a walled garden or a mellow townhouse in a well-heeled provincial town, guest accommodation is close to hotel standard in its professionalism. The character of the smaller places, however, is determined by their owners, whose tastes, hobbies, interests, backgrounds, aspirations and housekeeping skills are all reflected in the décor, furnishings and atmosphere. If you want to know the real England, stick to diamond-graded properties as opposed to starred hotels. But be wary of five-diamond properties, where the level of care is misplaced in gift-wrapped chocolates on pink satin pillows, and en-suite Jacuzzis. In four-diamond places the comfort and care matches the informality of the service. Three-diamond houses might be a real treat – a beautiful old house with threadbare rugs – or merely well-maintained with the right choice of breakfast cereals. Two- and one-diamond properties are clean and comfortable, and often take the form of delightful family homes, farmhouses or country pubs. You are unlikely to find en-suite bedrooms, but at least your room will have four-square proportions.

Working farmhouses are always memorable and welcoming, and remember what it is to be truly hospitable, perhaps knocking you up baked beans on toast with the children if you are too frazzled to go into town for dinner.

Best avoided in B&Bs is the temptation to stay awake all night glued to the television set on a high ledge in the corner of your room. It is no good feeling saturated with satellite TV the next morning, when you will need all your reserves to negotiate the indigestible ritual of social awkwardness that is the full English breakfast. The more impersonal inns can provide a welcome alternative to the awkward intimacies of B&Bs, but often the standard of the rooms is not all that high. 'Functional' is the word most often applied in this book to rooms above pubs.

Renting a House or Cottage

If there is more than one of you, it is worth exploring an area from a rented cottage or house. They are often the most attractive places to stay in the most enticing countryside, from remote moorland houses, seaside cottages and moth-eaten rectories to converted windmills, castles, Martello towers, lighthouses and Victorian coastal fortresses. You can also enjoy the slower-paced domestic side of places: eating locally smoked fish or cooking vegetables from the farmers' market, putting together picnics, reading the odd selection of books on the shelves and playing board games into the night.

Youth Hostels and Camping Barns

The YHA has 228 hostels in England and Wales ranging from 1960s city-centre blocks to rustic cottages and semi-ruinous medieval castles in the middle of a forest. These are no-

Holiday Cottages and Lighthouses

The National Trust, Holiday Cottage Booking Office, P.O. Box 536, Melksham, Wiltshire, SN12 8SX, **t** 0870 4584422, *www.nationaltrust.org.uk*. The National Trust has more than 250 holiday cottages in England for short-stay rental, as well as B&Bs, farmhouses and campsites all over England.

Distinctly Different, 4 Masons Lane, Bradford on Avon, BA15 1QN, **t** (01225) 866 842, *www.distinctlydifferent.co.uk*. Unusual places to stay in converted lighthouses, dovecotes, windmills galore.

Landmark Trust, Shottesbrooke, Maidenhead, Berkshire, SL6 3SW, **t** (01628) 825 925, *www.landmarktrust.co.uk*. A charity set up in 1965 to preserve historic buildings, partly funded by renting them out; 169 properties in Britain, including follies, forts, manor houses, mills, castles and cottages. When you send off for the *Landmark Trust Handbook* you get price and availability lists.

Vivat Trust, 70 Cowcross Street, London EC1M 6EJ, **t** 0845 0900194, or outside UK **t** 0044 207 336 8825, *www.vivat.org.uk*. Another charitable trust, which owns nine unusual holiday cottages and historic buildings.

Rural Retreats, **t** (01386) 701 177, *www.rural-retreats.co.uk*. The website has loads of photographs of beautiful properties, including 24 lighthouses around England. Provides welcome hampers, dinner delivery and logs for fires.

Holiday Cottages Group, *www.uk-holiday-cottages.co.uk* or try *www.easycottages.com* for self-catering cottages around England.

nonsense, cheap alternatives to guest accommodation for rugged outdoorsy types. The bedrooms and bathrooms are communal, divided only between the sexes. In some of them you cater for yourself, in others breakfast, dinner and packed lunches are available. One-year membership of the International Youth Hostel Federation entitles you to stay in YHA hostels all over England and the world. There is no age limit for members in England, and only occasionally are you expected to pull your weight with domestic chores. There are discounts for under-18s and families. With your membership card you receive the *YHA Go Accommodation Guide*, which details all the hostels in England and Wales. You can also request brochures including *Rent-a-Hostel* and *Family Breaks* (children under five are not allowed to stay in the dormitories, and not all hostels have family rooms). You can take out membership in any YHA hostel, and get a bed on the same night. Hostels are cheap, again with discounts for under-18s and families. You don't have to provide your own bedding.

There are also 50 camping barns or bunkhouses in the wilds of England, including the national parks of Dartmoor, the Peak District and the Lake District. These converted farm buildings are owned and operated by farmers. Communal bunk beds and showers and rudimentary cookers and fridges combine with remote rural locations to make these some of the more adventurous places to stay. You don't need to be a YHA member to stay, and dogs are often welcome. Ask for the YHA brochure *Camping Barns in England*.

YHA, Trevelyan House, Dimple Road, Matlock, Derbyshire DE4 3YH, **t** 0870 8708808, *www.yha.org.uk*; *www.hostelbooking.com* for international booking.

Camping and Caravanning

There is no longer such a thing in England as a charming patch of grass for you to pitch your tent on without getting into trouble. Ask the farmer in advance of pitching your tent in his field; he may well be pleased to help you, and might even point you in the direction of clean water or fresh produce. It also saves a lot of nervousness about getting rumbled in the morning. Otherwise you might just as well book into a campsite where there are washing facilities and toilets. Campsites are graded by VisitBritain from one- to five-star according to the standard and range of services – showers, toilets and convenience stores rank high in the ratings. VisitBritain produces *Camping and Caravanning* guides. The National Trust also has around 50 camping and caravan sites around England, listed on *www.national trust.org.uk* and in a brochure (*see* above). The Caravan Club, **t** (01342) 326 944, has more than 200 hundred sites around the country for members and non-members, with grass and all-weather pitches, waste disposal points, showers and laundry facilities.

London

07

1 km
½ mile
N
MAIDA VALE
PADDINGTON
BAYSWATER
NOTTING HILL
KENSINGTON
SOUTH KENSINGTON
FULHAM
CHELSEA
BROMPTON
KNIGHTSBRIDGE
BELGRAVIA
MAYFAIR
SOHO
CAMDEN
PIMLICO
BATTERSEA
WEST
Primrose Hill
London Zoo
Regent's Park
Euston
Marylebone
Paddington
John Lewis
Selfridge's
Liberty
Hamley's
Hyde Park
Kensington Gardens
Kensington Palace
Serpentine
Serpentine Gallery
Holland Park
Albert Hall
Science Museum
Victoria & Albert Museum
Natural History Museum
Harrods
St James's Palace
Green Park
Buckingham Palace
St James's Park
Victoria
Earl's Court
Battersea Park
PRINCE ALBERT ROAD
MAIDA VALE
ALBANY STREET
HAMPSTEAD RD
EUSTON
PARK RD
LISSON GROVE
EDGWARE
MARYLEBONE ROAD
PORTLAND PLACE
TOTTENHAM CT
HARROW ROAD
WESTWAY
GLOUCESTER PL
BAKER STREET
ROAD
PRAED STREET
SUSSEX GDNS
BISHOP'S BRIDGE RD
QUEENSWAY
OXFORD STREET
REGENT STREET
BAYSWATER ROAD
PARK LANE
PICCADILLY
THE
KNIGHTSBRIDGE
KENSINGTON GORE
KENSINGTON HIGH ST
BROMPTON ROAD
SLOANE STREET
BUCKINGHAM PAL RD
VICTORIA
KING'S ROAD
VAUXHALL BRIDGE
EARL'S COURT ROAD
CROMWELL ROAD
SLOANE SQUARE
BELGRAVE ROAD
OLD BROMPTON ROAD
FULHAM ROAD
KING'S ROAD
CHELSEA BR. ROAD
GROSVENOR
CHELSEA EMBANKMENT
CHELSEA BRIDGE
FINBOROUGH RD
ALBERT BRIDGE
BATTERSEA BRIDGE
ALBERT BR. RD
NINE ELMS
FULHAM ROAD
KING'S RD
BATTERSEA BRIDGE RD
BATTERSEA PARK ROAD

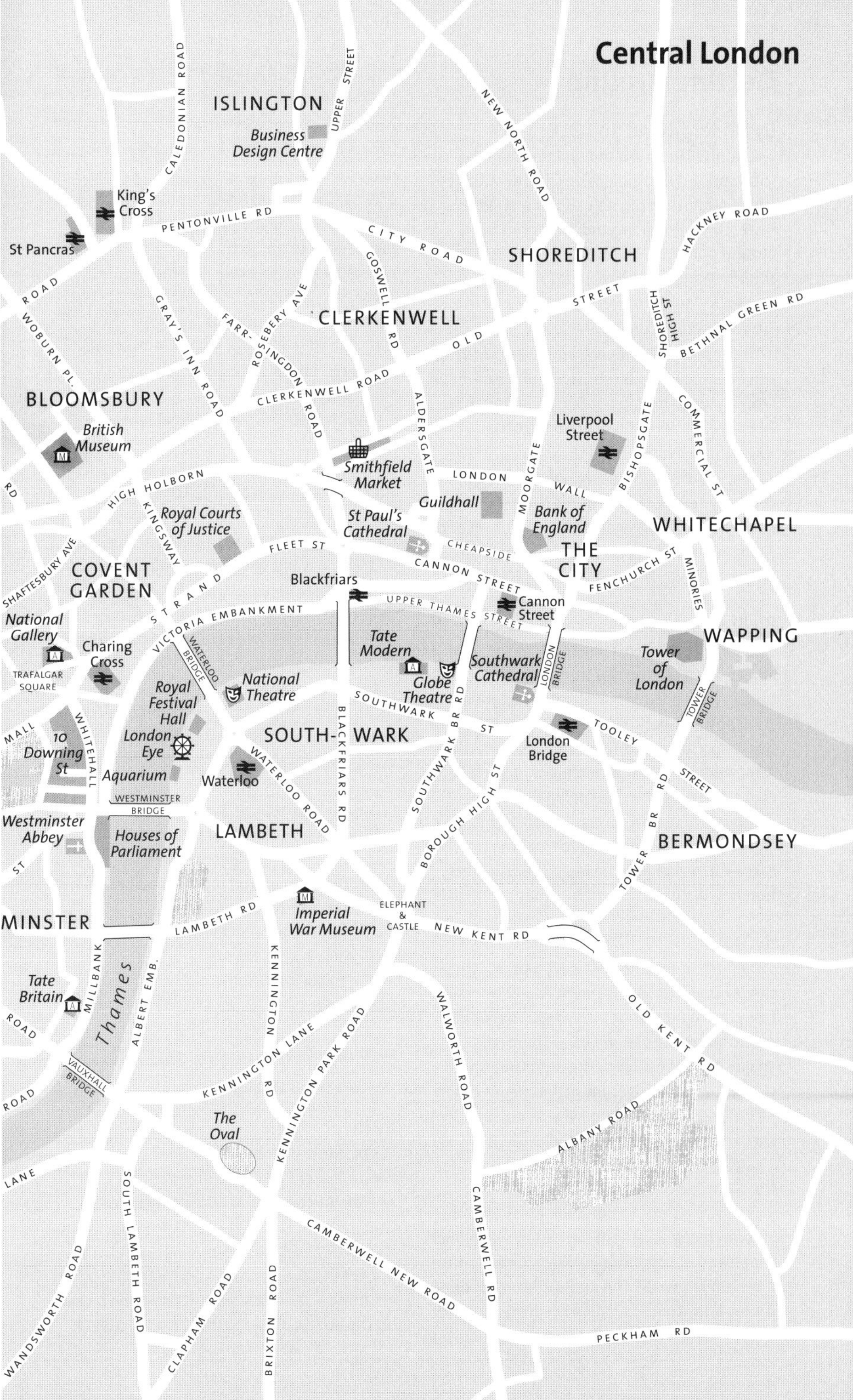

Central London
ISLINGTON
Business Design Centre
UPPER STREET
CALEDONIAN ROAD
King's Cross
St Pancras
PENTONVILLE RD
CITY ROAD
NEW NORTH ROAD
SHOREDITCH
HACKNEY ROAD
GOSWELL RD
ROSEBERY AVE
FARRINGDON ROAD
GRAY'S INN ROAD
CLERKENWELL
CLERKENWELL ROAD
OLD STREET
SHOREDITCH HIGH ST
BETHNAL GREEN RD
ROAD
WOBURN PL.
BLOOMSBURY
British Museum
ALDERSGATE
Smithfield Market
LONDON WALL
MOORGATE
Liverpool Street
BISHOPSGATE
COMMERCIAL ST
HIGH HOLBORN
KINGSWAY
Royal Courts of Justice
Guildhall
St Paul's Cathedral
Bank of England
WHITECHAPEL
SHAFTESBURY AVE
COVENT GARDEN
FLEET ST
CHEAPSIDE
THE CITY
FENCHURCH ST
MINORIES
STRAND
CANNON STREET
Blackfriars
Cannon Street
UPPER THAMES STREET
VICTORIA EMBANKMENT
National Gallery
Charing Cross
TRAFALGAR SQUARE
WATERLOO BRIDGE
Tate Modern
Globe Theatre
Southwark Cathedral
LONDON BRIDGE
WAPPING
Tower of London
TOWER BRIDGE
Royal Festival Hall
National Theatre
SOUTHWARK ST
SOUTHWARK BR RD
London Bridge
TOOLEY STREET
MALL
10 Downing St
WHITEHALL
London Eye
SOUTH-WARK
BLACKFRIARS RD
Aquarium
Waterloo
WATERLOO ROAD
WESTMINSTER BRIDGE
BOROUGH HIGH ST
TOWER BR RD
Westminster Abbey
Houses of Parliament
LAMBETH
BERMONDSEY
ST
MINSTER
LAMBETH RD
Imperial War Museum
ELEPHANT & CASTLE
NEW KENT RD
MILLBANK
Thames
ALBERT EMB.
KENNINGTON RD
Tate Britain
ROAD
KENNINGTON LANE
KENNINGTON PARK ROAD
WALWORTH ROAD
OLD KENT RD
VAUXHALL BRIDGE
ROAD
The Oval
ALBANY ROAD
LANE
SOUTH LAMBETH ROAD
CAMBERWELL NEW ROAD
CAMBERWELL RD
WANDSWORTH ROAD
CLAPHAM ROAD
BRIXTON ROAD
PECKHAM RD

Getting Around

By Underground and DLR

London's **Underground** system (the Tube) is 100 years old and expensive (the most basic single adult ticket costs £1.60) but still the fastest way to get around. Trains run from around 5.30am (Sun 7am) until at least 11pm.

London Transport, **t** (020) 7222 1234, *www.londontransport.co.uk*, *www.thetube.com*.

The East End, Docklands and Greenwich are served by the **Docklands Light Railway**, which links up with the Tube at Bank and Tower Hill.

DLR travel hotline, **t** (020) 7363 9700.

The fare system is organized in concentric zones, 1–6. For sightseeing buy an **Off-Peak One-Day Travelcard**, for as many zones as you need (from £4.10), available after 9.30am and valid on buses and trains too. For travel by bus only, buy a **One-Day Bus Pass** for just £2.

By Bus

London's buses are cheaper than the Tube, and you can see the city from the top deck. All bus services are integrated into the London Transport network. Prices are 70p–£1. Pick up a bus map, from main Tube stations, for routes. After midnight, N-prefixed **night buses** take over (radiating from Trafalgar Square).

A range of **tourist buses** stop all over central London. **Hop-on Hop-off**, **t** (01708) 631 122, takes you around all the main tourist sights, hopping on and off as many times as you like.

By Train

Overground trains are also integrated into the London Transport system. **Mainline trains** from the main stations may take you rapidly out to the suburban 'villages'. **Thameslink** snakes from West Hampstead to Greenwich via King's Cross; **Silverlink** rattles its way from Richmond to the East End via Hampstead. You can use your Travelcard on these trains.

By Taxi

Taxis are part of the mythology of London. You can recognize them by their old-fashioned shape and orange 'for hire' signs. Cabbies take an exam known as The Knowledge (of London routes and streets) to get a licence, and all licensed cabs are metered. They are expensive, but you'll take the fastest route and won't be ripped off. It's easy to hail a taxi in the day, unless it's raining, but at night they disappear (despite a massive price hike after 8pm). To order a taxi, call **Dial-A-Cab**, **t** (020) 7253 5000. Minicabs are cheaper, but less reliable. Never pick one up in the street, and try to identify a reputable firm (use your common sense). Some to try include:

Atlas Cars, **t** (020) 7602 1234.

Lady Cabs, **t** (020) 7254 3501. Run by women for women.

Town and Country Cabs, **t** (020) 7622 6222, *www.taxi.co.uk*. Male or female drivers.

By Car

Try not to bring a car into London: daytime traffic moves at an average of 8 miles an hour. Car parks cost a fortune. Street parking is near-impossible, with extortionate fines that vary wildly from borough to borough, as if to deliberately catch you out. The worst horror is having your car towed away: you pay at least £165 for the privilege of retrieving it (call **t** (020) 7747 4747 to find it). To top it all, you must pay a £5 daily 'congestion charge' to drive within a designated central zone; call **t** 0845 900 1234 or see *www.cclondon.com*.

On Two Wheels

Bicycle is a good way of getting around, if you can bear the danger and pollution. It is faster than by car, and more pleasant than the Tube, if you travel on back streets.

Contact **The London Cycling Campaign**, **t** (020) 7928 7220, *www.lcc.org.uk*, for advice and maps of safe routes.

Dial-a-Bike, 51 Marsham Street, **t** (020) 7234 4224.

On Your Bike, 52–4 Tooley Street, **t** (020) 7378 6669. Bike hire.

By River

A plethora of companies run services from Westminster Pier or Charing Cross Pier, both by Trafalgar Square. Services downriver to Greenwich and the Thames Barrier run every half-hour and take 45–50 minutes. Services upriver to Kew, Richmond and Hampton Court are more erratic. Buy your ticket at the pier or on the boat. Call **t** (020) 7222 1234 for details.

Tourist Information

Britain and London Visitor Centre, 1 Regent Street, Piccadilly Circus, SW1Y 4XT, **t** (020) 8846 9000, *www.visitbritain.com. Open Mon 9.30–6.30, Tues–Fri 9–6.30, Sat and Sun 10–4 (June–Oct Sat 9–5).*

Heathrow Underground Station (Terminals 1, 2 and 3). *Open daily 8–6.*

There are also offices at the main train stations, and local offices at **Greenwich, t** 0870 608 2000, and **Richmond, t** (020) 8940 9125.

The **London Tourist Board** has a recorded information service (48p a minute), or you can speak to a person on **t** (020) 7932 2000, or try *www.londontown.com*, which has details on restaurants, shops and attractions.

Clutching a **map** in London will not mark you out as a visitor: few Londoners venture out without a copy of the *London A–Z Street Atlas*, with all London streets indexed. Pick up bus and Tube maps at Underground stations.

The cost of living (or staying) in London is high, but most **museums** and **churches**, except St Paul's Cathedral and Westminster Abbey, are free. Look out for free concerts too.

Shopping

London...a kind of emporium for the whole earth.

Joseph Addison

London has been a cosmopolitan place to shop since Roman times. Below are some of the best areas for shopping.

Soulless **Oxford Street** is always packed with shoppers, thronging flagship high-street chain stores, like Top Shop or H&M, and department stores Selfridges and John Lewis. The side streets specialize in designer fashion (**South Molton Street, St Christopher's Place, Davies Place**). **Marylebone High Street** is now one of London's most glamorous shopping streets.

Regent Street, once the finest street in London, is now home to a few staid men's suit shops, Liberty, famous for its print scarves, and Hamley's, London's biggest toy emporium.

Three kinds of shopkeeper dominate **Bond Street**: fashion designers (all the big names, also Bruton Street and Conduit Street), art dealers, and jewellers like **Tiffany's, Cartier** and **Bulgari**, with flashy window displays.

The main attraction of Tottenham Court Road is its furniture stores – Heal's (classy), Habitat (once innovative, has lost its edge) – and discount computer and hi-fi shops.

Charing Cross Road is the traditional heart of the London book trade, although the old independents are going one by one. The most famous shop is Foyles, a chaotic, antiquated mess. Alongside modern chains are higgledy-piggledy second-hand bookshops such as Quinto (*84 Charing Cross Road*) and specialists like Zwemmer, London's leading art bookshop.

Jermyn Street boasts some of the best men's shirt shops in town, Paxton and Whitfield the cheese-seller, and the back of Fortnum & Mason, the ultimate English food shop.

North of Piccadilly is the quintessential address for men's bespoke tailoring, **Savile Row**. While some of the taylors look a bit fusty, Ozwald Boateng has updated the traditional suit to appeal to fashion icons.

High Street Kensington is a fun, easy place to shop, in mainly chain stores. For antiques, look around **Kensington Church Street** and the cobbled passage, **Church Walk**, that snakes behind Victorian St Mary Abbot's church.

Like Carnaby Street in Soho, the **King's Road** went hippie-chic in the 1960s. Most of the hip boutiques have gone upmarket or been replaced by the chains, but check out the Chelsea Antiques Market and Antiquarius. John Sandoe Books is worth a visit too.

It was the Great Exhibition that turned **Knightsbridge** into the home of the department store. Harvey Nichols is the most stylish (and the favourite of Patsy and Edina in *Absolutely Fabulous*), although Harrods still has the edge for fame.

Brompton Road and **Sloane Street** parade classy designer shops (many big names). Halfway down Brompton Road is **Beauchamp Place**, lined with tiny exclusive shops selling anything from jewellery to underwear (**Rigby and Peller** supplies the Queen's bras). Further down is Brompton Cross and **Walton Street**, another enclave of classy little shops

Covent Garden boasts not only its market, but countless offbeat shops from the New Age (lots of healing and astrology) to the gastronomic (Neal's Yard Cheese Shop). If London is the start of your English trip, stop at **Stanfords** in Long Acre for maps.

Where to Stay

London's hotels are overpriced and often shockingly bad (even dirty). A 'cheap' room is one that costs less than £100. At the top end, however, there are some excellent choices.

Try to book in advance. The **London Tourist Board** operates a booking service, **t** 09068 663 344 (*open Mon–Fri 9.30–6*). Otherwise you can line up outside a tourist office on arrival, or try *www.smoothhound.co.uk/hotels*. Haggle out of season, at weekends, or for longer stays.

Most hotels are in the West End, Kensington, Chelsea, Earl's Court and around west London. Bloomsbury often has good bargains.

Luxury

Brown's, Albemarle Street, W1, **t** (020) 7493 6020, *www.brownshotel.com*. Classic old-fashioned establishment, with impeccable, stiff service. ⊖ *Green Park*.

Claridges, Brook Street, W1, **t** (020) 7629 8860, *www.claridges.co.uk*. Art Deco bedrooms, black-and-white marbled foyer and class at this celebrated hotel. ⊖ *Bond St*.

Connaught, 16 Carlos Place, W1, **t** (020) 7499 7070, *www.the-savoy-group.com/connaught*. Attentive service and exclusive air command loyal devotees. ⊖ *Green Park, Bond St*.

Dorchester, 53 Park Lane, W1, **t** (020) 7629 8888, *www.dorchesterhotel.com*. Hyde Park views, marble and gold. ⊖ *Hyde Park Corner*.

Metropolitan, 19 Old Park Lane, W1, **t** (020) 7447 1000, *www.metropolitan.co.uk*. Cool, hip minimalism reigns in this designer hotel. Fashionable Nobu restaurant and Met bar are here. ⊖ *Hyde Park Corner, Green Park*.

Ritz, Piccadilly, W1, **t** (020) 7300 2308, *www.theritzlondon.com*. Marble and rococo carpets. *Ancien régime* luxury. ⊖ *Green Park*.

One Aldwych, 1 Aldwych, WC2, **t** (020) 7300 0500, *www.onealdwych.co.uk*. Contemporary chic at its most sophisticated. ⊖ *Holborn, Charing Cross*.

Sanderson, 50 Berners Street, W1, **t** (020) 7300 1400. Design team Ian Schrager and Philippe Starck have given a 1960s office block the minimalist makeover. ⊖ *Tottenham Court Road, Oxford Circus*.

Savoy, Strand, WC2, **t** (020) 7836 4343, *www.the-savoy-group.com/savoy*. Sleeker, more business-like luxury. The *fin-de-siècle* dining room is a favourite venue for afternoon tea. Actor Richard Harris spent his last years here. ⊖ *Charing Cross*.

Charlotte Street Hotel, 25 Charlotte Street, W1, **t** (020) 7806 2000, *www.charlottestreethotel.com*. Chic boutique hotel; big hit with media crowd. London's nicest staff. ⊖ *Tottenham Court Road, Goodge Street*.

Hempel, 31–5 Craven Hill Gardens, W2, **t** (020) 7298 9000, *www.the-hempel.co.uk*. Takes minimalism to its extreme, with a blank white foyer. ⊖ *Lancaster Gate*.

Portobello, 22 Stanley Gardens, W11, **t** (020) 7727 2777, *www.portobello-hotel.co.uk*. Victorian-Gothic furniture conceals all mod cons. ⊖ *Holland Park*.

Very Expensive

Durrants, George Street, W1, **t** (020) 7935 8131, *www.durrantshotel.co.uk* (*very expensive*). An 18th-century coaching inn with old-fashioned touches. ⊖ *Marble Arch*.

Hazlitt's, 6 Frith Street, W1, **t** (020) 7434 1771, *www.hazlittshotel.com*. Small Georgian rooms in essayist Hazlitt's former home. ⊖ *Tottenham Court Road*.

Aster House, 3 Sumner Place, SW7, **t** (020) 7581 5888, *www.asterhouse.com*. Silk walls and flowers adorn this award-winning hotel. ⊖ *South Kensington*.

Claverly, 13–14 Beaufort Gardens, SW3, **t** (020) 7589 8541. Lovingly detailed hotel, another award-winner. ⊖ *Knightsbridge*.

The Gore, 189 Queen's Gate, SW7, **t** (020) 7584 6601, *www. hazlittshotel.com/gore*. Gothic Edwardian décor, plus hundreds of old prints. ⊖ *Gloucester Road*.

Number Sixteen, 16 Sumner Place, SW7, **t** (020) 7589 5232, *www.numbersixteenhotel.co.uk*. Posh B&B in charming Victorian house with garden and fountains. ⊖ *South Kensington*.

Dorset Square, 39–40 Dorset Square, NW1, **t** (020) 7723 7874. Restored Regency building near Lord's Cricket Ground. ⊖ *Baker Street, Marylebone*.

Expensive

Hart House Hotel, 51 Gloucester Place, W1, **t** (020) 7935 2288, *www.harthouse.co.uk*. Superbly run hotel in a Georgian mansion overlooking Portman Square. ⊖ *Marble Arch, Baker Street*.

Academy, 17–21 Gower Street, WC1, **t** (020) 7631 4115, *www.etontownhouse.com*. Georgian townhouse atmosphere, with cosy library and paved garden. Antique charm. ⊖ *Goodge Street*.

Bonnington, 92 Southampton Row, WC1, **t** (020) 7242 2828, *www.bonnington.com*. Renovated Edwardian establishment with bland style but friendly staff. Relatively easy to book. ⊖ *Holborn*.

Russell, Russell Square, WC1, **t** (020) 7837 6470. Gothic Revival architecture and atmosphere, but friendly. ⊖ *Russell Square*.

Byron, 36–8 Queensborough Terrace, W2, **t** (020) 7243 0987, *www.capricornhotels.co.uk*. Friendly, smart hotel full of sunshine and flowers. ⊖ *Queensway*.

Five Sumner Place, 5 Sumner Place, SW7, **t** (020) 7584 7586, *www.sumnerplace.com*. Like a country home in the heart of London. Quiet. ⊖ *South Kensington*.

Tophams Belgravia, 28 Ebury Street, SW1, **t** (020) 7730 8147. Long-established favourite. ⊖ *Victoria, Sloane Square*.

Moderate

Fielding, 4 Broad Courtt, Bow Street, WC2, **t** (020) 7836 8305, *www.the-fielding-hotel.co.uk*. Opposite the Opera House. ⊖ *Covent Garden, Holborn*.

Edward Lear, 28–30 Seymour St, W1, **t** (020) 7402 5401, *www.edlear.com*. Small, homey, efficient hotel. ⊖ *Marble Arch*.

Georgian House Hotel, 87 Gloucester Place, W1, **t** (020) 7935 2211, *www.londoncentral hotel. com*. Spacious rooms with personality; high standards. ⊖ *Baker Street*.

Parkwood, 4 Stanhope Place, W2, **t** (020) 7402 2241, *www.parkwoodhotel.com*. Family-run hotel in charming Georgian mansion near Hyde Park. ⊖ *Marble Arch*.

Crescent, 49–50 Cartwright Gdns, WC1, **t** (020) 7387 1515, *www.crescenthoteloflondon.com*. Family atmosphere, with gardens. Old-fashioned good value. ⊖ *King's Cross, Euston*.

Abbey House, 11 Vicarage Gate, W8, **t** (020) 7727 2594, *www.abbeyhousekensington.com*. Simple, large rooms in delightful Victorian town house in quiet square. ⊖ *High Street Kensington, Notting Hill Gate*.

Ashley, 15–17 Norfolk Square, W2, **t** (020) 7723 9966, *www.ashleyhotels.com*. Maniacally clean, quiet hotel in a square full of simple, cheap hotels. ⊖ *Paddington*.

Gate, 6 Portobello Rd, W11, **t** (020) 7221 0707, *www.gatehotel.com*. Floral hotel in plum location. ⊖ *Notting Hill Gate*.

Garden Court, 30–31 Kensington Gardens Square, W2, **t** (020) 7229 2553, *www.gardencourthotel.co.uk*. Simple B&B with nice views over the square and gardens. ⊖ *Queensway, Bayswater*.

Hotel 167, 167 Old Brompton Rd, SW5, **t** (020) 7373 3221, *www.hotel167.com*. Attractive Victorian corner house with young clientele. ⊖ *South Kensington*.

Collin House, 104 Ebury Street, SW1, **t** (020) 7730 8031. Clean, hospitable B&B behind Victoria station. ⊖ *Victoria*.

Windermere Hotel, 142–4 Warwick Way, SW1, **t** (020) 7834 5163, *www.windermere-hotel.co.uk*. Delightful little hotel. ⊖ *Victoria, Sloane Square*.

County Hall Travel Inn Capital, Belvedere Rd, SE1, **t** 0870 238 3300/**t** (020) 7902 1608, *www.travelinn.co.uk*. A chain hotel in a prime location, with reasonably priced rooms near the river; excellent choice for families. ⊖ *Waterloo, Westminster*.

La Gaffe, 107 Heath Street, Hampstead, NW3, **t** (020) 7435 8965, *www.lagaffe.co.uk*. Charming B&B in a former shepherd's cottage. ⊖ *Hampstead*.

Cheap

Arran House, 77–9 Gower Street, WC1, **t** (020) 7636 2186, *www.london-hotel.co.uk*. Wonky floors and rose garden add charm to this no-frills guesthouse. ⊖ *Goodge Street*.

Avalon, 46–7 Cartwright Gardens, WC1, **t** (020) 7387 2366, *www.avalonhotel.co.uk*. No-frills, in a bright, old-fashioned Georgian house in a beautiful crescent packed with similar establishments. ⊖ *Euston*.

Manor Court, 7 Clanricarde Gardens, W2, **t** (020) 7727 5407, *www.visitbritain.com*. Simple B&B near Kensington Palace; seven family rooms. ⊖ *Notting Hill Gate*.

Huttons Hotel, 55 Belgrave Rd, SW1, **t** (020) 7834 3726, *www.huttons-hotel.co.uk*. Renovated family-run B&B. ⊖ *Victoria*.

Several agencies can also find you a room in a B&B, often in a stylish London home.

Bulldog Club, 14 Dewhurst Road, W14, **t** (020) 7371 3202, *www.bulldogclub.com*. Palatial surroundings in city or country – at a price.

Host and Guest Service, 103 Dawes Rd, SW6, **t** (020) 7385 9922, *www.host-guest.co.uk*. Agency with 3,000 homes on its books.

Uptown Reservations, 41 Paradise Walk, SW3, **t** (020) 7351 3445, *inquiries@uptownres.co.uk*. Homes in Knightsbridge and Chelsea.

Worldwide Bed and Breakfast Association, P.O. Box 2070, London W12, **t** (020) 8742 9123, *www. bestbandb.co.uk*. Rooms in upmarket private homes.

Eating Out

While London's hotels may still be struggling to match international standards, you can put away your prejudices about its food: London is a great gastronomic centre, cosmopolitan and with a wide variety of cuisines to sample. Not only can you eat excellent Italian, Spanish, Lebanese, Indian, Chinese, Thai, Polish and Russian food; some of the modern British restaurants are outstanding. The only drawback is the cost. Eating out in London is an expensive pleasure; you are lucky to get away with much less than £25–35 per head for a decent evening meal.

Very Expensive

Le Gavroche, 43 Upper Brook Street, W1, **t** (020) 7408 0881. Albert Roux, one of the most revered cooks in Britain, has delegated the cuisine to his son, Michel, but standards are still high. Dress smart. *Closed Sat, Sun.* ⊖ *Marble Arch.*

The Admiralty, Somerset House, The Strand, WC2, **t** (020) 7845 4646. In its setting by the river, this new restaurant has been snapping up awards. The views and elegant décor are matched by the French cuisine. Superb five-course vegetarian set menu too. *Closed Sun eve.* ⊖ *Charing Cross, Holborn.*

The Ivy, 1 West Street, WC2, **t** (020) 7836 4751. Oak panels and stained glass from the 1920s and salmon fishcakes on a bed of leaf spinach have conspired to make this an established favourite with celebrities. *Takes orders from 12–3 and 5.30–12, but book well in advance.* ⊖ *Leicester Square.*

Pied à Terre, 34 Charlotte Street, W1, **t** (020) 7636 1178. The neutral setting is an excellent foil for Tom Aiken's virtuoso modern French cuisine. *Closed Sat lunch and day.* ⊖ *Tottenham Court Road.*

Nobu, Metropolitan Hotel, 19 Old Park Lane, W1, **t** (020) 7447 4747. Dark glasses and a fat wallet are *de rigueur* at this glam minimalist Japanese. *Closed Sat lunch and Sun lunch.* ⊖ *Hyde Park Corner.*

Gordon Ramsay, 68–9 Royal Hospital Road, SW3, **t** (020) 7352 4441. It's hard to get a table here, but you can expect perfect modern French cooking from this temperamental footballer-turned-chef. *Closed Sat and Sun.* ⊖ *Sloane Square* and walk or taxi.

Bibendum, Michelin House, 81 Fulham Rd, SW3, **t** (020) 7581 5817. Ultra-rich French regional food, in restored Art Deco Michelin building. Cheaper oyster bar downstairs. *Closed Sun lunch.* ⊖ *South Kensington.*

Neat, 2nd Floor, Oxo Tower Wharf, Barge House Street, SE1, **t** (020) 7928 5533. Richard Neat's chi-chi new restaurant. Classy food and breathtaking views. The brasserie is cheaper and the lunch menu good value. *Closed Sat lunch and Sun.* ⊖ *Southwark.*

Expensive

Alastair Little, 49 Frith Street, W1, **t** (020) 7734 5183. One of the first and best of the modern British restaurants. *Closed Sun lunch.* ⊖ *Leicester Square, Tottenham Court Road.*

Richard Corrigan at Lindsay House, 21 Romilly Street, W1, **t** (020) 7439 0450. In elegantly ramshackle 18th-century rooms; modern Irish menu. *Closed Sat lunch and Sun.* ⊖ *Leicester Square, Tottenham Court Road.*

Criterion, 224 Piccadilly, W1, **t** (020) 7930 0488. Magnificent Art Deco, gold mosaic interior, opened in 1870. Marco Pierre White's brasserie draws big crowds. *Closed Sun lunch.* ⊖ *Piccadilly Circus.*

The Portrait Restaurant, National Portrait Gallery, 2 St Martin's Place, WC2, **t** (020) 7312 2490. Superb views of Whitehall and generous portions of modern European food. ⊖ *Leicester Square, Charing Cross.*

Quo Vadis, 26–9 Dean Street, W1, **t** (020) 7437 9585. Renowned chef Marco Pierre White's fine modern French food with Mediterranean influences in airy lime-green interiors. *Closed Sat lunch and Sun.* ⊖ *Tottenham Court Road.*

J. Sheekey, St Martin's Court, WC2, **t** (020) 7240 2565. Youngest sibling of the Ivy. Revamped fish restaurant in elegant wood-panelled rooms. ⊖ *Leicester Square.*

The Sugar Club, 21 Warwick Street, W1, **t** (020) 7437 7776. Innovative fusion cooking (duck with vanilla-scented flageolets). ⊖ *Oxford Circus, Piccadilly Circus.*

Christopher's, 18 Wellington Street, WC2, **t** (020) 7240 4222. American steaks and grills in a former brothel. ⊖ *Covent Garden.*

Orso, 27 Wellington Street, WC2, **t** (020) 7240 5269. High-quality Italian fare in a graceful terracotta Venetian dining room. ⊖ *Covent Garden, Charing Cross.*

Rules, 35 Maiden Lane, WC2, **t** (020) 7836 5314. The oldest restaurant in London (est. 1798), serving aristocrats as well as actors. Formal and old-fashioned. Specializes in game rarities such as ptarmigan. Dress smart. ⊖ *Covent Garden, Charing Cross.*

Bank Aldwych, 1 Kingsway, WC2, **t** (020) 7379 9797. A stylish restaurant in a converted bank, serving assured modern European cuisine. *Closed Sun eve.* ⊖ *Holborn.*

Blandford St Restaurant, 5–7 Blandford Street, W1, **t** (020) 7486 9696. Inventive modern European cuisine with excellent service. *Closed Sat lunch and Sun.* ⊖ *Baker Street, Bond Street, Marble Arch.*

Le Caprice, Arlington House, Arlington Street, SW1, **t** (020) 7629 2239. Eternally fashionable with high standards of modern British cooking and service. ⊖ *Green Park.*

The Greenhouse, 27/a Hay's Mews, W1, **t** (020) 7499 3331. Old English recipes resurrected (fillet of smoked haddock with Welsh rarebit). *Closed Sat lunch and Sun lunch.* ⊖ *Green Park.*

Quaglino's, 16 Bury Street, SW1, **t** (020) 7930 6767. Conran restaurant in a sunken ballroom. *Closed Sun lunch.* ⊖ *Green Park.*

Quilon, St James's Court Hotel, 41 Buckingham Gate, SW1, **t** (020) 7281 1899. Upmarket Indian near Buckingham Palace; exquisitely spiced fish and seafood. *Closed Sat lunch and Sun.* ⊖ *St James's Park.*

River Café, Thames Wharf Studios, Rainville Road, W6, **t** (020) 7381 8824. Simple, delicious Italian food in a riverside setting designed by Richard Rogers. Rogers' wife, Ruthie, and her friend Rose Gray, are the chefs. *Closed Sun.* ⊖ *Hammersmith.*

Kensington Place, 201 Kensington Church Street, W8, **t** (020) 7727 3184. Sleek, noisy, modern dining room with 'eclectic European' cuisine: venison, steak, wild sea trout, sorrel omelette. ⊖ *Notting Hill Gate.*

San Lorenzo, 22 Beauchamp Place, SW3, **t** (020) 7584 1074. Fashionable celeb hangout since the 1960s. Good, if overpriced, Italian food. *Closed Sun eve.* ⊖ *Knightsbridge, South Kensington.*

Dakota, 127 Ledbury Rd, W11, **t** (020) 7792 9191. One of the best in the area. Modern, elegant US cuisine (delicious cornbread). Impeccable service. ⊖ *Notting Hill Gate, Ladbroke Grove.*

40° at Veronica's, 3 Hereford Rd, W2, **t** (020) 7229 5079. Has unearthed historical and regional British dishes – spring lamb with crabmeat or calf's liver and beetroot. Elizabethan puddings. *Closed Sat lunch.* ⊖ *Bayswater, Notting Hill Gate.*

Pharmacy Bar and Restaurant, 150 Notting Hill Gate, W11, **t** (020) 7221 2442. The furore has long died down, but there are still queues for this restaurant and café/cocktail lounge designed by pill-box artist Damien Hirst. Waiters are dressed in hospital gowns designed by Prada. ⊖ *Notting Hill Gate.*

Moderate

Livebait Café Fish, 36–40 Rupert Street, SW1, **t** (020) 7287 8989. Fish and shellfish chargrilled, steamed, *meunière* or fried. Bustling atmosphere. ⊖ *Leicester Square.*

Andrew Edmunds, 46 Lexington Street, W1, **t** (020) 7437 5708. Simple dishes and excellent-value wine. Queues at the door. *Closed Sat eve and Sun eve.* ⊖ *Oxford Circus.*

Il Forno, 63–4 Frith Street, W1, **t** (020) 7734 4545. Popular Italian restaurant; imaginative food with a touch of class. *Closed Sat and Sun lunch.* ⊖ *Tottenham Court Road.*

French House Dining Rooms, 49 Dean Street, W1, **t** (020) 7437 2477. Dark, worn wooden rooms above atmospheric pub frequented by literati; modern European food. *Closed Sun.* ⊖ *Leicester Square.*

Fung Shing, 15 Lisle Street, WC2, **t** (020) 7437 1539. Delicate Cantonese food. ⊖ *Leicester Square, Piccadilly Circus.*

Randall & Aubin, 16 Brewer Street, W1, **t** (020) 7287 4447. Victorian butcher's shop converted into oyster and champagne bar, with a rôtisserie. Specializes in seafood and spit-roasts, also *langoustines*, crabs, whelks. *Open from 11am Mon–Sat, from 4pm Sun.* *⊖ Piccadilly Circus.*

Spiga, 84 Wardour Street, W1, **t** (020) 7734 3444. Chic modern Italian restaurant with pizzas made in *'forno a legna'*. *⊖ Tottenham Court Road, Leicester Square.*

Joe Allen, 13 Exeter Street, WC2, **t** (020) 7836 0651. American, modern British and European menu. Takes orders until 12.45am, attracting post-show actors and celebrities. Lively ambience. *Sun closes 11.30pm.* *⊖ Covent Garden, Charing Cross.*

Prospect Grill, 4–6 Garrick Street, WC2, **t** (020) 7379 0412. Low-key but stylish, with an American menu of grilled or roasted organic and free-range meats. *Closed Sun eve.* *⊖ Covent Garden, Charing Cross.*

Elena's L'Etoile, 30 Charlotte Street, W1, **t** (020) 7636 7189. Historic Fitzrovian locale. *Closed Sat lunch, Sun. ⊖ Tottenham Court Road.*

Maroush, 21 Edgware Rd, W2, **t** (020) 7723 0773. The best of the Middle Eastern restaurants on Edgware Road. A fun atmosphere with lively décor, wonderfully spiced dishes and excellent *meze*. Beware: if you turn up after 10pm the minimum charge is a startling £48 per person. *⊖ Marble Arch.*

Seashell, 49–51 Lisson Grove, NW1, **t** (020) 7723 8703. Arguably the best fish and chips in town. Café-style eating as well as takeaway. *Closed Sun. ⊖ Marylebone.*

Cambio de Tercio, 163 Old Brompton Rd, SW5, **t** (020) 7244 8970. Exuberant contemporary Spanish cooking: paella, skate wings, salt cod, octopus. Very popular, so book. *⊖ Gloucester Road.*

The Cow Dining Room, 89 Westbourne Park Road, W2, **t** (020) 7221 0021. The pseudo-countrified atmosphere at the upstairs room above the trendy pub belies the precision cooking. *Closed Sun eve. ⊖ Westbourne Park.*

Osteria Basilico, 29 Kensington Park Rd, W11, **t** (020) 7727 9372. Popular, nosiy restaurant serving new-wave Italian dishes like spaghetti with lobster and tomato. *⊖ Ladbroke Grove.*

Quality Chop House, 94 Farringdon Rd, EC1, **t** (020) 7837 5093. Superior English specialities like fishcakes, game pie and roast lamb, served in the atmospheric rooms of a former 19th-century working-class men's club. *Closed Sat lunch. ⊖ Farringdon.*

St John, 26 St John Street, EC1, **t** (020) 7251 0848. A converted smokehouse, still with an industrial feel to it. Hearty, meaty, ingenious British cooking with a difference. *Closed Sat lunch, Sun. ⊖ Farringdon.*

Café des Amis du Vin, 11–14 Hanover Place, WC2, **t** (020) 7379 3444 (*cheap*). A quiet French brasserie favoured by theatregoers. *Closed Sun. ⊖ Covent Garden.*

Cheap

Calabash, Africa Centre, 38 King Street, WC2, **t** (020) 7836 1976. Dishes from Africa such as *egusi* (stew of beef, melon and shrimps cooked in palm oil) from Nigeria. *Closed Sat lunch, Sun. ⊖ Covent Garden.*

Golden Harvest, 17 Lisle Street, WC2, **t** (020) 7287 3822. Outstandingly good Chinese food, including pomfret and carp. *⊖ Leicester Square, Piccadilly Circus.*

Café España, 63 Old Compton Street, W1, **t** (020) 7494 1271. Plain, authentic little Spanish restaurant. *⊖ Leicester Square.*

Kulu Kulu, 76 Brewer Street, W1, **t** (020) 7734 7316. Fresh, high-quality handmade sushi. *Closed Sun. ⊖ Piccadilly Circus.*

Mildred's, 45 Lexington Street, W1, **t** (020) 7494 1634. Eclectic vegetarian and organic fare. Good Sunday brunch. No bookings. *⊖ Oxford Circus.*

Poon's & Co., 26–7 Lisle Street, W1, **t** (020) 7437 4549. One of Chinatown's oldest, famous for its duck. *⊖ Leicester Square.*

Wagamama, 10/a Lexington Street, W1, **t** (020) 7292 0990. 'Positive eating, positive living' at this hi-tech Japanese noodle bar. *⊖ Oxford Circus, Piccadilly Circus.*

Alfred, 245 Shaftsbury Ave, WC2, **t** (020) 7240 2566. Modern angle on old British favourites. *Closed Sat, Sun. ⊖ Tottenham Court Road.*

October Gallery Café, 24 Old Gloucester Street, WC1, **t** (020) 7242 7367. Eclectic world food in a busy, cosy and friendly atmosphere. *⊖ Holborn, Russell Square.*

Mulligans, 13–14 Cork Street, W1, **t** (020) 7409 1370. Hearty Irish cooking, with lighter dishes alongside beef cooked in Guinness. Wicked puddings. *Closed Sat lunch, Sun.* ⊖ *Green Park, Piccadilly Circus.*

Chelsea Kitchen, 98 King's Rd, SW3, **t** (020) 7589 1330. Continental food and wine for less than £10. Known since the 1960s as a jostling, studentesque joint. ⊖ *Sloane Square.*

Stockpot, 6 Basil Street, SW3, **t** (020) 7589 8627. Three-course meals for little more than a fiver. Strains of school dinner, but not bad for the price. ⊖ *Knightsbridge.*

Geales, 2 Farmer Street, W8, **t** (020) 7727 7528. Superior fish and chips. *Closed Sun lunch.* ⊖ *Notting Hill Gate.*

Khans, 13–15 Westbourne Grove, W2, **t** (020) 7727 5420. Hectic Indian restaurant. ⊖ *Bayswater, Queensway.*

Micro Kalamaras, 76–8 Inverness Mews, W2, **t** (020) 7727 9122. Very friendly Greek basement restaurant, going strong since 1961. *Closed Mon–Fri lunch.* ⊖ *Bayswater, Queensway.*

Standard Tandoori, 21–3 Westbourne Grove, W11, **t** (020) 7229 0600. First-rate tandoori restaurant with excellent pickles. ⊖ *Bayswater.*

Satay House, 13 Sale Place, W2, **t** (020) 7723 6763. Small, intimate shop front serving delicious Malaysian food. ⊖ *Edgware Road, Paddington.*

Cafés and Tearooms

Bar Italia, 22 Frith Street, W1. The café with the best coffee and most authentic atmosphere in town and it knows it. The mirrored bar, complete with TV showing Italian soccer games, could have come straight from Milan or Bologna. Sit at the counter inside, or at a pavement table outside. *Open Mon–Sat 24hrs, Sun 7am–4am.* ⊖ *Leicester Square, Tottenham Court Road.*

Maison Bertaux, 28 Greek Street, W1. Mouthwatering pastries in a slightly cramped upstairs tearoom which is always crowded. *Open Mon–Sun 9am–8pm.* ⊖ *Leicester Square, Tottenham Court Road.*

Pâtisserie Valerie, 44 Old Compton Street, W1. Excellent French cakes and coffee. *Open Mon–Fri 7.30–10, Sat 8–7, Sun 9.30–6.* ⊖ *Leicester Square, Tottenham Court Road.*

Browns Hotel, 33–4 Albemarle Street, W1, **t** (020) 7518 4108. Tea served 3–5.45pm daily. Very traditional English hotel serving tea to all-comers, as long as you dress to fit the part. Set teas are expensive. ⊖ *Green Park.*

Harry's, 19 Kingly Street, W1. An all-night diner, with hearty fry-ups and reasonable coffee, featuring an eccentric cast of weirdos and insomniacs. During the day and early evening it serves Thai food. There's often a queue. *Open all night.* ⊖ *Oxford Circus.*

The Ritz, Piccadilly, W1, **t** (020) 7300 2308. Reserved tea sittings at 1.30, 3.30 and 5pm daily. The fanciest, most indulgent tea in town, served in the sumptuous Edwardian Palm Court. You'll definitely need to book. Set tea expensive. ⊖ *Green Park.*

Pubs

Dog and Duck, 8 Bateman Street, W1. Soho's smallest pub. Customers spill out on to the pavement in the summer, and huddle round the log fire in the winter. ⊖ *Oxford Circus, Piccadilly Circus.*

The French House, 49 Dean Street, W1. Meeting-place for De Gaulle's Free French during the Second World War; now adorned with pictures of famous Frenchmen. ⊖ *Leicester Square, Tottenham Court Road.*

Fitzroy Tavern, 16 Charlotte Street, W1. Dylan Thomas's main drinking haunt; literary mementoes on the walls. ⊖ *Goodge Street.*

Lamb and Flag, 33 Rose Street, WC2. One of few wooden-framed buildings left in central London, dating back to the 17th century, with low ceilings and a lively atmosphere. The pub was for a long time nicknamed the Bucket of Blood because it staged bare-knuckled fights. Now you just have to knuckle your way past the crowds at the bar to get yourself a drink. Spills over into the surrounding alleyways and yards in summer. ⊖ *Covent Garden, Leicester Square.*

The Eagle, 159 Farringdon Rd, EC1. New-wave pub with less emphasis on drinking and more on food, good atmosphere and general hanging out. Gets crowded. ⊖ *Farringdon.*

The White Cross, Cholmondeley Walk, Richmond. A pub that turns into an island at high tide. Enjoy the real fires and good food. Lots of outdoor seating by the river in summer. ⊖ *Richmond.*

Entertainment

To find out what's on in London buy a copy of listings magazine *Time Out*. Below are a few of the venues worth looking out for.

Theatre

Royal National Theatre, South Bank, **t** (020) 7452 3000, *www.nationaltheatre.org*. The National has three stages showing top-notch theatre. ⊖ *Waterloo*.

Royal Court, Sloane Square, **t** (020) 7565 5000. The major venue for experimental writing. ⊖ *Sloane Square*.

Young Vic, 66 The Cut, **t** (020) 7928 6363, *www.youngvic.org*. A studio theatre presenting plays old and new. ⊖ *Waterloo*.

Donmar Warehouse, Earlham Street, Covent Garden, **t** (020) 7369 1732, *www.donmarwarehouse.com*. Excellent venue where Sam Mendes cut his teeth. ⊖ *Covent Garden*.

King's Head, 115 Upper Street, Islington, **t** (020) 7226 1916. Serves a 3-course dinner in the theatre just before the show. ⊖ *Angel*.

Almeida, Almeida Street, Islington, **t** (020) 7359 4404, *www.almeida.co.uk*. A fringe theatre with a formidable reputation. ⊖ *Angel, Highbury and Islington*.

The Gate, 11 Pembridge Road, Notting Hill, **t** (020) 7229 0706, *gate@gatetheatre.freeserve.co.uk*. Excellent pub theatre. ⊖ *Notting Hill Gate*.

Regent's Park Open Air Theatre, Inner Circle, Regent's Park, **t** (020) 7486 2431, *www.open-air-theatre.org.uk*. Open-air theatre from May to Sept. Bring a blanket and umbrella. ⊖ *Baker Street*.

Opera and Ballet

Royal Opera House, Covent Garden, **t** (020) 7304 4000, *www.roh.org.uk*. Britain's leading opera venue. ⊖ *Covent Garden*.

London Coliseum, St Martin's Lane, **t** (020) 7632 8300, *www.eno.org*. Home of the English National Opera, which performs in English to high musical standards. *Closed for refurbishment*. ⊖ *Charing Cross*.

South Bank Centre, South Bank, Belvedere Rd, **t** (020) 7960 4242, *www.sbc.org.uk*. Three first-rate concert halls: the Royal Festival Hall; the Queen Elizabeth Hall and the Purcell Room. ⊖ *Waterloo*.

Barbican Centre, Silk Street, **t** (020) 7638 8891, *www.barbican.org.uk*. Home to the London Symphony Orchestra and English Chamber Orchestra. Excellent acoustics. ⊖ *Barbican*.

Royal Albert Hall, Kensington Gore, **t** (020) 7589 8212, *www.royalalberthall.com*. Hosts the Proms every year from July to early Sept; an eclectic platform for music old and new. The Last Night of the Proms is a raucous nationalistic affair at which the all-English orchestra plays all-English music, and the all-English audience sings along to the national anthem, 'Rule Britannia' and 'Land of Hope and Glory'. ⊖ *South Kensington*.

Wigmore Hall, 36 Wigmore Street, **t** (020) 7935 2141, *www.wigmore-hall.org.uk*. An intimate venue with excellent acoustics and solo performers. ⊖ *Bond Street, Oxford Circus*.

Sadler's Wells, Rosebery Ave, **t** (020) 7278 8916, *www.sadlers-wells.com*. Venue for all kinds of music, as well as dance and theatre; often avant-garde productions. ⊖ *Angel*.

St John's Smith Square, Smith Square, Westminster, **t** (020) 7222 1061, *www.sjss.org.uk*. One of the best lunchtime concert spots in town. Other good church venues include **St James Piccadilly** (Mon 1pm); **St Martin-in-the-Fields** in Trafalgar Square and **St Giles' Cripplegate**.

Dance

Everything from classical ballet to performance art. Covent Garden is home to the **Royal Ballet**. The **English National Ballet** performs at the Coliseum at Christmas (**t** (020) 7581 1245, *www.ballet.org.uk*). **Sadler's Wells** puts on an eclectic dance programme ranging from mime artist Lindsay Kemp to the National Ballet of Cambodia. **The Place Theatre** (17 Duke's Rd, Bloomsbury, **t** (020) 7380 1268, *www.theplace.org.uk*) is home of the **London Contemporary Dance School**. Every autumn London stages a festival called **Dance Umbrella**.

Jazz

One place that's always worth a visit is **Ronnie Scott's**, 47 Frith Street, W1, **t** (020) 7439 0747, *www.ronniescotts.co.uk*, the prime jazz venue in town, with a steady flow of big names and a low-key, laid-back atmosphere. Get there early (around 9pm) for a seat. *Open 8.30pm–3am, closed Sun*. ⊖ *Leicester Square*.

Oh thou, resort and mart of all the earth
Chequer'd with all complexions of mankind
And spotted with all crimes, in whom I see
Much that I love and more that I admire,
And all that I abhor...

William Cowper, *The Task*, Book III (1785)

London goes through drastic mood swings: grey, worthy and dull one minute, hip and happening the next. It has been accused of everything from provincialism to irredeemable sinfulness, and hailed as a cosmopolitan beacon of wealth and liberty. Just when it was being written off as the crumbling capital of a dead empire, the swinging sixties long over, London has come roaring back to life. After the ideological divisions of the Thatcher years, it is enjoying a renaissance: in Covent Garden, Notting Hill or Islington, you can barely move for people thronging to the latest art opening or the hottest ethnic restaurant. The capital is being redefined yet again by a creative generation of artists and designers, breaking down the fusty London of the past as others have done before. Suddenly, everything seems possible and Londoners are embracing the changes with barely a whiff of scepticism. Be warned, however. Amidst this creative frenzy, the old caveats about London still apply. It may be the most exciting city in Europe, but it is not the most beautiful, nor the easiest to get around. Visitors who expect too much too quickly come away disappointed.

Central London

Bloomsbury

Bloomsbury, according to *The Domesday Book*, was a breeding ground for pigs, but it has acquired a more refined pedigree since. Home to London University, the British Museum, the new British Library, bookshops and cafés, it is the intellectual heart of the capital. Marx and Lenin found inspiration in the British Library's Reading Room; Bertrand Russell and Virginia Woolf formed an artistic-intellectual movement here, the Bloomsbury Group, who met for tea and gossip in the area's Georgian town houses. Now it's a favoured location for the publishing trade and independent TV production companies. It's a quiet, slightly shabby but youthful quarter of London.

Bloomsbury Square was the original London housing development based on the leasehold system, and the model for the city's rapid 18th- and 19th-century growth. Now it is one of the more elegant squares in central London, with a ring of Georgian houses around a garden. It also has a plaque to the **Bloomsbury Group** (*see* p.196).

On the western side of the square looms **Senate House**, a sinister building, which stands at the heart of the **University of London**. Down the road you come to **Gower Street**, the blackened brick terraces which sum up everything the Victorians hated in Georgian building. Ruskin called it 'the *ni plus ultra* of ugliness in street architecture'. Along on the right, **University College** is a fine example of the Greek Revival style by

William Wilkins. Many Victorians hated it. Visitors head for the South Cloister in the far right-hand corner. Near the door is a glass cabinet with the stuffed body of **Jeremy Bentham**, the utilitarian philosopher and political reformer who died in 1832.

British Museum

Great Russell Street, **t** *(020) 7323 8299, www.thebritishmuseum.ac.uk; open Sat–Wed 10–5.30, Thurs and Fri 10–8.30*

In the 1770s, grumpy novelist Tobias Smollett complained that the fledgling British Museum was too empty and lacked a decent book collection. The museum has made up for both deficiencies since: stuffed with treasures from the British empire, and until recently boasting one of the finest libraries in the world, it has long been a magnet for visitors and scholars. With its stunning new Great Court, it is by far the most popular tourist attraction in London – proof that real quality wins the day.

Below is a guide to the museum's most famous and appealing artefacts.

On entering the museum, unsuspecting visitors stroll through the dim Victorian cavern of the South Portal and out into the luminous **Great Court**. Norman Foster's ingenious design, based on geometry and light, has attracted wide-ranging praise. In the centre of the Court is the Reading Room, wrapped in grand curving staircases. Drawn by the open space and dazzling light, you'll return here time and again from the relative gloom of the galleries, which lead off the court in all directions.

For the first time in its history, the **Reading Room** is open to the public. For more than a hundred years this was one of the best-loved rooms in the world, with a cavernous dome bigger in diameter than St Paul's. Designed by Sydney Smirke, it was the brainchild of Sir Antonio Panizzi, an Italian exile who invented the systems for labelling and cataloguing that are used in libraries to this day. A steady stream of the world's political thinkers came here, among them Marx (who wrote *Das Kapital* in Row G), Mazzini and Lenin. Other writers who have found inspiration, consolation and love among its eighteen million tomes include Thackeray, Hardy, Dickens and Yeats.

The new **Sainsbury African Galleries** on the north side of the Great Court house some of the finest African collections in the world, unusual in that they combine archaeological and contemporary material in a lively display.

Western Asian treasures are scattered throughout the museum, but the most accessible, the **Assyrian relics** of Nineveh, Balawat and Nimrud, are on the ground floor. The Assyrians constructed a civilization built on war with their neighbours, especially the Babylonians, between the 9th and 7th centuries BC. Their palaces were decorated with figures of wild animals, mythical creatures and magic symbols as well as depictions of soldiers. The most extraordinary artwork depicts a royal lion hunt. Upstairs is a sculpture, **The Ram in the Thicket** from Ur, birthplace of Abraham.

There are more lions in the **Egyptian** sculpture gallery, red and black ones carved in granite and limestone for the tombs of Pharaohs; Ruskin described them as 'the noblest and truest carved lions I have ever seen'. Among the ornate sarcophagi and Pharaohs' heads, look for the likeness of Amenophis III, and the gilded coffin of Henutmehit, the Chantress of Amen-Re, from 1290 BC. Many of the riddles of ancient Egypt were deciphered through the **Rosetta Stone**, a slab of black basalt discovered by

Napoleon's army in the Nile Delta in 1799, which reproduces the same text in three languages: Greek, demotic and Egyptian hieroglyphs.

The display of **Egyptian mummies and sarcophagi** is the most popular section of the British Museum, especially for children.

Two artworks overshadow the **Greek collections**: the Nereid Monument and the Elgin Marbles. The **Nereid Monument** is a reconstruction of a vast tomb found at the Greek colony of Xanthos in Asia Minor; it features remarkable frieze sculptures.

The **Elgin Marbles** have aroused so much controversy for being here rather than Greece that their artistic merit is sometimes overlooked. They are the frieze reliefs from the Parthenon, the temple to Athena on top of the Acropolis, and are considered some of the finest sculptures of antiquity; they reveal a remarkable mastery of detail and human feeling. Lord Elgin, the British Ambassador to the Ottoman Empire, discovered the stones in Athens in 1800. The Parthenon had been ruined in a skirmish between the Turks and a Venetian fleet besieging them in 1687. Elgin obtained a licence from the Turkish Sultan in 1802 to transport the treasures back home.

The highlight of the **Roman** collection is the **Portland Vase**, so called because the Barberini family sold it to the Dukes of Portland. The vase, made around the time of the birth of Christ, is of cobalt-blue glass and coated in an opaque white glaze depicting the reclining figures of Peleus and Thetis, with Cupid hovering overhead.

The most gruesome exhibit in the **Romano-British** section is **Lindow Man**, the shrivelled remains of an ancient Briton preserved in a peat bog. The body, dated between 300 BC and AD 100, shows evidence of extreme violence; all you see here is his torso and crushed head. A more pleasant surprise is the **Mildenhall Treasure**, 34 well-preserved pieces of 4th-century silver tableware dug up from a field in Suffolk.

You should not miss the medieval **Lewis chessmen**, a collection of 78 pieces in walrus ivory discovered in the Outer Hebrides in 1831. The farmer who first came across them fled thinking they were elves and fairies, and it was only the fortitude of his wife that persuaded him to go back for another look. The figures are thought to have been left by a travelling salesman some time in the 12th century.

The museum's vast collection of **prints and drawings** is displayed in rotation. On a good day you can find Michelangelo's sketches for the roof of the Sistine chapel, etchings and sketches by Rembrandt and anatomical studies by Albrecht Dürer. Look out for William Hogarth's satirical engravings, notably *Gin Lane*, which castigates the corrupting influence of drink on 18th-century London, and his series on cruelty.

British Library

*96 Euston Rd, **t** (020) 7412 7000, open Mon and Wed–Fri 9.30–6, Tues 9.30–8, Sat 9.30–5, Sun 11–5*

The British Library has been a surprise success. Construction of this new building began in 1978 and took longer to complete than St Paul's. Architect Colin St John Wilson overspent by £350 million, and the building was exposed to venomous criticism before its 1997 opening. Ironically, it's most vicious critics have been delighted by the spectacular interior, with its vast scale, open tracts of white Travertine marble, and complex and fascinating spaces flooded with light.

The big attraction is the library's **manuscripts**: from the sacred to the profane; from the delicate beauty of illuminated Bibles to the frenzied scrawl of Joyce's first draft of *Finnegan's Wake*; from musical scores to political documents to private letters. Among the greatest treasures are the **Lindisfarne Gospels** (*see* p.909) and the ***Magna Carta***. The British Library has two of the four surviving copies of this document, one of the founding texts of the modern democratic system, signed by King John at Runnymede under pressure from his barons in 1215. Among the other manuscripts are Lenin's reapplication for a reader's ticket under the pseudonym Jacob Richter. The extensive collection of literary manuscripts includes an illustrated version of Chaucer's *Canterbury Tales*, and Lewis Carroll's notebook version of *Alice in Wonderland*.

The City of London

The City is the heart of London, the place where the whole heaving metropolis began, and yet it is a strange, soulless desert – T. S. Eliot's 'Unreal City', wandered by the lost souls of limbo. Commuters stream in each morning, the bankers, brokers and clerks that oil the wheels of this centre of world finance; by early evening they have all vanished again. And yet it remains a fascinating place, full of echoes of the time when it *was* London. Its streets still follow the medieval plan, its fine churches and ceremonial buildings express the creation and loss of empire, and its business is still trade, as it was in the 14th century, even if it is trade of a most abstract sort.

Wren's churches, and St Paul's Cathedral in particular, grace the skyline, but the area is also characterized by the bloody carcasses of Smithfield meat market and the grim legacy of Newgate prison, now the Central Criminal Court. At the other end of the Square Mile, the Tower of London is a striking relic of medieval London. In keeping with London's new-found passion for all things big and tall, there are plans to construct a 728ft-high, 43-storey office block with a 128ft spire in Bishopsgate, and work has begun on a 180ft Norman Foster creation, nicknamed 'the erotic gherkin'.

In the Middle Ages the **Temple Bar** in Fleet Street controlled comings and goings into the City. Wren's arched gateway was removed in 1878 and replaced with a monument topped by a bronze **griffin**; one of the City's emblems, it was introduced by the Victorians, who remembered that the griffins of mythology guarded over a hidden treasure of gold. They presumably forgot that griffins also tore approaching humans to pieces as a punishment for their greed.

St Paul's Cathedral

St Paul's Churchyard; t (020) 7236 6883, www.stpauls.co.uk; open Mon–Sat 8.30–4.30; adm.

St Paul's is more than just a cathedral or famous landmark. It is an icon for the city. Get to know St Paul's and you understand London itself. For nearly 1,400 years, buildings on this site have sought to express the material confidence of a powerful capital, while at the same time delineating its spiritual aspirations. In the 7th century,

St Paul's was England's first major Christian temple; in its medieval incarnation it was the largest building in the land; Wren's version was hailed as an architectural masterpiece. Since then St Paul's has propped up national myths, as the burial place for heroes of empire, as a symbol of British endurance during the Blitz, and as the fairy-tale setting for Prince Charles's marriage to Lady Diana Spencer in 1981.

And yet St Paul's has often shared more with the commercial world outside than with the spiritual world celebrated within. In the Middle Ages, the cathedral was itself a kind of market, with horses parading down the nave and stallholders selling beer and vegetables to all-comers; today you are greeted by cash registers. While we may admire Wren's pure lines and lofty vision, we feel little warmth or sense of a living church community. St Paul's is a monument to wealth first, and God second.

Dilapidated old St Paul's was destroyed by the Great Fire of London on 4 September 1666, giving Christopher Wren his long-awaited chance to rebuild it from scratch. He set his heart on building a Baroque-style dome – considered excessively Popish in those religiously sensitive times. You can see a 20ft oak replica of his Great Model on display in the crypt. Wren got his dome through a mixture of guile and compromise. The royal warrant for his plan (with a steeple) granted him the liberty 'to make some variations rather ornamental than essential, as from time to time he should see proper'; when the cathedral opened 35 years later, Wren's dome was back.

The imposing scale of St Paul's is apparent as you approach the west front. A broad staircase leads up to a two-tiered portico upheld by vast stone columns and flanked by two clocktowers. Dominating the pediment is a statue of St Paul, with St Peter to his left and St James to his right; these three figures look down on the sovereign of the day, Queen Anne. The ensemble, the work of a single artist, Francis Bird, forges a clear mystical link between the City, the Crown and the Church.

The **nave** is vast but simple in its symmetries; concentrate on the harmony of the architecture and try to blank out the later and largely hideous statuary. On the marble floor beneath the dome you'll see the famous epitaph to Wren, added by his son after his death in 1723, '*Lector, si monumentam requiris, circumspice*' (Reader, if you seek a memorial, look around you). Look up to the **dome**, nowhere near as big on the inside as on the outside; in fact, Wren built a smaller second dome inside the first to keep the interior on a manageable scale. The story goes that the first stone of the dome was a relic from old St Paul's which bore the Latin word *resurgam* (rise up). Wren took it as a good portent and had the word inscribed in the pediment above the south door, adorning it with an image of a phoenix rising from the ashes.

For a small fee, you can climb up to the dome. The first stop is the **Whispering Gallery** 100ft up, so called because you can be heard with crystal clarity on the other side of the dome, 107ft away. Vertigo permitting, continue up to the Stone Gallery, the Inner Golden Gallery and the Outer Golden Gallery, with panoramic views of London from just below the ball and cross at a height of 365ft.

Down to the **crypt**, Wren's Great Model and the tombs of Britain's military leaders. Here you can find the Duke of Wellington in his porphyry casket and, directly beneath the dome, the black marble sarcophagus of Horatio Nelson.

Temple to Mansion House

Dr Johnson's House (*17 Gough Square, EC4,* **t** *(020) 7353 3745, www.drjh.dircon.co.uk; open May–Sept Mon–Sat 11–5.30; Oct–April 11–5; adm*) is the elegant 17th-century house where the Doctor lived from 1748 to 1759, compiling his famous dictionary.

Wren left the bulk of his 52 church renovations to subordinates, but **St Mary-le-Bow** (*Cheapside,* **t** *(020) 7248 5139; open Mon–Thurs 6.30–6, Fri 6.30–4*) bears all the signs of his own imprint. It is famous for its massive, distinctive 217ft steeple, and for its **Bow Bells**, whose peal persuaded Dick Whittington to return to London in search of fame and fortune. A true Londoner is said to be born within earshot of the pealing bells. The church has a magnificent Norman **crypt** too.

The **Guildhall** (*off Gresham Street;* **t** *(020) 7606 3030, www.cityoflondon.gov.uk; open Mon–Fri 10–4*) is the seat of the City government, headed by the Lord Mayor, his sheriffs and aldermen and composed of the 12 Great Livery Companies, or guilds, that nominally represent the City's trading interests. Nowadays the Corporation of London is little more than a borough council for the City, but in the Middle Ages it wielded near-absolute power over the whole of London, untouchable even by kings because of the guilds' wealth. Built in the 15th century, the hall has retained much from the medieval era, despite the Great Fire and the Blitz, but bears the mark of countless renovations. The pinnacled façade is a bizarre 18th-century concoction of classical, Gothic and even Indian styles. You can see the crypt by advance booking.

The **Guildhall Art Gallery** (*Guildhall Yard, off Gresham St;* **t** *(020) 7332 3700, www.guildhall-art-gallery. org.uk; open Mon–Sat 10–5, Sun 12–4; adm*) houses works collected by the Corporation of London since the 17th century. Most are of historical rather than aesthetic appeal: portraits of kings, queens and dignitaries and views of London. The star turn is John Singleton Copley's *The Defeat of the Floating Batteries at Gibraltar*, the largest oil painting in Britain.

The soaring gilt statue of Justice atop the **Old Bailey** (*Old Bailey and Newgate Street,* **t** *(020) 7248 3277; open Mon–Fri 10.30–1 and 2–4.30; no children under 14*) has become such a potent symbol of temperance in the English legal system that the site's barbarity has been forgotten; until 1902 it was Newgate Prison, a gruesome jail described by Henry Fielding as a prototype for hell: prisoners were left here, literally, to rot. The mood now could not be more different: its historical memory stretches back only as far as the famous trials of Oscar Wilde and 'Lord Haw-Haw'.

You can attend a **court hearing**, as good a spectacle as any, though sombre.

The church of **St Etheldreda** (*Ely Place,* **t** *(020) 7405 1061; open daily 8–6*) is dedicated to a 7th-century Anglo-Saxon princess who refused to have sex with her husbands. When Prince Egfrith of Northumbria made advances, she withdrew into holy orders at Ely, dying seven years later from a neck tumour. Disbelieving sister Sexburga had Etheldreda's coffin opened and found her skin unblemished. A miracle! This two-storey Gothic church, built in the 13th century as part of the Bishop of Ely's palace, has a fine stained-glass window, depicting the Holy Trinity surrounded by the Apostles and Anglo-Saxon and Celtic saints including Etheldreda. The **crypt** is much simpler.

The Brave New World architecture of the **Barbican Centre** (*Silk Street*, **t** *(020) 7638 8891, www.barbican.org.uk*) comes straight out of the 1950s, all high-rise concrete and labyrinthine walkways. The main reason for visiting is a trip to the **Arts Centre**, home to the London Symphony Orchestra, two theatres, three cinemas, two art galleries, two exhibition halls, a concert hall, a sculpture court and semi-tropical conservatory. **St Giles' Cripplegate** (**t** *(020) 7638 1997, www.stgilescripplegate.com; open Mon–Fri 11–4*), where John Milton was buried in 1674, is visible from the Barbican. The church itself was rebuilt after the Blitz. A stretch of Roman city wall can be seen behind it.

The ambitious **Museum of London** (*150 London Wall, EC2;* **t** *(020) 7600 3699, www.museumoflondon.org.uk; open Mon–Sat 10–5.50, Sun 12–5.50*) sets out to tell the story of London from prehistoric times to the present, drawing on a vast collection of documents and relics. It's a tremendous resource for the truly curious, although its archive of documents is far richer than its collection of artefacts. Many of the most fun displays are reconstructions: a 16th-century grocer's shop, a cell at Newgate Prison, a Victorian pub, a Second World War bedroom kitted out with a protective cage called a Morrison shelter. The undisputed centrepiece, however, is the Lord Mayor's Coach. Built in 1757 in blazing red and burnished gold, it is covered in allegorical paintings depicting the virtues of modesty and the glories of wealth.

Down the road, **Smithfield Market** has come a long way since the 14th century, when cattle were slaughtered in front of the customers; nowadays it's a civil, sanitized sort of place surrounded by restaurants and pubs.

By turns a centre for monks, clockmakers, gin-manufacturers and Italian labourers, **Clerkenwell** has the feel of a village with its squares, winding streets and pretty churches. Its proximity to the City made it an ideal headquarters for the knights of the Order of St John, who stayed here until the Dissolution of the monasteries in the 1530s. In the early 17th century the digging of the New River put Clerkenwell on the main freshwater route into London and so attracted brewers and distillers. In the 19th century Clerkenwell was slumland, and the Victorians built forbidding prisons there. After decades of neglect, it is now in full revival, its grimy backstreets filling with offices, converted lofts, attractive cafés and some of London's best restaurants.

The sites of Clerkenwell are all within easy reach from the **Green**, often used as a starting point for protest marches in the 19th century. The **Marx Memorial Library** at nos.37–8 (**t** *(020) 7523 1485, www.marxmemoriallibrary.sageweb.co.uk; open Mon 1–6, Tues–Thurs 1–8, Sat 10–1*) has the best private collection of radical literature in the city; Lenin wrote pamphlets here in 1902–3. Clerkenwell Close leads to the attractive yellow brick **St James's Church**, once part of a Benedictine nunnery.

Mansion House, the official residence of the Lord Mayor of London, is something of a failed Georgian experiment in the Palladian style. Designed by George Dance and completed in 1752, it's almost always shut (*call* **t** *(020) 7626 2500 if you're really keen*).

The Bank of England to the Tower

The eight huge Corinthian pillars of the **Royal Exchange** give the building a sense of importance to which it can no longer lay claim. It was home to all of London's stock and commodity exchanges until 1939. Designed by Sir William Tite in 1844, it is a rare example of Victorian neo-classical architecture. Notice the equestrian **statue of the Duke of Wellington**, made from the melted-down metal of French guns.

The playwright Richard Sheridan described the **Bank of England** as 'an elderly lady in the City of great credit and long standing'. Its record as prudent guardian of the nation's finances is well known; it rescued London from bankruptcy at the end of the 17th century, resisted the temptations of the South Sea Bubble and kept the country's economy buoyant throughout the Revolutionary wars against France. As the bank of last resort it played a crucial role in the development of Britain's capitalist system during the 18th and 19th centuries. But the Bank has had a tough time of it since the abandonment of worldwide currency controls in the 1970s; the rise of unfettered currency speculation has limited its control over the value of sterling, and the changing nature of international capital has made it hard for the Bank to monitor the commercial banks. In compensation, it has won independence from the Treasury and is now free to set interest rates as it sees fit, but the whole enterprise is under threat from the single European currency and its pan-European central bank in Frankfurt.

Architecturally, the Bank has a mixed record. A magnificent 18th-century building by Sir John Soane was destroyed in 1925 to create more space. All that remains of Soane's work is the curtain wall and a reconstructed **Bank Stock Office**. Beneath Soane's vaulted roof, the **Bank of England Museum** (*entrance on Bartholomew Lane;* ***t*** *(020) 7601 5545, www.bankofengland.co.uk; open Mon–Fri 10–5*) is surprisingly entertaining; most absorbing of all is a large transparent pyramid full of gold bars.

The City's most innovative building is Richard Rogers' **Lloyd's of London**, the world's biggest insurance market. On Leadenhall St you can see a fine façade from the 1925 Lloyd's. The entrance to the building is on Lime Street, a continuation of St Mary Axe.

Leadenhall Market is a whiff of real life among the office blocks, with plenty of bustle, live music, cafés and excellent food; game and exotic fish dominate. The **Monument** (***t*** *(020) 7626 2717; open 10–6; adm*) commemorates the Great Fire of London. On completion in 1677 it was the tallest free-standing column in the world.

Tower Bridge and the Tower of London

Just to the south of the City, Tower Bridge (***t*** *(020) 7403 3761; www.towerbridge.org.uk; open daily April–Oct 10–6.30, Nov–Mar 9.30–6; adm*) is one of the great feats of late Victorian engineering, half suspension-bridge and half drawbridge, linked to two neo-Gothic towers. Designed by an engineer, John Wolfe-Barry, and an architect, Horace Jones, in tandem, it has become one of London's most recognizable landmarks. Its fame was not instant, however; at its opening in 1894, the critics found its evocation of medieval style crude. *The Builder* called it 'the most monstrous and preposterous architectural sham that we have ever known...an elaborate and costly make-believe.' There is still a case to be made for all this. Its two bascules, the arms that rise up to let tall ships through, weigh 1,000 tonnes each. The bridge still opens at least once a day on average; call ahead (***t*** *(020) 7403 3761*) to find out the times.

At the southern tower is the **Tower Bridge Experience**, a hi-tech history of the bridge, plus a chance to enjoy the view from overhead walkways and admire the giant Victorian hydraulic engines that once operated the bridge.

The **Tower of London** (*Tower Hill; www.hrp. org.uk; open Mar–Oct Mon–Sat 9–6, Sun 10–6; Nov–Feb Mon–Sat 9–5, Sun 10–5; adm exp*) is one London sight that everyone knows but nobody likes. Ever since the monarchy moved out in the early 17th century, the Tower has existed principally as a stronghold of historical nostalgia. Modern Americans might want to compare it to the fantasy castles of Disneyland, especially if they follow the **Tower Hill Pageant** (entrance near All Hallows' Church) past tableaux of episodes in London's history.

The big attraction is the site, one of the best preserved medieval castles in the world. The **White Tower**, the keep at the centre of the complex, dates back to William the Conqueror and includes the 13th-century **St John's Chapel**. And the Tower corresponds to every myth ever invented about England. Its history is packed with tales of royal pageantry, dastardly baronial plots, grisly tortures and gruesome executions. The Tower is still guarded by quaint liveried figures, the Beefeaters, who conduct their Ceremony of the Keys at 9.45 each evening. And of course the Tower contains the fabulous **Crown Jewels**.

Covent Garden, Strand and Holborn

Covent Garden is home to the Royal Opera House, the old fruit and vegetable market, and is teeming with restaurants, boutiques and street performers.

Some find modern Covent Garden spoiled, yet looking into the past one should be relieved at how pleasant it is. When the wholesale market moved out to the south London suburbs in the 1970s, the London authorities wanted to build a major road through here. It was the local traders and residents who saved Covent Garden. If it all seems a little derivative, it is because it deliberately echoes its own past – a dash of Inigo Jones' original piazza, several measures of Charles Fowler's covered market, plus plenty of the eating, drinking and revelry that have always characterized this area.

Covent Garden Market has undoubtedly lost its rough edges – the main hall, once littered with crates and stray vegetables, is now spick and span, while the Flower Market houses transport and theatre museums – but the place has not lost its soul. You can still buy roast chestnuts from a street vendor, as Dickens did, or watch clowns in front of St Paul's where Punch and Judy shows first caught the public imagination.

The pedestrian alley of **Neal Street** is a mix of beads and wholefood shops vying for custom with designer boutiques. Down Shorts Gardens and you come to tranquil, New Age **Neal's Yard**, an oasis of cheap vegetarian food and natural therapies. Opposite is **Thomas Neal's Arcade**, a pseudo-Victorian arcaded emporia.

Trainspotters and families might like to visit the **London Transport Museum** (*39 Wellington Street, **t** (020) 7379 6344, www.ltmuseum.co.uk; open Sat–Thurs 10–6, Fri 11–6; adm; full disabled access*), which celebrates the system, from the red London Routemaster bus to the London Underground map, designed in 1931 by Harry Beck.

More entertainment is to be found at the **Theatre Museum** (*Tavistock Street, Covent Garden, WC2, **t** (020) 7943 4700, theatremuseum.vam.ac.uk; open Tues–Sun 10–6*), a collection of fabulous theatrical oddments – from Edmund Kean's death mask to the hand-printed costumes used by the Diaghilev Ballets Russes to premiere *The Rite of Spring in Paris* in 1913 – much enlivened by tours by actors.

Two of the most famous London theatres are a stone's throw away: the **Theatre Royal Drury Lane**, and the **Royal Opera House**, better known simply as Covent Garden. A redevelopment of the 1858 opera house building was completed in 1999. The political rows and financial problems that dogged the revamp have refused to go away (despite pledges to open up opera to the masses, tickets for some productions still cost up to £140) but the building itself has been hailed a success, with its beautiful Floral Hall and views across Covent Garden from the Amphitheatre restaurant.

Across Bow Street is the old **Bow Street Magistrates' Court**, where the Fieldings, Henry and John, held court in the 18th century. Henry, who was a barrister as well as the author of *Tom Jones*, used his tenure here to set up the Bow Street Runners; this informal plain-clothes police force cracked down on underworld gangs, challenging the infamous official marshals, or 'thief-takers', who were in cahoots with thieves. The Runners became famous for thwarting the Cato Street conspiracy in 1820. Until Robert Peel's 'bobbies' appeared in the 1830s, they were London's only police.

Don't be surprised if you feel you are sneaking up on **St Paul's Church** (*Inigo Place,* ***t*** *(020) 7836 5221; church and gardens open Tues–Fri 9.30–4.30, services Sun 11am*) from behind: you are. St Paul's is part of the original piazza that Inigo Jones built in mock-Italian style in the 1630s, but he and his low-church patron, the Earl of Bedford, reckoned they could get away with putting the altar at the western end. The Bishop of London ordered Jones to put the altar where it belonged, in the east, and flush against the planned main entrance. The interior is of disarminging simplicity: a double square, 100ft by 50ft. St Paul's won the affections of Covent Garden's theatre folk, who nicknamed it the Actors' Church; Ellen Terry, *grande dame* of late-Victorian theatre is buried here. St Paul's is one of few pre-Great Fire buildings left in London.

Across the Strand (not much of a beach these days) is the **Courtauld Institute**, now housed in Somerset House (*Strand, WC2;* ***t*** *(020) 7873 2526, www.courtauld.ac.uk; open daily 10–6; adm, free Mon; full disabled access*). The first Renaissance palace in England, it was demolished in the 1770s and replaced by a fine Georgian building by William Chambers, where the institute's exquisite collection of paintings, notably Impressionists and post-Impressionists, is now displayed. There is a magnificent *Adam and Eve* by Lucas Cranach the Elder and some fine Rubens, including his early masterpiece *The Descent from the Cross*. The Impressionists include a copy by the artist of Manet's *Le Déjeuner sur l'Herbe*, some wonderful Degas studies of dancers and moody Cézanne landscapes.

It's worth venturing a little further to the Inns of Court and **Sir John Soane's Museum** (*12–14 Lincoln's Inn Fields;* ***t*** *(020) 7405 2107, www.soane.org; open Tues–Sat 10–5; adm*). Soane (1753–1837) was a great English eccentric and architect, a fanatical student of antiquity and one of Britain's towering neo-classicists. In his three houses here he adapted each room to his quirky style and filled them with objects from his remarkable art collection. The whole collection was bequeathed to the public, with the stipulation that it be maintained as it was on the day of Soane's death. The Picture Room contains Hogarth's great satirical series of paintings, *The Rake's Progress*, and studies by Piranesi. Soane's other prize exhibit is the sarcophagus of the Egyptian Pharaoh Seti I (1303–1290BC) in the Sepulchral Chamber, but you will derive as much pleasure from Soane's classical colonnade along the upstairs corridor, his classical plaster casts or the use of mirrors to manipulate light in the house.

Trafalgar Square

Back in the 1810s and 1820s, when Britannia really did rule the waves and London was the capital of an empire, urban planning suddenly came into fashion. Previously, London had developed organically according to the whims of private landowners. But then industrialization arrived, threatening to stifle the capital in factory smoke, and Britain's victory in the Napoleonic Wars unleashed a desire for decent monumental architecture. The Prince Regent, an ardent patron of grand building schemes, was happy to sponsor major projects, and soon architects were putting forward proposals.

It was in this atmosphere that Trafalgar Square was conceived. The Prince Regent (later George IV) and John Nash wanted to create a vast open space glorifying the country's naval power. It was a fine idea, truncated by the vagaries of history. George developed a reputation as a spendthrift and, as economic crisis gripped the nation in the mid-1820s, his dreams were halted by a hostile parliament. Nash was dismissed when George died in 1830, and the square was left at the mercy of parliamentary committees who argued for the best part of a generation over its final form.

The whole Trafalgar Square project might have been abandoned had it not been for a determination to bestow honours on Horatio Nelson, the country's legendary naval commander who had died at sea during the Battle of Trafalgar in 1805. In 1808, the essayist William Wood proposed erecting a giant pyramid to his hero. Over the years 120 official proposals were submitted; **Nelson's Column** did not see the light of day until 1843. The Corinthian column, topped by a barely visible likeness of Nelson in his admiral's three-cornered hat, by E. H. Baily, was erected on a sloping basin prepared by the neo-classical architect Charles Barry. The bronze bas-reliefs at the base of the column represent Nelson's four greatest victories, at Cape St Vincent, the Nile, Copenhagen and Trafalgar. The two granite fountains arrived in 1845, while the bronze lions appeared a quarter of a century later.

The plinth at the northwest corner of the square remained empty for more than 150 years, a testimony to British inertia. In 1999 the Royal Society for the encouragement of Arts (RSA) stepped in with the Fourth Plinth Exhibition, a temporary display of contemporary sculpture. Mark Wallinger's *Ecce Homo* and Bill Woodrow's *Regardless of History* were followed by Rachel Whiteread's *Monument*, a direct-take on the plinth itself. Since its dismantling in May 2002, the plinth is once again empty.

Trafalgar Square is the point from which all measurements in London are drawn, as shown by a plaque on the corner of Charing Cross Road. On the eastern side of the square is South Africa House, where anti-apartheid protesters maintained a constant vigil through Nelson Mandela's 26-year imprisonment. Next door is James Gibbs' church of St Martin-in-the-Fields. In the southeastern corner stands a lamp-post known as the smallest police station in the world, with a telephone linked up to police headquarters at Scotland Yard.

The **National Gallery** (*Trafalgar Square;* ***t*** *(020) 7747 2885, www.nationalgallery.org.uk; open daily 10–6*) is an astonishing collection of West European painting from the 13th to the early 20th centuries, including masterpieces from virtually every major school. Its great names include Leonardo da Vinci, Piero della Francesca, Van Eyck, Raphael, Titian, Veronese, Rubens, Poussin, Rembrandt, Velázquez, Caravaggio, Turner, Constable, Delacroix, Monet, Van Gogh, Cézanne and Picasso. It's a 19th-century phenomenon: a catalogue of paintings from the Grand Tradition reflecting the pride and power of the collector nation. Pick up a floor plan from the information desk and you'll see that the gallery's four wings each concentrate on a different historical period, starting with early medieval Italian painting in the new Sainsbury Wing and moving gradually eastwards towards the 20th century.

Next door is the **National Portrait Gallery** (*St Martin's Lane, WC2;* ***t*** *(020) 7306 0055, www.npg.org.uk; open Sat–Wed 10–6, Thurs and Fri 10–9*), unique, and a true oddity. The portraits of Britian's kings, generals, ministers, pioneers, inventors and artists have not been chosen according to the quality of the painting, nor are there any radicals represented. The Victorian aristocrats who founded the gallery set it up as a stern kind of history lesson. The best paintings are probably Holbein's vivid Henrys VII and VIII and Sir Thomas More, and a Cubist T. S. Eliot by Jacob Epstein.

St Martin-in-the-Fields (***t*** *(020) 7839 8362, www.stmartin-in-the-fields.org; open Mon–Sat 10–8*) is the oldest building on Trafalgar Square. Its churchyard, now a junk market, contains the graves of Charles II's mistress Nell Gwynne and the 18th-century painters Reynolds and Hogarth. The church is popular for its free lunchtime and evening concerts and resident orchestra, the Academy of St Martin-in-the-Fields. As you walk up **St Martin's Lane**, you have already stepped into London's theatreland. Its theatres – the Albery and Duke of York's, as well as the Coliseum (home of the English National Opera) – were some of the last great playhouses to be built in London. But in the 18th century the street attracted such artistic residents as Joshua Reynolds, first president of the Royal Academy, and Thomas Chippendale, the furniture maker.

Mayfair

The May Fair was once just that: an annual festival of eating, drinking, entertainments and debauchery that took place in the first two weeks of May. It began in 1686, when the area was in its infancy; by the mid-18th century, the neighbourhood had gone so far upmarket that the residents described the fair as 'that most pestilent nursery of impiety and vice' and shut it down for good. Mayfair has been pretty staid ever since. There are some fine 18th-century houses around Curzon Street, and a few oddities, but Mayfair has not lived up to its early promise: it is cosmopolitan and expensive, but not fashionable; elegant and well maintained, but not sophisticated.

Start at **Apsley House** (*Hyde Park Corner,* ***t*** *(020) 7499 5676, www.apsleyhouse.org.uk; open Tues–Sun 11–5; adm*), dubbed Number 1 London by Wellington, who was given it as a reward for his victories against the French. Oddly enought, the highlight of the mucked-around Adam building is Canova's double-life-size sculpture of Wellington's nemesis Napoleon, stolen by the British hero from the Louvre after its megalomaniac subject rejected it.

Three kinds of shopkeeper dominate **Bond Street**: jewellers, art dealers and big-name fashion houses, whose gaudy shop fronts make for a diverting stroll. **Old Bond Street** is mainly jewellery and includes all the well-known names: Tiffany's, Cartier *et al.*, who seem to survive every recession. The street brought a rare piece of good luck to the 18th-century rake and gambler, Charles James Fox, who made a bet with the Prince of Wales on the number of cats appearing on each side of the street. No fewer than 13 cats appeared on Fox's side, and none on the Prince of Wales's. Maybe Fox should have taken his inauspicious number of cats as an omen and steered clear of the gambling dens of St James's, since he later went bankrupt.

Just after Stafford Street is the kitsch **Royal Arcade**. Through it, on Albemarle Street, is **Brown's Hotel**, one of the quintessential addresses of aristocratic London, founded by a former manservant in 1837. Franklin and Eleanor Roosevelt honeymooned here, while the Dutch government declared war on Japan from Room 36 in 1944. Come for tea, as classy but slightly cheaper than the Ritz; dress smart.

New Bond Street is the province of high-class designer clothes and accessory shops, plus the showrooms of well-established art dealers (there are more on Cork Street). Sotheby's, the famous auctioneer, is at nos.34–5; above the front door is an ancient Egyptian figure made of igneous rock dating back to 1600 BC.

There may not be any more May Fairs in Mayfair, but **Shepherd's Market**, a warren of cafés, restaurants and small shops, comes as a nice surprise after all the stuffiness. Back in the 17th century, this was where the fire-eaters, jugglers, dwarves and boxers would entertain the crowds in early spring. The entrepreneur Edward Shepherd turned the area into a market in 1735 (notice the attractive low Georgian buildings).

Berkeley Square is a key address for débutantes and aristocratic young bucks, who come for the annual Berkeley Square Charity Ball. The chief interest to visitors is the elegant row of Georgian houses on the west side. No.44, described by Nikolaus Pevsner as 'the finest terraced house in London', was built in 1742–4 for one of the royal household's maids of honour. It's now a private casino, the Clermont Club (once a haunt of Lord Lucan), and its stunning interior is out of bounds to the public.

St George's Hanover Square, a neo-classical church with a striking Corinthian portico, was built in 1721–4 as part of the Fifty New Churches Act. It is the parish church of Mayfair and enduringly popular as a venue for society weddings, including the match between Shelley and Mary Godwin.

Just north of Mayfair across Oxford Street, the **Wallace Collection** (*Hertford House, Manchester Square;* **t** *(020) 7935 0687, www.the-wallace-collection.org.uk; open Mon–Sat 10–5, Sun 12–5*) is a perfect monument to 18th-century aristocratic life, a sumptuous array of painting, porcelain and furniture housed in a period mansion called Hertford House. It's the setting that makes it so splendid, but highlights include works by Frans Hals (*The Laughing Cavalier*), Rembrandt (*Titus*), Rubens

(*Christ's Charge to Peter and The Holy Family*), Poussin (*Dance to the Music of Time*) and Titian (*Perseus and Andromeda*).

Piccadilly and Leicester Square

Piccadilly has long been considered vulgar. The name derives from the fortunes of Robert Baker, a tailor who made a fortune and built himself a mansion here in 1612. At the time, there was nothing here but a windmill. Baker's envious peers ridiculed his ostentation by calling his house Pickadilly Hall to remind him of his humble origins (a *pickadil* being a contemporary term for a shirt cuff or hem).

The 18th-century development of St James's and Mayfair made Piccadilly one of the busiest roads in London. The area continued to grow more crowded: in the late 19th century Shaftesbury Avenue and a flurry of new theatres were built; an Underground station was constructed, followed by vast advertising hoardings on the side of the London Pavilion music hall. Virginia Woolf and others found it marvellous, describing Piccadilly Circus as 'the heart of life...where everything desirable meets'. After the Second World War the ads went electric, adding a touch of modernity.

In the late 19th century, **Leicester Square** was *the* place to be seen of an evening, especially for middle-class men looking to flirt with 'actresses'. Attractions included the gaudy Alhambra Music Hall, Turkish baths, oyster rooms and dance halls. But all the fine buildings, including the 17th-century Leicester House, which gave its name to the square, are gone. The Blitz destroyed both buildings and the spirit of the place. Come here at more or less any time of day or night, however, and you will find a rough-and-ready crowd of cinema-goers, student tourists, buskers, street performers, portrait painters and pickpockets. For the dedicated star-spotter it's the place to catch A-list celebs treading the red carpet whenever there's a glitzy première at the Odeon.

The neon hoardings of **Piccadilly Circus** have become synonymous with London, along with red double-decker buses and the Queen. Quite why is a mystery. The best thing about it is the view down Lower Regent Street towards St James's Park. Two curiosities are nevertheless worth a moment's attention. The first is the **Criterion Brasserie**, which has a long dining room sumptuously adorned in neo-Byzantine style; the second is the **Eros statue**, a winged aluminium figure fashioned in memory of the Victorian philanthropist Lord Shaftesbury and unveiled in 1893. It is not in fact supposed to be Eros, the cherubic god of love, at all; artist Sir Alfred Gilbert intended it to be an Angel of Christian Charity, in memory of Lord Shaftesbury's good works.

Regent Street was once the finest street in London, but you wouldn't think it now. All it boasts are a few fine shops (men's clothes stores) and some stuffy buildings livened up once a year by electric Christmas decorations (and gawping crowds). Sadly the original plan, drawn up in 1813 by John Nash for the Prince Regent, never came to fruition. Nash's idea was to make Regent Street the main north-south artery linking the prince's residence at Carlton House on The Mall to Regent's Park; it would have been the centrepiece of an ensemble of squares, palaces and public thoroughfares.

The **Café Royal** (*t (020) 7437 9090; open Mon–Sat 10–11*) at no.68 has not changed much. A liveried doorman stands guard over one of the most fashionable addresses of the decadent years leading up to the First World War. Its extravagant mirrors, velvet seats and caryatid sculptures have remained as they were when Oscar Wilde, Aubrey Beardsley and Edward, Prince of Wales, held court here in the naughty 1890s.

From Piccadilly Circus to Green Park, **Piccadilly** is the southern edge of Mayfair. Here you can find **Fortnum & Mason**, the ultimate old-fashioned luxury English food shop (*t (020) 7734 8040, www.fortnumandmason.com; open Mon–Sat 10–6.30, Sun 12–6*), and the **Ritz Hotel**, where afternoon tea is an institution (*t (020) 7300 2308; daily 12–5*). Small high-class shops can be found in the streets to either side: Jermyn Street and Savile Row, and elegant arcades. Piccadilly is also home to the **Royal Academy** (*Burlington House, Piccadilly, W1; t (020) 7300 8000, www.royalacademy.org.uk; open 10–6 daily, 'til 10pm on Fridays; adm*), in Lord Burlington's Palladian villa (1720). It is one of London's most important exhibition venues, staging major historical shows as well as the famed Summer Exhibition, a traditional showcase for amateur British artists.

St James's Piccadilly (*t (020) 7734 4511; open daily*) is at odds with its neighbourhood, unmarked by pretension. From an architectural point of view, it is an object lesson in effortless grace and charm. It is the only church that Christopher Wren built from scratch in London, and as such most clearly expresses his vision of the church as a place where the relationship between priest and congregation should be demystified. St James's (1684) is airy and spacious, with the altar and pulpit accessible to all. An elegant gilded wooden gallery runs around the western end, supported by Corinthian pillars in plaster adorned with intricate decorations. There are beautiful carvings by Grinling Gibbons, on the limewood reredos behind the altar and on the stone font.

Burlington Arcade (1819) is the most famous of London's arcades, because of its top-hatted beadles who enforce quaint rules: no whistling, no singing and no running.

Soho and Chinatown

Here, halfway between the pomp of Westminster and the venal frenzy of the City, is where Londoners come to enjoy themselves. Soho still thrives off its reputation as a seedy, alluring hang-out for sozzled eccentrics who made the place famous after the Second World War. Nowadays the sleaze is disappearing, supplanted by the flashy cars and modish whims of advertising and media darlings.

Lowlifes and aristocrats have long dwelt side by side in Soho. In the 18th century it was fashionable with salon hostesses, artists and whores. In Victorian times it was full of cowsheds; for polite society, the area became a byword for depravity. In 1931 the Lord Chamberlain authorised nudity on stage for the first time at a revue at the Windmill Theatre, although he stipulated that the lighting had to remain low and the showgirls could not move, rules which were unchanged until the Second World War.

It was after the war that Soho came into its own. In the 1950s it became the centre of the avant-garde in jazz, new writing, experimental theatre and cinema, creating a subculture based on rebellion, permissiveness, *joie de vivre*, booze and drugs. Above all, Soho developed its own community of intellectuals and eccentrics, people of all classes mingling, borrowing money off each other and getting pleasantly tippled in pubs or illicit 'near-beer' bars that stayed open outside the stringent licensing hours.

Like all golden ages, 1950s Soho came to a sorry end. The liberalization of the 1960s and '70s brought peepshows and strip joints, which nearly destroyed the neighbourhood. The authorities, outraged by prostitutes soliciting on every street, threatened to bulldoze the whole district. It wasn't until the mid-1980s that new laws regulated the porn business and Soho regained some of its spirit. So attractive has Soho become that mainstream trendies have muscled in on the fun. Not a week goes by without a new bar, a new restaurant, a new fad: today it might be sushi served by robots; next week cafés that look like middle-class living rooms. Above all, Soho's main artery, Old Compton Street, is now the centre *par excellence* of London's gay café culture.

A contemporary statue of Charles II by Caius Gabriel Cibber stands in the gardens of **Soho Square**, behind a mock-Tudor toolshed. On the corner of **Greek Street** is a stern Victorian establishment, the **House of St Barnabas**, founded in 1846 to improve the lot of the poor through Christian teaching. This was where Gladstone would take prostitutes during night-time walks through the area in the early 1850s. His declared aim was to talk them out of their sinful ways, but cynical tongues wagged.

In **Frith Street** you will see **Ronnie Scott's** famous jazz club and a plethora of restaurants, including **Jimmy's**, a basement Greek café serving cheap moussaka and chips, which has changed little since the Rolling Stones ate there in the 1960s. Many phantoms also haunt **Dean Street**. The **French House** was the official HQ of the Free French forces under De Gaulle during the Second World War, and the unofficial HQ of literary Soho in the 1950s. Now it's a lively pub-cum-wine bar. Two clubs further down the street illustrate the changes in Soho. **The Colony** was once described as 'a place where the villains look like artists and the artists look like villains'. The **Groucho** – so called because of Groucho Marx's one-liner that he never wanted to join a club that would have him as a member – opened in 1985 and has been a hit with the world of television, music, comedy, publishing and film ever since.

The restaurant **Quo Vadis** became trendy in 1996 after it was bought from its Italian owners by Marco Pierre White (famous London superchef) and Damien Hirst (Young British Artist or 'YBA'-cum-restaurateur) and refurbished. Upstairs is where Karl Marx lived with his family in 1851–6 in a two-room attic flat in conditions of abject penury.

In many ways **Old Compton Street** is the archetypal Soho street, as well as the heart of gay London. Here you'll find cafés like **Pâtisserie Valerie**, restaurants, delis, gay clubs and bars, and modest-looking newsagents stocking every conceivable title on the planet. **Wardour Street** has been taken over by film companies.

Berwick Street Market always has fresh produce at incredibly low prices for central London. Ever since Jack Smith introduced the pineapple to London here in 1890, the market has had a reputation for unusual and exotic fruit and veg. The houses behind the stalls, like the market itself, date back to the 18th century. There are a couple of old pubs (The Blue Posts is the most salubrious), a scattering of noisy independent record stores and several excellent old-fashioned theatrical fabric shops specializing in unusual silks, satins, velvets, Chinese printed silks and printed cottons.

London's Chinese population came mostly from Hong Kong in the 1950s and '60s, victims of the cruel fluctuations of the Asian rice market. Back then Gerrard Street, like the rest of Soho, was cheap, run-down and welcoming to foreigners. It took more than a generation for the new community to be fully accepted, however, and it was not until the 1970s that this street was pedestrianized and kitted out with decorative lamps and telephone boxes styled like pagodas. Many of the older generation have only a rudimentary grasp of English, and remain suspicious of their adoptive home. The younger generation has integrated rather better; those born here are mockingly nicknamed BBCs (British-born children).

Chinatown extends round the block to Lisle Street and trades heavily in food: lots of restaurants – most cheap, some excellent – and supermarkets. There's always been a discreet business in gambling – underground dens for mah-jong, pai-kau and fan tan.

St James's and Royal London

St James's is a peculiarly British looking-glass world where everyone eats marmalade sandwiches and drinks tea from Fortnum & Mason, inhabited by kindly middle-aged gentlemen with bespoke tailored suits, where shopkeepers are called purveyors and underlings wear livery coats. What's more, this fairyland comes with a queen in a palace guarded by toy soldiers in busby hats and red, blue and black uniforms. St James's is the preserve of the Establishment, an old and rarefied pedigree that whiles away the hours in private clubs, and is endlessly lampooned on film.

A sense of occasion is invoked by the grand concave triple entrance of **Admiralty Arch**, the start of the long straight drive along The Mall to Buckingham Palace. You can appreciate St James's Park to your left, and, on your right, the white stone fronts of **Carlton House Terrace**, the remnants of one of London's more lavish building projects. The Prince of Wales (later George IV) commissioned architect Henry Holland to create a royal palace here, but 30 years and countless Corinthian columns later he had it demolished. John Nash constructed these elegant terraces in its place. They have housed many a club; now the most interesting is the **Institute of Contemporary Arts**, a surprising location for an avant-garde art centre with excellent café and bookshop.

Across The Mall is the home of the **Horse Guards**, the Queen's Household Division – seven regiments allocated the task of dressing up in toy-soldier costumes and parading in front of Buckingham Palace. Housed here and at Wellington Barracks are the Household Cavalry, Life Guards, Blues and Royals, Grenadiers, Coldstream Guards and the Scots, Irish and Welsh guards. The best time to see them is the first weekend in June, when they parade in front of the Queen in a ceremony known as **Trooping the Colour**. Otherwise you can make do with the **Changing of the Guard** (*outside the Horse Guards daily at 11am, or Buckingham Palace May–Aug daily at 11.30am*).

Buckingham Palace

On 7 August 1993, **Buckingham Palace** (*Buckingham Palace Road,* **t** *(020) 7799 2331, www.royal.gov.uk; open Aug and Sept daily 9.30–5.30; adm exp*) opened its doors to the public for the first time. For generations, royalists had invoked the need to preserve the mystery of the monarchy and refused, in the words of Walter Bagehot, to 'let daylight in upon its magic'. But by the early 1990s, after two royal marriage break-ups and a fire at Windsor Castle in what the Queen herself dubbed her '*annus horribilis*' (1992), the British monarchy needed to rally public opinion. As a PR coup, opening the doors of Buck House proved a flop, at least with media critics, but the public was more forgiving.

The tour takes in just 18 of Buckingham Palace's 661 rooms, stripped down to the bare minimum to ensure they are not sullied by the savage hordes: the original carpets are rolled away and replaced with industrial-strength red Axminster rugs that clash with the fake-marble columns, the greens, pinks and blues of the flock wallpapers, and the gold and cream ornamental ceilings. It is hard to imagine that anybody lives in such soulless surroundings, with not even a royal photo to welcome you.

The state rooms, filled with ostentatious chandeliers, chintzy furniture and ornate gilt and painted plaster ceilings, make you feel as though you are trapped in a Dairy Milk chocolate box. The real highlight is the 155ft-long **Picture Gallery**, crammed from floor to ceiling with the cream of the royal collection of some 10,000 paintings. The gems stand out easily enough: Van Dyck's idealized portraits of Charles I; Rembrandt's *Lady with a Fan*, *Agatha Bas* and *The Shipbuilder and His Wife*; landscapes by Ruisdael, Poussin and Claude Lorrain; portraits by Frans Hals; Rubens' underwhelming *St George and the Dragon*; Albert Cuyp's *Landscape with a Negro Page;* and much more besides. Apart from Charles I, the only royal to receive pictorial justice here is Victoria, whose family is cosily captured in Franz Winterhalter's 1846 portrait in the East Gallery.

You may linger and enjoy some fine views in the garden, before moving on to the highlight of the visit – the souvenir shop. This is the most telling part of the tour, with mugs, royal videos, Belgian chocolates moulded into the shape of the crown, or the attractive Buckingham Palace gold toothmug.

St James's

The curious name of **Pall Mall** derives from an ancient Italian ball game, *palla a maglio*, or ball and mallet; Charles II liked it so much that he built this pall mall alley. This is the high street of London's **clubland**. Former club *maître d'* Anthony O'Connor has defined the London club as a place 'where a well-born buck can get away from worries, women and anything that even faintly smacks of business in a genteel atmosphere of good cigars, mulled claret and obsequious servants'. However, the end of Empire and the emancipation of domestic servants brought about a sharp decline in clubland, from 120 clubs before the Second World War to 40 now. The most impressive is the **Athenaeum** on Waterloo Place, one of the best Greek Revival buildings in London. Look out for the brass plates of other clubs, including the Travellers', the United Oxford and Cambridge, the Army and Navy and the **Reform Club**.

Along with Pall Mall, **St James's Street** is clubland *par excellence*, with a reputation for its gambling dens. **White's**, the oldest London club, ran books on everything from births and marriages to politics and death in the 18th century. It was soon eclipsed by

Brooks down the road, where Charles James Fox ran up debts of £140,000, cadging money off the waiters before his father, Lord Holland, bailed him out in 1781.

For more than 300 years St James's Palace was the official residence of England's kings and queens; foreign ambassadors are still accredited to the Court of St James. Endowed with fine buildings, St James's Palace became known as a raucous place of debauchery under Queen Anne and the early Hanoverians, who held drunken banquets. Anne was known for her unseemly appetite for food and drink, particularly brandy, and for the bodily noises she frequently emitted at table. The Prince Regent celebrated his disastrous marriage with Caroline of Brunswick here in 1795, spending his wedding night fully dressed in a drunken slumber in the fireplace of the bridal chamber. When he moved into Carlton House, the palace's glory days were over. A fire destroyed the original buildings in 1809.

The gracious Palladian mansion of **Spencer House** (*27 Queen's Walk, www.spencerhouse.co.uk; open Feb–July and Sept–Dec Sun 10.30–5.45; adm; visit by guided tour only*) was born in sorrow: its original backer, Henry Bromley, ran out of money and shot himself moments after reading his will over with his lawyer. It was taken over by the Spencer family (ancestors of Princess Diana) who hired a bevy of architects, including John Vardy and Robert Adam, to produce one of the finest private houses in London. Completed in 1766, Spencer House boasts magnificent parquet floors, ornate plaster ceilings, gilded statues and furniture. The highlight is Vardy's Palm Room.

St James's Square was the start of a fashionable residential district. Just before the Great Fire of 1666, Charles II granted a lease to Henry Jermyn, Earl of St Albans, to build 'palaces fit for the dwelling of noblemen and persons of quality'. It set the tone for London's squares, but there are no private residences left in its Georgian houses; they have been replaced by clubs, libraries, embassies and offices.

Westminster and Political London

Westminster Abbey

Parliament Square, **t** *(020) 7222 5152, www.westminster-abbey.org for services or prayers; for visitors, Nave open Mon–Fri 9.30–4.45, Sat 9.30–2.45, late night Wed 6–7; Cloisters open daily 8–6; Royal Chapels, Statesman's Aisle and Poets' Corner open Mon–Fri 9.30–4.45, Sat 9–2.45; adm; Chapter House, Undercroft Museum and Old Monastery open daily 10.30–4; adm.*

It is impossible to overestimate the symbolic importance of Westminster Abbey in English culture. This is where monarchs are crowned and buried, where the Anglican Church derives its deepest inspiration, and where the nation as a whole lionizes its artistic and political heroes.

Architecturally the abbey derives its inspiration from the great cathedrals at Reims and Amiens and the Sainte-Chapelle in Paris. 'A great French thought expressed in excellent English,' one epigram has it. The abbey's origins go back to the Dark Ages, when it found a mystical patron in Edward the Confessor, saint and monarch. It was rebuilt in the finest Gothic traditions from the 13th to 16th century, and completed in

1745. Thus the abbey spans virtually the whole of modern English history. To be buried there, or even to have a plaque erected, is still the highest state honour for an English citizen. The tombs of the medieval kings and other relics bestow the legitimacy to which the modern monarchy lays claim. If St Paul's is a monument to the secular wealth of London, Westminster Abbey enshrines the mystical power of the Crown.

It was Westminster's association with the Crown that saved the abbey during the Dissolution of the monasteries in the late 1530s, when it escaped with just a few smashed windows and broken ornaments. The royal connection made it a target during the Civil War, when Cromwell's army used it as a dormitory and smashed the altar rails. Cromwell succumbed to its lure once he was Lord Protector, however, and had himself buried in the abbey after his death in 1658. His body was dug up at the Restoration and eventually reburied at the foot of the gallows at Tyburn. After the Civil War, the abbey was once again given over to burials and coronations. Aside from royals, the place is stuffed with memorials to politicians (in the Statesman's Aisle), poets (in Poets' Corner), actors, scientists and engineers.

The coronation ceremony is familiar thanks to television re-runs of the investiture of Elizabeth II in 1953, the first coronation to be televised. But ceremonies have not always gone as smoothly. Richard I had a bat swooping around his head during his coronation, Richard II lost a shoe in the abbey, while James II's crown wobbled and nearly fell off during his parade down Whitehall. George IV was so weighed down by his coronation garb that he nearly fainted and had to be revived with smelling salts.

Measuring 103ft from floor to ceiling, the **nave** of Westminster Abbey is the tallest in England; it's long too. The Purbeck marble columns grow darker towards the ceiling, deadening the effect of height, and the ceiling decorations push the eye not upwards, but forwards to the altar. Ornamentation is as important as effects of perspective. Note the 14th-century gilded painting of Richard II. The north aisle of the nave, **Statesman's Aisle,** is crowded with memorials to politicians. Scientists including Faraday and Newton are commemorated here too.

The **choir screen** is a 19th-century reworking by Edward Blore of the gilded 13th-century original. Note the heraldic shields commemorating families who gave money to construct the abbey in the 13th century. Behind the High Altar is **St Edward's Chapel**, the epicentre of the abbey with its memorials to medieval kings around the Coronation Chair.

The penny-pinching Henry VII managed one great feat of artistic patronage during his reign, the fan-vaulted **Henry VII chapel** which is nominally dedicated to the Virgin Mary but is in fact a glorification of the Tudor line of monarchs. Henrys VII and VIII, Edward VI, Mary and Elizabeth I are all buried here, along with a sprinkling of their contemporaries and successors. Elizabeth shares her tomb with her embittered half-sister Mary in a curious after-death gesture of reconciliation. The bodies of the two princes murdered in the Tower of London in 1483 also have a resting place here. The highlight of the chapel is the decoration. The ceiling resembles an intricate mesh of cobwebs, while the wooden choir stalls are carved with exotic creatures.

The south transept and adjoining St Faith's Chapel are part of the 13th-century abbey structure, and boast a series of wall paintings and some superbly sculpted figures of angels. Geoffrey Chaucer was buried in the south transept, known as **Poets' Corner**, in 1400; ever since other poets and writers have vied for a place next to him. When Edmund Spenser, author of *The Faerie Queen*, was buried here in 1599, several writers tossed their unpublished manuscripts into the grave with him. The playwright Ben Jonson asked modestly for a grave 'two feet by two feet' and so was buried upright. Few of the commemorated writers are actually interred here; among the 'genuine' ones are Dryden, Samuel Johnson, Sheridan, Browning and Tennyson. To free up more space in the corner, the abbey has installed a stained-glass window with new memorials to *parvenus* such as Pope, Robert Herrick and Oscar Wilde.

Houses of Parliament and Big Ben

Parliament Square, www.parliament.uk. Head for St Stephen's entrance to visit the Houses of Parliament; visiting arrangements are complicated and change all the time: overseas visitors may currently tour only in the summer recess; UK visitors should call t (020) 7219 3000 for details of entry and debates. To see the rest of the Palace of Westminster (Westminster Hall) apply for a permit about two months in advance from your MP or embassy. Dress formally, bring your passport and leave large bags behind. Once you're in, it's free.

Imagine the Palace of Westminster as a multi-layered onion. Most of today's building is the dizzy virtuoso work of Charles Barry and Augustus Pugin, two Victorian architects working at the height of their powers to replace the old parliament, which was destroyed by fire in 1834.

Westminster Hall has survived the centuries more or less intact. It was originally a banqueting chamber built by William Rufus, son of William the Conqueror, in 1097. The Hall was the meeting place of the Grand Council, a committee of barons that discussed policy with the monarch. Westminster Hall also became the nation's main law court. From about 1550, the lower house of parliament, known as the House of Commons, began meeting in St Stephen's Chapel in the palace. The juxtaposition of parliament and religion is curiously appropriate: since the Reformation, parliament has been a symbol of the primacy of Protestantism in English politics. Pugin and Barry recognized this, and incorporated the chapel into their design. It was only when St Stephen's was destroyed in the Blitz that the House of Commons became secular.

The inadequacies of the old Palace of Westminster were already recognized in the 1820s, but it took a calamity (fire) to force a change. On 16 October 1834 the Clerk of Works, a Mr Richard Wibley, was asked to destroy old talley-sticks in a cellar furnace. The fire raged out of control, and the whole palace was soon engulfed in flames. Pugin was an eyewitness to the 1834 fire and revelled in every minute of it. He was happy to see the neo-classical improvements to the old parliament go up in smoke. To forestall a neo-classical rebuild, Pugin put his name forward and, aged only 24, was named assistant to the older, more experienced Charles Barry. It was a near perfect partnership. Barry sketched out the broad lines of the design, while Pugin attended to the details of ornamentation. Some of Pugin's work was lost in Second World War air raids, but you can still admire the fervour of his imagination in sculpted wood and stone, stained glass, tiled floors, wallpaper and painted ceilings. Pugin gothicized

Barry's neo-classical design to his heart's content. The Palace of Westminster's blend of architectural restraint (Barry) and decorative frenzy (Pugin) is appealing.

Pugin went mad and died in 1852, before the clock tower known as **Big Ben** was built. The clock is renowned for its accuracy as it tolls the hour, but the story of its construction is one of bungling. The 320ft-high clock tower was finished in 1854, but because of a bitter disagreement between the two clockmakers, Frederick Dent and Edmund Beckett Denison, there was nothing to put inside it for another three years. Finally a great bell, made up according to Denison's instructions, was dragged across Westminster Bridge by a cart and 16 horses. But, as it was being laid out ready for hoisting into position, a 4ft crack suddenly appeared. Similar embarrassments ensued over the next two years, until a functioning (but still cracked) bell was at last erected at the top of the tower. It remains defective to this day. The most common explanation for the name is that the bell was named after Sir Benjamin Hall, the unpopular Chief Commissioner of Works who had to explain all the muddles to the House of Commons. The chimes are a bastardized version of the aria 'I Know That My Redeemer Liveth' from Handel's *Messiah*.

From the moment that Barry and Pugin's building opened in 1852, it set a new tone for proceedings in parliament. It was no longer just a legislative assembly, it was a *club*. Like so many British institutions, parliament is a place of rituals, established by a ruling order intent on protecting itself and its idiosyncratic ways; even if the institution has changed, many of the rituals have survived.

Whitehall and the Embankment

Downing Street, off Whitehall, has been home to British prime ministers on and off since 1735. Unfortunately, you won't be able to sidle up to the famous Georgian front door at no.10 without a security pass; the best you can hope for is a glimpse through the heavy iron gates installed in 1990. Next door, at no.11, is the house of the Chancellor of the Exchequer, the British equivalent of treasury secretary or finance minister, and next door to him, at no.12, is the government whips' office, where the party in power keeps tabs on its members in parliament.

This street, the scene of many a heated cabinet meeting and ministerial bollocking, was once an open venue for cock-fighting. A theatre for animals to tear each other apart with spurs, as entertaining as the politicians doing the same in the Palace of Westminster, stayed in business on this site until about 1675. It was more accident than design that led to Downing Street's lasting fame. When the prime minister, Robert Walpole, succeeded a certain Mr Chicken as tenant in 1735 he never meant to establish no.10 as an official residence. Only in the early 19th century was 10 Downing Street kitted out with proper facilities, such as John Soane's sumptuous dining room, and only in 1902 did it become the prime minister's home as well as office. When Tony Blair became prime minister in 1997 he installed his family in the more spacious No.11 next door, swapping places with his then unmarried Chancellor, Gordon Brown.

Down King Charles Street (Horse Guards Road) are the **Cabinet War Rooms** (***t*** *(020) 7766 0120, www.iwm.org.uk/cabinet; open Oct–Mar daily 10–6, April–Sept daily 9.30–6; adm*). Winston Churchill had the basement of several government buildings converted in preparation for war in 1938, and he, his cabinet and 500 civil servants worked here throughout the conflict, protected from the bombing by several layers of thick concrete. The floor below the present exhibition contained a canteen, hospital, shooting range and sleeping quarters. Churchill, whose office was a converted broom cupboard, kept a direct line open to President Roosevelt in Washington; all other phone connections were operated from an unwieldly old-fashioned switchboard, and scrambled, bizarrely, via Selfridges department store. The War Rooms, with their Spartan furniture and maps marking the British Empire in red, are a magnificent evocation of the wartime atmosphere.

Down the Embankment, past New Labour HQ, is **Tate Britain** (*Millbank*, **t** *(020) 7887 8000, www.tate.org.uk; open daily 10–5.50*). Founded at the end of the 19th century by sugar baron Sir Henry Tate, of Tate & Lyle, this is London's second great art collection after the National Gallery. It is now divided in two: international 20th-century art is across the river in the massive new **Tate Modern** at Bankside (*see* p.108); this gallery, renamed Tate Britain, is devoted to a survey of home-grown works from the Renaissance until the present day.

As well as the original neo-classical building, James Stirling's attractive **Clore Gallery** extension contains an outstanding collection of paintings by the great 19th-century artist J. M. W. Turner. The collection includes Stubbs, Gainsborough, Nash and Constable, as well as Turner. There are key works by William Blake, Hogarth and Joshua Reynolds, and the Tate is well known for its Pre-Raphaelites.

The South Bank and Southwark

Southwark, the London borough stretching from Waterloo Bridge to Tower Bridge, has seen it all: butchers, tanners, whores, corrupt bishops, coach drivers, actors, bear-baiters, railwaymen and dockers. Shakespeare's Globe Theatre was here, and so was the notorious Marshalsea debtors' prison. It is one of the most historic parts of London, used over and over by the city's novelists, particularly Dickens.

In the 17th century, Bankside and Southwark were bywords for a raucous good time. When the Romans built the first London Bridge in AD 43, Southwark developed as a small colony opposite the City of London, doing all its dirty work. In 1556 it came under the City's jurisdiction, and, for a while, theatres lifted the tone. Local industries sprang up: Bankside was bustling with wharves, breweries, foundries and glassworks.

The mid-18th century construction of Westminster and Blackfriars bridges sidelined Southwark, and the Victorian railways isolated it further. After the Second World War, as docks and warehouses closed, it became neglected and run down.

But since the year 2000 the South Bank has been through an astonishing revival and is now one of the most vibrant parts of the city. Museums have flourished on industrial sites, art galleries and restaurants moved into derelict wharves and warehouses. Even the **Globe Theatre** is back. And all the attractions are linked by a river walkway, thronged with people who until recently never set foot south of the river. The **London Eye** has established itself as a leading attraction, as has the **Tate Modern**.

Even the **Millennium Bridge**, initially beset by engineering problems, has worked its way into the public's affections.

Going back in time a little, the **South Bank Centre** was an earlier attempt to revive the area south of the river. It looks forbidding – dirty grey concrete blocks streaked with rain – but works as a cultural complex. The 1950s Royal Festival Hall is its main concert venue; there are also the National Film Theatre, Hayward Gallery, Queen Elizabeth Hall and Purcell Room (also concerts), and the Royal National Theatre. People come to hang out in its cafés too, browse in bookshops and listen to free music.

The **London Eye** (*Jubilee Gardens;* ***t*** *0870 5000 600, www.ba-londoneye.com; open May and Sept Mon–Thurs 9.30–8, Fri–Sun 9.30–9; June Mon–Thurs 9.30–9, Fri–Sun 9.30–10; July–Aug 9.30–10; Oct–April daily 9.30–8; adm*) is the world's biggest observation wheel. It provided as much entertainment during its construction as it has since it began operating; London watched in awe as the enormous wheel began to be hoisted into position, and in disbelief as industrial-strength winches snapped under the strain of raising the mighty load. The Eye has, since its maiden turn in February 2000, proved a resounding success, attracting rave reviews for its architecture and the striking impact the structure has had on the city's skyline – as well as for its stunning views: you can see for over 25 miles in almost every direction.

County Hall, a grey stone public building in pompous Edwardian 'Wrenaissance' style, was, until 1986, the headquarters of the Greater London Council, the elected city government that so threatened Margaret Thatcher she abolished it. Its basement now houses the **London Aquarium** (*Westminster Bridge Road,* ***t*** *(020) 7967 8000, www.londonaquarium.co.uk; open daily 10–6; adm*), one of the largest in Europe, with three subterranean levels of tanks seething with fish. The tanks take you through freshwater streams, rivers and ponds, coral reefs, mangroves and rainforests, and introduce you to the Picasso triggerfish, the tongueless albino African clawed frog and the electrical Peter's elephantnose. Highlights are lazy Pacific sharks, and a pool where you can stroke rays. It's all child-friendly and environmentally sensitive.

It's a short walk upstairs, from live sharks to Damien Hirst's pickled shark in the new **Saatchi Gallery** (*Westminster Bridge Road,* ***t*** *(020) 7289 4440; open Mon–Thurs and Sun 10–6, Fri and Sat 10–10*), the advertising mogul's much-hyped collection of Brit Art.

Beyond the South Bank Centre is the biggest, newest, most technically advanced **IMAX** cinema in Europe (***t*** *(020) 7902 1234, www.bfi.org.uk; adm*), **Gabriel's Wharf**, where you can eat, drink and browse in craft-style jewellery and fashion shops, and the **Oxo Tower** (*Bargehouse Street;* ***t*** *(020) 7401 2255, www.oxotower.co.uk*); an Art Deco warehouse that has been restored and converted into housing, design workshops and restaurants. There is a free public viewing platform at the top of its tower.

Tate Modern

Bankside, ***t*** *(020) 7887 8000, www.tate.org.uk; open Sun–Thurs 10–6, Fri and Sat 10–10.*

Next stop on the riverside cultural trail is Tate Modern, hailed as the cultural phenomenon of the Millennium; it surpassed all visitor-figure estimates within the first few months of its grand opening. Wide critical acclaim has been lavished on Swiss architects Herzog and de Meuron's understated transformation of the former power station, which has played as big a part in drawing the crowds as the collection itself. The massive Turbine Hall, escalators and balconies overlooking the Thames are always thronged with people.

There are seven floors in all, with most works spread out over six surprisingly poky gallery suites on the three middle floors. The exhibitions of modern works include pieces by the 20th century's most influential artists, Picasso, Matisse, Brancusi, Dalí, Pollock, Giacometti, Warhol and Hockney among them. The rooms are arranged thematically (still lifes, landscapes) rather than chronologically, the controversial idea being to interweave movements and draw out unexpected resonances. Thus you may find Claude Monet's *Water Lilies* next to Richard Long's mud wall paintings. Some find it liberating, others plain irritating (what if you want to explore Cubism?). Only half the permanent collection is on show at any one time, but it's a rich mix, with plenty of art works to get the blood of the ultra-conservative boiling, such as Carl André's *Equivalent VIII* (a pile of bricks) and Marcel Duchamp's *Fountain* (a urinal). The gallery's facilities are superb, with cafés, restaurants, reading points, bookshops and loos.

Connecting the brand new to the historic, the Norman Foster **Millennium Bridge** links Tate Modern to St Paul's Cathedral. The pedestrian 'blade of light' is central London's first new bridge since 1894. Around 150,000 people gathered for its opening in 2000; the bridge swayed alarmingly as they surged across. The wobbly bridge was promptly closed, and did not reopen until 2002, now wobble free.

Historic Southwark

Round the corner you can see the ruined foundations of the **Rose Theatre** (*56 Park Street,* ***t*** *(020) 7593 0026, www.rosetheatre.org.uk; open daily 10–5; adm*), the first Bankside playhouse (1587), which was rediscovered here in 1989. Perhaps more interesting really is the reconstructed **Globe Theatre** (*New Globe Walk;* ***t*** *(020) 7401 9919; www.shakespeares-globe.org; May–Sept two performances daily; exhibition and theatre tour daily Oct–April 9–4; May–Sept 9–12; exhibition and virtual tour daily 12.30–4; adm*). The original Globe was a few hundred feet away from this building, on the corner of present-day Park Street and Southwark Bridge Road. When London's first playhouse, The Theatre, was forced to move off its premises in Finsbury Fields in 1598, its manager, Richard Burbage, had it dismantled and reassembled here on Bankside where the Rose Theatre had taken root 12 years earlier. Shakespeare helped finance Burbage's enterprise and had many of his plays, including *Romeo and Juliet, King Lear, Othello, Macbeth* and *The Taming of the Shrew*, performed in its famous O-shaped auditorium for the first time. Bankside was the perfect location for theatre; the area was already notorious, among other things, for its taverns and whorehouses.

The Globe never recovered from a fire in 1613 and was finally demolished during the Civil War. This reconstruction was the brainchild of the late American actor Sam Wanamaker, who devoted most of his retirement to realizing the scheme, unfinished when he died in December 1993. The theatre finally opened four years later, following an extraordinary fund-raising effort.

The construction is faithful to the original, from the distinctive red of its brickwork, to its all-wooden interior and thatched roof (the first of its kind to appear in London since the Great Fire of 1666). If you are in London during the summer you should try to see a performance to appreciate the peculiarities of Elizabethan theatre. The huge stage, with its vast oak pillars holding up a canopy roof, juts out into the open area holding up to 500 standing members of the audience. The rest of the public is seated on wooden benches in the circular galleries, giving a peculiar sense of intimacy. There are a few concessions to modern sensibilities: the seating is more comfortable than in Shakespeare's day, and performances take place in the evenings.

The **Shakespeare Globe Exhibition** charts the building of both the original and the reconstructed theatre and offers a guided tour around the auditorium itself. It's more than just a venue for authentic performances of Shakespeare, however: there is also a study centre and library, open to scholars and theatre performers.

Ahead, **Southwark Cathedral** (*Montague Close, **t** (020) 7367 6700, www.dswark.org; open daily 8–6; donation requested*) has a past as chequered as its diocese, suffering fire and neglect since the 7th century. It started life as the parish church of St Mary Overie (over the river) and burned down twice before being incorporated into a priory in 1220. It was a Civil War bastion of Puritanism, where preachers denounced the evil Bankside playhouses. By the 19th century it was a wreck and had to be rebuilt. In the 20th century, Southwark was elevated to the rank of cathedral for south London. The architecture is Gothic, a rarity in London. The tower is 15th-century, although the battlements and pinnacles weren't completed until 1689.

The rest of the riverbank offers a mixed bag of attractions, old and new. The **Clink Prison Museum** (*Clink Street, **t** (020) 7378 1558, www.clink.co.uk; open Sept–mid-June daily 10–6; mid-June–Aug daily 10–9; adm*) is in the Bishop of Winchester's private prison, where anyone who challenged the extortion rackets he ran on Bankside would be locked up in gruesome conditions; for 400 years successive bishops acted as pimps to the local whores, known as Winchester Geese, and punished dissenters here. The macabre museum highlights the barbarism of life in medieval Bankside, especially for women, with scold's bridles, spiked iron gags and chastity belts. In 1537 Henry VIII ruled that women who murdered their husbands were to be boiled in a vat of oil; it was up to the executioner whether or not to boil the oil in advance.

If all this has been a bit much, stop off for a drink at the **George Inn** (*George Inn Yard, off Borough High Street*), an old coaching inn, where you may see morris dancing.

Now steel yourself again for **St Thomas's Operating Theatre Museum and Herb Garret** (*9/a St Thomas's Street, **t** (020) 7955 4791, www.thegarret.org.uk; open daily 10.30–5; adm*), a 19th-century operating theatre on the site of a 12th-century hospital. Nowhere else will you get such a graphic insight into the horrors of medicine before the modern age. Florence Nightingale, the legendary nurse of the Crimean War, set up London's first nursing school at St Thomas's in 1858.

'London Bridge is falling down' goes the nursery rhyme. In fact **London Bridge** has fallen down so often that there's nothing left to see. An American bought the previous incarnation of the bridge in the 1960s and had it reconstructed back home in Arizona – imagine his disappointment at finding Tower Bridge still bridging the

Thames. London Bridge lost its interest in 1661, when the spikes used to display the severed heads of criminals were removed. Interest may be renewed if Italian architect Renzo Piano gets permission to build a 1,016ft spire-shaped skyscraper next to it.

Beyond the bridge is the **London Dungeon** (*28–34 Tooley Street, **t** (020) 7403 7221, www.thedungeons.com; open Mar–mid-July 10–5.30; mid-July–Aug 9.30–7.30; Sept–Oct 10–5.30; Nov–Feb 10.30–5; adm*), a sort-of Madame Tussauds of medieval torture. **Hay's Galleria**, on the site of London's oldest wharf (1651), is now an arcade of bars, restaurants and shops for the yuppie crowd who inhabit the converted Victorian warehouses. Walk through it to the **Design Museum** (***t** (020) 7940 8790, www.design-museum.org; open daily 10–5.45; adm*), created by Terence Conran and Stephen Bayley, and devoted to industrial design and the cult of consumerism. It showcases such icons of mass production as the car (1928 designs by Le Corbusier), the vacuum cleaner (Dyson *et al.*), early radio and TV sets, telephones, tableware (by Enzo Mari) and chairs (by Charles and Ray Eames). The museum is in the heart of **Butler's Wharf**, as recently as the 1950s a hive of trade in commodities from tea and coffee to rubber, spices, wines and spirits.

Kensington and the Museums

Kensington is not just a desirable upmarket residential area, it is the home of London's great Victorian museums, and a de facto monument to Princess Diana, as well as the home of the more formal memorial to Prince Albert.

Since the death of Princess Diana, **Kensington Palace** (*Kensington Palace Gardens, **t** 0870 751 5170, www.hrp.org.uk; open daily Nov–Feb 10–5, Mar–Oct 10–6; adm*) has become something of a shrine to her memory; this was where she lived after the failure of her marriage to Prince Charles. The tour is divided into two sections: the historic apartments, and an exhibition of royal clothes, including the coronation robes worn by monarchs from George II onwards. The finest apartments are decorated by William Kent: a patterned ceiling in the Presence Chamber; *trompe l'œil* murals of court scenes on the King's Staircase; and painted episodes from the *Odyssey* on the ceiling of the King's Gallery. The Cupola Room plays clever optical tricks. From the King's Drawing Room there is a fine view over Kensington Gardens. It's a short walk from here to the **Serpentine Gallery**, famous for its shows of modern art. In the other direction is the **Round Pond**, where you can play with model boats, and George Frampton's famous statue of **Peter Pan**.

Kensington Gardens are a small part of **Hyde Park**, a large expanse of greenery for the centre of a big city. The park started out as part of the Westminster Abbey estate, becoming a Royal hunting ground after the monasteries were dissolved; it was not open to the public until the 17th century. William III hung lamps along Rotten Row (the sandy horse track along the southern edge, its name a corruption of the French *route du roi*) to deter highwaymen, which didn't stop George II being robbed of his purse, watch and buckles while out walking. In 1730 Queen Caroline created the **Serpentine** by having the underground Westbourne river dammed. The L-shaped lake is still the park's most prominent feature. The northeast corner of Hyde Park is the only place in Britain where demonstrators can assemble without police permission, a deal made in 1872 between the Metropolitan Police and demonstrators. The spot is known as **Speaker's Corner**, and every Sunday afternoon you can hear impassioned crackpots droning on for hours about the moral turpitude of the world.

A year after her beloved husband's death, the widowed Queen Victoria launched a competition for the **Albert Memorial** and picked George Gilbert Scott, nabob of neo-Gothic excess. The 175ft-high monument he built is an over-decorated stone canopy housing an indifferent likeness of Albert, but it was a big hit with the Victorians. Osbert Sitwell described it in 1928 as 'that wistful, unique monument of widowhood'. It took a writer as cynical as Norman Douglas to puncture the myth. 'Is this the reward of conjugal virtue?' he wrote in 1945. 'Ye husbands, be unfaithful!'

Opposite the memorial is the **Royal Albert Hall** (*Kensington Gore, **t** (020) 7589 8212*). As a concert venue the hall has an unforgivable flaw: an echo that has been the butt of jokes ever since the Bishop of London heard his prayers of blessing reverberate around the red-brick rotunda at the opening ceremony in 1871. But the Royal Albert Hall is still well loved. Visually, it is one of the more successful Victorian buildings in London. The high frieze around the outside depicts the Triumph of Arts and Sciences – an Albertian theme. The hall is huge (capacity 7,000) and hosts symphony orchestras, rock bands, and boxing matches. Every summer it hosts the Proms, a series of concerts the last night of which, in early September, is a national institution.

Natural History Museum

*Cromwell Road; **t** (020) 7942 5000, www.nhm.ac.uk; open Mon–Sat 10–5.50, Sun 11–5.50.*

Walk down Exhibition Road to the Natural History Museum. It looks for all the world like a cathedral until you come face to face with the giant dinosaur in the central hall. This skeletal creature, a 150-million-year-old plant-eating diplodocus, which warded off predators with its giant tusks and whiplash tail, sums up the best and worst of the Natural History Museum. Our prehistoric friend *looks* very impressive, but he's a fake; while the dinosaurs are the main attraction, there aren't many real bits to see.

Much of the museum resembles a science classroom: there are games explaining human perception and memory, interactive creepy-crawly displays, and a politically correct **Ecology Gallery** explaining the importance of the rainforests in the world's ecosystem. For adults, the museum gets going with the **Bird Gallery**, a remarkable collection of stuffed birds and wild animals from the 18th century onwards, and a geological section known as the **Earth Galleries**, filled with gemstones. A newer section is the **Earth Lab Datasite**, an educational resource where you can investigate UK geology using an extensive online database. And the museum has started opening its **Darwin Centre**: 22 million zoological specimens, including fish, reptiles, crustaceans and amphibians, all stored in alcohol, displayed with all the newest interactive computer technology.

Science Museum

*Exhibition Road, **t** (020) 7942 4446, www.nmsi.ac.uk, open daily 10–6.*

Next door is the Science Museum, which has done more than any other institution to make itself popular; one of the latest gimmicks is to allow children to sleep at the museum overnight. Anyone aged 8–11 with a sleeping bag will be treated to an after-hours tour and bedtime stories before lights out (children may also bring an adult).

For less privileged visitors, the **synopsis** on the mezzanine above the Ground Floor gives an overview of technological progress from Neolithic tools to the first aircraft. Here you can disabuse yourself of a few misconceptions: Jethro Tull was not just a bad 1970s heavy metal band but also an 18th-century agricultural pioneer who introduced rowcrop farming. The **Power** section gives a history of engines including models by Boulton and Watt from the 1780s. Then comes a **Space** section, complete with Second World War V2 rocket, satellites and a replica lunar landing module. Beyond, **Making the Modern World** traces the history of modern industry, from Stephenson's *Rocket* to the scorched Apollo 10 module. One of the highlights for children is a gallery full of interactive games called the **Launch Pad**, where they can learn the scientific rudiments of bicycle gears and what causes a hangover. Two further hands-on exhibits are **Garden** and **Things**.

On the first floor is **Challenge of Materials**, where a prototype pod from the London Eye dangles above a glass bridge supported by steel wires. **Time Measurement** traces clocks from the first Egyptian water-based timepieces to modern quartz and atomic clocks. **Food for Thought** explains everything you wanted to know about nutrition.

On the second floor, the **Chemistry of Everyday Life** explores the discoveries of such pioneers as Faraday. Under **Living Molecules** you'll find Crick and Watson's metal-plate model of the structure of DNA. You can also trace the development of computers and get an overview of nuclear physics. On the third floor, head for the **Flight Lab**, featuring simulators, a wind tunnel and a mini hot-air balloon. Equally intriguing is **Optics**, a collection of spectacles, telescopes, microscopes, lasers and holograms. The fourth and fifth floors are devoted to **medicine**.

The five floors of the new **Wellcome Wing** are bathed in otherworldly blue light so that it feels more like a space station, in keeping with the wing's aim to remain up to date with the latest in computer technology. The scanty exhibits, designed to shock and stimulate, include the computer on which the world wide web was conceived.

Victoria and Albert Museum (V&A)

*Cromwell Road and Exhibition Road; **t** (020) 7942 2000, www.vam.ac.uk; open Thurs–Tues 10–5.45, Wed 10–10.*

Across the road is the Victoria and Albert Museum, dedicated to applied art and design – but even such a broad definition does not cover the sheer vastness of its collections. Over the years it has become the nation's treasure trove, but the V&A has also kept bang up to date, displaying everything from Donatello to Dalí, from medieval reliquaries to Reebok sneakers. Its former director, Sir Roy Strong, once defined it as an 'extremely capacious handbag'. Unlike most large museums, you would be ill-advised to pick and choose your way around the V&A on a first visit. To get a proper feel of it, you should aim to get hopelessly lost along its seven miles of corridors. Pick up a museum plan at the reception desk to find your way out again.

A popular starting point is the **Dress Gallery**, dedicated to historical European fashion. See how the flamboyant clothes of the 17th and 18th century grew restricted by corsets and bodices, then blander and fussier in the 19th century, turned morose in the 1930s and '40s before exploding in new-found freedom and colour in the 1960s. Up a spiral staircase are **musical instruments**, a range of music boxes, virginals and a Dutch giraffe piano with six percussion pedals, as well as strings, wind and brass.

The V&A calls its **Italy 1400–1500** collection the greatest display of Renaissance sculpture outside Italy. The greatest treasures are two delicate reliefs by Donatello: the *Ascension With Christ Giving The Keys To St Peter*, commissioned for the Brancacci chapel in Santa Maria della Carmine in Florence, and *Dead Christ Tended by Angels*.

As you traverse the Italian section you pass the world's first museum café-restaurant. Each of the three rooms is a rich, highly decorated example of Victorian design.

The **Raphael Gallery** houses the series of cartoons painted by Raphael in 1514–15 as designs for tapestries to be hung in the Sistine Chapel.

Two of the **Plaster Rooms** are devoted to copies of some of the most famous sculptures and monuments in the world. The effect is surreal: try to get your mind around seeing Michelangelo's *David and Moses*, Ghiberti's *Gates of Paradise*, Trajan's Column from Rome, the *Puerta de la Gloria* from Santiago de Compostela, and chunks of Bordeaux, Aix-en-Provence, Amiens, York and Nuremberg cathedrals, all in one place.

The most famous piece in the section devoted to art from the Islamic world, India, China, Japan and Korea is **Tipu's Tiger**. This is an adjustable wooden sculpture dating from 1790 in which a tiger can be seen mauling the neck of an English soldier. There are Indian sculptures of deities dating back to the 1st century BC, and paintings and artefacts giving an overview of two millennia of Indian decoration. The **Japanese Art** galleries boast some fine lacquer work and ceramics, while the **Chinese Art** section focuses on fine objects used in everyday life, particularly ceramics and a collection of ornaments and figurines used in burial ceremonies, as does the **Korean Art** gallery. **Art in the Islamic World** contains a bazaar of carpets and prayer mats from Egypt and Turkey, and finely decorated bowls and earthenware from Persia.

Sandwiched in the middle of the oriental art sections is the **Medieval Treasury**, a beautiful collection of mainly religious artefacts from the 5th to the 15th century.

Upstairs, the **20th Century Gallery** is an engaging history of 20th-century design, with everything from Marcel Breuer's pioneering Bauhaus chair to Salvador Dalí's lipstick-pink sofa in the shape of one of Mae West's kisses. There is also a hi-tech **Silver Gallery**, with 500 years of British silver. Beyond is the medieval tapestry series known as the **Devonshire Hunt**. Famed for their beauty and wealth of detail, these tapestries were commissioned in the 15th century for Bess of Hardwick Hall.

In the **Henry Cole Wing** is the world's largest collection of **Constable paintings**, a clutch of Turners and a series of **Rodin sculptures**. Otherwise it's a mixed bag. Don't miss the **Frank Lloyd Wright Gallery** or the glittering **glass gallery**, with its staircase made entirely of green glass blocks.

In November 2001, the V&A opened the doors of the new **British Galleries**. The 15 galleries contain the most comprehensive collection of British design and art (from 1500 to 1900) anywhere. There are more than 3,000 objects on display but highlights are Henry VIII's writing desk, James II's wedding suit and the famous **Great Bed of Ware**, which was made for an inn and became instantly famous – Shakespeare and Ben Jonson both mentioned it in their plays. All of the top British designers are featured here – Morris, Gibbon and Adam – as well as famous manufacturers – Chippendale, Wedgwood and Liberty – in beautifully recreated settings.

London Villages

The London that stretches away beyond the centre is often described as a series of villages. Of course nothing within the London urban area is really comparable to village life, and each 'village' merges into the next in a continuous urban sprawl. But there are clearly distinct centres, around historic settlements (Highgate Village, to name one). The point at which central London ends and outer London begins is not clear, but places such as Notting Hill and Chelsea have their own sense of identity.

Notting Hill

The most central of the villages, Notting Hill conjures up images of imposing pastel-stuccoed Victorian houses, antique dealers on Portobello Road, Caribbean children dancing in the streets during its carnival, bohemian wannabes riffling through cheap jewellery and old clothes beneath the A40 flyover, and affluent professional families taking it all for granted. Notting Hill became an emblem of multicultural London after the big immigrant waves from the Caribbean in the 1950s; it is now so hip with the liberal middle classes that it is more exclusive than Kensington or Chelsea, and risks imploding. A rapid period of gentrification in the 1980s (after the original 100-year leases expired) has created barriers of class and status: the motorway flyover marks a neat divide between the spruced-up terraces to the south (Notting Hill proper), and the high-rise 1960s council estates to the north (North Kensington).

The success of the 1999 film *Notting Hill* led to huge rent increases and helped to destroy the very nature of the area it sought to eulogize on celluloid; the small independent shops and cafés that made the area fun are being pushed out by chain shops and coffee bars. Meanwhile, the influx of Amex bohemians continues in the wake of the 'trustafarians', and every other shop is now a designer emporium. If you want a glimpse of hip Notting Hill, you're best off renting a video of Nicholas Roeg's *Performance*, starring Mick Jagger.

Most visitors pile out of Notting Hill Gate station and head for Portobello Market. It's worth dallying, however, among the mews-style houses on Campden Hill, and the grandiose properties overlooking Holland Park, one of the most attractive residential areas in London, dotted with good pubs and restaurants. Carry on to **Leighton House** (*12 Holland Park Rd;* ***t*** *(020) 7602 3316, www.rbkc.gov.uk; open Mon–Sat 11–5.30*),

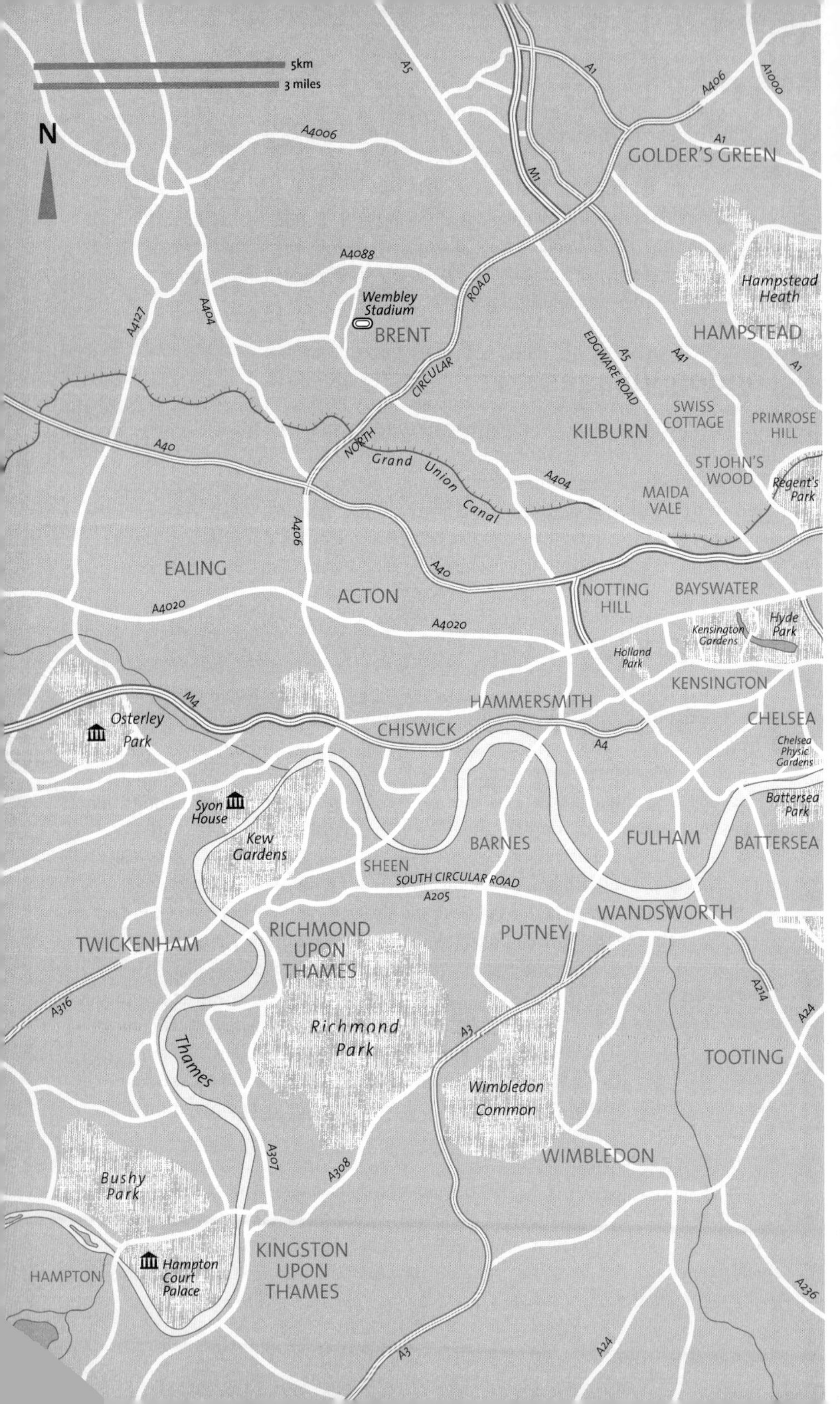

5km
3 miles
N
A5
A1
A406
A1000
A4006
A1
GOLDER'S GREEN
M1
A4088
Wembley Stadium
BRENT
NORTH CIRCULAR ROAD
A4127
A404
Hampstead Heath
HAMPSTEAD
EDGWARE ROAD
A5
A41
A1
SWISS COTTAGE
PRIMROSE HILL
KILBURN
A40
Grand Union Canal
A404
ST JOHN'S WOOD
MAIDA VALE
Regent's Park
A406
EALING
ACTON
A40
NOTTING HILL
BAYSWATER
A4020
A4020
Kensington Gardens
Hyde Park
Holland Park
KENSINGTON
M4
Osterley Park
HAMMERSMITH
CHISWICK
CHELSEA
A4
Chelsea Physic Gardens
Syon House
Battersea Park
Kew Gardens
BARNES
FULHAM
BATTERSEA
SHEEN
SOUTH CIRCULAR ROAD
A205
WANDSWORTH
RICHMOND UPON THAMES
PUTNEY
TWICKENHAM
A214
A316
A3
A24
Richmond Park
Thames
TOOTING
Wimbledon Common
WIMBLEDON
A307
A308
Bushy Park
KINGSTON UPON THAMES
Hampton Court Palace
HAMPTON
A236
A3
A24

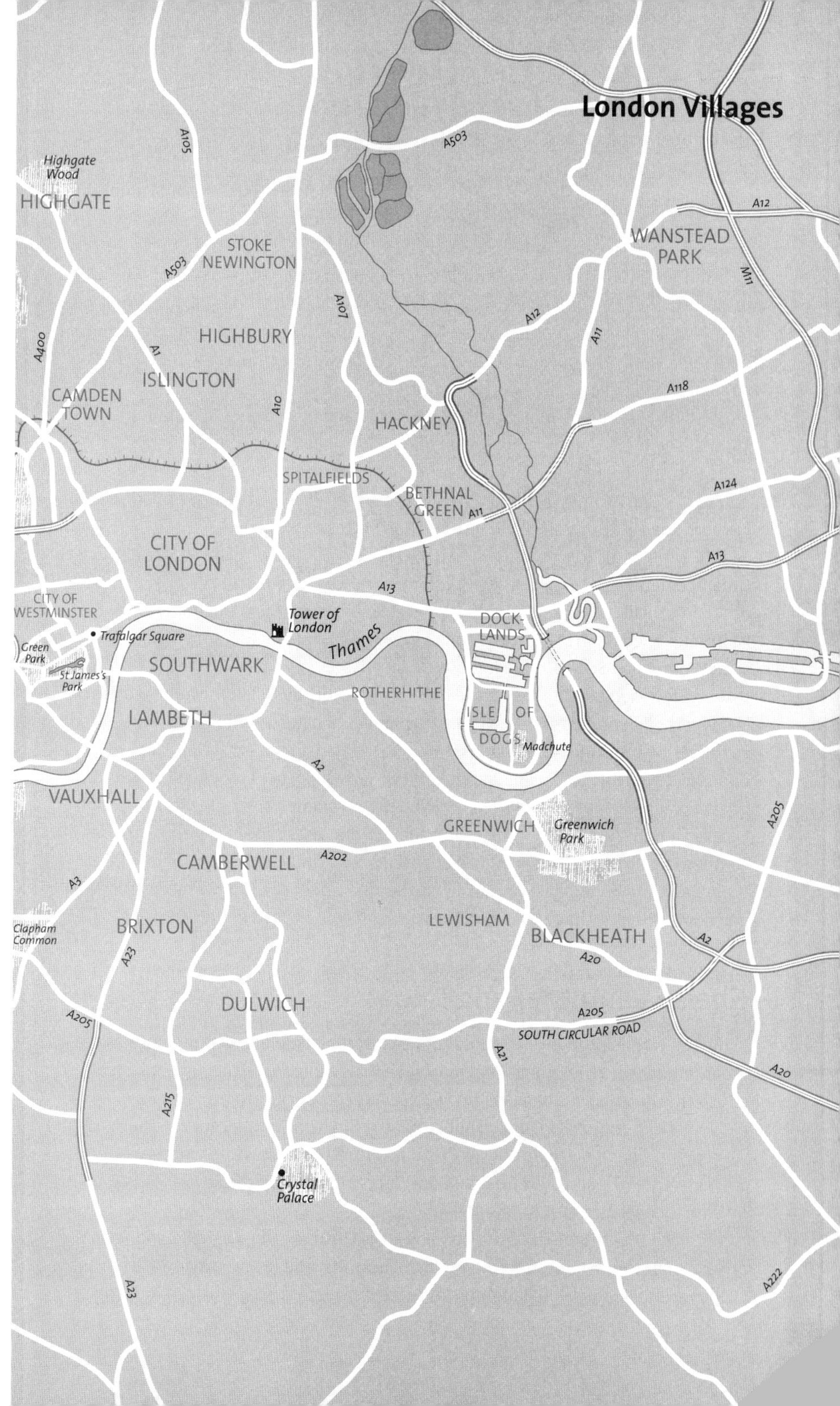

London Villages
HIGHGATE
Highgate Wood
STOKE NEWINGTON
HIGHBURY
ISLINGTON
CAMDEN TOWN
HACKNEY
WANSTEAD PARK
SPITALFIELDS
BETHNAL GREEN
CITY OF LONDON
CITY OF WESTMINSTER
Trafalgar Square
Tower of London
Thames
Green Park
St James's Park
SOUTHWARK
ROTHERHITHE
DOCK-LANDS
ISLE OF DOGS
Madchute
LAMBETH
VAUXHALL
GREENWICH
Greenwich Park
CAMBERWELL
LEWISHAM
BLACKHEATH
Clapham Common
BRIXTON
DULWICH
SOUTH CIRCULAR ROAD
Crystal Palace
A105
A503
A10
A107
A12
A11
M11
A118
A124
A13
A1
A400
A2
A202
A3
A205
A23
A20
A21
A215
A222

Pre-Raphaelite painter Lord Leighton's late-Victorian interior design extravaganza. The highlight of his astonishing Oriental palace is the Arab Hall, which has a stained-glass cupola and glorious floral tiles picked up in Rhodes, Cairo and Damascus.

If you're here for the shopping, you can start now: **Notting Hill Gate** and **Pembridge Road** have excellent second-hand record, book, furniture and toy stores and, towards Holland Park, the posy Damien Hirst bar Pharmacy.

The antique stalls start at the end of **Portobello Road** (*antiques and second-hand market Fri and Sat; fruit and veg market Mon–Sat*) nearest Notting Hill; the furniture, food, jewellery, cheap records, books, postcards, handmade and old clothes and funky bric-a-brac are at the north end, towards and under the A40 flyover. In between is a popular fruit and vegetable market. The street and its offshoots are also lined with quirky, individual shops, mainly rather expensive, and posh delis and restaurants. Right at the top is **Golborne Road**, a bustling Portuguese and Moroccan street.

The Portobello Road end of **Westbourne Grove** is home to expensive designer boutiques with an award-winning public-toilet-cum-flower-stall in the middle. **Ledbury Road** is also packed with fashion and accessory designers.

In the other direction, right up Ladbroke Grove and left down Harrow Road, is **Kensal Green Cemetery** (*open Mon–Sat 9–5.30, Sun 10–5.30, closes 4.30 in winter*). Eminent occupants include Thackeray, Trollope, Wilkie Collins, Leigh Hunt and Marc and Isambard Kingdom Brunel. It's also one of the few green spaces round here, other than **Wormwood Scrubs**, more famous for its prison.

After a few violent episodes in its early days, the **Notting Hill Carnival**, held on the last weekend in August, has become a permanent and peaceful fixture. For two days each year, on the Sunday and Bank Holiday Monday, the streets throb with steel bands as colourful Caribbean floats go by. Everywhere is the tangy smell of saltfish, goat curry, fried plantain and patties. Many of the middle-class residents of Notting Hill pack up the family Volvo and motor the hell out on Carnival weekend – not an eloquent testimony to their liberal credentials – but young crowds pour in to take their place. The impeccably liberal newspaper, the *Guardian*, once warned carnival-goers of 'a bassline that will reverberate through your ribcage for days'.

Chelsea and the King's Road

Chelsea was an attractive riverside community long before it was integrated into greater London. The humanist and martyr Thomas More made the district fashionable by moving here in the 1520s, and soon every courtier worth his salt, even Henry VIII himself, was building a house nearby. By the mid-19th century, Chelsea had turned into a bustling village of intellectuals, artists, aesthetes and writers as well as war veterans – the so-called Chelsea pensioners who lived in the Royal Hospital built by Christopher Wren for Charles II.

Chelsea in the early 20th century turned into little more than a sterile, snobbish annex of South Kensington. In the 1950s, it became a refuge of the dying aristocracy. In the 1980s, the sons and daughters of these last-ditch aristos mutated into an underwhelming social animal known as the Sloane Ranger – a special kind of upper-class twit with deeply misguided delusions about being trendy.

Chelsea's artistic streak never entirely disappeared, however, and in the 1960s and early '70s it flourished with a vengeance along the King's Road, the heart of swinging London. It let its hair down and filled with cafés and trendy boutiques selling mini-skirts and cheap jewellery. The Royal Court Theatre, in Sloane Square, came into its own as a venue for avant-garde writers like John Osborne (the original Angry Young Man), Edward Bond and Arnold Wesker. Mods, then punks, set the fashion tone.

During the 1960s, old-fashioned shops on the **King's Road** were superseded by the likes of Terence Conran, who opened his first **Habitat** household design store as a direct challenge to the fusty old **Peter Jones** department store. Since then all originality it had has been replaced by generic highstreet chainstores, and it could be a high street anywhere in England, if more monied than most. The **antiques markets** on the south side of the road is the only place where the old spirit lives on.

The heart of old Chelsea is down by the river. Just to the left of Battersea Bridge is **Chelsea Old Church**, which commemorates Sir Thomas More, author of the humanist tract *Utopia*. Its history goes back to Norman times, but most of it was rebuilt in classical style in the 17th century. The churchyard has been converted into a small park.

Stretching to the east are the delightful 18th-century brick houses of **Cheyne Walk**, one of London's most fashionable addresses for the past 200 years. Among the famous residents have been George Eliot, Henry James, Whistler and Turner. The Queen's House at no.16 was shared in the 1860s by a trio of poets, Dante Gabriel Rossetti, Algernon Swinburne and George Meredith, who kept a bestiary that included some noisy peacocks. The most interesting address is **Carlyle's House** (*open April–Oct Wed, Thurs, Fri 2–5, Sat, Sun 11–5; adm*). Few houses in London evoke such a strong sense of period or personality as this red-brick Queen Anne building, where historian Thomas Carlyle, author of *The French Revolution*, lived with his wife from 1834 until his death in 1881. It has been kept almost exactly as the Carlyles left it.

Docklands

To head downriver from the Tower is to enter a different world. The converted Docklands, practically an invention of Margaret Thatcher, are a Phoenix risen from the ashes of the derelict wharves and warehouses of a bygone age, disorientating and impressive, if not altogether successful.

The Docklands were built in the 1980s without a shred of planning or civic sense, in a free-for-all for speculators. The development failed to respect its environment and the wishes of local people; nobody thought to provide proper services or transport links, and when recession struck at the end of the 1980s, hundreds of developers went bust. It became a ghost town. However, with the opening of the DLR, and then the Jubilee Line extension, connecting Canary Wharf with Waterloo and London Bridge stations, City businesses have moved in, followed by their workers.

For visitors the area consists mainly of uninspiring office blocks with mirror-glass façades and luxury housing estates where the main luxury is anonymity. Among the shiny skyscrapers and flashy apartments, exists one of the poorest and most socially deprived areas in the country. It's worth a visit to muse on a wasted opportunity, and mull over the pros and cons of urban planning and unrestrained speculation.

Until the 16th century, when the land around it was drained, **Wapping** was a sliver of land hemmed in by swamps to the north and the river on the south. It has always been poor: John Stow described Wapping High Street in his *Survey of London* (1598) as 'a filthy strait passage, with alleys of small tenements or cottages'. Now it's a quiet, leafy residential area, with a sprinkling of traditional pubs and new restaurants. Most of the new architecture is soulless, but a few original features from Wapping's past still stand, like the old Customs House on the High Street and some more successful warehouse conversions. The waterfront near **Wapping Wall**, known as **Execution Dock**, earned its name because smugglers were hanged there and displayed in chains until three tides had washed over them, by which time the bodies had swelled to a 'whopping' size. The dock is now marked with an 'E' on the building at Swan Wharf, opposite Brewhouse Lane. It's a few minutes' walk from the **Prospect of Whitby** pub, once named 'The Devil's Tavern' and a haunt of bloodthirsty Judge Jeffreys (*see* p.318).

To build **St Katharine's Dock** and its commodity warehouses in the 1820s, the authorities knocked down 1,250 houses and made more than 11,000 people homeless. It lost money until its closure in 1968, and has now been prettified. Opposite the Murdoch empire that brought Wapping bitter fame in the 1980s is Nicholas Hawksmoor's church **St George in the East** (1714–29). The church was the site of an unholy 19th-century row about the liturgy; the congregation joined in the mayhem by blowing horns, whistling and bringing dogs into the Sunday service.

A more complete Hawksmoor church can be found past Limehouse Basin off the Commercial Road. The tower of **St Anne's Limehouse** has been a guide to ships coming ever since it was completed in 1724. In the 19th century the area was a den of vice, where people came to smoke opium. Oscar Wilde set the opium-smoking scene in *The Picture of Dorian Gray* in Limehouse. Along Narrow Street is a terrace of early Georgian houses and **The Grapes**, a 16th-century pub said to have been the model for the 'Six Jolly Fellowship-Porters' pub in Dickens' *Our Mutual Friend*.

The main attraction on the **Isle of Dogs** is the 812ft glass and steel tower block at the centre of **Canary Wharf**. Along with its two new sister towers on Canada Square (689ft and 653ft respectively), Cesar Pelli's monstrous tower (*tight security*) soars over the Docklands (and London's) skyline, the flashing light atop its pyramidal apex winking 40 times a minute. It is the tallest building in Britain. Clustered around it are a series of lower-lying buildings (hi-tech reworkings by American architects of Edwardian styles), courtyards, shopping plazas and waterside footpaths.

Hop back onto the DLR south to **Island Gardens** and **Greenwich**.

Rotherhithe was where the Pilgrim Fathers set out for America in *The Mayflower* in 1620. It's an unspoiled, little known part of riverside London. The old warehouses have been restored, but not tarted up. The narrow streets and green in front of St Mary's church lends a village-like air, attracting a modest number of artists and artisans. The church itself, attractively rebuilt in the 18th century, contains a plaque to Captain Christopher Jones of *The Mayflower* as well as remains of the *Fighting Temeraire*, the battleship whose demise was so poignantly captured by Turner.

Islington and Camden

In the 1950s you wouldn't have found much in **Islington** apart from a clapped-out old music hall, a few eel and pie shops and an extended series of slummy terraces. Now it is one of the liveliest districts in the capital, a Mecca for liberal-minded arty professionals who live in attractively refurbished Georgian townhouses and eat out in expensive ethnic restaurants. Its packed with pubs, cafés, designer bars and shops, and has its own alternative theatres.

During the 1980s Islington was associated with earnest left-wing politics that jarred utterly with the prevailing Thatcherite ideology of free markets and individual responsibility. Then it spawned New Labour Prime Minister Tony Blair, a Chianti, rocket and shaved-parmesan socialist.

In fact, the pleasures of Islington were interrupted only by the Industrial Revolution. In the 16th century it was popular as a royal hunting ground and noted for its pure spring water and dairy farms. The fields were dotted with mansions, gardens and orchards. Elizabeth I used to meet her favourites here, and people from all walks of life came to enjoy the bowling greens, dance halls and taverns. But the advent of the Grand Union Canal and the railways in the 19th century left the district dilapidated and dirty and Islington became a byword for everything that was *un*fashionable. In the 1950s and 1960s this was the home of the playwright Joe Orton and his lover Kenneth Halliwell. By 1964 the tide had turned again with the arrival of Camden Passage antiques market and pub theatres, led by the King's Head on Upper Street, and followed by the highly successful fringe Almeida Theatre. The best way to visit is to start at the Angel and work your way upwards, soaking up the atmosphere, and making diversions to the charming Georgian streets and squares to east and west.

Camden's modern identity was established in the 1970s, when the market started and the old Victorian warehouses were slowly converted into artists' studios, music venues and restaurants. Camden now is above all its buzzing open-air markets along the canal, a mix of cheap clothes and jewellery stalls, pubs and restaurants. At the weekends, traffic comes to a standstill. The atmosphere is young and trendyish. If you carry on drinking and eating long enough there are plenty of clubs to go on to.

Clear your head at **Regent's Park**, the most ornate of London's open spaces; a delightful mix of icing-sugar terraces, lakes and greenery. It was the brainchild of George IV's favourite architect, John Nash, who conceived it as a landscaped estate on which to build pleasure palaces for the aristocracy. Meant to be the culmination of a vast city rebuilding project, of which the centrepiece was Regent Street, the park comes closest to embodying the spirit of his plans (scuppered by lack of funds). Within the Inner Circle of the park is **Queen Mary's Rose Garden**. At the north end is the **Open Air Theatre** (***t*** *(020) 7486 2431; www.open-air-theatre.org.uk; open May–Sept*), a magical sylvan setting for summer productions of *A Midsummer Night's Dream* and other plays. Near the theatre is a **Boating Lake**, where you can rent boats.

The Zoological Gardens in Regent's Park are where the term 'zoo' originated. The abbreviation was immortalized in a music-hall song of the 1860s beginning: 'Walking in the zoo is the OK thing to do.' Zoos are not quite as OK as they used to be, but **London Zoo** (***t** (020) 7722 3333, www.zsl.org/london.zoo; open daily 10–5.30; adm exp*) has redeveloped itself to a pretty good state of animal correctness.

Hampstead

Hampstead is a pretty hilltop village of Georgian terraces and Victorian mansions, surrounded by the vast expanse of the Heath. Throughout its history, it has provided a refuge when life in the city has become too much. John Constable came here and painted some distant cityscapes that resembled rural idylls. Nowadays Hampstead, for all its liberal credentials, has an air of established comfort and is a staid and remarkably conservative place.

The real pleasure of **Hampstead village** is in getting lost in the winding back streets: **Judges Walk**, the legendary 'substitute' law court of the Great Plague; **Admiral's Walk**, which contains a multi-levelled Georgian house; Hampstead Grove, leading to **Fenton House**, a splendid brick mansion dating from 1693 (***t** (020) 7435 3471; open Mar weekends 2–5; April–Oct Wed–Fri 2–5, weekends 11–5; adm*); **Hollybush Hill**, a cul-de-sac lined with small houses including the 17th-century Hollybush pub; **Holly Walk**, a cobbled path flanked by fine houses and, at the bottom of the hill, **St John's**, an 18th-century church where Constable is buried; **Church Row**, from the church back to Heath Street, has some of the most elegant Georgian housing in London. **Heath Street** and the **High Street** are lined with shops and restaurants. Across the High Street is **Flask Walk**, with its second-hand bookshops, galleries, children's boutiques, and a posh tea and coffee merchant. It and **Well Walk** are where fashionable folk came to take the Hampstead spa waters in the 18th century.

The 16th-century **Spaniards Inn,** at the junction of Hampstead Lane and Spaniards Road, named after two Spanish proprietors who killed each other in a duel, owes its fame to the 18th-century highwayman Dick Turpin who used to stop for drinks here in-between coach hold-ups.

The main attraction of **Keats' House** (*Wentworth Place, Keats Grove, **t** (020) 7435 2062; open Tues–Sun 12–5; adm*) is the plum tree in the garden, under which Keats wrote 'Ode to a Nightingale' in 1819. In two years as a lodger here, Keats produced some of his most famous work, fell in love with Fanny Brawne, who lived in the other half of the house, and contracted the consumption that killed him at the age of 25.

The **Freud Museum** at 20 Maresfield Gardens (***t** (020) 7435 2002; open Wed–Sun 12–5; adm*) is in the house where Sigmund Freud set up his last home after fleeing the Nazis in Vienna in 1938. Six rooms have been left untouched since the founder of psychoanalysis died of throat cancer on the eve of the Second World War. You can see the couch where his patients free-associated during sessions, and Freud's collections of furniture and artefacts, including some extraordinary phalluses.

You can walk across Hampstead Heath to **Kenwood House** (*Hampstead Lane,* **t** *(020) 8348 1286; open April–Sept daily 10–5.30, Oct–Mar 10–4*), famous for its open-air summer concerts. The house was given a facelift by Robert Adam in the 1760s. The pictures include works by Rembrandt (a remarkable self-portrait), Vermeer (*The Guitar Player*), Van Dyck, Gainsborough, Guardi, Reynolds, Landseer and Turner.

Richmond

Richmond is a tranquil, affluent riverside community of attractive Georgian and Victorian houses, flanked by greenery. It is an ideal place to walk along the river, have a drink on the Green and catch a pre-West End play at Richmond Theatre, or a more fringey production at the Orange Tree.

In medieval times, the focal point of the district was Shene Palace, a manor house hunting lodge. The village green (**Richmond Green**) was a popular venue for pageants and jousting tournaments. Henry VII changed its name from Shene to Richmond, after his earldom in Yorkshire, and rebuilt the palace after a fire in 1497. The new Richmond Palace must have been quite something, a riot of spires and turrets which you can see reconstructed as a model in the Richmond Town Hall's small **museum** (*Red Lion Street,* **t** *(020) 8332 1141; open Tues–Sat 11–5, May–Sept also Sun 1–4*). Sadly, all that survives of medieval Richmond is a stone **gateway** off Richmond Green, and the **palace wardrobe**, or household office, just inside Old Palace Yard. In the yard is **Trumpeters' House**, built by a pupil of Christopher Wren and used as a refuge by Prince Metternich after the upheavals in Vienna of 1848. There are fine Georgian houses along Old Palace Terrace and Maids of Honour Row.

Today, as ever, the biggest attraction of Richmond is the riverside, which boasts the elegant five-arched **Richmond Bridge** dating from the 1770s and a neo-Georgian terrace of shops, restaurants and offices called **The Riverside**, opened in 1988. The architect was Quinlan Terry, a traditionalist chum of Prince Charles. Like it or not, it's waterfront terraces are crowded with strollers and sunbathers in summer. At the top of the bridge, Richmond Hill leads to wild **Richmond Park**, famous for its deer.

If you carry on along the river, you reach **Ham House** (*Ham Street, off Sandy Lane and Petersham Rd;* **t** *(020) 8940 1950; grounds open Sat–Wed 11–6; house open Sat–Wed 1–5; adm),* one of the grandest surviving Jacobean mansions in London. Built in 1610, and nicknamed the 'sleeping beauty' for its tranquil position, it became the home of William Murray, Earl of Dysart, a friend of Charles I. The gardens have retained their original 17th-century formal layout.

From the Twickenham side of **Richmond Bridge** (*Richmond Road, Twickenham;* **t** *(020) 8892 5115; open April–Sept daily 10–6; Oct daily 10–5; Nov–Mar Wed–Sun 10–4; adm*) you can enjoy a mile-long walk along a rural stretch of the Thames to **Marble Hill House**, a simple white Palladian villa built in 1729 for Henrietta Howard, the 'exceedingly respectable and respected' mistress of George II. Henrietta could not stand the pressure of life at court, where she had to negotiate a tricky path between her lover and her husband, and so, with a little help from the royal purse, she set up home here, some 10 miles out of central London.

A few miles upriver from Richmond is **Hampton Court Palace** (*East Molesey, Surrey,* ***t*** *0870 752 7777, www.hrp.org.uk; open Nov–Mar Mon 10.15–4.30, Tues–Sun 9.30–4.30; April–Oct Mon 10.15–6, Tues–Sun 9.30–6; adm*), one of the finest Tudor buildings in England, magnificently evoking the haphazard pleasures and cruel intrigues of Henry VIII's court. It started as the power base of Henry's most influential minister, Cardinal Thomas Wolsey, who bought the property from the Knights of St John in 1514, a year before he became Lord Chancellor of England. At its zenith the palace had 280 rooms and kept a staff of 500 busy entertaining European dignitaries. Seeing the grandeur to which his chief minister was becoming accustomed, Henry VIII threatened to knock Wolsey off his perch. Wolsey's panic response was to offer Hampton Court to the monarch; Henry snubbed him by refusing to take up residence. But when Wolsey failed to persuade the Pope to grant Henry a divorce from his wife, Catherine of Aragon, his possessions were seized by the crown and he was arrested for high treason, dying as he was escorted from York to London.

Henry then got interested in Hampton Court as a love nest for himself and Anne Boleyn. They removed Wolsey's coat of arms from the main entrance arch and renamed it **Anne Boleyn's Gateway** In 1540, Henry added an astronomical clock, and renamed the main courtyard Clock Court. The mid-1530s were Hampton Court's heyday. Henry built the **Great Hall**, with its 60ft-high hammerbeam roof and its stained-glass windows, including the crests of each of his wives, even the ones he repudiated or executed. The king also established the gardens and built a **real tennis court**. But Hampton Court turned sour for him after Jane Seymour died in 1538 while giving birth to his son and heir, Edward.

However, Hampton Court continued to thrive for a century after Henry's death. The Great Hall became a popular theatrical venue, and the state rooms filled with fine paintings, tapestries, musical instruments and ornaments. Charles I built fountains and lakes and accumulated an art collection including the *Triumph of Caesar* series by Mantegna. By William and Mary's time the apartments at Hampton Court were considered old-fashioned, and Christopher Wren was drafted in to build a palace to rival Louis XIV's extravaganza at Versailles. Wren's work centres around the cloisters of **Fountain Court**. New apartments were decorated by Antonio Verrio and Grinling Gibbons in sumptuous fashion. The **Chapel Royal** was also rebuilt, with only the original Tudor vaulted ceiling surviving. William III planted the famous **maze**.

Greenwich

Greenwich has been a place of pleasure since the 15th century, when Henry V's brother, Duke Humphrey of Gloucester, built the first royal palace. While neighbouring districts like Deptford and Woolwich have always had to live by wits and graft, Greenwich has long concentrated on hunting and jousting, or rarefied pursuits like astronomy. Thanks to the contributions of Jones, Wren, Hawksmoor and Vanbrugh, it also boasts a remarkable architectural heritage. It is an ensemble of great grace and proportion, which in recent years has spawned a community of well-off middle-class Londoners in fine Georgian houses up Crooms Hill or on the grassy verges of Greenwich Park and Blackheath.

Duke Humphrey's original palace was replaced by a fine red-brick construction named Placentia in 1427. It remained popular with the royal family and Henry VIII was born at Greenwich. He married his first wife, Catherine of Aragon, in the palace's private chapel and watched in frustration and rage as six of their seven children – four of them boys – died here within a few weeks of their birth. The latter half of Henry's reign, when Hampton Court became the 'in' palace, saw a decline at Greenwich. Edward VI was sent here to convalesce in 1553. Queen Elizabeth came here occasionally, and it was here that Sir Walter Raleigh magnanimously threw his cloak on a 'plashy place' (a puddle) so Her Majesty would not get her feet muddy. But it was the Stuarts who breathed new life into Greenwich.

At weekends the village is mobbed by bargain-hunters coming for the markets: crafts in the covered market off Nelson Road, and antiques, bric-a-brac and vintage clothing around Stockwell Street.

Much is made of the ***Cutty Sark*** (*by the pier,* ***t*** *(020) 8858 3445, www.cuttysark.org.uk; open daily 10–5; adm*) as the last of the great tea clippers that plied the route from England to the Far East. Built in 1869, it was one of the fastest sailboats of its time, winning the annual clippers' race in 1871. Steamships and the Suez Canal soon took over. Admire its magnificent gilded teak fittings, the rigging on its three masts and its fine collection of figureheads. The name comes from Robert Burns' poem *Tam O'Shanter*, in which a witch called Nellie wears only a *cutty sark*, a corruption of *courte chemise*, or short shirt. The female figurehead on the prow is dressed in this manner.

Next to the *Cutty Sark*, ***Gipsy Moth IV*** is the ketch in which the British mariner Sir Francis Chichester made his solo round-the-world voyage in 1966–7.

After Queen Mary witnessed the wounds inflicted on British sailors at the battle of La Hogue in 1692, she commissioned Christopher Wren to clear the ruins of the old palace of Placentia and build a naval hospital. Wren and his successors, Hawksmoor and Vanbrugh, were obliged to make a lot of compromises to come up with the current ensemble. The hospital was closed, and the **Royal Naval College** (*King William Walk,* ***t*** *(020) 8269 4747; open Mon–Sat 10–5, Sun 12.30–5*) moved here in 1873. In 1998 the site was leased to Greenwich University and Trinity College of Music. Only the **chapel** and **Painted Hall** are now open to the public.

The **National Maritime Museum** (*Romney Road,* ***t*** *(020) 8312 6565, www.nmm.ac.uk; open winter daily 10–5, summer daily 10–6*) reopened in 1999 after a £40-million overhaul and is now one of the most up-to date, interactive museums in the UK. Historical memorabilia, particularly that of Napoleon's era, still features, but the focus has shifted to the hi-tech world of modern shipping and cruise-liner travel.

The **Queen's House**, now part of the museum, was Inigo Jones' first experiment in Palladian architecture after his return from Italy in 1615. James I's wife Anne of Denmark was the queen, who wanted her own private villa as an extension to the

Palace of Placentia. After Anne's death in 1619 the house languished unfinished, but was taken up again by Queen Henrietta Maria in 1629. She nicknamed it her 'house of delights' and lived in it as Queen Mother after the Restoration. It is textbook Palladian classicism – simple and sober on the outside, and full of 'licentious imaginacy', as Jones put it, on the inside. The centrepiece is the **Great Hall**, a perfect 40ft cube. Note the **Tulip Staircase** at the eastern end of the hall, the wrought-iron helix staircase that twists up to the Queen's Bedroom. This was the first staircase in England to be built, as Jones put it, with 'a vacuum in the middle'. The floral decorations on its banister are fleurs-de-lys in honour of Henrietta Maria, daughter of King Henry IV of France.

Greenwich is a time as well as a place: Greenwich Mean Time, as measured at the **Old Royal Observatory** (*Greenwich Park,* **t** *(020) 8312 6565, www.rog.nmm.ac.uk; open daily 10–5; adm*), has synchronized the world's watches since 1884. As you approach the museum you see a metal plaque marking 0° longitude and a large red ball on a stick that lowers daily at 1pm precisely as a symbol of the accuracy and universality of GMT. Why Greenwich? First, because this was where England's first Astronomer Royal, John Flamsteed, built his home and observatory in 1675. And second, because Flamsteed and his successors did more than anyone to solve the oldest navigational problem in the book: how to measure longitude. Latitude could be ascertained from the angle of the Pole Star to the horizon, but longitude was something else. Scientists knew what they needed: a dependable and portable clock with which to work it out. In 1754, parliament issued a Longitude Act, offering a reward of £20,000 to the person who could crack the problem. The first proposals ranged from the sublime to the ridiculous. It was a Yorkshire clockmaker called John Harrison who eventually broke the impasse. He constructed his first marine clock in 1730 and continued perfecting it all his life; by the time he came up with the prize-winning model in 1772 he was 79 years old. Captain Cook took Harrison's clock to Australia and called it his 'trusty friend'. The observatory itself is worthy of note, particularly Flamsteed's original observatory, the **Octagon Room**, designed by Christopher Wren.

The Southeast
Surrey, Kent and Sussex

I'm just in love with all these three,
The Weald and the Marsh and the Downs countree.
Nor I don't know which I love the most,
The Weald or the Marsh or the White Chalk Coast!

Rudyard Kipling, 'A Three Part Song'

The Southeast, Kipling's beloved Weald, Marsh and 'Downs countree', is a distinctive corner of England. It extends nearly to France, the left foot of the running pig in the famous caricature of Britain, and, despite the dominating presence of

The Southeast

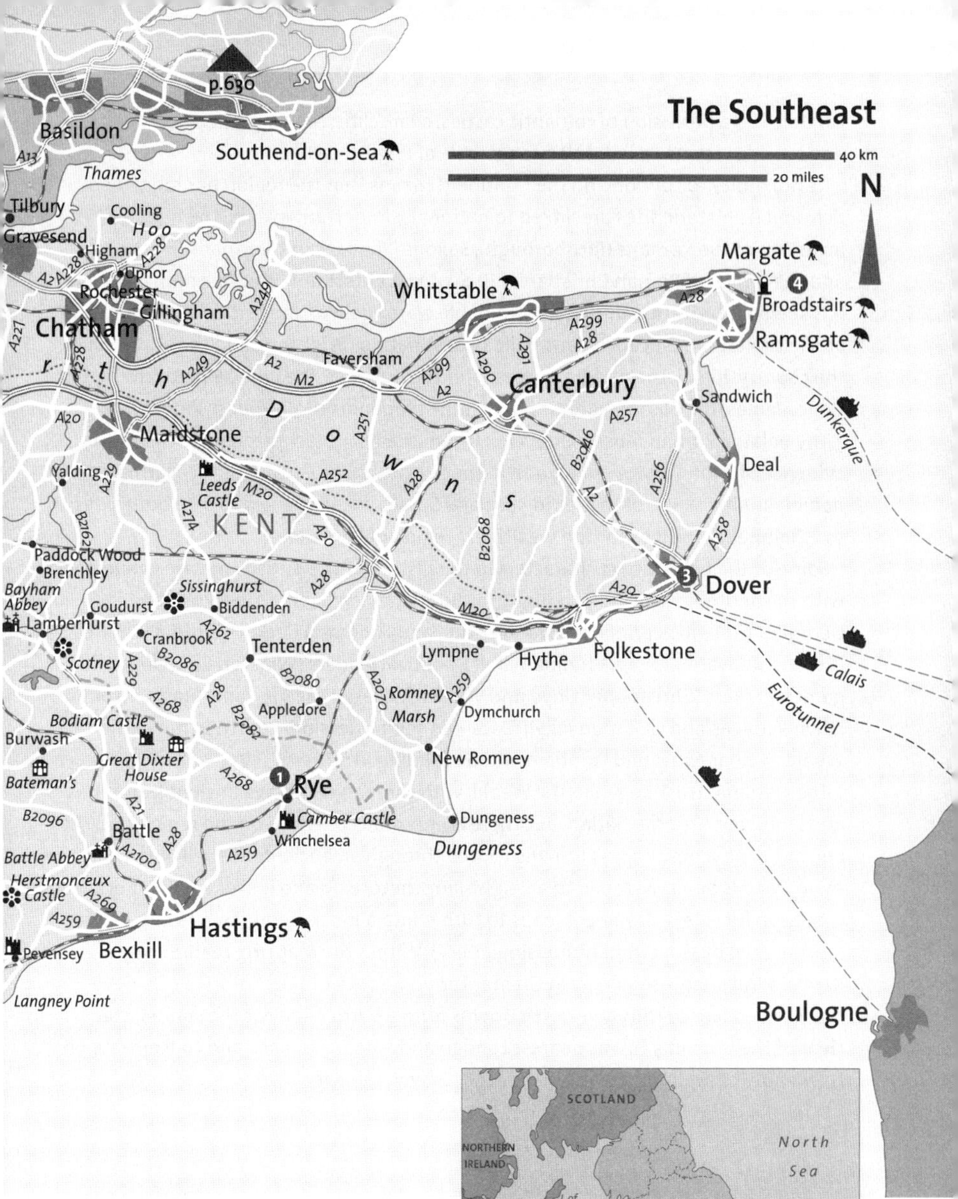

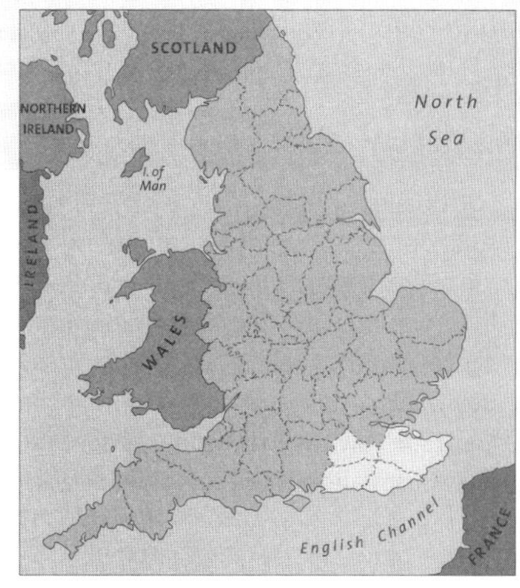

Highlights

1 Rye, for all-round interest on the edge of the marsh
2 Charleston Farmhouse, a Bloomsbury treasure trove
3 Dover Castle, bracing symbolism
4 Broadstairs beach, the eptiome of English seaside charm, with Dickensian knobs on

London, has a profusion of romantic castles, chalk cliffs, flower gardens, cathedrals and seaside resorts – all the classic symbols of English charm.

Its proximity to London and the Continent means that the region has long been rich, and its historic sites are linked to nationally important events: the military invasions of the Romans (**Richborough**), Saxons (**Thanet**) and Normans (**Hastings**); and the arrival of Roman Christianity in AD 495 (**Canterbury**). The southern coastline has seen militarization during interminable wars against France (**Dover**), jollification as the capital's most convenient holiday destination (**Brighton**), and the adoption of the countryside by the middle classes after the arrival of the railway (Rudyard Kipling, Henry James, the Bloomsbury Group and the gardeners of the Forest Ridge).

The palatial Roman mosaic floors at **Fishbourne** near Chichester are the earliest evidence of a long history of wealth in the Southeast. The cream of the Norman nobility built a string of castles in Kent and Sussex to oversee estates on both sides of the Channel. It's still by far the wealthiest region of England.

Some of the best-known characters in the history of the British Isles are connected with the Southeast, including kings (Harold Godwin, William I, Henry VIII and George III), religious primates (St Augustine and Thomas à Becket), writers (Charles Dickens, Rudyard Kipling, Virginia Woolf), political leaders (Winston Churchill), and garden makers (Christopher Lloyd and Vita Sackville-West). Arts-and-Crafts-inspired Edwin Lutyens and Gertrude Jekyll fostered their professional partnership in the Wealden villages around **Farnham** and **Godalming** in Surrey.

The National Trust began in the Weald, with campaigns to save ancient properties and landscapes for the nation, but there is enormous pressure on the region now. At any moment, a new bypass is being routed through an ancient bluebell wood or a minor road is being widened to an eight-lane motorway, and if ever a green field comes up for sale, a developer leaps to turn it into a mock-Georgian housing estate (encouraged by Government housing policy). Within the M25 ring road, Surrey and Kent are indistinguishable from Greater London. South of the motorway, however, the wooded **Surrey Hills** and **North Downs** form a barrier against the sprawl. Steer clear of the ungainly towns nearest London and along the coast, and concentrate on the beauty of Kipling's Weald, Marsh and 'Downs countree'.

Surrey

To outsiders, Surrey is suburbia, but south of the Surrey Hills it becomes green and rural. Some of the highest summits along the parallel **North Downs** and **Greensand Ridge** are in these hills, including **Box Hill** and **Leith Hill**. The North Downs Way begins in Farnham, climbing to Guildford over the famous **Hogsback**. In southwest Surrey, the loop of the Greensand Ridge creates **Hindhead Common** and the **Devil's Punch Bowl**. This corner is associated with architect Edwin Lutyens and garden designer Gertrude Jekyll, who lived in neighbouring villages and cut their professional teeth on the houses and gardens of middle-class incomers.

Landscapes of the Southeast

Parallel ridges of chalk and sandstone run across the Southeast. The **High Weald** forms the sandstone backbone of the region. For centuries this so-called Forest Ridge was a wooded, industrial and very poor upland, a long way from population centres. Now, it's a sought-after rural playground for wealthy Londoners. The **Greensand Ridge** runs south of the North Downs and north of the Low Weald through Kent, Surrey, Sussex and Hampshire. One of its summits, Leith Hill, is the highest point in the Southeast. The mixture of rugged heaths, hills and rolling pastoral scenery along the ridge has had a string of great country houses with deer parks built on it over the centuries – Knole, Petworth, Cowdray, Polesden Lacey and Leeds Castle. Between the ridges is the **Low Weald**, a wide clay vale crammed with windy country lanes and pretty villages as well as one or two unlovely market towns such as Maidstone, Tonbridge and Ashford. Where the valleys reach the sea, either side of the High Weald, you have marshland. **Romney Marsh** is an alien corner of the Southeast. Collectively, all of the above is known as the **Weald** and the whole thing is enveloped in chalk. The **North Downs** run from Farnham in Surrey to the East Kent coast where they end up as the White Cliffs of Dover. From Farnham southwards to Petersfield are the Hampshire Downs, which link up with the **South Downs**. This is the most famous landscape in the Southeast, smooth, rounded sheep-grazed hills. Where the chalk meets the sea at Beachy Head is one of Britain's most sensational white edges. The North Downs, Greensand Ridge, High Weald and South Downs all run east–west across the region.

Ridge-walking in the Southeast

Scenic ridges are just the thing for long-distance walks. The most famous is the **South Downs Way**, stretching 106 miles between Eastbourne and Winchester along the crest of the South Downs and onto the Hampshire Downs. As well as the views over the Weald there are intriguing diversions such as Chanctonbury Ring, the Long Man of Wilmington and Devil's Dyke. The best walking guide is the *Countryside Commission National Trail Guide*, and *OS Explorer Series Maps* 132 and 120–3. As rewarding, although lesser known,the **High Weald Landscape Trail** runs 89 miles between Horsham and Rye, taking in hop gardens, orchards, villages and historic gardens (*www.highweald.org*). You could walk it over three weekends, using public transport and B&Bs.

The **North Downs Way** is 153 mostly scenic miles and loosely follows the old route known as the Pilgrims' Way (diverting to avoid busy roads) between Farnham and Dover, with a detour via Canterbury. The **Greensand Way** is 108 miles along the Greensand hills of Surrey and Kent between Haslemere and Hamstreet, through woods, heaths, orchards and hop gardens. The best section is along the Surrey Hills between Hindhead and Leith Hill. Finally, the **Saxon Shore Way** travels 160 miles round the coast of Kent from Gravesend to Hastings in East Sussex, following the old shoreline as it was around 1,500 years ago, before the narrowing of the Wantsum Channel and the appearance of Romney Marsh and the North Kent Marshes.

Surrey Hills

The Surrey Hills around Dorking have been attracting day trippers and poets for centuries. They are a frontline Area of Outstanding Natural Beauty, forming a natural buffer against Greater London's sprawl. Dorking itself is congested and unappealing, although a good start for walks. But you can avoid it altogether, staying in Guildford instead. To the north of Dorking is **Box Hill**, a famous North Downs beauty spot. To the south, is **Leith Hill**, the highest point in Southeast England.

Box Hill

Daniel Defoe noted in the 1720s that 'an abundance of ladies and gentlemen from Epsom used to take the air, and walk in the boxwoods; and in a word, divert or debauch, or perhaps both' on Box Hill. Jane Austen set the picnic scene in *Emma* on Box Hill (564ft). The 17th-century diarist John Evelyn, who lived in Wotton (just west of Dorking along the A25) praised its yews and box trees for making it look like summer in winter. George Meredith lived in Flint Cottage, near Mickleham, for 30 years, writing *The Egoist* (1879) in a writing hut in the garden. 'I am every morning at the top of Box Hill – as its flower, its bird, its prophet,' he wrote. 'I drop down the moon on one side, I draw up the sun on t'other. I breathe fine air. I shout "ha ha" to the gates of the world. Then I descend and know myself a donkey for doing it.' Keats wrote the last 500 lines of 'Endymion' after a moonlit stroll on the hill in December 1817. He was spending a fortnight at the Burford Bridge Hotel, where Robert Louis Stevenson wrote part of the *New Arabian Nights*. The River Mole, which runs through the hotel's garden, has inspired poetry too – not all of it original – including Spenser ('like a nousling mole'), Milton ('sullen Mole') and Pope ('sullen Mole' again).

Above the river, a cliff known as **the Whites** rises 300ft, covered in box woods (hence the name). On top is oak and beech woodland, and grassland with views south into the Low Weald. From the car park near Burford Bridge, just off the A24 London to Dorking road, you can cross the Mole on picturesque stepping stones and climb up the Whites in the footsteps of Keats. Or you can join school groups and biker gangs at the National Trust car park, shop and restaurant. There are two recommended walks: The **Long Walk** is 8 miles and the **Short Walk** is just 1 mile long.

Where to Stay and Eat

Surrey Hills t (01306) –

On a fine day, head for the hills with a picnic and a rug. Failing that, try:

The Burford Bridge (foot of Box Hill), Dorking, **t** 0870 400 8283, *www.macdonald hotels.co.uk* (*very expensive*). A comfortable place to stay, at a famous beauty spot associated with Lord Nelson (who met Emma Hamilton here before the Battle of Trafalgar in 1815), and Keats, who finished his poem 'Endymion' in one of the rooms. The River Mole runs along the bottom of its delightful gardens, under the Whites.

The Plough Inn, Coldharbour, **t** 711 793. A 17th-century coaching inn, now a free house with two bars, restaurant and bedrooms (*moderate*). Home of the Leith Hill Brewery, which brews its own Crooked Furrow and Tallywhacker ales. Home-made bar food and excellent puddings.

The National Trust Servery (at the top of Box Hill), **t** 888 793 (*cheap*). Soft drinks and ice cream, soup, hot dogs and sandwiches for refuelling after the ascent.

Leith Hill Tower

t (01306) 711 777, www.nationaltrust.org.uk; open April–Sept Wed and weekends 10–5, Oct–Mar weekends 10–3.30; adm.

Leith Hill Tower crowns the highest point in the Southeast, bumping up its height to over a thousand feet. It was built in 1765 by Richard Hull, who is buried beneath the floor. To reach it, lanes climb the densely wooded lower slopes towards Coldharbour, where views open out over the Low Weald. There are several car parks on the road skirting Leith Hill, or you can walk up from Friday Street (south of the A25) through Abinger Bottom. The best short walk is from the Plough Inn in Coldharbour (*see* box).

Polesden Lacey

t (01372) 452 048, www.nationaltrust.org.uk; house open Easter–Oct Wed–Sun 11–5, gardens all year daily 11–6; adm.

Polesden Lacey resembles a luxurious Edwardian hotel. It was used by rich society hostess Mrs Grevel as a weekend retreat from her Mayfair home, to which she invited A-list celebrities (notably Edward VII and his mistress Mrs Keppel). She hired Mewes and Davis (architects of the Ritz Hotel in London) to transform the original Thomas Cubbitt house, inside and out, and filled it with expensive furniture and paintings as well as beautiful *objets* by Fabergé and Cartier (she inherited a fortune from her father, owner of McEwans brewery in Edinburgh, and her husband, who died in 1908).

Guildford

Guildford sprawls over low chalk hills either side of a gap in the North Downs carved out by the River Wey. At its heart, the old county town is lovely, with the hallmarks of an ancient town – ruined royal castle, 18th-century coaching inns and Tudor grammar school. It is lively too, with the University of Surrey; trendy bars cater for its youngish metropolitan population. Guildford High Street slopes down to the Wey, the Mount a perfect backdrop across the river. From the top of the street you can imagine you are in a rural town rather than an urban centre encircled by ring roads, half an hour from London. In 1927, Guildford became the centre of a new see, created out of the northeastern corner of the old diocese of Winchester. A brand new cathedral was built a short way from the town centre on land donated by the Earl of Onslow.

The old town centre is a handful of streets around High Street, Chapel Street, Castle Street and Quarry Street (the main shopping area). Start at the top of High Street and head down towards the river, branching off to the castle and museum. Inevitably, you will see the cathedral either first or last, as it's out of town.

The **High Street** is split into upper and lower, the lower part cobbled, pedestrianized and pretty. Between the two stands the statue of Guildford's favourite son, George Abbot, who rose through the ranks of Vice Chancellor of Oxford University and Bishop of London to become Archbishop of Canterbury, and founded the **Hospital of the Blessed Trinity** on Lower High Street. He was educated in the **Royal Grammar School**

Tourist Information

Guildford: 14 Tunsgate, **t** (01483) 444 333, *www.guildford.gov.uk. Open 9.30–5.*

Fri and Sat **market** on North Street. **Farmers' market** first Tues of the month on High Street.

Where to Stay

Guildford t (01483) –

The Angel Posting House and Livery, 91 High Street, **t** 564 555, *www.slh.com* (*very expensive*). A beautiful 16th-century coaching inn on the cobbled High Street, with 13th-century undercroft. Famous guests on the London–Portsmouth route have included Lord Nelson, Charles Dickens, Lord Byron and Jane Austen. Recently refurbished; 20 rooms and a dining room for guests. Features include a gallery overlooking the main reception hall, a Jacobean fireplace, 1655 clock, heavy old beams and floorboards.

Carlton Hotel, 36–40 London Road, **t** 303 030, *www.hotelengland.com* (*expensive*). Imposing cream brick Victorian building. Boasts 46 immaculate rooms since refurbishment. Comfortable bar named after local resident P.G. Wodehouse.

Crawford House Hotel, 73 Farnham Road, **t** 579 299, *www.crawfordhousehotel.co.uk* (*moderate*). Victorian house of local stone with comfortable rooms; near station.

Blanes Court Hotel, 4 Albery Road, **t** 573 171, *www.blanes.demon.co.uk* (*moderate*). Quality guesthouse off Epsom Road, in an Edwardian house with sunroom overlooking spacious grounds.

Hillcote, 11 Castle Hill, **t** 563 324 (*cheap*). Red-brick Victorian house near Lewis Carroll's house in quiet conservation area. Grade II listed building smothered in flower baskets.

Plaegan House, 96 Wodeland Avenue (off Farnham Road), **t** 822 181 (*moderate*). Charming, comfortable place to stay in a quiet corner of town. Short walk into town.

Mrs Hay's, 2 Woodland Avenue, **t** 451 142 (*moderate*). Busy, friendly family home with two rooms, both with view over the Downs.

Eating Out

The town centre has plenty of café-bars, including chains like Pizza Express. At the back of Guildford House art gallery is a café with a courtyard. Chapel Street, a narrow lane between High Street and Castle Street, is full of eateries including **Café Rouge** (*cheap*), 8–9 Chapel Street, **t** 451 221, for French brasserie-style food, coffee and drinks.

Café de Paris, 35 Castle Street, **t** 534 896, *www.cafedeparisguildford.co.uk* (*cheap*). Bustling family-owned French brasserie in an 18th-century building with Victorian floor tiles, serves charcuterie followed by coq au vin or salad Niçoise in a Parisian, yet nonetheless friendly, ambience. The more formal restaurant offers crayfish salad with rosti, confit de canard and variations on classic French desserts like crème brulée

on Upper High Street, founded in 1512 and re-endowed in 1553 by Edward VI, who gave it the 'Royal' prefix. The old grammar school is now part of a boys' private school, so you're unlikely to see the old chained library, but **Abbot's Hospital**, founded in 1619, is still an old people's home to this day, and you can enter the Jacobean gatehouse and peep into the courtyard, which resembles an Oxford college. This is no coincidence: Abbot's other foundation was Pembroke College. Opposite, the 18th-century **Holy Trinity Church** concludes the short tour of Abbot's life (1562–1633). His grand marble tomb stands in the north end near the organ. The church also contains a memorial to Arthur Onslow, one of three Onslow family Speakers of the House of Commons (*see* Clandon Park), buried at Merrow. The present church stands on the site of a medieval church, which collapsed in 1740, and now resembles a 1930s municipal building.

Further down the High Street you pass the **town clock**, which projects out from the 17th-century wedding-cake façade of the original Tudor **Guildhall**. **Guildford House** is with lavender or tarte tartin with clotted cream. *Closed Sun eve.*

Yellow River Oriental Restaurant, Chapel Street, **t** 503 100 (*moderate*). Stylish, minimalist Asian restaurant with specialities from China, Vietnam, Malaysia and Thailand.

Café Austria, 20 Chapel Street, **t** 537 979 (*cheap*). Traditional Austrian café serving strüdel, and Wiener schnitzel. *Closed Sun.*

Olivetto, 124 High Street, Tunsgate, **t** 563 277 (*moderate*). Italian guitar songs and the smell of garlic drift over the pavement. Pasta, grilled fish and meat, all cooked with olive oil. *Closed Sun.*

Olivo Ristorante & Focacceria, 53 Quarry Street, **t** 303 535 (*moderate*). Olivetto's sister, in a 16th-century Grade II listed building, full of character with wooden beams and floors, and al fresco terrace. Traditional Italian cooking includes chargrilled langoustines. *Closed Sun.*

Tudor Rose, 144 High Street, **t** 563 887 (*cheap*). Lovely 16th-century building with window seats and wooden bench tables overlooking cobbled High Street. Old-style English food: beans on toast, liver and bacon or roast lamb and mint sauce.

Zizzi, 272 Upper High Street, **t** 534 747 (*cheap*). Informal modern Italian restaurant.

fish!, Sydenham Road (near Castle Street on corner of Tunsgate), **t** (020) 8467 8866, *www.fishdiner.co.uk* (*moderate*). One of a chain. Shop on ground floor sells fresh fish. Minimalist stainless steel restaurant, up lift on top floor above multi-storey car park, has windows with views over town to cathedral. 'Choose your own' fish and preparation.

Rum Wong Thai Restaurant, 16 London Road (off Upper High Street opposite Civic Hall), **t** 536 092 (*moderate*). Traditional Thai food and beer. *Closed Mon.*

King's Head, on corner of Quarry Street near castle, **t** 575 004. Friendly pub with sunny courtyard full of flowers, and a roof terrace. Dark flagstoned bar. Baked potatoes all day.

The Withies Inn, Withies Lane, Compton, **t** 421 158. Just west of Guildford, signposted through village of Compton. Delightful cottagey pub in wooded setting with honeysuckle shading the garden. Popular with Aston Martin drivers and Downs walkers. Pub grub (*cheap*) and restaurant (*expensive*).

Compton Café, **t** 811 030. Tea rooms are in the old pottery buildings of Watt's Gallery. Attracts excursionists from London for breakfast, Welsh rarebit, buck and bacon or home-made scones and cakes. *Closed Christmas period.*

Entertainment

Yvonne Arnaud Theatre, Millbrook, **t** 440 000, *www.yvonne-arnaud.co.uk*. Venue for touring theatrical productions. The Mills Studio hosts local amateur and children's shows.

Concerts at Hatchlands, **t** 211 474, *www.cobbecollection.co.uk*. The home of the Cobbe collection of musical instruments hosts concerts from April to June and October to November.

one of the most striking domestic buildings along the High Street, built in 1660 by John Child, a lawyer and thrice mayor of Guildford. It is now a city council **art gallery** (***t*** *(01483) 444 740; open Tues–Sat 10–4.45*). To reach the **castle grounds** (***t*** *(01483) 444 715; open dawn–dusk*) go down **Tunsgate** or Chapel Street (where there are lots of restaurants). You can climb the ruined Norman keep in its pretty municipal gardens. From there, drop down to the museum on Quarry Street, passing **The Chestnuts**, the Dodgson family home at the bottom of Castle Hill, behind a clipped hedge (with a plaque on the gatepost). To find the **grave of Charles Dodgson** (aka Lewis Carroll), head up The Mount to Guildford Cemetery; the grave is behind the cemetery chapel.

Guildford Museum (***t*** *(01483) 444 750; open Mon–Sat 11–5*) was founded in 1898 by the Surrey Archaeological Society. Displays on 'Surrey through the Ages' include the society's collection of flints, coins and medieval church tiles. Other, more curious, displays include a case of the Dodgson children's wooden toys, and Gertrude Jekyll's

Lewis Carroll

Lewis Carroll, pseudonym of the Reverend Charles Dodgson, is the white rabbit in a hat of a trip to Guildford. His entire family, including seven unmarried sisters (aged 25–40), three younger brothers and his aunt Lucy, lived in a large Victorian house called Chestnuts at the bottom of Castle Hill. Carroll found it, paid the rent and supported his family out of the royalties from his books (*Alice in Wonderland*). He often visited, going on long walks over the Hogsback to Farnham and back by train. The idea for *The Hunting of the Snark* came to him while walking on the downs. He died at Chestnuts in 1898, aged 66, and is buried in Mount Cemetery.

own collection of Victorian cottage bygones (donated in 1911) assembled in a parlour scene with a ragrug in front of the grate and sewing kit on the table.

Everyone wants to get married in the atmospheric little church of **St Martha's**, overlooking the wooded Surrey Weald. Walk or drive up Pewley Hill, which leads uphill at the end of Tunsgate, and follow a track 2–3 miles across Pewley Downs to the church.

Guildford Cathedral

You can either drive there, taking the Farnham road from the city centre and following signs, or catch a bus from the Friary Shopping Centre. Sir Edward Maufe's mid-20th-century brick cathedral stands on a hilltop site known as Stag Hill, beside the modern Surrey University buildings. As you approach it off the A3, its sharp lines, flags and neat lawns have less in common with old cathedrals than with modern war memorials. Funnily enough, Maufe was Chief Architect and Artistic Adviser to the Commonwealth War Graves Commission, and built the famous Air Forces and Magna Carta memorials at Runnymede. The cathedral is not as modern nor as emotive as the more famous 20th-century cathedral at Coventry; the new diocese of Guildford simply needed a new cathedral (only the second Anglican cathedral on a new site since the Reformation). It took 25 years to build, from 1936 to 1961. Inside, it's all airy and bright: cream plaster matches the cream Doulting stone on prominent piers and arches.

Around Guildford

Compton

Compton is one Surrey's best days out. This tiny village west of Guildford has its own art gallery, Art Nouveau cemetery chapel and two superb places to eat. The **Watts Gallery** is a mile northwest of the village, signposted off the main road past the **Watts Cemetery Chapel**, on a hill above the road like a beacon of terracotta.

The Watts Gallery

t (01483) 810 235; open April–Sept 2–6, Wed and Sat also 11–1; winter until 4.

Not many people remember Victorian painter George Frederic Watts, or his wife Mary, a well known Arts and Crafts practitioner in her time. Watts barely gets a mention in art-history books and hasn't had a retrospective for decades, yet he was considered one of the great symbolist painters of his day. A solo exhibition of his work opened the Metropolitan Museum of Art in New York in 1883, and was so popular that it carried on for 14 months – eight months longer than planned. He had a studio in the Tate Gallery (where most of his work is now in storage) for 40 years. His most famous painting is the portrait of his first wife, Shakespearean actress Ellen Terry, holding a camellia. He was 47 when they married, she was 17, and it lasted only a year. His second wife, Mary, was also 30 years his junior. They built Limnerslease in Compton as a winter retreat, then moved permanently from London, building the Arts and Crafts-style Watts Gallery in the grounds to house Watts' collection of 300 pictures, including his first and last paintings. Watts lived just long enough to see it open in 1904. At one end is the curator's cottage, and at the other end the old pottery buildings of the Compton Potter's Art Guild (1900–54) founded by Mary Watts. The Compton decorative ware was sold at Liberty's, and now fetches high prices in the collectors' market. The buildings now house a commercial gallery and renowned café. Carry on through Old Compton for the **Withies Inn**.

Watts Cemetery Chapel

There are no Watts tombs inside the cemetery chapel (*open dawn–dusk*), but Mary Watts and the Compton potters designed it in folksy Art Nouveau style. Its red brick-work and terracotta decoration seem to glow. 'I always hoped that it would tone down,' Mary said. Every inch of the walls and ceilings is decorated in raised gesso relief and coloured gold, green and red. Mary called it 'glorified wallpaper'.

Clandon Park and Hatchlands

Clandon Park and Hatchlands are neighbours along the Epsom Road (A246), north-east of Guildford. You can see the two in an afternoon, starting with Clandon, and moving on to Hatchlands. The interesting interiors house two extraordinary private collections, which the National Trust has installed to fill the empty rooms.

Clandon Park

***t** (01483) 222 482, www.nationaltrust.org.uk; open April–Oct Tues–Thurs and Sun 11–5; adm exp, joint ticket for Hatchlands available.*

Clandon has been the home of the Onslow family since 1641. The 7th Earl still lives in a house in the grounds. His ancestors were politicians, three of them Speakers of the House of Commons. At one time the Onslows owned most of the land around Guildford, including the land on which the cathedral and Onslow village were built in the 20th century. The second Baron Onslow rebuilt Clandon out of the fortune of his wife, rich heiress Elizabeth Knight (whose nickname was 'the West Indian fortune'). Venetian architect Giacomo Leoni created a monument to English Palladianism with austere red-brick walls and lavish interiors. You enter from the back, via the famous two-storey **Marble Hall** – 40ft square, with vistas into the state rooms around it. The elaborate plaster ceiling by Italian stucco artists Artari and Bagutti features 3-D slaves with their feet hanging over the entablature. The marble chimneypieces are by Michael Rysbrack, the foremost sculptor in England in the early 18th century. There are more Rysbrack sculptures and ceilings depicting classical gods and naughty cherubs in the state rooms, which are decorated with paintings, brightly coloured Chinese birds on rococo gilt wall brackets from Mrs Gubbay's collection, and a fine collection of Meissen Italian comedy figures. Hannah Gubbay was a rich widow who amassed her collection in London auction houses in the early 1900s.

Hatchlands

t (01483) 222 482, www.nationaltrust.org.uk; park open April–Oct daily 11–6, house April–Oct Tues–Thurs and Sun 2–5.30, Aug also Fri; adm exp.

On the outside, Hatchlands is plain, going on drab. It was built by an architect called Stiff for Admiral Boscawen in the 1750s. The lavish nautical-style **interiors by Robert Adam** are more attractive. Boscawen's successors commissioned Humphrey Repton and Gertrude Jekyll to design the gardens, and Reginald Blomefield to add the domed Music Room in 1902. Some of the 18th-century glamour has been restored to the place, along with the Cobbe Collection of composers' keyboards. These include the piano on which Elgar composed 'Land of Hope and Glory', Chopin's pianoforte and Bizet's table piano, on which he composed *Carmen*. Hanging in the library is a curious painting recently identified as Shakespeare's patron, Henry Wriothesley, 3rd Earl of Southampton. The identification comes as a surprise, because the sitter is dressed as a woman, wearing lipstick, rouge and an earring – but tallies with recent scholarship on the 'master-mistress of my passion' to whom Shakespeare's early sonnets are addressed. Other paintings are by Van Dyck, Gainsborough and Poussin.

RHS Garden Wisley

t (01483) 224 234, www.rhs.org.uk; open Mar–Oct Mon–Fri 10–6, weekends 9–6; Nov–Feb Mon–Fri 10–4.30, weekends 10–4.30; adm.

The Royal Horticultural Society Garden Wisley, signposted off the A3, just south of junction 10 of the M25, is planted on 240 acres of mostly poor, sandy soil in the valley of the River Wey. On busy weekends, the popular plant centre, shop and restaurant heave. Start your tour in the formal gardens. From there, cross the conifer lawn to the **Mixed Borders** – one of the highlights – along a grass broad walk. The walk carries on up Battlestone Hill to the horticultural society's **Trial Grounds** (where new plant varieties are put to the test). The **Model Gardens** are the most popular section, with a series of small gardens to inspire domestic gardeners – a herb garden, courtyard garden and patio garden – and a fruit orchard, alpine meadow and rock garden.

Southwest Surrey

The southwest corner of Surrey straddles the **Greensand Ridge**. Its countryside is dramatic, with three large areas of open common land around Thursley, Witley and Hindhead; these are the wilds of Surrey. When Samuel Pepys travelled from Guildford to Petersfield in 1668 he hired a guide. A hundred and fifty years later, William Cobbett, who grew up in Farnham, deplored the 'villainous' heathland around the **Devil's Punch Bowl**. In the mid-19th century, the railway brought a rush of middle-class incomers, who commuted to work in London. One of them, Sir Robert Hunter, founded the National Trust, campaigning to preserve the Surrey Commons. Edwin Lutyens and Gertrude Jekyll, who both lived near Godalming, collaborated on the restoration and garden design of Wealden houses to suit the new owners. You can explore on foot along the Greensand Way from Haslemere, or by car.

Farnham

From Farnham, the chalk ridge known as the **Hogsback** runs 7 miles northeast to Guildford, carrying the North Downs Way and the A31. The River Wey runs along the south side of the ridge to the gap in the North Downs at Guildford.

William Cobbett (1763–1835)

William Cobbett was one of England's earliest and most opinionated travel writers. His epithets frequently crop up in quotation marks in travel guidebooks such as this one, dismissing great national landscapes such as the Devil's Punch Bowl or taking pot shots at the Establishment. Cobbett was a man who showed great integrity and heroic resilience to life's downers; his experiences would have done for most of us. He was born in Farnham in 1763. At 14 he ran away from home to work in Kew Gardens. At 19 he tried to join the navy, but failed. Two years later he joined the army, but had to flee the country after rashly accusing his officers of embezzlement. He ended up in America, where he set up as a bookseller, and wrote a string of prickly anti-Republican articles that earned him the nickname Peter Porcupine. He was fined $5,000 for an article accusing a doctor of killing his patients, and returned to England. He published his own newspaper, *The Porcupine*, which failed. His weekly Radical journal, the *Political Register*, was more successful, enabling him to buy a farm in Hampshire. But an article against flogging landed him in court for sedition. He defended himself, lost, and was sent to Newgate Prison, emerging two years later as a public hero. He stood as parliamentary candidate for Southampton, lost, and was offered £10,000 by the Government to retire from politics and stop publishing his *Register*. He refused the offer and fled to America again, returning two years later in 1819. He tried again to get into the House of Commons, for Coventry, lost, filed for bankruptcy, then lost two pending libel actions with costs and damages against him.

In 1821 he travelled on horseback around the country to find out the state of the English countryside and gather material for the *Register*; his writings were later compiled into the travel journal *Rural Rides*, one of the indispensable records of pre-Victorian England. At last, aged 70, he was elected to the Reform Parliament of 1832 as MP for Oldham, and spent the rest of his life making inflammatory speeches against corruption, injustice and inefficiency in the House of Commons. Even then he was rumoured to be the infamous 'Captain Swing' behind the barn-burning and machine-breaking of the Swing Riots against the mechanization of agriculture.

Tourist Information

Farnham: South Street, **t** (01252) 715 109, *www.waverley.gov.uk. Open Mon–Thurs 9.30–5, Sat 9–12.*

Where to Stay and Eat

Farnham t (01252) –

Farnham has many of the better chain café-restaurants (Caffé Uno, Pizza Piazza, Café Rouge). There is also a small cluster of eateries in Lion and Lamb Yard, off West Street, with tables outside: the **Cromwell Chocolate Bar and Coffee Shop** serves hot chocolate, coffee, cakes and toasted sandwiches with salad. Opposite, the **Lion and Lamb Bistro** serves sausages and chips or baked potatoes.

Little Twynax, 49 Burnt Hill Road, **t** 715 058, *www.smoothhound.co.uk* (*moderate*). A 300-year-old beamed cottage in a quiet spot a mile out of town. Garden overlooks paddocks. Nearby pub serves food.

The Vienna Restaurant, 112 West Street, **t** 722 978 (*moderate*). Wiener schnitzel is the only Austrian dish on offer, the rest is French/English. Smart presentation with crisp tablecloths. *Closed Sun.*

The Bishop's Table, West Street, **t** 710 222, *www.bishopstable.com*. Charming Georgian building in the centre of old Farnham, originally owned by the Marquis of Lothian and once a school for priests. Now hotel (*expensive*) and restaurant (*moderate*) with good local reputation, and lovely secluded walled garden. *Closed Mon lunch.*

Around Farnham

The Mariners Hotel, Millbridge, Frensham, **t** (01252) 792 050, *www.themarinershotel.co.uk* (*moderate*). Old smugglers' haunt in charming countryside between Portsmouth and London. Bar and Italian restaurant, **Genzianis**.

Anne's Cottage, Green Cross Lane, Churt, **t** (01428) 714 181, *www.bedandbreakfastnationwide.com* (*moderate*). Quiet country location 5 miles south of Farnham via A287. Lovely B&B in 16th-century cottage with sitting room on two floors; inglenook fireplace below and gallery above.

The Barley Mow, Tilford Green, Tilford, Farnham, **t** (01252) 792 205 (*cheap*). An 18th-century pub overlooking village cricket green. Darts and skittles, good beer, and home-cooked bar meals. Open fires in winter, riverside garden for barbecues in summer (Sun lunch). Restaurant serves traditional country pub food: duck, roasts, fish (*moderate*).

Godalming

The museum has a great little café. Otherwise pick up a pizza from the Mediterranean deli, **Kalimera**, next door, and picnic by the riverside. **Pizza Express** on the High Street can offer you a chair at a table too.

Haslemere t (01428) –

You can get coffee and lunch at **Durnsley's** on the High Street, or the usual at **Pizza Express** next door; both are close to the museum and put tables out on the pavement in summer.

Lythe Hill Hotel, **t** 651 251, *www.lythehill.co.uk* (*expensive*). Smart, privately-owned hotel and restaurant set in 20 acres of parkland; 41 bedrooms from 14th century to brand new.

Strathire, Grayswood Road, **t** 642 466 (*moderate*). Delightful period property set in an acre of landscaped garden; each of the four bedrooms is tastefully furnished and has a beautiful view. Warm welcome and wonderful walks.

Poachers Pocket, 14 Petworth Road, **t** 652 625 (*moderate*). Just off the High Street. Modern English menu: roasted cherry tomatoes on garlic bread with parmesan shavings, salmon fillet with pesto and parmesan crust on a bed of green salad. *Closed Sat lunch, Sun and Mon.*

Georgian House Hotel, High Street, **t** 656 644, *www.georgianhousehotel.com* (*moderate*). Dates back to the time of Queen Anne and takes its name from the American state of Georgia founded in 1733 by Haslemere man, General Sir James Oglethorpe. Thorpe's restaurant offers coffee, lunch and evening meals.

The bishops of Winchester built **Farnham Castle** as a stop on the London to Winchester Road. Farnham's cornmarkets were the greatest in England, according to Defoe, and Cobbett (a Farnham man born and buried) was proud of the delicate flavour of the local hops. Thanks to all the corn and hop money, the main streets are lined with beautiful 18th-century houses. But poor old Farnham is now a well-heeled military and stockbroker-belt town, with a few students from the Surrey Institute of Art and Design thrown into the mix. Castle Street is one of the prettiest streets anywhere, but the rest of the town is swamped by traffic. Aim for Waggon Lane and Maltings car park off South Street, which leaves you just where you want to be: **St Andrew's Church** is just down the lane, with Cobbett's tomb outside its main porch and a memorial plaque inside the tower. From there, you can go up Downing Street to The Borough – right to the castle, left to the museum.

Museum of Farnham

***t** (01252) 715 094; open Tues–Sat 10–5.*

This smashing little museum in Willmer House, an early Georgian townhouse built for a rich local hop merchant, has a handful of **Cobbett heirlooms** including his initialled chair, a Spanish mahogany table and his family chest. Running up the stairs is a series of paintings by Stephen Elmer (1715–96), a little-known local artist whose speciality was painting dead game. The reference library has lots of material on Cobbett. The upstairs loo is an exhibit in itself.

Farnham Castle

***t** (01252) 713 393, www.english-heritage.org.uk; open April–Oct 10–5; adm.*

Either walk or drive to Farnham Castle up Castle Street, an architectural set piece of Georgian townhouses with fanlights and decorative porches. The stone walls of the keep, mysteriously, enclose the motte, instead of sitting on top of it. Henry of Blois, Bishop of Winchester, built the first structure in 1138, since when countless additions have been made. Cobbett worked in the castle gardens as a 14-year-old boy. From 1926 until 1955 the castle was again the bishop's residence, for the diocese of Guildford.

The Blackwater Valley

North of Farnham is a string of military towns along the Blackwater Valley, an urban corridor flanked by Ministry of Defence land. The **Royal Military Academy Sandhurst** dates back to 1812, when William Pitt selected Sandown Park to keep officer cadets away from the distractions of London. The heaths around **Aldershot** were chosen as a new permanent training camp for the British Army in the mid-19th century. Aldershot became the first new military town in Britain since the Roman occupation, with its own schools, hospitals, sewage works, a sports centre and residential estates.

Waverley Abbey

A few miles southeast of Farnham on the Godalming road you come to the lonely ruins of Waverley Abbey (*open dawn–dusk*). This was the first Cistercian foundation in

Jekyll and Lutyens in Surrey

Gertrude Jekyll and Edwin Lutyens launched their careers in the countryside around Godalming, Farnham and Haslemere. Jekyll (1843–1932) grew up in Bramley, south of Guildford, and is buried in Munstead Church. She was fascinated by the traditional crafts of embroidery, silver work, drystone-walling and thatching. She is best known for her influential cottage gardening style, and for her association with Lutyens. Her garden designs found their way into stately homes, suburban gardens and the overseas cemeteries of the Imperial War Graves Commission. She eventually settled in Munstead, in a Lutyens house called Munstead Wood. Lutyens (1869–1944) grew up in Thursley and is buried in St Paul's Cathedral. His famous commissions included Castle Drogo in Devon, Hampstead Garden Suburb, Johannesburg Art Gallery, the British Embassy in Washington, New Delhi and the Cenotaph in Whitehall. His earliest jobs, however, were conversions for friends in Surrey. His trademark is a style of domestic architecture based on traditional English design and craftsmanship, yet highly individual – an updated, personalized vernacular. Waverley Borough Council publishes a touring leaflet (on sale in Godalming Museum), including 24 of his designs. The problem is that almost all his buildings are private houses, which can be glimpsed only surreptitiously over hedges. Munstead Wood is open one day a year as part of the National Garden Scheme (check at the tourist information centre).

England, founded in 1128 by the Bishop of Winchester (Tintern Abbey was close behind, in 1131). Across the river is a grand Georgian house. This was built in 1725 for Chancellor of the Exchequer Aislabie, who turned the river bank and abbey ruins into a romantic picture. Visitors have included Haydn, Florence Nightingale and Sir Walter Scott. The River Wey runs along the other side of the ruins, beneath the wooded ridge.

Godalming and Around

If you can make it to the Godalming car park signposted 'M' for museum, you will find a sleepy town centre. The High Street, which used to be the main Portsmouth road, and the riverside gardens are a haven, but the only real reason to visit is the **Godalming Museum** (***t*** *01483 426 510; open Tues–Sat 10–5, winter until 4*) on the High Street. It's a crucial stop on the Lutyens and Jekyll trail, with memorabilia including the tools of their trades – Jekyll's garden fork, sketchbook and old Gladstone bag, and Lutyens' T-Square. By the river is a memorial to Jack Philips, a Godalming man who was chief wireless operator on the *Titanic*. The cloister garden was planted by Jekyll.

Winkworth Arboretum

t *(01483) 208 477, www.nationaltrust.org.uk; open dawn–dusk; adm.*

Winkworth Arboretum is a few miles south of Godalming, down the Brighton road. It's at its best in autumn, when the Persian carpet effect of block planting in the autumn colour is spectacular. Dr Wilfred Fox bought the 100-acre valley site in 1937, and built up an awesome collection of exotic trees and shrubs over 20 years, inspired by the arboretums at Sheffield Park, Westonbirt and Exbury.

The Jekyll and Lutyens Trail

Thursley is a pretty one-street village on the edge of a great swathe of common land. It has a fabulous brown sandstone church with a timber-framed belfry. Two crosses in the churchyard mark the graves of Lutyens' father and his nephew (the architect himself is buried in St Paul's Cathedral). The Lutyens family home was Street House. The highlight along the trail is Busbridge Church, on the main road through the village of **Munstead**. Lutyens designed the war memorial, the wrought-iron chancel screen and Jekyll's tombstone in the churchyard, inscribed 'Artist, Gardener, Craftswoman'. There is a Burne-Jones stained-glass window. You can peep into Munstead Wood from Heath Lane, built by Lutyens in 1896–7; it looks 200 years older.

Haslemere

Haslemere is a busy, attractive country town set among hills. The **Greensand Way** begins down an alley next to the Georgian Hotel, striking across country to Gibbet Hill on **Hindhead Common**. Sir Robert Hunter, co-founder of the National Trust, campaigned for the preservation of Hindhead Common from Haslemere, where he lived, commuting to his day job as a solicitor in London. The **Educational Museum** (*t (01428) 642 112; open Tues–Sat 10–5*) on the High Street is a venerable Victorian institution behind a neo-classical façade, founded in 1888 by Sir Jonathan Hutchinson, a surgeon and another London commuter. The displays cover geology, zoology and human biology, local natural history and the Wealden glass and iron industries.

Black Down

Black Down (920ft) is the wettest place in the Weald. Once upon a time its slopes were used for pasture, then, as the nutrients drained from the soil, it became heathland and now it is largely pine woods with patches of open heath. The National Trust intends to return it to heathland. To walk on Black Down, take the B2131 (Petworth Road) from Haslemere, then the road signposted Black Down after half a mile, and look out for Tennyson's Lane.

Hindhead Common and the Devil's Punch Bowl

In September 1786, a sailor walking back to his ship in Portsmouth from London stopped for a drink at the old Red Lion in Thursley, then set off over Hindhead Common. Three men from the pub caught up with him at the Devil's Punch Bowl, murdered him for his money and rolled him over the edge. They were caught and hanged on **Gibbet Hill** on a 30ft pole. Cobbett on his *Rural Rides* took long detours to avoid Hindhead, which he called 'the most villainous spot God ever made'. Dickens' Smike listens 'with greedy interest' to Nicholas Nickleby reading the **Sailor's Stone** (erected 1786), which commemorates the murder. Sir Arthur Conan-Doyle lived in the old school in Hindhead for a while. Sir Robert Hunter acquired the common land around the Devil's Punch Bowl for the National Trust, to save it from development. It gets its name from the mist that swirls around it in the early mornings. Despite Hunter's efforts, the A3 goes straight through the common (there are plans to bury the road under the hill). Park next to the Devil's Punch Bowl Café and walk around the rim of the punch bowl along Highcombe Edge. Gibbet Hill and the Sailor's Stone are on the other side of the road.

Kent

Kent has 100 miles of coast and seven ports including the busiest roll-on, roll-off ferry port in the world. Almost a peninsula, Kent practically touches Continental Europe. It got its name from Caesar, who called it *Cantium*, meaning coastal district. Invaders have always targeted Kent, so Dover, Chatham and the windswept beaches of Romney Marsh have long been the most fortified places in England. When the invasion threat receded, proximity to the Continent brought foreign trade and influence. Towns like Cranbrook, Sandwich and Tenterden built handsome white weatherboard buildings with Dutch gables on the proceeds. Nowadays access to the Continent means the constant widening of roads and railways to carry traffic to and from Dover and the Channel Tunnel. The garden of England is once more under siege. The traditional orchards of cherries, wizened old apple and pear trees, and the dwindling Kentish hop fields already look like a nostalgic old postcard. But maybe the future's not that bleak: Kent still grows most of England's fruit. The **Medway Valley** around Teston, Yalding and West Farleigh, which Cobbett described as the 'very finest, as to fertility and diminutive beauty, in the whole world,' can still be breathtakingly beautiful. The views from the Eurostar train are so lush and green that you want to leap out before France.

To see the highlights of Kent, go straight to **Canterbury** and make excursions to **Faversham**, **Whitstable**, **Broadstairs**, **Sandwich** and **Dover**. The old spa town of **Tunbridge Wells** is an ideal base for the High Weald (as are Tenterden and Rye). Not even maps are sure where West Kent stops and Greater London starts, although the M25 runs through it. To the east of the M25, the **Greensand Hills** around Westerham and Sevenoaks are beautiful and packed with country houses and castles. The **North Kent Coast** has small pockets of Dickensian interest – just enough for a flying visit from London or Canterbury on the A2/M2.

Canterbury

I found the place where the frightened monks had first shuffled the inanimate victim of Moreville and Fitzurse out of reach of further desecration. While I stood there a violent thunder storm broke over the cathedral and made me feel as if I had descended into the very bowels of history.

Henry James, 1877

Canterbury is a small, scruffy city with a big reputation as the headquarters of the Anglican church. Its three oldest religious foundations – the **cathedral**, **St Augustine's Abbey** and **St Martin's Church** represent the origins of Roman Christianity in England. The cathedral is the main attraction, generating a Chaucerian buzz in the narrow streets around it. In winter, you're alone with the ghost of Thomas à Becket, whose head was lopped off in the cathedral. At the height of the cult of St Thomas, the city supported 22 parish churches, three friaries, three priories and countless religious hospitals providing rooms at the bottom end of the pilgrim market, in addition to the monastery. By the end of the 14th century, the pilgrimage over the North Downs to Becket's shrine, as depicted by Chaucer, was the package holiday of its day. When the monastery was dissolved in 1538 it took half a dozen ox carts to cart away the loot.

Before all that, in Romano-British and Germanic times, Canterbury was the tribal capital of Kent, connected to the Wantsum Channel on the River Stour and with good Roman roads marching through it from the ports to *Londinium*. St Augustine came to Canterbury as a missionary in 597 to convert the Jutish king, Æthelbert. The story is told in Bede's *Ecclesiastical History*. Æthelbert's Frankish wife, Bertha, was already a Christian so the King felt bound to receive Augustine, but as a worshipper of Thor, the Scandinavian god of thunder, he arranged to meet him in a field for fear of Christian magic. The magic worked nonetheless and Æthelbert's baptism set in motion a wave of conversions of kingly conversions, beginning with Ewin, King of Northumbria. Augustine became the first Archbishop of Canterbury, followed by church reformers like Adhelm, Dunstan and Thomas à Becket, all of whom became saints.

Around Town

There is a tight huddle of pedestrianized streets around the cathedral. **Palace Street**, leading to North Gate, has one of the most photogenic doors in England. Along the High Street, beside the River Stour, wander into the lovely **Hospital of St Thomas** (***t** (01227) 462 395*) with its vaulted crypt – a 12th-century bunkhouse for poor pilgrims. The three religious foundations are must-sees, while the museums cover the town's lively history. The **Museum of Canterbury** (*open Mon–Sat 10.30–5, summer also Sun 1.30–5; adm*) on Stour Street gives you an overview of 2,000 years of city history, plus Joseph Conrad memorabilia (Conrad lived nearby, 1919–24). The **Roman Museum** (*open Mon–Sat 10–5, summer also Sun 1.30–5; adm*) on Butchery Row is all about *Durovenum Cantiacorum*. It is built around three mosaic floors, a hypocaust and the foundations of a villa. The **Canterbury Tales** (***t** (01227) 454 888; open daily 10–5; adm exp*) takes you on a tour of 14th-century Canterbury with Chaucer as your narrator. At the top end of the High Street the **West Gate Museum** (***t** (01227) 452 747; open Mon–Sat 11–12.30 and 1.30–3.30; adm minimal*) is housed in a 14th-century gatehouse, a fortified entry into the city with portcullis, drawbridge and arrow slits.

Canterbury Cathedral

***t** (01227) 762 862; www.canterbury-cathedral.org; open Mon–Sat 9–5, Sun 12.30–2.30; closed for services.*

It is such a pleasure to pass the grand 16th-century gateway and enter the open space of the close that you feel as if you have been given the keys to the city. Your first view of the cathedral is the best, down the length of the church with its great Gothic bell tower. A fire in the old church a year after the murder of Thomas à Becket,

Getting There and Around

From London by **car** follow the M2 to the A2, then Canterbury is clearly signposted. From Dover, follow the A2. A more scenic route from London takes in the beautiful North Weald countryside (M20 from London to junction 8, then A20 through Leeds to Charing, where you pick up the A252 via Chilham to Canterbury).

By **train** from London Victoria direct to Canterbury West takes 1 hour 50 minutes and to Canterbury East 1 hour 30 minutes.

From Dover Priory to Canterbury East takes 25 minutes, and from Ashford International to Canterbury West takes 20 minutes. For all train information call National Rail Enquiries, **t** 08457 484950, *www.thetrainline.com*.

National Express **coaches** run regularly from London Victoria and take approx 2 hours. For all coach travel enquiries call **t** 08705 808080, *www.gobycoach.com*. For local transport information call **Traveline, t** 0870 608 2608.

The **Canterbury River Navigation Company**, West Gate Steps, West Gate, St Dunstan's, **t** (07885) 318 301, offers guided punt tours in summer on the willow-fringed backwaters of the River Stour. The company can also provide a picnic hamper and wine (otherwise bring your own picnic).

Tourist Information

Canterbury: 34 St Margaret's Street, Canterbury, **t** (01227) 378 100, *www.canterbury.co.uk*. *Open summer daily 9–5.30, winter Mon–Sat 9.30–5.*

A **'museum passport'** can be bought for entry to the Heritage Museum, Roman Museum and West Gate Museum.

The **Canterbury Festival, t** (01227) 452 853, *www.canterburyfestival.co.uk*, takes place over 2 weeks in mid-October. Opera, drama, dance, children's events, exhibitions, comedy, talks and concerts.

Where to Stay

Canterbury t (01227) –

Howfield Manor, Chartham Hatch (2½ miles west of Canterbury), **t** 738 294, *www.howfieldmanor.co.uk* (*expensive*). Homely, attractive country house, with some parts dating back to early medieval priory of St Gregory, set in 5 acres of gardens. There are 15 rooms and a restaurant. Look out for the priest hole in the bar.

The Falstaff Hotel, 8–10 St Dunstan's Street, **t** 462 138, *www.corushotels.com/thefalstaff* (*expensive*). Chain hotel in centuries-old coaching inn next to Westgate Tower with 47 slightly shabby rooms decorated in generic period style. Good restaurant.

The County Hotel, High Street, **t** 766 266, *www.macdonaldhotels.co.uk* (*expensive*). Timber-framed medieval coaching inn 5 minutes' walk from cathedral; king-sized and four-poster beds, very good 'fine dining' restaurant and lounge bar for cream teas.

The Ebury Hotel, 65–7 New Dover Road, **t** 768 433, *www.ebury-hotel.co.uk* (*moderate*). Elegant Victorian country-house hotel in large gardens, 10 minutes' walk from city centre. Indoor pool in the grounds. Also eight self-catering cottages (minimum one week's let).

The Grove Ferry Inn, Upstreet, **t** 860 302, *www.shepherd-neame.co.uk* (*moderate*). Stone Victorian ferry house beside River Stour, 4 miles northeast of Canterbury on the A28. Stripped floors, exposed brick and uncluttered feel. Eat on riverside deck.

The Cathedral Gate Hotel, 36 Burgate, **t** 464 381, *www.cathgate.co.uk* (*moderate*). Charming, rambling old hotel built in the early 15th century for pilgrims; full of character with great cathedral views.

The Coach House, 34 Watling Street, **t** 784 324 (*moderate*). Welcoming stuccoed Georgian townhouse 5 minutes' walk from the cathedral. Spacious bedrooms, but bathrooms shared.

brought a massive rebuilding (funded by the pilgrims to his shrine). The stacked tiers of Norman arches and columns were replaced in the nave with what Henry James called 'English points and perpendiculars'. The cathedral rises in three stages to the high altar and the shrine. The stone screen between nave and choir allowed the

Greyfriars House, 6 Stour Street, **t** 456 255, *www.greyfriars-house.co.uk* (*moderate*). Attractive brick family-run guesthouse, formerly the gatehouse of one of Canterbury's medieval monasteries; 2 minutes' walk from cathedral.

Tudor House, 6 Best Lane, **t** 765 650 (*moderate*). Friendly place in dead centre of town, in wonky, beamed 16th-century town-house with 6 rooms; garden backs onto river.

Eating Out

The old Canterbury of quaint teashops and monks' refectories is being replaced by chain café-bars and restaurants. Ideology aside, the quality is probably better.

Il Pozzo, 15 Best Lane, **t** 450 154 (*moderate*). Down steps between the cathedral and the High Street, a charming, long-established restaurant run by husband and wife; he is the Italian cook, she works front-of-house. Cannelloni parmigiana (pasta rolls filled with meat, spinach and ricotta) or prosciutto con melone followed by segato alla toscana (pan-fried calf's liver with caramelized onions and fresh sage). Italian wines on offer include vino nobile from Montepulciano. *Closed Sun and Mon.*

Jacques, 71 Castle Street, **t** 781 000 (*moderate*). Delightful, beamed restaurant with wooden tables and hop bines garlanding the walls, where you might be entertained by a pianist in the evenings. Fresh local produce served up as salads or steak on horseradish potatoes followed by chocolate desserts.

Tuo e Mio, 16 The Borough, **t** 761 471 (*moderate*). Welcoming restaurant with Mediterranean atmosphere, and seasonal specialities including game, Dover sole, calf's liver, and tiramisu. *Closed Mon, and Tues lunch.*

Bistro Viet Nam, 72 Castle Street, **t** 760 022 (*moderate*). Converted warehouse run by husband and wife; she is the Vietnamese chef, he works front-of-house. Lemongrass chicken and stir-fried chilli beef.

Café des Amis du Mexique, 93–5 St Dunstan's Street, **t** 464 390 (*cheap*). Upbeat, lively restaurant full of Latin beats; Mexican food, paella and lamb with Moroccan sausage.

Tapas, 13 Palace Street, **t** 762 637 (*cheap*). Jolly Spanish restaurant serving range of tapas.

The Old Weaver's House, 1 St Peter Street, **t** 464 660 (*cheap*). Extremely busy and popular, with black-and-white gabled front, dark-beamed interior and riverside location. Cream teas or traditional English food like roast beef and steak or chicken pie followed by apple pie and custard. *Open 11–11.*

Marlowe's Restaurant, 55 St Peter's Street, **t** 462 194 (*cheap*). Young, lively atmosphere with a choice of around 50 dishes – English, Mexican and American – including Marlowe Canterbury Pie (chicken, mushrooms, leeks and white wine in puff pastry) or teriyaki salmon followed by Alabama soft rock pie (chocolate mousse cake, marshmallow and ice cream with hot fudge sauce).

The Old Buttermarket, 39 Murgate, **t** 462 170 (*cheap*). Ye olde pubbe serving fish and chips and chocolate puddle pudding.

City Fish Bar, St Margaret's Street (*cheap*). Takeaway fish and chips.

Entertainment

Two venues offer a varied repertoire:

The Marlowe Theatre, The Friars (off the High Street), **t** 787 787, *www.marlowetheatre.com*. Popular theatre for touring productions of West End musicals, ballet and drama. Café-bar serves evening meals.

The Gulbenkian, University of Kent, **t** 769 075, *www.kent.ac.uk/gulbenkian*. A 1960s theatre on the university campus. Smaller, more sophisticated touring productions.

Canterbury Cathedral also hosts occasional evening performances by the Choral Society; the annual highlight is a candle-lit Christmas carol concert; **t** 762 862, *www.canterbury-cathedral.org* for details.

monks to sing and pray in privacy despite the continual flow of pilgrims, who gathered in the **nave**. The medieval pilgrims moved on their knees beneath the crossing to the **martyrdom transept**, leading out into the cloisters. There are various accounts of Thomas à Becket's last movements in the cathedral. According to one, the

St Thomas à Becket

St Thomas à Becket was a true English martyr, however many historians argue about the events that led up to his death. From a good but poor Norman family, Becket rose rapidly through the ranks of the Church to be appointed archdeacon of Canterbury in 1154. The following year the young Henry II appointed him chancellor. Becket became an intimate adviser of the King, his right-hand man. His religious functions did not stop him living magnificently, but his character and personal life were beyond reproach. So far so good. The trouble started when the King put him up for the archbishopric of Canterbury. The prescient Becket resisted, foreseeing a conflict of interest, but Henry insisted and Becket was consecrated archbishop in 1162. The merry chancellor became an ascetic archbishop and took his new role as champion of the Church very seriously. This set him head to head with the King. The relationship soured as Becket guarded the freedom and autonomy of the Church jealously against the King's attempts to assume its powers. It all escalated until a band of armed men came to Canterbury on 29 December 1172 and murdered Thomas à Becket in the cathedral. His death shocked Christendom, his tomb became a shrine overnight and he was canonized in 1173. Henry was forced by public opinion to do penance at the tomb in 1174. The cult of St Thomas à Becket continued at Canterbury, as immortalized in *The Canterbury Tales*, until it was destroyed by Henry VIII in 1538.

knights chased him around the cloisters, through the martyrdom door and into the northwest transept, where they killed him. Another version places Becket in the church preparing for vespers when the knights caught up with him in the northwest transept and urged him out into the cloister to arrest him. In either case there was a short struggle before one of the knights hacked off the top of the archbishop's head, at four-thirty in the afternoon of 29 December 1172.

The spot of Thomas à Becket's beheading is marked by the inscription THOMAS on the floor and a sculpture of bloodstained swords. The monks dragged his body to the eastern end of the crypt and buried him between two shiny Purbeck marble columns. He was dug up 50 years later and placed in an elaborate shrine in Trinity chapel, destroyed at the Dissolution. Thomas's bones were said to have been spirited away by the monks before Henry VIII's henchmen arrived, and reburied in the crypt; the burial spot was dug up in the 20th century and bones with long femurs (Thomas was tall) and a crack in the skull were found – but tests showed them not to be the saint's. The shrine is marked by a candle today. You can just about see the shallow groove worn in the reddish marble by the constant shuffle of pilgrims' knees for 300 years. Two royals – the Black Prince and Henry IV – were buried either side of St Thomas. It's an unkind arrangement, as Henry IV killed the Black Prince's son, Richard II, to become king. Spare a thought, as Henry James did, for the gallant young prince, heir to Edward III's throne, finished off by the plague. 'All gone are my beauty and grace, all wasted away is my flesh,' says the Latin inscription, 'very straight and narrow is my abode, in me there is nothing but truth...' James mused: 'and I too, as I stood there, lost the sense of death in a momentary impression of personal nearness to him.'

St Augustine's Abbey and St Martin's Church

St Augustine's Abbey (***t*** *(01227) 767 345;open April–Sept 10–6; Oct 10–5; Nov–Mar 10–4; adm*) is a 5-minute walk from the cathedral down Burgate and over the ring road. Augustine established a prestigious monastery for the 40 monks who came to England with him from Rome. Of the 26 known kings of Kent, six are buried in St Augustine's Abbey, including Æthelbert; Augustine was buried here too. The monastery grew, was knocked down to make way for a Norman abbey church, and grew again to house up to 80 monks. There are three Saxon churches (look for the recycled red Roman brick) beneath the ruined Norman abbey: St Pancras' Chapel is at the east end and the church of St Peter and St Paul at the west end, but there is no trace of St Mary's. The main gatehouse survived the Dissolution, and some of the domestic buildings were turned into a royal palace (now King's School). Around 250 artefacts (pins, coins, belt buckles) found on the site are on show; best is the mitre of Abbot Dygon (1496–1510).

It's another 5 minutes' walk to **St Martin's Church** (*open Tues and Thurs 10–3, Sat 10–1*), past the prison. Pretty in its churchyard, it is one of the oldest parish churches in use in England, with parts dating back to St Augustine's time – although no one can be sure which bits, due to endless rebuilding and Victorian restoration. The chancel is thought to incorporate sections of the chapel used by Bertha and St Augustine, while the nave with its odd west wall was built in the 6th century. For a long time the Saxon font was believed to have been the one in which Æthelbert was baptized.

East Kent

East Kent is bounded on three sides by the sea and on the west by an invisible line between the Swale and Romney Marsh. It's the green bit of Kent, along the ridge of the North Downs, with farmland and marsh to the north, but not one of the great English landscapes, with its ragged coastline and Brussels sprouts fields. For centuries this area has been targeted by enemies from Europe (it's only 22 sea miles from Dover to Calais). Military fortifications from all eras of English history are strung out around the coast, including the magnificent **Dover Castle**, Tudor castles at **Walmer** and **Deal**, and a Roman fort at **Richborough**. **Faversham** is pretty. **Whitstable** is becoming trendy for its fish restaurants and old-fashioned family holiday atmosphere. **Broadstairs** will be next, with the prettiest seaside in the whole of Kent and Sussex and its narrow streets and smugglers' pubs. There is even talk of **Margate** becoming an arty Hoxton Square on Sea, on the basis of its Turner and Tracy Emin connections – but only among people who have never been there. Turner came here to paint (*The Old Pier* and *Scary Sunrise with Sea Monsters*) and fell in love with his landlady. The teenage Tracy Emin had sex with every man in town and then got out (if her own accounts are to be believed). There are hopes that the £7-million **Turner Centre** (due to open in 2004) will do for Margate what the Guggenheim has done for Bilbao – turn a drab place into a hot cultural destination. In the meantime **Sandwich** is another delightful medieval town.

Getting There and Around

Faversham is just off the M2 by **car**, and on the A2 Dover–London road. For Whitstable, take the M2, then head east onto the A299 and follow signs.

Regular **trains** run from London Charing Cross and Margate to **Faversham**; from Canterbury, London Victoria and the Kent coast to **Whitstable**.

Tourist Information

Faversham: Fleur de Lys Heritage Centre, Preston Street, **t** (01795) 534 542, *www.faversham.org. Open Mon–Sat 10–4, Sun 10–1.*

Tuesday and Friday market in market place under the stilts of the old Guildhall.

Whitstable: 7 Oxford Street, **t** (01227) 275 482. *Open Mon–Sat 10–4, July–Aug until 5.*

A nine-day Whitstable **oyster festival** takes place in late July, with oyster landing and procession, and a seafaring production by the 'Walk the Plank Theatre Company' on their 'drama ship' in the harbour, morris dancing, laser light show on seafront and so on.

Where to Stay and Eat

Around Faversham

Wellbrook Farmhouse, South Street, Boughton, **t** (01227) 750 941, *www.wellbrookfarmhouse.co.uk* (*moderate*). Delightful timber-framed farmhouse 3 miles from town with mathematical tiles on front, set in 2 acres of pasture and gardens.

Preston Lea, Canterbury Road, **t** (01795) 535 266, *www.faversham.org* (*moderate*). Four pleasant bedrooms in Victorian house, half a mile out of town on the A2.

Twin Mays, Plumpudding Lane, Dargate, **t** (01227) 751 346, *www.twinmays.co.uk* (*moderate*). Comfortable B&B in small village 4 miles east of town. Foody **Dove** pub a few doors down.

There are one or two cafés in and around the market place, and several places to get lunch down Preston Street.

Whitstable t (01227) –

Hotel Continental, 29 Beach Walk, **t** 280 280, *www.hotelcontinental.co.uk* (*expensive*). Smart hotel on road to Tankerton Cliffs, with art deco front; eight beach huts and self-contained Anderson Shed with sea-facing sitting room.

Victoria Villa, 1 Victoria Street, **t** 779 191, *www.victoria-villa.i12.com* (*expensive*). Resplendent with tourist-board awards, hospitable B&B in conservation area back from harbour. Breakfast served in courtyard garden on sunny days, with Wedgwood china and newspaper.

Wheeler's Oyster Bar, 8 High Street, **t** 273 311 (*expensive*). The original eat-in or take-away

Faversham

In the Middle Ages, Faversham was a distinguished port with access to the sea via Faversham Creek. It became a subsidiary member of the Confederacy of Cinque Ports (as a limb of Dover), got rich on wool and oysters, and was favoured by kings: Stephen founded Faversham Abbey and was buried there, and Faversham fishermen picked up James II in the Swale (the Isle of Sheppey channel) as he tried to escape to France after the invasion of William of Orange. From the 17th to 19th centuries the town grew as a manufacturer of beer, gunpowder, barges and yellow London bricks, but the 20th century ignored it. Small and quiet, its late-medieval town centre has been immaculately restored and the Georgian façades of its townhouses freshly painted (there are 475 listed buildings). Pop into the **Fleur de Lys Heritage Centre** (*t (01795) 534 542; open Mon–Sat 10–4, Sun 10–1; adm minimal*) on Preston Street to pick up self-published booklets on this 'medieval gem of Kent'. In the market place stands the old **Guildhall**, atop even older stone pillars. West Street and Abbey Street, which leads down to Faversham Creek, are worth a look. The town is suffused in the smell of hops oyster bar, founded in 1856. Four tables in the cosy back parlour, or sit at the counter and gobble a plate of mussels or home-made crab and prawn tart. Book, and bring your own wine. Lobster risotto or crab cakes with apple and pear chutney, cod in saffron bouillon with mash and vegetable crisps, or baby lobster on herb pasta. Only in winter will you get the famous wild native Whitstable oysters. *Closed Wed.*

Copelands House, 4 Island Wall, **t** 266 207, *www.copelandhouse.co.uk* (*moderate*). Charming house – Georgian brick and sash windows at the front, white weatherboard at the back – on one of prettiest streets, backing onto beach.

Belmont House, 74 Oxford Street, **t** 266 911 (*moderate*). Handsome 1840s house set back from main road into town; short walk from beach and restaurants.

Royal Native Oyster Stores, Horsebridge, **t** 276 856 (*moderate*). Famous but expensive fish restaurant in Victorian oyster stores that once belonged to Whitstable Oyster Fishery Company (1793–1960). Warm cloud of wine-infused steam and range of seafood dishes. *Closed Mon.*

The Crab & Winkle Restaurant, South Quay, **t** 779 377 (*moderate*). Above wet fish shop on harbourside, in the old steam-train shed of the former Whitstable–Canterbury railway line. Growing reputation for good seafood; oysters feature prominently on a menu that also includes several fish dishes, whole crabs, lobster thermidor and seafood platters. Also coffee, breakfast and sandwiches.

Pearson's Crab and Oyster House, Sea Wall, **t** 272 005 (*moderate*). The old Pearson's Arms has renamed itself to cash in on the gastro trade. Serves IPA and Flowers, and fishy snacks like hot mussels, prawns and cockles. So-so restaurant upstairs, but excellent location for the beach.

Birdies Restaurant, 41 Harbour Street, **t** 265 337 (*moderate*). Behind lovely old Victorian balconied front; cheerful, quaint restaurant; not all fish. *Closed Mon lunch and Tues.*

East Quay Oyster Restaurant, East Quay, **t** 262 003 (*moderate*). Another plank in the raft of seafood eateries owned by the Whitstable Oyster Fishery Company; simple dishes.

Hotel Continental, 29 Beach Walk, **t** 280 280 (*moderate*). To the east of the harbour overlooking the beach; bar ideal for cold drinks or fish and chips; restaurant has a varied, fish-dominated menu.

Tea and Times, High Street, **t** 262 639 (*cheap*). Friendly café, good for toasted panini.

Entertainment

Imperial Oyster Cinema, Horsebridge, **t** 770 829. Tiny cinema and bar.

The Playhouse Theatre, High Street, **t** 272 042. Small, traditional theatre in old church; local amateur dramatics and touring productions.

from the **Shepherd Neame Brewery** on Court Street, the oldest brewery in England, dating back to 1698 (***t*** *(01795) 532 206 for tours*). You get a good view of the church's unusual crown spire down Church Street. **Arden House**, down Abbey Street, is named after Thomas Arden, the mayor of Faversham, whose 1551 murder became the subject of the anonymous Elizabethan play *Arden of Faversham*. Nothing survives of the abbey, nor of the tomb of King Stephen, the only Norman king buried on this side of the Channel. Take a stroll down to the old docks with their warehouses.

Whitstable

In summer marine gastronomes flock to this pretty seaside town for the oysters and sea-bathing. Whitstable's seafront houses have backyards running down to the beach, while the main street sweeps you down to the harbour. The most prominent building is the gravel works and there's no obvious place to go – no pier – but that is its appeal for those in the know. The famous Whitstable Oyster Company (est. 1793) stopped production 40 years ago, but Seasalter Shellfish on East Quay has its own

On the Invasion Coast

The landing of the first Roman invasion in 54 BC under Julius Caesar took place on the sandy beaches between Deal and Walmer. Ten miles north at Richborough are the foundations of the triumphal marble gateway of the real Roman Conquest, which took place a hundred years later under Aulus Plautius. Four Saxon Shore forts were built by the Romans along this vulnerable stretch of coast to guard against Germanic raiders. Nennius tells the story of Hengest and Horsa, mercenaries brought over by the overlord or Vortigern of the former Roman *Britannia* to help quash Pictish raids. They arrived in 449 at Thanet with several shiploads of Germanic toughs. In lieu they got Thanet, and conquered Christian *Cantium*, which became pagan Kent. After the Norman Conquest, Dover Castle became a royal castle, the 'key to England', a symbol of the Anglo-Norman monarchy. After his break with Rome in 1534, Henry VIII built a series of low, many-sided forts along the south coast to guard against anticipated invasion by a combined army of Catholic European countries. Deal Castle is the biggest. The vast 19th-century artillery fortress on Dover's Western Heights (guarding from landward attack) was the largest in a network of coastal fortifications stretching from Sussex to East Anglia to defend against Napoleon. It had to be big because an invasion force of 130,000 men with 200 boats had amassed on the cliffs at Calais, visible across the Channel on a clear day. In the Second World War, the blockhouses were turned into observation posts and anti-aircraft gun platforms, while 1,000-year-old Dover Castle remained a key operational headquarters.

oyster beds, and commercial fishing goes on from the West Quay. Eat at one of the fish restaurants, best of all the **Royal Native Oyster Stores**, wander down to the **harbour** with its black-tarred fishing stores, and browse along boutiques, craft shops and cafés of the High Street. **Whitstable Museum and Gallery** (***t** (01227) 276 998; open Mon–Sat 10–4, July and Aug also Sun 1–4*) on Oxford Street has a display on horror specialist Peter Cushing, for 40 years a resident of Whitstable. If you don't fancy the **shingle beach**, drive or walk up to **Tankerton Sea Parade** and swim beneath the green cliffs. On a rainy day, check out the **Imperial Oyster Cinema** (***t** (01227) 770 829*) above the Royal Native Oyster Stores in Horsebridge.

East along the coast from Whitstable, past Herne Bay, is a turn-off to **Reculver Roman Fort**. It is dominated by the two ruined towers of the Norman abbey, which stood in the old fort. Reculver was built a mile inland, but is now half underwater. The 600ft-long walls of the fort enclosed a grid of streets with the *principia* in the middle. To the east were barracks and bath houses, and to the north granaries. Have a drink in the King Æthelbert, by the car park, and walk west along the cliff to Bishopstone Glen.

Thanet

Thanet has a beyond-the-East-End atmosphere, windswept and forgotten with its disused airport and old power station. **Margate** is a playground for hyperactive teenagers, while **Ramsgate** is a playground for tanned yachties. **Broadstairs** is a big surprise with its beautiful bay, Italian restaurants and Bleak House, which Charles

Dickens rented as a holiday home. At low tide you can wander down the long sandy beach to Ramsgate on the trail of Gothic revivalist architect Pugin. Drive on to the spectacular Roman fort at **Richborough**, the front door of Roman *Britannia*.

Broadstairs

Broadstairs is a small fishing hamlet of 300 souls of which 27 follow the occupation of fishing; the rest seem to have no visible means of support! I am told the area is a hot bed of smuggling. When asked if this was so, the locals did give me the notion that if I persisted in this line of inquiry some serious injury might befall my person.

Daniel Defoe, 1723

In the right light, Broadstairs looks like a children's drawing of the seaside, with its quaint old smugglers' pubs, yellow sand and crisp line of chalk cliffs. On the cliff top is a promenade and a mishmash of Georgian and Victorian buildings. At the foot of the cliffs sits the old fishing harbour. Charles Dickens visited Broadstairs regularly for 14 years before his death, working on *The Old Curiosity Shop*, *Martin Chuzzlewit* and *David Copperfield* in various rented houses here. He rose at seven, started work at eight-thirty and finished by two, then went on brisk walks around the headlands with guests like Hans Christian Andersen. Dickens liked the sea air so much that he took a lease on Fort House, a castle of a building on the headland above the harbour, which was renamed **Bleak House** (***t*** *(01843) 862 224; open Feb–mid-Dec 10–6; adm*) after his

The Isle of Thanet

Then came three keels, driven into exile from Germany. In them were the brothers Horsa and Hengest. Vortigern welcomed them, and handed over to them the island that in their language is called Thanet.

Nennius 1:31

Upon this island Augustine came ashore with his companions... At the king's bidding they sat and preached the word of Life to him and to all his courtiers present... He gave them lodging in the city of Canterbury.

Bede, *Ecclesiastical History*

Thanet was known to the Romans as *Tanatus*. The Wantsum Channel, separating it from the mainland, was 2 miles wide at the time. Since then it has narrowed, and was first bridged in 1485. The old navigable sea channel, running between Minnis Bay and Pegwell Bay, was the route of the conquering Roman army under Aulus Plautius in AD 43. The Romans secured their foothold at Reculver and Richborough forts. Once they had gone, the Isle of Thanet was the first corner of former Roman *Britannia* to be settled by the Germanics: brothers Hengest and Horsa landed at Ebbesfleet, south of Ramsgate in 449. The Christian mission of St Augustine, 'Apostle of the English', landed at Ebbesfleet too, in 597, or it may have been Richborough. It's hard to tell, as Richborough is now 2 miles inland and Thanet is joined to the Kentish shore.

Getting There and Around

Broadstairs is reached by **car** via Ramsgate or Margate, both signposted from the end of the M2 and A299. **Trains** run from London Victoria or from London Charing Cross via Margate to Broadstairs.

Tourist Information

Broadstairs: 6/b High Street, **t** (01843) 583 334, *www.tourism.thanet.gov.uk. Open summer daily 9.15–1 and 1.45–4.45, Sun 10–4; winter closed Sun and Mon.*

The **Broadstairs Dickens Festival** takes place over nine days in June, with processions, dramatizations, Victorian music hall and talks. Visitors are encouraged to dress up in top hats and crinolines. Contact **t** (01843) 861 118, *www.dickensweekbroadstairs.co.uk* or **Dickens Festival Committee**, **t** (01843) 861 827.

Where to Stay

Broadstairs t (01843) –

The Royal Albion Hotel, Albion Street, **t** 868 071, *www.albion-bstairs.co.uk* (*expensive*). The hotel where Dickens stayed in 1842, with 19 bedrooms and views of the bay. Bar hosts jazz nights every Thurs.

Bay Tree Hotel, 12 Eastern Esplanade, **t** 862 502 (*moderate*). Friendly 1900s villa with sea views, 10 comfortable rooms and a small library for guests.

East Horndon Hotel, 14 Eastern Esplanade, **t** 868 306, *www.easthorndonhotel.com* (*moderate*). Welcoming hotel with five sea-facing rooms.

Dundonald House Hotel, 43 Belvedere Road (just off High Street, 2 mins from beach), **t** 862 236, *www.dundonaldhouse.co.uk* (*moderate*). This small family-owned hotel forms half of a Georgian mansion once owned by the Earl of Dundonald.

Hanson Hotel, 41 Belvedere Road, **t** 868 936, *hotelhanson@aol.com* (*moderate*). The other half of Dundonald's mansion, with cosy basement bar. Dogs and children welcome.

Eating Out

The hub of nightlife is Albion Street, which links Harbour Street with the High Street.

Citrus, 40 Albion Street, **t** 868 762 (*cheap*). Good English/French food in cosy restaurant with friendly service. Bruschetta followed by coriander lamb cutlet with potato dauphinoise and crème brulée. Tables in pretty walled garden. *Open eves only, winter closed Sun and Mon.*

Marchesi Restaurant, 12 Albion Street, **t** 862 481 (*cheap*). Marchesi's has been in the same Swiss-Italian family since the 1880s. The menu features local Dover sole and steak. *Closed Sun eve and Mon.*

Osteria Posillipo Pizzeria, 14 Albion Street, **t** 601 133 (*cheap*). Another link in the Italian connection. As good as, but more informal than, Marchesi's. Menu includes fish, pizza and pasta. *Winter closed Tues.*

Morelli's, 14 Victoria Parade, **t** 862 500, *www.morellis.com* (*cheap*). A Broadstairs institution, selling ice creams, coffees and snacks. The founder, Mario Morelli, walked from San Andrea in Italy to Britain in 1919, and his family business has been going strong since 1932 (third-generation Marino is now in charge). In December Morelli's makes Christmas-pudding flavoured ice cream, otherwise try stem-ginger or pink grapefruit sorbet.

Tartar Frigate Inn, Harbour Street, **t** 862 013 (*cheap*). With its wooden interior and nautical memorabilia, the Tartar Frigate was famous in Dickens' time for its strong tobacco and rum. Now you can get good beer (Masterbrew, IPA, Abbot) and a decent meal in the seafood restaurant upstairs.

death. His novel's connection with the house is tenuous. The ramshackle museum features memorabilia including Dickens' old writing desk. There are more bits and pieces in the **Dickens House Museum** (***t*** *(01843) 863 453; open April–mid-Oct daily 2–5, school summer holidays 11–5; adm minimal*) on the promenade, in the house that inspired Betsy Trotwood's house. Another writer, John Buchanan, set much of *The 39*

Steps in Broadstairs. At low tide you can walk along the beach, north to Margate (5 miles) and pretty Botany Bay, or south to Ramsgate (3 miles).

Ramsgate

Ramsgate's old harbour, surrounded by Victorian maritime buildings, still looks grand. It's a royal harbour, granted the title by George IV, who used to come here to get away from his second wife, Caroline of Brunswick, whom he loathed – hence the fine Regency buildings. All the grand old hotels are on the cliff top above the port. The **Maritime Museum** (*t (01843) 570 622; open Mar–Sept Tues–Sun 10–5, winter Thurs–Sun 11–4.30; adm minimal*) in the old clock tower on the harbour, displays models of boats and photos of whiskery old sailors. Stop for a drink, then head over the West Cliff beyond the harbour to explore Ramsgate's Pugin connection.

The Gothic revivalist architect and writer Augustus Pugin moved to Ramsgate when it was still a genteel place of Georgian squares and pleasure gardens. But Pugin had ambitions: he wanted to turn the West Cliff into a medieval-style community around a Roman Catholic church, school and almshouse. He got as far as **St Augustine's Church**, with its black flint exterior, and the **Grange**, which he built for himself. It was the first Gothic-style private house, and became the prototype for countless Victorian buildings around the country. To see the church, contact the Pugin Society (*t (01843) 596 401; open first Sun of every month 2–4*). Enter the churchyard from St Augustine's Road for views towards Ebbesfleet, where St Augustine landed in 597 (important to Pugin), and elaborate Catholic gravestones commemorating the nuns of the abbey and local Italian families. The Gothic **monastery** across the road was built by Pugin's son, Edward, who also built the enormous **Granville Hotel** on the East Cliff. It was planned as a terrace of private gentlemen's houses with shared facilities, but it bankrupted the architect and became a smart hotel with seawater on tap instead.

Pugin and the Gothic Revival

Augustus Welby Northmore Pugin (1812–52) kickstarted the Gothic revival. He erected numerous buildings, including churches, monasteries and convents, but his writings exerted greater influence than his architecture. His works *Contrasts* and *The True Principles of Pointed or Christian Architecture* are the textbooks of the Gothic revival. He also founded a successful metalwork and stained-glass business, but was too talented for his own good, overworking, going mad and dying young. At 15 he was already designing furniture for Windsor Castle; at 20 he was a single parent and bankrupt. He went on to design the interiors and fittings, down to the umbrella stands and ink wells, of the Houses of Parliament, making a huge name for himself. To Pugin, aesthetics were an issue of morality, and medieval Gothicism was all that stood in the way of the dreaded industrial Protestantism sweeping the nation. 'I rushed to the cathedral,' he wrote about a trip to Hereford. 'But horror! Dismay! The villain Wyatt had been there. The West Front was his!' He worked with crusading energy, converting to Catholicism and marrying a 'first-rate Gothic woman'. He spent his last 20 years at Ramsgate wearing sailor's clothes, and often took his 40ft lugger, *The Caroline*, out to the Goodwin Sands to rescue sailors.

Sandwich

This picturesque old Cinque Port is the image of a wealthy medieval town. A herring fishing fleet was based in the harbour, a passenger-ferry service shuttled important people to and from the Continent (Thomas à Becket began and ended his exile here), and the port had trading links with Flanders, Bordeaux and the Mediterranean. After the harbour silted up in the 16th century, the old port and thriving market town was buoyed up by an influx of Protestant refugees from the Netherlands, who brought weaving with them. The River Stour still laps against Strand Street, but where cargoes of timber, coal and salt once lumbered up the wide estuary there are now two golf courses. Have a look around the narrow lanes of The Chain and Fisher Street, the painted houses and medieval gate, pop into the churches and museum, and have lunch. There is a short walk along the Stour to Richborough Castle.

Richborough Castle (***t*** *(01304) 612 013, www.english-heritage.org.uk; open April–Sept 10–6, Oct 10–5, Nov–Feb weekends 10–4, Mar Wed–Sun 10–4; adm*) is just off the A256 south of Ramsgate. It's an imposing ruin of a key Roman fort, now marooned between a Pfizer factory and a power station. The changing coastline belies the strategic value of Richborough, which commanded the southern end of the Wantsum Channel and provided a safe haven for ships, serving as a supply base for the conquest of Celtic Albion. A monumental gateway clad in Italian marble and surmounted by triumphal bronze statues once straddled Watling Street, the road to the rest of *Britannia*; 20,000 tons of concrete went into its foundations – all that now survives. Raids from Gaul in the 3rd century turned the prosperous harbour into a fortress. By the 10th century Richborough was cut off from the sea by saltings and mudflats, and Sandwich had replaced it as the leading port of the southeast coast.

Deal and Walmer

Just south of Sandwich, **Deal** has a deal of charm. The quiet grid of old residential streets north of the pier is delightful, while south of it is a modest Victorian resort on the site of the old dockyard. Of the docks, only the **Timeball Tower** (1853) survives. The metal timeball was raised to the top of the mast at five to one and dropped on the hour so that ships at anchor would know the time – crucial to navigation. They say that the concrete pier is the same length as the *Titanic*. A small fleet of fishing boats launches off the shingle beach. **Deal Castle** (***t*** *(01304) 372 762, www.english-heritage.org.uk; open April–Sept daily 10–6, Oct daily 10–5, Nov–Mar Wed–Sun 10–4; adm*) stands at the end of the resort beach. It's the largest of the 10 blockhouses built by Henry VIII along the south coast, state-of-the-art Tudor military engineering: short, squat and menacing, with a 360-degree field of fire.

Walmer Castle and Gardens

t *(01304) 364 288; open April and Sept daily 10–6, Oct daily 10–5, Nov–Dec and Mar Wed–Sun 10–4, Jan–Feb weekends 10–4; adm.*

Walmer Castle, on Kingsdown Road, was built to defend the empty coastal strip south of Deal. Since the 18th century it has been the official residence of the Lord

Getting There and Around

Sandwich is 12 miles east of Canterbury by **car** on the A257. **Deal** lies halfway between Dover and Ramsgate on the Channel coast, and is well-connected to Folkestone, Dover, Thanet and Canterbury.

By **train** you have to change at Dover for **Sandwich**, which is a bit of a palaver; the train starts at Charing Cross and meanders for 2 hours 10 minutes via Paddock Wood, Dover and Deal. For **Deal**, the Margate train goes direct from London Charing Cross via Folkestone and Dover, or you can get a train from London Victoria via Medway and Faversham to Ramsgate and change .

From Canterbury, **bus** 113 runs hourly from the bus station to Sandwich.

A **Riverbus** cruises up the Stour from Sandwich to Richborough Fort, **t** (07958) 376 183, daily in summer, weekends only in spring and autumn .

Tourist Information

Sandwich: The Guildhall, **t** (01304) 613 565. *Open April–Oct daily 10–4*.

The **Royal St George's Golf Club**, Sandwich, **t** (01304) 613 090, hosts the Open every four years. Non-members can play Mon–Fri, and must have a handicap of 18 or under. The course is a challenge, featuring a 35ft bunker.

Deal: The Library, Broad Street, **t** (01304) 369 576. *Open Mon–Sat 9.30–5, Wed 9.30–1*.

Where to Stay and Eat

Sandwich t (01304) –

The Bell Hotel, The Quay, **t** 613 388, *www.princes-leisure.co.uk* (*expensive*). Friendly place to stay in 17th-century building with 6 bedrooms overlooking the river, 33 rooms altogether, and a restaurant.

King's Arms, Strand Street, **t** 617 330 (*moderate*). Friendly place to stay, in Sandwich's oldest pub, protected by its own gargoyle and a royal Tudor coat of arms. Six comfortable bedrooms. Real ales are Green King, IPA, and Youngs.

Fisherman's Wharf, Quayside, **t** 613 636. Downstairs brasserie serving fish and chips or mussels until 8pm (*cheap*). Upstairs cosy restaurant (*moderate*) with river views serves Dover sole with lemon butter or salmon with creamed leeks and horseradish. *Winter closed Sun eve*.

The George and Dragon, Fisher Street, **t** 613 106 (*moderate*). Excellent pub serving fish, and pizzas made in special pizza oven. Masterbrew, Youngs and Breakspear bitter.

Yummies, Strand Street, **t** 614 631 (*cheap*). Friendly place for sandwich and a cup of coffee or tea.

Deal t (01304) –

Dunkerley's Hotel, 19 Beach Street **t** 375 016 *www.dunkerleys.co.uk* (*expensive*). The run-down old pub has been converted into a comfortable hotel with 16 bedrooms. Dunkerley's seafood restaurant (*moderate*) has been going for 15 years and is highly rated locally. Seafood mélange with shellfish sauce or roasted sea bass with saffron mash.

The Royal Hotel, Beach Street, **t** 375 555, *www.theroyalhotel.com* (*moderate*). Smart, atmospheric hotel behind sea wall with 22 rooms. Built as a hotel in 1620, and boasts Georgian panelling, staircase and balconies. Elegant restaurant opens directly onto the beach, or you can have lunch in the bar.

Sondes Lodge, 14 Sondes Road, **t** 368 741, *sondeslodge@aol.com* (*moderate*). Two minutes' walk from seafront and town.

Hardicot Guesthouse, Kingsdown Road (on Walmer and Kingsdown borders), **t** 373 867 (*moderate*). Detached Victorian house with three bedrooms, and Channel views; 20-minute walk to Walmer Castle.

Hubert Guest House, 9 Castle Hill Road, **t** 202 253, *www.huberthouse.co.uk* (*moderate*). Attractive Georgian house with eight rooms in atmospheric part of Dover, near castle.

Deal Beach Parlour, 57 Beach Street, **t** 374 120 (*cheap*). Friendly old time-warp café serves sandwiches, light lunches and ice creams.

Vurley, South Court, High Street, **t** 360 207 (*cheap*). Home-cooked hearty food as well as tea, coffee and cakes. *Closed Sun, Mon and after 3pm*.

The Admiral Penn, Beach Street, **t** 374 279 (*cheap*). Next to Royal Hotel. Welcoming open fire on cool nights and Flegermeister beer, imported from Holland.

A Deal of History

Deal grew into a busy port between the 17th and 19th centuries for ships anchored in the water behind the Goodwin Sands, known as the Downs. The sands are a natural breakwater, 12 miles long, 5 miles wide and 3½ miles off the beach, and at low tide rise 6ft above the water, but more than a thousand ships have been wrecked on them. Sir Clowdisley Shovell (*see* p.398) lost 2,000 sailors – half the British naval fleet – here in a storm in 1703. Between the wrecks, however, the Downs served as anchorage for warships and merchant ships waiting for favourable winds to carry them into one of the English ports, or abroad. A naval dockyard was built to service and repair naval war ships. Deal got rich and rowdy supplying the fleets, their crews and passengers. Beach Street was the seamy district, full of disreputable pubs. The town was notorious. Almost everyone was involved in smuggling; the shifting sands were perfect for eluding customs boats and the beach ideal for secret landings. With the advent of steamships and the end of the wars, the dockyard closed, the sailors left town, and anti-smuggling laws closed down the secret trade. William Cobbett, passing through in September 1823, thought it horrible with 'tremendous barracks, partly pulled down and partly tumbling down, and partly occupied by soldiers.'

Wardens of the Cinque Ports, including the Duke of Wellington, Winston Churchill, William Pitt and the late Queen Mother. Wellington loved his castle by the sea and many of his belongings are there on show, including his famous Wellington boots. His bedroom is like a study with a camp bed for a visitor. This is where he died.

Dover

No promontory, town or haven in Christendom is so placed by nature and situation both to gratify friends and annoy enemies as this town of Dover.

Walter Raleigh, *A Discourse on Sea Ports*

Dover's white cliffs are emblematic of England. On top of them stands Dover Castle, the most magnificent castle in the country. The D-Day evacuation of stranded Allied troops from the beaches of Dunkirk in 1940 was launched from here (338,000 British, French and Belgium soldiers were evacuated to Dover in pleasure boats, cargo vessels, coasters, sailing barges and lifeboats). On a clear day you can see France from the cliffs. Dover is still the gateway to England from the Continent, but the town itself is sadly shabby. Second World War air raids did for two-thirds of its old buildings, and those raids were the last in 2,000 years of attacks. Only in Victorian times might you have visited Dover for its sea bathing, promenades and brass bands.

Dover Castle

t *(01304) 211 067; open April–Sept daily 10–6, Oct 10–5, Nov–Mar 10-4; adm.*

Dover Castle is the real thing. Castle Hill has been the 'key to England', a strategic military site, since the Iron Age. In 1066 William the Conqueror rushed to Dover after

Hastings, flattened the town and spent eight days building a new castle on the cliff top. It was always a royal castle, entrusted to the king's constable. By the 13th century it occupied the present site, dominated by Henry II's three-storey keep, the most costly of the great royal square keeps. The castle has adapted to advances in warfare over a thousand years. Capable of withstanding a siege for three months, it was manned and fortified during the Second World War. In May 1940 it was from naval headquarters in secret tunnels deep beneath the castle that the evacuation of Allied soldiers from Dunkirk was directed. A guided tour takes you through the tunnels to the old telephone exchange, coding and cipher centre, operations rooms and hospital. The 62ft-high Roman lighthouse on top is modelled on the 3 BC Pharos in Alexandria.

Along the White Cliffs

On the Western Heights are the remains of fortifications built to protect the castle from a Napoleonic land attack. From the White Cliffs car park, the cliff-top section of the **Saxon Shore Way** overlooks the passenger ferry docks and the Dover Straits, the busiest waterway in the world with more than 600 ships passing daily. Down a zigzag path (built by smuggling prevention officers in the early 1800s) is **Langdon Bay** with searchlights to catch the smugglers. It was from **South Foreland Lighthouse** (***t** (01304) 852 463, www.nationaltrust.org.uk;open Mar–Oct Thurs–Mon 11–5, July–Aug daily; adm*) that Marconi made the world's first international shore-to-ship radio transmission, on 24 December 1898, and the first international radio transmission, to Wimereux in France. **St Margaret's Bay** is quiet and picturesque. Noël Coward owned a house here between 1945 and 1951, entertaining Katharine Hepburn and later leasing it to Ian Fleming; the Kingsdown cliffs were the setting for Hugo Drax's rocket base in *Moonraker*, and Bond took on Goldfinger on the golf course. On Beach Road is an interesting little **museum** (***t** (01304) 852 764; open Easter, May Bank Holidays and June–Aug Wed–Sun 2–5; adm minimal*) with displays on Coward, the Dover Patrol and a Bronze Age woman called Marguerite.

Dover Port

Serious invaders all mashed Dover to a pulp, in return getting a safe natural harbour commanding the shortest route to and from the Continent. Archaeological evidence at two Roman forts suggests that Dover was the base of the Roman fleet in British waters (*Classis Britannica*). Excavations have unearthed barracks for up to 700 men, enough to man 10 warships, at Dover. (Similar squadrons at Boulogne and Lympne suggest the whole fleet was 90–100 warships.) Roman lighthouses on east and west cliffs guided ships into the harbour; one, the Pharos, is still there. Three Roman roads led out of Dover, one to Richborough, another to Lympne, and the third – Watling Street – to Canterbury and London.

Dover was one of the medieval Cinque Ports and two Ancient Towns, whose role was to defend the Straits of Dover. All the others were put out of action in the Middle Ages by changes in the coastline: Winchelsea and Hastings were already done for in the 13th century, Romney in the 14th, Sandwich in the 15th and Hythe and Rye in the 16th. Dover, however, was too strategically important to lose to silt: the Tudor monarchs first expanded and protected the docks; the Victorians made improvements to cope with steam ships the Navy used the western docks in both world wars; and the eastern docks were developed as a car ferry port in the early 20th century.

Dover Museum

t (01304) 201 066; open Mon–Sat 10–5.30; adm minimal.

The museum on Market Square is a reason to visit the town centre. It displays models of the harbour over the ages, Roman pots and godheads (although the most interesting Roman remains are *in situ* – the Pharos, the Painted House and the buried *Classis Britannica* fort). But the highlight of the museum is a 3,550-year-old Bronze Age boat, 30ft long, unearthed in 1992 by workmen in Townwall Street; its discovery was a huge surprise even to archaeologists supervising the works. More than 350 bronze tools and weapons, presumed to have been the cargo of a Bronze Age wreck, are displayed alongside.

Roman Painted House

t (01304) 203 279; open April–Sept Tues–Sun 10–4.30, July–Aug daily 10–4.30; adm minimal.

Two minutes' walk from the museum are some of the best Roman painted plaster walls to have survived in northern Europe. They are thought to have belonged to the *mansio* (staging inn) outside the north gate of the *Classis Britannica* naval fort, built in AD 200. In the 3rd century the fort was replaced by a new, larger army fort and these rooms were packed with rubble and earth to form a rampart – preserving them until the 1970s. The paintings are patchy, but you may be able to make out symbols related to Bacchus, the Roman god of wine.

The Middle Medway

The Medway is supposed to be the boundary separating the Men of Kent (to the east) from the Kentish Men (to the west), although you would be lucky to find anyone living in Kent who could tell you which was which. The Romans shipped rag stone from quarries on the Greensand Ridge to *Londinium* down the tidal reaches of the Medway. By the 16th century, the naval dockyards at Chatham were a big consumer of timber and iron carried down on barges from the High Weald. In the 18th and 19th centuries Tonbridge and Maidstone shipped Wealden goods – iron, timber and hops – downriver to the Thames. Above Maidstone the Medway can be lovely, a countryside of apple and pear orchards and hop fields between patchwork hills (the fields around **Teston Bridge** are excellent for picnics). From the pretty boating village of **Yalding**, where the Medway is joined by the Teise and Beult, the **Vale of Kent** drifts through scattered villages to Romney Marsh. This is the countryside of narrow sunken lanes between hedges of H.E. Bates' *The Darling Buds of May*, which was filmed in Pluckley.

Tonbridge is best known for its ruined motte and bailey castle above the Medway crossing and its smart public school, founded in 1553. The castle gatehouse is state-of-

Getting There and Around

By **car** from the M25 the A21 leads to Tonbridge and Paddock Wood.

By **train** from London Charing Cross regular services head south to Tonbridge and Paddock Wood. There is a branch line to Yalding and West Farleigh.

Tourist Information

Tonbridge: Tonbridge Castle, Castle Street, **t** (01732) 770 929, *www.heartofkent.org.uk*. *Open summer Mon–Sat 9–5, Sun 10.30–5; winter Sat 9–4, Sun 10.30–4.*

Where to Stay and Eat

Tonbridge and Around

Tonbridge is not known for its gastronomy, but there are several reasonable places to eat and drink at the north end of the High Street

The Rose and Crown, High Street, **t** (01732) 357 966, *www.bestwestern.co.uk* (*expensive*). Old coaching inn with 54 bedrooms and snug bar at attractive end of High Street.

Barn Cottage, Seven Mile Lane, Borough Green, near Sevenoaks, **t** (01732) 883 384, *suzifilleul@aol.com* (*moderate*). Graham and Susie will make you welcome at their lovely white-weatherboard Wealden house. Delicious food, a real treat.

The Swan, 35 Swan Street, West Malling, **t** (01732) 521 910 (*moderate*). Airy, sophisticated brasserie in smartly revamped old village just off the M20 near Maidstone.

The Swan on the Green, West Peckham, **t** (01622) 812 271 (*moderate*). Quality gastro pub beside quiet village green, off the B2016 'Seven Mile Lane' on edge of Mereworth Woods. Beers from micro brewery include Whooper Pale, Trumpeter Best, Swan on the Port Side, Bewick Swan and Swan Blonde lager. *No food Sun eve.*

The Chequers, Laddingford, near Paddock Wood, **t** (01622) 871 266 (*cheap*). Wonderful village pub in beautiful countryside with garden, Adnams beers and pub grub.

the-art 14th-century military technology, with drum towers, devilish portcullises and murder holes. Elegant council offices occupy an 18th-century townhouse next door.

All Saints' Church in **Tudeley**, 2 miles east of Tonbridge on the Paddock Wood road has a complete set of stained-glass windows by Marc Chagall. The East Window was commissioned by Sir Henry d'Avigdor-Goldsmid in memory of his daughter, who drowned in a sailing accident in 1963; it shows her being lifted out of the swirling sea up to Heaven. There are four smaller Chagall windows in the white-painted chancel.

Leeds Castle

t (01622) 765 400; grounds open April–Oct 10–5, Nov–Mar 10–3; castle April–Oct 11–5.30, Nov–Mar 10.15–3.30; adm exp.

Leeds Castle, easily reached by train or on the M20 from London, is a fairy-tale moated English castle, a place for romantic trysts. Edward I rebuilt the curtain walls of the original fort, added the gatehouse and gave the castle to his beloved queen, Eleanor of Castille. This began a tradition of queenly ownership, ending with Catherine of Valois, Henry V's queen. Henry VIII added the top floors before the castle passed out of royal ownership into the hands of the Legers, Culpepers, Fairfaxes and finally Wykeham Martins, who bankrupted themselves on improvements and gave it up. Wealthy 26-year-old Anglo-American Lady Baillie came to the rescue when English castles were going cheap post-war. She trawled the French antiques markets and commissioned French craftsmen to refurnish the rooms.

The Hop Farm Garden Country Park

t (01622) 872 068; open 10–5; adm.

Britain's largest group of Victorian oast houses stands north of Paddock Wood, now sadly reduced to a family attraction. You see oasts all over the Weald of Kent, with cylindrical walls and jaunty white cowls; here there are 25, all white weatherboard and mellow red brick. The first hops in England were grown at **Yalding** 400 years ago and added to beer as a preservative. For a long time no one liked their bitter taste; now hops are intrinsic to brewing. The oast houses are hop-drying rooms; the white cowls on the roofs are to stop down-draughts. In the 19th-century heyday the hop-growing villages of Kent were overrun with pickers from the East End at harvest time.

North to the Estuary

'The principal productions of these towns,' says Mr Pickwick 'appear to be soldiers, sailors, Jews, chalk, shrimps, officers and dockyard men...'

Charles Dickens, *The Posthumous Papers of the Pickwick Club*

Place names like **Gravesend**, **Deadman's Island** and **Gad's Hill** are redolent with Dickensian atmosphere, as is the twisting brown estuary with its dredgers, creeks and nameless islands. You will find the North Kent estuary towns either full of character, or depressing. **Rochester** is a delightful day's visit and **Chatham Historic Dockyard** unmissable, but try not to get bogged down in the endless carpet centres and sprawl of the Medway Towns. Buried in the urban jungle are fortifications dating back to the 16th century, built to protect the dockyard from both landward and seaward attack, but they've failed to prevent suburban encroachment. Some are open to the public, including **Fort Amhurst** (*t (01634) 847 747; open Easter–July Wed–Sun, Aug–mid-Sept daily, Sept-Christmas weekends 10.30-4 (an hour earlier in winter)*, an 18th-century installation of tunnels, batteries and magazines, and **Upnor Castle** (*t (01634) 718 742; open April–Sept 10–6, Oct 10–4; adm*), a 16th-century fort guarding the dockyard from across the river. On either side of the estuary is the open agricultural land of the **Hoo Peninsula** and **Isle of Sheppey**, breathing space in a cramped and untidy part of Kent.

Gravesend and the Hoo Peninsula

Gravesend developed in the Middle Ages through the export of woollen cloth and a lucrative monopoly of the London ferry, but the town's claim to fame is Pocahontas, the daughter of an American Indian chief, who died on a ship at Gravesend in 1617 and was buried there. Pocahontas, 'the playful one', had saved the life of captured Captain John Smith as he was about to have his head smashed in by her father, Powhatan, in America. She later converted to Christianity and married Englishman John Rolfe. On her trip to England with her husband in 1616 she was received as a princess and presented to the King and Queen, but fell ill and died shortly before setting off home. Despite this tragic, romantic story, there's nothing romantic about Gravesend. There's not even a grave of Pocahontas, just a modern statue in St George's churchyard. The

Beowulf, a Kentish Tale

Beowulf **tells the tale of Germanic warrior Beowulf, who travels to a foreign country to save King Hrothgar's hall – called Heorot – from the marsh monster Grendel. Known as the earliest European epic, it was written in Old English in the 11th century, after centuries of oral telling, and set in the 5th century. It was always assumed to be a mythical tale (monsters and underwater battle scenes), but references to historic characters and events, including Hengest, one of the first Germanic settlers of** ***Cantium*****, have convinced historians that there's reality in it. Topographical references in the poem suggest King Hrothgar's hall was on Harty Island, just off Sheppey; its main settlement in the 11th century was also called Heorot. The 'shining sea-cliffs' where Beowulf first sights land might have been Sheerness ('bright headland'), and the Roman road by which Beowulf is led to Heorot (a former Roman villa) can be found on Harty Island too. Beowulf defeats Grendel's mother in marshes surrounding Heorot. Even today, after widespread reclamation, Harty Island is flanked by marshes, particularly around the tidal Swale. But the real clincher is that the unpronounceable Old English name of the Romano-British settlement of Harty Island, Schrawynghop, translates as 'land surrounded by marsh haunted by malignant demons'.**

only reason to visit is to catch the ferry across the river to **Tilbury Fort** to get a good view of Victorian and Regency port buildings and have a drink in The Three Daws, a white weatherboard smuggling pub on the riverside.

Things get interesting on the A226 from Gravesend to Rochester. To appreciate how interesting, stop at the Sir John Falstaff pub in Higham, at the top of **Gad's Hill**. The hill was a notorious spot for highway robbery – in *Henry IV Part 1*, Shakespeare stages a double robbery on the hill (Falstaff's gang robs a couple of travellers, then Prince Hal and Poins rob Falstaff). Centuries later, Gad's Hill became the haunt of Dick Turpin. Across the road from the pub is **Gad's Hill Place** (***t*** *(01474) 822 366; Easter–Oct tours first Sun of month 2–5; adm*), now a school, where Charles Dickens lived for the last 13 years of his life (1857–70). The young Charles admired the grand, red-brick Georgian house as a child; his father told him to work hard and maybe one day it would be his – and it was. Dickens dug a tunnel from his front garden to the shrubbery across the road, where his Swiss Chalet used to be.

Drive on out to the **Hoo Peninsula**, following signs to Cooling and Cliffe on the B200, then the A228, where you get views over both Thames and Medway estuaries from lanes and fields. Aim for **St James' Church** in **Cooling**, past ruined Cooling Castle, a manor house fortified by John de Cobham in 1381. It is in this churchyard, in *Great Expectations*, that escaped convict Madgwick seizes young Pip beside the five little graves of his dead brothers and sisters as the mist slides off the marsh. There are in fact 13 lozenge-shaped body stones to the south of the church tower, the children of two local families whose names are listed just inside the church door. They were probably taken off by malaria, which plagued the peninsula into the 19th century.

Back on the A228, take a detour via **Upnor Castle** (*open April–Sept 10–6; adm*), on the outskirts of Strood. The first castle was built between 1559 and 1565, facing the Tudor dockyards on the opposite bank, to command the entrance to the anchorage. A few shots were fired from the castle in 1667 but failed to repel the Dutch fleet under Admiral de Ruyter, which sailed openly up the Medway, set fire to the royal fleet in the dockyards and stole the flagship, the *Royal Charles*.

Rochester

'Ah! Fine place,' said the stranger, 'glorious pile – frowning walls – tottering arches – dark nooks – crumbling staircases – Old cathedral too – earthy smell – pilgrims' feet worn away the old steps – little Saxon doors...fine place – old legends too – strange stories: capital.'

Charles Dickens, *The Posthumous Papers of the Pickwick Club*

Rochester is the oldest and prettiest of the Medway towns. It developed along Roman Watling Street, the main London–Dover road, and foundations of a wooden

Getting There and Around

By **car**, take the A2, which follows the Thames out of London to the Medway towns, or take the M25/M26, branching off at junction 6 on the A229.

Two **trains** an hour run from London Victoria to Rochester, and on to Whitstable, Broadstairs and Ramsgate.

There are regular Medway trips from Rochester pier on the 1924 paddle steamer *Kingswear Castle*, lasting from 45 minutes to 2½ hours. Bookings and enquiries **t** (01634) 827 648, *www.pskc.freeserve.co.uk*. Cruises run May–Sept.

Tourist Information

Rochester: 95 High Street, **t** (01634) 843 666, *www.medway.gov.uk. Open Mon–Sat 10–5, Sun 10.30–5.*

Rochester's **Dickens Festival** takes place at the beginning of June, around the High Street, castle and cathedral, with readings, entertainments and Dickensian characters. There is also a Dickensian **Christmas Weekend** which takes place early December.

Where to Stay and Eat

Rochester t (01634) –

Rochester's hotels are not up to much.

Gordon House Hotel, 91 High Street, **t** 831 000, *www.gordonhotel.free-online.co.uk* (*moderate*). Hotel in 17th-century townhouse with period decoration around stairs.

The Royal Victoria and Bull Hotel, 16-18 High Street, **t** 846 266, *www.rvandb.co.uk* (*moderate*). Centuries-old coaching inn whose guests have included Queen Victoria and members of the fictional Pickwick Club.

There is no shortage of cafés/tearooms on Rochester High Street.

Don Vincenzo, 108–110 High Street, **t** 408 373 (*moderate*). Very good glass-fronted modern Italian restaurant which serves wonderfully crisp pizzas. *Closed Tues.*

Mr Tope's Restaurant and Wine Bar, 60 High Street, **t** 845 270 (*moderate*). Friendly little restaurant beside College Gate. Sit outside, or in charming hotchpotch of brick and stonework, heavy timbers, dark panelling and low ceilings. Fri–Sun operates as a tearoom, Tues–Thurs French/English menu includes fillet steak or monkfish with asparagus followed by Belgian chocolate truffle cake or banoffee pie. *Live piano played Thurs eve.*

Williams of Rochester, 86 High Street, **t** 847 776 (*moderate*). Pretty old place with window like the back of a galleon. Traditional menu might include crusty mustard pork chops or roast followed by apple crumble. Children and families made particularly welcome.

Singapora, 51 High Street, **t** 842 178 (*cheap*). Long-established, popular restaurant serving Malaysian, Chinese, Indonesian and Thai food.

Charles Dickens' Medway

Charles Dickens' father, John Dickens, took a senior clerical position at the Chatham Dockyard just after the Napoleonic Wars. Charles was five. The family moved into a smart house in Ordnance Terrace, the best street in town, looking out over a cornfield to the docks. Things went badly for John, and four years later they were forced to move to the poorest part of Chatham. The children had a good time anyway. When a better job came up with the Navy Board in London the family upped and left again. But throughout his life Dickens returned to fond childhood memories of the Medway Towns. Chatham is described by Dickens' first biographer as 'the birthplace of his fancy', with its dingy, overcrowded streets, workhouses and convicts working on the docks. His first novel set in Medway was *The Posthumous Papers of the Pickwick Club*, with Samuel Pickwick putting up at the Royal Victoria and Bull Hotel on Rochester High Street. In *Great Expectations*, Pip lives on the Hoo Peninsula. In 1857 Dickens moved to the house he had always dreamed of, Gads Hill Place in Higham, where he died before finishing *The Mystery of Edwin Drood*.

Roman bridge have been found at the river crossing. Rochester is the second oldest diocese in England, after Canterbury, and its Norman castle was built by the architect of the Tower of London. Cathedral and castle stand on the High Street in a mishmash of black-and-white gables and coaching arches. There are enough bric-a-brac shops, art galleries, bookshops and tea shops to keep you going as long as a Dickens novel.

From the river, a cliff rises up to the magnificent rag-stone keep of the **castle** (***t*** *(01634) 402 276, www.english-heritage.org.uk; open Oct–Mar 10–4.15, April–Sept 10–5.15; adm*). 'What a study for an antiquarian!' exclaimed Mr Pickwick when he first set eyes on it. Its crumbling 12th-century keep rises 100 feet plus corner turrets.

The **cathedral** (***t*** *(01634) 401301; open daily 8.30–5.30*) stretches along the High Street behind a higgledy-piggledy line of shops. It is more rambling than the best, with its dinky spire and patchwork of stones from many restorations, but it scores highly for the lovely Norman sculpture around the west door. The carved figures on either side of Jesus in the tympanum represent Justus, one of St Augustine's fellow missionaries, and King Æthelbert, who together built the first church on this site; 400 years later, in 1077, the first Norman bishop, Gundulf, built the cathedral, then the castle. Inside, it resembles a large parish church. Have a look at Gundulf's fan-vaulting in the crypt and the worn steps leading up to the shrine of St William of Perth, a Scottish baker whose murder in Rochester in 1201, while on pilgrimage to Canterbury, earned him a sainthood and drew some of the lucrative pilgrim trade off the Canterbury road.

The High Street makes the most of its Dickensian connections, with plaques on the buildings that featured in Dickens' novels. At the far end of the High Street, Tudor **Eastgate House** had a minor role in *The Pickwick Papers* and *Edwin Drood*. Behind it you can see Dickens' **Swiss Chalet**, transplanted from Gad's Hill Place, now part of the **Charles Dickens Centre** (***t*** *(01634) 844 176; open April–Sept 10–4.45, Oct–Mar 10–3.15; adm*) – tableaux of Fagin's den, Scrooge's parlour and Cooling churchyard.

Chatham Historic Dockyard

t (01634) 823 800; open mid-Feb–Oct daily 10–6 (dusk if earlier); adm exp.

It's a short drive from Rochester to the dockyard, following signs past Fort Amhurst. Chatham was one of six royal dockyards in the country. Its heyday was in the Dutch Wars, when the fleet needed access to the North Sea. It closed in 1984, after 400 years; 80 acres of its unrivalled Georgian dockyard architecture has been preserved. Before the Industrial Revolution the royal dockyards were the largest manufacturing centres in the world; you can see this one as it looked in the age of sail, when boats like Nelson's *Victory* came off the production lines. Wealden oak, from up the Medway, was turned into naval battleships in the white weatherboard warehouses. Submarine *Ocelot*, launched in May 1962, was the last ever warship built for the Navy at the Royal Dockyard.

The Royal Engineers garrisoned the town to protect the dockyards. The **Royal Engineers Military Museum** (*t (01634) 406 397; open Tues–Fri 9–5, weekends 11.30–5; adm*), in Prince Arthur Road, Gillingham, traces their history from the King's Engineers, brought from Normandy in 1066 to build siege machines and castles for the conquest of England, to the sappers of modern campaigns.

West Kent

There is some lovely scenery in West Kent, south of the M25 and the North Downs from London. At its best it's an idealized English countryside, dotted with horses and oak trees. Some great country houses are concentrated here. The earliest owners of Hever, Knole and Penshurst were courtiers, located close to government but avoiding the damp, forested, pig-infested Low Weald. Winston Churchill adopted West Kent for the same reason – so that ministers could nip down from Westminster in half an hour for lunch. Octavia Hill, a founder of the National Trust, settled at Crockham Hill, campaigning to preserve local landscapes such as Toy's Hill. **Hever Castle** and **Penshurst Place** can be visited on the same day. The same goes for **Chartwell House** and **Quebec House** in Westerham, and **Knole House** and **Ightham Mote**, just a few country lanes away on the east side of Sevenoaks.

Westerham

A few miles south of the M25, Westerham's excellent restaurants and antique shops benefit from through-trade along the A25; its elegant Georgian architecture and views over the Weald of Kent make up for the trundling traffic. Although few of its coaching arches still belong to inns, it still feels like a coaching town. The road passes statues of Churchill and Major General Wolf on opposite corners of the town green, one fatter and grumpier looking than the other. Wolf grew up in Quebec House, just beyond the green, and became a schoolboy hero by dying in the night-time assault of Quebec that won Canada for the British in 1759.

Getting There and Around

Westerham is on the A25 between Sevenoaks and Reigate, and only half an hour by **car** from Gatwick airport.

Where to Stay and Eat

Westerham t (01959) –

The King's Arms Hotel, Market Square, **t** 562 990, *www.oldenglishinns.co.uk* (*expensive*). Handsome old Georgian coaching inn with 17 recently refurbished bedrooms. Popular with pilots flying at the Biggin Hill airshow.

The Grasshopper-on-the-Green, The Green, **t** 562 926. Friendly old-fashioned pub with menu of shank of lamb and smoked haddock (*moderate*). Real ales are Speckled Hen, Harveys and Courage Best.

Osteria Pizzeria Napoli, just off the Market Square, **t** 561 688 (*moderate*). Cosy restaurant offering good southern Italian food including pizza, pasta, fish and meat dishes. *Closed Mon.*

Rendezvous, 26 Market Square, **t** 564 245 (*cheap*). Airy, relaxed French brasserie with large windows and mirrors. Long menu includes peppered steak, omelettes or moules, as well as coffee and pastries.

Around Westerham

The Leicester Arms Hotel, High Street, Penshurst, **t** (01892) 870 551 (*moderate*). Handsome old creeper-clad inn with tiled roof and black-and-white beamed porch. Seven bedrooms decorated with tapestries. Modern-style restaurant might offer dressed Cromer crab salad or pork and herb sausages with mash, followed by pecan pie or lemon tart.

Moorden Farm, Chiddingstone Causeway (half a mile south of the station), **t** (01892) 870 334 (*moderate*). Beautiful old farmhouse just north of Penshurst with croquet lawn, tumble-down farm buildings and a profusion of wisteria and oak panelling. Guests' kitchen and oak-panelled bathroom.

The Mount House, High Street, Brasted, **t** (01959) 563 617 (*moderate*). Warm welcome at this handsome Georgian house in pretty little village 1½ miles east of Westerham on A25. Three double rooms, one with own private bathroom.

The Castle Inn, Chiddingstone (off B2027), **t** (01892) 870 247. Delightful old coaching inn in time-forgotten village between Penshurst and Edenbridge. Real ales include Larkins Traditional Ale and Chiddingstone Bitter. Classy restaurant (*moderate*) offers modern European food. *Closed Tues.*

Chartwell

***t** (01732) 866 368, www.nationaltrust.org.uk; open April–Oct Wed–Sun 11–5, July–Aug Tues–Sun 11–5; adm.*

Chartwell is a mile south of Westerham, signposted off the M25 and A25. The red-brick Churchill family home is a solid place with wooden floors and wide stairwells. When Churchill bought it in 1922, it was a Victorian pile with too many gables and bay windows. Fashionable architect Philip Tidden was hired to improve it. Churchill loved Chartwell, while his wife Clementine worried they could not afford it. At first it was a weekend retreat, but when Churchill was knocked out of ministerial office for 10 years he moved to Chartwell full-time, writing articles, books and speeches and redesigning the garden. It is this period that the house reflects, with invitations propped on the mantelpiece and a game of cards in progress. Churchill wrote about fifty books in his study, with epic titles like *Triumph and Tragedy*, *The Hinge of Fate* and *Gathering Storm*, not to mention the bestselling *History of the English Speaking Peoples* and his war memoirs. The walls are decorated with photographs of politicians and some of Churchill's own paintings of holiday landscapes. His little studio in the garden is full of paintings and walking sticks.

Hever Castle

t (01732) 865 224; open Mar–Nov, gardens 11–5, castle 12–5; adm exp.

The castle is tucked away beside the River Eden in acres of garden. Hever is one of the most visited castles in England, because of its connections with Anne Boleyn and the Astor family, and its proximity to London. The Bullens, as they started off, climbed the social ladder from Norfolk yeomanry to royalty in four generations. Their fall was faster still. Thomas Bullen was the real mover and shaker. He was born in 1477, married Elizabeth Howard, daughter of the Duke of Norfolk, in 1498, and installed his daughters, Mary and Anne, at Court. Anne was appointed lady-in-waiting to Henry VIII's first queen, Catherine of Aragon. Honours were heaped upon her father, including Earl of Wiltshire and Knight of the Garter. Henry's affair with Anne and break-up with Catherine (no heir) resulted in England's separation from the Roman Catholic Church, the end of monastic life in England and Wales, and the start of a long tradition of English isolationism. Anne was already pregnant with the future Elizabeth I when she married the King, and changed her name to Boleyn to suit her new status as queen. After her fall from Henry's favour, accused of adultery with her brother George, among others (he was executed before Anne), Henry took Hever. Thomas Bullen was thrown out of court and died soon after. The castle was close to dereliction in 1903 when American press baron William Waldorf Astor bought it. He transformed it into a luxurious Edwardian country pad with all mod cons. The castle sits in its square moat like a fairy cake on a plate. The perfection is all Astor's work, as is the mock-Tudor village behind the castle, which he built to accommodate his staff. The present Lord

Henry VIII's Wives

Henry VIII's first wife, **Catherine of Aragon**, gave birth to Mary, followed by a string of stillbirths. It was a traditional royal alliance: she was the daughter of Isabella of Spain and Ferdinand, and married to Henry for 19 years – but produced no son and heir. Countless people were hanged, drawn and quartered in the constitutional revolution that followed Henry's divorce from Catherine – which involved a break with the Roman Catholic Church – and secret marriage to **Anne Bullen** or **Boleyn**, who was already pregnant with the future Elizabeth I. Trumped-up charges of adultery and incest, and a double-edged sword at the Tower finished it all for Anne in 1538, and the Bullens were cast out of court. Henry's third wife, **Jane Seymour**, gave him a son – the future boy-king Edward VI – but died shortly after childbirth. His fourth wife, **Anne of Cleves**, was famously plain and too Germanic for the tastes of Henry, who ditched her after six months claiming the marriage had never even been consummated. Anne was given Hever Castle and eventually a royal burial – a pretty dignified end in the circumstances. **Catherine Howard** was Henry's pretty fifth wife, whom he doted on. But the jealousy of the by now fat and ageing king, and an alleged love affair, got her head chopped off. Eighteen months later Henry married **Catherine Parr**. She nursed him, didn't bother him and, incredibly, outlived him as queen. There is a rhyme to help you remember them all: divorced, beheaded, died; divorced, beheaded, survived.

and Lady Astor live less elaborately in Westerham, while the castle does corporate hospitality. Pop into **St Peter's Church** to see the stone tomb of Sir Thomas Bullen.

Penshurst Place

t (01892) 870 307; open Mar weekends, April–Oct daily, gardens 10.30–5, house 12–5; Sat closes at 4; adm exp.

The family home of the De L'Isles, near Tonbridge, is hidden behind high hedges in lovely Wealden countryside. The De L'Isles are direct descendants of the Sidneys, who were given Penshurst Place by Edward VI in the 16th century. Since then it has been extended, but not changed. It is not flamboyant: 'Thou art not, Penshurst, built to envious show/ Of touch or marble; nor canst thou boast a row/ Of polished pillars, or a roof of gold', wrote Ben Jonson.

The hammer-beamed 14th-century Barons' Hall was built by rich London merchant John de Pulteney. After de Pulteney died of the plague, Penshurst Place was taken over by Henry IV's third son, the Duke of Bedford; then Henry VI's youngest brother, Humphrey, Duke of Gloucester; followed by the Duke of Buckingham, who entertained Henry VIII in 1519 so extravagantly that the envious King had him executed on a charge of treason. Edward VI gave Penshurst to his tutor, Sir William Sidney, along with vast estates in Sussex, Hampshire, Lincolnshire and Nottinghamshire. His grandson, Sir Philip Sidney, is the famous one, remembered as the model of cultured Protestant chivalry. He was a brilliant poet who died of wounds received on the battlefield in Holland. His famous last words, 'Thy need is greater than mine', his posthumously published poetry and his lavish funeral at St Paul's cathedral made him an icon of the English Renaissance.

Philip became the preferred name for Sidneys. The first Philip's brother succeeded him, inheriting the Leicester earldom from uncle Robert Dudley and becoming Viscount De L'Isle. Ben Johnson, a friend and regular guest of the Sidneys, wrote a poem stating that even the partridges and fish on the estate considered it an honour to be eaten by the Earl of Leicester, his patron.

The Sidneys filled prestigious offices, including Governor of Ireland, Warden of the Cinque Ports and Constable of the Tower of London, but their poetry was never so good, nor their dying words so memorable, again. The present Viscount De L'Isle and his family – the 19th generation of Sidneys – live in the front of the house and own most of the village, subsidizing the post office and looking after the countryside in a way that would have made Johnson proud.

Tours start in the 60ft-high Barons' Hall (in the middle is the original octagonal fireplace and Henry VIII's feasting table) and carry on through the Duke of Bedford's hall and into the Long Gallery. The gardens feature the Tudor Italian garden of Henry Sidney, son of Edward VI's tutor, the first Sir William. Had the Sidneys not overstretched themselves by building an enormous London mansion on Leicester Square in the 18th century, Penshurst Place might have been landscaped. Have a look at the original Leicester Square in the village.

Down House, Home of Charles Darwin

t (01689) 859 119; open Feb–Mar Wed–Sun 10–4, April–Sept 10–6, Oct 10–5, Nov–Dec 10–4; adm.

Down House, in the village of Downe near Biggin Hill, is buried in the North Downs. Darwin was in his thirties and married when he moved into the house in 1842, with a reputation in natural science and geology gained on the *Beagle* voyage to South America six years earlier. The house is a solid white stucco Georgian-Victorian hybrid. Darwin lived here with his family for 40 years, until his death in 1882, and wrote *On the Origin of the Species* and *Descent of Man* in the study. Darwin was emblematic of the Victorian age in his domestic habits as well as his professional output: he wrote seminal works in the mornings and went on country rambles in the afternoons, all his needs attended to by a dutiful wife. Darwin came from a well-off Shropshire family: his grandfathers were Erasmus Darwin and Josiah Wedgwood, two of the most respected scientists of their day. Charles married his first cousin, Emma Wedgwood. A portrait of their common grandfather, Josiah, hangs on the study wall, between Darwin's two mentors, Kew botanist Joseph Hooker and geologist Charles Lyell. Memorabilia includes scientific paraphernalia in the study. Walk down the Sandwalk, which Darwin called his 'thinking path' and walked at least twice a day.

Sevenoaks

Sevenoaks is an affluent version of Tonbridge, with a public school at the smart end and a railway station at the other. Only 30 minutes from London by train, it's now a commuter town. A drive leads off the High Street through Knole Park to the home of the Sackvilles, earls of Dorset.

Knole House

A mile east of Sevenoaks, **t** *(01732) 450 608; house open April–Oct Wed–Sun 11–3.30; park open all year dawn–dusk; adm.*

Knole is a palatial Tudor house, in its time episcopal palace of the archbishops of Canterbury, royal palace of Henry VIII and ducal palace of the Sackvilles. 'It is not an incongruity like Blenheim or Chatsworth, foreign to the spirit of England,' wrote Vita Sackville-West in *Knole and the Sackvilles*. It is magnificent and austere. You enter through the oak door, on the other side of which is a turfed courtyard, the Green Court, and beyond that a paved court, the Stone Court, then five more courtyards. Around the seven courtyards there are supposed to be 52 staircases and 365 rooms, corresponding to the days of the week, weeks and days of the year. The Sackvilles still live in some rooms; visitors see a dozen show rooms, including three long galleries.

Elizabeth I gave Knole to her cousin Thomas Sackville in 1566. Thomas was a good poet, a contemporary of Spenser, Sidney and Shakespeare, and is credited with the first, achingly dull, English tragedy, *Gorboduc*. When he became 1st Earl of Dorset Thomas gave up poetry and set the best Renaissance craftsmen to work on Knole, adding plasterwork ceilings, carved chimneypieces, friezes and wall hangings. Knole is famous for its collection of 17th-century furniture, installed by the 4th Earl after the

Getting There and Around

By **car**, turn off the M25 at junction 5 and follow the A21 into Sevenoaks.

Sevenoaks is half an hour by **train** from London Charing Cross.

Tourist Information

Sevenoaks: The Library Building, Buckhurst Lane, **t** (01732) 450 305, *www.heartofkent.org.uk*. *Open Mon–Sat 9.30–5*.

The **Lakeside Theatre** at Hever Castle, **t** (01732) 866 114, *www.heverlakeside.co.uk*, hosts a 10-week summer festival from June to Aug, with jazz, classical and opera music, Gilbert and Sullivan and drama. The purpose-built theatre by the lake is covered, but bring warm clothes. Picnic by the lake, or have a pre-theatre supper at the **Wheatsheaf**, Bough Beach, **t** (01732) 700 254, the **Greyhouse**, Hever, **t** (01732) 862 221, or the **Henry VIII**, opposite the castle.

Where to Stay and Eat

Sevenoaks t (01732) –

The Royal Oak Hotel, High Street, **t** 451 109, *www.brook-hotels.co.uk* (*expensive*). Pleasant old hotel opposite Sevenoaks school; 37 comfortable rooms.

Beechcombe, 4 Vine Lodge Court, Holly Bush Lane, **t** 741 643 (*moderate*). Modern house in quiet area behind cricket green, a short walk from the station.

Loch Fyne, 63–5 High Street, **t** 467 140 (*moderate*). Top-quality seafood chain. The scrubbed floorboards and wooden tables reflect the good, honest menu. Fish pie, mussels, oysters or fresh Icelandic cod.

No. 5, The Royal Oak Hotel, High Street, **t** 455 555 (*moderate*). Sunny, modern décor; meat and fish dishes, plus bistro-style dishes like eggs Benedict and kedgeree.

Zizzi, 35 London Road, **t** 469 305 (*cheap*). Good pasta and pizza chain; upbeat atmosphere.

Spice Club, 57–9 High Street, **t** 456 688 (*cheap*). Very good Indian restaurant at top of town near cinema.

The Chequers Inn, High Street, **t** 454 377 (*cheap*). Traditional pub offering five or six real ales, recommended in the *Good Beer Guide*. Building dates back to 16th century, with dark beams to prove it.

Around Sevenoaks

The George and Dragon, The Street, Ightham, **t** (01732) 882 440 (*moderate*). Excellent, welcoming pub on delightful village square. Shepherd Neame beers include Masterbrew and Spitfire. Renowned for its food: fish of the day with butternut squash, sweet potato and green beans; delicious sauces and good vegetarian options.

The Chequers, Crouch (near Plaxtol and Borough Green), **t** (01732) 884 829 (*moderate*). Classy gastro pub. *Closed Sun eve and Mon*.

The Bottle House, Smarts Hill, **t** (01892) 870 306. Take Smarts Hill out of Penshurst, turn right at top towards Chiddingstone and 15th-century pub with well-worn brick floor tiles and terrace overlooking hills. Good food including fish; Harveys Best and Larkins on hand pump.

Entertainment

Stag Theatre, London Road, **t** 450 175. Small theatre hosting comedians and touring theatre productions, bands, orchestras and local am dram. Also two-screen cinema. Try the theatre's **Limelight Restaurant** (*moderate*) for pre-show suppers.

Civil War (when the Parliamentarians had looted the old stuff). As Royal Chamberlain, the 4th Earl was entitled to first pick of the royal cast-offs. The famous 'Knole Settee' gave its name to this style of sofa. Another treasure is the manuscript of Virginia Woolf's *Orlando*, inspired by Knole and by her lover, Vita Sackville-West, an androgynous aristocratic writer on whom the eponymous hero/heroine is based. As a woman, Vita was barred the inheritance of Knole and moved to Sissinghurst Castle, where she and her husband Harold Nicolson created the famous gardens (*see* p.177).

Ightham Mote

***t** (01732) 811 145; open Mar–Oct Sun, Mon and Wed–Fri 10.30–5.30; adm.*

Ightham Mote, one of the loveliest moated manor houses in England, is 3 miles east of Knole. Approach along the footpath from Shipbourne Church, passing Budds House and Wilmont Hill on the way, returning via the Chasers Inn. The Mote was built in the 14th century, when the Weald was wild and forested. Behind the walls it is domestic in feel, its squire owners living off fish, pigeons and vegetables from the garden. The courtyard appeared in an early *Country Life*, and, in 1951, when it was up for sale, a wealthy American remembered it from a cycling holiday and snapped it up.

Royal Tunbridge Wells and Around

You're on the High Weald in Royal Tunbridge Wells, a well-to-do old spa town on the Kent and Sussex border. The spa, known as the Pantiles after the pan-baked stones that paved its promenades, is at the bottom of town, surrounded by hill-top residential developments. **Mount Ephraim** was always the best address, overlooking the **Common** with its woods and rocky outcrops (now it's offices). **Mount Pleasant** is now the main shopping thoroughfare. Only **Mount Sion** is still residential. The railway station is at the bottom of town, a few steps from the old High Street.

A Wells Among -dens and -hursts

Tunbridge Wells grew gradually, with no formal planning like that of Bath, peaking between 1736 and 1755 during the reign of legendary impresario Beau Nash. The discovery of the wells is recounted in the first local history book, written by Thomas Benge Burr in 1766. Lord North, a member of James I's court, stumbled on a dark pool in the forest as he returned to London after a period of convalescence, took a sip of water, felt better and alerted his doctor who confirmed its medicinal properties. Lord North lived well into his eighties and his fashionable friends at court came down to try the waters. It's a stone-cold, iron-rich spring. At first people stayed in the nearby coaching town of Tonbridge or pitched a tent. (The spa town swapped its u for an o with the coming of the railway to avoid confusion, which it didn't.) Charles I's queen, Henrietta Maria, camped on the Common for six weeks to recover from the birth of her second son, Charles II. Some years later, Charles II and Queen Katherine stayed on Mount Ephraim while his retinue camped on the Common. Queen Victoria came twice, Edward VII gave the town its Royal prefix in 1909 and Princess Anne came three times. In the town's heyday, Beau Nash used to come down every year to open the season, staying a while to check that everything was running according to his rules.

Starting from Mount Pleasant, the scale of the town dwindles as you approach the Pantiles. Pop into the **museum** (***t** (01892) 554 171; open Mon–Sat 9.30–5, Sun 10–4*), in the 1930s Town Hall complex, to see the collection of Tunbridge Ware. The ornamental wooden boxes sold by local families as souvenirs developed into highly collectable stuff in the Victorian period. The old High Street leads down to Chapel Place and the Pantiles, passing **Halls Bookshop**, a local institution dating back to 1898; all the

Getting There and Around

By **car**, from London via the M25, follow A21 south towards Hastings, turning off on the A264 to Tunbridge Wells.

Two trains an hour leave from London Charing Cross to Tunbridge Wells via Sevenoaks and Tonbridge, taking about 50 minutes.

The **Spa Valley Railway** is a steam train from old Tunbridge Wells West station to Groombridge (for Groombridge Place Gardens) via High Rocks, a wooded country park famous for its sandstone rocks. West Station, off A26 Eridge Road, **t** (01892) 537 715. *Service runs Wed–Sun.*

Tourist Information

Royal Tunbridge Wells: The Old Fish Market, The Pantiles, **t** (01892) 515 675, *www.heartofkent.org.uk, www.visittunbridgewells.com. Open Mon–Sat 10–5, June–Aug also Sun 10–4.*

Ashdown Forest: **t** (01342) 823 583, *www.ashdownforest.org.uk, www.ashdownforest.co.uk. Open April–Sept Mon–Fri 2–5, all year weekends 11–5.* Maps and walking trails.

Where to Stay

Royal Tunbridge Wells t (01892) –

The Spa Hotel, Mount Ephraim, **t** 520 331, *www.spahotel.co.uk* (*very expensive*). Grand 18th-century mansion hotel in 14-acre gardens, with 69 bedrooms, tennis courts, swimming pool and all the health and beauty treatments known to woman.

The Royal Wells Inn, Mount Ephraim, **t** 511 188, *www.royalwells.co.uk* (*expensive*). Spa hotel that was favourite of Princess Victoria, who slept in every room. Nice period feel, with two restaurants and bar. Pleasant, airy first-floor conservatory restaurant (*moderate*) looking out across the common serves pan-fried salmon fillet, mushroom and parmesan risotto or sirloin beef. *Open Fri–Sat only.*

The Hotel du Vin, Crescent Road, **t** 526 455, *www.hotelduvin.com* (*expensive*). One of small chain of outstanding designer hotels and bistros, this one in an 18th-century sandstone building with 36 bedrooms, billiard room and boules court. The modern country-house bistro offers classic English dishes such as calf's liver and bacon with mash, traditional French dishes like chicken breast with Lyonnaise and leeks, and local produce such as smoked Flimwell salmon. Range of wines, cigars and cognac. Lovely terrace at back for lunch.

The Beacon, Tea Garden Lane, Rusthall, **t** 524 252 (*expensive*). Follow Mount Ephraim past Wellington Hotel towards Langton Green, turning off after a mile, to this Victorian house well-known for its views. Three bedrooms, bar and restaurant serving local produce and fish. Friendly service.

Mount Edgcumbe Hotel, The Common, **t** 526 823 *www.mtedgcumbe.com* (*moderate*). Small Regency summer house of the Plymouth Edgcumbe family, by common and a stone's throw from Pantiles; five bedrooms, brasserie and famous bar in a sandstone cave.

Ephraim Lodge, The Common, **t** 523 053 (*moderate*). Mr and Mrs Douchets welcome lucky guests into their lovely Georgian home on the common. Minimum two-night stay.

second-hand books cramming the shelves come from Tunbridge Wells homes, so what you see is a catalogue of local reading habits over the last century. Before crossing Neville Street into the Pantiles, have a look at the Restoration ceilings in the 17th-century church of **St Charles the Martyr**, the first 'chapel of ease' for spa visitors. The **Pantiles** was the first pedestrian precinct, laid out in Stuart times, its composition and scale lovely. The white colonnaded **Upper Walk** was the promenade from the **Bath House** via Beau Nash's **Assembly Rooms** to the **Pump Room**. Only the Bath House survives, occupied by a chemist who keeps the baths locked. Spring water bubbles up outside into a black marble bowl encrusted with iron deposits. Between April and September a dipper, wearing a frilly apron, will fetch you a glass of spring

The Crown Inn, The Green, Groombridge, **t** 864 742, *www.thecrowngroombridge.co.uk* (*moderate*). Five bedrooms, one en-suite, above a traditional pub a short drive west of Tunbridge Wells. It was once the haunt of Sir Arthur Conan Doyle and crops up in *Valley of Fear*: Watson and Holmes stay in Birlstone Manor, otherwise known as Groombridge Place. Real ales include Harveys (from Lewes), Larkins, Abbot Ale and IPA. Pub grub such as steak and ale pie (*cheap*). *No food Sun eve.*

Eating Out

Royal Tunbridge Wells

The Pantiles was designed for tea, coffee and light lunches, but no café or restaurant is outstanding. You may be better off picking up the tourist information centre's *Eating Out* booklet for the nearby High Wealden villages, including Cranbrook, Lamberhurst, Goudhurst and Biddenden.

Thackeray's, 85 London Road, **t** 511 921 (*moderate*). Tunbridge Wells' Michelin-starred restaurant. Suave, uncluttered setting and modern French cuisine: pan-fried scallops followed by roast fillet John Dory with risotto, grilled Aberdeen Angus steak with wild mushroom crust or asparagus and black truffle risotto with parmesan and poached egg. *Closed Sun eve and Mon.*

Signor Franco Ristorante, 5/a High Street, **t** 549 199 (*moderate*). Airy, bright first-floor Italian restaurant overlooking High Street. Ask for window table. *Closed Sun.*

Sankeys, 39 Mount Ephraim, **t** 511 422 (*moderate*). Leafy terrace and cellar bar decorated with old beer signs. Serves Guinness and Erdinger Weiss beer, and seafood including mussels, cod and chips or paella. *Closed Sun eve.*

La Casa Vecchia, 70–72 The Pantiles, **t** 544 700 (*moderate*). Mediterranean cooking on the edge of the Pantiles and regular live music (jazz, Latin and soul) in the bar upstairs.

Himalayan Ghurkha Restaurant, 31 Church Road, **t** 527 834 (*cheap*). Run by two ex-soldiers from the Nepalese Ghurkha regiment, including former engineer with an MBE. The Nepalese food is rice-based and similar to Indian but more subtly spiced. Try the Momo, a steamed dumpling, followed by Kukhura Chhoila, a chicken dish, marinated and mixed with herbs and spices, cooked in the Tandoori oven and served on a sizzling dish.

Ashdown Forest

Hatch Inn, Coleman's Hatch (near Hartfield), **t** (01342) 822 363. Picturesque ivy-clad weatherboard pub for lunch or a pint (Harveys). Rare beef salad and pan-fried farmed salmon.

There are two decent pubs in Hartfield, as well as the **Pooh Corner Shop**, **t** (01892) 770 456, *www.poohcorner.net*, which does all manner of Winnie the Pooh memorabilia.

Entertainment

The Trinity Arts Centre, Church Road, **t** 544 699. Outstanding local theatre, café-bar and gallery in converted Victorian-Gothic church.

Assembly Hall Theatre, Crescent Road, **t** 530 613. Prestigious touring productions.

The Parish Church of King Charles the Martyr, **t** 511 745. Lunchtime and evening concerts under impressive moulded ceiling.

water for a small fee. The **Lower Walk** was used as a market and is now antiques shops. The **Corn Market** arcade is a reconstruction of the former corn market, originally a theatre built in 1802. Here you can visit **A Day at the Wells** (*t (01892) 546 545; open April–Oct 10–5, Nov–Mar 10–4; adm*), an exhibition on Beau Nash's Wells where you can hear his rules on good taste and breeding: 'Boys and girls should dress as girls up to the age of five, after which the most rigorous differences should be observed.' Next door is the old **Royal Victoria and Sussex Hotel**, where the coat of arms of the Duke and Duchess of Kent commemorates the stay of Princess Victoria and her mother, the Duchess of Kent, in 1834. Cross the busy London road and climb up to the ancient Common, where Queen Henrietta Maria camped in 1629.

Ashdown Forest

Ashdown Forest is a small remnant of forest between East Grinstead, Tunbridge Wells and Uckfield, a Norman royal enclosure for deer-hunting, like most forests not all woodland but a mix of woods and heath (man-made by sheep-grazing and cutting birch for firewood over the years). It covers 4,000 donut-shaped acres, its unusual shape the result of illegal land enclosures in the 17th and 18th centuries. Almost everybody knows the forest from *Winnie the Pooh*. A.A. Milne lived in Hartfield, and the bear's adventures took place around Gills Lap ('Galleons Leap').

Several roads skirt the forest, including the Wych Cross–Coleman's Hatch Ridge Road, the B2026 and the busy A22. Head for the **Ashdown Forest Centre** (***t*** *(01342) 823 583; open weekends 11–5, April–Sept also Mon–Fri 2–5*), just east of **Wych Cross**, for maps. From there, the Ridge Road continues to **Coleman's Hatch** with views over the Weald of Kent. From the Hatch Inn, at the Coleman's Hatch junction, Kidd's Hill heads south to meet the B2026. Park here and walk north to **Gills Lap**, where A.A. Milne and E.H. Shephard are commemorated ('And by and by they came to an enchanted place on the very top of the Forest called Galleons Leap'). Further south, at the intersection of the B2026 and B2188, is the **King's Standing** car park, from where you can walk 2½ miles down to the river and back via Crow's Nest Clump. There are several car parks along the Crowborough Road from the B2026 to Nutley, including the Hollies and Ellison's Pond. **Hartfield** is a pretty, one-street village just outside the forest.

The High Weald to the Coast

Between Royal Tunbridge Wells and the coast lies beautiful countryside and marsh. When Rudyard Kipling found his home, **Batemans**, while touring the High Weald in his old car, he called it a place to 'raise the kids, build a wall, dig a well and plant a tree.' Vita Sackville-West and Harold Nicolson felt the same way about **Sissinghurst**, although probably planting more trees, as did Nathaniel Lloyd about **Great Dixter**.

Andredsweald

The ancient wildwood of Andredsweald, wild and impenetrable, covered three-quarters of the Weald, an area 75 miles by 30 miles. Celtic settlers preferred open chalk hills for forts, and the ridges served as early highways. The Romans christened the wood the Forest of *Anderida* after their port at Pevensey (Roman name *Anderida*) on the south coast. Roman military ironworks in the Weald produced around 550 tons of iron a year for 120 years. Germanic settlers turned the name into Andredsweald (-weald was Saxon for wood) and created clearings. These became the Wealden villages, the -hursts and -dens (-hurst means an inhabited clearing in the woods, -den relates to the ancient practice of 'pannage' by which pigs were driven into woodland pastures to be fattened on acorns for slaughter). Not until mass tree-fellings in the 16th century – to supply timber for the dockyard at Chatham and charcoal for the blast furnaces of the iron industry – did the wildwood of Andredsweald lose its menace .

Tourist Information

Tenterden: Town Hall, High Street, **t** (01580) 763 572, *www.ashford.gov.uk. Open April–Oct Mon–Sat 9.30–5.*

Getting There and Around

By **car**, turn off the M20 at Ashford and take the A28 Hastings road to Tenterden, or leave the M25 at junction 5 and take the A21 to Royal Tunbridge Wells, then the A262 Goudhurst to Biddenden road, picking up signs to Tenterden.

The nearest railway station is Headcorn, with **trains** from London Charing Cross. The no.12 bus shuttles back and forth to Tenterden.

A section of the old **Kent and East Sussex Railway** was reopened in 1974 and extended in 2000, operating restored steam locomotives from Tenterden Town Station (*t (01580) 765 155*) through Northiam to Bodiam Castle.

Where to Stay

Little Silver Country Hotel, Ashford Road, Tenterden, **t** (01233) 850 321, *www.little-silver.co.uk* (*expensive*). Friendly Victorian mock-Tudor affair with pretty garden.

Bettysland, 39 Swan Street, Wittersham, **t** (01797) 270 652 (*moderate*). Charming detached home between Tenterden and Rye with double room overlooking garden.

Bishopsdale Oast, Cranbrook Road, Biddenden, **t** (01580) 291 027, *www.bishopsdaleoast.co.uk* (*moderate*). Beautiful oast house in the middle of delightful countryside just north of Tenterden. Five bedrooms.

Sissinghurst Castle Farm, Biddenden Road, Sissinghurst, **t** (01580) 712 885, *www.kent-esites.co.uk/sissinghurstcastlefarm* (*moderate*). Grade II Victorian farmhouse on Sissinghurst estate. Beautiful views, and short walk to famous gardens.

Whitelands Farm, Grange Road, Tenterden, **t** (01580) 765 971 (*moderate*). Beautiful 16th-century farmhouse buried in countryside 5 minutes' drive from Tenterden in direction of Biddenden (or 20 minutes' walk). Lovely views of church from the bedrooms.

The Haven, 11 East Hill, Tenterden, **t** (01580) 766 805 (*cheap*). Modest, cheerful Victorian house with two bright and comfortable bedrooms and a shared shower room.

Old Burren, 25 Ashford Road, Tenterden, **t** (01580) 764 442 (*cheap*). Friendly, warm welcome awaits in 17th-century cottage with a pretty garden and two comfortable bedrooms at north end of High Street.

The Star and Eagle, High Street, Goudhurst, **t** (01580) 211 512 (*cheap*). Next to church at top of hill with a a large patio out back. Real ales include Flowers, Adnams and Bass. Upmarket pub nosh cooked by Spanish chef lunch and dinner. Also some bedrooms.

The Vine, High Street, Goudhurst, **t** (01580) 211 261 (*cheap*). Serves English and Thai food. Cosy bar offers Harveys and London Pride. Rooms upstairs.

Eating Out

The White Lion, High Street, Tenterden, **t** (01580) 765 077 (*moderate*). Behind white Victorian façade is a beamy old coaching inn with a dark bar and 15 bedrooms. Pub grub, Adnams and Green King IPA on tap.

The Whistlestop Restaurant, Coombe Lane, **t** (01580) 765 450 Tenterden, (*cheap*). Near Town Station, superb, friendly little café-restaurant with good home-made food from full English breakfasts and roast Sunday lunches to afternoon tea. *Closed Mon.*

The Lemon Tree, 29 High Street, Tenterden, **t** (01580) 763 381 (*cheap*). Old-fashioned restaurant in traditional Wealden hall house. Morning teas and coffees as well as full lunches with a roast every day, lots of fish and summer special of poached salmon, Pimms and strawberries and cream.

Thai Orchid, 75 High Street, Tenterden, **t** (01580) 763 624 (*cheap*). Thai favourites like Tom Yum soup, or traditional Mussaman lamb. Patio and garden seating. *Closed Sun.*

Ozgur, 126 High Street, Tenterden, **t** (01580) 763 248 (*cheap*). Cosy Turkish restaurant with mandolin music. Meze, char-grilled fish and meat, then baklava.

The Bell Inn, High Street, Burwash, **t** (01435) 882 304 (*cheap*). Delightful old pub by Brightling turn-off, sit outside on warm day opposite the church. Serves Green King ales including IPA and Speckled Hen, steak and kidney pie or fresh fish. One bedroom.

Sissinghurst, **Bodiam**, Batemans and Great Dixter are unmissable, but there are other more secret pleasures here. These include the charming village of **Goudhurst**, on a hill with a church paid for by the wool trade; **Biddenden**, with its medieval half-timbering; and **Burwash**, with its high street, pubs and views. **Cranbrook**, with its white weatherboard buildings, was a 14th-century cloth-making centre, with large merchants' houses, a big church and the **Union Windmill** (***t*** *(01580) 712 256; open April–Sept Sat 2.30–5, mid-July–Aug also Sun 2.30–5*), built during the Napoleonic wars when blockades increased demand for local flour. The garden at **Marle Place,** just off the A21 near Brenchley (***t*** *(01892) 722 304; open Easter–Oct 9–5.30*), has the charm of Sissinghurst, without the crowds; quirky touches include a life-sized papier-mâché old lady stroking her cat. Everyone loves **Bayham Abbey**, signposted from Lamberhurst; its ruined sandstone walls are often photographed. A crusading knight built it in the early 1200s and installed a community of White Canons to pray for his troubled soul. **Scotney Castle** (***t*** *(01892) 891 081; castle open May–Oct, gardens Mar–Oct Wed–Sun 11–6; adm*) is charming too, with picturesque gardens.

Tenterden

Tenterden is within easy reach of the gardens of the High Weald and Romney Marsh, has good places to stay and eat, and a magnificent High Street lined with white weatherboard buildings behind plane trees and little gardens. The church and grand houses were built on the fruits of the medieval wool trade. Tenterden was also a limb of the Cinque Port of Rye (its coat of arms features a three-masted ship). Until the late Middle Ages an arm of the Rother Estuary extended fingers inland to Tenterden; Small Hythe and Reading Street supported a ship-building industry. Look at **St Mildred's Church** and the **museum** (***t*** *(01580) 764 310; open Tues–Sun Easter–June 1.30–4.30, July–Sept 11–4.30, Oct 1.30–4.30; adm*) down Station Road which, among old farm tools, has a display on Tenterden's days as a port. In summer, a steam train chugs from Tenterden Station to Bodiam Castle. A few miles south on the road to Rye is **Smallhythe Place** (***t*** *(01580) 762 334; open Easter–Oct Sat–Wed 11–4.30; adm*), the half-timbered home of Victorian actress Ellen Terry.

Sissinghurst Castle Garden

t *(01580) 710 701, www.nationaltrust.org.uk; Easter–Oct Mon, Tues and Fri 11–6.30, weekends 10–6.30; quieter after 3pm on weekdays; adm.*

The National Trust is trying to lower the profile of Sissinghurst because it attracts more visitors than it can cope with. Everyone loves its sagging tiled roofs, mottled brick walls covered in honeysuckle and old roses, and romantic association with Vita Sackville-West and Harold Nicolson. He designed it, with its yew hedge walls; she filled the 'rooms' with meadow flowers and plants mentioned in Shakespeare's plays.

Harold and Vita were a couple of upper-class drifters until they found Sissinghurst. She had been turfed out of her family home at Knole; he had led a roaming life as the son of a diplomat, and at 40 was working as a journalist for the *Evening Standard* in London. Like Kipling, they drove around the High Weald looking for somewhere to settle. What they found was the decaying range and tower of a Tudor mansion. They cleared some rubble and laid out 10 separate gardens around the tower, framed by the old moat. Beyond are meadows, lakes and woodland. The couple wrote novels, biographies, poems and magazine articles, gardening in every spare moment. In 1946 Vita began a column in *The Observer* chronicling the garden's progress, and Sissinghurst shot to fame. Climb the tower to Vita's dusky study lined with bookshelves to get a view of the garden's layout. One of the most famous yew-walled gardens is the white garden.

Great Dixter House and Gardens

t (01797) 252 878; open April–Oct Tues–Sun 2–5; adm exp.

The gardens of Great Dixter in Northiam, above the Rother Valley off the A28, rank with Hidcote and Sissinghurst. In the middle stands the rambling, timber-framed Wealden house of famous horticulturalist Christopher Lloyd. His father, Nathaniel, commissioned Edwin Lutyens to extend the medieval hall house in 1910, after retiring early from his London printing business and taking a shine to the High Weald. Everything to the right of the wonky old porch is the old manor house; to the left is Lutyens' extension. A second medieval hall, picked up for £75 in Biddenden, has been tacked on. Lutyens laid out the framework of the garden, incorporating the old farm buildings. Christopher planted the garden, began the nursery business and writes countless books and articles on gardening (including 30 years of contributions to *Country Life*). The 6-acre gardens are arranged on terraces around the house, again divided into a series of 'rooms' by yew hedges. The famous herbaceous borders are planted with naturalistic clumps, and the wildflower meadows are punctuated with Nathaniel's topiary. In winter you can see through the trees to Bodiam Castle. Tours of Lutyens' interiors are fitted around Christopher's daily routine. In winter, he tends to write in the snug parlour of the original mid-15th-century hall.

Bodiam Castle

t (01580) 830 436; open Mar–Oct daily 10–6, Jan–Feb weekends only 10–4; adm.

Bodiam Castle, across the valley from Great Dixter, near Robertsbridge, was built to guard the Rother Estuary when it was vulnerable to invasion. It looks like a fairy-tale castle reflected in its moat and appears to perfectly combine the roles of baronial residence and fortress. During one visit, Henry James said 'Summer afternoon – summer afternoon; to me those have always been the two most beautiful words in the English language'. Bodiam is a nostalgic sort of castle, barely defensible even when it was built in the late 14th century.

Batemans

Open April–Oct Sat–Wed 11–5, gardens also Mar weekends 11–4; adm.

Just south of Burwash, Batemans stands in a beautiful spot at the bottom of the wooded Dudwell Valley, a handsome Jacobean house with lichen-encrusted ironstone gables. Rudyard Kipling and his American wife, Carrie, discovered Batemans on a summer driving tour and bought it in 1902. Kipling is supposed to have shouted 'That's her! The only She! Make an honest women of her, quick!' He was famous by then, having already written the *Jungle Books* and *Just So* stories, and wanted somewhere peaceful to write books and raise his children, John and Elsie. They stayed here for the rest of their lives, entertaining friends such as Rider Haggard, Henry James and Bonar Law. The dark wooden panelling and oak furniture is how Kipling liked it, 'alive with ghosts and shadows'. His study is furnished as he left it, with his big old sofa, window-facing desk covered with writing materials, and shelves of reference books – more than 500, including several on Sussex. Beyond the little corn mill at the end of the garden, you can follow the brook over the stile to the setting of *Puck of Pook's Hill* (1906), a natural hollow 'overgrown with willow, hazel and guelder-rose' where two children conjure up the long-eared Puck, who takes them magically into stories of old Sussex. The setting of Batemans helped to establish Kipling's identity as the archetypal Englishman of his era, born in Bombay (1865), married to an American, but nonetheless the Sussex squire.

You can see the 65ft-high **Brightling Needle** on the skyline. It was one of Jack Fuller's follies around his Brightling Park estate, built to celebrate the Battle of Waterloo in 1815. Mad Jack was an outspoken MP for East Sussex – once thrown out of the House for calling the Speaker an 'insignificant little fellow in a wig' – and a local legend. One of the most bizarre of his follies is his pyramid mausoleum in **Brightling church**, supposed to contain Mad Jack himself with a glass of claret in his hand.

Sussex

I have seen no wretchedness in Sussex...the gardens are neat, and full of vegetables of the best kinds...and as to these villages in the South Downs, they are beautiful to behold...

William Cobbett, *Rural Rides*

Sussex is dominated by the tumbled hills of the High Weald and Kipling's 'blunt, bow-headed, whale-backed downs'. The downland scenery emerged out of the Neolithic shift from foraging in the forest to farming and settlement; arable on the low hills and pasture on the upper slopes. The burial mounds, tracks, chalk figures and Celtic hill forts – the **Trundle**, **Devil's Dyke** and **Caburn** – are remains of a civilized society. After the Norman Conquest, Sussex became a strategically important corridor between England and Normandy. William I's most trusted knights were entrusted with narrow strips of land called *rapes*, around the castles at **Arundel**, **Bramber**, **Lewes**, **Pevensey** and **Hastings**, and later on **Chichester**. In the 16th and 17th centuries, a new breed of Sussex aristocrats, grown rich on the redistribution of monastery lands, breathed new life into these fading dependencies. The great houses (no longer castles) in their manicured estates at **Cowdray**, **Petworth** and **Goodwood** perpetuated the quasi-feudal world with tied cottages and colour-coded gate posts.

When William Cobbett travelled through Midhurst and Petworth in August 1823, the sight of so many well-fed labourers and vegetables sent him into a rage against the brutal factories of the north. Elsewhere the Sussex Weald was already post-industrial (and a wasteland in the 18th century). The great historic episodes of working-class lawlessness – the Swing riots and peasant revolts – started in the Weald. By the end of the 19th century, most rural areas of England were in decline and a well-off urban middle class was growing nostalgic for an imagined old rural England – the one Kipling was writing poems about. The tumble-down barns, broken gates and overgrown tracks looked picturesque to their eyes, and the land was cheap. The new money could get there on the London–Brighton road and railway, transforming ancient farmhouses into lavish mansions with exotic gardens such as **High Beeches**, **Nymans** and **Leonardslea**. The Bloomsbury Group adopted the Sussex Downs as their seaside retreat in the first few decades of the 20th century, when it was still an out-of-the-way sort of place, where Virginia Woolf could write of 'a week end of no talking, sinking at once into a deep safe book reading; and then sleep...and then to wake into the hot still day, and never a person to be seen, never an interruption: the place to ourselves: the long hours.' She and Leonard were the first of the group to come down here, in 1910, first to the village of West Firle, then Beddingham, **Lewes** briefly and finally Monk's House in **Rodmell**, four miles from the sea. In 1916 Virginia's sister Vanessa Bell and her household moved into **Charleston**, a rambling farmhouse about 7 miles away over the Downs from Monk's House. Today you can visit both houses, decorated with Bloomsbury furniture and paintings.

Meanwhile, the railway turned the coastal resort towns of **Brighton** and **Eastbourne** – formerly remote fishing villages – into the main centres of population.

The coastal plain around **Chichester** has always been prosperous. At the time of the Roman Conquest it was the base of the Atrebates tribe under King Cogidubnus. **Selsey** grew into a powerful religious centre in Saxon times: it is where King Cnut tried to hold back the waves. Cnut's daughter is buried at **Bosham** church. After the Norman Conquest, the bishopric was moved from Selsey to Chichester, the market town of the plain, which got a new cathedral and became the sixth *rape* of Sussex.

Rye and the Marsh

The 'Ancient Town' of Rye is perched on a small sandstone promontory in the marsh. It has an extraordinary number of famous residents, past and present (mostly writers and artists) including Henry James and Spike Milligan. From the High Weald, the main road (A268) passes the medieval Landgate and circles the hill. Walk into town up the steep lane through the Landgate. Where there is marsh now there used to be sea, and in 1155 maritime Rye became part of the Confederation of Cinque Ports (along with Winchelsea) which was duly renamed the Confederation of Cinque Ports and Two Ancient Towns. The seagulls and fishing boats in Strand Quay on the River Tillingham remind you that the open sea is not far away. The Cinque Ports all suffered French raids and Rye was burned to the ground in 1377. The charming town you see now, with

Getting There and Around

By **car**, leave the M20 at Ashford, following the A2070 to Rye, or if you are travelling south on the A21, take the B2089 to Rye; this slow, rambling route through the Wealden villages is the most attractive way.

By **train**, go to Ashford International from London Charing Cross or London Victoria, then connect with the south-coast line to Rye.

The one-third full-size steam and diesel locomotives of the **Romney, Hythe and Dymchurch Railway** (**t** *(01797) 362 353*) run the 13½ miles between Hythe and Dungeness at 25mph on rails only 15 inches apart, the longest miniature steam railway in the world. It opened in 1927, not long after the L'al Ratty in Cumbria, and grabbed a few headlines during the Second World War when it was used by the army. Trains run Easter–Sept daily, Mar and Oct weekends only.

Tourist Information

Rye: Strand Quay, **t** (01797) 226 696, *www.visitrye.co.uk. Open Mar–Oct daily 10–5, winter Mon–Sat 10–4.*

Festivals

Rye Festival, **t** (01797) 224 442, *www.ryefestival.co.uk*. Talks including celebrity speakers on history, art and literature, and top-quality music from blues guitar to classical. First two weeks of Sept in various venues around town including St Mary's Church, the Methodist church, George Hotel and Rye Community Centre. Always lively and interesting mix.

Where to Stay

Rye t (01797) –

Rye Lodge Hotel, Hilder's Cliff, **t** 223 838, *www.ryelodge.co.uk* (*expensive*). Relaxing hotel – formerly a Victorian school – with views across the marsh and estuary. Black-and-white exterior, light interior; 19 comfortable bedrooms. Indoor 'Venetian pool' decorated with mural of Venice. 'Fine dining' restaurant.

Jeake's House, Mermaid Street, **t** 222 828, *www.jeakeshouse.com* (*expensive*). A smashing place to stay, in the former home of American poet Conrad Aiken. The house incorporates a 17th-century wool store (built by the Jeake family) and 18th-century Quaker Meeting House, bolted together on a steep hill.

King Charles II Guesthouse, 4 High Street, **t** 224 954, *www.ryetourism.co.uk/kingcharles* (*moderate*). Beautiful 15th-century town-house, former home of Victorian novelist Radclyffe Hall, author of *The Well of Loneliness* and other potboilers. Ancient fire-places, beamwork and front door. Charles II used to drop in on clandestine visits during his long exile in France (or so they say).

The Benson, 15 East Street, **t** 225 131, *www.bensonhotel.co.uk* (*moderate*). Queen Anne house built for wealthy wool merchant and named after former mayor of Rye E.F. Benson, best known for his Mapp and Lucia books. Four sweet bedrooms with four-poster beds and marsh views.

Durrant House Hotel, 2 Market Street, **t** 223 182, *www.durranthouse.com* (*moderate*). Homely place to stay with seven rooms, three with river views.

its cobbled lanes, fish-scale-tiled fronts and Georgian brick façades with neat sash windows, is the new Rye.

As you pass the **Landgate**, look back at the view over the marsh before you enter the pretty cobbled streets and lanes, lined with galleries, second-hand bookshops and ancient pubs. Blue plaques tell you where all the famous residents lived. **Mermaid Street**, with its famous old smuggling inn (the Mermaid Inn) used to be the main street into town from the anchorage outside Strand Gate. It takes you to **St Mary's Church** and **Ypres Castle** (**t** *(01797) 226 728; open April–Oct Thurs–Mon 10.30–1 and 2–5; adm*), part of the medieval wall defences, past **Lamb House** (**t** *(01892) 890 651; open April–Oct Wed and Sat 2–6; adm*), where Henry James moved in 1898. It's one of the

The Old Vicarage, 66 Church Street, **t** 222 119, *www.oldvicaragerye.co.uk* (*moderate*). Pretty little pink-painted Georgian building with floral bedrooms in picturesque heart of Rye, facing church behind profusion of pink-flowering roses. Breakfast includes home-made bread and scones.

The Old Borough Arms, The Strand, **t** 222 128, *www.oldborougharms.co.uk* (*moderate*). Pretty, white-painted, blue-shuttered 17th-century house at the bottom of Mermaid Street, overlooking the Strand; nine bedrooms. Cream teas and light lunches served at weekends.

Cliff Farm, Iden Lock, **t** 280 331 (*cheap*). About 1½ miles out of Rye on Military Road towards Appledore, turning right after railway bridge. Pretty little spot, nestling beneath prehistoric sea-cliff overlooking the marsh; three bedrooms.

Eating Out

Rye

The Mermaid Inn, Mermaid Street, **t** 223 065, *www.mermaidinn.com* (*very expensive*). Old smuggling haunt of the notorious Hawkhurst gang. Two cosy sitting rooms with fireplaces and 31 bedrooms. The restaurant serves fish, grills and pot-roast partridge, or you can eat something lighter at the fireside in the public bar (baguettes, fish pie, moules). Henry James, Rupert Brooke, Ellen Terry and the Bensons have all tippled here.

The Copper Kettle, The Mint, **t** 222 012 (*moderate*). Olde-worlde beamed restaurant with hanging baskets and bottles crammed into every ledge and cupboard. Specializes in Whitstable oysters and game including 'locally shot hare'. *Open eves only, summer Thurs–Mon, winter Fri–Sun only.*

The Flushing Inn, 4 Market Street, **t** 223 292, *www.theflushinginn.com* (*moderate*). Behind the heavy oak door is traditional restaurant which has been in the same family since 1960. The building was rebuilt in 1420 shortly after the French destroyed the town, and features blackened panelling and oak doors. The big thing here is local seafood – lobster, crab, Dover sole, scampi, as well as local Romney lamb. *Closed Mon eve and Tues.*

Fletcher's House, Lion Street (off Market Street), **t** 222 227 (*cheap*). The front room is a great spot for a morning coffee or glass of wine, on a cobbled lane leading up to the church. Greek salads, quiches and pies, delicious cakes, deep-fried brie with redcurrant jelly. *Closed Mon and Tues.*

Old Bell Inn, The Mint, **t** 223 323 (*cheap*). An appealing spot on a sunny day with its pretty terrace shaded with wisteria and green umbrellas. Inside beamed and cosy. Real ales include Courage Directors and Level Best. Pub grub at lunchtime.

Romney Marsh t (01797) –

The Britannia, Dungeness, **t** 321 959 (*cheap*). Fish and chips overlooking the power station. The hanging sign creaks forbiddingly in winter, but it's friendly, offering Spitfire and Masterbrew.

The Pilot Inn, Battery Road, Dungeness, **t** 320 314 (*cheap*). Just outside the Dungeness estate, a popular spot for fish fresh from the sea and chips.

smartest Georgian buildings in the town. James loved it, especially the old garden house, 'which is simply the making of a most commodious and picturesque detached study and workroom' (sadly destroyed in the Second World War). Here he wrote *The Wings of the Dove*, *The Ambassadors* and *The Golden Bowl*. On the hall wall are photos of writer friends, among them Thomas Hardy and Hugh Walpole, who once said that he loved James, was staggered by his wisdom, yet was sometimes so bored that he had pins and needles in his legs and arms. Down on **Strand Quay**, the old black timber warehouses have been converted into cafés and bric-a-brac shops.

Camber Castle

***t** (01797) 223862; open July–Sept weekends 2–5; adm.*

You can walk from Rye to the atmospheric ruins of Camber Castle, or drive towards Rye Harbour and park just after the River Brede, following the path along the river (a lovely walk). The castle stands in the middle of fields miles from the sea, but once stood on the edge of the Rother Estuary guarding Rye Harbour. It is one of Henry VIII's south-coast artillery castles, its clover-leaf shape, thick round stone bastions and massive central tower virtually unchanged since it was abandoned in 1642 due to the changing coastline; the sea has retreated a couple of miles from the fortress.

Winchelsea

The 'Ancient Town' of Winchelsea is a few miles south of Rye on the A259, perched on sandstone above the marsh. Drive straight through the medieval gate into the tree-lined grid of wide streets. The present town of Winchelsea was built by Edward I after old Winchelsea was swept away during the great storm of 1287, which also re-routed the River Rother south of the Isle of Oxney, right outside Rye. Old Winchelsea supplied a quarter of the Cinque Ports fleet, which is why Edward I didn't hesitate to build a new town. It grew rich on the wine trade until the 15th century, when the harbour silted up. Its magnificent church is partly ruined. Opposite is a small museum. From the old windmill on the east of town there is a sensational view.

Romney Marsh

Have you ever bin in the Marsh?
Only as far as Rye, once, Dan answered.
Ah, that's but the edge. Back behind of her there's steeples settin' beside churches, an' wise women settin' beside their doors, an' the sea sittin' above the land.

Rudyard Kipling, *Puck of Pooks Hill*

Four hundred years ago, Rye, Winchelsea, Tenterden, Appledore, Lympne and Hythe all looked out over the sea at high tide. Today, the 40 pumping stations on Romney Marsh still have to work hard to clear the flood waters after a wet winter. In Roman times, Port Lympne was one of the main harbours of Roman *Britannia*, known as *Portus Lemanis*, and Tenterden had wharves. It took centuries of labour to reclaim the 100 square miles of marsh from the sea, aided by falling sea levels and accumulating silt behind the shingle bar known as Dungeness. Even in the 16th century the high tide came up to the foot of Rye Hill, forming a shallow harbour between Rye and Winchelsea. About a mile south, Camber Castle stood on a shingle spit on the edge of the harbour. When the tide receded, expanses of Rother Estuary were left behind.

The 50,000 acres of arable and grassland of the marsh, famous for its sheep, have always been a military zone. It's so flat and open it's clearly vulnerable to invasion. In the Second World War there were plans to flood the marsh at the first sign of trouble. In the Napoleonic Wars, a string of Martello Towers with interlocking fields of fire were built along the **Royal Military Canal**, zigzagging 23 miles along the inland edge

Cinque Ports, Two Ancient Towns and Some Limbs

From the southeast coast you can see France on a clear day across the Channel, 22 miles away at the closest point. In the Second World War artillery fired straight across from the cliffs. So close, France was long a threat to English national security. To counter this menace, in the Middle Ages the five biggest southeastern ports – Sandwich, Dover, Hythe, Romney and Hastings – were brought into a defensive confederation in exchange for special rights and privileges, including freedom from taxes and trading duties. These were the Cinque (pronounced 'sink') Ports – the forerunners of the Royal Navy – bound to provide the king with a fighting fleet of 57 ships for 15 days each year, longer at a price. Each port was allowed members or limbs to help bump up the number of ships. Winchelsea and Rye joined Hastings, but their fleets grew bigger than Hastings' and the confederation was renamed the Cinque Ports and Two Ancient Towns. They continued to chase herring down the east coast in the season, raising a naval fleet only when pressed. The height of the confederation was the 13th–16th centuries, until the confederates' harbours became choked with silt and they were superseded by a purpose-built Royal Navy based around the Thames and the southern ports. Today the confederation is a ceremonial entity whose Lord Warden was, until recently, the Queen Mother.

of the marsh like a moat and flanked with gun emplacements. In the 18th century, smugglers like the Hawkhurst Gang exploited the marsh. Spooky stories about the marsh include the Dr Syn books by Russell Thorndike. It is atmospheric, hemmed in between ancient sea cliffs and the fortress-like sea wall at Dymchurch – behind which the high tide comes in above head height. Arriving from London via the A262, turn onto the B2000 through the pretty village of **Appledore** to Dungeness. From Rye, follow the canal to Appledore. When you get to the T-junction at Appledore, turn sharp right, then right again onto the Fairfield Road to see lonely **Fairfield Church**. Fetch the key from Becket's Barn, on the right before the church.

Dungeness

People either love **Dungeness** or want to get out as fast as they can. It's a pebbly subcontinent of migrating sea birds, shingle-loving plant life, lighthouses, nuclear power stations, night fishermen and film students. It's a scruffy place whose residents – pensioners, fishermen, nuclear workers, loners – live in bungalows along the coast road or in one of the sought-after fishermen's huts and converted railway carriages on the shingle. The garden at **Prospect Cottage**, a black weatherboard building with bright yellow windows off the Dungeness Road, was created by film-maker Derek Jarman before his death in 1994 (and helped to bring the place notoriety). Jarman came here for the lack of fences and the bleakness; the garden of driftwood sculptures and shingle-loving plants blends into the shingle wilderness. The road comes to an end at a cluster of buildings including the power station, two lighthouses and the Britannia pub. At night the **nuclear power station** is lit up like Las Vegas. You can climb up the old lighthouse to appreciate the desolation, then ground yourself with chips at the Britannia.

The **Romney, Hythe and Dymchurch Railway** (*Mar–Oct weekends, Easter–Sept also Mon–Fri*) is the longest miniature steam railway in the world. It opened in 1927, and made the headlines when it was used by the army during the war. Jump aboard at **Hythe**, after looking at **St Leonard's Church** (***t*** *(01303) 263 739; open 10–5, crypt May–Sept 10.30–noon and 2.30–4*) with its famous ossuary containing the bones of some 4,000 people. Stop at **New Romney** to climb another lighthouse.

The Mid-Sussex Forest Ridge

The Forest Ridge is another name for the High Weald; you can still find clumps of ancient woodland. Gideon Mantel discovered the bones of the iguanodon on the ridge, in a quarry north of Cuckfield. He called it the iguana-saurus, until a friend suggested that iguanodon sounded better. At the turn of the 20th century the ridge was adopted by a handful of wealthy gardeners, who created the gardens at **Leonardslea**, **Wakehurst**, **Nymans** and **High Beeches**. **Standen** is equally exciting, but for the house instead of the garden; the house was built for a London solicitor by the Arts and Crafts architect Philip Webb and furnished by Morris and Co.

From the M25, the M23 and A23 Brighton road make the Forest Ridge a bit too accessible from London. The ridge towns of Crawley, East Grinstead, Uckfield, Hayward's Heath and Horsham are no great shakes. Hilaire Belloc lived near Horsham and loathed the suburbanization of it. He once bribed the guard on his train to shout out Hors-ham instead of Horsham, the correct pronunciation of the ancient horse-trading town (he said). All the attractions are well signposted round here.

Steam trains chuff back and forth on the **Bluebell Line** (***t*** *(01825) 722 370*) between Kingscote Station, a few miles south of East Grinstead, and Sheffield Park, a 100-acre garden laid out by Capability Brown and transformed in 1909 by Arthur Gilstrap Soames into fabulous woodland garden around four lakes.

Gardens of the West Sussex Forest Ridge

A group of rich amateur enthusiasts created these gardens with exotic plants brought back to Britain from around the British Empire. Around their big old houses, these men created romantic landscapes out of conifers and rhododendrons.

Ludwig Messel was a wealthy London stockbroker, typical of the new money coming into the Weald. At **Nymans** (***t*** *(01444) 400 321, www.nationaltrust.org.uk; open Mar–Oct Wed–Sun 11–6, Nov–Feb weekends 11–4; adm*) in Handcross he started a collection of rhododendrons and planted a heath garden.

The hub of the West Sussex horticultural coterie was the garden of Robert Loder at **High Beeches** (***t*** *(01444) 400 589; open Easter–Oct Thurs–Tues 1–5; July–Aug Fri and Sun–Tues; adm*), a few miles from Nymans on the B2110 East Grinstead road. The garden – 20 acres of landscaped woodland – is a place of pilgrimage. Loder had three sons. The youngest, Wilfred, remained at High Beeches, handing over to his own son, Giles, who planted the greatest number of trees and shrubs from western China anywhere outside of that region.

The eldest Loder son, Edmund, married into **Leonardslea** (**t** *(01403) 891 212; open April–Oct 9.30–6; adm*) in Lower Beeding near Horsham. Here he developed one of the most varied woodland gardens in England, with palm trees, redwoods, bamboos, rhododendrons and camellias flourishing on the steep valley sides like natives. Across the road from Leonardslea lived the naturalist Frederick Goodman, who went on plant-hunting expeditions to Guatemala and edited a book describing 19,000 new species. Loder and Goodman produced the Rhododendron *Loderi*, one of the most successful hybrids. Ten miles from Leonardslea lived William Robinson, an influential writer whose magazine *The Garden* promoted a naturalistic style of gardening.

In 1903 Gerald Loder bought **Wakehurst Place** (**t** *(01444) 894 000, www.nationaltrust.org.uk; open 10–7; adm*), a Tudor mansion with a 180-acre garden that boasts a winter garden as well as spring and autumn colour. It is managed informatively by the Royal Botanic Gardens, with national collections of birch and hypericum. Wakehurst is the home of the Millennium Seed Bank; its underground vault is intended to preserve a seed from every British species.

Standen

***t** (01342) 323 029, www.nationaltrust.org.uk; house open Mar–Oct Wed–Sun 11–5; gardens Mar–Oct 11–6, Nov–Dec Fri–Sun 11–3; adm.*

Standen, on West Hoathly Road, 2 miles east of East Grinstead, was built in 1892–4 by leading Arts and Crafts architect Philip Webb and decorated by Morris and Co. It was built as a holiday home for James Beale, a London solicitor based in Holland Park, who retired here with his seven children and their children. The house was cleverly designed in a rambling L-shape to give the impression that it grew naturally over time. Webb incorporated an old cottage into his scheme, blending old and new in a mishmash of vernacular styles. Inside, the beds are from Heals, the lighting by Webb, the fabrics by Morris and Co. and the ceramics by William de Morgan.

Hastings and 1066 Country

Hastings

White chalk cliffs characterize most of the south-coast resorts. Not Hastings, which has dirty grey-brown sandstone cliffs and an edgy Wealden air. Hastings is about fish: it comes in fresh onto the beach and is sold wet or battered in town. Ignore the battered resort and head to the old town with its medieval streets, and the bustling fishing beach known as the Stade, beneath the cliffs. There are about 40 fishing boats all told (some of which hardly ever put out to sea, there are so few fish left), the largest beach-launching fleet in Europe.

The Old Town

Modern trawlers still operate off the Stade. The catches are brought in tubs to the fishmarket on Rock-a-Nore Road and auctioned before most people are out of bed. At the far end of the road is a sealife aquarium, **Underwater World** (**t** *(01424) 718 776;*

The Men of Hastings

The 'Men of Hastings' got a special mention in the *Anglo-Saxon Chronicle*, marking their independence from the Germanic kingdoms beyond the marshes. The Norman conquerors arrived on the long sandy beach to the west of Hastings, near Pevensey, camping out on West Hill before marching north to fight Harold in 1066. The ensuing battle borrowed its name from Hastings, the nearest town. The maritime community was preserved in the creation of the fifth Norman *rape*, centred on Hastings. The reversal of fortunes experienced by all the Cinque Ports visited Hastings in the 13th century. The sea inundated the harbour and the town degenerated into a small fishing village around a scrap of shingle, beneath the East Hill. Its fleet of wooden clinker-built boats launched off the beach and returned on the surf with hauls of sole, plaice and cod. The fishing nets were dried in huts on the beach made out of fishing boats, sawn off and upended. This is still the case.

open Oct–Mar 11–4, April–Sept 10–5; adm) and **Shipwreck Centre** (***t** (01424) 437 452; open Aug–Sept 10–6, Oct–July 11–5; adm*). The **Fishermen's Museum** (***t** (01424) 461 446; open April–Oct 10–5, Nov–Mar 11–4; adm*), in the old fishermen's church, has a small collection of real old fishing memorabilia, such as the sailing lugger *Enterprise*. The water-powered **Funicular Railway** (*open summer 10–5.30, winter 11–4*) climbs up East Hill. The old town developed in the valley of the Bourne between the East and West Hills. It's picturesque, particularly **All Saints' Street,** with blue plaques commemorating famous ex-Hastings Men like the Pre-Raphaelite painter Dante Gabriel Rossetti and the 17th-century naval admiral Sir Clowdisley Shovell. On High Street little shops sell bric-a-brac, old furniture and second-hand books. From shabby George Street you can take the **West Hill Railway** (*open summer 10–5.30, winter 11–4*) up to the scanty ruins of **Hastings Castle** and the **1066 Story** (***t** (01424) 781 112; open Nov–Feb 11–3.30, Mar 11–4, April–mid-July 9–5, mid-July–Aug 9–5.30, Sept 9–5, Oct 11–4; adm*) and **St Clement's Caves** (***t** (01424) 422 964; open winter 11–4.30, summer 10–5.30; adm exp*), a network of tunnels used by smugglers for storing contraband.

Battle

It's not often the average civilian can say he is going to Battle. The small town is on the site of the Battle of Hastings. The gatehouse of Battle Abbey faces a picturesque market square, and the infamous battlefield is preserved, a slab marking the spot where King Harold Godwinson died. The battle changed the course of English history: English people were left speaking the wrong language in their own country. After the Norman Conquest, the site of the annihilation of Saxon-Danish England was turned into a monument to the new king. **Battle Abbey** was built by William the Conqueror as an act of atonement for the bloodshed, a ploy to win acceptance from the people. The abbots were among the greatest baronial landowners in Sussex, their estates amounting to a sixth *rape*. At the Dissolution, the abbey went to Henry VIII's master of the horse, Sir Anthony Browne, who knocked down the church and converted the abbot's lodgings into a swanky new house. **Hastings Battlefield and Abbey Visitor Centre** (***t** (01424) 773 792; open April–Sept 10–6, Oct 10–5, Nov–Mar 10–4; adm*) now

Getting There and Around

From the M25 by **car** follow the A21 all the way south to Hastings.

Regular **trains** run from London Victoria to Hastings via Lewes. To reach Battle, trains from Hastings take 15 minutes, or you can catch a **bus** from the train station, which takes 35 minutes and drops you outside the abbey.

Tourist Information

Hastings: Queens Square, **t** (01424) 781 111, *www.hastings.gov.uk. Open Mon–Fri 8.30–6.15, Sat 9–5, Sun 10–4.30.*

Battle: Battle Abbey Gatehouse, High Street, **t** (01424) 773 721, *www.battletown.co.uk. Open daily summer 9.30–5.30, winter 10–4.*

Where to Stay and Eat

Hastings t (01424) –

Royal Victoria Hotel, Marina, St Leonards-on-Sea (short walk from Old Town), **t** 445 544, *www.royalvichotel.co.uk* (*very expensive*). Grand old hotel on the seafront with 52 rooms. First-floor English/French restaurant overlooks the Channel.

Lionsdown House, 116 High Street, *www.lionsdownhouse.co.uk*, **t** 420 802 (*moderate*). Attractive old building with three bedrooms.

Lavender and Lace, 106 All Saints Street, **t** 716 290, *lavendarlace1066@aol.com* (*moderate*). Long-established B&B in 16th-century building with two rooms to let and an oak-beamed old-world character. Short walk from fishing harbour. *Closed Jan–Mar.*

64 High Street, 64 High Street, **t** 712 584 (*cheap*). Modest, friendly B&B in Old Town with two double rooms and shared bathroom. No smoking.

There are masses of pubs in the Old Town, many older than even their façades suggest. Restaurants too, including a Spanish tapas bar and a French bistro.

The Stag, All Saints Street, **t** 425 734. Traditional pub, offering Shepherd Neame ales like Spitfire and Golding, with open fire on cool nights, and live music Tues, Wed and Thurs including folk. Small restaurant (*moderate*) offers dishes from tagliatelle to rump steak.

The Coach House Restaurant, All Saints Street, **t** 428 080 (*moderate*). Classy, friendly place with an unpretentious menu: fillet of beef with mushroom and brandy sauce or pork tenderloin with Kentish apple fritter and local cider and mustard sauce. Local ingredients include British cheeses with home-made apple chutney, and fish bought off the Stade. *Open Thurs–Sun.*

Porters Wine Bar, 56 High Street, **t** 427 000 (*moderate*). Pleasant, dark woody bar with prints, mirrors and the odd trumpet on the wall, selling foreign bottled beers and reasonably priced wines. Bistro menu includes smoked cod and broccoli gratin, beef and Guinness pie or fresh fish. *Closed Sun lunch.*

Pissarro's, 10 South Terrace (opposite main shopping centre), **t** 421 363, *www.pissarros.*

occupies the abbey gatehouse. There are no battle scars; the thing to grasp is that the Saxons had the strategic advantage at the top of the hill, but the Normans won through a cunning ruse (or superior tactics, depending which side you're on).

Pevensey

Pevensey has an old town, a modern town and a ramshackle shingle beach with a mix of sunbathers, dog-walkers and fishermen. The old town is a mile inland, backed by the low-lying Pevensey Levels, full of history and marsh atmosphere. It began as the Roman port of *Anderida*. William the Conqueror led his army ashore at Pevensey in 1066 and camped overnight within the walls of the old Roman fortress. To secure the beachhead, a castle was built, and later rebuilt in stone. In the Middle Ages, the town outside its walls became a limb of the Cinque Ports until the harbour silted up. Today old Pevensey is a classic one-street town: the High Street leads to the castle *co.uk* (*cheap*). Lively, swinging pub with live blues and jazz Thurs–Sat eves and Sun afternoon. The restaurant offers a mix of African, Moroccan, Mexican, Greek and Spanish dishes. Also 17 rooms to let, some en-suite.

Blue Dolphin, High Street (off George Street), **t** 425 778 (*cheap*). Well-known fresh fish and chip shop.

Cinque Port Arms, All Saints Street, **t** 444 758 (*cheap*). Cosy and full of character. No food, just booze including Harvey and Fullers ESB.

The FILO (First In Last Out), High Street, **t** 425 079 (*cheap*). Pub with character offering home-brewed ales, including Crofters, Cardinal and Gold. Lunches Mon–Sat include roasts, ploughman's and fish.

Battle t (01424) –

The Pilgrim's, 1 High Street, **t** 772 314 (*expensive*). Opposite the abbey gates, built in the 15th century as a guesthouse for the abbey. Excellent new restaurant and bar already listed in the *Good Food Guide*. All the produce comes from local farms, market gardens and kitchen gardens: Hastings fish, Brightling venison, Tenterden and Seddlescombe wines. Cheaper lunch menu, or you can have afternoon tea of home-made scones and strawberries, or just a drink at the bar.

The Food Rooms, 53–5 High Street, **t** 775 520 (*moderate*). Deli-cum-restaurant/café owned by The Pilgrim's, with same line in local produce and same chef. Stock up here for a picnic or have a snack: soup and bread, local cheeses or stir-fried king prawns.

The George Hotel, 23 High Street, **t** 774 466, *www.thegeorge-battle.com* (*moderate*). Georgian coaching inn with 23 bedrooms that are gradually being refurbished by new owners. New bar and restaurant in old cottage and stables at back promise to do well too.

The Bull Inn and Wine Bar, 27 High Street, **t** 775 171 (*cheap*). A 17th-century coaching inn built from Battle Abbey stone, and haunt of the infamous Hawkhurst Gang of Sussex smugglers, with inglenook fireplace. Now plays live blues and jazz on Tues and Thurs evenings and Sun afternoon and can put you up for the night in one of five slightly old-fashioned bedrooms.

The King's Head, off High Street, **t** 772 317 (*cheap*). Good, traditional pub for pint of Ruddles or Directors, or pub grub.

High Hedges, North Trade Road (A271 from Battle towards Eastbourne), **t** 774 140 (*cheap*). Pleasant 18th-century family house, 10 minutes' walk from town.

Entertainment

Hastings

White Rock Theatre, White Rock, Seafront (opposite the pier), **t** 781 000. Hosts touring productions including musicals, pop groups, comedians, tribute bands and opera. Café.

The Stables Theatre and Art Gallery, The Bourne, **t** 423 221. Top-notch am dram includes Christmas panto.

gateway past flint cottages, pub and the old church of St Nicholas, the patron saint of sailors. **Pevensey Castle** (***t*** *(01323) 762 604, www.english-heritage.org.uk; open April–Sept 10–6, Oct 10–5, Nov–Mar Wed–Sun 10–4; adm*) is on the site of one of the chain of Saxon Shore Forts. The impressive moated and drum-towered medieval castle stands within the old Roman walls, which still stand to about 30ft.

Herstmonceux Castle

t *(01323) 833 816; gardens open April–Sept 10–5, Oct 10–6; guided tours of castle Sun–Fri (call ahead to book); adm.*

Three miles north of Pevensey, magnificent Herstmonceux Castle was built by Roger de Feinnes in the 15th century. Until recently it sheltered the Royal Greenwich Observatory, which moved here to escape the bright lights of London.

The Battle of Hastings, 1066

There was no clear successor to Edward the Confessor in 1066, but three claimants. Harold Hardrada, King of Norway, was a descendant of Cnut (994–1035). William (Guillaume) the Bastard was a cousin of the late King. Both had better claims to the throne than Harold Godwinson, the most powerful earl in the kingdom, but not a royal. Both rivals pressed their claims in the same week in October 1066. First came Harold Hardrada with 300 Viking ships and 12,000 men, marching through the north of England and taking the heads of the northern lords as souvenirs. Godwinson raced thousands of men nearly 200 miles in four days to meet him at Stamford Bridge. He arrived earlier than expected and tore the Viking army to pieces. A day later, William set sail for the south coast of England. Harold's army trudged back down the Great North Road to London, planning to cut William off before he could reach the forest track into Kent and London. Harold's army consisted of 5,000 noble men, 13,000 farmers and a hardcore elite of a few thousand professional soldiers trained to use the double-handled axe. They commanded the high ground, forcing the Normans to fight uphill. William fought with warhorses and archers, while Harold's men were on foot with swords and axes. The Norman strategy was one of attrition, alternating volleys of arrows with horseback assaults. The decisive moment came when William's cavalry charged and swerved at the last moment, giving the impression of a long-awaited break in the Norman ranks. Saxon organization broke down and the Norman knights burst through the wall of shields at full gallop. Harold took an arrow in the eye. The English fled into the forest pursued by horsemen. All this is recounted in the Bayeux Tapestry, but you have to cross the Channel to see that.

1066 Country Walk

The 31-mile-walk follows in the footsteps of William the Conqueror after he landed at Pevensey on 28 September 1066. The route between Pevensey and Rye includes Herstmonceux Castle, Battle Abbey, and an optional detour to Hastings. There are way-markers but you will need a map (*OS Explorer 124: Hastings & Bexhill*). The going is easy, through the low-lying Pevensey Levels and valleys of the Tillingham and Brede. You can catch a train back to your starting point (Pevensey or Rye) at the end.

The South Coast: Eastbourne and Around

Eastbourne with its pier and grand hotels is an archetypal Victorian seaside resort, at the foot of **Beachy Head**. On the downs to the west are the chalk figure of the **Long Man of Wilmington**, the Bloomsbury Group's country houses and a couple of pretty downland villages. East of Eastbourne, you are back in 1066 Country.

Eastbourne

Eastbourne was developed by William Cavendish, Earl of Burlington, who owned the land at the foot of the downs. It took off in 1851, when he became the 7th Duke of Devonshire and one of the richest men in England. There's a statue of him at the sea end of Devonshire Place. Nowadays it is to the long-stay hotels on the seafront that characters in Terence Rattigan plays come to escape failed marriages, but on sunny days the atmosphere of boiled-cabbage drear evaporates, the brass bands come out to play and visitors promenade with ice creams. The **pier** is the hallmark of the Victorian resort, with its blue and white fairy-tale domes that shimmer into ordinariness as you approach. At its end is a Martello Tower. In the old town, the **Towner Gallery** (*relocating to a new building near the Congress Theatre;* **t** *(01323) 417 961; open April–Oct Tues–Sat 12–5, Sun 2–5, Nov–Mar closes at 4; adm free*), has 21 Victorian genre paintings, a room devoted to Eric Ravilious (1903–42), watercolours, wood engravings and Wedgwood designs.

Eastbourne Downland

Walk or drive up to the Beachy Head car park, where the South Downs meet the sea. From here you can climb down stepped cliffs to the sea. Further along the cliff path is **Beachy Head**, a dramatic 600ft cliff topped by an old red-and-white striped lighthouse. The name is an anglicization of *Beau Chef* – beautiful headland. It's falling into the sea at a rate of 1.6ft a year. The headland continues west to **Seaford Head** in a ribbon of white cliffs known as the **Seven Sisters**.

The South Coast Resorts

Apart from Beachy Head and the Seven Sisters, the Sussex coastline is unromantic. It's one long, straight shingle beach, with the odd sandy bit. This unexceptional coast is lined with 18th- and 19th-century white stucco houses with bay windows. In the 1840s, the *Times* declared that 'so infallible and unchanging are the attractions of the ocean that it is enough for any place just to stand on the shore.' No one would have said this before the 18th-century resort boom. When seaside propagandist Dr Russell of Lewes started sending people to the coast for their health, the cry went out 'Oh I do like to be beside the seaside,' and the holidaying classes took up the cause. Everyone who could afford it trooped down to the south coast to drink the water and immerse themselves in it. Margate was the first sea-bathing resort, then Brighton, in 1736, and in the 1750s Seaford, Eastbourne, Littlehampton and Worthing. They built concert halls, libraries, assembly rooms and promenades, squares, crescents and terraces of housing. Each resort got a reputation: Brighton was racy, Eastbourne sedate, Hastings romantic and Bexhill convalescent. Bognor Regis never took off. Developed as a classy resort for royalty, it achieved a measure of immortality as the place where George V came to die, but his last words, 'Bugger Bognor', did for it. By 1770 Margate, Brighton and Weymouth, in Dorset, were the most successful resorts. For a decade Brighton was the fastest-growing town in Britain: in 1837, 50,000 people arrived on public stage coaches; 10 years later the railway brought as many in a week. It set the pace. In the 1890s Londoners began to buy holiday homes on the coast based on a style imported from British India, called bungalows. Developers copied them everywhere and the whole thing went downmarket. Many of the resorts became retirement havens. Brighton has recently enjoyed a renaissance as a metropolitan, bohemian centre by the sea.

Getting There and Around

By **car**, the A22 goes all the way to Eastbourne from the M25.

There are one or two **trains** an hour from London Victoria to Eastbourne via Gatwick and Lewis.

The Cookmere Cycle Company, The Granary Barn, Seven Sisters Country Park, near Seaford, **t** (01323) 870 310. *Open daily 10–6, winter closed Mon.* Bicycle and canoe hire.

Tourist Information

Eastbourne: Cornfield Road, **t** (01323) 411 400. *Open Easter–Sept Mon–Sat 9.30–5, July–Aug also Sun 10–1; Oct–Easter 9.30–4.*

1812 Nights at the Redoubt Fortresses, **t** (01323) 412 000, take place every Wed and Fri at 8pm: military band concerts build up to Tchaikovsky's 1812 overture as a grand finale, with cannon fire and fireworks.

Military bands also play in the **bandstand** at weekends, daily in high summer, at 11am and 3pm. Look out for 'Sunday night at the Proms' concerts too, where the Elgar classics are given a run for their money.

Where to Stay

Eastbourne t (01323) –

There are a number of guesthouses and country hotels scattered around the Eastbourne Downs.

The Grand Hotel, King Edward's Parade, **t** 412 345, *www.grandeastbourne.com* (*very expensive*). Enormous seafront hotel with 152 rooms and two restaurants. Serves the best afternoon tea, including scones, sandwiches and a pot of tea. At dinner, men must wear a jacket and tie.

Hydro Hotel, Mount Road, **t** 720 643, *www.hydrohotel.com* (*very expensive*). Further along the parade from the Grand, pebble-dashed façade belies sumptuous interior. You can have afternoon tea beside the croquet lawn and enjoy sea views from the bedrooms.

Lansdowne Hotel, King Edward's Parade, **t** 725 174, *www.lansdowne-hotel.co.uk* (*expensive*). Large seafront hotel opposite the Western Lawns with 110 bedrooms, including 32 singles, and sea views. Has been in the same family since 1912 and remains independently run. Traditional English restaurant and period décor.

Chatsworth Hotel, Grand Parade, **t** 411 016, *www.chatsworth-hotel.com* (*expensive*). Traditional family-run seafront hotel with old fashioned lift, period décor and sea views from the 47 bedrooms.

Riverdale House, Seaford Road, Alfriston, **t** 871 038, *www.riverdalehouse.co.uk* (*moderate*). Perched on hill next to identical house (built for two brothers in late 1800s) on southern edge of village with lovely views of downs and Cuckmere Valley. *Closed Dec.*

Chalk Farm Hotel, Coopers Hill, Willington (2 miles out of Eastbourne), **t** 503 800, *www.chalkfarm.org.uk* (*cheap*). Ivy-clad hotel with restaurant. Ask about the connection with George Orwell's *Animal Farm*.

Eating Out

Most seafront hotels do a good cup of tea. Carlisle Road is full of restaurants and café-bars. There are no fewer than three popular Italian restaurants on Cornfield Terrace.

Dukes, 11 Carlisle Road, **t** 737 399 (*moderate*). Organic meat and salads from the owner's farm in Heathfield: lamb with mint sauce and roast duck with cabbage. *Closed Mon.*

Tiger Inn, East Dean, **t** 423 209 (*moderate*). Walk up to this traditional pub on the Downs overlooking flinty downland village East Dean's green (about 3 miles). High-quality food made from local ingredients like Hastings fish, downland meat and eggs. No bookings for dinner, no credit cards, no mobile phones, big wine list, Harvey's Best, no children inside and 'subtle dogs' only.

Martini Restaurant, Cornfield Terrace, **t** 736 635 (*moderate*). Smarter Italian restaurant with pasta dishes, veal and beef, fish, duck and lamb. *Closed Mon.*

Pomodoro and Mozzarella Pizzeria Ristorante, Cornfield Terrace, **t** 733 800 (*cheap*). Friendly, bright Italian restaurant where you can get pizza, pasta, meat, fish and vegetables.

Pizzeria Italia, Cornfield Terrace, **t** 737 177 (*cheap*). Cheerful, with plastic tablecloths and limited pizza and pasta menu.

Martello Towers

One hundred and three Martello Towers were built along the coast from Seaford in Sussex to Aldeburgh in Suffolk between 1805 and 1812, in response to the threat of an invasion by Napoleon. They were modelled on a gun tower at Martello in Corsica which had repelled the Royal Navy in 1794. Each was armed with a long-range cannon. The Martello coastline was the first part of Britain to be mapped using triangulation, the start of Ordnance Survey.

The Long Man of Wilmington

The best place to see the Long Man is from the car park of ruined 14th-century Wilmington priory, a few miles north of Eastbourne. He is one of two chalk giants in Britain (the other is Cerne Abbas in Dorset, *see* p.269), cut into the steep escarpment of Windover Hill for no apparent reason. He stands 230ft tall, arms outstretched and each holding a staff. He was redrawn in 1874, but his true age is unknown.

Alfriston

The downland village of Alfriston on the Cuckmere River is all charm with its narrow main road, stumpy old market cross, 14th-century beamed pubs and village green. On the far side of the green stands the church and next to it the picturesque, thatched **Clergy House** (***t*** *(01323) 870 001; open Mar weekends 11–4, April–Oct Sat–Thurs 10–5, Nov–Dec Wed–Sun 11–4; adm*), the first building bought by the National Trust, in 1896. The South Downs Way passes through, and even if you're not walking the Way you could climb up onto the downs for views of Cuckmere Haven. Back in the village, the old George Inn with its smuggling connections serves real ale. The brick-tiled Old Saddlers Tea Shop, half café and half music shop, plays Edith Piaf.

Lewes and Around

The county town of Lewes looks and feels like a traditional old county town. It's small enough to get around on foot, boasts a handsome flint castle, fine architecture in its High Street, Harvey's Brewery down by the river and important civic buildings. It started life as a medieval new town around the castle of the Warennes, at the centre of one of the five feudal *rapes* of the Norman Conquest. Daniel Defoe described its setting as 'the most romantic I ever saw'. Its buildings are peppered with blue plaques commemorating famous residents. Lewes is an ideal base for an exploration of the Bloomsbury Group houses, including Virginia Woolf's in Rodmell and Charleston Farmhouse, tenanted by Duncan Grant and Vanessa Bell.

Lewes

You will find Britain's oldest outdoor pool, or lido, in Lewes, dating back to 1860. Six hundred years earlier, **Simon de Montfort** defeated and captured Prince Edward (future Edward I) at the **Battle of Lewes** in 1264. The next day Henry III signed the famous *Mise of Lewes*, dictated by De Montfort, advocating that power be vested in

Getting There and Around

By **car**, Lewes is just off the A27 Brighton to Eastbourne road. The A275 and A26 roads, linking East Grinstead and Tunbridge Wells with the south coast, also pass through Lewes.

Regular **train** services from London Victoria to Lewes take 1 hour. Trains also run from Brighton, Eastbourne and Newhaven.

Tourist Information

Lewes: 187 High Street, **t** (01273) 483 448. *Open Mon–Fri 9–5, summer also Sat 10–5 and Sun 10–2, winter Sat 10–2.*

Where to Stay

Lewes t (01273) –

Shelleys Hotel, High Street, **t** 472 361, *www.shelleys-hotel.com* (*very expensive*). Countryhouse hotel associated with the poet Shelley's family, in a beautiful 17th-century manor house; 19 extremely comfortable bedrooms. Restaurant ('country-house style with modern accent') has won numerous awards.

White Hart Hotel, High Street, **t** 473 794, *www.whitehartlewes.co.uk* (*moderate*). Handsome stuccoed coaching inn garlanded with flower baskets. A blue plaque explains that 'Thomas Paine 1737–1809 here expounded his revolutionary politics' in the Headstrong Club. Of the 52 comfortable bedrooms, 33 are in a new block. All mod cons and carvery.

Berkeley House Hotel, 2 Albion Street (just off School Hill), **t** 476 057, *www.berkeleyhousehotel.co.uk* (*moderate*). Three smart, comfortable rooms in this rather snooty establishment.

Miller's B&B, 134 High Street, **t** 475 631, *www.hometown.aol.com/millers134* (*moderate*). Pretty 16th-century townhouse at top end of High Street.

Number 6, Gundreda Road, **t** 472 106, *www.stayinlewes.co.uk* (*cheap*). Delightful family home in quiet surroundings 10 minutes' walk from town centre, with three rooms to let.

Eating Out

Circa, 145 High Street, **t** 471 777 (*moderate*). Modern, trendy glass-fronted restaurant. Menu includes six wild mushroom tortellini and squash velouté. Excellent reputation. *Closed Mon, and Sun eves.*

Lazatti's, 17 Market Street, **t** 479 539 (*moderate*). Informal, bright, cheery Italian restaurant. Large menu includes pizza and pasta as well as meat, fish and vegetarian. Also coffee and pastries. *Closed Sun.*

Pailin Thai, 20 Station Street, **t** 473 906 (*moderate*). Excellent Thai food. *Closed Mon.*

Snow Drop Inn, South Street, **t** 471 018 (*moderate*). Award-winning vegetarian food in relaxed theatrical atmosphere complete with masks, murals, plastic grapes, flowers and candles.

Bills, Cliffe High Street, **t** 476 918 (*cheap*). Large, open-fronted grocer's-cum-café just over the bridge, its wooden shelves stacked with fruit, veg and jars of pickles. Menu includes pizza with green herb salad, and coffee with hot milk. *Closed Sun.*

Pelham Arms, High Street, **t** 476 149 (*cheap*). Great atmosphere and food including scampi and chips for lunch and Pelham Pie (steak, ale and mushroom) for dinner. *No food Mon eve.*

Lewes Arms, Mount Place (off Fisher Street), **t** 473 152 (*cheap*). The real thing: a small, crowded pub with several small rooms around bar. People in corridor served through a hatch. Real ales include Green King and Harveys.

an assembly of knights, churchmen and burgesses. He was the first advocate of parliamentary rule in England. Five hundred years later, the same issues of democracy were debated by writer and revolutionary Thomas Paine at the meetings of the Headstrong Club in the **White Hart** on Lewes High Street. Eighteen months after leaving Lewes for the American colonies, Paine wrote his first radical work, *Common Sense*, picked out by George Washington as catalyst for the independence struggle, followed by *The Rights of Man* and *The Age of Reason*. Paine was one of two foreign contributors to the drafting of the French Constitution. In 1987 the Headstrong Club was revived; it now meets fortnightly in the Royal Oak. The old surgery of Dr Richard Russell is on the High Street; his writings on the medicinal uses of seawater led to the surge in popularity of seaside resorts. Gideon Mantel, who lived opposite, was an early dinosaur hunter known as the 'Wizard of the Weald'. He not only named iguanodon, but mapped out the earliest chronology for the Age of Reptiles (now known as the Mesozoic Era), at a time when both theologians and scientists still believed that the world was only a few thousand years old and the first humans were called Adam and Eve. Mantel's vision of southern England roamed by monsters such as megalosaurus and iguanodon (published in 1831) was deeply shocking. Virginia Woolf spent some time in Lewes before buying a house in Rodmell.

The High Street is the town's main axis, spanning the River Ouse, and lined by white weatherboard and flint cobbled houses. The castle is on the west hill. Numerous little shops sell prints, second-hand books and antiques. Chief of these are the **Star Brewery Workshops** (*t (01273) 480 218; open Mon–Sat 10.30–5.30*) on Castle Ditch Lane, with its art gallery and craft workshops, and the more touristy **Old Needlemakers Craft Centre** (*t (01273) 472 322; open Mon–Fri 9.30–5.30, Sun 10–4*), off Market Lane (pick up an illustrated map of the town from the tourist information centre). There are two museums in Lewes. On Castlegate, a pretty paved lane leading to the castle gatehouse, is the **Barbican House Museum** (*t (01273) 486 290; open Tues–Sat 10–5.30, Sun–Mon 11–5.30; adm*), where local archaeology is displayed alongside a library full of books about Sussex, and the journals of Gideon Mantel. The diaries are nicely human – excited references to fresh boxes of fossils from Wealden quarries, pride at being visited by great fossil-hunters like William Buckland and Charles Lyell, and embittered asides about his arch-rival Richard Owen (who coined the name 'dinosaur'). The museum ticket also allows you to climb up the motte to the ruined keep.

Mantel's house, **Castle Place**, is next to Castlegate on the High Street. Its pilasters with ammonite capitals are just the thing for England's leading dinosaur hunter. Further along High Street is 15th-century **Bull House**, where Thomas Paine, 'founder of American independence with pen and sword', lived for eight years, working as an excise officer and writing revolutionary pamphlets. Down cobbled Keer Street is the former suburb of Southover, which grew up around the old priory. At its foot stands **Southover Grange**, a 16th-century mansion built from the stones of the demolished priory, with a blue plaque commemorating diarist John Evelyn (1620–1706), who stayed here when 'a pupil at the grammar school'.

Anne of Cleves House (*t (01273) 474 610; open Tues–Sat 10–5, Mar–Oct also Sun–Mon 11–5; adm*) is further down on Southover Street. This old building of gables and hanging tiles is full of dark oak furniture, heavy beams and sturdy chimney breasts, as well as displays on local history and Wealden industries. Henry VIII's fourth wife never lived here, but it was given to her as part of her divorce package. You can walk to the ruins of the old **Lewes Priory**, the English headquarters of the French Cluniacs (*guided tours leave from Anne of Cleves House Tues and Thurs 2.30; adm*).

Monk's House

t (01892) 890 651, www.nationaltrust.org.uk; open April–Oct Wed and Sat 2–5.30; adm.

Two miles south of Lewes at the end of a flint-walled lane in the downland village of Rodmell is the pretty white weatherboard cottage of Virginia and Leonard Woolf, who moved here in 1919. Virginia couldn't resist the fruit trees around the house and called it 'an unpretending house, long and low, a house of many doors'. Her study was built at the end of the garden, French windows opening on to the Ouse Valley. From there you can follow her steps down to the river, where she drowned herself on 28 March 1941, the pockets of her fur coat weighted with stones, while Leonard was working in the house. Her ashes were buried under an elm tree on the edge of the garden.

The Abergavenny Arms in Rodmell is a popular stop-off for walkers.

Charleston Farmhouse

t (01323) 811 265; open April–June and Sept–Oct Wed–Sun 2–6, July–Aug Wed–Sat 11.30–6, Sun 2–6; adm.

At the end of a farm track off the A27 Lewes–Eastbourne road, at the foot of Firle Beacon, you find Charleston. The farmhouse is a monument to the creative impulses of the Bloomsbury Group, who gathered here around Vanessa and Clive Bell, Duncan Grant and their children (Maynard Keynes came so often he had his own bedroom). Inside, every surface is decorated by hand, including filing boxes, toilet seats and furniture. The influences are French Post-Impressionism, Italian fresco painting and folksy southern European art. Vanessa Bell, Grant and Roger Fry did most of it, while others mucked in. On the walls hang portraits of the family and friends (painted and photographed by each other), snuck in among them the odd Sickert or Renoir. There are plates designed by Grant, curtains painted by the children Quentin and Angelica, and Clive Bell's bookcases decorated by Grant. Fry made one or two small architectural changes, opening up fireplaces, converting rooms and designing the studio for Grant and Vanessa Bell. Initially Charleston was a holiday cottage, later a permanent home. Every room has a history, such as the Garden Room where Vanessa Bell told her daughter Angelica that Grant, not Clive Bell, was her father. Grant stayed on until 1978, outliving the rest of his generation, and his daughter Angelica remained until 1980, when the Charleston Trust was formed to restore the somewhat shabby house.

Berwick Church

Berwick Church, 3 miles down the road from Charleston, is a tiny flint church at the end of a long lane. The religious murals inside, painted by Duncan Grant, Vanessa Bell and Quentin Bell, are the last public work of the Bloomsburys, commissioned during the Second World War. The effect is cheerful and bright. An actress friend of Angelica posed for the Angel Gabriel, and the angels above the chancel arch appear to be wearing fitted dresses. The nearby Cricketers Arms is a good pit stop.

The Bloomsbury Group

The Bloomsbury Group brought bohemia and a reflection of modernism to England. At the heart of this unconventional group of upper-class artists, writers and philosophers, who lived in and around Bloomsbury in the early 20th century, were the sisters **Virginia Woolf** and **Vanessa Bell**. Virginia was the intense one, constantly in search of a room of her own or on the brink of suicide, whereas Vanessa was the Mrs Dalloway of the group, hospitable and warm, filling her house with children and eccentric guests. She married **Clive Bell,** had a love affair with **Roger Fry** and formed a relationship of some sort with the painter **Duncan Grant** at Charleston. Clive Bell and Fry were art critics and historians, who introduced Post-Impressionism into Britain by exhibiting Gauguin, Matisse and Van Gogh in several major shows in 1910 and 1912. Fry, Vanessa Bell and Grant set up the **Omega Workshops** in Bloomsbury in 1913, employing young artists to decorate and design furniture, textiles and decorative schemes in the spirit of William Morris. In 1917 the Woolfs (Virginia and Leonard) set up the **Hogarth Press** in their basement, publishing **T.S. Eliot**, **E.M. Forster**, **Vita Sackville-West** and anyone else they approved of, while Vanessa did the cover designs. Other members of the group included the economist **John Maynard Keynes**, who moved into the farmhouse of Tilton, about half a mile away from Charleston, with his wife in 1925 (and also had an affair with Grant), Forster, Eliot and the writer **Lytton Strachey**, a cousin and yet another one-time lover of Grant. **Angelica Bell** married her father's ex-lover **David Garnett**, the author of *Aspects of Love*. The group was introverted, socially and professionally, hanging out together on the Sussex downs, and painting the same views and each other, publishing, exhibiting and reviewing each other's work, and writing each other's biographies. They attracted both admiration and envy, of course. After spending a weekend with the Bloomsburys, D.H. Lawrence said he 'was nearly driven mad and dreamt that black beetles were attacking him'.

Brighton

Brighton earned itself an early reputation for 'idleness, sensuality, and nearly all the ramifications of social imposture.' The town became an issue of morality, with George, Prince of Wales, at the heart of the debate. Brighton's fashionable reputation was already established by the time of his first visit in 1783, but his liking for the place stimulated a flurry of Regency architecture and licentiousness. Now the assembly rooms have been replaced with nightclubs, but coffee houses still proliferate and Brighton wears its historical obsession with lifestyle and self-gratification as lightly as it did two centuries ago.

Few English seaside resorts have reinvented themselves quite like Brighton, so metropolitan it has been dubbed London by the Sea. The universities bring students into town, along with trendy shops, cafés and clubs. Brighton also has a famous gay scene, the hub of which is Kemp Town. The town has long attracted artists, too, but also has a gargantuan homeless population. Brighton and its smart residential suburb, Hove, gained city status in 2000. It's an almost obligatory day or weekend trip

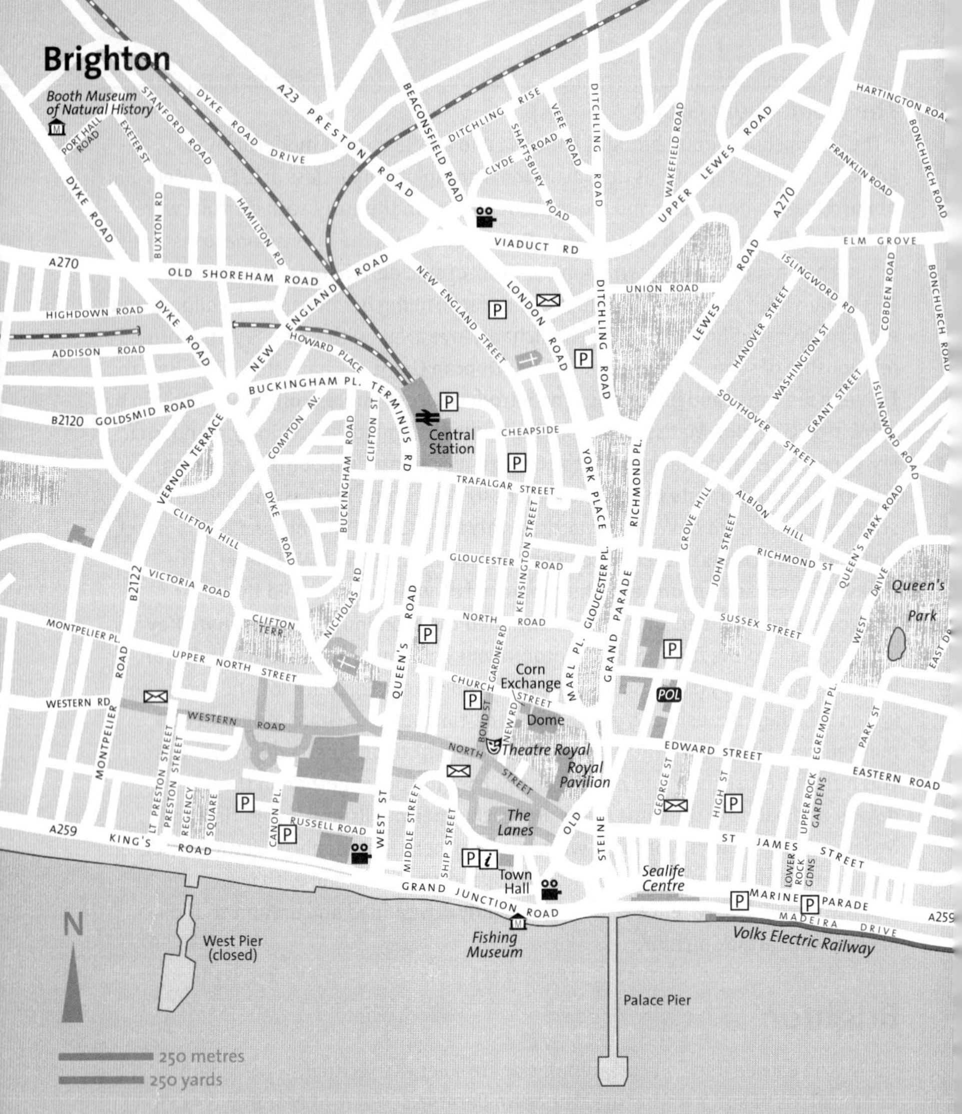

for Londoners aged 18 to 40 – those of them who don't live there already. Ken Livingstone, Mayor of London, has a house here. The French Surrealists loved Brighton for its three-sided seafront squares, with one side open to the sea (and the imagination). But the town is better known for its seamy reputation, as depicted in Graham Greene's *Brighton Rock* and the 1980s film, *Mona Lisa*.

Orientation

The main roads into Brighton – the A23 from London or A27 from Lewes – converge on the seafront at the Royal Pavilion, one of the silliest buildings in England.

Old Steine is your best orientation point, at the end of the two main roads into the town (the A23 and A27) and down the hill from the railway station, although you

Getting There and Around

By **car**, the M23 connects Brighton to the M25 in about 45 minutes. From London allow 2 hours. The fast **train** from London Victoria takes 50 minutes and the National Express coach from London Victoria takes 2 hours.

Tourist Information

Brighton: 10 Bartholomew Square, **t** 0906 7112255, *www.visitbrighton.com*. Press 4 to speak to someone; it's a premium-rate call. *Open Mon–Fri 9–5, Sat 10–5, Sun 10–4.*

Brighton International Festival, **t** (01273) 700 747. Hundreds of events theatrical and musical over first three weeks in May.

Saltdean Lido, Saltdean Park Road, **t** (01273) 880 616. A beautiful art-deco open air pool resembling a cruise liner, just off the main road east of Brighton, between Rottingdean and Saltdean. *Open May–Sept daily 10–6*, weather permitting.

Where to Stay

Brighton t (01273) –

Check *www.tourist.brighton.co.uk/ accommodation* for alternatives.

The Grand, King's Road, 224 300, *www. grandbrighton.co.uk* (*luxury*). The most palatial hotel in town, with 200 rooms, and worth the experience if you can afford it. Prime ministers and celebrities stay here. Classical style with lovely staircase; rooms with sea views from wrought-iron balconies. The hotel was built in 1867, and ripped apart by an IRA bomb in a 1983 attack on Prime Minister Margaret Thatcher and her Conservative party, but has now been restored to its former glory.

Hilton Brighton, West Pier, King's Road, **t** 775 432, *www.hilton.com* (*very expensive*). Another large, grand Victorian hotel on the seafront (built in 1890).

Old Ship Hotel, King's Road, **t** 329 001, *www.paramount-hotels.co.uk* (*very expensive*). Large seafront hotel in the midst of bustling cafés, bars, antique shops and boutiques. Its origins go back to 1559 and in the 19th century it was a favourite haunt of the wealthy, the aristocracy and smugglers alike. The Prince Regent was a regular. Brasserie-style café on the ground floor. Most of its 152 bedrooms have a sea view.

Paskins Town House, 18–19 Charlotte Street, **t** 601 203, *www.paskins.co.uk* (*expensive*). On one of Brighton's pretty Regency streets with wrought-iron balconies and bow fronts, off Upper St James' Street, Paskins is an environmentally friendly hotel, which also has awards from The Vegetarian Society. A Grade II listed building, one of a row of tall Georgian townhouses in a conservation area that runs off Marine Parade. Tasteful bedrooms and sturdy showers. Excellent organic breakfasts, using local produce: home-made tarragon and sun-dried tomato sausages; nut, seed and spice fritters. Bar also serves sandwiches, tea and coffee.

Hotel Twenty One, 21 Charlotte Street, **t** 686 450 (*expensive*). Brisk, friendly and business-like small hotel in prime position at the top of Regency Square. Seven of its 12 rooms have sea view across the lawns.

New Steine Hotel, 12/a New Steine, Marine Parade, **t** 681 546 (*expensive*). One of the smaller private hotels in Brighton's original town square of 18th-century Georgian terraced houses. Welcoming atmosphere and lounge with newspapers, magazines, books and board games. Parisian bistro serves traditional French dishes (*cheap*).

probably won't want to spend much time here. The long green stretching down its valley to the sea ends up at the **Palace Pier**. Most of the action is west of the pier, around the tangled **Lanes** and the regimented **North Laine** with its trendy shops and bars. The road along the seafront is lined with hotels, some quite grand. Steps lead down to the beach, lined with café-bars and nightclubs under the old fishermen's arches. **Madeira Drive**, often thronged with bikers, extends east to the Marina. Half a mile west, around Brunswick Square, you enter **Hove**, a more placid, well-to-do suburb

The Prince Regent Hotel, 29 Regency Square, **t** 329 962, *www.princeregent.com* (*expensive*). In another centre for hotels, a classic seafront square opening onto the derelict West Pier. Regency townhouse with elaborate plaster mouldings inside.

Brighton House Hotel, 52 Regency Square, **t** 323 282, *www.brightonhousehotel.co.uk* (*expensive*). A Grade II listed Regency townhouse that shares a curving balcony with the hotel next door. Genteel and friendly. Original fireplaces in some of the 12 rooms, all with power showers. No smoking.

Ascott House Hotel, 21 New Steine, Marine Parade, **t** 688 085 (*moderate*). Sparklingly clean and friendly hotel in a Regency townhouse. Some rooms have sea views.

The Ambassador Hotel, 22–3 New Steine, Marine Parade, **t** 676 869 (*moderate*). Small, comfortable hotel. Rooms at the front have sea views.

Trouville Hotel, 11 New Steine, Marine Parade, **t** 697 384 (*moderate*). Another highly recommended Regency townhouse. Small and select, with delicious breakfasts and personal service.

Adelaide Hotel, 51 Regency Square, **t** 205 286 (*moderate*).A beautiful old-fashioned hotel in an elegant Regency townhouse with bow windows. Welcoming and friendly; 12 pretty bedrooms.

Eating Out

Brighton is full of places to eat and drink. Streets like Preston Street, St James' Street and The Lanes are entirely given over to food. The possibilities are endless, but it is all too easy to end up in one of countless café-bars, eating mediocre ciabatta sandwiches; battered fish and chips on the seafront are probably a better bet, but when they pall, here are some good alternatives.

Restaurants

Terre à Terre, 71 East Street, **t** 729 051 (*moderate*). Lively, award-winning vegetarian restaurant. Café atmosphere, with imaginative global menu. Crispy cakes of fried potato with onion or Jerusalem artichoke mousse. *Closed Mon lunch.*

Gingerman, 21/a Norfolk Square, **t** 326 688 (*moderate*). Modern European restaurant serving bruschetta of baby squid with crispy pancetta followed by fillet of Buchan beef with potato and pea purée or grilled venison with spiced apples and potato and celeriac gratin. *Closed Sun and Mon.*

English's, 29–31 East Street, **t** 327 980 (*moderate*). Here since 1945, on the edge of the Lanes overlooking the main square. Housed in fisherman's cottages, it's an informal, intimate seafood restaurant, proud of its reputation. Oysters or fish of the day.

Regency Restaurant, 131 Kings Road, **t** 325 014 (*moderate*). Traditional English food with locally caught fish a speciality. Always busy, with pavement seating under gas heaters.

Troggs Restaurant, George Street, Kemp Town, **t** 687 821 (*moderate*). Downstairs from Troggs Café, 2 minutes' walk from the pier. Organic vegetarian menu. Spinach and chives frittata with Wensleydale cheese, topped with a lemon and chervil hollandaise followed by aubergine and chick pea chermoula with sweet potato and coriander risotto ball. *Open Wed–Sat eves only.*

Bankers, 116/a Western Road (just beyond Norfolk Square), **t** 328 267 (*cheap*). Worth the walk for Brighton's best fish and chips, which you can eat in or take away to the seafront nearby.

Food For Friends, 17–18 Prince Albert Street, **t** 202 310 (*cheap*). One of the earliest vegetarian restaurants, with a student-canteen atmosphere, serving freshly squeezed juices, organic wines and classic vegetarian fare.

of Brighton with grander squares and crescents, including more than 500 listed buildings, and a quieter beach. **Kemp Town** is the same distance in the other direction – more grand squares and crescents. It's the home of Brighton's gay community; its main commercial thoroughfare is St James' Street, where you find a mix of bars, barbers and grocery stores. The shingle **beach** stretches all along the seafront. The town stretches back from the sea up the downs, getting less interesting as you go.

Moshi Moshi, Opticon, Bartholomew Square, **t** 719 195 (*cheap*). Modern Japanese restaurant and sushi bar with good local reputation. *Closed Mon.*

Kambis, 107 Western Road (main street linking Brighton and Hove, parallel to the seafront), **t** 327 934 (*cheap*). Highly recommended Lebanese restaurant.

Pinocchio, 22 New Road, **t** 677 676 (*cheap*). An Italian restaurant that deserves a mention if only for its long opening hours. Lots of pizzas and pasta dishes.

Al Duomo, 7 Pavilion Buildings, **t** 326 741 (*cheap*). Central, family-run friendly Italian pizzeria and restaurant.

Cafés

The Tin Drum, 43 St James' Street, **t** 624 777 (*cheap*). Big wooden tables and bare boards. Perfect, sunny brunch joint, with full vegetarian or carnivore breakfasts and chips.

The Mock Turtle, Pool Valley, **t** 327 380 (*cheap*). Near the Palace Pier, where students take their mums and dads on Graduation Day. Try the Welsh rarebit, buck rarebit or bacon and bean soup .

Grinder Café, North Lane, Kensington Gardens, **t** 684 426 (*cheap*). The terrace is ideal for people watching.

The De Vere Grand, King's Road (on the central seafront), **t** 224 300 (*cheap*). Buffet breakfast or high tea. You can take your time here, reading newspapers or watching the sea from wicker chairs.

Royal Albion Hotel, 35 Old Steine, **t** 329 202 (*cheap*). Also on the seafront, close to the pier and The Lanes. Breakfast at Jenny's, morning coffee or afternoon tea in the lounge. Featured in *Mona Lisa*.

Cafe Puccino's, 1 Bartholomew's (opposite the Town Hall), **t** 204 656 (*cheap*). Mellow, with comfy sofas on wooden floors and stacks of newspapers and magazines to read. Breakfast, hot chocolate and coffee, a little jazz and friendly service.

The Sanctuary Café, 51–5 Brunswick Street East, **t** 770 006 (*cheap*). Once a church, then a gallery and tearoom, now a relaxed café. Coffee and vegetarian treats, soothing music and local artists' work. Vegan soup with organic soda bread.

The Meeting Place, Brighton and Hove Boundary, Kings Road, **t** 206 417 (*cheap*). A café on the beach, just beyond the West Pier. Breakfast, juices, tea and coffee, toasted sandwiches and cake. *Open 7am–dusk if fine.*

Troggs Café, George Street, Kemp Town, **t** 687 821 (*cheap*). Two minutes' walk from the pier and seafront. All vegetarian and organic; try the hot baked homity pie with melted cheese topping.

Pubs and Bars

The Dorset Street Bar, 28 North Road, **t** 605 423 (*cheap*). A lively, informal bar and restaurant; lovely place to sit outside with a drink on a summer's day. Breakfast, sandwiches, fresh fish, wild boar sausages and so on.

The Colonnade, 10 New Road, **t** 328 728 (*cheap*). Theatre-going pub next to Theatre Royal; 1930s-style décor with dark wood, red curtains and carpet.

Jim Thompson's (by the Sea Life centre), **t** 666 933 (*moderate–cheap*). Somewhat outlandish, and worth popping into, if only for a drink at the bar and a look. Ceiling hung with Indonesian wood carvings, masks and golden suns, Chinese lanterns and illuminated Buddhas. Pacific Rim menu with vegetarian options.

Side Winder, 65 Upper St James' Street (opposite the big church), **t** 679 927 (*cheap*). Excellent for Sunday lunch in winter and light fish lunches in summer.

Alfresco, The Milkmaid Pavilion, King's Road Arches, **t** 206 523 (*cheap*). A pleasant place

Along the Seafront

The Palace Pier

The Palace Pier opened in 1899 – 400 yards of oriental domes and arches, benches and fairground rides. To give you energy for the walk to the end, and ballast for the stomach-churning rides, you can buy bags of donuts from kiosks. Next to the pier on Marine Parade, the **Sealife Centre** (*open 10–5; adm*) occupies the Victorian aquarium.

for a drink on the terrace, and a welcoming Italian seafood restaurant designed to look and feel like a cruise ship. Pizza or pasta and sea views.

The Lion And Lobster, 24 Silwood Street, **t** 327 299 (*cheap*). West of West Pier, traditional, lively, atmospheric pub for all ages, serving standard pub grub.

Entertainment

The Brighton Dome, 29 New Road, **t** 709 709, *www.brighton-dome.org.uk*. The Prince Regent's stables are now a concert venue, re-opened in 2002 after a £22 million refurbishment. The Berlin Philharmonic Orchestra, Jimi Hendrix and the Rolling Stones have all played here and Abba won the Eurovision Song Contest here with 'Waterloo' in 1974. Regency exterior, Art Deco interior and new improved acoustics.

Theatre Royal, New Road, **t** 328 488. Star-studded entertainment at Brighton's pre-West End theatre.

The Komedia Theatre, Gardner Street, **t** 647 100. Drama, comedy and **Curve**, **t** 603 031, a pleasant brasserie and bar.

Gardner Arts Centre, University of Sussex, Falmer, **t** 685 861. Drama, film, comedy and music during academic year (*Sept–July*).

Sallis Benney Theatre, University of Brighton, Grand Parade, **t** 643 010. Music, drama – and lectures.

Duke of York's Cinema, Preston Circus, **t** 602 503. Historic arthouse cinema.

Nightlife

Brighton has a lively club scene. *This is Brighton Magazine*, a free listings magazine you can pick up at Brighton Station or nearby pubs/cafés, or *www.magazine.brighton.co.uk*, are good places to check out what's on. *The Source* is an alternative, or *G-scene* (gay).

Bands play most nights at **The Freebutt**, Phoenix Place, **t** 603 974 and **Concorde 2**, *www.concorde2.co.uk*, on Madeira Drive as well as numerous pubs. The iconic Brighton night is the burlesque cabaret known as **Vavavavoom!** where the crowd as well as the artists are the stars in themed spectacles such as Bollywood nights or Roman orgies. The venue varies; go to *www.vavavavoom.co.uk* for details.

The Honeyclub, King's Road Arches, **t** 202 807. Two rooms by the sea. Different music every night. Hosts super-club brand Cream on Fridays. Dress like the beautiful people.

Wild Fruit at Creation, West Street, **t** 321 628. Gay and gorgeous. Uplifting house, techno and garage first Sunday of every month. Dress gregarious.

Volks Club, Madeira Drive (by the beach), **t** 682 828. Reggae, jungle, jazz, funk, house and hip hop.

The Joint, West Street, **t** 770 095. Try Thursday nights for Dynamite Boogaloo trashy beats. Always mixed and happy crowd.

Funky Buddha Lounge, 169–70 King's Road Arches, **t** 725 541. All genres from funk to chunky house.

Revenge, 32–43 Old Stein, **t** 606 064. Glam and disco.

Casablanca, 3 Middle Street, **t** 709 710. From funk to samba.

Catfish Club at Madeira Hotel, 19–23 Marine Parade. Soul and Motown, lots of fun.

Enigma/Jazz Place, 10 Ship Street, **t** 328 439. Try Phonic Hoop on Saturdays with live dance and jazz breaks.

Club Fuk (formerly Zanzibar), 129 St James' Street. From groove to gay pop.

Hanbury Ballroom, St Georges Road, **t** 605 789. Opulent ballroom with creative nights like 'lap-top jam' (punters make music with their lap tops).

Funky Fish at Madeira Hotel, 19–23 Marine Parade. Groovy and unpretentious.

Artists' Quarter and Fishermen's Museum.

At beach level is a series of former fishermen's stores under the arches of the promenade, known rather pretentiously as the Artists' Quarter (the old stores are artists' studios or nightclubs now). Under one arch is a **Fishermen's Museum** (***t*** *(01273) 723 064; open 10.30–5*), full of interesting old flotsam and jetsam.

The West Pier

The West Pier was once England's finest pier, 'the queen of piers' and a Grade I listed building. It featured in Richard Attenborough's *Oh What a Lovely War* and the film of *Brighton Rock*. In the winter of 2002–3, however, the pier was destroyed by strong winds, high tides and arson. While many saw its end as a happy release after a long period of dilapidation, some still cling to the hope of resurrection. Built in 1866 by architect and engineer Eugenius Birch, an 'architectural fantasia' with oriental decoration, its walkway was tactically blown up in the Second World War, to prevent 'invasion via the ice-cream kiosk'. Patched up post-war, the West Pier had a strict dress code, classical music concerts and plays starring John Gielgud, while the Palace Pier kept the hoi polloi happy. It was closed in 1975, and since then locals, developers, Brighton council planners and heritage boffins bickered about what to do with it. And while they argued, dereliction continued. The approved £30 million restoration scheme, half funded by lottery money, seems less likely than ever after the recent collapse. Meanwhile starlings use it as a nesting ground, swirling and darting above it flocks at dusk.

The Royal Pavilion

t *(01273) 290 900; open Jan–Mar 10–5.15, April–Sept 9.30–5.45, Oct–Dec 10–5.15; adm.*

The Royal Pavilion is absurdly wonderful; a pastry-mix confection. A late 18th-century visitor said it looked like 'a mad house or a house run mad as it has neither beginning, middle, or end.' It was the seaside house of George, Prince of Wales. Originally just a farmhouse overlooking the Steine, it was rebuilt and altered in 1787 and 1801 by Henry Holland, and again in 1813 by John Nash, who turned it into a kitsch maharajah's palace with minarets and domes. The decorative scheme involves serpents, Chinese boatmen, palms, bamboo, and sugared-almond pinks and greens. The Music Room made the Prince weep for joy when he first set foot on its carpet, beneath coiled golden dragons and a *trompe l'oeil* dome from which are suspended nine lotus-shaped chandeliers. Po-faced Queen Victoria refused to set foot in her uncle's pleasure palace and, after removing the best furniture, gave it to Brighton.

Brighton Museum and Art Gallery

t *(01273) 290 900; open Tues 10–7, Wed–Sat 10–5, Sun 2–5.*

The Museum and Gallery is to the north of the Royal Pavilion, next door to a domed concert hall on Church Street. The complex was built in 1803 by William Porden as the stables and riding school for Prince George's horses. The first Indian-influenced building in England, it inspired the revamp of the Royal Pavilion. Inside are exhibitions of 20th-century design and a computerized encyclopaedia of local history.

North Laine and the Lanes

If you tire of the seaside, wander into North Laine and the Lanes, a pedestrianized area of cafés and bars with pavement tables, and shops.

North Laine is the trendiest shopping area of Brighton; its grid of streets extends from the railway station to the Pavilion, and crosswise to the Lanes – a tight huddle of medieval streets. At the top, nearest the station, Sydney Street specializes in comics, old records and retro clothes. Next down, Kensington Gardens feels like a street market, with shops selling fabrics and flowers. On Gardner Street, shops sell vegan shoes, and kites; here you'll find the Komedia theatre. On Bond Street there are larger shops selling furniture. Across busy North Street (home of old-fashioned department store Hanningtons) you enter the Lanes, which get very crowded at weekends. Shops here mainly sell tacky jewellery, fudge, teddy bears and candles, apart from Dukes Lane, which is all expensive designer clothing chain stores. There are lots of places to sit and drink, and buskers play in the East Street square. Nile Street and Prince Albert Street have interesting shops dealing in Art Nouveau antiques and paintings.

Around Brighton

Brighton Downs

The South Downs stretch east from Brighton to Beachy Head. North of Brighton, off the A27, a narrow lane over the downs leads to **Ditchling Beacon**, with views over the Weald. Beneath the beacon, in Ditchling village, you can visit **Wing's Place**, another handsome Tudor property left to Anne of Cleves as part of her divorce settlement.

West of Brighton, a minor road off the A27 leads over the downs to **Dyke Hill**, an Iron Age fortress where the deep gash of **Devil's Dyke** forms a natural defence. Nothing remains of the fort itself apart from a small section of the bank and ditch (topped by a trig point), but the views are breathtaking. According to legend, the dyke was the work of the devil, who tried to drown the parishes of the Weald by digging a channel through the downs to the sea. His plans were foiled by an old woman who, hearing his curses, lit a candle at her window. The devil mistook it for the rising sun and fled. There is a family restaurant on the summit, or a walk down to the Shepherd and Dog in Fulking, along the lane to Poynings, and back along the dyke's bottom footpath.

Bramber and Steyning and Upper Beeding

The Devil could have saved himself trouble by using the gap in the downs through which the River Adur flows to the sea, west of Devil's Dyke. The three villages of Bramber, Steyning and Upper Beeding now fill the gap. Bramber and Steyning are on the west side of the Adur, Upper Beeding on the east. The remains of **Bramber Castle**, headquarters of the *rape* of William de Braose, stand on a hill next to the Norman church. The quiet village of **Steyning**, on the other side of the A283, started life as one of the strongholds of Alfred the Great, with its own mint. There are wonky timber-framed buildings along Church Street; its main street is pretty and flinty.

Above Steyning are two Celtic hill forts, **Chanctonbury Ring** and **Cisbury Ring**. To reach Chanctonbury (smaller and crowned with beech trees) on foot, head west along the South Downs Way, or drive up a narrow lane (signposted) off the A283 west of Steyning. Grander Cisbury Ring is reached from the end of a narrow lane off the A24

Worthing road. The dents in the ground around it are the remains of Neolithic flint mines. From the top you can see the Isle of Wight and Beachy Head.

Arundel

Driving from Brighton along the A57 through sprawling coastal towns, you come to the wonderful Arun Valley and **Arundel**. Its focal point is **Arundel Castle**, its tremendous grey stone turrets and chimney stacks rising above the trees. The town is full of antiques and tea shops, quiet lanes and alleyways and crenellated towers. From the Arun bridge the main street climbs uphill between old flint buildings to an enormous French Gothic **cathedral**, built in Bath stone at the end of the 19th century by the man who designed the hansom cab. It contains the **tomb of St Philip Howard**, an ancestor of the 15th Duke of Norfolk, who built the first cathedral on the site to celebrate his coming of age (the Catholic cathedral in Norwich is another one of his). Up the road is an entrance to **Arundel Park**, 1,000 acres of downland enclosed by the 10th Duke in the 18th century (the other entrance is at Swanbourne Lake by the river). Arundel has been a tourist attraction since 1800, when the castle and grounds were first opened to the public on a regular basis, and the river was much admired for its mullet.

Arundel Castle

t (01903) 883 136; open April–Oct Sun–Fri 12–5, grounds 11–5; adm exp.

Arundel Castle looks too good to be genuine, and it's not. It was built by architect Charles Alban Buckler for the antiquarian 15th Duke. From the 1580s to the 1780s the Norfolks had preferred to live anywhere but their crumbling, owl-infested castle at Arundel, although they liked to be buried in its chapel. The last one to live in the castle was the 13th Earl, St Philip Howard, who made his decision to return to Catholicism as he paced the Long Gallery. When Buckler started building, it was on 18th-century foundations; the Tudor brick ranges had been demolished. The castle plan is U-shaped, opening onto the ruined Norman keep and encircled by restored 12th-century curtain walls. The castle tour takes you through the armoury and the chapel. Incredibly ornate, the chapel is decorated with Purbeck marble columns, stained glass and stone carvings. The battlemented mock-medieval Barons' Hall, 133ft long and 50ft high, has a hammer-beam roof modelled on Penshurst Place (*see* p.169). Look for an 18th-century painting, *The Earl of Surrey defending his allegiance to Henry VII after the Battle of Bosworth*. The Earl fought alongside his father, who led the vanguard for Richard III, and wound up in the Tower of London, stripped of his titles and estates. He was the first but not the last Howard to fight for the ancestral rights. The dining room, drawing room and library were built in mock-Norman or early-medieval Gothic style, and filled with ancestral portraits, tapestries and heraldry. You can see the full family line-up in chronological order in the picture gallery. These include the poet Earl of Surrey, who was beheaded for incorporating the royal coat of arms into his own (treachery). In the dining room are mementoes of Mary Queen of Scots, who for a time was engaged to the 4th Duke. There are a handful of portraits

Tourist Information

Arundel: **t** (01903) 882 344. *Open Mon–Sat summer 10–6, winter 10–3; Sun 10–4.* Try *www.arundel.org.uk* or *www.sussexbythesea.co.uk* for more information on where to stay and eat.

Where to Stay and Eat

Arundel and Around t (01903) –

Bailiffscourt Hotel, Climping, **t** 723 511, *www.hshotels.co.uk* (*very expensive*). A beautiful 1930s manor house in 30 acres of parkland and walled gardens 3 miles south of Arundel, 100 yards from Climping beach, this is a luxurious sanctuary. Restaurant menu might include delicacies such as smoked haddock risotto with poached egg and mustard dressing.

The Burpham Country Hotel and Restaurant, **t** 882 160, *www.johansens.com* (*expensive*). Country hotel in quiet village of Burpham 2½ miles from Arundel. Restaurant (*eves only*) offers an English menu with French overtones: Cornish scallops and prawn cassoulet with saffron, cognac and cream followed by roast fillet of Sussex beef with truffle and Madeira sauce (*moderate*).

Byass House, 59 Matravers Street, Arundel, **t** 882 129, *www.byasshouse.co.uk* (*moderate*). An elegant Georgian townhouse on a lovely street. Dinner parties for up to 10 people can be arranged as part of the service.

The White Hart, Market Square, Arundel, **t** 882 374 (*moderate*). If you enjoy a pint of real ale, this is the place for Harveys, a traditional Sussex brew, and a quiet meal; local fresh fish is the speciality (*no fish Mon*). Traditional pub grub at lunchtime (sandwiches, ploughman's, battered fish), full English menu in the evening.

St Mary's Gate Inn, London Road, **t** 883 145, *www.stmarysgate.co.uk* (*moderate*). Typical English inn with restaurant and bar just down from Arundel cathedral, dating from 1527. Five bedrooms too. Light meals and snacks in the bar. Restaurant serves traditional English meat and fish dishes such as lamb shank with mint gravy.

Black Rabbit Inn, Mill Road, **t** 882 828. A fabulous riverside pub, a mile east of Arundel bridge along an avenue of lime trees. Food includes steaks and roasts (*moderate*).

Arden Guest House, 4 Queen's Lane, Arundel, **t** 882 544 (*cheap*). A Victorian family house near the castle. Convenient, friendly and efficient.

The King's Arms (*cheap*). On a cobbled lane on the corner of King's Arms Hill, in a lovely part of town, this is a pleasant pub to sit outside with a drink on a sunny day.

Arundel is well supplied with tearooms. Most of them are on Tarrant Street. Try the **Copper Kettle**, 21 Tarrant Street, **t** 883 679, with its tinkling doorbell, Earl Grey tea and lamb chops, delicious home-baked cakes, buns and cream teas.

by Van Dyck and Mytens in the drawing room, including a portrait of the collector earl with his grandson, later the 5th Duke. In the Ante Library is another Van Dyck portrait, of the collector earl and his wife, poring over a globe, his finger on Madagascar, where he thought of emigrating until he was told that it was infested with fleas. The library, a splendid long room of red velvet and Honduras mahogany, was converted from the old Elizabethan long gallery by the 11th Duke in 1801, and refurbished for the visit of Queen Victoria in 1846. This is where St Philip Howard opted for Catholicism.

Bignor Roman Villa

***t** 01798 869 259; open Mar–April Tues–Sun 10–5, May and Oct daily 10–5, June–Sept daily 10–6; adm.*

A narrow lane leads west off the A29 north of Arundel to the remains of Bignor Roman Villa, uncovered in 1811 when a plough chucked up fragments of broken floor

Arundel and the Norfolks

Arundel goes back to the Norman Conquest castle of Roger de Montgomery, one of the most powerful Norman barons in England. The Fitzalans, who became earls of Arundel, had estates in the Welsh Marches, around Clun and Oswestry, but preferred to live in Arundel. One of them married Edward I's niece, two were beheaded and the rest commanded armies against Scots and French. In the 16th century, the Fitzalan heiress married Thomas Howard, the 4th Duke of Norfolk – bringing the Norfolks to Sussex. The first four dukes of Norfolk established one of the most powerful dukedoms in the country, as important as the duchies of Lancaster or Cornwall. To them, Arundel Castle was a bijou residence compared to East Anglian holdings – palatial castles at Framlingham and Castle Rising. The Norfolks ranked alongside the Percys of Northumbria or the Mortimers of the Welsh Marches, their actions at the heart of English history.

The 1st Duke of Norfolk (the first four dukes were all called Thomas Howard), whose mother was descended from Edward I, led the vanguard at Bosworth Field and died alongside Richard III. The 2nd Duke won the Battle of Flodden for Henry VIII. The 3rd Duke, who married the daughter of Edward IV, was the uncle of two queens, Anne Boleyn and Catherine Howard. He loyally presided at the trial and execution of his niece Anne, which didn't stop Henry VIII executing his daughter Catherine to rid himself of the influence of the Howards; the Duke only escaped beheading alongside his son, Henry Howard, Earl of Surrey, because the King died first. The Dukes of Norfolk have remained Roman Catholics to the present day – in opposition to the Protestantism of the royal house.

Henry Howard was the original English Renaissance man, a soldier and brilliant poet who advocated the simple life in his poetry. The poet's son, the 4th Duke, was the richest peer in the country. He was a favourite of Queen Elizabeth I, but was imprisoned for planning to marry Mary Queen of Scots, and later beheaded for his role in the Ridolfi Spanish plot to overthrow the Queen. His son, St Philip Howard, deprived of the Norfolk dukedom, spent the last 10 years of his life in the Tower of London on trumped-up charges of being pro-Spanish at the time of the Armada. He was canonized by Pope Paul VI in 1970.

St Philip's son, the collector earl (the dukedom had not been restored), recovered the family fortune by marrying a Shrewsbury heiress, with estates in south Yorkshire, Derbyshire and Nottinghamshire, and a 'prodigy' house by Robert Smythson in Worksop. He was the greatest early English patron and art collector, establishing the model of the collector-connoisseur taken up by the Grand Tourists. His unrivalled collection of around 700 pictures, antique marbles, gems, prints and drawings was dispersed in the Civil War. Some of it is traceable: the Leonardos and Holbeins at Windsor Castle, the Raphaels at Chatsworth and the Arundel marbles in the Ashmolean Museum. A few pieces still hang in the stone corridors of Arundel Castle, next to ancestral portraits. In the 19th century the 15th Earl of Norfolk decided to revive the family's glorious history by rebuilding the castle at Arundel.

tiles. The hypocausts, hot baths and mosaics of cupids dressed as gladiators are modest compared with the palace at Fishbourne, but the setting is much more memorable, under a thatched barn in a field at the foot of the South Downs. In the late 3rd and early 4th century, the villa stood at the centre of a wealthy farming estate on the edge of Stane Street, which ran from *Noviomagus* to *Londinium*.

Chichester

To Neptune and Minerva, for the welfare of the Divine House by the authority of Tiberius Claudius Cogidubnus, great king in Britain, the guild of smiths and those therein give this temple from their own resources.

The Cogidubnus Inscription, AD 1

This handsome old town developed at the southern end of Stane Street, linking *Londinium* and the south-coast port of *Noviomagus*. Now the roads converge on an elaborate medieval market cross and a cathedral with a detached belfry, the only one in England. There are some handsome Georgian streets, within the inevitable ring road. Chichester's pulse beats to a small-town drum for most of the year, but picks up a faster rhythm during the summer music festival.

Start from the medieval **market cross** in the centre of town. It stands at the crossroads of four wide pedestrianized streets – North, South, East and West Streets – which run along the course of the old Roman roads. That is all you will find of *Noviomagus*. The Roman public baths are underneath the Army and Navy shop on West Street, and beneath the junction of Lion Street and North Street is a temple dedicated to Neptune and Minerva. Above ground are Georgian streets and beautiful medieval monuments, including the pinnacled market cross and the cathedral.

Chichester Cathedral

St Wilfred established Christianity among the South Saxons at Selsey in 681. Four hundred years later the Normans moved the Christian base eight miles north to Chichester. Their church was up and running by 1123; the cloisters and bell tower were added three hundred years later. Today the cathedral and detached bell tower are set among pretty cottages and gardens. The steeple is a landmark for miles. Henry James thought the three-sided cloisters the prettiest thing in the town. Inside, the cathedral is hung with some outstanding works of modern art, including Hans Feibusch's *Baptism of Christ* (1951), *Mother and Child* by Henry Moore and *Crucifixion* by Graham Sutherland. There is also stained glass by Marc Chagall. Two political paintings in the transepts reveal the agenda of 16th-century Bishop Robert Sherburne, illustrating the close relationship of the bishops of Chichester with the monarch: one is decorated with medallions of all the English kings from William the Conqueror on; the other portrays all the bishops of Chichester from St Wilfred to Bishop Sherburne. Philip Larkin fans will know about the **Arundel Tomb** (from his poem 'Arundel Tomb': 'Side by side, their faces blurred/ The earl and countess lie in stone'). It is thought to be a monument to the 13th Earl of Arundel (1307–76) and his second wife. They're lying

Tourist Information

Chichester: 29/a South Street, **t** (01243) 775 888, *www.chichester.gov.uk. Open Mon–Sat 9–5, summer also Sun 10–4.*

Chichester Harbour Office, Itchenor, **t** (01243) 512 301, *www.conservancy.co.uk.* Information on nature walks and **Chichester Harbour Water Tours** (booking **t** (01243) 786 418). The **Itchenor Ferry** operates April–Sept to Smugglers' Hard, from where it's a 20-minute walk to Bosham.

Chichester Arts Festival, **t** (01243) 785 718, *www.chifest.org.uk.* Takes place first two weeks in July, with exhibitions, shows and celebrity speakers. Candle-lit concerts in the cathedral, chamber music in the ballroom of Goodwood House and performances in the Festival and Minerva theatres (**t** (01243) 781 312, *www.cft.org.uk*) are the highlights.

Where to Stay

Chichester t (01243) –

The Ship Hotel, North Street, **t** 778 000, *www.shiphotel.com* (*expensive*). Handsome 18th-century hotel with airy Brooks Brasserie (*cheap*). Some of the 36 rooms have been refurbished in clean modern style, others have been left chintzy.

Suffolk House Hotel, East Row, **t** 778 899, *www.suffolkhousehotel.co.uk* (*expensive*). Small family-run hotel in former Georgian townhouse of dukes of Richmond, short walk from cathedral.

The Coach House, Binderton (near West Dean), **t** 539 624 (*moderate*). Lovely place to stay in flint-walled stables of old manor house.

Eating Out

George and Dragon, 51 North Street, **t** 785 660, *www.georgeanddragoninn.co.uk* (*moderate*). Lively, family-run pub with conservatory dining room. Also 10 comfortable bedrooms in separate building behind pub garden.

Woodies Wine Bar and Restaurant, 10–11 St Pancras, **t** 779 895 (*moderate*). Long-established and recently expanded, Woodies is a friendly restaurant with new bar next door. Menu might include fish-cakes, risotto or fillet steak followed by summer pudding.

Comme Ça, 67 Broyle Road, **t** 788 724 (*moderate*). High-quality French food in old Georgian inn on A286, a short walk from Festival Theatre. *Closed Sun and Mon.*

The Buttery at the Crypt, 12/a South Street, **t** 537 033 (*cheap*). In early medieval stone-vaulted cellars of the old guildhall you can get an atmospheric cooked breakfast, ploughman's, omelette or afternoon tea served by a waitress in the traditional black dress with white collar.

Café Coco, 13 South Street, **t** 786 989 (*cheap*). Pleasant stop for coffee or lunch with brasserie-style menu.

St Martin's Tea Rooms, St Martin's Lane (off East Street), **t** 786 715 (*cheap*). Another local institution, offering organic teas, coffees and light lunches such as soup and potato cakes. Nice garden. *Closed Sun.*

Shepherds Tea Rooms, 35 Little London, **t** 774 761 (*cheap*). Much-loved local tea rooms offering teas, coffees, cakes and scones as well as more substantial poached salmon with new potatoes, Welsh rarebit or quiches.

side by side, he in armour; the touching detail that inspired Larkin was his ungloved hand holding hers, leading the poet to conclude: 'What will survive of us is love'.

Pallant House

t (01243) 774 557, www.pallant.org.uk; call for post-renovation opening hours.

Just off South Street is a cluster of 18th-century residential streets known as the Pallants. Pallant House, a beautiful Queen Anne building, houses a surprisingly high-powered city art gallery, specializing in 20th-century paintings and sculpture. It opened in 1982 to house the collection of Dean Walter Hussey (the man who filled the cathedral with art treasures), including paintings by Paul Nash, Graham

Noviomagus

Chichester, known as the 'City of the Plain', sits in the middle of flat alluvial countryside between the South Downs and a deep natural harbour, now known for its scenery and birdlife. In the 3rd and 4th centuries, the countryside immediately around *Noviomagus* was some of the most productive and wealthy in Roman Britannia. Chichester Harbour is thought to have been the back door of the Roman invasion, opened by Cogidubnus, king of the Regnenses and a friend of Rome. Not much is known about Cogidubnus, which makes the contents of the Cogidubnus Inscription, uncovered in 1723 on the corner of Lion Street and North Street, all the more intriguing. The Latin inscription says that a temple was built at *Noviomagus* by the authority of 'Tiberius Claudius Cogidubnus, great king in Britain' (*rex magnus Brit*). Nobody knows exactly how much power is signified in the phrase 'great king'. It has been suggested that Cogidubnus was the governor of the whole province. Certainly, he gave Vespasian a secure base from which to campaign in the south and west without watching his back. The Regnenses would have got a ready market for their agricultural produce and Wealden iron, and a steady flow of goods from Italy and Gaul coming in through the port. When the II Augusta moved west in AD 44–45, the old legionary fortress became the regional capital, *Noviomagus* or 'new market', and Cogidubnus got his swanky palace at Fishbourne.

Sutherland, Henry Moore, Glyn Philpot and Howard Hodgkin, Frank Auerbach, David Bomberg, Lucien Freud, John Piper, Bridget Riley and Gino Severini. In 1989 Charles Kearley, whose modernist house is at the centre of Sculpture at Goodwood (*see* p.212), left Pallant House another good collection. Recently, a third great donation by the architect Sir Colin St John Wilson (who built the new British Library at Kings Cross) has bolstered the museum further. Sir Colin was the associate designer of the new wing by architects Long and Kentish (builders of the Maritime Museum in Falmouth), with new galleries to show off the combined collections of Hussey, Kearley and St John Wilson.

Around Chichester

Chichester Harbour

There is no harbour in Chichester itself, nor even sea. Chichester Harbour is the name for 11 square miles of tidal creeks and channels south of Chichester. A designated Area of Outstanding Natural Beauty, it is popular with wading birds and yachties. **West Itchenor** is the most popular sailing village, with its flint cottages. You can catch the Itchenor–Bosham ferry (*April–Sept 10–6*) or go on guided nature walks and boat trips. In summer there are long queues to the seaside at **West Wittering**, with its 54 acres of pebbles and dunes backed by grass and beach huts, one of the nicer beaches on the south coast.

Fishbourne Roman Palace

Salthill Road, 1½ miles west of Chichester on A259, railway station 5-minute walk, buses 700 and 11; **t** *(01243) 785 859; open Feb and Nov–mid-Dec daily 10–4, Mar–July and Sept–Oct 10–5, Aug 10–6, mid-Dec–Jan weekends 10-4; adm.*

On the southern outskirts of *Noviomagus*, and on the edge of its harbour, the grandest villa in Roman *Britannia* is thought to have belonged to Cogidubnus, whose territory stretched as far as *Aqua Sulis* (modern Bath). He had his palace built by Italian craftsmen on the site of the legionary supply depot of the II Augusta. Its opulent layout included a hundred centrally heated rooms around courtyards decorated with wall paintings and elaborate mosaic floors, irrigated gardens, bathhouses and a guest wing. According to archaeological evidence, it was destroyed by fire in the 3rd century, and the occupants retreated into the wings, until the whole place was abandoned in the 4th century. Twenty floor mosaics have been uncovered since its discovery in 1960, at the back end of a modern housing estate. It is an extraordinary treasure in humdrum surroundings. Visit after 2.30 to avoid school groups.

Bosham

Bosham (pronounced Bozzam) is one of the most popular villages around the harbour. The architect Sir Colin St John Wilson (*see* Pallant House) has a house here. The pretty cottages have high steps to keep the water out. Bosham Harbour had superseded Fishbourne by the 11th century. The legend of Cnut failing to push back the waves with his staff originated at Bosham. Harold Godwinson set sail for Normandy from Bosham in 1064. From the 13th century onwards Bosham flourished as a wool port. The church with its steeple is a popular place to get married. It is mainly Saxon, and contains the bones of a tiny Saxon child; another Cnut legend is that his youngest daughter drowned in the mill stream behind the church in 1035, and was buried in the church.

Goodwood House

t *(01243) 755 040, www.goodwood.co.uk; open Easter–Oct Sun–Mon 1–5, Aug Sun–Thurs 1–5; adm.*

The Goodwood estate, on the downs north of Chichester, is one of the great English sporting estates. The Goodwood Races rank high in the racing calendar. It also hosts motor-racing events, a flying school and golf courses. These sporting attractions are all run by Lord March, son of the present Duke of Richmond. The Dukes of Richmond got Goodwood after the Restoration, when the 1st Duke, son of Charles II and his French mistress Louise de Querouaille, joined one of the first and most fashionable hunts in the country in nearby Charlton. The earliest house was a hunting lodge, belonging to the Earl of Northumberland at Petworth; Goodwood has always been recreational. The present house was built by James Wyatt in 1790 for the 3rd Duke. Its flint façade conceals the Regency exoticism of the interior. Set against Egyptian pillars and crimson drapes are sporting paintings – *The Charlton Hunt, Racing Scene in Goodwood Park, Racehorses Exercising, Shooting at Goodwood* – some of them by

George Stubbs, who spent nine months at Goodwood painting for the 3rd Duke. For lunch, try the Fox Goes Free, in the village of Charlton.

Sculpture at Goodwood

***t** (01243) 538 449; open Mar–Nov Thurs–Sat 10.30–4.30; adm exp.*

Sculpture at Goodwood was set up in 1994 by Wilfred and Jeanette Cass, South African collectors of British sculpture, to boost contemporary British sculptors. They commission a dozen new works a year and exhibit them in a 20-acre woodland setting with views over Chichester Cathedral. Works include familiar names like Bill Woodrow, Anthony Caro, David Nash and Andy Goldsworthy. The works are all for sale. The trail takes about an hour and a half.

The Weald and Downland Open Air Museum

***t** (01243) 811 348; open Jan–Feb 10.30–4, Mar–Oct 10.30–6, Nov–Dec weekends only 10.30–4; adm exp.*

Signposted off the A286, in Singleton, the museum looks like a lost village of ancient, half-timbered houses with thatched roofs and wattle-and-daub walls. It is in fact a sanctuary for endangered vernacular buildings, rescued from modern roads and reservoirs. It's the place to get to grips with traditional building techniques from the Weald and Downland region.

Petworth

Petworth has a feudal air, crammed in under the wall of the great house. The handsome old buildings of the market square and Lombard Street, East Street, High Street and Middle Street have more good antiques shops than anywhere else in the southeast (but don't expect to find bargains). On the High Street, the **Petworth Cottage Museum** (***t*** *(01798) 342 100; open April–Oct Wed–Sun 2–4.30; adm*) is an antidote to the high tone of it all. A tied cottage, number 346 on the Leconfield estate register, it has been left as it was between 1901 and 1930, when a seamstress lived there.

Petworth House

***t** (01798) 342 207; open Mar–Oct Sat–Wed 11–5.30; adm exp.*

The boundary wall of Petworth House encloses one of the best Capability Brown parks in the country. The house stands on the edge of it, dominating the town. Inside it are 300 paintings including 20 Turners and 20 Van Dycks, and hundreds of antique sculptures. The 10th Earl of Northumberland (1602–68), the 6th 'proud' Duke of Somerset (1662–1748) and the 2nd and 3rd Earls of Egremont were some of England's greatest private art collectors. They had the house grandly redesigned several times by the most fashionable architects, artists and craftsmen of the period. The golden age at Petworth, recreated by the National Trust, was the 74-year reign of the 3rd Earl of Egremont (1763–1837), who turned Petworth into a drop-in centre for young and talented British artists like Turner and Constable. He built roads, hospitals and

Tourist Information

Petworth: Market Square, **t** (01798) 343 523, *www.chichester.gov.uk*, *www.sussexlive.com*.

Where to Stay and Eat

Petworth t (01798) –

There are plenty of excellent real-ale pubs around Petworth, all of which provide good food and a place to stay.

The Horse Guards Inn, Tillington, **t** 342 332, *www.horseguards-inn.co.uk* (*moderate*). A 17th-century free house renowned for its food, 5 minutes west of Petworth off the A272. Menu might include rack of lamb, fillet of beef or roast sea bass with couscous. Real ales are London Pride and Youngs. Some rooms.

Badgers Inn, Coultershall Bridge, **t** 342 651. Pleasant, well-to-do pub with popular restaurant (*moderate*).

Black Horse, Byworth, **t** 342 424. A lovely unspoiled real ale pub in quiet village 1½ miles out of Petworth in Pulborough direction. Four real ales include Pedigree and Cheriton Pots. Food served in cosy back room (*moderate*). Book at weekends to eat.

Half Way Bridge Inn, Lodsworth, **t** 861 281, *www.thesussexpub.co.uk* (*moderate*). Despite unpromising roadside location on A272 west of Petworth, this is a very hospitable place to stay with eight bedrooms in a barn conversion, excellent food – shoulder of lamb; steak, kidney and Guinness pudding; or venison and red wine casserole – and real ales.

The Old Railway Station, **t** 342 346, *www.oldstation.co.uk* (*cheap*). On the A285 by the Badgers Inn, formerly Petworth's railway station (built 1894). Unusual night's sleep in one of three carriages, each split into two double rooms, or the station house. Breakfast is taken on the old platform or in the guest lounge.

schools, and contributed to the building of the first pier in Brighton. At Petworth, he added contemporary British art to the Old Masters, Dutch and Italian art already on its walls, rehanging them as he pleased, 'all mixed up together, good and bad.'

In the mid-12th century Petworth was a far-flung castle on the estates of the Percys, earls of Northumberland, whose main holdings were in Northumberland. Generations of Percys died in the Tower or on a battlefield fighting the king, until the 10th Earl broke the cycle, becoming a connoisseur of the arts instead. He started the picture collection at Petworth in the 1630s, commissioning the Van Dycks and collecting Old Masters. The 6th Duke of Somerset inherited the Percy castle by marrying an heiress, and turned it into a glittering ducal palace, decorated by royal craftsmen such as Louis Laguerre and Grinling Gibbons. Most of the elaborate interior design is his, including the sensational baroque chapel; his main contribution to the picture collection was the so-called Petworth Claude. His successor, the 2nd Earl of Egremont, was one of the great 18th-century collectors, specializing in antique sculpture and building a sculpture gallery.

Midhurst

Midhurst is a few miles west of Petworth on the A272. On a sunny day, Cowdray Park is a perfect picnic spot. If you are lucky there will be an afternoon polo match on the Lawns. Cowdray is a small corner of the 17,000-acre estate of the Pearsons, media tycoons (owners of the *Financial Times*, *Penguin* and *Dorling Kindersley*) and polo fanatics, who bought the Cowdray estate in 1908 and have turned Midhurst into the country's polo capital. Cowdray hosts the British Open Championship – known as the

Tourist Information

Midhurst: North Street, **t** (01730) 817 322.

Cowdray Park Polo Estate Office, **t** (01730) 813 257. The polo season takes place from mid-April to September. The highlight is the Gold Cup, the British Open Championship, which attracts international teams in July. The Lawns is the main ground, with five polo fields. Anyone can watch matches for free midweek, or for a charge at weekends, during the Gold Cup and Goodwood Week (which comes directly after the final).

Where to Stay and Eat

Midhurst t (01730) –

Spread Eagle Hotel, South Street, **t** 816 911, *www.hshotels.co.uk* (*very expensive*). Beautiful old hotel with delightful mix of Georgian brick and sagging timberwork, the crowning glory of the old town. Formal dining in main restaurant and lighter meals either in the bar, conservatory or terrace. Pool, gym and saunas too.

Angel Hotel, High Street, **t** 812 421, *www.theangelmidhust.co.uk* (*expensive*). A 15th-century coaching inn behind late Georgian façade complete with hanging baskets and tall decorative chimneys. Bar meals include pasta, salads, char-grills and 'sizzlers', or you can eat in the restaurant. There are 28 bedrooms including five 'feature' rooms.

Elsted Inn, Elsted Marsh, **t** 813 662 (*moderate*). A few miles west of Midhurst, this is a friendly pub in the middle of nowhere, with four modest bedrooms.

Gold Cup – one of the most prestigious polo tournaments in the world. In the middle of the park are the ruins of **Cowdray House** (*t (01730) 812 423; closed awaiting funds for restoration*), once a fortified Tudor mansion. The house burned down in 1793, around the time that the last Lord Montague drowned going down the Rhine Falls in a canoe. His sister resurrected the family fortunes by marrying into the wealthy Poyntz family, but her two young heirs died in a freak boating accident in Bognor Regis in 1815, and the Cowdray estates were sold on. You can see why there is talk of a Cowdray Curse, supposed to have been invoked by a disgruntled monk at Battle Abbey after Sir Anthony Browne grabbed the abbey lands at the Dissolution. The family line, said the monk, would come to a horrible end by fire and water.

The South
Hampshire, Isle of Wight, Wiltshire and Dorset

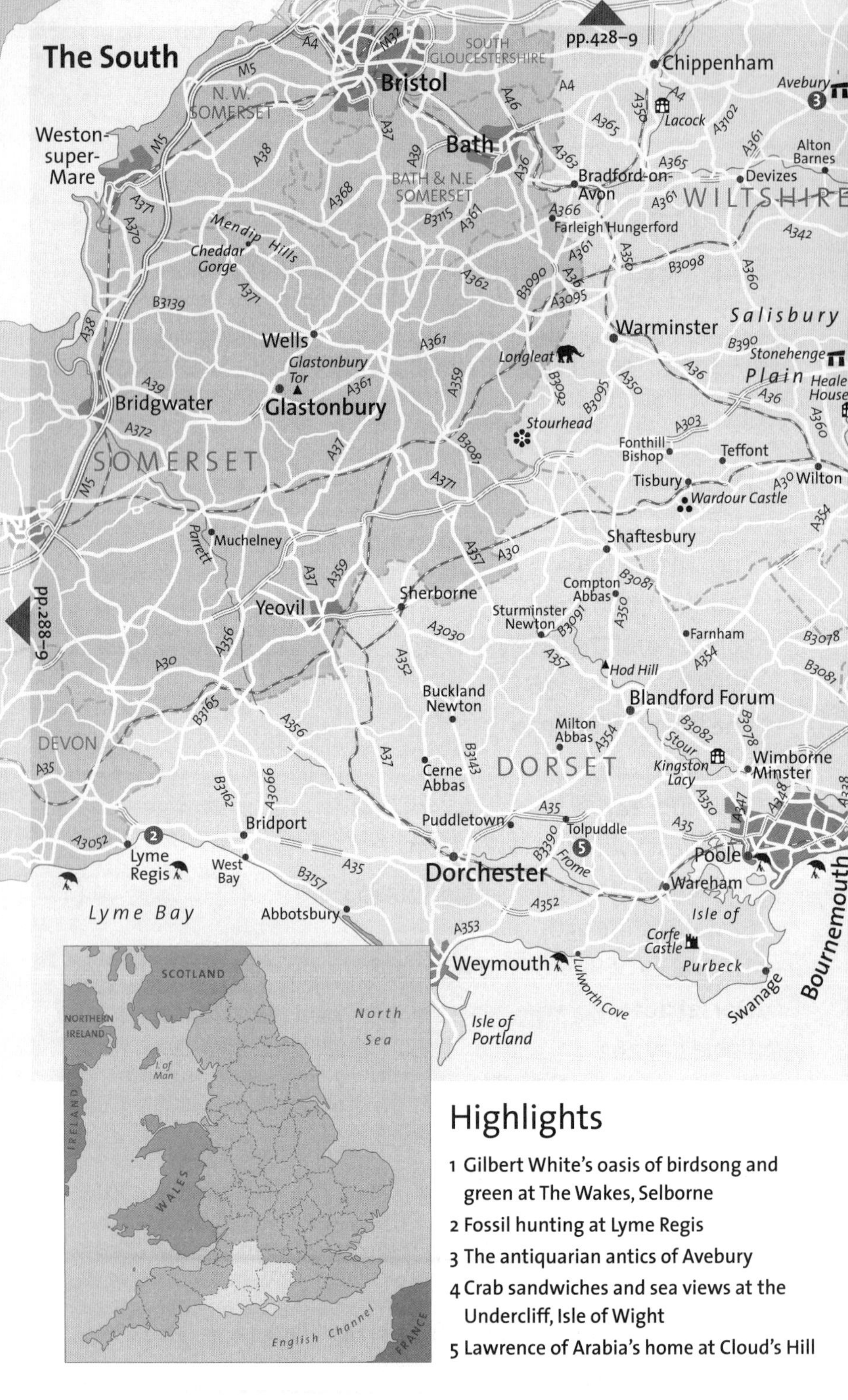

Highlights

1 Gilbert White's oasis of birdsong and green at The Wakes, Selborne
2 Fossil hunting at Lyme Regis
3 The antiquarian antics of Avebury
4 Crab sandwiches and sea views at the Undercliff, Isle of Wight
5 Lawrence of Arabia's home at Cloud's Hill

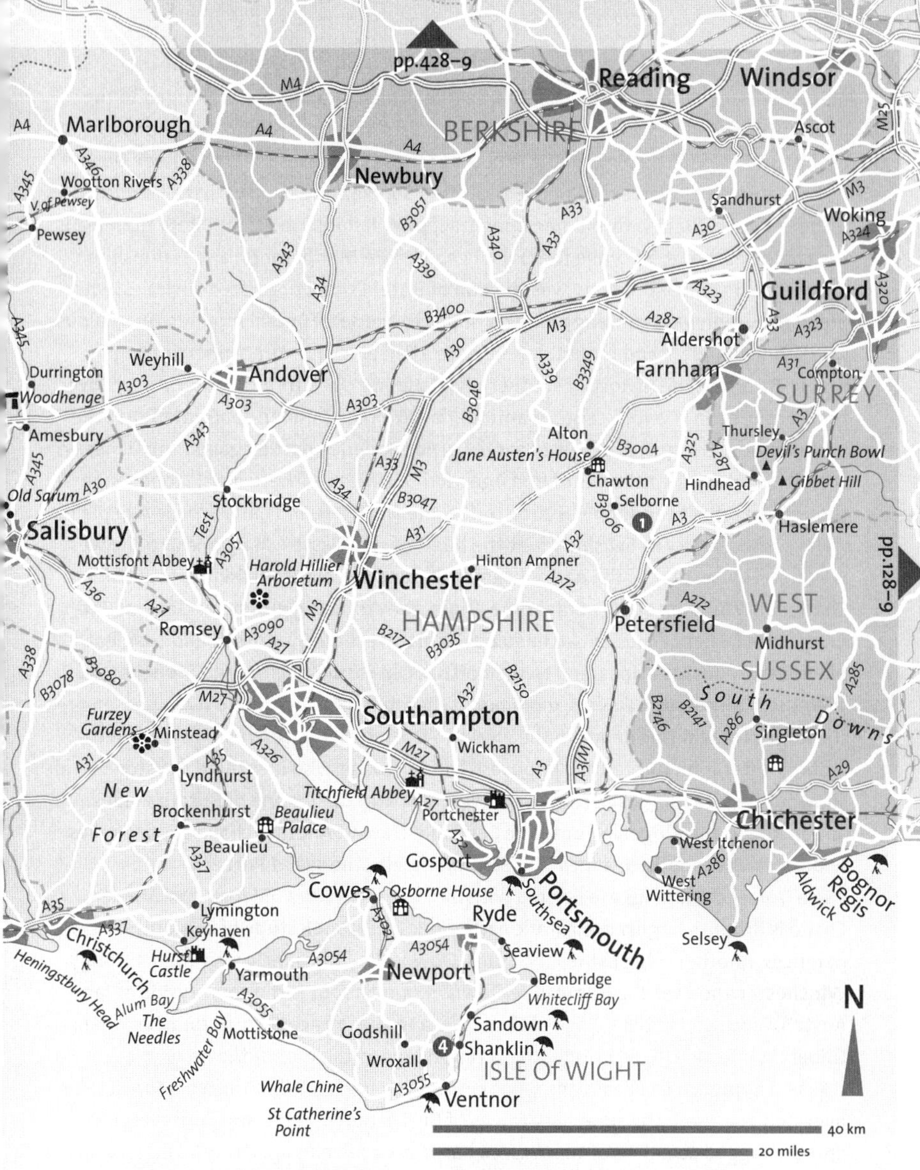

There are some heights in Wessex, shaped as if by a kindly hand,
For thinking, dreaming, dying on...

Thomas Hardy, *Wessex Heights*

The South of England – **Hampshire**, **Wiltshire**, **Dorset** and **the Isle of Wight** – has an idealized double known as Wessex, which follows the same contours as central southern England, includes the same towns and villages, even shares its history, but has none of the humdrum congestion of the region today. Thomas Hardy called it 'a partly real, partly dream country' and perpetuated the illusion by creating his own map of Wessex with fictional place names. Real, historical Wessex belonged to the 9th-century West Saxon kings. The archaeologists' Wessex encompasses hundreds of prehistoric sites in the region. At the heart of these Wessexes are the Wessex Downs. (What those other Wessexes, Prince Edward and Sophie, have to do with it all is unclear.)

The **Salisbury Plain**, a forbidding open tract of Wiltshire used for military training, is the chalk heart of it all, while the Dorset chalklands, Marlborough and Hampshire downs are its limbs. The plain was the hub of Britain's first organized societies, with prehistoric highways running along its ridges to the sea. Funeral mounds, anomalous sandstone boulders and chalk figures create a Tolkeinesque atmosphere of pagan magic. Bizarrely, the history of southern England has aged three thousand years over two centuries. In the 16th century, antiquarian William Camden speculated that the mounds were the graves of West Saxon warriors killed in battle against the Danes. In the 18th century the talk was of Iron Age sacrificial rituals. These days, Stonehenge is thought to reflect the sophistication of the late Neolithic and early Bronze Age plain.

The cathedral city of **Salisbury** is at the heart of the Wessex chalklands. To the west is Wilton House, seat of the earls of Pembroke, and the old stone hilltop town of Shaftesbury. To the south is Cranborne Chase, the stomping ground of General Pitt-Rivers, 'the father of modern archaeology'. Northwest are Stourhead and Longleat, old houses in lush gardens, and to the north is Old Sarum hill fort and Stonehenge.

On the **Marlborough Downs**, more burial chambers cluster around Avebury Henge, the largest megalithic henge in the world. In the 17th century, Avebury was called 'Aubrey' after John Aubrey, the impoverished aristocrat who identified the stones and showed them to Charles I. From Avebury a chalk arm carries one of Britain's oldest 'green' roads, the Ridgeway, onto the Berkshire Downs. Another chalk leg, 12½ miles wide, stretches southwest into Dorset, running into the sea at Purbeck.

The **Dorset chalklands** are littered with burial mounds and hill forts too. Maiden Castle is Britain's largest prehistoric earthwork, a textbook study of concentric defences. Another ridge carries the South Downs Way, another 'green' road, through Winchester and over the Hampshire Downs. Round about is the countryside of Jane Austen, who lived in the village of Chawton, and the 17th-century natural historian Gilbert White, who lived in Selborne, a tiny village at the foot of the downs.

As you approach the coast, the woodland and sandy heaths of the **New Forest** take over, and you reach the sprawling towns of Christchurch, Poole and Bournemouth, and the ragged coastline of the Wessex basin. It's a mixed bag. The workmanlike old naval towns of **Southampton** and **Portsmouth** are soused in bracing maritime history, but the rim of their deep harbours is all built up. If you stand on Hengistbury Head overlooking Christchurch Harbour, or look through mist at Brownsea Island in Poole Harbour, the coast gains atmosphere. Purbeck and the Isle of Wight are scenic gems.

The Jurassic Coast of Dorset became a World Heritage Site in 2001. Here, 190 million years of the earth's history can be seen laid out along 95 miles of coastline: between Exmouth and Purbeck you can see the whole of the Mesozoic Era, spanning the Triassic, Jurassic and Cretaceous periods. Jurassic fossils literally fall out of the cliffs at **Lyme Regis**. All the Victorian geologists studied here.

Alfred the Great

In this year Alfred son of Æthelwulf died six days before All Saints' Day. He was king over the whole English people, except for that part which was under Danish rule; and he held that kingdom for twenty-eight and a half years.

Anglo-Saxon Chronicle, AD 900

Wessex is the site of the Alfredian myth. Alfred the Great became King of the West Saxons in 871, inheriting a kingdom with two Viking armies camped in it. Over the next seven years there were two further large-scale invasions of Wessex, and minor skirmishes too. Alfred resisted by fighting and diplomacy (baptisms, hostage-takings, pay-offs). Northumbria and Mercia fell to the Vikings in 876 and 877, and Alfred's luck ran out too at Chippenham in 878: the Vikings 'occupied and settled the land of the West Saxons, and drove a great part of the people across the sea...except King Alfred,' writes the *Anglo-Saxon Chronicle*. Alfred hid in the Somerset marshes, rallied his men, burned some cakes and launched a counter-offensive that sent the Vikings packing. His victory, at Edington, secured a decade of peace, culture and education. When the Vikings attacked again in 892 they were defeated by defences structured around *burhs*, each one no more than a day's march from the next. Alfred enlisted scholars from Wales, Mercia and Gaul (including Asser, his biographer) to restock the libraries. He learned Latin and translated four books, including *Pastoral Care* by Pope Gregory. Alfred also wrote down a new code of law, borrowing from the old laws of the West Saxon, Kentish and Mercian kings, and adding a few of his own. We know all this precisely because it was written down, in the *Anglo-Saxon Chronicle* and Asser's *Life of Alfred*. It's all from the West Saxon point of view, but you do get a sense of the Saxons being a united people under Alfred, 'King of the Anglo-Saxons'.

Hampshire

Hampshire is too close to London to be unspoiled, the New Forest notwithstanding. The M3 cuts straight through to the coast, passing unlovable commuter satellite towns like Basingstoke, Andover, Petersfield and Alton. Its chalk scenery is appealing in places; William Cobbett called Hampshire 'the best of all landscapes for living in' (*Rural Rides*, 1830). **Winchester** has the charisma of Alfred the Great and its cathedral. East of the town are the homes of Jane Austen and Gilbert White – literary shrines in nostalgic English countryside. South of it are the Test and Meon rivers, a shrine to fly fishermen (first and foremost Izaak Walton, who is buried in the cathedral).

The county has serious military connections, from the training schools at **Aldershot** and **Sandhurst** and the military towns of the **Blackwater Valley** in the north, to the maritime coastline in the south, with its deep estuaries, fed by an unusual double tide that sweeps around the Isle of Wight at different speeds, so that Portsmouth and Southampton get 17 hours of deep water a day. **Portsmouth** has its old naval dockyard and **Southampton** its ocean cruise liners. To the west of Southampton Water, you can lose yourself (rare in the south of England) in the woodland of the **New Forest**, where wild ponies roam and you may see unicorns *couchant* under ancient oaks.

Getting There and Around

By **car**, turn off the M3 at junction 9 or 10 and follow signs to city centre.

Freqent **trains** from London Waterloo take 50 minutes. For all train information contact National Rail Enquiries, **t** 08457 484950, *www.thetrainline.com*.

National Express runs regular **coach** services from London Victoria. For all coach enquiries call **t** 08705 808080, *www.gobycoach.com*.

Tourist Information

Winchester: The Guildhall, The Broadway, **t** (01962) 840 500, *www.visitwinchester.com. Open summer Mon–Sat 9.30–5.30, Sun 11–4; winter Mon–Sat 10–5.*

Winchester Arts Festival takes place over two weeks in July with classical and jazz music, talks, walks and exhibitions in various city venues including the cathedral, Guildhall, Theatre Royal and St Cross Water Meadows. Visit *www.winchesterfestival.co.uk* for details.

Where to Stay

Winchester t (01962) –

Hotel Du Vin, Southgate Street, **t** 841 414, *www.hotelduvin.com* (*luxury*). The first of a suave, upmarket chain of hotels, this one in a handsome 17th-century red-brick town-house with a beautiful walled garden; full of antique French-style furniture, rugs on polished floorboards and fresh flowers. The deliberate effect is charmingly faded.

The Wessex Hotel, Paternoster Row, **t** 861 611, *www.macdonald-hotels.co.uk* (*very expensive*). This large 1960s hotel has 94 bedrooms, some with views of the cathedral. Its location, on the edge of the cathedral precinct, is the best in town.

The Wykeham Arms, 75 Kingsgate Street, **t** 853 834 (*expensive*). Dating back to the 18th century and tucked away in the quietest, oldest and most charming part of town, between the college and cathedral; log fires, real ales, quirky memorabilia and old-fashioned charm; 14 cosy bedrooms nicely furnished with pictures and books include seven more modern rooms across the road.

The Winchester Royal Hotel, St Peter Street, **t** 840 840, *www.marstonhotels.com* (*expensive*). Handsome, extended 17th-century coaching inn with 75 bedrooms (most in modern part) and traditional restaurant.

Five Clifton Terrace, 5 Clifton Terrace, **t** 890 053, *chrissiejohnston@hotmail.com* (*moderate*). Two large rooms with king-sized beds in elegant Georgian terraced house 5 minutes' walk west of city centre.

Dawn Cottage, Romsey Road, **t** 869 956, *dawncottage@hotmail.com* (*moderate*). Friendly, cottagey guesthouse set back from busy road, 15 minutes' walk or quick bus ride from city centre. Three bedrooms.

Eating Out

Winchester has some top-notch restaurants: the Hotel Du Vin and Wykeham Arms feature prominently on any good-food list.

The Chesil Rectory, 1 Chesil Street, **t** 851 555 (*very expensive*). At the east end of the High Street, across the bridge, this 15th-century townhouse turned rectory offers modern English food with an emphasis on local produce – British cheeses, New Forest mushrooms and game, smoked trout from the Test, and Brixham sea fish. *Open Tues–Sat dinner, also Sat lunch.*

Hotel Du Vin Bistro, Southgate Street, **t** 841 414 (*expensive*). Elegant French-style bistro where you might have crab chowder or potted shrimps followed by roasted monkfish or steak and frites.

The Wykeham Arms, 75 Kingsgate Street, **t** 853 834 (*expensive*). You can eat on old, graffiti'd Winchester College desks in the bar or in the more formal restaurant. The high-quality menu might include smoked haddock kedgeree for lunch, Hampshire downland lamb or Thai-style beef for dinner.

Winchester Cathedral Refectory, Cathedral Close, **t** 857 258 (*cheap*). Modern visitor centre next to cathedral, offering light lunches such as jacket potatoes.

Cadogan and James, 31/a The Square, **t** 840 805 (*cheap*). Great little deli, which puts out a couple of pavement tables when the sun shines. Coffee and sandwich/soup. *Closed Sun.*

Winchester

Winchester is one of the country's most distinguished old towns, just an hour from London and near a Continental port, which means excellent restaurants (and sky-high house prices). The story of Winchester runs like a golden thread through the country's history. It was the heart of King Alfred's Anglo-Saxon kingdom and it remained the Norman capital until the 11th century. The Norman cathedral dominates. If you like military museums, you are in heaven (there are six). The national memorial of Alfred the Great 'the founder of the kingdom and nation' is here, a statue of the king glaring proudly with hand on shield.

At one end of the High Street is the 18th-century bridge over the Itchen and mill. The statue of King Alfred stands nearby, glowering at the West Gate. At the other end is the ruined castle. In-between stands the cathedral, behind it Winchester College and the Wykeham Arms (a good lunch stop). Downriver from the bridge you come to the water meadows, which inspired Keats' 'Ode To Autumn' (1819), Wolvesey Castle and St Cross Hospital. Cadogan and James deli is one of the nice shops on The Square and Great Minster Street.

Winchester Cathedral

Approach the cathedral from High Cross (the 15th-century market cross), passing under an old timber-framed house beside the church of St Lawrence. The cathedral close is dominated by the Isle-of-Wight-stone cathedral. It is magnificent. Pause at the site of the three great Saxon minsters. Alfred was buried in the Old Minster, moved to the New Minster and then to Hyde Abbey on the outskirts of town, where his tomb was destroyed at the Reformation. The Norman cathedral was unprecedented in scale, at 531ft long. A shrine was built in it for St Swithun, bishop of Winchester from 852 to 862, and the bones of the old Saxon kings were reinterred here.

The interior was remodelled in the 14th century in Perpendicular Gothic style. The west wall was knocked out to create an airy window, and an elaborate stone vault was suspended from the Norman roof beams. It was paid for by William of Wykeham, bishop of Winchester from 1366 to 1404, twice lord chancellor of England, and founder of Winchester College and New College, Oxford. His chantry chapel is on the south of the nave. On the north of the nave is the **tomb of Jane Austen**, who died in Winchester on 18 July 1817 aged 41. The inscription by her clergyman brother Henry oddly neglects to mention her writing; a memorial plaque was added in 1901 to fill the gap. Next to it is a 12th-century Tournai marble **font** acquired by art connoisseur Bishop Henry de Blois, with the story of St Nicholas carved around the sides (including the three boys chopped up in a pie). Fisherman Izaak Walton (1593–1683) is buried in a chapel in the south transept – the most atmospheric Norman part of the cathedral. Best known for *The Compleat Angler* (1653), which dramatizes the simple, pious delights of fishing through the songs and chatter of his central character, Piscator, he was married twice, first to the great-grand-niece of Thomas Cranmer, then to the half-sister of the canon of Winchester, and was friends with Bishop George Morley (1662–84). From here you can climb up to **Bishop Morley's library**, with

Winchester's Royal Connections

Winchester calls itself the 'ancient capital of Wessex'. So too do Wilton, Hindon, Somerton, Shaftesbury and Chippenham. All boast old royal palaces (buried). Alfred was buried in Winchester, but there is only one documentary mention (in the *Anglo-Saxon Chronicle*) of him visiting – to hang some Danes. In fact the Saxon royal house was mobile, camping wherever it could get a decent meal. Southampton was the biggest urban centre until Alfred founded 30 *burhs* in the 9th century. Winchester did not urbanize until late in the 800s, when it became one of the biggest *burhs*, safe behind the walls of *Ventna Belgarum*, the fifth largest town in Roman *Britannia*. It boomed in the 10th century (after Alfred's death); the names of its streets reflect its trades: food, leather, wood and iron. The Itchen and its tributaries powered mills, and 10 parish churches served its growing population. Alfred's cultural reform of the 880s were centred on religious houses; by the 10th century Winchester had three big ones. The **Old Minster** was the main cathedral in Wessex and the largest pre-Conquest cathedral. The **New Minster** (founded by Edward the Elder, Alfred's son) was an even larger monastery, whose hymns drowned out those of the Old Minster. On the south side was the **Nunminster**, founded by Alfred's queen. A distinctive **Winchester School** of arts and crafts emerged from the Old Minster under Bishop Æthelwold – manuscript illumination, metalwork, pottery and sculpture (stone and ivory). The most famous artwork is a book of blessings called *The Benediction of St Æthelwold*.

There were royal burials at Winchester too, but there were also royal burials at Wareham, Malmesbury, Sherborne, Wimborne and Shaftesbury. Winchester, however, looked like an important enough city for William the Conqueror to take it seriously. He built a castle, demolished the Saxon palace and built a new Norman palace. He

its barrel-shaped stone ceiling. Next door is a room devoted to the 12th-century **Winchester Bible**, one of the best Romanesque lectern bibles in existence. The four volumes took one monk 25 years to make. Henry de Blois paid for it. Carry on up the stairs to the triforium gallery, which houses fragments of sculpture rescued from the 15th-century great screen, smashed up at the Reformation.

The cathedral is thick with **tombs**, not all easy to identify. The tomb in the choir is thought to belong to **Henry de Blois**. The bones of **Saxon kings** are contained in six wooden mortuary chests in the chancel. There is **Cynegils** (611–43), the first Christian king of Wessex and his son, **Cenwalh**; then **Egbert**, whose defeat of the Mercians at the Battle of Ellendun in 825 made Wessex the dominant Anglo-Saxon kingdom; **Æthelwulf**, the father of Alfred the Great; **Canute** and his wife, Emma. And a Norman too: William I's second son, **Rufus**, who was killed in the New Forest in a peculiar hunting accident. He was the last king to be buried in Winchester. **St Swithun's shrine** at the east end of the cathedral is marked with a plaque.

Winchester College

By the west front of the cathedral are the massive wooden doors of **Kingsgate**, abutting half-timbered Cheyney Court – once the Bishop of Winchester's courthouse. Kingsgate leads into a part of town dominated by the flint walls of **Winchester** levelled the three Minsters to make way for one big cathedral; no other church in England or Normandy came close in size until the late 12th century. Coronations and royal births, christenings and burials, not to mention the recoronation and ritual bathing of Richard I after a disastrous crusade, established Winchester as an early medieval city with credentials. The findings of Domesday were delivered to Winchester and the royal treasure was kept in the palace there.

But after the royal centuries, power shifted to the bishops of Winchester – four treasurers and 10 lord chancellors among them. The most powerful of them all was **Henry de Blois** (1129–71), brother of King Stephen, grandson of William the Conqueror and Abbot of Glastonbury, builder and patron of the arts. He asked the Pope to elevate Winchester to a metropolitan see of Wessex, with him as archbishop. **William of Wykeham** (1367–1404) was another big bishop, lord chancellor and founder of Winchester College and New College, Oxford. Of the 21 dioceses in medieval England and Wales, the Diocese of Winchester was by far the richest. **St Giles' Fair** was the most renowned of the half dozen great annual fairs in England and took place in Winchester on St Giles Hill, owned by the bishop. He owned the river too, with all its mills, and he had his own courts and a palace with a moat and keep.

The Reformation did for Winchester. The bishops lost power, and it became the object of royal nostalgia, the Camelot of Tudor kings. It was in the 16th century that Alfred was first called the Great, like Charlemagne. In the 17th century Charles II commissioned Wren to design a summer palace here in the style of Versailles, but he died before it was built. Winchester seemed all washed up. But royal interest rekindled during the Napoleonic Wars, when Winchester became an assembly point for troops embarking at Portsmouth and the chief army barracks of the southwest.

College, one of the oldest schools in England, founded in 1382 by Bishop William of Wykeham. Guided tours of the chapel, hall and cloisters begin from the entrance on College Street. Jane Austen died of a diseased kidney in the yellow house on College Street. Because you are here anyway, or to mourn the early death of the great writer, stop for a quiet drink in the **Wickham Arms**.

From the end of College Street follow the riverside footpath over the meadows to **St Cross Hospital**. A branch of the river path leads a mile southeast to **St Catherine's Hill**, the old Iron Age hill fort that preceded the Roman town.

Wolvesey Castle

www.english-heritage.org.uk; open April–Sept 10.30–6, Oct 10–5; adm.

The medieval bishops of Winchester were a powerful bunch, Henry de Blois the most powerful of them all. His main abode was Wolvesey Castle. The keep-like kitchens are still standing, and a couple of towers; otherwise all you can see is the layout of the old buildings, marked in flint. Numerous state occasions took place at Wolvesey, including the wedding feasts of Henry IV in 1403 and Queen Mary in 1554. In 1415 the French ambassador met Henry V here to dissuade him from invading France – as dramatized in Shakespeare's *Henry V* – with a gift of tennis balls.

St Cross Hospital

t (01962) 851 375; open Mon–Sat, April–Oct 9.30–5, Nov–Mar 10.30–3.30; adm.

Cows graze around the walls of St Cross Hospital, in water meadows on the south of the city. It is the oldest 'almshouse of noble poverty' in England, founded in 1136 by Henry de Blois for 13 lucky beggars, and extended in 1446 by Cardinal Beaufort, son of John of Gaunt. Today 25 inmates are housed in 15th-century accommodation around a grass courtyard. On the wall of the Brothers' Hall is inscribed the 18th-century poem, 'O blest retreat retired from noise and strife,/ Could I but spend the evening of my life within these courts.' Why wait until evening? With its vegetable gardens, dovecote and 12th-century vaulted chapel it's a paradise on earth.

City and Westgate Museums

The **City Museum** (*t (01962) 848 269; open April–Oct Mon–Sat 10–5, Sun 12–5; Nov–Mar Tues–Sat 10–4, Sun 12–4*) in the square by the cathedral tells you all about the Roman, Saxon and medieval town, with Roman mosaics, an 11th-century tombstone from the Old Minster ('Here lies Gunni, the earl's companion') and medieval pots. There is a copy of the *Blessings of Æthelwold*, one of the best things to come out of the famous Winchester School of art. The story continues (16th–17th centuries) in the **Westgate Museum** (*t (01962) 848 269; open Feb–Mar Tues–Sat 10–4, Sun 2–4, April–Oct Mon–Sat 10–5, Sun 12–5*) at the end of the High Street.

The Great Hall and Round Table

t (01962) 846 476; open summer daily 10–5, winter weekends 10–4.

There's not much left of the Norman castle where Henry III was born and William I's treasury kept. Only the **Great Hall** survives, built by Henry III in Gothic style, with Purbeck stone columns, pointed arches and tracery windows. Everybody comes to see the **Round Table** on the wall, 18ft across and weighing a ton. It's proof of the nostalgia of English kings for their semi-legendary forebears: it was made by either Henry III or Edward I, both big fans of King Arthur, and repainted by Henry VIII in Tudor colours for the visit of Emperor Charles V.

The Military Museums

Open daily 10–4; some close for lunch.

Most of these museums are in the Peninsula Barracks. The **Royal Green Jackets** have a long association with Winchester. They were the SAS of the 1800s, their motto 'first into the field and last to leave'. The **Royal Hampshire Regiment** moved to Winchester in 1881. Until then, infantry regiments were numbered and had no base. Their headquarters are on Southgate Street. The **King's Royal Hussars** (*closed Mon*) are more recent arrivals. Their history includes charging down a Crimean valley towards the big Russian guns in what Tennyson romantically termed the 'Charge of the Light Brigade'. The most modern exhibitions are the **Light Infantry Museum** (*closed Sun*) and the **Ghurkha Museum** (*closed Sun*). The light infantry were trained to skirmish, at first wearing breeches and stiff red tunics, replaced by khaki and camouflage in the 1750s. The Ghurkhas were Nepalese soldiers enlisted by the British for their toughness.

East Hampshire

'This is not a great farming land and there are no famous country houses,' said Ralph Dutton of Hinton Ampner. The triangle of countryside between Winchester, Basingstoke and Petersfield is rolling, open chalkland. The houses are less interesting than their occupants, who have included Jane Austen. **New Alresford** is a perfect lunch stop, its market street lined with handsome lime trees and Georgian houses. It is at the end of the **Watercress Line** steam railway, which runs 10 miles to Alton.

Jane Austen's House

Open Mar–Nov daily 11–4; Dec–Feb weekends 11–4; adm.

Jane Austen was a Hampshire girl, although she avoids Hampshire in her novels, preferring the West Country (*Sense and Sensibility*), Hertfordshire and Derbyshire (*Pride and Prejudice*), Northamptonshire (*Mansfield Park*), Bath (*Persuasion*) and the Welsh Marches (*Northanger Abbey*).

The author grew up in her father's rectory in a village outside Basingstoke, and, on his retirement, moved with the family to Southampton, after five unhappy years in Bath. In 1809 Jane, her mother, sister Cassandra and friend Martha Lloyd moved into this pretty brick house in the village of Chawton, just south of Alton. It's all sash windows, white-painted doors with brass knobs and narrow corridors with creaky floorboards. All six of the writer's major novels were finished during her eight years in Chawton. Memorabilia includes her three-legged writing desk and a patchwork quilt she made with her mother out of scraps of old frocks.

Selborne

A few miles south of Chawton is Selborne, a little thatched village dripping with wisteria where the much-loved naturalist Gilbert White was born in 1722 and lived until his death in 1793. To the west of the village is a chalk hill, or hanger, covered in beech woods. To the east is gentle greensand stone countryside.

White's *Natural History of Selborne* was first published in 1789. Darwin said that it was the book that inspired his interest in zoology. William Cobbett made a detour through Selborne in August 1853, having recently read it. 'Nothing can surpass in beauty these dells and hillocks and hangers,' he wrote in *Rural Rides*, 'which last are so steep that it is impossible to ascend them, except by means of a serpentine path,' and he jumped off his horse to measure the circumference of a yew tree trunk in the churchyard (23ft 8in). From the Selborne Arms you can walk in the footsteps of the naturalist, up the zig-zag path he and his brother cut up Selborne Hill in 1753. The descent to Love Lane is more gentle. Gilbert is buried in the churchyard (by the stump of Cobbett's yew) behind the village green. The Gilbert White House tearoom serves home-made lemonade and homity pie, or mushroom and chestnut pasties.

The Gilbert White House

t (01420) 511 275; open daily 11–5; adm.

Gilbert White's house, the Wakes, looks as it might have done when he lived in it – thanks to careful restoration. Rosemary and honesty grow by the back door, yellow roses climb up the walls and a magnificent cypress stands in long meadow grass. You can see the original manuscript of *The Natural History of Selborne*, the book that made White a cult figure and suffused Selborne in perpetual sunshine and birdsong. It's all about the little things, like the 'little party of swallows' playing around horse-riders on the downs and the 'skulking insects' kicked up by their trampling hooves, and full of superstitious country folk, naughty boys and gamekeepers' anecdotes.

Hinton Ampner Manor House

t (01962) 771 305; open Easter–Sept Sat–Wed 12–5, Aug weekends 1.30–5; adm.

East of Winchester, the tiny hamlet of Hinton Ampner is hidden from the busy A272 on the edge of the South Downs. The red-brick manor house (*open summer Tues–Wed, Aug also weekends*) is covered in magnolia and honeysuckle, and its gardens are the work of the quietly extraordinary Ralph Dutton, last Lord Sherborne, who remodelled the house in Regency style and wrote a book about it called *A Hampshire Manor*. Dutton often said that he should have been born in the 18th century, instead of 1936.

Old Winchester Hill

Old Winchester Hill is the last summit along the South Downs before Winchester. To reach it, go down the A32 and take the lane before West Meon for a mile. It is crowned with an Iron Age hill fort built 2,500 years ago. You can see as far as the Isle of Wight from the summit, a short walk along the rim of the chalk bowl.

Portsmouth

The town is bare, and little occupied in time of peace.

John Leland (1502–52), Henry VIII's antiquarian

Portsmouth, on the island of Portsea, is a naval town between the Portsdown Hills and the sea, but not as romantic as it sounds. The island is linked to the mainland by major roads (the M275 and A27) and the town was flattened in the Second World War. Its history, however, is all about the defence of the realm. Portsmouth is still a naval town: 60 percent of the surface fleet is based here, including all the Royal Navy Destroyers. There are four navy training schools around Portsmouth (called HMS Collingwood, HMS Dryad, HMS Saltern and HMS Temeraire, although they are no longer ships), and the headquarters of the Royal Marines are on Whale Island, just inside the harbour. John Dickens, an employee of the Naval Pay Office, brought his wife Elizabeth to Portsmouth in 1809, and a few years later Charles Dickens was born here. They lived in a house on the main road into Portsmouth and briefly in Southsea, a smart new seaside development for senior naval staff. Charles was two when the family moved back to London, but still remembered the place well.

Commercial cargo and passenger ferries to France, Spain and the Channel Islands, and the Isle of Wight car ferry have been established on the site of the old dockyards. Portsmouth Harbour includes Gosport and Portchester, and three official naval museums: the **Royal Submarine Museum** in Gosport, and the **Royal Naval Museum** and **Royal Marine Museum** in Portsmouth. But the biggest draw is the historic ships in the naval base: ***Mary Rose***, **HMS *Victory*** and **HMS *Warrior***.

The Historic Dockyard

t (023) 9286 1533; open 10–4.30; adm exp.

The historic dockyard is still a working naval yard, so expect drilling and hammering. Each of the ships on display is a pioneer of a new technology, from the Middle Ages to the 19th century. The ***Mary Rose*** (1511–45) was an early example of the new type of Tudor battleship, featuring heavy cannon; until then ships had been used as floating castles to get as close to the enemy as possible for hand-to-hand fighting. The *Mary Rose* sank off Southsea in an unmemorable skirmish with the French, and all but 40 of the 400 sailors drowned. Henry VIII stood screaming on the shore as it sank due to a failure to close the lower gun decks, which flooded.

When Nelson went to sea in the 1770s, the 'line of battle' concept had developed, and ships of the line had evolved into distinct classes distinguished by the number of guns. The ***Victory***, the most famous first-rate ship, was Nelson's flagship at Trafalgar in 1805, a symbol of the supremacy of the Royal Navy. Nelson lost an eye in Corsica, an arm at Tenerife, was shot in the stomach at St Vincent and wounded in the head at the Nile, and returned from Trafalgar in a barrel of brandy guarded by marines. He is the consummate schoolboy naval hero. A brass plaque marks the spot where he died.

In 1859 France launched *La Gloire*, the first warship to be armed with iron plates, making all wooden-hulled ships obsolete. Britain responded with **HMS *Warrior***, the first iron-framed and iron-clad battleship using both steam and sail.

Old Portsmouth

From the motorway, follow signs to Old Portsmouth. The **cathedral** is worth a look: the nave with its round columns and white Purbeck stone looks like a children's-book Roman villa. It was added in the 1930s, when the old church of St Thomas was elevated to cathedral status. The new building incorporates the original 12th-century chapel built by Jean de Gisors, a rich merchant who also built himself a quay. De Gisors' quay developed into the medieval dockyard, or camber, under Richard I, Henry VII, Henry VIII and Charles II; the town grew around it. The camber is now crowded with pleasure boats, and a defensive sea wall protects Old Portsmouth and its streets – Grand Parade, Battery Row, Tower Street and Capstan Square. The Point used to be the seamy place where sailors got into fights; it still has a couple of good pubs where you can get a plate of chips with your beer. Broad Street extends between the camber sea wall and Governor's Green, at the centre of which is the 12th-century **Royal**

Getting There and Around

By **car**, take the M3 from London, the M27 from the west, the A34 from the Midlands or the A27 along the coast from Chichester.

Portsmouth Harbour station is the terminus for a regular **train** service from London Waterloo, which also stops at Portsmouth and Southsea station on Commercial Road, near the modern High Street. For all train information call **National Rail Enquiries**,**t** 08457 484950 or go to *www.thetrainline.com*.

National Express runs several **coaches** a day to Portsmouth coach station on The Hard. Stage Coach, **t** 01903 237 661, runs local **buses** between the south-coast resort towns.

Brittany Ferries and P&O run **ferries** to France and Spain from Portsmouth's Continental Ferry Port, 10 minutes from the town centre.

Wightlink Ferries, **t** 0870 5827744, operate from the old harbour, off The Hard, running car ferries to Fishbourne and passenger ferries to Ryde on the Isle of Wight.

Tourist Information

Portsmouth: The Hard, near Victory Gate (entrance to Historic Dockyard). *Open 9.30–5.30.*

Southsea: Clarence Esplanade, **t** (023) 9282 6722. *Open 9.30–5.30.*

Festivals

The **Tall Ships Festival** took place for the first time in Portsmouth in August 2002, and should be back in 2005. Historic boats from all around the world moor in the harbour, accompanied by street entertainment and jollities on the seafront. Go to *www.joliebrize.com* for the latest.

Where to Stay and Eat

Portsmouth t (023) –

There is plenty of basic accommodation in Portsmouth. Base yourself in the atmospheric Old Town if you can, or stay on Wickham's delightful market square, 9 miles north of Portsmouth. Your best bet for food is fish and chips or pub grub.

The Queen's Hotel, Clarence Parade, Southsea, **t** 9282 2466, *www.queenshotel-southsea.co.uk* (*very expensive*). Magnificent Edwardian hotel overlooking the Common, with ornate stone-carved balconies and countless neoclassical decorative flourishes. There are two bars, a restaurant (*moderate*) and 74 rooms, including large rooms with sea views.

Garrison Church (*open April–Oct Mon–Fri 11–4*), built as a charitable hospital and taken over by the army in the 16th century, when a Governor's House was built too.

Charles Dickens Birthplace Museum

t *(023) 9282 7261; open April–Sept 10–5.30, Oct 10–5; adm.*

Since it opened in 1903, Dickens' birthplace at 393 Old Commercial Road has been an object of pilgrimage. The terraced Victorian street to which John Dickens brought his new wife Elizabeth in summer 1809 used to be on the outskirts of town. They stayed here until late spring 1812, giving birth to their first child, Fanny, in 1810 and Charles on 7 February 1812. Charles remembered the front garden in later life. The rooms are furnished in the style of a lower middle-class family of 1812, with Dickens memorabilia including the sofa on which he died 58 years later in Gad's Hill Place (*see* p.163).

Southsea

Southsea grew up as a suburb of Old Portsmouth, then became a Victorian seaside resort. **Southsea Castle** (***t*** *(023) 9282 7261; open April–Oct 10–5; adm*), one of Henry VIII's forts, retains its Tudor keep and design. From its turrets, Henry VIII

Sally Port Inn, High Street, **t** 9282 1860 (*moderate*). A 16th-century timber-framed townhouse opposite the cathedral with a magnificent Georgian cantilevered staircase and 10 modest, cheerful bedrooms with personal showers and hand basins. First-floor restaurant serves fish (*Thurs–Sat*). Bar meals served daily.

Fortitude Cottage, 51 Broad Street, **t** 9282 3748, *fortcott@aol.com* (*moderate*). Charming cottage overlooking the old quayside. The bright breakfast room has a bay window and pretty blue-and-white china.

The Seacrest Hotel, 12 South Parade, **t** 9273 3192, *www.seacresthotel.co.uk* (*moderate*). Comfortable, old-fashioned seafront hotel with white portico opposite the D-Day Museum; 12 of the 28 cheerful bedrooms look out towards the Solent. There's a restaurant too (*cheap*).

The Still and West, 2 Bath Square, **t** 9282 1567 (*cheap*). Old-world brass and dark wood pub with ships painted on the ceiling. Bar meals served downstairs, cheerful restaurant upstairs specializing in fish. Big windows make you feel like you're on a boat.

Spice Island, Bath Square, **t** 9282 4293 (*cheap*). Modern-style family pub on two floors; downstairs fish and chip shop and bar; upstairs restaurant serving pub grub.

Wickham t (01329) –

The Old House Hotel and Restaurant, The Square, **t** 833 049, *www.theoldhousehotelandrestaurant.co.uk* (*expensive*). Stylish Georgian hotel in delightful little country town 9 miles north of Portsmouth, with an interesting mix of contemporary and period décor. Lovely bedrooms, some with original fire grates or wooden panelling, and several dining rooms, including one in converted stables overlooking the garden. Lunches and dinners of local, seasonal produce might include roast pigeon, green-herb-crusted brill or steak Rossini, all topped off with a traditional bread and butter pudding and lashings of cream.

The Wickham Wine Bar and Restaurant, The Square, **t** 832 732 (*moderate*). A late 15th-century timber-framed building with creaking floorboards and a rare 16th-century wall painting upstairs. The cooking is modern international, with an unusual mixture of delicious dishes such as smoked chicken Caesar salad followed by Cajun spiced pork belly, or butter-roasted, oak-smoked cod and dark Belgian chocolate and butterscotch tart with home-made ice cream. *Closed Sun.*

watched the *Mary Rose* sink. The **D-Day Museum** (***t*** *(023) 9282 7261; open April–Sept 10–5.30, Oct–Mar 10–5; adm*) has a tapestry of the Second World War.

Follow the coast road east from Southsea to the **Royal Marines Museum** (***t*** *(023) 9281 9385; open June–Sept 10–4.30, Oct–May 10–4.30; adm*) in Eastney. The marines were first trained in 1664 for the Dutch Wars, in response to the changing nature of sea warfare. The prime exhibit is a Bond-style motorized submersible canoe known as the 'sleeping beauty', developed for the SBS (the marine SAS) to take divers armed with boat mines into enemy harbours; it was used only once, in 1944, in Operation Rimau; none of the 23 divers returned.

Portchester and Gosport

The Romans built **Portchester Castle** (***t*** *(023) 9237 8291; open Mar–Sept 10–6, Oct 10–5, Nov–Mar 10–4; adm*) on a chalk hill behind the harbour, which they named *Portus Magnus*, the Great Port. King Alfred's son Edward established a *burh* with a garrison of up to 650 men. It was converted into a Norman castle with a keep and inner bailey in 1120. The small town outside the walls produced salt and fed the castle. The harbour was deep enough for shipping until the 12th century. It's lovely today.

Gosport is across the harbour from Portsmouth. The **Royal Navy Submarine Museum**

The Royal Dockyards

The early medieval period was the era of the Cinque Ports of Kent and Sussex, which provided ships and men to kings of England in return for trading privileges. Later, Southampton was used for naval duties by King John, Edward III and Henry V, ferrying soldiers off to interminable wars in France. The royal dockyards developed in the south of England in the Tudor period. This is when Portsmouth came into its own, along with Deptford and Woolwich on the Thames, Chatham on the Medway, and Devonport on the south coast. Henry VIII is credited with the foundation of the first permanent standing fleet. He commissioned 46 purpose-built warships (built in the Thames dockyards), including the innovative *Mary Rose* with its complete line of gun ports. It kept the French and Spanish fleets at bay, but could never have launched an attack on the scale of the Spanish Armada. The 16th-century Anglo-French and Anglo-Spanish wars, and the three 17th-century Dutch Wars saw the Royal Navy humiliated on more than a few occasions, notably in the Dutch blockades of the Thames and De Ruyter's capture of the Royal naval flagship at anchor in the Medway. It was not until the long European wars against Louis XIV that the Navy began to regain mastery of the seas for the first time since the Armada, climaxing in the glorious victory of Vice-Admiral Horatio Nelson against the Franco-Spanish fleet off Cape Trafalgar in 1805. Portsmouth's dockyard boomed in the 19th century, building 150 warships with names such as *Devastation* and *Inflexible*. Lord Palmerston said that 'it would be better to lose Gladstone than to run the risk of losing Portsmouth'. Britannia ruled the waves.

there (***t** (023) 9252 9217, www.rnsubmus.co.uk; open April–Oct Mon–Sun 10–5.30, Nov–Mar Mon–Sun 10–4.30; adm*) occupies the old HMS Dolphin submarine naval base. You can reach it from the A32 to Fareham or on the Gosport ferry from Portsmouth. *Holland I* (1901–13) was the navy's first submarine and the forerunner of all future designs. HMS *X-24* is a rare example of the midget X-craft submarines used in the Second World War. They would be released from the mother submarine, and divers would swim from them to clamp explosives onto the bottom of enemy ships. HMS *Alliance* (1945–73) is one of a type of submarine used right through the Cold War.

Around Portsmouth

The roads around Portsmouth Harbour are busy, but there are a few sights to see. Between the A27 and M27, seek out the ruins of **Titchfield Abbey** (***t** (01329) 842 133; open dawn–dusk*), founded in 1232 for Premonstratensian monks. At the Dissolution, Thomas Wriothesley, Earl of Southampton and a favourite of Elizabeth I, converted it into a Tudor mansion. Wriothesley was the patron to whom Shakespeare dedicated his poems 'Venus and Adonis' (1593) and 'Rape of Lucrece' (1594); he is thought to have been the 'fair youth' of Shakespeare's sonnets. North of the M27, the A32 heads into the **Meon Valley** via the market town of **Wickham**, birthplace of William of Wykeham, Bishop of Winchester. Its 18th-century brick houses and shops make it a pleasant stop, before the prettiest stretch of the valley. A narrow lane just before West Meon leads to **Old Winchester Hill** with its Iron Age fort and views (*see* p.226).

Southampton

Southampton sprawls between the Itchen and Test rivers on Southampton Water. Big motorways tie ugly knots around the town, urging you to leap onto the Cowes ferry. Southampton's history is all Venetian wine merchants, Cunard and White Star liners. Today it's all cars, containers and cruise ships. The Eastern Docks, where the *QEII* is berthed, developed in the mid-19th century; the Western Docks in the 1920s.

The Old Town

Head straight down Above Bar Street to medieval Bargate, the main gate into the old town from the north. This is the watery setting for James Cameron's film *Titanic*. Sections of the medieval walls and old town gates, including **God's House Tower**, a

Getting There and Around

By **car** from the north follow the M3 onto the A33 into the centre. From the west, turn off the M27 at junction 3 onto the M271, then the A36 into the centre. From the east, turn off the M27 at junction 7 onto the A334.

There is a direct, regular, frequent **train** service from London Waterloo.

National Express **coaches** run several times daily from London Victoria to Harbour Parade.

Red Funnel **ferries, t** 0870 4448898, *www.redfunnel.co.uk*, run from Town Quay to East Cowes on the Isle of Wight.

Southampton is the UK's major **cruise-liner** port with P&O liners docking at the Mayflower Terminal and Cunard using the Ocean Terminal near Ocean Village Marina.

Blue Funnel, **t** (02380) 223 278, run various **mini-cruises** from Ocean Village Marina, including a 4½-hour trip to West Cowes and back, a 3-hour three-river (Hamble, Test and Itchen) cruise and a 1-hour harbour tour.

Tourist Information

Southampton: 9 Civic Road, **t** (02380) 221 106. *Open Mon–Sat 8.30–5.30.*

Test Valley: 13 Church Street, Romsey, **t** (01794) 512 987. *Open summer 9.30–5, winter 10–4.*

The **International Boat Show, t** (01784) 473 377, takes place around Town Quay in mid-September, with tents full of the latest boats and boating equipment on Mayflower Park and around Town Quay.

The **Hot Air Balloon and Flower Festival** takes place on Southampton Common, The Avenue (A33), **t** (02380) 832525, over the first weekend of July; mass hot-air-balloon take-off at 6am and 6pm, and stalls selling arts and crafts, flowers and vegetables.

Where to Stay

Southampton t (02380) –

De Vere Grand Harbour Hotel, West Quay Road, **t** (02380) 633 033, *www.deveregrand harbour.co.uk* (*luxury*). Snazzy modern hotel with pyramid-like glass façade, on perfectly flat reclaimed land on site of old west quay; spacious marble reception area, exotic foliage, space and daylight. Facilities include two restaurants, bar and leisure club. Some of the 172 bedrooms have balconies.

The Dolphin Hotel, 34–5 High Street, **t** 339 955, *www.thedolphin.co.uk* (*very expensive*). Exciting things are afoot for this attractive stucco-fronted coaching inn with its distinctive two-storey bay windows. Millions of pounds have been spent on top-to-bottom refurbishment in contemporary style. The 70 bedrooms are to have laminated maple wood floors, and buttermilk walls hung with contemporary art. Restaurants, bars and boutique shops are planned off the courtyard, through the coaching arch.

The Star Hotel, 26 High Street, **t** 339 939, *www.thestarhotel.com* (*moderate*). Handsome cream-stuccoed coaching inn with grand central archway and ornate iron

15th-century artillery fort, and two water gates, survive. Leave the wall via the famous **West Gate**, where wine and wool used to come in and go out. Henry V led his army through it to Harfleur and Agincourt. The Pilgrim Fathers embarked here for America in 1620. **Bugle Street** is the main street of the old town, with striking old buildings. Container ships glide uncannily past the end of the street.

The medieval fish market took place in **St Michael's Square**, where a half-timbered house, now the **Tudor House Museum** (***t*** *(023) 8063 5904; closed for restoration*), shows the wealth generated by Southampton merchants. In a 15th-century wool warehouse is the **Maritime Museum** (*open Tues–Fri 10–1 and 2–5, Sat 10–1 and 2–4, Sun 2–5*), with models of cruise liners. Across the road in Mayflower Park is a memorial

balcony on first floor; 45 bedrooms and a pleasant panelled restaurant and bar.

The Elizabeth House Hotel, 42–4 The Avenue, **t** 224 327, *www.elizabethhousehotel.com* (*moderate*). Less than a mile from the city centre in a pleasant and leafy part of the city near the university. Two late Victorian/early Edwardian creeper-clad buildings; 28 fresh, bright bedrooms; restaurant and bar.

Eating Out

Ennio's Al Porto, Town Quay Road, **t** 221 159 (*moderate*). Welcoming Italian restaurant on ground floor of five-storey red-brick Victorian warehouse opposite the Red Funnel terminal. Strong on fish. *Closed Sun.*

Buon Gusto, 1 Commercial Road, **t** 331 543 (*cheap*). Popular pre-theatre Italian restaurant close to Mayflower Theatre, where you can start with whitebait or calamari, followed by pasta and steak. *Closed Sun.*

The Olive Tree, 29 Oxford Street, **t** 343 333 (*cheap*). Contemporary Mediterranean-style restaurant with live jazz on Sunday nights.

The Duke of Wellington, 36 Bugle Street, **t** 234 688 (*cheap*). Gentle old pub in old town with long pavement benches where you can plonk yourself down on a sunny day and feel you have been spirited back to old Southampton. Serves decent pub grub.

The Red Lion, 55 High Street, **t** 333 595 (*cheap*). Atmospheric pub below Bargate, said to have been the setting for the trial of the three conspirators against Henry V just before he sailed for France in 1415. Lunch, dinner and Sunday carvery.

Test Valley

Berties, 80 The Hundred, Romsey **t** (01794) 830 708 (*moderate*). Twin brother of Berties in Winchester; same upmarket Mediterranean-style cooking in contemporary setting. *Closed Sun.*

The Greyhound, 31 High Street, Stockbridge, **t** (01264) 810 833 (*moderate*). Traditional Georgian coaching inn with rooms offering trout fishing on the Test and excellent upmarket bar meals using seasonal local ingredients, mainly fish. *Closed Sun eve.*

Entertainment

Mayflower Theatre, Commercial Road, **t** 711 811. Glitzy productions of West End musicals in a recently refurbished 1928 auditorium with several bars.

Turner Sims Concert Hall, University of Southampton, **t** 595 151, *www.turnersims.co.uk*. Purpose-built hall on campus north of the centre (take Burgess Road off The Avenue (A33) and then University Road) hosts two classical/jazz/world/folk concerts a week.

Nuffield Theatre, University of Southampton, **t** 671 771. Next door to Turner Sims; four productions a year by resident director, and amateur student dramatics. Theatre bar for light meals.

Harbour Lights Cinema, Ocean Village, **t** 335 533. Superbly designed modern arts cinema.

to the Pilgrim Fathers. Ferries cross to the Isle of Wight and Hythe from the modern **Town Quay**. Past the Eastern Docks on Albert Road South is the **Southampton Hall of Aviation** (*t (023) 8063 5830; open Tues–Fri 10–5, Sat 10–4, Sun 12–5; adm*), devoted to early aircraft companies like Avro, Vickers-Supermarine and De Havilland, which set up around the Solent. The centrepiece is a legendary Battle of Britain Spitfire.

From Merchants and Warmongering Kings to Cruise Liners

Southampton was once Hamwic, the chief Saxon port of the south of England, connected by river with Winchester. **West Quay** was the earliest centre of trade in the town, importing as much wine as London and exporting wool to Flanders. This is where a French raiding party landed in 1338, leading to massive fortification of the city walls. In the 15th century, Southampton had a monopoly on metal exports, notably Cornish tin. The new **Watergate Quay** was built at this time. Henry V launched his military campaigns in France from Southampton – an army of 6,000 soldiers and 24,000 archers. The Italian trade brought wealth and glamour to the town: rich merchants from Genoa, Venice, Catalonia and Aragon built big houses. The end of the Italian trade in the 16th century and the prohibition on wool exports began two centuries of decline. But between 1870 and 1930 Southampton was transformed into a passenger port to rival Liverpool. This was the golden age of sleek, white-funnelled luxury liners with magnificent names like *Oceanic*, *Olympic*, *Carpathia* – and *Titanic*.

The Golden Age of the Luxury Liner

By day, Harris Tweed, Chanel jerseys, indolent conversation and energetic sport. By night, a sudden increase in tempo, a blaze of jewels, the gleam of ivory shoulders.

Cunard publicist

When the railway came to the docks in 1892, Southampton began its rise as a passenger port. People were clamouring to emigrate and money was poured into the docks. In 1907, White Star transferred its big ships *Cedric*, *Celtic*, *Baltic* and *Adriatic* from Liverpool to Southampton. These super-liners were grand hotels of the sea with private cabins, passenger decks and ornate lounges. The ship was as important as the destination. Cunard's *Lusitania* and *Mauretania* were 'the largest, most powerful, and by intention the fastest ocean liners ever constructed' in their time. White Star responded with *Olympic*, which had electric lifts and daily newspapers printed at sea. And *Titanic*, which was fast enough for a weekly transatlantic service – in theory. Cunard's *Carpathia*, *en route* from New York to Gibraltar, picked up *Titanic*'s distress signal, three days out of Southampton on her maiden voyage to New York in 1912. *Carpathia* raced 58 miles in three hours, by which time *Titanic* had sunk along with 1,503 of the 2,206 people on board. The mania for transatlantic liners carried on regardless until cheap flights messed it all up. Now cruise liners are being built again.

Romsey and the Test Valley

The Test Valley is known for its market gardens and trout fishing. **Romsey** is its main town, and its main attraction is the Norman abbey church. It was founded by Alfred the Great's son Edward in 907 and rebuilt in the 12th century by Bishop Henry de Blois of Winchester with three storeys of Romanesque arches and zigzag decoration. The nave is 250ft long and 70ft high. A memorial marks the grave of Earl Mountbatten of Burma, who lived at Broadlands over the bridge. In the market place is a bronze statue of Palmerston (1784–1865), responsible for the string of naval blockhouses around the south coast known as Palmerston's Follies, in political debating mode.

Outside Romsey is the **Harold Hillier Arboretum** (*t (01794) 368 787; open 10.30–6; adm)*. Hillier called his 180-acre arboretum a 'stamp collection of plants'.

Broadlands

t (01794) 505 010; open mid-June–Aug 12–5.30; adm.

The elegant Palladian mansion of Broadlands by Henry Holland and Capability Brown was the home of Henry John Temple, 3rd Viscount Palmerston. Twice prime minister (1855–8 and 1859–65), Palmerston switched sides from Tory to Whig early in his career, over the issue of parliamentary reform, and is remembered for a liberal and reckless foreign policy (helping Italy to achieve unity, and fighting the Crimean War). Earl Mountbatten retired to the house after the Second World War and opened it up to the public before he was assassinated in Ireland in 1979. The great-great-grandson and godson of Queen Victoria, he held the posts of Supreme Allied Commander of Southeast Asia, Viceroy of India and Lord Lieutenant of the Isle of Wight. Both Queen Elizabeth II and Prince Charles began their honeymoons in the first-floor portico room.

Mottisfont Abbey

t (01794) 340 757; open Easter–Oct Sat–Wed 11–6, June daily house 11–6, grounds 11–8.30, July and Aug also Thurs; adm.

A little further up the Test is Mottisfont Abbey, a 16th–18th-century mansion on the site of a 12th-century Augustinian priory. At the Reformation the old monastery was given to William, Lord Sandys, lord chamberlain to Henry VIII, in exchange for the villages of Chelsea and Paddington. Lord Sandys converted the priory church into his home, and it was extended again in the 1740s. The collection of old-fashioned roses in the walled garden is at its best in June. Inside, only the *trompe l'oeil* drawing room painted in 1938 by Rex Whistler is open to visitors.

The river and A3057 continue north to Andover through delightful countryside. Stop at the attractive little town of **Stockbridge**, whose attractive High Street has lots of places to eat including the Michelin-starred Greyhound.

Getting There and Around

By **car**, the M27 from Winchester and London ends at Brook on the northeast edge of the forest, then you're soon lost in the forest.

There is a mainline **train** service from Bournemouth, Southampton and London Waterloo to Ashhurst, Beaulieu Road, Sway and Brockenhurst.

National Express **coaches** run regularly to Southampton from London Victoria.

Tourist Information

Lymington and New Forest Visitor Centre, New Street, Lymington, **t** (01590) 689 000. *Open winter Mon–Sat 10–4, summer Mon–Sat 10–5.*

Lyndhurst and New Forest Visitor Centre, car park, Lyndhurst, **t** (02380) 282 269. *Open winter 10–4, spring 10–5, summer 10–6.*

Where to Stay and Eat

There are 10 Forestry Commission camping sites scattered around the forest, **t** (0131) 314 6505 or *www.forestholidays.co.uk* for details.

Minstead t (02380) –

The Trusty Servant, Minstead, **t** 812 137 (*moderate*). Excellent pub with menu ranging from pies and ploughman's to hearty steaks, roast duck, beef and Yorkshire pudding. Six comfortable bedrooms.

Eugenie Cottage, Seamans Corner, **t** 813 325 (*cheap*). Welcoming, in a lovely setting.

Brockenhurst t (01590) –

Rhinefield House Hotel, Rhinefield Road, **t** 622 922, *www.rhinefieldhousehotel.co.uk* (*very expensive*). Magnificent grey-stone Victorian stately home with crenellations in middle of forest. Big show trees – redwoods and copper beeches – on either side of long drive; elegant lounge, dining room and ample grounds. Two nights minimum stay at weekends.

Thatched Cottage, 16 Brookley Road, **t** 623 090 (*expensive*). Five double bedrooms in this 17th-century oak-beamed, thatched former farm cottage; next door is an excellent restaurant in a barn-like extension, open Wed–Sat for breakfast, lunch and dinner. Its three-tier cream tea has won awards; it comes with sandwiches, scones (plain, sultana and wholemeal, and walnut), cakes and a pot of tea, or champagne if you prefer. Dinner might be sautéed New Forest wild mushrooms with crayfish mousse and champagne sauce followed by roasted Romsey lamb, New Forest venison or perhaps Brixham shellfish.

The Cloud Hotel, Meerut Road, **t** 622 165, *www.cloudhotel.co.uk* (*expensive*). Elegant cream-painted hotel – formerly three 1900s terraced cottages – on edge of delightful expanse of forest lawn, with 18 cheerful bedrooms, 10 overlooking the forest. Restaurant and comfortable lounges.

Cottage Hotel, Sway Road, **t** 622 296, *www.cottagehotel.org* (*moderate*). Former forester's cottage set back from Sway Road with white walls, bright yellow front door and plants; snug and welcoming with fire, books and photos in lounge bar; six comfortable bedrooms.

Simply Poussin, The Courtyard, Brookley Road, Brockenhurst, **t** 623 063 (*moderate*). Small, relaxed restaurant with emphasis on seasonal local ingredients. The menu might include roast wood pigeon, pot-roasted pork, rare sirloin beef. *Closed Sun and Mon.*

Beaulieu and Buckler's Hard t (01590) –

The Montagu Arms Hotel, on main road through Beaulieu village, **t** 612 324, *www.montaguarmshotel.co.uk* (*luxury*). Flash hotel with wisteria dripping off its walls; 23 bedrooms with stylish fabrics and handsome furniture, fine dining restaurant and informal brasserie with sofas where meals include burgers and chips or lamb with mashed potato, gravy and green beans.

The Master Builder's House Hotel, Buckler's Hard, **t** 616 253, *www.themasterbuilders.co.uk* (*luxury*). This newish swanky hotel occupies a beautiful Georgian house built for the master builder – Henry Adams – of the 18th-century ship-building industry that developed here on the west bank of Beaulieu River. The popular Yachtsman's Bar is decorated with yachting photographs by Beken of Cowes. The restaurant is top-class.

Forest Enclosure

In 1079, William I enclosed a huge area of rough, wooded countryside, including villages and fields, and called it *Novo Foresta*, after which he brutally turfed villagers out of their houses and poked out their eyes for poaching. The forest was governed by Forest Law and had its own courts. The commoners had rights to graze sheep and livestock (pasture), turn out pigs to feed on autumn acorns or beech nuts (mast), cut turf (turbary) and wood for fuel (estovers) and dig clay marl for fertilizer (marl). The king had the right to blind anyone who stole his deer. In 1100 King Rufus, the Conqueror's son, was killed by an arrow while hunting in the New Forest. Some said it was the forest's revenge. Others pointed the finger at the King's brother Henry, who rushed straight to Winchester to bury Rufus and have himself crowned, then threw his other brother Robert in jail for ever.

Through the centuries the forest has gone from royal hunting-ground to producer of timber for shipbuilding. In the 1970s, when the Forestry Commission took over its running from the Crown, a Verderer's Court was set up to protect commoners' rights to turn out ponies in the forest, and, less popularly, to dig marl.

The New Forest

Quite suddenly, coming off the M27 from Southampton, the trees begin to thicken. In no time at all you enter the forest, a place where you could still, really, get lost. The New Forest is not all trees, however: there are thousands of acres of open heathland roamed by wild ponies; arable farmland; pasture; villages; towns, conifer plantations – and large tracts of broadleaf woodland. The oak woods are the real thing – great old trees growing out of the spongy forest lawn like something out of *A Midsummer Night's Dream*. On sunny weekends, thousands of cars with mountain bikes on their roofs are absorbed by the forest. The main centres, **Lyndhurst** and **Brockenhurst**, are congested and dreary. **Lymington** and **Christchurch**, on the coastal fringes, or any of the smaller villages, are much more interesting. If you intend to go walking, get an OS map and the Forestry Commission's booklet *Explore the New Forest*.

There are one or two honey-pot attractions in the New Forest. At the junction of five main roads is unavoidable Lyndhurst, where the only reasons to stop are to get maps at the visitor centre and to visit the grave of Mrs Reginald Hargreaves, better known as Alice Liddell, the heroine of Lewis Carroll's *Alice in Wonderland*, outside the south transept window of the church of St Michael's and All Angels.

To get you into the spirit of things, take the **Rheinfield Ornamental Drive** between Brockenhurst and the A35, a scenic drive laid out in the mid-19th century with rhododendrons and azaleas, towering Douglas firs, redwoods and Wellingtonias. The **Bolderwood Arboretum**, north of the A35, is full of exotic species from North America and the Far East. Beyond that, you enter the windswept northern heaths. A good short walk is the waymarked **Tall Trees Walk**, between Black Water and Brock Hill car parks.

National Motor Museum and Palace House, Beaulieu

t (01590) 612 345; open April–Oct 10–6, Nov–Mar 10–5; adm exp.

In 1952, 25-year-old Edward Douglas-Scott-Montagu inherited **Palace House**, one of the homes of the dukes of Buccleuch, on the River Beaulieu. He installed five old cars in the front hall and called it the Montagu Motor Museum in memory of his father, one of Britain's motoring pioneers. Fifty years on it's a roaring success, with acres of glinting vintage cars and motorbikes. A monorail shuttles visitors to and from Palace House, the old gatehouse of the pre-Reformation abbey, remodelled in the 1870s by Gothic revivalist Arthur Blomfield in exuberant Victorian style.

Across the river, Beaulieu is just the place for tea. There is an easy walk along the river to **Buckler's Hard** (4½ miles there and back), a tiny, unspoilt village.

Minstead to Furzey Gardens

Minstead is one of the loveliest villages in the forest: a pub, church and village shop clustered around a green, and a handful of thatched cottages. Beside the church with its sagging tiled roof, a stone cross marks the **grave of Sir Arthur Conan Doyle** – 'Patriot, Physician and Man of Letters' – who owned a cottage in nearby Bignell Wood. A footpath leads 2¼ miles to the colourful tree heathers of **Furzey Gardens** (***t** (023) 8081 2464; open daily 10–5; adm*).

Rufus Stone to Lower Canterton

Rufus Stone, off a narrow lane north of the A31, commemorates the death of Rufus in the New Forest in 1100 (*see* p.236). The memorial has been on the tourist trail since 1745. Walk through woodland to **Lower Canterton** (1½ miles), another tiny hamlet.

The New Forest Coast

Lymington

Lymington was the port of the New Forest, in the salt marshes on the estuary of the Lymington river. Until the mid-19th century, salt-panning and boatbuilding were the mainstay of the local economy. Now it has a jaunty quayside, good restaurants and river walks, and a lively Saturday market. It's a short hop across the Solent to the Isle of Wight. From the quay, ferries go to **Hurst Castle** (***t** (01590) 642 500; open daily April–Oct 10–5.30; adm*), one of Henry VIII's forts, on the end of Hurst Spit, jutting into the Solent. The fort faces Yarmouth Castle on the east of the Solent.

The Solent Way goes to **Keyhaven**, a quiet fishing village behind the spit.

Christchurch

Christchurch has enough geology and history for any school field trip: the prehistoric headland, Avon and Stour rivers forming a V-shape around the old town (the Saxon town was called Twynham or 'between-ham'), and the Norman priory church that gave the town its name. The sprawl is grim, but the centre is pretty. The long arm of Hengistbury Head leaves a crack for boats to negotiate the sandbanks and salt

Getting There and Around

Bournemouth Boating Services, t (01202) 429 119, run boat trips around the New Forest coast from Easter to October. Motor launches go every day (weather permitting) from Tuckton Bridge via Christchurch Quay to Mudeford Bridge, where there is a quiet beach with safe swimming, sought-after beach huts. and a little café called The Hut. From there you can catch another ferry to Mudeford Quay, the 'noddy train' up to Hengistbury Head or walk round the peninsular to the sea shore.

Tourist Information

Christchurch: 23 High Street, **t** (01202) 471 780. *Open Mon–Fri 9.30–5, Sat 9.30–4.30; July–Sept Mon–Fri 9.30–5.30, Sat 9.30–5.*

Where to Stay and Eat

Lymington t (01590) –

Stanwell House Hotel, 14–15 High Street, **t** 677 123, *www.stanwellhousehotel.co.uk* (*expensive*). Classy Georgian townhouse hotel with flagstone and wooden floors, colonial-style furniture with bold, colourful cushion fabrics, old prints on the walls and bright conservatory with soft sofas for afternoon tea. There are 31 bedrooms, including three suites. *Bar and bistro open daily, restaurant weekends only.*

Mooses, Ashley Lane (off High Street), **t** 675 370 (*moderate*). Bright, airy, buzzing Mediterranean-style restaurant. Live jazz or acoustic music on Wed eve, hanging pianist harnessed to wall on Fri and Sat eves.

Egan's, 24 Gosport Street, **t** 676 165 (*moderate*). Cheerful, colourfully decorated restaurant behind picket fence with about 14 tables. The cooking is Anglo-French with a sprinkling of Thai spices. Fish and meat are local; New Forest game in season. *Closed Sun and Mon.*

The Ship Inn, Quay Street, **t** 676 903 (*cheap*). From the terrace there are views of the marina. Standard pub grub all day.

The Gun Inn, Keyhaven, **t** 642 391 (*cheap*). Welcome refreshment if you have walked from Lymington along the sea wall, serving crab salad, and roast dinners on Sun.

Christchurch t (01202) –

The Avonmouth Hotel, 95 Mudeford Quay, **t** 483 434, *www.avonmouth-hotel.co.uk* (*expensive*). Large white-painted hotel with 40 bedrooms, many with views over Mudeford Bay and Hengistbury Head; traditional English restaurant.

Druid House Hotel, 26 Sopers Lane, **t** 485 615, *www.druid-house.co.uk* (*moderate*). Pleasant, small family-run hotel on busy road, enlivened in spring and summer by hanging baskets and climbing plants; eight fresh, bright bedrooms.

The King's Arms Hotel, 8 Castle Street, **t** 484 117 (*moderate*). Handsome old inn with large, comfortable bedrooms and nice, firm comfortable chairs. The view from your window might be the priory church, river, bowling green or castle ruins. Good carvery restaurant or bar snacks.

You can catch the ferry or drive (10 minutes) to Mudeford Quay (pronounced Muddy-ford), where you can buy fresh fish, oysters and whelks as well as other fishy snacks. A ferry crosses back and forth to Mudeford Beach.

Splinter's Restaurant, 12 Church Street, **t** 483 454 (*moderate*). Classy restaurant with three contrasting dining rooms including one with wooden pews, another with stylish blue furniture. The modern international cooking might include fillet of beef with shallot and garlic purée and herb potatoes or sea bass served with fennel, asparagus, new potatoes and creamed spinach. *Closed Sun and Mon.*

FishWorks, 10 Church Street, **t** 487 000 (*moderate*). Small chain with siblings in Bristol, Bath and Chiswick; fresh-fish counter downstairs and restaurant upstairs. Simple décor with white walls, wooden tables and no clutter. Set menu might include crab salad, cod fillet with mashed potatoes and parsley sauce, oysters and mussels, plus specials. *Open lunch and dinner.*

The Boat House, Quay Road, **t** 480 033 (*cheap*). Lively, child-friendly restaurant overlooking park and river. *Open daily 9am–midnight.*

Haven House Inn, Mudeford Quay, **t** (01425) 272 609 (*cheap*). Small, cosy and atmospheric. Pub grub until 4pm.

marshes of the harbour. The best views are from the head (by ferry or footpath) or from Mudeford Quay (by car), a good place for lunch or a drink.

Christchurch Priory (*t (01202) 485 804; open 9.30–4.45*) is a Norman masterpiece. Features include blind arcading in the north transept, the view down the nave to the 14th-century carved stone reredos and the fan-vaulted Salisbury Chantry, which was built in 1529 for the Countess of Salisbury, and defaced on Henry VIII's orders after the 76-year-old countess was accused of treason and beheaded standing up.

On Quay Road near the church is the **Red House Museum** (*t (01202) 482 860; open Tues–Sat 10–5, Sun 2–5*), where you can mug up on the archaeology of **Hengistbury Head**. The peninsula has archaeological traces of human settlement stretching back to the last Ice Age, when Britain was joined to the Continent.

The Isle of Wight

A waterlily on a blue lake

Alfred, Lord Tennyson

The Isle of Wight has been its own county since 1890, with its own motto and crest and county hall in Newport. The island fits tidily into the Hampshire coastline like a piece of a puzzle that has come away; in fact it was once part of the mainland. The south of the island is the most scenic, with thatched villages, rolling chalk downs and streams that have cut deep wooded ravines, known as chines. On the beaches you can search for dinosaur bones; several **dinosaur skeletons** have been found between Compton Bay and Atherfield Point. Landslips between Bonchurch and St Catherine's Point have created a jumbled Undercliff whose vegetation resembles the Côte d'Azur. At the western tip of the island are the Needles, one of Britain's most unusual coastal chalk shapes. At **Alum Bay** you can see layers of coloured clay and sand squeezed into vertical stripes in the 150ft-high cliff. The Victorians discovered the rural charms of the island: Queen Victoria and Alfred, Lord Tennyson both moved here. **Ryde**, **Sandown**, **Shanklin** and **Ventnor** are busy resorts, but most visitors come to walk, cycle, sail and look at historic buildings.

Cowes

Cowes is famous for its annual regatta in the first week of August. **Cowes Week**, the world's longest-running sailing event (since the 1820s), brings 8,000 sailors to race up to 1,000 boats, and thousands more spectators throng the Solent. The starting line is in front of the Royal Yacht Squadron in Cowes Castle. Landlubbers can watch from the Green. There are lots of good small shops, including **Beken of Cowes** on Birmingham Road. Since 1888, the Bekens have made yacht prints and calendars.

Getting There and Around

By Boat

Wightlink, **t** (01705) 827 744. Operates car ferries from Portsmouth to Fishbourne and Lymington to Yarmouth, as well as catamarans for foot passengers from Portsmouth to Ryde. A **Wightlink Rover** ticket combines the ferry and one day's bus and railway travel.

Red Funnel, 12 Bugle Street, Southampton, **t** 0870 4448898, *www.redfunnel.co.uk*, run car ferries and the 'red jet' hydrofoil from Southampton to Cowes in just 18 minutes.

By Car

You can take your car on the ferry, or rent one when you reach the island.

Solent Self-Drive, 32 High Street, Cowes, **t** (01983) 282 050.

Esplanade Ltd, 9–11 George Street, Ryde, **t** (01983) 562 322.

By Train

Portsmouth and Southampton are linked to London Waterloo and the Midlands by fast intercity trains, with boat services connecting for the island. From Ryde you can catch a train to Shanklin via Sandown.

The **Isle of Wight Steam Railway**, **t** (01983) 882 204 – part of the original Ryde–Newport line – chuffs back and forth from Smallbrooke Junction to Wootton via Havenstreet. The two-way trip lasts about 55 minutes.

By Bicycle

The island is flattish and a good size to explore by bike. Bring your own, or hire one.

Isle Cycle Hire, Wavells, The Square, **t** (01983) 760 738. Mountain bikes by the day or week.

Autovogue, 140 High Street, Ryde, **t** (01983) 812 989.

Extreme Cycles, Church Street Motors, Church Street, Ventnor, **t** (01983) 852 232.

On Foot

The **Tennyson Trail** explores West Wight. It starts at Freshwater Bay, just behind Farringford Hotel, Tennyson's former home, and heads west to the Needles, then round to Carisbrooke Castle. It is one of several inland trails, but the **coastal walk** is the most popular walking route. You can order a booklet of island walks, *The Isle of Wight Coastal Footpath and Trails*, by mail from the main tourist information centre.

Tourist Information

Isle of Wight: **t** (01983) 813 818, *www.islandbreaks.co.uk. Open Mon–Fri 9–5, Sat 9–4.*

A **Walking Festival** takes place over two weeks in May with a programme of guided walks around the island.

Cowes: 9 The Arcade, Town Quay. *Open Mon–Sat 9.30–1 and 2–5.30, Sun 11–4, closes earlier in winter.*

The famous **Cowes Week** regatta takes place during the first week in August. As well as the sailing-boat races, there is a festival on land.

Sandown: 8 High Street. *Open Mon–Sat 9.30–5.30, Sun 10–4.*

Shanklin: 67 High Street. *Open Mon–Sat 9.30–5.30, Sun 10–4.*

Ventnor: Salisbury Gardens, Dudley Road. *Open summer Mon–Sat 9.30–4.30, winter shorter hours.*

Yarmouth: The Quay. *Open Mon–Sat 9.30–5.30, Sun 10–4.*

Where to Stay and Eat

Cowes t (01983) –

The New Holmwood Hotel, Queen's Road, Egypt Point, **t** 292 508, *www.newholmwood.co.uk* (*expensive*). Victorian house built 1872 by pharmaceutical tycoon Charles Maw and

Osborne House

***t** (01983) 200 022; open April–Sept 10–6, Oct 10–5; adm exp.*

Italianesque Osborne House, on the edge of East Cowes overlooking the Solent, was the seaside home of Queen Victoria and Prince Albert. Here they indulged in family life. 'It is impossible to imagine a prettier spot,' enthused Victoria after her first visit, rented out to Continental royalty, whose guests included Kaiser Wilhelm II and his cousin King Edward VII; 26 rooms in fresh seaside colours with sea views; three guest lounges; upmarket restaurant serving Anglo-French food (*moderate*). Heated outdoor pool in summer.

The Anchor Inn, 1 High Street, **t** 292 823 (*moderate*). A lively yachting pub. Small, bright twin rooms overlook the High Street.

Baan Thai, 10 Bath Road, **t** 291 917 (*moderate*). Friendly and relaxed, serving delicious home-made Thai food. *Open eves only; book.*

Tonino's, Shooters Hill, **t** 298 464 (*cheap*). Well-established Italian restaurant with bright Mediterranean décor. *Open summer daily, winter closed Sun and Mon.*

Pierview, 25 High Street, **t** 294 929 (*cheap*). Welcoming traditional pub with open fire in winter.

Seaview and Around t (01983) –

The Priory Bay Hotel, Priory Drive, **t** 613 146, *www.priorybay.co.uk* (*luxury*). Just south of Seaview, a beautiful mix of Tudor and Georgian buildings with terraced gardens, tennis courts, a croquet lawn, outdoor swimming pool (*summer only*) golf course and private bay. Restaurant serves modern English food (*moderate*).

Seaview Hotel, High Street, **t** 612 711, *www.seaviewhotel.co.uk* (*expensive*). Delightful small hotel with 16 colourful bedrooms (some furnished with locally made quilts and curtains) and two excellent, contrasting restaurants – one crisp and subdued, the other bright and modern with models of boats – offering the same French/English menu with melt-in-the-mouth local beef and fresh local seafood (*moderate*). *Closed Sun eve.* Old-fashioned public bar decorated with nautical theme.

Northbank Hotel, Circular Road, **t** 612 227, *northbank@netguides.co.uk* (*moderate*). Delightful white-painted Victorian house with French windows steps from the sea. Eighteen bedrooms and pleasant restaurant offering Aga-cooked traditional English meals using local produce when possible; vegetables grown in hotel allotment.

Xoron Floatel, Embankment Road, Bembridge Harbour, **t** 874 596, *www.xoronfloatel.aol.com* (*moderate*). Restored 112ft Second World War gunboat filled with foliage and daylight; three cabins offering double, twin and family accommodation; great views of the harbour and Solent from upper deck lounge.

Khrua Thai Restaurant, High Street, **t** 568 899 (*cheap*). Intimate, high-quality Thai restaurant in old wine cellar of the terracotta-tiled Watson's Brothers grocers that once catered for well-to-do Victorian holiday-makers.

Sandown t (01983) –

The town is full of hotels with patio cafés where you can get a glass of cold beer and big English meals of roast beef and Yorkshire pudding, steak and kidney pie, or fish and chips. If you can't face all that, try **King's Bar and Café**, **t** 406 445, which has a balcony overlooking the bay and serves decent food.

Shanklin t (01983) –

Glenbrook Hotel, 6 Church Road, **t** 863 119 (*moderate*). Small thatched hotel tucked away behind a stout wall with quaint beamy interior, six very comfortable bedrooms and a wooded garden incorporating the upper section of the Shanklin Chine. Its old-world restaurant – Henry VIII's Kitchen – is popular in town for good-value steaks and grills. *Open eves only, closed Sun.*

Holliers Hotel, Old Village, **t** 862 764, *www.holliers-hotel.com* (*moderate*). Old coaching house with pleasant atmosphere;

'we have a charming beach quite to ourselves – we can walk anywhere without being followed or mobbed'. The Queen's mother, the Duchess of Kent, their nine children and dozens of grandchildren kept things lively with songs, charades, *tableaux vivants* and racing around in the sunshine. The house is not like other royal palaces: it's light and creamy with Italian-style bell towers, surrounded by ornamental Italian gardens. Parkland sweeps down to the Solent, which reminded the Prince of the Bay of Naples.

30 modest bedrooms. Meals such as roast duck, chicken Kiev and omelettes served in the restaurant. *Open eves only.*

The Brunswick Hotel, East Cliff, **t** 863 245, *www.brunswick-hotel.co.uk* (*moderate*). Period décor, indoor and outdoor pools, good restaurant for guests and modern rooms.

Fisherman's Cottage, **t** 863 882 (*cheap*). At the foot of the Chine, serves large pub meals.

Bonchurch t (01983) –

Winterbourne House, Bonchurch Village Road, **t** 852 535, *www.winterbournehouse.co.uk* (*expensive*). Delightful creeper-clad country house formerly owned by the Reverend James White, a friend of Charles Dickens. The novelist visited in July 1849, played rounders on the beach, made daily ascents of Boniface Down and busied himself writing *David Copperfield*. Seven bedrooms, including doubles, four-posters and suites; superb restaurant (*moderate*) and 4 acres of landscaped gardens overlooking the sea. Guests have a key to the gate at the bottom of the garden, which leads out onto the cliff path and down to the beach.

The Royal Hotel, Belgrave Road, Ventnor, **t** 852 186, *www.royalhoteliow.co.uk* (*expensive*). Impressive Victorian hotel set back from cliff in its own gardens with 55 rooms and a large restaurant with French windows and excellent service. On the English/French menu you might find pan-fried sea bream with seared scallops, Mediterranean vegetable tart tatin or 'pan-fried breast of chicken filled with Parma ham, brie and sun-blushed tomatoes'.

The Horseshoe Bay House, Shore Road, **t** 856 800, *www.horseshoebayhouse.co.uk* (*moderate*). Utterly charming family-run seaside hotel with four bedrooms, two with sea views, and excellent seafood restaurant, where you can also get a light lunch of ciabatta, mixed-leaf salad and French fries. From the terrace, steps drop straight down to the sea wall, where a small beach hut serves refreshments to walkers on the coastal path.

The Lake Hotel, Shore Road, **t** 852 613, *www.lakehotel.co.uk* (*moderate*). Excellent, inexpensive accommodation with 22 bedrooms at foot of the Undercliff, with purple-flowering trumpet vine over the verandah and a south-facing lawn.

The Bonchurch Inn, Bonchurch Shute (up hill from duck pond), **t** 852 611 (*cheap*). Wonderful old stone pub furnished with wooden deckchairs from the *Queen Mary* cruise liner, and family photographs. Built in 1854 as the coach house to the Bonchurch Hotel, now private apartments next door. Sit out in the old courtyard in the summer. The friendly Italian manager Nino provides Italian bar meals.

Beach Café, Steephill Cove (*cheap*). From the back of the beach at this impromptu café you have the best sea views, delicious crab sandwiches, freshly baked cinnamon rock cakes and a good cup of tea.

The Boathouse, Steephill Cove, **t** 852 747 (*cheap*). The menu is shellfish caught in the morning by the owner, Mark. The dining area is on the roof terrace, which means that it doesn't open if the catch or the weather is too bad. Book early.

The Spyglass, Ventnor, **t** 855 338 (*cheap*). Popular, noisy pub down on the beach with live music and chip-based bar meals.

Farringford and Freshwater t (01983) –

Farringford Hotel, Bedbury Lane, Freshwater Bay, **t** 752 500, *www.farringford.co.uk* (*expensive*). Creeper-clad Victorian country house in middle of 33 acres of parkland with croquet lawn and nine-hole golf course. This was the home of the poet Alfred, Lord Tennyson for

Albert brought in Thomas Cubitt, who had developed the smart London districts of Bloomsbury, Belgravia and Pimlico, to work on the house, and his German art adviser, Ludwig Grüner, to consult on the Victorian-Renaissance interiors and paintings. Many of the rooms reflect the imperial aspirations of the Victorian age: a statue of the Prince in Roman armour; a fresco of Neptune surrendering the seas to Britannia; the Indian-style Durbar wing. Touching touches include a life-sized statue of Noble, the

39 years. In the restaurant (*moderate*), which looks out onto the grounds towards the Afton Downs, the cooking is modern English with a hint of the Mediterranean. The menu might include pork tender loin and sweet potatoes or pan-fried cod and minted pea purée. *Dinner dance most Sats.*

The Clarendon Hotel and Wight Mouse Inn, Military Road, Chale, **t** 730 431 (*moderate*). A 17th-century coaching inn at the foot of St Catherine's Down, catering for families. The child-friendly pub (with games rooms) is noisy and packed in school holidays, but quietens down with live music in the evenings. Real ales, 365 whiskies and a good restaurant.

Chale Bay Farm, Military Road, Chale (on coast road between Blackgang and Freshwater), **t** 730 950, *www.chalebayfarm.co.uk* (*moderate*). Offers high-quality, purpose-built rooms around Japanese-style water garden with views of Needles on a clear day.

The Lodge, Main Road, Brighstone, **t** 741 272, *www.thelodgebrighstone.com* (*moderate*). Three-quarters of a mile from the coast, a handsome Victorian country house built in hunting-lodge style with arched windows and a lofty hall; seven bedrooms, most with bathrooms, and a large garden.

2 Tollgate Cottages, Wilmingham Lane, **t** 756 535, *www.tollgatecottages.com* (*cheap*). Small, friendly private house at foot of Tennyson and Afton Downs, about a mile from Freshwater Bay; private suite with sitting room and two bedrooms.

Yarmouth t (01983) –

The George Hotel, Quay Street, **t** 760 331, *www.thegeorge.co.uk* (*luxury*). Stuccoed 17th-century townhouse, built for the Governor of the Isle, abutting the castle walls on one side and Solent on the other. Gorgeous and homely, furnished with antiques and fresh flowers. There are two dining rooms – the formal restaurant (*expensive*) and a bright, cheerful brasserie (*moderate*); both are excellent.

The Bugle Hotel, The Square, **t** 760 272 (*moderate*). Large, recently refurbished brasserie-bar in atmospheric old inn with seven bedrooms, including two suites with sitting rooms.

Wavells, The Square, **t** 760 738 (*moderate*). Accommodation in flat above bakery in centre of town with five sunny, modern bedrooms, including the Harbour Suite with its own kitchen.

Salty's, Quay Street, **t** 761 550 (*cheap*). You can get snacks including large baskets of chips in the bar downstairs. Very busy in summer. The fish and shellfish restaurant upstairs is barn-like with oars, rudders and a boat providing nautical flavour. *Open winter Thurs–Sun, summer Tues–Sun.*

Newport t (01983) –

Burrs, 27/a Lugley Street, **t** 825 470 (*moderate*). Intimate and well-established little fish restaurant. Princess Anne was a recent diner. Your starter might be smoked haddock mash with horseradish and pesto bread or crab and spinach brûlé followed by fresh sea bass. *Open eves only, closed Sun and Mon.*

Frasers, St Thomas Square, **t** 530 001 (*cheap*). You can easily squander an hour or more among arthouse prints and fresh coffee smells in this friendly café-bar. Live music in summer at weekends.

Entertainment

Shanklin Theatre, Prospect Road, **t** 868 000. Traditional theatre with 520-seater auditorium and repertory company putting on mainly musicals.

queen's collie dog; a chintzy private suite; a painting of Hercules giving up his power and becoming a slave to Omphale, Queen of Lydia and photos of dressing-up parties. Albert spent most of his time organizing grand garden schemes from the roof of the clock tower. He taught the children to cook and garden in the Swiss Cottage.

When Albert died of typhoid in December 1861, the grief-stricken Victoria retreated to Osborne. The Landseer painting *Sorrow in the Horn Room* shows the Queen in mourning on a black horse, held by her Highland servant John Brown (as portrayed by Billy Connolly in the film *Mrs Brown*). She died at Osborne on 22 January 1901.

East Wight

Ryde is 15 minutes from Portsmouth on the catamaran. It's a real seaside resort, with beach, arcades and theatre. Thackeray once bumped into the Dickens family on the pier, and thought they looked 'abominably coarse, vulgar and happy.' The Edwardian resort of **Seaview** is quieter, with a small sandy beach. The best walking country is on the chalk headland around **Bembridge**. The road skirts around jolly **Bembridge Harbour**; stop here for the **Maritime Museum** (***t** (01983) 872 223; open April–Oct 10–5; adm*) and a bowl of seafood chowder at the Square Rigger. Stout **Bembridge Windmill** (*open April–Oct Sun–Fri 10–5, July–Aug also Sat; adm minimal*) is the last windmill remaining on the island. It's a pleasant walk from here to quaint **Brading** (2½ miles). A narrow lane off the Sandown road takes you to the **Bembridge and Culver Downs**. Walk down to **Whitecliff Bay**. The cliffs are highly fossiliferous: keep your eyes peeled for sea urchins and belemnites (Cretaceous), gastropods and bivalves (Tertiary).

Sandown and Shanklin

Sandown Bay, once the home of dinosaurs, now has two resorts. **Sandown** is a buckets-and-spades family resort with a sandy beach, pier and palm trees. Its geology museum has dinosaur relics and huge ammonites. **Shanklin** is a pleasant seaside hybrid with a thatched old village at the top of the cliff and a Victorian resort at the bottom, where holiday-makers jostle for space on the pavements in summer. Go to the beach down **Shanklin Chine** (***t** (01983) 866 432; open April–May and Oct 10–5, June–Sept 10–10; adm*), a ferny gorge lit up with twinkly lights. A lift runs up the cliff again from the Victorian esplanade. Keats visited.

South Wight

From Shanklin, you reach the jungly terraces of the **Undercliff**. Henry James called the 3-mile coastal footpath between Shanklin and Ventnor 'the prettiest part of the Undercliff, or in other words to the prettiest place in the world'. Stop off in **Bonchurch**, with its rocky bay and old church on the wooded cliff top, and eat shrimp sandwiches at the Horseshoe Bay Hotel. James found Bonchurch 'simply delicious...like a model village; the turf might be of green velvet and the foliage of cut paper'. Dickens spent the summer of 1849 working on *David Copperfield* in **Winterbourne House**; in the afternoons he walked or played rounders on the beach. Walk along the sea wall to the old Victorian resort of **Ventnor**, which has a faded glamour. In its heyday it had two stations to cope with all the visitors spluttering their way here to find relief from bronchial ailments. The little beach is happily old-fashioned: fishing boats on the shingle and dated shops. A mile further along the coastal path is **Steephill Cove**, a row of cottages on the sea (one a lobster restaurant) with little gardens full of buoys, at the foot of a wooded cliff. Sandcastles are supervised from the beach café. Another half mile along the coastal path is the delightful **Ventnor Botanic Garden** (**t** *(01983) 855 397; open dawn–dusk, visitor centre open Mar–Oct 10–6, winter weekends 10–4)*.

Inland from Ventnor, near Wroxall, is **Appuldurcombe House** (**t** *(01983) 852 484; open April–Oct 10–1 and 2–6; adm*). The ruined Palladian mansion of the Worsleys, one-time governors of the island, sits in a chalk bowl of Capability Brown landscape. Walk from crumbling Freemantle Gate to the obelisk, or north to quaint **Godshill**.

The coast road west of Ventnor heads into open countryside. Walk from Buddle Inn to **St Catherine's Lighthouse** (**t** *(01983) 867 979; open April–Oct Tues–Fri and Sun 1–4.30*) on **St Catherine's Point**, the southern tip of the island. A rutted chalk track leads to **St Catherine's Down**, crowned by **St Catherine's Oratory**, a pepperpot-shaped medieval chapel. There are views as far as the Needles. Continue north to the **Hoy Monument**, built in 1814 to mark the visit of Tsar Alexander I of Russia.

Further west still along the coast road, you come to lovely **Mottistone Manor Garden** (**t** *(01983) 741 302; open Easter–Oct Sun 2–5.30, Tues–Wed 11–5.30; adm*) and the Neolithic Longstone longbarrow.

West Wight

The cliff road west of St Catherine's Point has footpaths leading off it down steep chines to beaches. The cliffs between **Atherfield Point** and **Whale Chine** are fossil-hunting territory. You can find bivalves, brachiopods and ammonites, and even black bone fragments of iguanodon in the shingle.

Farringford and Freshwater Bay

Tennyson lived at **Farringford** for 39 years. He and photographer Julia Margaret Cameron did to **Freshwater Bay** in the 1860s what the Bloomsbury Group did to the Sussex Downs in the 1920s. Cameron, as it happens, was Vanessa Bell's aunt, and Virginia Woolf's only play was called *Freshwater*. The cliffs are flanked by two pillars of rock, the Stag and Mermaid. Tennyson ('one of the finest looking men in the world,' according to Carlyle) composed poems walking on the downs. Cameron, a pioneering photographer, lived at Dimbola Lodge (named after family estates in Ceylon), halfway between the bay and Farringford, and welcomed the cream of Victorian society: Darwin and Thackeray lived locally; guests included Lewis Carroll, Robert Browning, Holman Hunt, Edward Lear and the actress Ellen Terry. Cameron photographed them all, in costume. Carroll (an amateur photographer) thought her pictures pretentious. She has been recognized, however, as one of the most experimental photographers of the 19th century. You can see some of her work and take tea in the old ball room (**t** *(01983) 756 814; open Tues–Sun 10 –5, summer holidays daily; adm*).

There is a glorious 3-mile hike from Freshwater over Tennyson Down (where the poet composed 'Charge of the Light Brigade') to the Needles. Betjeman described the walk as 'like a thrilling and terrifying dream'. From the thatched church built by Hallam, Tennyson's son, ascend to the 1897 **Tennyson Monument**. Beyond are the

Needles, three chalk pillars protruding from the sea. You get a good view from the 19th-century **Old Battery** (*t (01983) 754 772; open Mar–Oct 10–4.30; adm*). A cable car runs down the cliff on the far side to Alum Bay with its bands of coloured sand.

Yarmouth

Ferries ply the Solent from Lymington to Yarmouth, a robust, hearty old seaside town at the mouth of the Yar. On the quayside is **Yarmouth Castle** (*t (01983) 760 678;* **open** *April–Sept 10–6, Oct 10–5; adm*), built in 1547 by Henry VIII to defend the west of the island. Its most advanced feature is the landward arrow-shaped bastion.

Newport

Newport is the county town of the island, with statues of Queen Victoria and Lord Mountbatten in the town square. At the geographic heart of the island, Newport has no sea but it has appeal, with its stone church and cafés. **Carisbrooke Castle** (*t (01983) 522 107; open April–Sept 10–6, Oct 10–5, Nov–Mar 10–4; adm*), the official residence of the governor from 1293 to 1944, is a short trip away. With its motte and bailey and curtain walls, it is a classic picture-book Norman castle on a charming scale. Charles I was imprisoned here at the end of the Civil War, until his beheading in London.

Wiltshire

Holiday-makers tend to race through Wiltshire *en route* to the West Country, leaping out at Stonehenge. But off the rat runs – the M4 and A303 – minor roads follow charming valleys. It's known as the 'chalk and cheese' county: sheep graze on the chalk hills and cows in the valleys. At its heart is **Salisbury Plain**, a military zone and prehistoric holy ground, sifted and revealed by the great antiquarians of the 16th–19th centuries, including local landowner John Aubrey, eccentric country parson (and arch-druid Chyndonax) William Stukeley, and Richard Cunningham and Richard Colt Hoare (who together excavated 140 barrows on the plain).

Neolithic and Bronze Age Wiltshire

All that we know about Neolithic people is from their graves: we know a lot about their deaths, but not much about their lives, so a lot of speculation goes on. The latest theory is that small, scattered groups came together to practice rituals. Neolithic people are believed to have lived a mobile existence, following herds and cultivating temporary fields; an advance on hunting and sleeping in damp caves, but not the good life. By the early Bronze Age (3000–2000 BC) Wessex was the most populous part of the country. This was the period of great monumental building, culminating in the great sarsen trilithons at Stonehenge. In 1938, archaeologists poking around in round barrows noted how often certain unusual miniature pots, elaborate gold ornaments and distinctive grooved bronze daggers cropped up, and named the style of burial 'Wessex Culture'. You find Wessex burials all over Europe, but the number of them around Avebury and Stonehenge show this was a des res.

How Salisbury Superseded Old Sarum

Medieval Salisbury started life on a hill two miles north of the present town. Old Sarum had a Norman cathedral and castle, but the clergy complained about the rude soldiers until Bishop Poor petitioned the Pope to move the cathedral down to the lush meadows of the Avon and Nadder. In 1220 his new cathedral got underway. It took 60 years to complete, by which time a grid of streets lined with canals had been laid out. The town's markets did well trading wool; there were fulling mills up and down the valleys powered by stream water. The old Saxon market town of Wilton complained bitterly about all this. It alleged that Salisbury's market was being held daily instead of on Tuesdays, as stipulated in the Bishop's Charter. In turn Salisbury complained that Wilton traders were grabbing merchants on their way to market. The moaning made no difference. Salisbury's cathedral remained towerless because of its watery foundations until the 14th century, by when the town was so rich that it built one anyway, 400ft high. By the 15th century Salisbury was one of the richest wool-manufacturing towns in England. Old Sarum was forgotten. But in time the canals became open sewers channelling disease around the town, and by the 17th century Salisbury was a backwater too.

Above the plain are the attractive **Marlborough Downs**, especially nice where they overlook the **Vale of Pewsey**, and in the sarsen (sandstone) boulder fields north of Avebury. Sarsens are an anomalous feature of chalk countryside, used in the megalithic monuments of **Avebury** and **Stonehenge**. These uplands were lively in the late Neolithic period and early Bronze Age: there are so many prehistoric sites that they start to seem commonplace. The story of Stonehenge starts up the River Avon at **Woodhenge** and **Durrington Walls**, and includes the complex of prehistoric structures at Avebury.

Northwest Wiltshire is the southern tip of the oolite Cotswolds, with pretty stone villages along the Avon. Otherwise the Avon Valley is dull until **Bradford-on-Avon**, where the river cuts a deep gorge – the stunning **Limpley Stoke Valley**.

Salisbury

The famous spire of Salisbury cathedral broadcasts its greatness over low-rise 20th-century housing for miles in all directions, while the grid of streets in the town centre – Fishrow, Salt Lane and Poultry Cross – retain a medieval flavour. From Salisbury, you can head off downriver into the Vale of Wardour (River Nadder), Broad Chalk Valley (River Ebble) or Avon Valley, heading north to Stonehenge.

There are two parts of Salisbury: tranquil cathedral close and busy commercial town. All the museums are grouped around the cathedral; once you hit town you can devote yourself to lunch and shopping. There is a superb **market** on Tuesdays and Saturdays (better than Wilton's), when the market square is crammed with fresh fish, fruit and vegetables, and rolls of fabric. The old streets around the square – Salt Lane, Butchers' Row, Silver Street – are good for a mosey. **St Thomas' Church** guards a

Getting There and Around

By **car** from London the M3 motorway runs southwest towards Winchester and Southampton. Turn off at junction 7, south of Basingstoke, onto the A30, which guides you straight into Salisbury city centre.

There is a fast **train** service from London Waterloo, at least once an hour.

National Express **coaches** run several times a day from London.

Tourist Information

Salisbury: Fish Row, **t** (01722) 334 956. *Open Mon–Sat 9.30–5, summer also Sun.*

Market days are Tues and Sat. The whole of Market Square is filled with fruit and vegetable stalls, clothes, pillow cases, fresh fish, crockery, tea towels and so on. Once or twice a year you will find a French market with stalls selling bread and cheeses.

Salisbury's **performing arts festival** takes place over two weeks from May to June in venues all over town, including the cathedral, Playhouse, City Hall and Guildhall. For details call **t** (01722) 332 977, box office **t** (01722) 320 333, or go to *www.salisburyfestival.co.uk*.

Where to Stay

Salisbury t (01722) –

The Red Lion Hotel, Milford Street, **t** 323 334, *www.the-redlion.co.uk* (*expensive*). Old town-centre coaching inn with creeper-clad courtyard through high carriage archway and peculiar 'skeleton-and-organ' grandfather clock in the lobby. Sadly the overall atmosphere is rather corporate.

The White Hart, St John Street, **t** 327 476, *www.whitehart-salisbury.co.uk* (*expensive*). Behind magnificent columned portico, the interior has largely been restored after a fire in 1994 with an eye on corporate clients; 68 bedrooms and a high-quality contemporary English-style restaurant, lounge and bar.

The Old Mill Hotel, Town Path, Harnham, **t** 327 517, *www.comeoninn.co.uk/oldmill* (*moderate*). Former 18th-century warehouse with 11 bedrooms, half with cathedral views, and gardens next to 16th-century paper mill on edge of water meadows. Constable must have painted his classic view of the cathedral from close by. It's a 10-minute walk into Salisbury over the meadows. The restaurant is in the mill itself, and the mill stream still runs through the middle.

Cricket Field House Hotel, Wilton Road (A36), **t** 322 595, *www.cricketfieldhousehotel.co.uk* (*moderate*). A 19th-century gamekeeper's cottage with 10 rooms in modern extension, a mile from the city centre. It takes its name from the South Wiltshire cricket grounds on the other side of the garden fence.

The Clovelly Hotel, 17–19 Mill Road, **t** 322 055, *www.clovellyhotel.co.uk* (*moderate*). Pleasant, cottagey place set back from Mill Road near the station, 5–10 minutes' walk from city centre, with 14 pretty bedrooms.

The Old Rectory, 75 Bell View Road (on corner of Swaynes Close), **t** 502 702, *www.theoldrectory-bb.co.uk* (*moderate*). You will be made at home at this 1919 former rectory with three bedrooms.

Websters, 11 Hartington Road, **t** 339 779, *www.websters-bed-breakfast.com* (*cheap*).

treasure: over the chancel arch is the largest surviving 15th-century doom painting in England. Most of these medieval paintings of the Last Judgement were destroyed at the Reformation; this one was rediscovered under whitewash in the 19th century.

The Cathedral Close

When the medieval cathedral planners stood on the banks of the Avon in 1220 they were looking at an empty meadow; they could do what they wanted, and they created a perfect cathedral in its own 50-acre close. The close is lovely, with its Georgian and medieval buildings clustered around the cathedral. In 1327 it was fortified with a high stone wall and three gatehouses.

Small, bright rooms in a colourful Victorian terraced house in a cul-de-sac, 15 minutes' walk from cathedral.

Meadow Croft, Great Durnford, **t** 782 643 (*cheap*). Charming private house in pretty little village with two double bedrooms. *Open Mar–Oct.*

Wilton t (01722) –

The Pembrook Arms Hotel, Wilton Road, **t** (01722) 743 328, *www.pembrookarmshotel.co.uk* (*expensive*). Quiet, dignified old coaching inn with simply furnished rooms.

Eating Out

Salisbury and Around

The Jade, 109 Exeter Street, **t** 333 355 (*moderate*). Small Cantonese and seafood restaurant. Very popular and busy, getting through 110 lobsters, 25 dozen scallops and buckets of live oysters and mussels a week. Or you could stick to crispy, aromatic duck. *Closed Sun.*

La Gondola, 155 Fisherton Street, **t** 324 856 (*moderate*). Friendly, good-quality Italian restaurant serving home-made dishes.

Le Herisson, 90 Crane Street, **t** 333 471 (*moderate*). Superb deli and brasserie (in conservatory overlooking garden) serving delicious European-style food including tapas and risotto. *Closed Sun.*

Harpers, 6–7 Ox Row, Market Place, **t** 333 118 (*cheap*). Friendly, long-established, family-run restaurant with large, airy dining room offering unpretentious modern English food including Poole fish and local sausages. *Closed Sun in winter.*

The Haunch of Venison, 1 Minster Street (opposite the Poultry Cross), **t** 322 024 (*cheap*). Ancient, characterful, smoke-stained inn built for builders working on St Thomas' church, with pewter-top bar, red-cushioned oak benches and 300-year-old mummified hand of a card player caught cheating by the butcher in the back bar. Upstairs, restaurant offers traditional English fish and meat dishes followed by spotted dick or sticky toffee pudding.

Michael Snell Tea Rooms, St Thomas' Square, **t** 336 037 (*cheap*). Michael Snell served a five-year apprenticeship in a Swiss bakery and patisserie, and now makes his own pastries, chocolates and ice cream, and roasts his own coffee. Lunches served too, including casseroles, soup and bread. *Closed Sun.*

LXIX Bar and Bistro, 69 New Street **t** 340 000 (*cheap*). Easy to miss, in listed building; ground-floor wine bar and upstairs bistro with painted brickwork, wooden floorboards and seating. *Closed Sun.*

Horseshoe Inn, Ebbesborne Wake, **t** 780 474 (*cheap*). Delightful pub in beautiful Broad Chalk Valley, about 10 miles west of Salisbury in the direction of Shaftesbury. Two snug bars, decorated with tools hanging from low beams, and farmers leaning against the bar. Good traditional country pub meals served in the bar and conservatory. The food is '90% home made', with favourites including liver-and-bacon casserole, pies and local faggots. Sunday roasts come with heaps of vegetables. Real ales come directly from the barrel, including Ringwood Best and local Stonehenge Ales. Two double rooms for B&B (*moderate*). *Closed Mon.*

From High Street you come to the battlemented old north gate. Beyond, a narrow lane of brick houses leads into a square of 18th-century townhouses, with roofs like Dutch hats, wisteria and magnolia over the front doors and iron railings. Stop at **Mompesson House** (***t*** *(01722) 335 659; open April–Sept Sat–Wed 11–5; adm*), a Queen Anne house named after the wealthy merchant who built it in 1701. The rooms were redecorated in 1740 with baroque plasterwork and panelling, and an elegant staircase added. Kate Winslet had a fit of tears on the four-poster bed in *Sense and Sensibility*.

King's House, home of the **Salisbury and South Wiltshire Museum** (***t*** *(01722) 332 151; open Mon–Sat 10–5, July–Aug also Sun 2–5*), also has its place in fiction. It featured in Thomas Hardy's *Jude the Obscure* as Melchester Training College, from which Sue

Bridehead swims to freedom across the river. It is now a major archaeological museum, with about five thousand objects on display, including all of Old Sarum and quite a bit of Stonehenge.

The **Royal Gloucestershire, Berkshire and Wiltshire Infantry Regiment** (***t*** *(01722) 414 536; open April–Oct daily 10–5; adm*) occupies a medieval grey stone house known as the **Bishop's Wardrobe**. Among campaign memorabilia and the like is a stuffed rough-haired terrier called Bobbie who received an Afghan Medal for bravery in the Battle of Maiwand. Next door in the **Medieval Hall** (*open April–Sept daily 11–5*) is an audio-visual show on life in medieval Salisbury.

Salisbury Cathedral

Salisbury cathedral lifts your eyes up to the Heavens with its tiers of arched windows, pinnacled gable ends and magnificent spire. The **spire** is the tallest in England, rising 400ft from its Gothic tower. One of the few English cathedrals built from scratch without rebuilding, it is as perfect now as in 1280, when building was completed. Enter through the **west front**, a 13th-century wall of saints and bishops. Bishop Poor, who founded the cathedral in 1220, is in the bottom left-hand corner. The **cloisters** were an indulgence of the non-resident canons, who could have walked outside the walls; they are the biggest in England. The Perpendicular Gothic **interior** is perfect. For proportion, scale and design, everything is as it was intended. Columns lead you visually up to the ribbed fan-vaulting, drawn with a thick-nibbed pen compared to Winchester's thin pencil lines.

The faceless 14th-century **clock** at the west end is one of the oldest mechanical clocks in the world. At the east end is the **shrine of St Osmund** (bishop 1078–99), the founder of the original cathedral at Old Sarum. From the south transept you enter the cloisters. On one side is the octagonal **chapter house**; a single Purbeck marble column in the middle shoots a fountain of ribs over the vaulted ceiling. A sculpted medieval frieze around the walls depicts scenes from Genesis: Adam and Eve, Cain and Abel, and Noah's Ark. It houses one of four surviving calf-skin editions of the *Magna Carta* (signed in 1215; Lincoln Cathedral and the British Museum have the others).

Old Sarum

t *(01722) 335 398; open April–Sept 10–6, Oct 10–dusk, Nov–Mar 10–4; adm.*

Old Sarum, north of Salisbury above the Avon Valley, was once a prestigious Norman hill-top town with a castle and cathedral (*see* p.247). An aerial photo shows it off most eloquently: the castle ruins on the flat-topped mound, ringed by a wide outer bailey and an Iron Age ditch. The Norman castle was built in neat blocks of dressed Chilmark stone and the walls limewashed to dazzling effect. It was here that William the Conqueror summoned the nobles of England in 1086 to swear an oath of allegiance to their new king. William II, Henry I and Henry II also held councils here, but the end for Old Sarum came when its cathedral was abandoned for a flashy new one by the river in the 13th century. The town became a famous 'rotten borough', returning an MP to parliament despite having no population (William Pitt the Elder started his career as MP for Old Sarum). It's a good picnic spot, but don't expect much of the ruins.

The Ancient Capital of Wilton

Wilton crops up in the *Anglo-Saxon Chronicle* as one of the royal towns of the West Saxon kings (the palace is under Kingsbury Square) and the scene of Alfred's defeat by the Vikings in 871. According to a 15th-century poem, Alfred founded Wilton Abbey. The kings of England were benefactors of the abbey, and the abbesses daughters or sisters of the very top brass: Edward the Elder's wife and daughters were buried here; Edward the Confessor's wife was educated here; Gunhild, a daughter of Harold, was a nun here. At the time of the Norman Conquest, the abbey had the highest income of any nunnery in England. It had slipped to fourth position by 25 March 1539, when it was dissolved. After the nuns had gone, the new town of Salisbury eclipsed Wilton.

Wilton

From Salisbury it is a short drive to Wilton, passing a statue of the dashing Earl of Pembroke on a tall plinth *en route* to the centre, where Georgian houses stand back from the road behind pollarded trees. Wilton is a major tourist stop; the coachloads come for the great house and the shopping village in the 18th-century factory buildings of Royal Wilton Carpets. West out of town is the 19th-century Italianate church of **St Mary and St Nicholas**, built in golden sandstone; with its twisted rope columns, arches and lions it resembles a Lombardic basilica. Precious antiquities incorporated into the design include mosaics from Santa Maria Maggiore in Rome, French medieval stained glass and 2nd-century BC marble columns from the Gulf of Spezia.

Wilton House

***t** (01722) 746 729; open April–Oct Tues–Sun 10.30–5.30; adm exp.*

Sir William Herbert (made 1st Earl of Pembroke in 1551) built Wilton House on the abbey lands at the Dissolution. Painter Hans Holbein advised on the plans. In the early 17th century the house became a cultural Mecca, where all the rich, talented and royal gathered around Mary Sidney, Countess of Pembroke, and her illustrious brother, Sir Philip Sidney. Only a small portion of the Tudor mansion survived a fire. In 1647 a new house was built by Inigo Jones and John Webb. Their **Double Cube Room** (60ft by 30ft), extravagantly painted with cherubs and gold fruit, is renowned (it was the ballroom in a film of *Sense and Sensibility*). As part of the 18th-century landscaping of the gardens, the Nadder was diverted and spanned by a **Palladian Bridge**. The two-storey cloisters were part of Gothic alterations between 1801 and 1814, mostly undone since. The walls are dripping with paintings by Rubens, Reynolds and Van Dyck, the rooms full of furniture by Chippendale and Kent.

The West Wiltshire Downs

West of Salisbury, rivers cut through the West Wiltshire Downs to **Shaftesbury** and the stately homes of **Stourhead** and **Longleat**, just north of the A303. Broad Chalk Valley takes you to Cranborne Chase (*see* p.268). A side road leads via the Horseshoe

Where to Stay and Eat

The West Wiltshire Downs

Howards House, Teffont Evias, **t** (01722) 716 392, *www.howardshousehotel.co.uk* (*very expensive*). Ten miles west of Salisbury, this is the 17th-century dower home (with 19th-century Swiss-style eaves) of the mansion, whose chimneys peep out over a yew hedge across the road. Rescued from dereliction in 1989, the décor is modern and elegant. You can stop for lunch or dinner (*moderate*) or stay in one of nine bedrooms with floral-patterned fabrics and queen-sized beds.

The Angel Inn, Hindon, **t** (01747) 820 696, *www.theangelhindon.fslife.co.uk* (*moderate*). Characterful 18th-century coaching inn in pretty stone village just off A303, 16 miles west of Salisbury, with seven bedrooms, restaurant and flagged bar with stout wooden tables offering traditional country-inn cooking.

Beckford Arms, Fonthill Gifford (5 miles from Shaftesbury and 9 miles from Wilton), **t** (01747) 870 385 (*moderate*). Delightful, bright and airy gastro pub with big wooden tables and cushioned wooden seats, scattered magazines, candles and interesting pictures on the walls. Meals include seared scallops or blue-cheese fritters with basil mayonnaise followed by beer-battered cod or game. Four double rooms and one single.

Inn onto the A30, which takes you to Shaftesbury past the Fovant Regimental Badges, cut into the downs by soldiers in 1916. Otherwise head down the B3089 into the quiet **Nadder Valley** (or Vale of Wardour). Make a detour to the tiny village of **Teffont Evias**, with its slender spire, thatched cottages and turreted manor. Drive through the stone gateway at Fonthill Bishop into **Fonthill Park**. This was the heart of the estate of eccentric 18th-century millionaire William Beckford. The remains of Fonthill Abbey, which fell down, are private. Follow signs to the ruins of **Old Wardour Castle** (***t*** *(01747) 870 487; open April–Sept daily 10–6, Oct 10–5, Nov–Mar Wed–Sun 10–1 and 2–4; adm*), the home of the Arundell family (*see* p.380). The castle was ruined in the Civil War, starting with a nine-day siege in which Lady Blanche Arundell and 25 men took on a 1,000-strong Parliamentarian army, and finished by her son besieging the Parliamentarians to get it back. It was turned into picturesque gardens in the 18th century.

Stourhead House and Gardens

t *(01747) 841 152, www.nationaltrust.org.uk; gardens open 9–7 or dusk if earlier; adm; house open Easter–Oct Fri–Tues 11–5; adm exp.*

The ducks of Stourhead are some of the luckiest in England. In 1754 the wealthy London banker Henry Hoare dammed the valley of the river Stour and gave them a lake to die for: steep wooded slopes, soft banks and romantic follies by Henry Flitcroft. Approach from the village of Stourton. By the old church, the rocket-shaped Bristol High Cross (poached in 1762) ushers you into an idealized landscape. A walk around the **serpentine lake** (1 mile) takes you past Flitcroft's neo-classical **Pantheon**, **Temple of Flora** and **Temple of Apollo**. Stourhead is the apotheosis of the 18th-century landscape garden. It is a painting by Laguerre brought to life and a pocket-sized Grand Tour all in one. In the house, paintings of pyramids, crumbling Roman arches and waterfalls show Hoare's influences. Widowed antiquarian Sir Richard Colt Hoare inherited Stourhead in 1785 and wrote archaeological tomes: his two-volume *Ancient Wiltshire* is in the library, one of two wings he added to the Palladian house.

Two miles west of Stourhead on Kingsettle Hill, **King Alfred's Tower** (*open Easter–Oct daily 12–5 or dusk if earlier; adm minimal*) is one of the most imposing of Flitcroft's monuments. It marks the spot where Alfred is thought to have mustered his troops before defeating the Danes at Edington in 878.

Longleat House and Safari Park

***t** (01985) 844 400; Longleat House and Safari Park open Easter–Oct daily; call for hours of all 12 different attractions; adm exp, joint ticket better value.*

Longleat is one of the most splendid country houses in England. The architect was Robert Smythson (of Hardwick Hall and Wollaton Hall in the East Midlands, *see* p.591 and p.589). The view down the drive across Capability Brown parkland is memorable, but Longleat is not everyone's cup of tea: the commercialism and African animals put many people off. In 1949 Longleat became the first stately home to open its doors for commerce. Its **safari park** was the first in Europe, opening in 1966. Longleat also boasts the longest hedge maze, a butterfly garden, adventure castle, boat and train rides, etc. Tours of the house begin in the Great Hall with its hammer-beam roof and hunting trophies, one of the few rooms not to have been modernized in the 19th century, when the 4th Marquis redecorated in lavish Italian style: elaborate gilt ceilings, embossed leather walls and ornate picture frames. There is a big portrait of the present Marquis, the 9th Viscount Weymouth Alexander Thynn, surrounded by his family and girlfriends. His private apartments – decorated with *Karma Sutra* murals – promise 'key-hole glimpses into my psyche', for anyone that interested.

Up the Avon to Stonehenge

From Salisbury on the A345, turn left after Old Sarum down Philips Lane following the sign to Stratford Sub-Castle and Wilton, and bearing right at the T-junction along the Avon. Soon you reach **Heale House Gardens** (***t** (01722) 782 504; open Tues–Sun 10–5; adm*). This 8-acre garden has the sort of rambling charm loved by period-film-makers (*Portrait of a Lady* and *Damage*). At the front of the house – all mellow red brick and magnolia – self-seeded plants grow between the flagstones, and moss and old roses grow over the stone balustrades of steps leading down to the river. Charles II hid here for six nights before his escape to France. Lucky old him.

From the garden, head to Great Durnford, the start of a 5-mile **walk to Stonehenge**. The path passes **Normanton Down barrow**, amid a cluster of Bronze Age burial mounds including the **Bush barrow**, the largest and richest of the early Bronze Age.

Salisbury Plain and Stonehenge

Salisbury Plain is the most densely packed archaeological landscape in England. In the 94,000 acres owned by the army there are 2,300 archaeological sites, including Stonehenge. The plain is the junction of chalk ridges that were early roads across the country, making it a hub of trade and culture in the late Neolithic and early Bronze Age.

Hengeworld

In his book *Hengeworld*, archaeologist Mike Pitts makes the case for Stonehenge, Durrington Walls and Woodhenge being related, the scene of large-scale funerary processions which took place on the summer and winter solstices, ritually enacting the journey of life into death. The theory is quite convincing, one part archaeology and three parts imagination: feasting and dancing at Durrington Walls, first rituals at Woodhenge, followed by a journey downriver and up the avenue to Stonehenge. Stonehenge is the house of the ancestors – think of the dead man killed by arrows and the ring of bluestones (from the west of Britain, where the sun sets). A funeral is also the birth of an ancestor – think of the carved penises found at Stonehenge, common symbols of rebirth – so the culmination of the ceremonies is the rising sun driving a corridor of light through the stones and striking the altar stone.

Stonehenge

t (01980) 624 715, www.english-heritage.org.uk; open Easter–May daily 9.30–6, June–Aug 9–7, Sept–mid-Oct 9.30–6, mid-Oct–Mar 9.30–4; adm.

Stonehenge looks smaller than the photos suggest, hemmed in at the junction of the A303 and the A344, but its outer circle of 25-ton sarsen stones capped with slabs forms an instantly recognizable silhouette. After years of contention, the roads that thunder past are to be hidden underground and, if all goes ahead as planned, by 2008 you'll walk half a mile to the stones from a brand-new visitor centre.

Until radiocarbon tests were conducted on the stones in 1993, Stonehenge was assumed to belong to the Bronze Age; it turned out to be a millennium older, begun in the late Neolithic period. These days, it is no longer seen as a rigid monument, but as the site of evolving rituals and technologies.

Five major 20th-century excavations produced the main revelations. In 1901 Gowland found deer antlers worn down by pounding the megaliths into dressed stones. He also saw that the sun had a role to play. In 1919–26 Hawley turned the site inside out and proposed a 'multiple building phase' theory, but everyone was too bored by his chips of rock to take any notice. In the 1950s, Atkinson resurrected Hawley's theory, and took the credit. In 1993 English Heritage decided it wanted dates, and shattered everyone's beliefs by proving that Stonehenge had been constantly changing since the Neolithic period.

The first signs of activity were about 5,000 years ago, when a bank and ditch were dug. At this time the plain was a pastoral landscape of grazed turf, woodland and scattered houses by fields. There were still no round barrows, Durrington Walls or Woodhenge. After a few hundred years wooden posts were set in the middle of the henge and cremated bodies (possibly 240 of them) suggest it was used as a crematorium. The site underwent its most complex developments 4,550–3,600 years ago. A man was killed with arrows at close range (perhaps ritual or sacrifice) and given a grand burial in the ditch. Stones were introduced to the henge; eventually they were aligned with the rising midsummer sun. The sarsens were cut into shape using carpentry techniques; 82 bluestones, each weighing 4 tons, were brought over land

and sea 250 miles from southwest Wales and set in a horseshoe at the centre of the monument, and an avenue was constructed linking Stonehenge to the Avon.

A mile upstream are two even more mystifying prehistoric structures. Excavations at **Woodhenge**, off the A345 (follow signs to Durrington off the A303), revealed six concentric oval rings of 168 posts enclosed by a deep ditch and bank (the tallest post may have stood 25ft). The body of a child with its skull split in two was discovered in the middle. Like Stonehenge, Woodhenge was orientated on the midsummer sunrise and midwinter sunset. It is easy to find. The concentric rings are now marked with concrete posts so you can see the complexity of the site. Next to it, bissected by the road, is the biggest henge of them all. **Durrington Walls** is 1,725ft across, 300ft bigger

Getting There and Around

There are regular **buses** between Marlborough and Avebury, dropping off outside the Red Lion pub in Avebury Henge.

Tourist Information

Marlborough: **t** (01672) 513 989, *www.marlboroughwilts.co.uk. Open summer Mon–Sat 9–12.30 and 1.30–5.30, winter Mon–Sat 10–12.30 and 1.30–4.30.*

Market day is on Wed and Sat, with stalls along the High Street.

Where to Stay

Marlborough t (01672) –

The Ivy House Hotel, High Street, **t** 515 333, *www.ivyhousemarlborough.co.uk* (*expensive*). Ivy-covered Georgian townhouse hotel, with elegant public rooms and garden restaurant. The 35 bedrooms are quaint with all mod cons.

The Castle and Ball Hotel, High Street, **t** 515 201, *www.oldenglish.co.uk* (*moderate*). Pleasant, gentle hotel with handsome r ed-brick front; 32 bedrooms, and a restaurant lounge serving cream teas, sandwiches or steak and kidney pies amid the rustle of newspapers and the tinkle of tea things.

Fisherman's House, Mildenhall village (2 miles from Marlborough), **t** 515 390 (*moderate*). Delightful accommodation in mellow brick Georgian house with lawns sloping down to the River Kennet. Antique pine furniture and sea-grass matting.

Ash Lodge, Chopping Knife Lane, **t** 516 745, *www.ashlodge.co.uk* (*moderate*). Large 1936 private house on edge of Savernake Forest, about 15 minutes walk from the High Street. Friendly atmosphere.

Monk's Rest Lodge, Salisbury Road, **t** 512 169 (*moderate*). New purpose-built guesthouse at end of garden.Comfortable and efficient.

The Red Lion Pub, Red Lion High Street, Avebury, **t** 539 266, *redlion.avebury@laurelpubco.com* (*moderate*). Thatched pub serving pub grub in the middle of the stone circle. Pretty rooms with prehistoric views.

Eating Out

Coles Bar and Restaurant, 27 Kingsbury Street, **t** 515 004 (*moderate*). By far Marlborough's best restaurant, a short walk up the hill beyond the town hall. Stylish, relaxed décor, in which European/Asian fusion cooking is served: you might have cold Thai fishcakes with bean shoots and sweet chilli jam followed by traditional English roast duck, cod or lamb. *Closed Sun.*

2XS, 7 Kingsbury Street, **t** 514 776 (*moderate*). In a 300-year-old building furnished in contemporary style just down the hill from Coles. Bistro-style, with bangers and mash for lunch and deep-fried risotto cakes with basil, mozzarella and 'sun-blushed' tomatoes for dinner. *Closed Sun eve.*

Zafferini's, 48 Kingsbury Street, **t** 513 353 (*cheap*). Lively Italian restaurant. No pizza.

The Sun Inn, High Street, **t** 512 081 (*cheap*). Robust, old-fashioned pub with oak beams.

The Royal Oak, 111 High Street, **t** 512 064 (*cheap*). Marlborough's most reliable pub for food; crowded on Thurs and Fri eves.

than Avebury. It hosted grand celebrations with lavish feasting (8,500 animal bones, mainly pigs, have been dug up). But don't try to find it, it's too difficult to work out.

East Wiltshire

The interesting part of east Wiltshire is south of the M4, around the **Marlborough Downs**, **Devizes** and the **Vale of Pewsey**. The stone monuments around **Avebury** are unrivalled in their complexity and scale, but the landscape is speckled with dykes, tumuli, earthworks, field systems and longbarrows.

Marlborough

Marlborough stands on the River Kennet, its Downs rolling away to the north and the Savernake Forest stretching to the southeast as far as the Kennet and Avon Canal. The town's colonnaded **High Street** leads from church to town hall. Novelist William Golding (*Lord of the Flies*) spent his childhood in a house on the **Green**. William Morris and John Betjeman went to **Marlborough College**. Merlin is said to lie beneath a Neolithic mound in the college grounds. It served as a motte for the Norman castle, built by Bishop Roger of Old Sarum and a favourite of King John's in the 13th century.

The 6-mile walk to **Avebury** across the downs is a good approach to the monuments. The sarsen fields of **Fyfield Down** are littered with sandstone boulders. The name of the stones may come from old English for Saracen, which came to mean pagan after the crusades against the Arabs, or Saracens; they were the pagan stones.

Avebury

Avebury is 20 miles north of Stonehenge on the Marlborough Downs. The stone circle is so big that you can't see the whole thing at once, and it is only one of many prehistoric boxes here. Archaeologists' picture of what went on here is hazy to say the least. Around 5–6,000 years ago there was something happening on top of Windmill Hill: cattle may have overwintered here, and vast numbers of animal bones in the ditches suggests feasting. Over the next 1,500 years a bewildering range of monuments spread around the vast embanked stone circles. The whole site is most impressive from the air, almost illegible from the ground. William Stukeley came up with the image of a hieroglyphic snake stretching between the Sanctuary (the head) and an unmarked site on Beckhampton Hill (the tail) with the stone circle representing its coiled body – a 3-D symbol of prehistoric belief. Rich playboy archaeologist Alexander Keiller bought the whole site in 1934 and tidied it up, re-erecting stones and replacing missing ones with concrete stumps. His finds are the core of an excellent **museum** (*open summer 10–6, winter 10–4; adm*).

The bus from Marlborough drops you outside a pub in the middle of **Avebury Henge** – not as ludicrous as it sounds. The massive bank and ditch enclose 28 acres (14 times larger than Stonehenge), and the earthworks were once 70ft high, built by up to 400 labourers digging with antlers and stones. The stone circles arrived later: an outer circle of 98 standing stones and two inner circles of 27 and 39 stones. Stukeley

Getting There and Around

By **car**, Devizes is just south of the M4.

Bus no. 49 leaves from the Market Place to Swindon, stopping at Avebury, where you can catch no. 48 to Marlborough.

It's a 1½-mile **walk** along the towpath to Caen Hill Locks from Devizes wharf.

Tourist Information

Devizes: Cromwell House, Market Place, **t** (01380) 729 408. *Open summer Mon–Sat 9.30–5, winter 9.30–4.30; closed Sat 1–2.*

A big **general market** takes place on Thurs in the Market Place and Shambles. Otherwise, there's a **bric-a-brac market** in the Shambles on Tues, a **farmers' market** on the first Sat of the month in the Market Place, and a smaller **general market** in the Shambles on Sat.

Where to Stay and Eat

Devizes t (01380) –

Places to stay in Devizes are disappointing. The hotels are old-fashioned and chintzy. There are, however, plenty of places to eat and drink. The pubs have most to offer, both in town and around the Vale of Pewsey.

The Bear Hotel, High Street, **t** 722 444, *www.thebearhotel.net* (*moderate*). Dominating the market square, with its name emblazoned across its façade and a columned porch supporting a statue of a black bear, this 17th-century coaching inn has counted George III and Edward VII among its guests. Comfortable, although both décor and restaurant (*closed Sat lunch and Sun eve*) could do with a revamp.

The Elm Tree, High Street, **t** 723 834 (*moderate*). Decent Italian-style pub grub.

Franco's, Basement, 6 Old Swan Yard, High Street, **t** 724 007 (*cheap*). Cosy, friendly basement Italian restaurant and pizzeria, with gingham tablecloths and murals of Italian scenes on the walls. Dolce Pani on the ground floor serves cakes, sandwiches and coffee. *Closed Sun.*

Edwin Giddings, The Chequers (just off High Street), **t** 723 355 (*cheap*). On sunny days, this little deli sets a couple of tables on the pavement. Good coffee and rolls.

The Healthy Life, 4 The Little Brittox, **t** 725 558 (*cheap*). This wholefood shop with its modest café is planning to extend into a café-bistro at no. 7 across the road. For now, eat in the vegetarian café or take away pasties and pizzas, soups and salads.

The Vale of Pewsey t (01672) –

The Barge Inn, Honey Street (near Pewsey and Alton Barnes), **t** 851 705 (*cheap*). Attractive Victorian inn built on the towpath beside the Kennet and Avon Canal to serve the canal traffic, now popular with walkers, canoeists, horse-riders and crop-circle fanatics – the back room is a local crop-circle HQs, with an elaborate mystical mural on the ceiling, photos on the walls and an Ordnance Survey map patterned with coloured dots marking the sites of crop circles. You can see the Alton Barnes White Horse on the valley side. From the wharf, Sarsen stones were sent by barge to Windsor for the repair of the castle. Pub grub served daily.

The Royal Oak Inn, Wootton Rivers (15 miles from Devizes), **t** 810 322, *www.wiltshire-pubs.com* (*cheap*). Hearty food in thatched Tudor inn with oak beams in the middle of the walking countryside of Pewsey Vale, a stone's throw from the Kennet and Avon Canal. Six bedrooms in separate house with kitchen and sitting room.

identified two stone avenues leading to a stone circle on Overton Hill, known as the Sanctuary, and Beckhampton Hill. The Sanctuary is a smaller version of Woodhenge, with evidence of six rings of post holes and an extra inner circle of stones. An adolescent was buried at the foot of one of the stones.

There's no mistaking the form of **Silbury Hill**, a 130ft-high truncated chalk pyramid, 550ft across. It's the largest artificial mound in prehistoric Europe, but again no one knows why it was built. The best guess is that it was built 4,600 years ago, the same time as the stone circles. **West Kennet longbarrow**, just over the A4 from the hill, is more than 300ft long, with five burial chambers holding the skeletons of 46 people, along with pottery, beads and animal bones. It may have been a shrine as well as a tomb. There are two oval enclosures beside the stream between the Sanctuary and Silbury Hill, camps fenced with 25ft-high oak posts.

The Vale of Pewsey

The Vale of Pewsey cuts through the chalk between Devizes and Wootton Rivers, the Kennet and Avon Canal wiggling along the valley floor. The escarpment on the north side is famous for the horses cut into its chalk. There are good ridge walks from **Alton Barnes**. One path meets the Wansdyke dyke, constructed in the 6th century to mark the limits of the Kingdom of Wessex. From Wansdyke Path you get good views of **Alton White Horse** (cut in 1812). Other good walks are along the towpath to **Pewsey Wharf** and Wootton Rivers. Alton Barns' Barge Inn is a hub of crop-circle information.

Devizes

The prosperous old market town of Devizes has a brewery, market square, Victorian covered marketplace and shambles. On market day the square is full of stalls selling old-fashioned produce. The canal, which brought trade in the 19th century, is now a recreational waterway. The **Kennet and Avon Canal Museum** (***t*** *(01380) 729 489; open summer 10–5, winter 10–4; adm minimal*), in an old warehouse on the quayside, tells the story of the canal. **Devizes Museum** (***t*** *(01380) 727 369; open Mon–Sat 10–5, Sun 12–4; adm minimal*) has some good archeological stuff, including most of the 'Wessex Culture' barrow goods (*see* p.246) excavated around Avebury and Stonehenge. You can see Bronze Age jewellery made of gold, amber, jet and shale; weapons and tools made of copper and bronze; and high-quality pottery.

Two miles west of Devizes, the Kennet and Avon Canal drops 237ft down **Caen Hill Locks** into the Avon Valley. Engineers built a stairway of 16 locks, which canal boats climbed one step at a time, to get around the drop.

The Valley of the Bristol Avon

The Bristol Avon (as opposed to the Salisbury Avon) starts near Tetbury in the Cotswolds and winds uneventfully to Melksham, where it turns west through the gorge of the Limpley Stoke Valley between Bradford-on-Avon and Bath. In the Middle Ages, sheep on the hills and fulling mills on the river made Bradford, Lacock and Castle Coombe rich on cloth and wool. Now the valley is sadly cut in two by the M4.

Bradford-on-Avon

All the town of Bradford stondith by cloth-making.

Leland, 1540

The warm Cotswold-stone buildings of Bradford-on-Avon climb steeply up from the Avon between high stone walls. It's so steep that some of the houses have street-level

Tourist Information

Bradford-on-Avon: 50 St Margaret's Street, **t** (01225) 865 797. *Open summer daily 10–5, winter 10–4.*

Bike and Canadian Canoe Hire, Lock Inn Cottage, Bradford-on-Avon, **t** (01225) 867 187. Explore the Kennet and Avon Canal, 2 miles to Avoncliff and 10 to Bath. *Open all year daily 9–6.*

Lacock: contact the Chippenham office, **t** (01249) 706 333, *open Mon-Sat 9.30–5pm*, or try *www.thisislacock.co.uk* for more places to stay.

Lacock Abbey Recitals, Lacock Abbey, **t** (01249) 730 042. Classical concerts all year.

Where to Stay and Eat

Bradford-on-Avon t (01225) –

Woolley Grange Hotel, Woolley Green, **t** 864 705, *www.woolleygrange.com* (*luxury*). Relaxed, informal, child-friendly Jacobean manor-house hotel on edge of town with Bath stone gables and tall chimneys, set in large gardens. Antique furniture and well-worn rugs on floorboards. Good views over Wiltshire Downs and heated outdoor pool. Excellent restaurant with long-standing chef cooking up hearty Mediterranean/ English cooking that might include pan-fried chicken, fillet of beef or John Dory.

The Georgian Lodge, 25 Bridge Street, **t** 862 268, *georgianinnlodge.hotel@btinternet.com* (*moderate*). Simple, pleasant place to stay in the centre of town; 10 bedrooms around a leafy courtyard with modern English restaurant (*moderate*). *Closed Mon lunch.*

The Priory Steps, Newtown, **t** 862 230, *www.priorysteps.co.uk* (*moderate*). Six 17th-century weavers' cottages converted into gorgeous bedrooms in delightful part of town. All guests sit down together for dinner in elegant dining room.

Clifton House, 198 Bath Road, **t** 865 994, *www.bradfordonavon.net* (*moderate*). Gabled Jacobean property with grand entrance hall, three bedrooms with Victorian fireplaces and a courtyard with pond.

The Thai Barn, 24 Bridge Street, **t** 866 443 (*moderate*). Set in old forge with rough-stone walls and big black beams, a popular restaurant that always seems to be busy (*book in advance*), serving high-quality Thai food. *Closed Mon, and Tues lunch.*

29 Tory, 29 Tory, **t** 864 935, *music@themutual.net* (*cheap*). Charming, modestly furnished cottage built into the hillside. Top-floor bedroom with amazing views over rooftops.

The Dandy Lion Inn, Market Street, **t** 863 433 (*cheap*). Attractive pub with friendly atmosphere. Pub lunches include a pint of prawns.

The Bunch of Grapes, 14 Silver Street, **t** 863 877 (*cheap*). Friendly pub offering evening meals in bar or farmhouse-kitchen restaurant.

doors on all three stories. Street names reflect the town's wealthy past in the wool and cloth trade: Silver, Market, Woolley, Shambles. The side roads are delightful.

Start beneath the copper beech tree in Westbury Gardens, in the centre of town. The medieval stone bridge has an unusual 17th-century lockup. Across it is Westbury House, an elegant neo-classical townhouse. A five-storey Victorian warehouse stands by the river. Uphill are straight rows of weavers' cottages. Steep flights of stone steps climb between the terraces, and springs gush out of the rock in mossy passages.

At the foot of the hill is the Saxon **chapel of St Laurence** (*open Mar–Oct 9.30–6*), thought to be the successor to Adhelm of Sherborne's 8th-century chapel. This building is mainly 11th century. Rather than demolish it, the Normans built **Holy Trinity** over the road. Put to many uses over the centuries, the old chapel was spotted by a sharp-eyed vicar in 1856 and stripped back to the rough stone walls and narrow windows. From there, climb up to the picturesque **chapel of St Mary** (*open 9–4*).

In the other direction the river leads to a 14th-century **Tithe Barn** (*open 10–dusk*), property of the Abbess of Shaftesbury. Its chief glory is a cruck-beam roof, resembling the upturned hull of a ship. Walk along the canal to the Cross Guns pub in Avoncliff.

The Lock Inn Café, Frome Road, **t** 868 068 (*cheap*). Smashing, busy little place on canal side where you can watch the boats and fill up on the boatman's all-day breakfast (huge). Also serves bistro-style meals of kedgeree or bangers and mash (*Thurs–Sat*).

Lacock **t** (01249) –

At the Sign of the Angel, 6 Church Street, **t** 730 230, *www.lacock.co.uk* (*expensive*). Beautiful 15th-century half-timbered coaching inn with ancient tiled floors, antique furniture, oak panelling and six cosy stout-beamed bedrooms in old building. Restaurant offers traditional English roasts and Cornish fish. *Closed Mon lunch*.

The George Inn, West Street, **t** 730 263 (*moderate*). One of two good places to eat in Lacock, with old books, maps and prints on the walls and an unusual dog-powered spit roast by the fire. Duck sausage and orange, steak and kidney pie, breaded lobster tails or plain ploughman's.

Lacock Pottery, 1 The Tanyard, **t** 730 266, *www.lacockbedandbreakfast.com* (*moderate*). Large, beautiful place strewn with rugs and decorated with ceramics and antique furniture; three bedrooms, one in cottage with its own walled garden.

King John's Hunting Lodge, 21 Church Street, **t** 730 313 (*moderate*). Delightful bedrooms and tea room in one of the oldest houses in Lacock, with quaint little stairways and doors around a massive cruck beam and 13th-century stonework.

Appletree Cottage, Bewley Common (just up the hill from Lacock), **t** 730 373 (*moderate*). All rustic charm in old stone and thatch.

Limpley Stoke **t** (01225) –

The Cliff Hotel, Cliff Drive, Crowe Hill, **t** 723 226, *www.cliffhotel.co.uk* (*expensive*). Victorian country-house hotel tucked peacefully away among the trees with a terraced garden and small open-air pool; 11 bedrooms including two with four-posters and a pleasant restaurant offering whole-some country-house cooking (*moderate*) including local specialities such as game casserole, wild-boar sausages or Wiltshire lardy cake with custard.

Avon Villa, Avoncliff, **t** 863 867 (*cheap*). Modest, friendly rooms beside the aqueduct.

The Inn at Freshford, The Hill, Freshford, **t** 722 250 (*cheap*). Perfectly located pub by the Avon. Real ales include Devizes-made 6X.

The Cross Guns, Free House, Avoncliff, **t** 862 335 (*cheap*). Superb, delightfully located country pub with gardens stretching right down to the river bank. A hundred malt whiskies and an Italian ice-cream machine. Pub meals of steak and ale pie, game casse-role or fish in the restaurant or garden, while the bar is left for drinkers and pre-booked diners with dogs. Eight rooms (*moderate*) with river views.

Great Chalford Manor

***t** (01225) 782 239, www.nationaltrust.org.uk; open April–Oct Tues–Wed for tours; adm.*

Moated Great Chalford Manor, a few miles north of Bradford-on-Avon, shows how much money there was in wool. Wealthy clothier Thomas Tropnell built it and the adjacent parish church in the mid-15th century. The farm buildings on the third side of the courtyard were added in the next century. It's a satisfying ensemble, with church, manor house and farm buildings all in the same lichen-encrusted stone.

Lacock

North of Bradford-on-Avon off the A350 is the unusually well-preserved village of Lacock, entirely owned by the National Trust. There are no traces of modernity, just old stone buildings with sagging roofs. **Lacock Abbey** (***t** (01249) 730 227, www.nationaltrust.org.uk; open Mar–Oct daily 11–5; adm*) is famous as the ancestral pile of William Henry Fox Talbot, a pioneer of modern photography. He was one of those Victorian men who were interested in everything, publishing as many Assyrian translations as scientific papers. His six-part book *The Pencil of Nature* (1844–6) was the first published text illustrated with photographs. You don't see many of Fox Talbot's images because the chemicals were so sensitive to light, but since the oriel window of the abbey was the subject of so many, here you've got the next best thing.

The Limpley Stoke Valley

The River Avon, Kennet and Avon Canal and the railway jog side by side along the Limpley Stoke Valley, the remains of the valley's industrial past (fulling mills, breweries and quarries). Hidden from the rest of the world behind hills and trees, the stone hillside villages are lovely, and the towpath is ideal for walks and cycle rides. **Avoncliff** is tucked into the bottom of the valley, 1½ miles from Bradford-on-Avon. It's a great spot for a pub lunch, with its 18th-century stone aqueduct carrying the canal over the river.

Harold Peto's Garden

t *(01225) 863 146; open April and Oct Sun 2–5, May–Sept Tues–Thurs and weekends 2–5; adm.*

The village of **Iford** at the confluence of the Avon and Frome rivers seems to belong in a romantic tale. Architect Harold Peto created the atmosphere. He believed that sculpture in a natural setting can 'carry one's mind back to the past in a way that a garden of flowers only cannot do', and to prove it he bought an old manor beside the river in 1899 and laid out an Italianesque hillside garden full of classical sculpture. He also gave the old stone bridge its statue of helmeted Britannia. In summer, opera is staged in the Byzantine stone cloister, encrusted with treasures poached by Peto from Italy. The walk from the Freshford Inn along the river to Iford is magical.

Farleigh Hungerford Castle

t *(01225) 754 026; open daily April–Sept 10–6, Oct 10–5; Nov–Mar Wed–Sun 10–4; adm.*

Thomas Hungerford's small castle stands above the River Frome, south of the Limpley Stoke Valley. Thomas got rich on wool and marriage, and became the first parliamentary speaker in 1377. He bought the estate, and illegally castellated the manor house. It looks impressive, but would have been useless against attack.

Dorset

More than half of Dorset is designated an 'Area of Outstanding Natural Beauty'. The prehistoric landscape of the Dorset chalklands is littered with 1,500 ancient monuments. Maiden Castle near Dorchester is Britain's largest prehistoric earthwork, with 2 miles of ramparts; it is one of 30 Iron Age hill forts in the county. Today Dorset is a strip of holiday coast and lots of hidden villages. Thomas Hardy spent most of his life in the county. Born at High Bockhampton, he was apprenticed to architects in Dorchester, and lived in Weymouth, Swanage, Sturminster Newton, Wimborne

Pious West Saxon Kings

Dorset had stacks of pre-Norman-Conquest religious foundations. The medieval abbeys that succeeded them took over the estates, which had been acquired through royal patronage. Some of these abbeys survive as ruins or parish churches. Sherborne, Shaftesbury and Wimborne were the richest foundations, and the burial places of West Saxon kings. Sherborne is associated with saints Adhelm and Asser, super-monks of the 8th and 9th centuries who belonged to the Wessex royal house. It became the seat of the southwestern diocese of the Kingdom of Wessex, governing Dorset, Somerset, most of Wiltshire, Devon and Cornwall. Adhelm, Abbot of Malmesbury, was the first bishop. In the 9th century, Alfred the Great's brothers **King Æthelbald** (d. 860) and **King Æthelbert** (d. 865) were buried at Sherborne, and Asser, Alfred's biographer, became bishop. When Asser died the diocese was divided into the three smaller bishoprics of Sherborne, Wells and Crediton, serving Dorset, Somerset and Devon. **King Alfred** himself founded two religious houses: a monastery at Athelney (in thanks for his defeat of the Danes at Edington) and a nunnery at Shaftesbury (his daughter was abbess). It was one of six Wessex nunneries including Amesbury, Romsey, Wherwell, Wilton and Winchester that were successful before the Conquest. Kings of Wessex showered gifts of land and property on Shaftesbury's nunnery. **Æthelred the Unready** gave it the relics of St Edward the Martyr, murdered in 978, attracting hordes of pilgrims, and **King Cnut** died there in 1035. Wimborne also benefited from royal associations dating back to the 8th century. This is where King **Æthelred**, yet another of Alfred's brothers, was buried. It is also where Æthelred's son **Æthelwold** made a stand against the accession of his cousin Edward the Elder to the throne after Alfred's death: the nuns of Wimborne were famous all over Europe for their discipline; Æthelwold stole one of them and took her to Northumbria; under Alfred's Law Code, nun-stealing was forbidden, incurring a fine of 150 shillings.

Minster and Dorchester again. Dorset is the most closely mapped region of Hardy's fictional Wessex, and the setting for most of his stories. From the Hardy sites of **Dorchester** you can make trips to the resort of **Weymouth** and to **Poole Bay**, although the bay towns of Bournemouth, Poole and Christchurch may be busier than your ideal image of Dorset. Visit the gentle **Vale of Blackmoor**, flanked by the handsome stone abbey towns of **Shaftesbury** and **Sherborne**, and the hills of **Cranborne Chase**. The Southwest Coastal Path begins on the **Isle of Purbeck**. West of Purbeck there are no coastal towns along **Chesil Beach** until **Lyme Regis**, one of the most delightful coastal towns in England, in terrific coastal scenery.

Poole Bay: Sand, Sea and Oil

Christchurch, Poole and Bournemouth fall into the hollow of the Hampshire Basin, a landscape of sand, clay and gravel, its heaths and harbours fringed with creeks and salt marshes. The basin is fast disappearing under suburbs; it has never been any good for growing things, so it's ideal for dreary residential developments.

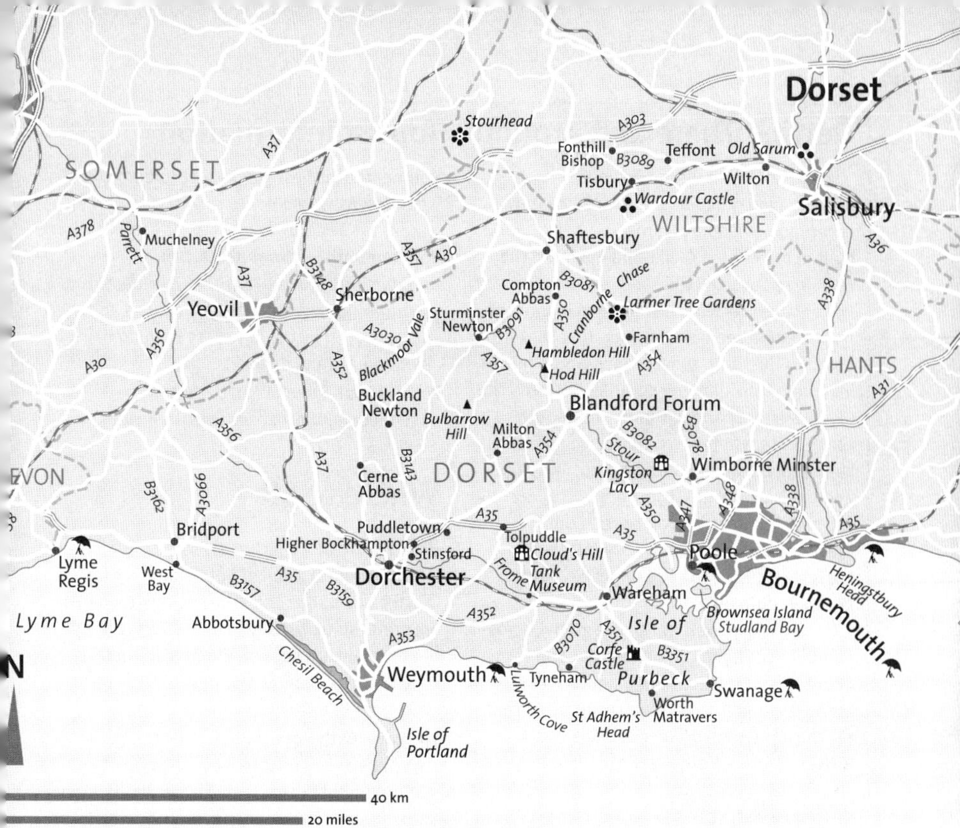

The Victorians started the suburbanization, planting pine trees and building villas. **Bournemouth** became a high-class invalid resort; the pines were said to turn the air into pure aromatherapy. Today, the resort's glory is its sandy beach, a 7-mile curve of soft yellow sand so fine it gets into your mouth. Hardy called the town 'Sandbourne' in his books. At either end of this golden crescent are the harbours of Christchurch and Poole. **Christchurch Harbour** is tiny, while **Poole Harbour** is a haven of scattered islands and creeks filled with little boatyards. West of Poole, a Roman pottery industry was built on the clay; the distinctive black burnished ware was exported as far as Hadrian's Wall. Today, there are a dozen British Petroleum oil wells near Wareham, known as **Wytch Farm**. One of the most productive is in the middle of the harbour on Furzey Island. The oil wells are discreet; the sprawling suburbs are more of a blot on the landscape.

Bournemouth

Bournemouth was built for the feel-good factor. The original resort attracted invalids and holiday-makers; today it attracts students, clubbers and surfers. The bay, backed by sandy cliffs, is still beautiful, and Victorian gardens form green lungs. The town is keen to promote itself as an idyllic seaside resort, but you have to duck under a high-

Getting There and Around

Poole Bay is best visited by boat.

The **Waverley Paddle Steamer** is the only ocean-going paddle steamer left in the world, built in 1947 on the Clyde, and operated there until 1974. Saved by the Paddlesteamer Preservation Society, she has been in more or less constant service ever since, first venturing down to the south coast in 1978. She is much in demand, dividing her summer between the Clyde, Bristol Channel, Thames and south coast, and spending 10 days every September steaming between Bournemouth, Swanage and the Isle of Wight. There are two bars and a self-service restaurant on board. Contact **Waverley Excursions**, Waverley Terminal, Glasgow, **t** 0845 130 4647, or get tickets at Bournemouth Pier.

From the **Hamworthy Ferry Terminal**, across Poole Harbour, you can go on a day trip to Cherbourg or the Channel Islands and return in the evening. The two ferry companies that ply the route both do special deals.

Brittany Ferries, **t** 0870 908 1281. Just over two hours to Cherbourg.

Condor Ferries, **t** 0845 3452000, *www.condorferries.co.uk*. Services to Guernsey and Jersey.

There are also three ferry companies based at the quay running seasonal trips to Brownsea Island, around the bay and further afield to the Isle of Wight, Swanage and Old Harry Rocks.

Brownsea Island Ferries, **t** (01929) 462 383, *www.brownseaislandferries.com*. The main operator for Brownsea Island.

Blue Line Cruises, **t** (07802) 435 654, *www.bluelinecruises.co.uk*. One-hour round trips at weekends to Old Harry Rocks and summer excursions to Swanage.

Crowsands *Dorset Belles*, **t** (01202) 330 305, *www.dorsetbelles.co.uk*. Summer trips to Swanage, where you can take the steam railway to Corfe Castle, or the Isle of Wight, where you can join a sightseeing tour bus around the island or take a cruise around the Needles.

Fishing is another option.

Sea Fishing Poole, **t** (01202) 679 666. Operates from a hut on the quayside, where you can buy crab lines, fishing tackle and bait; variety of fishing trips from the harbour.

Tourist Information

Bournemouth: Westover Road, **t** (01202) 451 700, *www.bournemouth.co.uk. Open Mon–Sat 9–5.30, summer also Sun 10–5.*

Bournemouth Seafront Beach Office, Undercliffe, **t** (01202) 451 781. *Open daily 9–5.* Here you can hire chalets (four chairs and a little cooker) by the day or week, deckchairs, windbreaks and parasols.

Poole: 4 High Street, **t** (01202) 253 253, *www.pooletourism.com. Open daily 10–5.*

Where to Stay

Bournemouth t (01202) –

Bournemouth is full of hotels catering for coach parties and conference delegates. All are pretty similar, many offer leisure facilities but few are truly special. The Eastcliff hotels have the advantage of sea views and a zigzag path or lift taking you down to beach.

The Royal Bath Hotel, Bath Road, **t** 555 555, *www.devereroyalbath.co.uk* (*luxury*). Bournemouth's first resort hotel was built in the 1800s in the gleaming white neo-classical style. Its guests have included Queen Victoria, Oscar Wilde and Disraeli (not all at once). In 1876 Russell Cotes bought it and filled it with his collections. There are 140 bedrooms, a 'fine dining' restaurant, cocktail bar, garden restaurant and leisure facilities.

Hotel Miramar, East Overcliff Drive, **t** 556 581, *www.miramar-Bournemouth.com* (*luxury*). Handsome red-brick Edwardian hotel behind terraced gardens, with 40 rooms, uniformed porters and sea views.

The Carlton, East Overcliff Drive, **t** 552 011, *www.bookmenzies.co.uk* (*very expensive*). Handsome seafront hotel with 73 rooms, indoor and outdoor heated swimming pools and leisure complex.

East Cliff Court, East Overcliff Drive, **t** 554 545, *www.bookmenzies.co.uk* (*very expensive*). Stylish, with 70 bedrooms, outdoor pool, bar and restaurant.

Highcliff Marriott Hotel, St Michael's Road, Westcliff, **t** 557 702, *www.marriotthotels.com/bohbm* (*expensive*). Plush, civilized hotel refurbished to the tune of £10 million in 2001, with palms and flags out front. Some of the 157 bedrooms have sea views; all have access to the facilities – indoor and outdoor pools, tennis court and restaurant.

The Grove Hotel, 2 Grove Road, **t** 552 233, *hotel grove@aol.com* (*moderate*). Attractive white-painted Victorian building with green louvred shutters, climbing plants and wall flowers, in the middle of town yet happily secluded in acres of lovely gardens. It has been in the same family for 40 years, so has a more personal atmosphere; 35 rooms.

Poole t (01202) –

The Mansion House, Thames Street, **t** 685 666 (*expensive*). Poole's best hotel; 32 bedrooms in a creeper-clad Georgian townhouse just off the Quay, built by an 18th-century merchant and later home to the mayor of Poole. The elegant cherry-wood-panelled restaurant (*moderate*) offers English/French food with emphasis on local ingredients like Poole fish, New Forest game and Somerset cheeses. *Closed Sat lunch and Sun eve.* Residents' bistro for quicker meals (*cheap*).

The Quay Thistle Hotel, The Quay, **t** 666 800 (*expensive*). Fortress-like modern brick hotel with 70 bedrooms. Two bars, including the American Bar, and Harbour View restaurant.

The Salterns Hotel, 38 Salterns Way, Lilliput, **t** 707 321, *www.salterns.co.uk* (*expensive*). Superb location on Salterns yachting marina, 2 miles east of Poole around the harbour, with waterside restaurant and bar; 20 light bedrooms.

The Saltings, 5 Salterns Way, Lilliput, Sandbanks, **t** 707 349, *www.pooletourism.com* (*moderate*). Attractive Art Deco marine-style home with sloping roof and gravel garden in exceptionally smart corner of the south coast. Two lovely bedrooms.

Eating Out

Bournemouth

Oscars, Royal Bath Hotel, Bath Road, **t** 555 555 (*moderate*). Gourmet repertoire of English/French cooking in a romantic setting with red roses on tables. Dinner might include fillet of Welsh black beef with potatoes, monkfish with saffron mash or sea bass with mushroom ravioli; lunch Dorset lamb with rosemary mash or pan-fried salmon. *Closed Sun eve and Mon.*

Edwards, 19–21 Exeter Road, **t** 292 697 (*cheap*). Pleasant place to grab quick, filling lunch: ciabatta and filled baguettes with fried potato coils, bangers and mash, fish and chips, burgers or steaks.

Bar Vin, 165–7 Old Christchurch Road, **t** 316 664 (*cheap*). Civilized, popular wine bar catering for young professional types with bistro-style menu.

O'Neil's Irish Bar, 231 Christchurch Road (on the Lansdowne roundabout), **t** 786 591 (*cheap*). Friendly Irish pub. Live music Fri and Sat. *Open until 2am.*

Poole

The Custom House, Poole Quay, **t** 676 767 (*moderate*). An imposing Georgian building with its columned portico and Union flag. In the à la carte restaurant upstairs, roast sea bass, steaks and Dorset lamb shank might be on the menu; the ground-floor bar offers cheaper meals of mussels and seafood. On a fine day, sit outside at pavement tables.

Guildhall Tavern, Market Street, **t** 671 717 (*cheap*). Friendly pub with excellent French-style bar meals. The speciality is seafood, including crab, lobster and bouillabaisse.

Blue Boar, Dear Hay Lane (just off Market Close), **t** 682 247 (*cheap*). Pleasant locals' pub away from quayside.

Entertainment

BIC, **Pavilion** and **Pier Theatre**, **t** 456 456.

Bournemouth International Centre (BIC), Exeter Road. A large, modern, multi-purpose seafront venue with facilities for conferences, exhibitions and concerts. The largest of three halls accommodates big-name pop bands with audiences of 4,500.

The Pavilion Theatre, Westover Road. Traditional theatre hosting comedy, the Chippendales, celebrity TV cooking shows, opera and smaller bands.

The Pier Theatre. Similar repertoire to Pavilion, but summer only.

Seaside **brass bands** play May–Sept at Pinewalk Bandstand, Lower Gardens and Pier Approach. Call **t** 451 195 for details.

speed flyover to reach the beach. You can hire deck chairs and beach huts just like the old days, but you're overlooked by a brand-new conference centre as you bathe. There are, however, young people in Bournemouth. In the graveyard of **St Peter's Church**, east of the main square, are the tombs of William Godwin, his wife **Mary Wollstonecraft** and their daughter **Mary Shelley**, author of *Frankenstein*. Percy Bysshe Shelley's heart, brought back from Italy, is buried in his wife's grave.

The **Russell Cotes Art Gallery and Museum** (***t*** *(01202) 451 858; open Tues–Sun 10–5*) is housed in a Scottish baronial Italianate villa, built for the pretentious Annie and Merton Russell-Cotes. The house is emblazoned with heraldic emblems, on tiles, woodwork and stained glass, to show off Merton's great status. The eclectic collections range from Maori woodcarvings to Dante Gabriel Rossetti's *Venus Verticordia* and a Constable in the lavatory. The grounds incorporate a cliff-top Japanese garden.

Poole

From Poole Quay it's hard to make sense of the harbour's creeks and bays, headlands and islands. **Brownsea Island** (***t*** *(01202) 707 744; open Easter–Oct daily 10–5, winter 10–4; adm*) is the largest, its 500 acres of heath and woodland a haven for wading and nesting birds; most of the northern side is owned by Dorset Wildlife Trust but the rest is open to the public, including quiet beaches and fabulous southern views. Below the harbour is a reservoir of crude oil about 10 miles long, drilled from Furzey Island. Behind the quay are warehouses, alleys and little shops selling Purbeck pottery. The names of the streets – Market Street, Cinnamon Lane, Buttons Lane and Paradise Street – reflect centuries of trade, also visible in the **Customs House** and **St James'** church, built of Purbeck stone with columns of Newfoundland pine inside. **Poole Pottery** has been going since 1873, the most successful firm to exploit the local clay. At first it manufactured tiles and mosaic floors for shops, pubs and civic buildings, then in the 1920s it got a reputation for Art Deco tableware. Now it's a huge attraction, with a shop and restaurant (***t*** *(01202) 668 681*). The **Waterfront Museum** (***t*** *(01202) 262 600; open April–Oct Mon–Sat 10–5, Sun 12–5, Nov–Mar Mon–Sat 12–3; adm*) inhabits the medieval customs warehouse and tells the story of the lucrative Newfoundland fishing trade.

Dorchester

The county town of Dorchester is the epicentre of Hardy country. Just about every town and inch of countryside within a 20-mile radius has some connection with his life or fiction. Hardy's 10th novel, *The Mayor of Casterbridge*, which he wrote in a rented house on Shire Hall Lane, was set in Dorchester, and the King's Arms Hotel, Maumbury Rings, Maiden Castle and the county museum all get a mention.

There is a statue of Dorchester poet William Barnes in the churchyard of St Peter's at one end of High Street West, and of Thomas Hardy at the other. Between them are

Getting There and Around

By **car**, the M3 heads southwest from London to Southampton, joining the M27 and then the A31 through the New Forest to Poole and Bournemouth, where you can join the A35 into Dorchester. Or you can leave the M3 at junction 7, picking up the A30 to Salisbury and the A354 to Dorchester.

Dorchester has two **train** stations, both on the edge of town. Direct services from London Waterloo run to Dorchester South, from where a local bus runs into town once an hour. Trains from Bristol and Bath go to Dorchester West, a short walk from the town centre.

Tourist Information

Dorchester: 11 Antelope Walk, **t** (01305) 267 992. *Open April–Oct Mon–Sat 9–5, May–Sept also Sun 10–3, Nov–Mar Mon–Sat 9–4.*

Where to Stay

Dorchester t (01305) –

Westwood House Hotel, 29 High West Street, **t** 268 018, *www.westwoodhouse.co.uk* (*moderate*). Large, friendly Georgian house with lovely bedrooms; wicker furniture, spa baths and proper bedspreads. Sunny breakfast room but no restaurant.

The Casterbridge Hotel, 49 High East Street, **t** 264 043, *www.casterbridgehotel.co.uk* (*moderate*). Enter flagstone hallway into upmarket Georgian hotel with handsomely decorated public rooms and comfortable bedrooms, including four-posters.

Yalbury Cottage Hotel, Lower Brockhampton, **t** 262 382, *www.yalburycottage.com* (*moderate*). Charming thatched cottage 2 miles east of Dorchester along River Frome (a pleasant walk) and a mile from Hardy's birthplace cottage, with eight good rooms, a good restaurant and rural views.

Keeper's Cottage, West Stafford, **t** 264 389, *www.keeperscottage.net* (*moderate*). Lovely little cottage with roses climbing up the old stone walls and bedrooms furnished with antique furniture and old German and French beds with lovely quilts. The cottage, a short walk from Hardy's birthplace, featured in Hardy's short story 'The Waiting Supper'. Aga-cooked breakfasts should set you up for the great walks around here. Good pub and Yalbury Cottage restaurant nearby.

Eating Out

Potters Café-Bistro, 19 Durngate Street, **t** 260 312 (*moderate*). By day it is a pleasant café offering the usual sandwiches, baguettes and jacket potatoes, as well as maybe a warm goats' cheese salad. On Thurs–Sat eves it metamorphoses into a 'fine dining' restaurant where you might have seared scallops in a Vietnamese soup followed by sea bass or pork tenderloin with beetroot *jus*, all prepared from scratch, down to the meat and fish stocks.

The King's Arms, 30 High East Street, **t** 265 353 (*cheap*). With its portico rising up to a two-storey bay window, the King's Arms cuts quite a dash on the High Street. It is underwhelming inside, despite the historical interest of a minor role in Thomas Hardy's *Mayor of Casterbridge*. Bar food.

Judge Jeffreys', High East Street, **t** 264 369 (*cheap*). Traditional provincial restaurant near the Dorset Museum, serving hearty meals of beef stroganoff, mixed grills and salmon in olde-worlde, low-ceilinged, oak-beamed atmosphere. The building lodged Judge Jeffreys during the Bloody Assizes in 1685. *Open daily for lunch, Fri–Sat dinner.*

La Caverna, 57 Icen Way (off High Street), **t** 262 500 (*cheap*). Nice little Italian restaurant near the Dinosaur Museum, serving mainly pizza. *Open eves only.*

The Mock Turtle, 34 High West Street, **t** 264 011, *www.themockturtle.com* (*cheap*). Modern English restaurant in old building with yellow-painted walls and exposed brick. Starters might be toasted goats' cheese or air-dried ham and parmesan salad, followed by fricasseed scallops and monkfish or braised lamb shank. *Open Tues–Fri lunch, Mon–Sat dinner.*

the town's shops and attractions. The **Old Court Room** (*open Mon–Fri 10–12 and 2–4*) in the Shire Hall is where the Tolpuddle Martyrs were tried in 1834 for forming an illegal trade union. All six were transported to Australia for seven years, but brought back two years' later with unconditional pardons (after a public outcry).

The **Keep Military Museum** (***t*** *(01305) 264 066; open April–Sept Mon–Sat 9.30–5, Oct–Mar Tues–Sat 9.30–5, July–Aug also Sun 10–4; adm*) on Poundbury Road is housed in the Victorian gatehouse of the old training depot of the Devonshire and Dorset Regiment. There are some remains of the original Roman settlement of *Durnovaria*: walk around the 4th-century **Roman walls**, marked by an 18th-century avenue of trees and visit the remains of a **Roman town house** with mosaic floors. Just outside the walls is a Roman amphitheatre known as **Maumbury Rings** since excavations revealed a late-Neolithic henge monument (2500 BC) beneath it. In the Civil War the rings were used as an artillery redoubt.

Opened by Pitt-Rivers in 1886, the **Dorset County Museum** (*open Mon–Sat 10–5, summer also Sun 10–5*) houses important **archaeological collections**: relics of Maiden Castle's 3,000 years of occupation and an Iron Age skeleton with a Roman *ballista* bolt lodged in its spine, plenty of 'Wessex Culture' grave goods (*see* p.246), tableware, a carved Roman table leg and some of the black burnished Poole ware mass-produced

Where to Stay and Eat

The Dorset Chalklands

The New Inn, 14 Long Street, Cerne Abbas, **t** (01300) 341 274, *www.thenewinnca.co.uk* (*moderate*). About eight miles north of Dorchester in delightful Cerne Valley, old flint and brick inn with cobbled entrance way and eight bedrooms furnished with pine and attractive bed spreads.

The Swan Inn, Market Place, Sturminster Newton, **t** (01258) 472 208 (*moderate*). Large Georgian coaching inn with five clean, comfortable bedrooms furnished in pine. Restaurant too.

Stourcastle Lodge, Gough's Close, Sturminster Newton, **t** (01258) 472 320, *www.stourcastle-lodge.co.uk* (*moderate*). Long white 18th-century house just off market square with friendly atmosphere, five comfortable bedrooms, some with whirlpool baths and brass bedsteads, Aga-cooked breakfasts and excellent dinners (*moderate*), using local meat and dairy produce.

Newton House, Sturminster Newton, **t** (01258) 472 783 (*moderate*). Georgian house of the pioneering archaeologist General Pitt-Rivers. Lovely garden and interiors.

Holyleas House, Buckland Newton, **t** (01300) 345 214, *www.holyleashouse.co.uk* (*moderate*). Delightful place to stay halfway between Dorchester and Sherborne on the B3143 with floorboards, rugs, antiques and a football-playing terrier called Poppy.

Whiteways Farmhouse, Bookham, Alton Pancras (8 miles north of Dorchester), **t** (01300) 345 511, *www.bookhamcourt.co.uk* (*moderate*). Large, handsome farmhouse built in 1998 with recycled old beams and doors. Glorious views over the Blackmoor Vale. Also three self-catering holiday cottages. Nice walk to the Gaggle of Geese pub in Buckland Newton, a mile away.

Lamperts Cottage, Sydling St Nicholas, **t** (01300) 341 659, *www.bedandbreakfastnationwide.com* (*cheap*). You cross a footbridge over the Sydling stream to reach the front door of this charming thatched cottage with its flagstone floor, scrubbed pine furniture and friendly atmosphere.

Smiths Arms, Godmanstone (on A352 between Cerne Abbas and Charminster), **t** (01300) 341 236 (*cheap*). Low flint and thatch building, a charming spot for a drink (try the Stowford Press cider), particularly if it's warm enough to sit out on the banks of the River Cerne and enjoy the views. *Closes 5.30pm.*

in Roman times. The **Writer's Gallery** shows off Dorset's literary pedigree: Adhelm, one of the greatest scholars of the late 7th century, ended his career as Bishop of Sherborne; Wordsworth met Coleridge and wrote 'Ruined Cottage' while living near Lyme Regis in 1795–7; Jane Austen moved to Lyme Regis for a while in 1804; and of course there were the home-grown talents of William Barnes and Thomas Hardy. Hardy's study in Max Gate is reconstructed here, alongside books and manuscripts. The **Geology Room** is strong on Jurassic and Cretaceous fossils, including three-toed iguanodon footprints.

The Dorset Chalklands

This chalklands stretching from Dorchester to Salisbury are all prehistory. The classic aerial photograph of **Maiden Castle**, showing Iron Age bank and ditch fortifications, has made it one of the best-known prehistoric sites in the British Isles. **Cerne Valley** has a prehistoric nude giant etched into its chalk slope. **Cranborne Chase**, the tract of downland between Salisbury, Wimborne, Blandford Forum and Shaftesbury, is a treasure trove: the Chase was a hunting forest, owned by the earls of Gloucester, which passed through several lords of the Chase to the Pitt-Rivers family. General Pitt-Rivers, the archaeologist, devoted himself to its excavation. You could spend days tracking down its ancient past. The A354 Salisbury–Blandford Forum road follows the line of the old Roman road from Old Sarum to Dorchester through the Chase (there's a good section near Cobley). East of Sixpenny Handley down a farm track off the A354 is Neolithic **Wor Barrow**, where Pitt-Rivers exhumed a skeleton of a man with a flint arrowhead in his side. South of it are the **Larmer Tree Gardens**, Pitt-Rivers' pleasure grounds. At Coombe Bissett, just before you reach Salisbury on the A354, a minor road follows the lovely Broad Chalk Valley beside the River Ebble. (A good walk is along the high ridge to Tollard Royal and back through Ashcombe Bottom.)

Maiden Castle

The castle, a mile south of Dorchester, grew from a Neolithic camp to a massive Iron Age hill fort with perfectly formed ramparts – and came to a horrible end in AD 44 at the hands of Vespasian's 2nd Legion: 38 Celtic skeletons have been found outside the east entrance with fragments of Roman ammunition embedded in their splintered bones. *Durnovaria*, the new Roman town down the hill, took over from the tribal capital of the Durotriges, and Maiden Castle became a religious backwater with a temple and priest's house. Approach through the west entrance. By 200 BC this was the most heavily defended part of the hill fort.

Cerne Valley

The A532 from Dorchester follows the River Cerne into beautiful chalk countryside. North of the pretty village of **Cerne Abbas** is the famous **Cerne Giant**. He is 180ft long with a 120ft club over his shoulder and a 22ft erect penis. No one knows when or why he got there; AD 1 is the best guess. Some archaeologists think he is the Roman god

Hercules, although the primitive deity Helith is another contender (he was big around these parts). After St Augustine converted England to Christianity and made water spring from the dry ground to baptise them, the giant god lost his powers. Edwold, brother of murdered King Edmund of East Anglia, retired to Cerne and set up as a hermit beside **St Augustine's well**. His relics became the foundation for a new monastery in 987. **Cerne Abbey** was dissolved in 1539; the ruins are in the grounds of Abbey House. The well is along a steep cobbled path past the graveyard. You can wish for a husband here, if you want one. A path leads on up Giant Hill to the giant and an ancient earthwork called the **Trendle**, 150ft above the giant's outstretched arm.

Blandford Forum

Despite the name, it was never a Roman settlement; in fact the Roman road went via Badbury Rings a few miles east. The old name, Chipping Blandford, was Latinized in the 13th century. The town was rebuilt in 1731 after a fire and is now famous for the harmony of its Georgian buildings and its delightful river setting. Local builders John and William Bastard made quite a name for themselves, building the town hall and church, and a line of shops decorated with urns, grapes and foliage. The Bastards' old workshop was in Beres Yard. Off the market place, the **Cavalcade of Costume Museum** (*open Thurs–Mon 11–5*) occupies one of their grandest mansions.

On the downs at Blandford Camp is the **Royal Signals Museum (*t** *(01258) 482 248; open weekends 10–4, Easter–Oct also Mon–Fri 10–5*). The army first pitched tents on the downs in the mid-18th century. The tents became permanent and in 1967 the Royal Signals School relocated here from Yorkshire.

Hod Hill

Three miles northwest of Blandford Forum along the A350, turning left towards Hanford, you come to Hod Hill, an Iron Age hill fort of the Durotriges tribe overlooking Blackmoor Vale. It covers 35 acres within a double bank and ditch. A number of Roman ballista bolts were found in the chieftain's hut. Unusually, the second legion built its own fort inside the old hill fort; no other hill fort in Britain hosted a permanent Roman garrison. From here you can walk to Hambledon Hill, also once a hill fort.

Kingston Lacy

***t** (01202) 883 402; open Mar–Oct Wed–Sun 10.30–6; adm.*

Between Blandford Forum and Wimborne Minster, along the B3082, you drive down an avenue of 200-year-old beech trees, one of four tree-lined avenues leading into the park of Kingston Lacy, a Roman-style palazzo belonging to the Bankes family. The old Restoration house was transformed in 1834 by Egyptologist William John Bankes, with the help of architect Charles Barry. The year before, Bankes had been acquitted of lewd behaviour with a private in the Guards in a public loo near Westminster Abbey. In 1841 he did it again, with another guardsman, in Green Park. He didn't reckon he'd get off again, and fled to Italy, leaving Kingston Lacy with relatives. Bankes' lewdness was the low point of a life spent digging in Egyptian tombs. One or two monuments ended up back at Kingston Lacy; in front of the house stands the Philia obelisk, erected here as a monument to the man and his passion for Egyptology.

Badbury Ring, off the beech avenue, is another Iron Age hill fort of the Durotriges. It was sacked and abandoned by the Romans in favour of the new town of *Vindocladia* down the hill. *Vindocladia* did not outlive Roman rule; the old hill fort was stronger than the Roman town when fighting resumed in the 5th century. Edward the Elder camped here on his way to turf out his cousin Æthelwold (Alfred's nephew) from the royal palace at Wimborne. Æthelwold was upset about Alfred's will, which still survives, so you make up your own mind if he was right to be peeved. There are three Bronze Age round barrows and a section of the old Roman road.

Blackmoor Vale

Travel writer Bill Bryson calls the view from Bulbarrow Hill over the Blackmoor Vale one of the best in England, and he is renowned for his cynicism. Looking down on it is the best way to appreciate Hardy's 'Valley of the Little Dairies'.

Sturminster Newton is the market town of the vale, where both Thomas Hardy and General Pitt-Rivers lived. The locals (mainly retired) buy fish and pillowcases at the tiny Monday market, garden tools in the large stores behind the market square, and never need to leave the place. Hardy lived at 'Riverside' from 1876 to 1878, after marrying Emma Gifford, and wrote *The Return of the Native* there. General Pitt-Rivers lived at Newton House. The council offices can give you vale walks leaflets; one good short walk (1½ miles) is to Newton along the river and back over the town bridge.

Shaftesbury

The A30 used to be the old Great West Road carrying horse-drawn coach traffic into the West Country. The grand old towns of Shaftesbury and Sherborne were staging posts between Salisbury and Exeter, and both have coaching inns and handsome townhouses built of locally quarried stone. The town hall, church and townhouses along Shaftesbury's High Street are greensand stone, and the town stands on a dramatic greensand spur. On the escarpment stands a ruined abbey (*open April–Oct 10–5; adm minimal*) founded by King Alfred. (Alfred founded two religious houses in Wessex, the other at Athelney.) Shaftesbury was one of the safest *burhs* in Wessex, just 30 miles from the cathedral at Sherborne. Alfred installed his daughter Æthelgifa as the first abbess, the nuns were Wessex aristocrats' daughters, and the endowment of land by kings of Wessex in the 10th and 11th centuries made Shaftesbury the richest of nine Benedictine nunneries in England by the end of the Saxon period. The cult of St Edward contributed to the vast wealth, after Æthelred (the Unready) brought his murdered brother's relics to the abbey in 979. People used to say that if the abbess of Shaftesbury and the abbot of Glastonbury (the richest monastery) got together, their heir would own more land than the king of England.

Tourist Information

Shaftesbury: 8 Bell Street, **t** (01747) 853 514. *Open summer daily 10–5.30, winter Mon–Wed 10–1, Thurs–Sat 10–5.30.*

Where to Stay and Eat

Shaftesbury t (01747) –

The Salt Cellar, Gold Hill Parade, **t** 851 838. Incredibly popular with its classic, picture-postcard views down cobbled Gold Hill. Serves cakes and light lunches.

Bell Street Café, 17 Bell Street, **t** 850 199. Ancient building with impressive stone fireplaces and door arches, and a staircase made out of wooden railway sleepers. Offers wholesome light lunches, teas and coffees at scrubbed pine tables with bits of art for sale around the walls. *Open Mon–Sat.*

The Knoll, Bleke Street, **t** 855 243, *www.pick-art.org.uk* (*moderate*). The Pickards let out one double bedroom in their charming red-brick Victorian house, hidden away behind a thick hedge with a pretty garden and clifftop views over the Vale of Blackmoor.

Grosvenor Hotel, The Commons, **t** 852 282 (*moderate*). Handsome cream-painted old coaching inn which has got a little shabby around the edges. The carriage doors lead into a pleasant courtyard where you can drink tea. The 35 bedrooms are always clean. Bar meals include sandwiches, liver-and-bacon pies and steaks.

Museum Inn, Farnham, **t** (01725) 516 261, *www.museuminn.co.uk* (*moderate*). This thatched building dates back to the 17th century. In 1898 it was rebuilt to accommodate the hoards of visitors to the Pitt-Rivers museum and pleasure gardens. It is now a classy restaurant with eight delightful bedrooms, beautifully refurbished with old beams, flagstones and fire places set off by smoothly plastered cream and yellow painted walls.

The Old Forge, Fanners Yard, Compton Abbas, **t** 811 881, *theoldforge@hotmail.com*. Charming spot just below Fontmell Down. Classic car restoration and rooms to let. It's all decorated with bits and pieces from auctions. The breakfast room has a log-burning stove, and is stocked with board games, maps and local guide books. The old smithy has been converted into a self-catering cottage, with a galleried double room above the old workshop floor.

Chettle t (01258) –

Castleman Hotel, Chettle (8 miles northeast of Blandford off A354), **t** 830 096, *www.castlemanhotel.co.uk* (*moderate*). Excellent country-house hotel in former 16th-century dower house with eight large bedrooms, some furnished with antiques, set in old-world village on Cranborne Chase. The dining room serves dinner every eve and Sun lunch in modern English style with emphasis on local produce and game.

Shaftesbury is a good base for Cranborne Chase and the vales of Wardour and Blackmoor, or a good stop for lunch and a quick tour of the abbey ruins. There are craft shops and a town museum clustered around the steep cobbled lane of **Gold Hill**, thatched cottages down one side and the hefty abbey wall on the other. The wall is the most imposing relic of the old nunnery: 30ft high and buttressed, it runs 100 yards down the lane. Carry on down Gold Hill to the tiny village of St James and back up to the **abbey ruins**. The medieval ground plan has been turned into a pretty garden, and a little museum at the entrance displays archaeological fragments.

Around Shaftesbury

Follow signs to Tollard Royal, climbing the Zig Zag Road onto Cranborne Chase. From Win Green Hill you can walk along the ridge to Tollard Royal and back through Ashcombe Bottom. General Pitt-Rivers' Larmer Tree Gardens are just to the south.

Larmer Tree Gardens

***t** (01725) 552 300, www.larmertree.co.uk; open Aug–June Sun–Fri; adm; music festival 3rd week in July; box office open Mon–Fri 9–5.*

The best time to visit the Larmer Tree Gardens is on a Sunday afternoon in summer, when bands play in the colonial-style tea room or the small wooden open-air theatre against a painted classical backdrop. The musical Sundays were established during the garden's heyday in the 1890s, when the Pitt-Rivers Band was a regular part of entertainments that included skittles, bowls, golf and a small zoo – 'inducements' organized by General Pitt-Rivers to make his new 'educational museum' attractive to the public. Pitt-Rivers was a pioneer of museums, arranging his displays thematically (rather than chronologically) to stave off the public listlessness he had observed. 'The outing,' he said, 'is in itself an important accessory to a visit to a country museum.' People came from up to 20 miles away – as many as a thousand on a Sunday – by bicycle. The **Museum Hotel** was built in Farnham to cope with them all. The museum has since been shared out between the Salisbury Museum and the Pitt-Rivers Museum in Oxford, but the 11-acre pleasure gardens are surrounded by rolling chalk hills and tiny villages, with terrific views over Cranborne Chase. The annual music festival (*see* box) carries on in the original spirit of the place.

Sherborne

Sherborne is built of golden Ham stone, dug from the Ham Hill quarries 13 miles away. The warm stone is put to magical use in the abbey. Boys from the public school wander alongside the ghosts of Walter Raleigh and bishops Adhelm and Asser.

Who Killed King Edward?

When King Edgar died on 8 July 975 the succession was disputed between his eldest son, Edward (the Martyr), and his youngest, Æthelred (the Unready). Edward became king, but two and a half years later was murdered while visiting Ethelred and his stepmother, Elfrida, at Corfe. Æthelred got the crown, although he was only 12. Edward's body mysteriously vanished for a while, then reappeared a year later and was taken to Shaftesbury for a royal burial. Miracles were reported, and Edward was given a shrine and called a saint. No one was charged, but everyone blamed the stepmother. Æthelred encouraged the cult of the Martyr to strengthen his own support, and the kingdom, against renewed Viking attacks at the end of the 10th century. During excavations of the abbey church in the 1930s a small lead box was found containing the bones of a heavily mauled Saxon teenager – if not Edward, at any rate the bones Æthelred brought to Shaftesbury to be venerated. Two other Saxon princes (Æthelbert of East Anglia and Kenelm of Mercia) went the same way, knocked off by evil stepmothers during social visits.

Getting There and Around

By **car**, follow the M3 southbound to junction 8, where you can join the A303 to Wincanton and follow signs to Sherborne.

London Waterloo to Sherborne takes 2½ hours by **train**. The Bristol–Weymouth line stops at Yeovil Pen Mill station, 3 miles away.

National Express **coaches** run a daily service through Sherborne from London Victoria.

Tourist Information

Sherborne: 3 Tilton Court, Digby Road, **t** (01935) 815 341. *Open summer Mon–Sat 9.30–5.30, winter Mon–Sat 10–3.*

Where to Stay

Sherborne t (01935) –

The Eastbury Hotel, Long Street, **t** 813 131, *www.theeastburyhotel.co.uk* (*expensive*). Elegant Georgian townhouse with 15 bedrooms, including six singles, and an upmarket conservatory restaurant overlooking a lovely walled garden; 5 minutes walk into town.

The Antelope Hotel, Greenhill, **t** 812 077, *antelopesherborn@aol.com* (*moderate*). Former 18th-century coaching inn on the A30 at the top of town with friendly and attentive service, a locals' bar and restaurant serving roast monkfish with mashed potatoes, char-grilled fillet steak and venison with ratatouille.

The Pheasant Guest House, 24 Greenhill, **t** 815 252 (*moderate*). Civilized accommodation in 18th-century townhouse at top end of town on raised pavement above busy road; three big bedrooms, one with a window seat.

Eating Out

The Green, 3 The Green (off the top of Cheap Street), **t** (01935) 813 821 (*moderate*). Buzzy little place serving modern European cooking, such as goats' cheese and cherry tomato tart followed by Cornish cod or lamb with spring onion mash. The décor is pleasant with cream-painted walls and antique tables and chairs. On warm days you can eat in the garden courtyard. *Closed Sun and Mon.*

Caffé Fiore, 82 Cheap Street, **t** (01935) 812 180 (*cheap*). Small family business that calls itself an Italian-style bistro and coffee shop. Serves breakfast until 11am, lunches including large hot and cold salads, and all-day panini and sandwiches. *Closed Sun.*

Digby Tap, just off Digby Road (*cheap*). Traditional drinkers' pub with wooden settles, stone floors and open fireplaces. Attracts friendly mixed crowd.

Sherborne Abbey

Sherborne Abbey (*open summer 8.30–6, winter 8.30–4*) stands at the centre of town surrounded by monastic buildings (now Sherborne School) and a 15th-century almshouse complex. Its fan-vaulting and medieval wood-carving are stunning. The rubble belongs to the Saxon church, which was built in the 11th century to the east of St Adhelm's original cathedral. The low boundary wall between the close and Sherborne School was once a wall of the old parish church of All Hallows. To the right of the west door you can see the infamous door between the two churches (*see* box). At the east end are stones reddened by the heat of the blaze. After the fire, the Norman church was rebuilt in Perpendicular style. The spray of fan vaulting covers the entire roof with geometric patterns of stone ribs. It took about a century to build, which explains variations in the design. The choir vault came first, then the nave, culminating in the fireworks of the north transept. Carved bosses at the intersections of the angular ribs depict a mermaid with a mirror and comb, and green men with mouths full of leaves. Have a look at the medieval miserichords in the choir, including a woman beating her husband and a man birching a boy. The Raleighs had a private pew in St Catherine's Chapel and the Digby vault lies under the south transept.

Sherborne's Castles

Sherborne's **Old Castle** (*t (01935) 812 730; open April–Sept 10–6, Oct 10–5; adm*) and **New Castle** (*open April–Oct Tues–Thurs and weekends 11–4.30*) stand on the east of town on either side of the River Yeo. The ruins of the medieval castle stand opposite the endless chimney pots of the ancestral seat of the Digby family, set in grounds by Capability Brown. The Digbys still live on the estate (though not in the castle) given to Sir John Digby by James I as a reward for his diplomatic efforts at the Spanish court. Ironically, the previous owner, Sir Walter Raleigh, had been one of Elizabeth I's chief instruments in upsetting Anglo-Spanish relations in the first place. Raleigh moved into the Old Castle in 1592. After a couple of shivering years he built himself the New Castle, where he intended to start a great dynasty with numerous heirs and titles, having already collected a string of lucrative posts including Captain of the Queen's Guard and Lord Warden of the Cornish Stannaries. But things didn't go according to plan. He secretly married Elizabeth I's maid of honour, Elizabeth Throckmorton, and the couple were banished from Court for the union. Raleigh was not cut out for

Sherborne Abbey, Castles and Town

In AD 705 the country's leading scholar, Adhelm, who had earned his reputation at Canterbury and Malmesbury, became Bishop of Sherborne. He was already in his seventies and his best days were over, but he remained a key figurehead in the religious life of the country. He built the cathedral, and over the next few centuries the town grew up around it with royal favourites such as Asser, King Alfred's biographer, at the helm. In 1075, when the diocese moved to Old Sarum, Bishop Roger rescued Sherborne by turning the old cathedral church into an abbey and granting it land. He built one of his trademark castles above the River Yeo, and rebuilt the church in the Norman style. The abbey did alright, but the monks got on badly with the rest of town. In the late 14th century, a new parish church (All Hallows) was tacked on to the western end of the abbey church. No one liked this arrangement: the monks complained that the parishioners rang their bells erratically, and the parishioners complained that the monks had moved their font and narrowed the door between abbey and parish church. The Bishop of Salisbury ordered the parishioners to restrain their bell-ringing, and the monks to replace the font. A riot broke out anyway and part of the abbey church was burned down in 1437. The stunning fan vaulting – one of the thrills of Perpendicular church architecture – was the result of the rebuilding at the expense of the town. After the Dissolution, the town took over the abbey church that it had built. Sherborne School took over some of the monastic buildings. Sir Walter Raleigh got hold of Bishop Roger's castle in 1594 and built himself a new one across the river. He married Elizabeth I's lady in waiting, and lived at Sherborne for the rest of his life, between bouts in prison or fighting the Spanish at sea. Sir John Digby – James I's ambassador in Spain – got the estate after Raleigh's execution.

provincial life. Instead he entertained philosophers and scientists with dangerously modern ideas, and went on trial in Cerne Abbas for anti-religious behaviour. He was eventually readmitted into Court, became embroiled in plots against James I and was executed. Raleigh's house (built in 1594) was the cross-beam of the existing H shape. John Digby added the four wings in 1625 and a grand flight of steps. Capability Brown turned the Yeo into a serpentine lake and got rid of the formal gardens. The New Castle bristles with Dutch gables, elaborate chimneypots, quoins and griffins. The dark cement rendering can look gloomy, but was fashionable in the 17th century. Visitors are allowed into a dozen state rooms, adapted by generations of Digbys – Jacobean fireplaces, Victorian wallpaper and Georgian furniture. On the plaster ceilings in the Green Drawing Room and Lady Bristol's Bedroom you will see Raleigh's coat of arms and heraldic buck; in the museum is Raleigh's pipe.

The Frome and Piddle Valleys: Hardy Country

East of Dorchester along the A35, following the rivers Frome and Piddle towards Wareham, you enter Hardy country, the setting of many events in the author's life and books. You're in the Hampshire Basin, Hardy's ragged Egdon Heath, where you'll wish the A35 wasn't humming in the background. You can get hold of books and guides to Hardy's Wessex in the Dorset County Museum in Dorchester, among other places.

Hardy's Birthplace Cottage

***t** (01297) 561 900, www.nationaltrust.org.uk; open April–Oct Thurs–Mon 11–5; adm.*

A mile off the A35 you come to Higher Bockhampton. Hardy's Birthplace Cottage is down a rough bridleway on the edge of Thorncombe Wood. The old brick cottage in which he lived with his parents and grandmother has a thatched roof and three chimneys, and a garden full of herbs. Hardy was born in the attic room. When he was a boy, the garden backed onto the open heathland of Thorncombe Wood – Egdon Heath, in his books. Hardy left home at 22, to work in Arthur Blomfield's architectural practice in London. But he regularly returned to visit his mother, finishing his first novels, *Desperate Remedies* (1871) and *A Pair of Blue Eyes* (1873), in his old bedroom, and starting *Under the Greenwood Tree* (1872), in which the cottage became Upper Mellstock. You can walk to the Rain barrow, a prehistoric burial mound which features prominently in *The Return of the Native*.

Max Gate

www.nationaltrust.org.uk; open April–Sept Sun, Mon and Wed 2–5; adm.

Hardy designed Max Gate, on the edge of the heath by Dorchester, and his father and brother built it. Visitors may be surprised at how suburban it looks, but this is where Hardy finally settled down with his first wife, Emma, in 1883, and remained with his former mistress and second wife, Florence Dugdale, after Emma's death in 1913. Here he wrote *Tess of the D'Urbervilles*, *Jude the Obscure*, *The Dynasts* and most of his poetry. You can see the dining room with Hardy's bookcases and sofa, and the drawing room. Hardy's domestic life in Max Gate was not happy, but a frequent visitor was T.E. Lawrence of Arabia. In the shrubbery is the pet graveyard, where Florence's terrier Wessex is buried among birds and cats.

Hardy used to walk from Max Gate to **Stinsford church** (a mile east of Dorchester), where he had sung in the choir as a boy. His ashes were buried in Westminster Abbey, but his heart was brought to the churchyard to be with his first wife, Emma, next to his father and mother. (Cecil Day Lewis, a Hardy fan, is buried in the same row.) It is to Stinsford church that Tess is headed in *Tess of the D'Urbervilles*, when Angel Clare carries her across the flooded road.

Tolpuddle

The River Piddle runs off Puddleton Down north of Dorchester and heads for Poole Harbour, taking in a string of piddling, puddling villages. **Tolpuddle**, just off the A35 between Alfpuddle and Puddletown (Weatherbury in *Far from the Madding Crowd*), seems the most unlikely birthplace of modern trade unionism. The July festival brings about 4,000 people into the village to see brass bands and marching trade unions. In 1831, six farm labourers met under the sycamore tree on the village green and decided to join forces and ask for an increase in wages together. After three years of fruitless negotiations, they were arrested under an obscure law, marched 7 miles to Dorchester and sentenced to seven years' transportation. Their harsh treatment provoked a public outcry, and they were repatriated from Australia two years later. The sycamore tree is still standing – just. Across the road are six cottages built by the TUC in 1934 to mark the centenary of the Tolpuddle Martyrs, as they became known. The small **Tolpuddle Martyrs Museum** (*open Mar–Oct Tues–Sat 10–5.30, Sun 11–5.30, Nov–Feb Tues–Sat 10–4, Sun 11–4*) tells their story.

Cloud's Hill

***t** (01929) 405 616, www.nationaltrust.org.uk; open April–Oct Thurs–Sun 12–5.*

This old gamekeeper's cottage on the edge of rhododendron woods, south of Tolpuddle, was the home of the legendary Lawrence of Arabia. It was, he wrote to a friend in August 1924, 'very quiet, very lonely, very bare', but nothing was superfluous to the need to 'dream, or write or read by the fire' and keep out of the public eye. He enlisted with the Bovington Tank Corps and entertained Thomas Hardy here.

From here, you can follow a Lawrence trail to **Bovington Tank Museum** (***t** (01929) 405 096; open daily 10–5; adm exp*), St Martin's Church in Wareham and St Nicholas' church in Moreton, where he was buried on 21 May 1935 in the presence of Winston Churchill, among many others.

Wareham

The small town of Wareham sits between the Frome and Piddle on the west of Poole Harbour, surrounded by heath and marsh. By the 9th century it had grown into a fortified port with a nunnery where a Wessex king was buried. The Saxon street grid

Getting There and Around

Wareham is on the London Waterloo to Weymouth **train** line

There are **buses** to and from Weymouth to Corfe, Swanage and Poole. Call **Poole Bus Station**, **t** 673 555.

Tourist Information

Wareham: Holy Trinity Church, South Street, **t** (01929) 552 740. *Open Feb–Oct Mon–Sat 9.30–5, July–Sept also Sun 10–4, Oct–Feb 10–3.*

There is a small **market** on Thurs at Cottees Auctioneers on East Street.

Where to Stay and Eat

Wareham t (01929) –

The Priory Hotel, Church Green, **t** 551 666, *www.theprioryhotel.co.uk* (*luxury*). Lichen-encrusted old stone former priory with sagging roof-tiles, flagstone courtyard and beautiful gardens sloping down to the river. Two dining rooms. Lunch in the upstairs Garden Room or garden, dinner – beef Wellington, roast duck with ratatouille, lobster – and Sunday lunch in the cosy old vaulted cellar (*expensive*).

The Old Granary, The Quay, **t** 552 010 (*expensive*). Mellow red-brick Georgian building on the quayside with popular restaurant offering a range of dishes including fish and chips, steak-and-ale pie, gammon, stroganoff and a dozen fresh fish dishes. Four bedrooms.

Anglebury House, 15–17 North Street, **t** 552 988 (*moderate*). Lawrence of Arabia is said to have stopped for tea in the tea rooms and stayed overnight above the butcher's shop, now the restaurant. You can do the same. The menu includes 10 fish dishes, stroganoff, curries, stir-fries, pasta, steak and mixed grills. The olde-worlde tea shop (*open daily 9–5*) serves tea, coffee and snacks. There are seven bedrooms. *Restaurant open Tues–Sat eves only*.

Belle Vue, West Street, **t** 552 056 (*moderate*). Three homely bedrooms in Victorian private house by Saxon town wall.

La Trottolina, The Quay, **t** 551 662 (*cheap*). Cheerful Italian restaurant on quayside with varied menu, and lively atmosphere complete with accordion player.

Raj Poot, North Street, **t** 554 603 (*cheap*). Long-established Indian restaurant with good local reputation. *Open eves only*.

and sections of the old turf walls survive. Aim for the pretty quay by the old town bridge. A 6-mile walk to Corfe Castle begins here. Behind the quayside you can see the grey stone tower of **St Lady Mary's Church**. Inside it are Romano-British inscriptions, dating from the 7th century (long after the West Saxon invasion). At the end of North Street is the late Saxon **church of St Martin's** (*open in summer; in winter get the key from A.F. Joy Men's Outfitters, 35 North Street, or Horsey's Newsagents, 27 North Street*), which houses a life-sized Purbeck marble effigy of T.E. Lawrence, sculpted by his friend Eric Kennington, showing the leader of the Arab Revolt in Arab dress. Lawrence is buried in the churchyard of St Nicholas in Moreton. **Wareham Museum** (*open Easter–Oct Mon–Sat 10–4*) on East Street is packed with town history.

The Isle of Purbeck

The Isle of Purbeck is really a peninsula. The only road to its remote villages and striking coast leads from Wareham to Swanage. The Purbeck Hills, a whaleback ridge of rolling chalk scenery, run across the middle between Old Harry Rocks and Lulworth Cove. Buttressing Purbeck from the sea is a rampart of limestone through which runs

Tourist Information

Lulworth Cove: The Heritage Centre, West Lulworth, **t** (01929) 400 587. Geology and local history museum, which can provide local information. *Open April–Sept 10–6, Oct and Mar 10–5, Nov–Feb 10–4.*

Where to Stay and Eat

Corfe Castle t (01929) –

Mortons House Hotel, East Street, **t** 480 988, *www.mortonshousehotel* (*expensive*). Gabled Tudor manor backed by Nine Barrow Down, with 17 rooms, an oak-panelled sitting room and a pretty walled garden. The upmarket restaurant might serve smoked salmon, roast duck or pan-fried salmon fillet.

The Old Curatage, 30 East Street, **t** 481 441, *oldcuratage@aol.com* (*moderate*). This delightful stone building is at least 350 years old. Three cottagey rooms, the largest with views over the Purbeck countryside. Comfortable and friendly.

The Fox Inn, West Street, **t** 480 449 (*cheap*). Friendly 16th-century pub with garden and cosy bar with old well inside. Pub grub.

Studland t (01929) –

Fairfields Hotel, Swanage Road, **t** 450 224, *fairfieldshotel@tiscali.co.uk* (*expensive*). You will be well looked-after in this relaxed, child-friendly hotel with 12 bedrooms and views over Ballard Down and the sea. 'Home from home' atmosphere. Early tea for children. Dinner (*moderate*) might be lobster followed by Studland Bay plaice or Dorset lamb, and home-made profiteroles with fresh strawberries, crumbles and cheesecakes.

The Bankes Arms Country Inn, Manor Road, Studland, **t** 450 225 (*moderate*). Beautiful old stone building with sea views from five of the nine bedrooms and cliff-top garden. Wholesome country-inn fare served in the bar: beef bourguignon, game casserole, Somerset pork and fish.

Rectory Cottage, Rectory Lane, **t** 450 311, *www.rectorycottage.co.uk* (*moderate*). The older half of an old rectory, 5 minutes' walk from the beach; three comfortable rooms, one with balcony and sitting room.

Lulworth Cove t (01929) –

None of the hotels in Lulworth is special, but they are friendly and straightforward.

Lulworth Beach Hotel, Main Road, **t** 400 404, *www.lulworthbeachhotel.com* (*moderate*). Comfortable hotel opposite duck pond with 12 bedrooms. Good quality fish and game restaurant (*moderate*). Nice garden overlooking pond.

Gatton House, Main Road, **t** 400 252, *www.gattonhouse.co.uk* (*moderate*). Edwardian greystone house on hill above road with eight cheerful bedrooms, some with views of Purbeck Hills. *Open Mar–Oct.*

Graybank, Main Road, **t** 400 256 (*cheap*). Ten minutes' walk from the cove, this greystone Victorian house has seven modest, sweet-smelling bedrooms with hand basins, and a bathroom just down the hall. *Open Feb–Nov.*

The Old Barn, Main Road, **t** 400 305 (*cheap*). Old stone building with six bright upstairs bedrooms (one en-suite). *Open all year, including Christmas day.*

Beach Café, Lulworth Cove, **t** 400 648 (*cheap*). On the beach, this is a charming little café selling ice cream and sandwiches all day. On Fri and Sat eves in summer the Lulworth Beach Hotel takes over the café as a seafood restaurant (*t 400 404*), with two sittings: 7.30–9 and 9 until late. As the evening wears on the music gets louder and the atmosphere jollier. Don't miss it.

Castle Inn, Main Road, **t** 400 311 (*cheap*). Quaint, thatched real-ale pub with copious bar menu of 50–60 meals, including mixed grills, pies, sausage and chips, and salmon steaks.

a thin vein of coloured Purbeck marble, quarried in the Middle Ages for the pillars, fonts and effigies of English abbeys and cathedrals, including Westminster Abbey, Salisbury Cathedral, and the tombs of King John and Richard Beauchamp. Between Worth Matravers and Swanage, the cliffs have been quarried since the Great Fire of

London for the façades of public buildings. The faded resort of Swanage developed as a quarry town in the 17th century.

The Isle of Purbeck is the youngest end of the Jurassic Coast. Fossils abound in the cliffs and quarries, from the period when the Jurassic sea beat the retreat. Among the ammonites and marine creatures are dinosaur footprints.

Corfe Castle

t (01929) 481 294; open April–Sept 10–6, Oct 10–5, Nov–Feb 10–4, Mar 10–5; adm.

The A351 travels through a gap in the Purbeck Hills, guarded by Corfe Castle (*open Mar–Oct daily 10–5.30, Nov–Feb daily 11–3.30; adm*); the romantic medieval ruins stand silhouetted on a conical hill above the road. Beyond, the road narrows through the picturesque grey-stone village *en route* to the coastal cliffs. 'The gap at Corfe' first gets a mention in the *Anglo-Saxon Chronicle* in AD 978, as the place where Edward the Martyr was murdered, by his stepmother and half-brother, the future King Æthelred the Unready (*see* p.272). The site was fortified by King William I after the Norman Conquest. Henry I built the keep, John built the outer bailey defences and Henry III built both gatehouses. The castle was destroyed after the Civil War, but the ruins remain. You can walk around the curtain wall to the village, and over a stone bridge to the outer gatehouse with its portcullis grooves and murder holes.

Corfe Village and Around

The arrangement of streets, market place and church in **Corfe village** is medieval, although most of what you see dates from the 17th century. In the Middle Ages, Corfe was where Purbeck marble was shaped and polished. There are dinosaur footprints in the museum on West Street.

Beyond Corfe on the edge of the bay, **Studland** is the start of a path to Old Harry Rocks, once joined to the Isle of Wight Needles by a chalk ridge. The little stack beyond is known as Old Harry's Wife. Carrying on over Ballard Down to Swanage, the ridge is renowned for its butterflies. An obelisk marks the western end of the down.

The only way to reach the picture-postcard village of **Worth Matravers** is down twisty lanes and paths. The cluster of limestone houses around a duck pond, the old Square and Compass pub (with its tiny archaeology museum) and sea views are the start of walks along dramatic cliffs to the old Purbeck-stone cliff quarries at Winspit and Seacombe.

Another walk takes you to **St Adhelm's Head** with its Norman chapel and coast-guard station, past medieval terraced fields, wild flowers and quarrymen's cottages.

Lulworth Cove

Lulworth Cove is a perfect seaside village, set against dramatic cliffs, lobster pots on the shingle beach and fishing boats bobbing on the water. Into this 'miniature Mediterranean' plunged Sergeant Troy in *Far From the Madding Crowd*. Nowadays the madding crowd is here on a sunny day. A footpath leads up and along the cliffs to Durdle Dor, an archway of Portland Stone guarding an excellent swimming beach.

The Jurassic Coast

The 95-mile stretch of coast between Exmouth in east Devon and Old Harry Rocks on the Isle of Purbeck is known as the Jurassic Coast. It is the only place in the world displaying unbroken evidence of the Mesozoic Era (251–66 million years ago). By walking the coast from east to west you can trace the evolution of the species from fish to dinosaur to mammals – over a period of 185 million years. In the Jurassic period the shallow seas that covered the region were abundant in marine life: giant ammonites, long-necked plesiosaurs and dolphin-shaped ichthyosaurs; their fossilized remains are now falling from the cliffs onto the sand around Lyme Regis. Towards the end of the period the sea levels dropped and trees grew; then the sea rose again, swamping the forest under a salty lagoon. In the cliffs a mile east of Lulworth Cove you can see the fossil forest. The swamps and lagoons of the late Jurassic–early Cretaceous period were roamed by dinosaurs, who left footprints. A hundred sauropod footprints were discovered at Keat's Quarry near Reton in 1997.

The Lulworth Range

Don't be alarmed at the occasional boom from a hillside; a 7,000-acre army firing range stretches along the coast from Kimmeridge Bay and Lulworth Cove, so that the unspoiled scenery is out of bounds much of the time. It's open most weekends and August (*to check dates call the range officer,* ***t*** *(01929) 404 819*). In the ghost village of **Tyneham** – evacuated in 1943 'for the duration of the emergency' – you can pick up walks information. Five hundred yards east of the cove, on the other side of the **Fossil Forest Gate**, steps leads down the cliff to the fossilized remains of a prehistoric forest. The doughnut-shaped structures, known as burrs, are where the trees once stood. The forest took root on newly exposed land at the end of the Jurassic period, when sea levels dropped. They were swamped, and fossilized, when sea levels rose again.

Weymouth and Chesil Beach

Weymouth is south of Dorchester, at the end of a congested road. The bay has a long sandy beach and a handsome old Victorian harbour, but the resort is no great shakes. The River Wey runs out to sea beneath the Nothe, a headland topped with gardens and a Victorian fort (***t*** *(01305) 766 626;* open *May–Sept 10.30–4*), one of Palmerston's forts built in the 1860s. The harbour is the place to be, with fishing boats and quays backed by Victorian warehouses. Until the Victorian quay was built, the river was fringed with marshes. The seafaring communities of Melcombe and Weymouth developed on either side and were joined under one name in 1571. The best bit of beach is at the harbour end.

The Isle of Portland

Portland is an 'island' connected by a narrow isthmus to the coast. It is the Alcatraz of Dorset: three prisons, one in a Victorian army barracks, another in a Napoleonic fortress, and a third floating in the harbour. But Portland is best known for its stone,

Getting There and Around

Regular **trains** run direct to Weymouth via Dorchester from Bristol or London Waterloo. There are frequent **buses** from Dorchester to Weymouth.

Tourist Information

Weymouth: King's Statue, The Esplanade, **t** (01305) 785 747. *Open April–Oct 9.30–5, Nov–Mar 10–4.*

Bridport: 47 South Street (a mile from West Bay), **t** (01308) 424 901. *Open summer Mon–Sat 9–5, winter Mon–Sat 10–3.*

The young professional **Garden Opera Company** performs for a couple of nights in June in the garden of Abbey House in Abbotsbury, accompanied by a live quartet. Call Abbotsbury Music, **t** (01305) 871 475 or go to *www.abbmusic.org.uk* for details.

Where to Stay and Eat

Weymouth t (01305) –

Hotel Rex, 29 The Esplanade, **t** 760 400, *www.kingshotels.co.uk* (*expensive*). Thirty-one pink bedrooms and a steak and seafood restaurant in this large, efficient Georgian stuccoed hotel.

The Chatsworth Hotel, 14 The Esplanade, **t** 785 012, *www.thechatsworth.co.uk* (*moderate*). Georgian townhouse with seafood restaurant and pleasant rooms. Harbour and esplanade views.

Perry's, 4 Trinity Road, The Old Harbour, **t** 785 799 (*moderate*). Superb fish restaurant with sultry ground-floor dining room where mirrors reflect the harbour view, and more formal dining upstairs with a fiercely contested bay-window seat. Roasted sea bass, grilled sole and gratin of white crab meat, topped off by sticky toffee pudding. *Open every eve and Tues–Fri and Sun lunch.*

Mallams, 5 Trinity Road, **t** 776 757, *www.mallamsrestaurant.co.uk* (*moderate*). Pretty harbourside cottage restaurant next door to Perry's with crisp tablecloths and understated nautical décor. *Open Mon–Sat eves, in summer also Sun.*

The Red Lion, Hope Square, **t** 786 940 (*cheap*). Good family pub where you can sit outside on a warm day. Pub grub.

The Ivy Coffee House, 7 Cove Row, **t** 789 737 (*cheap*). Quaint former pub with old wood

which has been quarried since the 17th century to clad prestigious buildings, including St Paul's Cathedral, Waterloo Bridge and the UN building in New York. (The British Museum's decision to use a substitute French stone for its millennium extension caused quite a furore.) You can catch a bus from Weymouth to Portland and walk around the side of the Verne Citadel and down to the harbour, catching a boat back.

Chesil Beach and Abbotsbury

From Portland, a ruler-straight bar of pebbles runs for 10 miles parallel to the mainland. This is **Chesil Beach**. Behind it is a lagoon, known as the **Fleet**, which supports flora and fauna common in southern Europe. The thatched yellow stone cottages of **Abbotsbury** village are where the beach joins the mainland. It began as the market of the 11th-century Benedictine abbey and an excellent place to begin walks. Two miles northwest is **Abbotsbury Castle**, an Iron Age hill fort with double ramparts. It was one of a string of fortresses of the Durotriges tribe. A footpath by the Ilchester Arms leads to the buttressed 14th-century **St Catherine's Chapel** on the top of Chapel Hill. At the western end of the Fleet is the 600-year-old **Swannery** (***t*** *(01305) 871 858; open mid-Mar–Nov 10–5; adm*), which has the largest colony of managed swans in the world (up to 700 swans). They feed off a seaweed (*zortera marina*) abundant in the lagoon, and were encouraged to nest in Abbotsbury by the monks. The best time to come is 12 panelling, wooden settles and bar. Serves breakfast, light lunches, home-made cakes and cream teas.

Abbotsbury t (01305) –

Abbey House, Church Street, Abbotsbury (9 miles from Weymouth, Bridport and Dorchester, a pebble's throw from Chesil Beach), **t** 871 330, *www.theabbeyhouse.co.uk* (*moderate*). Lunch, afternoon tea or a night's stay is a treat in the former infirmary of the Benedictine abbey with its garden, thatched tithe barn and views of St Catherine's Hill. Fresh Bridport fish dishes including the 'Dorset Smokey' – smoked haddock with white wine and cheese sauce topped with shaved parmesan, and toasted under the grill – and vegetarian dishes such as 'Abbotsbury Mushroom' – button mushrooms in stilton and port sauce. *Open for lunch 12–2.30; cream teas, sandwiches and tea cakes until 5*. Five pretty rooms to let.

Bridport and West Bay t (01308) –

Riverside Restaurant, West Bay, **t** 422 011 (*moderate*). It began as a fish and chip shop 40 years ago, and is now an acclaimed seafood restaurant. The décor is airy, with bare stripped wooden floorboards, simple furniture, fresh flowers and views of the river and harbour. Everything on the menu is home-made, including the elaborate desserts. The fresh fish includes stalwarts like baked cod and grilled brill fillet with crispy spinach and sorrel. *Closed Mon and Sun eves, Dec, Jan and half Feb. Booking essential.*

Bridport Arms Hotel, West Bay, **t** 422 994, *adriancollis@westdorsetinns.co.uk* (*moderate*). Thatched pub on beach owned by local Palmers brewery offering weak 'BB' or Bridport Bitter (originally made to keep agricultural workers sober) and strong '200' brew; 13 bedrooms, to be refurbished 2004.

Haddon House Hotel, West Bay, **t** 423 626 (*moderate*). Welcoming 'country house hotel' 300 yards from West Bay. Regency-style décor, 12 comfortable bedrooms, and an intimate restaurant.

The George Hotel, 4 South Street, Bridport, **t** 423 187 (*moderate*). Friendly pub opposite the guildhall, 15 minutes' walk from the harbour. Palmers beer and home-made bar meals including old favourites like shepherd's pie, bubble and squeak, and liver and bacon.

noon or 4pm, when they are fed. A mile and a half away are the **Subtropical Gardens** (**t** *(01305) 871 387; open daily 10–5 or dusk if earlier; adm*), founded in 1765 by the Countess of Ilchester as a kitchen garden, and replanted with camellias, magnolias and rhododendrons over the last two centuries. You can drive to the **Hardy Monument** above the village on Black Down Hill; it commemorates the admiral, Nelson's flag captain at the Battle of Trafalgar, not the more famous writer.

Between Burton Bradstock and West Bay the beach is littered with rock falls, packed with the fossilized fruits of the Jurassic seas: ammonites, sea urchins, brachiopods, gastropods and bivalves. **West Bay** (the setting of TV series *Harbour Lights*) is the harbour of charming **Bridport**, an excellent base for the coast.

Lyme Regis

And a very strange stranger it must be who does not see charms in the immediate environs of Lyme, to make him wish to know it better.

Jane Austen, *Persuasion*

Lyme Regis is a perfect seaside town, with its mix of colourful 18th-century cottages, quaint tangled streets, and massive stone walls retaining the cliffs. The town grew up

Getting There and Around

The nearest **railway** station is Axminster, 6 miles northwest on the A35, on the Plymouth to London Waterloo line. **Buses** to Lyme Regis meet the trains.

Tourist Information

Lyme Regis: Guildhall Cottage, Church Street, **t** (01297) 442 138. *Open winter Mon–Sat 10–4, Sun 10–2; summer Mon–Sun 10–5, Sun 10–4.*

Where to Stay

Lyme Regis t (01297) –

Hotel Buena Vista, Pound Street, **t** 442 494 (*expensive*). Attractive Regency house at the top of town with sea views from the garden, decorated with prints and old photos; 18 bedrooms. Room at top of narrow, steep stairs has best view.

The Alexandra Hotel, Pound Street, **t** 442 010, *www.hotelalexandra.co.uk* (*expensive*). Former 18th-century home of a dowager countess, it has been a hotel for a hundred years. Views of the bay from the lawns; a path leads down through civic gardens to the Cobb. Cosy décor and friendly uniformed staff; 26 bedrooms. Good restaurant, south-facing conservatory and a sitting room stocked with board games.

The White House Hotel, 2 Hillside, The Street, Charmouth, **t** 560 411 (*expensive*). Attractive white-painted Regency Hotel set back from road behind palm trees. Elegant interior with excellent restaurant serving wholesome country-house cooking using organic meat and local fish. Eight bedrooms, all carefully decorated. It takes about an hour to walk along the beach or cliff path to Lyme Regis.

The Mariners Hotel, Silver Street, **t** 442 753, *mariners@ukgateway.net* (*moderate*). Former coaching inn at mouth of River Lyme. Warm, friendly atmosphere, with creaky floorboards and low ceilings; 12 pretty rooms and a good restaurant using fresh, local produce.

Old Lyme Guesthouse, 29 Coombe Street, **t** 442 929, *www.oldlymeguesthouse.co.uk* (*moderate*). Three minutes from sea in centre of old town, this 300-year-old stone cottage has five cheerful bedrooms, all furnished to a very high standard. The

around the Cobb, a curved stone pier as famous as the ammonites of Lyme Bay. Two fictional heroines have behaved dramatically on the Cobb: Jane Austen's Lydia in *Persuasion*, who knocks herself out on the steps, and the heroine of John Fowles' *The French Lieutenant's Woman*, in her black hooded cloak. The 18th-century resort developed when the harbour went into decline. Jane Austen visited in 1803 and 1804, enjoying coastal walks over Black Ven to Charmouth and writing with enthusiasm about the place in her books and letters.

The cliffs of Lyme Bay are famous for Jurassic marine fossils. There are zillions of them, including the occasional scary ichthyosaur or plesiosaur. The fossils are literally falling out of the eroding cliffs onto the beach.

There's a lot to see in the quaint streets of Lyme, all on a delightful scale. There are two fossil shops on Broad Street, one or two art galleries and a couple of second-hand bookshops. On Cockmoile Square at the top of fortress-like Gun Cliff stands the Guildhall and the red-brick Victorian **Philpot Museum** (***t** (01297) 443 370; open Easter–Oct 10–5; adm minimal*), named after the mayor of Lyme Regis who built it in 1900. Mary Anning, the inspiration for the tongue-twister 'she sells sea shells on the sea shore', was born on the site of the museum, and John Fowles was curator in the 1980s. Mug up on the town's geological and literary connections, and join a fossil-hunting walk. The museum not to miss, however, is **Dinosaurland** (***t** (01297) 443 541;*

proprietor is full of helpful information about the town.

Eating Out

Rumours, 14–15 Monmouth Street (on corner of Coombe Street), **t** 444 740 (*moderate*). Small, unpretentious fish restaurant with big reputation; eight tables, Big Band jazz music and daily menu. The local Thai crab cakes are a popular starter, followed by John Dory on roasted butternut squash risotto or plaice stuffed with crab poached in light parmesan cream. All home-made, including bread and ice cream. *Summer closed Wed, spring and autumn closed Tues and Wed, winter open Fri and Sat eves only. Booking essential.*

The Millside Restaurant, 1 Mill Lane, off Coombe Street, **t** 445 999 (*cheap*). Morning coffee, lunches and evening meals in this superb restaurant on the resort side of Lyme, run by a husband and wife team (he cooks, she works front of house). Lunch is served in the wine bar, with murals of climbing flowers, or on the sun-trap patio. Evening meals are served in the pastel restaurant next door. Fresh fish, steaks and other favourites.

Antonio's Trattoria, 7 Church Street (near the Philpot Museum), **t** 442 352 (*cheap*). Atmospheric Italian restaurant in the spirit of the traditional Italian trattoria, where the whole family mucks in. Lots of pasta, fresh local fish and meat from the Coombe Street butchers. National flag napkins, red and green tablecloths, pictures of rural Italian scenes on the walls, Italian music, beer and wine. *Open eves only, closed Sun and Dec–Mar.*

Lyme Fish Bar, 34 Coombe Street, **t** 442 375 (*cheap*). Excellent fish and chip shop near Dinosaur Land; serves fresh battered Brixham fish, eat-in or take-away.

For pubs you are spoilt for choice. You might try **The Volunteer**, 31 Broad Street, **t** 442 214, a small, cosy traditional pub at the landward end of Broad Street, serving good fish; **The Pilot Boat** at the bottom of Broad Street, on the seafront, next door to the Philpot Museum, **t** 443 157, is a friendly, larger pub, serving food all day, including fresh fish; **The Cobb Arms**, Marine Parade, **t** 443 242, almost on the Cobb, opposite the Life Boat House, is a lively family pub.

open 10–5, July–Aug until 6; adm), in a neo-classical brick church on Coombe Street behind Gun Cliff. This private collection of fossils includes an ichthyosaur skeleton and a baby ichthyosaur dug up by the owner's 11-year-old son. Steve, the owner, is an expert on fossils and the best fossil-hunting guide.

En route to the fossil beach (*see* p.283), pass through the churchyard, where you can see the grave of Mary Anning and her memorial stained-glass window. She supplied all the early geologists with fossils, lived on the bread-line, and complained that she was being exploited by the scientists, who took all the credit for her discoveries. When she died, a eulogy was given at the Geological Society in her honour.

To get to the old harbour, walk along a crescent of sandy beach backed by a parade of concrete shops, built to hold up the cliff after a landslide in 1962 took out the old cottages. The two stone piers are Lyme's only protection against the sea. About a dozen fishing boats are based in the harbour; in summer they take tourists fishing.

The **Cobb** protects the inner harbour from the full force of the sea. You can walk along it when the sea is calm, just like Meryl Streep did in the film version of *The French Lieutenant's Woman*. From here, you can look back at the cliffs and the painted houses of Lyme. In one of the fisherman's stores is a little **aquarium** (*open Easter–Oct; adm minimal*), full of local fish, including lobster, crab, dog fish, conger eel and sea mice. To the west of the Cobb is **Monmouth Beach**. It gets its name from the

Fossil-hunting

West of the Cobb, on Monmouth Beach, huge ammonites are visible in the limestone pavement, well worth the short walk in the direction of Pin Hay Bay. The best beach for fossil-hunting, however, is east of Lyme Regis below Black Ven, the cliff of grey Jurassic shale and limestone beds. You can reach it either from Lyme Regis or from Charmouth at low tide. At high tide the limestone slabs beneath Church Cliffs – where unsung fossil-gatherer Mary Anning found an ichthyosaur and a plesiosaur – are impassable. Black Ven is in a permanent state of slow collapse, bringing fossils cascading down with it, so you can get away without a fossil hammer. Where the mudflow reaches the sea is the fossil-hunting ground, not the cliff, which is dangerously prone to sudden falls (Mary Anning's father, Richard, was almost washed out to sea in a landslide beneath the cliffs). Look in the dark patches of sand for ammonites, belemnites and shells.

Looking up at Black Ven you can see the geological layers. At the bottom are the shales, no good to fossil hunters. The dark layer of **Black Ven marls** above is one to be interested in – full of fossils. Chunks of it fall onto the beach and the light grey limestone splits easily to reveal ammonites (their distinctive spiral shells can be up to a yard across). Above the Black Ven marls are the **belemnite marls**, full of the bullet-shaped remains of belemnites (primitive cephalopods, of the octopus family). The golden top layer is **upper greensand**, deposited in the Cretaceous period 100 million years after the Jurassic beds.

Duke of Monmouth, who sailed into Lyme from Holland in 1685 to overthrow Catholic King James II and re-establish a Protestant monarchy (*see* p.318). Along the beach you can see the ammonite pavement in the Blue Lias rock. Alternatively, from the Cobb, you can follow the path to the **Undercliff**, a lush terrain created by landslides (8 million tons of soil and rock fell down in 1839). You will hardly see the sea until you get to **Seaton**, 5 miles along the cliff path.

West Country
Bristol, Bath, Somerset, Devon and Cornwall

The West Country

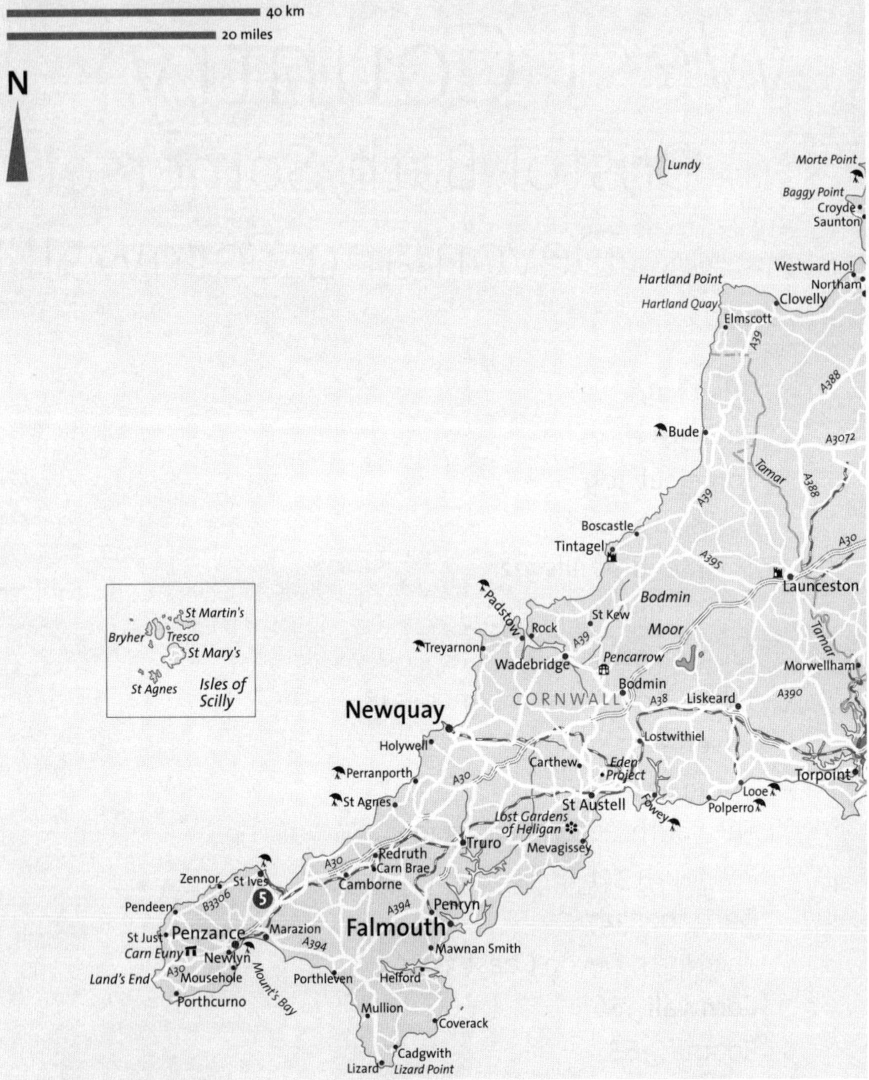

All beyond Sarum or Dorchester is to us 'terra incognita' and the map makers might, if they pleased, fill the vacuities of Devon and Cornwall with forests, sands, elephants or savages or what they please.

An essay on English roads, 1752

The West Country is a world apart, and the Great Western Railway is a magic-carpet ride that shows off the reasons why: the Somerset hills, the River Exe, the red cliffs of Dawlish and Teignmouth, the creamy Devonshire countryside – rivers, patchwork

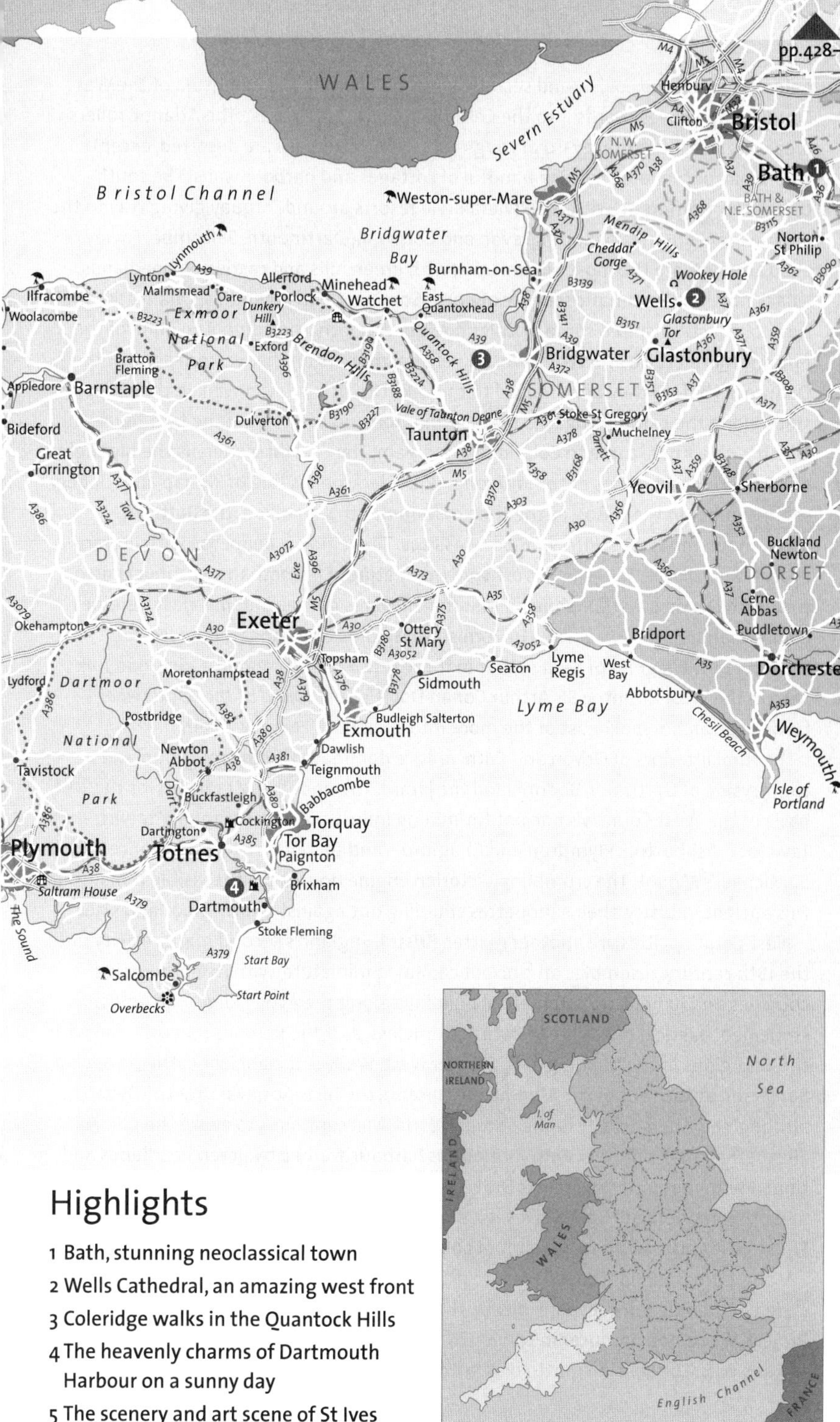

Highlights

1 Bath, stunning neoclassical town
2 Wells Cathedral, an amazing west front
3 Coleridge walks in the Quantock Hills
4 The heavenly charms of Dartmouth Harbour on a sunny day
5 The scenery and art scene of St Ives

fields, cottages and cows – and secretive, green Cornwall. The peninsula of the West Country tapers westwards into the Celtic Sea. On its north coast, the Atlantic rollers break over a sailors' graveyard of rough rocks; long stretches are deserted, except where narrow valleys shelter a handful of cottages and harbour walls. The south coast is very different, with the Riviera-style resorts around Torquay giving way to the deep-water estuaries of South Devon and Cornwall; Dartmouth, Salcombe, Fowey and Falmouth are the most picturesque, with green hills and castles on headlands.

Back north, the dramatic scenery of north Somerset – the Mendips, Quantocks and Exmoor coast – inspired some of Coleridge's best poetry, including 'The Rime of the Ancient Mariner'. He and Wordsworth were neighbours on the western edge of the Quantocks before they both moved to the Lake District; you can walk in their footsteps along the Exmoor coast as far as Lymington and even locate the farmhouse in which 'Kubla Khan' came to Coleridge in a dream. The coastal scenery is the highlight of Exmoor, with its hints of *Lorna Doone* – R.D. Blackmore's tale of kidnap and robbery set in Exmoor in the 1680s, at the time of Monmouth's rebellion, the Battle of Sedgemoor and Judge Jeffreys' Bloody Assizes. The region is peppered with literary evocations: Charles Kingsley's *Westward Ho!* features Elizabethan swashbuckling on the north Devon coast; Daphne du Maurier ensnares genteel middle-class heroines (*Rebecca* and *My Cousin Rachel*) in Cornish smuggling and danger; Tennyson's retelling of the legend of King Arthur in the *Morte d'Arthur* created a Victorian folk hero in the West Country; Sir Arthur Conan Doyle's *The Hound of the Baskervilles* turned the archetypal beast of the moor into a Sherlock Holmes villain.

The rural interiors of Devon and Cornwall are dominated by the rough, upland countryside of Dartmoor, Bodmin and the Lizard. The underlying granite was the basis of the West Country's ancient tin-mining industry with its stannary towns – Tavistock, Ashburton, Plympton and Chagford – and tin ports such as Penzance and St Michael's Mount. The crumbling Victorian engine houses are the visible remains of this ancient industry, their silhouettes standing out against empty moorland skies.

West Country cities are another matter. **Bristol**, England's second maritime city until the 18th century, resembles an 'ancient capital in miniature' with its harbourside churches and handsome commercial buildings along the Avon Gorge. The golden stone neo-classical buildings of **Bath** are timeless, as if the Romans had colluded with the Georgians in the building of it. Further west, **Wells** is the ancient cathedral city of Somerset, at the foot of the Mendips. **Plymouth**, the historic naval town of Devon, although bombed heavily in the Second World War, continues to evoke the golden Elizabethan maritime era, with its glorious harbour, framed by green headlands and tinged with memories of Francis Drake. **St Ives** has Barbara Hepworth, Ben Nicholson and other modernists; Tate St Ives is a metropolitan gallery with a Cornish flavour. **Padstow** is abuzz with the restaurants of TV chef Rick Stein.

Many a dreamer has moved west to play out his or her fantasy. Tim Smit, the self-styled gardening guru responsible for **The Lost Gardens of Heligan** and the **Eden Project**, was a pop producer in London in the 1980s before moving down to Cornwall to keep pigs. The seaside grotto of **A la Ronde** in South Devon, the cliff-cut **Minack**

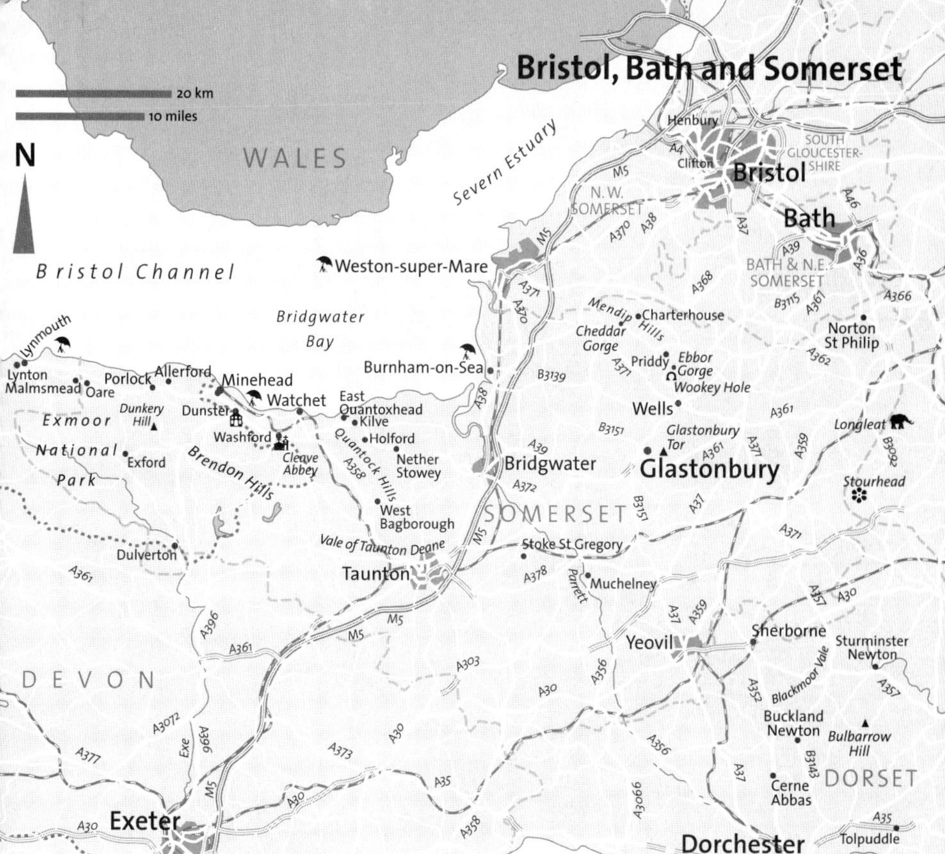

Theatre on the Land's End Peninsula and the quasi-feudal **Castle Drogo** on the edge of Dartmoor are all the work of genuine eccentrics.

However the apparent softness of the West Country – the buttery patchwork fields, clotted cream, Cheddar cheese and the dialect – disguises all sorts of interesting tensions and contradictions: dreamy Somerset has thrice been a platform for rebellion and invasion; folksy Devon boasts some of the most radical examples of modernity in architecture and urban planning in the 20th century; and many Cornish people still do not think of themselves as English.

Bristol

Bristol is the metropolitan presence in the west of England. 'It is a genuine city...an ancient capital in miniature,' wrote J.B. Priestley in 1933. The city evokes nostalgia for the maritime age. Eight twisting miles of the River Avon separate the old town quays from the open sea, passing through a gorge worthy of Sinbad the Sailor. In the Middle Ages, woollen goods were shipped out and the ships returned with dried cod from Ireland, Scotland and Iceland, and wine and olive oil from the Mediterranean. In the 17th and 18th centuries, Bristol prospered from the Atlantic trade and trafficking of

West African slaves to the New World. By the time Daniel Defoe visited in the 1720s it was 'the greatest, the richest and the best port of trade in Great Britain, London only excepted'. The downturn came with bigger ships, which could not negotiate the twists and tides of the Avon. In the 19th century Liverpool superseded Bristol, thriving on the industrialization of the northwest and leaving Bristol isolated in the south-west. The enduring image of Victorian Bristol is not its docks, but the one-off engineering feats of Brunel – the SS *Great Britain* and Clifton Suspension Bridge. But by 1898, shipbuilding too had died out in Bristol. The docks shifted downriver to the mouth of the Avon, and by the time of Priestley's visit were exporting soap powder and cigarettes, and importing cars. Nonetheless the river remains the key to modern Bristol and the derelict harbour is being regenerated as apartments and bars.

Orientation

The city centre has long been a choked road junction, but as part of a millennium regeneration programme major roads have been diverted and the old quay extended with wooden decking. Up the hill are the **cathedral** and **Museum and Art Gallery**, while many attractions give onto the **Floating Harbour**. Old quayside stores along **St Augustine's Reach** have been converted into bars, and beyond them is **@Bristol**, a £97-million complex of cultural attractions on a derelict wharf. The cone-shaped **Pero Bridge** leads to the **Contemporary Art Gallery**, **Industrial Museum** and **SS *Great Britain***, or you can carry on through Queen Square to **St Mary Radcliffe**.

Bristol and its Rivers

Medieval Bristol sprung up where the rivers Frome and Avon met. Riverside marshland was used by Bristol Abbey for sheep-grazing, while merchants' houses backed onto Frome Quay and the castle stood on the north bank of the Avon. In the early 18th century the wealthy moved into Queen Square, built on the reclaimed marshland, then further up the hill to Clifton. In the 19th century the old course of the Avon was turned into the Floating Harbour (to improve port facilities) and the tidal river was diverted along the New Cut. The Frome was channelled under the expanding town; all that is left of it is a branch of the old quayside called St Augustine's Reach.

@Bristol

***t** (0117) 921 0529, www.at-bristol.org.uk; open 10–6; adm exp.*

@Bristol, Bristol's newest attraction, has transformed the harbourside through its integration of old and new buildings. It consists of three separate attractions – Explore, Wildscreen and IMAX – linked by public spaces. **Explore** is housed in the 1903 GWR railway goods shed and calls itself a 21st-century science centre (interactive multimedia). Highlights include a walk-through tornado and a total-surround planetarium called the Imaginarium. **Wildscreen** is a virtual zoo, presenting wildlife on film.

Over Pero Bridge

Just over the bridge, **The Architect Centre and Gallery** (*open Tues–Fri 11–5, Sat and Sun 12–5; adm free*) aims to interest the wider public in contemporary architecture through its exhibitions. Further down, in an 1830s warehouse, the **Arnolfini Centre** (*closed until 2005*) is one of the main contemporary arts venues in the West Country, its café-bar a good hang-out.

The **Industrial Museum** (***t** (0117) 925 1470; open April–Oct Sat–Wed 10–5, Nov–Mar weekends 10–5; adm*) is in an old transit shed on Prince's Wharf, the last berth used in the city; the rusty old bits and bobs date from the days when Bristol manufactured Bristol Commercial Vehicles, Douglas Motorcycles and hand-built 'Bristol' cars. Displays in the museum narrate Bristol's industrial life since the slave trade.

It is a 10-minute walk along the quayside to the **SS *Great Britain*** and the full-sized replica of the **SS *Matthew***, built in 1997 to celebrate the 500th anniversary of Cabot's

Getting There and Around

By Car

Leave the M4 from London or Wales at junction 19, taking the M32 into the city centre. Aim for the big car park under Millennium Square. The M5, to Birmingham and the West Country, also passes Bristol.

By Train

There are direct services from London Paddington to Bristol Temple Meads; the journey takes less than two hours. There are also services from Bath Spa, Cardiff, Birmingham New Street and the North. Temple Meads station is a 25-minute walk from the city centre and harbourside. You can take a Water Taxi, which runs all year from behind the station (clearly signposted). For all train information call **National Rail Enquiries**, **t** 08457 484950, *www.thetrainline.com.*

By Coach and Bus

National Express **coaches** run regularly from London Victoria (approx 2hrs 20mins) and London Heathrow (approx 2hrs 15mins) to Marlborough Street Coach Station, Bristol. For coach enquiries call **t** 08705 808080 or go to *www.gobycoach.com.*

Open-top buses run from April to Sept for an overview of the city centre (with commentary). Your 'hop-on-hop-off' ticket lasts 24 hours, or the whole trip lasts just over an hour.

Tourist Information

Bristol: The Annexe, Wild Screen Walk, Harbourside, **t** 0906 711 2191, *www.visit-bristol.co.uk. Open summer daily 10–6; winter Mon–Sat 10–5, Sun 11–4.*

An **International Balloon Festival** is held over three days in early August, on the estate of Ashton Court, 3–4 miles from the city centre.

Where to Stay

Bristol t (01179) –

Marriott Royal Hotel, College Green, **t** 255 100 (*expensive*). Handsome neo-classical stone building with shiny marble floors.

The Berkeley Square Hotel, 15 Berkeley Square, Clifton **t** 254 000 (*expensive*). The Georgian square is one of the loveliest spots in town. Architectural drawings hang in the corridors between warm, cosy bedrooms.

The Avon Gorge Hotel, Sion Hill, Clifton, **t** 738 955 (*expensive*). Modern, hi-tech hotel. Amazing views over the gorge from the breakfast room, Rib Room restaurant (speciality Scotch beef), White Lion Bar and terrace; 82 bedrooms.

Hotel du Vin, The Sugar House, Narrow Lewins Mead, **t** 255 577, *www.hotelduvin.com* (*expensive*). The most stylish place to stay in the city, in an old sugar refinery behind a leafy courtyard. Elegant bar with rugs on floorboards and 40 loft-style bedrooms with own CD players and free-standing baths.

The Victoria Square Hotel, Victoria Square, Clifton, **t** 739 058, *www.vicsquare.com* (*expensive*). Best Western hotel in two gracious Victorian townhouses on tree-lined square, 10 minutes' walk from town past the Victoria Rooms and university. Restaurant (*open Mon–Thurs*) serves traditional dishes like braised knuckle of lamb.

Naseby House Hotel, 105 Pembrook Road, Clifton, **t** 737 859 (*moderate*). Small, family-run Victorian house around the corner from

voyage of discovery. From its deck you can see the tower on Brandon Hill, built to mark the 400th anniversary a century earlier. The SS *Great Britain* sits in the original Great Western Dry Dock where it was built in the 1830s. Brunel's ship is known as the first modern ocean liner for its combination of different technologies – iron hull, screw propeller and steam engine – and its size, 100 feet longer than any ship built before. Brunel envisaged a passenger steamer service from London to Manhattan, with customers transferring from the train to his ship at Bristol; in the end, the SS *Great Britain* proved too big for Bristol's docks and sailed from Liverpool. After five years, an extra deck was inserted to transport emigrants (900 on a single voyage) to Australia.

Bristol Zoo and a short walk from the city centre. Friendly and efficient.

The Rodney Hotel, 4 Rodney Place, Clifton, **t** 735 422 (*moderate*). Part of a Georgian terrace built in 1789. The guests are mainly commercial, but its 31 bedrooms are cheerful enough. Restaurant and bar.

Westbury Park Hotel, 37 Westbury Road, **t** 620 465 (*moderate*). Detached Victorian house with many original features, overlooking Durdham Down, 2 miles from city centre; nine bedrooms.

Downland House Hotel, 33 Henleaze Gardens, **t** 621 639 (*moderate*). Elegant Victorian house on the edge of open parkland 2 miles from city centre.

Downsview Guest House, 38 Upper Belgrave Road, **t** 737 046 (*moderate*). Another Victorian townhouse on the park.

Sunderland Guest House, 4 Sunderland Place, Clifton **t** 737 249 (*cheap*). Conveniently situated family-run guesthouse.

Eating Out

The quaint old thoroughfare of **King Street** is full of timber-framed buildings converted into cafés and restaurants. It leads to Welsh Back, the Bristol Old Vic and Harbourside. The whole area has been revamped since the '80s.

Hotel du Vin Bistro, The Sugar House, Narrow Lewins Mead, **t** 255 577 (*moderate*). It's a pleasure to eat in the elegant dining room of this 18th-century sugar refinery, its panelled walls hung with pictures. The French/Mediterranean menu also features traditional British favourites like roast pigeon followed by rhubarb crumble.

Ha Ha Bar & Canteen, 20/a Berkeley Square, Clifton, **t** 277 333. Hidden away down steps off Queen's Road, this conservatory-style building with sunken patio, attracts a young professional crowd at lunchtime and after work. Very crowded Fri and Sat nights. Pub grub (*moderate*).

Ristorante Da Renato, 19 King Street, **t** 298 291 (*moderate*). Cosy and intimate, serving traditional Italian food. A few steps from the Old Vic, it's ideal for pre- or post-theatre meals, and plays to the gallery with old photos of actors on walls. *Closed Sun.*

Byzantium Restaurant, 2 Portwall Lane, Radcliffe, **t** 221 883 (*moderate*). Converted warehouse opposite St Mary Radcliffe Church, with Moroccan arches, North African décor and rustic French menu with Mediterranean influences. Belly dancers add to the flavour at the weekend. *Closed Sun.*

Rajdoot Tandoori, 83 Bark Street (near the City Museum), **t** 268 033 (*moderate*). North Indian food. Excellent service and presentation. Very smart. *Closed Sun lunch.*

La Taverna dell' Artista, 33 King Street, **t** 297 712 (*cheap*). Renato's sibling, directly opposite, in an early 17th-century building. Lively bar with pizzeria downstairs, quieter restaurant upstairs, plastered with theatrical posters. *Open eves only, bar area until 2am.*

The Llandoger Trow, King Street, **t** 260 783 (*cheap*). By the river, and named after a late-17th-century two-masted trading barge or 'trow' from the Welsh village of Llandogo on the River Wye, this is a restored Jacobean inn with original flagstones, beams and ceiling friezes. Where writer Daniel Defoe met Alexander Selkirk, the real-life Robinson Crusoe. Pub grub in bar, or you can eat in the restaurant (*cheap*).

The Duke, 45 King Street, **t** 277 137 (*cheap*). Excellent jazzy pub with a black-and-white-

It was towed back to Bristol for conservation 30 years ago; £7 million of lottery money have hastened its restoration.

Queen Square to St Mary Radcliffe

In the loop of the two rivers, recently restored **Queen Square** represents the first phase of the city's Georgian expansion. Across the square, **Welsh Back** is the original tourist area on the west bank of the Avon, with its restaurants, pubs and, on King Street, the 18th-century **Theatre Royal**, which claims to be Britain's oldest still in use.

tiled floor, trumpets on the walls, live jazz and blues every evening at 8pm, Sun also at 12 noon. Pub grub *Mon–Fri lunch* (*cheap*).

Marriott Royal Hotel, College Green, **t** 255 100 (*cheap*). Handsome Georgian building where you can get cream teas.

Mud Dock Café, 40 The Grove, **t** 349 734 (*cheap*). Hip café-bar and bike shop in converted riverside warehouse. Mediterranean-style food – sandwiches, salad, pasta, risotto and tapas – for brunch, lunch and dinner.

Riverstation, The Grove, **t** 144 434 (*cheap*). Modern, airy restaurant in the old river police station at the entrance to the floating harbour. Deck overlooks the river,with views of St Mary Radcliffe Church. The old slipway is now the deli counter, serving pizza and meze (*9am–10pm*). In the restaurant upstairs you might get a warm salad of Jerusalem artichokes followed by grilled sea bass.

Browns, 38 Queens Road, Clifton, **t** 304 777 (*cheap*). Bistro-style restaurant and bar in a miniature 19th-century Doge's Palace. Sit out on the terrace under twinkling fairy lights. Very lively early evening with after-work crowd making most of happy hour (*4–8*). Serves breakfast, lunch, afternoon tea and dinner, with burgers and plenty of vegetarian options.

Entertainment

St George's, Great George Street, **t** 230 359. A 19th-century Greek Revivalist church, now offering a classical concerts by international artists, and jazz, world music and folk. Five minutes' walk from city centre. Bar and restaurant (*cheap*).

Victoria Rooms, Queen's Road, **t** 545 032. Another Greek Revivalist venue, built in the 1830s. Roomy concert hall where Jenny Lind, the 'Swedish Nightingale' sang in 1848 and Charles Dickens gave a reading in 1852, and a smaller room where Ellen Terry once gave a recital. Occasional evening concerts and Wed lunchtime concerts by students, open to all comers.

Hippodrome, St Augustine's Parade, **t** 0870 607 7500. In the heart of city centre, a large Georgian building with a 3,000-seater auditorium; shows the usual mix of touring West End musicals, and big, glitzy opera and popular ballet productions.

The Bristol Old Vic, King Street, **t** 877 877. A Grade I listed building, Britain's oldest still-existing theatre has been in continuous use since 1766 (electricity was installed in 1905). Three theatres in one: the **Main House** seats 650 and stages both classical and popular plays by the repertory company; the **Studio** seats 140 for in-house and amateur drama; and the tiny 50-seater **Basement** shows new plays or works by first-time directors. Restaurant and café-bar for snacks, lunch and evening meals (*cheap*) until 7.30pm, when the evening's show begins. Bars upstairs and down.

IMAX Theatre@Bristol, Anchor Road, Harbourside, **t** 155 000. Films shown daily, every 75 minutes.

Arnolfini Arts Centre, 16 Narrow Quay, **t** (01179) 299 191. Overlooks the harbour. Exhibitions, talks and events, dance, arthouse films and music. An excellent venue. *Closed for refurbishment until spring 2005.*

Watershed Media Centre, 1 Canyons Road, Harbourside, off Augustine's Reach, **t** 276 444. Foreign and arthouse films.

South of the Avon, above the ring road and surrounded by grim tower blocks, is the beautiful, grime-stained church of **St Mary Radcliffe** (*t (01179) 291 487; open summer 9–5, winter 9–4*), 'the fairest, the goodliest and most famous parish church in England', according to Elizabeth I. St Mary's once stood right above the harbour; its spire greeted Bristol merchants after sea voyages, and it was also the last opportunity to offer a prayer to God on the way out. The merchants – men like William Canynges (1402–74), who owned 10 ships and has been called England's first 'merchant prince' – were the church's greatest benefactors. The subtly Oriental-style north porch with its seven-pointed entrance arch, the monuments of the merchant princes, and the whale bone at the entrance to St John's Chapel brought back by John Cabot in 1497, are all relics of the old city's cosmopolitan past. Inside, the soaring Gothic arches create surprising perspectives. In the 15th-century north transept is a chaotic pendulum driven by a flow of recycled water, installed in 1997 by a physics professor; the water flows into the middle of a cross beam, which tips in a 'chaotic' direction to spill the water. The father of boy poet Thomas Chatterton was choir master of St Mary's. Young Thomas claimed to have discovered a collection of poems by an unknown 15th-century monk called Thomas Rowley in the muniment room above the north porch. Written on medieval parchment (cut from the edges of 15th-century legal documents), they fooled everybody. Chatterton sent Rowley's poems to Horace Walpole, who thought they were beautiful until it turned out he had been conned, when he turned hostile. Chatterton, the real author, killed himself in an attic room in London aged 17. His tragedy was not lost on *bona fide* poets Southey and Coleridge, who were married to the Fricker sisters in St Mary's in 1795. The statue of Chatterton outside was removed on the grounds of his suicide.

The Heart of the Old City

The heart of the old city is north of Queen Square, around the 18th-century commercial buildings and medieval churches of Clare Street and Corn Street. It is still the business district. On Corn Street used to be the bookshop of Joseph Cottle, who introduced Wordsworth and Coleridge. In the 1700s, business was conducted in either

John Cabot, Bristol and the Discovery of America

John Cabot, credited with discovering the North American mainland, set sail for the west from Bristol. Born Giovanni Caboto in Genoa in 1450 (same time and place as Columbus) he grew up in Venice and lived in Spain before moving to Bristol to secure backing from Bristol merchants for Atlantic exploration. He was not the first person to set foot on North American soil – the Vikings had already been there – but he was the first with official letters from Henry VII in his pocket entitling him 'to seeke out, discover, and finde whatsoever isles, countreys, regions or provinces of the heathen and infidels whosoever they be...' He was actually looking for a northwest passage across the Atlantic to the spices and riches of Asia – the idea being that since the earth was round, it was possible to travel westwards to the Far East. Although this is true, the confusion was the fault of 15th-century mappers, whose estimation of the circumference of the globe was about 7,000 miles short and did not reckon on a new continent and the Pacific Ocean in between. Cabot's first voyage failed. The second attempt, a year later in a boat called the SS *Matthew* (after his Venetian wife Mattea) was a roaring success. He set off with 18 crew in May 1497 and just over a month later, very early in the morning, sighted land. Cabot landed, but didn't venture inland; instead he leapt back aboard, after a brief walk along the beach, to chart the coastline. He returned without any cargo, let alone Oriental spices, but the Bristol merchants were pleased to have a charted sea route to a new cod fishing ground. Henry VII was pleased too, and christened the newly found land Newfoundland.

the coffee houses (Coleridge gave a lecture against slavery in one on the quayside in 1795) or the **Corn Exchange**, built in 1753 by John Wood. All the city's merchants used to trade here, in spite of the name. Figures carved on the façade represent Africa, America, Asia and Europe – the range of Bristol's trading interests. The four objects resembling bronze bird baths are the old **Nails**, used by merchants in Bristol's heyday for their cash transactions ('pay on the nail').

At the junction of Corn Street, High Street, Wine Street and Broad Street once stood a tall and elaborate medieval cross; it now beautifies Henry Colt Hoare's gardens at Stourhead. Walk down Broad Street and under an archway beneath St John's church onto Quay Street. **St John's** is the only surviving church of four built atop the town wall in the 12th century; the gate once lead directly onto Frome Quay. Across the road are the 17th-century **Christmas Steps**, a worn flight of steep steps leading nowhere.

The New Room

The area northeast of the old city, around the Broadmead shopping precinct, is grim – the area was flattened in the Second World War and rebuilt as a concrete jungle – but steel yourself against orange brick to see Wesley's New Room, which survived the bombs. Methodist preacher John Wesley arrived in Bristol in March 1739, and began building at once. From Broadmead, you approach the Methodist complex through a courtyard, passing an equestrian statue of Wesley. The statue at the far end is Charles Wesley, also an ordained Methodist preacher, who came to Bristol with his brother. The lime-green walls, columns supporting a gallery, ticking clock and daylight pouring in through a lantern window make it easy to imagine yourself at an early Methodist gathering. John Wesley preached from the top pulpit. His July 1791 sermon on the immorality of slavery was halted for five minutes when he broke out in shaking.

Bristol Cathedral

From the city centre, the main road climbs up to College Green *en route* to the Georgian squares and Victorian cultural institutions at the top of town. Facing each other across the green are the mid-20th-century Council House and the cathedral. Fragments of the original Norman abbey church survive, such as the **Abbey Gatehouse** leading down to the cathedral school in the old monastery buildings. The rest was rebuilt in the 13th and 14th centuries, except the nave and its two west towers, which date from G.E. Street's 19th-century restoration. Inside, the style is Gothic, but where your mind expects to be ushered indefinitely upwards, it soon hits the low roof of this hall church: the nave, choir and aisle roofs are all the same height and the pier arches rise to full height, giving the impression of one large room. Look into the **Elder Lady Chapel** – the oldest part of the church (1215) – for the carved monkey heads and vaulting, and take a peek at the steps on the south side of the church leading to the old dormitory, flattened by monks' feet into a slope. The richly carved Norman **chapter house** is fine too.

Carrying on past College Green up Park Street you come to **Great George Street**, uniform black railings on one side and handsome old trees on the other, leading off to

Bristol and the Slave Trade

Bristol was well placed to exploit 18th-century colonial links with North America and the Caribbean which, at the time, consumed more than half of British exports and supplied a third of its imports. The main Atlantic trade was conducted in a notorious triangle between European, West African and American markets: European goods were shipped to the West African coast and traded for African slaves, who were shipped across the Atlantic on the infamous 'middle passage' and bartered for commodities such as tobacco, rice, sugar and rum in the American colonies. The slaves were rarely seen in the slave ports of London, Liverpool and Bristol, but it has been estimated that 2.7 million Africans were transported to the plantations on English ships alone; for a complete figure you would have to add in the black cargoes of the Spanish, Portuguese, Dutch, French, Danish and American ships too.

Many of Bristol's most notable benefactors, such as Edward Colston, made their personal fortunes out of the slave business. Bristol merchants were involved in the slave trade from the moment the monopoly of the London-based West African Company expired until the abolition of slavery in 1807. Shocking as we now find it, the trade was a risky business with no guarantee of returns. Voyages on the triangle took a year; 'success' depended on landing in the right place on the 2,000-mile West African coast and carrying the right selection of goods to bargain for the best slaves (healthy black men between 10 and 25 years old). Disease and violence were so common on the middle passage that slaves often jumped overboard to near-certain death in order to escape the dire conditions *en route* to Jamaica, the British Empire's leading slave market.

a clean horizon at the top of a hill. About halfway up, **Georgian House** (*open April–Oct Sat–Wed 10–5; adm free*) was built in 1790 for a rich sugar merchant. It has been refurnished in period style to show how master and servants lived together in the same house. At the top of the street in Brandon Hill are good views of the city. You can climb up the 105ft-high **Cabot's Tower**, built in 1897.

Queen's Road

On the fringes of Clifton, Queen's Road used to be Clifton's cultural district. The Greek Revivalist Victoria Rooms opened at the very top in 1842, for political, social and cultural events. The Fine Arts Academy opened opposite in 1854 and, 16 years later, further down Queen's Road, a museum and library opened in a Venetian Gothic building (all now owned by the university). The present **City Museum and Gallery** (***t** (0117) 922 3571; open daily 10–5*) opened in 1904, devoted to art, science and history. The strong art collection has works by 20th-century British painters from the St Ives School (Hepworth and Nicholson) and the Bristol School (Avon Gorge paintings). A display of Bristol maps traces the city's development since the 16th century.

Next door, the towering **Wills Memorial Building** (1914–25) commemorates the tobacco-rich Wills family, who poured money into the university.

Clifton

At Clifton you have both a natural and a man-made wonder in a suburban setting. The Avon Gorge – a mile long and 300ft deep – is bridged by Brunel's single-span road bridge measuring 702 feet from pier to pier. The competition for the bridge coincided with the early suburban development of Clifton. **Clifton Village**, as it is quaintly known, has always been the most desirable residence in Bristol. Brace yourself for the hills to explore the architectural set-piece of **Victoria Square** (1830–55), perfectly uniform **Caledonian Place** and, overlooking the Avon, **Royal York Crescent** (1791–1820). A few hundred yards from the village centre on foot, following signs to the bridge, you reach Zion Place and the **Clifton Suspension Bridge Visitor Centre** (*open summer daily 10–5; winter Mon–Fri 11–4, weekends 11–5; adm minimal*) on one corner. Here you can see Thomas Telford's rival design for the bridge, a clumsy Gothic structure, which he – as competition judge – selected; Brunel persuaded the committee to change its mind.

Clifton Suspension Bridge

When Bristol wine merchant William Vick died in 1784 he left £1,000 to the Society of Merchant Venturers for a bridge across the Avon Gorge from Clifton Down to Leigh

Brunel (1806–59)

When Isambard Kingdom Brunel got a coin stuck in his throat he invented a machine that would hold him upside down and shake him to dislodge it. Brunel was one of the Victorian greats. He built iconic structures of iron, using new technologies to make them bigger and better. His long association with the West Country began when he won the competition for a new bridge over the Avon Gorge. His design for the iron **Clifton Suspension Bridge** was carried out against the recommendations of Thomas Telford, whose own Menai Suspension Bridge had nearly been destroyed by cross winds. Brunel was appointed chief engineer of the new **Great Western Railway**, laying down 118 miles of tracks from Bristol to London with stations at Bath, Chippenham, Swindon, Maidenhead and Reading, and the longest tunnel in the country at Box. He built three great ships (two at Bristol), each the largest in the world at its launching. The **SS *Great Western*** (1837) was the first transatlantic passenger steamship to provide a regular service (Bristol to New York in 15 days). The **SS *Great Britain*** (1843) was the first iron-hulled, propeller-driven steamship (*see* p.xxx). The **SS *Great Eastern*** (1858) was the first ship with a double iron hull, and unmatched in size for 40 years; it was designed to make the round trip to Australia without being re-coaled, thought impossible. Brunel also built the spectacular **Royal Albert Bridge** over the River Tamar at Saltash near Plymouth, which opened in 1859, the year of his death. Other projects included his **Atmospheric Railway** in South Devon, which pioneered a new faster system of propulsion; his use of compressed-air techniques to sink the pier foundations for **Maidenhead Bridge** – a technique now widely used in underwater and underground construction; and the design of a complete **pre-fab hospital** which was shipped out in parts to the Crimea in 1855.

Woods. There was no need for a bridge, but the idea caught on. The competition was won by 23-year-old Brunel (*see* box), whose deceptively simple bridge is strung 250 feet above the gorge on massive iron chains. The chains are threaded through elegant stone piers and anchored 56 feet below the road at either end. It was designed for horse-drawn carriages but now handles four million vehicles rumbling across it every year. Don't contemplate a dramatic finale here: attempted suicides usually end up stuck in the mud waiting for the tide.

The best view of the bridge can be seen reflected in a metal dish about 5 feet across, beamed down through a hole in the roof of the oldest *camera obscura* in the country. When it first opened, a man with flag was hired to run into the view to prove it was not a trick. The apparatus was installed in the old windmill above the suspension bridge in 1829, now known as the **Observatory** (*open afternoons; adm minimal*).

Bath

> *They arrived at Bath. Catherine was all eager delight; – her eyes were here, there and everywhere, as they approached its fine and striking environs, and afterwards drove through those streets which conducted them to the hotel. She was come to be happy and she felt happy already.*
>
> Jane Austen, *Northanger Abbey*

The thermal baths of Bath are one of England's oldest tourist attractions, dating back to the Roman Empire. 'Bath,' wrote J.B. Priestley in *English Journey*, 'has the rare trick of surprising you all over again. You know very well it is like that, yet somehow your memory must have diminished the wonder of it, for there it is, taking your breath away again.' The combination of neo-classical buildings in golden Cotswold stone and the scenery around the Avon is irresistible. The town looks as though the Romans, who warmed their feet in the hot springs and prayed to the goddess Sulis Minerva for sunshine, gave place directly to the Georgians, who packed out the assembly rooms and found everything 'most agreeable': the Romans built a fine set of classical buildings around the spa, and so did the Georgians – about 16 feet higher. Now that the Roman Great Bath has been unearthed, it sits comfortably in the middle of the Georgian town.

The new Nicholas Grimshaw spa building has been controversial for its refusal to blend in with the general harmonies, but Bath is more patchwork than first impressions suggest. 'Wondrous is this wall-stone; broken by fate,' said the Saxon poem 'The Ruin', of *Aqua Sulis*, the Roman town. 'Stone courts stood here; the stream with its great gush sprang forth hotly; the wall enclosed all within its bright bosom; there the baths were hot in its centre.' After Alfred the Great's victory against the Danes in 878, Bath was rebuilt on the present grid-plan. Some streets were lost under the enormous Norman cathedral (120ft longer than the present church) and bishop's palace, which stood on the site of the old Saxon abbey and incorporated the sacred spring within its walls. When the cathedral moved to Wells, the church was pulled down in favour of the present smaller structure. By the 17th century, Bath was at a low ebb. The traveller Celia Fiennes was appalled at how sordid the place had become, 'thick and hot' with the fumes from the baths, dogs splashing around among the sick people. The narrow streets and closely packed buildings in the centre of town retain the scale of early Bath, while the thrust of Georgian expansion was on the surrounding hills.

You can see Bath in a day (many coach trips do), but it doesn't do it justice. Must-sees are the Roman baths, Pulteney Bridge and the architecture of the John Woods, father and son. Take a walk through the promenades, gardens, colonnades and vistas – designed for strolling, and locate all those Jane Austen locations. The heart of it all is the public space between the abbey and the Roman Baths. You can get quite a good impression of the Georgian spa complex too: the Concert Hall and Pump Room used to belong to King's Bath, demolished to reveal the Roman archaeology underneath.

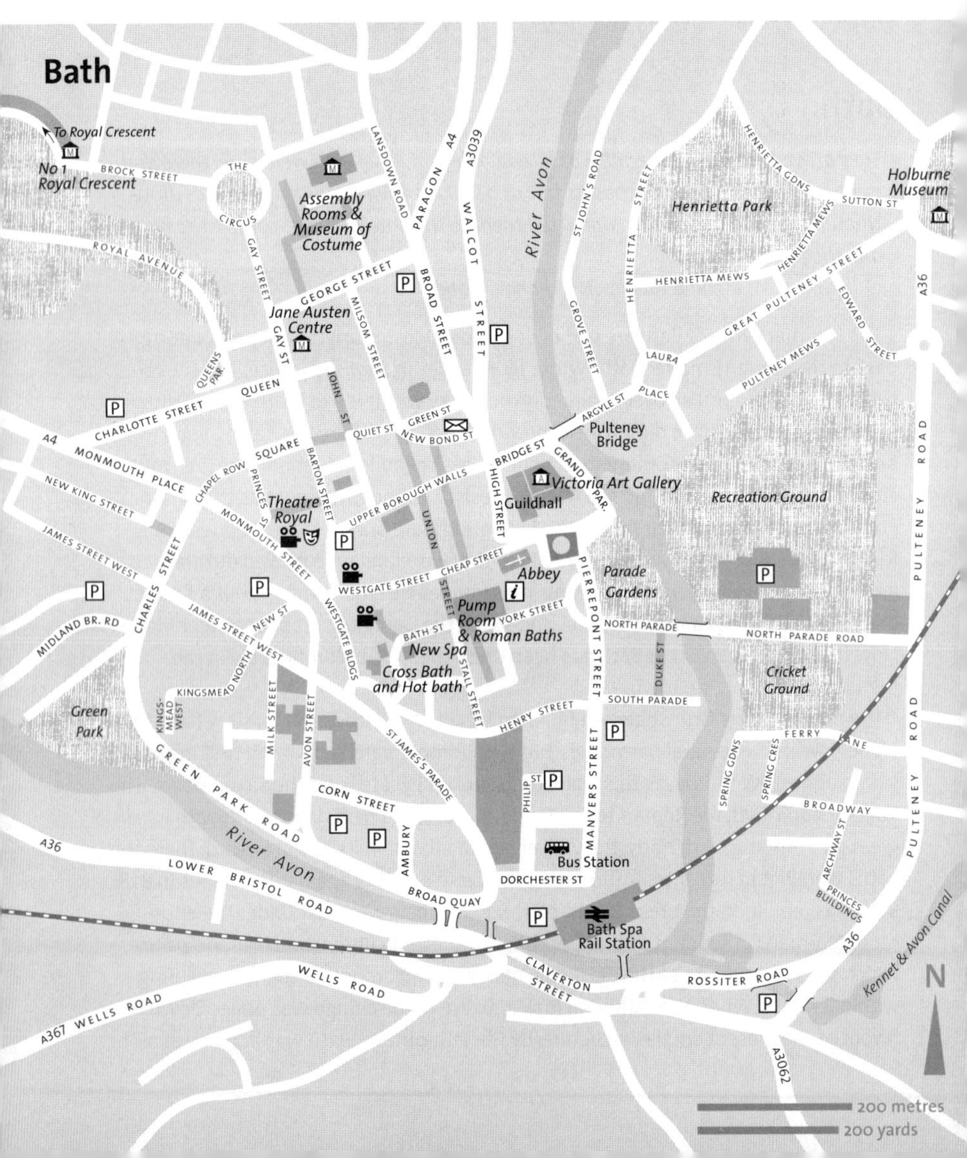

Getting There and Around

By **car**, leave the M4 at junction 18 and follow the A46 south to Bath, joining the A4 into the city.

It takes 60–90 minutes to reach Bath by **train** from London Paddington.

National Express **coaches** run a regular service from London Victoria.

Walks and Tours

A free two-hour **walking tour** begins at the Abbey Churchyard, taking in all Bath's architectural hot spots. *Starts daily 10.30am, Sun–Fri also 2pm.*

The Jane Austen Museum runs a **Jane Austen Walking Tour** starting outside the Abbey Churchyard. It lasts 1½ hours, and visits places associated with the author's life, *Persuasion* and *Northanger Abbey*. *All year Sat and Sun 1.30pm, July and Aug daily 1.30pm, starting at the museum.*

There are about five companies running **open-top bus tours** of the city centre, some with guides. They make stops all around the city, including High Street and York Street on either side of Bath Abbey. Tickets valid all day, hop-on-hop-off.

Boat Trips

Pleasure Boat Trips lasting 50 minutes go down the River Avon from Pulteney Bridge to Bathampton Weir. *Easter–Oct every hour from 11am to dusk.*

Bath Boating Station, Forester Road, **t** (01225) 466 407. An old Victorian boating station in gardens with punts and canoes for hire. *Open April–Sept daily 10–6.*

Tourist Information

Bath: Abbey Chambers, Abbey Church Yard, **t** 0906 711 2000, *www.visitbath.co.uk. Open Mon–Sat 9.30–6 (winter closes at 5), Sun 10–4.*

Bath boasts both a literature and a music festival. The **Music Festival** is the bigger and better established of the two (it's been going for more than 50 years). The two-week festival starts in mid-May, at venues including the Pump Rooms, Forum, Guildhall, Assembly Rooms, Abbey Church and Wells Cathedral. The emphasis is classical, with world music, jazz and contemporary music too. The festival opens with a free concert in Victoria Park.

The **Literature Festival** lasts nine days at the beginning of March, with storytelling, readings of poetry and novels, workshops, debates and talks by literary figures.

Bath Festival Box Office, 2 Church Street, Abbey Green, **t** (01225) 463 362. *Open Mon–Sat 9.30–5.30, also Sun during festivals.*

Where to Stay

Bath t (01225) –

The Royal Crescent, 16 Royal Crescent, **t** 823 333, *www.royalcrescent.co.uk* (*very expensive*). Mid-crescent, a grand yet relaxed hotel with excellent Pimpernel's restaurant in Georgian dower house down garden path.

The Queensberry Hotel, Russell Street, **t** 447 928, *www.bathqueensberry.com* (*very expensive*). Smart townhouse hotel with bowls of fruit and fresh flowers, thick carpets and

Aqua Sulis

The natural spring at the centre of Bath pumps up 1,170,000 litres of mineral-rich water daily at a constant temperature of 46.5 degrees centigrade. By the end of the first century the Romans had enclosed the warm spring within a stone wall and built a temple next to it dedicated to Sulis Minerva – a goddess conflating Sul, the Celtic guardian of the waters, with Roman Minerva, goddess of the arts. The warm waters were channelled from the sacred pool into a series of swimming baths, which were constantly altered over the next 350 years. At the turn of the 5th century the Roman spa complex was destroyed by the Germanics, who didn't have time for cleanliness. The Anglo-Saxon abbey was built from stone lifted from the ruins. The hot spring continued to bubble up through the rubble, now paved over at the centre of the four courtyard gardens. Its **Olive Tree Restaurant** is one of the best in town.

The County Hotel, 18–19 Pulteney Road, **t** 425 003, *www.county-hotel.co.uk* (*very expensive*). A few minutes' walk from the city centre, this handsome Bath-stone hotel has elegant public rooms and 22 comfortable bedrooms. No smoking.

Lansdowne Grove Hotel, Lansdowne Road, **t** 483 888 (*expensive*). Large, cream-painted hotel with gardens, conservatory cocktail bar and restaurant; 50 bedrooms.

The Carfax Hotel, Great Pulteney Street, **t** 462 089 (*expensive*). Occupies three Georgian townhouses between the Holburne Museum and Pulteney Bridge. Owned by the Salvation Army, it has no bar and is non-smoking. Its 38 bedrooms overlook the cricket ground or Henrietta Park.

Duke's Hotel, Great Pulteney Street, **t** 463 512 (*expensive*). A Georgian hotel with period decoration and some superb original features, like the staircase.

The George's Hotel, 2–3 South Parade, **t** 464 923 (*moderate*). Friendly, informal place to stay, with the atmosphere of an old coaching inn. Cheerful pavement café sets out its tables in summer.

The Lodge Hotel, Bathford Hill, Bathford, **t** 858 575, *www.lodgehotelbath.co.uk* (*moderate*). Two miles out of Bath on the A4 towards Chippenham, a superb family-run Georgian hotel in a peaceful location. Hand-picked flowers in each room, and you can help yourself from the decanter of sherry in the snug. Heated swimming pool May–Oct.

Number 14, Raby Place (on Bathwick Hill as it slopes down to Pulteney Street), **t** 465 120 (*moderate*). A Regency house with a very welcoming atmosphere.

Eating Out

FishWorks, 6 Green Street, **t** 448 707 (*moderate*). One of a superb chain of seafood restaurants. The upstairs dining room is bright and bustling, the cooking simple and scrumptious. *Closed Sun eve and Mon.*

The Olive Tree Restaurant, Russell Street, **t** 447 928 (*moderate*). Excellent reputation for its Mediterranean/English menu. *Closed Sun eve and Mon.*

Moody Goose, 7/a Kingsmead Square, **t** 466 688 (*moderate*). Low-key restaurant tucked away in the vaulted cellars of a row of Bath-stone buildings. High-quality English food.

Le Clos, 1 Seven Dials, Saw Close, **t** 444 450 (*moderate*). Next door to the Theatre Royal, overlooking Kingsmead Square. A smart little restaurant offering modern French cooking. *Closed Sun eve.*

The Beaujolais, 5 Chapel Row, near Queen Square, **t** 423 417 (*moderate*). French provincial cooking in pleasant setting with walled garden. Dishes from omelette with salad to roast pork with the works. *Closed Mon lunch.*

Tilley's Bistro, 3 North Parade Passage, **t** 484 200 (*moderate*). French and Greek cooking.

Rajdoot Tandoori, 83 Park Street, **t** (01179) 268 033 (*cheap*). Near the city museum, a long-established Indian restaurant of excellent quality, offering original recipes. Friendly service. *Closed Sun lunch.*

The Pump Room Restaurant, Abbey Churchyard, **t** 444 477 (*cheap*). A memorable

medieval cathedral precincts. In the 12th century, a bath known as the King's Bath stood on top of the sacred spring. Aqua Sulis was rediscovered in 1727 by workmen digging along the centre of Stall Street, who unearthed the gilded bronze head of Minerva in a sewer trench and a Roman hypocaust 16 feet below street level. In 1755 part of the east end of the Roman baths was found (beneath a Saxon cemetery) during construction of the Duke of Kingston's Bath. Fragments of a temple pediment with a sculpted Gorgon's head were discovered in 1790 when the Pump Room was being built. It was not until 1878 that the Roman sacred spring full of votive offerings was unearthed beneath the King's Bath. The 18th-century baths, including the King's Bath and Duke of Kingston's Bath, were demolished in favour of the ruined Roman baths – at the time more fashionable.

Georgian setting for morning coffee, afternoon tea or lunch, it was the scene of the endless balls and assemblies so detested by Jane Austen and her more sensible heroines. Now serves lunches of lemon and garlic chicken, roast loin of lamb, hake with herb linguini, tarte provençal.

Sally Lunn's Tea House, 4 North Parade Passage, **t** 461 634 (*cheap*). Behind the 18th-century stone façade is the old Tudor townhouse in which Sally Lunn created her famous bun in the late 1600s. Morning coffee plus refills, light meals and afternoon teas are served to gentle classical music.

Adventure Café, 5 Princes Buildings, George Street, **t** 462 038 (*cheap*). Trendy sandwich shop. Gourmet snacks include tortilla wraps and English-breakfast bagels.

The Old Green Tree, 12 Green Street, **t** 448 259. Snug, oak-panelled city-centre pub. Real fire and real ales. Pub grub at lunchtime, from ploughman's to beef and ale pie (*cheap*).

Paragon Wine Bar, Paragon Street, **t** 466 212 (*cheap*). A warren of small rooms crammed with wooden tables; popular with the intellectual crowd.

The Walrus and the Carpenter, 28 Barton Street, **t** 314 864 (*cheap*). Well-established bar and restaurant near Queen's Square and Theatre Royal. Selection of burgers and vegetarian dishes served in two small candle-lit rooms with gingham tablecloths. *Closed Sun eve.*

The Bell Inn, 103 Walcot Street, **t** 460 426 (*cheap*). Bustling pub with table football and courtyard. Jazz on Mon, Wed and Sun.

Around Bath

The George Inn, Norton St Philip, **t** (01373) 834 224 (*moderate*). Superb drive (following the A367 Exeter signs) on the B3110, a pretty road with views, to this ancient pub 6 miles southeast of Bath. The picturesque old inn with a garden on a hill has excellent views over the cricket field towards the medieval-Gothic church and hills. The George is one of the best-preserved early half-timbered inns in the country, complete with old galleried courtyard. Travellers and merchants stayed over on the way to cloth fairs, encouraged by the enterprising monks of nearby Hinton Charterhouse. Early visitors would have shared rooms and probably beds. You won't have to do that: the oak-furnished rooms are charming. Very popular restaurant.

Packhorse Inn, Southstoke, **t** (01225) 832 060 (*cheap*). Take the A367 towards Shepton Mallet, then B3110 towards Frome, and at Crosskeys pub turn right – a glorious drive through twisty lanes. The inn dates from 1489, and its two rooms are divided by a tiled passageway leading to the church: it once served as a thoroughfare for funeral processions. Old-world atmosphere with blazing hearth and traditional pub games. Varied menu.

Entertainment

Theatre Royal, Sawclose, **t** 448 844. Big all-purpose theatre which hosts West End productions, opera, ballet and concerts.

Pump Room

Open April–Sept 9–6, Oct–Mar 9.30–5; adm.

The Pump Room was the social hub of Georgian Bath, where Jane Austen heroines rushed in search of husbands. For a few coins you can have a glass of the foul-tasting spring water there. Then walk under the colonnaded walkway along Stall Street and Bath Street to Cross Bath and Hot Bath. The restoration of these baths as part of a multi-million pound spa complex (***t** (01225) 331 234, www.thermaebathspa.com*) has been the most exciting, and controversial, change in Bath since the unearthing of the Roman baths. At the heart of the controversy is the new 'symphony of stone, metal and glass' spa building designed by Nicholas Grimshaw and Partners.

The Makers of Georgian Bath

Despite the apparent architectural uniformity of the Georgian city, its development was piecemeal and speculative. The names of Ralph Allen, John Wood and Richard 'Beau' Nash stand out in early Georgian Bath: they all capitalized on the enthusiasm of the upper classes for spa towns. **Ralph Allen** (1694–1764) started his career as a Bath postal worker and made a fortune by reforming the national postal system (re-routing cross-country mail to avoid London). With his wealth, he bought the Combe Down quarries above Bath, and built a railway with an ingenious windlass system to transport stone down to the town – so that his stone was the cheapest and most readily available for Bath's expansion. He built his home, Prior Place, near the quarries, with a garden planned by his friend, the poet Alexander Pope. The architect was **John Wood the Elder** (1704–54), who bought large chunks of land and developed them in Palladian style. His son, **John Wood the Younger** (1728–81), finished the Circus and continued building in the same style. Willing investors swarmed in under the influence of **'Beau' Nash** (1674–1761), the stylish son of a Swansea glass manufacturer, who moved to Bath in 1705 and was elected master of ceremonies. He organized subscription balls and assemblies, devised rules for dress and behaviour, and created a safe, ordered and exclusive environment for genteel society – the setting for Jane Austen's novels.

Roman Baths Museum

Open April–Sept 9–6, Aug also 8–10; Oct–Mar 9.30–5; adm exp.

As with many Roman remains, it is hard to visualize the baths in their heyday from the assortment of old stones you can see today, but the Great Bath is evocative. All the baths lead off the central Circular Bath, among them the Great Bath, Turkish-style baths, religious precinct containing the sacred spring and a sacrificial altar, with steps up to the temple building; its façade of four 27ft-high Corinthian columns once supported the **Gorgon's head pediment** – now on display on your way down to the Roman level The Gorgon looks barbaric with wild eyes, flowing hair and beard and deeply furrowed brow. The **Sacred Spring** is surrounded by some of the thousands of votive offerings found by archaeologists, including curses scratched on rolled-up sheets of lead. The 300ft-long **Great Bath** is open to the sky, and full of steaming green water channelled from the spring through lead box piping. The **Circular Bath** was inserted into the original Entrance Hall as a cold plunge pool for the saunas. From a walkway over the Roman courtyard to the **Temple** you look down on the gilt bronze head of the goddess Minerva, part of the cult statue in the temple. You are underneath the Pump Room now; the rest of the temple remains buried beneath the abbey yard and streets outside.

Bath Abbey

Next to the Pump Room is the west front of Bath Abbey, surrounded by medieval lanes. This masterpiece of the late Perpendicular style was the third church on the same site. King Edgar, wistfully known as the first true King of England, was crowned in the original Saxon church. Edgar is revered as a great empire-building West Saxon king, who married three times – killing the previous husband of one of his wives – and raped a nun. The present church was begun in 1499, just before the Reformation. The carved stone angels climbing up and down ladders on the west front illustrate the dream that inspired Bishop Oliver King to replace the crumbling old Norman church – too big to maintain once the bishopric was restored to Wells. He dreamed these heavenly ladders were standing on a crown and an olive branch, an allegory of his own name, and a voice commanded 'a king to restore the church'. In the 18th century lean-to houses were built against the south wall of the church, on the site of the old abbey cloisters. The skeletons of 25 monks were found in their cellars, now the **Bath Abbey Heritage Vaults Museum** (*open Mon–Sat 10–4; adm minimal*).

While you are in the old city, stop for a bun in **Sally Lunn's Tea Room** on North Parade. For a small donation (free with tea) you can visit the old kitchens.

Pulteney Bridge

The High Street leads north from the abbey, past the old Guildhall, to the **Victoria Art Gallery** (*open Tues–Fri 10–5.30, Sat 10–5, Sun 2–5; adm free*) on Bridge Street. The highlight of the collection is the display of 18th- and 19th-century Bath artists based on two paintings by Gainsborough, who lived in Abbey Street between 1758 and 1774. The long upper gallery is decorated with a plaster frieze of the Elgin marbles.

Pause by the Avon beside Pulteney Bridge to enjoy the classical architecture. The bridge – built by the Adam brothers after seeing the Ponte Vecchio in Florence – is one of England's best, with shops on both sides. It was part of a grand plan by William Pulteney to build a new town on the east bank of the Avon, but economic depression stymied the scheme. Only Great Pulteney Street materialized, leading from the bridge to the old Sydney Hotel. You can see how the side streets were truncated when the

The Bath of Jane Austen

Jane Austen (1775–1817) visited Bath for the first time aged 19, staying with her uncle and aunt at **no. 1, The Paragon** and again five years later, staying with her mother at **13 Queen Square**, downhill from the Royal Crescent (the smartest address in town). In 1801 the whole family moved from Steventon to Bath on her father's retirement as rector. They lived in four different houses over five years, during which time she wrote nothing except an unfinished novel, *The Watsons* – too busy with all the social finagling. The Austens' first home was **4 Sydney Place**, a new development on the east side of the river over Pulteney Bridge. In 1804 they moved to **27 Green Park Mansions**, on the west side of town overlooking the park. Shortly after her father died in January 1805, she and her mother spent a few months at **25 Gay Street** before moving to their last and humblest home, in **Trim Street**. In 1806, Jane, her mother and sister left Bath for good and joined her brother Frank in Southampton. Bath was not conducive to writing. She disliked it totally, and found the constant round of socializing a bore, but it features in every one of her novels except *Pride and Prejudice*, and was the main setting of *Northanger Abbey* and *Persuasion*.

money ran out. The hotel was built purely for entertainment, with a ballroom, tea room and card room. It was famous for its lozenge-shaped pleasure gardens, where public breakfasts were served in summer until the Kennet and Avon Canal and then the railway were routed through the middle. It is now the **Holburne Museum of Art** (*t (01225) 466 669; open mid-Feb–mid-Dec Tues–Sat 10–5, Sun 2.30–5.30; adm*), housing the eclectic art collection of Sir William Holburne (1793–1876), whose claim to fame was serving on the HMS *Orion* aged 12 at the Battle of Trafalgar (1805). After the Napoleonic Wars, he returned to Bath, inherited a baronetcy, lived with his three unmarried sisters and collected 17th- and 18th-century fine and decorative art: silver, ceramics, bronzes and sculpture, and portrait paintings, including a couple of eminent Bath doctors painted by Gainsborough, allegedly in lieu of payment for the treatment of his syphilis.

Queen Square, The Circus and Royal Crescent

Start the John Wood tour with **Queen Square**, the first major development on the edge of the old city, begun in 1728 by John Wood the Elder. The novel idea, which has been so widely copied that it now seems commonplace, was to create the impression of great urban palaces around a central square, while cramming numerous houses affordable to the middle classes behind the sweeping neo-classical façades. The Austens stayed here in 1799. 'We are exceedingly pleased with the house,' Jane wrote to her sister Cassandra. 'It is far more cheerful than the Paragon, and the prospect from the drawing-room window, at which I now write, is rather picturesque.' From here Gay Street takes you up to the Circus.

The **Jane Austen Centre** (*open Mon–Sat 10–5.30, Sun 10.30–5.30; adm*) is on Gay Street, not far from no. 25 where Jane and her mother lived for a few months in 1805. Here you can flesh out the Bath of Jane Austen, with details of Pump Room balls, unscrupulous sedan-chair men and impractical swishy dresses. The guides here can tell you anything you want to know about the books or the city.

The **Circus** was begun in 1755 by John Wood the Elder and finished by his son. The theatrical Roman-style columns were designed by playful Wood the Younger. The **Costume Museum** (*open daily Jan–Dec 10–5; adm*) is housed in the Assembly Rooms, designed by John junior in 1771 as a social venue. It was the most expensive building in Georgian Bath and put the rival rooms in the lower town out of business. The parade of costumes dating from 1660 to the present will make you wish you'd dressed better.

Finally you come to the **Royal Crescent** at the top of town, the summit of Palladian achievement in Bath. Thirty houses are incorporated into a crescent of Ionic columns overlooking a pastoral rural slope.

The show house, **Number One Royal Crescent** (*open mid-Feb–Oct Tues–Sun 10.30–5, Nov Tues–Sun 10.30–4; adm*) has been filled with period furniture of the Crescent's heyday, when the Duke of York rented for the season.

Don't leave this part of town without visiting the **Building of Bath Museum** (*open mid-Feb–end Nov Tues–Sun 10.30–5; adm*) in an old Methodist chapel on The Paragon. The masons, planners, architects and carpenters are the heroes of this exhibition.

Around Bath

In 1741 Ralph Allen built the Palladian mansion of **Prior Park** (*t (01225) 833 422, www.nationaltrust.org.uk; open Easter–Sept Wed–Mon 11–5.30, Oct–Nov Wed–Mon 11–5.30, Dec–Jan Fri–Sun 11–dusk; adm*) on a hill about a mile south of the city, with the help of John Wood and Alexander Pope (*see* p.306). Capability Brown later landscaped the gardens in the Romantic style. The in-crowd of the day all visited – Horace Walpole, William Pitt and Henry Fielding (who based Squire Allworth in *Tom Jones* on Allen). The restored **gardens** (*open Easter–Sept Wed–Mon 11–5.30, Oct–Nov Wed–Mon 12–5.30; adm*) make an ideal trip from Bath (take the no. 2 or 4 Badger Line bus from the city centre). The mile-long circuit walk takes in the Palladian Bridge, one of only four in the world (*see* Stowe Gardens and Wilton House).

Somerset

The reclusive county of Somerset got its name in Saxon times, meaning 'the people of the summerland' and referring to the custom of bringing livestock down from the hills to pasture in summer. The Somerset Levels stretch flat and green from the Mendip Hills to the sea, peppered with Jurassic hills and mystery: prehistoric lake villages, King Alfred burning the cakes and kooky Glastonbury. The dramatic limestone Cheddar Gorge is a world away from the waterlogged Levels and the deep, wooded valleys and dramatic coastline of Exmoor. The cathedral city of Wells is the best base for Somerset, in easy reach of Mendips and Levels. Glastonbury will appeal to New Age nuts; for all others, an afternoon is enough to see the abbey and climb the Tor. The wild and windswept Quantocks and Exmoor National Park, populated by the ghosts of Wordsworth and Coleridge, will appeal to rugged literary types.

The main West Country road (A303) cuts diagonally through the South Somerset Hills, past Iron Age Cadbury Hill Fort (the traditional site of King Arthur's Camelot), the pretty market town of Castle Carey and a handful of stately houses including Barrington Court and Montacute House. An enjoyable stop-off is **RNAS Yeovilton Fleet Air Arm Museum** (*open daily 10–4.30; adm exp*), a 6-acre naval museum with a simulated helicopter flight that lands you, Top Gun-style, on the deck of an aircraft carrier full of noise, blinking lights and loudspeaker announcements.

Wells

I can wish the traveller no better fortune than to stroll forth in the early evening with as large a reserve of ignorance as my own, and treat himself to an hour of discoveries.

Henry James

Henry James called Wells, at the southern foot of the Mendips, 'a cathedral with a little city gathered at the base.' Like Bath, it sprung up around natural springs. Before the Norman Conquest, the bishop's seat was in Wells; later it moved to Bath, then back again. This indecision caused an architecturally productive rivalry between the

Getting There and Around

By **car**, leave the M5 at junction 22, heading north on the A38 towards Cheddar and Wooky Hole, then join the A371 to Wells.

There are direct **train** services to Bristol Temple Meads and Bath Spa, where you can pick up regular **buses** to Wells.

National Express **coaches** run from London Victoria once a day.

Tourist Information

Wells: Town Hall, **t** (01749) 672 552. *Open April–Oct daily 9.30–5.30, Nov–Mar 10–4.*

There is a **general** and **farmers' market** on Wed in the old Market Place, and a general market on Sat.

The **cathedral** holds a range of classical and choral **concerts**, including daily evensong. The programme is available from most tourist information centres, or call **t** (01749) 832 201.

Where to Stay and Eat

Wells t (01749) –

Wells is well-supplied with old-fashioned inns, including the **White Hart**, the **Star**, the **Crown** and the **Ancient Gatehouse Hotel**. They have coaching arches, modest restaurants and reasonable accommodation.

The Swan Hotel, Sadler Street, **t** 836 300, *www.bhere.co.uk* (*expensive*). Wells' biggest hotel was originally a medieval posthouse. The 35 bedrooms are furnished in period style and the restaurant is oak-panelled. The Swan has recently taken over the neighbouring **Star Hotel**, whose 15 bedrooms (*moderate*) have been revamped to a good standard.

Beryl, Hawkers Lane, **t** 678 738, *www.beryl-wells.co.uk* (*expensive*). Swanky B&B in a Victorian-Gothic mansion on a hill, set in 13-acre gardens. Grand wooden hallway, impressive stairway and cathedral views from at least some of the nine richly decorated bedrooms.

Canon Grange, Cathedral Green, **t** 671 800, *www.canongrange.co.uk* (*moderate*). Behind 20th-century pebble-dashed façade, a creaky old house with flagstone hallway and beams dating back to 1450. Lovely guesthouse with six bedrooms, some with cathedral views. Very friendly.

Furlong House, Lorne Place, St Thomas Street, **t** 674 064, *www.johnhowardwells@aol.com* (*moderate*). Homely Georgian house

two towns, culminating in Bishop Jocelin's 13th-century cathedral with its astonishing west front. His successors, who stayed put in Wells, are the bishops of Bath and Wells.

Town and Cathedral

Start in the market square. Two crumbling stone gateways lead off it. Beggars used to sit by **Pennyless Porch**, which leads into the cathedral green, and collect money from passing church-goers. The other leads into the grounds of the Bishop's Palace. The lozenge-shaped cathedral green is surrounded by pretty houses and battlemented stone walls.

The magnificent **west front** of Wells Cathedral is built in warm yellow stone and perfectly framed by the sky. The 13th-century **statues** decorating every inch of space are its chief glory. There used to be around 400, but many are now missing. At the top is Christ flanked by angels, and beneath him in descending hierarchical order are apostles, saints, bishops and kings lined up as a Christian sinner might expect to see them on Judgement Day. Originally they were painted. Above the main door is a row of little round **singing holes** – a unique design feature to amplify the music of choristers and trumpeters during processions. The sculpture gallery continues inside, in the carvings on **capitals**; the most complete of them is the cautionary tale of the fruit set in lovely walled gardens at end of pretty mews off St Thomas Street. Three rooms decorated with William Morris wallpaper and antique wooden furniture.

Infield House, 36 Portway, **t** 670 989, *www.infieldhouse.co.uk* (*moderate*). Pleasant Victorian townhouse backing onto old railway line, 10 minutes' walk from High Street and cathedral. The guest lounge is well stocked with maps and local guides. All three bedrooms have Victorian fireplaces with blazing fires in winter. Views of Mendips from rear bedroom, town and Glastonbury Tor from twin room.

The Crown Hotel, Market Place, **t** 673 457, *www.crownatwells.co.uk* (*moderate*). Behind its Victorian façade are several houses of different ages combined, with 15 bedrooms down narrow corridors. Bar and lounge overlook the market place. **Anton's Bistro** serves pub-style lunches; à la carte menu for dinner.

The Ancient Gatehouse Hotel, 20 Sadler Street, **t** 672 029, *www.ancientgatehouse.co.uk* (*moderate*). As the name suggests, this hotel forms part of the old cathedral wall, and incorporates the west gatehouse. Although desperately crying out for refurbishment, it is still a great place to stay – the atmosphere is off the scale. A stone staircase spirals up to the gatehouse room with a four-poster bed and shower squeezed in. Four other bedrooms overlook the cathedral green. The Italian restaurant (*moderate*) offers lunches and dinners. In summer you can sit out to eat on the cathedral green.

The Fountain Inn and Boxer's Restaurant, 1 St Thomas Street, **t** 672 317 (*cheap*). Old pub downstairs serves local Butcombe bitter, among other ales. Upstairs, there is a high-quality modern English-style restaurant, with pine tables and flowery wallpaper (*moderate*).

Ritcher's Patisserie-Café, 5 Saddler Street, **t** 673 866 (*cheap*). Small café-restaurant, a short walk from the market square, with bar stools at the front and tables at the back. Serves salads, Italian-style sandwiches and coffee. Modern English **restaurant** next door, **t** 679 085 (*moderate*) serves excellent meals based on staples such as lamb and beef.

Cloister Restaurant, Wells Cathedral, **t** 676 543 (*cheap*). Morning coffee and light home-made lunches served under the stone vaults of the old cloisters. *Open lunch only.*

stealers in the south transept. The chances are that you have never before seen anything like the **scissor arches** on all four sides of the crossing. In a high-up corner is a late 14th-century **mechanical clock**, still with its clock face: the hour hand carries the sun up to midday at the top and down to midnight at the bottom, shadowing its movement across the sky; every 15 minutes, wooden knights joust around a castle, one gets knocked off his horse, and Jack Blandifer whacks the bell with his hammer.

There is another clock outside the north transept, to summon the choristers from their rooms. The choristers were known as the Vicar's Choral and were employed to sing the services when the canons were away on cathedral business. From 1348 on they lived in the **Vicar's Close**, a self-contained college with a communal dining hall, 42 houses and a little chapel. The raised bridge spanning the road between the cathedral and the close kept the corruptible male choristers away from the temptations of the town. When the bell struck, they would hurry to the cathedral, emerging down a flight of stone steps into the choir. Nowadays, you can retrace their route up the steps – taking a detour into the **Chapter House** with its fan vaulting – across the chain bridge. The close is an example of a complete medieval street, closed off at the far end by the chapel and tapered to give an illusion of length. It reminded Henry James of 'one of those conventional streets represented on the stage, down whose impossible vista the heroes and confidants of romantic comedies come swaggering arm in arm and hold amorous converse with heroines perched in second-storey windows.' Today the cathedral choir consists of boys and girls from Wells Cathedral School and men – the Vicar's Choral – who live in the Vicar's Close.

In the old chancellor's house on the cathedral green is the **town museum** (*open winter Wed–Mon 11–4, summer Wed–Mon 10–5.30; adm minimal*), full of interesting stuff, including the remains of Herbert Bolsch's 'witch of Wookey' dug out of the cave mouth in the early 1900s. Beautiful old museum cabinets display prehistoric hippo tusks from the Mendips. There are some original stone angels from the cathedral's west front too, and plaster casts of other carvings, made for the Great Exhibition.

Next door to the cathedral, the moated **Bishop's Palace and Gardens** (***t*** *(01749) 678 691; open April–Oct 10.30–6, Sun–Fri 2–6; adm*) stands feudally behind its circuit of walls and fortified gateway. Once over the drawbridge, you can visit the old upstairs rooms and chapel of the 13th-century palace, and wander around the 14-acre gardens.

The Mendip Hills

North of Wells, the rolling plateau of the Mendip Hills stretches to the coast, its carboniferous limestone scenically carved by water. **Cheddar Gorge** is one of the most scenic parts, packed with coach parties. **Ebbor Gorge** down the road is quieter. The Mendips are known for their tunnels and caves too, most famously the **Wookey Hole Caves**. Coleridge visited Wookey; those 'caverns measureless to man' and 'caves of ice' in 'Kubla Khan' bear a striking resemblance to the show caves of the Mendips.

On the plateau top, the moorland fields are hemmed in by grey stone walls and the weather is harsh: the upland villages of **Priddy** and **Charterhouse** were built around lead and zinc mines. Charterhouse now boasts a 70-acre nature reserve scarred with two millennia of lead workings and the remains of a small Roman fortress. The **Charterhouse Centre** (***t*** *(01761) 462 267; open Mon–Fri 9–5*) has walks information.

The pretty village of **Lower Stanton Drew** is just off the A368 in the middle of red marl countryside. In the garden of the Druid's Arms pub is a group of late Neolithic to

Tourist Information

Mendips: The Cheddar Gorge, **t** (01934) 744 071. *Open Easter–Oct daily 10–5, rest of year Sun 11–4 only.*

Where to Stay and Eat

The Mendip Hills

Glencot House, Glencot Lane, Wookey Hole, **t** (01749) 677 160, *relax@glencothouse.co.uk* (*expensive*). Mock Jacobean stone mansion built by the Victorian paper mill owner of Wookey Hole, set in 18-acre gardens beside the River Axe. Ornate fireplaces, oak and walnut panelling, stripped wooden floors, chandeliers and 13 bedrooms. Traditional country house hotel restaurant open for dinner only.

The New Inn, Priddy, **t** (01749) 676 465 (*cheap*). So-called since 17th century when it first became an inn; before that it was a farm cottage. In a remote spot up in the Mendips, with only an old farmhouse for company. Overlooks green with wooden sheep hurdles and pens for August sheep fair.

Cox's Mill, The Cliffs, **t** (01934) 742 346 (*cheap*). Opposite Cox's Cave, good pub for lunch, with flagstoned bar.

early Bronze Age **megaliths** known as the Cove. Further on, down a cul-de-sac off the main village road, are three impressive **stone circles** in a field.

Wookey Hole Caves

t (01749) 672 243, www.wookey.co.uk; open winter 10–4, summer 10–5; adm exp.

The Wookey Hole Caves are well signposted from Wells. Try to avoid them during school holidays, when they're packed. As it's always 11 degrees Celsius underground, winter is the best time to visit. The caves have been attracting visitors for centuries – famously Coleridge and Alexander Pope, who shot down stalactites for his home in Twickenham – but it wasn't until 1904 that Herbert Bolsch found evidence of Romano-British habitation. There are 25 interconnecting chambers, nine of which can be visited without getting wet and cold. The early cave dwellers lived in the cave mouth and buried their dead 600 feet down. It's all so spooky that when the skeleton of an arthritic woman was uncovered by Bolsch she was at once nicknamed the **Witch of Wookey**. A little cave known as the **Hyena Den** is where William Dawkins found ancient hyena bones. A **museum** houses Bolsch's finds and Dawkins' bones, as well as masses of information on the archaeology and geology of Mendip potholes.

Cheddar Gorge and Show Caves

t (01934) 742 343; open May–mid-Sept 10–5, mid-Sept–April 10.30–4.30; adm exp.

Although commercially over-exploited, the 3 miles of Cheddar Gorge retain their scenic majesty. This is where the famous **Cheddar Man** was discovered in 1903 – the oldest complete skeleton yet found in Britain, buried 9,000 years ago before Britain became an island. In 1996, DNA testing linked him directly with Adrian Targett, the Cheddar village school history teacher. The best access to the gorge is from the Mendip plateau, following the Ice Age meltwater torrent that carved the gorge out of the rock, and dodging the tourist buses as you go. There are three caves, two of them the mouths of underground Pleistocene riverbeds, the third an artificial cave quarried by Richard Pavey to emulate those found by rival mill owners George Cox and Richard Gough, all in the 19th century. These days it is all exploited for tourism by the Marquis of Bath at Longleat: the old cottages and mills are now tea rooms and pubs or shops selling Cheddar cheese and souvenirs. **Gough Cave** is the most spectacular of the caves, its lofty chambers stained by iron oxide. Smaller **Cox Cave** has some enchanting stalagmites and stalactites reflected in rock pools like fairy grottos. The Tolkeinesque **Crystal Quest** in **Pavey's Cave** is fun. On a clear day, it's worth climbing up the 274 steps of Jacob's Ladder to **Pavey's Lookout Tower**, start of the 4½-mile Gorge Walk.

The Somerset Levels

The tides of the Bristol Channel rise up to 23 feet above mean sea level – the second highest tidal surge in the world. A low ridge of shingle, sand and clay along the coast between Weston-super-Mare (a very ordinary resort town) and Bridgwater keeps the

History and Legend: the Once and Future King, and Saints

One legend goes that Joseph of Arimathea built the first Christian church in the British Isles at Glastonbury in AD 63, another that he was the uncle of Jesus Christ and brought him on a trip to Glastonbury, returning alone to bury the Holy Grail of Christ's blood and sweat under the Tor. It is also told that there is a Romano-British monastery at Glastonbury where Arthur was taken by boat after being mortally wounded at the Battle of Camlann, and where he and Guinevere lie buried.

A real, historical abbey was founded by Saxon King Ine, which grew renowned under Dunstan in the 10th century, and was the richest monastery in England in the Middle Ages. Both abbot of Glastonbury and archbishop of Canterbury, Dunstan revived the English monasteries by restoring the strict Benedictine Order. He also brought Glastonbury under the patronage of English kings, leading to massive endowments. Three late Saxon kings were buried at Glastonbury Abbey: Edmund I in 946, Edgar in 975 and Edmund Ironside in 1016. By Domesday, Glastonbury Abbey owned an eighth of Somerset.

Dunstan was not the only power here. The 12th-century abbot Henry of Blois was one of the most influential men of his age – grandson of Henry I, brother of King Stephen and bishop of Winchester. William of Malmesbury dedicated *Glastonbury Chronicles* to him. At the Dissolution there were 47 monks at the abbey under Abbot Whyting; the library contained 400 books and the income from the abbey estates equalled Westminster Abbey. Whyting refused to surrender and was hanged on the Tor for treason. His head was stuck on the abbey gateway, and other parts of his dismembered body were posted to Wells, Bath, Bridgwater and Ilchester.

Glastonbury's enterprising monks promoted a string of lucrative cults on the back of legends and history. Seven years after the abbey burned down in May 1184, the Glastonbury monks unearthed the bodies of legendary **King Arthur and Queen Guinevere** near the old church. Pilgrims flocked to the town to pay homage. In 1278 the bodies were dug up and enshrined in a marble tomb in the presence of Edward I. The inscription read *REX QUONDAM REXQUE FUTURUS* – 'the Once and Future King'. The monks also promoted the cult of **St Dunstan** around a dubious pile of old bones. They claimed to have rescued Dunstan's bones from his tomb at Canterbury in 1012 during Viking raids. In 1508 the Archbishop of Canterbury intervened to put a stop to the false idolatry. But no sooner had St Dunstan's image been banished than the cult of **St Joseph of Arimathea** peaked, with the monks building a new chapel of St Joseph. Thanks to the promotional skills of the monks, King Arthur, the Holy Grail, Avalon and Camelot are all now part of the same story.

sea out of Somerset and holds in the marshland known as the Levels. The flood silt has preserved ancient traces of settlement: two Iron Age **'lake villages'** have been unearthed, and the wooden planks of the 6,000-year-old **Sweet Track**. In 1693 the **Alfred Jewel**, with its inscription 'Alfred ordered me to be made', was found in the Levels four miles northwest of Athelney, where Alfred encamped in 878 and planned his campaign to reconquer Wessex from the Danes. The flatness is partly alleviated by the **Polden Hills**, which divide the northern **Vale of Avalon** from the southern **Basin of Sedgemoor**. **Glastonbury Tor**, the largest of a cluster of strange conical hillocks, is visible for miles around, topped by the tower of St Michael's Church.

Glastonbury

From every approach to Glastonbury the 525ft-high summit of the Tor stands out. Glastonbury is a place of Christian mythology and earth magic, and assorted New Age cults hybridizing Arthurian legend, Christianity, paganism and fantasy galore. Among its residents are magicians, rune readers, soul therapists and shamanic healers. There is a 'heart-centred' guesthouse whose proprietor is 'the note-taker for a spirit guide called White Cloud'. where you can stay for the Glastonbury Goddess

Getting There and Around

By **car**, leave the M5 at junction 23 and follow A39 to Glastonbury.

The nearest **railway** station is at Castle Cary, but the most convenient is Bristol Temple Meads. A bus goes from the station to Glastonbury, taking about 1½ hours.

Tourist Information

Glastonbury: The Tribunal, 9 High Street, **t** (01458) 832 954. *Open summer daily 10–5, winter 10–4.*

If you're here in June, the place to be is the **Glastonbury Festival** – in fact the area is best avoided unles you're a festival-goer. To get the vibe and for specific details of what's on, how to get there, camping and so on, visit *www.glastonburyfestivals.co.uk*.

Where to Stay and Eat

Glastonbury t (01458) –

For all its pseudo-spiritual mumbo-jumbo, Glastonbury leaves the inner child crying out for a decent meal and a good night's sleep. There are no great cafés or restaurants, and only one or two nice places to stay.

Number 3 Hotel, Magdalene Street, **t** 832 129, *www.numberthree.co.uk* (*expensive*). Handsomely furnished house next to abbey grounds with five bedrooms including three in old coach house behind pretty garden.

The George and Pilgrims Hotel, 1 High Street, **t** 831 146, *www.georgeandpilgrims.activehotels.com* (*moderate*). Impressive stone-fronted medieval inn, built for pilgrims visiting the abbey, with an oak-beamed bar, open fireplace and stone-mullioned bay window with a seat.

Melrose, Coursing Batch, **t** 834 706 (*cheap*). On approach to Glastonbury Tor, this is Glastonbury's classiest B&B. A beautiful, bright Georgian house with two bedrooms and views across the Somerset Levels.

Tordown, 5 Ashwell Lane, **t** 832 287, *www.tordown.com* (*cheap*). Large Victorian house on slopes of Glastonbury Tor. Offers hydrotherapy spa, higher-self communication sessions and healing treatments; or you can just sleep in one of seven bedrooms.

Hawthorne's Hotel and Brasserie, Northload Street, **t** 831 255 (*moderate*). Popular, informal 70-seater brasserie where the menu might include grilled goats' cheese and honey followed by stir-fried duck. Front bar for drinks. *Open Tues–Sat eves*. The new owners are gradually improving the 11 bedrooms.

Abbey Tea Rooms, 16 Magdalene Street, **t** 832 852 (*cheap*). Pleasant old-fashioned tea shop offering cream teas, meat-and-two-veg lunches, cakes and sandwiches.

Café Galatea, High Street, **t** 834 284 (*cheap*). Range of vegetarian snack lunches and dinners, including mushroom pancakes.

Entertainment

Assembly Rooms, High Street, **t** 834 677. Live acoustic music Thurs and Sun 7pm, as well as theatre, Christmas pantomime and crop-circle conventions.

Festival in July. Most concrete, at the heart of the old town, is the abbey, whose foundation is said to date back to the time of Christ.

Start in the town, then visit the abbey and climb the Tor for the views. When you've had your fill of New Age paraphernalia, **Glastonbury Lake Village Museum** on the High Street (*open summer 10–5, winter 10–4; adm minimal*) charts the excavations of an Iron Age village on a small island northwest of Glastonbury. There is part of a boat made of a single piece of oak. Stop for a drink at the **George and Pilgrim Inn**, built in the 1450s for the wealthy pilgrims to the monastery. Behind the medieval gatehouse, **Glastonbury Abbey** (*open 9.30–6 or dusk if earlier; adm*) is a fabulous ruin. The medieval church was 581 feet long, the longest in England. The **Lady Chapel** is all that survives of the Norman church, built after a fire in 1184 destroyed the abbey with all its treasures, books and relics; note the decorated round arches and plants growing up the walls. The grave of Arthur and Guinevere is clearly marked. Bits and pieces of the rest of the monastery survive, such as the 14th-century abbot's kitchen. Don't miss the **holy thorn tree**, behind St Patrick's Chapel. Joseph of Arimathea planted his staff in Wearyall Hill and it blossomed into a thorn tree; this one is said to be descended from the original, and blossoms twice a year, in spring and midwinter.

It's a 15-minute walk or bus-ride up the Vale of Avalon to the foot of the **Tor**. Just before Well House Lane on Chickwell Street is the entrance to **Chalice Well and Gardens**, where water flows from a well said to be the burial place of the Holy Grail of Christ's blood and sweat. Atop the Tor are remains of the 15th-century **St Michael's Church** where Abbot Whyting was hanged, drawn and quartered at the Dissolution. There are breathtaking views back over the vale.

Muchelney

There's another abbey ruin south of the Polden Hills at **Muchelney**. Its founder is supposed to have been King Athelstan, but in spite of this auspicious beginning the abbey never grew very big (at most 15 monks) or rich. In 1335 the Muchelney monks got into trouble with the Bishop of Shrewsbury for having too much fun, sleeping in king-sized beds instead of cubicles in the dormitory, snacking in private and riding around the countryside on horseback. Nothing is left of the church, but the abbot's lodging survives intact, decorated with some of the best pieces to come out of the **Muchelney Pottery** (*open Mon–Sat 9–1 and 2–5*) of John Leach (grandson of the famous Bernard Leach), south of the village. The pottery specializes in simple, wood-fired, domestic items.

Taunton

Taunton, on the southern edge of the Quantocks, is the county town of Somerset, but has little of interest. During the reign of James II, Taunton had a reputation for Protestant dissent. The Duke of Monmouth made its castle the headquarters for his rebellion in 1685. The town's chief glory is **St Mary Magdelene Church**, one of the biggest Perpendicular churches in England.

Getting There and Around

By **car**, Taunton is 5 miles from the M5, off junction 25.

Regular inter-city **trains** from London Paddington stop at Taunton, continuing to Plymouth and Penzance. Virgin trains operate from Newcastle, stopping at Durham, York, Leeds, Sheffield, Derby, Birmingham, Bristol and Taunton.

Six or eight National Express **coaches** a day go to Taunton from London Victoria.

Tourist Information

Taunton: The Library, Paul Street, **t** (01823) 336 344. *Open 9.30–5.30, later in summer; winter Mon–Sat only.*

Where to Stay

Taunton t (01823) –

The Castle Hotel, Castle Green, **t** 272 671, *www.the-castle-hotel.com* (*very expensive*). This magnificent hotel incorporates part of the medieval castle's east gate. High standard of hospitality.

The Corner House Hotel, Park Street, **t** 284 683, *www.corner-house.co.uk* (*moderate*). Medium-sized hotel in turreted Victorian building, 500 yards from town centre; 28 bedrooms and bistro serving Brixham fish and local Somerset produce.

Forde House, 9 Upper High Street, **t** 279 042 (*moderate*). Lovely Georgian house with beautiful garden a few minutes' walk from town centre. Five comfortable bedrooms.

Orchard House, Fons George, Middleway, **t** 351 783, *orch-hse@dircon.co.uk* (*moderate*). Handsome red-brick Georgian house with pedimented door, just a few minutes' walk south of the town centre, with six lovely bedrooms to let.

Eating Out

The Castle Hotel, Castle Green, **t** 272 671 (*expensive*). Top-notch restaurant where TV chef Gary Rhodes earned his first Michelin star. He's moved on, but it still features in all the food guides. *Closed Sun eve.*

The Sanctuary, Middle Street, **t** 257 788 (*moderate*). Wine bar and candle-lit restaurant downstairs, brighter dining room and roof terrace upstairs. Vegetarian cooking, warm salads and daily fresh Brixham fish.

Brettons, 49 East Reach, **t** 256 688, *www.brettonsrestaurant.com* (*moderate*). Friendly brasserie with a pretty courtyard garden. English/French-style cooking might include duck breast glazed with clover honey, potatoes and sage rosti, or fresh Brixham fish catch. Light lunch menu of panini, salads or kedgeree. *Open Tues–Fri lunch, Mon–Sat dinner.*

Brazz, Castle Bow, **t** 252 000 (*cheap*). Upbeat brasserie next door to Castle Hotel with art on walls. Serves coffee and pastries until midday, then mushroom risotto or sausages and mash.

Sally Edwards, The Crescent, **t** 326 793 (*cheap*). Lovely café offering tea and coffee, home-made pastries and Somerset apple cake, fishcakes, salads and ciabattas.

There is a cluster of attractive buildings around the **Georgian Market House**, built by Bampfyld of Hestercombe, and nearby **Bath Place**, a narrow lane of Georgian houses and shops. **St Mary Magdalene Church**, with its warm red Ham Stone tower at the far end of Hammet Street, is almost as wide as it is long, with an unusual double row of aisles on either side of the nave. The poet Coleridge used to walk over the Quantocks from his cottage in Nether Stowey to preach here. Behind Castle Hotel, the **Somerset County Museum** (*open Tues–Sat 10–5; adm free*) is in the Great Hall used by Judge Jeffreys during the Bloody Assizes. There's an intriguing hotchpotch of stuff in the museum, from Monmouth's pistols to a decorated 3,000-year-old ceremonial shield found at South Cadbury, and a stretch of prehistoric track.

The Monmouth Rebellion

The Duke of Monmouth was the tragic hero of a Protestant rebellion against his Catholic uncle, James II, in 1685. His credentials as a rebel leader were impeccable: he was the first-born of Charles II's many illegitimate children; he was a successful general of the English army in the Low Countries in the 1670s; he was popular and looked good on a horse. His romantic rebellion, however, was a fiasco, remembered mainly for the brutality of the reprisals. Monmouth landed with three ships and 83 followers at Lyme Regis. They had no money and few arms, and wandered around Somerset without any clear plan, trying to recruit a rebel army. The ragtag army was defeated by the Royal army at the Battle of Sedgemoor on 6 July 1685; Monmouth was captured despite trying to escape dressed up as a farmer. He begged for lenience on the grounds that he didn't mean it, but nonetheless had his head chopped off by Jack Ketch; it took the executioner five strokes of the axe and then a sword to sever it. The Monmouth Rebellion was the last large-scale popular rebellion in English history and Sedgemoor the last battle on English soil. The reprisals are in fact more renowned than the rebellion: Judge Jeffreys had 250 rebels hanged, drawn and quartered (Charles II executed only 30 after the Civil War). All of which did nothing for James II's reputation.

You can visit Sedgemoor battlefield in the village of Westonzoyland. Park at the Sedgemoor Inn and have look around the church next door (where Monmouth's troops sheltered) before following Monmouth Road to the battlefield.

The Quantocks and Exmoor

In the west of Somerset is the ridge of the Quantock Hills. Exmoor rises above the Brendon Hills on the other side of the Vale of Taunton Deane. This parallel range of hills is where Wordsworth returned to poetry after adventures in revolutionary France, and where Coleridge wrote his best poems. Together, their long walks produced the *Literary Ballads*, a defining text of the Romantic Movement. Coleridge's 'Kubla Khan' and 'The Rime of the Ancient Mariner' were the result of two separate walks in 1797. On the first, he headed alone to Porlock Weir with a copy of the 1614 book *Purchas his Pilgrimage*, which includes the line 'In Xanada did Cublai Can build a stately Palace.' Soon after, he headed west over the moors with the Wordsworths to write a poem about a doomed ship. They stayed the night in Watchet – from where the Mariner set sail – continuing to the Valley of Rocks and across Exmoor to Dulverton.

Nether Stowey and Around

The village of Nether Stowey, at the northern foot of the Quantocks, is a low-key literary shrine. The only obvious reference to the Romantic poets who stayed here is the **Ancient Mariner pub** opposite **Coleridge's Cottage**. Coleridge moved to the village in 1797, aged 25, with his wife Sarah and son Hartley, and stayed for 13 years. His cottage is now let by the National Trust; the poetic tenants open it up to visitors. It is still the modest little place it was in Coleridge's day, with a few bits and pieces of Coleridge memorabilia including his ink stand – inlaid with gilt and ebony – and a

Getting There and Around

West Somerset Railway, **t** (01643) 704 996, operates a steam train down the Vale of Taunton Deane on the west side of the Quantocks between Bishops Lydeard and Minehead via Watchet and Dunster. The round trip takes 3 hours. Otherwise you'll need a car and/or shanks' pony.

Tourist Information

Bridgwater: 50 High Street, **t** (01278) 427 652, *www.somersetbythesea.co.uk. Open summer Mon–Fri 10–5, Sat 9.30–4.30; winter Mon, Wed and Fri 10–1 and 1.45–4.* The eastern side of the Quantocks as far as Kilve.

Minehead: 17 Friday Street, **t** (01643) 702 624. The Quantocks and Exmoor, especially the coastal section. *Open summer Mon–Sat 9.30–5, Sun 10–1; winter Mon–Sat 10–4.*

Taunton: Paul Street, **t** (01823) 336 344. The western Quantocks.

Where to Stay and Eat

The Quantocks and Exmoor

Rising Sun, West Bagborough, **t** (01823) 432 575 (*expensive*). The picture of an old-fashioned pub, but it's all brand new and very smart, since a fire on 9 January 2003 gutted the place. Food is the main emphasis, with a Michelin-starred chef cooking delicious bar meals (sandwiches, a bowl of soup or chips, Cumberland sausages with onion gravy and mustard-glazed ham with fried eggs) and dinners such as mackerel with roasted tomatoes or shank of lamb with pot-roasted vegetables. Art gallery and two delightful bedrooms upstairs, one with a four-poster bed, the other with 19th-century French décor. *Closed Mon.*

Alfoxton Park Hotel, about 1½ miles through woods from Holford, **t** (01278) 741 288, *www.alfoxtonpark.co.uk* (*moderate*). William and Dorothy Wordsworth rented this secluded, white-painted Queen Anne house for about a year in 1797–8. It stands at the end of a long wooded drive surrounded by parkland and woods, looking out to the Bristol Channel.

Winsors Farm, Holford, **t** (01278) 741 435, *www.winsors-farm.co.uk* (*moderate*). Attractive white-painted house with large garden. Two lovely bedrooms and a semi-detached cottage with its own sitting room for guests. Friendly and welcoming.

Tilbury Farm, West Bagborough, **t** (01823) 432 391 (*moderate*). Rough golden stone 17th-century farmhouse surrounded by farm buildings and 20 acres, 5 minutes' walk from the pub. Three bedrooms furnished with rush matting and pine. Aga-cooked organic breakfasts. Views over the Vale of Taunton Deane towards the Brendon Hills, and walks from the back garden onto the Quantocks ridge.

Bashfords Farmhouse, West Bagborough, **t** (01823) 432 015, *www.bashfordsfarmhouse.co.uk* (*moderate*). Delightful 18th-century farmhouse with the biggest lintel above the fireplace you have ever seen. Three cheerful, piney bedrooms.

Esplanade House, The Esplanade, Watchet, **t** (01984) 633 444 (*moderate*). Former Georgian farmhouse on the harbour with tea garden. Three pretty bedrooms with window seats. Welcoming hosts.

Chantry Tea Gardens, Sea Lane, Kilve, **t** (01278) 741 457 (*cheap*). Warm welcome on a brisk walk, next to the ruins of a medieval chantry and a pebble's throw from the sea. Delicious cream teas and ploughman's.

Blue Ball, Triscombe (southwest side of the Quantocks), **t** (01984) 618 242 (*cheap*). Traditional thatched pub with inglenook and beams. Strong emphasis on food: lunch might be Moroccan lamb with cous cous, dinner lemon sole with lemon grass.

The Star Inn, Mill Lane, Watchet, **t** (01984) 631 367 (*cheap*). Popular locals' pub serving good-quality bar meals (*cheap*): fresh cod and chips, sausage and mash or steak and kidney pudding. Local real ales like Gone with the Whippet and Hound Dog, brewed by the Cottage Brewery in Castle Cary. In summer you can drink in the beer garden.

The Corner House, 1 Market Street, Watchet, **t** (01984) 631 251 (*cheap*). Café under new management that promises to upgrade the menu with quiches, soup, warm filled rolls, hot fish and meat dishes with fresh vegetables. *Open summer daily, winter Wed–Sun.*

letter to his brother George which goes into great detail about all his aches and pains. A regimental sword among the memorabilia commemorates a Coleridge escapade in the army under the name Silas Tomkyn Comberbache.

A short walk takes you through steep wooded **Hodder's Combe** between Nether Stowey and Alfoxton, a favourite of the poets who often took their guests (luminaries like Hazlitt and Lamb). Starting from Holford, it re-enacts Coleridge's poem 'This Lime-Tree Bower My Prison', crossing 'springy heath, along hill-top edge'. You can peep through a fence at Alfoxton Park (where Wordsworth lived). Then continue to a 'roaring dell, o'erwooded, narrow, deep', which, as Coleridge described, is 'fanned by the waterfall'.

The rocky stretch of coast at East Quantoxhead – **Kilve's Delightful Shore** – is composed of tilting sheets of fossil-rich limestone pavement a foot and a half thick.

The **Lydeard Hill** car park, off the A358 beyond West Bagborough, is one of the most popular starting points for walking and cycling in the Quantocks. It is the second highest point of the range (1,200ft) with a great heathery ridge walk to Wills Neck (the highest point, 1,260ft) and on to Crowcombe. There are fantastic views across the Bristol Channel to Wales, and as far as Dartmoor, Exmoor and the Brecon Beacons.

Watchet

The ship was cheered, the harbour cleared,
Merrily did we drop,
Below the kirk, below the hill,
Below the lighthouse top.

Coleridge, 'The Rime of the Ancient Mariner'

Coleridge composed the first few lines of 'The Rime of the Ancient Mariner' in the pub at Watchet, while on a long walk with William and Dorothy Wordsworth. The

The Southwest Coastal Path

The Southwest Coastal Path is Britain's longest national trail, stretching roughly 600 miles around the peninsula from Minehead in Somerset to Studland Bay in Dorset. The footpaths hugging the cliff tops were beaten out in the last few centuries by coastguards patrolling the smugglers' coves, beaches and headlands and now take you round some of the most varied coastal scenery in the country. There are plenty of places to stay and get refreshments *en route*. The Southwest Coastal Path Association recommends late spring, early summer or early autumn as the best times to walk it, before and after the busy holiday season, but when the sea may be warm enough for swimming. The annual handbook contains a full list of accommodation. You will need two weeks to do it in one go, but most people prefer to do it in shorter sections over longer periods. Check the SWCP Association website, *www.swcp.org.uk*, for itineraries with walking times and distances, or for practical advice and information contact the Association Secretary, Eric Wallis, Windlestraw, Penquit, Ermington, Devon PL21 0LU, t (01752) 896 237, *info@swcp.org.uk*.

houses here are small and brightly painted. In summer, you may hear sea shanties in the boat museum, but the fishing is dead. and the shops all sell souvenirs.

The dreary house of **Hestercombe** is surrounded by two extraordinary gardens (*open daily 10–5pm; adm*). In the front is a formal garden laid out by Edwin Lutyens and planted by Gertrude Jekyll, which appeared twice in *Country Life*. In a wooded combe behind the house is the restored 18th-century landscape garden of Coplestone Warre Bampfylde – who designed the cascade for Colt Hoare at Stourhead.

Exmoor National Park

Exmoor is tamer than Dartmoor, all winding country lanes and fields. It covers 267 square miles and 34 miles of coast. Its highlight is the steep valleys in the north. The Southwest Coastal Path gets interesting between the towering gritstone cliffs and slate coves west of Lynmouth Bay, where the villages of Lynmouth and Porlock are squeezed into narrow, rocky coastal inlets. In the south, the gentler countryside between Dulverton and Bampton is worth exploring. Base yourself at Porlock, Dulverton, Lynton or Dunster for walking, horse-riding or cycling .

The Exmoor Coast

The best approach to Exmoor is along the coast road from the Quantocks, the route that Coleridge and Wordsworth took on their walking tours along the coast to Lynton. It's also the route taken by Cromwell's men as they marched on Dunster Castle in the Civil War. **Dunster** is a charming old town of red stone, thatched cottages, cobblestones, a mill, bridge and beautiful church; the battlements are not of the castle, but of an 18th-century folly. **Minehead** calls itself the gateway to Exmoor: pass through it

Coleridge in the Quantocks

The poet Samuel Taylor Coleridge had been living in Bristol for a while with Robert Southey when the cottage in Nether Stowey was given to him at a knockdown rent by a local admirer called John Pool. William Wordsworth and his sister Dorothy were living close by at Racedown in north Dorset. That is where they first met, through an introduction by a Bristol bookseller. The Wordsworths moved to Alfoxton, just down the road from Nether Stowey, to be near their new friend, and the three of them got into the habit of country rambling and round-the-clock talks, breaking off now and again to write a poem. Some of the locals thought they were spies. A government official came down from London to check up on them, tailing them on their nocturnal walks and noting what they said – but concluded that they were merely nutters. Coleridge's contemporaries all felt inferior to him, although his health and laudanum addiction wrecked his potential. Nevertheless, he managed to write an awful lot of poetry, literary criticism, journalism, something like 2,000 letters and 70 notebooks, and a few plays including one called *Remorse* (a hint of his mental condition at the time), as well as lecturing on philosophy and literature, and preaching. No one seems to have a bad word to say about Coleridge, unlike Wordsworth, probably because he was much more likable for all his failings.

Getting There and Around

You can reach Taunton or Exeter by **train**, and then catch a **bus** to Exmoor.

There is a **circular moorland bus** between Minehead Peak and Porlock, via Dunster and Wheddon Cross, Exford to Porlock (*Easter–Sept weekends only, July–Aug also Tues and Thurs*). For information call **t** (01823) 251 140.

First Somerset and Dorset, t (01823) 272 033, also runs a seasonal bus service along the Exmoor coast from Taunton (*summer daily, winter weekends only*) to Lynton via Butlins Minehead, Bishop's Lydeard, Watchet, Dunster and Porlock. **First North Devon, t** (01271) 376 524, runs a year-round bus service from Butlins Minehead (*daily*) to Lynton via Porlock and Lynmouth. For timetable enquiries contact **Traveline, t** 0870 608 2608.

Tourist Information

Porlock: West End, High Street, Porlock, **t** (01643) 863 150, *www.porlock.co.uk*. *Open Easter–Oct Mon–Fri 10–1 and 2–5, Sat 10–5 and Sun 10–1; winter Mon–Fri 10.15–1, Sat 10–2.*

Lynton and Lynmouth: Town Hall, Lynton, **t** (01598) 752 225.

Exmoor National Park Visitor Centres are at:

Dunster: Dunster Steep, **t** (01643) 821 835. *Open Easter–Oct daily 10–5, winter weekends 11–3.*

Lynmouth: The Esplanade, **t** (01598) 752 509. *Open Easter–Oct 10–5, winter weekends and school holidays.*

Dulverton: Fore Street, **t** (01398) 323 841. *Open Easter–Oct daily 10–5, winter daily 10.30–3.30.*

The *Exmoor Visitor* is published in March with a calendar of events for the whole year (talks, shows, horse rides), guided walks and lists of places to stay.

The best walkers' map is the Ordnance Survey, *Outdoor Leisure 9, Exmoor 1:25,000.*

Where to Stay and Eat

Dunster t (01643) –

The Yarn Market Hotel, High Street, **t** 821 425, *www.yarnmarkethotel.co.uk* (*expensive*). Some of the 25 bright bedrooms overlook the ancient market cross; two get a glimpse of the castle. Restaurant has character.

Dunster Water Mill, Mill Lane, **t** 821 759 (*moderate*). 18th-century mill with two simple bedrooms, tea room and garden (*closed Fri except July–Aug*). Guests have free access into the castle grounds.

Spears Cross Hotel, West Street, **t** 821 439, *www.smoothhound.co.uk/hotels/spearsx* (*moderate*). Warm welcome in this small, snug hotel with three bedrooms, a fireplace in the guest's lounge and oak-panelled rooms. The pretty, terraced garden dotted with model houses was created by Mr Pluck, the first owner of hotel.

Hathaways of Dunster, West Street, **t** 821 725 (*moderate*). Intimate candle-lit restaurant with a menu of fresh Weston Bay fish and Somerset pork with cider-apple sauce. *Open*

as quickly as you can. It's the home of Butlins holiday camp. The main road continues into the delightful **Vale of Porlock**. On the east side are the chocolate-box villages of **Bossington**, **Allerford** and **Selworthy**. On the west side are **Porlock**, the main town, and **Porlock Weir**, a jumble of houses at the foot of a wooded cliff behind an old stone harbour. Coleridge dreamed a fully formed poem, of which 'Kubla Khan' is a fragment, at Ash Farm near Porlock. When he awoke he started to write it down, but was interrupted mid-flow by 'a person on business from Porlock'. By the time the intruder had gone, the poet had forgotten the rest. Beyond Porlock, the road twists 1,300 feet up **Porlock Hill** through fabulous combe landscapes. South of Porlock, **Dunkery Beacon** (1,700ft) is the highest point on Exmoor. Between Porlock and Lynton the road to Malmshead narrows over **Robber's Bridge** and passes **Oare Church**, where Lorna Doone was shot, in **Badgeworthy Water**.

dinner only, Easter–Oct Mon–Sat, rest of year Tues–Sat.

Stags Head, West Street, **t** 821 229 (*cheap*). Snug, friendly pub serving local beers including Exmoor Ale, and bar meals.

Porlock t (01643) –

The Anchor Hotel, Porlock Weir, **t** 862 753, *www.exmoor.biz* (*expensive*). Victorian hotel with 14 big, bright double bedrooms, most with views over the harbour. Another six rooms in the old pub next door.

The Oaks Hotel, Porlock, **t** 862 265, *www.oakshotel.co.uk* (*expensive*). Pretty Edwardian country house hotel off the main Minehead–Lynton road with eight clean, comfortable bedrooms. Gentle, period feel and terrific views towards Bristol Channel and Porlock Weir.

West Porlock House, West Porlock, **t** 862 880 (*moderate*). Half of handsome 1920s manor house in wooded hillside above Porlock Bay; overgrown gardens full of rhododendrons and azaleas. Five charming bedrooms, most with sea views. *Open Mar–Oct only.*

Silcombe Farm, Culbone, **t** 862 248 (*moderate*). Lovely, clean Victorian farmhouse with pretty gardens on edge of Silcombe Combe. Amazing views up the combe and over the Bristol Channel. Three bedrooms and Aga-cooked breakfasts. Bar meals served at the **Culbone Inn**, 2 miles' drive or walk.

The Castle Hotel, High Street, West Porlock, **t** 862 504, *castlehotel@btconnect.com* (*moderate*). Small hotel with firm beds and inviting bar offering meals (*cheap*).

Seapoint, Upway, Porlock, **t** 862 289 (*moderate*). In a quiet spot above the village, just behind the Ship Inn, Seapoint is in a large Edwardian house with four attractive bedrooms and beautiful guest lounge; fire-place, and window seat overlooking the bay. Dinner available too.

Exmoor Falconry and Animal Farm, Allerford, **t** 862 816, *www.exmoorfalconry.co.uk* (*moderate*). Pretty yellow farmhouse with ancient beams. Three little bedrooms and garden. Cream teas and home-made cakes.

The Ship Inn, Porlock, on main village road, **t** 862 507 (*cheap*). Atmospheric thatched pub with snug bar, where Southey wrote an abysmal sonnet during one of his walks. Serves ploughman's lunches.

Ash Farm, Porlock, **t** 862 414 (*cheap*). Take the Lynmouth road out of Porlock, and turn off after 4 miles towards Yearnor. This homely farmhouse above Culbone Combe in the midst of the best walking countryside is where Coleridge wrote 'Kubla Khan'.

Lynmouth and Lynton t (01598) –

Hewitt's Hotel, North Walk, Lynton, **t** 752 293 (*very expensive*). Rambling 19th-century house overlooking Lynmouth Bay. From the grand hall, an oak staircase sweeps up past a Burne-Jones stained-glass window.

The Rising Sun Hotel, Harbourside, Lynmouth, **t** 753 223, *www.risingsunlynmouth.co.uk* (*expensive*). Thatched 14th-century smugglers' inn with a terraced garden and 16 comfortable bedrooms (some with views of the East Lyn River), including a detached

Lorna Doone Country

R.D. Blackmore's novel *Lorna Doone* (1869) is set on Exmoor in the 1680s, at the time of the Monmouth Rebellion. It's full of wild scenery and the tangy Somerset dialect. Judge Jeffreys, John Churchill and James II all make a brief appearance. The narrator is John Ridd, a local boy seeking vengeance for the murder of his father by the violent outlaw clan of the Doones, camped out in a remote Exmoor valley. He falls in love with Lorna of the Doones, who turns out to be their prisoner and the daughter of a London grandee. It all ends with a gallant rescue and a gun shot at a wedding in Oare church. 'A Doone Country Walk' booklet (on sale everywhere in the area) guides you into the 'deep green valley carved from out the mountains in a perfect oval', where John Ridd first set eyes on Lorna Doone.

cottage where the poet Shelley honeymooned with his teenage bride in 1812. You can eat lunch in the bar, or dinner in the oak-panelled restaurant. Traditional English/French dishes include Lynmouth seafood and Exmoor game.

Lynton Cottage Hotel, North Walk, Lynton, **t** 752 342, *www.lynton-cottage.co.uk* (*expensive*). Cream-painted 19th-century hotel with grandstand views over the bay. Elegant double flight of stairs leads up to 17 bedrooms. Restaurant (*open eves only*).

Le Bistro, Watersmeet Road, Lynmouth, **t** 753 302 (*moderate*). Traditional English menu of fish and game. *Open Fri–Sun lunch, Tues–Sun dinner.*

Riverside Cottage, Riverside Road, Lynmouth, **t** 752 390, *www.riversidecottage.co.uk* (*moderate*). Cheerful townhouse with six bedrooms. *Closed Dec–Jan.*

The Crown Hotel, Market Street, Lynton, **t** 752 253, *www.thecrown-lynton.co.uk* (*moderate*). Traditional old town hotel with 12 bedrooms and pleasant atmosphere. Snooker room, reading room, bar and restaurant. Friendly. Good food.

Southcliffe, Lee Road, Lynton, **t** 753 328, *www.southcliffe.co.uk* (*moderate*). Victorian-Gothic resort architecture, 5 minutes' walk from funicular. Clean and welcoming with home-cooked breakfasts and dinners.

Hunter's Inn, Heddons Mouth, Parracombe, **t** 763 230 (*cheap*). Large Victorian Swiss chalet at top of Heddon Valley, 15 minutes' drive from Lynton. Good place for a cup of tea, a pint, or hot and cold food.

Dulverton t (01398) –

The Lion Hotel, Bank Square **t** 323 444 (*moderate*). Traditional 19th-century coaching hotel with friendly bar and decent restaurant; 13 bedrooms.

Town Mills, High Street, **t** 323 124, *www.townmillsdulverton.co.uk* (*moderate*). Handsome creeper-clad Georgian house beside the old mill leat. Breakfasts brought to your room. Two bedrooms have log fires.

Highercombe Farm, 2–3 miles north of Dulverton, **t** 323 616, *www.highercombefarm.co.uk* (*moderate*). New farmhouse with large country-style bedrooms. Green views over 350 acres of working beef and sheep farm. *Open Mar–Oct.*

Lewis's Tea Rooms, 13 High Street, **t** 323 850 (*cheap*). Delightfully old-fashioned tea room with log fire and a table laden with cakes, jam and honey. Loose-leaf tea served by the pot. Light lunches include Welsh rarebit or ham and eggs.

Exford t (01643) –

The Exmoor Whitehorse Inn, Exford, **t** 831 229, *www.exmoor-hospitality-inns.co.uk* (*expensive*). Old-world 16th-century coaching inn beside the River Exe with 26 bedrooms. Traditional restaurant and good locals' bar.

The Crown Hotel, **t** 831 554, *www.crownhotelexmoor.com* (*expensive*). Attractive old coaching inn in the heart of Exmoor hunting countryside. Rifles, foxes' heads and tails adorn the walls of the bar, and the fire blazes away in winter. High-quality restaurant too.

Lynmouth is the only resort on the Exmoor coast. In 1812 Shelley brought his young bride here and noted that 'all shows of sky and earth, of sea and valley are here'. Many residents still remember the night of 15 August 1952, when a 24-hour rain storm dumped a freakish 9.1 inches of rain onto sodden moorland, sending 114,000 tons of mud cascading onto the town and killing 34 people. It's hard to imagine on a still day amid the award-winning geraniums.

There's a funicular railway up to **Lynton**, and good walks around **Watersmeet** and the headland north of Countisbury. The **Valley of Rocks**, west of Lynmouth Bay, was one of England's 18th-century picturesque landmarks. It's a full day's walk along it from Lynton to **Heddon Point**, or you can drive to Heddon Valley and walk down to the beach at Heddon's Mouth Cleave.

South Exmoor

From the neat little market town of **Dulverton** in the Barle Valley you can walk along a wooded valley or drive along the B3223 through open moorland to **Tarr Steps** – 17 drystone slabs resting on gritstone piers, known as a clapper bridge – across 180 feet of the River Barle. Further north on the River Exe is the stag-hunting village of **Exford** – the heart of Exmoor – the start of walks south into the beautiful Exe Cleave.

Devon

Devon can still appear to be the old country of *Westward Ho!*, *The Hound of the Baskervilles* and *Tarka the Otter*: the rugged cliffs and surfing beaches of the north coast, the 'Riviera' resorts and yachting marinas of the south coast and creamy countryside crisscrossed by winding lanes; Dartmoor a dark presence in the middle. All this is lovely, but in other respects rural Devon has kept up with the times: the massive 19th-century seaside development of Exmouth, Teignmouth and Torquay turned parts of the south coast into one long resort; it's only south of Tor Bay at Salcombe and Dartmouth that you get back to unspoiled scenery. Ilfracombe is the only resort on the north coast, while Barnstaple Bay is where everyone lives. Plymouth harbour takes you back to the Elizabethan age of exploration, when the great seafaring adventurers were Devon sea dogs such as Drake, Grenville, Frobisher (who searched in vain for the Northwest Passage), Hawkins (Sir John, slaver, spy and comptroller of the navy, and his son Sir Richard) and Gilbert (who took possession of Newfoundland, England's first colonial possession, in 1583) – the captains who defeated the Armada. But Plymouth still has the largest naval base in western Europe, and its modern city centre ushered in a brave new world of post-war inner city planning. The Dartington Project was radical too in its way. Devon is not so backward after all.

Exeter

Devon's cathedral city is separated from the coast by the Exe estuary. Its origins are Roman: it was the legionary fortress of II Augusta under Vespasian, becoming *Isca Dumnoniorum in* AD 75. Its defensive wall was one-and-a-half miles long, enclosing the Saxon and medieval towns; much of it survives, as does the old Roman street plan. Exeter prospered as the centre for Devon wool until the Napoleonic Wars destroyed European trade, when the city slipped into decline. Much of its architectural heritage was destroyed by Second World War air raids, and post-war reconstruction has left it stark. City planner Thomas Sharp thought that neo-Georgian brick buildings would 'best stand the test of time...being well-proportioned and honest'. Time is still testing.

Exeter has three centres of interest: the cathedral close; west of the High Street, including the museum; and Rougemont Castle and the Quay. The handsome timber-framed and Georgian buildings of the **cathedral close** are now smart shops, hotels

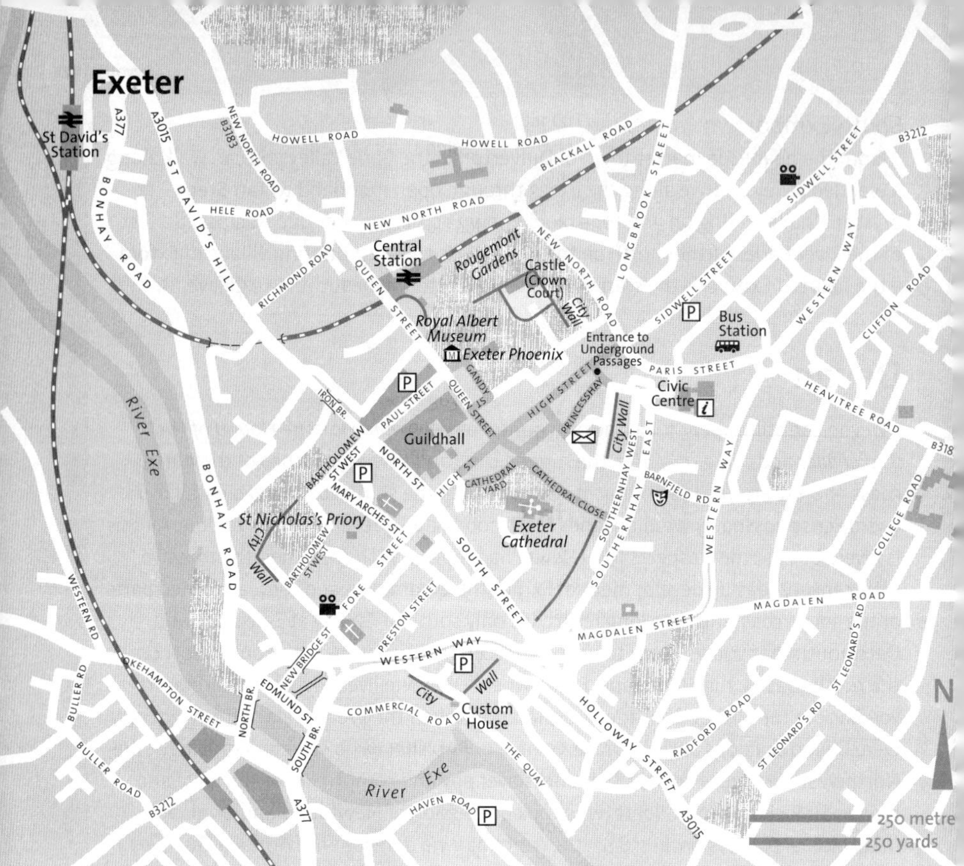

and restaurants. **Exeter Cathedral** is one of England's most distinctive, with its two Norman towers, and the elaborate west front decorated with a triple row of sculpted figures. The cathedral got a Gothic makeover in the 14th century: down the nave to the choir is the longest stretch of vaulting in the world (300 feet). Interesting features include the minstrels' gallery, where 12 carved figures play medieval instruments, and a 15th-century mechanical clock; the golden ball in the centre of the clock face is the earth, and the *fleur de Lys* represents the sun moving around it once every 24 hours. Beyond the carved stone screen is the choir, crammed with effigies of knights and tombs of bishops. The 60ft-high rocket-shaped medieval oak canopy over the bishop's throne is the tallest of its kind in Britain; the 19th-century choir stalls echo its shape.

On your way to the old part of town across the **High Street** you pass the **Guildhall**, dating back to 1330 and projecting a 16th-century pillared façade over the pavement (***t** (01392) 265 500 to arrange a visit*). If you get in, look at the Tudor oak panelling and collar-braced roof of the Great Hall.

The **Royal Albert Memorial Museum** (*open Mon–Sat 10–5; adm*) down Queen Street is a fabulous late-Victorian confection, with galleries devoted to geology, ethnology, local history, ceramics, glass – and stuffed animals (including a Tasmanian giraffe). It also houses mosaics from the Roman city and items from the last millennium including a painted wooden sculpture of St Peter trampling the devil, which once

Getting There and Around

By **car**, leave the M5 at junction 30, following signs to Exeter and Dawlish (A379).

Regular **trains** run from London Paddington to Exeter St David's, and on to Penzance.

There are eight National Express **coaches** a day from London Victoria.

Free **guided walks** start outside the Royal Clarence Hotel throughout the year, and seasonal port tours start outside Quay House.

Tourist Information

Exeter: The Civic Centre, Paris Street, **t** (01392) 265 700, *www.thisisexeter.com. Open 9–5 Mon–Sat, summer also Sun 10–4.* Also Quay House, **t** (01392) 265 213. *Open summer daily 10–5, winter weekends only 10–4.*

Exeter Arts Festival, t (01392) 265 205, *www.exeter.gov.uk/festival*, takes place over two weeks in July. The repertoire includes music and drama, with celebrity guests.

The **Northcott Theatre Company, t** (01392) 493 493, puts on a month of Shakespeare in Rougemont Gardens from July to Aug.

Where to Stay

Exeter t (01392) –

The Royal Clarence Hotel, Cathedral Yard, **t** 319 955, *www.regalhotels.co.uk* (*expensive*). Swish 56-bedroom city-centre hotel opposite the cathedral, whose classy restaurant and café-bar are a franchise of Michael Caine's (*see* below).

St Olaves Court Hotel, Mary Arches Street, **t** 217 736, *www.olaves.co.uk* (*expensive*). Medium-sized, family-run Georgian townhouse hotel with walled garden; decanters of sherry in the 15 bedrooms. High-class, intimate restaurant.

The White Hart Hotel, 66 South Street, **t** 279 897, *www.roomattheinn.info* (*moderate*). Traditional coaching inn with snug bar; modern 1970s extension at the back houses 40 of the 55 bedrooms.

Topsham t (01392) –

Reka Dom, 43 The Strand, **t** 873 385, *www.rekadom.co.uk* (*moderate*). White townhouse built around a gravel yard. Delightful home with old wisteria over the front door, rugs and pictures, and two sunny bedrooms. Tower with double bedroom, kitchen and panoramic views of the Exe.

The Galley, 41 Fore Street, **t** 876 078, *www.galleyrestaurant.co.uk* (*expensive*). Four bedrooms above restaurant with views over the Exe, and three cottagey rooms in old bakehouse cottage, five doors down. Breakfast of smoked salmon, bagels and fresh croissants.

Globe Hotel, Fore Street, **t** 873 471 (*moderate*). Comfortable place to stay. The cosy wood-panelled bar is fire-lit in winter.

Eating Out

Exeter

Michael Caine's at Royal Clarence Hotel, Cathedral Yard, **t** 310 031 (*expensive*). Stylish

stood on High Street. Behind the museum is the 1960s concrete library and revamped **Phoenix Arts Centre**, with a smart café-bar.

The scanty remains of the Norman castle are in **Rougemont Gardens**, around a grand Georgian mansion (now the crown court) built on the old motte. The **city walls** are well preserved; look at the impressive section with bastions on Southernhay. Off Fore Street an alley leads to the **Benedictine Priory of St Nicholas** (*t (01392) 265 858; open Easter–Oct Mon, Wed and Sat 3–4.30; adm minimal*). The church was demolished at the Dissolution and the rest sold to merchants who converted it into a lavish house.

SPACEX (*t (01392) 431 786, www.spacex.co.uk; open Tues–Sun 10–5; adm free*) on Preston Street near the Quay is one of the best contemporary art venues in the West Country.

setting for upmarket modern French cooking, including honeyed duck or calf's liver with sage. **Café-bar**, **t** 310 130, serves bistro-style food.

Well House, Cathedral Green (next door to the Royal Clarence), **t** 22 3611 (*moderate*). Good old country pub with black-stained planks, also owned by Michael Caine's. Range of West Country real ales including Cathedral Cask, Honey from the Well, Wellhouse Bitter and Well Water. Bar meals come from Michael Caine's kitchen. Popular dishes are Well House pie – a steak pie with Well House Ale gravy – and fish and chips made with real-ale batter.

Brazz, 10–12 Palace Gate (just off South Street), **t** 252 525 (*moderate*). Lively, modern place to eat, one of a small West Country chain. Hearty brasserie mix of fishcakes, steak and chips or Caesar salad, served by upbeat staff.

Thai Orchid, 5 Cathedral Yard, **t** 214 215 (*moderate*). Elegant, friendly Thai restaurant serving Tom Yum soup, green chicken curry and exotic fresh fruit salads with mangos and pineapples carved into flowers. *Closed Sat lunch and Sun.*

The Ganges, 156 Fore Street, **t** 272 630 (*cheap*). Good Indian restaurant, with a wide range of dishes for vegetarians.

Cathedral Refectory, 1 The Cloisters, **t** 432 735 (*cheap*). Good hot stews and pies, filled rolls and cakes. *Closed Sun.*

Boston Tea Party, 84 Queen Street, **t** 201 181 (*cheap*). Large tea room with the atmosphere of a community drop-in centre. *Closed Sun.*

The White Hart Hotel, 66 South Street, **t** 279 897 (*cheap*). Exeter professors plot in the dark corners of the White Hart bar. Serves Bass ale and bar meals.

Topsham

The Galley, 41 Fore Street, **t** 876 078 (*moderate*). Excellent small seafood restaurant with shellfish specialities from Brixham in marine-style décor. *Closed Sun and Mon.*

La Petite Mason, 35 Fore Street, **t** 873 660 (*moderate*). Small family-run restaurant with homely atmosphere behind old shop-front. Top-quality menu of English/French dishes such as lamb infused with rosemary and red wine, all home-made on the premises including petit-fours and bread. *Closed Sun and Mon, summer lunch only.*

The Bridge Inn, 4 Bridge Hill, **t** 873 862 (*cheap*). A 16th-century former maltings above the River Clyst, with a huge range of real ales and river views from the bar and garden. Ploughman's, pasties, sandwiches and soup.

Entertainment

Northcott Theatre, Stocker Road, **t** 493 493. Exeter's main theatre, on Exeter University campus, 2 miles out of town (regular buses from Exeter bus station). Challenging, serious drama. Bar serves food.

Phoenix Art Centre, Bradninch Place, **t** 667 080. Touring productions of drama, comedy, ballet and music. The **Phoenix Café-Bar** serves lunch and evening meals. *Open 10.30am–11.30pm.*

The old **port** of Exeter lies on a wide bend in the River Exe. With the 17th-century Customs House and handsome Victorian warehouses, it's a honeypot on sunny days, with antiques and craft shops, canoe and bike hire and towpath walks.

From Exeter Down the River Exe

You can see the Exe by train from Exeter to **Teignmouth** or **Dawlish** and back. The railway travels along the waterfront to the two faded old resorts. You can also get a train down the other side of the estuary, getting off at **Topsham**, a handsome old seafaring town. This was Exeter's port from Roman times on. In the late 13th century the Countess of Devonshire built a weir upriver of Topsham to cut off trade to Exeter; four centuries later Exeter built a canal parallel to the river to bypass it. Its colourful Dutch gabled houses along the strand reflect trading links with the Low Countries.

A la Ronde

Open Easter–Oct Sun–Thurs 11–5; adm.

This tiny 16-sided cottage on the outskirts of Exmouth is utterly eccentric. It was built in 1798 for the Parminter sisters, who had spent 10 years touring the Continent and wanted to display their souvenirs. The arrangement of the interior is right down the rabbit hole, with eight doors leading off a central octagon into tiny rooms, all painted shades of green and embellished with embroidery, paintings, and sea-shell friezes. The shell gallery in the galleried cupola at the top is decorated with shells, feathers, moss, broken pottery, bones and paintings.

The South Devon Coast: Sidmouth to Tor Bay

The scenery along the south coast of Devon is sunny. Red cliffs and blue-green sea give life to the resorts. The towns of **Tor Bay** – once called the 'English Riviera' without irony – are fused into one by bay-windowed Victorian terraces and fish and chip shops. This is the tourist hub of Devon: **Torquay**, **Paignton** and the bustling harbour

The South Devon Resorts

In 1760 it took four days on abysmal roads to travel 170 miles from London to Exeter, but only a day to get from London to Brighton – the popular seaside resort of the era. The South Devon coast took off in the 1780s, when the French Revolution shut down Europe, forcing the English upper classes out of their Continental resorts. Devon seemed more exclusive than the busy seaside towns of Kent and Sussex, and its resorts became the first in England to have a winter season. Fishing had previously been the main source of income at Teignmouth, Dawlish, Sidmouth and Exmouth. By 1800, however, scenery and climate were the money-spinners. In 1794 an Exeter newspaper called Teignmouth the 'Montpellier of England' and compared Tor Bay with 'the scenery on that part of the coast of the Mediterranean on which Monaco and other picturesque places are situated.' In spring 1806 the Princess of Wales paid an extended visit to the new resorts. **Sidmouth** was the first to get its own seawater baths. The South Devon resorts had all the traditional attractions – lending libraries, theatres, promenades and summer regattas – but they targeted a classier holiday crowd, who could afford the long journey. Once the Continent reopened, they fell into decline, but the invalid market saved them: the mild Devon air was publicized by the medical profession. By 1840, **Torquay** was the country's leading winter health resort, specializing in nervous and consumptive complaints. One leading contemporary medical authority described it as 'the southwestern asylum for diseased lungs' filled with 'people who looked like muzzled ghosts'. In the late 19th century the railway brought middle- and lower-class holiday-makers to join the upper-class convalescents. **Brixham**, **Dartmouth** and **Salcombe** retained an air of exclusivity, attracting walkers and sailing enthusiasts rather than all the sea bathers. Sidmouth stopped growing, preserving its Georgian and Regency character.

Getting There and Around

Regular **trains** from London Paddington go to Newton Abbot, where you can change for Torquay, and there are some direct trains to Torquay.

The **Brixham Belle Company, t** (01803) 528 555. Runs ferries from North Quay to Brixham, Paignton and Dartmouth Mar–Oct, evening cruises in high summer. Buy tickets on Torquay's North Quay.

Paignton and Dartmouth Steam Railway, t (01803) 555 872, travels 7 miles from Paignton Steam Station, just beside the mainline railway station, to Kingswear following the coast and the River Dart. From Kingswear, you can cross on the ferry to Dartmouth. Trains run all day, and you can get on and off wherever you like with your return ticket. *Easter–Oct.*

Tourist Information

Sidmouth: Ham Lane, **t** (01395) 516 441, *www.visitsidmouth.co.uk. Open winter Mon–Sat 10–1.30; spring Mon–Thurs 10–4, Fri–Sat 10–5, Sun 10–1; May–July Mon–Sat 10–5, Sun 10–4; Aug Mon–Sat 10-6, Sun 10–5, Sept–Oct Mon-Sat 10–5, Sun 10–4.*

Torquay: Vaughan Parade, **t** 0906 6801268. *Open Mon–Sat 9.30–5; high summer Mon–Sat 9–6, Sun 10–5.*

Brixham: Old Market House, Quayside, **t** (01803) 852 861. *Open winter Mon–Fri 9.30–5, summer 9.30–6.*

Brixham Heritage Festival is held at Whitsun, starting and ending with a display of fireworks on the quay. In between you can see maritime heritage displays, folk singers, storytelling, parades, all sorts of live music and Morris dancing.

A **Trawler Race** is held in mid June, in which local and visiting sailing trawlers race around the bay as crowds watch from the breakwater.

Where to Stay and Eat

Sidmouth t (01395) –

The Hotel Riviera, The Esplanade, **t** 515 201, *www.hotelriviera.co.uk* (*luxury*). Behind iron railings and potted palm trees, this is Sidmouth's most attractive seafront hotel, with traces of its former Georgian elegance; 27 bedrooms. Panoramic painting of the early days of the bay in the lounge.

The Belmont Hotel, The Esplanade, **t** 512 555, *www.belmont-hotel.co.uk* (*very expensive*). One of attractive group of red-brick Regency and Georgian buildings around cricket field, with period décor.

The Victoria Hotel, The Esplanade, **t** 512 651, *www.victoriahotel.co.uk* (*very expensive*). Sibling of the Belmont, its sunny lounge decorated with old prints of Sidmouth. Indoor and outdoor pool and putting green.

The Royal Glen Hotel, Glen Road, **t** 513 221, *www.royalglenhotel.co.uk* (*expensive*). Old-fashioned Regency hotel, 100 yards back from The Esplanade. Baby Queen Victoria spent her first Christmas here in 1819 with the Duke of Kent, who later died here. Leather armchairs and indoor pool.

Clock Tower Tea Room, Connaught Gardens, **t** 512 477 (*cheap*). An attractive mock castle and clock tower with walled garden. Serves tea, coffee, sandwiches, cakes and cream teas, as well as hot dishes such as lasagne.

Ottery St Mary t (01404) –

Normandy House Hotel, Paternoster Road, Ottery St Mary, **t** (01404) 811 088,

scene of **Brixham**. Agatha Christie was born in Torquay, and Miss Marple's adventures took place around here. South of Torquay, **Salcombe** and **Dartmouth** are small, pretty boating centres with unbeatable coastal walks.

Sidmouth and Ottery St Mary

The old-fashioned resort of **Sidmouth** lies scattered down a patchwork Devon valley, with its tea shops and floral displays. Along the seafront, the strip of cream hotels with wrought-iron balconies is elegant against red cliffs capped with woods. Look around the handsome Georgian streets and Fields, the local department store. Six *www.normandyhousehotel.co.uk* (*moderate*). Smallish Georgian townhouse beside St Mary's Church with five bedrooms. Elegant and comfortable. Good restaurant, lounge bar and patio beer garden.

Torquay t (01803) –

The tourist information centre can give you an extensive list of B&Bs.

The Imperial Hotel, Park Hill Road, **t** 294 301, *www.paramount-hotels.co.uk/imperial torquay* (*luxury*). Behind box-like 1950s sea-facing façade lurks the original 1864 Victorian grand hotel on the seafront, 5 minutes' walk from Torquay harbour; 155 bedrooms, two restaurants, two pools, tennis and squash courts and a hairdresser.

The Osborne Hotel, Hesketh Crescent, Meadfoot, **t** 213 311 (*very expensive*). Around the corner and over the hill from Torquay harbour, 10 minutes' walk into town. On the sea with perfect views. Two restaurants, brasserie and à la carte (*moderate*). Has style in a town otherwise lacking it.

The Balmoral Hotel, Meadfoot, Sea Road, **t** 293 381, *www.hotel-balmoral.co.uk* (*expensive*). Striking sky-blue hotel in beautiful location looking out to sea.

Number 7 Fish Bistro, 7 Beacon Terrace, **t** 295 055 (*moderate*). Smallish, family-run seafood bistro with simple, bright décor, and fresh fish and shellfish on the menu. *Open lunch all year Wed–Sat, dinner winter Tues–Sat, summer daily.*

Brixham t (01803) –

The Quayside Hotel, 41–9 King Street, **t** 855 751, *www.quaysidehotel.co.uk* (*expensive*). Friendly terracotta-painted hotel in six 18th-century fishermen's cottages,with 29 bedrooms and an excellent seafood restaurant. Lunches in the bar, evening meals in the restaurant.

The Blue Anchor, 83 Fore Street, **t** 859 373 (*cheap*). Old sail loft partly dating back to the early 16th century, just off the harbour. Now a cosy pub with log fires in winter and serving real ales, including Green King and Dartmoor Best. Bar meals. *Closed Sun eve in winter.*

Ziggy's Fish Bar, 3 The Strand, **t** 853 357 (*cheap*). Fish and chips on the quayside to eat in or take away.

The Poop Deck, 15 The Quay, **t** 858 681 (*cheap*). One of several long-established, cheerful restaurants around the quay. Informal, bistro-style. Specializes in locally caught seafood, including lobster, Dover and lemon sole, mullet and mussels.

Shores, 13/a the Quay, **t** 853 131 (*cheap*). Another cheerful, family restaurant with a large menu.

Entertainment

The Princess Theatre, Torbay Road, Seafront, **t** 0870 2414120. Large modern theatre (1,500 seats) hosting touring productions of West End musicals, glitzy opera, popular ballet and mainstream drama. Two or three weeks a year Torbay's local amateur groups TOPs (Torquay Operatics Society) and TOADs (Torbay Operatic and Amateur Dramatic Society) put on shows. Large bar and restaurant.

Babbacombe Theatre, Cary Point, Babbacombe Down, **t** 328 385. Small, old-fashioned variety theatre, 2 miles out of Torquay up the Babbacombe Road from the harbour. The summer show starts Feb and ends Oct, then the Christmas variety show begins.

miles inland along country lanes is the tiny old market town of **Ottery St Mary**, with more pretty Georgian buildings and a tight cluster of steep, narrow streets. Samuel Taylor Coleridge was born here and baptized in **St Mary's Church**, where his father was vicar. The church looks like a smaller version of Exeter cathedral; in fact the old parish church was rebuilt in 1337 by the Bishop of Exeter, who founded a collegiate church for 40 members, with links to the cathedral. After the Reformation it went back to being a parish church. Inside, you find all the detail of a cathedral squeezed into a church, complete with narrow fan-vaulted side aisle and mechanical clock.

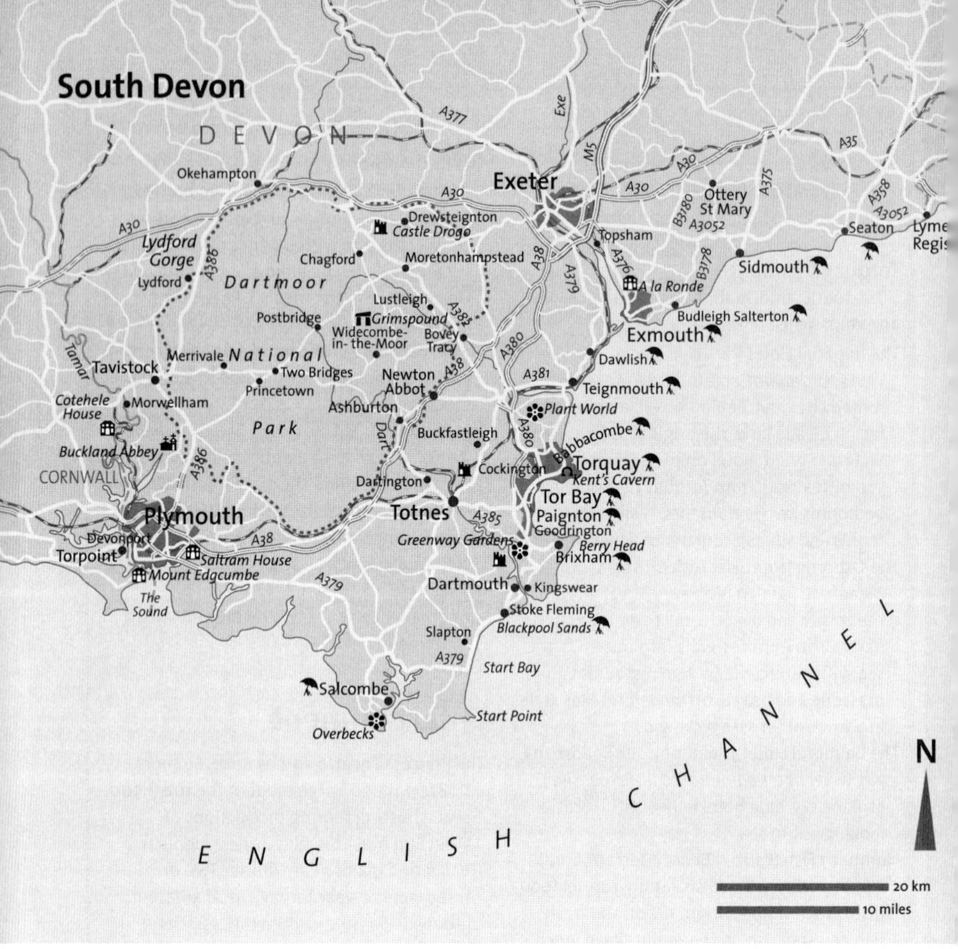

Tor Bay

The resorts of Torquay, Paignton and Brixham merge into one sprawl around the Riviera crescent of Tor Bay. It can just about muster charm on a sunny day. The seaside suburb of **Babbacombe** is popular with pensioners. **Babbacombe Model Village** (*open all year, June–Sept 9am–10pm, Oct–May 9–dusk; adm*) depicts, on a scale of one to 12, tableaux such as a county cricket match. The 31,000-year-old fossil of a human jaw, northwest Europe's oldest man, was found among the bones of long-extinct animals in **Kent's Cavern** (*open daily 10–4; adm*), between Babbacombe and Torquay.

Torquay

Drive along Ilsham Marine Drive into **Torquay harbour**. Here you can see how the English Riviera got its name, with gleaming white buildings poking out of wooded hillsides. The coast is rocky, the sea turquoise green and white surf splashes around rocky outcrops. There are some lovely coves, such as **Anstey's Cove**. The harbour, when you get there, is large and full of yachts, but shabby. Here the tourists look dispirited and the net curtains and twee lawns remind you that this is England. **Torquay**

Museum on Museum Road (*open Mon–Sat 10–5, summer also Sun 1–5; adm minimal*) has finds from Kent's Cavern, including the 31,000-year-old human jaw.

From **Tor Abbey Gallery and Museum** (*open daily Easter–Oct 9.30–5; adm*) down on the seafront the bay looks beautiful. The 12th-century Premonstratensian abbey was remodelled into a Georgian house in the 18th century. Its 20 rooms display furniture (1750–1900), 19th-century art (Blakes and Pre-Raphaelites), landscapes and seascapes including a painting of Torquay in 1780. There's also an Agatha Christie room, where the writer's typewriter, bookcases, desk, ornaments and manuscripts are displayed.

Around Torquay

On a hillside between Torquay and Newton Abbot is **Plant World** (***t*** *(01803) 872 939; open April–mid-Oct daily 9.30–5; adm minimal*). Its proprietor, Ray Brown, has been called the most important inventor of new plants, unleashing creations like the hardy geranium Purple Haze and a poppy named Muriel Brown after his mother. The hillside garden is designed as a giant map of the world and the five continents are planted with rare and exotic indigenous trees, shrubs and flowers.

Along the coast road towards Paignton, follow the signs down an unspoiled green valley to the thatched village of **Cockington** with its old granary and gamekeeper's cottage. Cockington Court, the manor house, is surrounded by acres of parkland. Edwin Lutyens built the ungainly thatched Drum Inn, part of a plan for a larger village that never happened, and regarded as one of his least successful projects.

There are 19 **beaches** and countless **coves** along the 22 miles of Tor Bay and its headlands. At Torquay you have Abbey Sands and pebbly Meadfoot. Paignton, Preston and Goodrington all have sandy beaches.

Brixham

Brixham is a working harbour and fish market – the third largest fishing port in the UK, with 140 fishing boats, including 40 big trawlers. The narrow, colourful houses up and down the hillside seem to cover every inch of it. You often see classic tall ships in

Brixham, William of Orange and the Glorious Revolution

In the winter of 1688 William of Orange invaded England, at the invitation of prominent English nobles unhappy with their autocratic Catholic king James II. William landed at Brixham with 500 boats, one of the largest fleets ever – four times bigger than the Spanish Armada – carrying 14,000 troops. At the head of the procession that marched to London were 200 English cavalry, 200 Africans from the Dutch colonies, 200 Laplanders, 300 Swiss, 500 volunteers drawn from Anglo-Scottish regiments and banners proclaiming the motto 'for the Protestant religion and liberties of England'. Then came the Dutch army. Dutch *stadtholder* William called himself 'William of Orange' – Orange being a tiny independent sovereignty in France – better to play the part of an independent Protestant sovereign prince at the head of an international liberation force coming to rescue England from a Catholic tyrant. It worked. He ascended the throne with his consort, Mary, as William and Mary.

the harbour, including a replica of Raleigh's *Golden Hind* (*open summer*), and you can hear the clinking masts of the yacht club. At the end of the harbour is a statue of William of Orange, commemorating his landing here on 5 November 1688. The quay-side is always crowded with artists painting the bustling scene, especially between 5 and 7.30pm when the fishing fleet returns. You can buy fresh fish from Perrett and Sons, as well as seafood sandwiches and tea. Various companies also offer fishing excursions and pleasure trips to Paignton and Dartmouth. There is an interesting **museum** (***t*** *(01803) 856 267; open Nov–Mar Mon–Sat 10–1; April–Oct Mon–Fri 10–5, Sat 10–1; adm minimal*) in the old (1904) police station, devoted to local maritime history, with displays on the two Napoleonic forts and Victorian cottage on Berry Head.

South of Tor Bay

South of Tor Bay all the way to the Lizard Peninsula, the coast of Devon and Cornwall has been carved out of faulted and folded Devonian rocks, its edges frayed by winding inlets. These wooded estuaries are the distinctive features of the south coast, providing deep-water harbours and the setting for celebrated semi-tropical gardens.

Dartmouth

It's hard not to gush about Dartmouth, especially if it's your first port of call. It has a wide, serpentine estuary with sandy coves, set against a backdrop of green hills dotted with white buildings; plenty of boating activity (yachts, car ferries, fishing trawlers and the occasional cruise liner); and turquoise sea water. The harbour views are stunning. Dartmouth has ancient riverside fortifications as well as the Royal Naval College, the country's principal training school for young naval officers – up to 500 23-year-olds at once. In term time you see them in town wearing jackets and ties. Upriver are pretty villages like Dittisham, and charming Totnes at the Dart's bridge.

You'll probably come down to the harbour along Victoria Road, experiencing a rush of pleasure as you first see it. In front of you is an oddity: the **Boat Float** marina is linked to the estuary by a water tunnel under the road. The Embankment is lined with Victorian buildings and peppered with kiosks advertising river trips. You are standing on reclaimed land here; a muddy tidal creek known as 'the pool' once ran behind the four colonnaded merchants' houses on Duke Street called the **Butterwalk**. The houses were built in the 17th century by a rich Newfoundland merchant; goods were unloaded directly into ships at high tide. In one of the four houses, **Dartmouth Museum** (*open Nov–Mar 12–3, April–Oct 11–5; adm minimal*) shows off plasterwork ceilings and oak panelling. The highlight of its exhibition is the boat models.

Behind the Embankment, narrow lanes and long flights of steps climb uphill past little shops. Walk south along the river to **Bayards Cove**, with its pretty quayside cottages along the river wall. The *Mayflower* and *Speedwell* stopped off here in August 1620 *en route* to Plymouth. **Bayards Cove Fort** was built in the early 1500s to guard the narrowest point of the estuary. Beyond it is an old Victorian paper mill, awaiting redevelopment.

Getting There and Around

If you are coming by **car** from Torquay you will have to finish the journey on the car ferry over the River Dart from Kingswear, or go inland via Totnes.

The nearest **railway** station is Totnes, which links up with mainline services from London Paddington and Bristol. Regular buses run from Totnes to Dartmouth. If you catch a train to Torquay you can continue by **steam train** and then the ferry over the Dart.

Tourist Information

Dartmouth: Newcomen Engine House, Mayor's Avenue, **t** (01803) 834 224. *Open all year Mon–Sat 9.30–5, Easter–Sept also Sun 10–4.*

The **Port of Dartmouth Regatta** takes place over three days including the last Friday in August, but there are activities all week including a fair, Red Arrows displays, market stalls along the Embankment and the Regatta Ball in Coronation Park.

The **music festival** takes place over three days in May, with a variety of music including rock, salsa, classical, flamenco and pop tribute bands. The main venues are pubs and gardens.

Where to Stay and Eat

Dartmouth t (01803) –

Long steep Victoria Road – the valley road into town – has plenty of B&Bs to offer. Or you could do worse than **The Ship in Dock Inn**, Ridge Hill, **t** 835 916 (*moderate*), on the corner of Coronation Park, about 50 yards from the centre, looking out over the River Dart. It is friendly, with a snug bar and five small rooms.

The Royal Castle Hotel, The Quay, **t** 833 033, *www.royalcastle.co.uk* (*very expensive*). An inn since the 17th century, the Royal Castle is much older than Victorian castle façade. Cosy flagstone bar and pleasant seafood restaurant upstairs overlooking the river; 25 designer bedrooms.

Barrington House, Mount Boone, **t** 835 545 (*expensive*). Large, white-painted house with cool, sunny rooms. Views over the harbour; 5 minutes' walk into town.

The Little Admiral Hotel, Victoria Road, **t** 832 572, *www.little-admiral.co.uk* (*expensive*). Comfortable townhouse hotel with stylish décor. Tapas restaurant, *open Thurs–Sat.*

The Carved Angel, 2 South Embankment, **t** 832 465 (*expensive*). Glass-fronted restaurant overlooking estuary. Classic French/English menu, including smoked ham hock and foie gras followed by rump of Devon lamb or fillet of turbot. *Closed Sun dinner, Mon lunch.*

Warfleet Lodge, Warfleet Road, **t** 834 352 (*moderate*). Victorian-Gothic house set above the road behind a battlemented wall. It used to belong to Sir Charles Freake, who moved in royal circles and once had Prince Edward VII to stay. Dark wood panelling, a grand staircase with gargoyles on the posts and a large stained-glass window on the landing. Three lovely big bedrooms and views over the river and woodland; 10 minutes' walk into town.

Café Caché, 24 Duke Street, **t** 833 804 (*moderate*). Zingy Mediterranean-style restaurant and café serving lunches and dinners of Thai crab cakes, smoked prawns and spicy baby squid and rice. B&B too (*moderate*). *Closed Sun in winter.*

The Carved Angel Café, 7 Fosse Street, **t** 834 842 (*cheap*). Small, welcoming café offering filled baguettes, omelettes and quiches at lunchtime, as well as more substantial hot meals and sweet desserts. *Open Mon–Sat lunch, Fri–Sat dinner; winter closed Mon.*

The Cherub Inn, Higher Street, **t** 832 571 (*cheap*). Beamy old free house, dating back to the 14th century, with tiny windows and little fire-lit rooms. Eat in the upstairs restaurant or in the bar from a menu including steak and Guinness pie, venison, and locally caught fish.

Dartmouth Arms, Bayards Cove, **t** 832 903 (*cheap*). Delightful old pub on the water's edge, backed up against great retaining wall; popular with young naval officers. Home-made pizzas.

Café Alf Resco, Lower Street, **t** 835 880 (*cheap*). Murals and burning torches enliven the patio of this ever-popular café. Big breakfasts, good coffee and grilled open sandwiches. *Open Wed–Sun 7–2.30, July–Sept 'rustic suppers' followed by live flamenco or jazz on Sat and Sun.*

In summer a ferry tos and fros to **Dartmouth Castle** (*open April–Sept 10–6, Oct 10–5, Nov–Mar 10–4; adm*), which guards the mouth of the estuary, facing 15th-century **Kingswear Castle** on the opposite headland. There are good walks in the woods.

You can see the **Royal Britannia Naval College** (*open Easter and summer holidays Mon–Fri for 2–2½-hour tours*), with its striped chimneys and clock tower, from all over town. It was built in 1899–1905 by Aston Webb (architect of Pall Mall) to resemble a ship. The main hall is the 'quarter deck' with the 'poop deck' gallery around it; outside the terrace is the 'bridge' with a flagstaff at the prow. That puts the parade ground in the sea, but never mind. Since 1863 every male heir to the throne has attended here.

Around Dartmouth

Some of the best coastal walks in England are around Dartmouth. From the castle there's a 5-mile walk along the cliff path to **Warren Point**. From **Kingswear**, across the river, it's a hilly 2 miles to **Coleton Fishacre Garden** (*t (01803) 664 500*) with its rare shrubs and trees, and **Berry Head**. The **Dart Valley Trail** links Totnes with Dartmouth on the west bank, and Greenway with Kingswear on the east bank. Totnes to Dartmouth is 12 miles; Dittisham–Greenway–Kingswear–Dartmouth 9 miles.

Greenway Gardens (*Churston Ferrers, Brixham,* **t** *(01803) 842 382; open Mar–Sept Wed–Sat 10.30–5; adm, discount if you arrive by any means other than car*) on the east side of the Dart, opposite Dittisham, was the birthplace of Sir Humphrey Gilbert (1539–83). Its 34-acre woodland gardens drop down to the Dart, where the old Boat House contains an unusual tidal bath, and a salon upstairs for tea. Agatha Christie used Greenway as a holiday home for 30 years. The excellent café serves cream teas and lunches supplied by local smokehouses, organic bakeries, farms and fishermen. At low water you can see the Anchor Rock where Sir Francis Drake smoked his pipe.

Totnes

At the highest point of navigation on the River Dart, Totnes started life as a busy port and market town. Now it is a perfect tourist town with a bohemian reputation. Visitors come by car, ferry, train and coach (15 a day in summer), or by foot along the Dart Valley Trail. Its handsome buildings now house alternative therapists, vegetarian cafés, unusual shops (one selling 'environmental' shoes), a renowned fishmonger's and cheese shop, some excellent bakeries and a guitar-making school. New Age and old age rub along very well together: young couples move here and join art co-ops, while the old folk of the Elizabethan Society dress up in tights and bonnets and sell knitted toilet roll covers in the (seasonal) Tuesday market. In this esoteric olde worlde atmosphere, the largest and most hi-tech catamaran in the world, the *Goss Challenge*, was built; it was destined for world domination in the round-the-world race, until it sank mid-Atlantic. Nearby Dartington Hall, renowned for its mid-20th-century social experiments, may have something to do with the atmosphere of Totnes. Two private schools were set up in the 1980s to maintain Dartington's alternative educational philosophies: the Sands School in Ashburton, where the pupils joint-manage the school and participate in decorating and repair work; and the Rudolf Steiner school.

Getting There and Around

By **car**, leave the M5 at Exeter and follow the A38 Plymouth road south to the A384, which leads into Totnes.

Direct **trains** run to Totnes from London Paddington.

The South Devon Railway Trust operates a seasonal **steam train** between Totnes and Buckfastleigh, which jogs 7½ miles along the River Dart, stopping once at the village of Staverton, where you can get off and have lunch in the **Sea Trout Inn**, **t** (01803) 762 274 and go off on lovely walks. **Buckfastleigh–Totnes Steam Train**, **t** 0845 3451420.

Riverlink, **t** (01803) 843 235, operates the River Dart ferries between Totnes and Dartmouth on the tides. A **Round Robin** ticket takes you to Dartmouth by ferry, but gives you an alternative route back, via the foot ferry to Kingswear, catching the steam train back from Kingswear to Paignton and returning to Totnes on an open-top double-decker bus, stopping off, if you want, at Agatha Christie's Greenway Gardens, opposite Dittisham on the north bank of the River Dart. You can buy a ticket and start the journey at any point.

Tourist Information

Totnes: The Town Mill, Coronation Road, **t** (01803) 863 168. *Open Mon–Sat 9.30–5.*

There is an old-fashioned **market** in the Civic Square on Fri and Sat, selling organic produce, and a **farmers' market** every fourth Sat in the Civic Hall. The tiny **Elizabethan market** takes place May–Sept on Tues in the Civic Square. Members of the Elizabethan Society in period costume sell home-made produce. Call Mrs Crang, **t** (01803) 863 714, for details.

Intriguing events in Totnes include the **August Orange Race** down the High Street, commemorating a visit by Francis Drake. The **October Raft Race** takes place on the first Sunday of the month: all comers race home-made craft down the 9-mile stretch of river between Buckfastleigh and Totnes, over rocks, weirs and shallows.

Ways With Words, a 10-day literature festival, takes place at Dartington Hall in mid-July, with 200 speakers – writers, actors, politicians and miscellaneous celebrities – and more than 100 events. Accommodation and meals available, or you can just drop in for a single event. Particularly strong on non fiction: themed days on science, psychology, philosophy and history run alongside the main programme. For information call **t** (01803) 867 373, *www.wayswithwords.co.uk*.

The **International Summer School and Music Festival**, lasting five weeks, follow on from the literature festival at Dartington. Information **t** (01803) 847 080, *www.dartingtonsummerschool.co.uk*, box office **t** (01803) 847 070, summer school enrolments **t** (01803) 847 077. There are three high-calibre professional concerts every evening (classical, jazz and rock); book well in advance.

The quayside is where you arrive by ferry from Dartmouth, but it's all happening on the High Street, which ascends from the river to the medieval town gate at the top, getting steeper and narrower on the way. Ticklemore Street, at the bottom, has two excellent fishmonger's, a local cheese shop and two little galleries.

Totnes Museum (*open April–Oct; adm minimal*) is housed in an Elizabethan merchant's house with historic rooms and an exhibition about Totnes man Charles Babbage, who invented the computer. Stone steps beside East Gate Arch lead up to the pillared 16th-century **Guildhall**. Beyond is 15th-century **St Mary's Church**, with its massive red sandstone bell tower and extra fourth aisle, added in the 19th century to cope with the growing congregation. Its highlight is the rood screen.

The High Street continues up to **Totnes Castle**, a perfect motte and bailey, topped with a 14th-century circular stone keep.

Where to Stay and Eat

Totnes t (01803) –

The Royal Seven Stars Hotel, The Plains, **t** 862 125, *www.smoothhound.co.uk/hotels/royal7* (*moderate*). Totnes' only hotel is an old 17th-century coaching inn. Its glassed-over flagstone yard serves as the reception area; 16 faded bedrooms, most en-suite, and a restaurant.

King William IV, High Street, **t** 866 689 (*moderate*). Handsome bow-fronted pub. Five clean, simple bedrooms.

The Old Forge, Seymour Place (Bridgetown side of Totnes), **t** 862 174, *www.oldforgetotnes.com* (*moderate*). Old stone building dating back to the 15th century with cobbled yard and 10 lovely bedrooms. Very friendly.

The Elbow Room, North Street, **t** 863 480, *elbowroomtotnes@aol.com* (*moderate*). Centuries-old barn conversion in cluster of townhouses at the foot of Totnes Castle with two attractive bedrooms and lovely first-floor lounge decorated with wooden elephants. Another friendly place.

Old Follaton, Plymouth Road (a mile out of Totnes), **t** 865 441, *www.oldfollaton.co.uk* (*moderate*). Unspoiled rural spot with box-hedged pathway leading up to front door and impressive staircase sweeping up to the bedrooms. Wonderful views out over the countryside through bay windows.

Ticklemore Fish Shop, 10 Ticklemore Street, **t** 867 805 (*cheap*). Seafood sandwiches, a pot of cockles, seafood cocktail or fresh peeled prawns. *Closed Sun.*

Willow Vegetarian Garden Restaurant, 87 High Street, **t** 862 605 (*cheap*). Vegetarian café with sunny garden and protest notice board plastered with anti-GM information and details of every sort of holistic happening, crop circle forum or opportunity for enlightenment in the Totnes region. Menu favourites include mushroom crumble, falafel and 'celestial pie'. Sometimes live sitar and tabla accompany Wed curry nights. Live folk or jazz every Fri. *Open Mon–Sat 10–5, Wed, Fri and Sat also dinner.*

Rumour Wine Bar, 30 High Street, **t** 864 682 (*cheap*). Happy, relaxed café-bar and restaurant with art on the walls. Range of bistro-style dishes, including fish, steaks, savoury pancakes, salad, pasta and stir-fried noodles. *Closed Sun lunch.*

Greys Tea Shop, High Street, **t** 866 369 (*cheap*). Traditional tea room at the top of town. Tea, coffee, cakes and light lunches including omelette, salads and sandwiches. *Closed Wed and Sun.*

Entertainment

Dartington Arts Centre, Dartington Hall, **t** 865 864, *www.dartingtonarts.co.uk.* Barn Theatre and Cinema (*screenings Tues–Sat*) and musical performances in the Great Hall.

Dartington Hall

Underlying the whole conception is the assumption that modern conditions have revolutionized life.

Christopher Hussey

At the heart of Dartington is romantic, grey stone Dartington Hall, built around a medieval courtyard and surrounded by landscaped gardens. Nowadays it is best-known as an arts college with a good music summer school. But the diversity of building styles – medieval, mock-Tudor, neo-Georgian and high modernist – indicates its unusual origins. The **Dartington Project** was one of the most radical Utopian experiments in 20th-century Britain. In 1925 the derelict, overgrown Dartington estate was bought by the inordinately rich Dorothy and Leonard Elmhurst, who spent the rest of their lives trying to create an integrated vision of modern Britain. Their big idea was that all aspects of modern life – the arts, industry, agriculture and education – could coexist in a rural environment. The Elmhursts planned to bring the cultural and industrial activities of the city into the countryside and make them compatible – at a time when rural life was in crisis and country house estates seemed anachronistic. They set up a new farm employing modern farming practices, and businesses including the largest building company in the southwest, a school (where Barbara Hepworth sent her children) with radical teaching methods (hardly any classroom work), and built a range of working-class and executive housing. As things turned out, its true radicalism was the association of industry with some of the biggest creative lights of the day on the international arts scene: American landscape architect Beatrix Ferrand, international modernist architect William Lescaze, Dutch choreographer Kurt Jooss, studio potters Bernard Leach and Marianne de Trey, and musician Imogen Holst were all involved. The experiment failed for many reasons, but Dartington carried on making headlines in the post-war period and greatly influenced the national debate on issues of modernity such as urban planning and the role of the arts.

Arriving from Totnes, you will pass the **Cider Press Centre** (*open Mon–Sat 9.30–5.30, Easter–Christmas also Sun 10.30–5.30*), one of the only enterprises to survive from the original Dartington Project. There are also 12 craft shops selling Dartington Crystal, cheese and kitchenware, and two restaurants. **Dartington Pottery** is part of the complex too. It has been on the site since Bernard Leach arrived in the 1930s and is where he wrote his famous *Potter's Book*. The pottery is still highly respected, based on the reputations of potters Janice Tchalenko, Steve Course and Roger Law.

Turn right at the church to Dartington Hall, following signs to **High Cross House** (*open June–Oct*). You can't miss it: although it's more than 70 years old it still looks modern with its long, rectangular blue-painted block, and living rooms, painted gleaming white, stacked against it. Built in 1932 by Lescaze for the headmaster of Dartington Hall School, it was acclaimed in the architectural press as cutting-edge domestic architecture and a showpiece of the international modernist movement. It now houses the Dartington Trust's archive and art collections, including work by Ben and Winifred Nicholson, Alfred Wallis, Christopher Wood, Bernard Leach, Shoji Hamada and Marianne de Trey. Just before it, the lane to the right leads to the once progressive **Foxhole School** (1931–2), built by Oswald Milne; note the neo-Georgian building where Bernard Leach once taught. **Dartington Hall** itself is at the top of the drive. Pevsner called it one of the best examples of domestic medieval architecture in England, with its glazed great hall around a wide courtyard, landscaped by Beatrix Ferrand. It has been heavily modernized inside, but the 25-acre gardens were laid out around the steep valley by Ferrand, with long views across fields, thatched Arts-and-Crafts-style huts, a tilting lawn and sculptures by Henry Moore. You can get a light lunch in the White Hart Bar. Before you leave, drive up Park Road, leading into **Warren Lane**, where you can see something of the clash of styles and visions going on at Dartington. Note the modernist house and dance studio built for Kurt Jooss next to a group of modernist workers cottages.

Getting Around

From the ferry steps on Fore Street you can take the **foot ferry** to East Portlemouth and explore the beaches on the east side of the estuary. Seasonal ferries run from Whitestrand Quay to South Sands and Kingsbridge.

There are **fishing trips** from the quay every day in summer (weather permitting).

Tourist Information

Salcombe: Market Street, **t** (01548) 843 927, *www.salcombeinformation.co.uk. Open summer daily 10–5, winter Mon–Sat 10.30–4.*

Where to Stay

Salcombe **t** (01548) –

The Marine Hotel, Cliff Road, **t** 844 444, *www.menzies-hotels.co.uk* (*very expensive*). Top-class Menzies hotel on the water's edge; huge 1960s lounge with big windows and grand piano; 53 bedrooms, pool and gym.

The Tides Reach Hotel, South Sands (20 minutes' walk into town, or regular ferry off the beach), **t** 843 466, *www.tidesreach.com* (*very expensive*). Restful 1930s hotel overlooking the beach; 35 bedrooms with coordinated colour schemes. Dinner, bed and breakfast deals.

Devon Tor Hotel, Devon Road, **t** 843 106, *www.salcombeinformation.co.uk* (*moderate*). Comfortable, clean and modest with six flowery bedrooms, four looking out to sea.

Ria View, near the Baptist church apartments, **t** 842 965 (*moderate*). Simple friendly B&B with great views over town.

Burgh Island **t** (01548) –

Burgh Island Hotel, Bigbury-on-Sea, **t** 810 514, *www.burghisland.com* (*luxury*). In the 1920s the smart set weekended in this glistening white Art Deco hotel on Burgh Island, just west of Plymouth. Noël Coward and friends danced the Charleston in evening dress under the peacock dome of the Palm Court. Other guests included Lord Mountbatten, Edward and Mrs Simpson and Agatha Christie, who wrote *Evil under the Sun* and *And Then There were None* on the island, which also provided the settings. At low tide it is joined to the mainland by a narrow strip of sand; at high tide, guests are ferried to and from the mainland by sea tractor; 21 rooms, including 14 suites.

Eating Out

Salcombe is popular and the pubs and restaurants get very busy, so book ahead.

The Galley Restaurant, **t** 842 828 (*moderate*). Excellent food. Ask for a window table. *Open April–Oct eves only.*

Restaurant 42, Fore Street, **t** 843 408 (*moderate*). Tasteful, oak-floored dining room and lounge with leather sofas, and sunny terrace with teak furniture and parasols. Modern English cooking includes local seafood; delicious West Country bouillabaisse. *Closed Sun eve and Mon.*

Dusters Bistro, 51 Fore Street, **t** 842 634 (*moderate*). A lively bistro. *Open April–Oct Thurs–Tues eves, weekends for breakfast; live jazz Sun.*

The Ferry Inn, Fore Street, **t** 844 000 (*moderate*). In a prime position by the ferry, this pub has stunning views. Ideal spot for outdoor eating . Good food includes local fresh fish and crab sandwiches.

Captain Morgan's, Whitestrand Car Park, off Fore Street, **t** 843 646 (*cheap*). Small café, very good breakfasts and chip-based lunches. Hot tea and comfort food on a wet day.

The Victoria Inn, Whitestrand car park, **t** 842 604. Snug traditional pub with pictures of yachts and Queen Victoria. Lunch and evening meals (*cheap*). **The Kings Arms**, opposite, also has good food.

Fortescue Inn, Union Street, **t** 842 868. Good traditional pub near the water. Very popular, so it can get crowded. Good food (*cheap*).

Catch 55, 55 Fore Street, **t** 842 646 (*cheap*). Seasonal bistro serving fillet steak, mussels and scallops, burgers and pasta. *Open Easter–Oct eves, July–Aug also lunch.*

South to Salcombe

The road from Dartmouth to Salcombe follows the coast to **Slapton Sands**, a 3-mile beach in Start Bay. The sands were used for battle training for the Normandy landings. There is a memorial at Torcross village to 749 soldiers killed in the sinking of two American landing ships by German U-boats travelling to the sands from Portland harbour. The Ley is a nature reserve, where migrating birds rest in spring and autumn. Public footpaths include a short nature trail between Slapton Bridge and Deer Bridge, and guided walks in summer from the **Field Study Centre** (***t*** *(01548) 580 466*). It's also an excellent swimming beach, although **Blackpool Sands** (between Stoke Fleming and Strete on the A379 from Dartmouth) is better equipped, with showers and a café.

Salcombe is a condensed version of Dartmouth, a couple of lanes at the water's edge then a steep climb up to the village. Fore Street has shops selling expensive yachting clothes, a yacht club and boat hire. There are lots of pleasant walks round about, and almost as many books about them; the National Trust leaflet 'Walks around the Salcombe Estuary' is the best. It includes the **Snape walk**, an easy 2 miles around Batson Creek and down into the Kingsbridge Estuary. The **Bolt Head coastal walk** is a dramatic one; head for Overbecks and Sharp Tor.

Overbeck's Museum and Garden (*museum open April–Sept Sun–Fri 11–5.30, Aug also Sat, Oct Sun–Thurs 11–5; gardens daily*) on the headland just south of Salcombe is part youth hostel, part Mediterranean garden, and part museum of curiosities. The museum (1913) houses the collections of Otto Christoph Joseph Gerhardt Ludwig Overbeck, the madcap research chemist who bought it in 1928. The garden was laid out in terraces in 1901 by Eric Hopkins (who also built the house) and since then has been planted up with semi-tropical plants, including more than 200 hairy palms.

Plymouth

The rivers Tamar and Plym flow off Dartmoor into the wide bay of Plymouth Sound. Between them is Plymouth, a sprawling modern city with a **naval base** called HMS Drake, and grisly outskirts. At the heart of town is the **Barbican**, the ancient harbour of the Elizabethan golden age of maritime exploration and privateering by Drake, Raleigh, Frobisher, Gilbert and the Hawkins. It was the launch pad for England's most celebrated voyages of exploration: Sir Francis Drake's circumnavigation of the globe in 1577; the Australasian expeditions of Captain James Cook; Darwin's scientific survey of the southern hemisphere in the *Beagle* in 1831; and the Antarctic expeditions of Captain Scott. It was also the final stop for the Pilgrim Fathers in 1620, before making history in America (there are 43 new Plymouths in the world). Drake (1540–96) stands above them all in Plymouth's affections, the captain of the fleet who famously finished off his game of bowls before finishing off the Spanish Armada in 1588. The precise location of the audacious game is thought to be under the **Citadel**, built in the reign of Charles II during a fresh round of wars with a new enemy, the Dutch.

Getting There and Around

By Car

Take the M5 to Exeter, then follow the A38 round the south of Dartmoor to Plymouth.

By Train

There are direct trains from London Paddington to Plymouth, and on to Penzance.

The **Tamar Valley Line, t** (01752) 221 300, a 14-mile scenic branch line on the east bank of the River Tamar, passes the dockyard and Brunel's bridge, then crosses the Tamar on the Calstock viaduct into Cornwall to the old mining village of Gunnislake. You can combine a short section with a walk (*www.carfreedaysout.com*). Calstock is a good place to break the journey; you can walk a mile uphill to Cotehele House through woods from the station.

The **Devon Rail Rover** ticket is a 3- or 8-day ticket offering free rail access to the whole of Devon, including the Tamar Valley line; available from staffed stations.

There is also a **Cornish Rail Rover** and **Freedom of the Southwest** ticket, offering unlimited travel around the region. For credit-card booking call **t** 0870 900 2323 or go to *www.wessextrains.co.uk*.

By Boat

Passenger ferries to Spain and France depart from Millbay Docks on Grand Parade.

Tamar Cruising and **Plymouth Boat Cruises** run cruises from the Barbican. Ask for information at the dockside booths. The one-hour **harbour cruise** takes you round the outside of the Royal Navy dockyard. The **River Tamar cruise** takes 4 hours and stops at Calstock, where you can get off if the tide is right.

From Stonehouse you can get the **Cremyll foot ferry** to Mount Edgcumbe House (*see* p.346). It is a good walk along the coastal path to the pretty villages of Kingsand and Cawsand, from where you can catch a (seasonal) ferry back to Plymouth.

A **roll-on-roll-off chain ferry** goes back and forth day and night over the River Tamar between Devonport and Torpoint, from where you can continue to Antony House.

Tourist Information

Plymouth: Island House, 9 The Barbican, **t** (01752) 304 849. *Open summer Mon–Sat 9–5, Sun 10–4, winter Mon–Fri 9–5, Sat 10–4.*

A **Fireworks Festival** takes place over two days at the beginning of August, best viewed from the Hoe, which is also the venue for festivals and shows throughout the year, including vintage car shows and concerts.

On alternate years (2004, 2006) the **Royal Dockyard** (signposted off the A38) opens its doors to the public on August Bank Holiday.

Where to Stay

Plymouth t (01752) –

The Grand Hotel, Elliot Street, The Hoe, **t** 661 195, *www.plymouthgrand.com* (*expensive*). Grand Victorian hotel in prime position on the Hoe, with 70 bedrooms, many with balconies and sea views. **Promenade Restaurant** and bar.

The Duke of Cornwall Hotel, Millbay Road, **t** 275 850, *www.thedukeofcornwallhotel.com* (*expensive*). Magnificent Victorian-Gothic

Around Town

Armada Way forms the axis of the modern city centre, running from the railway station in the north to the war memorial in the south. It is wide and pedestrianized, lined with fountains and chestnut trees, and flanked by bright, smooth Portland-stone-clad buildings, which contrast with the dark, rough stone buildings of the Barbican. The intersecting grid of streets creates zoned sections, all according to the plan: the **commercial zone** north of Royal Parade; the **civic zone** (the guildhall, law courts and civic centre) between the parade and Notte Street; and the **hotel zone** at the southern end, nearest the Hoe.

hotel west of the Hoe; 72 'individually styled' bedrooms, good restaurant on ground floor.

Bowling Green Hotel, 9–10 Osborne Place, Lockyer Street, The Hoe, **t** 209 090, *www.bowlingreenhotel.com* (*moderate*). Lovely place to stay overlooking the Hoe; 12 pleasant bedrooms, friendly atmosphere.

Invicta Hotel, 11–12 Osborne Place, Lockyer Street, The Hoe, **t** 664 997, *www.invicta hotel.co.uk* (*moderate*). Attractive family-run hotel with period-style décor. Oblique views of the Hoe from the front rooms. Very clean and friendly.

Mayflower Guest House, 209 Citadel Road East, The Hoe, **t** 667 496, *www.mayflower guesthouse.co.uk* (*cheap*). Friendly, basic place to stay with small bedrooms, two minutes' walk from the Hoe.

Caradus Guest House, 25 Athenaeum Street, The Hoe, **t** 664 635 (*cheap*). Another friendly, basic place to stay, with faded period-style décor. No en-suite rooms.

Eating Out

Piermasters, Southside Street, The Barbican, **t** 229 345 (*moderate*). Popular rustic-style seafood restaurant on two floors of tall Victorian townhouse. Paella or moules marinières for lunch, scallops or oysters followed by roast monkfish or poached fillets of lemon sole for dinner. *Closed Sun*.

Bites, Quay Road, **t** 254 254 (*cheap*). Popular sandwich bar. *Closed Sun*.

The Minerva, Looe Street (*cheap*). Cosy old-fashioned locals' pub near Plymouth Arts Centre, decorated with old photos and fishing paraphernalia.

Jaipur Palace, 146 Vauxhall Street, The Barbican, **t** 668 711 (*cheap*). Good Indian. *Closed Sun lunch*.

The Baba Indian Restaurant, 134 Vauxhall Street, The Barbican, **t** 256 488 (*cheap*). Tandoori, Balti and curry dishes, including some seafood and vegetarian. *Open eves only, Sun also lunchtime buffet*.

Cap'n Jaspers, Whitehouse Pier, The Barbican, **t** 262 444 (*cheap*). Small kiosk with outside seating for tea with fried egg and bacon roll. *Open 7.30am–11.45pm*.

Entertainment

Depending how rough and tough you are, it is probably best to avoid the night clubs and drinking holes of Union Street on Friday and Saturday nights, when it gets pretty rowdy.

The Theatre Royal, Royal Parade, **t** 267 222. The largest theatre in the southwest. Hosts a popular repertoire of large-scale musicals, drama, ballet and opera (mainly touring productions).

The Barbican Theatre, The Barbican, **t** 267 131, *www.barbicantheatre.co.uk*. Old 18th-century seamen's club which hosts small-scale touring productions including dance, drama and comedys. Theatre bar puts on comedy, cabaret and live music on Fri and Sat eves, sometimes midweek too.

Plymouth Arts Centre, 38 Looe Street, **t** 206 114. Arthouse cinema with screenings daily at 6pm and 8pm. Good vegetarian restaurant, **t** 202 614 (*cheap*), which serves quiche, salad, soups and the like. *Closed Mon eve and Sun*.

Royal Parade was the first street of new Plymouth to be built and gives you a sense of the elegance and modernity of the 1950s town, especially the eastern end between Thomas Tait's **Dingles Department Store** on one corner of Armada Way ('proud to have been the first store to be built in Britain after the war and the first ever modern store to be built in the West Country') and the old **National Provincial Bank** (now the National Westminster) designed by B.C. Sherren, the bank's own architect. Post-war planner Abercrombie (*see* p.344) stipulated a style of architecture that would 'recapture the wonderful continuity of the street scene obtained by Nash and Wood the Younger but in the modern idiom'. These buildings have been called 'the grandest ensemble of early fifties buildings in the country'.

The Plan for Plymouth

The commercial heart of Plymouth was blitzed by Second World War German air raids as devastating as those on Coventry and London. The post-war plan for its reconstruction was one of most influential planning documents of its day. It was put together by Abercrombie and Watson with complete disregard for the old street plan and architectural styles. The radical Plan for Plymouth recommended that 'a design in outline for the whole architectural treatment in the reconstruction should be prepared' to achieve uniformity of style. The chief architects were William Crabtree, who had been taught by Abercrombie at Liverpool University, and Thomas Tait, famous for designing buildings that resembled sculptural blocks set against tapering towers. The result is one of the most complete statements of the ideals and priorities of the 1950s city in Britain. The plan was all about an integrated zoned city and encouraged rather than threatened the preservation of the Barbican as the 'historic precinct', the yachting facilities around the Sound and the recreational Hoe.

Armada Way rises gently to **Plymouth Hoe** ('hoe' meaning high place), an open headland with fabulous views over the Sound. It's a superb climax to the boulevard. In the mid-19th century a **bandstand**, **Promenade** and **statue of Drake** were built here. A lower promenade and art deco-style outdoor pool (now derelict) were added in the 1920s and 1930s. The Hoe has retained its Victorian seaside atmosphere. **Smeaton's Tower** was relocated to the Hoe when Eddystone reef began to disintegrate. You can see Drake's Island, a mile or so out to sea, and beyond it the mile-long breakwater built of Dartmoor granite between 1812 and 1841. On a clear day you can even see the Eddystone Lighthouse, 14 miles out to sea. **Plymouth Dome**, built in the mid-1980s, tells the story of Plymouth and its heroes.

There is a railway bridge by Brunel over the River Tamar at Saltash. The **Royal Albert Bridge** has two spans of 139 meters and a central pier. It opened in 1859, the year of Brunel's death. You'll get your best view of it as you cross it on the train going south.

Barbican

From the Hoe, walk around the headland on Madeira Road, beneath the sheer walls of the Citadel. **Sutton Harbour** is the site of the original town. In the 14th century it was guarded by a small fort or barbican, which gave its name to the waterside area from Hoe Street to Lambay Hill. This is the heart of Plymouth today: big old quayside warehouses and townhouses converted into bars and cafés look out across the cobbles at the wooden pontoons and battered old fishing boats in the harbour, and the fresh air is tinged with the reek of sludge on the harbour bottom. On **West Pier**, you can see the worn stone steps down which the Pilgrim Fathers embarked on their voyage to America in 1620. Their names are inscribed on the wall of **Island House**, where they stayed, and the **Mayflower Stone** set in the harbour wall commemorates them. Other plaques commemorate Sir Humphrey Gilbert's voyage to Newfoundland in 1583, where he established England's first colony in the name of Queen Elizabeth I, and Cornish emigrants shipped out to Australia in the 19th century.

On the old industrial side of the harbour is the modern fish market (1995) and the £15-million new **National Aquarium** (***t** (01752) 220 084, www.nationalaquarium.co.uk; open daily April–Oct 9–6, Nov–Mar 9–5; adm exp*), with displays on the local marine habitat as well as exotic fish. Beyond is the high-tone Great Western yacht club. Behind the Barbican, walk down **New Street**, one of the oldest in Plymouth, with its granite cobbles and tall 16th-century townhouses, built for sea captains and merchants who needed to be close to the quays. You can look inside the atmospheric **Elizabethan House** (*open daily 10–5; adm minimal*). The Jacobean **Merchant's House** on St Andrews Street, a short walk from the Barbican down Notte Street, was once owned by William Parker, a privateer like Drake, who became mayor of Plymouth. You can join a guided tour around the **Citadel** (*ask at the Tourist Information centre*), built in 1666, visiting the ramparts, chapel and parade ground.

Galleries and Museums

At the top of town, the **City Museum and Art Gallery** (***t** (01752) 304 774; open Tues–Fri 10–5.30, Sat 10–5; adm free*) has an interesting exhibition on the history of porcelain. The discovery of China clay – the secret ingredient of fine porcelain, which eluded Europeans for a thousand years – and the opening of a factory on Coxside (on the other side of the harbour) in 1768 led to the explosion of inexpensive blue and white 'china' in Britain. Another room is decked out in period style with a collection of prints, books, furniture and several Reynolds paintings.

There are a surprising number of small **commercial galleries** around the Barbican area. Beryl Cook was from Plymouth. You will find her paintings of fat-legged, raucous women in one or two galleries on Southside Street. On the same street is a mural, ***Last Judgement*** (1985), by the late Robert Lenkiewicz, best known for working with vagrants, one of whom he kept perfectly preserved in a drawer after he died; you can sometimes see his paintings – life-sized portraits – in his studio at the north end of the Barbican.

Plymouth Arts Centre is a lively Plymouth institution, tucked away near the harbour in the old part of town. Go past the old Customs House and through the arch at the top of Buckwell Street (beside the Breton Arms) on Looe Street. Its three small galleries exhibit contemporary art and craft, and first brought fame to Cook in 1975.

Around Plymouth

The Sound is enclosed by the green hills of Mount Edgcumbe on one side, and Statton Heights on the other. In every direction is a string of beautiful old mansions.

Antony House

***t** (01752) 812 191, www.nationaltrust.org.uk; open April–Oct Tues–Thurs 1.30–5.30, June–Aug also Sun; adm.*

You can easily reach Antony House on Torpoint by car ferry from Devonport. Since the late 15th century this has been the Carew family home. The current house, a pale grey Georgian mansion with low wings of red brick, was built between 1711 and 1721. Humphrey Repton laid out the lawns, which sweep down to the estuary of the River

Lynher where it joins the Tamar, and hundreds of acres of woodland. Richard Carew was born in Antony House in 1555 and became member of parliament for Saltash, treasurer to Sir Walter Raleigh and High Sheriff of Cornwall, among other things. He is best known for his *Survey of Cornwall* (1602) which, though historically unreliable, is full of funny stories about the Elizabethan gentry.

Mount Edgcumbe House

***t** (01752) 822 236; house open April–Sept 11–4.30; adm; park and formal gardens all year dawn–dusk.*

To reach Mount Edgcumbe, take the Torpoint car ferry over the Tamar from Devonport or the Cremyll foot ferry from Admiral's Hard in Stonehouse. Richard Edgcumbe moved his main family seat from Cotehele House to the mouth of the estuary in 1553. His new house was supposed to have been so beautiful that the Spanish Duke of Medina Sidonia, who led the Spanish Armada in 1588, wanted to live there after the conquest. The Spaniard didn't get it, but it was destroyed by an incendiary bomb in the Second World War. Completely rebuilt in the 1950s, Mount Edgcumbe House looks like a Tudor mansion, but is not; many pieces of old furniture and paintings survived, however, and are on display. The real attraction is the country park, from which you can follow the Southwest Coastal Path to the old smuggling villages of Kingsand and Cawsand at the end of the Rame peninsula.

Saltram House

Open Easter–Oct Sun–Thurs; house 12.30–6; kitchen, garden and gallery 11–6.

Saltram House is to the east of Plymouth (and just south of the A38) on the edge of the tidal estuary of the Plym. This large mid-18th century mansion was partly built by Robert Adam for John and Lady Catherine Parker around the remains of a group of Tudor and Stuart buildings. The rooms display all the original contents, including carved gilt-wood furniture by Chippendale, a dozen portraits by Reynolds (who was born in Plympton St Maurice and often visited the house), Axminster carpets and Chinese wallpapers. The Victorian garden was laid out by the 3rd Earl, with exotic ornamental trees. The deer park was landscaped in the 18th century with vistas and follies. You can walk down the valley to Blaxton Quay, along the estuary to Saltram Point and back across the park.

The Tamar Valley Line to Cotehele House

***t** (01579) 351 346; open April–Oct.*

The Tamar was the border between Saxon Devon and Celtic Cornwall delineated by Athelstan in 926. From Plymouth station – at the north end of Armada Way – grab a window seat on the Tamar Valley Line, a 14-mile branch line along the Tamar to Gunninslake. The magnificent 1,300-acre Cotehele estate is a mile-and-a-half's walk through Cotehele Wood from the station at Calstock, a charming 19th-century port with one or two pubs, a fish and chip shop and a café-bar. Otherwise you can catch the ferry from the quay, where tin, copper and arsenic were transported by boat to the rest of the world. Cotehele House is the most perfectly preserved Tudor house in Cornwall, abandoned in 1553 by the Edgcumbe family, who left it to the care of widows and elderly relatives. If you are arriving by car, Cotehele is 15 minutes up the A388 and lanes from the Tamar Bridge.

Crownhill Fort

Crownhill Fort was the main link in the chain of Palmerston's defences of Plymouth, overlooking the Plym and Tamar valleys as well as the main road to Tavistock. It is also the only one left intact and open to the public. Architecturally it is one of Plymouth's most important buildings, a stunning piece of Victorian military engineering.

Dartmoor

A long, low moan, indescribably sad, swept over the moor. It filled the whole air, and yet it was impossible to say whence it came...

The Hound of the Baskervilles, Sir Arthur Conan Doyle

Anyone who's ever read *The Hound of the Baskervilles* will be afraid of Dartmoor, especially the notorious valley bogs, such as Grimpen Mire, into which stray walkers and ponies may sink. Dartmoor is the largest granite moorland of the south, with the highest peak of the southern uplands, High Willhays (2,037ft).

Orientation

The high moor is carved into three sections – north, south and east – by the main moorland roads. The B3357 runs east–west across the moor between Tavistock and Dartmeet, where it unravels into a tangle of lanes. The B3212 runs from Moretonhampstead in the northeast to Yelverton in the southwest. Where the two roads cross, at Princetown, is the heart of the moor – marked by an infamous prison. The high moor is so bleak that most tourists head for the honeypots near the roads: Becka Falls (a commercialized nightmare); the reservoirs (particularly Burrator); Bovey Tracey's Guild of Craftsmen; Lydford Gorge; the clapper bridge at Postbridge; and Haytor. But you can only really get to know Dartmoor if you venture out on foot.

Walking

The open moor is treacherous so most walks follow landmarks – tors, stone monuments, industrial ruins, river valleys and man-made watercourses called leats. Parts of the moor are army firing ranges; red flags on prominent hill tops indicate when the ranges are in use. For longer walks, you need an OS map (the yellow-covered 1:25,000 is the best), compass (serious walkers favour the Silva), a basic idea of orientation, wet- and cold-weather clothes, and proper walking shoes or boots. The Dartmoor mist can descend fast, deadening sound, and, in winter, roads and trails are often obliterated by snow. But there are good walks even for the casual wanderer.

Getting There and Around

By Car

The fast A38 Plymouth–Exeter road skirts the southern and eastern edges of the moor, with views of the big hills and turn-offs to moorland villages. The western peripheral road (A386) between Plymouth and Okehampton is virtually a moorland road, and particularly atmospheric between Tavistock and Okehampton. But the trans-moor roads are the best: the B3357 and B3212, which cross at Two Bridges.

By Train

The South Devon Railway Trust operates a seasonal steam train between Totnes and Buckfastleigh, which jogs 7½ miles along the River Dart and stops once at the village of Staverton, where you can get off and have lunch in the Sea Trout Inn, **t** (01803) 762 274, and go on walks. For details call **t** 0845 345 1420

By Bus

Sunday, when there are regular bus services, is the best day to get around the moor by bus. The no. 82 **Transmoor Link** crisscrosses the moors between Plymouth and Exeter, stopping at all the beauty spots including Moretonhampstead, Postbridge and Princetown. Buy your ticket on the bus and hop on and off as you choose. *Operates summer daily, winter weekends only*. For information call **First Devon, t** (01752) 402 060 or **Traveline, t** 0870 608 2608.

The **Dartmoor Sunday Rover** ticket is excellent value. It includes a network of 19 buses and the Plymouth–Gunnislake branch railway, though services are much reduced in winter. You can get a bus to the moor, then walk to another bus stop to catch a bus home. Call **Traveline, t** 0870 608 2608, for full details.

On Foot

The **Abbots' Way** runs from Buckfastleigh to Tavistock through southern Dartmoor via Princetown, Nuns Cross Farm and Merrivale. The **Two Moors Way** stretches 100 miles from Ivybridge on Dartmoor to Lynmouth on Exmoor cutting right across both moors.

There are several other long-distance walking trails, including the **West Devon Way**, **Two Castles Trail** and **Dartmoor Way**.

In summer the Dartmoor National Park Authority runs two or three **guided walks** daily. For details and times contact the National Park information points or go to *www.dartmoor-npa.gov.uk*.

Tourist Information

The High Moorland Visitor Centre: Tavistock Road, Princetown, **t** (01822) 890 414. *Open summer 10–5, winter 10–4.*

Postbridge: on B3212, **t** (01822) 880 272. *Open Easter–Oct 10–5.*

Haytor: at lower car park on main road, **t** (02364) 661 520. *Open Easter–Oct 10-5.*

Okehampton: Museum Courtyard, 3 West Street, **t** (01837) 53020, *www.okehamptondevon.co.uk* and *www.discoverdartmoor.com*. *Open Nov–Easter Mon, Fri and Sat 10–4.30; April–July Mon–Sat 10–4.30; Aug daily 10–5; Sept–October Mon–Sat 10-4.30.*

Tavistock: Town Hall, Bedford Square, **t** (01822) 612 938. *Open summer Mon–Sat 9.30–5, high summer daily 9.30–5, winter Mon, Tues, Fri and Sat 10–4.*

Moretonhampstead: 11 The Square, **t** (01647) 440 043.

Ashburton: Town Hall, **t** (01364) 652 142. *Open Mon–Sat only.*

The **Ministry of Defence ranges** at Okehampton, Merrivale and Willsworthy Ranges, in the northwest of Dartmoor, are often closed to walkers for live firing. Call **t** 0800 458 4868 or go to *www.dartmoor-ranges.co.uk* to find out if the ranges are safe. The boundaries are clearly marked on Ordnance Survey maps and on the ground with red and white posts and warning notices. Red flags are hoisted at the boundary in the day and red lamps at night.

Tavistock historic charter market takes place on Fri in the purpose-built Victorian Pannier Market, with a mix of food, clothing and Women's Institute stalls. You will usually find stalls selling bric-a-brac and craftwork on Tues, Wed, Thurs and Sat.

Spirit of Adventure, Powder Mills, Postbridge, **t** (01822) 880 277, *www.spirit-of-adventure.com*. Organizes climbing, abseiling, cycling, orienteering and kayaking activities for groups and individuals. Book in advance.

Where to Stay and Eat

East Dartmoor

The Edgemoor Country House, Haytor Road, Lowerdown Cross, Bovey Tracy, **t** (01626) 832 466, *www.edgemoor.co.uk* (*expensive*). Less than a mile out of Bovey Tracy on the Widecombe road, this attractive creeper-clad former 19th-century school caters for well-heeled tourists who like their comforts; 14 rooms and excellent restaurant.

The Cleave Inn, Lustleigh, **t** (01647) 277 223. Pleasant village pub dating back to the 15th century, offering good quality food (*moderate*).

Brookside, Lustleigh, **t** (01647) 277 310, *www.brooksidedartmoor.co.uk* (*moderate*). Charming house in staggering distance from pub.

Hele Farm, North Bovey, **t** (01647) 440 249 (*moderate*). A 17th-century farmhouse with garden room, sitting room, open fire, fresh flowers, pretty garden with own stretch of River Bovey, tennis court, 128 acres of farmland and a golden retriever.

Chagford t (01647) –

Gidleigh Park Hotel, **t** 432 367 (*luxury*). Gabled, 1929 mock-Tudor house, 2 miles out of Chagford, surrounded by woodland. Lawns sweep away to an 18-hole putting green. Porch full of green Wellington boots and golfing umbrellas. The lounge and bar overlook the gardens, and some of the best food in England is served in two small dining rooms (*lunch moderate, dinner expensive*). If you're on a restricted budget you could just have cream tea.

The Mill End Hotel, Sandy Park, **t** 432 282 (*expensive*). This 18th-century former mill house beside the River Teign has been a hotel for more than 70 years. Several cosy lounges and 15 old-English-style bedrooms. High-quality restaurant offers modern English dishes.

The Three Crowns Hotel, High Street, **t** 433 444, *www.chagford-accom.co.uk* (*moderate*). Has 22 rooms, serves a good selection of bar meals, and the restaurant does à la carte or set meals (*cheap*).

22 Mill Street, **t** 432 244 (*moderate*). Small, glass-fronted restaurant with modern European menu. *Open Wed–Sat lunch, Mon–Sat dinner*. Also two homely bedrooms for B&B.

The Globe Inn, High Street, **t** 433 485 (*moderate*). Home-made pies at the bar, dining room (*cheap*) and rooms upstairs.

Glendarah House, Lower Street, **t** 433 270, *www.glendarah-house.co.uk* (*moderate*). Attractive late-Victorian house backing onto open countryside, on main road into Chagford from Moretonhampstead. Three pretty bedrooms with glorious views.

Parford Well, Sandy Park (1½ miles from Chagford in direction of Drewsteignton), **t** 433 353 (*moderate*). Beautiful modern house furnished with old pine furniture; three bedrooms.

Drewsteignton t (01647) –

The Drew Arms, The Square, **t** 281 224 (*moderate*). Cosy bar with wooden floorboards, long bench seats around sides and cream-painted wooden panelling in the landlady's kitchen. Old photos on wall, small coal fire. Great food like hock of ham, belly pork and homity pie; real ale through hatch. Three rooms.

Moretonhampstead t (01647) –

The White Hart Hotel, The Square, **t** 440 406 (*moderate*). Handsome, old-fashioned town-centre hotel. Cosy, friendly bar, offering pub grub. Ask for room in main building.

Great Sloncombe Farm, Moretonhampstead (off the A382 from Chagford), **t** 440 595, *www.greatsloncombefarm.co.uk* (*moderate*). A 13th-century Dartmoor farmhouse and busy working farm of Aberdeen Angus beef cattle. Own eggs and organic vegetable garden. Three cottage bedrooms with patchwork quilts and lovely views. Warm, friendly atmosphere. Guest lounge with wood-burning stove.

Sloncombe House, Moretonhampstead, **t** 440 903 (*moderate*). Victorian granite house in a tiny hamlet. Beautiful tiled entrance hall, big windows, conservatory, gleaming bathroom and splendid garden with tor in middle of perfect lawns. Bog garden in old sheep dip.

Great Wooston Farm, Mardon Down (2 miles north of Moretonhampstead), **t** 440 367, *www.greatwoostonfarm.com* (*moderate*). Large 1900 farmhouse with three pretty old-fashioned bedrooms. Wonderful, rural feel and walk along the Teign Valley to Castle Drogo in Drewsteignton.

Buckfastleigh

The White Hart, Plymouth Road, **t** (01364) 642 337 (*cheap*). Traditional 400-year-old pub serving real ales, including Beachcomber and White Hart from the Teignworthy brewery in Newton Abbot, and Sam's Medium draught cider. Bar meals, restaurant to be built at the back.

The Singing Kettle, 3 Kistor Place, Belgrave Road, **t** (01803) 299 489 (*cheap*). Old tea shop that serves excellent breakfasts, morning coffee, lunches and afternoon teas.

Lydford **t** (01822) –

The Castle Inn, Lyford, **t** 820 241 (*moderate*). Nine cottagey bedrooms with window seats and patchwork throws. One balconied double overlooks Lydford Castle. The restaurant is furnished with high-backed wooden settles. Bar meals include ploughman's or bubble and squeak. The restaurant menu features lots of game and fish. Short walk to Lydford Gorge.

Lydford House Hotel, Lydford, **t** 820 347, *www.lydfordhouse.co.uk* (*moderate*). The Dartmoor artist William Widgery built himself this country house in 1880, and lived in it for 10 years. In 1887 he erected the large granite cross on the top of Brat Tor to commemorate Queen Victoria's Golden Jubilee. Twelve comfortable bedrooms, a large sitting room with some of Widgery's paintings of Dartmoor, fresh flowers and ornaments over the fireplace. The bus stops at the bottom of the drive. Morning coffee, light lunches and cream teas served in conservatory or on the lawn.

The Dartmoor Inn, Lydford, **t** 820 221 (*moderate*). Top-notch gastro pub on main Tavistock–Okehampton road, a mile from Lydford village. Bar and dining areas with high-backed settles and old log-burning stove. Farmhouse sausages with onion gravy and mash or wild mushroom risotto for lunch. Traditional country-inn menu in the evening with emphasis on seasonal local produce. *Closed Sun, and Mon lunch.*

Tavistock **t** (01822) –

Horn of Plenty, Gulworthy (3 miles west of Tavistock in the direction of Gunnislake), **t** 832 528, *www.thehornofplenty.co.uk* (*very expensive*). Georgian country-house hotel overlooking the Tamar Valley, originally built for the captain of the Duke of Bedford's mines. Now has 10 bedrooms and a renowned Michelin-starred conservatory restaurant (*lunch moderate, dinner expensive*) with views. Delicious, high-quality fusion cooking.

Browns Hotel and Wine Bar, 80 West Street, **t** 618 686, *www.brownsdevon.co.uk* (*expensive*). Warm, welcoming Victorian coaching inn on site of much older hostelry, with 18 comfortable bedrooms. The conservatory, which spills out into a pretty garden, is a pleasant setting for a light lunch. The informal restaurant serves goats' cheese tartlets, chargrilled monkfish and steak.

The Bedford Hotel, 1 Plymouth Road, **t** 613 221, *www.warm-welcome-hotels.co.uk* (*expensive*). Imposing Victorian-Gothic hotel on the town square, with traces of former elegance; 29 bedrooms. Morning coffee and light lunches served in the Duke's Bar, where the grand piano is played on Fri and Sat eves.

Peter Tavy Inn, Peter Tavy (near Tavistock), **t** 810 348 (*moderate*). Hearty dishes of eggs and ham or traditional Devonshire cheese ploughman's followed by bread and butter pudding or chocolate tart, all served in the flagstoned bar.

Mallard's Guest House, Plymouth Road, **t** 615 171 (*moderate*). Set back behind a neat garden in grand Victorian style.

Eko Brae, 4 Bedford Villas, West Street, **t** 614 028, *www.smoothhound.co.uk/tavistock* (*moderate*). One of two Victorian villas, in pleasant spot with views over town.

Higher Rowes Farm, Horndon, **t** 810 816, *hrowesfarm@eurobell.co.uk* (*moderate*). A rough stone track leads to this 17th-century Devon longhouse with friendly atmosphere and a yard full of pigs, turkeys, rabbits, dogs and horses. Three bedrooms looking out over the moor.

The Coffee Mill, 44 Brook Street, **t** 612 092 (*cheap*). All-day breakfasts and simple lunches. *Closed Sun.*

The Duke's Coffee House, 8–11 The Pannier Market, **t** 613 718 (*cheap*). Small coffee shop serving good coffee and snack lunches – panini, nachos and pizza. On a warm day you can sit outside and watch the market. *Closed Sun.*

The Elephant's Nest, Horndon, **t** 810 273 (*cheap*). Follow the signs from the A386 at Mary Tavey to hamlet of Horndon. Excellent pub with local ales, scrumpy cider and good snacks.

The Heart of the Moor t (01822) –

Two Bridges Hotel, Two Bridges, **t** 890 581, *www.warm-welcome-hotels.co.uk* (*expensive*). Slate-roofed country-house hotel at junction of transmoor roads, looking out at the West Dart River. Views to the tors beyond Princetown. Famous guests have included Vivien Leigh. Victorian atmosphere with stuffed birds in cases and leather sofas; 33 bedrooms, some with four-poster, half-tester and antique brass beds. Afternoon tea served in the lounge.

Lydgate House Hotel, Hartyland, **t** 880 209, *www.lydgatehouse.co.uk* (*expensive*). Cream-painted Victorian country house on steep wooded valleyside of the East Dart River, with smashing views down the valley. Seven bedrooms nicely furnished in period style. Home-cooked evening meals for guests only, but anyone can stop off here for cream teas with scones and strawberry jam or light lunches.

Cherrybrook Hotel, Two Bridges, **t** 880 260, *www.cherrybrook-hotel.co.uk* (*moderate*). Former early 19th-century farmhouse set in 3½ acres, surrounded by small fields hemmed in by drystone walls. Cosy lounge and bar with log-burning stove. Seven simply furnished bedrooms. Good, honest atmosphere. Evening meals prepared using local produce, with delicious desserts like trifle and steamed syrup pudding, and Devon cheeses. Wistman's Wood 20 minutes' walk away.

East Dart Hotel, Postbridge, **t** 880 213, *www.dartmoorhotels.com* (*moderate*). A 19th-century coaching inn less than 100 yards from the river; 11 comfortable bedrooms. Fox heads above Huntsman's Bar, pitchers, horse brasses and a hunting mural around the room. Good bar meals served lunch and dinner.

Duchy Guest House, Tavistock Road, Princetown, **t** 890 552 (*moderate*). A Victorian house looking out over road onto the moor, a rope's throw away from Dartmoor Prison. Very friendly, with three cheerful bedrooms.

The Plume of Feathers, Princetown, **t** 890 240 (*cheap*). Cosy bar with log fire, worn flag-stones and sign creaking in the wind outside. Real ales include Jail Ale and Dartmoor IPA by the Princetown brewery. Campsite and bunk houses.

Warren House Inn, **t** 880 208 (*cheap*). Standing alone on remote Postbridge to Moretonhampstead road, miles from anywhere. Beamed bar, comfy settles, a log fire at either end of the snug, blazing away summer and winter alike. Particularly cosy when the weather closes in. Steak and ale pie or rabbit pie.

The moor is not as old as the Devonian lowlands around it, but more menacing, formed over thousands of years from molten magma bubbling up through the earth's crust. Its clitters, bogs, cleaves and DANGER AREAS shroud it in dark mystery. From the gentle Devon farmland you are suddenly up on the moor, surrounded by a heathery wilderness of grass flattened by the wind. The weather on the high moor can close in suddenly; the mist, in particular, is perilous to walkers.

The plateau is not picturesque, but it is dotted with fantastic granite shapes on the crests of hills called tors, planted by giants. You may, however, feel as the author of *A Gentleman's Walking Tour of Dartmoor* did in 1864: 'To a stranger on the moor, the country round seems almost exactly alike; there are tors in every direction, and with very little apparent difference between them, too. The whole country round consists of moorland hill-and-dale; you toil over one hill and down the other side, cross a brook (just like the one at the foot of the last hill), and then up another steep ascent, and on looking round, you seem to be pretty much where you were about an hour before.'

The uplands are covered in peaty bog, but the real danger is the valley bogs, where soggy moss collects in liquid mud. Around the fringes of the granite dome you may breathe a sigh of relief as you return to scattered villages, enclosed farmland, and deep wooded gorges where the rivers Dart, Tavy, Teign and Plym tumble off the top.

It is surprising, then, that somewhere so harsh shows so much evidence of human activity: the moor was more populous 5,000 years ago than it is today. Bronze Age villages such as Grimspound were built on the lower slopes, and the dead were buried in monumental stone tombs called cists and cairns incorporating standing stones. The **prehistoric monuments** are good to aim for on walks, as are the **industrial remains**. Over the last thousand years Dartmoor has been Europe's major source of tin and copper; its 19th-century granite quarries supplied stone for London Bridge, the British Museum, Nelson's Column and Plymouth's breakwater. The moor is littered with quarries, tin workings, tramways, mills and tinners' cottages. Medieval tinners 'tin-streamed' the river beds – digging out tin ore from beneath the silt and working their way upstream to the tin source. The tin was smelted and taxed in the stannary towns of **Tavistock**, **Ashburton**, **Plympton** and **Chagford**, which grew rich on it. The 19th-century copper boom brought more prosperity to the western fringes around the **Tamar Valley** and **Mary Tavy** mines.

Eastern Fringes

East Dartmoor is the most densely populated part of the moor, dotted with villages along the Teign and Bovey rivers and their tributaries.

Buckfastleigh, just off the busy A38 at the southeastern foot of the moor, was a thriving mill town in 1900, and is now enjoying a modest regeneration based around the **Valiant Soldier** (*open Easter–Oct Mon–Sat 10.30–4.30; adm minimal*), a fossilized 1950s pub on the High Street. One day in 1965 the widowed landlady locked the door, disappeared into an upstairs bedroom and never reopened it again. The poor old thing gradually declined behind closed curtains until 1996. It's a sad story for the old lady, but the pub has been preserved intact, down to the old money in the cash till.

Buckfast Abbey

***t** (01364) 645 500; church open 9am–9.30pm, gift shop 9–5.30, produce shop and restaurant 10–4.30; all close earlier in winter.*

In summer a special bus runs from Buckfastleigh to Buckfast Abbey, a Roman Catholic monastery of about 40 Benedictine monks. The huge complex – church, shops and restaurant – attracts half a million visitors a year. It stands on the site of a 12th-century Cistercian monastery which was abandoned at the Dissolution. The new monks arrived in 1882, in response to an advert in the Catholic newspaper *The Tablet*; the French Government had thrown them out of their monastery near Avignon and they were looking for a new home. It took them 31 years (1907–38) to build the new church, which they did themselves. Four monks worked at a time, cutting and dressing the stone by hand and using wooden scaffolding lashed together with ropes. The early-medieval-style grey limestone church is imposing, but unsoftened by time and use. A few of the old monastic buildings survive, including the old south gate (now a retreat centre) and guesthouse (now the bookshop). In the early 19th century a wealthy miller flattened the rest of the ruins and built himself a neo-Gothic mansion and mill. In the old mill, the monastic produce shop sells goods made by monks in Europe. Buckfast specialities are candles, honey and Tonic Wine.

Bovey Tracey

Bovey Tracey, a busy little market town on the eastern edge of Dartmoor, is home to the showrooms of the **Devon Guild of Craftsmen** (*open daily 10–5.30*). The guild was set up in 1955 by a small group of local craftsmen including Bovey potter David Leach (son of the great Bernard Leach) to promote the best regional crafts. In 1986 the guild bought the Victorian riverside mill, and converted it into a gallery and craft shop, stacked with furniture, ceramics, glass, clothes, wood and metalwork.

The B3387 climbs about 300 yards out of Bovey Tracey onto the east moor. **Haytor Rocks** (1,500ft) are a honeypot for the holiday crowds – classic Dartmoor scenery, easy to reach. Hay Tor has a distinctive twin-peaked profile.

Up the road, the grey stone market town of **Widecombe-in-the-Moor**, made famous by the folk song 'Widecombe Fair', hugs the hillside beneath its 240ft-high church tower. The fair still takes place on the second Tuesday of September, but on any weekend you will see crowds wandering around the old market square looking for it.

North of Bovey Tracey the A382 goes to **Lustleigh**, a pretty village with a good pub on the edge of the dramatic **Lustleigh Cleave** (carved out by the River Bovey). There is a lovely 5-mile walk along the top of the cleave to **Hunter's Tor** (1,070ft).

Moretonhampstead, a handsome, down-at-heel market town with some good old buildings – coaching inns and a Victorian library – is on the edge of the high moor at a big junction of minor roads. Lutyens is thought to have built the neo-Georgian bank, now the elegant Lion Gallery, specializing in equestrian art.

As you enter **Chagford** off the moor, you are squeezed down its narrow lanes into the small, sloping town square. This old stannary town, on the lower slopes of the moors above the River Teign, is one of the prettiest on Dartmoor, bustling with creaky pubs, and old-fashioned shops. It was a popular Victorian centre for expeditions onto the moor and is still a popular starting point for the late-Neolithic **Grey Wethers** stone circles, or the famously inaccessible **Cranmere Pool letterbox**.

In the northeast corner of Dartmoor, **Drewsteignton** is a typical old Dartmoor village on a windy hill, with a square of painted houses and an excellent pub. It takes its name from Drogo de Teign, the Norman baron who owned the parish in the 12th century. A few miles south, **Castle Drogo** (*open April–Oct Sat–Thurs 11–5; adm*) sits dramatically on a crag 853ft above the Teign Gorge. Despite its pretensions, it is not medieval and has nothing to do with Drogo de Teign. It was built between 1911 and 1930 by Edwin Lutyens for millionaire Julius Drew. The landings, stairways and halls are stark, with bare granite walls, but the main rooms are stylized in the atmosphere of different periods: the library 1930s, the drawing room 18th century, the dining room Jacobean, and the kitchens Victorian. Lutyens also laid out the granite structure of the formal terraced gardens to the northeast.

There is a 3½-mile walk along the Teign Gorge from Castle Drogo to Fingle Bridge.

Western Fringes

Between Tavistock and Okehampton, the A386 skirts the north moor, the most inhospitable part of Dartmoor and almost entirely incorporated within three MoD firing ranges. Only experienced walkers are advised to venture here.

Okehampton

Okehampton is a busy market town, cut off from the moor by the busy A30. South of the road is some of the bleakest, boggiest moorland, and 2,037ft-high High Willhays. For the daring, there's a 6-mile walk between Yes Tor, High Willhays, Dinger Tor and East Mill Tor that sticks largely to military roads. Just outside Okehampton is its ruined medieval **castle**, overlooking the West Okement River. On West Street, the **Museum of Dartmoor Life** (***t** (01837) 52295; open Easter–Oct Mon–Sat 10–4.30*) tells the social history of the moor. There is a pleasant, hilly 5-mile walk known as the **Two Museum Trail** to the **Finch Foundry** (***t** (01837) 840 0046; open April–Oct Wed–Mon 11–5; adm*) at Sticklepath. Pick up the leaflet 'Okehampton Countryside Walks East' in town.

Tavistock

Tavistock is easily reached off the A386 periphery road and the B3357 moor road, and has lots of places to stay. It's an old-fashioned market town with hand-painted shop signs and a Victorian market stacked with local cheeses, bread and fresh produce. The town grew up around the 10th-century Benedictine Abbey. In the early Middle Ages it became one of four stannary towns built around the edge of the moor, where tin was smelted and taxed. Tavistock's glory days came in the 19th-century copper boom, when one of the biggest copper lodes in the world was discovered between the Tavy and Tamar valleys. The **Devon Great Consuls copper mine** became the richest copper mine ever, its shares rising from £1 to £800 in a single year. The 7th Duke of Bedford owned the mineral rights and became hugely wealthy. Visit the **market** on Bedford Square (*closed Mon*) for Devon cheeses. There's a little **museum** (*open Easter–Oct Wed*

2–4, Fri–Sat 10–1 and 2–4; adm minimal) devoted to local history, and two statues: one of the 7th Duke, the other of Sir Francis Drake, born down the road in Crowndale.

Six miles south of Tavistock, at the highest point of navigation on the River Tamar, **Morwelham Quay** (*open Easter–Oct 10–5.30; winter 10–4.30; last admission two hours before closing; adm exp*) was the port of the west Dartmoor tin and copper mines. Its fortunes took off when the Tavistock canal was opened in 1816, anticipating the opening of the copper mine in 1844. The decline of the mine, coinciding with the arrival of the railway line, marginalized Morwelham into obscurity. Since 1969 it has been restored and turned into a popular industrial attraction: costumed staff work the old equipment; tram rides take you into the George and Charlotte copper mine; restored buildings include the fully licensed Ship Inn, and a salvaged ketch called the Garlandstone in the Devon Great Consuls docks.

Buckland Abbey

Open April–Oct Fri–Wed 10.30–5.30; adm.

Buckland Abbey, a former Cistercian monastery in the Tavy Valley between Tavistock and Plymouth, is known as the home of Sir Francis Drake. Drake bought it off Richard Grenville, another swashbuckling maritime type who famously took on 15 Spanish ships after the rest of his fleet had beaten a retreat. Tennyson turned Grenville into a national hero in the poem 'Revenge'. The old abbey is a charming, rustic place. Unusually, Grenville ignored the cloisters and abbot's lodgings – the traditional favourites for an abbey conversion – and turned the church tower into his Tudor mansion, so there's none of the formality of a conventional country house. The **Drake Gallery** exhibits memorabilia, including a flag thought to have flown on the *Golden Hind* and Drake's drum (which is said to beat by itself when England is under threat).

Lydford Gorge

North of Tavistock, dramatic, wooded **Lydford Gorge** is one of the 'natural wonders' of Dartmoor. It has been a tourist attraction since the 18th century when the fashion for the picturesque attracted travel writers and painters. From the village of Lydford it is a 3-mile walk along the River Lyd past the Devil's Cauldron and other potholes to the 90ft-high White Lady Waterfall and back. The town of Lydford, now a handful of roadside cottages, was once the centre of stannary and forest law. The courts were held in the 12th-century keep of the castle. One prisoner, Richard Strode, was locked up without trial for objecting that the waste products of the tinners were choking the estuary at Plympton and obstructing the fishing boats – although he was MP for Plymouth and protecting the rights of Plymouthians was his job. In the churchyard on the right of the church door, is the epitaph of George Routleigh, watchmaker, who died 'aged 57, wound up, in the hopes of being taken in hand by his maker and of being thoroughly cleaned, repaired and set agoing in the world to come'.

From the Dartmoor Inn at the Lydford junction of the A386 you can walk into the rock-strewn Tavy Cleave to Willsworthy Bridge. Another good walk is from the Mary Tavy Inn into Tavy Cleave and around Ger Tor to Deadlake Foot and Hare Tor.

The Heart of Dartmoor

The B3357 between Tavistock and Princetown climbs onto the high moor. Check your petrol gauge before you set out. To either side are the rugged outlines of tors: to the north Cox Tor, Great Staple Tor and Middle Staple Tor; to the south Feather Tor, Pew Tor, Vixen Tor and King's Tor. The road continues to **Merrivale**, a gentle valley (with a good pub – the Dartmoor Inn) where a group of prehistoric stone monuments stands near old quarries and tin mines. It's an easy 2-mile walk to the standing stones from the Four Winds car park. Two rows of Bronze Age granite stumps of stone form an avenue 200 yards long. A cairn on the line of the southern row is thought to mark the burial place of an important person; about 20 yards beyond that is a cist, an enormous slab of granite with a chamber underneath used for burying the dead. Fifty yards south-west is a small Bronze Age cairn circle. Further southwest again is a monumental Neolithic circle. From Merrivale the road runs on to Princetown and Two Bridges.

Princetown straddles the crossroads on top of the moor, the prison at its heart. Near the prison gates is the **Prison Museum**, with a display of items confiscated from prisoners, such as a tattoo gun made out of a biro, and a tape-recorder motor. The **High Moorland Visitors' Centre** (*open daily Easter–Oct 10–5, rest of year 10–4*) was built in 1809 as a barracks for prison officers, later becoming the Duchy Hotel where Sir Arthur Conan Doyle wrote *The Hound of the Baskervilles*. A 5-mile walk takes you along the old railway line to Foggintor Quarries.

Foxtor Mire, or the Great Grimpen Mire

'That is the great Grimpen Mire,' said he. 'A false step yonder means death to man or beast.'

The Hound of the Baskervilles, Sir Arthur Conan Doyle

Foxtor Mire was the moorland setting for *The Hound of the Baskervilles*, with fictional Baskerville Hall on the site of Whiteworks cottages, facing across the mire to Fox Tor (High Tor in the book). Seldon, the escaped convict, made signals across the mire to Barrymore in the Hall from Fox Tor. A treacherous mire path leads between Whiteworks and Fox Tor; it's not as dangerous as Conan Doyle suggests, but do try to avoid the bright green patches. Below Fox Tor you can see a cross known as **Childe's Tomb**, which commemorates a 14th-century huntsman called Amyas or Ordulf Childe who got lost in a blizzard, killed his horse and slept inside it for warmth, but died anyway in the snow. He was laid in the Bronze Age cist beneath the cross.

Two Bridges

On top of the moor, at the crossing of the B3212 and B3357, the pub at Two Bridges is a cheerful place to break your journey. You could go up to the top of Crockern Tor, just off the B3212 Postbridge road, where the stannary parliament met in the 15th century; you can still see the seats cut into the rock. Some of the most popular Dart Valley walks begin further along the B3357 at Dartmeet, where the East and West Dart rivers converge amid terrific scenery (with a shop and café).

Postbridge

Along the B3212 northeast from Two Bridges to Moretonhampstead the moor looks darker than ever. Postbridge, in the fertile valley of the East Dart, alleviates the gloom. It's a popular base for the central moor. Day-trippers come to see the medieval clapper bridge on its granite pillars above the Dart. There are plenty of good walks starting here too.

The **Warren House Inn** sits high up on the lonely road in the middle of nowhere. It's a Dartmoor legend, where there's always a cosy fire blazing. From here it's 3 miles across the moor to **Grimspound**, a well-preserved Bronze Age settlement of 24 huts in an enclosure on the north slope of Hambledon. Although it looks defensive, with its massive paved entrance and 6ft-high walls, it was almost certainly a farming village. The thresholds are the most evocative detail.

The North Devon Coast

With its rocky headlands raked by the full force of the Atlantic, North Devon has some of the most dramatic coastal scenery in Britain, with small coastal settlements at the mouths of steep wooded combes. Charles Kingsley in *Westward Ho!* describes these combes as 'like no other English scenery. Each has its upright walls, inland of rich oak wood, nearer the sea of dark green furze, then of smooth turf, then of weird black cliffs which range out right and left into the deep sea, in castles, spires and wings of jagged iron stone.' Writing in the 1920s, Henry Williamson, author of *Tarka the Otter*, was equally effusive about the inland scenery. Avoid built-up Barnstaple Bay and the resorts of Ilfracombe Westward Ho! if you can.

Ilfracombe

Ilfracombe is on the northern headland of Barnstaple Bay, a typical English resort with a whiff of boiled cabbage and stewed tea. Its built on the steep sides of a combe, above a sheltered river harbour, with no seafront, as such. Its beaches are reached through tunnels blasted in the rock, at the foot of massive grey cliffs. You won't want

Elizabethan Sea Dog Sir Richard Grenville

The land between Bude and Bideford once belonged to the Grenville family. Sir Richard Grenville (1542–91) was Sir Walter Raleigh's cousin and Queen Elizabeth I's sheriff in Cornwall, with the task of keeping the Spanish out. In 1588 he chased Spanish ships out of the Irish Channel. In 1591 he was captain of the *Revenge* – full of Bideford sailors – and second in command of Lord Thomas Howard's fleet, which went to capture Spanish treasure ships homeward bound. Lord Thomas withdrew on finding the odds against him too heavy, but the *Revenge* became separated from the rest of the fleet and Grenville tried to break through the Spanish line. He fought 15 Spanish ships all night, was mortally wounded and finally captured. His exploit is celebrated in Tennyson's poem, 'The Revenge'.

Getting There and Around

By **car** from the north exit the M5 at junction 27, following the A361 to Barnstaple, Braunton and Ilfracombe. From Exeter, the A377 travels to Barnstaple, joining the A361 to Braunton, Ilfracombe and Croyde. You'll need a car to get around too, unless you plan to walk or cycle.

Tourist Information

Ilfracombe: Landmark Theatre, Wilder Road, **t** (01271) 863 001, *www.ilfracombe-tourism.co.uk. Open winter 10–5, summer 10–5.30.*

Woolacombe: The Esplanade, **t** (01271) 870 553. *Open Mon–Sat summer 10–5, winter 10–1.*

Where to Stay and Eat

Ilfracombe t (01271) –

Most of Ilfracombe puts out a B&B sign in the summer, particularly along Brannocks Road. The nicest places are on Torr Park Road, running half way down the Torrs. One of these to look out for is **The Glen Torr**, Torr Park Road, **t** 862 403 (*cheap*).

Norbury House Hotel, Torr Park Road, **t** 863 888, *www.norburyhousehotel.co.uk* (*moderate*). Friendly hotel in pretty part of Ilfracombe with views over town and out to sea; eight bedrooms.

The Orchard, Lee (3 miles from Ilfracombe over the Torrs), **t** 867 212, *ginnypotts@hotmail.com* (*moderate*). Red 17th-century converted barn with three bright bedrooms. The owners will pick you up after a long walk, and you can throw your wet clothes into a drier. Thirty seconds' walk to the **Grampus Inn**, which does home-cooked bar meals.

Rose Cottage, Lee, **t** 863 257 (*moderate*). Airy, bright one-bedroomed thatched cottage with rough slate walls, flagstone floor and sitting room. Close to pub.

The Angel, 23 Church Street, **t** 866 833 (*moderate*). Excellent small restaurant in old butcher's shop, with wooden church pews, bookshelves and the original Victorian wall tiles. High-quality individual style of cooking using local fish and produce. *Open eves only.*

Woolacombe t (01271) –

The Woolacombe Bay Hotel, South Street, **t** 870 388, *www.woolacombe-bay-hotel.co.uk* (*luxury*). The hotel resembles a Disney town nestling beneath the downs with gables, chimneys and timber-work; 64 bedrooms, two pools, tennis courts and putting green.

The Watersmeet Hotel, Mortehoe, **t** 870 333, *www.watersmeethotel.co.uk* (*luxury*). Medium-sized, cream-painted hotel in small cove near Woolacombe with pool and grass tennis courts on terrace above cliffs. Steps lead down to the cove. Dining room has white linen and panoramic sea views. Airy

to linger, but it's a good base for Lundy Island and coastal walks. Park in the harbour car park, and climb **Lantern Hill** (on the seaward side of the harbour) to the romantic 13th-century stone chapel with its sea light on top. The views are fabulous. The **Tunnel Beaches** (*open summer 9–9, winter 9–5*) boast grey sand and appealing Victorian touches, such as striped deckchairs and a swimming pool carved out of the rocks.

From the headland to the west of the town, you can join the zigzagging Torrs Walk to **Lee Bay**, 3 miles west, dominated by Lee Bay Hotel and its fuschsia-filled gardens.

Lundy Island

Lundy Shore Office, **t** *(01237) 470 422; The Quay, Bideford.*

This lonely island, three miles long and half a mile wide, has a dozen inhabitants, no shops and no roads. It's popular with breeding seabirds including puffins (Lundy is Old Norse for puffin) and oystercatchers, and with seals. On the south and west side are rugged grey cliffs, on the east side steep, grassy slopes; in between it's flat and

and pleasant, with coordinated fabrics and efficient staff.

The Castle Hotel, The Esplanade, **t** 870 788, *www.woolacombe-web.net/thecastle* (*moderate*). Small, family-run Victorian hotel (Woolacombe's first) above the road and behind the beach. Eight bedrooms with window seats and old-fashioned décor.

Little Beach Hotel, The Esplanade, **t** 870 398, *www.surfedout.com* (*moderate*). Friendly family-run Edwardian hotel with 11 en-suite bedrooms, three with sea views and balconies. Refurbished in 2003. Evening meals and bar.

The Board Walk Bar and Restaurant, The Esplanade, **t** 871 115 (*moderate*). Bright, fun, small seafront restaurant serving Clovelly seafood as well as traditional meat dishes. *Open April–Oct only*.

The Red Barn, Beach Road, **t** 870 982 (*cheap*). Happy, lively family surfers' bar with surfing videos on TV, surfboards hanging from barn-like rafters and a surfer mural. Pool table in winter, table football in summer. The restaurant offers omelettes, burgers, steak, chilli and the like.

Croyde t (01271) –

Croyde Bay House Hotel, Moor Lane, **t** 890 270 (*expensive*). Small, old-fashioned hotel with seven bedrooms and a sun lounge overlooking the bay. *Open Fri–Sun, closed Dec and Jan*.

Croyde Manor, **t** 890 350 (*moderate*). Beautiful Georgian manor house 10 minutes' walk from Croyde beach. Hall full of oars, fishing rods and walking sticks.

Combas Farm, Putsborough, **t** 890 398 (*moderate*). Pretty white-painted 17th-century farmhouse in colourful garden in secluded valley, near Baggy Point, a mile from Putsborough Sands. Four comfortable rooms to stay in.

The Thatched Barn Inn, **t** 890 349 (*cheap*). Bar snacks, lunches and full evening menu served. B&B too (*moderate*).

Entertainment

Landmark Theatre and Cinema, The Seafront, Wilder Road, Ilfracombe **t** 324 242. ßBuilt in the 1990s, and resembling a sand-castle, the Landmark caused a fracas for its architectural style when it opened – but, like it or loathe it, it is nonetheless a cultural beacon on the North Devon Coast. One upturned bucket holds the auditorium (which doubles up as theatre and cinema). The repertoire includes good touring companies and old-time music hall. Arthouse films are shown Thurs–Sat if nothing else is on. Airy café-bar. *Open summer daily 10–5, staying open in the eves when there's a show on, winter Tues–Sat 10–4 and Sun 10–2.*

green. Habitation is in the south, around St Helena's Church, Marisco Tavern and the jetty. The island's ship, MS *Oldenburg*, takes less than two hours from Bideford (*all year*), Ilfracombe and Clovelly (*summer*), four or five times a week in summer, less often in winter. You can go on a day trip or stay in one of 23 properties, including a cottage, a schoolhouse, a lighthouse and a medieval castle (*all owned by the Landmark Trust;* **t** *(01628) 825 925 for bookings*).

Morte Point to the Taw

South of Ilfracombe, Morte Point heralds west-facing sandy beaches, good for swimming and surfing. The rollers come straight into 2-mile **Morte Bay** between rocky headlands. The small resort town of **Woolacombe** is full of hotels. Just around the headland is **Barricane Beach,** famous for the Caribbean shells that wash up. **Putsborough** shelters behind the long arm of Baggy Point. You can walk along the beach from Woolacombe, or drive down narrow lanes. **Croyde** straggles along the coast road on the other side of Baggy Point. It's a big surfing centre. **Croyde Bay** is

Rock Pools

'It is not very much use in coming to Ilfracombe unless you have some little taste for natural history,' wrote a visitor in 1867. 'Socially it is everything here. You are hardly fit to live unless you know something about anemones. Nearly every house has got its aquarium.'

Lacking royal patronage or the endorsement of leading physicians, the remote North Devon coast failed to attract early holidaymakers. Instead it appealed to a few upper-class travellers who followed writers like Wordsworth and Coleridge, searching for the picturesque. Mainstream popularity came later, when Charles Kingsley's *Westward Ho!* (1854) and Richard Blackmore's *Lorna Doone* (1869) made the North Devon coast a place of romantic adventure. At around the same time a series of books entitled *A Naturalist's Rambles on the Devon Coast*, *Seaside Pleasures* and *Land and Sea* turned Ilfracombe into the home of the new amateur science of marine biology – one of the more enduring seaside pursuits invented by Victorian holiday-makers hungry for self-improvement. The author of these books, Philip Gosse, can be credited with the discovery of the rock pool. He set in motion an invasion of the coast by enthusiastic collectors who observed, sketched and, of course, cleaned out all the living organisms left behind in the tidal pools. Nowadays Gosse is best remembered as the father of Edmund, in his memoirs, *Father and Son* (1907).

wonderful, with its yellow sand. The café above the beach has a webcam focused on the waves, so internet surfers can decide whether to come and surf for real. **Saunton** has a 4-mile beach backed by the grassy dunes of Braunton Barrows, which reach 100ft high in places. The beach is popular with longboarders.

Barnstaple Bay

The ports of Barnstaple Bay caught the Atlantic trade in the 17th-century, then cod, herring and mackerel until the 18th century, and local trade after that. Now the ports are dead. Barnstaple and Bideford are the main towns, at the lowest crossings of the rivers Taw and Torridge. The coastal footpath and road divert inland here; you may want to skip the estuary *en route* to the spectacular landscape north and south.

Barnstaple is a large market town, worth visiting on market day (almost every day). The **Pannier Market**, built in 1885, leads out onto Butcher's Row, a lovely street of small shops. On Friday, main market day, the market hall fills up with more than 300 stalls of country ladies selling cream, butter, chickens and pies. Saturday is a commercial market, with a hotchpotch of stalls selling shoes, clothes, groceries, tools and kitchen-ware. Tuesday is plants and flowers and Wednesday bric-a-brac.

The town has two museums too. In the square next to the bridge, the **Museum of North Devon** (*open Tues–Sat 10–4.30; adm free*) exhibits local slipware; the 1900s pottery of the Branhams factory is particularly interesting. Beside the old quayside, in an attractive Queen Anne Building (once a merchants' meeting place), the **Heritage Centre** (*open Mon–Sat 10–5; adm*) can tell you all about the town's maritime history.

Bideford is a smaller version of Barnstaple. Its charm is its location on the steep valley side of the Torridge River. Climb up Bridge Street to the handsome Pannier Market (not much to buy). The quayside still looks the part, with boats and cranes and the 24-arched Long Bridge spanning the wide river. The **Burton Museum and Gallery** by the river has an excellent collection of Fishley slipware, including harvest jugs with yellow glazes decorated with sgraffito (scratched) words and leaves, or childish figures. The downstairs galleries host contemporary art exhibitions. There is a craft shop and café too. Just off the Quay, up Rope Walk, is **Bideford Pottery**, a traditional pottery which makes sgraffito-decorated slipware pots, including harvest jugs.

The **Torridge Valley** between Bideford and the old railway station is beautiful, with tidal water, marshes, reedbeds and woods. The best way to see it is by bicycle along the Tarka Trail, following the old railway line. The road runs along the river to **Great Torrington**, an amiable market town with a colonnaded town hall and an elegant pink Pannier Market (general market on Thurs and Sat). Look in on **Nick Chapman's**

Getting There and Around

From Exeter St Davids the **Tarka Line train** runs to Barnstaple in just over an hour, 12–14 times a day. The railway station is on the south side of the river, half a mile from the centre.

You can hire a bike in the station at **Tarka Trail Cycle Hire**, **t** (01271) 324 202. The Tarka Trail heads north and south from Barnstaple: if you are heading north to Bideford, you spend the first 2 miles negotiating the town (on cycle lanes). If you go south towards Instow you are straight into the countryside, and you can continue to Great Torrington and Petrocstow, the end of the Tarka Trail.

Another place to hire a bike and join the trail is **Otter Cycle Hire**, Station Road, Braunton, **t** (01271) 813 339. From here you can cycle the north bank of the Taw to Barnstaple, cross to the right bank and pick up the trail to Instow and Bideford, the Torridge Valley and Great Torrington. Or hire a bike at **Bideford Cycle** Hire, Torrington Street, **t** (01237) 424 123, and go south along the river to Petrocstow.

Tourist Information

Taw Estuary: The Bake House, Caen Street, Braunton, **t** (01271) 816 400.

Barnstaple: The Square, **t** (01271) 375 000, *www.staynorthdevon.co.uk*. *Open Mon–Sat 9.30–5.*

Bideford: Victoria Park, The Quay, **t** (01237) 477 676.

Great Torrington: **t** (01805) 626 140. *Open Mon–Fri 10–4.30, Sat 10–1.*

Where to Stay and Eat

Taw Estuary t (01271) –

Crowborough Farm, Georgeham (pretty old stone village, where Henry Williamson wrote *Tarka the Otter*), **t** (01271) 891 005 (*moderate*). Quiet track off coastal road leads to old farmhouse in beautiful green valley. Short walk to Rock Inn behind the church and down valley to Croyde Bay. Relaxed and friendly with three sunny bedrooms.

Fairlinch, edge of Braunton, near Lobb, **t** (01271) 812 508 (*moderate*). Romantic Regency manor farmhouse in glorious position atop Lobb Hill overlooking the Taw Estuary. Interesting features include priest hole, oak panelling and an extraordinary fire surround decorated with the carved figures of Justice, Hope, Charity and Faith. One of the three bedrooms has a French Renaissance-style plasterwork ceiling.

Barnstaple t (01271) –

Cappuccino, Guild Hall, Pannier Market, **t** 327 227 (*cheap*). Colourful market café. Serves a range of good coffees, doorstep 'gourmet'

pottery in Porch House (**t** *(01805) 622 842*) as you drive in from Bideford. Just outside town is **Dartington Crystal** (*open Mon–Sat 9.30–5, Sun 10.30–4.30*), which emerged in 1967 out of the Dartington Project. It is one of the leading glass manufacturers in the country; the factory shop pulls in the coach loads.

Tarka Country

> *The eels of the Two Rivers were devourers of the spawn and fry of salmon and trout, and the otters were devourers of eels. Tarka stood on the shillets of the shallow stream while they twisted and moved past his legs.*
>
> *Tarka the Otter*, Henry Williamson

Author Henry Williamson moved to North Devon in 1921, after the First World War, and lived there for 14 years, writing stories about the world of 'otters, deer, salmon, water, moonshine...the only world in which perhaps there was consistency, form,

sandwiches, delicious cakes, cream teas, and pasta bowls. *Closed Sun.*

Pannier Market Café, Pannier Market, **t** 327 227 (*cheap*). Good working man's caff with views of the market stalls. Serves all-day breakfasts, big mugs of tea and coffee, toasted sandwiches, bacon sandwiches and ham, egg and chips. *Closed Sun.*

Bideford t (01237) –

The Royal Hotel, Barnstaple Street, **t** 472 005, *www.brend-hotels.com* (*moderate*). Victorian hotel at the eastern end of old Bideford Bridge looking out over the River Torridge. Charles Kingsley wrote part of *Westward Ho!* while staying at the hotel. The atmosphere is warm.

Cappuccino Plus, 25–6 Mill Street, **t** 473 007 (*moderate*). Colourful Mediterranean-style restaurant and wine bar; wide-ranging menu from sandwiches to fresh fish. *Closed Sun, and Mon eve. Wine bar open late. Book at weekends.*

The Swan Inn, Torrington Street, East the Water, **t** 473 460 (*moderate*). Friendly, unpretentious place to eat scampi and chips or fresh fish.

Great Torrington and Around

Half Moon Inn, Sheepwash, **t** (01409) 231 376 (*expensive*). Robust fishermen's inn on pretty town square in Torridge Valley, surrounded by thatched houses; 14 comfortable rooms. The hotel offers game-fishing on 10-mile stretch of the River Torridge (salmon, sea trout and brown trout); rod room, drying facilities and tuition. Traditional English-style restaurant.

The Black Horse Inn, High Street, **t** (01805) 622 121 (*cheap*). Cosy inn with fire, serving fish pie, sausage and chips or mushroom pie. Three guest rooms (*moderate*).

Browns Delicatessen, 37 South Street, **t** (01805) 622 900 (*cheap*). Lovely little place for takeaway rolls or good strong coffee. Three tables at the back for afternoon teas and more substantial English lunches. *Closed Sun.*

Entertainment

Queens Theatre, Boutport Street, Barnstaple, **t** (01271) 863 001. Auditorium in the old town hall with an atmosphere. Hosts touring theatre.

The Plough Arts Centre, Fore Street, Great Torrington, **t** (01805) 622 552, *www.plough-arts.org*. Busy little arts centre with small auditorium offering mix of local and touring theatre and bands, world music and arthouse cinema. Café serves wholesome home-cooked dinners. Friendly bar with bottled ales; gallery upstairs exhibits the work of local artists. *Open Wed–Sat.*

The North Devon Potteries

North Devon has been a pottery centre since the Middle Ages. The traditional manufacturing style is either earthenware (low-fired rustic clay pots) or slipware (earthenware that has been dipped in a solution of water and clay and decorated). The main potteries were at Barnstaple and Bideford, exploiting the rich seam of red earthenware clay at Fremington and the supply of wood in the river valleys to fire kilns. A huge export trade flourished with Wales, Ireland and America (where the 17th-century slipware pots are now major archaeological prizes). For collectors, there are three important periods. First, the late 18th century, when elaborate harvest pitchers, unique to this area, were made on commission for wealthy families; these now fetch thousands of pounds at auction and are filling the display cases of the V&A and Fitzwilliam museums, as well as the Burton in Bideford. In the mid-19th century there was a revival of slipware manufacturing, which was sustained until the early 20th century in the work of the Fishley family. From the early 1800s until the First World War four generations of Fishleys worked in the same rural pottery in Fremington; their work is now also exhibited in museums all over the country. After the Industrial Revolution, the pottery industry moved north to Stoke on Trent, near the coalfields; the clay still came from Devon, but the North Devon families could no longer compete with businessmen like Josiah Wedgwood. So the third period was a reaction against the industrialization of pottery in the north. In the 20th century, a number of renowned craft potters set up workshops in North Devon, to be near the materials and for the way of life. Important potters like Michael Leach, Clive Bowen, Svend Bayer and Sandy Brown moved into the area. Some can be visited today.

Clive Bowen trained with Michael Leach and set up his pottery in Shebbear in 1971 (***t** (01409) 281 271*). He is one of the best of his generation of potters, producing wood-fired Fremington clay tableware. Svend Bayer, who was trained by Michael Cardew, has a workshop 2 miles out of Sheepwash on the Torrington Road (***t** (01409) 231 282; open daily 8.30–6, but ring first*), producing large wood-fired pots. Sandy Brown works in Appledore and is well-known for artistic tableware. Others include Harry Juniper at Bideford Pottery (***t** (01237) 471 105*), who makes traditional slipware pots including big harvest pitchers; Philip Leach, son of Michael and grandson of Bernard, who has worked with Clive Bowen and now runs the Springfield Pottery in Hartland (***t** (01237) 441 506*); and Tim Slope, who works in Tapley House in Instow.

integrity' and earning himself a reputation as England's favourite nature writer. His bestseller *Tarka the Otter* (published in 1927) follows Tarka's adventures up and down the rivers Taw and Torridge. The otter's journey can be retraced along the Tarka Trail, a 180-mile walking route stretching from the North Devon coast to the top of Dartmoor in a figure of eight centred on Barnstaple, and touching Lynmouth and Ilfracombe in the north, and Bideford, Great Torrington and Okehampton in the south. The trail takes you through moors, cliffs, wooded river valleys and sandy bays. The stretch of the trail between Braunton and Petrocstow follows an old railway line and is popular with cyclists. You can hop on the scenic Tarka Line train to Barnstaple at Exeter St Davids. It takes just over an hour and weaves up the Exe and Tor, crossing and re-crossing the river. You can hire a bicycle at Barnstaple Station, and then you're off on a good cycle path in either direction. Any North Devon tourist information centre or bookshop can supply you with leaflets and guide books. Otherwise contact the **Tarka Country Tourism Association** (***t** (01271) 345 008; tcta@www.devon-cc.gov.uk*), or phone **Coast and Countryside** in Bideford (***t** (01237) 423 612*) for more details.

Appledore

At the confluence of the Taw and Torridge rivers about two miles from the sea, Appledore has a long history of boatbuilding. In 1970 the largest covered shipbuilding docks in Europe were opened here; recent commissions include two Royal Navy survey ships, HMS *Echo* and HMS *Enterprise*. All this goes on out of sight of the pretty Victorian quayside and Georgian terraces. From the quay, there are wide views across the estuary to Instow. Narrow alleyways lead uphill from the quayside, open doors leading into galleries, craft shops and fishing shops. Sandy Brown on Marine Parade (*ring the doorbell*) is a noted potter (*see* p.363). In summer a ferry goes to **Instow**, which has a long sandy beach. From the coastguard's hut, you can see **Northam Burrows**, an estuarine marsh protected by a shingle ridge. At the top of the town in a grand Georgian house is the excellent **North Devon Maritime Museum** (***t** (01237) 422 064; open Easter–Oct 2–5; adm minimal*) on Odun Road with models of ships.

Avoid the dreary resort of **Westward Ho!** which was developed in the mid 19th century on the back of Charles Kingsley's book – but without his backing. Kingsley wrote to the resort company: 'How goes on the Northam Burrows scheme for spoiling that beautiful place with hotels and villas? I suppose it must be, but you will frighten away all the sea-pies and defile the Pebble Ridge with chicken bones and sandwich scraps.' It must be the only place in England with an exclamation mark.

It feels good to get back on the coast road, leaving the busy estuary behind. The picture-postcard village of **Clovelly** in its steep wooded combe is part of a private estate that has never been modernized or developed (it charges visitors for entry). A steep cobbled street leads down past immaculately preserved fishermen's cottages to the stone harbour. Charles Kingsley lived in Clovelly for many years (his sister married the rector), and a small room in one of the cottages has been turned into a Victorian study and dedicated to him. At the bottom of a wooded cliff, around the quayside, are a pub, some cottages and piles of crab nets. In the harbour are a handful of rowing boats (which sit on the grey shingle at low tide trailing rusted metal chains).

There is a good walk 2 miles east along the beach (at low tide) to **Buck's Mills**, another tiny village with a tea shop. In summer there are boat trips (1½ hours) to Lundy Island, just off the coast.

At **Hartland Point** the coastline turns south. The walk between Hartland and Bude is one of the toughest sections of the Southwest Coastal Path, with some of the wildest coastal scenery. There are few pubs and only a few farmhouses to stay in. There are good walks from wind-battered **Hartland Quay** – all that survives of a port which stopped operating in 1860. The narrow street of old fishermen's cottages and quay

Getting There and Around

The **Appledore–Instow ferry** runs between May and Oct approximately every 15 minutes. Run by **Tarka Cruises**, **t** (01237) 477 505, *enquiries@appledore-letting.co.uk*. The company also runs 2-hour fishing trips (sea bass, mackerel) from 10am (tide depending).

To reach Hartland, follow signs off the A39 along the B3248, continuing to Stoke. The road ends a mile further on at Hartland Quay.

Tourist Information

Clovelly: car park, **t** (01237) 431 781. *Open daily summer 9–5.30, winter 10–4.*

Where to Stay and Eat

Appledore **t** (01237) –

There are a couple of pleasant pubs and a good fish and chip shop on the corner of Market Street.

Bradbourne House, Marine Parade, **t** 474 395, *vlampen@virtus.demon.co.uk* (*moderate*). B&B in an elegant Georgian house overlooking the River Torridge with fantastic wooden spiral stairs and two lovely bedrooms with private bathrooms. Friendly and helpful owners.

Greysands, Watertown, **t** 479 310 (*moderate*). A lovely half-mile walk along the beach into Appledore.

Regency House, Marine Parade, **t** 473 689 (*cheap*). Overlooks the sea. Six rooms.

Clovelly **t** (01237) –

Red Lion Hotel, The Quay, **t** 431 237, *www.clovelly.co.uk* (*expensive*). Excellent, renowned for its food. Bar meals available, book for restaurant (*eves only*).

New Inn Hotel, High Street, **t** 431 303, *www.clovelly.co.uk* (*expensive*). A short walk up from the quay. Bar meals and restaurant.

Hartland **t** (01237) –

2 Harton Manor, The Square, Hartland **t** 441 670, *merlynl@email.com* (*moderate*). Beautiful house with oak floorboards, big fireplace and golden labrador. Walls hung with photographs of rocks, and woodcut prints. Small studio full of books and paintings. Twin and double.

West Titchberry Farm, Hartland Point, **t** 441 287 (*moderate*). An 18th-century Devon longhouse with three bedrooms; board games and woodburning stove in lounge. Follow Hartland Point signs from Hartland village. Walkers will appreciate the offer of a packed lunch and lift home at the end of a walk. About 5 minutes' walk from coastal path.

Hartland Quay Hotel, Hartland, **t** 441 218, *www.hartlandquayhotel.com* (*moderate*). Lonely hotel above the old Elizabethan quay with 15 functional bedrooms. Great atmosphere and Wreckers beer.

Stoke Barton Farm, Stoke, **t** 441 238 (*cheap*). Farmhouse tea room offering arguably the best cream tea in the West Country. Try and organize a walk that brings you here around lunch time. You can wear your muddy boots on the flagstones without feeling sheepish. Also light lunches. *Open Easter–Sept. Closed Mon and Fri.*

The Old Farmhouse, Hescott Farm, **t** 441 709, *oldfarmhouse.hescott@virgin.net* (*cheap*). About 3 miles from Hartland Point and Clovelly, with flagstone floor and big pine breakfast table. Three simple bedrooms with comfortable beds.

Coombe House, Stoke, **t** 441 427 (*cheap*). Warm, welcoming place to stay, 5 minutes' walk from Hartland Quay. The bathroom looks out to sea. Three simple rooms.

stores leads down a slipway to the ruined harbour. Inland, there are two good potteries in Hartland, including **Springfield Pottery** (*t (01237) 441 506; open Mon–Sat 9–5*) run by Philip (and Frannie) Leach, son of Michael Leach and grandson of Bernard Leach.

Cornwall

The Cornish peninsula juts southwest into the Atlantic, cut off from England to the north by the River Tamar. The Tamar was established as the border between Saxon England and Celtic Britain by Athelstan in the 10th century; for Cornish people it is still where England ends. To all the world, however, Cornwall looks like England's southwestern tip. It has a county town, county courts, a 'Royal' Cornwall Museum and even a statue of Athelstan in Bodmin town square. But until the late Middle Ages it did look like a separate part of Britain: it had its own language, government, head of state (the Duke of Cornwall), saints, weights and measures. Henry VIII styled himself 'King of England and France, Gascony, Guienne, Normandy, Anjoue, Cornwall, Wales and Ireland' at his coronation – and did for Cornwall: he stamped out the Cornish language and Celtic-Catholic religious life, closed down the Cornish University of

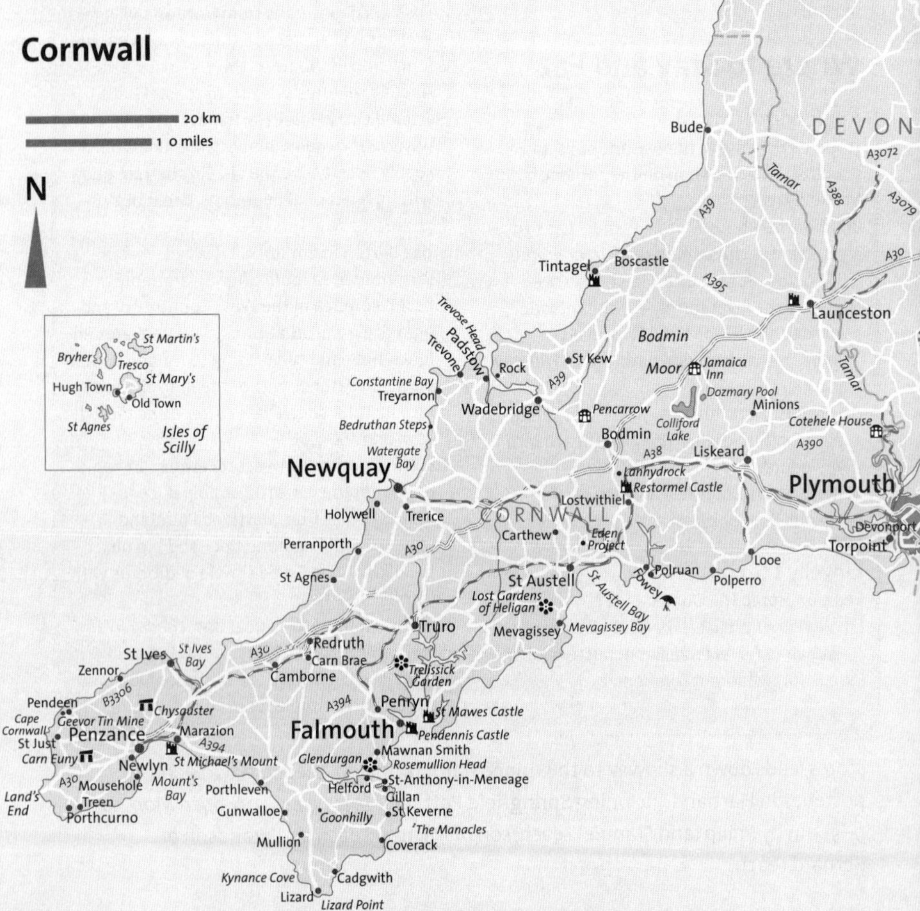

Cornwall's Case for Being Kernow

Cornwall's view of itself as a separate British nation – rather than a county of England – has a sound historical basis. The series of conquests and invasions that instilled unity in England, for better or worse, failed to assimilate Cornwall. There are no Roman villas or Saxon burghs in Cornwall because there was no Roman conquest or Saxon colonization. In the first millennium AD, until the defeat of King Hywell of Cornwall by Athelstan in 926, Cornwall developed its own language, Celtic-Catholic religion, and laws enforced by indigenous kings. 'From earliest times Cornwall was distinct from the kingdom of England, and under separate government... Cornwall, like Wales, was at the time of the Conquest, and was subsequently treated in many respects, as distinct from England,' wrote the Attorney General to the Duchy of Cornwall in the 1855 Foreshore Case. The Norman kings of England made Cornwall an earldom which became, under Edward I, a duchy, the first ever created by an English monarch (held by Prince Charles). This is at the heart of Cornwall's special situation. According to the Attorney General its creation 'referred on the occasion, not to the many recent occupiers of the Honor, or even to the greater Earls who had held the Great Honor of Cornwall from the Conquest, but to the remoter period when the territory was a separate kingdom, and was governed by Rulers and Dukes of its own'. The duke was heir to the old kings of Cornwall, with regal powers and a palace in Lostwithiel. Tin-mining was regulated by the Stannary Parliament, which had its own law-making powers and was exempt from the laws and taxes of Westminster; in practice, all Cornish life came under its jurisdiction. Cornish history is one of collisions between the Stannary Parliament and English monarchs. Henry VII's suspension of stannary government, confiscation of stannary charters and attempts to raise Cornish taxes to fund his own wars in Scotland led to an uprising in 1497; Michael Joseph *An Gof* (The Smith) led a Cornish peasant army of 15,000 men to London, meeting the King's army (raised for the Scottish wars) on Blackheath. The rebels were no match for the professional soldiers, and *An Gof* was executed at Tyburn. There was a second Cornish uprising in the same year, when a 6,000-strong Cornish army attacked Exeter. As part of the clampdown, an English force was sent into Cornwall to put an end to the flagrant privateering, smuggling and independent sea battles of the Cornish captains; ships were impounded with all their gear, victuallers arrested and captains executed in London. The Charter of Pardon in 1508, however, reaffirmed the legislative independence of the Stannary Parliament: 'No act or statute shall have effect in the stannaries without the assent and consent of the 24 stannators.' The beginning of the end of self-government came with the 1549 Act of Uniformity, which ordered that all church services must be conducted in English instead of Latin. Following a petition to the king – 'And so we the Cornish men utterly refuse this new English' – Humphrey Arundell raised another Cornish army, whose defeat was followed by reprisals: 'Henry VIII's mobsters were the real conquerors of Cornwall,' writes Cornish historian John Angarrack in *Our Future Is History*.

Glasney, murdered a significant proportion of the population, redrew the map and revised history to suggest that Cornwall had been an English county since Athelstan.

Rebellious Cornwall is now fighting back. The Cornish language, Kernewek, which was supposed to have died with Dolly Pentreath in 1777, was officially recognized by the Council of Europe as a British minority language in 2002.

English Heritage, which controls tourism in Cornwall, is under fire for sending out misleading messages about England's ownership of Cornwall's heritage. The history books are being rewritten again. For so long the rural backwater loved by metropolitan second-home owners, the poor appendage of a rich country, Cornwall is re-emerging as Kernow, the central pier of a community of Celtic nations including Scotland, Ireland, the Isle of Mann, Wales and Brittany. But for now Cornwall remains something of a cultural no-man's land, deprived of identity for centuries. It is also one of the poorest regions in northwest Europe, on the receiving end of the highest level of European Union grant aid available (£600 million between 2000 and 2006).

None of this gets in the way of its beauty. The shattered headlands and deep sandy coves of the Atlantic coast contrast with the buttery south coast, where sinuous tidal inlets wind inland. The narrow twisting roads are banked by hedges and turf walls. The towns and villages are compact and clean-edged. The underlying granite has produced windswept heathery scenery on Bodmin Moor, the Penwith peninsula and the Isles of Scilly, dotted with the relics of prehistory and the tin-mining industry.

Tin, which has been mined here since the Bronze Age (tin plus copper makes bronze), was long Cornwall's economic bargaining tool against would-be conquerors – Romans, Saxons, Danes and Normans. By the mid-19th century Cornwall was producing half the world's tin and two-thirds of its copper. It was the testing ground for engineering inventions, producing three of the biggest names of the Industrial Revolution: Thomas Savary, Richard Trevithick and Humphrey Davy. Now the tin mines have closed, fish have been fished to near-extinction, and Cornwall relies heavily on its tourist trade for survival.

Bodmin

Bodmin developed around St Petroc's monastery, the biggest medieval church in Cornwall. It is neither pretty nor coastal and is a paradox, the most English of Cornish towns: in its square stands a statue of Athelstan, the Saxon king who 'ethnically cleansed the Cornish', in the words of Bodmin-based historian John Angarrack. On the imposing town square is the Shire Hall, so-called even though Cornwall has never been a shire (it's a Saxon term). Old Bodmin Gaol stands near the centre, a macabre Victorian building with crenellated granite walls.

Pencarrow House and Gardens, 5 miles northwest of Bodmin off the A389, is a lovely Palladian-style mansion, its gardens stocked with rare trees and peacocks. Sir William Molesworth, the 8th Baronet (1810–55) built the mile-long approach drive embanked with rhododendrons, and laid out the formal Italian gardens around the house. He also planted ornamental woodlands around an Iron Age fort.

Lanhydrock House and Gardens nestle at the back of a park on the western slope of the Fowey valley. A tree-lined avenue runs through the 17th-century gatehouse and

Getting There and Around

By **car**, the main A30 route into Cornwall cuts across Bodmin Moor, narrowly bypassing Bodmin town.

Bodmin Parkway station is a major stop on the London Paddington to Penzance mainline **railway**.

The **Bodmin and Wadebridge Railway**, built by Sir William Molesworth of Pencarrow to carry lime sand from Wadebridge up the Camel Valley as compost, now conveys passengers on 3-mile steam-train rides. *Runs Easter and June–Sept daily; Easter–May Tues, Wed and Sun*. Call **t** (01208) 73666 for times and prices.

The **Camel Trail** is a popular cycling route, following the old railway line beside the River Camel between Bodmin, Wadebridge and Padstow (12 miles), with a 7-mile extension to Camelford. You can rent a bicycle at **Bridge Bike Hire**, Eddystone Road, **t** (01208) 813 050, at the start of the trail near Padstow.

Tourist Information

Bodmin: Shire Hall, Mount Folly, **t** (01208) 76616. *Open summer Mon–Sat 10–5, winter Mon–Fri 10–4*. Information on Bodmin, the moor and Cornwall more generally.

Where to Stay and Eat

Bodmin

Priory Cottage, 34 Rhind Street (off Priory Road), **t** (01208) 73064 (*moderate*). Friendly, centuries-old cottage in quiet, secluded part of town. Two bedrooms.

Hotel Casi Casa, 11 Higher Bore Street, **t** (01208) 77592, *www.hotelcasicasa.co.uk* (*moderate*). Pretty, central little white-fronted hotel with flower baskets and a door bell that chimes like Big Ben. Seven bedrooms, comfortable bar and lounge.

Berrio Bridge House, **t** (01566) 782 714 (*moderate*). On eastern side of Bodmin Moor, halfway between Launceston and Liskeard, pretty white cottage B&B beside River Lynher with three neat, pretty bedrooms.

Maple Leaf Café, Honey Street, **t** (01208) 72206 (*cheap*). Friendly small café with courtyard at back. Good wholesome lunches – home-made soups, cauliflower cheese, pasta bakes – and an espresso machine.

knocks on the front door of the splendid neo-Jacobean house, its walls covered in magnolia *grandiflora*, camellia and ivy. It was one of the largest houses in Cornwall when built in the 1630s by Sir Richard Robartes on the land of St Petroc's. Since then much of it has been demolished, leaving only the north wing and its barrel-vaulted long gallery. The 2nd Lord Robartes refurbished the old place in Victorian style. Now it has everything but charm: vintage car rides, 910 acres of parkland and meticulously presented interiors. A highlight is Tommy Agar Robartes' dressing-case, laid out on the bed as if he were about to return to the Front Lines in 1915 (he never did).

Bodmin Moor

The main West Country road (A30) whizzes straight through the middle of Bodmin Moor. **Jamaica Inn** (of the Daphne du Maurier novel) is a popular but tacky pit-stop. A mile down the lane is quaggy **Dozmary Pool**, where, according to legend, St Bedevere chucked Excalibur.

Tempting as it is to rush on to the coast, the moor is an unspoiled world of hedged lanes and footpaths, granite tors and free-ranging cows. For the best of the moor, head for **Minions** in the southeast corner, where there's a good 5-mile walk around **Cheesewring Tor** and past the **Hurlers prehistoric stone circles**. Another good short

Cornish Saints

While travelling in Cornwall you'll come across all sorts of saints you've never heard of before or since. In the 5th century, Christianity retreated to the western, Celtic fringes of Britain in the face of the Germanic invasions. This chilled-out, open-air, non-hierarchical version of Christianity imported from Ireland (Eire) was also strong in the north of Britain at the time Augustine started working on the King of Kent in Canterbury (AD597). The two brands of Christianity came head-to-head at the Synod of Whitby in 664, and Roman Christianity emerged victorious. The key figures of Celtic Christianity were the Irish monk St Aidan (d. 651), who set up the monastery of Lindisfarne on Holy Island, and his disciples SS. Cuthbert, Chad and Cedd, who helped spread the word. In the land of Kernow, west of the River Tamar, Celtic Christianity thrived under a colourful set of churchmen and women like St Piran, who sailed across the Irish Sea on a millstone, and St Ia, who arrived on a leaf. Little is known about these early martyrs, but their lives are commemorated in place names including St Austell, St Meryn, St Ervan, St Erth, St Mabyn, St Mawes and St Ewe.

walk takes you from St Berward's church in Churchtown to **King Arthur's Hall** in the middle of lonely King Arthur's Down. On the northwest moor, you can clamber up to the summit of **Rough Tor** (1,312ft) for staggering views.

The Camel Trail

The Camel Trail is a popular cycling route, following the old Bodmin and Wadebridge Railway line beside the River Camel between Bodmin, Wadebridge and Padstow (12 miles), and on to Camelford (7 miles). The line was built by Sir William Molesworth of Pencarrow to convey limey sand from Wadebridge up the Camel as manure. You can take a steam-train ride (*17 June–Sept daily, Easter–mid-May Wed and Sun;* ***t*** *(01208) 73666*), or hire a bike from Pedal Power at 15 Honey Street (***t*** *(01208) 72557*).

The South Coast: Looe to Fowey

Once through the moor you feel like you're in Cornwall proper at last, with pretty coastal villages and ports lined up before you.

Looe

The south-coast town of **Looe** is pretty, while its workaday harbour still functions as a busy port bringing in coal, timber and fish, and exporting stone and minerals. The East Looe River divides the town into East and West Looe, linked by a seven-arched bridge. **East Looe** has the working Fish Quay, its fishing fleet moored against the river wall, the fish market and packing houses on the quayside. Fore Street, behind the quay, leads to a cluster of sea-front streets. The medieval Guildhall on High Market Street houses a museum full of flotsam and jetsam such as an old pilchard press and a pair of leather seaboots. The buckets-and-spades sandy beach is jolly, but you might

Getting There and Around

If you're arriving by **car**, you can park by the river at West Looe or park at Liskeard and continue to Looe by train.

The mainline London Paddington to Penzance **trains** stop at Liskeard, from where you can catch a local train to Looe: the scenic **Looe Valley Line**, **t** (01752) 233 094, runs a regular service on the old quarry line; the journey takes half an hour.

If you're ready for a walk after the trip down, ask for the **Looe Valley Trails** leaflet at the Tourist Information centre. Mark Camp at **Walkaboutwest**, **t** (01503) 273 060, is a Blue Badge guide for day or evening walks.

Boat trips depart from East Quay around the bay to the Looe Island bird reserve with its smugglers' caves. Ask at the Tourist Information centre. The **Shark Angling Club**, **t** (01503) 262 642, runs seasonal fishing trips: two-hour mackerel trip, half-day shark or reef fish (ling, pollock, conger) trip, or an all-day shark or reef fish trip.

Tourist Information

Looe: The Guildhall, Fore Street, East Looe, **t** (01503) 262 072, *www.looecornwall.co.uk*. *Open summer daily 10–5*.

Fowey: 4 Custom House Hill, **t** (01726) 833 616, *www.fowey.co.uk*. *Open Mon–Fri 9–5.30, weekends until 5*. Sells bus, train, boat, theatre and festival tickets.

The **Daphne Du Maurier Week** arts and literary festival takes place mid-May with many celebrities and literary figures invited. Du Maurier's family home, Ferryside at Bodinnick, is private, but can clearly be seen from the ferry quay.

Fowey Regatta Week in mid-August has races, Red Arrow jets and entertainment every evening including events at The Fowey.

Where to Stay

Looe t (01503) –

Pentylys, West Looe Hill, **t** 262 583 (*moderate*). The best place to stay in West Looe: friendly, with two spotless, quiet bedrooms, pretty garden on hillside behind house and little patio garden. Two minutes from quay.

Tidal Court, 3 Church Street, **t** 263 695 (*moderate*). Modest and old-fashioned in great location.

Fowey t (01726) –

Fowey Hall, Hanson Drive, **t** 833 866, *www.foweyhall.co.uk* (*luxury – but children free with adults*). This vast Victorian country house was the model for Toad Hall in *The Wind in the Willows*, with its columns, onion-shaped corner towers and long windows. Right at the top of town in secluded grounds, it was built by Charles Hanson, who made his fortune in the Canadian lumber trade and rose to become Sheriff of Cornwall and Lord Mayor of London.

The Fowey Hotel, The Esplanade, **t** 832 551, *www.thefoweyhotel.co.uk* (*very expensive*). Large cream-painted Victorian hotel built by Great Western Railway with pretty garden at mouth of estuary. Period-style furnishings. The public dining room (*moderate*) has huge bay windows and mirrors.

The Marina Hotel, The Esplanade, Fowey, **t** 833 315, *www.themarinahotel.co.uk* (*very expensive*). Handsome yellow-painted Georgian waterfront house with wrought-iron balconies and patio garden just behind the river wall. Restaurant (*expensive*) specializes in seafood. Some rooms and restaurant have harbour views.

The King Of Prussia, Town Quay, **t** 833 694 (*moderate*). The nickname of a local smuggler. Clean, bright rooms overlooking quay. Bar meals (*cheap*). Live music Sat eve.

Trevanian Guest House, 70 Lostwithiel Street, **t** 832 602, *www.trevanianguesthouse.co.uk* (*moderate*). Friendly, old-fashioned guest

prefer to go east along the coast path to **Millendreath Beach**, which is smaller and nicer. Children crab off the harbour wall and burly men drink tea outside the **Shark Angling Club of Great Britain** on the Fish Quay. It's less fussy than some of the rest of house behind net curtains with dried flower displays dotted around the rooms.

The Old Exchange, 12 Lostwithiel Street, **t** 833 252 (*moderate*). Owned by the Old Town Crier, whose breakfasts are legendary.

Eating Out

Looe

Osborne House, Lower Chapel Street, **t** 262 970 (*moderate*). A 30-seater restaurant with four rooms to let. Seafood, lobster, crayfish, crab and local produce. Traditional English/French menu. Good wine list.

The Old Malthouse, Fore Street, West Looe, **t** 264 976 (*moderate*). A 350-year-old brewery, close to the harbour, with free parking; three double rooms too.

Trawlers-on-the Quay, The Quay, **t** 263 593 (*moderate*). Long-established seafood restaurant right on the working quay. Dinner all year, summer light lunches too. Todd, the Surfin' Chef, is from Baton Rouge, Louisiana.

The Salutation Inn, Fore Street, **t** 262 784 (*cheap*). A good traditional pub (1612) with tiled floor, leather bench seats, old photos, a small coal fire and low beams. Bar snacks.

Anne's Sandwich Shop (*cheap*). Tiny seasonal shop just off Fore Street on way to quay. Huge filled baps, baguettes and sarnies.

Emile's, The Barbican (at top of town near St Martin's Church), **t** 262 932 (*cheap*). Fish and chips. *Open Tues–Sat eves.*

Around Looe t (01503) –

Talland Bay Hotel, Talland-by-Looe, **t** 272 667, *www.tallandbayhotel.co.uk* (*very expensive*). Lovely old-world country-house hotel at end of a long track, on coastal path between Looe and Polperro; 21 bedrooms, pool, croquet lawn, small putting green and patio overlooking coastal path. Tall conifers dapple the lawn with shade and its colourful garden drops down to the sea.

St Aubyn's, Marine Drive, Hannafore, **t** 264 351, *www.staubyns.co.uk* (*moderate*). Victorian house with eight rooms overlooking the headland on the west side of Looe, on the coastal path to Polperro. Beautiful tiled porch with stained-glass windows and terrific sea views. Small beach down cliff path.

Annaclone, Marine Drive, Hannafore, **t** 265 137 (*moderate*). Friendly and open with three bedrooms. The breakfast room is small, but there is a snooker room with full-sized table.

Cardwen Farm, Pelynt, **t** 220 213 (*moderate*). A lovely setting in a beautiful garden by the River Poll. Converted early 18th-century slate outbuildings are snug with cavernous open fire, ancient charred lintel and sooty stone. Breakfast room is bright and fresh.

Fowey

Food For Thought, The Quay, **t** 832 221, *www.restaurantfoodforthought.co.uk* (*moderate*). Consistently excellent restaurant with emphasis on fish and shellfish. *Closed Sun eve.*

Sam's, 20 Fore Street, **t** 832 273, *www.samsfowey.com* (*moderate*). Steamy warmth and jazzy music hit you on entering this popular bistro. You may have to wait an hour at the bar to be seated, but they will get to you in the end. Specials include big bowls of fresh mussels or oysters. No credit cards or reservations.

Taipan Restaurant, **t** 833 899 (*moderate*). Delicious smells and good local reputation.

The Ship Inn, Trafalgar Square, **t** 627 208, *www.smallandfriendly.co.uk* (*moderate*). A very old St Austell Brewery inn built by Elizabethan privateer Sir John Rashleigh, a contemporary of Drake and Raleigh. Snug bar and separate dining room; five comfortable bedrooms.

The Other Place, 41 Fore Street, **t** 833 636 (*cheap*). Downstairs ice creams and take-away fish and chips. Upstairs deep blue walls, lilies and blue-mosaic tiled bar. *Closed Jan–Feb.*

The Lugger Inn, Fore Street, **t** 833 435. A pub that does great fish and chips (*cheap*).

the Cornish coast. You can take the ferry or cross the bridge to **West Looe**, which is quieter than East Looe; it has a few small shops and Just Jennies tea shop.

Marine Drive climbs up around the coast for half a mile to a gate, beyond which the coastal footpath carries on west to **Polperro** ($4\frac{1}{2}$ miles; stop for lunch at the Five Pilchards Inn in Porthallow and catch the bus back). In its secluded bay, the little fishing port of Polperro has a history of fishing and smuggling; now it's one of Cornwall's picturesque ancient harbours, whose higgledy-piggledy whitewashed cottages are all second homes and holiday lets. A 15-strong fishing fleet of netting boats, trawlers and scallopers bring catches of mackerel (and scallops) into the covered fish market on the quay, but the fishermen can't afford to live in the old village and they don't even use the pubs. There's a museum in an old fisherman's store on the slipway at the end of the west quay, showing photos of the bay when boats used to unload pilchards directly from their boats into the quayside fish stores.

West of Polperro, the coastal path continues strenuously along cliffs to the secluded, shingly beach at **Lantivet Bay** ($3\frac{1}{2}$ miles), then on to **Polruan** ($3\frac{3}{4}$ miles), where you can take the pedestrian ferry to Fowey.

Fowey

Fowey is Cornwall's grandest old harbour town. Its shops sell expensive nautical gear, it has some excellent restaurants and it's surrounded by green hills preserved for centuries by the local gentry. In the Middle Ages, Fowey was as prosperous as any south-coast port; it traded tin and cloth, ferried pilgrims to Santiago, supported the English in various military campaigns and initiated a few private ones of its own; the medieval Fowey Gallants gained notoriety for their acts of daredevil piracy, terrorizing the ports of France and Spain and the Cinque Ports of southeast England. Today, the harbour is busy with pleasure boats and container ships heading for the china-clay docks. Despite its compactness, the town is imposing; its narrow lanes and flights of steps echo your footsteps. Large Victorian buildings on the quay include an **aquarium**, a **museum** and the **Daphne du Maurier visitor centre** (*all open daily 10–5*). The author lived west of Fowey at Menabilly and used the area as a setting for many of her novels. The town is stacked up the hillside behind the quay, with the Gothic mansion of the Treffy family halfway up. The **church** has a handsome tower and a fabulous peal of bells. Sir Arthur Quiller-Couch is buried in the churchyard.

Around Fowey

There are numerous walks around Fowey; pick up a National Trust leaflet. The best short walk is the **Hall Walk**, taking the Bodinnick ferry from Fowey and walking from Bodinnick to Penleath Point along a private promenade, laid out in the 16th century by a member of the local gentry. Another walk takes you from Coombe Farm down to Poldrimouth, with its Du Maurier associations, and east along the cliff to **Catherine's Point**, which guards Fowey harbour with its Tudor castle and Rashleigh mausoleum. Just beyond the point is **Readymoney Cove**, once a landing place for smugglers, at the end of a secret wooded valley. The old trading route between Fowey and Padstow is a popular walk, known as **Saints Way**.

A few miles north of Fowey is **Castle Dore**, an impressive Iron Age fortress guarding the mouth of the River Fowey, occupied into the Roman period. **Restormel Castle**, a mile northeast of the old market town of Lostwithiel, is the castle's Norman successor, protecting the river crossing and collecting tolls from traders. Restormel later became the administrative centre of Cornwall and a stannary court.

St Austell and Around

The only industry left in Cornwall is the extraction of china clay, or kaolin, discovered in England around 1746 by a Plymouth chemist called William Cookworthy in west Cornwall and around St Austell, and sold to Staffordshire potteries like Wedgwood. The industry has been boosted recently by the use of kaolin in paper-making; around 18–20 clay pits are still working. All this is great for the local economy, but makes it a less attractive area visually: mining villages like Foxhole, Nunpean and St Denis are surrounded by white spoil heaps, known as the Cornish Alps. The **Wheal Martyn Discovery Centre** (*open Easter–Oct daily 10–6*) in Carthew tells you all about china-clay extraction, in the setting of the old refinery. The Wheal Martyn pit was reopened in 1971 and continues to be worked today.

The Eden Project

t (01726) 811 900; open daily 10–5; adm exp.

Three miles east of St Austell, an old pit is the home of the most talked-about greenhouse in the country. It is the second brainchild of Tim Smit (whose first baby was Heligan, *see* below). It's a 21st-century update of the Victorian wrought-iron glasshouses, but everything about it is bigger, including the mission to excite the populace about 'the vital relationship between plants, people and resources'. £86 million and 14,000 tons of tubular steel have gone into Eden's three space-age 'biomes'. Each biome replicates a climatic zone and its flora, including a tropics biome with a huge waterfall crashing through palms, mangroves and rubber trees, and an open-top temperate biome. Two more are planned, one for arid sand-loving plants. Although the gardens are still young, it all looks smashing and it's hard to begrudge the price or the queues. The benefits for Cornwall of large-scale tourist attractions like Eden are debatable. It certainly brings in the punters, some of whose cash seeps into the poor local economy. Opponents would argue, however, that it further clogs up the rural landscape and pushes up house prices at the expense of the local people.

Mevagissey

Narrow lanes wind down through green hills into this tiny fishing harbour. The fishing boats, stacked plastic crates of ropes and nets, and men in gumboots busying between the two are the signs of a small but active fishing community. Otherwise Mevagissey is a tourist town, with streets reeking of chips and pasties. Have a walk around the harbour wall, where there are great views back into town and along the headlands. An **aquarium** in the old lifeboat shed shows the fish that end up in the fishermen's nets. At the end of the quay there's a little **museum**, full of local interest.

Tourist Information

Mevagissey: St George's Square, **t** (01726) 844 857, *www.mevagissey-cornwall.co.uk. Open summer daily 9–5, winter Mon–Fri 11–3.*

Where to Stay and Eat

Mevagissey and Around t (01726) –

The Fountain Inn, Cliff Street, **t** 842 320, *www.fountain.inn.cwc.net* (*moderate*). A 15th-century inn with smugglers' bar and oak-beamed, slate-flagged front bar. Upstairs restaurant specializes in fish; several bright bedrooms.

Corran Farm, St Ewe (1½ miles from Mevagissey), **t** 842 159, *www.corranfarm.co.uk* (*moderate*). Trim, cream-plastered farmhouse looking out over green hills. Tastefully furnished rooms. Borders Lost Gardens of Heligan.

Higher Kestle Farm, St Ewe, **t** 842 001 (*moderate*). Cream-painted Victorian farmhouse next door to Corran Farm with three pretty and spotless bedrooms and fabulous views of swelling hills. Cosy guests' sitting room. Easy walk to Heligan.

The Salamander Restaurant, **t** 842 254 (*cheap*). Menu includes seafood chowder and locally caught fish.

Mevagissey Walks

There is an excellent stretch of coastline west of Mevagissey, dominated by the two headlands of **Dodman Point** and **Nare Head** and crinkled with sandy coves. The modest village of **Gorran Haven** is a good place to begin a walk around Maenease Point to Hemmick Beach via Dodman Point, with its massive Iron Age cliff castle. Further west, on the cliffs above Porthluney Cove, **Caerhays Castle** is a romantic pile built by John Nash in 1808 on the site of the medieval fortress of the Trevanion family, who went broke building it. John Charles Williams stepped in, and was one of the first gardeners to make use of early 20th-century plant discoveries, raising successful hybrids such as the entirely new Camellia *x williamsii* group (J.C. Williams, Caerhays and Cornish Snow are all varieties). West again, there is a walk from the unspoilt fishing village of Portloe east to Tregenna and back along the coastal path. Nare Head is another 2½ miles along the coastal path from Portloe, or you can drive there.

The Lost Gardens of Heligan

t (01726) 845 100, www.heligan.com; open daily summer 10–6, winter 10–5; adm.

At the head of the Mevagissey valley, the 'lost' gardens were once at the heart of the Tremayne family estate. Their 'rediscovery' in 1990 sparked massive media interest and funds poured into their restoration. In their Edwardian heyday the gardens were hugely diverse, growing exotic fruit in glasshouses and the latest specimens of plants and trees brought back by plant hunters George Forrest, Robert Fortune and Ernest 'Chinese' Wilson. In 1914 all the gardeners disappeared to fight in the First World War, the gardens became derelict and overgrown and were eventually forgotten. Their restoration has been as exciting as the rediscovery. The location is unbeatable. Walled fruit gardens trap the sun and boast rare examples of horticultural innovation from the 18th and 19th century, such as manure-heated pineapple pits and a prefab fruit house designed by Joseph Paxton (a pioneer of modern horticulture). A jungly arm shoots down the valley; the crowds thin out here and you can feel the romantic spirit of the secretive pools, paths and views.

The North Coast: Boscastle to Padstow

From Hartland Point to Padstow light
Is watery grave by day or by night.

The stretch of coastal path between Boscastle and Padstow on the north coast follows a magnificent section of cliffs. At low tide you can climb down to the sandy beach at **Lundy Bay** with its caves and rock pools. Of the ports of Porthquin, Port Isaac and Portgaverne – once busy fishing pilchards and exporting ore and slate from the nearby mines – only **Port Isaac** has kept its spark. At low tide its beach is littered with seaweed, rusty chains and lobster pots. The village climbs uphill along narrow lanes and alleys; buy a pot of prawns, cockles or lobster scraps from one the shell-fish shops and go for a wander. The coastal path leads off enticingly in both directions.

Getting There and Around

The nearest mainline **railway** station is Bodmin Parkway, 17 miles away. A regular **bus** service runs from Bodmin to Padstow throughout the day.

National Express **coaches** stop at Wadebridge, from where you can catch the same onwards bus

Tourist Information

Boscastle: Cobweb car park, **t** (01840) 250 010. *Open summer 10–5, winter 10.30–4.30.*

You can book **fishing trips** (*Easter–Oct*) at the Rock Shop, on the main street next to the bakery, **t** (01840) 250 527. Two hours (mackerel and pollock), 4 hours (bass and deep-sea fish), 8 hours (reef fishing, shark). Rod, reel and bait all included in the deal.

Padstow: The Redbrick Building, North Quay, **t** (01841) 533 449, *www.padstowlive.com*. *Open summer daily 9.30–5, winter Mon–Fri 9.30–4.30.*

Where to Stay and Eat

Port Isaac t (01208) –

Slipway Hotel, The Harbour Front, **t** 880 264, *www.portisaac.com* (*expensive*). A 16th-century building at the bottom of narrow streets winding down to the harbour. Wonky rooms and views of the harbour. Cosy bar and restaurant which cooks seafood coming off the boats (*moderate*) for breakfast, lunch and dinner.

The Anchorage Guest House, 12 The Terrace, **t** 880 629 (*moderate*). Faces the sea.

Boscastle t (01840) –

The Olde Manor House, The Bridge, **t** 250 251 (*cheap*). Fresh fish, either brought over from Plymouth and Newlyn, or caught by local Boscastle fishermen. You can also get a cream tea or snack lunch.

The Harbour Restaurant, **t** 250 380 (*cheap*). Best carvery in village, plus own steak and kidney pies and local seafood. Also morning coffee, lunch and afternoon tea with home-made scones and strawberry jam. *Open Easter–Oct and Christmas.*

Padstow t (01841) –

The Seafood Restaurant, Riverside, **t** 532 700, *www.rickstein.com* (*luxury*). The fish come straight off the fishing boats into the kitchen and onto the plate. The restaurant has a huge reputation thanks to TV celebrity chef Rick Stein. Dinner might include grilled tuna salad with guacamole and lemon grass followed by monkfish vindaloo or grilled Padstow lobster; 13 bedrooms (*luxury*), most overlooking the harbour. Minimum stay of two nights at weekends.

St Petroc's Hotel and Bistro, 4 New Street, **t** 532 700, *www.rickstein.com* (*very expensive*). Pretty white-painted hotel behind a hedge. Beautifully furnished and decorated, with attentive staff and relaxed atmosphere. Reading room with cream-painted wooden

Boscastle

You feel as if you're still in North Devon here, with the wooded valley and links with Richard Grenville (*see* p.357), who rebuilt the quay prior to the Spanish Armada. From the old village, it is a short walk down the steep valley to the harbour. Where the river opens out into the sea, a double breakwater shelters a handful of boats; whitewashed fishermen's cottages huddle around the slipway.

From the old village, a footpath leads two miles inland up the wooded Valency valley to **St Juliot Church** (2 miles), famously restored by Thomas Hardy after he met his first wife, Emma Gifford.

Heading south to Willapark headland, the coastal path leads across **Forrabury Common** where you can see the rare, preserved remains of an Iron Age arable-strip-farming system. The views are magnificent from the cliff castle.

panelling and sea-grass matting. Ten bedrooms with ornate wrought-iron beds and chairs. The Mediterranean-style **Bistro** (*expensive*), Rick Stein's second restaurant, serves mussels, steak, salads and chips.

Cross House Hotel, Church Street, **t** 532 391, *www.crosshouse.co.uk* (*expensive*). Cream-painted, blue-shuttered Georgian house at the top of Cross Street. Elegantly furnished with rich period colour schemes; 11 bedrooms and a pretty patio garden at the back overlooking the town and estuary.

Tregea Hotel, 16-18 High Street, **t** 532 455, *www.tregea.co.uk* (*expensive*). Elegant, comfortable 17th-century townhouse hotel, 5 minutes' walk uphill from the harbour. Airy interior, all cream-painted and colour-washed wood, with pretty wallpaper and window seats. Breakfasts of croissants, hams, cheese and perfect eggs.

Armsyde, 10 Cross Street, **t** (01841) 532 271, *www.armsyde.co.uk* (*moderate*). Beautiful 18th-century townhouse hotel with period furniture, stripped wooden floorboards and rush matting. Fresh and attractive bedrooms. A little stairway leads up to the top room, which has a French cast-iron bed and sloping ceiling.

The Ebb Restaurant, 1/a The Strand, **t** 532 565 (*moderate*). Stylish restaurant specializing in local produce including Fowey oysters, Padstow crab and lobster, Cornish beef, sea bass and cheese. Two airy, bright dining rooms, one with tables, benches and bar, the other more formal with smart linen and tableware. *Open eves only*.

Margot's, 11 Duke Street, **t** 533 441 (*moderate*). Informal, friendly restaurant with eight tables, pink marbled walls hung with paintings for sale. Seared scallops with bacon followed by confit of duck with spring-onion mash and mustard cream sauce topped off with sticky toffee pudding or saffron-poached pears. *Open Wed–Sun lunch, Wed–Mon dinner*.

Rick Stein's Café, 10 Middle Street, **t** 532 700, *www.rickstein.com* (*moderate*). If you can't afford his restaurants you will be pleased with the café, just next door to his delicatessen. Good coffee and pastries, as well as light lunches of mussels. Upstairs there are three lovely bedrooms (*expensive*).

The Shipwrights, North Quay, **t** 532 451 (*cheap*). Good for a pint and a game of pool.

London Inn, Lanadwell Street, **t** 532 554 (*cheap*). Good old-fashioned drinking pub 50 yards from quay with flagstone snugs, bench seating and Tinners beer. Pub grub and restaurant.

Watergate t (01637) –

Watergate Bay Hotel, **t** (01637) 860 543, *www.watergate.co.uk* (*moderate*). Large Victorian slate hotel with white gables, bays and modern glass annex – the poolside café lounge. One of several big hotels up valley.

The Beach Hut, on the beach, **t** (01637) 860 877 (*moderate*). Colourful bar with painted driftwood counter, fire in winter, funky music (jazz, Latin) and photos of surfers on walls. Seafood the speciality. *Open for breakfast, light meals and dinner in the bistro upstairs*.

Tintagel

This rugged, wave-battered headland is one of the main sites of Arthurian legend. It was here, according to Geoffrey's *History of the Kings of Britain*, that King Arthur was born. As if to support his case, mounds of 5th–6th-century imported pottery found on the headland suggest Tintagel was a Romano-British stronghold, maybe the seat of the kings of *Dumnonia*. Ignore the village and join the procession of people to the headland. The dramatic ruins on **Tintagel Head** belong to the 13th-century cliff-castle of Richard, Earl of Cornwall. Now it's run by English Heritage, making Celtic blood run hot – Arthur, scourge of the Anglo-Saxon invaders, in the hands of the English. The ruins straddle a collapsed rock causeway linking island to mainland. Follow the track down to the haven below the headland, where Tennyson described Merlin scooping baby Arthur out of the sea. Then climb the wooden steps up to the exposed top of the headland, 250ft above the sea. There are plenty of medieval remains to explore, but you really need a good storm to savour the atmosphere.

Padstow and Around

At the mouth of the Camel Estuary, Padstow is a great base for the north coast, with good restaurants, decent places to stay and some of the most beautiful stretches of coastline to north and south. From the grey slate quayside there are views of rolling green hills across the river, which at low tide becomes a huge expanse of yellow sand, leaving the boats in the harbour grounded in sludge. The town's name was originally Petrocstow, after a monastery founded here by Irish missionary St Petroc in the 6th century. These days, people call it Padstein, since fish-loving TV chef Rick Stein moved in with a chain of eateries, which have turned the sleepy old port into gastronomy-on-sea. If you're not just here for the food, the heart of Padstow is the **inner harbour**, always full of boats – visiting beam trawlers between January and April (after the Dover sole) and pleasure boats in summer. There is only a tight huddle of little streets to explore, but it is easy to get lost here, in narrow lanes where the old shops have been replaced by gift shops, pasty shops and craft shops. There is an interesting little **museum** (*open Easter–Oct 10–5; adm minimal*) in the old Victorian institute.

Padstow is famous for its May Day celebrations, held annually on 1 May. A red and a blue ''obby 'oss' dance through the town, stopping at houses and pubs on the way; the crowds follow, trying to touch the 'osses' masks (which have magic properties), buoyed up by accordions and primeval drums. The whole drunken procession ends up at **Prideaux Place** (*open Easter and June–Sept Sun–Thurs 1.30–5; adm*), the grand Elizabethan house of the Prideaux family at the top of town, in its own deer park overlooking the Camel Estuary.

A foot ferry goes back and forth all day across the estuary to **Rock**, a sailing village with swimming beaches and the haunt of rowdy public school boys on holiday. From there, you can walk across the golf course to **St Enodoc's Church** and visit the grave of poet laureate John Betjeman. Continue to the unspoilt, fish-tail-shaped **Pentire peninsula**, where there is an Iron Age fort called the Rumps, or walk to **Stepper Point** and **Trevose Head** on the opposite headland.

King Arthur

In his *History of the English-speaking Peoples*, great rationalist Winston Churchill is in no doubt about the reality of Arthur: 'Somewhere in the Island a great captain gathered the forces of Roman Britain and fought the barbarian invaders to the death...Twelve battles, all located in scenes untraceable, with foes unknown, except that they were heathen, are punctiliously set forth in the Latin of Nennius.' Nennius was a 9th-century chronicler who compiled a history of the old kings of Britain. His work was the main source of the *History of the Kings of Britain* by Geoffrey of Monmouth, a 12th-century Welsh scholar working in one of the religious houses in Oxford. The *History*, which catalogues the reigns of 99 British kings over 2,000 years up to the year 689, is the great source of Arthurian legend, bringing the 6th-century King Arthur and Merlin into popular consciousness – heroic, romantic, civilized and magical. And it is almost entirely made up. There were so few sources for Geoffrey to go on. He does, however, mention 'a certain very ancient book written in the British language' – untraced and most likely cited to give his yarn authenticity. During the Middle Ages, further romantic tales were spun around Geoffrey's *History*, encouraged by Tudor monarchs keen to show off their heroic Welsh pedigree. The most famous, *Morte d'Arthur*, was written by Sir Thomas Mallory, a disreputable Warwickshire knight whose recorded crimes included theft, cattle-rustling and abduction. It was probably written during one of Mallory's spells in prison. The action roams all over Britain, from Wales to Northumbria and Cornwall. It was Mallory's Arthur who entered the modern world, capturing the imagination of the poet Tennyson, who penned his own *Morte d'Arthur*, sparking the 19th-century explosion of Arthurian poems and stories, and the proliferation of Arthurian sites in the West Country.

If you were touring Arthurian sites, you might start at **Cadbury Castle**, a Somerset hill fort named as Camelot by the 16th-century antiquarian John Leland, where archaeology is on the side of the Arthurians: digs in the 1960s identified it as one of the largest 6th-century fortifications in Britain. From there, you could head north-west to the North Devon village of **Morwenstow**, home of eccentric vicar and Arthurian scholar Robert Hawker (1803–74). Tennyson visited him anonymously in 1848, wearing a long black cloak. You can follow Tennyson's footsteps with Hawker, who took him along the cliffs to see his little retreat, built of driftwood into the cliff-face. Another Arthurian hotspot is the lake into which Sir Bedevere throws the sword Excalibur, and an arm 'clothed in white samite' rises up to catch it. There are several contenders, including **Dozmary Pool** on Bodmin Moor (*see* p.369) and **Loe Pool**, on the west of the Lizard Peninsula near Porthleven (*see* p.388), Tennyson's choice.

Newquay and Around

South of Trevose Head, the coast turns west for a while, so you get sunsets over the sea, fast-changing weather and the big Atlantic rollers that are popular with surfers. The tide goes way out, leaving expanses of beach littered with washed-up slate, particularly at **Constantine** and **Treyarnon**. The long beach at **Porthcothan Bay** is the only un-raked beach on the north coast; it still gets fertilized by seaweed when the tide comes in, and the sand dunes are allowed to spread. At low tide there are caves to explore around the headland (but beware the tides, which come in very fast) and the cliff walks in either direction are unbeatable. Further south, the **Bedruthan Steps** are a distinctive series of rocks marching across the green bay between headlands. Bedruthan was a giant and the rocks kept his feet dry across the bay. At high tide, they look like shark fins breaking the surface. At low tide you can climb down to the wet, sandy beach and explore the rock pools.

Further down the coast, **Watergate** is a great beach for beach-combing; come in winter about 15 months after a hurricane in South America for the richest pickings of sea beans, swept across the ocean by the Gulf Stream. It is also a popular surfing beach. A shop on the beach sells and hires surfing and power-kiting gear.

Newquay itself is to be avoided. The main street, Fore Street, is lined with arcades and lager lads. The harbour is on one side of Towan Head, and on the other side – a short walk from the centre – is wide, sandy Fistral Beach, which calls itself 'Europe's premier surfing beach'. Surfing competitions are held here four times a year.

A few miles inland from Newquay, **Trerice House** (***t*** *(01637) 875 404; open Easter–Oct Sun–Mon and Wed–Fri 11–5; adm*) was home to a branch of the Arundells, one of Cornwall's foremost families from the mid-14th to the 17th century. All the heads of the Arundell family were called John, except Thomas who got his lands confiscated for his involvement in the Duke of Buckingham's rebellion against Richard III. A younger brother of one of the Johns married the sister of Henry VIII's fifth wife, Catherine Howard, and bought some monastic estates in Wiltshire at the Dissolution. He founded a junior branch of the family in Wardour, which outlived the quieter Cornish lot. Now you can look around the gardens.

Industrial Cornwall: Camborne and Redruth

The short stretch of the north coast between Perranporth and Hayle is the heart of industrial Cornwall. **Camborne** was the centre of engineering, while **Redruth** was the financial and administrative centre. When South Crofty mine shut down in 1998, Cornish tin-mining and the engineering industry vanished. Camborne and Redruth have merged into a conurbation of old miners' terraces and light industry. Behind them is towering **Carn Brae**, one of the richest archaeological sites in Cornwall, with remains of a Neolithic fortified settlement which, on the evidence of burnt remains and flint arrowheads, came to a sudden and violent end.

Stop at the **Cornish Mines and Engines Discovery Centre** (***t*** *(01209) 315 027, www.nationaltrust.org.uk; open April–Oct Sun–Fri 11–5, Aug daily; adm*) on the site of East Poole Mine, owned by the Agar Robartes of Lanhydrock. The visit takes you on a tour of mining that is now firmly in the past. From the engine house you can see South Crofty, Europe's last working tin mine, closed in 1998. Turn right out of the centre and follow signs to the 1970s **Cornish School of Mines Geological Museum** (*open Mon–Fri 10–4; adm free*). The mines school was set up in 1859 to provide engineering skills to the tin- and copper-mining industries, which at the time produced half of the world's tin and copper. The mineral collection is based on local specimens.

There is a gentle 7-mile walk around **Carn Brae**. Follow signs to the **Mineral Tramway Centre** (**t** *(01209) 613 978; open Sun–Fri 10–4*) in Penhallick, where you can pick up a walking trail. The 2-mile stretch along the Basset Tramway from Carnkie follows the **Great Flat Lode**, considered the best-preserved mining landscape in Europe.

Gwennap Pit, just south of Redruth following signs off the A393 Redruth–Falmouth road, is the original amphitheatre in which John Wesley preached 18 times between 1762 and 1789. Down on the coast, **St Agnes** has a sweet surfing cove, an antidote to the spoil tips and ruined engine houses. At **Trevaunance Cove**, the crumbling brown cliffs enclose a ruined harbour, exposed at low tide, and a shingle-topped sandy beach. You could stop for lunch at the Driftwood Spa Inn, lively in the evenings.

Truro

Truro has all the hallmarks of an English county town – a Victorian-Gothic cathedral, county courts and a county museum, but of course it's really Cornish. It's a fine old

Getting There and Around

By **car**, take the A30 west off the M5 at Exeter; Truro is off the A3076 about 1½ hours beyond Exeter.

Trains on the main London Paddington to Penzance line stop at Truro.

National Express **coaches** operate from Truro Bus Depot on Lemon Quay via Plymouth and Exeter to London.

Boat trips to Falmouth sail from the town quay, *May–Oct*. The crossing takes an hour.

Tourist Information

Truro: Municipal Buildings, Boscawen Street, **t** (01872) 274 555, *www.truro.gov.uk. Open Mon–Fri 9–5.30, summer also Sat 9–5.*

Where to Stay

Truro t (01872) –

Alverton Manor, Tregollis Road, **t** 276 633, *www.connexions.co.uk* (*expensive*). Amazing stone Gothic-Victorian building on edge of town, formerly owned by the Bishop of Truro, with a bell tower, mullioned windows and crenellations; 33 comfortable bedrooms and a traditional restaurant.

The Royal Hotel, Lemon Street, **t** 270 345, *www.royalhotelcornwall.co.uk* (*expensive*). Big, old town-centre hotel. The 35 rooms are old-fashioned with dark furniture.

Cliftons Guest House, 46 Tregolls Road, **t** 274 116, *www.cliftonsguesthouse.co.uk* (*moderate*). In tall Victorian townhouse with bay windows set above main road into town. Six rooms. Friendly and comfortable.

The Townhouse, 20 Falmouth Road, **t** 277 374, *www.trurohotel.com* (*moderate*). An easy-going private hotel with 12 rooms, 5 minutes walk from cathedral. Food 24 hours, help yourself whenever you like.

Bay Tree Guest House, 28 Ferris Town, **t** 240 274 (*cheap*). A Georgian townhouse with four rooms.

Eating Out

Mandarin Garden, 14/a Kenwyn Street, **t** 272 374 (*moderate*). Looks unpromising, but serves excellent Chinese food. *Open eves only.*

Piero's, Kenwyn Street, **t** 222 279 (*moderate*). Large, long, airy Italian pizza-pasta restaurant with lively music. *Closed Sun.*

The Feast, 15 Kenwyn Street, **t** 272 546 (*cheap*). Small, friendly vegetarian restaurant with sunny décor. *Open Mon–Sat 10–5.*

Mannings at The Royal Hotel, Lemon Street, **t** 247 900 (*cheap*). Brasserie and bar with gentle background music. Sizzling platters, hot chicken salad, Thai steamers for two.

town, originally one of the Cornish stannaries, now jolliest on Saturdays when its four markets – the covered Pannier Market, Food Market, Tinner's Court Market and Farmer's Market – coincide. There are winding streets, elegant Georgian buildings, interesting little shops, the museum and cathedral to explore. It's a shame, though, that the river has been expunged from the centre of town, and the old quays look at each other across an ugly car park.

The old **Coinage Hall** on Boscowan Street was the source of Truro's early wealth and status. Tin ingots from the local mines were stored here to await the industry's quality-control tests and get the Duchy's stamp before the tin could be traded and shipped out from the quays. **Truro cathedral**, a mighty Gothic rocket shooting right out of the town, was built on the site of the old parish church when Cornwall got its own diocese in 1876. It seems rather big and pompous. Crossing Lemon Street from Lemon Quay, you can pick up the river, which ducks and dives to the attractive **Victoria Gardens** near the railway viaduct. The main shopping streets are Boscowan Street and River Street, where the **Royal Cornwall Museum** (*open Mon–Sat 10–4; adm*) in an old Georgian bank will detain you longer than anticipated. It tells an Anglo-centric version of the story of Cornwall. The mercifully unpartisan Rashleigh Gallery has models of beam engines and colourful mineral displays.

Falmouth

We are in a very wild and barbarous place which no human being ever visits, in the midst of a most barbarous race, so different in language and custom from the Londoners and the rest of England that they are as unintelligible to these last as to the Venetians.

The Venetian ambassador, Falmouth, 1506

Falmouth is the once-mighty port of the ria coastline, tucked into the third largest natural harbour in the world (after Sydney and Rio). Its name tells only part of the story, as it sits on the mouth not only of the River Fal, but also the rivers Percuil, Tressilian, Truro and Restronguet and several other creeks. The wide open estuary is always full of little sailing boats cutting across the path of huge containers; dotted around the green edges are tiny hamlets, and some of the best walks in Cornwall.

Falmouth's dramatic history of piracy, privateering and lawlessness, which once gave visiting ambassadors the jitters, is viewed by the Cornish not as barbaric but as an unofficial Cornish foreign policy whose enemies and allies were often at odds with those of the government in Westminster. In the 1550s Falmouth went to war against Spanish shipping; the men of the Killigrew family – who feature prominently in the town's swashbuckling history – amassed private fortunes by plundering Spanish ships in the harbour and provisioning pirates and privateers who operated from the Helford River. In the 18th century, the town began to develop along more respectable lines as a Royal Navy base and packet station, acting as the Royal Mail's point of departure for its overseas mail services. The Fox family of Quaker traders came to

Getting There and Around

Flights to Newquay from London Gatwick take just over an hour, then you'll need to hire a car or taxi for the 40-minute drive to Falmouth.

By car you carry straight on down the peninsula on the A30 from the M5.

A shuttle **train** continues to Falmouth from Truro, on the mainline.

Boat trips leave from the Prince of Wales Quay to Truro, Fal & Helford rivers, Flushing and St Mawes, as well as fishing trips (enquire at the quay).

Tourist Information

Falmouth: 28 Killigrew Street, **t** (01326) 312 300, *www.go-cornwall.com. Open daily 9.30–5.30.*

Where to Stay

Falmouth t (01326) –

The Greenbank Hotel, Harbourside, **t** 312 440, *www.greenbank-hotel.com* (*expensive*). Large cream-painted 17th-century hotel on the water's edge, looking out towards Flushing and St Mawes. Tiled entrance lobby; beautifully decorated and furnished with period furniture. Enjoy the views from the **Harbourside Restaurant**, where seafood is the speciality.

Dolvean Hotel, 50 Melville Road, **t** 313 658, *www.dolvean.co.uk* (*moderate*). Award-winning B&B, definitely the best in Falmouth; 11 fresh, comfortable bedrooms. Short walk into town centre.

Cotswold House Hotel, 49 Melville Road, **t** 312 077, *cotswoldhousehotel@fsnet.co.uk* (*moderate*). Just across the road from the Dolvean; homely, extra friendly and efficient. Sea views from some bedrooms.

Melville House, 52 Melville Road, **t** 316 645, *www.melville-house-falmouth.co.uk* (*cheap*). Pink Victorian townhouse with views over Falmouth Estuary.

St Mawes t (01326) –

Hotel Tresanton, Harbourside, **t** 270 055, *www.tresanton.com* (*luxury*). White-walled Mediterranean-style hotel comprising a cluster of houses. It began on a small scale in the 1940s, earning its reputation among the well-to-do yacht crowd, and was reopened in 1999 after some costly improvements. Features local artwork and driftwood picture frames. The gorgeous mosaic-tiled

Falmouth in 1762 and over the next hundred years developed the docks and shipbuilding industry, pouring profits into flamboyant gardens around the Helford River.

The town itself is workaday, although the new **National Maritime Museum** in Discovery Quay (***t*** *(01326) 313 388, www.nmmc.co.uk; open daily 10–5; adm*) has added some zest to the place. Leave your car outside town at the Ponsardon car park and try the Park and Float, 20 minutes' float via the Prince of Wales Quay (*float price includes museum entry*). The hands-on museum has lots of boats. There are a few knick-knack shops and restaurants on High Street and Church Street, parallel to the quays, getting more glamorous the nearer you get to Customs House Quay, built by John Killigrew in 1670 and now a pleasant maritime spot.

The Ria Coastline

This fabulous coastline is shaped by rias – drowned river valleys formed when the sea level rose in Neolithic times. These long, narrow, deep-water inlets, flanked by woodland that comes right down to the water's edge, are used as a harbour by vast container ships, an uncanny juxtaposition.

restaurant spills out onto a sunny terrace on warm days. Book well in advance for lunch (*moderate*) and dinner (*expensive*).

The Idle Rocks Hotel, Harbourside, **t** 270 771, *www.richardsonhotels.co.uk* (*expensive*). Right on the seawall. Restaurant with brasserie bistro, cocktail bar and terrace looking out over the harbour. *Open eves only.*

The Victory Inn, Victory Hill, **t** 270 324, *www.roselandinn.co.uk/victory* (*moderate*). On hill behind quay, friendly and quaint.

Helford River t (01326) –

Accommodation in the Helford River area is mostly self-catering. Contact *www.falmouth-sw-cornwall.co.uk* or **Falmouth Tourist Information**, **t** 312 300. One place to try is **The Riverside**, Helford (*moderate*), a delightful large cottage with terraced gardens which can accommodate 12 adults and five children. Cooked breakfast, dinners and wine are provided, as well as a motor launch and sailing dinghies. Available for weekends in winter, by the week in summer. Charged per head, minimum eight people.

The Shipwright's Arms, Helford Village, **t** 231 235. Thatched pub with terraced patio overlooking water or mudflats, depending on the high and low tides.

Eating Out

Falmouth

Powell's Cellar, at the bottom of the High Street, **t** 311 212 (*moderate*). Seafood and steaks, deep-fried vegetable parcels with tomato coulis or stilton crumble with broccoli and sweetcorn. *Open eves only.*

The Seafood Bar, Quay Street, **t** 315 129 (*moderate*). Tucked away in a basement halfway down with a good local reputation. Try the sardines, crab soup and crab cakes, mussels and calamari. *Open eves only.*

The Chainlocker, Quay Hill, **t** 311 085 (*cheap*). Right on the quay, serves fish and chips.

The Quayside Inn, **t** 312 113 (*cheap*). Sit outside and enjoy the views across the harbour towards Flushing and St Mawes. Wonderful food: try the hand-carved ham, beef and stilton pie or huge hands of bread. Live music Fri and Sat nights.

Spencers Coffee House and Restaurant, Arwenack Street, **t** 313 983 (*cheap*). Tea and coffee, jacket potatoes, grills, full English and vegetarian breakfasts, gammon, fried fish, baguettes, sandwiches, omelettes. *Open daily, summer until 8pm, winter until 3pm only.*

You can walk to **Pendennis Castle** (***t** (01326) 316 594; open daily April–Sept 10–6, Oct–Mar 10–5; adm*) past Falmouth Docks, or drive. The castle was captained by the John Killigrews, father and son. Pendennis retains a military atmosphere; its defensive position was so good that it was expanded to face new threats over the centuries. From **Flushing** there is a 4½-mile walk around Trefussis Point to Mylor Bridge and back down quiet lanes, or on to Restronget and the Pandora Inn, by the water.

There are regular foot ferries from the Prince of Wales Quay in Falmouth to Truro, Flushing, St Mawes and up the Helford River. You may want to base yourself in one of the smaller places.

Roseland Peninsula

One of the most staggeringly lovely corners of Cornwall is the Roseland Peninsula on the eastern shore of Falmouth Haven, almost cut off by the sinewy tidal arm of the River Fal and dissected by the River Percuil. If you are driving from Truro or Falmouth, the **King Harry Ferry** shuttles between the beautiful, densely wooded banks of the River Fal past ships docked in its incredibly deep waters. **Trelissick Gardens** (*open Jan–mid-Feb Thurs–Sun 11–4, mid-Feb–Oct daily 10.30–5.30, Nov–Dec daily 11–4; adm*) are on the western side of the ferry crossing. The gracious 18th-century parkland drops steeply down to the Fal estuary, while the fabulous gardens of rhododendrons and camellias were planted by the Copelands, a Staffordshire Spode china family who moved down to Cornwall and bought the neo-Georgian mansion in 1937.

Taking the foot ferry from Falmouth to **St Mawes**, there is a beautiful 2½-mile walk from St Mawes to St Just in Roseland church via **St Mawes Castle** (*open April–Oct daily 10–6, Nov–Mar Fri–Tues 10–1 and 2–4; adm*), a miniature clover-leaf Tudor fortress on the clifftop, built at the same time as Pendennis on the opposite headland to guard the entrance to Falmouth Haven against the Spanish. It is almost homely, with its elaborate coat of arms, Latin inscriptions and waterside garden of spiky exotic plants. Continue along the coastal path to **St Just church**, located beside a wide, salty creek. People come for miles just to see its flamboyant churchyard, with not a sinister old yew tree in sight but palms, rhododendrons and enormous cabbage swamp plants by ponds instead. The last ferry back to Falmouth is at 5.30pm.

In summer a second foot ferry from St Mawes crosses the Percuil River to **Place**, from where you can pick up the coast path to **St Anthony's Point** at the southernmost tip of the peninsula, with interesting 19th-century and Second World War fortifications. Walk from there around the cliffs to **Porthbeor Beach**, and back to the ferry.

Helford River

The Helford River is the westernmost of the rias, tucked in behind Lizard Peninsula. It is also the most unspoilt, with its little pirate coves and secretive wooded creeks. There are some grand private houses on either side whose gardens slope down to the water. The wide river presents a serious obstacle to travel; only a foot ferry crossing connects the southern villages – collectively known as the Meneage – with urban centres like Falmouth and Truro. The coast path cuts inland from **Rosemullion Head** to the ferry crossing, then back along southern side and around **Gillan Creek**. The best way to see the river is on a boat trip from Falmouth (*Falmouth Pleasure Cruises, **t** (01326) 211 100*) to Gweek (the limit of navigation), or by hiring your own sailing or motor boat (for anything from an hour to a week). If you are coming by car from the north, park in **Mawnan Smith** and walk down to the shore, then west along the coast path to **Glendurgan Gardens** (*open Tues–Sat 10.30–4.30; adm*) or east to Rosemullion Head. Glendurgan was built in the 1840s by Quaker Alfred Fox, but the valley gardens date back to the 1820s. As Falmouth's chief shipping agents, the Foxes were perfectly placed to get hold of exotic trees and shrubs from as far afield as China. Alfred's nephew Robert raised hybrid rhododendrons at Glendurgan. A gate leads from the gardens to the village of **Durgan**, the limit of navigation at low tide. In the 1850s Charles Fox created another little paradise in a steep ravine to the west called **Trebah**. A stream tumbles through the gardens to a small beach at the mouth of the Helford.

From Helford Passage there is a seasonal ferry service (*summer 9–5*) to **Helford**, an idyllic village in a quiet inlet. These days every house in Helford is a holiday home, so there's not even a semblance of normal life, although it was once such a busy port that it had a Customs House of its own. From Helford, you can walk via Kestle to the head of **Frenchman's Creek**, one of the most enchanting creeks of all, especially at high tide, when the water laps the trees. It was made famous by Daphne du Maurier, who gave the creek its name. A path leads down its east side through woods.

Gillan Harbour, a late medieval port in Gillan Creek, is separated from the Helford River by **Dennis Head**, where the ramparts of an Iron Age cliff castle are mixed up with Royalist fortifications from the Civil War. Look at the lovely 15th-century **St Anthony's church** in the village of the same name on the north bank of the creek.

The Lizard Peninsula

South of the intimate wooded fringes of the Helford River, you emerge onto the flat, windswept plateau of the Lizard Peninsula. The serpentine rock of which it is made is exposed around Kynance, Mullion and Coverack in the form of contorted black, red and green cliffs. **Lizard Point** separates the sheltered harbours on the east side of the peninsula from the wave-battered bays on the west. You can walk round.

The B3293 skirts around the Helford River and its creeks to **Coverack** on the eastern coast. Unusually for a Cornish harbour village, Coverack sits above a wide bay. Its small harbour is sheltered behind Dolar Point. From here, looking north you can see Lowland Point (a 1½-mile walk from Coverack), an Ice Age beach. From the point you can see the **Manacles** reef, where many a ship has been wrecked. Nowadays divers flock to the reef in search of treasure. You can continue to **St Keverne**, cutting inland to a narrow lane. The leaders of the 1497 Cornish uprising, Michael Joseph *An Gof* (The Smith) and the lawyer Thomas Flamank are commemorated in St Keverne with a plaque on the church wall, adapted from *An Gof*'s famous last words at Tyborne:

MICHAEL JOSEPH *AN GOF* AND THOMAS FLAMANK LEADERS OF THE CORNISH HOST WHO MARCHED TO LONDON AND SUFFERED VENGEANCE THERE JUNE 1497. THEY SHALL HAVE A NAME PERPETUAL AND FAME PERMANENT AND IMMORTAL.

Up the hill (in the direction of London's Blackheath, where the peasant 'host' met Henry VII's 25,000-strong army) are statues of the Cornish patriots – *An Gof* depicted rallying his men – erected in 1997 in the spirit of Cornish revival.

A vertiginous lane leads down to **Cadgwith**, a workmanlike fishing village of thatched cottages with crab boats pulled up on the tiny beach, a good fish shop and singing in the pub. You can walk north along the coastal path to **Carleon Cove**, at the foot of the Poltesco valley. The ruins behind the beach once belonged to a pilchard factory (1,347,000 fish were caught in two days in 1908), later a serpentine works. Or you can head south on the coastal path to Lizard Point. It's a fabulous section of coast-line. On **Bass Point** stands the old Lloyds Signal Station, which telegraphed London ship-owners news of their ships entering the Channel, and a lookout that logs all passing shipping. You can stop for tea or drinks on the terrace of the old Housel Bay Hotel, whose guests have included George Bernard Shaw and Lewis Carroll.

From Lizard village green, footpaths lead south to **Lizard Point**, where there are two cafés and a shop selling serpentine trinkets. The Lizard is the gateway into the English Channel, and the first sight of England for ocean shipping – not always a welcome one: hundreds of boats have been wrecked on the submerged rocks that extend more

Where to Stay and Eat

The Lizard Peninsula t (01326) –

The Polurrian Hotel, Mullion, **t** 240 421, *www.marine-hotel-leisure.com* (*expensive*). Big, bright hotel with 39 bedrooms, outdoor pool and gardens sloping down towards the headland. Also indoor pool and leisure club, tennis and squash courts.

The Housel Bay Hotel, Housel Bay, **t** 290 417, *www.houselbay.com* (*expensive*). Family-run Victorian hotel on headland, looking out towards the Lizard lighthouse and Lizard Point. Short walk down cliff path to Housel Cove.

The Bay Hotel, Coverack, **t** 280 464, *www.thebayhotel.co.uk* (*expensive*). Comfortable family-run hotel in own gardens, on coastal path behind the sea wall, overlooking the bay. Quick walk down steps to the beach.

The Old Vicarage, Mullion, **t** 240 898, *www.smoothhound.co.uk* (*moderate*). Dates back to Elizabethan times, extended in 1834 with money provided by Queen Anne's bounty. Sir Arthur Conan Doyle used the house as his inspiration for the vicarage in *The Devil's Foot*. Tucked away behind a leafy hedge with four lovely bedrooms, 5 minutes' walk from pubs and shops.

Mullion Cove Hotel, Mullion, **t** 240 328, *www.mullioncove.com* (*moderate*). Pleasant 1900s hotel on coastal path overlooking Mullion Harbour; 30 rooms, with every luxury and smashing sea views. Airy conservatory bar and bistro (*cheap*) and outdoor solar-heated pool. Atlantic View Dining Room (*moderate*).

St Mellans House, Meaver Road, Mullion, **t** 240 172, *www.stmellans.co.uk* (*moderate*). Pretty Edwardian house on way into village, next to charming cream-painted Catholic church. Three bedrooms with views. Good breakfasts: kippers, smoked haddock, eggs any way you like and summer-fruit pancakes

Valley View House, Porthallow, St Keverne, **t** 280 370, *www.smoothhand.co.uk* (*moderate*). Charming house in picturesque cove. Has pretty Cockle Island cottage for weekly let 100 yards from sea.

The Paris Hotel, Coverack, **t** 280 258 (*moderate*). Edwardian hotel on the quay, named after the SS *Paris* passenger liner which foundered on the Manacles in May 1893. The bar is cosy, sea views panoramic and fish served in the restaurant (*cheap*) fresh and simply prepared.

Penmenner House Hotel, Penmenner Road, **t** 290 370 (*cheap*). An 1850 house just off the coastal footpath, visited by the poet Rupert Brooke on his circuitous way to a romantic rendezvous with the under-age Noël Olivier in the New Forest. He met up with the gang of so-called Cambridge Apostles here and put the world to rights over dinner; a letter from Brook to Noël bears testimony. Clean, bright and family-run. Six bedrooms, all with sea views.

Top House, Lizard Village (*cheap*). Photos of lifeboats and wrecks decorate the walls. Serves local Sharps ale, brewed near Padstow.

The Caerthillian, Lizard Village, **t** 290 019, *www.caerthillian.co.uk* (*cheap*). Victorian house with four bedrooms a few steps from village pub.

The Old Cellars, Cadgwith, **t** 290 727 (*cheap*). Morning coffee and cream teas in courtyard, with delicious home-made doughnuts. Lunches of local crab, cod and fresh pollock caught off the beach.

Cadgwith Cove Inn, Cadgwith, **t** 290 513 (*cheap*). Forty rooms, and pub meals of fish from cove, including monkfish and lobster.

than a mile out to sea. In the days when the French and Spanish were always about to invade, its beacon was the first in a chain of communications flashing along the south coast. A concrete path zigzags down to the old lifeboat shed in **Polpeor Cove**, which operated from 1859 until 1961. In heavy seas, the lifeboat men used to crawl down so as not to get swept off. You can see the slipway where the lifeboat was hauled up off the beach to the shed in bad weather.

On the headland stands the old twin-towered **lighthouse** (***t*** *(01209) 210 900; open April–Sept Sun–Thurs 11–5, July–Aug also Fri; adm*), built in 1752 by Trinity House. It's the biggest lighthouse complex in the world, once accommodating six keepers' families. You can see the engine room where a powerful fog horn was operated by three enormous steam engines – two blasts a minute when visibility drops below three miles.

East of the lighthouse is the **Lion's Den**, a hole in the cliff top created by a collapsing sea cave, west is **Kynance Cove**. Steps lead down to the serpentine cove, its sandy beach guarded by crags and caves, completely inundated at high tide; boulders are piled up by the sea beneath the red-black cliffs.

Mullion, a mile or so from the sea, is a complete toy-town village with its own one-way system, council estates, fire brigade, school and shops. From Mullion, three roads shoot down three valleys to Mullion Cove, Poldhu Cove and Polurrian Cove. The harbour at **Mullion Cove** is a perfect green square basin that looks like a swimming pool. Beyond the cove Mullion Island – a bird sanctuary – forms a natural breakwater. There's a good 1½-mile walk south from the harbour up Mullion Cliff to Bosvean. North of Mullion, **Poldhu Cove** is a lovely spot, its dunes enclosed by headlands. The first long-distance radio signal was sent across the Atlantic from Marconi's cliff-top wireless station here. The coastal path leads on to **Helzephron Cliff** ('Hell's Cliff') via **Gunwalloe church**, dramatically sited on the cliff with a detached rock belfry.

Helston and Porthleven

Helston is the Lizard's most serious town. It was once a stannary town and has handsome Georgian townhouses, large civic buildings and banks to prove it. It's at its jolliest in May, when bunting is flung up across the steep high street and, on 8 May, the Furry (or floral) Dance attracts big crowds as couples dance through the streets. For the rest of the year it's less exciting, but drop into the Blue Anchor, which has its own brewery making lethal 'Spingo' beer. **Porthleven**, just past Helston, has a terrific man-made harbour, built in the early 19th century after crowds had helplessly watched the man o' war HMS *Anson* being wrecked a mile east. On the water's edge are Victorian warehouses and a scientific and literary institute with a clock tower. To the south, there are good walks around **Loe Pool**, a lake separated from the sea by a shingle bar (park at Penrose, Highburrow, Chyvarlow, Degibna or Helston). It is one of the contenders for the 'great water' into which Bedevere throws Excalibur in Tennyson's *Morte d'Arthur* – 'a dark strait of barren land:/On one side lay the Ocean, and on one/Lay a great water, and the moon was full.'

Penzance and Mount's Bay

Penzance

Penzance is the main port of Mount's Bay, a stepping stone to Land's End and the Scilly Isles. It can strike you as dreary, characterized by busy roads and industrial estates, or quaint in a workmanlike way – especially around the old harbour. Mount's Bay has been busy for thousands of years. Today it's all go, from the old dockside

Getting There and Around

The A30, the major trunk road of the West Country, which continues on from the M5 (from Bristol and Birmingham) and A303 (from London) at Exeter, takes you all the way to Penzance by **car**.

Great Western **trains** run regularly from London Paddington, via Bristol Temple Meads, Exeter and Truro; you can leave bags in the hotel near the station.

Harry Safari, **t** (01736) 711 427, does minibus tours for eight people around the peninsula, stopping at ancient sites.

Tourist Information

Penzance: Station Approach, **t** (01736) 362 207. *Open summer Mon–Sat 9–5, Sun 9–1; winter Mon–Fri 9–5, Sat 10–1.*

Where to Stay

Penzance t (01736) –

The Summer House, Cornwall Terrace, **t** 363 744, *www.summerhouse-cornwall.com* (*expensive*). Charming Regency corner house tucked behind Queens Hotel on Newlyn Promenade. Beautifully furnished and decorated with dark wooden floorboards and sunshine-yellow walls, twigs placed artistically in enormous vases and comfy old sofas. Five fresh, summery bedrooms. Extremely good-value restaurant, *open summer only, Tues–Sat eves.*

The Georgian House Hotel, 20 Chapel Street, **t** 365 664, *www.theaa.co.uk/hotels* (*moderate*). Formerly the Portuguese Embassy. You are slap in the middle of Penzance's tourist thoroughfare, near restaurants and pubs. Bedrooms pleasant and old-fashioned.

Kimberley Guest House, 10 Morrab Road, **t** 362 727 (*moderate*). Tall, gabled Victorian house in quiet street opposite Penlee Park. Eight rooms and cheerful breakfast room.

Estoril Hotel, 46 Morrab Road, **t** 362 468, *www.estorilhotel.co.uk* (*moderate*). Attractive Victorian house, clean and comfortable.

Penzance Arts Club, Chapel Street, **t** 363 761, *www.penzanceartsclub.co.uk* (*moderate*). Four B&B rooms, the best of them with floorboards and art on walls. Showers in glass boxes in corners. All very easygoing – old sofas around the house, paintings stacked up against walls, breakfast whenever you like.

warehouses behind Wharf Road beneath the pinnacled tower of the church along the arms of the bay to the detached islet of St Michael's Mount, boats, cars, helicopters and trains are in a state of constant activity. In the Bronze Age St Michael's Mount was the local hub of activity, later it was Mousehole and Newlyn. Penzance itself was a late bloomer, the major tin port and administrative centre for West Cornwall in the 16th century; 300 years later half of Cornwall's tin was exported from Penzance, to Turkey, Portugal, Spain, Prussia, Norway and Sweden, all of which had vice-consuls in the town. It seems disinterested in tourists, leaving all that to Mousehole, St Michael's Mount, and St Ives. I am too busy mending boats, catching fish and selling it all to the French, and getting people to and from the Scilly Isles, it seems to be saying. What if I am a bit shabby?

Park in the large car park by the railway station, once part of the old harbour. Down on the **harbourside**, along Wharf Road, it is busy with boat builders, marine engineers and warehouses. **Trinity House National Lighthouse Centre**, housed in an old buoy repair warehouse on the quayside, is easy to spot. It's full of disused lamps and optics, including the Bishop Rock light, one of the largest ever built, dating back to 1880. It also tells classic lighthouse lore, including the story about Henry Winstanley's Eddystone Lighthouse, off Plymouth, built in 1698 and the first lighthouse to inhabit

Ednovean Farm, Perranuthnoe, **t** 711 883 (*moderate*). Roomy, arty place in a stunning, secluded location.

Ennys, St Hilary, **t** 740 262, *www.ennys.co.uk* (*moderate*). Lovely house in a delightful spot. Go for a dip through the flower garden to the heated pool. *Open April–Oct.*

Eating Out

The Summer House, Cornwall Terrace, **t** 363 744, *www.summerhouse-cornwall.com* (*moderate*). Attractive, airy restaurant, spilling out onto leafy patio on warm evenings. Delicious Mediterranean-style home cooking, such as fillet of red mullet with black olives and fresh basil followed by warm apple tart. Open Tues–Sat eves, by prior booking only Nov–Feb.

Michelangelo's, Market Jew Street (near Wharfside shopping centre), **t** 331 113 (*cheap*). Homely, old-fashioned, busy coffee-house and restaurant, offering traditional comfort food like macaroni cheese, cottage pie, cod and chips and hot chocolate fudge cake. Good selection of teas and coffees.

Turks Head, Chapel Street, **t** 363 093 (*cheap*). Friendly, good pub food, lots of fresh fish and fresh vegetables.

Bar Co Co's, 12 Chapel Street, **t** 350 222 (*cheap*). Tapas bar, with walls brightly painted with dancing women, flowers and fish. Also cake and coffee, brunch Sat am. *Closed Sun.*

The Renaissance Café, **t** 366 277 (*cheap*). At the Wharfside near the railway station overlooking the harbour. High ceilings, fans, lamps and big bright paintings. Friendly and welcoming; you can slump on a sofa with coffee and a bun, or sit by the window with a drink from the bar. Good place to while away hours between trains.

Entertainment

The Acorn, Parade Street, **t** 365 620, *www.acorntheatre.co.uk*. The old Victorian chapel has housed the arts centre for more than 30 years. It now hosts mainly comedy, music and films, with some drama, in its 255-seater auditorium.

Penzance Arts Club, Chapel Street, **t** 363 761, *www.penzanceartsclub.co.uk*. Established in 1994, the arts club puts on regular art exhibitions in this Georgian townhouse house. You will find art hanging even in the loo.

a wave-swept rock. The trouble was that it was swept off the rock in the storms of 1703, along with the keepers and Winstanley himself, who had boasted that he would like nothing more than to be in his lighthouse in a storm.

Several streets take you into town. From the lighthouse centre, **Chapel Street** leads past the church (there are superb views from the churchyard over the bay) with a pleasant mix of shops, restaurants and interesting buildings such as the flamboyant Egyptian House; the chocolate house tearoom with its seafaring sign, candy-twist columns and nude nymphs; and the Admiral Benbow pub with a smuggler crouched on the roof with his shooter. The **Union Hotel** used to be the assembly rooms. It was there that the news of Nelson's death and the victory of Trafalgar was first told on the mainland. A Penzance fishing boat intercepted the British warship HMS *Pickle* that was carrying the good-bad news to Falmouth. It was immediately passed on to the Mayor of Penzance, who let everyone know in what is now the Nelson Bar. The **Maritime Museum** has sadly closed, losing its excellent seafaring collection, including salvage from the 1707 wreck of Sir Clowdisley Shovell's fleet off the Scilly Isles and a life-sized section of an 18th century man o' war, to the new, glossy National Maritime Museum in Falmouth.

Penlee Gallery and Museum (*open May–Sept Mon–Sat 10–5, Oct–April 10.30–4.30; adm*) on Morrab Road, off Chapel Street, is in a handsome Italianate mansion that once belonged to an 18th-century Penzance merchant. Permanent exhibitions cover farming, mining and fishing, as well as one or two extraordinary events in local history such as the Spanish raid of 1595, seven years after the Armada, when 200 troops set fire to Newlyn, Mousehole, Penzance and Paul before being chased off by soldiers from Plymouth. Temporary exhibitions with a local flavour frequently include Newlyn School paintings (*see* below). There is a good café too.

Market Jew Street is the main shopping street at the top of town, its unusual name apparently deriving from the Cornish 'marghas yow', meaning Market Thursday. The shops are mainly down-at-heel, but at one end is the magnificent green domed and porticoed Victorian guildhall (now a bank). In front of it stands a statue of local inventor Humphrey Davy holding up his greatest invention – the miner's safety lamp. One or two lanes lead on uphill to little galleries, selling crafts and art.

Newlyn

Newlyn is best known for its modern fishing harbour and market, and its turn-of-the-century regional arts scene. There are one or two things to detain you here. On New Road, **Newlyn Art Gallery** (*open Mon–Sat 10–5*) is the best contemporary art gallery west of Exeter and Bristol. It was built in 1885 at the height of the Newlyn art scene; its three most popular exhibitions are those of local painters and sculptors of the Newlyn Society of Artists, at Christmas, Easter and in July–August. Take a right at the end of New Road up the Coombe to the **Pilchard Works** (*open Easter–Oct Mon–Fri 10–6; adm*),the only surviving pilchard factory in Britain. By turning itself into a heritage attraction, it avoids EU regulations requiring new stainless steel equipment and polystyrene packaging boxes (which would almost certainly close it down) instead of the traditional wooden crates. The works process 102 tons of pilchards a year, exporting almost entirely to Italy, and tell the story of the Cornish pilchard industry in the days when 10,000 tons were caught annually. There are a few shops and galleries at the head of the quay around the **Fisherman's Mission**, with its ship weathervane made by Newlyn Copper. To get a sense of the old fishing harbour that

The Newlyn School

The heyday of the Newlyn School was 1880–1930, just before St Ives took off. The earliest Newlyn painters had studied Impressionism in France and thought that Newlyn looked just like the little French fishing villages they had been painting. **Walter Langley** (born in Birmingham) was the first of the Newlyn painters to settle, in 1882, followed by his friend **Edwin Harris**. **Stanhope Forbes**' *Fish Sale on a Cornish Beach*, painted in a gale on a beach between Newlyn and Penzance, drew national attention to Newlyn. The group painted in the open, depicting ordinary life laced with a bit of Victorian melodrama, and often annotated with lines of poetry or Shakespeare. In the 1880s **Newlyn Copper** achieved some success too, teaching metal-working to young men.

enraptured the Newlyn painters, walk along the narrow road between the modern fishmarket and the Victorian Iceworks to the old quay, as painted by Walter Langley; it's now a little green at the foot of a village area known as the Fradgen. Most of the Newlyn artists lived in the colourful cottages in the Fradgen and Trewarveneth Street.

St Michael's Mount

***t** (01736) 710 507; open Mar–Oct 10.30–5.30, Nov–Feb Mon, Wed and Fri tours only (depending on weather); adm.*

St Michael's Mount is a couple of miles east of Penzance along the coast road, a few hundred yards offshore from Marazion. At low tide you can reach it on foot along a stone causeway across the mud, but at high tide the castle is marooned on its cone of granite. The fairy-tale battlements belong to the Aubyn family home. Colonel John Aubyn bought the old Benedictine priory turned post Dissolution barracks in 1659; subsequent refurbishments have retained its Gothic appearance, with the addition of some Chippendale furniture and an Old Master painting here, and a new Victorian wing there. The harbour at the foot of the hill was rebuilt in 1727 to stimulate trade in tin and copper. Summer crowds trek across the causeway like the medieval pilgrims to the priory (who came to see the jawbone of St Appolonia of Alexandra, patron saint of toothache). Get yourself up to the 14th-century priory church at the top of the island, where the views rekindle any magic lost in the crowds.

Back in **Marazion** there are a few galleries near the seafront and a couple of good restaurants, including the Godolphin Hotel, which serves lunches on the terrace overlooking St Michael's Mount.

St Ives

Pretty, white-washed St Ives wraps itself around the rocky headland of St Ives Head on the western rim of St Ives Bay, the last stop before Land's End Peninsula. Tate Gallery St Ives arrived like a starship on the seafront in 1990, reversing the fortunes of the declining harbour town and its seasonal seaside attractions. Due to the Tate's success, small commercial galleries are flourishing all over town and restaurants are improving (B&Bs, however, stubbornly refuse to change). The harbour, tucked into the headland, adds grit to the galleries, while the town's three sandy beaches jolly it all along. In the height of the summer the place heaves.

Ditch your car *en route* into town, as the small centre gets jam-packed in summer. Beneath the main road into town, east-facing **Porthminster Beach** is the main family beach of St Ives, but you are more likely to drift from the quayside to **Porthgwidden Beach** – in a sheltered rocky niche in the headland – or **Porthmear Beach** on the other side of the headland, which is north-facing and gets the big Atlantic rollers. In the old fisherman's mission above the harbour, **St Ives Museum** (*open summer daily 10–5, winter weekends 10–4*) is full of interesting everyday old flotsam and jetsam from the old town before it caught art fever.

Tourist Information

St Ives: Street-An-Pol, The Guildhall, **t** 796 297. *Open Mon–Sat 9–6, Sun 10–4.*

Where to Stay

St Ives t (01736) –

Lots of pretty average B&Bs, mostly dowdy and old-fashioned; all the creative energy seems to have been directed away from interior design.

Porthminster Hotel, The Terrace, **t** 795 221, *www.porthminster-hotel.co.uk* (*expensive*). Overlooks the bay above subtropical gardens; 47 bedrooms, bar, lounge and restaurant. Heated outdoor and indoor pools, and fitness centre.

The Garrack Hotel, Burthallan Lane, **t** 796 199, *www.garrack.com* (*expensive*). A 1920s house, blanketed in Virginia creeper and set in gardens high above Porthmeor Beach; 24 rooms. Very good evening meals in restaurant (*moderate*).

Skidden House Hotel, Skidden Hill, **t** 796 899, *www.skiddenhouse.co.uk* (*moderate*). Centuries-old, in excellent position just up from the sea. Red-painted shutters, white walls and flower baskets.

The Anchorage, 5 Bunkers Hill, **t** 797 135, *www.theanchoragebb.fsnet.co.uk* (*moderate*). Six rooms, just off the quay.

Cobbles, 33 Back Road West, **t** 798 206 (*moderate*). Super, friendly B&B in centre with parking space.

Norway House, Norway Square, **t** 795 678 (*moderate*). Pretty white cottage near harbour with three rooms.

Kynance Guest House, The Warren, **t** 796 636, *www.kynance.com* (*moderate*). Cheerful blue-shuttered building, perfectly located on the edge of Porthminster Beach and a short walk to the town centre. Clean and comfortable.

The Belyars Croft Hotel, The Belyars, **t** 796 304, *www.belyarscrofthotel.co.uk* (*moderate*). Victorian house with big views over the bay, a steep 5-minute walk into town. Period décor, 13 bedrooms, some with sea views.

Eating Out

The Alba Restaurant, **t** 797 222 (*moderate*). Run by a Rick Stein protégé with good seafood and modern English dishes.

Porthminster Beach Café, **t** 795 352. Excellent seafood restaurant right on the beach. Open summer only, daily from 10am, for morning coffee, lunch (*cheap*) and dinner (*moderate*). Book well ahead.

Café on the Square, Island Square, **t** 793 621 (*cheap*). Tucked away in a back street up stone steps. Pleasant, informal and airy. *Open breakfast, lunch and dinner until late.*

Porthgwidden Beach Café, **t** 796 791. Fresh local produce, lots of seafood (*cheap*). *Open summer only, breakfast from 8am, lunch, tea and dinner.*

Café Pasta, The Wharf, **t** 796 447 (*cheap*). Modest pizza and pasta restaurant on the quayside.

To get your bearings, stand on the end of St Ives Head (otherwise known as The Island) and look back. Beneath you, **Tate Gallery St Ives** (*open daily 10–5*) looks like the starship enterprise in disguise; striking and monolithic, but like a jumble of houses full of balconies and small windows. It was built to exhibit the work of the St Ives School – which it does – but its five diverse gallery spaces also feature changing displays of 20th-century art, usually with a Cornish connection. Behind it in the hillside cemetery is the tiled **grave of Alfred Wallis** (near the chapel) made by Bernard Leach, who had lived on and off in St Ives since 1920. The inscription reads ALFRED WALLIS/ARTIST & MARINER, with a picture of a man climbing up steps through a lighthouse door. Wallis was a fisherman who took up painting when he retired, and caught the attention of Ben Nicholson with his naïve paintings of boats on old bits of

Modern Art in St Ives

Artists have been painting St Ives since Turner first sketched it in 1811. By the 1890s they were coming down in hordes on the railway and using old sail lofts as studios. By 1920, when **Bernard Leach** set up his pottery with **Shoji Hamada**, there was a small community of artists living in the town, who came together to form the St Ives Society of Artists in 1927. **Alfred Wallis**, a retired fisherman with a local rag-and-bone business, is the unofficial patron saint of St Ives artists past and present. He had no art training and didn't pick up a paint brush until he was widowed at the age of 72; then he couldn't stop, painting on bits of wood and old marmalade jars. In the 1920s **Ben Nicholson** and **Christopher Wood** discovered him while on a trip and started to copy his unsophisticated style, turning their back on art-school conventions like perspective. Nicholson married the abstract sculptor **Barbara Hepworth** in London in 1933 and they moved down to St Ives at the outbreak of the Second World War. Hepworth bought her Trewyn Studio in 1949, the year of the famous split in the St Ives Society of Artists over abstraction in art. The avant garde broke off and formed the **Penwith Society**, leaving the figurative painters to their own devices. Artists like Nicholson, Wood, Hepworth and Naum Gabo were internationalist in outlook, but shared enough common values, and the landscape of St Ives, to be called a school. The St Ives School is considered Britain's most international 20th-century art scene.

cardboard. There is a plaque on the wall of his old cottage in Back Road West, just along from the Tate Gallery.

Barbara Hepworth's old studio, at the bottom of Barnoon Hill, became the **Barbara Hepworth Museum and Sculpture Garden** (*open Oct–Mar Tues–Sun*) shortly after her death in 1975. The complex of delightful, ramshackle workshops with low, sloping roofs turns its back to the town, facing into Hepworth's garden. In 1951, three years after setting up studio, she came to live here too when her marriage with Ben Nicholson broke down. There is a small exhibition in her old living rooms (stripped of all domestic memories), while her workshops and garden are a sculpture gallery and her memorial. Her dusty, whitewashed stone workshop is kept just as she left it – old hand-tools lying around, her overalls on a hook and notes to herself pinned to the walls. She produced more than 600 original pieces in wood, stone and metal, lived alone, and set fire to herself smoking in bed, aged 72.

Expensive contemporary art is now sold at the **Wills Lane**, **New Millennium** and **Belgrave** galleries, while a raft of others sell a hotchpotch of local work.

About a mile out of town, taking the steep road called the Stannack from the top of the High Street, the **Bernard Leach Pottery** (*t (01736) 796 398; may be shutting up shop for good*) has a workaday atmosphere, which belies the quality of work produced here. Leach founded the pottery in 1920 with Shoji Hamada, who slept on a camp bed in the workshop, and developed a craft tradition that has influenced every studio potter since. It is still a working pottery, under Trevor Corser and Joanna Wason, whose wares are on sale. The house is filled with pieces by the entire Leach family and Shoji Hamada,and items donated by ex-students like Michael Cardew. Look out for the fire-place decorated with Bernard Leach tiles.

Land's End Peninsula

Land's End Peninsula, also known as Penwith, is the western extremity of Britain, beyond the deep bays of St Ives and Penzance. Although the interior is a patchwork quilt of fields dotted with farmhouses, the battered north coast between St Ives and Pendeen is harsh, backed by rough hills, scree slopes, moors and the shattered relics of prehistoric life. You would hardly believe it, but Bronze Age Penwith was the most populous part of Cornwall and St Michael's Mount was its port. On the western rim of the peninsula there are more than a thousand known archaeological sites, most still prominent in the landscape: stone circles, cliff castles, burial chambers (quoits) and Bronze Age villages with strange tunnels called fougous. The prehistoric structures echo the natural tors and rocking stones so that it is often hard to tell them apart. They could be confused with Hepworth sculptures too. Not all of the archaeology is ancient: along the cliffs there are also the ruined engine houses and chimney stacks of 19th-century tin mines. At that time the bays were busy with pilchard fisheries too. The main shoals would appear in mid-July, southwest of Land's End, swimming into the Channel in oily swarms (the last great pilchard catch was at St Ives in 1907). To tour Penwith, base yourself in St Ives, Penzance, or a farmhouse B&B further west, and explore on foot where you can.

Mousehole

Mousehole, just around the southern headland of Mount's Bay, is yet another picturesque granite fishing village. (*In summer leave your car before the hotel.*) It is remembered as the home of Dolly Pentreath (d. 1777), the last native speaker of the Cornish language (until its revival), and the Penlee lifeboat disaster of 19 December 1981, when eight Mousehole men – the entire crew of the *Solomon Browne* lifeboat – drowned trying to save a coaster in mountainous seas beyond Lamorna Cove. The

Where to Stay and Eat

Land's End Peninsula t (01736) –

The Old Sunday School, Cape Cornwall Street, St Just, Penwith, **t** 788 444, *www.oldsundayschool.co.uk* (*moderate*). Nicely converted 200-year-old chapel, now art gallery and guesthouse.

The Gurnard's Head Hotel, Treen, Zennor, **t** 796 928 (*moderate*). An old pub standing alone on coastal road between St Ives and Land's End, short walk from the Celtic hill fort. Good food. Paintings for sale on the walls. Live folk music Wed and Fri eves.

The Old Coast Guard Hotel, Mousehole, **t** 731 222, *www.oldcoastguardhotel.co.uk* (*moderate*). Fabulous, stylish place to stay. Antique grey woodwork, scrubbed wooden wardrobes and sea views. Half the hotel's 20 bedrooms are in the lodge with double doors opening out onto the garden. Restaurant (*moderate*), brasserie and bar.

The Ship Inn, Mousehole, **t** 731 234 (*moderate*). Both bars overlook the water. Bar snacks lunch and dinner.

Gear Farm, Zennor, **t** 795 471 (*cheap*). Through Boswednack, just before Gurnard's Head Hotel. Wonderful farmhouse, best bathroom in Cornwall with long views over dry-stone-walled fields. Very friendly. Three rooms. Breakfast in conservatory at long, scrubbed wooden table.

Old Coast Guard Hotel is a fabulous place to stay, with antique grey woodwork, scrubbed wardrobes and sea views. There is an excellent walk south along the cliffs to rugged Lamorna Cove (where a café serves pizza, pasta and good breakfasts) with its granite quarries, up the Lamorna Valley and back via Kemyel.

Over the Top and Around the Coast from Mousehole

The Newlyn–Treen road crosses the Lamorna Valley and soon you'll see a sign to the **Merry Maidens**, the best-preserved of Cornwall's stone circles, dating from the late Neolithic era–early Bronze Age. Treen, with its general shop, pub and car park, is the starting point for a walk to the most famous *logan* or rocking stone in Cornwall. The path heads south through the stone gateway of Iron Age cliff castle **Treryn Dinas** on the rocky headland. The **Logan Rock** is inside the castle. All these headlands are fabulous to explore, with their smooth, grey anthropomorphic rocks and cliff-top views. You can follow the coast path east to **Penberth Cove** or west to Porthcurno.

The road sweeps down the valley to **Porthcurno**, past a complex of 1950s buildings – all that is left of the training college for the telegraphy station at the back of the beach which, at its height in the early 20th century, was the largest in the world and the hub of the British imperial communications network; 14 buried cables ran up the beach. Eastern Telegraph Company chose the site in 1870 because it was out of the way of major shipping lanes, with deep sand to bury the cables. In 1929 it merged with the radio telegraphy side of the Marconi Company to form Cable and Wireless. Now there's a **Museum of Submarine Telegraphy** (*open Jan–Mar Sun–Tues 10–4, April–June Sun and Fri 10–5, July–Aug daily 10–5, Sept–Oct Sun–Fri 10–5, Nov–Dec Sun–Mon 10–4; adm*). Mug up on telegraphy in the Wiring the World exhibition in the telegraph station. There is a working replica of Marconi's spark transmitter, which sent the first Morse radio signal across the Atlantic in 1901. The small hut on the beach was the physical terminus of the cable links with the former colonies; from here the 14 cables stretch underwater as far as Gibraltar, Bombay, Azores and Brest.

Up the headland above Porthcurno is the open-air **Minack Theatre**, cut into a rocky gully in the cliff in the 1930s by Rowena Cade, daughter of a Derbyshire industrialist. You can visit all year, although productions (usually Shakespeare) are staged only in summer. It looks like it has strayed from ancient Greece, with its amphitheatre of stone seats; behind the stage, it's a sheer drop to the sea.

Land's End

The theme park on **Land's End** is one of England's most depressing tourist spots; why ruin a spectacularly beautiful headland and landmark, England's southwestern extremity, in this way? By approaching on foot from Sennen Cove along the coastal path, however, you can still appreciate the natural grandeur of the site. On a clear day you can see the wave-battered lighthouse on Wolf Rock, nine miles off shore. It is one of the most remote lighthouses in Britain; a keeper was once driven mad with fear during a sustained storm, leading to a rule that there should always be two keepers.

To the north of Land's End, behind the long sandy sweep of **Whitesand Bay,** is the most popular beach on Penwith; amenities are at the southern end, at Sennen.

Not far away, taking the Sancreed turn off the A30, is the excavated Iron Age village at **Carn Euny**. The existence of round houses and a more elaborate courtyard house indicate to those who know that the village developed between 200 BC and AD 400, although there was a settlement on the site as early as the Neolithic era. You can see a stone tunnel, or fougou, here; it's about 15 yards long and built of drystone walls, the earthern roof supported by granite lintels. No one knows why the fougous were built, but smugglers later found them useful for hiding contraband.

The North Coast

St Just is the centre of the now defunct tin- and copper-mining district of Penwith, stretching north to Pendeen. **Cape Cornwall** is a dramatic place to begin a cliff walk north to the headland of Pendeen Watch, taking in ruined engine houses dotted along the cliffs. **Geevor Tin Mine** (*open Mar–Oct Sun–Fri 10–5, Nov–Feb Mon–Fri 10–4; adm*) was the last working mine in West Cornwall, closing in 1992. It is a huge and complex mine, where you can see the complex process of ore extraction through crushing, sifting and purifying processes. It's all quite modern and not very romantic, but a fascinating glimpse of the real Cornwall. In the museum, a model of the underground workings shows 70 miles of levels under the sea, the furthest extending more than a mile from the shore. In the 1960s, Geevor took over the old workings of neighbouring **Levant Mine** (*open June–Aug Sun–Fri 11–5, Sept–May Fri 11–5; adm*), a Victorian cliff mine disbanded in 1930 because miners were no longer prepared to descend 2,000 feet underground on a ladder. The crumbling brick chimneys around the site are known as calciners; they are where the arsenic and sulphur were burned off to leave tin and copper compounds. The 1840 engine house contains the only steam-driven Trevithick beam engine in Cornwall.

You could spend an entire holiday tracking down Stone Age–Iron Age antiquities here. From a car park east of **Pendeen**, on the B3318, a track leads along the Tinner's Way across the moor to **Chun Quoit**, a perfectly preserved Stone Age chamber tomb built of four upright megaliths supporting a massive capstone. From here, a path leads up to the stone ramparts of **Chun Castle** on the top of the hill. It is the only Iron Age hill fort in Cornwall built of stone. On the slopes beneath it you can still see the outlines of the prehistoric fields.

Chysauster Iron Age Village (*open April–Sept 10–6, Oct 10–dusk; adm minimal*), just off the Gulval–Gurnard's Head road between the A30 north of Penzance and the B3306 coast road, is not to be bettered archeologically anywhere in England, and is also intensely atmospheric, wild and overgrown. The nine excavated courtyard houses, preserved with thresholds and fire grates, date from the first three centuries AD, when the rest of Britain was increasingly Romanized.

From the tiny stone farming village of **Zennor**, a few fields away from the cliffs, you can walk up Zennor Hill to **Zennor Quoit**, a Stone Age chamber tomb with a monumental entrance. In Zennor there is a café in the old chapel (or you can drink beer in the Tinner's Arms). The lane between the church and the pub leads to **Zennor Head**, following the coastal path around the sheer headland, with terrific views back towards the dome of the granite moorland. The longer walk south to Pendeen is one of the most dramatic, empty and wild sections along the South-West Coastal Path.

The Scilly Isles

The Scilly Isles are an archipelago of about 50 islands and countless rocky islets 30 miles beyond Land's End. Five are inhabited: St Mary's, Tresco, St Martin's, St Agnes and Bryher. You could walk around the coast of St Mary's, the biggest, in an afternoon. The rest, with Tolkeinesque names like the Biggal of Gorregan, are left to seals, birds and gales. The isles are said to be the drowned land of Lyonesse of Celtic legend, home of Tristram and the Lady of Lyones. They are in fact sinking; in the early Middle Ages the islands were connected at low water, now they're divided by narrow sea channels with romantic names like Garden of Maiden Bower.

There are hundreds of miles of Scilly coastline, with deserted sandy beaches and rocky coves to explore. The inland heathland is peppered with prehistoric remains, including a Neolithic chambered tomb particular to Scilly. The climate is particular too, warm even in winter, filling the fields with daffodils and lacing hedgerows with wild flowers – the fleshy mesembryanthemum, pink sea-thrift and dwarf pansy – which don't grow on the mainland. The cut-flower industry started in 1868 and is now the mainstay of the island's economy, along with tourism. Fishing and wrecking, the traditional sources of income, are more or less extinct. The rocky islands guarding the English and Irish channels are notorious ship-wreckers; take a boat trip around Bishop's Rock lighthouse to see the lethal Western Rocks. Scilly is the main landfall for many migrating birds, far from extinct, who stop off here in spring and autumn. In October the islands are overrun with birdwatchers, B&Bs are booked up months ahead, launches are packed out, and every evening the birdwatchers' log is brought out in the Scillonian Club in Hugh Town, and sightings recorded. The twitchers long for wild westerlies to blow vagrant American birds across the Atlantic.

Scilly is a remarkable place to be outdoors, so pack wet weather clothes at any time of year. Base yourself in Hugh Town, the main population centre on St Mary's, and explore the islands by boat and on foot. By the end of your stay you'll have a ruddy-cheeked glow.

On a rainy day pop into the **museum** (*open summer Mon–Sat 10–4.30 and 7.30–9; adm*) in Hugh Town to see the archaeological finds – most impressive of all a 2½ft-long Iron Age sword in its ornate bronze scabbard. Salvaged wreckage includes a Greek vase from HMS *Colossus*, Nelson's store ship at the Battle of the Nile, wrecked off Samson in 1798, and flotsam from Sir Clowdisley Shovell's fleet, wrecked off the Western Rocks in October 1707 returning from the Wars of the Spanish Succession. On the ground floor is a fully rigged 19th-century pilot gig.

On a sunny day no one sticks around in town; everyone is out walking in remote places and finding deserted beaches. St Mary's is at the hub of the islands and by doing a complete lap of it you glimpse them all: the bare hills of Samson; the southern beaches of Tresco and St Martin's to the north; the scattered islets to the east; the mouth of the English Channel to the southeast; and waves churning over St Agnes and Annet to the west. From the half-hour Garrison Walls Walk, at its best in the early evening, you get a panorama of the western islands. Stay on the lower path, where you get views of Bishop's Rock lighthouse over Annet, the twitchers' paradise of St Agnes and the Gugh, and down into Porthcressa Bay. If you head north to Porthmellon, you can follow the coastal path past mesembryathemum-covered walls

Getting There and Around

There is a regular **helicopter** service to the Scilly Isles from Penzance Heliport, **t** (01736) 363 871.

The ***Scillonian* ferry** runs a return service from Penzance to St Mary's most days in summer, twice weekly in winter. It takes about 3 hours. Contact **The Isles of Scilly Travel Centre**, Quay Street, Penzance, **t** 08457 105555. Once you're there, the **St Mary's Boatman Association** has 10 passenger launches motoring around the islands in summer. Tickets from kiosk on St Mary's Quay. **Tim Fortey 'Calypso'**, **t** (01720) 422 187 after 5.30pm, has four smaller tour boats.

You can catch a **bus** from Hugh Town across the island and walk back, or do the same by taxi.

Bicycles can be hired on St Mary's from **Buccaboo Cycle Hire** at Porthcressa, **t** (01720) 422 289.

Guided wildlife and archaeological **walks** around the island are run by **Island Wildlife Tours**, **t** (01720) 422 212 or **Scilly Walks**, **t** (01720) 423 326, *www.scillywalks.co.uk*.

Tourist Information

Scilly Isles: Wesleyan Chapel, Well Lane, Hugh Town, St Mary's, **t** (01720) 422 536, *www.simplyscilly.co.uk. Open summer Mon–Fri 8.30–6, Sat 8.30–5, winter Mon–Fri only 8.30–5.*

There are twice-weekly **gig races** in summer (*Wed and Fri, 7.45pm*) from St Mary's Quay.

Where to Stay and Eat

There are plenty of places to stay, both luxurious and down-to-earth, and a number of good restaurants.

Hugh Town t (01720) –

Star Castle Hotel, **t** 422 317, *recep@star-castlescilly.demon.co.uk* (*luxury*). In the 16th-century fort above Hugh Town, an atmospheric place. Small cosy bar in the old dungeon serving good local beers.

Atlantic Hotel, High Street, **t** 422 417, *atlantichotel@brinternet.com* (*very expensive*). About 100 yards from the quay, a marvellous place with panoramic ocean views.

The Harbourside Hotel, The Quay, **t** 422 352, *www.harbourside-scilly.co.uk* (*expensive*). Clear views of the islands from a spot overlooking the ferry docks.

Evergreen Cottage, The Parade, **t** 422 711 (*moderate*). A beautiful 1700s captain's cottage with a garden overflowing with flowers.

Hazeldene, Church Street, **t** 422 864 (*cheap*). A typical old Scillonian cottage with a friendly atmosphere.

The best pubs are **The Mermaid,** The Bank, **t** 422 701 and the **Atlantic Inn**, High Street, **t** 422 323, both of which do fisherman's pie and the like in harbour-view restaurants.

Chez Michel, The Parade, **t** 422 871 (*moderate*). The best restaurant, run by a Swiss-French cook relying on local produce: Cornish asparagus, Scilly crab, lobster and freshly caught fish, strawberries with syllabub or home-baked shortbread. Also open for coffee and tea.

The Galley Restaurant, The Parade, **t** 422 602 (*cheap*). Tiny, long-established restaurant in cottage attached to fishmonger's: skate, John Dory, lemon sole, mackerel, bass.

Juliet's Garden Café and Restaurant, Seaways Flower Farm, **t** 422 228 (*cheap*). On headland above Porthloo beach. Sandwiches and cakes in garden with views of Gough.

round the west side of the island to Harry's Walls and the 16th-century fort, an excellent lookout towards the bare hills of Samson and the golden sands of Tresco, with Bryher in between. From Porthloo beach aim for the telegraph mast nearest the shore and you'll come to the prehistoric sites on Halangy Down. The stone remains of a Bronze Age village are built on terraces up the hill. At the top of the hill, Bant's Carn chambered tomb is about 1,500 years older.

The northern face of the island lacks all habitation and roads. Bar Point on the northernmost tip is a wild spot backed by dunes, ferny slopes and angular pine trees. The sandy coastal path towards Toll's Island takes you to Innisidgen Carn. Further south, you can reach remote, sandy Pelistry beach over a sand bar at low-tide.

Porth Hellick beach, on the southeastern coast, is all scrunchy shingle and shells. At the back of the beach is a monument marking the spot where the body of Sir Clowdisley Shovell, admiral of the British fleet, was found after his boat HMS *Association* was wrecked off the Western Rocks in 1707. You can follow a nature trail up the Holy Vale stream, along a magical path where the embanked roots of trees part like processional swords to guide you over quaggy ground.

Between Porth Hellick and Old Town the coastal path crosses heathland past huge rocks projecting into the sea. Take note of the 'Warning Aircraft Stop' sign; continue with a green light over the runway of St Mary's Airport, or stop if it's red.

Plain Old Town sits on a beautiful green headland. It was once called Porthenor and boasted a castle, quay and church, but fell into decline when Hugh Town grew in the 16th century. It now boasts two cafés and a churchyard packed with sailors' graves; detailed epitaphs include one 'who died at Rio de Janeiro of Yellow Fever on his voyage to the Cape of Good Hope aged 21' among the shipwrecked. The obelisk at the top belongs to Louise Holzmaister, one of 300 fatalities of the 1875 wreck of the *Schiller*, a New York-bound German liner which ran onto the Western Rocks in fog.

Beside the modern lighthouse on Peninnis Head, the rocks resemble Hepworths. On Tresco, you can walk to **Cromwell's Castle** and **King Charles' Castle**, continuing on to the lush subtropical Tresco Abbey Gardens (*open daily 10–4; adm exp*).

Another trip could take you to St Agnes and The Gugh (pronounced 'goo'), to see the **Old Man of Gugh**, an isolated Bronze Age standing stone, 9ft high.

North of London

Bedfordshire, Hertfordshire and Buckinghamshire

11

Highlights

1 Stowe Gardens, which set the standard for the classical age of gardening
2 Wartime code-breaking Bletchley Park
3 Shaw's Corner, the idyllic retreat of Henry Moore and George Bernard Shaw
4 Palladian West Wycombe Park

Bedfordshire, **Hertfordshire** and **Buckinghamshire** are three unassuming counties, but not without their own quirky charms. The 17th-century religious writer John Bunyan is the presiding spirit of Bedfordshire: he was born in **Elstow**, often to be seen tramping the roads between prayer meetings, and imprisoned in Bedford Jail, where he wrote *The Pilgrim's Progress*. Another 17th-century religious writer, John Milton, spent months in political exile in south Buckinghamshire, writing his famous 'justification of the ways of God to man', *Paradise Lost*. He was brought to **Chalfont St Giles** by a Quaker friend, part of the meeting at **Old Jordons** near Amersham, along with the movement's founders William Penn and George Fox. The 18th-century religious poet and writer of hymns William Cowper of **Olney** in north Buckinghamshire once said that the first book he ever picked up was Bunyan's *Progress*. Cowper's most famous non-religious poem, 'John Gilpin', tells the tale of a madcap horse ride from London to Ware in south Hertfordshire and back. His co-writer of hymns was the vicar of Olney, John Newton, who, like Bunyan, was dramatically converted to evangelical Christianity. The jailbird of Bedford, the blind religious poet of Chalfont, the depressive hymn-writer and his friend, the slave-trader turned vicar of Olney, all give the region historical character.

When Socialist writer George Bernard Shaw came to Hertfordshire in 1906, in search of peace and quiet, he was in good company. Buckinghamshire is a political county, which has produced numerous prime ministers and Establishment figures. Indeed 19th-century Bucks was nicknamed Rothschildshire: the entire London banking tribe settled in neighbouring houses in the Vale of Aylesbury – **Ascott House**, **Waddesdon** and **Tring**. Queen Victoria's prime minister Benjamin Disraeli, who lived at **Hughenden Manor** near High Wycombe, borrowed heavily off them to buy shares for the country in the Suez Canal. Like the Rothschilds, Disraeli remodelled his house in grand style, harking back to the days when the stately homes of the region – Knebworth, Stowe, Hatfield House and Woburn Abbey – were the engines of government. Disraeli was a friend of Edward Bulwer Lytton of **Knebworth** (whom he made viceroy of India in 1876), and wrote the same kind of silver-fork novels about the gilded aristocracy. **Hatfield House** – Elizabeth I's childhood home – was rebuilt in fabulous Renaissance style by Robert Cecil, James I's chief minister. It looks like the headquarters of a powerful corporation, which is just what it was – the family firm of the Salisburys. The gardens of **Stowe**, created by a succession of Whig politicians, are the landscape equivalent of an essay by Pope, filled with allegorical features and classical allusions. The Bedfords of **Woburn Abbey** were at the heart of the old aristocratic order, owning copper mines in Devon, estates in central London, and large swathes of Lincolnshire; Woburn is one of the great treasure houses of England. The unalloyed 18th-century neo-classicism of **West Wycombe Park** was created by another, more eccentric, politician, Sir Francis Dashwood, a great clubman.

These are some of the pluses of the region's proximity to London; another is the Second World War intrigue of the **Bedford Triangle**, an area of covert government activities including the code-breaking headquarters at **Bletchley Park,** and spy-dropping airfields of **Tempsford** and **Twinwoods**. The last fifty years have been less kind, particularly in the south. Hertfordshire fares the worst, with major motorways bissecting its mild countryside, while Buckinghamshire comes off better, squeezed between the M40 and M1. However, closeness to London was the deciding factor in the distribution of garden cities and new towns around the region. The first of them was **Letchworth**, founded in 1903 with Arts and Crafts-style houses and a panache missing from the later developments of **Milton Keynes**, **Stevenage** and **Hatfield**. In fact, towns are not the area's strong point. The only larger town of note is **St Albans**, in south Hertfordshire, with its superb cathedral and Roman remains. In the north of the region, the **Chilterns**, like the North Downs on the other side of London, have miraculously preserved the qualities of an ancient landscape. In the south the region blends into London's sprawl.

Bedfordshire

Bedfordshire is easily missed, but has interesting corners. North Bedfordshire is beautiful, especially along the upper reaches of the Ouse and Nene valleys, with pretty stone villages and the remains of Second World War airfields and 'hush hush' houses. The south merges with London and the Buckinghamshire chalklands. In the middle, on the rolling Greensand Ridge, are the big old Bedfordshire estates: Old Warden, Woburn Abbey and Wrest Park. This is John Bunyan country too: the author of *The Pilgrim's Progress* was born in Elstow and ended up in Bedford Jail. William Cowper read Bunyan's work in Olney. All of which gives Bedfordshire a particular atmosphere.

Bedford

Bedford's greatest asset is its river, the Great Ouse, and its main interest is its connection with John Bunyan, the Bedford Nonconformist preacher and author of *The*

Espionage, Subterfuge and Code-breaking

Bedford is surrounded by Second World War sites: secret airfields and stately homes used for espionage, subterfuge and code-breaking. An extraordinary number of covert operations took place within the **Bedford Triangle**, between the spy-dropping airfields of **Harrington** near Kettering, **Tempsford** to the east of Bedford, and **Bletchley Park**, just south of Milton Keynes. Chicksands Priory, Woburn Abbey, Milton Ernest Hall and North Crawley Grange were all commandeered by the British and American military for covert operations. Tempsford and Harrington airfields were used to launch propaganda 'white leaflet' raids and drop agents into Occupied Europe, as well as munitions and supplies for Resistance groups. **Woburn Abbey** became the headquarters of the British propaganda service. **Chicksands Priory**, just west of Shefford, was a listening post and the country home of the BBC during the Blitz, intercepting enemy radio traffic and broadcasting encoded messages to Resistance groups in France. In the middle of the triangle, northwest of Bedford, **Milton Ernest Hall** became the US Air Force Service Command headquarters. It probably also had something to do with the Psychological Warfare Division of the OSS (Office of Strategic Services, the forerunner of the CIA).

At the heart of the triangle is the mysterious disappearance of the American band-leader Glen Miller, who spent four months at Milton Ernest Hall, using the old Twinwoods airfield to take his music to US airbases around England. On 15 December 1944 he left the hall and boarded a Norseman at Twinwoods for Paris; he was never seen again. You can visit the old control tower of the **Twinwoods** airfield, which has been turned into a Glen Miller museum. You can also visit **Bletchley Park Manor**, codenamed 'Station X', which was the headquarters of the British government code and cipher school – exactly half way between the university cities, and recruiting grounds, of Oxford and Cambridge. The code-breaking operation is famous for breaking the German Enigma codes.

Tourist Information

Bedford: 10 St Paul's Square, **t** (01234) 215 226. *Open Easter–Oct Mon–Sat 9.30–5, Sun 11–3.*

Getting There and Around

By **car**, take the M1 to junction 13, then the A421 to Bedford, following signs onto the A6 into town.

London Thameslink **trains** run to Bedford from London Bridge and King's Cross Thameslink. Intercity trains run from London St Pancras. For all train information contact National Rail Enquiries, **t** 08457 484950, *www.thetrainline.com.*

Contact National Express, **t** 08705 808080 (within the UK) or **t** (+44) 121 625 1122 (from abroad), *www.gobycoach.com*, for regular coach links from London, and **Traveline**, **t** 0870 6082608, for local transport services.

Where to Stay

Bedford t (01234) –

The Swan Hotel, The Embankment, **t** 346 565, *www.bedfordswanhotel.co.uk* (*expensive*). Elegant town-centre hotel built in 1794 by the Duke of Bedford with a stairway imported from Houghton House, oak panelling and mirrors; 110 bedrooms.

The Embankment Hotel, The Embankment, **t** 261 332, *www.embankmenthotelbedford.co.uk* (*moderate*). Victorian black-and-white hotel with 20 modest bedrooms and a carvery restaurant, beside Great Ouse.

The Queen's Head, 2 Rushden Road, Milton Ernest, **t** 822 412 (*moderate*). Handsome old pub in lovely countryside 4 miles north of Bedford, with arrow slits in thick stone walls. Newly refurbished bedrooms and delicious bar meals: fishcakes or potato wedges with salsa dips.

De Parys Guest House, 48 De Parys Avenue, **t** 261 982 (*cheap*). Grand Victorian house on quiet tree-lined street leading to Bedford Park; large and friendliest hotel of several on same street.

The Oakley Arms, 100 High Street, Harrold, **t** 720 478, *theoakleyarms@aol.com* (*cheap*). A 400-year-old thatched pub with modest bedrooms in a pretty ironstone village 9 miles north of Bedford.

Eating Out

Nicholls Brasserie, 38 The Embankment, **t** 212 848 (*cheap*). Roast summer vegetables, fish-cakes, steaks and spicy falafels with aubergine ragout; good bruschetta with green leaf salad and French dressing. Patio seating. *Closed Sun.*

Mamma Mia's, 4 Kimbolton Road, **t** 353 470 (*cheap*). Friendly, busy little place at end of St Peter's Street; filling pasta dishes.

Grand Indian, 39 Tavistock Street, **t** 359 566 (*cheap*). Bedford's best Indian restaurant.

Café Crema, 69 High Street, **t** 330 518 (*cheap*). Quiet place for coffee, panini or cakes.

The Golden Cross, 2–4 Bedford Road, Great Barford, **t** 871 727 (*cheap*). Old village pub just outside Bedford on A421 serving excellent Peking and Cantonese food. You can drink in the bar until your table is ready. *Closed Mon and Tues lunch.*

Horse and Jockey, Church End, Ravensden (follow B660 Kimbolton Road out of Bedford, and after a few miles turn off following signs to Church End), **t** 772 319 (*cheap*). Very good pub food including salmon and herb fishcakes. Skittles table.

The Jackal, Thurleigh, **t** 771 293 (*cheap*). Take Kimbolton Road out of Bedford and turn left at Blacksmith's arms. Restaurant-style pub food in lounge bar; small public drinking bar.

Entertainment

Corn Exchange, St Paul's Square, **t** 269 519. Multi-purpose venue with repertoire ranging from Beethoven to comedy. Week-long **beer festival** takes place here in Sept.

Pilgrim's Progress. The county town is otherwise unmemorable. The southern skyline is dominated by the enormous green Cardington hangars, built for airships R100 and R101: the latter crashed on its maiden flight in 1930, killing all but eight people. The hub of town is St Paul's Square, flanked by the church and town hall. At one end of the High Street stands a bronze statue of John Bunyan with shackles around his legs, and relief scenes from the Progress around the pedestal. The statue was given to the town in 1874 by the 9th Duke of Bedford, who also commissioned the bronze reliefs on the doors of the Bunyan Meeting Free Church (*open summer 10–4, winter 10–3*) on Mill Street, just off High Street. It is the third church on the site since 1672, when meetings took place in a converted barn and Bunyan was minister. The second was built in 1707, and the present classical-style church in 1850. The 20th-century stained-glass windows depicting scenes from Bunyan's religious journey include the author in Bedford jail. A postcard of this window was the only communication to reach Terry Waite during his four years as a hostage of Islamic Jihad in Beirut (1987–1991). Behind the church is the **John Bunyan Museum** (***t** (01234) 213 722; open Mar–Oct Tues–Sat 11–4*). Memorabilia includes the flute he took with him into prison, his tinker's anvil (marked JB) and the old door of Elstow abbey church supposed to have been the 'wicket gate' through which Christian the pilgrim fled for refuge.

At the top of High Street, continuing up De Parys Avenue, is beautiful **Bedford Park**. At the bottom end, you can walk on the Embankment and hire a rowing boat. Close to the Embankment is the **Bedford Museum and Cecil Higgins Art Gallery** (*Castle Lane, **t** (01234) 353 323; open Tues–Sat 11–5, Sun 2–5; adm*). The gallery houses brewery owner Cecil's collection of pre-Victorian decorative art, while the old Higgins family mansion has been restored in the style of a Victorian family home. One of the bedrooms is dedicated to Victorian architect William Burges (1827–81) and his exuberantly painted Gothic furniture, including the decorated mahogany bed on which he died. On display in the gallery are British watercolours and drawings, including Turner, Cotman, Rossetti and Burne-Jones; displays of 17th-century glass, such as unusual Jacobite and

John Bunyan (1628–88) and *The Pilgrim's Progress*

Bunyan was born in 1628 in the village of Elstow, two miles south of Bedford, and became a tinker like his father. At the age of 16 he enlisted in the parliamentarian army and spent two years fighting in the Civil War. In 1653 he joined a Bedford independent church, found his faith and began preaching all over the Midlands; he got a name for eloquence and religious zeal. After the restoration of Charles II, new laws made it illegal to preach to separatist congregations. Bunyan ignored the laws and spent most of the period from 1660 to 1672 in Bedford jail. The old jail was on the corner of High Street and Silver Street (where Debenhams now stands). *The Pilgrims Progress* was written during a second six-month imprisonment in 1677, and was published in 1678. Bunyan's allegory of the journey from sinfulness to God features a pilgrim called Christian who meets, on his journey to the Celestial City, characters called Obstinate, Pliable, Faithful and Mr Worldly Wiseman, and towards the end enters a town called Vanity, where he attends the fair. Coleridge called it 'that admirable allegory' and pointed out that 'the interest is so great that in spite of all the writer's attempts to force the allegoric purpose on the Reader's mind by his strange names – Old Stupidity of the town of Honesty, etc. – his piety was baffled by his genius...we go on with his characters as real persons.'

anti-Jacobite toasting glasses (one engraved 'Glorious memory of King William' another 'The King across the Water'); ceramics and Victorian tiles by William de Morgan and Pugin.

Around Bedford

Elstow Church

The old abbey church of Elstow stands next to the half-timbered moot hall (*open Sun and Tues–Thurs 1–4; adm minimal*) on the village green. It used to be twice as long, but much of it was demolished at the Reformation. John Bunyan was born in the village and baptized in the church in 1628; he continued to worship here for the next twenty years. On the west wall of the church are the remains of the 'wicket gate' immortalized by Bunyan; in his autobiography, *Grace Abounding*, he explains that whenever he entered the gate as a boy he was convinced that the devil was watching him from the bell tower. In *The Pilgrim's Progress* Christian knocks on the gate, and a 'grave person' called Goodwill pulls him inside to protect him from Beelzebub's arrows. Inside there are two Victorian stained-glass windows in memory of the author. The font is the one in which Bunyan and his two daughters were baptized more than 300 years ago. In the south aisle there is a curious brass of one of the last abbesses, Elizabeth Hervey, in full Benedictine robes and crosier.

Houghton House

The shell of the red-brick Jacobean mansion of Mary, Dowager Countess of Pembroke, sister of the poet Philip Sydney, stands in a beautiful setting a mile north of Ampthill. It was the inspiration for 'Palace Beautiful' in *The Pilgrim's Progress*, where Christian knocks after climbing 'Hill Difficulty'. He is shown in by four beautiful damsels – Discretion, Prudence, Piety and Charity – and looks out over a heavenly country that bears no resemblance to the present surroundings. The Duke of Bedford dismantled the house and flogged its contents in 1794.

About a mile west of Ampthill on the A507 is the **Great Park** (*open dawn–dusk*), enclosed in the 15th century around the castle of Sir John Cornwall, Agincourt commander and uncle of Henry V. On his death, the castle passed to the crown. Henry VIII visited at least once a year for the hunting. Nothing is left of the castle today, but there are good views of Houghton House over the Greensand Ridge.

Woburn Abbey

t (01525) 290 666; open Mar–Oct daily 11–4, Jan–Feb weekends 11–4; adm.

Woburn Abbey is one of the great treasure houses of England, the ancestral home of the dukes of Bedford (although the present duke, the 13th, lives in Paris). His son, the Earl of Tavistock, and grandson, Lord Howland, run the place. The Bedfords, it was once said, owned some of everything between East Anglia and Southampton, from the Bedford Levels in Cambridgeshire, drained by the 4th Earl, to Bedford Square and Russell Square in Bloomsbury, developed on the grounds of the family's old London

Where to Stay and Eat

Woburn t (01525) –

The Inn at Woburn, George Street, **t** 290 441 (*very expensive*). Handsome cream-painted golfers' hotel with flag and old hotel sign above door; 58 bedrooms, most in modern extension. Atmospheric old bar (for snacks) and restaurant (*moderate*).

The Bell Hotel, Bedford Street, **t** 290 280, *www.oldenglish.co.uk* (*moderate*). Attractive Georgian red-brick building with pleasant, old-fashioned atmosphere and 24 recently refurbished bedrooms. The bar and restaurant are across the road. Bar meals include leek and pork sausages, or you can eat Dover sole, salmon or beef in the restaurant.

Market Place, Market Place, **t** 290 877 (*moderate*). Bright restaurant run by Lord Tavistock's second son; serves stone-baked pizza, risotto and guacamole, all organic and free range. *Open Tues–Sat eves, Fri–Sun lunch.*

mansion. The great ancestor, John Russell, a high-flying Tudor courtier, was given the lands of Woburn Abbey in the will of Henry VIII and made 1st Earl of Bedford by Edward VI. The old abbey was converted into a house in the 17th century – possibly by Inigo Jones, who was building the Piazza in Covent Garden for the 4th Earl at the time – and remodelled by Henry Flitcroft and Henry Holland in the 18th century. Humphrey Repton landscaped the 3,000-acre deer park. As you approach the house up the long, winding drive, you catch a fleeting view of Flitcroft's Palladian west front.

The 4th Duke created an impressive series of **State Rooms**, which were soon filled with paintings collected on the Grand Tour. His portrait by Gainsborough hangs above the doorway of his bedroom. In the Paternoster Row corridor (along the old cloisters) is a painting of the old Bedford mansion in London. Up Flitcroft's cantilevered staircase are the rooms where all the best art is kept: 16th- and 17th-century Dutch art, 21 Canalettos (in one of Henry Holland's interiors), nine Reynolds and, in the **Blue Drawing Room**, paintings by Poussin. It is here that the 7th Duchess, Anna Maria Stanhope, first sat down to a light meal of tea, cakes and sandwiches at 5 o'clock – to alleviate the achingly long interval between lunch and supper – beginning the fashion for afternoon tea in smart society. Out of the state room windows you can see the statue of the late Lady Tavistock's black mare Mrs Moss standing by the lakeside; she produced 12 winners for the Bloomsbury stud in the 1970s. In the **Long Gallery** is the famous portrait of Elizabeth I, showing the queen as empress of the world. Collections of porcelain, silver and gold are kept in the crypt. A grotto takes you into the garden; look for Lady Tavistock's coffin among the shells and rocky alcoves.

Woburn Abbey Antiques Centre (*open daily 10–5.30*) in the south stable has around 60 shops behind reclaimed 18th-century shop fronts. The entrance to the 300-acre **Woburn Safari Park** (***t*** *(01525) 290 407; open mid-Mar–mid-July and Sept–Oct daily 10–4, July–Aug daily 10–5, Nov–mid-Mar weekends 11–3; adm exp*) is a mile further along the A4012. It takes about an hour to drive through the enclosures of free-roaming animals.

Woburn village is untiringly beautiful: every time you travel along its Georgian main street it seems lovely all over again. At the top end is the town hall and cobbled market place; the rest is full of hotels, restaurants and antiques shops.

Wrest Park Gardens

t 01525 860152; www.english-heritage.org.uk; open April–Oct weekends 10–6; adm.

The magnificent French neo-classical home of the 2nd Earl de Grey stands on the site of the ancestral home of the Greys, earls of Kent. Its **gardens** stretch from the front of the house to an Italianate pavilion designed by Thomas Archer, the builder of Birmingham cathedral. They retain an elegant Victorian French-style parterre, 17th-century long canal and formal 18th-century woodland gardens of the Duke of Kent.

Tempsford

The secret RAF airfield at Tempsford, codenamed Gibraltar Farm, was the main base for 'Carpetbagger' operations in 1943 to supply Resistance groups in Occupied Europe; you can find its remains north of Sandy, just off the A1, where a barn stands as a memorial to the men who flew from Tempsford in black Lysanders and Liberators. The assassination of Reinhard Heydrich, the Reichsprotektor of Bohemia and Moravia, was carried out on 27 May 1942 by Czech agents flying from here. The 23-year-old SOE agent Volette Szabo, the first woman to receive the St George Cross (posthumously) flew her last mission from here on 7 June 1944. She was dropped over France with three other agents, ambushed by the SS in Salon-la-Tour three days later, fought bravely to help the others escape, was captured and tortured in Paris, and executed in Ravensbruck concentration camp in January 1945.

Following the Great Ouse

The rolling farmland to the north and west of Bedford is peppered with pretty stone villages like **Harrold**, **Odell** and **Pavenham**, wonderful stretches of river, and a long stone footbridge that crosses the flood plain at **Felmersham**.

The handsome old stone linen town of **Olney** has plenty of places to eat, drink and browse on its wide main street. The home of poet William Cowper from 1767 to 1780 stands on one side of its market square, and is now the **Cowper and Newton Museum** (*t (01234) 711 516; open Mar–Dec Tues–Sat 10–1 and 2–5; June–Aug also Sun 2–5; adm*). In fact it is two small houses joined by a grand façade: Cowper lived on one side with his fiancée, Mrs Unwin, and three pet hares (Puss, Bess and Tiney); his 'servants and a thousand rats' on the other. John Newton, slave-trader turned curate of Olney, lived in the vicarage. Both the angst-ridden, depressive Cowper and the bullish, over-confident Newton experienced dramatic midlife conversions to Christianity – Cowper after 18 months in St Albans' mental asylum, Newton on board a slave-ship in a storm. They collaborated on the *Olney Hymns*, which include 'Amazing Grace' and 'God Moves in a Mysterious Way'. Unlike Newton, Cowper was plagued with doubts, according to one biographer 'suffering particularly from the conviction that he, uniquely among mankind, had been selected for an irrevocable, special damnation'. His best poems, including the still-funny 'John Gilpin' and 'The Task', a proto-Romantic poem admired by Wordsworth and Coleridge, were written in London, away from the doctrinaire

Eating Out

Olney t (01234) –

Café Brio, Market Place, **t** 717 000 (*cheap*). Bright, cheerful Italian café-bar, through arch off Market Place. Full range of excellent coffees and very good pasta and pizza. Live jazz Mon eve.

Tea Pot, High Street, **t** 712 392 (*cheap*). Old-fashioned tea room with sandwiches cut into four and served with watercress and good cakes. *Closed Sun.*

influence of Newton. Among the Cowper memorabilia on display here are a shoe buckle, handkerchief, sofa, coffee pot, a curious letter cabinet with doors disguised as book spines, books and letters. Cowper used to smoke in the summer house in the garden. Newton's grave is at the back of the church; a window is dedicated to Cowper.

North of Olney are the gardens of **Castle Ashby** (*t (01604) 696 187; open 10–dusk; adm*), home of the earls of Northampton. The house was built in 1574 to impress Elizabeth I, and adorned by the Victorians with Latin inscriptions in terracotta. The Italian garden has handsome stone-framed glasshouses at either end of its sunken lawn; one features a triumphal arch and flanking stone colonnades. An arboretum leads to the lake, landscaped by Capability Brown who was so pleased with his own work he uttered 'Thames, Thames, thou wilt never forgive me!' from the bridge.

From Clapham, near Milton Ernest, Twinwoods Road climbs up to the recently restored **Twinwoods Airfield Control Tower** (*t (01234) 824 773; open weekends 10.30–4; adm*). It was from here that Glen Miller disappeared in 1944; he waited for the fog to clear before taking off in a Norseman, never to be seen again. Now you can see his piano, RAF paraphernalia and military vehicles.

Hertfordshire

Too close to London for interest, Hertfordshire has sadly changed since the writer George Bernard Shaw and the sculptor Henry Moore came here in search of peace, the latter imagining that his bronzes 'exported a bit of the peace of this corner of Hertfordshire to the many cities, at home and abroad, where they now stand.' Another writer, E.M. Forster, was born in north Hertfordshire – 'a district which I still think the loveliest in England' – and based *Howard's End* on his childhood memories of Stevenage. Forster's town became a 'new town' in the 1950s, as Letchworth, further north, had become the world's first 'garden city' – a self-contained town with its roots in post-industrial ideology – in the 1910s. All of which does nothing for the rural charms of the area, further dissected by major roads and the M25. Visit **St Albans** with its Roman history and cathedral, **Shaw's Corner**, the village of **Much Hadham** (Moore's base) and the stately homes of **Knebworth** and **Hatfield House** nearby.

St Albans

The busy old cathedral town of St Albans, 20 minutes from central London by train, feels like a smart north London suburb, but it's an ancient place, with its old **abbey church**, raised to cathedral status in 1877, and the ruins of ***Verulamium***, one of the largest towns in Roman *Britannia*. Unusually, the site of the *municipium* was not built on after its 5th-century demise: Saxons and Normans quarried the stone (the Norman cathedral tower was built of Roman tiles), but the foundations remained. A Roman theatre, forum, gate, temple and townhouses have been unearthed, and a museum shows off all the bits. Recent digs indicate that *Verulamium* was burned to the ground in the Boudiccan Revolt. The abbey church stands on the site, outside the Roman walls, of the execution of St Alban, who became Britain's first Christian martyr in AD 209. Bede tells how Alban, a prominent Roman citizen, refused to make an offering to pagan Roman gods after converting; it was the Romans who erected the first shrine to St Alban on the spot where they martyred him. Five hundred years later King Offa endowed the monastery, and the Normans rebuilt it on a grand scale.

There are three parts to St Albans: town, cathedral and *Verulamium*, all in walking distance. Park outside the Verulamium Museum. The **town** has a charming triangle of streets outside the old Waxhouse Gate of the abbey: High Street, Chequers Street, Market Place and French Row. On Wednesdays and Saturdays, market stalls run the length of Market Place to the flinty old clock tower, built in 1403–12 to sound a nightly curfew. The lower end of the High Street boasts a few cafés, boutiques, antiques and craft shops. Down around the cathedral in George Street and Fishpool Lane is the prettiest part of town. Busy Chequers Street and Holywell Hill were once lined with coaching inns; you can see some of the old coaching arches among the shops. The **town museum** (***t*** *(01727) 819 340; open Mon–Sat 10–5, Sun 2–5*), down Hatfield Road, has bits and pieces from the Saxon and medieval town to the modern commuter city.

St Albans Cathedral

The cathedral of the diocese of Bedfordshire and Hertfordshire stands on Holywell Hill. It is a patchwork of Roman tiles, salvaged from *Verulamium*, flint, Bedfordshire sandstone and modern brick. The **abbey gateway** is all that remains of the medieval monastery, which fostered 13th-century historian Matthew Paris. The Norman abbey was founded on the site of King Offa's 7th-century church of St Alban, whose shrine was reassembled from fragments during Victorian restoration. It stands at the east end, in **St Alban's Chapel**, overlooked by a medieval watching loft to ensure that pilgrims contributed to, rather than took from, the offerings. On its south side is the **tomb of Humphrey, Duke of Gloucester**, the youngest brother of Henry V.

Verulamium

Verulamium* Museum** (t*** *(01727) 819 339; open 10–5; adm*) is at the crossroads of Fishpool Street and Watling Street in *Verulamium*. On one side stood the basilica and forum; the theatre and temple were not far away. Themed rooms – 'merchants and markets', 'food and farming' – interpret the archaeology of everyday Roman life found on the site. There are forges of gold, bronze and iron smiths, medical instruments and tools, loaded dice and gaming counters and a bronze statuette of the goddess Venus. Wall paintings and mosaics feature a dolphin, geometric patterns and a tail-less lion.

The **Roman theatre** (***t*** *(01727) 835035; open Mar–Oct 10–5, Nov–Feb 10–4; adm*) was built in the mid-2nd century, facing onto Watling Street. Plays, religious devotions and

Getting There and Around

St Albans is 10 minutes by **car** from junction 7 of the M1 and junction 21a or 22 of the M25.

It takes 20 minutes by train from London King's Cross Thameslink.

Tourist Information

St Albans: The Town Hall, Market Place, **t** (01727) 864 511. *Open summer 9.30–5.30, mid-July–mid-Sept also Sun 10–4; winter Mon–Sat 10–4.*

Where to Stay

St Albans t (01727) –

St Albans is the sort of place where you should stay in an old inn, preferably on Holywell Hill or Fishpool Street.

St Michael's Manor Hotel, Fishpool Street, **t** 864 444, *www.stmichaelsmanor.com* (*very expensive*). Large Georgian house set in 5 acres of manicured gardens backing onto park. Pleasantly airy and spacious with plump cushions and chandeliers. If you don't stay in one of the 23 bedrooms, you can still have coffee, light lunch or modern English dinner (*expensive*) in the conservatory restaurant overlooking the lake.

Comfort Hotel, Ryder House, Holywell Hill, **t** 848 849, *www.choicehotelseurope.com* (*expensive*). Behind the interesting 1911 façade is a pattern-book reception, bar and restaurant, and 60 identical bedrooms.

The Black Lion Inn, Fishpool Street, **t** 851 786, *www.theblacklioninn.com* (*moderate*). Handsome 17th-century red-brick pub with two rows of white windows; unbeatable location.

The White Hart Hotel, 25 Holywell Hill, **t** 853 624 (*moderate*). Classic coaching inn with carriage arch and yard; the dark-wood-panelled front bar dates back to the 14th century and creaks like a boat. Rooms vary, not all have shower.

Ayot St Lawrence t (01438) –

The Old Rectory, **t** 820 429, *www.ayotbandb@aol.com* (*moderate*). You're guaranteed a welcome at this pretty five-bedroomed rambling house covered in climbing plants, near Shaw's Corner.

The Brocket Arms, **t** 820 250, *www.brocketarms.com* (*moderate*). Ancient beamy pub near Shaw's Corner, with a large open fire, good home-cooked pub grub, restaurant (*moderate*) and a handful of bedrooms.

Eating Out

The streets of St Albans are paved with café-bar and restaurant chains such as **Café Rouge**, **Café des Amis**, **Zizzi's** and **Café Vicolo**. Here is a

readings would have been staged in this theatre in the round. ***Verulamium* Park** incorporates the northern section of the Roman city, defined by the line of trees at its southern end. The lake was dammed in the Middle Ages to supply fish for the abbey.

Gorhambury House, at the end of Gorhambury Drive (***t*** *(01727) 854 051; open May–Sept Thurs 2–5; adm*), the home of Lord Verulam, was built in 1784, and features elaborate chimney pieces, family portraits and a magnificent great hall.

North of St Albans

Shaw's Corner, Ayot St Lawrence

t *(01438) 820 307; house open Easter–Oct Wed–Sun 1–5, gardens 12–5.30; adm.*

North of St Albans, down winding country lanes, the home of Nobel-prize-winning writer George Bernard Shaw from 1906 until his death in 1950 is hidden behind trees and climbing plants. Shaw's Corner provided privacy for the celebrated author of *Arms* selection of the more atmospheric pubs, cafés, bars and eateries.

Kyriakos Greek Taverna, 30 Holywell Hill, **t** 832 841, *www.kyriakostaverna.co.uk* (*moderate*). One of St Albans' stalwarts; moussaka, dolmades or stifado and seafood, or an 18-dish meze including cold dips, charcoal grills and casserole. *Open eves until late.*

Giovanni's, The Black Lion Inn, Fishpool Street, **t** 851 786 (*cheap*). Pleasant Italian restaurant in old-world atmosphere of pub, serving pasta, fish, grills, breast of chicken and duck. *Open Mon–Sat eves.*

Sultan, 23 George Street, **t** 812 507 (*cheap*). Popular, long-established Balti restaurant serving good fresh Indian food.

Claude's Crêperie, 15 Holywell Hill, **t** 846 424 (*cheap*). In a setting of bare floorboards, candles and pot plants you can get a croissant, omelette, salad and filled baguette, or choose sweet and savoury crêpes from a long list, all washed down with French bottled beers and ciders. *Closed Mon.*

The Waffle House, Kingsbury Watermill, St Michael's Street, **t** 853 502 (*cheap*). Waffles with toppings including pecan nut with butterscotch sauce or ham with cheese and mushroom, in white weatherboard building with tall chimneys or at wooden tables by the mill race.

Rose and Crown, St Michael's Street (near Roman museum and St Michael's Church), **t** 851 903 (*cheap*). Old-fashioned pub with two small bars, serving American deli-style sandwiches at lunchtime with gherkins, crisps and potato salad.

Ye Olde Fighting Cocks, Abbey Mill Lane, **t** 865 830 (*cheap*). Friendly old pub near park with heavy, low beams, chipped walls, oak pews and real ales. One of England's oldest pubs.

The Lower Red Lion, 36 Fishpool Street, **t** 855 669 (*cheap*). Friendly real-ale pub (nine beers on the go at one time) with two cosy bars; seven standard bedrooms (*moderate*), not all en-suite.

Entertainment

There is often live music in Café des Amis, Horn of Plenty and Rose and Crown.

The Alban Arena, Civic Centre, off St Peter's Street, **t** 844 488. The town's main multi-purpose auditorium, seats 800; touring musicals, pop concerts, comedians and films.

The Abbey Theatre, Holywell Hill, **t** 857 861. Small theatre purpose-built in the 1960s by and for resident Company of Ten amateur theatre company, set up in St Albans in 1930s. Ten productions a year, from Shakespeare to contemporary drama.

The Maltings Arts Theatre, Maltings Precinct, **t** 844 222. Small, professional arts venue set up in 1988; mix of contemporary and period drama, one-man shows, children's theatre, jazz, blues and world music.

and the Man (1894), *Man and Superman* (1903) and *Major Barbara* (1905), within striking distance of London, where he also kept a townhouse. Shaw spent most weekends here with his wife, Charlotte, and five servants, working on *Pygmalion* and *St Joan*. His last published work was a *Rhyming Guide to Ayot St Lawrence*, which included the lines 'This is my dell, and this is my dwelling/ Their charm so far beyond my telling/ That though in Ireland is my birthplace/ This house shall be my final earthplace'. He died on the dining-room couch aged 95 (seven years after Charlotte). The couch is still in the dining room, and his many hats and sticks hang on the stand in the hall. He had two workrooms: the study, with his typewriter, spectacles and pens on the desk, and photographs of old friends like William Morris and G.K. Chesterton on the walls; and the summer house, hidden behind a clump of trees at the bottom of the garden, where he worked if the weather was good enough at a fold-down writing table hinged to the wall, with a large wicker wastepaper basket, telephone on the wall, and bed, where he would nap in the afternoons reading a book. The whole room could be turned to catch the sun.

Devil's Dyke, Wheathampstead

Just south of Ayot St Lawrence, take the B653 from Wheathampstead for half a mile, turning right down narrow Dyke Lane just before the Wicked Lady pub. After a mile is a grand iron gate, which leads onto a footpath down the dyke – a 40ft-deep ditch with steep wooded banks. A sign reads 'this entrenchment is part of a British city built 1 BC; probably here that Julius Caesar defeated British king Cassuvalalaunus 454 BC'.

East Hertfordshire

Knebworth House

***t** (01438) 812 661; open June–Sept daily, Oct–May weekends only; gardens, park and playground 11–5.30, house 12–5; adm exp.*

South of Stevenage, you shoot off junction 7 of the A1(M) into Knebworth House, home of the Lytton family for 500 years and occasional venue of rock concerts since 1974 (the Rolling Stones and Oasis have played here). The fairy-tale palace overlooks Lutyens gardens and a deer park. It is a great family house, home to more stories than treasures. Sir Robert Lytton, who fought with Henry Tudor at Bosworth and became one of the new king's leading courtiers, built the core of the present house in 1490 – a Tudor red-brick palace around a quadrangle. Three ranges were demolished in 1810 and the remaining one transformed by the Victorian novelist Edward Bulwer Lytton ('it was a dark and stormy night'), who inherited in 1843. Architect H.E. Kendall added Gothic domes, battlements, gargoyles and orange stucco; John Crace redesigned the interiors in high Victorian style, with lashings of Lytton family heraldry and dark oak. It works, particularly the state drawing room with its stained-glass window of the first Tudor king, Henry VII, and a chandelier that looks like a crown.

Shortly after the 2nd Earl of Lytton moved into Knebworth in 1908, young architect Edwin Lutyens – his brother-in-law – was employed to tone things down. Entrance hall, dining parlour and library (containing Bulwer Lytton's collection of books) have Lutyens interiors: plain oak panelling, elegant fireplaces and restrained furnishings. Bulwer Lytton was popular in his day and admired by Charles Dickens, who named his tenth child Edward Bulwer Lytton Dickens. The magnificent banqueting hall, with its 17th-century oak screen and pine panelling, became a theatre for one of Dickens' amateur theatricals in 1850: Ben Johnson's *Every Man in His Humour*, in which Dickens played Bobadil to an audience of local county gentry. The success of *Every Man* inspired Dickens and Lytton to found The Guild of Literature and Art for actors and writers. To raise money, Dickens performed in a special production of Bulwer Lytton's comedy *Not So Bad As We Seem* at Devonshire House in London 'in the presence of Her Majesty and His Royal Highness The Prince Albert'. Another time, Dickens stayed at Knebworth while he revised the proofs of Bulwer Lytton's *A Strange Story* – which was to be serialized in his periodical *All the Year Round* – while his friend read the last chapters of *Great Expectations*. Bulwer Lytton found the ending too harsh. Dickens agreed, and returned to Rochester where he rewrote it in four weeks. Up the double flight of oak stairs is Bulwer Lytton's old study, as depicted in the painting above the fireplace, with the novelist smoking a pipe at his desk. On the table is his crystal ball.

The **gardens** include Lutyens' formal gardens, a Victorian wilderness and a pet cemetery. Lutyens sunk the lawn and planted the avenue of lime trees and thick yew hedges with alcoves for statues. Gertrude Jekyll planned the herb garden at the front.

Much Hadham and Perry Green

The delightful village of Much Hadham is on the B1004 between Ware and Bishop's Stortford. The bishops of London owned the manor house beside the church until the early 19th century, attracting wealthy people to the village who built houses in all the best styles: wisteria-covered thatched cottages, Georgian mansions and weather-board townhouses. Henry V's widowed queen, Katherine, was dumped on the bishop here after her indiscretion with Owen Tudor. The sculptor Henry Moore lived in nearby Perry Green until his death in 1986. Moore designed the long-chinned king and queen who flank the west door of the church. The small **Forge Museum** (*open Fri–Sun 11–5; adm minimal*) has a resident blacksmith and a charming Victorian cottage garden.

In the nearby hamlet of **Perry Green** are the studios of the **Henry Moore Foundation** (***t*** *(01279) 843 333; tours April–Sept Sun–Fri at 10.30 and 2.30, by appointment only; adm exp*), next to the Moore family home, Hoglands. Moore and his wife, Irina, moved here in 1940 when their Hampstead home and studio were damaged in the Blitz, gradually buying up the whole village. Hoglands is private, but you can visit the Bourne Maquette Studio, containing many of the artist's plasters, terracottas and found objects, including flints and fragments of bone. The Sheep Field Barn Galleries exhibit works on paper, working models, and tapestries based on Moore's drawings.

Hatfield House

t *(01707) 287 010; open Easter–Sept, house 12–4 (guided tours Mon–Thurs), gardens 11–5; adm exp.*

Too close for comfort to the new town of Hatfield, Hatfield House nonetheless has a a magical quality. Elizabeth I received the news of her accession sitting under an oak tree in the park. She and her brother Edward spent their childhood in Old Hatfield House; a wing of it stands next door to the Jacobean prodigy mansion of the Cecils. The south front has splendid Renaissance touches – a white stone colonnade and domed corner towers – while the north front is studded with bay windows. In the magnificent **marble hall**, with its panelled ceiling and marble floor, are famous portraits of Elizabeth I – the *Rainbow Portrait* and *Ermine Portrait*. A carved oak staircase leads up to the oak-panelled **long gallery**, which runs the entire length of the south front (180ft) between the wings. Elizabeth I's hat, gloves and silk stockings are displayed here. In the **library**, dominated by the mosaic portrait of Robert Cecil, 1st Earl of Salisbury, you can see letters from Elizabeth I and Mary Queen of Scots. There is a breathtaking **chapel**, and an **armoury** in the portico; the armour was salvaged from the defeated Spanish Armada. Gardens and a 4,000-acre park surround the house.

Wander through the archway into the handsome old town. The **Eight Bells** pub at the bottom of the Georgian main street was visited by Dickens, who came to Hatfield as a reporter for the *Morning Chronicle* in November 1835 after a fire broke out in the west wing of Hatfield House, killing the 85-year-old Dowager Lady Salisbury. In *Oliver Twist*, published a year later, Bill Sikes flees to Hatfield after the murder of Nancy, but is given away in the pub by a peddler who spots blood on his hat.

Letchworth

Founded in 1903, Letchworth – the world's first garden city – is an achievement of grand ideological and architectural merit that set in motion an international movement to provide new housing and employment in a town and country setting. The concept was formulated in *Tomorrow: A Peaceful Path to Real Reform* (1898) by Ebenezer Howard, who moved to Letchworth in 1905 (361 Norton Way South) with his wife and four children, and on to Welwyn Garden City in 1921. Sadly the architectural legacy of Letchworth has been endless overblown pastiches of its vernacular style of housing, so that the post-war new towns – Hatfield, Harlow, Hemel Hempstead and Stevenage – have become shorthand for dreary pattern-book nonentities. Take a walk around Letchworth and you'll see how delightful suburban housing can be: rough-cast walls, clay-tiled roofs, dormer windows, elegant cream and green colour schemes. The developers aimed to achieve a 'high standard of beauty' by constructing 'simple, straightforward buildings' in 'good and harmonious materials'. Architects Barry Parker and Raymond Unwin were greatly influenced by Arts and Crafts. Parker's thatched studio – now the **First Garden City Heritage Museum** (***t*** *(01462) 482 710; open Mon–Sat 10–5; adm minimal*) – is derived from the East Anglian tradition of hall and solar; it's the place to find out about housing reform.

Buckinghamshire

The long, thin county of Buckinghamshire stretches between the Thames and the Great Ouse with its ends cut off by the M1 and M40. 'All the great statesmen of the period were born, or bred, or lived, in this county,' said Disraeli, who obviously included himself among them. It was home to six prime ministers: the Marquis of Lansdowne (1737–1805), the 3rd Duke of Portland (1738–1809), George Grenville (1712–70), Lord Grenville (1759–1834), Lord John Russell (1792–1878) and Benjamin Disraeli himself (1804–81). **Chequers**, in the Chilterns, is the official country residence of prime ministers today. The renowned gardens of **Stowe**, home of the Grenvilles, and **Hughenden Manor**, where Disraeli adopted the life of a county gent in 1848, are open to visitors. The arrival of powerful European bankers the Rothschilds in the 1840s turned the Vale of Aylesbury into Rothschildshire, home of what Disraeli called the new aristocracy 'of virtue, ability and power'. Nathan Mayer Rothschild, third son of the great banking ancestor Mayer Amschel of Frankfurt (1744–1812), moved to England in 1798. Nathan's three sons all bought properties within five miles of each other: Lionel at Tring, Mayer Amschel at Mentmore Towers and Anthony at Aston Clinton. The third generation, enthusiastic art collectors, natural historians and horticulturists, built houses at Halton, Ascott and Waddesdon. The only Rothschild properties open to the public are **Ascott**, **Waddesdon** and the **Walter Rothschild Zoological Museum** in Tring.

All these rich Establishment types were complemented by a Bucks tradition of political and religious nonconformity. Pennsylvania founder William Penn and his friends set up a Quaker meeting at **Old Jordons** near Amersham. Another Quaker, Thomas Ellwood, brought poet John Milton to **Chalfont St Giles** during an outbreak of the plague in London. You can visit his cottage, which has barely changed. Disraeli thought there was 'something in the air of Bucks favourable to political knowledge and vigour' – maybe as simple as its proximity to London in delightful countryside. The **Chiltern Hills** are known for their creaking beech woods and downland; the caves, church, Dashwood house and mausoleum at **West Wycombe** are their highlight. North of Aylesbury, around the old county town of **Buckingham**, you can tour the country lanes, stopping off at stately homes and churches – but avoid Aylesbury, Amersham, High Wycombe and Milton Keynes if you can.

Buckingham and Around

The handsome old county town is in the middle of lovely countryside, ringed by the houses and gardens of Stowe, Claydon House, Waddesdon and Bletchley Park. Buckingham stands in the loop of the Great Ouse, its long pastoral history tied to the patronage of the Cobhams and Temples of Stowe. It slipped into decline, losing its county town status to Aylesbury in the 16th century, burning down in 1725 and failing to industrialize in the 19th century. Today you can see the unspoiled Georgian town rebuilt after the fire, brought to life by the students of its small 1970s university. There's no drama, just 18th-century coaching inns, old shops fronts and quiet streets.

The long, narrow market place is dominated by the towers and battlements of the **old gaol**, built by Lord Cobham of Stowe in 1748 to woo back the summer assizes from Aylesbury (the plan failed). In it a **museum** tells the story of the town. The Georgian **town hall** with its neat little clock on top closes off the south side of the square. On one side, Castle Street climbs up to the **church**, which was built in 1781 with the stone of its medieval predecessor. Wander back along the river or through narrow lanes.

Stowe Gardens

Still follow sense, of every art the soul,
Parts answ'ring parts shall slide into a whole,
Spontaneous beauties all around advance,
Start even from difficulty, strike from chance;
Nature shall join you; Time shall make it grow
A work to wonder at – perhaps a STOWE.

Pope's 'Epistle to the Earl of Burlington' on landscape gardening

Back in the 18th century Stowe (***t*** *(01280) 822 850, www.nationaltrust.org.uk; open Mar–Oct Wed–Sun 10–5.30, Nov–Feb weekends 10–4; adm*) set the standard for gardens; now it is a monument to the heroic age of gardening. There are no flowers to speak of, but pastoral valleys, serpentine lakes and great monuments – a vision of Britain as heir to the Greek and Roman empires. Its creator, Richard Temple

Tourist Information

Buckingham: The Old Gaol Museum, Market Hill, **t** (01280) 823 020. *Open Mon–Sat 10–4*.

The main **market** is on Tues (farmers' market first Tues in the month) and Sat, when there is also a flea market behind the Old Gaol.

The **North Bucks Show**, a one-day agricultural show in Stowe Park, takes place on a Sat in July. It features show-jumping, best-of-breed competitions, rural crafts, stalls selling gardening tools, and a children's fairground.

Where to Stay

Buckingham t (01280) –

Villiers Hotel, 3 Castle Street, **t** 822 444, *www.villershotel.com* (*very expensive*). Much modernized old coaching inn with leather armchairs, bookshelves and prints; carriage arch leads into long, narrow courtyard; 46 bedrooms with antique-look cupboards, marble around sinks and large armchairs.

5 Bristle Hill, 5 Bristle Hill, **t** 814 426 (*moderate*). Friendly cottage guesthouse in quiet part of town near church.

Churchwell, 23 Church Street, **t** 815 415, *www.churchwell.co.uk* (*moderate*). Quaint and homely with three rooms.

Around Buckingham

The north Buckinghamshire countryside is so beautiful, you may be inspired to stay in a guesthouse out of town.

Field Cottage, Hillesden Hamlet, **t** (01280) 815 360 (*moderate*). Beautiful 17th-century stone farmhouse in middle of fields, with thatched roof, tiled floors and exposed stone and brick interior. Lovely, rural spot, about 3 miles from Buckingham.

Hickwell House, Botolph Claydon, **t** (01296) 712 217, *www.hickwellhouse.co.uk* (*moderate*). Near Winslow, 10 minutes' drive from Buckingham; rambling 17th-century thatched house with massive stone chimney running through middle, tiny doorways, sloping floors, full-sized snooker table and lovely garden.

Rolling Acres, Water Stratford (2 miles west of Buckingham, and 1½ miles from Stow Gardens), **t** (01280) 847 302 (*cheap*). Warm welcome at handsome modern house in pretty thatched village; by beautiful river-bend beneath bridge – ideal for picnics.

Folly Farm, Padbury, **t** (01296) 712 413 (*cheap*). Brick farmhouse next to enormous farm buildings set back from A413, 3 miles south of Buckingham on way to Winslow; friendly, with cake-baking proprietor.

The Congregational Church, 15 Horn Street, Winslow, **t** (01296) 715 717 (*cheap*). Beautiful converted chapel in attractive market town. Every bedroom has its own church window; delicious breakfasts.

Eating Out

Henry's at **Villiers Hotel**, 3 Castle Street, **t** 822 444 (*moderate*). Excellent restaurant where you might start with leek and potato soup or tiger prawn and crab tortellini followed by loin of pork and sage, poached salmon and monkfish roulade or roast beef. Pleasant atmosphere. *Closed Sun eve*.

White Hart Hotel, Market Square, **t** 815 151, *www.millhouseinns.co.uk* (*moderate*). Handsome 18th-century front with white portico; huge dusky bar lined with old prints; popular in evening, when the music is loud. Some basic rooms.

Dipalee, 18 Castle Street, **t** 813 151 (*cheap*). Popular Balti restaurant.

Cheng-Du, Meadow Walk, **t** 815 898 (*cheap*). Long-established Chinese restaurant.

Meadow Row Tea Rooms, Meadow Row, **t** 814 031 (*cheap*). Pleasant tea shop serving all kinds of tea and good strong coffee, as well as baguettes, sandwiches, cottage pie or steak and kidney pie, on quaint pedestrian shopping walkway off High Street opposite the Old Gaol. *Closed Sun*.

(1675–1749), was a soldier and Whig politician. Twice pensioned off, he threw himself into redesigning house and garden, employing first Sir John Vanbrugh (the architect of Blenheim Palace) and the royal gardener Charles Bridgeman, then, 20 years later, William Kent and Capability Brown, who remained head gardener for 10 years.

From Buckingham, you approach up the 1½-mile-long grand avenue laid out by Richard's nephew, Earl Temple (1711–79), who extended the gardens in celebration of victory against the French in the Seven Years War and the political success of his brother-in-law, William Pitt the Elder. The Temple fortune was dissipated by 1848, forcing the family to sell up; the gardens are all that remains to be seen. Start at the neo-classical Temple of Concord and Victory, embellished with patriotic friezes in 1763. The Grecian Valley below it was one of Capability's creations, landscaped from a flat field and planted with trees. Its pioneering naturalism was a far cry from William Kent's stylized Elysian Fields, created about 10 years earlier – a 3-D Arcadian painting by Poussin, with temples and allusions to classical myths. The Alder stream was dammed to create the River Styx, running between gloomy wooded banks from a ferny grotto. On its mortal side is the Temple of British Worthies, with busts of Whig heroes from King Alfred to Walter Raleigh by Rysbrack and Scheemakers. The Ionic rotunda on the immortal side is the Temple of Ancient Virtue. Up Hawkwell Field is James Gibbs' Gothic Temple; sheep graze around it for pastoral effect. Gibbs also built the neo-classical Temple of Friendship on the far side of the lake, where Lord Cobham and his political cronies met to plot against the Tories, crossing the covered Palladian Bridge to get there. Over the lake you have one of the most perfect views of a country house – the neo-classical portico above sweeping lawns framed between wooded hills. You can see the village church where Capability Brown was married in 1744. Beyond the ha-ha are views of Buckingham through a Corinthian Arch.

Milton Keynes and Around

The new town of Milton Keynes was created in 1970, incorporating three old towns (Stoney Stratford, Bletchley and Wolverton) and 13 villages, one of which was Milton Keynes. A grid of tree-lined V (vertical) and H (horizontal) roads joined by roundabouts binds it all together. At its centre are shopping malls, restaurants, bars, cinemas and a ski centre with real snow. Despite the good intentions of the planners, the town has the atmosphere of an airport terminal. By comparison, the old coaching town of Stoney Stratford is all old world charm, and your best base in the area.

Bletchley Park

t (01908) 640 404; open weekends 12.30–6, tours at 2; adm exp.

Bletchley Park is one of Britain's most interesting Second World War survivors. Known as Station X, it was the country's code-breaking HQ. It is located half way between Oxford and Cambridge universities, the wartime recruiting grounds for code-breakers.Rather dilapidated now, the Victorian mansion and decaying sheds held a staff of 12,000 people by 1945. They still have a particular atmosphere, but the main reason to visit is the Cryptology Trail. One of the first recruits, Cambridge computer pioneer Alan Turing, developed a machine known as the Bombe, which successfully cracked the codes of the German military cipher machine Enigma. The Enigma machine resembles a typewriter with two sets of keys – but was capable of producing 150 million million million code variations in any message by a highly complex substitution of letters with ciphers. The code-breakers searched day and night for a crib – if they knew the meaning of one message they could crack the code. Enlightened guesswork applied to simple messages (weather reports), mistakes (a U-boat operator who sent the same message twice in different ciphers) and acts of daring (the salvage of a naval weather code book from a scuppered German U-boat in the Atlantic) gave them just enough to work on. By the end of the war the British Type X machine was decoding 3,000 messages a day. The trail features original Enigma and Type X machines and the Colossus, built to crack the most highly encrypted messages of the German High Command.

Grand Houses of Buckinghamshire

Ascott House and Gardens

Southwest of Leighton Buzzard on the A418, near Wing, **t** *(01296) 688 242, www.nationaltrust.org.uk; open Mar–Sept Tues–Sun 2–6; adm.*

Ascott House – formerly a farmhouse on Mayer Rothschild's Mentmore estate – was bought in the 1870s by his nephew Leopold Rothschild, who extended it in neo-Tudor style. It faces Ivinghoe Beacon and Dunstable Downs over the Vale of Aylesbury . Leopold was one of the third generation of Rothschilds in England. His main house was Gunnersbury Park in Middlesex, but he came to Ascott House for stag-hunting in autumn and winter. Famous Chelsea gardener Sir Harry Veitch laid out the gardens to look their best in the hunting season, with evergreen holly, blue firs, golden and green yew. Leopold inherited a collection of French furniture and English paintings, which he brought to Ascott. His son Anthony added collections of 18th-century English furniture and Chinese porcelain spanning a thousand years. From the gardens, you can see Mentmore Towers – another Rothschild property. It was built for Leopold's uncle Mayer by Joseph Paxton, and modelled on Wollaton Hall in Nottinghamshire.

Nearby, pop into the churches at Wing and Stewkley. **All Saints', Wing** is one of three Saxon churches in England, built in the 10th century. The rectangular building, semi-circular apse and crypt are all Saxon, as is the 21-foot-wide chancel arch. The medieval carvings on the roof include angels, saints, kings and gargoyles. In the chancel are 16th–17th-century monuments to the Dormer family of old Ascott Hall. Three miles up the road, **St Michael's, Stewkley** is a Norman *tour de force* of zigzag decoration.

Waddesdon Manor

West of Aylesbury on A41; **t** *(01296) 653 203, www.nationaltrust.org.uk; open Wed–Sun, house 11–4, gardens 10–5; Bachelor's Wing Thurs–Fri 11–4; adm exp.*

The dreamy French château of Ferdinand de Rothschild stands amid parterres and fountains. With its Bath-stone towers and arched windows, Waddesdon outdoes all the other Rothschild houses, including those of cousins Lionel (Tring), Mayer (Mentmore) and Anthony (Aston Clinton). The architect was Destailleur, a Frenchman who had already worked for the Rothschilds in Austria. Building began in 1874, the year that Ferdinand (an Austrian Rothschild) received his vast inheritance. His life's work was Waddesdon. A specially built steam railway brought the materials from Quainton Station, a few miles north. Bare Lodge Hill was planted with mature trees dragged up by teams of horses. The rooms are crammed with 17th- and 18th-century Savonnerie carpets, Sèvres and Meissen porcelain, and Dutch, English and Italian paintings. The Bachelor's Wing holds a collection of European weapons. The grounds feature formal French gardens, an aviary and a rose garden.

Claydon House

t (01296) 730 349, www.nationaltrust.org.uk; house open Easter–Oct Sat–Wed 1–5, grounds 12 –6; adm.

South of Buckingham, in Middle Claydon, the 18th-century mansion of the Verneys stands within sheep-grazed parkland next to the old parish church. The architect was Luke Lightfoot, a brilliant and eccentric woodcarver who was also a bit of a rogue. His interiors, though, are something else: wild Rococo carvings around the doors and chimney pieces of the North Hall and Chinese Room; sumptuous neo-classical ceiling decorations and the chimneypiece in the Salon; the domed stairwell with an elaborate wrought-iron balustrade and mahogany stairs inlaid with box, ebony and ivory. The 2nd Earl Verney wanted to create a rival to Stowe, home of his long-standing political opponent, Earl Temple, in Buckinghamshire. The undertaking bankrupted him. The rotunda and Egyptian ballroom were demolished by his niece Mary after his death in 1791 and Claydon House was never so sparkling again. It ended up in the Calvert family, stolid army and navy men who later settled as MPs for Buckinghamshire. A frequent guest at Claydon then was Florence Nightingale, sister-in-law of Sir Harry Calvert, who was known in Parliament as the 'Member for Florence Nightingale'. Next to the house stands All Saints church. It is full of Verney monuments, including that of Charles I's standard-bearer Sir Edmund Verney, who acquired the house in 1620; his tomb is said to contain nothing but the hand that held the flag in the Battle of Edgehill – all that was found of his remains after the battle.

The Chilterns: North of the M40

The chalk hills of the Chilterns range 400 square miles southwest from Luton to Reading, where the River Thames cuts them off. The clay-with-flints topsoil supports ancient beech woods and arable farmland, while the long scarp slope down to the Vale of Aylesbury is chalk downland. The scarp carries the Ridgeway, a prehistoric 'green road', from Ivinghoe Beacon to Avebury in Wiltshire. Away from the main roads are delightful walks. South of the M40, the results are heavenly (*see* p.430).

From the pleasant scarp-foot town of **Wendover** it is a short walk over the A413 onto the Ridgeway, which climbs to the top of Coombe Hill, classic open downland. From the war memorial on top you look down over the Vale of Aylesbury and the prime-ministerial estate at Chequers. Just north of the neighbouring black-and-white town of Tring – another good base – Ivinghoe Beacon is a great place for picnics, kite-flying and inspecting prehistoric remains. **Ashridge Park** – 5,000 acres of chalk grassland, woodland and farms – once belonged to the dukes of Bridgewater. Francis Egerton, the 3rd Duke, collaborated with the Staffordshire engineer James Brindley on the first canals. There are views of his old house from the top of the Bridgewater Monument (*open Easter–Oct weekends 12–5*), a memorial to him built in 1832. Next to the monument, the **Ashridge Estate Visitor Centre** (***t*** *(01422) 851 227; open Easter–Dec Mon–Fri 1–5, weekends 12–5*) has leaflets for the 3½-mile woodland walk to **Ivinghoe Beacon** and a 1½-mile stroll down the wooded ridge to the picturesque village of **Aldbury**, perfect for lunch or a pint.

Tring Park and the Walter Rothschild Zoological Museum

t *(020) 7942 6171; open Mon–Sat 10–5, Sun 2–5.*

On the edge of Tring Park, the Victorian museum of Lionel Walter Rothschild opened to the public in 1892. It was a present from his father Nathaniel Mayer. Lionel Walter was a natural historian, who sponsored the expeditions of Henry Palmer to the Galapagos Islands and harnessed zebras to his carriage. An inventory of his collection at his death lists 2,400 mounted animals, including 13 gorillas and 25 chimps, 2,400 birds and 680 reptiles and amphibians – the largest natural history collection assembled by one man. His brother, Nathaniel Charles, a senior partner in N.M. Rothschild & Sons, was an expert on fleas. The beautiful Victorian galleries of polished wooden and fancy ironwork are now a branch of the Natural History Museum in Kensington. Sadly the Tring bypass cuts off the old Rothschild mansion (now an arts school) from its landscaped park at the foot of the Chilterns escarpment, where Lionel Walter used to keep zebras, emus and wallabies. There are two 18th-century monuments – a 50-foot obelisk and the classical façade of an old summer house – built by James Gibbs.

Old Beaconsfield and Bekonscot Model Village

Hidden away down quiet Warwick Road in the busy commuter hub of Beaconsfield, just about all of old England is packed into half an acre in the **Bekonscot Model Village** (*follow signs to 'Model Village' off A40 and A355;* ***t*** *(01494) 672 919; open mid-Feb–Oct 10–5; adm*). This, the oldest model village in the world, first opened to the public in 1929. There is a castle and manor house, villages of black-and-white timber-framed houses, cricket on the green, boats in the harbour, tigers and polar bears in the zoo, and a train chuffing over bridges. It was built by Roland Callingham, a London accountant who had moved from Ascot to Beaconsfield in 1910 (the name 'Bekonscot' is an ugly combination of the two names).

You might want to stop in **Old Beaconsfield**, the historic town centre, which developed around the coaching trade at the junction of the old Oxford–London and Aylesbury–Windsor roads. There used to be 26 coaching inns around the crossroads of Windsor End, London End, Aylesbury End and Wycombe End (now a roundabout). The poet Robert Frost lived at The Bungalow in Reynolds Road from 1912 to 1915. It's a busy junction, but the church and houses stand back behind greens, and there are one or two places to stop for a drink. Try the Charles Dickens pub, or the George coffee room.

Getting There and Around

Tring is just off the A41 between Aylesbury and Hemel Hempstead, easy to reach from the M1, M40 and M25 by **car**. It takes 40 minutes by **train** to Tring Station from London Euston on the Northampton line.

Tourist Information

Wendover: The Clock Tower, High Street, **t** (01296) 696 759. *Open Mon–Sat 10–4.*

Tring: 99/a Akeman Street, **t** (01442) 823 347. *Open Mon–Fri 9.30–3, Sat 9–1.*

Where to Stay and Eat

Wendover t (01296) –

The Red Lion Hotel, High Street, **t** 622 266, *www.wizzardinns.co.uk* (*moderate*). Charming old coaching inn with hanging pub sign and lamp on black-and-white timbered front; some of the 24 bedrooms are swanky, others in need of refurbishment. The bar has a flagstone floor and inglenook.

Le Bistro Restaurant and Bar, 4 Pound Street, **t** 622 092 (*moderate*). Lively and relaxed atmosphere with soft background jazz. Caesar Salad or deep-fried brie with mango followed by beef stroganoff, roast cod or tagliatelle with roasted vegetables. *Open Mon–Sat eves, Sat also lunch.*

Rossini, 20 High Street, **t** 622 257 (*cheap*). Stylish modern Italian and Mediterranean restaurant with burgundy walls and black beams. *Closed Sun eve and Mon.*

Tring and Around

The Rose and Crown, High Street, Tring, **t** (01442) 824071, *www.roseandcrowntring.co.uk* (*moderate*). Hundred-year-old Rothschild built and owned black-and-white fronted hotel with 20 rooms and a good restaurant.

The Old Forge, 5 High Street, Ivinghoe, **t** (01296) 668 122, *www.ivinghoe.co.uk* (*moderate*). Modern, motel-style with four new bedrooms, each with a power shower.

The Greyhound Inn, Stocks Road, Aldbury, **t** (01442) 851 228 (*moderate*). Friendly old-fashioned pub with 3 bedrooms upstairs.

2 Church Cottage, Aldbury, **t** (01442) 851 207 (*cheap*). Pretty beamed cottage opposite the church with one double bedroom.

Stocks Farmhouse, Aldbury, **t** (01442) 851 397 (*cheap*). Farmhouse built in 1906, looking out over fields to wooded ridge, down leafy lane from Aldbury village on the Ivinghoe road; homely and relaxed atmosphere; four bedrooms.

Around the Chilterns

The Crown, 16 High Street, Amersham, **t** 0870 400 8103, *www.macdonaldhotels.co.uk* (*very expensive*). Charming old coaching inn with cobbled yard full of potted flowers and wrought-iron furniture; 19 bedrooms including suites and four posters, one of which (room 101) made a cameo appearance in *Four Weddings and a Funeral* (the post-wedding scene with Hugh Grant and Andie MacDowell).

Old Jordons Quaker Guest House, Old Jordons, near Beaconsfield, **t** (01494) 879 700, *www.oldjordons.org.uk* (*moderate*). You don't have to be a Quaker to stay in this restful complex including the old farmhouse where early Quakers George Fox and William Penn secretly met, and a late 17th-century meeting house; 28 bedrooms, some en-suite.

The George and Dragon, West Wycombe, **t** (01494) 464 414, *www.george-and-dragon.co.uk* (*moderate*). Delightful early 18th-century coaching inn through cobbled archway in heart of conservation area.

Chalfont St Giles and John Milton's Cottage

Chalfont St Giles, where Milton spent almost a year completing *Paradise Lost* and beginning *Paradise Regained*, has grown into a small town. It's not quite the rural retreat that it once was (it's too close to the M40), but **Milton's cottage** (*21 Deanway, Chalfont St Giles;* **t** *(01494) 872 313; open Mar–Oct Tues–Sun 10–1 and 2–6; adm*), built in the 16th century, is unspoiled, with creaky wooden floorboards, low beams and a big old fireplace. It is the only surviving building in which Milton – a Londoner born and bred – is known to have lived. The garden has been replanted with flowers named in his poems. Milton wrote in many languages on a range of subjects and made himself blind reading; chief propagandist for Cromwell's government, the Restoration turned his world upside down. He was turfed out of his Westminster home, imprisoned and narrowly escaped execution thanks to powerful friends. The blind poet's reader in London, Thomas Ellwood, found him a 'pretty box' at Chalfont St Giles – which belonged to the Fleetwoods, a good local Puritan family – to escape the London plague. He is said to have composed 40 lines of *Paradise Lost* a day and dictated them to his secretary in the evening. There are only three small rooms on show, but the curator brings the place to life, with the help of a lock of hair stolen from his grave in St Giles' Cripplegate, a high-backed chair and 20 first editions. Milton arrived here in June 1665 and returned to London the following spring.

Amersham and Old Jordons Meeting House

> *...under pretence of Religious Worship, [Quakers] do often assemble in great numbers in several parts of the Realm, to the great endangering of the publick peace and safety, and to the terror of the people.*
>
> The Quaker Act, 1662

It is said that dissent and Nonconformity were fostered in Buckinghamshire's ancient beech woods, and Quakerism arrived down the old northwest road. In the mid-17th century, Amersham and the neighbouring villages were Quaker strongholds. Among the early friends who met in the old kitchen (now the dining room) of William Russell's farm **Old Jordons** (*Meeting House open Mar–Oct Wed–Mon 10–1 and 2.15–6; Nov–Feb weekends 10–1 and 2.15–dusk, Wed–Fri by appointment,* **t** *(01494) 874 146) Mayflower Barn and Old Farmhouse kitchen by appointment only,* **t** *(01494) 879 700*) were the founders of the movement: George Fox, William Penn (also founder of Pennsylvania), James Naylor and Thomas Ellwood (who set up Milton in Chalfont St Giles). It is a Quaker landmark, with the old farmhouse (now a Quaker guesthouse and conference centre) and barns grouped around the garden, and the old red-brick meeting house, built after the Toleration Act of 1688 with money left by another leading Buckinghamshire Quaker, Isaac Pennington. Outside are the graves of William Penn (1641–1718), Isaac Pennington (1616–79) and Thomas Ellwood (1639–1713).

West Wycombe

Just off the M40, High Wycombe is a sprawling town of detached villas and estates. Avoid it. But a mile west down the Oxford Road is West Wycombe, a village of mellow brickwork, saggy roofs and wonky exposed timber. Above it rises beautiful West Wycombe Hill, the golden ball of St Lawrence's church poking out of the woods, which also conceal a Roman-style mausoleum. The ensemble has rural charm, impressive architecture and a healthy dose of eccentricity. The madcap behind it all was Sir Francis Dashwood, Lord le Depencer, chancellor of the exchequer from 1762 to 1763, Grand Tourist, connoisseur collector, enthusiastic builder of neo-classical buildings and member of numerous societies, including the notorious Hell-Fire Club (*see* below). West Wycombe Park is his Palladian mansion, in glorious landscaped gardens with a bizarre series of caves occupied by tableaux of Sir Francis' circle of friends.

Hell-Fire Caves

***t** (01494) 533 739; open Mar–Oct daily 11–5.30; adm.*

A fake ruined abbey provides the Gothic entrance to the caves, dug between 1748 and 1752 by 100 unemployed farm workers in a work-creation scheme to quarry chalk for the road between High Wycombe and West Wycombe. A gloomy tunnel takes you 1,300 feet into the hill, past mannequins of the Hell-Fire Club members: John Wilkes (MP for Aylesbury and Lord Mayor of London); Lord Sandwich; the poet Paul Whitehead; and Dashwood's friend and frequent guest Benjamin Franklin. The club, also known as the 'Monks of Medmenham' and the 'Society of St Francis of Wycombe' started meeting in 1742 at the old Cistercian abbey at Medmenham on the Thames, about 8 miles from West Wycombe, and is believed to have met in the caves too. The elected 'abbot' wore a crimson gown, while the 'monks' wore flowing white robes. The meetings were secret, but there was talk of profane mock-Satanic rituals and Byronic orgies. The club disbanded in 1763, owing to political disagreements and an incident involving a baboon dressed as the devil, let loose by John Wilkes during a ceremony conducted by Lord Sandwich.

You can climb up the hill from the caves to the **Dashwood Mausoleum**, which was the last of the Sir Francis' buildings, completed in 1765. The hexagonal structure was modelled on Constantine's Arch in Rome. Next to it stands **St Lawrence's church** (*open April–Sept weekends 2–5, June–Aug Mon–Fri 1–4*), a medieval building lavishly remodelled by Sir Francis with imitation marble, Rococo wall friezes and a ceiling painted with classical decoration. The golden ball on top of the tower could apparently sit ten people for supper. From the balcony beneath there are wonderful views over the hills.

West Wycombe Park

***t** (01494) 513 569; grounds open April–May Sun–Thurs 2–6, house and grounds June–Aug Sun–Thurs 2–6; adm.*

With its porticos and colonnades lined up against ochre walls, the Dashwood family home looks like another of the neo-classical temples dotted around the park. Flamboyant 18th-century dilettante Sir Francis Dashwood remodelled his father's house over 40 years, inspired by regular trips to Italy and Greece. He employed draughtsmen to realize his ideas, rather than architects who might have toned them down. The colonnaded south front was the work of John Donowell. Patron and draughtsman fell out in 1764, and Nicholas Revett took over, adding the west portico – the 'Temple of Bacchus' – and monuments. The painted ceilings were the work of Milanese artists Giuseppe Borgnis and his son Giovanni, brought to England by Dashwood for the job. From the Roman atrium-style entrance hall, with its polished stone floor, marbled walls and columns and busts of Roman emperors, you enter the main rooms. Among the gilt-framed paintings collected by Sir Francis on Grand Tours of Italy are portraits of the man himself in fancy dress. The Borgnis ceilings steal the show: the designs are taken from celebrated interiors in Rome and illustrations in Robert Wood's *Ruins of Palmyra*, such as the *Council of Gods* in the Saloon and *Triumph of Bacchus and Ariadne* in the Blue Drawing Room. From the north portico, the 18th-century vistas have been preserved; down the avenues between the trees you glimpse the Donowell and Revett monuments, including the Temple of the Winds and Temple of Apollo. This is the antiquarian paradise of a seasoned Grand Tourist.

Hughenden Manor

***t** (01494) 755 573; open Mar weekends 1–5, April–Oct Wed–Sun 1–5; adm; numbers limited, so book at weekends.*

Hidden away on a hill above the A4128 a few miles north of High Wycombe, the red-brick country house of Queen Victoria's favourite prime minister, Benjamin Disraeli, and his wife, Mary Anne, stands in formal gardens surrounded by pasture. The Disraelis moved here in 1848, after 10 years of marriage. He was 44 years old, MP for Buckinghamshire and the successful author of four novels. She was 12 years his senior, a wealthy widow who had cleared his premarital debts (around £60,000), and now managed the finances and ran the household so that he could get on with his career. 'Whether in town or country,' said Prime Minister Lord Derby, visiting in 1851, 'politics constitutes his chief, almost his sole, pleasure'. The ambitious couple borrowed money to buy Hughenden, a rather plain Georgian house, and remodelled it – with another loan – in imposing neo-Gothic style. The architect was Edward Buckton Lamb, who had worked on Chequers. He stripped away the stucco to reveal the blue and red brickwork, jazzed up the roofline with battlements and pinnacles and added a loggia between the wings on the front. The rooms were Gothicized before Mary Anne decorated them in lush mid-Victorian style – richly patterned flock wallpaper, yellow silk drapes and terracotta walls. The Disraelis did not collect furniture or art, but surrounded themselves with portraits of family, friends and royals, and gifts from Queen Victoria such as a statuette of John Brown with the Queen's pony and border collie. The library is stocked with 4,000 books. Hughenden was inherited by Disraeli's nephew Coningsby, named after the hero of his second novel. About a mile southwest of the house is the 50ft-high Disraeli Monument, commissioned by Mary Anne as a surprise to commemorate Benjamin's father Isaac. Outside the church are the graves of Disraeli, Mary Anne and Coningsby.

Thames Valley and Cotswolds

Berkshire, Oxfordshire and Gloucestershire

12

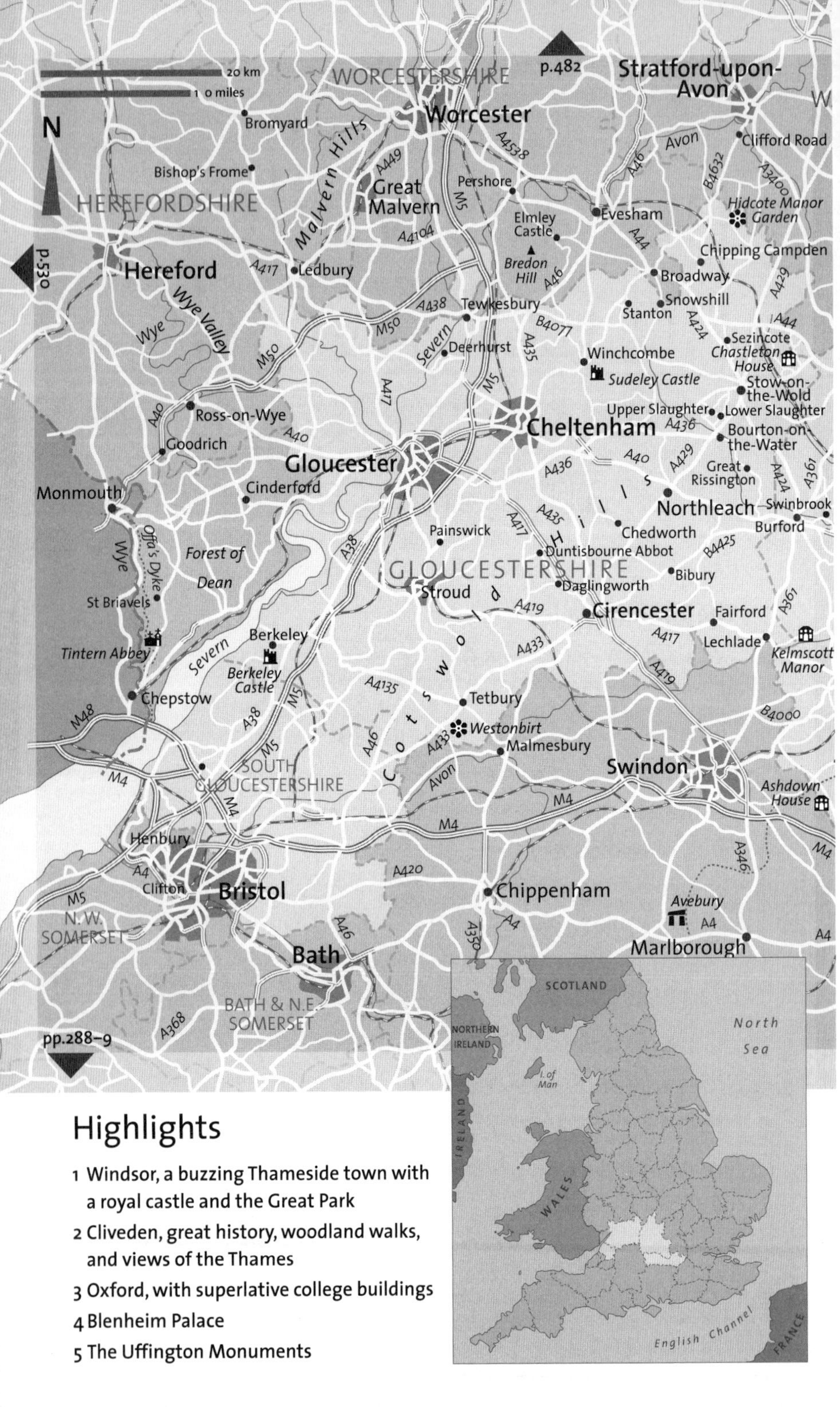

Highlights

1 Windsor, a buzzing Thameside town with a royal castle and the Great Park
2 Cliveden, great history, woodland walks, and views of the Thames
3 Oxford, with superlative college buildings
4 Blenheim Palace
5 The Uffington Monuments

The Thames takes you all the way from the affluent western suburbs of London upstream to its source at Cirencester. In its lower reaches it passes Royal palaces and great houses, briefly becoming the Isis as it passes through the ancient university town of Oxford. Near its source it meanders through the gentle, rolling countryside of the Cotswolds, with their particular landscape and villages of honey-coloured stone. This has long been a fertile, rich corner of England – never more so than now that the M4 and M40 motorways have brought it all in easy reach of London.

The Thames Valley

Most of my life I have dwelt in the neighbourhood of the river. I thank Old Father Thames for many happy days. We spent our honeymoon, my wife and I, in a little boat. I knew the river well, its deep pools and hidden ways, its quiet backwaters, its sleepy towns and villages.

Jerome K. Jerome

The River Thames is liquid history, from its source in the Cotswolds near Cirencester all the way down its 135-mile course through London to the North Sea. You pass great houses like **Buscot Park** and **Cliveden**, inhabited by the councillors of monarchs whose preferred countryside residences were **Windsor Castle** and Hampton Court Palace (*see* p.124), and delightful riverside settlements. **Marlow** and **Henley**, **Wallingford** and **Abingdon** are buzzing Thameside towns with picturesque bridges over the Thames, grassy riverbanks and busy restaurants and hotels.

Here the Thames is all charm and good humour, sporting green wooded banks and overlooked by Edwardian villas; it is the Thames of bare-chested river captains on shiny white motor-launches, competitive oarsmen from the Marlow and Henley clubs and romantic couples zigzagging in rowing boats. This is the jaunty Victorian Thames of Jerome K. Jerome's sell-out novel *Three Men in a Boat*, which tells the adventures of three foolish men and a Scots Terrier called Montmorency travelling upriver from Kingston to Goring in the early summer of 1889. It is also, on occasions, the dreamy Edwardian Thames of *Wind in the Willows* (1908), where various old manor houses purport to be the 'original' Toad Hall; Kenneth Grahame first told the story of Ratty and Toad to his son on the Thames footpath.

The historic towns of Windsor and Eton face each other across the Thames on the east side of the Chilterns (*see* pp.421–2), an island of old-world charms in a swelling sea of suburban sprawl. Here, Windsor Great Park and a touch of royal glamour provide an effective force-field against the urban turmoil.

The Thames has a split personality, however, and the contrast between the upper and lower reaches is stark. In the same decade that Charles Dodgson (aka Lewis Carroll) narrated the adventures of *Alice in Wonderland* on a boat trip from Oxford, and 20 years before the publication of Jerome K. Jerome's *Three Men in a Boat*, Dickens described London's midnight 'slime and ooze', trawled for human flotsam by the Gaffer in *Our Mutual Friend*: 'at every mooring-chain and rope, at every stationary boat or barge that split the current into a broad arrowhead, at the offsets from the piers of the Southwark Bridge, at the paddles of the river steamboats as they beat the filthy water, at the floating logs of timber lashed together lying off certain wharves, his shining eyes darted a hungry look.'

The river that witnessed Elizabeth I's 'heart and stomache of a man' speech at Tilbury on the eve of the Spanish Armada, and King John's endorsement of *Magna Carta* on the Thameside meadow of Runnymede in 1215 is now the river of the Henley Royal Regatta and boozy corporate gin palaces.

Getting There and Around

A web of motorways (the M3, M4, M25 and M40) and A-roads serve the Thames Valley.

There are railway stations in all the main towns along the valley to Oxford; Reading is the key junction on the network. Direct trains run from London Waterloo to **Windsor & Eton Riverside** station via Ascot; the journey time is 55 minutes. Thames Trains run from London Paddington to **Windsor & Eton Central** station, changing at Slough. For all train information contact **National Rail enquiries, t** 08457 484950, *www.thetrainline.com*.

Green Line runs a regular **bus** service from London Victoria to Windsor. Contact **Traveline, t** 0870 608 2608. A direct bus runs between Windsor and Heathrow Airport Central Bus Station, Mon–Sat every half hour, Sun hourly. Contact **Airoute Link, t** (01628) 796 666.

An **open-top tour bus** circulates Windsor constantly, starting outside the castle.

On **foot**, the Thames Path runs 184 miles from the Thames Barrier to Teddington, then it's more patchy. Contact the **National Trails Office, t** (01865) 810 224, *www.nationaltrails.gov.uk* for details. For the free leaflet *Reach a Range of Riverside Walks by Train, Bus and Boat*, send an sae to the National Trails Office, Cultural Services, Holton, Oxford OX33 1QQ.

Boat Trips and Hire

Boat trips from Windsor are run by **French Brothers, t** (01753) 851 900.

For rowing-boat hire try:

John Logie Motor Boats, Barry Avenue, The Promenade, Windsor, **t** (07774) 983 809. Rowing and motor boats by the hour. *Open Easter–Oct.*

Hobbs and Sons, Station Road, Henley, **t** (01491) 572 035, *www.hobbs-of-henley.com*. Long-established family-run boating business; runs passenger cruises on the Regatta Course and hires out rowing boats from the river front.

J Hooper, Riverside, Henley, **t** (07770) 937 132.

And for cruiser hire:

Kris Cruisers, The Waterfront, Southlea Road, Datchet, **t** (01753) 543 930, *www.kriscruisers.co.uk*.

Swancraft, Benson Waterfront, Benson, **t** (01491) 836 700.

Tourist Information

Windsor: 24 High Street, **t** (01753) 743 907, *www.windsor.gov.uk. Open summer 10–5.30, winter 10–4*. You can buy the *Thames Path National Trail Companion* and maps of the town and Windsor Great Park here.

Marlow: 31 High Street, **t** (01628) 481 717. *Open Mon–Fri 9–5, Sat 9.30–5 (4 in winter).*

Henley-on-Thames: King's Arms Barn, King's Road, **t** (01491) 578 034. *Open Mon–Sat 9.30–5, Sun 11–4.*

Festivals and Sporting Events

Ascot Racecourse, Ascot, **t** (01344) 876 876. Royal Ascot, in June, is a fashionable social event with racing as the excuse. Over-the-top hats obligatory. Posh picnics in the car park *de rigueur*.

Royal Windsor Racecourse, Maidenhead Road, **t** 08702 200 024. Regular race days and occasional evening meetings. *April–Oct.*

Henley Women's Regatta, t (01491) 572 153. Third weekend in June.

Henley Royal Regatta, t (01491) 572 153. One of the highlights of the English social calendar. In the first week of July the riverside lawns are packed with blazer-clad boaties, women in floral frocks and Pimms-swilling corporate types as rowers whiz by on the river.

Henley Festival, t (01491) 843 404, *www.henley-festival.co.uk*. Straight after the Regatta, in the festival grounds. Classical, jazz, rock, folk and world music. Outside the festival, it's always worth catching a performance at the **Kenton Theatre**, New

Windsor and Around

The classic approach to Windsor – if you don't come by boat – is on the A308 Windsor Road, passing through the green buffer-zone of Runnymede, the fairy-tale castle dead ahead of you. Despite the motorways that snake around it, and the dreary towns round about, Windsor remains a world apart. Watered by the Thames and

Street, Henley-on-Thames, **t** (01491) 575 698, a lovely old theatre on a picturesque street in between two good pubs.

Marlow Regatta. Takes place on a Saturday in the third week of June. Serious racing takes place on Eton College's rowing course at Dorney Lake, Taplow, **t** (01628) 525 977, while the fun town regatta takes place a week earlier at Marlow, **t** (01628) 488 950.

Windsor Festival, **t** (01753) 740 121. Themed walks, talks and book signings in second half of September. Venues include old Windsor Royal Station, the Waterloo Room of the castle, St George's Chapel and Windsor Great Park.

Where to Stay

Windsor t (01753) –

The Castle Hotel, 18 High Street, **t** 0870 400 8300, *www.macdonald-hotels.co.uk* (*very expensive*). Smart Georgian building with well-decorated public rooms and two restaurants, one formal à la carte, the other serving upmarket sandwiches and salads, bangers and mash, fish and chips.

Hart & Garter Hotel, High Street, **t** 863 426, *www.hartandgarter.com* (*expensive*). Imposing Victorian red-brick hotel opposite Garter Tower, just the right side of quaint and old-fashioned. The colonial-style café-bar overlooks the castle wall. The Victorian Restaurant upstairs has a traditional carvery overlooking the old Royal Station.

Sir Christopher Wren's House Hotel, Thames Street, **t** 861 354, *www.sirchristopherwren.co.uk* (*expensive*). Attractive red-brick neo-classical house reputedly designed by Wren for his uncle. Many of its 92 rooms inhabit neighbouring buildings on Thames Street. Elegant reception and leisure facilities.

The Christopher Hotel, 110 Eton High Street, **t** 852 359, *www.christopher-hotel.co.uk* (*expensive*). Victorian tiled hotel and restaurant divided by coaching arch. Pleasant, small bar with big windows on High Street. **Renata's Restaurant** (*closed Sun*) has modern art on the walls and crisp linen tablecloths; the organic, seasonal food includes all the modern classics, from Thai fishcakes to poached fillet of lamb.

Fairlight Lodge, Frances Road, **t** 861 207, *www.fairlightlodge.webjump.com* (*moderate*). A life-sized model of a Grenadier guard stands to attention in the hallway of this attractive 19th-century townhouse on a quiet residential street near Long Walk. Clean bedrooms. Relaxed and friendly.

Marlow t (01628) –

The Compleat Angler, Marlow Bridge, **t** 0870 400 8100, *www.heritage-hotels.com* (*luxury*). Set back from the river next to the suspension bridge, it is named after Izaak Walton's book on the joys of angling, written in 1653 at Marlow. Both restaurants are excellent. **Walton's Brasserie** (*expensive*) is an elegant conservatory restaurant with river views and a terrace, serving leg of lamb and rosemary kebabs and seared swordfish, or afternoon teas. The high-class **Riverside Restaurant** (*luxury*) feels like a boat. Recent guests have included Jim Carey, Bill Clinton and Rod Stewart. *Also open for breakfast. Live music played on Saturday night.*

Cliveden Hotel, Taplow, **t** 668 561, *www.clivedenhouse.co.uk* (*luxury*). Cliveden was the home of a prince, three dukes, an earl and the Astors until 1966. It has entertained royalty, politicians, writers, the rich, beautiful and powerful. Now there are 38 swanky bedrooms, and elegant dining rooms (*luxury*), including Waldo's, a brick-vaulted cellar, the French dining room and the Terrace. The cottage on the riverside comes with a butler.

nourished by droves of tourists, the castle at its heart is flanked by the green lungs of Windsor Great Park and Runnymede. The royal family appropriated the name during the First World War, and created a great brand. You could see all of Windsor in half a day *en route* to Heathrow airport, or spend a happy few days touring the riverbanks and villages roundabout.

Henley-on-Thames t (01491) –

You are spoiled for choice in and around Henley, except during the Regatta.

Red Lion Hotel, Hart Street, **t** 572 161, *www.redlionhenley.co.uk* (*very expensive*). Traditional, wisteria-clad coaching inn overlooking the river with bedrooms named after famous guests (Charles I, Dr Johnson and the Duke of Marlborough).

Thamesmead House Hotel, Remenham Lane, **t** 574 745, *www.thamesmeadhousehotel.co.uk* (*expensive*). Upmarket six-bedroom hotel overlooking cricket ground, furnished in airy minimalist style. Scandinavian chic.

The Leander Club, Riverside, **t** 575 782 (*expensive*). Upmarket B&B with 11 bedrooms and a rowing theme. Excellent restaurant, whose chef trained under Marco Pierre White.

Phyllis Court Club, Phyllis Court Drive, **t** 570 500 (*expensive*). Quirky, fuddy-duddy private members' club on the riverside with 17 public bedrooms.

Lenwade, 3 Western Road, **t** 414 232 (*moderate*). Immaculate B&B in quiet Victorian family home near town centre. Faultless service.

Old School House, 42 Hart Street, **t** 573 929 (*moderate*). Down little drive opposite the church, a converted Victorian school building offering good standard accommodation and breakfasts in walled patio.

Dutch Barge Rival, P.O. Box 4553, mobile **t** (07976) 390 416, *www.rivalbarge.com* (*moderate*). Traditional Dutch barge with wooden interior, wood-burning stove and sun deck. Three bedrooms and laid-back atmosphere.

Around Henley

Fyfield Manor, Benson (near Wallingford), **t** (01491) 835 184 (*moderate*). Next to the airfield. Extraordinary house going back to 12th century, with 19th-century Italianate front and water garden. Two large en-suite bedrooms, one with wooden panelling.

Fords Farm, Ewelme (near Wallingford), **t** (01491) 839 272 (*moderate*). Location and modest charms recommend this working farm by church and almshouses in the Chiltern foothills.

Apple Ash, Woodlands Road, Harpsden Woods, **t** (01491) 574 198 (*moderate*). Edwardian family home with convivial hosts and friendly dogs, a mile south of Henley. Home comforts include power showers and cast-iron Gothic-style bedheads.

Riviera, Bolney Road, Lower Shiplake, **t** (0118) 940 1263 (*moderate*). Black-and-white-fronted Edwardian boathouse on riverside, 2½ miles out of Henley but only 200 yards from local station, with trains on the hour to Paddington and Oxford, and staggering distance from a good pub. Indoor heated pool downstairs.

Larch Down Farm, Whitehall Lane, Checkendon, **t** (01491) 682 282 (*moderate*). Naturalistic garden surrounds B&B, 6 miles from Henley. Good pub nearby.

If you find all the above booked, try:

Holmwood, Shiplake Row, Binfield Heath, **t** (0118) 947 8747 (*cheap*). Decent B&B.

The Knoll, Crowsley Road, Shiplake, **t** (0118) 940 2705 (*cheap*). Another pleasant B&B.

Orchard Dene Cottage, Lower Assenden, **t** (01491) 575 490 (*cheap*). More pastoral B&B.

Eating Out

Windsor t (01753) –

Windsor is crammed with eateries, including most of the better chain cafés and restaurants, packed in behind the Guildhall and old Royal Windsor Station.

Strok's Riverside Restaurant, Thames Street, **t** 861 354 (*expensive*). Upmarket but informal hotel restaurant overlooking the river and bridge. Serves delicacies such as warm goats' cheese and asparagus tart, followed by pan-fried red mullet with creamed

The heart of the town is in the few streets around the imposing statue of Queen Victoria, from where the castle rises up the hill, the arcades of Wren's exquisite Guildhall stretch out over flagged pavements and the elegant mishmash of Georgian and Victorian houses lead off down Peascod Street. Wren, no less than the architect of St Paul's Cathedral and president of the Royal Society, was apparently told by the

Jerusalem artichoke, topped off by peach Bakewell tart with clotted cream.

Castello Restaurant, 4 Church Lane, **t** 858 331 (*moderate*). Pizza, pasta and specials such as aubergine bake behind old shopfront.

Browns, Barry Avenue, **t** 831 970 (*moderate*). Bar and restaurant overlooking the river, with terrace seating. Brasserie-style food.

Monty's, Windsor Bridge,**t** 854 479, *www.montys-riverside-restaurant.co.uk* (*moderate*). French restaurant named after Montmorency, the scurrilous cat worrier in *Three Men in a Boat*. The pleasant nautical-style dining room overlooks the river. Good grills. *Winter closed Sun eve.*

The House on the Bridge, Windsor Bridge, **t** 790 198 (*moderate*). Victorian red-brick building opposite Monty's (owned by the same people) with elegant interior. Similar French-style menu. Also does afternoon tea in summer.

Antico Restaurant, 42 High Street, Eton, **t** 863 977 (*moderate*). Cosy, cluttered dining room behind old shop front. Lots of meat dishes. *Closed Sat lunch and Sun.*

Crooked Tea Rooms, High Street (*cheap*). A crooked old building serving light lunches and teas.

Marlow t (01628) –

This lively town is well provided with cafés, pubs and restaurants too. The High Street leading into Spittal Street is lined with tempting restaurants wafting delicious cooking smells onto the pavement, as well as decent chains like **Zizzi**, **t** 890 200 (*cheap*), where you can get an excellent selection of pasta, pizza and salads.

Jasmine Peking, Market Square, **t** 475 035 (*moderate*). Sesame prawn toast, spring rolls and aromatic crispy duck.

Don Lorenzo, 101 High Street, **t** 482 180 (*moderate*). Homely, old-fashioned Italian restaurant beneath blue and white awnings.

Bell and The Dragon, High Street, Cookham , **t** 521 263 (*moderate*). The snug bar opens up into a cosy restaurant with patio garden. Watercress and mozzarella salad, followed by chargrilled haddock.

George and Dragon, The Causeway, **t** 483 887 (*cheap*). Lively pub with pavement tables by bridge. Modern-style pub grub, and lively music in evenings.

Henley t (01491) –

The range of restaurants on Market Place and Hart Street includes chains such as Café Rouge.

The Henley Tea Rooms. Riverfront Italian-run café-restaurant with quick service; fish and chips, egg and chips, teas and coffees.

Loch Fyne, Market Place, **t** 845 780 (*moderate*). Loch Fyne fishcakes, dressed Cromer crabs, herb-crusted cod steak. You can eat outside on Market Place with a glass of white wine. *Open 10–10.*

Villa Marina, 18 Thameside, **t** 575 262 (*moderate*). Just behind the Angel, off the main road. Elegant old-fashioned Italian restaurant, an oar's length from the river, decorated with fulsome flower baskets.

Antico, 49–51 Market Place, **t** 573 060 (*moderate*). Old-world Italian restaurant near Town Hall. Try the home-style *zuppa di verdure*.

Dorchester-on-Thames t (01865) –

The White Hart, 26 High Street, **t** 340 074, *www.oxford-restaurants-hotels.co.uk* (*expensive*). Pleasantly furnished former coaching inn with an old well. Pleasant bar and comfortable bedrooms.

Fleur de Lys, High Street (*cheap*). Cosy bar with leafy garden. Serves pub grub and real ales.

Abbey Tea Room, Abbey Gatehouses (*cheap*). You can get a cup of tea and find out more about Dorchester in the little museum here. *Open Easter–Sept weekends.*

town councillors to add the central columns to the **Guildhall** for extra support. Wren gave in to their fussing, building the columns an inch short of the roof to make his point. Pop into the Georgian church of **St John the Baptist** (*open daily 10.30–4.30*) to see the *Last Supper* by Flemish painter Frantz de Cleyn. You can find some decent places for lunch, tea or drinks in among the souvenir shops behind the Guildhall.

Windsor's serious shopping goes on in the old **Windsor Royal Station** off High Street, a wonderful iron-girdered and glass-vaulted warren of upmarket clothing boutiques.

At the **riverside** you can join a boat trip, or cross the bridge to **Eton High Street**, a jolly old-fashioned thoroughfare of antiques and smart souvenir shops, restaurants and pubs leading directly to **Eton College** (*t (01753) 671 177; tours daily at 2.15 and 3.15; adm*). This, the most famous of England's old 'public' boys' schools, is reminiscent of an Oxford or Cambridge college – not surprising, as it was founded in 1440 by Henry VI to supply scholars to his other foundation, King's College, Cambridge. Before you start fantasizing about sending your offspring here for an upper-class education, consider the costs: about 1,300 boys between the ages of 13 and 18 spend three terms (called 'halves') each year at Eton, and their parents pay an annual fee of at least £20,691 for the privilege. School uniform is the traditional black tailcoat and pin-striped trousers. Princes William and Harry recently attended Eton, coming away with the relaxed, hearty social manner for which the public school sector is renowned (and enough good exam grades to get them into university).

Windsor Castle

t (020) 7766 7304; open Mar–Oct daily 9.45–5.15, Nov–Feb 9.45–4.15; state apartments sometimes closed for Royal business; St George's Chapel open daily, Sun and religious holidays to worshippers only; adm exp.

The splendid view of Windsor Castle from the M4 might be of an Italian hill village of grey stone towers and high, crenellated walls. Around 250 people including administrators, the deans and canons of St George's Chapel, restorers of the Royal Collection and soldiers live and work in its three 'wards', comprising 13 acres, a post office and a doctor's surgery. One of the Queen's official residences, it is said to be much preferred to Buckingham Palace, her goldfish bowl in the city. You will find her here most weekends (if the Royal Standard is flying from the Round Tower), all of April and part of June, when the Court decamps *en masse* from London, and for official state visits of foreign leaders held in the esteem of the Government.

The main castle builders were William the Conqueror, who chose the strategic site above the Thames; Edward III, who made the castle a stronghold worthy of the name and founded St George's Chapel; Charles II, who turned Edward's fortress into a baroque palace; George IV, whose architect Geoffrey Wyatville built St George's Hall and created the fairy-tale skyline by adding crenellations and raising Henry II's Round Tower to an imposing height; and the present Queen Elizabeth II, who presided over a £37-million restoration after a fire in 1992 destroyed nine state rooms.

At 11am daily from April to the end of June, and then on alternate days excluding Sunday, the military band ceremoniously accompanies the new guard from Victoria Barracks up the High Street and through King Henry VIII Gate into the Parade Yard of the Lower Ward. There they perform for half an hour while the guard changes, and then accompany the old guard back to the barracks.

Visitors to the castle enter the Middle Ward through St George's Gate (after airport-style security check). The path curves around the artificial motte of the Round Tower (which contains the royal archives), past the interesting Castle Exhibition Centre. The state apartments are in the Upper Ward, while St George's Chapel is in the Lower Ward, from which you exit via King Henry VIII Gate.

Pause on the **North Terrace**, with its views over the Thames towards Eton College. The 16 state rooms display arms (including the lead bullet that killed Nelson at Trafalgar in 1805) and masterpieces by Rembrandt, Rubens, Holbein, Canaletto and Van Dyck. The smaller apartments were built for Charles II, and house some of the best works, including a triple portrait of Charles I by Van Dyck and a Rembrandt self-portrait. The **Queen's Audience Chamber** and **Queen's Presence Chamber**, with painted ceilings by Verrio and wood carvings by Grinling Gibbons, are the climax of Charles II's sumptuous baroque decorative scheme. The splendid **Waterloo Room** was built like a ship to celebrate the defeat of Napoleon in 1815. **St George's Hall**, a Gothic banqueting hall by Wyatville, is adorned with Garter heraldry and suits of armour. In the **State Dining Room** and **Octagon Dining Room** are one or two pieces of Gothic furniture designed by a 15-year-old Pugin, working with his father for Morel & Seddon.

You may want to make a detour to **Queen Mary's Doll's House**, a 1-in-12 scale model given to Queen Mary in 1924. The architect was Edwin Lutyens, architect of New Delhi, the Whitehall Cenotaph and Castle Drogo. The garden is by Gertrude Jekyll, the sewing machine by Singer, the cars by Rolls Royce, and the books on the library shelves by their own authors, including Kipling, Conan Doyle and Hardy.

The Queen goes to **St George's Chapel** in the Lower Ward for matins on Easter Day and the annual ceremony of the Order of the Garter, England's highest chivalric order, founded in 1348 by Edward III. The 25 Knights of the Garter are matched by the same number of canons, and both knightly and ecclesiastical orders look to the chapel as their spiritual home. The present Perpendicular Gothic chapel was built by Edward IV in 1475 and 10 monarchs are buried here, including Henry VIII, who commissioned the fan vault. The Queen Mother and Princess Margaret are buried in the King George VI Memorial Chapel, visible from the north Quire aisle. In the dark, oak-carved Quire the current knights hang their banners and swords over their personal stalls, while 670 stall plates commemorate former knights all the way back to 1390. The gold mosaic-encrusted **Albert Memorial Chapel** was built for Queen Victoria in memory of her beloved husband, who died in the castle in 1861. Both Victoria and Albert are buried in the royal mausoleum at **Frogmore House** (*__t__ (020) 7321 2233; open some days in May and Aug*), a royal retreat in Home Park off Long Walk.

Windsor Great Park

Pick up a map of the Great Park at the tourist information centre on the High Street, then walk down Park Street to the entrance of the **Long Walk**. This straight 3-mile avenue was laid out by Charles II from the castle to the *Copper Horse*, an equestrian statue of George III added by his son, George IV, to complete the vista. There the park widens into a 4,800-acre tract of open countryside where you can walk, cycle and picnic to your heart's content. For a longer walk or ride, turn right at the horse statue along the path to the village, where you can get a cup of tea or an ice cream at the

The Order of the Garter

The motto of the Order of the Garter, *Honi soit qui mal y pense* was minted by Edward III (1327–77) during the Hundred Years War, meaning shame on him (who thinks evil of Edward's claim to the French throne). The monarch, obsessed with the legend of King Arthur, founded the chivalrous order to bolster morale in the protracted campaign. The garter worn by the knights to fasten their battle armour became the symbol of the order. With the king as its head and St George as its patron, it was one of the highest orders of chivalry founded in the courts of Europe during the Middle Ages, but is unusual for having survived to the present day.

post office shop and watch the cricket. Then circle to **Bishop's Gate** and back to the statue. On the edge of the park is **Saville Garden** (*open Mar–Oct 10–6, Nov–Feb 10–4,* **t** *(01753) 847 518; adm*), a 35-acre all-year garden with a plant centre and restaurant. At the south end of the park, towards Ascot, is **Virginia Water**, a serpentine lake created by the Duke of Cumberland, son of George II, and featuring a 100-foot totem pole and artificial waterfall. On the northern banks are the **Valley Gardens**, and above them **Smith's Lawn**, home to the Guard's Polo Club, where matches take place from April to September on Sunday afternoons, culminating in the Queen's Cup.

Runnymede

Rowing past Runnymede in the summer of 1849, Jerome K. Jerome grows unusually poetic and imagines the meeting between King John and the 25 barons on 15 June 1215. He pictures the action on Magna Carta Island, according to popular tradition, rather than on 'Runnymede meadow between Windsor and Staines', as specified on the original parchment of 49 articles signed by the king (copies of which can be seen in the British Museum, and at Lincoln and Salisbury cathedrals). The *Articles of the Barons* were quickly reassembled by legal experts into *Magna Carta*, which effectively reined in the king's power. The most famous article is this: 'No free man shall be arrested or imprisoned or disseised [legally dispossessed of his land] or outlawed or exiled or victimized in any other way...except by the lawful judgement of his peers or by the law of the land'. The integrity of the Runnymede estate has been protected since 1929 by the National Trust.

Dorney Court

t *(01628) 604 638; open May Bank Holidays and Aug Sun–Fri 1.30–4.30; adm.*

Ten minutes' drive from Eton through pretty countryside is the warm pink-brick manor house of the Palmer family, who have lived there since the 16th century. It stands pretty as a picture beside the Tudor church tower, encircled by yew hedges, its exposed timbers pockmarked with age. Inside, the rooms are infused with the smoke of four centuries of wood fires in the Great Hall, lined with Palmer portraits (including the late Peregrine Palmer) and horned animal skulls. The location scouts of *Lock Stock and Two Smoking Barrels*, *Sliding Doors* and *Elizabeth* all found inspiration here.

Marlow and Around

Jerome K. Jerome described Marlow as 'one of the pleasantest river centres I know of. It is a bustling, lively little town; not very picturesque on the whole, it is true, but there are many quaint nooks and corners to be found in it.' His words are still apt. Its buzzing High Street crosses the Thames over a suspension bridge built by William Tierney Clark in 1832. The Shelleys were living in West Street from 1817 to 1818 when Mary wrote *Frankenstein*. The five-times Olympic gold-medal winner and Leander Club oarsman Sir Steven Redgrave is a Marlow man; his statue stands way above average height in the riverside gardens.

Cookham

The artist Stanley Spencer (1891–1959) lived and worked in Cookham, a beautiful, well-heeled riverside village of Georgian cottages and climbing plants on the south side of the Thames, about two miles east of Marlow. He was born in Fernlea on the High Street, the 10th of 11 talented children. The village was frequently the setting for his New Testament paintings, among them *Christ Preaching at Cookham Regatta*, *Listening from Punts* and *Last Supper*, showing eight pairs of feet protruding from under the table of the malthouse down School Lane.

Stanley Spencer Gallery

t (01628) 471 885; open mid-April–Oct daily 10.30–5.30, Nov–Dec weekends 10.30–5.30, Jan–mid-April weekends 11–5; adm minimal.

This smashing little gallery devoted entirely to the work of Stanley Spencer opened in 1962 in the old Victorian Methodist chapel, where he worshiped as child. His paintings are shown in rotation, but the Cookham works are always on display. The gallery can give you a leaflet to trace the sites of the artist's inspiration around the village.

Cliveden

t (01628) 605 069, www.nationaltrust.org.uk; estate and garden open mid-Mar–Oct 11–6, Nov–Dec 11–4; adm; house and Octagon Temple April–Oct Thurs and Sat 3–5.30; woodlands April–Oct 11–5.30, Nov–Dec 11–4; adm exp.

Twenty-five miles from Westminster, five from Windsor and ten from Ascot and Henley, commanding glorious chalk-cliff-top views over the Thames Valley, Cliveden has been the play home of the filthy rich and absurdly well-connected for 400 years. Since 1985 it has been a luxury hotel leased by the National Trust to the Cliveden Hotel Company, continuing a long tradition of upper-crust hospitality. Its first occupant, the profligate 2nd Duke of Buckingham, 'lord of useless', built Cliveden for his mistress in the 1660s. Its next owner, the Earl of Orkney, hero of the Spanish Wars of Succession, entertained King George there in 1724. George II's frivolous son and heir, Frederick Louis, Prince of Wales, took over Cliveden for 14 years; estranged from his father's Court, he established a merry Whigite coterie at Cliveden, where he was killed by a cricket ball in 1751. The 2nd Duke of Sutherland, one of the wealthiest men in Victorian Britain, bought Cliveden for his wife in 1849. Two fires precipitated the complete rebuilding in Roman cement-rendered Italian style by Charles Barry, the architect of the Houses of Parliament. Fabled guests of that era included Alfred, Lord Tennyson, Sir Joseph Paxton and Garibaldi. The Derby-racehorse-owning Duke of Westminster, whose London property portfolio made him one of the richest men in England, owned Cliveden for a while. He sold it to William Waldorf Astor, a fantastically rich American europhile who turned himself into an art connoisseur and collector while serving as the US Ambassador in Rome. He gave Cliveden as a wedding gift to his son Waldorf and new wife Nancy, who immediately slung out the musty old hangings in favour of bright chintz fabrics, and established herself as the first female member of parliament, representing Plymouth. During Nancy's ebullient reign, Cliveden became the gravitational centre for writers, performers and politicians like Henry James, Rudyard Kipling, Winston Churchill, Charlie Chaplin and King George. A secluded riverside cottage belonging to a Harley Street doctor in the grounds of Cliveden was the setting for the notorious Profumo affair in the early 1960s; in the heightened mood of the Cold War, the tabloid story of Cabinet war minister John Profumo and society prostitute Christine Keeler, who was also having an affair with a Russian spy, led to the downfall of the Macmillan Government.

From the car park, walk to the house down the Grand Avenue, the setting of the enormous *Fountain of Love* by Thomas Waldo Story. The magnificent river-and-woodland view from the Upper Terrace is rivalled only by the view of the Italianate south front from the parterre. The grounds are dotted with Roman antiquities collected by the Duke and Duchess of Sutherland and William Waldorf Astor, and classical buildings like the open-air theatre.

Henley-on-Thames and Around

Thirty-five miles west of London between Oxford, Windsor and Reading, backed by the wooded hills of the Chilterns, Henley is a classy riverside town most famous for its summer regatta. The shops are smart, restaurants inviting and the old-fashioned **Kenton Theatre** appealing. From the riverside up Hart Street or New Street to **Market Place** the old town is delightful, and the new **River and Rowing Museum** is excellent. North of the old town bridge on the Remenham bank are the lawns of the **Festival Grounds**, where corporate entertainers get sozzled on Pimms in a tent city during the Regatta and Henley Festival. The dead-straight **Regatta Course** runs a mile and a quarter north of the bridge from Temple Island to the Phyllis Club grandstand. Beneath the bridge is the white-gabled **Leander Club** of Olympic gold-medal-winners Sir Steven Redgrave and Matthew Pincent, the world's oldest rowing club, founded in London in 1818. South of the bridge, the riverside promenade is backed by Victorian and Edwardian villas and lawns. The view of the town from the elegant five-arched bridge is all old-world charm.

River and Rowing Museum

t (01491) 415 600; open summer 10–5.30, winter 10–5; adm.

Statues of Olympic rowers Steven Redgrave and Matthew Pincent should by now be welcoming visitors to this elegant modern building of glass and planks standing on concrete pillars above the Thameside meadows. The **Rowing Gallery** looks at the history of rowing from the fearsome Athenian war boats of 400 BC to the Redgrave and Pincent coxless pair in the 1996 Sydney Olympics. The **Thames Gallery** interprets the river from source to sea in terms of archaeology, wildlife, transport and leisure. The **Henley Gallery** tells the story of the town from its 12th-century origins as an inland port shipping timber and grain to London, to its Regatta heyday. *Henley From the Walgrave Road* by Jan Siberechts, painted in 1768, shows how little it has changed. For children there is a **Wind in the Willows Gallery**.

Greys Court

t (01491) 628 529; house open April–Sept Wed–Fri 2–5.30; garden Mar and Oct Wed 2–5.30, April–Sept Tues–Sat 2–6; adm.

Hidden away down country lanes, the crumbling flint walls and crenellated towers of Greys Court are penetrated only by the sounds of sheep and wood pigeons. Set behind the 14th-century walls and vegetable gardens, a handsome gabled manor house sits comfortably in place of the medieval hall. Greys Court gets its name from the first Lord Grey, one of Edward III's original Knights of the Garter, whose medieval walls remain. The house was largely built by Sir Francis Knollys, a Tudor courtier based in Surrey whose son William is believed to have been the inspiration for the vain dolt Malvolio in *Twelfth Night*.

Fawley Court

t (01491) 574 917; open May–Oct Wed, Thurs and Sun 2–5; adm.

Downriver from Henley, this 17th-century red-brick mansion, built by Christopher Wren and upgraded by James Wyatt, has a strange atmosphere thanks to the green barrack huts and overgrown basketball court bordering the drive. In 1953 Father Josef Jarzebowski of the Polish Congregation of Marian Fathers bought Fawley at auction and founded a school for Polish boys and a museum of Polish history, with artefacts smuggled out of a museum in occupied Poland during the Second World War. The school has closed but the museum continues to grow. The showrooms also boast magnificent ceilings by James Wyatt and Grinling Gibbons.

St Mary's Church, Ewelme

Several miles of twisting lanes east of Wallingford bring you to this dear little church with Chaucerian connections, buried in the hillside in a timeless arrangement above four-square almshouses and a school. The manor belonged to Thomas Chaucer, son of the poet, and his daughter Alice, who married William de la Pole, the first Duke of Suffolk, a nasty piece of work who got his head chopped off on a boat as he headed for exile in France. The Suffolks endowed the church, almshouses and school. An alabaster effigy of the Duchess shows her as a Lady Knight of the Garter, attended by weepers and angels. Thomas is buried in exquisite **St John's Chapel**, its ceiling decorated with carved wooden angels like an East Anglian church. This, and the 10-foot rocket-shaped font lid, reveal the Suffolks' East Anglian connections. Covered steps lead directly down into the almshouses.

Dorchester-on-Thames

Eight miles south of Oxford, the painted timber-framed buildings of Dorchester's High Street lean forward as if to get a better look at the picturesque village in the water meadows of the rivers Thames and Thame. Dorchester started out as a Roman fort on the road between Silchester (near Basingstoke) and Alchester (near Stratford-upon-Avon), the successor to an Iron Age fort above the valley in the Sinodun Hills (a good short walk). In the 18th century it enjoyed a brief revival as a coaching centre on the Oxford–London route with two coaching inns.

Park beside the elongated bridge spanning the flood plain and head for the **Dorchester Abbey Museum** *(open May–Sept Tues–Fri 1–5, Sat 11–5, Sun 2–5)* in the old abbey church, a large building with eight pointed windows throwing light into an airy nave. There are treasures, like the gnarled Norman lead font decorated with 11 apostles (it probably survived the iconoclasts because it was too heavy to lift), and the tree of Jesse window tucked away beside the east window, the mullions of which are carved into twisted branches. It is the palpable age and scale of the barn-like interior, however, that makes it special. St Birinus brought Christianity here and founded a cathedral in the 7th century but the bishopric moved to Winchester and then Lincoln and the abbey church was left for the parish after the Dissolution.

Oxford

And that city with her dreaming spires,
She needs not June for beauty's heightening.

Matthew Arnold

Oxford inhabits the bull's eye of lowland England. Old roads, waterways and railway lines converge on its Thames crossroads from all directions. In Oxford 'the industrial energies of England...meet with a roar of exhausts in an environment of moist green languor', wrote Jan Morris in her book *Oxford*. The town's origins go back to the Saxons. It has its Market Street, Norman motte, modest cathedral, county hall, manufacturers of cars and agricultural parts and – tucked into this sturdy civic fabric – England's oldest university. The influence of eight hundred years of **Oxford University** runs through the town's fabulous buildings.

The university comprises 35 autonomous colleges, named after patron saints (St John, St Edmund, St Peter), wealthy benefactors (Exeter, Lincoln and Hertford), the souls of the dead English soldiers (All Souls) and even the shape of a door knocker (Brasenose). Prospective undergraduates apply to a college, not to the university, for

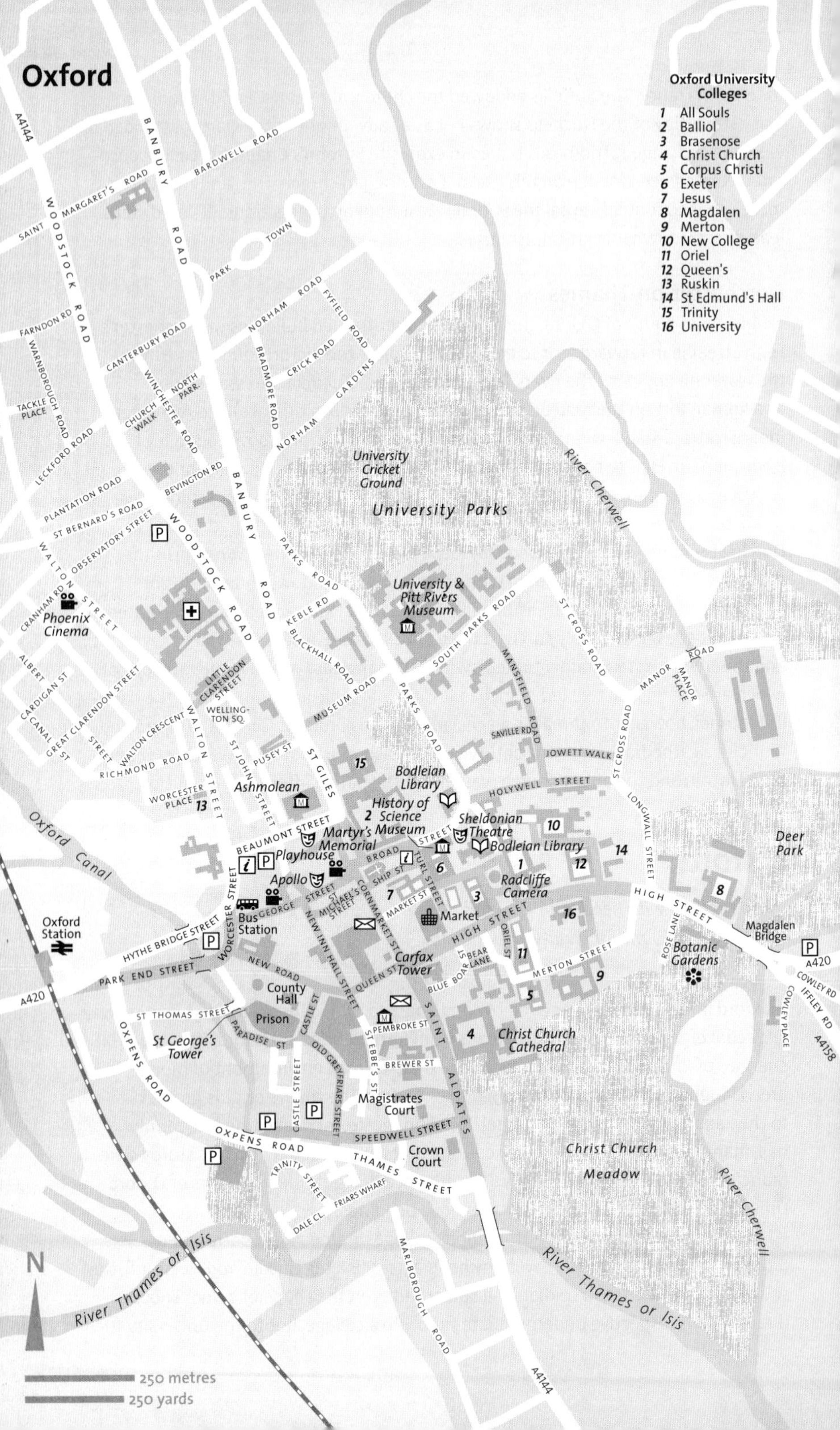

Oxford
Oxford University Colleges
1 All Souls
2 Balliol
3 Brasenose
4 Christ Church
5 Corpus Christi
6 Exeter
7 Jesus
8 Magdalen
9 Merton
10 New College
11 Oriel
12 Queen's
13 Ruskin
14 St Edmund's Hall
15 Trinity
16 University
University Cricket Ground
University Parks
River Cherwell
University & Pitt Rivers Museum
Phoenix Cinema
Bodleian Library
History of Science Museum
Sheldonian Theatre
Ashmolean
Martyr's Memorial
Playhouse
Apollo
Radcliffe Camera
Deer Park
Oxford Canal
Oxford Station
Bus Station
Market
Carfax Tower
County Hall
Prison
St George's Tower
Christ Church Cathedral
Botanic Gardens
Magdalen Bridge
Magistrates Court
Crown Court
Christ Church Meadow
River Thames or Isis
N
250 metres
250 yards

Getting There and Around

Roads and railway lines come into Oxford from all over the country. Oxford is just off the M40 at junction 8, roughly 1½ hours by **car** from London and 1 hour from Birmingham.

Trains from London Paddington take an hour. For all train information contact **National Rail Enquiries**, **t** 08457 484950, *www.thetrainline.com*.

National Express runs frequent **coaches** from London Victoria and Birmingham, and several other companies offer competitive rates on the London–Oxford route, with pickups in north and west London. For all coach information contact National Express, **t** 08705 808080 (within the UK) or **t** (+44) 121 625 1122 (from abroad), *www.gobycoach.com*.

Tourist Information

Oxford: 15–16 Broad Street, **t** (01865) 726 871. *Open Mon–Sat 9.30–5, Sun 10–3.30.*

Where to Stay

Oxford t (01865) –

Randolph Hotel, Beaumont Street (opposite Ashmolean Museum), **t** 0870 400 8200 (*luxury*). Impressive Victorian-Gothic hotel with 119 bedrooms and uniformed staff.

Eastgate Hotel, High Street, **t** 0870 400 8201 (*luxury*). A 17th-century coaching inn overlooking Examination Schools, with 63 bedrooms and a French-style café-brasserie which plays jazz in the afternoon.

Old Bank Hotel, 92–4 High Street, **t** 799 599, *www.oxford-hotels-restaurants.co.uk* (*luxury*). Modern and stylish, with fashionable restaurant attached; 43 bedrooms.

Old Parsonage Hotel, 1 Banbury Road, **t** 310 210, *www.oxford-hotels-restaurants.co.uk* (*luxury*). The 16th-century parsonage of St Giles' Church, behind old stone wall and under lichen-encrusted roof. Friendly, extremely welcoming hotel with 30 flowery bedrooms and excellent restaurant.

Cotswold Lodge Hotel, 66/a Banbury Road, **t** 512 121, *www.cotswoldlodgehotel.co.uk* (*luxury*). A Victorian pile built for an Oxford don, now a spacious, sunny hotel behind trees, with one of the loveliest stone-flagged receptions in the city. Attractively furnished and comfortable.

Bath Place, 4–5 Bath Place, **t** 791 812, *www.bathplace.co.uk* (*expensive*). Oxford's most charming hotel, a cluster of pretty-coloured 17th-century cottages around a tiny, leafy courtyard; down cobbled lane off Holywell, between New and Hertford colleges. Mentioned in *Jude the Obscure*.

14 Holywell Street (opposite New College), **t** 721 880 (*moderate*). Cosy, unpretentious sort of place on one of Oxford's loveliest roads, right in the middle of town. No en-suite bathrooms.

St Michael's Guesthouse, 26 St Michael's Street, **t** 242 101 (*moderate*). Modest, functional city-centre accommodation.

All the main roads into town (Iffley Road, London Road, Cowley Street, Woodstock Road and Banbury Road) are lined with B&Bs. Here is one to try.

Brown's Guesthouse, 281 Iffley Road, **t** 246 822, *brownsgh@hotmail.com* (*moderate*). Friendly and small, all stripped pine.

On the London Road in Headington there are several clean, neat, moderately priced guesthouses.

Pickwick's, 15–17 London Road, **t** 750 487.

Sandfield, 19 London Road, **t** 762 406.

Red Mullions, 23 London Road, **t** 742 741.

Eating Out

There are two reliable French-style café-restaurants on Little Clarendon Street: **Pierre Victoire**, **t** 316 616, and **Café Rouge**, **t** 310 194. **George and Davis'** ice-cream café is down the road, **t** 516 652, for mini-pizzas, tea and coffee (*open 8am until midnight*).

admission, and if they are accepted it is the college that defines their world at Oxford. Each college manages its own finances – some are considerably wealthier than others – and has its own tutors, sports teams, dining room, halls of residence, art treasures, strengths, weaknesses and reputation. Oxford University is the umbrella

Le Petit Blanc, 71–72 Walton Street, **t** 510 999 (*moderate*). One of chef Raymond Blanc's restaurants, providing high-quality quick lunches and high teas, as well as all-day tea and cakes.

Gees, 61 Banbury Road, **t** 553 540 (*moderate*). Stylish modern English cooking with Mediterranean twist, dished up in Victorian conservatory. Pleasant walk from centre.

Old Parsonage Hotel Restaurant, 1 Banbury Road, **t** 310 210 (*moderate*). Civilized, chatty and informal, with old-fashioned paintings on walls. Varied menu includes Thai fillet salad or calf's liver with bacon.

The Chiang Mai Kitchen, Kemp Hall Passage, 130/a High Street, **t** 202 233 (*moderate*). Popular Chinese restaurant tucked away off High Street. Authentic cooking includes excellent tom yum soup, noodles and salads.

Cherwell Boathouse, 50 Bardwell Road, **t** 552 746 (*moderate*). Beside River Cherwell, snazzy revamped restaurant serving modern English/French meals, including breast of wood pigeon.

Chutney's, 36 St Michael's Street, **t** 724 241, (*cheap*). Colourful open-plan Indian, with lots of vegetarian dishes. *Closed Sun.*

Aziz, 228–30 Cowley Road, **t** 794 945 (*cheap*). Top-notch Bangladeshi restaurant on hectic street, short walk from city centre.

Cafés

Georgina's Cafe, Covered Market, **t** 249 527 (*cheap*). Friendly little place with raffish rustic décor, the haunt of students and young mothers. Serves ciabatta sandwiches and cakes. *Closed Sun.*

Heroes, Ship Street, **t** 723 459 (*cheap*). City-centre café where you can eat filled baguettes and coffee to groovy music.

News Café, Ship Street, **t** 242 317 (*cheap*). Spacious café, serving drinks and snacks upstairs, hot food downstairs. Good breakfasts. *Open until 9pm.*

Try the **Randolph Hotel**, Beaumont Street, **t** 0870 400 8200 or the **Old Parsonage Hotel**, 1 Banbury Road, **t** 310 210, for tea.

Pubs and Bars

Quad Bar and Grill, 92–4 High Street, **t** 202 505 (*cheap*). Trendy café-bar of Old Bank Hotel, decked out with contemporary art. Stone floors and wooden deck.

Turf Tavern, **t** 243 235 (*cheap*). One of oldest pubs in the city, reached down high-walled alleys from either New College Lane or Holywell Street. Its three flagstone beer gardens are packed out on warm evenings. Inside, its small rooms are dimly lit, with stone, wood and tile floors. Classic pub grub and Sunday roasts.

The Bear, Alfred Street (behind Museum of Oxford), **t** 728 164 (*cheap*). Small, atmospheric old pub. A panelled room houses a handsome display of ties, all neatly arranged in glass-fronted cabinets and labelled on yellowing paper.

Lamb and Flag, Giles Street, **t** 515 787 (*cheap*). Good pub for idling in several cosy rooms.

Eagle and Child, Giles Street, **t** 302 925 (*cheap*). Old haunt of the Inklings, a literary group including Tolkien and Lewis Carroll. A long, dark, wood-panelled corridor with snugs on either side takes you into the bar and the Rabbit Room, where the Inklings met between 1939 and 1962.

King's Arms, Holywell Street, **t** 242 369 (*cheap*). Endless nooks, crannies and wooden booths, as well as a large front bar. Pub grub.

Freud Restaurant-Bar, 119 Walton Street, **t** 311 171 (*cheap*). Live music almost every night – jazz, blues, Bavarian folk bands – in a converted neo-classical church. *Bar open until 2am Thurs–Sat.*

Entertainment

Apollo Theatre, **t** 0870 606 3501. Popular repertoire of touring comedians, musicals and family shows.

Oxford Playhouse, **t** 305 305. More serious and innovative drama.

Phoenix Picture House, Walton Street, **t** 554 909. Arthouse cinema.

name for the committees, boards, councils and miscellaneous staff that binds it all together, running libraries and museums, staging final exams and awarding degrees. It even has its own police force, four men in bowler hats, known as bulldogs.

'Nobody knows everything about Oxford University,' wrote Morris – 'why Magdalen college is pronounced 'Maudlin' but the church of St Mary Magdalen just down the road is said as you would expect, why Oxford's terms are called Michaelmas, Hilary and Trinity, why the porters of Christchurch wear bowler hats though they are not bulldogs, what the Hebdomadal Council gets up to, what sort of person actually calls the Oxford section of the Thames 'the Isis'.' Its beginnings are mysterious. The story goes that groups of English scholars turfed out of Paris University in 1167 settled in the town, which already had an infrastructure of learning based on its monasteries. By the end of the 12th century the university was well established, with its halls of residence and peculiar customs. The first colleges were Merton, University and Balliol, founded in the 13th century with large endowments for poor scholars. Next came Exeter, Oriel, Queen's and New College in the 14th century. By the 16th century Oxford had established itself as one of the major intellectual centres in Europe, along with Padua, Paris, Bologna and Cambridge. Henry VIII founded Christchurch, by far the biggest of the Oxford colleges, fit for the next generation of Renaissance courtiers.

That the university dominates Oxford is self-evident, but 'town and gown' are inseparable. Swathes of the town were bought up and streets of houses demolished to make way for enormous college buildings. The dons dominated the town like the Italian Mafia (but speaking Latin), with their wealth, intelligence and friends in high places. The traders, lodging houses, theatres and police were firmly in their pocket, and if a scholar broke the law his case would be heard not in a civil court but by members of the university. As the fortunes of the town declined in the late Middle Ages, the tension between town and gown increased. There were regular fights, occasional deaths, and in 1355 on St Scholastica's day, the massacre of more than 60 students. In the Civil War, with the royal headquarters and the king himself based in the university, the city remained stubbornly Parliamentarian.

Charles I stayed in Christchurch deanery. Two centuries later the deanery was the home of Alice Liddell, daughter of the dean, who inspired the *Alice in Wonderland* stories. Charles Dodgson (aka Lewis Carroll) lived across the quad. He was the maths tutor and first told the story of Alice in a rowing trip up the Thames with the Liddell girls. Oxford is riddled with interlinking stories. Pre-Raphaelite artist William Morris married Jane Burden (his model for Guinevere) in St Michael's Church, which also has connections with the Protestant martyrs Cranmer, Ridley and Latimer. As an undergraduate T.E. Lawrence (of Arabia) explored an ancient underground waterway at night in a canoe. Christopher Wren, the Savilian professor of geometry, built grand edifices around the town. The poet Shelley wrote atheist pamphlets and was thrown out only a year into his degree. Edmund Halley (of Halley's comet) observed the stars from an observatory atop of his house in New College Lane. In various Oxford colleges the Merton tutor J.R.R. Tolkien wrote the *Lord of the Rings* trilogy, C.S. Lewis wrote the *Narnia* books, Robert Boyle developed Boyle's law on the expansion of gases, the Wesley brothers invented Methodism and 19th-century geologist William Buckland cooked battered mice and panther for his guests. Come during term time if you can, when there are more students than tourists.

Oxford Highlights

There are four panoramic views of Oxford: from the towers of **Carfax**, **St Mary's** and **St Michael's**, and the top of the **Sheldonian**. If you have to choose, go up St Mary's tower, which overlooks **Radcliffe Square**, the heart of the university, built by Wren, Hawksmoor and Gibbs. Back at the bottom, go on a guided tours of Duke Humphrey's library, the core of the **Bodleian** and one of the most beautiful rooms in Oxford. As for the colleges, **Christchurch's Tom Quad** is the grandest, **Merton's Mob Quad** the most evocative of the Middle Ages, **St Edmund's Hall** one of the smallest and prettiest, and **New College** the best all-rounder. The **Ashmolean Museum** needs time and patience. If you have neither, go instead to the **Pitt Rivers Museum**, whose setting enhances an incredible collection. Try to get to a lunchtime concert in the **Holywell Music Rooms**, evensong in **Christchurch Cathedral**, or a performance by the renowned Christchurch, Magdalen or New College choirs. You can usually find summer performances of Shakespeare in one of the college quads. There are delightful green spaces (although the college gardens are closed to visitors): go on the **Magdalen College river walk**, around the Botanic Gardens, to Christchurch Meadow for a picnic or, best of all, hire a punt by Magdalen Bridge. When you need a drink, try the **Turf Tavern**, hidden away down a narrow alley off Holywell Street, or the snug bar of the **Eagle and Child** on St Giles', where Tolkien and Lewis met to discuss their books.

The college buildings are the glory of Oxford. 'She is old, and private,' wrote Jan Morris in Oxford, 'and embeds her beauties in gardens behind high walls.' Visiting hours are usually in the afternoons, but vary between term-time and holidays. The most popular colleges charge an entrance fee, while others are more welcoming. If you walk purposefully with a book under your arm you can get in almost anywhere.

Southeast Oxford

Carfax

Oxford's four main streets meet at **Carfax**, the historic hub of the city. Dominating the crossroads is the ancient tower of **St Martin's Church**, known as **Carfax tower**. From the top you have one of the great views of Oxford – the town hall, cathedral spire, county courts and prison, and in all directions college quads with their Gothic pinnacles, crenellations and towers. The town has nothing to compare architecturally with the colleges, one of the reasons it has a chip on its shoulder; the overweening presence of hoity-toity Oxford undergraduates is another. The worst incident of student bashing started in the old Swyndlestock Tavern on the corner of Queen's Street opposite Carfax on 10 February 1355 – coincidentally St Scholastica's day. When the bar-room brawl spilled out into the streets, the bell of Carfax tower was rung to summon men from the fields. The students, who rallied to the bell of St Mary's, were outnumbered, beaten up, 63 killed and their lodgings trashed. For 500 years afterwards on St Scholastica's day the mayor and 63 citizens were made to process to the vice-chancellor and pay a penny fine each to the university.

Christchurch College

The main entrance from St Aldgate's, under Wren's bell tower, is closed to tourists, so carry on down to Broad Walk and enter through the **cloisters** around the back. This is the smallest of five quadrangles in Christchurch. The largest is **Tom Quad**, grand, stern, guarded by men in black bowler hats, and four times the size of any other Oxford quad. Domed **Tom Tower** dwarfs the flanking ranges. Its 7-ton bell – **Great Tom** – is the loudest in Oxford; it rings 101 times every evening at five past nine – one for every undergraduate at its founding, on Oxford time (five minutes behind GMT). The great hall resembles a church with its arched windows and pinnacles. An archway leads past the deanery, where Charles I stayed during the Civil War.

Illustrious old boys include William Buckland (1784–1856), a pioneering geologist who kept a hyena in his rooms and claimed to have eaten his way through half the animal kingdom – mole apparently tasted the worst. Buckland said he could identify anything by taste. Once, dining at Nuneham Manor, he was given a strange morsel, which he popped into his mouth and swallowed; it turned out to have been the pickled heart of the Sun King, Louis XIV. Charles Dodgson (aka Lewis Carroll), was maths tutor at Christchurch, living for the last 30 years of his life in the northwest corner of Tom Quad, looking out onto St Aldgate's.

Christchurch Cathedral stands on the site of the 8th-century priory church of St Frideswide, dissolved in 1524 by Henry VIII's lord chancellor, Cardinal Wolsey, to make way for the new college. It was going to be called Cardinal College, until Wolsey fell out of favour first. The king kept the old Norman priory church and in 1546 made it the cathedral of the new Oxford diocese. In the **Lady Chapel** is the reassembled shrine of St Frideswide, destroyed at the Reformation. The saint miraculously escaped from an unwanted swain (a lightning bolt got him right between the eyes) to found the priory. The window above the shrine is by Burne-Jones. Christchurch choir is one of Oxford's three top choirs.

Go through neo-classical **Peckwater Quad** and into **Canterbury Quad** with its James Wyatt gatehouse. A small doorway on the south side leads into the **Picture Gallery** (*adm minimal*), a collection of Old Master paintings and Lewis Carroll memorabilia.

Oriel, Corpus Christi and Merton Colleges

From Christchurch you emerge into Oriel Square, where Oriel, Corpus Christi and Merton colleges are all clustered, slightly off the beaten track. Famous undergraduates of **Oriel** (*open Mon–Sun 2–5*) include Elizabethan explorer Sir Walter Raleigh, 18th-century naturalist of Selborne Gilbert White, and imperial colonizer and politician Cecil Rhodes, who bequeathed £100,000 to Oriel, and endowed the Rhodes scholarship for foreign students (famous scholars include Bill Clinton). Across the road, **Corpus Christi** (*open Mon–Sun 1.30–4.30*) was founded in 1512 by Richard Foxe, bishop of Winchester, and Hugh Oldham (pronounced 'Owldham'), bishop of Exeter; for years a chained fox and three owls reminded students of the founders. **Merton** (*open Mon–Fri 2–4, weekends 10–4*) is down cobbled Merton Street; its **Mob Quad**, dominated by the medieval library (*guided tours 2–4; adm*) and the pinnacles of the chapel, takes you back to the Middle Ages. J.R.R. Tolkien (1892–1973), author of *The*

Hobbit and the *Lord of the Rings* trilogy, was Merton professor of English, and died in his old college rooms in 1973.

High Street

The long sweep of the High Street – known simply as the High – between Carfax and Magdalen Bridge is famously beautiful, flanked by six stone colleges, St Mary's church and pastel-painted townhouses. Wordsworth praised its 'stream-like wanderings,' Turner painted it, and Pevsner called it 'one of the world's great streets'. To get the best impression, start at the bridge and walk westwards.

University College

Closed to visitors.

On the south side of the High, just beyond the Victorian façade of the Examination Schools – where finals are held in May – is University College, or Univ. A plaque marks the site of 17th-century scientist **Robert Boyle's house**, where he developed Boyle's Law of the expansion of gases. If you can brazen your way into the college, you'll see a life-size nude figure of the drowned poet Shelley lying on a marble slab, bathed in watery light from a cupola above. Shelley spent less than a year at Univ, filling his head with the ideas of Tom Paine and William Godwin, growing his hair long and refusing to participate in university life; he was expelled on suspicion of circulating atheist pamphlets. The overblown memorial was created for Shelley's grave in Rome, but the cemetery declined it as too lurid, so in 1894 it was put up here instead.

All Souls

Open Mon–Fri 2–4.

The entrance to All Souls is opposite Univ on the High. All Souls is the academic pinnacle of Oxford. It was founded for secular monks after Agincourt in remembrance of the English dead in the Hundred Years Wars, and has evolved into the only post-graduate, all-male college in the university. You can't apply for a place; if you have done exceptionally well in your degree, you are invited to take the exam, a crucial element of which is how you perform at the dinner. There are sixty fellows, two-thirds of them academics, the rest honorary. Illustrious former fellows include **Christopher Wren**, who built the sundial on the wall of the Codrington Library in the great quad. If you can't get in, peep through the locked gates in Radcliffe Square.

Magdalen College

***t** (01865) 276 000; open daily 2–dusk.*

Magdalen (pronounced 'Maudlin') stands on the city side of the River Cherwell (pronounced 'Char-well'), at the east end of the High. If Christchurch was built for bishops and kings, Magdalen, with its deer park and riverside gardens, was built for hunting types. **Magdalen Tower**, above the bridge, is one of Oxford's most beautiful buildings. For hundreds of years, at dawn on May Day, Magdalen choristers have sung an invocation to summer from atop the tower – while bleary-eyed students crowd the street and punts in the river below. Magdalen's secluded 15th-century **cloisters** are on your right as you go through the main entrance. The gargoyles, which include monsters, hippopotami, wrestlers and biblical figures, are said to have inspired the stone statues in Narnia. **C.S. Lewis** (1898–1963) studied at University College, getting a brilliant degree in Greats and English, before landing the job of English professor at Magdalen. His sudden conversion to Christianity happened one day in 1929 on a bus: 'I gave in and admitted that God was God, and knelt and prayed: perhaps, that night, the most dejected and reluctant convert in all England.' J.R.R. Tolkien was a friend, and they used to meet in pubs to discuss their writing. In 1930 Lewis moved out of college and started writing books on Christian, fantasy and academic subjects. The *Lion, the Witch and the Wardrobe*, the first of his Narnia series, was finished in 1949, and the others followed in less than a year. From the cloisters you step out onto lawns in front of the 18th-century **New Building**, from where you can glimpse the deer park. The building stands on top of the vegetable plots, fishponds and orchards of the old kitchen gardens. Go through the wrought-iron gate to the banks of the Cherwell. There is a mile-long walk around Magdalen meadow, called **Addison's Walk** after the essayist Joseph Addison (1672–1719), who was the first to write about the merits of the natural as opposed to formal garden.

Botanic Gardens

***t** (01865) 286 690; open daily April–Sept 9–5, Oct–Mar 9–4.30; adm minimal.*

The university's Botanic Gardens are some of the oldest scientific gardens in Europe, along with Pisa and Leiden. Behind its 17th-century walls and bordering the river, the 5-acre garden was developed by the Earl of Danby in 1621 to grow medicinal herbs. The first keepers, the Jacob Bobarts, father and son, built up the collection to more than 1,000 species, and published catalogues and seed lists. It now boasts 8,000 plant species, nearly 300 species of herbaceous plants in the old walled garden, rockeries and a bog in the new garden, and glasshouses full of exotic flowers and plants.

The Heart of the University

Catte Street, between Broad Street and the High, passes the main university buildings and takes you through the most remarkable architectural cluster anywhere in England. The first university building was St Mary's Church, where degree ceremonies and meetings of the governing body – the Congregation – originally took place. In 1320, university business moved into an annexe, but it was not until the 15th century that the first independent university buildings – the divinity school and Duke Humphrey's library – were built, and it was another two hundred years before the schools quadrangle – the old lecture rooms, labs and exam rooms – took shape alongside. Degree ceremonies took place in St Mary's until Wren's Sheldonian Theatre was built in 1669. Nearly a hundred years later, the new university library and reading room – the domed Radcliffe Camera – was built by James Gibbs, and the university's publishing arm moved into the Clarendon Building by Nicholas

Hawksmoor. The old schools quadrangle is now the hushed heart of the Bodleian Library (which also now incorporates the Radcliffe Camera, the new Bodleian Library, vaults beneath Radcliffe Square and specialist libraries around town).

Radcliffe Square

Cobbled Radcliffe Square is a superb public space. The stone buildings defining the square – Brasenose, All Souls, the old schools quadrangle and St Mary's Church – are collectively outstanding. All these buildings were already here when a competition for a new library building was launched with the bequest of London medical practitioner John Radcliffe (1650–1715). Nicholas Hawksmoor cleared the ragged old buildings of the square, recommended a circular building then lost the competition to James Gibbs. Domed **Radcliffe Camera** is outstanding; the round neo-classical library is now an undergraduate reading room (*closed to visitors*).

St Mary's Church

The glorious 150ft spire of the old university church, rising out of clustered Gothic pinnacles, is the mainstay of the Oxford skyline. Enter the church from the High, through the flamboyant candy-twist columns of the **baroque porch**, added to the old church in 1630. It works remarkably well, relating more to the heterogeneous High than the Gothic building behind. It was here in 1556 that the Protestant martyrs of Mary I's reign – Archbishop Cranmer and bishops Ridley and Latimer – were sentenced to burn in Broad Street for their parts in the Reformation. The bishops went first. The wood was green and Ridley was heard to say, 'Lord have mercy upon me: I cannot burn...I cannot burn'. The archbishop, cowed, was brought to St Mary's and asked to repeat his recantation for the crowd; instead he found the strength that had deserted him under interrogation, and declared that the hand that wrote the recantation 'shall be first burned'. Don't feel too sorry for him: he was responsible for the worst kind of English Protestant fundamentalism, and the deaths of thousands of Catholics. From the tower of St Mary's you get the best views of the university.

Brasenose College

Open daily 10–11.30 and 2–4.30.

On the west side of Radcliffe Square is the crenellated Tudor entrance tower of Brasenose, named after the bronze knocker like a snout on the main door. The knocker was stolen in the turbulent 14th century by a group of migrating students and professors, and attached to a building in Stamford, Lincolnshire. It was not until 1890 that Oxford got it back; the real knocker hangs above the high table in the dining hall.

The Old Schools Quadrangle and Divinity School

From Radcliffe Square, an archway leads into the Old Schools Quadrangle, a narrow, flagged enclosure. It was built in 1613 as an extension to the 15th-century divinity school. The entrance **tower**, from Catte Street, is one of Oxford's most extraordinary pieces of architecture: Jacobean, it rises five storeys high, each storey representing a different order of architecture (Tuscan, Roman, Doric, Corinthian and Composite). Near the top is a statue of the enthroned James I handing out books to fame and the university. One of the main benefactors was **William Herbert**, 3rd Earl of Pembroke, whose armour-clad and dashing bronze statue by Hubert Le Sueur stands in the middle. The **divinity school**, built between 1420 and 1483, looks like a cathedral chapel with its superb lierne vaulting, pendants, bosses and Gothic windows. A second storey was added later to house the library of Humphrey, Duke of Gloucester, Henry VI's youngest brother (*guided tours morning and afternoon; adm*). Surrounding the quad are the wooden doors of the old schools with their Latin names – '*schola moralis philosophiae*' and so on. They now form the core of the university's library, named after Thomas Bodley, a retired diplomat who in 1602 refounded the library founded by Duke Humphrey and destroyed by the Reformation. The **Bodleian** is one of three English copyright libraries (along with the British Library and Cambridge University Library) entitled to a free copy of every book published in Britain.

Sheldonian Theatre and Clarendon Building

t (01865) 277 299; open summer Mon–Sat 10–12.30 and 2–4.30; winter closes at 3; adm minimal.

A passage from the Old Schools Quad leads into an open space surrounded by the Sheldonian Theatre, the Clarendon Building and the famous Venetian-style stone bridge over Catte Street. The **Sheldonian Theatre** was one of Wren's earliest designs, built like a Roman theatre between 1664 and 1669 for matriculation and graduation ceremonies. No one knows who the heads on the Broad Street front represent – Roman emperors, apostles or philosophers. Next door, the neo-classical portico of the **Clarendon Building** fronts onto Broad Street; statues of the nine muses decorate the roof. This magnificent Nicholas Hawksmoor building was built for the printworks of the Oxford University Press; the money for it came from the royalties of the Earl of Clarendon's 18th-century bestseller, *History of the Great Rebellion*. It is now the registry of the university (the OUP is now located in grand 19th-century premises in the outlying area of Jericho).

The Museum of the History of Science

t (01865) 277 280; open Tues–Sat 12–4 and Sun 2–5.

Next door to the Sheldonian stands the old Ashmolean, which opened in 1683 as a museum with a few science-teaching rooms. The Museum of the History of Science opened here in 1924. Its collection of scientific instruments includes Dr Lewis Evans' portable sundials and microscopes; astrolabes (medieval instruments for making astronomical measurements) and optical tools. You can see the original penicillin apparatus, Lewis Carroll's photographic equipment, Robert Hook's drawings of fleas, and the blackboard – chalked equations intact – used by Albert Einstein at a lecture on the theory of relativity.

New College

From Catte Street, opposite the Clarendon Building, one of the most atmospheric lanes in Oxford zigzags down to the High, between New College, Hertford, All Souls, Queen's and St Edmund Hall. Curiosity leads you under the pseudo-Venetian stone **Bridge of Sighs**, along the fortress-like cloister wall of New College and past the pretty house of astronomer **Edmund Halley** (1656–1742). He left Queen's without a degree, spent two years mapping the southern skies in St Helena, returned to Oxford as Savilian professor of geometry, and in 1705 identified the 76-year orbit of the comet named after him: he said it would return in 1758, and it did. You can see his observatory on top of the house. New College was founded in 1379 by William of Wykeham, bishop of Winchester, to fast-track boys from the school he had founded in Winchester straight into the clergy, whose numbers had been decimated by the black death. William of Wykeham's other foundations included Winchester cathedral and Windsor castle. He built New College like a fortress-monastery, incorporating the old town wall into the design. Peer through the gate into the college garden, called 'a sweet, sacred, stately seclusion' by Nathaniel Hawthorne. The **front quad** is said to have been the model for all the other Oxford college quads, with the chapel, dining hall and residential buildings facing each other on four sides. Go into the old **cloisters**, built around 1400, and **chapel**, as near to perfection as any in Oxford. Look out for the west window by Sir Joshua Reynolds, who appears as a shepherd in the top half, and the statue of *Lazarus* by Jacob Epstein (1880–1959). New College choir is renowned.

If you leave by the main entrance you emerge onto **Holywell Street**, a delightful part of Oxford with stone cottages and elaborate porches. The Holywell Music Rooms are said to be the oldest in Europe, and are a good venue for lunchtime recitals.

The University Museum of Natural History and Pitt Rivers Museum

A short walk up Parks Road takes you into the university's science area. The University Museum of Natural History (*open daily 12–5*) and Pitt Rivers Museum (***t** (01865) 272 950; open Mon–Sat 12–4.30, Sun 2–4.30*) are shrines of the Victorian religion of evolutionary science – a church-like building crammed with geological specimens, dinosaur bones and stuffed animals like so many sacred relics. Around the walls are statues of eminent scientists instead of saints. The museum was founded in 1855, four years before the publication of Darwin's *On the Origin of the Species*, and it was here in 1860 that the zoologist Thomas Huxley defended the evolutionary argument of man's descent from apes against Bishop Samuel Wilberforce of Oxford and the anatomist Richard Owen. The debate might have been forgotten if it had not been so heated; at one point the bishop asked Huxley if the ape in question was on his grandfather's or grandmother's side. Most of the geological material came from the private collection of William Buckland (*see* p.447), who found and identified the first dinosaur in the world, the megalosaurus. You can see casts of the teeth and thumb spike of Gideon Mantell's iguanodon, the second species of dinosaur known to man, found in the Sussex Weald. From this scant evidence Mantell was able in 1824 to conjure up the creature whose immense skeleton dominates the museum; this one is the cast of a fossil skeleton found in Belgium in 1877.

The **Pitt Rivers Museum** was built in 1884 to house the ethnological collections of General Pitt Rivers. Black-framed display cabinets pack it out like a warehouse. Pitt Rivers started collecting in 1851, realizing that he could understand civilizations in evolutionary terms through their fundamental objects – weapons, pots, clothes and so on. He organized his vast assortment of stuff – African drums and Eskimo boots – so as to marvel at the progress of civilizations. There are musical instruments, carved figures, clothing, weapons, pots, bags, jewellery, masks, shrunken heads and skulls.

When you leave, carry on down Museum Road to St Giles' Street and back into town past St John's College, the Ashmolean and the Martyrs' Memorial.

Broad Street

You will wander up and down Broad Street many times on a trip to Oxford, and never tire of it: the old-fashioned façade of Blackwell's bookshop, founded in 1883; the wrought-iron gates of Trinity College; the iron cross where the Protestant martyrs were burned and the old stone walls of Balliol, Trinity and Exeter colleges.

Balliol, one of the oldest colleges, dates back to 1282, although its nondescript buildings are Victorian. Famous old boys include poets Robert Southey, Matthew Arnold, Algernon Charles Swinburne, Gerald Manley Hopkins and novelist Graham Greene (1904–91), who claimed he used to play solitary games of Russian Roulette with a revolver to relieve the tedium of college life.

Trinity, founded in 1555, educated William Pitt the Elder (1708–78), who presided as prime minister over of the expansion of the American colonies, and Lord North (1732–92), who lost them again. It has always been a popular college for aristocratic wastrels like John Aubrey (1626–97), whose gambling debts forced him out of town into the countryside, where redemption came in the discovery of Avebury Henge. He is buried in St Mary Magdalen Church, at the end of Broad Street abutting the **Martyrs' Memorial**; the blackened memorial by Sir George Gilbert Scott, erected 300 years after the execution of Cranmer *et al*, is the traditional coach drop-off point.

Turl Street leads from Broad Street to the Victorian covered market – all iron girders and glass. *En route* is the entrance to **Exeter College**, whose 19th-century chapel houses the *Adoration of the Magi* tapestry by old Exetonians William Morris (1834–96) and Edward Burne-Jones (1833–98). Exeter's ancient rivalry with **Jesus College**, across Turl Street, erupted in 1979 with the Turl Street Riots. Exeter's Welsh scholars have included Lawrence of Arabia (1888–1935), who took crusader castles as a special subject. Take a detour down Ship Street to see the gargoyles on Jesus College of scholars vomiting and defecating into the gutter. On the corner of Ship Street and Cornmarket Street is the old rubble tower of the church of **St Michael's** at the North Gate, Oxford's oldest Saxon structure. From the 13th to 18th centuries, the town prison stood beside the tower. This is where Archbishop Cranmer was held in 1556. He was made to watch the executions of his bishops from the top of the tower before his own turn. It is one of Oxford's four panoramic viewpoints.

Ashmolean Museum

t (01865) 278 000; open Tues–Sat 10–5, Sun 2–5.

The Ashmolean was founded in 1683 on Broad Street and moved into its grand, Greek-style premises in 1845. Its core collection was built up by the John Tradescants, father and son – gardeners to Charles I – and acquired by Elias Ashmole after the death of John the younger in 1662. Ashmole, a Brasenose graduate and solicitor, presented the collection to the university as his own in 1677. Today the neo-classical portico fronts a terrific collection of archaeology, classical sculpture and art. The largest piece is the **shrine of a Nubian king** who died in the Sudan, aged 55, nearly 3,000 years ago. Upstairs, one of the highlights is a room full of the **Tradescants' curiosities**: a Russian boot, 'divers things cut on plum stones', Cromwell's warty death mask, James V's sword blade, Guy Fawkes' lantern, Cranmer's shackles, and a deer-skin robe supposed to have belonged to Powhatan, the father of Pocahontas. Another highlight is **King Alfred's Jewel**, an exquisite enamel piece inscribed 'Alfred had me made', which was found in Athelney in Somerset in 1693. Rooms of astonishing art works include drawings by Raphael and Michelangelo, Rubens sketches, Pre-Raphaelite paintings, landscapes by Lorraine, Turner and Constable (including Turner's view of Oxford High Street), and Renaissance paintings in carved wooden frames and hinged panels, including Uccello's *The Hunt in the Forest*.

Around Oxford: Woodstock and Blenheim Palace

The old town of **Woodstock**, five miles northwest of Oxford, is small, handsome, well-to-do and shot through by the busy A44. It is the place for a languorous lunch in one of several good restaurants, *en route* to a Cotswolds adventure. Blenheim Palace is on its doorstep.

Blenheim Palace

t (01993) 811 325, www.blenheimpalace.com; bus no. 20 runs every half hour from Oxford train station or Gloucester Green bus station; open mid-Feb–Oct daily 10.30–4.45, Nov and Dec Wed–Sun 10.30–4.45; adm exp.

Approach the Duke of Marlborough's grandiose soldier's palace from the town of Woodstock; that is the way he wanted you to see it, over the bow-shaped lake spanned by Vanburgh's bridge, Capability Brown's parkland merging with the fields. Blenheim was built to wow you. It's a three-sided square, the fourth side opening onto the lake. Corner towers thrust up 30ft battlemented finials and the central portico might belong to a Roman temple. Blenheim was built for the glorification of a national hero, who saved Europe at the head of an allied army in the gruelling Spanish Wars of Succession. The house is named after Marlborough's greatest victory, in Austria on 14 August 1703, which involved a 250-mile march across Europe from the Netherlands to the Danube in the rain and a brilliant battle that annihilated most of the French army. Marlborough already had the dukedom; Queen Anne promised him the house. Monumental architect John Vanburgh built it, assisted by Nicholas Hawksmoor, Grinling Gibbons, Louis Laguerre and James Thornhill. The nation footed the bill. Then foreign policy changed, political loyalties shifted, the tidal wave of public affection unleashed after Blenheim petered out, and so did the state subsidy. The Duchess got involved in cost-cutting negotiations with Vanburgh and Gibbons, both of whom left in a huff. Before you enter, look back over the lake towards the 134ft **Doric Column of Victory**, surmounted with a statue of the young, heroic Duke of Marlborough. The Duchess erected it five years after her husband's death at 72.

Inside, the rooms endlessly recapitulate Marlborough's victories. In the great hall an allegorical painted ceiling by Thornhill depicts Marlborough showing Britannia the plan of the battle of Blenheim. One wall of the Green Writing Room is taken up by a tapestry showing the duke on horseback accepting Marshal Tallard's surrender at Blenheim. And so on. Note the elaborate ceilings by Hawksmoor and Laguerre, family portraits by Romney and Reynolds, Van Dycks, Chippendale chairs, Gibbons carvings and treasures beyond your wildest dreams. The magnificent marble monument to the duke and duchess in the chapel is by Rysbrack. Pause in the **Winston Churchill Room** (Churchill was born here, nephew of the 8th Duke, in 1874, and lies buried in the family vault at Bladon church) to see memorabilia, including affectionate letters to his father: 'I will take your advice about the cigars,' he writes, 'and I don't think I shall often smoke more than one or two daily.'

The grounds are wonderful. Walk around the lakeside to the temple of Diana, where Churchill proposed to his wife Clementine in 1908. There is a restaurant overlooking the water terraces, an elegant addition to the gardens by the 9th Duke in the 1920s.

Wantage and the Berkshire Downs

South of Oxford and the Thames Valley is an escarpment marked by the ancient Uffington White Horse. It is one of several archaeological remains on the Berkshire Downs known as the Uffington monuments. Base yourself in **Wantage**, a good, solid market town with a handsome square, to explore them. The **Vale and Downland Museum on Church Street** (***t*** *(01235) 771 447; open Mon–Sat 10.30–4.30, Sun 2.30–5; adm minimal*) explains the local geology, history and archaeology. This is Alfred the Great country. Alfredian tours of Wessex start in Wantage, where, according to Asser's *Life of King Alfred*, the king was born in 849. (Thomas Hardy's fictional name for Wantage was 'Alfredston'.) The statue of Alfred in the market square (1877), shows him carrying a scroll and sword. January 871 saw a series of Alfredian battles on the downs. 'The opposing ranks met in conflict, with great shouting from all men – one side bent on evil, the other side fighting for life and their loved ones and their native land,' wrote Asser, adding that Alfred attacked 'like a wild boar'. This was the first time the Danes had been beaten in open battle. Since the 18th century the downs have been used for training race horses; there are 40 stables in Lambourne.

Getting There and Around

By **car**, Wantage is just north of the M4, off junction 13, or down the A338 from Oxford.

There are regular **bus** services from Oxford.

The nearest railway station is Didcot Parkway (8 miles), with frequent **trains** from London and the west, then bus.

The **Ridgeway**, an ancient 'green road' or prehistoric trackway, is one of Britain's most popular long-distance walks (85 miles), linking Avebury Henge and the Chilterns. Leaflets from the Vale and Downland Museum in Wantage describe shorter walks around the Uffington monuments and Berkshire Downs.

Tourist Information

Wantage: Vale and Downland Museum, Church Street, **t** (01235) 77147. *Open Tues–Sat 10.30–4.30, Sun 2.30–5.*

Market on Wed and Sat in the market place.

Where to Stay

Wantage and Around t (01235) –

The Bear Hotel, Market Place, **t** 766 366, *www.biznet.maximizer.com/thebear* (*expensive*). Handsome old coaching inn on market place with flagged courtyard and old-fashioned restaurant. Comfortable.

White Horse, Woolstone (near Faringdon), **t** (01367) 820 726, *www.whitehorsewoolstone.co.uk* (*expensive*). Charming country pub associated with Thomas Hughes, author of *Tom Brown's School Days*. Pretty, clean, bright bedrooms.

The Star Inn, Watery Lane, Sparsholt, **t** 751 001 (*moderate*). Good pub with rooms in converted barn.

Quince Cottage, Letcombe Regis, **t** 763 652 (*moderate*). Delightful thatched cottage offering a warm welcome to visitors.

The Old Vicarage, Letcombe Regis, **t** 765 827 (*moderate*), just opposite the pub, decorative checkered brickwork and beautiful, large garden, pretty double bedroom with antiques and fresh flowers.

Ridgeway Youth Hostel, Court Hill (near Letcombe Regis, well signposted off A338), **t** 760 253 (*cheap*). Superb base for walking, with dormitories in converted old barns.

Eating Out

Time and Plaice, 8 Newbury Street, **t** 760 568 (*moderate*). Homely and unpretentious. Mixed menu might include clam and haddock chowder or gnocchi with spinach and pinenuts. *Closed Sat lunch, Sun and Mon.*

The Star Inn, Watery Lane, (4 miles out of Wantage in Sparsholt), **t** 751 539 (*moderate*). Excellent restaurant-style pub grub (honey-roast duckling, steak and ale pie, Thai vegetable curry).

The Royal Oak, Newbury Street, **t** 763 129 (*cheap*). The place for a drink, with real ales and grown-up crowds.

The Uffington Monuments

Take the B4507 five miles west of Wantage to Uffington Castle car park. Climb up to **Uffington Castle**, an Iron Age hill fort on the crest of White Horse Hill, dating from the 7th century BC. About 200 yards from the castle is the **Uffington White Horse**, 111 yards from ear to tail. The best view of the horse is from the B4508 between Fernham and Longcot, or from the White Horse pub near Woolstone. Its origins are mysterious. Following the Ridgeway from the castle you come to **Wayland's Smithy**, a Neolithic longbarrow built with massive sarsen stones, which takes its name from Wayland, the Saxon smith god.

Ashdown House

t (01494) 528 051, www.nationaltrust.org.uk; house open April–Oct Wed and Sat 2–5; woodland all year Sat–Thurs dawn–dusk; adm.

Two miles south down the B4000 is this delightful, small Dutch-style house in grounds dotted with sarsen stones. It was built in the 17th century by the 1st Earl of Craven. Guided tours takes you up the magnificent staircase to rooftop views.

The Cotswolds

Villages, manor houses, farmsteads, built of such a magical material...
J.B. Priestley, *An English Journey*, 1933

The Cotswolds hills extend 40 miles from Chipping Campden to the Severn Vale, an island north of the M4, east of the M5, southwest of the M40 and encircled by Gloucester, Cheltenham, Banbury and Oxford. One pretty village succeeds another in this gentle countryside, nestled into the landscape like so many sleeping cats with curious names: Moreton-in-the-Marsh, Stow-on-the-Wold, Bourton-on-the-Water, the Slaughters, Chippings, Guitings, Ampneys, Colns and Duntisbournes. Here is Merry England in microcosm, with megalithic monuments, Iron Age hill forts, Roman mosaics, wool churches, and stately homes. The uplands do not make you sit up and take notice so much as the villages in the valleys. The vernacular architecture can be outstanding and never sinks below the charming; the typical Cotswold building is long and narrow with a steep stone-tiled roof, tall chimneys, and a decorated stone porch to keep off the rain. It's all built from locally quarried Cotswold stone, easy to shape, hardened by air, and slightly glowing even under a grey English sky; Laurie Lee called it the colour of crystallized honey.

'A man bringing a single red tile or yard of corrugated iron into these two symphonies of grey stone,' said J.B. Priestley of the villages of Upper and Lower Slaughter, 'should be scourged out of the district.' This sentiment lies behind the Cotswolds' too-cute reputation. Tourists pour in by the coach load, demanding fudge and antiques. Bourton-on-the-Water looks as unreal as the 1:10 scale model village of it behind the Old Inn. But there is much of real interest off the beaten track. The valleys, including the Windrush, Evenlode, Churn, Leach and Coln, hog much of the region's natural beauty and are home to undiscovered villages, Saxon and medieval churches (Duntisbourne, Fairford, Chipping Camden) and Roman villas (Chedworth, Great Witcombe, Sudeley). The dramatic scarp is beaded with Iron Age hill forts (Uleybury and Cleeve Hill) and Neolithic burial mounds (Hetty Pegler's Tump and Belas Knap).

Cirencester

The ancient market town of the southern Cotswolds stands at the crossroads of the Roman Fosse Way and Ermine Street, three miles northeast of the source of the Thames. Cheerful and busy, it has a museum crammed with Roman archaeology, a

Arts and Crafts in the Cotswolds

Part of the Cotswolds' present-day appeal is a result of its adoption as the natural home of the Arts and Crafts movement in the late 19th and early 20th century. The movement was an ideological quest for morally sustaining creative manual work, which harked back to an idealized, pre-industrial, rural life. It was a direct reaction to the dehumanizing mechanization of industry. From prehistoric sites to the medieval wool industry, the Cotswolds perfectly fitted the ideologies of William Morris, Ernest Gimson, Charles Ashby and Michael Cardew; for them, noble pre-industrial values infused the Cotswolds, an island of tradition amid roaring industrial England. When they first adopted it, the region was in steep decline: agriculture and the cotton industry were dying out, and the market towns and rural hamlets were haunted by unemployment, emigration, even starvation; but the young socialist idealists of the London Arts and Crafts guilds gravitated to it as the last bastion of the Middle Ages.

William Morris led the way in 1871, buying Kelmscott Manor outside Oxford. Then furniture makers Ernest Gimson and the Barnsley brothers set up in Sapperton, 5 miles west of Cirencester, baking their own bread, brewing cider and keeping hens and goats. They used Cotswolds elm, ash and fruit woods and the odd piece of English oak and walnut tree, and employed the traditional techniques of the country wheelwright. In 1902 one of the leading lights of the London Guild and School of Handicraft, Charles Robert Ashby, launched a full-scale social experiment in Chipping Campden. His aim was to 'bring out the artist in the ordinary working man'. Ashby dragged 70 London craftsmen and their familiies off to the Cotswolds to make affordable jewellery and metalwork. The star of the guild was George Hart, who made medieval-style flower designs in twisted wire. Ashby organized dances, plays and readings and set up the Campden School of Arts and Crafts, which ran evening classes in cookery, gardening, literature and history. A lack of commissions, and cheaper mass-produced imitations, forced the guild out of business in 1906.

The revolution failed, but a new generation of Cotswolds craftsmen inherited the Arts and Crafts ethos, if steering clear of the social engineering. In 1911 Gordon Russell set himself up as a furniture designer in Broadway. Like Ashby, he organized talks, evening classes and theatricals for his employees. He employed the same blacksmiths who had worked for Ernest Gimson in Sapperton, and also created furniture with simple solid forms and unstained wood. He was not shy of using machines (an economic advance), and supplemented his income by selling antiques to American tourists. By the 1920s and '30s handicrafts had become the luxury items of the upper-middle classes. Pottery was the most successful craft, because its materials were cheap and its end products of domestic use. In 1926 St Ives potters Bernard Leach and Michael Cardew came to the Cotswolds on motorbikes to attend a week-long demonstration of crafts at Russell's workshops. Cardew fell in love with an old pottery just outside Winchcombe, which 'gave out a feeling of generosity and good old fashioned country ways of working'. He moved in right away and established a reputation for slipware. In 1936 he was joined by Ray Finch, who in the 1960s designed rustic-style pottery for Cranks wholefood restaurants.

Tourist Information

Cirencester: Corn Hall, Market Place, **t** (01285) 654 180. *Open 9.30–5.*

Where to Stay

Cirencester and Around t (01285) –

Fleece Hotel, Market Place, **t** 658 507, *www.relax@fleecehotel.co.uk* (*expensive*). Grand, family-run hotel.

Cripps House, Coxwell Street, **t** 653 164 (*expensive*). Warm welcome at wealthy clothier's house in quiet back street, beautifully furnished with antique furniture.

Abbeymead Guesthouse, 39/a Victoria Road, **t** 653 740 (*moderate*). Friendly guesthouse on a road lined with B&Bs. No smoking.

Manor Farm, Middle Duntisbourne, **t** 658 145, *www.smoothhound-hotels-manorfarm.html* (*moderate*). Welcoming 16th-century farmhouse set in 160 acres.

Eating Out

Harry Hare's Brasserie, 3 Gosditch Street, **t** 652 375 (*moderate*). Behind the church, all scrubbed wood charm. Serves pork and leek sausages or braised ham with mushy peas.

Black Jacks Coffee House, 44 Black Jack Street, **t** 640 888 (*cheap*). Delicious coffee, snacks and lunches. *Closed Sun.*

Swan Yard Café, 9–13 West Market Place, **t** 641 300 (*cheap*). Good homity pie and vegetarian flans. *Closed Sun.*

Tatyan's Chinese, 27 Castle Street, **t** 653 529 (*cheap*). Cheerful Cantonese restaurant with fresh flowers on the table.

Entertainment

Brewery Arts Theatre, Brewery Court, **t** 655 522. Small theatre in complex of craft workshops with gallery and café. Music from folk to chamber orchestras and touring drama.

celebrated wool church and streets of painted pink, cream and blue cottages. Its atmosphere, unusually for the Cotswolds, is lively. The Romans founded *Corinium Dubunnorum*, the second largest town in *Britannia*, here. Roman highways from Lincoln, Gloucester, Bath and Colchester entered its four main gates. It was a city of large-scale marble-faced public buildings, monumental columns topped with statues of Roman gods and centrally heated stone houses with painted walls and mosaic floors. Remains of the longest Saxon church in England lie in the grounds of the 12th-century abbey, founded by Henry I. The abbey lands were sold off at the Reformation, and in 1695 passed to Lord Bathurst, whose estate includes vast Cirencester Park.

The magnificent **parish church** dominates the market place. The ornate three-storey south porch, busy with Gothic niches, panelling and oriel windows, was built in 1490 by the abbey for the merchant guilds to meet and do business. In turn the guilds paid for the church tower and Perpendicular nave, where they installed angels carrying their coats of arms. Craftsmen continue the Arts and Crafts guild tradition down narrow backstreets. **Brewery Arts** (***t** (01285) 657 181; open Mon–Sat 10–5*) on Cricklade Street has a coffee shop, workshops and gallery selling high-quality crafts.

Behind the church are the **abbey grounds**, where you can see a Norman arch and a scrap of Roman wall. For town history go to ***Corinium* Museum** (***t** (01285) 655 611; open Mon–Sat 10–4, Sun 2–5; adm*) on Park Street. It displays six mosaic pavements, and Roman sculpture on a grand scale: there is a fragment of a Corinthian capital once attached to a 70ft column. Further up Cecily Hill you reach **Cirencester Park** (*open 8–5*), laid out in the 18th century by the first Lord Bathurst with the help of Alexander Pope. It's a short drive from here to the remains of a Roman amphitheatre (*open dawn–dusk*).

Around Cirencester

The Churches of the Dunt Valley

The Dunt Valley, northwest of Cirencester, is one of the most lovely in the Cotswolds, with its river path and narrow lanes. Take a picnic, as there are no pubs or cafés, to visit the valley's three tiny churches. Off the A417 (Ermine Street) you come first to **Daglingworth church**, with its 15th-century porch, Saxon oak door and arch, and four simple sculptures representing the crucifixion, St Peter with the key to heaven and Christ on his throne. Next stop is **Duntisbourne Rouse**, a grey stone church with a Saxon nave and 18th-century box pews. Stone steps lead down into a dark crypt. Follow signs past the ford at Duntisbourne Leer to **Duntisbourne Abbot**, a 12th-century church by a cluster of cottages.

Chedworth Roman Villa

t (01242) 890 256, www.nationaltrust.org.uk; open Tues–Sun Mar and Nov 11–4, April–Oct 10–5; adm.

The A429 (Fosse Way) shoots northeast from Cirencester, crossing the River Coln near Chedworth. Here, in the wooded upper reaches of the Coln Valley is the 4th-century Roman villa. Floor mosaics, bath houses, a hypocaust heating system and natural spring shrine were all uncovered after rabbits revealed its existence.

Bibury

Irresponsibly, William Morris called Bibury 'the most beautiful village in England', which means that everyone goes there. Follow the Coln from Chedworth or Fairford. The village is clustered around its **church**, set amid crumbling old table graves and climbing roses, but many visitors go straight to photogenic **Arlington Row** on the riverside, a medieval wool store converted into weavers' cottages in the 17th century. It's one of the defining biscuit-tin images of the Cotswolds.

Fairford Church

The bridge at Fairford carries the A417 Cirencester–Lechlade road over the Coln. Upstream is the church, a treasure trove of medieval art where you can see the only complete set of **medieval stained glass** in England. In a ragged churchyard and adorned with gargoyles, the church was built at the end of the 15th century by Cirencester cloth merchant John Tame and his son Edmund. Come at dusk, when the 28 windows designed by Flemish glaziers seem to catch fire in the gloomy interior. They tell the whole Christian story from the Old Testament prophets to the life of Christ, New Testament apostles, saints and the Last Judgement – in the west window – with web-footed demons and pitchforks. The 14 carved miserichords were brought from Cirencester abbey after the Dissolution. In the churchyard near the south porch is the table **tomb of Valentine Strong**, founder of the family of master masons who worked on St Paul's cathedral. You can walk along the riverside through delightful water meadows.

Tetbury

Ten miles southwest of Cirencester down the A433, Tetbury is another quintessential Cotswolds town that owes its beauty to the wool trade, Cotswolds stone and a timely decline when other towns took off with the new railways. In the 18th century, Tetbury was a fashionable hunting centre with its own assembly rooms. A mile away is **Highgrove House**, Prince Charles's country home. The photogenic showpiece here is **Chipping Steps**, a long flight of ancient worn stone steps flanked by old weavers' cottages with pretty walled gardens. The market place, pillared market hall and prosperous 17th-century townhouses (now all expensive antiques shops) on the main streets are all vividly Cotswolds too. Five miles south down the A433, **Westonbirt Arboretum** (***t*** *(01666) 880 220; open 10–8 or dusk if earlier; adm*) has a renowned collection of exotic trees and shrubs.

Malmesbury

On the edge of the Cotswolds, Malmesbury is busier than Tetbury, with an abbey church on the hillside above the Avon. It's a good, solid West Saxon town associated with Bishop Adhelm, Alfred the Great and King Athelstan, whose tomb is in the abbey church. Malmesbury got rich on wool, then woollen cloth in the 16th century. Now it is a pleasant backwater, slightly removed from Wessex and Cotswolds mayhem.

Malmesbury Abbey Church

t *(01666) 824 339; open summer 10–5, winter 10–4.*

The grand ruins of the abbey church stand at the top of town above the Avon. This is all that is left of the prestigious Saxon foundation of **Bishop Adhelm**, one of the great scholars of the 7th century. The 12th-century librarian **William of Malmesbury** wrote famous histories of the kings of England here; it was William who told the story of Eilmer the Flying Monk, who threw himself off the top of the church tower in a home-made flying contraption and broke both legs in the High Street. Neither Adhelm nor William would recognize the present abbey church, which was built by Bishop Roger of Old Sarum in 1170. The spire, added in the 14th century, was as tall as Salisbury's; when it fell down a hundred years later, it brought down the chancel and crossing too. The west tower followed suit in the 17th century, crushing the west end of the nave. After the Reformation wealthy cloth merchant William Stumpe had built himself a grand house in the grounds, and used the remains of the Norman nave as a cloth factory. He eventually gave it to the town as a parish church. Look at the amazing sculpted reliefs decorating the **Norman porch**, which depict scenes from the Old Testament, the Life of Christ and the apostles of the Pentecost. In the north aisle is the greatest treasure, the **tomb of Athelstan**, King of England 924–39. He was Alfred the Great's grandson, and is known, rightly, as the first king of all England. Climb up the stone spiral stairs to the treasury, which has a 15th-century lectern bible.

Burford

From Oxford on the A40 Burford is the eastern gate of the Cotswolds. Its High Street drops down to the River Windrush; here merchants' houses are complemented by the

Getting There and Around

Burford is halfway between Cheltenham and Oxford on the A40.

Burford Bike Hire, Woolland, Barns Lane, **t** (01993) 823 326. *Open summer weekends and all other times by prior booking.*

Painswick is on the A46, halfway between Bath and Stratford-upon-Avon, and not far from **Stroud**, which has a direct rail link with London Paddington.

Tourist Information

Malmesbury: Town Hall, **t** (01666) 823 748. *Open Mon–Thurs 9.30–4.*

Burford: The Brewery, Sheep Street, **t** (01993) 823 558. *Open Mon–Sat 9.30–5.30.*

Painswick: **t** (01452) 813 552. *Seasonal opening, depends on volunteers.*

Stroud: George Street, **t** (01453) 760 960.

Market on Wed, Fri and Sat in Shambles; Sat market in Cornhill.

Stroud Fringe Festival, first week of Sept, features all kinds of music in venues around the town.

Where to Stay and Eat

Tetbury t (01666) –

The Close Hotel and Restaurant, Long Street, **t** 502 272, *www.theclosehotel.co.uk* (*very expensive*). Luxurious 16th-century mansion with Cotswold stone turrets. Full of antique furniture, with walled garden and croquet lawn. Restaurant (*moderate*) serves rabbit, venison, pigeon and veal.

The Snooty Fox, Market Place, **t** 502 436, *www.hatton-hotels.co.uk*, (*expensive*). A 16th-century coaching inn with a pleasant oak-panelled restaurant and bar.

Avon Cottage, 6 Gumstool Hill, **t** 503 272 (*moderate*). Pretty 18th-century stone cottage with modest little rooms.

Malmesbury t (01666) –

The Old Bell Hotel, Abbey Row, **t** 822 344, *www.oldbellhotel.com* (*very expensive*). Attractive clematis-covered building beside old abbey, with medieval stone fireplace and ferny patio. Restaurant serves dishes such as smoked chicken risotto with mange tout, asparagus and goats' cheese.

Smoking Dog, High Street, **t** 825 823 (*moderate*). Bright, chunky place with varied menu of smoked wood pigeon and the like.

black-and-white coaching inns of the old London–Midlands road. Some of the best stone was quarried in the Windrush Valley, the best of all at Taynton (used for Windsor Castle and Blenheim Palace). In the 17th century, two families of Burford stonemasons, the Strongs of Taynton and the Kempsters of Upton, made their fortunes supplying stone to London after the Great Fire of 1666. Thomas Strong won the contract to rebuild St Paul's and laid the foundation stone in the presence of the bishop and chapter. In 1690 Kit and William Kempster worked on the dome and clock tower. In 1691, Kit was elected master of the Worshipful Company of Masons in London. 'I have used him in good works, he is very careful to work true to his design and strong, and I can rely on him,' wrote Wren of Kit, recommending him to the Bishop of Oxford for the building of Tom Tower.

The hectic **High Street** is lined with craft shops and galleries. There is the market house, built in 1500, known as the **Tolsey** after tolls paid by traders to the guild of merchants that controlled the town's affairs in the Middle Ages, with a handful of stalls on the open ground floor most days. Upstairs, the interesting little **museum** (***t*** *(01993) 823196; open April–Oct Tues–Fri and Sun 2–5, Sat 11–5*) contains the maces, seals and charters of the merchant guild, and bits and pieces to do with stonemasonry and local trades. It's quieter down **Sheep Street** and around the magnificent

Burford and Around t (01993) –

There are some grand places to stay in this old coaching town, but none quite perfect.

The Golden Pheasant, High Street, **t** 823 223 (*expensive*). Charming old-fashioned Cotswold stone inn with 12 bright bedrooms. Popular traditional English restaurant.

Upper Farm, Clapton-on-the-Hill (9 miles northwest of Burford, near Bourton-on-the-Water), **t** (01451) 820453 (*moderate*). Delightful 17th-century farmhouse with smashing views over Windrush Valley and 140 acres of mixed farmland.

Painswick t (01452) –

Painswick Hotel, Kemps Lane, **t** 812 160, *www.painswickhotel.com* (*very expensive*). Elegant former rectory with 19 bedrooms and fabulous views from two drawing rooms, terrace and croquet lawn. Light lunch or coffee on terrace. Dinner (*expensive*) in restaurant might include Evesham asparagus and Cotswold lamb.

Cardynham House, The Cross, **t** 814 006, *www.cardynham.co.uk* (very *expensive*). Unusual place to stay with themed bedrooms, one with heated courtyard pool.

The Falcon Inn, New Street, **t** 814 222, *www.falconinn.com* (*expensive*). Handsome grey stone inn with 12 cheerful rooms, some overlooking the churchyard. Oldest functioning bowling green in England.

Damsells Lodge, The Park, **t** 813 777 (*moderate*). Just outside Painswick, looking out over hills. Creaky and charmingly haphazard.

Hambutts Mynd, Edge Road, **t** 812 352 (*moderate*). Friendly place to stay in lovely old house with three bedrooms, and views towards Stroud

The Royal Oak, St Mary's Street, **t** 813 129 (*moderate*). Cosy bar crammed with furniture and brasses. Pretty courtyard. Pub grub to fish cakes with sautéed potatoes and vegetables.

The March Hare, **t** 813 452. Small restaurant, serves delicious Thai food with fondue nights on Tues. *Closed Sun and Mon. Book.*

Stroud t (01453) –

Mills Café, Withey's Yard (off High Street), **t** 752 222 (*cheap*). Long-established café in leafy yard, serves wholesome broccoli and cheese bakes. *Closed Sun.*

Sunshine Health Shop, Church Street, **t** 763 923 (*cheap*). Buy a picnic here.

Mother Nature, Bedford Street, **t** 758 202 (*cheap*). Health food store where you can also get filled baguettes.

church, built of Taynton stone. The zigzag decoration around the west door and the rounded arches holding up the tower belong to the Norman church, much added to over the centuries by Burford merchants. In the 15th century the tower was finished off with the spire, the fan-vaulted south porch was erected, and the free-standing guild chapel incorporated into the church as the lady chapel. In the chapel of St Thomas is a mysterious stone slab with three pagan figures cut into it; they date back to the second century. There is another curious carving on the Norman font – an inscription, 'Anthony Sedley, prisoner'; in 1649, eight hundred disaffected Parliamentarian soldiers – Levellers – rebelled in Salisbury against Cromwell's orders to embark on a fresh campaign in Ireland. They marched north to Burford, where they were attacked at night by Cromwell and Fairfax. Some escaped, but 340, including Anthony Sedley, were imprisoned in the church for four days. The ringleaders were shot in the churchyard. Seventeenth-century Burford stonemason Kit Kempster is buried in the south transept. The weeping cherub on his memorial stone was designed by his son. William Morris visited the church in 1876, and complained to the vicar about the clumsy restoration work, to which the vicar replied: 'The church is mine and if I choose to I shall stand on my head in it.'

Following the Windrush

The Windrush runs from Burford through a delightful valley of woodland, meadows and fields. The villages here are not twee; weeds can sometimes be spotted growing in their pavements. Ideally, you could hire a bike and head west to the **Barringtons** and **Rissingtons**, or set off on foot east to the villages of **Asthall**, **Widford** and **Minster Lovell** (William Morris's second favourite village after Bibury). Behind the church at Minster Lovell, the imposing ruin of **Minster Lovell Hall** (*open dawn–dusk*) is a pleasant surprise, with its pointed gable-ends and stairless spiral staircase. It was built by Lord William Lovell in the 1440s, and dismantled in 1747 when its new owners, the earls of Leicester, moved to Holkham Hall in Norfolk. The village of **Swinbrook** was once owned by the Fettiplaces. Their Elizabethan mansion is long gone, but look into the church of St Mary. Along the north chancel wall are two 17th-century monuments, each featuring three effigies of Fettiplace men, lying propped up on one elbow. The tiny, forgotten church of St Oswald in **Wideford**, half a mile away in the direction of Burford, incorporates the mosaic of a Roman villa in the chancel floor.

Kelmscott Manor

***t** (01367) 252 486; open April–Sept Wed 11–1 and 2–5, some Sats 2–5; adm.*

Kelmscott Manor, near Lechlade, is an old farmhouse of grey Cotswold stone and lichen-caked tiles, surrounded by tumble-down outbuildings, dovecotes, old-fashioned shrubs and flowers and a boathouse on the Thames. William Morris called it his 'heaven on earth'. He spent his summers here from 1871 to 1896 with his family and his friend Rossetti, until Rossetti's affair with his wife turned heaven into hell. The house is full of home-made furniture and furnishings: tapestries, paintings, carpets, fabrics, wallpapers, tiles and books, in the medieval style of the Arts and Crafts movement. There are curtains inspired by a doodle in the margin of a 15th-century French manuscript, coloured chalk pictures by Rossetti of Morris's daughter May and his wife Jenny looking like the Lady of Shallot, an Arthurian round table by Philip Webb and a Breughel painting of a medieval village.

Just south of Kelmscott Manor on the A417 is **Buscot Park** (***t** (01367) 240 786, www.nationaltrust.org.uk; open April–Sept Wed–Fri and most weekends 2–5.30; adm*), a beautiful 18th-century Renaissance-style house with a fabulous garden.

Painswick

High on a spur between two valleys, the village of Painswick is an ideal base for the western Cotswolds. It is beautiful, full of excellent places to eat and drink in scenic surroundings. Old grey stone houses line narrow lanes between high retaining walls, and the rocket-like **church steeple** – added in the 17th century during a late boom in the cloth industry – reaches halfway to the stars. The churchyard is occupied by the magnificent carved table tombs of the wealthy clothiers whose mansions surround the churchyard, and 99 sculpted yew trees. Painswick also boasts craft shops, galleries and wonderful walks south into the Slad Valley, where Laurie Lee wrote *Cider with Rosie* and drank at the Bullpack. (He is buried in the church.) There are views across the Severn Vale from the top of **Painswick Beacon** (off the A46 Cheltenham road).

The Rococo Garden

t (01452) 813 204; open mid-Jan–Oct 11–5; adm.

Painswick's Rococo Garden is quite a curiosity, marking an obscure phase in the development of the English landscape garden between 1720 and 1760; symmetry and balance were out, but naturalistic parkland was not yet in. Instead you have humorous long vistas and geometric patterns offset by wandering paths and the occasional folly. The gardens of Painswick House are the most intact to survive of this period; painted in 1748 by local artist Thomas Robin, they were completely restored in 1984. The house was built in the 1740s by Charles Hyett, an asthmatic who chose the spot for the fresh air and called it 'Buenos Aires'. His son Benjamin designed the 6-acre garden; its centrepiece is a geometric **Kitchen Garden** incorporating neat lines of fruit trees, a circular pond and a freestanding Gothic fantasy wall.

Stroud

At the foot of the Cotswold scarp south of Painswick, Stroud is a town of steep streets surrounded by 19th-century cloth mills and major roads. The Golden Valley, once crammed with fulling mills and now very built-up, carries the railway from Swindon to Gloucester and Bristol. All this will jolt you out of your Cotswolds reverie, but it's worth a look. On George Street stand the neo-classical **Subscription Rooms**, now the Tourist Information centre. Threadneedle Street leads to Union Street and a **market building** with covered colonnades around an open courtyard. Off the High Street is the **old Shambles**, a narrow street ending in the churchyard. On Fridays and Saturdays, market traders set up their trestle tables under the stone colonnade on one side. The gardens beneath the churchyard are delightful, with views over the Severn Vale to the Forest of Dean. There is a predominance of 'green' cafés, organic food and craft shops: Stroud is a centre of environmental living; the country's first green councillor was John Marjoram of Slad. Made in Stroud on Kendrick Street showcases local craftwork.

The Southern Scarp

There are 17 Iron Age hill forts along the Cotswold scarp, with its massive views over the Severn Vale. Five miles south of Stroud on the B4066, **Uleybury** is a good one. Follow the footpath from beside the church to the hump, smothered in wildflowers and butterflies. North of Uleybury, the Neolithic longbarrow known as **Hetty Pegler's Tump** is just off the road. A few miles north along the same road, **Coaley Peak** enjoys the same views over the Severn Vale to the Brecon Beacons, but without the climb. It is a romantic place to watch the sun set on a summer evening.

Stow-on-the-Wold and Around

Stow is slap in the centre of the Cotswolds, at the junction of old roads heading southwest to Bristol and Bath, south to Salisbury, northwest to Worcester, northeast to Warwick and Coventry. Unlike the other Cotswolds towns and villages, it is on top

Tourist Information

Stow-on-the-Wold: **t** (01451) 831 082.

Where to Stay and Eat

Stow-on-the-Wold t (01451) –

Stow is well-off for tea and coffee shops, inns and hotels.

The Grape Vine Hotel, Sheep Street, **t** 830 344, *www.vines.co.uk* (*luxury*). Three Cotswold stone buildings overlooking old market. Plush inside, with 22 bedrooms. Conservatory restaurant (*moderate*) serves classic English food with Mediterreanean touches, such as venison or fillet of turbot on squid-ink pasta.

The Royalist Hotel, Digbeth Street, **t** 830 670, *www.theroyalisthotel.co.uk* (*very expensive*). Ancient building with hefty beams; eight bedrooms; two restaurants, one formal (*expensive*) and another brasserie (*cheap*) serving posh bangers and mash.

Number 9, 9 Park Street, **t** 870 333 (*expensive*). Utterly charming ivy-covered family home with vases of fresh flowers and Indian antiques; only three rooms, so book well in advance.

Crestow House, Hunts Hill, **t** 830 969 (*expensive*). A good-quality Stow guest-house; two nights minimum stay.

The Talbot Brasserie and Bar, The Square, **t** 830 631 (*moderate*). Vegetarian pâtés and Italian ham. Eight tidy rooms; breakfast is delivered in a wicker hamper.

Queen's Head, The Square, **t** 830 563 (*cheap*). Attractive flagstone pub with cosy niches and solid oak benches.

Around Stow

Kings Head Inn, Bledington, **t** (01608) 658 365, *www.kingsheadinn.net* (*expensive*). Traditional village green pub with high-backed wooden settles, beams and inglenook fireplace. Country-inn-style menu includes stews, venison, duck and fresh fish. Twelve cosy bedrooms.

Lords of the Manor, Upper Slaughter **t** (01451) 820 243 (*expensive*). West of Stow, sumptously furnished 16th-century mansion in 8-acre gardens including lake and park, built on the site of a medieval priory. Lunch on the terrace or in the bar (*moderate*), or dinner in the restaurant.

The Old Mill Lodge, Mill Lane, Lower Slaughter, **t** (01451) 822 127, *www.oldmill-lowerslaughter.com* (*expensive*). Spacious, beatifully furnished place with stylish breakfast hampers.

The Fox Inn, Lower Oddington, **t** (01451) 870 555 (*moderate*). Just east of Stow, stylish, lively pub with flagstone floor, sturdy wooden furniture, two huge fireplaces and contemporary art on the walls. Wholesome country cooking includes beef and ale pie, venison, pheasant or guinea fowl.

of a hill. 'Stow on the Wold where the winds blow cold,' they say; in 1762 five soldiers died of exposure in a blizzard. 'Stow-on-the-Wold where antiques are sold' is more like it these days. Despite cold and commerce, Stow, with its market square enclosed by handsome buildings of warm yellow Cotswold stone, is an ideal Cotswolds base.

The Slaughters

The villages of the delightful tree-lined valley of the River Eye were not the site of historical carnage; they owe their name to the Saxon 'slough', meaning wetlands. Upper and Lower Slaughter are honey-coloured beauty spots, as neat and tidy as their chocolate-box image. In **Lower Slaughter**, where old cottages cluster around the green and the brook is spanned by clapper bridges, there is an early 19th-century watermill with a café inside. From beside the mill, you can pick up the Warden's Way to **Upper Slaughter**. Here, next to the picturesque churchyard, are cottages remodelled by the architect Edwin Lutyens. The old ford is like a Constable painting.

Chastleton House

t (01608) 674 355; open by appointment only, April–Sept Wed–Sat 1–5, Oct Wed and Sat 1–4; call ahead.

This Tudor mansion is a few miles east of Stow off the A436. It was built for wealthy lawyer Walter Jones by Robert Smythson, of Hardwick Hall and Longleat fame. Jones bought it from Robert Catesby in 1604, a year before the Gunpowder Plot. He aspired to the ranks of the gentry, and got off to a good start by marrying off his son to one of the Fettiplace daughters, but his descendants were impecunious. As a result, the chipped, scuffed, faded, ripped, creaking house has an agreeably lived-in atmosphere.

The Rollright Stones

A few miles northeast of Chastleton House is a famous group of Bronze Age megaliths, including the King's Men stone circle, the King Stone and a burial chamber known as the Whispering Knights. The legend is that they are the petrified remains of a king and his followers, who ran into trouble with a local witch. Park near the **King's Men**, which is a perfect circle of 73 stones on a hill top. Across the road is

the **King Stone**, a wonky slab of limestone 5ft high. A short walk up the road, the **Whispering Knights** burial chamber is older than the other monuments, constructed around 4000 BC. Four stones remain upright, while the capstone lies where it fell.

Sezincote

t (01386) 700 444; house open May–July and Sept Thurs–Fri 2.30–6; garden open Jan–Nov Thurs–Fri 2–6; adm.

Ten miles north of Stow on the A424 Broadway road a narrow lane brings you to the Indian-style palace of Charles Cockerell, built in 1805 from his fortune made in the East India Company. The Prince Regent visited in 1807, and the onion domes, carved orangerie and Brahmin bulls on the bridge inspired the Brighton Pavilion, built in 1815. The whole thing is offset by English oak woods.

Winchcombe and Around

The handsome brown stone houses of Winchcombe nestle snugly in the hills. Within walking distance of the village are a Neolithic longbarrow, a Roman mosaic, a ruined abbey and a great manor house associated with Henry VIII. Winchcombe was a provincial capital of Mercia, and Winchcombe abbey – of which nothing remains – was founded by the Mercian king Kenwulf. The **church** preserves fragments of the abbey, including a stone coffin said to belong to Kenwulf. Forty gargoyles with moon faces and crooked smiles guard it. They are the 'Winchcombe worthies', said to resemble the more disreputable monks of the abbey; the one outside the south aisle wearing a helmet and splendid moustache is Ralph Boteler, 15th-century Lord of Sudeley and benefactor of the church. The treasure of the church is an old altar cloth, believed to have been embroidered by Catherine of Aragon, who stayed at Sudeley; the border shows her pomegranate emblem.

Where to Stay and Eat

Winchcombe t (01242) –

Wesley House, High Street, **t** 602 366, *www.wesleyhouse.co.uk* (*expensive*). Beamy 15th-century townhouse with six tasteful bedrooms. Dinner might include roast loin of venison with beetroot fondant and bitter chocolate sauce.

Old White Lion Inn, 37 North Street, **t** 603 300, *www.theoldwhitelion.com* (*expensive*). Comfortable, friendly old coaching inn.

The Plaisterers Arms, High Street, **t** 602 358 (*moderate*). Dusky old bar with an unusual wooden darts cubicle and basic rooms.

Ireley Farm, Broadway Road, **t** 602 445, *warmingtonmaggot@aol.com* (*moderate*). An 18th-century working farmhouse with three lovely rooms.

Pilgrim House, Hailes (near Hailes Abbey), **t** 603 011 (*moderate*). Lovely 18th-century farmhouse on site of old pilgrims' inn, full of character (inglenooks and woodburning stoves). Delicious breakfasts; also art classes.

Sudeley Castle

***t** (01242) 602 308; open Mar–Nov daily, house 11–5, garden 10.30–5.30; adm exp.*

Sudeley is just over the river from Winchcombe, down a street of pretty stone cottages and pollarded limes. Looking back you can see the row of **Victorian almshouses** and the old **Temperance Hall** set up by Emma Dent of Sudeley. The castle was built by Ralph Boteler, admiral of the fleet under Henry V and Henry VI. There are plenty of royal connections here, especially, and almost incestuously, with the wives of Henry VIII. The house was given by Edward VII to his nephew Thomas Seymour, brother of Henry VIII's third wife, Jane. Thomas married Henry's widow Catherine Parr, who died soon after. He then tried it on, unsuccessfully, with the 15-year-old Princess Elizabeth. He ended up dead in the Tower. Good riddance. During the Civil War, Prince Rupert based himself at Sudeley, which was wrecked by Cromwell's soldiers and languished into the 18th century as a romantic ruin. The Dent brothers, Worcestershire glove-makers, bought the property in 1837 and commissioned George Gilbert Scott to restore it. It passed to nephew John Dent, whose wife Emma continued the restoration work, as well as doing good works around the town. The interiors are mostly Victorian with furnishings by Morris and Co, but the library has the atmosphere of the 16th-century castle, and there is a bed slept in by Charles I during the Civil War. There are pretty raised flowerbeds around the old stone chapel, where you can see **Catherine Parr's coffin**, and an old-fashioned rose garden.

Belas Knap

There are more than seventy Neolithic longbarrows in the Cotswolds, and this is the best. It is 177ft long and 59ft wide, and consists of turf-covered slabs. Excavations suggest it was reused at least thirty times for burials, and was in constant use as a shrine. Mysteriously, the grand main portal leads nowhere; the real entrances are around the sides. It's a lovely walk south from Winchcombe along the Cotswolds Way.

Hailes Abbey

***t** (01242) 602 398; open April–Sept 10–6, Oct 10–5; adm*

The ruins of Hailes Abbey are 3 miles northeast of Winchcombe, reached via the B4632 or on foot along the Cotswolds Way. Hailes was founded in the 13th century by

Richard, Duke of Cornwall, brother of Henry III, after he survived a sea-storm on his way home from the crusades. A nearby village was done away with, so that the order of Cistercian monks might live in peaceful isolation. Their prize possession was a small **bottle of Christ's blood**, which drew in the pilgrims. In the *Canterbury Tales*, the Pardoner swears 'by the blode of Christ that is in Hayles'. It was one of the richest Cistercian abbeys in England by the time of its Dissolution, when the building was looted, the monks turfed out and the 'holy blood' denounced as 'oily, coloured gum'. There is not much left to see, but the setting goes a long way, particularly if you arrive, pilgrim-like, on foot. The old church is worth looking into for its early 14th-century wall paintings.

Winchcombe Pottery

***t** (01242) 602 462; open Mon–Fri 9–5, May–Sept also Sat 10–4, Sun 12–4.*

North of Winchcombe on the B4632, just before Hailes Abbey, this tumbledown farmyard pottery with its old bottle kilns, log piles and rusting bits of machinery buried in the undergrowth enjoyed renown in the early 20th century. In 1926 Michael Cardew, the first pupil of Bernard Leach in St Ives, fell in love with the abandoned Victorian pottery, which he came upon by chance during a trip to the Cotswolds. He revived it, producing a range of medieval-style domestic slipware; his stated intention was to make pots for middle-class families to use every day. In 1936 Cardew was joined by Ray Finch, whose wares eventually ranked alongside the factory potteries at Poole and Royal Doulton. In the 1960s Finch produced the tableware for Cranks wholefood restaurant in London. By the 1970s his simple designs and iron-flecked glazes had become part of a domestic style much illustrated in interior décor magazines. Finch still works away with his pipe, and you can buy hand-thrown pots. Hunt out the old bottle kilns at the back, covered in weeds, next to the ruin of Michael Cardew's cottage.

Chipping Campden and Around

Chipping Campden, the northern gate of the Cotswolds, is the height of Cotswolds charm. The perfectly curved wide main street with its merchants' houses, market hall, almshouses and church, all of the same gorgeous honey-coloured stone, look as if they were all built at once, not over centuries. A work of exquisite harmony, there is no better monument to medieval wool wealth than this. The Guild of Handicraft – the boldest social experiment of the Arts and Crafts movement – was set up in Chipping Campden in 1902, attracted by the manifest skill of the local stonemasons. Behind it was Robert Ashby, who convinced 70 families of craftsmen from the east end of London to move here and show the world that traditional rural handicrafts could be economically viable (they couldn't). He renovated **Braithwaite House** (now Lloyds and the British Legions Club) for the bachelors of the guild, and chose the **Woolstaplers Hall**, opposite the townhouse of Campden's greatest medieval wool merchant, William Grevel, for himself, regularly hosting amateur dramatics.

Tourist Information

Chipping Campden: Old Police Station, High Street, **t** (01386) 841 206. *Open summer 10–5.30, winter 10–5.*

Cotswold Country Cycles, Longlands Farm Cottage, Chipping Camden, **t** 438 706.

Country Lanes Cycles, Moreton in the Marsh railway station, **t** (01608) 650 065.

The **Cotswolds Way** is a 104-mile long-distance walking trail from Chipping Campden to Bath.

Where to Stay and Eat

Chipping Campden t (01386) –

The Cotswold House Hotel, **t** 840 330, *www.cotswoldhouse.com* (*luxury*). Magnificent 17th-century hotel overlooking market square; 20 beautifully furnished bedrooms, elegant sitting rooms, lovely 2-acre gardens, informal bar-brasserie and Garden Restaurant serving modern English food. Old-fashioned charm married to modern luxury.

The King's Arms Hotel, High Street, **t** 840 256, *www.thekingsarmshotel.com* (*very expensive*). Thirteen bedrooms with patchwork quilts, solid farmhouse furniture. Brasserie-style meals include ragout of monkfish, scallops and king prawns or roast rack of English lamb.

Seymour House Hotel, High Street, **t** 840 429, *www.seymourhousehotel.com* (*very expensive*). Handsome Georgian hotel. Top-notch restaurant serves Italian, English and French-style cooking.

Badger's Hall, High Street, **t** 840 839 (*expensive*). A 17th-century building with quaint tea shop downstairs, and two rooms upstairs with old pine furniture.

Caminetto Restaurant, High Street, **t** 840 934 (*moderate*). Excellent Italian in old King's Arms pantry. *Closed Sun, and Mon lunch.*

Dragon House, High Street, **t** 840 734, *www.dragonhouse-chipping-campden.com* (*moderate*). Formerly George and Dragon pub, now a quiet place to stay.

The Churchill Arms, Paxford (near Chipping Campden), **t** 594 000, *www.thechurchillarms.com* (*moderate*). Popular bar-restaurant; top-quality modern English food. Four rooms upstairs.

The Eight Bells, Church Street, **t** 840 371 (*cheap*). Oldest pub in Chipping Campden. Real ales and good food.

Maylambs Delicatessan, High Street, **t** 840 903 (*cheap*). Arm yourself with sandwiches and drinks here.

Numerous other buildings were turned into family homes. **Elm Tree House**, opposite Robert Welch's studio, became the **Campden School of Arts and Crafts**, where evening classes and summer courses were held to broaden the minds of the craftsmen. The redundant **Silk Mill** on Sheep Street was turned into workshops, including gold and silversmiths, jewellers, furniture designers, wood carvers and blacksmiths. The craftsmen were encouraged to take an interest in each other's work. When the experiment failed, for economic reasons, including competition from cheap imitations, most of the craftsmen moved back to London, but a few stayed on. The furniture maker Jim Pyment kept the ground floor of the Silk Mill and the silversmith George Hart kept the first floor. The **Guild of Handicraft Trust Exhibition** (*open Mon–Fri 9–5*) is on the ground floor, with a display of objects made by the guild. Upstairs, you can visit **Hart's Gold and Silversmiths**. George Hart was one of the guild's most successful craftsmen, specializing in relief decoration on silver. He was joined by his son Henry in 1930, then his grandson David, who still works there today. The worn oak benches and tools date back to Ashby's time. With its bold shapes and simple flowing lines, Arts and Craft-style domestic silverware is fashionable again: a silver tankard with leaf chasing that cost £5 in 1903 is worth £13,000 a century later, or £500 new.

St James's Church is best approached from out of town to the north, its tower soaring above an avenue of centuries-old lime trees. The wide, bright interior houses impressive monuments to its benefactors. A brass in front of the altar depicts **William Grevel** (d. 1401), 'flower of the wool merchants of all England,' who retired to the Cotswolds after a career in London. The grandest monument is to **Sir Baptist Hicks**, another rich London merchant, who traded in silks, damasks, velvets and satins and lent money to Charles I; it stands in the south chapel and features the reclining life-sized effigies of husband and wife, with naturalistic hands and shoes. Sir Baptist bought Campden manor in 1610 and built a palatial Italianate house beside the old church, which was destroyed in the Civil War. The domed **gatehouse** is one of the glories of Campden. Hicks also endowed the **market hall** and the row of **almshouses**.

Dover Hill

Dover Hill is a few miles west in the direction of Weston-sub-Edge. It is a lovely natural amphitheatre and the start of the Cotswolds Way. It was also the venue of the **Cotswolds olympick games** until the last meeting in 1852, by which time it had grown out of all proportion, with strapping lads coming down on the trains from Birmingham and Coventry. This was the year of the famous backsword fight described by Ashby in *The Last Records of a Cotswolds Community*: 'In this fight with the left hand tied to the hocks the two champions fought till one lost an eye and the other was so badly bruised that he died a fortnight after, but, says tradition, it was the Campden man that one.' The hill is named after Robert Dover, who founded the games in 1612. He complained of the men of Campden: 'so base they grew that at this present day, they are not men but moving lumps of clay'. There was wrestling, boxing, running, jumping, dancing, horse-riding, hammer-throwing and – one that didn't catch on – shin-kicking with iron-tipped boots (training involved toughening the shins by beating them with planks of wood).

Hidcote Manor Gardens

t (01386) 438 333, www.nationaltrust.org.uk; open Easter–Oct Sat–Wed 10.30–5; adm.

Lawrence Johnson, the founder of these gardens, north of Chipping Campden near Mickleton, was a Jamesian character. A rootless, over-educated fin-de-siècle American loner, he was born in Paris in 1871 to parents from Baltimore, brought up by relatives in Europe, educated at Cambridge, and fought in the Boer and First World wars. In 1907 he moved into Hidcote, creating within two decades 'the most influential garden of the century'. His idea of enclosed garden 'rooms' off hedged 'corridors' was a big innovation. Hidcote appeared twice in *Country Life*. The gardens at Sissinghurst were planned on the same lines: 'a series of separate autonomous gardens linked by long alleyways, so that although when standing at one end of a vista you could see to the bottom of it, surprise gardens would successively come into view as you progressed' (Vita Sackville West). The garden rooms are full of flowers planted to look as natural and abundant as if they had blown in on the wind.

Broadway and Around

Broadway sits at the northwestern foot of the Cotswolds, in the Vale of Evesham but unquestionably a Cotswolds town with its wide main street and golden stone. In the 16th century it was a stop on the Worcester–London coaching road, before the big uphill climb onto the Cotswolds. The spectacular **Lygon Arms** was one of the coaching inns. When the railway was routed via Moreton-in-the-Marsh, Broadway slid into picturesque decline. It has been attracting tourists since the 19th century, when Henry James wrote a rave travel piece about its sagging roofs and crumbling gables in *Harpers Magazine*. Now tourists arrive by the coach load, and it is a bit too smart for its own good. J.B. Priestley hit the nail on the head: 'Broadway is at Ye Olde game'.

One mile south of Broadway off the A44, **Beacon Hill** is the second highest peak in the Cotswolds (1,023ft). An extra hundred feet are gained by climbing to the top of the folly built for the Earl of Coventry in 1799, known as **Broadway Tower** (**t** *(01386) 852 390; open April–Oct daily 10.30–5, Nov–Mar weekends 11–3; adm*). The dark Gothic stone turrets were the work of James Wyatt. In 1827 it became the printing house of Sir Thomas Phillips, and later was home to Carmel Price, friend of Pre-Raphaelite artists Rossetti, Burne-Jones and Morris. May Morris described finding the four of them bathing on the roof in a wind so brisk that soap suds flew from the tub.

Snowshill Manor

t (01386) 584 528, www.nationaltrust.org.uk; gardens open Easter–Oct Wed–Sun 11–5.30; manor house closed for refurbishment 2004;adm.

A minor road leads south of Broadway into the hills, following a stream. 'You have only to take a turn or two from a main road into one of these enchanted little valleys,'

Tourist Information

Broadway: **t** (01386) 852 937. *Open Mar–Oct Mon–Sat 10–1 and 2–5.*

Where to Stay

Broadway t (01386) –

Lygon Arms, High Street, **t** 852 255, *www.savoy-group.co.uk* (*luxury*). A 16th-century coaching inn which once put up Oliver Cromwell (on the eve of the Battle of Worcester, 1651). Endless, cosy oak-beamed rooms crammed with faded tapestries, antiques and Gordon Russell furniture.

Cowley House, Church Street, **t** 853 262 (*expensive*). Beautiful old stone farmhouse set back from road behind pretty garden.

The Barn House, 152 High Street, **t** 858 633, *www.karenbrown.com/England/barnhouse.html* (*moderate*). Large 17th-century house with lovely bedrooms, big garden and heated pool.

The Olive Branch Guest House, 78 High Street, **t** 853 440, *www.theolivebranch-broadway.com* (*moderate*). Warm and friendly with seven rooms.

Eating Out

Lygon Arms, High Street, **t** 852 255 (*expensive*). Settle into an armchair for afternoon tea, pop in for a drink at the bar or dine on Cotswold lamb in the medieval-style restaurant. *Open dinner daily, lunch weekends.*

Oliver's Brasserie, High Street, **t** 854 418 (*moderate*). Lygon Arms' brasserie: salmon and haddock cakes.

Jardines, 16–19 The Huntings, Church Close (*cheap*). Good cream teas and filled rolls.

wrote J.B. Priestley in *English Journey*, 'and you are gone and lost.' After 4 miles you come to the hamlet, church and manor of Snowshill, sitting in its own valley amid fields and woods. It is preserved as the late owner, the eccentric Charles Paget Wade, left it. The house is all grey stone gables and roofs, separated by a courtyard from an outhouse, where Wade ate and slept. It is crammed with Indonesian masks, model boats, weapons, spinning wheels, bicycles and Japanese armour. The gardens are the perfect foil. Wade chose the gardener on the basis of his name, which was Hodge, and his hat, 'which was mauve' and 'that he knew nothing about gardening beyond cabbages and cauliflowers, so here was the very man.'

A few miles west along narrow lanes is the many-gabled hamlet of **Stanton**, as picturesque as Bibury. The batsman on the cricket pitch looks out over the whole of the Vale of Evesham towards the Malverns. At the foot of the scarp, **Stanway House** (*open June–Sept Tues and Thurs 2–5; adm*) blazes away in golden stone, its magnificent Tudor gateway beside the church creating a perfect Cotswolds ensemble.

Cheltenham

Forget the stone drip-courses and butter-crosses of the Cotswolds, and think stuccoed squares and terraces, shops, theatres and assembly rooms. While the Cotswolds villages look as natural as if they had grown out of the rock, Cheltenham is all about planned development. Between 1790 and 1840 it was the number one British spa town, its nitrous waters a magnet to overfed, fashionable society. They came to get well and have fun. It doesn't have the coherence of Bath, but it does boast some handsome terraces and crescents.

The Spa Resort

The single event that made the spa town beside the River Chelt was the five-week visit of George III in 1788. He was known as the farmer king because he talked livestock prices and dressed like a country squire. Cheltenham suited him, with its hills and woods where he could walk the dogs and watch cricket. The legend is that in 1718 pigeons drew attention to the waters by pecking away at the crusty salt deposits. A well was sunk for the town, and eminent men of science wondered that the old men could drink so much without any ill effects. 'They had no rule, but to drink till the water passed clean through them,' wrote Dr Lucas in his *Essays on Waters*. The water was bottled and sold in London as a treatment for headaches, watery eyes, asthma, digestive disorders, colic, sterility and 'nests of worms in the bowels'. Its healing properties were renowned above Bath's. The well was paved and enclosed under a dome, and tree-lined paths were laid out to connect it to the town. Visitors began to arrive in summer – recommended doses between one and three pints in the morning – and were treated to traditional country entertainments like cock-fighting and baiting bulls with dogs. Before long, the High Street was paved and lamp-lit, music was played at the well in the mornings, and in the evening there was tea and card-playing in the purpose-built long rooms on either side of the approach to the well. By the

Tourist Information

Cheltenham: 77 The Promenade, **t** (01242) 522 878. *Open Mon–Sat 9.30–5.15.*

Festivals

Cheltenham International Festival of Music (mainly classical) is held over three weeks in July. **Cheltenham Festival of Literature** lasts nine days in October; talks, readings and debates by leading writers. For both, **t** (01242) 227 979, *www.CheltenhamFestivals.co.uk.*

The **National Hunt Festival** takes place over three days in March with 20 horse-racing meetings featuring Champion Hurdle and Cheltenham Gold Cup; **t** (01242) 513 014; *www.cheltenham.co.uk.*

Where to Stay

Cheltenham t (01242) –

Queen's Hotel, **t** 0870 400 8107 (*luxury*). Magnificent hotel with neo-classical portico at top of tree-lined promenade on site of old Imperial Spa. 'Fine dining' and **Le Petit Blanc** restaurant (*see* below).

Willoughby House Hotel, 1 Suffolk Square, **t** 522 798, *www.willoughbyhouse.com* (*expensive*). Beautiful, welcoming neo-classical Regency hotel in smartest part of Cheltenham with period-style décor and eight bedrooms.

Lypiatt House, Lypiatt Road, **t** 224 994, *www.lypiatt.co.uk* (*expensive*). Tasteful, relaxed Victorian house, set back behind gravel drive; 10 bedrooms with patchwork quilts, and a pretty conservatory.

Milton House Hotel, 12 Royal Parade, Bayshill Road, **t** 582 601, *www.miltonhousehotel.co.uk* (*expensive*). Handsome Victorian townhouse full of plants; eight comfortable rooms.

Lonsdale House, Montpellier Drive, **t** 232 379 (*moderate*). In half-built Victorian terrace; nine bedrooms, three en-suite; civilized.

Eating Out

Le Petit Blanc, The Queen's Hotel, The Promenade, **t** 266 800 (*moderate*). In the old hotel ball room; top-notch 'rustic French with some Asian influences' brasserie-style menu. Afternoon tea in the lounge of the Queen's is a Cheltenham tradition; tinkling tea cups, chandeliers and Regency gold and crimson décor.

Daffodil, 18–20 Suffolk Parade, Montpellier, **t** 700 055 (*moderate*). In a 1930s art deco cinema; light modern cooking. *Closed Sun.*

La Champignon Sauvage, 24–6 Suffolk Road, **t** 573 449 (*moderate*). Elegant, with delicious contemporary cooking: roast Whitby cod, pea and barley risotto or pork with black pudding. *Closed Sun, Mon and June.*

Mayflower, 32–4 Clarence Street, **t** 522 426 (*cheap*). Long-established Chinese restaurant serving traditional Cantonese, Pekinese and Szechuan dishes like crispy duck and beef with cashew nuts in yellow bean sauce. *Closed Sun.*

Moka, 14 Suffolk Parade, **t** 263 646 (*cheap*). Good coffee, pastries and classical music.

Montpellier Wine Bar, Montpellier Street, **t** 527 774 (*cheap*). Suave place for evening drinks.

Entertainment

The Everyman Theatre, Regent's Street, **t** 572 573. Variery of touring drama, comedy and music in Frank Matcham auditorium.

Pittville Pump Room, **t** 523 852 and **Town Hall**, **t** 227 979. Classical concerts.

time of King George's visit, Cheltenham was a chink of civilization in a rustic setting. The **Royal Old Well** where George took the waters soon proved inadequate to the demand. Landowners bored hundreds of new holes, and where the water tasted salty new wells were sunk. However it was not until the Enclosures Act of 1801 did away with common land that the estate owners were able to start building. The **Montpellier Spa** was the most popular, with its domed pump room and pleasure gardens. In 1818 the **Imperial Spa** was built, with beautiful terraced gardens. Then in the 1820s Joseph Pitt started on the **Pittsville Pump Room** on the north side of town.

Around it he envisaged a new town to rival Cheltenham, with a church and 600 houses. But the fashion for inland spa resorts was already on the way out, in favour of sea bathing. The **Pump Room** opened in July 1830 to music and fireworks, but the rest of Pitt's adventurous building scheme was abandoned. The Victorians built schools rather than pump rooms, including **Cheltenham Ladies College** – founded as 'an institution for the daughters and young children of Noblemen and Gentlemen' – and **Cheltenham College for Boys**. One of its pupils was Gustav Holst, whose father was the music master. At 17 Holst became choir master and organist at Rissington church, going on to study at the Royal College of Music and to compose *The Planets*. Today, Cheltenham is probably best known for its racing track. Thousands flock to the March meeting, which is the climax of the steeplechase season.

Around Town

Start at the top of town in the cluster of streets known as the Suffolks, move downhill through Montpellier and over the High Street to Pitt's 100-acre commercial flop.

The **Suffolks** won't keep you long, but here there are Regency terraces; attractive small shops selling antiques, jewellery and pine furniture; a good café and several restaurants. **Montpellier**, calling itself the Continental Quarter, bustles, specializing in chic women's boutiques. This was the heart of the spa town. The long main street, the **Promenade**, runs downhill to the High Street, on one side the pleasure gardens, on the other Regency terraces. **Montpellier Gardens**, once famous for its funfair and balloon rides, is now mostly tennis courts, but the **Imperial Gardens** are lovely. The old Imperial Spa became the **Queen's Hotel** in 1837, at the time that the grand terraces of townhouses were built. The main spa buildings are prominent: the old green-domed **Montpellier Spa** is now a magnificent-looking bank, and set back from the wide pavement is a striking neo-classical terrace with caryatids balancing the shopfronts on their heads. Through the buildings you can glimpse the Gothic-style **Cheltenham Ladies College**, on the site of the Old Royal Well. There is also a pretty Victorian shopping arcade. Further down the Promenade are Cheltenham's grandest terraces. Next to the grandiose Neptune Fountain is a little green statue of the Antarctic explorer Edward Wilson in a woollen hat.

Not far away on Clarence Street is the excellent **Art Gallery and Museum** (*open Mon–Sat 10–5.20, Sun 2–4.20*) with a café and shop. Exhibitions include a social history of Cheltenham from Anglo-Saxon to Victorian times. In the **Cotswolds Arts and Crafts Room** there is furniture by the Barnsley brothers and Ernest Gimson – practical high-backed rush-seated chairs, traditional settles, and oak dressers – and silver plates and pepper pots by Ashby.

By the time you reach the High Street the town is starting to lose steam. Many of its more interesting old buildings have gone, such as the Victorian grammar school and the Assembly Rooms where Paganini and Strauss gave concerts, and Dickens, Wilde and Thackeray gave readings. **Gustav Holst's Birthplace** (***t** (01242) 524 846; open Feb–Dec Tues–Sat 10–4; adm*), a small Regency house on Clarence Road, has the piano on which he composed *The Planets*. It is also a museum of Regency and Victorian domestic life. When Holst was born in 1874, the street was called Pitville Terrace; here you are already on the fringes of the Pittville estate. On sunny days **Pittville Park** is nice. On the high ground around the elegant **Pump Room** *(open Wed–Mon 11–4)* are grand detached villas, painted and decorated in stucco. The **race course** is yet further away, on the northern edge of town (best reached by car).

Gloucester

Gloucester has everything going for it, but is a disappointment. The setting is magnificent, at the foot of the Cotswolds and the head of the River Severn, bordering the Forest of Dean and the Welsh Marches. Its cathedral and Victorian docks are things of greatness; if only the 20th century hadn't happened to the town. Gloucester began as the Roman fortress town of *Glevum* at the lowest crossing of the Severn, guarding the military road into Wales, and later became one of four *coloniae* in *Britannia* including Lincoln, Colchester and York, where retired soldiers ended their days. The city's four main streets follow the old Roman thoroughfares to the central crossroads, known as the Cross. Gloucester's long and prosperous career as an inland port began in the Middle Ages. The city achieved its full flowering pre-Reformation, when the thriving Severn trade jostled with the booming religious life based on the Norman abbey and friaries. The New Inn on Northgate Street, with its perfectly preserved courtyard and balconies, was built to accommodate the droves of pilgrims visiting the shrine of Edward II in the abbey church.

Gloucester Docks

The ring road on the south side of the city passes the main entrance to the docks (**t** *(01452) 311 190, info@glosdocks.co.uk*) on Southgate Street. With its red-brick warehouses and docking basins it's a symbol of the Victorian era when Britain exported manufactured goods around the world. The docks are at the head of the **Gloucester and Sharpness Canal**, linking Gloucester to the Severn estuary where it widens; 19th-century Gloucester was also linked by canal with the potteries of Stoke-on-Trent, the metal works of the Black Country and the textile factories of Leicester and Nottingham.

Tourist Information

Gloucester: 28 Southgate Street, **t** (01452) 421 188. *Open Mon–Sat 10–5.*

Eating Out

Gloucester t (01452) –

There are several cheap and cheerful restaurants around Gloucester Docks.

Orchid at the Undercroft, **t** 308 920 (*cheap*). The cathedral restaurant serves wholesome snacks and lunches, such as soups and flans, as well as tea and coffee.

The New Inn, Northgate Street, **t** 522 177 (*cheap*). One of the best-preserved medieval courtyard inns in the country, built for pilgrims to the shrine of Edward II; old wooden coaching doors lead into galleried courtyard and dusky bar, where lanterns hang from blackened beams.

The Fountain Inn, Westgate Street (opposite the cathedral), **t** 522 562 (*cheap*). Another medieval courtyard inn, its pleasant courtyard full of hanging baskets and plant pots.

Old Bell Winebar, Southgate Street, **t** 332 993 (*cheap*). Timber-framed Jacobean townhouse with oak-panelled bar featuring a carved chinmey-piece.

The warehouses have been converted into shops and restaurants, and the **National Waterways Museum** (**t** *(01452) 318 054; open 10–5; adm*), and the basins are packed with painted narrow boats. The **museum of the Gloucester Regiment and Royal Gloucester Hussars** (**t** *(01452) 522 682; open summer daily 10–5, winter Tues–Sun 10–5; adm*) is housed on the ground floor of the regimental headquarters of the Gloucestershire, Berkshire and Wiltshires.

Gloucester Cathedral

You get a good view of the Gothic cathedral tower from the docks, a 10-minute walk away. The cathedral close is a quaint alley of weatherboard shops selling fudge; the little shop at the end, abutting the pilgrims' arch, was the model for Beatrix Potter's *Tailor of Gloucester*. The four-pinnacled tower of the cathedral is 225ft high, built of Painswick stone, and decorated with Gothic embellishments to make it soar. The church was founded in 1089 for the monks of St Peter's Abbey and converted into a cathedral after the Reformation as the shrine of Edward II, gruesomely murdered in Berkeley Castle. Something of almost every architectural period survives inside: chunky old Norman pillars run down the nave under the low roof, and Victorian stained-glass windows throw pools of colour onto the stone floor.

The **tomb of Edward II** has always been the main attraction. It stands on the north side of the choir, remodelled after the death of Edward in sensational Perpendicular style. The intricately carved stone screen offered pilgrims fleeting glimpses into the monastic inner sanctum. The east window, which is the hallmark of the style, fills the entire wall and glows with the colours of the stained glass. The tomb of Edward II features an effigy of the king in a long robe.

Head for the **cloisters**, behind a wall of stone tracery which rises up to some of the earliest fan vaulting in England. On the south side are little arched alcoves where the monks worked, and at the other end are their wash basins with recesses for their towels. 'Even at this day,' wrote Nathaniel Hawthorne in his *English Notes*, 'if I were a canon of Gloucester, I would put that dim ambulatory to a good use.'

Town Museums

After the cathedral, there are two museums worth popping into. The **City Museum and Art Gallery** on Brunswick Street (**t** *(01452) 524 131; open Tues–Sat 10–5; adm minimal*) displays carvings of Roman gods, a chunk of a 30ft high Roman column and all sorts of pottery, keys, brooches and bracelets. The **Folk Museum** on Westgate Street (**t** *(01452) 526 467; open Tues–Sat 10–5; adm*), in a group of Tudor and Jacobean buildings, tells the history of Gloucester . The nursery rhyme 'Humpty Dumpty' originated in the town during the Civil War as a Parliamentarian taunt.

Berkeley Castle

***t** (01453) 810 332; open Tues–Sat 11–4. Sun 2–5; adm.*

Halfway between Bristol and Gloucester, west of the M5, the ancient castle of the earls of Berkeley dominates the banks of the River Severn. It looks magnificent, with its round Norman keep and 14th-century buildings around a courtyard. It has its great hall, drawing room, dining room and chapel, all very stately and grand, but the main attraction is 'the unspeakably ghastly chamber of Edward II's murder', which the 19th-century diarist Augustus Hare remembered visiting as a boy. Peer through the grille into the gloomy cell 'with a floor of unplaned oak, and the light falling from two stained windows upon a white head of Edward in a niche, and an old bed with a sword lying upon it in the position in which it was found after the murder.' His captors were Queen Isabella and her lover, Roger Mortimer. To make the king's death look natural, the gaolers wanted to kill him without leaving a mark on his body. They succeeded on 21 September 1327 'with a hoote brooch [red-hot poker] putte thro the secret place posterialle.' The shrieks of the king were heard in Gloucester.

Tewkesbury

At the confluence of the rivers Severn and Avon, cut off from the Vale of Evesham by the M5, Tewkesbury is an olde worlde town of small, timber-framed bric-a-brac shops and tea shoppes. The old **abbey church** is its attraction. Southwest of town, on the banks of the Severn, is the **site of the Battle of Tewkesbury** in 1471, where Edward IV defeated the Lancastrian queen, Margaret, and secured 14 years of Yorkist rule. There are some lovely spots by the river too, including the 19th-century abbey mill.

The Battle of Tewkesbury

The battle of Tewkesbury took place on the morning of 4 May 1471 a mile south of town. It was the last battle of the Wars of the Roses, at which Edward IV defeated Margaret, the queen of Lancastrian King Henry VI (probably already dead). What followed was 14 years of Yorkist rule under Edward IV and Richard III, ending abruptly at the Battle of Bosworth. Pick up a leaflet from the tourist information centre and explore the battlefield on foot. The Lancastrian army, 6,000 men under Margaret and Prince Edward, had sailed from France to Portland in Dorset. The plan was to restore the house of Lancaster by putting Edward on the throne. They marched through the West Country towards pro-Lancastrian Wales, stopping at Exeter and Bristol to gather men and weapons. At Gloucester the gates were locked, forcing them to use another bridge over the Severn further north. At Tewkesbury they received news that Edward IV's army of 4,000 men was on their tail. Realizing they would never reach the bridge, they camped in the water meadows of the Swilgate, south of Tewkesbury. The king camped at Tredington, a few miles away. The next day, the Lancastrians were annihilated, some of them in the abbey where they had sought sanctuary. Edward, the young pretender, was killed in battle. Margaret was imprisoned, and eventually ransomed to the king of France. Edward IV spent 22 years on the throne, and was succeeded by his brother, Richard of Gloucester, who murdered the young princes – and you probably know the rest.

Tourist Information

Tewkesbury: 64 Barton Street, **t** (01684) 295 027, *www.visitcotswoldsandsevernvale.gov.uk*. *Open April–Oct Mon–Sat 9–5, Sun 10–4.*

The **Battle of Tewkesbury Fair** takes place over the second weekend in July, behind the Gupshill pub on the A38. Demonstations of falconry, jousting and juggling, followed by trial and executions of battle villains with baying crowds around the abbey.

Where to Stay

Tewkesbury t (01684) –

The Bell Hotel, 52 Church Street, **t** 293 293 (*expensive*). Creaky 17th-century hotel backing onto river, opposite the abbey; 25 modest bedrooms.

Jessop House Hotel, 65 Church Street, **t** 292 017, *www.jessophousehotel.com* (*expensive*). Handsome Georgian townhouse down alley. Stone-flagged hall with grand stairway; eight bedrooms with pretty fireplaces.

Abbey Hotel, 67 Church Street, **t** 294 247, *www.the-abbey-hotel.co.uk* (*expensive*). Delightful Victorian tiled hallway and breakfast room hung with paintings; 13 bedrooms all shapes and sizes; warm atmosphere.

Malvern View Guest House, St Mary's Road (off Church Street), **t** 292 776 (*moderate*). Helpful proprietor and ideal location compensate for cramped quarters.

Two Back of Avon, Riverside Walk (off High Street), **t** 298 935 (*moderate*). Cheerful riverside house with flower baskets, looking out at mill and willow trees.

Carrant Brook House, Rope Walk, **t** 290 355 (*cheap*). Homely semi-detached red-brick house, short walk from abbey. Three bedrooms, supplied with chocolate biscuits and nice soft pillows.

Eating Out

My Great Grandfathers, 84–85 Church Street, **t** 292 687 (*cheap*). Stalwart English dishes including roast dinners, steak and ale pie, fisherman's pie, apple pie or treacle tart. *Closed Mon.*

Abbey Tea Rooms, **t** 292 215 (*cheap*). Small, friendly café opposite abbey with lace tablecloths, serves soup, ploughman's and breaded plaice.

Pickwicks Tea and Coffee House, Church Street, **t** 290 397 (*cheap*). Small café but no hot food. *Closed Sun.*

Berkeley Arms, Church Street, **t** 293 034 (*cheap*). Welcoming old-fashioned pub.

Rajshahi, 121 High Street, **t** 273 727 (*cheap*). Friendly Indian restaurant specializing in Balti dishes.

Tewkesbury Abbey Church

t (01684) 850 959; open daily 8–6; adm.

This was the church of the Benedictine abbey of Tewksbury, founded at the end of the 11th century by Robert Fitzhamon, one of William the Conqueror's knights, and sold to the town after the Reformation. The building is dominated by the huge Norman tower, the biggest in England, decorated with round arches and zigzags. Rising to the top of the west front is a 65ft-high round Norman arch with multiple recessed arches within it. At the east end, six chapels cluster around the ambulatory. Holding up the roof of the nave are Samsonian columns, 30ft high and 6ft wide. Above them, the 14th-century vaulting looks like an elaborate canopy. This is the burial place of Prince Edward, son of Henry VI, who died in 1471 at the Battle of Tewkesbury, and of countless medieval knights: Roberts, Guys and Hughs; Clares, Despensers and Beauchamps; the lords of the 'honour of Tewkesbury', whose effigies and chantry chapels give the place its pre-Reformation atmosphere. The 14th-century remodelling of the nave roof, choir and ambulatory was done by Eleanor de Clare, after her husband, Hugh le Despenser, a favourite of Edward II, was executed at Hereford. Her nephew Edward le Despenser built the fan-vaulted Holy Trinity chantry; he features on top of it in the painted, life-size 'kneeling knight' statue. Her granddaughter married Richard Beauchamp, Earl of Worcester; on his death she married his cousin, another Richard Beauchamp, this time Earl of Warwick. The Warwicks were one of the most powerful families in the country. Their daughter Anne married Richard Neville, 'the kingmaker', whose backing of Lancastrian and Yorkist kings by turns in the Wars of the Roses earned him the sobriquet. He didn't make it to the Battle of Tewksbury, as he was killed first at the Battle of Barnet. Among the victors at Tewkesbury were the king's brothers, Richard of Gloucester, who would later become Richard III and marry Anne, and George, Duke of Clarence, who is buried behind the high altar, having been drowned in a barrel of malmsey wine in the Tower (according to Shakespeare).

Deerhurst

A short drive south of Tewkesbury on the A38 you come to Deerhurst, a hamlet of several farms and two ancient churches. It is a lovely spot, surrounded by meadows, cows and footpaths. The priory church of St Mary here dates back to the 8th century. A farmhouse abuts the south aisle, incorporating part of the old cloisters. Around the back, in a dank recess, you can see the barely legible Saxon carving known as the **Deerhurst Angel**. The double-headed window at the west end and the small triangular windows are distinctive Saxon features.

About 50 yards beyond the priory, the lane ends at a gate, beyond which is the flood plain of the River Severn. Here is Odda's chapel, a small late Saxon chapel that was discovered in 1885, embedded in rambling farm buildings. Its original dedication stone was found in 1675, explaining that it was built by Odda, a kinsman of Edward the Confessor, in memory of his brother Elfric, who died in Deerhurst in 1058. A gated arch leads into the thick-walled, barn-like building, which has survived largely intact in its rustic setting: the nave and square-ended chancel behind a solid chancel arch.

West Midlands

Worcestershire, Warwickshire, Birmingham and Staffordshire

13

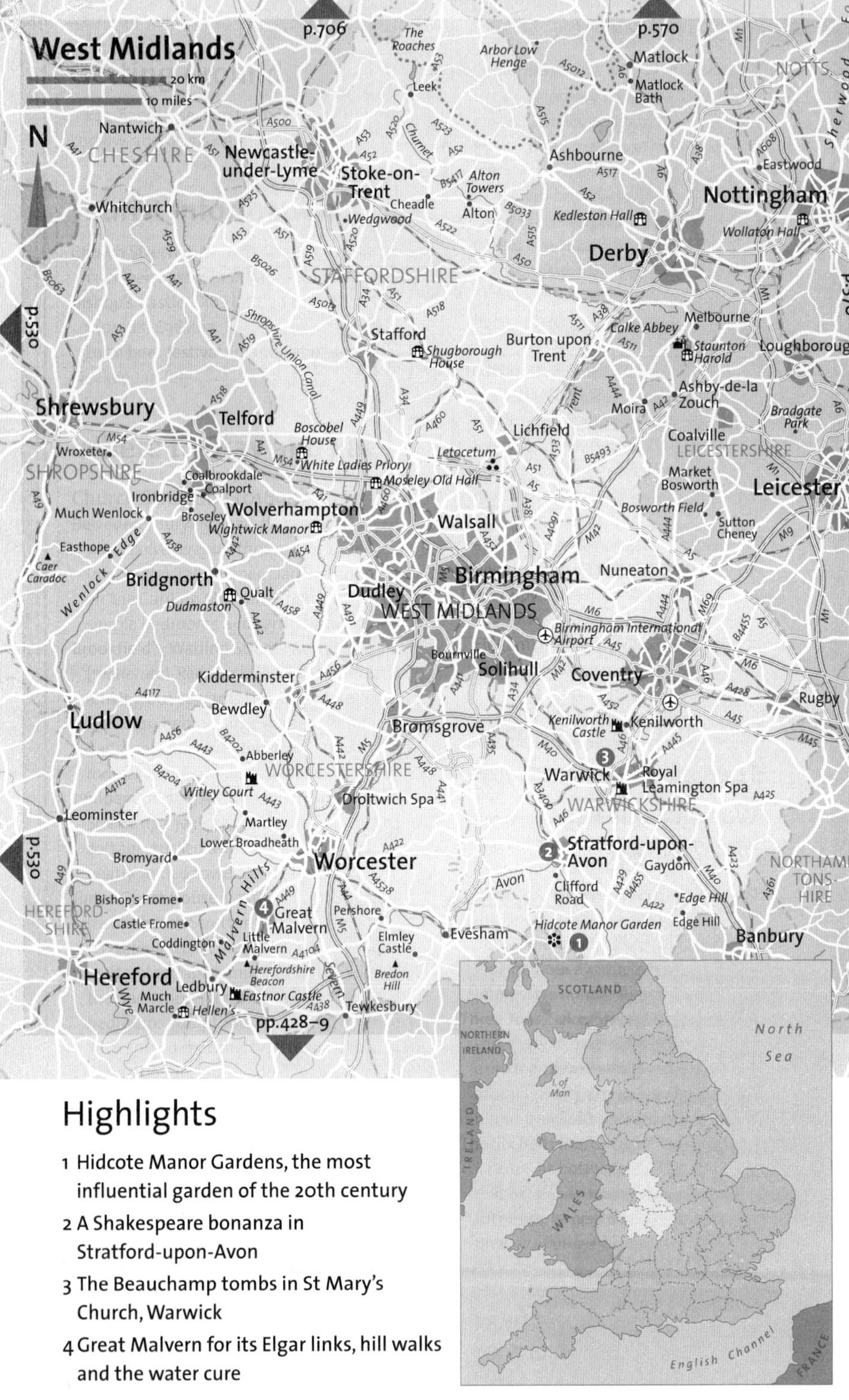

Highlights

1 Hidcote Manor Gardens, the most influential garden of the 20th century
2 A Shakespeare bonanza in Stratford-upon-Avon
3 The Beauchamp tombs in St Mary's Church, Warwick
4 Great Malvern for its Elgar links, hill walks and the water cure

Here is some of the best and the worst of England, threaded together along the M5, M6 and M40 motorways. Two of the most densely concentrated Victorian manufacturing centres in the world, in north and south Staffordshire, have turned into sprawling urban areas. The prosaically named West Midlands conurbation combines Birmingham and the Black Country, while the new city of Stoke-on-Trent features the six pottery towns of Stoke, Hanley, Burslem and, well, three more. But it is not all bad. England's second largest city, the metropolis of the west and home to the downwardly inflected Brummy accent, Birmingham dominates the West Midlands; its suburbs spread into neighbouring counties and dormitory villages. J.B. Priestley passed a 'City of Birmingham' sign on a rural approach road in 1933 and 'entertained a wild hope that this really was the City of Birmingham, and that the town had been pulled down and carted away.' Like most people, he didn't expect to like it, but these days you might warm to the lively old manufacturing town: more money is being spent on improving Birmingham than anywhere else in Britain. Old Brummy horrors like the elevated ring road are being knocked down and new attractions are springing up in their place – among others, two superb metropolitan art galleries, the New Gallery Walsall and the Barber Institute.

The south of the region is a contrast: you move into the stomping grounds of Shakespeare and Elgar, who have given their names to a brand of idealized English countryside. 'A country life I find absolutely essential to me,' wrote Elgar of the Malvern Hills and Worcestershire's River Severn, which flows from Celtic hills through the Marches to Worcester, the 'faithful city' of the Civil War and burial place of King John. Warwickshire never misses a chance to remind you that it is 'Shakespeare's county'. Stratford-upon-Avon, the Shakespearean castles of Warwick and Kenilworth and the countryside of meadows, woods and farmland, gently rolling into the Cotswolds and Vale of Evesham, all look the part.

Worcestershire

Whether the countryside makes the genius or however that may be, it is certain that no one was ever more imbued with the very spirit and essence of his own country than Elgar, it was in his very bones. Worcestershire was everything to him – the very look of spring coming, the cottages, the gardens, and fields and fruit orchards...

Carice Elgar Blake, daughter of the composer Edward Elgar

Worcestershire, the countryside of the River Severn and Malvern Hills, is Elgar country, the home of the greatest British composer since the 17th century. You can follow the Elgar Trail from the cottage where Edward Elgar was born, in Lower **Broadheath**, to the cathedral where 'I drew my first ideas of music', and the scruffy churchyard in **Little Malvern** where the family is buried. 'I am still at heart the dreamy child who used to be found in the reeds by the Severn side,' he said in 1921, aged 64.

The mighty **Severn** flows north to south through Worcestershire, gouging out a near-perfect wooded valley at **Bewdley** before reaching the county town of **Worcester** and the plain. West of the Severn, in the more intimate, hilly countryside of the River

Teme, where hop fields and orchards hug the valley slopes, are the sombre ruins of **Witley Court**, the Victorian palace of the Dudley family. (The Dudleys owned Black Country mines, and factories in the West Midlands conurbation, which extends into Worcestershire, Staffordshire and Warwickshire.) You may prefer to ignore the northern towns of Kidderminster, Bromsgrove, Redditch and Stourport-upon-Severn, sticking to the countryside of the south and west instead. In the southeast the River Avon meanders through the market gardens of the **Vale of Evesham**. Hill-lovers, for whom the checkerboard fields of the vale and plain are lacking, should climb **Bredon Hill** to see the glory of the lowlands. The **Malvern Hills** are the highlight of Worcestershire, a Precambrian upland of hill forts and views 9 miles long, visible from all around. They form a natural border between the Midlands plains and the Marches to the west. **Worcester**, the county town, would be an ideal base if its hotels were better. As it is you are best off basing yourself in **Great Malvern**, a Victorian spa town in the shadow of the Worcestershire Beacon, and nipping over the ridge to Ledbury for dinner.

Worcester

Worcester is a riverside county town, and there on the banks of the river is the cathedral. Despite some bad planning decisions in the last 40 years (replacing fine old chunks with shopping arcades) it remains a town of church spires, modest Georgian streets and one or two handsome thoroughfares. Once upon a time Worcester was an affluent town of creaking timber-framed buildings, tucked away from the turbulent Welsh borders behind the Malvern Hills and called 'the faithful city' for its loyalty to unpopular kings: King John, who is buried in the cathedral, and both Charleses in the Civil War (Charles II was bustled out of the north gate, narrowly evading capture by Cromwell's army after the Battle of Worcester in 1651). Georgian Worcester must have been quite something too, with gracious new streets of brick townhouses built on the back of booming porcelain- and glove-manufacturing industries, boosted by the arrival of the Worcester–Birmingham Canal in 1815. When William Cobbett rode into Worcester in September 1826 he found 'one of the cleanest, neatest, and handsomest towns I ever saw,' emphatically adding 'indeed I do not recollect to have seen any one equal to it'. Elgar, the city's most famous son, wrote of his 'undimmed affection' for the city where he learned his love of music. Worcester is now the hub of the Elgar Trail.

Worcester Cathedral

A bronze statue of composer Edward Elgar (1857–1934) stands at the end of the High Street, near the site of the old Elgar family music shop, across a noisy road from the cathedral. The luxuriant moustache, Cambridge gown and Order of Merit around his neck show the quintessential local boy done good. 'I drew my first ideas of music from the cathedral,' he once said. The young Elgar rushed to catch the organ playing out the evening services, and borrowed books from the music library.

William Cobbett called the cathedral 'a poor thing, compared with any of the others'. It has two saints, St Oswald and St Wulfstan, both former bishops. Oswald

Getting There and Around

Worcester is just off the M5 from the south or Birmingham by **car**.

There are direct **train** connections from London and Birmingham to Foregate Station. For all train information contact **National Rail Enquiries**, **t** 08457 484950, *www.thetrainline.com*.

Coaches either drop you off at the Warndon Coach Stop on the motorway, from where you can catch a local bus into the city centre, or take you to the central Crowgate Bus Station. For coach information call **National Express**, **t** 08705 808080 (within the UK) or (+44) 121 625 1122 (from abroad), *www.gobycoach.com*.

River trips lasting 45 minutes depart from South Quay, behind the cathedral, in summer.

Tourist Information

Worcester: The Guildhall, High Street, **t** (01905) 726 311. *Open Mon–Sat 9.30–5.*

Festivals

The **Three Choirs Festival** of music is held in Worcester every three years, in rotation with Gloucester and Hereford (Worcester's next turn is 2005). The cathedral is the main venue, but the programme may include barber-shop, brass and jazz as well as the festival chorus and orchestra. Contact the tourist information centre or go to *www.3choirs.org* for details.

Where to Stay

Worcester t (01905) –

Diglis House Hotel, Severn Street, **t** 353 518, *www.diglishousehotel.co.uk* (*expensive*). This much-extended Georgian townhouse, in a lovely, quiet spot on the banks of the river, is the best place to stay in Worcester. It's a short walk from the cathedral and Royal Worcester Porcelain Factory and Museum, with restaurant and bar.

Ye Olde Talbot Hotel, Friar Street, **t** 23573 (*expensive*). Tired-looking but comfortable place to stay over beamy old pub in the social hub of town.

The Fownes Hotel, City Walls Road, **t** 613 151, *www.fownes-hotel.activehotels.com* (*expensive*). Former Victorian glove factory with clock on pediment and 61 bedrooms, cocktail bar and restaurant. Drab décor on busy road, but only two minutes' walk from cathedral.

The Giffard Hotel, High Street, **t** 0870 400 8133, *www.macdonaldhotels.co.uk* (*moderate*). Ugly modern block facing the cathedral, with 102 bedrooms and a first-floor restaurant.

Burgage House, 4 College Precinct, **t** 25396 (*moderate*). Pretty Georgian townhouse overlooking the cathedral with patchwork quilts and floral-patterned curtains.

The White House, 8 Green Hill, off Bath Road, **t** 356 970, *bandb@trade-events.co.uk*

founded the Saxon cathedral under King Edgar, and brought in the monks; Wulfstan, one of the monks, became bishop in 1062 held on to his job after the Norman Conquest by rebuilding Oswald's cathedral in the grand Norman style. The money generated at the shrines of the two former bishops was spent rebuilding Wulfstan's cathedral bit by bit. The **west front** of the cathedral drops straight down to the river, a sight to see from the opposite bank. Have a look around the back before you go in, through the medieval gateway of **Edgar's Tower**, into the old monastic precincts. Here, standing on College Green in front of the Norman doorway, is where the old Benedictine monastery comes to life. The door leads to the old refectory, watergate and ferry crossing, and the ruins of the **Guesten Hall** – a guesthouse built by the monks in 1320. Another deeply recessed Norman doorway takes you into the **cloisters** and **chapter house**, the first in England to be built with a single central pillar supporting a vaulted roof, like the spokes of an umbrella. Inside, the cathedral is a sumptuous Gothic space with thin columns climbing up the walls of the **nave** and arching over the top like creepers. The exuberance is largely thanks to Victorian restorers, who painted the roof, installed stained glass and black-and-white paving on (*moderate*). You can be sure of a warm welcome at this delightful white-painted Georgian house in quiet private gardens; 5 minutes' walk from cathedral, riverside and restaurants.

Osborne House, 17 Chestnut Walk, **t** 22296, *www.osborne-house.freeserve.co.uk* (*moderate*). Attractive, friendly house with four modest bedrooms, not all en-suite; 15 minutes' walk from cathedral.

Eating Out

King Charles II Restaurant, 29 New Street, **t** 22449 (*moderate*). Large oak-panelled timber-framed townhouse at Cornmarket end of New Street. Charles II escaped through its back door after the Battle of Worcester in 1651. The menu is divided into 'Chicken and Duckling', 'Veal, Liver and Kidney', 'Beef', 'Pasta' and 'Sea'. *Closed Sun.*

The Glass House, Church Street, **t** 611 120 (*moderate*). Swish modern restaurant on two storeys with a cellar bar, decked out with stained-glass windows and art. Food might include wok-fried seafood and noodles or pan-roast monkfish on olive-oil mash. *Closed Mon.*

Saffron's Bistro, 15 New Street, **t** 610 505 (*moderate*). Bare polished floorboards and rugs, sturdy pine kitchen furniture and Mediterranean yellow walls. Serves Thai green curry, lamb and Mediterranean vegetable kebabs, or tiger prawns.

Browns, 24 Quay Street, **t** 26263 (*moderate*). Traditional French/English restaurant in stylishly converted old grain warehouse beside the Severn. Serves grilled sardines followed by roast guinea fowl, fresh fish, or calf's liver and mash, all with plenty of vegetables and delicious bread. *Open Wed–Fri and Sun lunch, Tues–Sat also dinner.*

Drucker's Vienna Patisserie, Chapel Walk, Crown Gate, **t** 616 870 (*cheap*). Cheerful chain café overlooking Huntingdon's Hall.

Alternatively, for a coffee try the cafés in the museum and gallery, cathedral and Royal Worcester Porcelain Factory and Museum.

King's Head, 67 Sidbury, **t** 731 243 (*cheap*). Good, clean family pub next door to the Commandery where you can get light lunch.

Puccini's Pizza-Pasta, 12 Friar Street, **t** 27770 (*cheap*). Opposite Greyfriars, stylish and informal with one or two pavement tables, good toppings and freshly cooked pasta sauces. *Open Wed–Sun.*

Entertainment

Huntingdon's Hall, Crown Gate, **t** 611 427. Beautiful Georgian Methodist chapel, now a venue for concerts – classical, jazz, acoustic rock, folk and blues.

the floor, and completely overhauled the early English choir. The **monuments** are the real highlights. **King John's tomb** is here, in front of the high altar, although he died in Newark-upon-Trent on the other side of the Midlands. In 1218 his carved Purbeck marble effigy was placed on a plain stone tomb, rebuilt grandly in 1529. It is the oldest royal effigy in England. On the south side of the altar is the **chantry chapel of Prince Arthur**, the elder son of Henry VII. Arthur's death in Ludlow in 1502 aged 16 (possibly from plague), shortly after wedding Catherine of Aragon, led to the reassignment of Catherine to his younger brother, the future Henry VIII. The prince's tomb is in a richly glorified stone cage up worn stone steps. The **Duke of Hamilton**, Royalist commander in the 1651 Battle of Worcester, who died of wounds shortly after, is in front of the altar. The early 17th-century effigies of the **Wyldes**, who lived in the Commandery for two centuries, are in the south nave. The Norman **crypt** is the oldest part of the cathedral, built in 1084 by Wulfstan. The largest of its era in England, it is a forest of short, squat columns.

Around Town

After the cathedral, pop into the Royal Worcester Porcelain Factory and Museum, take a walk or boat trip along the river, and a stroll around the town. On **Foregate Street**, which leads from the cathedral into town, you find impressive public buildings including the old **Victoria Institute**. Now the museum and a gallery hosting temporary exhibitions, it is a proud-looking building with mosaic tiles and arched windows. In narrow, tree-shaded **High Street** is the **Guildhall**, a Queen Anne building of brick and stone. The painted statues of Charles I, Charles II and Queen Anne around its doorway were an affirmation of the city's royalist position in the Civil War, which had taken place sixty years earlier; Cromwell appears above the fanlight nailed up by the ears. You can get a roast dinner with gravy in the old **Assembly Room** upstairs. Walkways lead off the High Street into the modern Crowngate shopping precinct, where 'heritage' plaques on the modern shopfronts taunt you with the historical gems knocked down in the 1960s. Only the early 18th-century Nonconformist chapel known as the **Countess of Huntingdon's Hall** was spared. It hosts lunchtime concerts.

Worcester's social hub of pubs and restaurants is Friar Street, a medieval thoroughfare of black-and-white timber-framed buildings. Down the road is a Tudor house, once the home and workshop of a weaver, a barber and a dentist. Further down, you pass the double doorway of **Greyfriars** *(www.nationaltrust.org.uk; open Mar–Oct Wed–Fri 2–5, Sat 1–5; adm)*, Worcester's best medieval house, leads into a cobbled courtyard of oak-panelled rooms hung with tapestries and antiques. It was built in 1480 for a wealthy brewer, but took its name from the Franciscan monastery that stood next door until its suppression in the 16th century.

A short walk down busy College Road from the cathedral, the **Commandery Civil War Centre** (*open Mon–Sat 10–5, Sun 10.30–5; adm*) extends along the canal. The Commandery was used as Royalist headquarters in the 1651 Battle of Worcester. The Civil War Centre traces the battle, with displays of wide-brimmed Civil War hats.

From the cathedral, Severn Street leads down to the red-brick buildings of the **Royal Worcester Porcelain Factory and Museum** (*open Mon–Sat 9–5.30, Sun 11–5; adm*), based here since 1840. Businessman Dr. John Wall founded the company in 1751, having perfected a secret recipe for soft-paste porcelain (*see* p.525). It got a royal warrant from George III in 1788. Now you can take factory tours, visit the museum displaying 250 years of Worcester ware, and shop at the discount porcelain shops.

Along the Rivers Severn and Teme

The A443 north of Worcester in the direction of Tenbury Wells follows the rolling red-earth countryside of the Teme Valley, passing hop fields and greenhouses as the road twists and climbs. You could spend an hour at Witley Court and stop off for a drink at the Mason Arms in the hill village of **Abberley**, a few miles further north. Either loop back along the B4197 ridge road with its magnificent views towards Martley, dropping down to the Elgar Birthplace Museum in Lower Broadheath, or pick your way along the country lanes to the Severnside town of Bewdley.

The Elgar Trail

Edward Elgar was born on 2 June 1857 in a pretty brick cottage, now the **Elgar Birthplace Museum** (*open Feb–Nov 11–5; adm*), at Lower Broadheath, above the Severn Valley 3 miles northwest of Worcester. This was the first of twenty houses that Elgar lived in, but he never moved far from the Severn. 'A country life I find absolutely essential to me,' he wrote in 1930. Elgar is known as the national composer, and considered the most important British composer since Purcell and Handel. He produced choral works, orchestral works, concertos, chamber music and songs to suit every occasion, most famously the first of his *Pomp and Circumstance* marches, which, to the words of 'Land of Hope and Glory', plays out the quintessentially English Last Night of the Proms to encores and ovations ('a tune that comes once in a lifetime'). Here you see the man behind the music, fond of cycling and golf – some of his best tunes came to him on the golf course – and foreign travel. His old writing desk is set out as he liked it: inkpots, cigarette case, family photos and score paper. Like Dickens, he maintained a strict routine of work in the mornings and exercise in the afternoons, heading back to his desk before dinner. Next door is the modern **Elgar Centre**, which exhibits Elgar memorabilia relating to his life as a composer – press cuttings, concert programmes and photos – including manuscripts of *Salut D'Amour*, with its dedication to 'a Carice' upon his engagement (Carice is a combination of the first two names of his wife Caroline Alice Roberts) and *Froissart*, his first concert overture, performed in Worcester Cathedral in 1890. Elgar requested that his birthplace cottage be his memorial.

Elgar used to pedal around the lanes on an old Sunbeam bicycle which he called Mr Phoebus, breathing in the music that filled the fresh Malvern air for him – 'you simply take as much as you require'. The Elgar Trail takes you to a handful of his houses: **Birchwood Lodge**, a rented summer cottage in Storridge which overlooks half the world, and **Craeg Lea** in Great Malvern where he composed *The Dream of Gerontius*. The views were of absolute importance to him. Each move to a bigger house was associated with a fresh success, musical (Craeg Lea on the back of the *Enigma Variations*) or honorary (knighthood in 1904 and Order of Merit in 1921).

Witley Court

***t** (01299) 896 636, www.english-heritage.org.uk; open April–Sept daily 10–6, Oct daily 10–5, Nov–Mar daily 10–4; adm.*

The ruins of Witley Court, clearly signposted off the A443 a mile out of Great Witley, are a monument to a lost era; the Victorian palace of the earls of Dudley was a prodigy house of the industrial age. The 1st Earl Dudley was a millionaire industrialist, one of the richest men in Britain, the owner of Black Country coal mines and ironworks. He commissioned architect Samuel Daukes to transform the neo-classical home of the Foleys into an Italianate palace, surrounded by William Nesfield formal gardens. The John Nash porticoes were left as they stood, while a crescent-shaped wing was added, ending in a conservatory. The whole building and the 18th-century baroque church were clad in creamy Bath stone, and the rooms were filled with French and Italian furnishings. At extravagant hunting weekends with royal guests

The Severn Valley Line

'The men that live in West England,' wrote Hilaire Belloc, 'They see the Severn strong,/A-rolling on rough water brown Light aspen leaves along.' This is modest praise for the once-great English river, the main artery of the industrial West Midlands and busier in its day than the Thames. The old steam trains of the Severn Valley Line (*t (01299) 403 816; train connections at Kidderminster to Birmingham, Stratford-upon-Avon, Worcester, Leamington Spa and Malvern; car parking at both Bridgnorth and Kidderminster stations*) run between Bridgnorth and Kidderminster with stops at Bewdley and the charming riverside village of Arley.

the Perseus and Andromeda fountain played twice a week, sending a jet of water 100 feet into the air. But a fire gutted the house in 1937, and now the view of the south front from the fountain is the best: the Ionic portico, the sweeping southwest wing extending to the skeletal remains of the conservatory, the stone temples on the edge of the lawns, and beyond them fields.

The Italian baroque interior of the **parish church of Great Witley**, by James Gibbs, is sensational, with ceiling paintings of the *Resurrection* by Antonio Bellucci (1654–1726), taken from the demolished chapel of the Duke of Chandos in Edgware, and gilded relief decoration in *papier mâché* all over the walls. In the south transept is the towering Rysbrack memorial to the 1st Lord Foley, the patron of the church. It is one of the most splendid baroque monuments in the country.

Bewdley

Between Shrewsbury and Bewdley, the Severn is the model of a perfect river, flowing between steep wooded banks. The declining Georgian riverside town of Bewdley drops picturesquely down to the stone Telford Bridge. Handsome red-brick townhouses are set back from the water on either side. Bewdley was a major inland port until the new town of Stourport-on-Severn was chosen as the terminus for the Staffordshire and Worcestershire Canal. From then on, the industrial trade from the Potteries and Black Country towns bypassed Bewdley. The old riverside town slipped even further with the arrival of the railway. For all its pre-industrial charm, there's little to keep you here. From the river, Load Street leads up to the guildhall; behind it is the old shambles, which now houses a **museum** (*open April–Sept 11–4.30*) where craftspeople – including a woodcarver and stained-glass maker – work away in the old arcades. Stop at Dinglespout, next to the old George Hotel, to enjoy the décor over coffee, cakes or meat and two veg followed by syrup sponge pudding: at the front are William Morris wallpaper, hanging lamps, polished wooden tables, bookshelves, and comfortable old leather armchairs.

Stretching 4 miles northwest of Bewdley is the **Wyre Forest**, formerly the hunting chase of the Mortimers of Wigmore. There are four waymarked walks through broadleaf and conifer woods from the Wyre Forest Visitor Centre (***t** (01299) 266 302*) on the A456, 3 miles west of Bewdley.

Droitwich Spa

Towards the end of the 19th century, John Corbett (1817–1901), the salt king, developed Droitwich as a spa resort. The black-and-white Victorian spa buildings include the magnificent derelict **Worcestershire Brine Baths Hotel**. The modern **Brine Baths** (*t (01905) 794 894; open Mon–Fri 11.30–7, weekends close earlier; adm exp; booking essential*) stand on the site of Corbett's baths, built in 1888. The natural brine has 2.5lbs of salt in every gallon; you can float easily in the warm healing water.

Great Malvern

Great Malvern is the largest of the spring-water settlements along the lower east side of the Malverns, an old spa town of large Victorian villas and public gardens at the heart of Worcestershire and Herefordshire walking country. Behind the town is the hump of the Worcestershire Beacon, the highest point of the Malverns.

Malvern emerged as a spa resort in the middle of the 18th century, boosted by the analysis of the local spring water by the local doctor John Wall, founder of Worcester Porcelain. 'The Malvern water, says Dr John Wall, is famed for containing nothing at all,' went the jingle. The absence of minerals in the Malvern spa water meant that it was ideally suited to the newfangled hydropathy or water-cure treatments coming out of Germany in the early 19th century. Eminent Victorians Charles Darwin, Florence Nightingale and Charles Dickens took the cure here. Abstinence was the word once you checked into one of the hydropathy hotels: Gräfenberg (after the Czech original) and, grimly functional, the Establishment. They were run by doctors James Gully and James Wilson, water treatment pioneers, one with huge whiskers, the other bald. They set up a detox regime of early mornings, water treatments, fresh air, boiled meat and early to bed – modern health farm meets pre-war boarding school. Sex was frowned upon, especially by Dr Gully, who ran two separate hotels, one for men and another for women, linked by a footbridge known as the Bridge of Sighs. This was the cure, as much for profligate metropolitan lifestyles as any ailment. If all went well you reached the 'crisis' or turning-point and broke out in spots and diarrhoea. 'But the large boil, the boil was the thing,' wrote one of Wilson's patients. 'The patients took quite an artistic delight in beholding one.'

The composer Elgar lived in Malvern for 13 years, and was buried in Little Malvern.

Around Town

The main Wells–Worcester road runs along the wooded base of the hills with grandstand views over the plain, and Church Street runs steeply downhill at a right angle towards the river, 4 miles away. The priory church, its magnificent tower struggling to impose itself against the awesome backdrop of the Malvern Hills, and Malvern Museum are at the top of town. The **Foley Hotel**, named after the main landowners of Witley Court, was one of the earliest resort buildings, built in 1810. The plain Doric columns fronting the street belonged to the old **Coburg Baths**, built four years later. Wilson and Gully came to Malvern in 1842, setting up together in the **Crown Hotel** on

Getting There

The M5 passes close by from Birmingham and the south; take the Worcester turn-off.

There are direct **trains** from Birmingham and London Paddington.

Tourist Information

Great Malvern: 21 Church Street, **t** (01684) 892 289. *Open daily 10–5.*

There is something on most weekends at the **Three Counties Show Ground**, 3 miles southeast of Great Malvern in the direction of Upton, at the junction of the B4208 and B4209. Events include dog, horse and motor shows, and antique fairs. **Three Counties Agricultural Society**, **t** (01684) 584 900.

Where to Stay

Great Malvern **t** (01684) –

The Foley Arms Hotel, Worcester Road, **t** 573 397, *www.foleyarmshotel.com* (*expensive*). Delightful white-painted Georgian hotel at top of town with elaborate cast-iron balcony carrying the coat of arms; 28 attractive bedrooms, many with views of Severn Valley.

The Abbey Hotel, Abbey Road, **t** 892 332, *www.sarova.com* (*expensive*). A civilized Victorian-Gothic hotel with 106 bedrooms next to the priory gatehouse and church.

The Great Malvern Hotel, Graham Road, **t** 563 411, *www.great-malvern-hotel.co.uk* (*expensive*). Old-fashioned Victorian hotel with relaxed atmosphere; 14 bedrooms, bar food and restaurant.

Mount Pleasant Hotel, Belle Vue Terrace, **t** 561 837, *www.mountpleasanthotel.co.uk* (*expensive*). A wisteria-clad Georgian hotel in one of the top spots in town, at the foot of the 99 steps to the Worcestershire Beacon; décor in need of a revamp, but nonetheless winning charm, clean and informal. Room One overlooks the Malvern Hills and vale.

The Red Gate, 32 Avenue Road, **t** 565 013 (*expensive*). Red-brick house set back from quiet tree-lined avenue to the station, with six pine, lace and patchwork bedrooms; a few minutes' walk from town centre.

St Just, Worcester Road, **t** 562 023 (*expensive*). Attractive house opposite common, with balcony on two fluted columns over front door, and elegant breakfast room.

Bredon House Hotel, 34 Worcester Road, **t** 566 990, *www.bredonhousehotel.co.uk* (*expensive*). Special place to stay with friendly hosts and grandstand views over Severn Valley; bedrooms simply and elegantly furnished.

Wyche Keep, 22 Wyche Road, **t** 567 018, *www.jks.org/wychekeep* (*expensive*). Pebble-dashed mock castle on hillside up narrow drive off Ledbury road; dinner available.

The Pembridge Hotel, 114 Graham Road, **t** 574 813 (*moderate*). Squarely built Victorian townhouse with eight large bedrooms.

Sidney House, 40 Worcester Road, **t** 574 994 (*moderate*). Gorgeous white house on cliff top enjoying fantastic views; extremely hospitable, with tasteful pine furniture, delicious breakfasts and local information.

Eating Out

The White Season, 27 Church Street, **t** 575 954 (*moderate*). Malvern's best restaurant. A friendly husband and wife team serve up a mainly seafood menu and elaborate puddings. Lunches might include risotto, fishcakes and grilled fish. *Open Wed–Sat.*

Anupam, 85 Church Street, **t** 573 814 (*moderate*). Well-regarded Indian restaurant.

Red Lion Inn, St Anne's Road, **t** 564 787 (*cheap*). Ideal for walkers' refreshment.

St Anne's Well Café (up St Anne's Road), **t** 560 285 (*cheap*). Cosy, woody, vegan café. Green herb salads, home-made soups and herbal teas. *Winter open weekends only.*

The Vineyard Bar and Restaurant, Malvern Theatres, Grange Road, **t** 567 751 (*cheap*). A big, bright place for coffee or glass of wine.

The Malvern Hills Hotel, Wynds Point, **t** 540 690 (*cheap*). Join the crowds at pub tables after climbing British Camp Hill.

Entertainment

Malvern Theatres, Grange Road, **t** 892 277. Airy modern complex on the site of the old winter gardens, with a lively programme of drama, opera, dance, concerts and comedy.

Belle Vue Terrace and renaming it **Gräfenberg**. Three years later Dr Gully bought **Holyrood House** on Wells Road and built **Tudor House** next door in the same Gothic style: men in Tudor House, women in Holyrood. Next door is the old Warwick House department store, for years a Malvern institution. Steps lead down to Abbey Road and the green-painted **Establishment** – the purpose-built hydropathic palace of Dr Wilson. The **Festival Theatre** complex opens its doors onto the old Victorian **winter gardens**.

Malvern Museum

***t** (01684) 567 811; open Easter–Oct 10.30–5; adm minimal.*

Housed in the mighty 15th-century gatehouse of the old Benedictine monastery, this smashing little museum has only a handful of tiny rooms. Each one tells an aspect of the Malvern story, from its geology through monastic times to the Victorian heyday and beyond. You can find out about water treatments such as the 'douche' – gallons of water dumped on you from a height –and the 'sitz bath' – sitting in cold water to sort out abdominal problems.

Priory Church

The old Benedictine priory church, now the parish church, stands next to the stone gatehouse. The exterior is decorated with the airiness of the Perpendicular style: big windows, ornamental battlements and finials on the tower and roof, in colourful stone. Inside the nave, it is surprising to find the stubby columns of the old Norman church. The late 15th-century **stained glass** is ranked with the best in England, and the church is packed with museum pieces. The **miserichords** are worth a good look, carved with the *Labours of the Months*: weeding in April, haymaking in June, bringing home the fruit harvest in September and so on. Worn medieval floor and wall tiles, rescued by Victorian restorers, are on display. Next to the altar is the alabaster **Knotsford Tomb** with the effigy of John Knotsford, responsible for the demolition of the monastery buildings after the Dissolution.

St Anne's Well

Open weekends 10–5 or dusk if earlier, Easter–Sept also Mon–Fri 10–5; adm.

It's three-quarters of a mile from Belle Vue Terrace to St Anne's Well. The hillside is dotted with Victorian villas with little terraced gardens and views over Malvern. Follow the zigzag path to the octagonal Victorian pump room (now a café), where you can help yourself to the spring water from the overflowing fountain. Gully and Wilson sent their patients to the well daily before breakfast. You can carry on up to the top of the Worcestershire Beacon, the highest point of the Malverns.

The Malvern Hills

The long angular range of the Malvern Hills rises abruptly out of the Worcestershire plain, sloping down on the other side to the wooded hills of Herefordshire. Nine miles long, a mile wide and 1,400ft at its highest point, it is an island of Precambrian otherness in the English lowlands.

Base yourself in Great Malvern, or Ledbury on the Herefordshire side. Steep pass roads between the hills enable you to conquer the peaks on foot from car parks halfway up. You can walk along the whole ridge, or parts (the tourist information centre in Great Malvern has walks leaflets). **Worcestershire Beacon** to the **British Camp** is an interesting section. The views all along are superb: pick out landmarks such as the Wrekin to the north and Bredon Hill in the Vale of Evesham to the east.

To get a feel for the hills, take the Wyche road south from Great Malvern through the cutting onto Jubilee Drive (a scenic road constructed to mark Queen Victoria's 1887 Jubilee), stopping at the British Camp car park midway along the range; have a drink at the Malvern Hills Hotel and climb the **Herefordshire Beacon** (known as British Camp on account of the Celtic hill fort on top). To north and south you can see the ridge walk lunging up and down from peak to peak, should you feel tempted.

Back in the car, continue along the main pass road (A449) to **Little Malvern** and loop back to Great Malvern, stopping at the **Elgar graves** (signposted) at St Wulfstan's Roman Catholic church in Little Malvern. It's a gloomy church next to a gloomier Victorian vicarage. Elgar is buried with his wife and daughter at the edge of the graveyard. Sadly a stand of conifers blocks the view for which he loved the spot.

The Vale of Evesham

The Vale of Evesham, sandwiched between the Cotswolds and the Severn plain, is one of England's main fruit-and-vegetable-growing regions. The River Avon meanders through it from Stratford-upon-Avon to Tewkesbury, with its lovely abbey (*see* p.478). The vale is most lovely viewed from the Cotswolds or Bredon Hill, spread out before you like a dream of old rural England – especially after a drink in the pub at Elmley Castle. In spring, the effusion of pink and cream blossom brings brilliance to the orchards; you can follow a **Spring Blossom Trail** (by car or bicycle). In other seasons, you can buy seasonal local produce (asparagus, strawberries, plums, apples and pears) from farm shops by the roadside. The agricultural market towns of Evesham and Pershore are quietly interesting.

Evesham and the Abbey

Evesham is the pilgrimage site of **Simon de Montfort**, 'pioneer of representative government'. A handsome group of church buildings overlooks the Avon as it loops around the town, although the abbey church has long gone. Its outline has been marked out in Abbey Park, and here a modern memorial stone shows the position of the tomb of Simon de Montfort (1208–65). His death in the 1265 Battle of Evesham, trapped in the bend of the Avon by the royalist army under Prince Edward (future Edward I), turned him into a political martyr and his tomb became a destination for pilgrims. One of the monks of Evesham Abbey – an eyewitness to the battle – recorded how de Montfort died: he was hacked through the neck by Sir Roger de Mortimer, a baron of the Welsh Marches, then his head, hands, feet and genitals were cut off. The rest of his army was killed as it fled over bridge and across field, or seeking sanctuary in the abbey church. Prior to his martyrdom, de Montfort was leader of the most fundamental attempt to redistribute power within England before the 17th century, attempting to remove arbitrary power from the king and give it to parliament. His statue still stands outside the Houses of Parliament in London. A year before his death, he defeated royalists at the Battle of Lewes in Sussex and took King Henry III and Prince Edward prisoner. It was Edward's escape at Hereford in May that led to renewed fighting at Evesham, and ended that civil war.

Before the Reformation, the abbey encompassed two parish churches, **All Saints** and **St Lawrence**, as well as the detached **bell-tower** of 1513, a towering Perpendicular Gothic structure with magnificent pealing bells. Today the churches form an imposing ensemble, through which gateways lead into the old market square and Vine Street. Here stands the pre-Reformation almonry, a stone cottage behind a tiny herb garden. It used to be the home of the abbey almoner, who distributed relief (alms) to the town's needy. Now it houses a museum, where you can see models of the abbey and battlefield, before ambling along the riverside between Workman Bridge and Abbey Park.

Pershore

Coming into Pershore from Evesham the A44 turns straight into the lovely Georgian High Street, which runs parallel to the Avon; many of the houses have jetties in their back gardens. Broad Street leads off to the old **abbey church**. Minus the nave (which was demolished at the Reformation), it stands in the middle of a green, thrusting up a decorated tower supported by flying buttresses. In the early Gothic chancel clusters of slender shafts shoot up the arcading from floor to vaulted roof.

Have a drink in the riverside garden of the Star Inn on the High Street, or head to the picnic site by the old Pershore Bridge, off the A44 on the southern edge of town.

Bredon Hill

Bredon Hill (*OS Explorer 190, Malvern Hills and Bredon Hill, 1:25000*) rises out of the checked floor of the vale, round, green and begging to be climbed, although it does not even hit 1,000ft. It is a benign presence in the vale (A.E. Housman wrote a love poem entitled 'Bredon Hill'), 12 square miles, with dramatic edges to match those of

Tourist Information

Evesham: The Almonry, Abbey Gate, **t** (01386) 446 944. *Open summer Mon–Sat 10–5, Sun 2–5; winter Mon–Sat only.*

Where to Stay and Eat

Evesham t (01386) –

Northwick Hotel, Waterside, **t** 40322 (*expensive*). Some of the best accommodation in Evesham, set back from busy road with a large courtyard. Falcans Bar, on one side, does decent food.

Ye Olde Red Horse, Vine Street (opposite The Almonry), **t** 442 784 (*cheap*). Has a bizarre mock-medieval courtyard with goldfish pond in middle, plus several bar rooms.

Lantern Eating House, 62 Bridge Street, **t** 47726 (*cheap*). Cheerful restaurant for battered fish. *Open Mon 10–3, Tues–Fri 10.30–6, Sat 11–8, Sun 12–4.*

the Cotswolds. Ascend from any one of the villages around its base. Elmley Castle is a good one, with its pretty black-and-white cottages and old-fashioned pub. The summit is marked by a stone tower and the remains of a Celtic hill fort.

Warwickshire

But a great thought keeps you company as you go and gives character to the scenery. Warwickshire – you say it over and over – was Shakespeare country.

Henry James, 1870s

Warwickshire is a small diamond-shaped county in the middle of England and Wales. This is '**Shakespeare Country**' and the Bard is the reason most visitors come here. The classic English farming countryside helps to illuminate what a boy like Shakespeare was doing in a place like this. 'There is something as deeply attuned to human needs in the Warwickshire pastures as there is in the underlying morality of the poet,' wrote Henry James, who speculated that Shakespeare's genius fed off the rich countryside like a golden ear of wheat or a fat, healthy cow. James was on his way to **Warwick Castle**, one of two great medieval castles on the young Shakespeare's doorstep. The other one is **Kenilworth Castle**, which enjoyed its heyday back in the 1500s. Shakespeare was 11 years old during Queen Elizabeth I's celebrated two-week stay at Kenilworth with Robert Dudley, the darling of her court, who took her hunting every day in the Forest of Arden. **Stratford-upon-Avon**, birthplace and later home of Shakespeare, is of course the heart of the Shakespeare myth (and commercialization of his image). A hundred years before the playwright was born, Warwickshire was embroiled in the Wars of the Roses. Coventry was the Lancastrian headquarters of Henry VI and his queen, Margaret, while Richard Neville, known as the kingmaker for his endorsement of both the Yorkist and Lancastrian kings at different times, operated out of Warwick Castle. Two major battles took place nearby, at Tewkesbury and Mortimer's Cross – heady stuff on the doorstep of the playwright of *Henry VI* (which begins with Warwick: 'I wonder how the king escaped our hands') and *Richard III*.

Coventry might have been on the tourist map too had it not been bombed to smithereens by German air raids in the Second World War. Northern Warwickshire is now the sprawling dormitory hinterland of Coventry and Birmingham, where the attractive towns of **Warwick** and **Royal Leamington Spa** are joined by dreary ribbon development along A-roads.

Coventry

Coventry is a vision not of a dream city, but of a practical accomplishment and operational usefulness, catering for the needs of a rising democratic and progressive nation.

The Mayor's *Foreword* in Coventry's post-war planning document

The phoenix is the symbol of post-war Coventry, which rose from the ashes of a single night of bombing – 14 November 1940 – that reduced the city to rubble, including the cathedral. Coventry was the only British city to lose its cathedral, in spite of the best efforts of the Luftwaffe. The decision to build a new one in its place was taken the very next morning. The architect commissioned was Basil Spence, whose controversial modernist-Gothic structure of reinforced concrete and steel reflected the 1950s manufacturing city of motor cars and electrical gadgets rather than historic Coventry, compared by Hawthorne to the old timber-framed towns of Stratford, Warwick and Chester. Post-war, the phoenix was incorporated into the city's coat of arms and Coventry became a symbol of reconstruction (it is twinned with Dresden and Sarajevo). The old Coventry legend of Lady Godiva found new meaning too. According to the 13th-century chronicler Roger of Wendover in his *Flores Historiarum*, Godiva rode naked through the town at noon in 1049, her modesty concealed only by her long hair, to persuade her stubborn husband, Leofric, Earl of Mercia, to relax his taxes on the people of Coventry. Her bronze statue, unveiled in 1949, conveys her self-sacrifice and humanity. However it's hard not to feel sad in Coventry. Priestley, visiting in 1933, called it 'genuinely picturesque', but now you just feel the shame of boring flat roofs, ugly 1960s buildings and the lethal ring road. English Heritage has listed the 1950s two-storey shopping precinct – the prototype for precincts all around the country – but it doesn't compensate for the loss. Head for the Cathedral Quarter, incorporating three cathedrals: the inspired modern cathedral standing next to the bombed-out shell of old St Michael's, and the site of the pre-Reformation cathedral of St Mary, founded by Leofric and Godiva. Coventry is not a dream city, but the millennium Phoenix Initiative may enliven it with public squares and Italian-style cafes. Operationally useful? A practical accomplishment? How about just pleasant?

Coventry Cathedral

Sir Basil Spence's modern cathedral of steel and reinforced concrete is fused by a canopied forecourt to the Perpendicular ruins of the old one. The impression here is of a prosperous old town, post-war precincts screened behind a knot of narrow cobbled lanes and red Coventry sandstone buildings. The medieval spire of the bombed-out cathedral of St Michael rises to 300ft (surpassed in height only by Salisbury and Norwich); somehow it survived 11 hours of bombing by 500 tons of explosive and

Getting There and Around

Coventry is right in the middle of the country, in between the M40 and M6.

National Express **coaches** run from major cities to Pool Meadow Bus Station.

There are direct inter-city **train** services to Coventry station from London Euston, and lots of connections via Birmingham.

Tourist Information

Coventry: Bayley Lane, **t** (02476) 227 264. *Open Mon–Fri 9.30–4.30, weekends 10–4.30.*

Where to Stay and Eat

Coventry t (02746) –

You most probably won't choose to stay in Coventry, but there's at least one decent place for lunch.

Browns, Earl Street, **t** 221 100 (*cheap*). Nothing to do with the Browns chain; cool, modern canteen-style restaurant (you queue up and choose and they bring it to your table) with balcony seating and some pavement tables on sunny days. You get a full plate of food (three vegetables and a main dish).

more than 40,000 firebombs in 1940. 'This was such an eloquent symbol,' Spence said in 1974. So he left it as it was, including the cross of charred wood set up as a makeshift altar after the bombing. The modern cathedral, with its 1½-ton metal spire, resembles one of the mechanical parts that came off the assembly lines of Coventry's car industry in the 1950s, its slatted windows like industrial vents. Entering through John Hutton's engraved glass doors, you are in a traditional long nave with side aisles and mock fan-vaulting. Spence incorporated the work of leading 20th-century artists, including a 75ft-high tapestry by Graham Sutherland, a stained-glass window by John Piper and Jacob Epstein's bronze statue of *St Michael and the Devil* outside above the steps. It is an amazing place, but deeply unfamiliar and off-putting in many ways.

St Mary's Hall (*open Easter–Sept Sun–Thurs*) was the combined headquarters of the medieval merchant guilds and the borough, built in 1340 and enlarged over the next few hundred years. The worn red sandstone northern front faces the cathedral over Bayley Lane. Courts, ceremonials, signings, auditings, swearings-in and receptions of nobles and royal visitors including Henry VI, Henry VII, and Mary Queen of Scots were held here. The great hall was built by the stonemasons and woodcarvers of old St Michael's. Its treasure, a 15th-century Tournai tapestry, hangs on the wall for which it was made when Henry VII and his queen, Elizabeth, came to visit. The courtiers of Henry VI are shown clustered around the king, who is shown kneeling with chains around his neck to signify his double term of imprisonment in the Tower of London before his murder in 1471 by the Yorkists. (A Tudor cult developed around Henry VI, but the Reformation interrupted the process that would have made him a saint.)

The **Priory Visitor Centre** (*open Mon–Sat 10–5.30, Sun 12–4*) on the site of the cloisters, houses finds including a painted glass fragment of the face of Lady Godiva.

The Phoenix Initiative

To the west of the cathedral, the town drops steeply down from Holy Trinity Church and the revamped site of the Saxon priory of Leofric and Godiva to the ring road. Here the Phoenix Initiative is turning one of Coventry's bleakest hillsides into a string of piazzas. The **Transport Museum** (*open daily 10–5*) showcases Coventry's place at the heart of 20th-century British car manufacturing: the town was the base for 140 car makers including Daimler, Standard Triumph and Jaguar. (Peugeots, Jaguars and black London cabs are still made in Coventry.) The reason Coventry was targeted in the Blitz is explained too: the town became a wartime military production centre.

South of the cathedral, off Earl Street, the **Herbert Art Gallery and Museum** (***t** (024) 7683 2381, www.coventrymuseum.org.uk; open Mon–Sat 10–5.30, Sun 12–5*) showcases Coventry's early enterprise. The town has produced cutlery, cloth, gloves, buttons, clocks, ribbons and sewing machines, and there are examples of them all here. The gallery has works by Henry Moore, Jacob Epstein and L.S. Lowry, and a roomful of Lady Godivas. The highlight is Graham Sutherland's cartoons for the cathedral tapestry.

The listed 1950s shopping precinct leads to Spon Street, where the town's surviving timber-framed buildings have been relocated to form a convincing medieval street. Here is the bronze equestrian statue of Lady Godiva. Peeping Tom – who appeared in the tale a century after its first telling in 1235 – peers out from the Cathedral Lanes; for this indiscretion the poor lad was blinded. His eyes, wrote Tennyson in his romantic poem 'Godiva', 'shrivell'd into darkness in his head'. The historical Lady Godiva owned large estates in the Midlands including, Coventry, which appears in Domesday as a hamlet of 69 families around the priory founded by her husband Leofric.

Kenilworth Castle

***t** (01926) 852 078; open April–Sept 10–6, Oct 10–5, Nov–Mar 10–4; adm.*

Kenilworth Castle, 4 miles southwest of Coventry along the A429, is at its best just before dusk, when its crumbling sandstone walls glow in the setting sun. The original castle was built by the chamberlain of Henry I, Geoffrey de Clinton, since when it has passed in and out of royal hands. King John spent a huge sum of money improving it. He flooded surrounding meadows so that in 1266 when Henry III besieged the castle – by then occupied by rebel-baron Simon de Montfort – he had to send for boats from Chester. De Montfort's garrison held out for nine months until an outbreak of dysentery forced it to surrender. Elizabethan courtier Robert Dudley turned Kenilworth into a sumptuous Tudor palace fit to entertain the Queen, building a new gatehouse, stables, private apartments for visitors and a tiltyard for jousting tournaments. The visit of Elizabeth I in July 1575 lasted 19 days and, according to pageant-master George Gascoigne, consisted of hunting, musical entertainments and fireworks over the water. A fictionalized description of the whole thing features in Sir Walter Scott's romantic novel *Kenilworth*. Dudley died in 1588, shortly after the defeat of the Spanish Armada, on his way to Buxton to take the waters. His body was brought to Kenilworth and taken on to St Mary's in Warwick, where you can see his garish Renaissance tomb.

It's a short walk from Leicester's Gatehouse to the remains of the 14th-century abbey and Henry V's 'pleasaunce (or pleasure-house) in the marsh' (*le Plesaunz en Marys*), which originally stood on the edge of the mere and could be reached by boat.

Where to Stay and Eat

Kenilworth t (01926) –

Clarendon House Hotel, 6 High Street, **t** 857 668 (*expensive*). Well-modernized 15th-century inn ideally located, with pretty oak-beamed bedrooms and good brasserie.

Old Bakery Hotel, 12 High Street, **t** 864 111, *www.theoldbakeryhotel.co.uk* (*expensive*). Old-fashioned hotel in picturesque old town with 14 attractive bedrooms and bar.

Castle Laurels Hotel, Castle Road, **t** 856 179, *www.castlelaurelshotel.co.uk* (*moderate*). Attractive Victorian townhouse with foliage, black-and-white beamwork, bay windows and tiled entrance hall almost opposite Kenilworth Castle; very pleasant and helpful.

Simpson's, 101–103 Warwick Road, **t** 864 567 (*moderate*). A busy, loud, glass-fronted restaurant with bare floorboards, white tablecloths and a big reputation; the contemporary French menu might include foie gras, scallops and black pudding and slow-braised pork with turnips. *Closed Sun and Mon.*

Harrington's on the Hill, 42 Castle Hill, **t** 852 074 (*moderate*). Delightful, cosy, rustic-style restaurant in pretty white-painted cottage with flower baskets and big bay windows, only a slingshot's distance from the castle. For lunch sandwiches and baguettes, for dinner steak, mushroom tagliatelle, lots of fish. *Closed Sun.*

Restaurant Bosquet, 97/a Warwick Road, **t** 852 463 (*moderate*). Unassuming but highly recommended traditional French restaurant on busy road. Run by friendly husband and wife team (he cooks, she meets and greets).

Royal Leamington Spa

'Baths?' said the young lady inside the office, with professional charm. 'There are all sorts you can have. Natural Saline, Zotofoam, Massage Douche, Plombiere Douche, Vichy, Nauheim and Needle, Scotch Douche or Turkish. If you want electrical treatment, you can have high frequency D'Arsonval, Ionisation, Diathermy or Thermo Penetration...'

Warwickshire County Book, 1950

Fifty years ago, you might still have come to Leamington for a spa treatment in the old Victorian Pump Rooms and drunk tea in one of the hotel lounges, or listened to German brass bands in the public gardens alongside retired colonial types and elderly spinsters. 'They come to Leamington to die,' began the 1950 *Warwickshire County Book* emphatically. Things have changed since then. The Pump Rooms are now a smart new library and museum, and the average age in town seems to be that of the Warwick University students and new IT executives.

Leamington is a Warwickshire upstart. It was an unheard-of village in 1800; by 1838, its natural saline springs were at the heart of a new town of cream stucco villas with tall sash windows and ornate wrought-iron balconies. Queen Victoria visited the town before her accession in 1837 and gave it the royal prefix. Hydropathic doctor Henry Jephson doled out the cure, insisting that his patients take regular exercise, eat good plain food and go on historical jollies to Kenilworth Castle. The attractions of the spa town are its parks and the gardens on either side of the River Leam, which flows through the middle of town. There is always something pretty to look at: vistas of Regency terraces and handsome Victorian villas. A handsome grid of broad streets make up the town centre, whose main thoroughfares are The Parade, Regent Street and Warwick Street. Architectural set pieces include Lansdowne Circus (Hawthorne stayed at no. 10) and Clarendon Square.

Any trip to Leamington will revolve around the Royal Pump Rooms on The Parade, home to the **Leamington Art Gallery and Museum** (***t*** *(01926) 742 700; open Tues, Wed, Fri and Sat 10.30–5, Thurs 1.30–8, Sun 11–4*). The imposing stone colonnade facing the road belongs to the old Assembly Rooms. You can still sample the salty healing water from a tap just to the left. In the old spa treatment rooms behind them is the new gallery, museum and library, with a modern café. No water cures now, but you can find out all about the cranky treatments. The art gallery, in the former ladies swimming pool, has a collection of 19th- and 20th-century paintings including works by L.S. Lowry and Stanley Spencer.

The riverside park was laid out only for private patrons of the Pump Rooms. The **Jephson Gardens**, on the other hand, were laid out on the old riverside meadows in 1832 by property developer Edward Willes to enhance the value of his townhouses on Newbold Terrace. Recently, £3 million of lottery money has rescued the gardens from a long, slow decline. Spruced-up monuments include a marble statue of Dr Jephson. On the south side of the Leam, off Priory Terrace, is an oddity: an old elephant wash, a cobbled slipway into the river where circus elephants used to be taken to bathe.

Getting There and Around

Follow signs for A452 Leamington off the M40, 3 miles away.

National Express **coaches** from London and other major cities stop at Hamilton Terrace.

Trains run direct from London Paddington or Marylebone and Birmingham.

Tourist Information

Royal Leamington Spa: The Royal Pump Rooms, The Parade, **t** 742 762. *Open summer Mon–Sat 9.30–5, Sun 10–4; winter Mon–Fri 9.30–5, Sat 10–4, Sun 11–3.*

Where to Stay

Royal Leamington Spa t (01926) –

The Royal Leamington Hote, 64 Upper Holly Walk, **t** 883 777, *www.meridianleisure.com* (*expensive*). Beautiful cream-stuccoed building with polished floorboards and decorative plasterwork, framed prints on walls, old books on shelves; 30 pleasant bedrooms with big beds and fluffy towels.

The Lansdowne Hotel, Clarendon Street, **t** 450 505, *www.thelansdowne.co.uk* (*expensive*). Green-painted, gabled Regency building on end of terrace, draped in creeper; inside friendly and comfortable with bright, elegant hallway, pine furniture in bedrooms and framed prints and posters on walls.

8 Clarendon Crescent, **t** 429 840 (*expensive*). You are guaranteed a warm welcome in this open private house in a Regency crescent, stocked with antique furniture; five rooms like posh home-from-home.

The Adams Hotel, Avenue Road, **t** 450 742, *www.adams-hotel.co.uk* (*expensive*). One of Leamington's prettiest detached Regency townhouses, set back behind an old cypress tree, with 14 comfortable bedrooms, some recently revamped, and plenty of elegant period features.

York House Hotel, 9 York Road, **t** 424 671 (*moderate*). Handsome red-brick Victorian villa on quiet road overlooking river and Pump Room Gardens, attractively furnished with floral wallpaper and pretty fabrics.

Eating Out

Love's, 15 Dormer Place, **t** 315 522 (*moderate*). Unassuming décor of this small restaurant in terraced row belies the imaginative and ambitious modern English cooking. *Closed Sun and Mon.*

Wilds, 7 The Parade, **t** 336 732 (*moderate*). Long-established wine bar in old cellars with thick arched walls and flagstone floor; candle-lit in evenings, dusky and cool in day; guests are encouraged to stay at table after dinner and carry on with bottle of wine. *Closed Sun.*

Solo, 23 Dormer Place, **t** 422 422 (*moderate*). Fresh-tasting modern cooking in awkward-shaped restaurant. A meal might start with goats' cheese tart with vine tomatoes or salmon on crushed peas, followed by Scotch beef and lemon tart or chocolate fondant.

Moo Bar-Restaurant, Russell Street, **t** 337 763 (*moderate*). Trendy, glass-fronted 1970s-style bar with lime green swivel seats, hanging orange and yellow ball-shaped lamps and young super-cool staff; light lunch might include tiger prawns, Greek salad or bangers and mash.

Royal Pump Rooms Café, **t** 742 750 (*cheap*). Elegant and airy, and handy for the Art Gallery and Museum.

Sozzled Sausage, 141 Regent Street, **t** 831 111 (*cheap*). Cheerful bar and restaurant with pasta, panini and vegetarian meals on the menu as well as sausages. *No food Fri and Sat eves.*

The Thai Elephant, 20 Regent Street, **t** 886 882 (*cheap*). Very popular Thai restaurant with good service; book to avoid disappointment.

Rhubarb Rhubarb, 50 Warwick Street (on corner of Bedford Street), **t** 425 005 (*cheap*). Half café and half craft shop, selling African wooden knick-knacks, pots, candles and wicker baskets; a great place to idle away a rainy afternoon with newspapers; big sofa and vegetarian snacks including bagels, nachos, French bread with interesting cheeses and beanburgers. *Closed Sun.*

Warwick

The ancestral castle of the earls of Warwick looms above the old county town. The River Avon washes the base of its plunging medieval walls like a moat, giving none of its benefit to the town, which seems in every respect at a disadvantage, in the shadow of one of the country's best medieval castles. Warwick Castle is the model of a great feudal stronghold, with towers, dungeons and links with Richard Neville (d. 1471), known as the kingmaker for his high-handed part in the Wars of the Roses. With its elegant brick buildings, built after a fire destroyed the core of the Tudor town in 1694, and powerful stone gates Warwick is very nearly a gem, but ruined by traffic.

Wander up High Street between the old town gateways, and look around **Lord Leycester's Hospital** (*open Tues–Sun summer 10–5, winter 10–4; adm*), whose chapel stands on top of the West Gate. The hospital was founded by Robert Dudley of Kenilworth, Earl of Leicester, as a home for old soldiers in 1571. Before that, the crooked timber-framed buildings, were the headquarters of the town's merchant guilds. 'I presume there is nothing else so perfect in England, in this style and date of architecture, as this interior quadrangle of Leicester's Hospital,' wrote Hawthorne of the old halls, chapel and galleried courtyard in 1857. The Queen's Own Hussars have a regimental museum in the hospital.

North of the High Street is a disappointing market place surrounded by a tangle of old shopping streets. At one end is the stone market hall, now the **Warwickshire Museum** (*open Tues–Sat 10–5, May–Sept also Sun 11.30–5*), a good one that has grown out of several private collections. The highlight is the *Sheldon's Tapestry Map of Warwickshire*, one of five maps of the Midlands counties (Worcester, Gloucester, Oxfordshire and Berkshire) woven by the Sheldon firm. William Sheldon learned tapestry weaving in Flanders on a grand tour, and set up looms in about 1569 in Warwickshire and Worcestershire, making these maps and floral-patterned tapestries and selling them to English gentry, who had previously had to import Continental tapestries for their country mansions. **St John's Museum** (*open Tues–Sat 10–5, May–Sept also Sun 11.30–5*) of Victoriana and local history is housed in a splendid Jacobean mansion set back from St John's Street, near the station.

St Mary's Church

Three quiet lanes lead into sleepy Old Square, one of them burrowing through the 18th-century bell-tower of St Mary's Church. The tower dwarfs everything in the square. It was built shortly after Warwick's great fire of 1694, which destroyed the old nave and tower; the Norman crypt, 14th-century chancel and Beauchamp Chapel – the glories of the church – were spared. The vaulted **crypt** houses a rare ducking stool. Above is the small **chapter house** where lies the massive tomb of Fulke Grenville (d. 1628), 'servant to Queen Elizabeth, councillor to King James, and friend to Sir Philip Sydney', as the inscription reads. He was given Warwick Castle by James I and killed by a servant in its Watergate Tower, which he is said to haunt to this day. In the **chancel** is the tomb of Thomas Beauchamp (d. 1369), 1st Earl of Warwick, and his countess, Katherine, daughter of Roger de Mortimer, Earl of March. Thomas was one of the

Tourist Information

Warwick: The Courthouse, Jury Street, **t** (01926) 492 212. *Open daily 9.30–4.30*.

Getting There and Around

By car, leave the M40 at Junction 15, and follow the A429 into Warwick.

Warwick has direct **rail** connections with Birmingham, Leamington Spa, London and Stratford-upon-Avon, and **coach** services from most of those places.

Where to Stay

Warwick t (01926) –

The Lord Leycester Hotel, Jury Street, **t** 491 481, *www.lord-leycester.co.uk* (*expensive*). Georgian brick building with columns and pediment over door, and slate steps up to the dusky, lamp-lit hotel with panelling and period features; all bathrooms new, and many of its 50 bedrooms in good condition.

The Warwick Arms Hotel, 17 High Street, **t** 492 759 (*expensive*). Grand stone hotel whose atmosphere and décor could do with a bit of a revamp.

Forth House, 44 High Street, **t** 401 512 (*expensive*). Wonderful, civilized place to stay, with a long hall leading straight out into delightful courtyard garden overlooked by rooms; friendly dogs, Biggles and Bonnie.

The Aylesford Hotel, 1 High Street, **t** 492 799, *www.aylesfordhotel.co.uk* (*moderate*). Small, pretty Georgian townhouse with yellow-painted walls and all kinds of classical details in white; eight bedrooms lead off spiralling staircase. The little brasserie at the front becomes a restaurant (*moderate*) in the evenings, along with the no-smoking cellar restaurant.

The Tilted Wig, 11 Market Place, **t** 410 466 (*moderate*). Pine-furnished town-centre pub with four newish small, comfortable rooms, cells 1–4. Its bar is the best pub for a pint or glass of wine in the evening.

Eating Out

Fanshawes, 22 Market Place, **t** 410 590 (*moderate*). Good honest English cooking in long, narrow restaurant. Fixed-price menu includes a choice of eight main courses which might include stuffed quail with duck and chestnut mousse, poached trout fillet with watercress and rocket sauce and a vegetarian dish. *Open eves only, closed Sun.*

Findons, 7 Old Square, **t** 411 755 (*moderate*). Homely, intimate upmarket restaurant overlooking St Mary's Church. Modern English menu might include venison, poached sea bass with mustard and fennel, and a good bread and butter pudding. *Closed Sat lunch and Sun.*

Saffron, Westgate Shopping Centre, Market Street, **t** 402 069 (*moderate*). Good-quality Goan cooking.

Lloyds Number One, 3–7 Market Place, **t** 402 747 (*cheap*). Chain café-pub for coffee and cake at patio tables.

most powerful magnates of his day, fighting alongside the Black Prince and Edward III at Crécy and Poitiers, and building Caesar's Tower in Warwick Castle with the booty from captured French nobles. Around the tomb are 36 carved alabaster weepers in 14th-century costume. Thomas's son, another Thomas and the 2nd Earl, completed the rebuilding of the chancel and the nave. His tomb stood in the nave and was destroyed in the great fire. In the mid-15th century, the 3rd Earl, Richard Beauchamp (d. 1439), built the magnificent **Beauchamp Chapel** on the corner of the church for his own tomb, which lies in the middle of the chapel in a cage. His gilded, armour-clad effigy is shown in an attitude of prayer, his feet resting on a bear and griffin and his head on a swan. Richard was one of the paragons of medieval chivalry, a dying breed in his own lifetime. He fought in Henry IV's Welsh campaigns, and captured Owen Glendower, went on a pilgrimage to Rome and a crusade to Jerusalem (jousting his way across Europe), campaigned with Henry V in France, became Captain of Calais, Governor of Normandy (where he burned Joan of Arc in Rouen in 1431) and Regent of France in 1437. When Henry V died, in 1422, Richard was made carer of his son Henry VI. The weepers around the sides of his Purbeck marble tomb include Richard Neville, Wars of the Roses kingmaker, who married his sister. The other three garishly coloured tombs in the chapel were added a century later. They belong to the Dudleys: Ambrose Dudley (d. 1589), the Elizabethan Earl of Warwick; his brother Robert Dudley of Kenilworth (d. 1588), Queen Elizabeth's favourite; and Robert's wife Lettice (d. 1634) and infant son, Robert (d. 1584).

Warwick Castle

Open April–Oct 10–6 Nov–Mar 10–5; adm exp.

South of the High Street, behind high battlemented walls, is the castle of Thomas and Richard Beauchamp and 'Warwick the kingmaker'. Two kings – Edward II and Edward IV – were held prisoner in this castle and another, the future Richard III, secured his throne from Warwick Castle by ordering the murder of the young princes. It's a legendary castle – its history brought to life in waxworks by the Madame Tussauds people.

Immense stone walls and craggy towers – **Guy's Tower**, **Caesar's Tower** and **Clarence Tower** – encircle it all. On one side is the **Great Hall**, flanked by an imposing range of apartments – the **State Rooms** – and in the corner is the old Norman motte (great views). Henry James, who visited Warwick shortly after an 1871 fire destroyed some of the old interiors, found it 'the very model of a great hereditary dwelling'. The **king-maker exhibition**, for all its overblown theatrics, effectively tells the tale of Richard Neville, who got the castle by marrying the daughter of the 3rd Earl, Richard Beauchamp. In doing so he became Earl of Warwick, one of wealthiest barons in country and a law of his own, pushing Edward IV onto the throne instead of Henry VI, then backing Henry when Edward proved ungrateful, and finally getting his comeup-pance on a foggy battlefield at Barnet, 10 miles north of London.

You could easily spend a sunny afternoon in the landscaped castle grounds, with their river island, rose garden and peacocks.

Stratford-upon-Avon

Local boy made good William Shakespeare has spawned a robust tourist industry in the well-to-do market town of Stratford-upon-Avon, where he was born in 1564, the son of a glover. and retired to Stratford. His birthplace is one of five Shakespearean properties in and around town; our unholy fascination with Shakespeare evidently knowing no bounds. Yet in spite of the apparent wealth of information, England's national bard remains an elusive character, an unrecognizable, chinless identikit compiled out of birth, marriage and death certificates. These are the facts: born in Henley Street in 1564, married (local girl) Anne Hathaway in 1582, left for London soon after and joined the Lord Chamberlain's Company in 1594, wrote 38 plays and reams

Tourist Information

Stratford-upon-Avon: Bridgefoot, **t** (01789) 293 127. *Open winter Mon–Sat 9–5, Sun 10–3; summer Mon–Sat 9.30–5.30, Sun 10.30–4.30.*

Market on Fri and second Sat of month around Shakespeare monument and riverside.

Where to Stay

Stratford-upon-Avon t (01789) –

The Shakespeare Hotel, Chapel Street, **t** 0870 4008182, *www.shakespearehotel.net* (*very expensive*). Impressive black-and-white-fronted Tudor building occupying most of the street. Business-oriented with conference rooms, 86 mostly en-suite bedrooms and two restaurants, one brasserie-style with Mediterranean menu, the other traditional with a pianist playing.

The Falcon Hotel, Chapel Street, **t** 279 953, *www.regalhotels.co.uk/thefalcon* (*very expensive*). Another black-and-white-fronted 16th-century old town inn, with large 1960s extension housing 53 of the 84 en-suite bedrooms; piped olde-worlde atmosphere.

Thistle Hotel, Waterside, **t** 294 949, *www.thistlehotels.com* (*very expensive*). Attractive red-brick building well located near theatres on quiet road, decorated in sickly mock-Victorian style, with around 60 bedrooms.

The Dukes Hotel, Payton Street, **t** 269 300, *www.dukes-hotel.co.uk* (*expensive*). In a quiet conservation area, only a few minutes' walk from the theatres; its imposing cream-painted Georgian façade has round-headed windows and wrought-iron benches on raised pavement; beautiful tiled hallway and 30 comfortable bedrooms.

The Payton Hotel, 6 John Street, **t** 266 442, *www.payton.co.uk* (*expensive*). Opposite the Dukes, pretty Georgian townhouse with cheerfully decorated bedrooms and free parking in any of city-centre car parks.

Caterham House Hotel, 58–59 Rother Street, **t** 267 309 (*expensive*). Delightful, long-established small hotel with 12 individually decorated bedrooms (only one with en-suite bathroom), fresh flowers, large patterned rugs, and sunny corners.

Eastnor House, 33 Shipston Road, **t** 268 115, *www.eastnorhouse.com* (*expensive*). Another grand detached Victorian villa with an impressive tiled hallway and old polished woodwork; friendly and efficient.

The Marlyn Hotel, 3 Chestnut Walk, **t** 293 752, *www.marlynhotel.co.uk* (*moderate*). Pretty and perfectly located on quiet lane in old town; eight bedrooms.

Parkfields, 3 Broad Walk (just off busy Evesham Place), **t** 293 313, *www.parkfield-bandb.co.uk* (*moderate*). Attractive red-brick Victorian house with unusual round dormer windows, old pine doors leading into rooms, deep red-painted walls and unusual carpets; affable proprietor.

Virginia Lodge, 12 Evesham Place, **t** 292 157 (*moderate*). Set behind unrivalled flower gardens, friendly Victorian townhouse with beautiful, wide, tiled hallway; bright and comfortable bedrooms, canopies over beds and solid furniture. An extremely narrow flight of stairs leads to twin room at top.

Craig Cleeve House, 67–9 Shipston Road, **t** 296 573, *www.craigcleeve.com* (*moderate*). Handsome Victorian pile on south side of Avon, on Cotswolds road, with swirly wall-paper patterns in the hall and up the stairs; calm and professional atmosphere.

of poetry, returned to Stratford in 1613 and died there. All this and still we are no closer to finding our man. Shakespeare's contemporary playwrights had much more juicy personal lives: Ben Jonson narrowly escaped the death penalty for killing a fellow actor; Christopher Marlowe, a government spy, was murdered in a pub brawl; Thomas Kyd was tortured for information after Marlowe's death and died impoverished. Hence, perhaps, the popularity of theories that Shakespeare was a fiction or cipher, the product of an Elizabethan empire which needed a poet of comparable stature to

Eating Out

The Vintner, 4–5 Sheep Street, **t** 297 259 (*moderate*). Large, lively café-bar and restaurant with shiny flagstones, creaky floorboards and oak rafters; lots of rooms on two floors. Open for morning coffee (and croques monsieur or panini), light lunch and dinners of steak, veal, fish pie and pasta.

Margaux, 6 Union Street, **t** 269 106 (*moderate*). Lively, loud, garish restaurant behind unassuming shopfront in terrace row; décor doesn't prepare you for classy modern English/Mediterranean cooking that comes out of the kitchen. *Closed Sun.*

Russons, 8 Church Street, **t** 268 822 (*moderate*). An old shopfront in old town, offering an unpretentious, delicious menu which might include fresh pasta with asparagus, pine nuts, sun-dried tomatoes and cream; roasted rump of English lamb with vegetable and rosemary kebab and new potatoes; or baked sea bass with Greek salad and new potatoes. *Closed Sun and Mon.*

Lambs of Sheep Street, Sheep Street, **t** 292 554 (*moderate*). The setting is a timber-framed 16th-century coaching inn with solid wooden furniture; the food salads and fish-cakes or heavier meals of steak, chicken breast, pork, lemon sole or risotto.

Havilands, 5 Meer Street, **t** 415 477 (*cheap*). Little café with tiny courtyard at back, pavement seating and a handful of pine farm tables in shop, all bright and cheerful; excellent cakes and sandwiches.

Drucker's Vienna Patisserie, Hall's Croft, **t** 297 848 (*cheap*). Highly civilized tea shop in beautiful surroundings.

Marco Italian, 20 Chapel Street, **t** 292 889 (*cheap*). Good deli where they'll make you a delicious sandwich.

Desports, Meer Street, **t** 269 304 (*cheap*). Café with a black-and-white checked floor where you can get ciabatta, baguettes with brie or something called a 'Danwich' with a glass of wine or individual cafetière – all to the reassuring sounds of the coffee grinder.

Dirty Duck, Waterside, **t** 297 312 (*cheap*). Up steps to delightful little terrace with wrought-iron garden furniture under a mulberry tree; inside bar menu chalked up on boards; pre- and post-theatre dinner in restaurant (book). In the small bar are portrait photographs signed by actors such as Richard Burton, Brian Blessed (wearing armour) and Jeremy Irons on a ski holiday.

The Opposition, Sheep Street, **t** 269 980 (*cheap*). Décor is stylish with dark wooden furniture and fitted carpets; menu is more bistro-ish than Lambs next door, including sausage and mash, pizza and pasta, as well as steaks. Caters for a younger crowd.

Entertainment

Royal Shakespeare Theatre, Waterside, **t** 403 403. Enormous 1960s brick building with line of square windows and central tower. It houses the main stage of the Royal Shakespeare Company, which puts on usually excellent productions of Shakespeare's plays (many of England's best actors have cut their teeth here, and return for the big roles) and Quarto Restaurant, **t** 403 415 (*expensive*).

The Swan Theatre, Waterside, **t** 403 403. Church-like Victorian building next door to the Royal Shakespeare Theatre, since 1986 dedicated to the plays of Shakespeare's contemporaries, such as Christopher Marlowe and Ben Jonson.

ring its praises. The only whiff of scandal is the 'fair youth' and 'master-mistress of my passion' of Shakespeare's sonnets, now believed to be his patron, Henry Wriothelsey, Earl of Southampton.

Stratford, with its handsome old timber-framed houses and riverside gardens, makes Shakespeare a wholesome country boy. 'Those who think that a great genius is something supremely ripe and healthy and human may find comfort in the fact,' wrote Henry James, contemplating the fruitfulness of Shakespeare country through his train window.

The various elements of the Bard's family, Ardens, Hathaways, Shakespeares and Halls, were a well-to-do propertied crowd, as you will discover by visiting William Shakespeare's birthplace, his Stratford home (site of) and resting place, and the houses and farms of his mother, wife, daughter and granddaughter. There is a suspicious sense of completion about the walk from Shakespeare's birthplace to his grave at Holy Trinity Church via the family home. Anne Hathaway's Cottage is about a mile away in the village of Shottery, via footpaths, and Mary Arden's House 3½ miles away in Wilmcote. To make the most of the Shakespeare experience, try to get tickets to a Royal Shakespeare Company production in one of Stratford's two theatres – the Royal Shakespeare Theatre and the Swan Theatre – on the riverside.

Shakespeare's Birthplace

***t** (01789) 204 016; open April–May and Sept–Oct 10–5, June–Aug 9–5, Nov–Mar 10–4; adm exp.*

When the last private owner died in 1847, the birthplace, by then a pub and butcher's shop, already boasted 7,000 visitors a year. The Shakespeare Birthplace Trust (motto: 'To do honour to William Shakespeare') was set up to preserve the house bought by William's father, John Shakespeare, in 1556. Hawthorne, visiting in 1855, before its restoration, found it 'not very easy to idealize', after which the Trust knocked down the neighbouring houses that had welded this rather grand, detached property (John Shakespeare was mayor of Stratford) into an anonymous terrace. Looking at it from Henley Street – sturdy exposed timbers, dormer windows, steeply sloping tiled roof – Shakespeare is supposed to have been born in the upstairs room behind the large middle window. Across the garden is the **Shakespeare Centre**, with an excellent exhibition that fleshes out the man behind the Folios – his family, his career with the Lord Chamberlain's Men and his properties in and around Stratford.

Victorian photos of the birthplace cottage from the time the Trust took it over show a house with little in common with this one – now restored to its 'authentic' origins. Hawthorne thought it gave 'a depressing idea of the humble, mean, sombre character of the life that could have been led in such a dwelling as this – the whole family, old and young brought into too close contact to be comfortable together'. The whole family consisted of seven people, Mary, John and five children, the third of whom was William. Downstairs are the parlour, hall and kitchen: flagstone floors, soot-blackened fireplaces – all filled with period furnishings. You can see an old window, scratched with the names of visitors including Dickens and Tennyson. The 19th-century tradition of signing names on tourist sights extended to the ceiling and walls of the birth room ('I did not write my own name,' says Hawthorne, who 'felt no emotion whatever in Shakespeare's house'), but they have been covered up by zealous restorers.

New Place and Nash's House

Open April–May and Sept–Oct 11–5, June–Aug 9.30–5, Nov–Mar 11–4; adm.

From the end of Henley Street, High Street leads into timber-framed Chapel Street. There is an eloquent gap where New Place, Shakespeare's family home from 1597 (aged 33) until his death in 1616, used to be. It is supposed to have been beautiful, one of the largest houses in Stratford, with ranges around a courtyard and a long garden stretching away at the back. After William's death, the family of his eldest daughter Susanna (husband John Hall and daughter Elizabeth) took over the property. The end is said to have come in 1759, when owner Rev. Francis Gastrell demolished it to get rid of the tourists. The Trust has recreated the gardens in Tudor style. You reach them through the house next door, once owned by Elizabeth's first husband, Thomas Nash. A photo of the house in 1876, when the Trust acquired it, shows a very different place: a handsome brick front with a portico and sash windows; soon after, the old timbers were uncovered or replaced, and the rooms filled with heavy oak furniture.

Hall's Croft

Open April–May and Sept–Oct 11–5, June–Aug 9.30–5, Nov–Mar 11–4; adm.

Hall's Croft is a short walk from New Place in the direction of the church in Old Town. It too is timber-framed, with a magnolia tree in front. It is presumed that Susanna, Shakespeare's daughter, and her husband, doctor John Hall, lived here before moving into New Place in 1616. Hall came to Stratford in the early 1600s and did very well for himself as the only doctor. His case notes are kept in the British Museum. The interior is impressive: shiny flagstones downstairs, wide sloping floorboards upstairs, tiny windows and stone fireplaces. You will be pleased to find out about old medicine and forget the Bard for a moment.

Holy Trinity Church

Old Town and the river lead to the church that contains the Shakespeare family graves. Shakespeare died on 23 April 1616, aged 52, and was buried in the chancel, an indication of his standing in his own lifetime. His grave bears the inscription: 'Good friend for Jesus sake forebear to dig the dust enclosed here, blest be the man who spares these stone, and cursed be he who moves my bones.' The bust of Shakespeare on the chancel wall was made shortly after his death, probably commissioned by family members. On display is a copy of the parish register, proof of his baptism and death. His wife Anne joined him here. Next to them are John Hall and Susanna, Elizabeth and Thomas Nash.

Anne Hathaway's Cottage

Open April–May and Sept–Oct 10–5, June–Aug 9–5, Nov–Mar 10-4; adm.

The family home of Shakespeare's wife, Anne Hathaway, is in the village of **Shottery**, a mile west of the town centre. You can reach it along a footpath from Evesham Place – or by car. The cottage is one of the highlights of Stratford. It remained in the Hathaway family until the Trust took it over in the 1890s. One or two heirlooms, including a four-poster oak bed dating from Anne's time, had been handed down through 13 or so generations and remain *in situ*. The cottage, nestled in its gently sloping gardens, is a perfect combination of old stone, timber and brickwork under a thatched roof covered by climbing roses, with little windows peeping out from under the eaves. The small garden manages to swallow up visitors down sunken paths between banks of flowers and box hedges. Inside, after a talk on 16th-century domestic life, you duck under low beams and tread carefully over uneven flooring. The cottage was smaller in Anne's day, the upper section at the orchard end added by Anne's brother Bartholomew in the 17th century. Anne was one of eight children living under the same roof from her father Richard's two marriages. Despite the hordes, restaurant, gift shop and café, you can imagine the teenage William Shakespeare coming to visit his future wife (eight years his senior) here and charming the family over dinner.

Mary Arden's House

Open April–May and Sept–Oct 10–5, June–Aug 9.30–5, Nov–Easter 10–4; adm.

Shakespeare's mother, Mary Arden, was the youngest of eight girls. Her father, Robert, a wealthy Wilmcote farmer, died in 1556, shortly before she married John Shakespeare and moved to Stratford. The house in Wilmcote (signposted from Anne Hathaway's Cottage) passed to Robert's widow Agnes, his second wife of only a few years, with four children of her own; nonetheless William might have visited as a child. Here you have the Arden family farmhouse and neighbouring Palmer's Farm, along with a museum of rural life in the outbuildings. **Palmer's Farm** is a black-and-white timber-framed house, each beam seeming to pull in a different direction. Around the back, it is a rural idyll: dirt paths, stone farmbuildings, trailing plants, old wooden barn doors hanging open. **Mary Arden's House** is a more muted affair. Its old timbers are clad in Victorian brickwork on the outside and plaster on the inside, and the downstairs rooms are furnished in Victorian style – rag rugs and an old iron kitchen range. The joke is that until November 2000 everybody thought that Palmer's House was the Arden family home; for 70 years the Trust had been showing millions of visitors around a house that had nothing to do with the Ardens or Shakespeare, until a surprising document turned up in the Sussex Records Office showing that the Ardens in fact lived next door in Glebe Farm. Luckily the Trust owned Glebe Farm too.

Edge Hill

On 23 October 1642 around 14,000 Royalist troops came to blows with a similar number of Parliamentarians led by the Earl of Essex beneath Edge Hill, an L-shaped ridge 4 miles long skirting the battlefield at Radway. The king was heading to London from Shrewsbury, where he had raised an army. He had rested at Bridgnorth, Wolverhampton, Aston Hall near Birmingham and Kenilworth Castle, plundering the countryside on the way. Essex came west from Northampton to cut him off, garrisoning Banbury, Warwick, Worcester and Hereford. This, the opening battle of the Civil War, was a bit of a shambles. Most of the soldiers had never fought before and the only way to tell them apart was a coloured scarf; the Royalists wore red, the Parliamentarians orange. The men became disorientated as it grew dark and that night there were massive desertions. The battle was not resumed in the morning. Charles claimed a victory, retiring to Oxford.

After all this, you'll probably be glad to get back to Shakespeare's plays, the good, the bad and the indifferent. The poet Dryden complained that Shakespeare 'often obscures his meaning with words'. A.C. Bradley, one of the godfathers of Shakespearean criticism, called his language 'obscure, inflated' and 'pestered with metaphors'. Frank Kermode calls him 'a very good but sometimes not so good poet' and 'sometimes but not always clearly a writer of genius'. Book yourself into a play at one of the RSC theatres (*see* box) and make your own mind up.

Birmingham

Birmingham was once the city of canals and 1960s elevated ring roads. 'It made a great many articles, chiefly in metal,' wrote J.B. Priestley in 1933, 'but so far in my life not one of these articles had gained any hold over my affections'. He visited the art gallery and museum, which he thought outstanding, and mooched around the centre, which seemed imposing and dignified to him, but all in all he was not taken by the place: 'I had never said, "Good old Birmingham" myself, and had never heard anybody else say it.' Brummies, however, defend their city with pride. It was civic pride that made Birmingham great in the 1870s and '80s, when the city hogged the industrial limelight as Manchester had in the 1840s. Birmingham was a town of small workshops and diverse trades. The town's strong and public-spirited council saw local politics – conducted with a blend of municipal pride and Nonconformist religious zeal – as the major force of change in society. 'I have an abiding faith in municipal institutions,' said the mayor, Joseph Chamberlain, laying the foundation stone of the new Council Building in 1873, 'an abiding sense of the value and importance of local government.' Chamberlain was an idealist and champion of the civic gospel – bringing gas and water companies under the control of the Corporation, building dignified municipal buildings and raising the moral tone of local government. 'The town will be parked, paved, assized, marketed, gas-and-watered and improved – all as a result of three years' active work,' he said before leaving to join Gladstone's Cabinet. At the end of the Victorian period, Birmingham was fêted as the best-governed city in the world, and home to the household names of industry: Cadburys, Austin motor-cars, Birds and Dunlop.

The ring road, with its *Clockwork Orange*-style underpasses, was another, albeit misguided, instance of modernizing municipal action (aimed to make the city car-friendly). Happily it's on its way out. Over the last 10 years Birmingham has been busy reinventing itself as a modern city of newly branded cultural institutions (the NEC, ICC, NIA, MAC and BM&AG), shops, restaurants and large-scale schemes to improve the built environment, involving huge investment and fashionable architects like Nicholas Grimshaw and Richard Rogers.

New Street and the Bull Ring

From the end of High Street, a walkway leads over the ring road to the revamped **Bull Ring**, the historic market centre of Birmingham, which has been the focus of

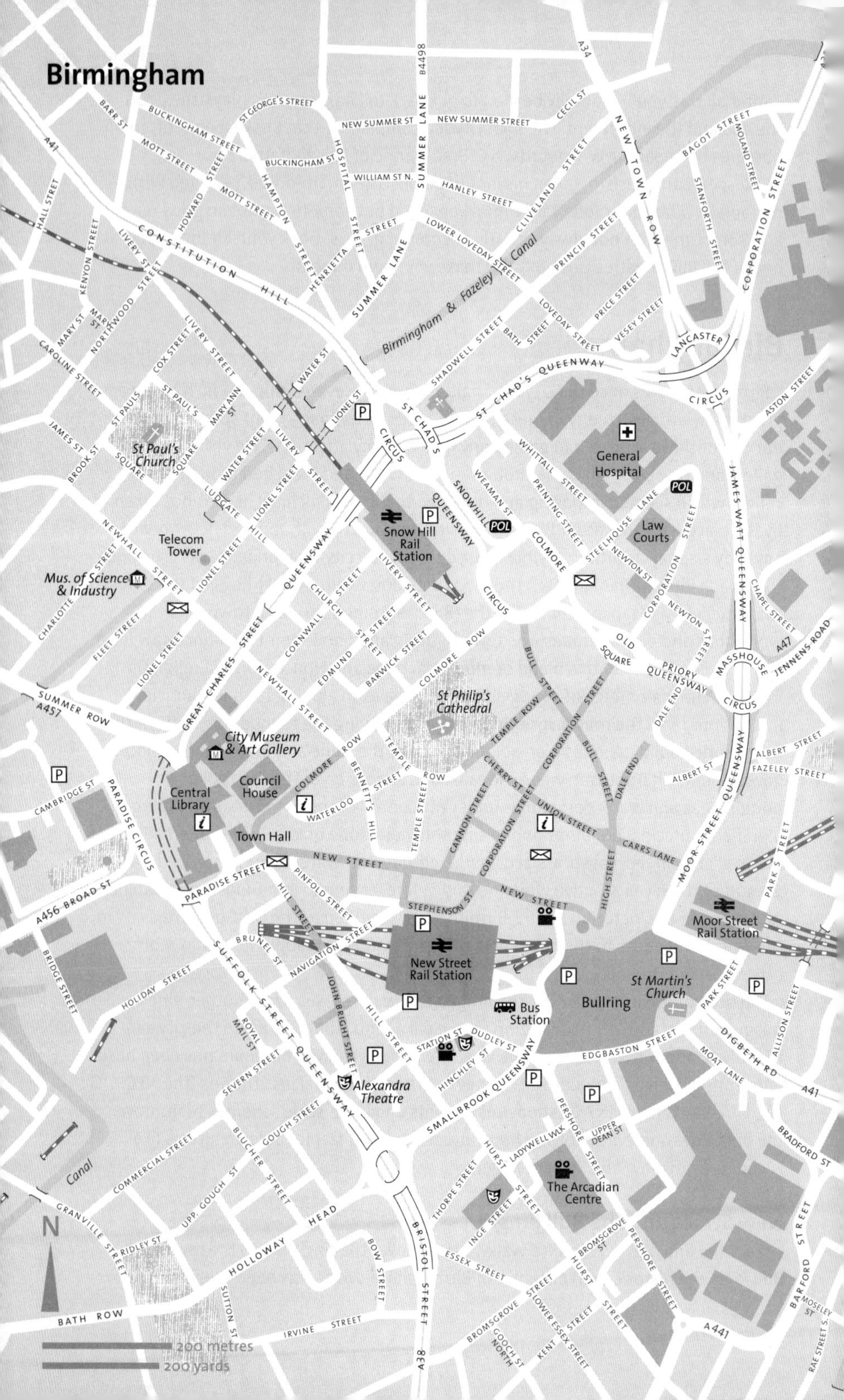
Birmingham
BARR ST
BUCKINGHAM STREET
ST GEORGE'S STREET
NEW SUMMER ST
NEW SUMMER STREET
B4498
A34
CECIL ST
A41
MOTT STREET
BUCKINGHAM ST
HOSPITAL STREET
WILLIAM ST N.
SUMMER LANE
HANLEY STREET
CLIVELAND STREET
NEW TOWN ROW
BAGOT STREET
MOLAND STREET
STANFORTH STREET
CORPORATION STREET
HALL STREET
KENYON STREET
HOWARD STREET
MOTT STREET
HAMPTON STREET
LOWER LOVEDAY STREET
PRINCIP STREET
CONSTITUTION HILL
LIVERY ST
NORTHWOOD STREET
HENRIETTA STREET
Birmingham & Fazeley Canal
PRICE STREET
VESEY STREET
LOVEDAY STREET
BATH STREET
SHADWELL STREET
MARY ST
MARY ST
CAROLINE STREET
LIVERY STREET
COX STREET
WATER ST
LANCASTER CIRCUS
ST CHAD'S QUEENWAY
ASTON STREET
ST PAUL'S
MARY ANN ST
LIONEL ST
ST CHAD'S CIRCUS
JAMES ST
ST PAULS SQUARE
St Paul's Church
SQUARE
WATER STREET
LIVERY STREET
General Hospital
BROOK ST
WHITTALL STREET
WEAMAN ST
SNOWHILL QUEENSWAY
POL
JAMES WATT QUEENSWAY
PRINTING STREET
LUDGATE HILL
LIONEL STREET
Snow Hill Rail Station
STEELHOUSE LANE
Law Courts
NEWHALL STREET
Telecom Tower
QUEENSWAY
COLMORE CIRCUS
NEWTON ST
CORPORATION STREET
Mus. of Science & Industry
LIONEL STREET
CHURCH STREET
LIVERY STREET
CHAPEL STREET
CHARLOTTE STREET
NEWTON STREET
FLEET STREET
CORNWALL STREET
BARWICK STREET
COLMORE ROW
OLD SQUARE
A47
JENNENS ROAD
LIONEL STREET
EDMUND STREET
BULL STREET
PRIORY QUEENSWAY
MASSHOUSE CIRCUS
SUMMER ROW
A457
GREAT CHARLES STREET
NEWHALL STREET
St Philip's Cathedral
TEMPLE ROW
DALE END
City Museum & Art Gallery
COLMORE ROW
TEMPLE ROW
CORPORATION STREET
BULL STREET
ALBERT STREET
ALBERT ST
FAZELEY STREET
CAMBRIDGE ST
PARADISE CIRCUS
Central Library
Council House
BENNETT'S HILL
CHERRY ST
DALE END
MOOR STREET QUEENSWAY
WATERLOO STREET
TEMPLE STREET
CANNON STREET
UNION STREET
Town Hall
CORPORATION STREET
CARRS LANE
PARK STREET
NEW STREET
HIGH STREET
PARADISE STREET
A456 BROAD ST
PINFOLD STREET
STEPHENSON ST
NEW STREET
HILL STREET
Moor Street Rail Station
BRUNEL ST
NAVIGATION STREET
BRIDGE STREET
SUFFOLK STREET QUEENSWAY
JOHN BRIGHT STREET
New Street Rail Station
Bullring
St Martin's Church
PARK STREET
HOLIDAY STREET
Bus Station
ALLISON STREET
ROYAL MAIL ST
HILL STREET
STATION ST
DUDLEY ST
EDGBASTON STREET
DIGBETH RD
MOAT LANE
A41
HINCHLEY ST
SEVERN STREET
Alexandra Theatre
SMALLBROOK QUEENSWAY
GOUGH STREET
BLUCHER STREET
PERSHORE STREET
UPPER DEAN ST
LADYWELL WLK
BRADFORD ST
Canal
COMMERCIAL STREET
UPP. GOUGH ST
HURST STREET
THORPE STREET
The Arcadian Centre
GRANVILLE STREET
N
HOLLOWAY HEAD
BRISTOL STREET
INGE STREET
BROMSGROVE ST
PERSHORE STREET
BARFORD STREET
RIDLEY ST
BOW STREET
ESSEX STREET
HURST STREET
SUTTON ST
BATH ROW
BROMSGROVE STREET
LOWER ESSEX STREET
MOSELEY ST
IRVINE STREET
A441
200 metres
200 yards
A38
GOOCH ST NORTH
KENT STREET
RAE STREET S.

Getting There and Around

Domestic flights and charters fly to and from Birmingham airport, **t** 0870 733 5511, *www.bhx.co.uk*.

By car, Birmingham is at the hub of several motorways: the M5 from the south; M40 from London; M6 from the east, heading on north to Liverpool and Manchester; and the M54 northwest into Wales. The M42 links them all.

There are frequent trains from London, via Oxford or Coventry, and the Northwest. There are good connections into the Welsh Marches and East Midlands too.

Regular coach services run from London to Birmingham and the Northwest, and from Birmingham to the rest of the Midlands.

Tourist Information

Birmingham: 2 City Arcade, off Corporation Street, **t** (0121) 202 5099. *Open Mon–Sat 9.30–5.30, Sun 10.30–4.30.*

Where to Stay

Birmingham t (0121) –

The Burlington Hotel, Burlington Arcade, 126 New Street, **t** 643 9191, *www.burlington-hotel.com* (*very expensive*). Reached down an attractive Victorian arcade off New Street, this swanky Victorian hotel used to be the Midland; now it caters largely for a business clientele, with 112 period-style bedrooms and a split-level restaurant in the old ballroom.

Malmaison Hotel, The Mailbox, Royal Mail Street, **t** 246 5000, *www.malmaison.com* (*very expensive*). Part of trendy new complex of designer shops near New Street; small, swish northern city chain of hotels, including stylish brasserie (*moderate*) serving eggs Benedict or onion soup followed by salmon fishcakes, poached halibut or thyme-roasted wood pigeon; hi-tech gym.

City Inn, 1 Brunswick Square, Brindley Place, **t** 643 1003, *www.cityinn.com* (*expensive*). Right in the heart of the convention quarter, a modern hotel with 238 bedrooms equipped with CD players, power showers, fluffy bathrobes, air conditioning and sound proofing. Modern European restaurant.

Hotel du Vin, 25 Church Street, off Culmore Row, **t** 200 0600, *www.birminghamhotelduvin.com* (*expensive*). Small, charming French-style chain of hotels; 66 bedrooms; excellent bistro (*moderate*) serving foie gras, steak with frites, risotto of smoked salmon with broad beans and mint, followed by French cheeses or rice pudding.

Copperfield House Hotel, 60 Upland Road, Selly Park, **t** 472 8344 (*expensive*). Small, family-run Victorian townhouse 3 miles south of city centre, near the university and cricket grounds; comfortable bedrooms feature classic film collections; pleasant dining room (*moderate*).

The Birmingham Marriott Hotel, 12 Hagley Road, Five Ways, **t** 452 1144, *www.marriott-hotels.com* (*expensive*). Don't be deterred by the rumbling roundabout, this swanky Edwardian-style hotel has an Egyptian-themed swimming pool, marble bathrooms, spacious double-glazed bedrooms and two restaurants.

The Regency Hotel, Stratford Road, Shirley, Solihull, **t** 745 6119, *www.regalhotels.co.uk/regency* (*expensive*). Large, business-oriented, Regency-fronted hotel set back from main road behind trees, with Irish bar and restaurant and 112 bedrooms; bus no. 6 takes you to Shirley station, from where you can get into centre.

Old Farm Hotel, 108 Linden Road, Bournville, **t** 458 3146 (*moderate*). Near Bournville cricket pitches; nine small pine bedrooms on ground floor and three larger rooms upstairs with views across wooded Bournville gardens; bar opens onto big back garden; 5 miles from city centre.

Eating Out

Bank, 4 Brindley Place, **t** 633 7001 (*expensive*). Walk through revolving door to enter this trendy, design-conscious restaurant, one of the corner stones of the Brindley Place scene, providing breakfast, pre- and post-theatre supper, weekend brunch and full English/ French/ Italian-influenced menu including pea and Gorgonzola risotto, seared scallops, sausage and mash, and grilled meat and fish.

La Toque d'Or, 27 Warstone Lane, Hockley, **t** 233 3655 (*expensive*). Combines industrial-chic décor with expert French cooking using Brixham fish, Perigordian foie gras, beef from the Welsh borders; relaxed, informal and hidden away from the Brindley Place crowds down an alleyway among jewellery shops. *Open Tues–Fri lunch, Tues–Sat dinner.*

Shimla Pinks, 214 Broad Street, **t** 633 0366 (*moderate*). Swanky westernized Indian chain with scuffed pine floors.

Le Petit Blanc, 9 Brindley Place, **t** 633 7333 (*moderate*). Stylish, modern brasserie-style restaurant around oval stainless-steel bar; also outside tables and gas heaters. Serves herb pancakes, pan-fried salmon, coq au vin with French beans and green salad, as well as a 'fast fresh food' menu for early lunches and a children's menu.

The Mongolian Bar-Restaurant, Ludgate Hill, **t** 236 3842 (*moderate*). Fill a bowl with your chosen raw ingredients and watch them being flash fried on a huge flat hotplate in appropriate sauce

Chung Ying Garden Cantonese Restaurant, 17 Thorp Street, **t** 666 6622 (*moderate*). Vast restaurant reached up flight of twinkly stairs; air conditioning and fans, big round tables and patterned carpets.

Rose Villa Tavern, Worstone Lane, Hockley (next to Clock Tower), **t** 236 7910 (*cheap*). Friendly old-fashioned Victorian-style pub in striking distance of Jewellery Quarter Museum; jukebox stocked with nostalgic old songs like 'Tell Norma I love her'.

Tap and Spile, Gas Street (off Broad Street), **t** 236 7910 (*cheap*). Pleasant old-fashioned canalside pub with scuffed wooden furniture and old floorboards.

Royal Al Faisal, 130–40 Stoney Lane, Spark Brook, **t** 449 5695 (*cheap*). Heart of Balti land. Come early on Saturday for traditional Balti dishes – cooked in two-handled metal woks – which you eat with naan bread. The restaurant is friendly, lively and no-frills with paper table cloths and napkins, about 20 heated vats of buffet dishes and photos of a garlanded Prince Charles on a visit.

Canalside Café, Gas Street, **t** 248 7979 (*cheap*). Charming former lock-keeper's cottage with canalside tables enlivened by red-and-white checked tablecloths and canal boats moored picturesquely alongside. Offers humus and pitta, all-day breakfasts, roasts, curries and some vegetarian dishes.

Out-of-town Pubs

The Boot, Lapworth. Cosy, groovy old pub; outside tables under awning warmed by gas heaters; beautiful white-painted restaurant in rafters with pale pine floor and menu of pasta, fish and braised Moroccan lamb.

Fleur de Lys, Lowsonford. On Birmingham–Stratford canal, with big inglenook fireplace and comfortable old wooden bar; serves good food (*moderate*) and real ales.

Entertainment

Symphony Hall, International Convention Centre (ICC), Broad Street, box office **t** 780 3333, *www.symphonyhall.co.uk*. Home of City of Birmingham Symphony Orchestra and venue for touring orchestras and soloists. The Symphony Hall is one of 11 halls in the ICC, the other 10 used for conferences. It's all part of the Birmingham NEC empire, whose other venues include the National Exhibition Centre (a huge exhibition hall) and the NEC Arena (pop concerts), both near Birmingham airport, and the National Indoor Arena (top sports), in Brindley Place. For information, call the ICC, **t** 644 6012, or go to *www.necgroup.co.uk*.

The Jam House, 1 St Paul's Square, **t** 200 3030. Jools Holland' split-level live-music bar and restaurant gets packed on weekends, so you need to book.

Glee Comedy Club, Hurst Street, Arcadian Centre, **t** 693 2248, *www.glee.co.uk*. Live comedy, followed by disco Fri and Sat. Reserve table. *Open Mon–Fri 9.30–5, Sat 11–5.*

Alexandra Theatre, Suffolk Street, box office **t** 0870 607 7533. Big glitzy performances of touring London musicals and family shows.

If none of the above appeals, take a walk around the **Chinese Quarter**, centred on the Arcadian; its attractions include a couple of naff-trendy bars, secure 24-hour car park, Virgin Cinema, Chinese supermarket, and Chinese, Italian and Indian restaurants.

some of the most strenuous efforts to heal the ghastly wounds of the 1960s and '70s. It's now at least safe. Ahead of you, Victorianized **St Martin's Church** served the original medieval settlement. Turn back, and head up **New Street**, Birmingham's smartest shopping street, which leads to the municipal heart of town. 'So long as you keep within a very narrow limit in the centre, Colmore Row, New Street, Corporation Street, Birmingham has a quite metropolitan air,' wrote Priestley in the 1930s, 'and you could imagine yourself in the second city of England'. **Corporation Street**, which leads off New Street to the Victorian-Gothic Law Courts, was part of Mayor Chamberlain's Improvement Scheme. He envisaged 'a great street, as broad as a Parisian boulevard from New Street to Aston Road,' in the place of overcrowded slums. Built in sections by different developers to avoid flooding the property market, it fell short of Haussmann's flair, but it does have a grand, metropolitan feel.

St Philip's Cathedral and Around

Between Corporation Street and Colmore Row, Birmingham's small Italianate cathedral sits in the middle of a large tree-shaded green, surrounded by handsome iron lamp-posts and railings. It was built in the early 1700s, graduating to cathedral status in 1905 after minor Victorian alterations. Architect Thomas Archer toured Renaissance Europe for inspiration. When it was built, his baroque domed tower marked the heart of new Birmingham, which had expanded uphill from the old market centre around St Martin's. Inside, all things are bright and beautiful, including the Victorian chancel with its painted marble-effect columns, the Art Nouveau hanging lamps and four spectacular Burne-Jones windows, depicting the *Nativity*, *Ascension* and *Crucifixion* (east end) and *Last Judgement* (west end). The benefactor was Emma Chadwick Villiers-Wilkes, the wealthy heiress of a Birmingham wire company.

New Street and Colmore Row lead into **Victoria Square**, a fan-shaped municipal square of trees, old-fashioned lamp-posts and modern statues of mythical beasts. Here you see buildings of Victorian stucco and columns; it's where all the banks, building societies and offices have their premises in the centre of town. The oldest building is the old **town hall**, an impressive early 19th-century building encased in rows of neo-classical columns. Architects Hansom and Welsh were inspired by the temple of Jupiter Stator in Rome. Pre-Chamberlain, the town hall was a venue for large political meetings and musical concerts; a poky backroom was provided for council meetings (which took place in the pub instead). In 1874 Chamberlain laid the foundation stone for the new **Council House**, which opened in 1879. On the central pediment above the entrance is a sculptural group representing 'Britannia rewarding the Birmingham Manufacturers' – or Victorian pride in its local industries. Ten years later the **Chamberlain Memorial** was unveiled, a Gothic fountain of Portland stone dedicated to the great man 'during whose mayoralty many great public works were notably advanced,' reads the inscription. It stands in Chamberlain Square, the continuation of Victoria Square, where the 1970s concrete Birmingham Museum and Art Gallery and Central Library set the tone. There are two Victorian statues of eminent 18th-century Brummies: a marble figure of engineer James Watt and a bronze of Joseph Priestley, unveiled on the 1874 centenary of his discovery of oxygen. Both of the men belonged to the Lunar Society (*see* Soho House). When the Central Library moves into the Richard Rogers building at Millennium Point, there is hope that the grim old building in Chamberlain Square will be demolished.

Birmingham Museum and Art Gallery (BM&AG)

t *(0121) 303 3442, www.bmag.org.uk; open Mon–Thurs and Sat 10–5, Fri 10.30–5, Sun 12.30–5; adm for special exhibitions.*

The council gave the city a museum and art gallery in 1885 out of the profits of 10 years' running of the water department. The original building consisted of the Round Room, hung floor-to-ceiling with Victorian paintings, and the Industrial Gallery, where examples of Birmingham's manufactured products were shown alongside those of the rest of the world. To that, the Edwardian tea room was added. Since then, the collections – including Birmingham history, the ancient world and world cultures – have expanded into the 1913 Feeney extension (John Feeney, who gave £50,000 for the new art gallery, owned the *Birmingham Daily Post*) and, more recently, the old offices of the gas and water departments.

From Chamberlain Square, steps lead up to the old **Round Room**, still crammed with Victorian paintings. Leading off it is still the **Industrial Gallery**, an ornate, sunny Victorian arcade with iron columns supporting a large upper gallery. It remains one of the highlights, its applied art collections as wonderful as the room itself. There are examples of Pre-Raphaelite stained glass, products of the Soho Manufactory, Wedgwood pottery and 20th-century studio pottery. One of the first objects acquired by the museum was the **Sultanganj Buddha**, a 6th-century copper cast of a standing Buddha dug up by British railway engineers in northern India in 1862. The tea room beyond is one of the treats of the BM&AG. Retrace your steps to the Pre-Raphaelite paintings and drawings and late 18th-century British watercolours in the Feeney extension. The collection of Millais, Holman Hunt, Rossetti and the rest of them grew almost by chance, from a few oils poached from local collectors by the first curator, including ***The Last of England*** by Ford Madox Brown. Further gifts and bequests contributed to what is now the largest collection of Pre-Raphaelite works on paper in the world (only a fraction on display at any time). There is a whole room devoted to large paintings by Burne-Jones, who was born in Birmingham but called it 'a hole of a place'. Priestly wrote glowingly of Turner, Cox, Cotman and De Wint, 'who, whatever their private lives may have been, always impress me as being about the happiest set of men who ever lived in this country.'

The modern art gallery in the **Waterhall** (separate entrance), contains works by Barbara Hepworth, Ben Nicholson, Henry Moore and Francis Bacon. The **Gashall** (entrance on Edmund Street) is a venue for major loan art exhibitions.

Centenary Way

From Chamberlain Square a hump-backed footbridge over the ring road leads to Centenary Square and on to Brindley Place. Centenary Way proved, back in the early 1990s, that there was life beyond the 'concrete collar'. It leads to a swathe of attractions on the western side of the inner ring road: fountains, sculptures, lawns and the impressive Hall of Memory war memorial, which looks like a Roman temple. Past a group of modern buildings – the International Convention Centre (ICC), Symphony Hall and Repertory Theatre – you can stroll to the red-brick wharf buildings of Brindley Place. On parallel Broad Street, you can just about see, between the traffic, statues of three large men in frock coats; this is William Bloye's bronze *Conversation Piece* (unveiled in 1956) between Boulton, Watt and Murdoch of the Soho Foundry.

Brindley Place

You pop out the back of the ICC building at the junction of Birmingham's canals, flanked by mock warehouses with Dutch gables and gantries and numerous café-bars. This is the city's most popular social hub, heaving on a Friday or Saturday night and lively on a sunny day. The canals were everything to 18th- and 19th-century Birmingham. They placed the Victorian manufacturing town squarely in the centre of the country, connected to the major seaports of Bristol and London. Now you can ride on a narrow boat or drink in a canal-side pub. The **National Sea Life Centre** (***t** (0121) 633 4700; open daily 10–5; adm exp*) – of all things in an inland city without even a river – stands on the water's edge. Displays include an underwater tunnel. On Oozells Street, just off Brindley Place, is the **Ikon Gallery** (***t** (0121) 248 0708; open Tues–Sun 11–6*), an important contemporary art gallery housed in the shell of a Victorian-Gothic primary school (converted with £3.7 million of lottery money in 1995–8). It hosts temporary exhibitions and has a good bookshop and café-bar.

The Jewellery Quarter

From Brindley Place, walk to the Jewellery Quarter along the canal, joining the towpath at the National Indoor Arena (NIA) and climbing back up to road level at Newhall Street. St Paul's Square marks the southern end of the quarter. This is the old industrial part of town, boasting factory buildings in various states of repair, many now protected by preservation orders. It stretches to the top of Vyse Street, the direction of Birmingham's 18th-century expansion out of the over-industrialized town centre and slums. At first the metalworkers – makers of buttons, pen nibs, cheap jewellery and trinkets – converted townhouses into workshops, only later moving into purpose-built factories. Metal products are still manufactured here, and the Assay Office and Jewellery School still function. Visit on a weekday, when the quarter is busy at work. English Heritage has mapped out a walk, taking you past the best Gothic, Italianate and Art Nouveau façades. It starts at the **Museum of the Jewellery Quarter** on Vyse Street (***t** (0121) 554 3598, www.bmag.org.uk; shop open Tues–Sun 10–4; guided tours 11.30–4*), in the old Smith and Pepper gold jewellery factory. Smith and Pepper were not notable other than for a failure to adopt any of the new technologies and business practices of the 20th century – leaving an intact workshop; in 1981 the owners, by then as ancient as their belt-driven polishing machines, locked up the factory doors and never came back. It is a glimpse of the old order – paper bills on spikes, petty-cash books, work-worn peg benches on the factory floor. The walk goes right out of the door to Great Hampton Street (look out for the Pelican Works) and back along Hockley Street to the clock tower, built in 1903 to commemorate Chamberlain's visit to South Africa as colonial secretary. Walk along Warstone Lane, where there are one or two ornate factories, and down Caroline Street into **St Paul's Square**, a handsome Georgian development around St Paul's, 'the jewellers' church'. Birmingham's Assay Office – where precious metals have been hallmarked since 1878 – stands on Newhall Street, just off the square.

Eastside and Thinktank: The Museum of Science and Discovery

From the city centre, it's a 10-minute walk to **Millennium Point**, a bold new public square between Curzon Street and Jennens Road, skirting around the demolition and redevelopment of Masshouse Circus. This is the heart of Eastside, billed as a '£6 billion new media, learning and technology quarter', east of the inner ring road.

Millennium Point was the first phase of regeneration. Fronting onto it is **Thinktank: The Museum of Science and Discovery** (***t*** *(0121) 202 2222, www.thinktank.ac.uk; open 10–5; adm exp*), a Nicholas Grimshaw and Partners building. Thinktank has it all: a working Victorian beam engine, pumping a ton of water at every stroke; two Second World War fighter planes; the 1930s winner of the land speed record; and more than 250 interactive, futuristic exhibits. Next to Thinktank's glass and terracotta louvre-tiled façade is a new **IMAX** cinema boasting a 50ft-high screen, 42 speakers and '385 luxury stadium-style seats'.

The worst section of the ring road is next to go in the regeneration of Eastside. Over the next 10 years the whole area will get a makeover: offending buildings will be demolished, main roads humanized and new housing, business and educational centres built. Birmingham Central Library is moving from Chamberlain Square to a brand-new Richard Rogers building, scheduled to open in 2008. The **University of the First Age** (***t*** *(0121) 202 2345*), **Young People's Parliament** ('with video conferencing and web casting facilities'), **New Technology Institute** and **Technology Innovation Centre** (***t*** *(0121) 331 5400*) are all moving in too.

Birmingham's Suburbs

Soho House Museum is north of town, surrounded by dreary suburbs and best reached by car. The Botanical Gardens, Barber Institute and Bournville are in the other direction, all stops on the same railway line south of the city centre.

Soho House Museum

Soho Avenue, off Soho Road, Handsworth, **t** *(0121) 554 9122; take the metro from Snows Hill to Benson Road, or by car aim for West Bromwich on the A41 and follow signs; open Tues–Sat 10–5, Sun 12–5; adm.*

Soho House was the elegant neo-classical home of Matthew Boulton, Birmingham's most famous son, one of few great men in a town of small-scale manufacturers and civic heroes. Boulton made things out of metal: small things like buttons and buckles, beautiful things like silver dress swords and tableware, and stonking great industrial steam engines in partnership with James Watt. He invented a steam engine to make copper coins, and centrally heated his own house with hot air, like the Romans. Boulton almost bankrupted himself by building his Soho works outside the established Jewellery Quarter, on what was then heathland ('soho!' was an old hunting call). The Soho Manufactory, which resembled an Italian palace, is long gone, along with its parkland, canals and lakes, and workers' cottages (Boulton employed 700 workers in 1770). A watercolour in the museum shows it as it was, Boulton's house in a pastoral valley, with the works chimney poking out of the woods; now Soho House has been swallowed up by Birmingham's sprawl. Boulton and Watt built the Soho Foundry in 1795, a mile away in Smethwick, to build steam engines. Boulton was at the centre of a group of scientists called the Lunar Society, who met on the full moon. The members, some of the greatest scientists of the day – Erasmus Darwin, Joseph Priestley, James Watt and Josiah Wedgwood – met around Boulton's mahogany dining-room table, mixing wine, food and science. The house has been restored to the style of 1805 and filled with furniture by Gillow of Lancaster and James Newton to evoke the cluttered home of a restless inventor whose interests included metallurgy, astronomy, geology, meteorology, chemistry and electricity. Upstairs is a display of silverware made at the Soho Manufactory and copper coins made at the Soho Mint.

Boulton diehards can arrange a visit to the old **Soho Foundry** and William Murdock's cottage in Smethwick (*call Avery Berkel Limited,* **t** *0870 903 4343*) and the Watt, Boulton and Murdock monuments in **St Mary's Church** on Hampstead Road (*call the rector of St Mary's* **t** *(0121) 554 3407*).

Birmingham Botanical Gardens and Glasshouses

***t** (0121) 4541 860; open 9–dusk.*

The Botanical Gardens in Edgbaston make a nice trip from the city centre (get off the train at Five Ways). Edgbaston has always been a desirable suburb, large detached houses behind high walls; its wealthy 19th-century citizens were generous donors to its Botanical Society. The striking, wrought-iron glasshouses were added later. You can have tea and cakes at the Pavilion restaurant on Loudon Terrace. The 'Ernest "China" Wilson Border' commemorates the famous plant hunter who trained here in 1893–7.

Barber Institute of Fine Arts

University of Birmingham, Edgbaston, **t** *(0121) 414 7333; open Mon–Sat 10–5, Sun 12–5.*

Lady Barber, the wife of a wealthy Birmingham businessman, founded the Barber Institute in 1932 to redress an imbalance: the university was too fond of business and industry and not enough of art, she felt. Her chosen architect was Robert Atkinson, whose brick and stone building stands near the East Gate of the university. It is one of the most comprehensive small picture galleries anywhere. All new acquisitions must be at least 30 years old, and there's one of each of the greats – Tintoretto, Poussin, Monet, Rubens, Rembrandt, Van Dyke, Gainsborough, Degas – to illustrate the key developments of European art since the Renaissance.

Bournville

Bournville is 4 miles south of the city centre, beyond Edgbaston (there are regular trains from Birmingham New Street to Bournville). The major attraction is Cadbury's chocolate factory. Bournville village was the big idea of George Cadbury, the reforming half of the chocolate partnership with his brother Richard. The Cadburys moved their factory out of industrial Birmingham in 1878 to this then-rural site close to the Worcester Canal and the railway. In 1895, George started building a village around it, giving it a Frenchified name out of sheer fancy. Five years later he handed over the property to the Bournville Village Trust, setting out stringent planning guidelines to preserve open space in the village. You can still tell the village apart from the city sprawl that has encompassed it. It is distinguished by red-brick semi-detached Victorian villas and a quaint English style of building. There are no pubs, as the Cadbury brothers were committed teetotal Quakers. Pause on **Bournville village green**, 'one of the small outposts of civilization, still ringed round with barbarism,' in Priestley's words. The small building, modelled on Dunster's butter market in Somerset, was erected by the factory workers in 1913 as a memorial to George Cadbury, who gave them a five-and-a-half-day week, public holidays, works outings and other benefits. There are two old timber-framed buildings on the green, brought to Bournville in the early 1900s to give the place a bit more cachet: 14th-century **Selly Manor** (***t*** *(0121) 472 0199; open Tues–Fri 10–5, April–Sept also weekends 2–5*) was poached by Cadbury from Selly Oak in 1907. Next door is the 13th-century **Minworth Greaves Hall** (*open same hours*), a hall-house from Sutton Coldfield.

Cadbury World

t *(0121) 451 4159; open Feb–Oct daily, Nov–Jan closed Mon and Fri, for tours; adm exp; booking essential.*

Chocolate is England's favourite treat, and Cadbury's the biggest manufacturer of it (although the European Union would say that most of what Cadbury's produces isn't chocolate), so book to avoid queues into Cadbury World, next door to the Bournville factory, to see how bars of Dairy Milk, Flakes, Cream Eggs and Crunchies are made. If you don't have any children with you, go round the back to the Cadbury Collection museum (*free*) to find out about Bournville village and the Cadbury family.

The Black Country

The Black Country, north and west of Birmingham either side of the M6, should be renamed the grey country. The coalmines and choking industrial grime that gave the region its notoriety in the mid-19th century have gone, and the old Black Country towns of Walsall, Wolverhampton, Dudley and Stourbridge have woven themselves into one urban carpet of concrete and brick. 'I felt that I was not looking at this place and that,' wrote J.B. Priestley in 1933, 'but at the metallic Midlands themselves, at a relief map of a heavy industry.' Looking down at the smoking factory chimneys from the ruins of Dudley Castle, Priestley imagined a different future: 'I would keep a good tract of this region as it is now, to be stared and wondered at; but I would find it difficult to ask any but a few curators to live in it.'

Priestley was a visionary. The **Black Country Living Museum** (**t** *(0121) 557 9643; www.bclm.co.uk; open Mar–Oct 10–5, Nov–Feb Wed–Sun 10–4; adm exp*) does just what he recommended. This open-air industrial museum in **Dudley**, which opened its doors in 1978, is a convincing re-evocation of an industrial community as it was, with coalmine and canal-side village. All the houses, shops and workshops are authentic Black Country buildings, painstakingly reconstructed here over the last 25 years. The 26-acre site covers two centuries of industrial history, from a working replica of the Newcomen engine – the world's first steam engine, built in 1712 to pump water from one of Lord Dudley's mines – to the early 20th-century electric trolley buses that buzz visitors around. Wander, poke your nose around doors, watch craftsmen working away in foundries, and eat fish and chips from the village shop (between 12 noon and 3). At the Race Course Colliery you can go underground with torch and helmet, or take a canal boat trip into Lord Dudley's subterranean limestone workings in Castle Hill.

West of Wolverhampton on the A454, **Wightwick Manor** (**t** *(01902) 761 400; www.nationaltrust.org; open Mar–Dec, house Thurs and Sat 1.30–5, gardens Wed, Thurs and Sat 11–6; adm*) boasts a parlour decorated in Pre-Raphaelite style, a medieval hall with Morris wallpapers, textiles and carpets, William de Morgan tiles, books from the Kelmscott Press, and paintings by Madox Brown, Hunt, Millais and Burne-Jones.

Walsall

The New Art Gallery is Walsall's barnstorming new attraction; the old Leather Museum won awards of its own in its day. Both are signposted off main roads into town, or within walking distance if you come by train from Birmingham New Street. A minor attraction *en route* is the **Jerome K. Jerome Birthplace Museum** (**t** *(01922) 653 116; open Sat 12–2 or by appointment*) in a Georgian townhouse on Bradford Street, just south of the centre. The author of *Three Men in a Boat* was born here in 1859, but spent only four years in Walsall before the family moved to Stourbridge and then London, where he worked as a clerk at Euston Station until trying his hand at writing. One room contains the author's writing desk and First World War Red Cross uniform.

The **Leather Museum** (**t** *(01922) 721 153; open April–Oct Tues–Sat 10–5, Sun 12–5; Nov–Mar closes at 4*) takes you on a tour of one of the town's oldest trades, which developed from a good supply of Staffordshire hides and Black Country metal (horse bits, buckles and so on). There are still saddlers and leather goods manufacturers in Walsall, including the Queen's handbag makers. The museum is in an old Victorian loriner's workshop on the north side of town, and displays designer bags and belts.

The **New Art Gallery, Walsall** (**t** *(01922) 654 400, www.artatwalsall.org; open Tues–Sat 10–5, Sun 12–5*) opened in February 2000, a terracotta-tile-clad high-rise in the middle of town that looks modest and a little unusual compared with the other millennium buildings around the country. It was designed by architects Adam Caruso and Peter St John to house the Garman Ryan art collection, which had been gathering dust in its old gallery since 1973. Kathleen Garman, lover and wife of the artist Jacob Epstein, and the American sculptress Sally Ryan accumulated art eclectically to suit their tastes, favouring the works of family and friends – Epstein, of course, Modigliani and Lucian Freud among others. There is no shortage of big names here either, with paintings by Monet, Rembrandt, Constable, Van Gogh, Picasso and Matisse. The works are displayed thematically – birds, flowers, still lifes and so on – in a series of small pine-clad rooms with windows and low ceilings that suggest a living space rather than a conventional gallery. Through the windows you look down on the canal and a town of chimney stacks, low warehouses and high-rises. On the top floor is a restaurant.

Staffordshire

Staffordshire, stretching uneventfully north of Birmingham, won't be top of any visitor's list of places to go in England, but if you're passing through there are several places worth visiting. The theme park at Alton Towers is the county's biggest draw. Travellers with a more historical bent should stop off at the delightful cathedral town of Lichfield, birthplace of Samuel Johnson. Keen shoppers may consider a day's shopping at the factory shops of the old Stoke-on-Trent potteries. In the far north of the county, Leek and the Churnet Valley take you into the Peak District (*see* pp.572-84).

Lichfield

The old cathedral town of Lichfield is no more than 5 miles north of the West Midlands conurbation – yet utterly apart from it. The medieval grid pattern of streets, the cathedral in its close and the Georgian refinements of its architecture are perfect.

The medieval town was developed by the bishop on the other side of Minster Pool, which, along with Stowe Pool, had been dammed as a fish- and mill-pond. The street names – Dam Street, Wade Street, Frog Street – reflect their watery background. The medieval diocese of Lichfield was one of the oldest and largest in the country, dating back to the original Saxon foundation of St Chad. The town itself, at the junction of major old roads (including Roman Watling Street), developed as a staging post. Both Civil War armies seized on its strategic value, thrice smashing the hell out of the Cathedral Close in an attempt to gain control of the town. The 18th century was the town's heyday, with money coming in from the coach and catering trades, smart brick houses replacing the old wooden buildings, balls and musical events in the Swan and George, cultural societies and one or two celebrity residents. Samuel Johnson (1709–84), the son of a Lichfield bookseller, started his life here, establishing a school that was attended by his friend, the young David Garrick. In 1737 they left Lichfield together for London, where Johnson wrote his famous dictionary and Garrick established a reputation as one of the greatest actors of his generation. In 1756 Erasmus Darwin (1731–1802) began a successful medical practice in Lichfield. He was a founder member of the Lunar Society (*see* p.517), but is best known for *Zoonomia* in which he presents the evolutionary argument developed by his grandson Charles Darwin. The daughter of the canon of Lichfield cathedral, **Anna Seward** (1747–1809) wrote the biography of Erasmus Darwin and advised Boswell on his *Life of Johnson*.

Tourist Information

Lichfield: Donegal House, Bore Street, **t** (01543) 308 209. *Open April–Oct Mon–Fri 9–5 and Sat 9–2.*

Lichfield hosts an **International Arts Festival** over 10 days in early–mid-July, during which the town heaves with orchestral and chamber music, film, medieval mystery plays, poetry, jazz and talks. For information call the festival office, **t** (01543) 306 543.

Where to Stay

Lichfield t (01543) –

George Hotel, Bird Street, **t** 414 822, *www.thegeorgelichfield.co.uk* (*expensive*). Handsome stuccoed Georgian building in middle of town, much-used for conferences. Bedrooms with dark wooden furniture and very ordinary en-suite bathrooms.

Bogy Hole, 23 Dam Street, **t** 264 303 (*expensive*). Despite its name, an attractive yellow-painted building; inside friendly and cheerful, with a collection of wooden clogs and a pretty paved backyard. Lovely conservatory breakfast room; bedrooms small and comfortable.

Angel Croft Hotel, Beacon Street, **t** 258 737 (*moderate*). Georgian house on busy road with plain bedrooms; another 12 rooms in Westgate House, another Georgian town-house on the other side of the car park.

The Little Barrow, 62 Beacon Street, **t** 414 500 (*moderate*). Medium-sized 1970s hotel on busy street into town, with 24 en-suite bedrooms, restaurant and bar.

8 Cathedral Close, 8 The Close, **t** 418 483, *gilljones@talk21.com* (*moderate*). Ideal location with three bedrooms, next door to cathedral bookshop, one room overlooking Darwin's herb garden and two facing the west front of the cathedral.

23 Cathedral Close, 23 The Close, **t** 306 142 (*moderate*). Beautiful large Georgianized medieval house with fabulous wooden stairs and grandly proportioned bedrooms; furniture seems flimsy by comparison.

Eating Out

Pizza By Golly, 63 Tamworth Street, **t** 250 916 (*moderate*). Busy Italian pizza restaurant, where you need to reserve a table even on a weekday.

Cathedral Coffee Shop, 19/a The Close (near Bird Street gateway), **t** 306 125 (*cheap*). Sweet cakes, dainty sandwiches and jacket potatoes; stout section of the old curtain wall in the garden.

Pig and Truffle, Tamworth Street, **t** 262 312 (*cheap*). Friendly café-bar. *Serves food 12 noon–2.30pm and Mon–Thurs eves.*

Eastern Eye, Bird Street, **t** 254 399 (*cheap*). Popular, long-established Indian restaurant.

Ruby, St Johns Street, **t** 251 144 (*cheap*). Good Cantonese restaurant.

Around Town

Lichfield is small and easy to get around, with a ladder of streets leading to the cathedral and Beacon Park over the town bridge. The Market Square and Cathedral Close both have a church and celebrity house to visit. In the middle of **Market Square**, in contrasting attitudes, are the statues of Samuel Johnson, slumped in a chair his head resting on his fist ('a ponderosity of stone,' wrote Hawthorne), and his friend and biographer James Boswell, upright with cane and notebook tucked under his arm. Around the pedestal of Johnson's statue are carved scenes from his life including his Penance, described in Boswell's biography: in old age Johnson was tormented by his petulance as a young man in refusing to cover for his sick father, who kept a book-stall in Uttoxeter; to punish himself he spent the night outdoors in the square in the wind and rain without his hat. **St Mary's Church** is now a Heritage Centre, with local history displays and a viewing platform up the spire.

Samuel Johnson's Birthplace Museum

t (01543) 264 972; open April–Sept daily 10.30–4.30, Oct–Mar 12–4.30; adm.

Johnson was born above his father's bookshop in the three-storey building with a projecting front on the corner of Market Square. He spent 25 years in this house, working for his father, teaching, and reading everything he could lay his hands on. He moved to London aged 28 and built his reputation as a scholar, writing articles in the *Gentleman's Magazine* and shooting to fame on the back of his dictionary, published in 1755 after eight years' compilation. Boswell's *Life of Johnson* was an instant success, and bequeathed us a number of witty Johnson quotes prefixed by 'Sir'. Memorabilia on display includes Garrick's walking stick.

Erasmus Darwin Centre

t (01543) 306 260; open Tues–Sat 10–4.30, Sun 12–4.30; adm minimal.

Erasmus Darwin moved to Lichfield in 1756 with his new wife, extended the front of the house facing Beacon Street, planted a botanical garden at the back leading on to the Cathedral Close, and quickly established himself as a brilliant physician, inventor and writer. In the old house there are models of his inventions, such as a speaking machine that said 'ma ma', a copying machine that enabled two documents to be written simultaneously and an undercarriage for horse-drawn coaches that anticipated modern steering. Before you leave poke your head into the delightful Vicar's Close, a perfect medieval square to one side of the herb garden.

St Chad's Cathedral

Lichfield cathedral is one of the early pre-Reformation foundations, reaching all the way back to the original 8th-century cathedral of St Chad, Bishop of Mercia. By the end of the 12th century, the Norman cathedral was too small for all the pilgrims to St Chad's shrine. A new cathedral was built between 1195 and 1285 in local pink sandstone, with three pointed spires. In 1299 the close was fortified with a towered curtain wall and a strong new set of gates. Pilgrims were sent down Dam Street through South Gate, which remains the main approach. This gate was the main target of the first Parliamentarian siege of the cathedral in the Civil War; the central tower of the cathedral was destroyed in the prolonged final siege and the interior was plundered by each army as it gained the upper hand. The cathedral was rebuilt, but restoration continued for two centuries. Gilbert Scott replaced the statues in niches around the outside. Samuel Johnson crops up on the south face, reading a book as usual, among a host of kings and saints. Through the double doors on the west front you get a view down arch after arch of the nave to the stained-glass window of the Lady Chapel. The interior is busy with wall tablets (Anna Seward inside the entrance), busts (Johnson and Garrick in the south transept), medallions (Erasmus Darwin in the south choir aisle) and stone monuments. One of the oldest cathedral treasures, exhibited in the arcaded Chapter House, is the **Lichfield Gospels**; it, a handwritten and decorated copy of the gospel of Mathew, Mark and part of Luke, completed in AD 730 in the intricate style of the Book of Kells and Lindisfarne Gospels.

Wall and *Letocetum*

In the village of **Wall**, south of Lichfield on the A5 (Watling Street) are the remains of the small Roman town of ***Letocetum*** (*t (01543) 480 768, www.english-heritage.org.uk; open April–Sept 10–6, Oct 10–5; adm*). Roman finds were first discovered at the end of the 17th century, and the Roman walls were plundered for stone in the 18th century, according to antiquarian William Stukeley. *Letocetum* was Lichfield's predecessor, an early staging post that developed into a small provincial town. Pottery and building debris have been found for a mile along Watling Street and 650ft back from the road, showing the extent of the town at its 3rd-century peak. What is left are the massive stone foundations of the bathhouses and *mansio* with the road running between them. A small collection of finds is displayed in a museum next to the site.

Burton-upon-Trent

The main landmarks in Burton-upon-Trent, midway between Lichfield and Derby, are the Bass Brewery chimney and water tower. Burton is all about beer. Brewing took off here in the 18th century, benefiting from the pure Trent Valley spring water and the canalization of the River Trent, which enabled speed of delivery and export. William Bass bought his first brewery on the High Street in 1777. By the end of the 19th century Bass was one of the biggest of more than 30 breweries, all crammed into the town centre along with associated industries. A 1921 model of Burton in the Bass Museum shows a town of densely packed industrial buildings and terraced housing in a tangle of railway lines. In the last 50 years the industry has shrunk, but not died.

The **Bass Museum** (*t 0845 600 0598; open 10–4; open 10–4; adm*) inhabits the old Victorian brewery. Next door are the prefab sheds and lorries of the modern brewery. Its beers include Tennants, Staropramen and Bass Ale. Some beer is still made in the old Brewhouse. The history of Burton and Bass is told in the old joinery.

Around Stafford

Izaak Walton's Cottage

I have laid aside business, and gone afishing

Izaak Walton, *The Compleat Angler*

A few miles north of Stafford off the A5013, near the village of Shallowford, is the thatched cottage of the 17th-century writer and fisherman Izaak Walton (*t (01785) 760 278;*

Where to Stay and Eat

Burton-upon-Trent t (01283) –

Woodhouse Farm, t 812 185 (*moderate*). Three en-suite rooms, overlooking lovely countryside where horses graze. Friendly, helpful and fun hosts.

Ye Olde Dog and Partridge, High Street, Tutbury, t 813 030. For lunch, drive out of Burton-upon-Trent to **Tutbury**, a pretty little town with a castle in good walking countryside, a striking black-and-white pub with a good lunch-time carvery (*cheap*) and a brasserie-style menu in the evening.

open Easter–Oct Wed–Sun 1–4.30; adm). The upstairs windows peep out from under the thatch like twinkly eyes and the small garden is a profusion of summer flowers and herbs set in farmland. Walton's famous book, *The Compleat Angler* (1653), published when he was 60, is a conversation between a fisherman (Piscator) and a huntsman (Viator) about the relative merits of their sports, intermingled with songs and poems. It is set on 'Totnam Hill' in London, one May morning. A fowler (Auceps) joins the conversation in a second edition. Charles Cotton, a close friend of Walton, wrote a supplement on fly-fishing in 1676. A third part – *The Experienced Angler* – was later added under the collective title *The Universal Angler, made so by Three Books of Fishing*. The cottage places the bucolic anti-Civil War writer in context.

Shugborough House

***t** (01889) 881 388, www.staffordshire.gov.uk/shugborough; open April–Sept daily 11–5, Oct Sun 11–5; adm.*

A short drive east of Stafford towards Lichfield, within the boundaries of Cannock Chase, a wooded drive banked with rhododendrons leads into the landscaped park of the earls of Lichfield. The estate was the work of Thomas Anson, who inherited a fortune from his elder brother, Admiral Lord Anson, the second Englishman to circumnavigate the globe. He commissioned James 'Athenian' Stuart to build romantic follies around the park, extended the house, collected Old Master paintings and antique sculpture, was a founder member of the Society of Dilettanti, hobnobbed with Josiah Wedgwood and Matthew Boulton and went on Grand Tours; did everything, in other words, to put Shugborough on the map. The estate passed to Thomas's great-nephew, who hired architect Samuel Wyatt (elder brother of the famous neo-classical architect James Wyatt) to smarten up the house, cladding it in stucco and adding a long columned portico. Sadly all the furniture, Old Masters and sculpture were sold in 1842. There is now a **County Museum of Rural Life** in the stables and kitchens, but the most interesting part of the house is the small exhibition of portraits of the rich, royal and famous taken in the 1960s by photographer Lord Lichfield, the 5th Earl. There is a lovely walk from the grounds over Essex Bridge – an old stone packhorse bridge – to the Lock House pub on the banks of the Staffordshire and Worcestershire Canal.

The Pottery Towns of Stoke-on-Trent

And do you really think we may make a complete conquest of France? Conquer France in Burslem. My blood moves quicker, I feel my strength increase for the contest.

A letter from Josiah Wedgwood to business partner Thomas Bentley, 1769

The six towns of Stoke, Hanley, Tunstall, Burslem, Fenton and Longton that comprise the city of Stoke-on-Trent are synonymous with a declining pottery industry and, now that two-thousand giant bottle ovens have been removed from the skyline, a dreary urban horizon. It is here, however, that insanely beautiful pottery and porcelain dishes and ornaments have been manufactured since the 17th century. You can see them in the Museum and Gallery in Hanley and at Spode, Wedgwood and Royal Doulton.

The pottery towns of Stoke-on-Trent, built on local clay, abundant coal and a ready water supply, were already referred to as the Potteries in the 18th century. The local clay produced a mottled red pottery, which was alright for the 'slipware' popular in the 17th century, but not for the elegant white tableware fashionable in the 18th century. To keep up with the fashion, white clay was imported from Cornwall by sea, canal and railway. The end of the 18th century was dominated by Josiah Wedgwood, best known for his unglazed blue Jasper ware, and Josiah Spode, credited with perfecting the composition of bone china (or English porcelain).

The Stoke-on-Trent tourist information centre (*Quadrant Road, Hanley,* **t** *(01782) 236 000*) has details of all the Potteries tours.

Potteries Museum and Art Gallery, Hanley

***t** (01782) 232 323, www.stoke.gov.uk/museum; open Mar–Oct Mon–Sat 10–5, Sun 2–5; Nov–Feb Mon–Sat 10–4, Sun 1–4; adm.*

The Ceramics Gallery has a staggering collection of English pottery and porcelain, mainly from Staffordshire. The collections are grouped historically: Wedgwood, Spode, the Arts and Craft Movement, 20th-century Studio Potters (Leach, Cardew and co.), and collections including the Keiller Collection of mid-18th-century cow creamers and

The Quest for Perfect Porcelain

The refinement of pottery into perfect porcelain was an English national obsession for much of the 18th century, inspired by imports of hard, semi-translucent and beautifully decorated Chinese porcelain wares.

All pottery is made of clay and water, combined with other raw materials to give it its unique qualities. The most primitive clay pots are made of **earthenware**, which is opaque, porous and needs to be glazed to retain liquids. A lead-glazed, decorated earthenware known as slipware put the Staffordshire Potteries on the map in the mid-17th century. Slipware is made by trailing liquid clay – 'slip'– in patterns over finished pots before glazing and firing; sometimes a pattern is scratched through the slip to reveal the colour of the body underneath. The composition of earthenware has gone through many refinements; in the mid-18th century, creamware, a beautiful white earthenware, was made in Staffordshire as a cheaper alternative to porcelain.

Salt-glazed **stoneware**, developed in Europe, was perfected by Staffordshire potters in the early 18th century. It is much more durable than earthenware, made of the same ingredients but fired at much higher temperatures to make it hard and vitreous. Wedgewood's Jasper is a version of stoneware, stained with metal oxides (blue is the most popular colour) and unglazed.

The recipe for **porcelain** with its hard, semi-translucent body eluded European potters until the early 18th century, when huge reserves of kaolin or china clay (half the mix) were discovered in Cornwall. Bone china, perfected by Josiah Spode, is considered the most refined form of pottery. The secret ingredient is ground animal bone, giving a degree of plasticity to the china clay and making it translucent, intensely white and very hard.

the frog service made in 1773–4 for Catherine the Great by Wedgwood and Bentley, each piece bearing Catherine's badge, a green frog in a shield.

Gladstone Pottery Museum, Longton

*Uttoxeter Road, **t** (01782) 319 232; open daily 10–5; adm.*

Alongside the big household names, Stoke-on-Trent produced hundreds of ordinary 'pot banks' with one or more giant coal-fired bottle oven and workshops around a courtyard, making everyday tableware for the lower middle classes. Gladstone Pottery (which has four coal-fired ovens) is a working museum, with potters in Victorian costume demonstrating the processes; the atmosphere is Dickensian.

The Potteries

The World of Spode Visitor Centre

*Spode Works, Church Street, Stoke, **t** (01782) 744 011; visitor centre and shop open Mon–Sat 9–5, Sun 10–4; adm; factory tours Mon–Thurs 10 and 1.30, Fri 10; adm; booking essential.*

Spode has been operating from the same blackened brick buildings for more than two hundred years. The innovations of the Josiah Spodes, father and son, transformed the tableware industry. In 1784, Josiah senior mastered the technique of reproducing hand-painted designs in blue print under a glaze. The willow pattern was the most popular blue under-glaze pattern of all time and is still produced today. In 1800, Josiah junior perfected and popularized the formula for bone china, renowned for its whiteness and translucency. He was appointed 'Potter and English Porcelain Manufacturer to His Royal Highness the Prince of Wales' in 1806. Nowadays Spode has 'diversified' into pottery demonstrations, factory shopping and cream teas.

The Wedgwood Story

*Barlaston, **t** (01782) 204 218; open Mon–Fri 9–5, weekends 10–5; call for factory tour times; adm exp.*

Josiah Wedgwood was king of the potters. His experiments (as recorded in his book) led to a number of new and improved ceramic bodies and glazes. His first success was an improved cream-coloured earthenware, named Queen's Ware after Queen Charlotte bought a tea service in 1766. His restrained, hand-painted border patterns set the trend for decorated tableware. He kept a catalogue of his wares and marked his wares WEDGWOOD – none of which anybody else was doing at the time. His international reputation was based on the invention of a ceramic body called jasper, the classic Wedgwood; blue was the most popular colour, although it also came in green, lilac and black. In 1938, the sixth Josiah Wedgwood left the Etruria factory (built on the Trent and Mersey Canal in 1769) and moved to a greenfield site outside the main conurbation of Barlaston. Refreshments in the bar and restaurant are served on Wedgwood china.

Royal Doulton Visitor Centre

*Nile Street, Burslem, **t** (01782) 292 434; visitor centre and shop open daily 9–5; factory tours Mon–Sat 9.30–5, Sun 10.30–4.30; adm; booking essential.*

Doulton originated in Lambeth, south London, and moved to Burslem in 1878, specializing in fine bone china. In 1901 Edward VII gave the 'Royal' prefix to the company. Doulton's most famous design is the Bunnykins range, introduced in 1934. Around a thousand ceramic figurines are displayed in the museum.

Leek and Around

The old silk-weaving town of **Leek** in the northern corner of Staffordshire is a good base for the Staffordshire moors and Churnet Valley; buy a picnic here and stop off for a drink. On market days the old cobbled market square bustles. Pop into **Brindley Mill** (***t** (01538) 381 446; open Easter–Sept weekends 2–5, July–Aug also Mon–Wed*), a handsome Georgian corn mill on Macclesfield Road. James Brindley (1716–72) is best known as a canal builder, but started out as a Leek millwright, with a workshop on Mill Street. The old mill was attributed to Brindley in 1970, on account of the legend '*1752 JB added*'. It proudly displays one of his notebooks and his theodolite.

The Churnet Valley

Head southeast to the Churnet Valley between Alton and Oakmoor for a day's walking along the wooded paths of **Dimmings Dale**. Head for the Rambler's Retreat on the River Churnet, and walk up the old industrialized valley, transformed in the 19th century by the Earl of Shrewsbury into a romantic woodland with carriage drives and a series of ponds. Further along the valley you glimpse the square towers of Alton Castle, built by Pugin for the 16th Earl. But if it's adrenaline you're after, head straight for the **Alton Towers** theme park (***t** 0870 500 1100, www.altontowers.com; open April–Oct daily 9.30–5.30; adm exp*), and rollercoasters Nemesis and Oblivion. The newest attraction is HEX, built into the ruined mansion of the 15th Earl of Shrewsbury at the centre of the park.

The slender Gothic spire of Pugin's church of St Giles in **Cheadle** rises out of a nest of pinnacles, studded all the way to up the weathervane, soaring above the red roofs of the small Victorian market town. 'Pugin was prouder of Cheadle church than of any of his other buildings,' wrote Pevsner. He called Cheadle the 'real thing'; it most perfectly recreated his idea of a pre-Reformation church of the Middle Ages. In a letter

The Roaches Walk

The Roaches ('rocks' in old French) form the dramatic southwestern edge of the Pennine Moors, and create varied walking countryside in the Dane Valley. There's a good 4-mile walk starting from Gradbach (3 miles west of the A53 Leek–Buxton road), with an interesting detour to Lud's Church, a narrow rocky gorge once used as a hiding place by a group of Lollards, 14th-century religious dissenters.

Tourist Information

Leek: 1 Market Place, **t** (01538) 483 741. *Open Mon–Fri 9.30–5, summer also Sat 9.30–5, winter Sat 10–4.*

Where to Stay and Eat

Leek t (01538) –

Peak Weavers Hotel, King Street, **t** 383 729, *www.peakweavershotel.com* (*moderate*). Large red-brick townhouse up stone steps.

Hotel Rudyard, Lake Road, Rudyard Lake, **t** 306 208, *www.hotelrudyard.com* (*moderate*). Handsome Victorian hotel by wooded lakeside 1½ miles from Leek along the A523 road towards Macclesfield, then left at the sign.

Den Engel, Bodkin House, Bodkin Court, Stanley Street, **t** 373 751 (*moderate*). Belgian bar and restaurant serving up steaming dishes of moules frites, guinea fowl cooked in strong Belgian beer or cod with shrimp sauce, with a range of Belgian beers to drink. Some outside seating.

Primo Piano, Sheep Street, **t** 398 289 (*cheap*). Pizza and pasta. *Closed Sun and Mon.*

Coffee Beans, Derby Street, **t** 383 165 (*cheap*). Modest little tea shop serving ragamuffins and oak cakes, teas and coffees.

The Churnet Valley t (01538) –

The Bank House, Oakmoor, **t** 702 810, *www.smoothhound.co.uk/hotels/bank.html* (*expensive*). Delightful gabled and columned house overlooking Churnet Valley, with courtyard at back and beautiful terraced garden with series of ponds.

The Rambler's Retreat, Dimmingsdale, near Alton, **t** 702 730 (*moderate*). Friendly, superbly located restaurant and coffee shop in an old Victorian mill in a wooded valley. Superb cakes and lunches.

The Talbot Inn, Alton, **t** 702 767 (*moderate*). Old coaching inn, now gastro pub with riverside garden beneath old town bridge. Baguettes, mussels in wine, steak and stilton pie.

Crowtrees Farm, Oakmoor, **t** 702 260, *www.crowtreesfarm.co.uk* (*moderate*). Lovely old farmhouse overlooking Churnet Valley, with fresh and bright interior, tasteful furniture and big beds.

The Bulls Head Inn, High Street, Alton, **t** 702 307, *www.thebullsheadinn.freeserve.co.uk* (*moderate*). Friendly, characterful pub with eight bright, clean rooms, matching curtains and bedspreads and home-cooked pub grub.

The Old School House, Castle Hill Road, Alton, **t** 702 151 (*moderate*). Victorian school house next to church in conservation area, with three bedrooms and a breakfast room overlooking the churchyard.

to his patron, the 16th Earl of Shrewsbury, he referred to 'perfect Cheadle, Cheadle my consolation in all afflictions'. Put a coin in the light metre of the church and it bursts into brilliant medieval Gothic colour, not an inch of the ceiling or walls without decoration. Next door are cloisters (now a private house) and a school, both of them also built by Pugin in the Gothic style.

For a bit of fun, pop into **Les Oakes & Sons General Dealer** at Hales View Farm on Oakmoor Road (***t** (01538) 752 126; open Mon–Fri 9–5.30, weekends 9–4.30*). 'You are now entering a fool's paradise' says a sign outside. Around the back are sinks and baths, trolley wheels, bicycles, windows and school desks. Ask to have a look at the private collection upstairs: typewriters, cash registers, old advertising billboards, wagons, rocking horses and a full-sized plastic horse.

Welsh Marches

Shropshire and Herefordshire

14

Highlights

1 The ruined Roman *civitas* of Wroxeter
2 Ludlow, the classy town of the Earls of March, with Michelin-starred chefs
3 Stone carvings, from the sublime to the rude, at Kilpeck church
4 Caer Caradoc, for the great outdoors (on a hill)

Getting There and Around

The Welsh Marches are most easily reached by **car** off the M54 (north) and M50 (south).

The region is not well-connected by rail. For all **train** information contact **National Rail Enquiries, t** 08457 484950, *www.thetrainline.com.* The scenic **Severn Valley Railway** is a good way to see some riverside landscape.

Coaches travel to the main towns from London and Birmingham. For all coach routes and times contact **National Express, t** 08705 808080, *www.gobycoach.com.* Infrequent local **buses** can take you between places. Call **Traveline, t** 0870 608 2608 for details.

You're best off with a car, a bicycle or on foot. There are two long-distance walking routes (Offa's Dyke path and the Wye Valley Path).

Happy is the eye
'Twixt Severn and Wye.

Touring the Welsh Marches it feels like you've gone back in time. The roads are quiet, towns small and scenery lovely, even around the remains of early industry at **Ironbridge** and the **Forest of Dean** coalfields. This is the nostalgia-tinted landscape of A.E. Housman, the Dymock poets and Elgar; of magical hills, rich pastures, dewy orchards, meandering rivers and red-earth fields below the dark Welsh mountains.

The Marches have a long history of turbulence, peppered with the romantic names of Roger de Montgomery, Llywellyn (Prince of Wales), Edward of March and Owen Glendower. The region got its name after the Norman Conquest (marches means borders): to the west was wild Wales and to the east Norman England. William I divided the Marches into three powerful earldoms around the old Saxon towns of Chester (Hugh d'Avranches), **Shrewsbury** (Roger de Montgomery) and **Hereford** (William FitzOsborn). The Marcher lords exercised kingly powers to establish towns and forests, wage war on the Welsh and build as many castles as they wanted. A main line of Marcher castles runs from north to south: Chester, Shrewsbury, **Ludlow**, Hereford and **Chepstow**; others (**Wigmore**, **Clun** and **Bishop's Castle**) occupy a second range of hills; and there are countless other motte and bailey castles dotted around the borderlands (70 between Shrewsbury and Hereford alone). **Stokesay Castle** is a lovely fortified manor house. In fact these hills had been a frontier long before the Normans: there are Celtic forts on every hill top (**Old Oswestry**, **Caer Caradoc** and the **Wrekin**); the remains of a Roman legionary fortress at **Wroxeter**; and **Offa's Dyke**, the famous bank and ditch boundary built by King Offa at the end of the 8th century.

In the 18th century a host of Williams followed in the footseps of the Conqueror to colonize the region: travellers and tourists including William Gilpin (who published *Observations on the River Wye*) followed by painters and poets including Joseph Mallord William Turner and William Wordsworth, came to the Marches in search of the picturesque, especially around the **Wye Valley** with its ruined abbeys and castles. Elegant country houses appeared at **Berrington Hall** and **Attingham Park**, commanding views of the mountains from parks landscaped by Capability Brown and Humphrey Repton. **Hawkstone Park**, an 18th-century pleasure garden north of Shrewsbury, has at its heart the ruined castle of the **de Audleys**, who fought in the Welsh campaigns of Henry II, Edward I and Henry IV.

Shropshire

Edward IV and [his queen] Elizabeth indeed are still to be met almost anywhere in the county; as regards domestic architecture, few parts of England are still more vividly old-English.

Henry James, 1877

The mighty **Severn** is Shropshire's main river, giving Shrewsbury, the Ironbridge Gorge and Bridgnorth their character as it flows across a wide plain. Out of the flat valley rise the **Shropshire Hills**. Pioneering geology was conducted here by Sir Roderick Murchison, whose 1839 book *The Silurian System* introduced a 40-million-year new chapter into the history of the earth. The *Silures* were an Iron Age tribe who lived in the border lands, but most Shropshire hill forts were built by the *Cornovii* tribe, whose capital was the **Wrekin** until the Romans moved them to the *civitas* of **Wroxeter**. When the Romans left, the Mercians pushed the *Cornovii* west behind **Offa's Dyke**, the famous earthworks named after the King of Mercia who dominated 8th-century England. **Shrewsbury** became the new border capital. After the Norman Conquest it became the Marcher stronghold of the new earl, Roger de Montgomery, with a motte and bailey castle and walls. By the late Middle Ages, Shrewsbury had a monopoly on Welsh wool and medieval wool merchants ploughed money into handsome churches and townhouses. In the surrounding countryside are the elegant 18th-century properties of **Hawkstone** and **Attingham**, built by the Hill cousins, and the industrial remains of the **Ironbridge Gorge**, picturesque cradle of the Industrial Revolution.

Elsewhere, the Norman Marcher lords established new towns around castles to control the borders. Some, like **Ludlow** and **Bridgnorth**, have prospered; others, like remote **Clun** and **Bishop's Castle**, have barely grown since. They were the first to be raided by the legendary princes of Wales: Llywelyn the Great (1173–1240), his grandson Llywelyn the Last Leader (1228–82) and Owen Glendower (1355–*c*.1416), whose conspiracy with Henry Percy and Edmund Mortimer to defeat Henry IV and divide England and Wales three ways features in Shakespeare's *Henry IV Part 1*. These towns are all interesting to visit. Ludlow is a gem: it boasts a fabulous castle and Michelin-starred restaurants. The upland walks on the **Long Mynd**, **Stiperstones** and **Church Stretton Hills** are some of the high points of south Shropshire. North Shropshire is more ordinary, although **Oswestry**, on the border, has a certain fascination.

Shrewsbury

Shrewsbury sits on a sandstone hill in an unassailable loop of the Severn where the London–Holyhead road crosses. Its streets are a jolly old tangle best explored on foot, with a rich mix of red and grey stone, black-and-white timber-framed and Georgian brick buildings. 'I never knew such pleasant walking,' wrote Nathaniel Hawthorne after a visit to the town in 1885. Shrewsbury was a prosperous centre of the medieval wool and cloth trade, profiting from the rich sheep pastures of the Welsh hills and road and river links to England. There are three ways in: down the narrow neck of land from the north, guarded by the sandstone castle of Marcher potentate Roger de Montgomery; over English Bridge from the east; or over Welsh Bridge from the west. In Shrewsbury the old stories come alive: the execution in June 1283 by hanging, drawing and quartering of the Welsh prince Dafydd, brother of Llywelyn ap Gruffud, Prince of Wales, at the orders of Edward I; the overnight stay of Henry Tudor, future King of England, *en route* to the Battle of Bosworth; the exhibition of the corpse of 'Hotspur' in the market square after the Battle of Shrewsbury; and the manoeuvres of Charles I, who launched his Civil War campaign in Shrewsbury. Shrewsbury was also the home town of such great men as Robert 'Clive of India' (1725–74) and Charles Darwin (1809–82), who both appear as statues around town.

Shrewsbury Castle and Shropshire Regimental Museum

t (01743) 358 516; open May–Sept Tues–Sat 10–5, Sun–Mon 10–4; Oct–mid-Dec and mid-Feb–April Wed–Sat 10–4; adm.

Opposite the entrance to the castle grounds is the old **Shrewsbury School** building, now the public library. On either side of the arched entrance, atop ornamental pillars, are statues of 16th-century schoolboys wearing ruffs and baggy knee breeches. Note the bearded bronze **statue of Charles Darwin**, the school's most famous old boy.

Across the road, you enter the old inner bailey of the **castle** through heavy Civil War gates.The castle guards the only land approach to town. What you see today is the result of centuries of construction, from the Norman militarization of the border through the Welsh campaigns of Henry II and Edward I to the Civil War and the domestication of the site by bridge builder Thomas Telford in the 18th century.

The oldest part of the castle, Roger de Montgomery's motte, collapsed into the river in 1271; its stump is surmounted by Laura's Tower, an 18th-century folly. Roger's rebellious son forfeited the Montgomery estates to Henry II, who used the castle as a launch pad for his military campaigns into Wales, rebuilding the curtain walls and great hall in stone. After Edward I annexed Wales, the castle at Shrewsbury became redundant and fell into ruins. Charles I did not stay here at the beginning of the Civil War, basing himself instead in the Council House, off Castlegates. Telford turned the great hall into the neo-Gothic home of Sir William Pulteney, MP for Shrewsbury. It now houses a **museum of county regiments**, the biggest of which was the King's Shropshire Light Infantry. War trophies include a lock of Napoleon's hair (snipped by the 53rd Regiment on St Helena) and the blue-velvet-covered baton of Hitler's right-hand man, Grand Admiral Karl Dönitz, captured at Flensburg in May 1945.

Town Centre

From the railway station climb up Castlegates; otherwise find your way into the town centre from one of the car parks outside the walls. It takes about 20 minutes to circumnavigate the town on foot, but maps are misleading; they give no idea of the hills. **St Alkmund's Place** inhabits one of the highest points, the original market place. Medieval timber-framed buildings squeeze into its cobbled confines alongside black-and-white Victorian fakes and two old churches, one a pre-Conquest foundation. The

Getting There and Around

The M54 **motorway** takes you west from the West Midlands and after Telford turns into the A5, which leads you straight into Shrewsbury. Park outside the city walls at Gay Meadows, across English Bridge, or the Frankwell car park, across Welsh Bridge.

Shrewsbury is on the Cardiff–Manchester railway line, and there are direct **trains** from Birmingham and Chester. From London, change at Birmingham.

National Express runs at least two **coaches** a day from London, and more from Birmingham.

Tourist Information

Shrewsbury: The Music Hall, The Square, **t** (01743) 281 200. *Open summer Mon–Sat 9.30–5.30, Sun 10–4; winter Mon–Sat 10–5.*

Historical Walking Tours depart from the tourist information centre, summer daily 2.30, winter Sat 2.30.

Where to Stay

Shrewsbury t (01743) –

The Lion Hotel, **t** 353 107 (*expensive*). Ancient coaching inn on main road into town which counts Charles Dickens among its former guests; four buildings of different ages bolted together, ranging from beamy medieval to functional 1960s; 58 bedrooms; comfortable bars, lounges and restaurant.

Prince Rupert Hotel, Butcher Row, **t** 499 955, *www.prince-rupert-hotel.co.uk* (*expensive*). Central black-and-white 17th-century townhouse; 70 generic period-style rooms, oak-panelled restaurant and anodyne ambience.

Tudor House, 2 Fish Street, **t** 351 735, *www.tudorhouseshrewsbury.com* (*expensive*). Black-and-white townhouse opposite St Alkmund's church; five pretty bedrooms.

Bellstone Hotel, Bellstone, **t** 242 100, *www.bellstone-hotel.co.uk* (*moderate*). Tastefully modernized city-centre hotel with 18 rooms and contemporary café-bar and brasserie.

The Shrewsbury Hotel, Bridge Place, Mardol, **t** 236 203 (*cheap*). New 'Wetherlodge', with busy chain pub attached; friendly staff; 22 neat pine-furnished bedrooms.

College Hill Guesthouse, 11 College Hill, **t** 365 744 (*cheap*). Friendly, long-established B&B in Georgian-fronted Tudor house behind the Square; six twin bedrooms.

The Golden Cross Hotel, 14 Princess Street, **t** 362 507, *www.goldencrosshotel.co.uk* (*cheap*). Quaint Civil War pub in quiet spot overlooking St Chad's Green; six double rooms with bathroom down hall.

Eating Out

Shrewsbury is not a great gastronomic town like Ludlow, nor have the big chain café-bars

market was relocated in the early Middle Ages to a square down the hill; you can still see the old butchers' hooks hanging off Abbot's House on **Butcher Row**. Photogenic **Bear Steps** lead down to Fish Street. **Grope Lane**, one of several medieval alleyways or 'shuts' around town, leads on down to High Street. To the north, the 222ft-high tower of **St Mary's church** rises from a delightful old close, including **Drapers' Hall**, the headquarters of the town's early 17th-century cloth company. A plaque on the west tower wall of the church commemorates steeplejack Robert Cadman (1711–39) who fell to his death trying to walk a tightrope over the Severn between the tower and Gay Meadow. ''Twas not for want of skill or courage to perform the task he fell. No, no, a faulty cord being drawn too tight hurried his soul on high to take her flight...' The medieval stained glass was imported from north European churches by the incumbent vicar in the 19th century. **St Mary's Water Lane** runs down to the only remaining watergate in the old town walls between sandstone walls.

The grey stone **market hall** of 1595 dominates the **market square**. It stands on a sturdy set of stone pillars with an open ground floor. On the north front is an armour-

and restaurants yet made a big impression, but the hotels, pubs and cafés do reasonable nosh, and there are one or two homely long-established restaurants.

Osteria Da Paolo, Hills Lane, **t** 243 336 (*moderate*). Tucked away down an alley near museum; friendly proprietor mingles with the guests. Basic hearty Italian food.

Cromwell's Hotel, 11 Dogpole, **t** 361 440. Friendly, recently revamped pub-restaurant and wine bar; in the small brick and wicker restaurant (*moderate*) you could eat king prawns followed by baked fillet of monkfish on pesto mash and sticky toffee pudding. The wine bar menu features toasted panini and salads. Upstairs are six rooms in modern, beige, minimalist style (*expensive*).

Sol Brasserie-Bar, 82 Wyle Cop, **t** 340 560 (*moderate*). Behind narrow shop front is a long, breezily decorated restaurant with imaginative, elaborate international-style cooking. *Closed Sun and Mon.*

Philpots, Butcher Row (*cheap*). Good takeaway sandwiches.

Owens Café-Bar and Bistro, Butcher Row, **t** 363 633 (*cheap*). Lively, fun 'jazz bar' for a toasted sandwich, Italian-style coffee or full meat or fish meal. Musical instruments on colourful walls. *Open late Wed–Sat, with live music on Thurs (acoustic) and Fri (local bands) eves.*

Three Fishes, Fish Street, **t** 344 793 (*cheap*). No-smoking pub with quiet crowd, real ales including Hobson's locally brewed beer and standard pub grub.

Bellstone Brasserie, Bellstone, **t** 242 100 (*cheap*). Attractive sunny café-bar-brasserie, perfect for an early evening drink and nibbles or breakfast.

The Pantry, Golden Cross Passage (off High Street), **t** 344 929 (*cheap*). Restaurant and café, with open kitchen where you can see your quiche being made.

Bear Steps Coffee House, **t** 244 355. Charming place for coffee, tea or light lunch at top of Bear Steps in the heart of old Shrewsbury. Seating outside, under covered arcade.

The Armoury, Victoria Quay, Victoria Avenue, **t** 340 525 (*cheap*). Airy brick-walled former military depot on the river road between Welsh Bridge and park, now a pub and restaurant with contemporary pub-grub-style menu.

Entertainment

The Music Hall, The Square, **t** 281 281. Victorian music hall, now small film theatre showing arthouse films, and occasional theatre, amateur opera, jazz and classical music, tribute bands or Christmas pantomime.

Buttermarket, Howard Street, **t** 231 142. Club which holds jazz evenings in the cellar once a week.

Shrewsbury Castle, **t** 361 196. Summer theatre, mainly Shakespeare.

clad **statue of Richard of York**, father of Edward IV, salvaged from the Welsh Bridge in 1791. Opposite is a bronze **statue of Robert 'Clive of India'**, born in Shrewsbury, erected in 1860. The grand buildings on the stone-flagged square belonged to Shrewsbury's wealthy wool and cloth merchants, who conducted their business in the market. 'They have an indescribable charm for me,' wrote Nathaniel Hawthorne of the houses in 1855, 'the more, I think, because they were wooden – but, indeed, I cannot tell why it is that I like them so well, and am never tired of looking at them.'

The Georgian and Victorian town stretches south of the market square between the old and new **St Chad's churches**. The old collegiate church collapsed in 1788, leaving a red sandstone ruin. Its magnificent neo-classical successor is one of Shrewsbury's architectural showpieces. It was built in 1790–2 by George Steuart, the architect of Attingham Park, with a portico attached to a round nave that rises to a three-tiered tower and cupola. Painted glass windows by local artist David Evans, installed in the 1840s, illuminate the interior. The overgrown churchyard featured in a 1980s film of Charles Dickens' *A Christmas Carol*.

Shrewsbury Museum and Art Gallery on Barker Street (***t*** *(01743) 361 196; open May–Sept Tues–Sat 10–5, Sun–Mon 10–4; Oct–April Tues–Sat 10–4*) occupies the 17th-century mansion of wealthy William Rowley, on the west of town. Everyone calls it Rowley's House. It houses archaeological finds from Wroxeter: Roman tombstones, javelin tips and buckles; a dedication to Hadrian ('son of the deified Trajan, grandson of deified Nerva...') inscribed in stone; and a replica of the solid silver Wroxeter mirror.

Shrewsbury Abbey

t *(01743) 232 723; open Easter–Oct 10–4.30, Nov–Easter 10.30–3.30.*

The old **Shrewsbury Abbey church**, a mass of red sandstone, guards the southern road out of town. In 1083, when Roger de Montgomery founded the Benedictine abbey, there was no English Bridge, and the river flowed past its doors. The 12th-century abbey provided the realistic setting and inspiration for Ellis Peter's 'Brother Cadfael' detective stories. In *A Morbid Taste for Bones*, Cadfael goes to the Welsh town of Gwytherin to negotiate for the bones of St Winefride. *One Corpse Too Many* takes place in the summer of 1138, with the fall of Shrewsbury Castle to the army of King Stephen, and the execution of the defenders. The abbey's early prosperity, boosted by St Winefride's bones, brought new building in the 14th century, when the west tower was added and the interior remodelled in Gothic style. The armoured statue of Edward III on the west front dates from this period. At the Dissolution, the nave became the parish church; transepts, chapels and monastic buildings were demolished. The rough stonework on the exterior is Victorian: John Loughborough Pearson rebuilt the east end, blending the Norman and Gothic elements of the medieval church; little of what you see is original. In a niche of the south aisle is the headless stone monument of a knight, believed to be de Montgomery, who died in the abbey in 1094. The tomb of Richard Onslow, speaker of Elizabeth I's House of Commons, and his wife, was moved into the church after old St Chad's collapsed in 1788.

Around Shrewsbury

Battlefield Church

Two miles north of Shrewsbury, down a track off the A49 Whitchurch road, you come to **St Mary Magdalene Church** (*open Sun 2–5, or pick up the key from the lawn-mower shop next door to Davenport garage, 100 yards down the A5112 Shrewsbury road from the roundabout*), founded in 1408 to commemorate the Battle of Shrewsbury, fought here in 1403. Five chaplains were employed to pray for Henry IV and the souls of the battle dead (5–9,000 men died). Henry's stone effigy stands above the east window, minus his sword. The battle is the climax of Shakespeare's *Henry IV Part 1*: dashing Prince Hal puts an end to his profligate ways by killing Sir Henry Percy, 'Hotspur', on his way to join Owen Glendower's Welsh army ('Three times hath Henry made head against my power; thrice from sandy-bottomed Severn have I sent him bootless home'). Edmund Mortimer, brother-in-law of Hotspur and son-in-law of Glendower, sided with the rebels. All three were fed up with King Henry, and signed an agreement (the 'Tripartite Indenture') proposing to carve up England and Wales between them. A lot was at stake in the three-hour battle. Hotspur was killed and staked up in Shrewsbury market. Prince Hal was wounded by an arrow in the face, but carried on fighting (and became king). Edmund Mortimer escaped, dying in 1409. Glendower fought other battles – he invaded England as far as Worcester – but with decreasing hopes of winning Welsh independence. He was never captured, however.

On the day of battle,the King's army lined up on the ridge near **Haughmond Abbey** (*off the B5062, northeast of Shrewsbury;* ***t*** *(01743) 709 661; open April–Sept 11–5; adm*), now in ruins. The Augustinian abbey was founded by the Fitzalans, earls of Arundel and Clun. The abbot's hall was burned down in the Civil Wra, but the chapter house has an impressive stone-carved entrance arch and old timber ceiling.

Hawkstone Park

...it excels Dovedale, by the extent of its prospects, the awfulness of its shades, the horrors of its precipices, the verdure of its hollows and the loftiness of its rocks...

Samuel Johnson, 1774

Fourteen miles north of Shrewsbury up the A49 are the newly restored 18th-century pleasure gardens of Sir Rowland Hill and his son Richard. Their grand neo-classical house (now a Christian centre) opens to visitors in August. Hawkstone Park (***t*** *(01939) 200 611; open Jan–Mar weekends 10–4, Easter–Oct Wed–Sun 10–5, July–Aug daily 10–6; adm*) stretches over four wooded sandstone hills. Richard cut the paths and steps into the hillside, excavated caves and tunnels, built follies and created views of Redcastle Rock – on which you can pick out the ruins of the medieval castle of the de Audleys, Marcher warlords involved in the Welsh campaigns of Henry II, Edward I and Henry IV.

Attingham Park

t *(01743) 708 162; open Easter–Oct, house Fri–Tues 12–5, grounds daily 10–8; Nov–Dec grounds daily 10–5; adm.*

The austere neo-classical portico of Attingham Park, 4 miles southeast of Shrewsbury on the B4380, looks south over Humphrey Repton parkland to the Shropshire Hills. The unusual Palladian plan by architect George Steuart was designed to enclose the house of Noël Hill, a cousin of the Hawkstone Hills. In 1782, the year building started, Noël inherited a fortune. Two years later he was made the 1st Lord Berwick by Pitt the Younger, for his work as MP for Shropshire. Steuart designed the wings in the French fashion: one masculine for the Lord and one feminine for the Lady. The west wing is decorated in dark heavy wood; the east wing is light and exotic. The 2nd Lord Berwick added the Repton grounds and glazed picture gallery by John Nash before he went bankrupt and sold the contents. The classic Grand Tour paintings were added by the 3rd Lord, who spent 25 years as a diplomat in Italy.

The **Mile Walk** was laid out in 1770 by a little-known landscape designer called Thomas Leggett. It takes you to the 12-acre walled garden, which hasn't been in use for years – a real Frances Hodgson Burnet-style *Secret Garden*, complete with gardener's bothy, derelict glasshouses and vegetable stores.

Wroxeter or *Viroconium Cornoviorum*

t (01743) 761 330; open April–Sept 10–6, Oct 10–5, Nov–Mar 10–4; adm.

Across the B4380, adjoining the Attingham estate, are the remains of the tribal capital of the *Cornovii* and fourth largest Roman city in Britain. The legionary fortress, forum colonnade and public baths have been excavated. The strategic position, where Watling Street crossed the Severn, provided a base for the Welsh campaigns of the XIVth and XXth legions. In AD 90, when the army moved to a new fortress at Chester, *Viroconium* became a civilian town. Major public buildings were erected for Emperor Hadrian's British tour in AD 121. 'Old Work' was part of the entrance from the exercise hall (*palaestra*) into the bath-house. Across the lane, the column bases once formed the portico of the forum. In the small **museum** a replica of the Hadrianic dedication stone records the building of the forum by the *civitas Cornoviorum* in AD 130.

The Wrekin

Three miles east of Wroxeter rises the Wrekin, 1,335ft of ancient volcanic rock, above the Shrewsbury plain. On top are the double ramparts of a massive Iron Age hill fort, the home of the *Cornovii* tribe at the time of the Roman Conquest, when the tribal capital moved to *Viroconium Cornoviorum*. The views of the Shropshire countryside are staggering, with the distinctive shapes of Wenlock Edge and Caer Caradoc to the southwest. Take the minor road that branches off the A5 at the M54 junction as you head east from Shrewsbury; a steep footpath leads to the summit.

On the Trail of the Fugitive King

The story of the six weeks King Charles II spent on the run in England would make a great comic film. He went on the run after an unsuccessful attempt to reclaim the throne at the head of a Scottish army, three years after the execution of his father, Charles I, in 1649. The Royalists marched south from Scotland down the west of England, recruiting as they went. The Parliamentarian army caught up with them at Worcester in 1651, inflicting a crushing defeat. Charles was bundled to safety through the city gates and taken 30 miles north to the Shropshire manor house of the Giffords, loyal Catholic supporters, 10 miles northwest of Wolverhampton. From there his plan was to go west to the Welsh coast and flee to France. It proved impossible because all the Severn ferry crossings were being watched by Parliamentarians. It was also impossible to return to the Giffords' house, so he was brought to their old hunting lodge in the oak woods at Boscobel. There he spent the next two days, one of them up a tree while the Parliamentarians searched the house. Then he moved 10 miles east to Moseley Old Hall, on the outskirts of Wolverhampton, from there moving slowly southwest between Catholic safe houses via Stratford-upon-Avon to Bristol, spending much of his time crammed into secret cupboards. He crossed Somerset to Lyme Regis, where for the second time he failed to set sail. The last leg of his fugitive tour of England was east through Dorset, Wiltshire and Hampshire to the Sussex coast, where he finally escaped on a coal barge.

Oswestry and Around

In the northwest of the county, between the Welsh hills and the Shropshire plain, the old market town of Oswestry serves a scattered rural population on both sides of the border. It is a classic border town, frequently burned to the ground in border raids. The modern town took shape in the 19th century, when Cambrian Railways moved in – a building explosion in red brick. There's not much to keep here; it's the countryside around that is the big attraction, with views over the plain and west towards the Berwyn hills. Just over the border are the attractions of Llangollen and the Dee Valley.

Old Oswestry

Less than a mile north of Oswestry is a magnificent Iron Age hill fort. It takes 40 minutes just to walk around the ramparts, which were built between the 5th and the 3rd centuries BC, when Old Oswestry became the regional base of the *Cornovii*.

Tourist Information

Oswestry: Heritage Centre, 2 Church Terrace, **t** (01691) 662 753. *Open April–Oct Mon–Sat 9.30–5; Nov–Mar Mon–Sat 10–4.*

Big Wed and Sat **markets** spill out from Market Hall.

Ellesmere: Mereside, **t** (01691) 622 981. *Open Easter–May and Oct 11–4, June–Sept 10–5.*

Ellesmere Info Link, Wharf Road, **t** (01691) 624 488. *Open Mon–Wed and Fri 10–4, Sat 10–1.*

Where to Stay and Eat

Oswestry t (01691) –

The Wynnstay Hotel, Church Street, **t** 655 261 (*expensive*). Handsome Georgian coaching inn with porticoed entrance, run by Best Western; 29 formulaic but tidy bedrooms; lounge bar and restaurant (country-inn style of cooking with Mediterranean flavour).

Sebastian's Hotel and Restaurant, 45 Willow Street, **t** 655 444, *www.sebastians-hotel.co.uk* (*expensive*). Oswestry's finest 'restaurant with rooms'. Five-course set menu (including appetizer and sorbet) of hearty, unfussy French cooking including Fleetwood fish and Welsh lamb. Eight charming bedrooms, some in stables, with oak floorboards.

The Walls Restaurant, Welsh Walls Road, **t** 670 970 (*moderate*). Old school house. Dishes include chicken breast, lamb shank, roasted red pepper and pasta.

The Oak Inn, Church Street, **t** 652 304 (*cheap*). Real-ale pub opposite church, no music or pub grub; quiet and civilized. *Open eves only.*

Jack Mytton, Hindford, **t** 679 861 (*cheap*). A mile out of Whittington on Ellesmere road, a welcoming family restaurant named after legendary Mad Jack, who rode a bear. *Closed Mon in winter.*

Shropshire Poacher, Heritage Centre, 2 Church Terrace, **t** 671 323 (*cheap*). Pretty patio at back; offers light lunches such as leek and mushroom crumble and sandwiches.

Ellesmere t (01691) –

The Black Lion Hotel, Scotland Street, **t** 622 418 (*moderate*). Old-fashioned town-centre hotel; three bedrooms with patchwork quilts. Open all day in summer for hearty four-square lunches.

Mereside Farm, opposite Moors car park, **t** 622 404 (*moderate*). Warm welcome with pot of tea on arrival, two bedrooms with pretty fire surrounds and cosy sitting room with log fire; stone's throw from mere.

The Boat, Erbistock (follow A528 Wrexham road north of Ellesmere, turning left at Dee Bridge), **t** (01978) 780 666 (*cheap*). A picturesque riverside pub at the end of a winding lane; sausage and horseradish mash for lunch in the bar or garden, which tumbles down to the Dee, and French/English country-inn-style evening meals of beautifully prepared and presented duck, cod, lamb and steak in airy restaurant (*moderate*).

Catholic Hideaways of Eastern Shropshire

Between the A5 and the M54 east of Telford, **Boscobel House** (**t** *(01902) 850 244, www.english-heritage.org.uk; open Mar–Oct daily 11–5, Nov Wed–Sun 11–4; adm*), a shambolic black-and-white timber-framed farmhouse enclosing a dusty courtyard, incorporates the 17th-century hunting lodge of the Giffords, where Charles II hid from the Parliamentarians in priest holes and oak trees at the end of the second Civil War. Not much survives of the 12th-century church of **White Ladies Priory** – Shropshire's only nunnery – just south of Boscobel, and nothing at all of the Giffords' old house.

Moseley Old Hall (**t** *(01902) 782 808; open Easter–mid-Oct weekends and Wed 1–5; Nov–mid-Dec Sun 1–4; adm*), off junction 1 of the M54, was the home of Thomas Whitgreave and his widowed mother Alice. It was Charles II's second stopover. Thomas was a staunch Catholic Royalist, who had fought at Naseby. Charles arrived on 8 September 1651 and stayed two days. You can see the four-poster bed in which he slept when he wasn't hiding in the compartment under the trap door in the cupboard next to the chimney breast. The cupboard used to be concealed behind panelling too.

Ironbridge Gorge

The Severn runs south of the 'new town' of Telford through the Ironbridge Gorge, named after its elaborate cast-iron bridge. The old market town of **Ironbridge** is the heart of the gorge. The old riverside settlements were 18th- and 19th-century centres of industrial activity: contemporary depictions of the gorge resemble traditional portrayals of hell for the smoke, noise and fire. With the development of steam power and the railways, the gorge slipped back into rural obscurity, but since the 1960s a series of industrial museums has been developed around the old iron, tile and pottery works. The historic epicentre is the valley of **Coalbrookdale**, where Quaker ironmaster Abraham Darby established his ironworks in 1709, and developed the revolutionary technique of smelting with coke, rather than the more expensive charcoal. Darby mass-produced cheap cast-iron cooking pots; his son and grandson, also Quakers, manufactured boats, steam engines and bridges – backed by Quaker financiers such as William Reynolds.

The Iron Bridge, Tollhouse and Museum of the Gorge

Start with the **Iron Bridge** itself. It was the first large-scale iron bridge in the world, built in 1779 at the Coalbrookdale works by Abraham Darby III to the design of Thomas Pritchard, a Shrewsbury architect. It was needed to carry men and materials to and from the industrialized south bank of the river, but it was also a great PR coup, exciting interest in cast iron. There is an exhibition about the bridge in the old **toll-house**. A 10-minute walk from the bridge is the **Museum of the Gorge** (**t** *(01952) 433 522; all Ironbridge museums and sites open Mar–Oct 10–5, main sites stay open in winter, same hours; smaller sites close; adm; joint ticket for all museums and sites*) located in the old neo-Gothic warehouse of the Coalbrookdale Company, where you can get your bearings; its highlight is a large-scale model of the gorge in 1796.

Getting There and Around

Take the M54 **motorway** to Telford, then follow Ironbridge Gorge Museum signs, which guide you into Ironbridge via the A442, past Blists Hill Victorian Town.

Trains run to Telford, from London Euston via Birmingham, from the north via Wolverhampton, and from the west via Shrewsbury.

National Express **coaches** also go to Telford, direct from London or via Birmingham.

You can pick up **local buses** from **Telford Bus Station** to Ironbridge. For information call **Telford Travel Link**, **t** (01952) 200 005.

A **shuttle bus** runs between the museums in summer. In winter you really need a car.

Tourist Information

Telford: **t** (01952) 238 008.

Ironbridge Gorge: The Wharfage, **t** (01952) 432 166. *Open Mon–Fri 9–5, weekends 10–5.*

A good-value 'passport ticket' lets you into all 10 Ironbridge Gorge museums.

Where to Stay

Ironbridge t (01952) –

The Valley Hotel, **t** 432 247, *www.valleyhotel.co.uk* (*expensive*). Originally an 18th-century country house, this hotel comprises a cluster of chimneyed buildings and converted stables around a courtyard; tile manufacturer Arthur Maw owned the house, and installed decorative tiles in the hall and stairwell; 35 neat, bright rooms.

The Old Vicarage, Church Road **t** 432 525 (*expensive*). Large red-brick 1901 building nestling above Coalbrookdale with wide corridors and elegant high-ceilinged rooms.

Coalbrookdale Villa, Paradise, **t** 433 450, *www.coalbrookdalevilla.co.uk* (*moderate*). Wonderful Victorian-Gothic ironmaster's house tucked away in the trees above the dale; long pointed-arch windows, beautiful airy hallway and four pleasant rooms.

The Grove Hotel, 10 Wellington Road, **t** 432 240, *www.fat-frog.co.uk* (*moderate*). Friendly Georgian coaching inn with four modest rooms and the popular **Fat Frog Restaurant**.

The Library House, Severn Bank, **t** 432 299, *www.libhouse.enta.net* (*moderate*). Haven of old-world charms half a minute's walk from the bridge down a stone-flagged alley of pot plants. Interior crammed with prints and photos. Dining room has quarry-tiled floor, old pine kitchen table and dresser full of shiny copper pots; four bedrooms.

Thorpe House, Coalport (a mile from Ironbridge following the river), **t** 586 789, *thorpehouse@tiscali.co.uk* (*moderate*). Rambling Victorian riverside house with dusky breakfast room and four bedrooms. Strong coffee served at breakfast in nice china cups and saucers.

Eating Out

Ironbridge Brasserie and Wine Bar, 29 High Street, **t** 432 716 (*moderate*). Bistro-style menu featuring fillet steak and (Brixham) fish dishes; wine bar downstairs and patio garden overlooking river and bridge. *Book.*

Oliver's Vegetarian Bistro, 33 High Street, **t** 433 086 (*cheap*). Menu includes cashew and carrot roast. *Open Tues–Sat eves, weekends and school holidays also lunchtime.*

Horse and Jockey, 15 Jockey Bank, **t** 433 798 (*cheap*). Small family-run Victorian pub just off Madley road out of gorge. It has won a national 'best steak and kidney pie' award.

The Malthouse, The Wharfage, **t** 433 712, *malthse@globalnet.co.uk* (*moderate*). Calls itself a 'country pub restaurant and bar with rooms'; stylish and modern. Bar snacks include soup or sausage and mash; restaurant offers grilled salmon or honey-roast pork belly; live jazz nights Thurs–Sun; six tasteful, bright bedrooms.

The Fat Frog Restaurant, Grove Hotel, 10 Wellington Road, **t** 433 269, *www.fat-frog.co.uk*. Continental restaurant in basement with murals, gingham table-cloths and candles. *Closed Sun eve.*

Coalbrookdale Inn, 12 Wellington Road, **t** 433 953 (*cheap*). Excellent old-fashioned real-ale pub, serves pub grub until 8pm.

The Butcher's Bar, 70 High Street, Broseley, **t** 884 410 (*cheap*). Popular bar in old butcher's shop with *trompe l'oeil* figures on the walls, including a woman sitting in a corner and a man using the phone.

Coalbrookdale and Darby Houses.

Before the Iron Bridge was built the whole gorge was known as Coalbrookdale, the name used for the side valley in which Darby established his ironworks in 1709. At one end of the complex is the Great Warehouse, now the **Museum of Iron** (***t*** *(01952) 433 522; open 10–5; adm*), packed with cast-iron cauldrons. A model of Coalbrookdale in 1885 helps to make sense of the lifeless site, with its Long Warehouse, on stilts so that trains could be loaded underneath, and the Old Furnace, surrounded by ruined workshops and a derelict waterwheel.

The speed of their own industrial expansion overtook the mansions of the Darbys, swallowed up in workers' terraces up the valley sides: **Dale House**, built by Abraham Darby I, and **Rosehill House**, built by Richard Ford. Rosehill (***t*** *(01952) 433 522; open 10–5; adm*)has been refurnished in mid-Victorian style, as it might have looked when Abraham Darby III's youngest son Richard lived there, and filled with Darby heirlooms.

Coalport, Hey Inclined Plain and Tar Tunnel

Start at the **Coalport China Museum** (***t*** *(01952) 433 522; open 10–5; adm*) in the old china works, founded in 1800. Some of the Coalport china produced here is displayed inside an old bottle kiln. The works was the largest employer in the 'new town' of **Coalport** at the junction of the Severn and the Shropshire Canal. Boats were lowered down the steep valley side to the river by the **Hey Inclined Plain**, a 1,000ft track with boat hoists. It's a short walk to the **Tar Tunnel**. It was built in 1786 to get coal from the mines to the river, but abandoned when bitumen began to ooze from the walls.

Jackfield

Jackfield developed around the china works, expanding with the arrival of the railway. From Coalport, walk to **Maw's Craft Centre** and the **Jackfield Tile Museum** (***t*** *(01952) 433 522; open 10–5; adm*). In 1900 Maw's and Co. Encaustic Tile Works was the biggest decorative tile factory in the world. The museum occupies the old Craven Dunhill premises, with its ornate wall and floor tiles, from Roman mosaics to romantic scenes and flowery Gothic patterns. Custom-made designs include a map of the British railway network commissioned by North-Eastern Railways for stations.

Broseley

Of all the old industrial villages along the gorge, only Broseley still looks the part. The old King Street Pipeworks, now the **Clay Tobacco Pipe Museum** (***t*** *(01952) 433 522; open Mar–Oct 1–5; adm*), tells a tale of pipe-making. The entrance is opposite the **Quaker Graveyard** where Abraham Darby I is buried. The Roses, who developed the china works, lived in **The Lawns** on Sycamore Road, designed by Thomas Pritchard.

Blist Hill Victorian Town

t *(01952) 433 522; open 10–5; adm.*

Blist Hill Victorian town, half a mile up the Madeley road from Coalport, is populated by characters in waistcoats and soft hats driving horse-drawn carts. Carpenters and blacksmiths work away in workshops. This 'living museum' was developed on the derelict Blist Hill coalfield. At the end of the 19th century 500 people worked here in the mines, small blast furnaces, brick and tile works, and operated the canal system.

Buildwas Abbey

Following the River Severn west out of the Ironbridge Gorge, across the A4169, is the ruined Cistercian monastery of Buildwas. Founded in 1135, the abbey got along quietly until the Welsh revolts of Owen Glendower in the reign of Henry IV, when raiders wasted the abbey. The ruined church is Norman, with stout round piers on both sides of the nave supporting round arches and clerestory windows. Only the vaulted chapter house *(www.english-heritage.org.uk; open April–Sept 11–5; adm)* still stands.

Bridgnorth

The Severn flows south from Ironbridge Gorge through red sandstone countryside, past the old inland ports of Bridgnorth and Bewdley towards the cathedral city of Worcester. Bridgnorth is a market town with spice, where you can board a steam train

Getting There and Around

The steam locomotives of the **Severn Valley Railway**, **t** (01299) 403 816, chug back and forth between Bridgnorth and Kidderminster. Four stops include Arley and Bewdley. With a day ticket, you can get on and off as often as you like. Weekends all year, May–Sept and school holidays daily.

Tourist Information

Bridgnorth: The Library, Listley Street, **t** (01746) 763 257. *Open Mon–Wed and Fri–Sat 9.30–5, April–Oct also Thurs 10–1 and 2–5.*

Where to Stay

Bridgnorth t (01746) –

The Old Vicarage Hotel, Worfield (3 miles northeast of Bridgnorth), **t** 716 497, *www.theoldvicarageworfield.com* (*very expensive*). Edwardian red-brick vicarage with conservatory and gardens; delightful bedrooms and top-notch restaurant offering modern English fare in charming setting.

Severn House, 38 Underhill Street, **t** 766 976 (*moderate*). Attractive riverside Georgian townhouse with six good rooms.

The Croft Hotel, St Mary's Street, **t** 762 416 (*moderate*). Spruce old-fashioned family hotel with dark wood furniture and low black beams. Bar, restaurant and 14 rooms.

The Friars Inn, St Mary Street, just of High Street, **t** 762 396 (*moderate*). Friendly pub accommodation. Neat and tidy rooms.

Sandward Guest House, 47 Cartway, Low Town, **t** 765 913 (*moderate*). Roomy no-frills place to stay with some excellent river views.

Eating Out

The Habit, East Castle Street, **t** 767 902 (*moderate*). Contemporary rustic-chic brasserie and bar; bubble and squeak or sweet-and-sour vegetable filo pastries.

Bamber's, 65 St Mary's Street, **t** 767 364 (*moderate*). French/English meat cooking in an atmospheric restaurant with red velvet high-backed settles, table lamps, dark wood bar and furniture, log fire and alcoves.

Castle Tea Room, West Castle Street, **t** 763 161 (*cheap*). Old-fashioned tea room.

Entertainment

Theatre on the Steps, Stoneway Steps. Small theatre in old Methodist church.

to Kidderminster. **Low Town**, astride the handsome stone bridge, sprung up around the quay and is now mainly pubs. **High Town** stretches back from the cliff above the river, with a view of **St Mary's Church**, a green-domed Italianate building by engineer Thomas Telford. Ascend via the Victorian Cliff Railway, stone steps or the steep zigzag Cartway to the planned 'new town' of Robert de Boleme, Roger de Montgomery's son, in a grid beneath the Norman castle. All but the layout was destroyed in the Civil War, and rebuilt after the Restoration. **Castle Walk**, a Victorian promenade around the old castle walls, has views of the Severn Valley. A shard of the old **castle** stands in the municipal garden. You can see the station of the **Severn Valley Railway** at the foot of the hill. **Pampudding Hill** across the tracks was a Parliamentarian cannon platform in the Civil War. From Castle Hill, West Castle Street and Georgian East Castle Street converge on the **High Street**. At its top is the **market hall**, a Victorian building of multi-coloured brickwork, decorative tiles and iron beams manufactured at Ironbridge. It was meant to lure traders away from the old **Town Hall**, which straddles the road on sandstone legs, but you still find stalls holding up the traffic there on Saturdays.

Much Wenlock and Wenlock Edge

Much Wenlock

A few miles southwest of Ironbridge is the market town of Much Wenlock, whose ruined priory and black-and-white timber-framed, brick and limestone buildings reflect its wealth, built on tanning, brewing and farming. In the middle of town is a farm, with chickens in the courtyard – a rare sight in England these days. When Abraham Darby founded his iron works in Coalbrookdale the wealth shifted there, pushing Much Wenlock into early retirement, leaving it unchanged and delightful.

The one-room **museum** (***t*** *(01952) 727 679; open April–Oct Mon–Sat 10.30–1 and 2–5, June–Aug also Sun 2–5*) has displays on Wenlock Edge, including a wooden geological time machine, and Wenlock sports enthusiast Dr William Penny Brookes, who promoted amateur athletics through the Wenlock Olympian Games in 1850.

A short walk from the main square brings you to the ruins of **Wenlock Priory** (***t*** *(01952) 727 466; open April–Sept daily 10–6, Oct daily 10–5, Nov–Mar Wed–Sun 10–4; adm*), founded by Roger de Montgomery after the Norman Conquest. The priory church must have been magnificent, going by the dimensions of the remains. You can still see intricate carvings in the chapter house and fragments of medieval tiles on the floor of the old library on the east side of the cloister.

Wenlock Edge

Wenlock Edge is known to geologists the world over, having given its name to a six-million-year period of geological time: rocks aged between 424 and 430 million years, wherever in the world, are Wenlockian. It's a perfect escarpment too: the crest of the scarp falls away like a cliff to the west and slopes gently into Corve Dale to the east.

Interesting walks explore Hope Dale and Corve Dale. Pick up a National Trust walking leaflet in the tourist information centre. There are two car parks on the ridge,

Tourist Information

Much Wenlock: The Museum, The Square, **t** (01952) 727 679. *Open April–Oct Mon–Sat 10.30–1 and 2–5, June–Aug also Sun 2–5.*

Where to Stay and Eat

Much Wenlock t (01952) –

The Talbot Inn, High Street, **t** 727 077 (*expensive*). Atmospheric country inn that once put up guests of Wenlock Abbey. Good bar food includes chops, sandwiches and soup. Sturdy, clean rooms in converted 18th-century malthouse off old courtyard.

The Raven Hotel, **t** 727 251, *www.ravenhotel.com* (*expensive*). Stylishly revamped Georgian coaching inn with tiled floors, wicker and cream décor and 15 glorious bedrooms. Top-quality restaurant.

Reynolds Hotel, 46 High Street, **t** 727 292 (*moderate*). Traditional pub with beams and dart board. Eight rooms with nice quilts.

Copper Kettle Teashop, High Street, **t** 728 419 (*cheap*). Quaint little teashop with delicious cakes and sandwiches.

Wenlock Edge t (01746) –

The Wenlock Edge Inn, Hill Top, **t** 785 678, *www.wenlockedgeinn.co.uk* (*expensive*). Cosy, old-fashioned, dog-friendly pub on the wooded escarpment of Wenlock Edge, a minute's walk from Ippkin's Rock. Offers good home-cooked warm food using fresh ingredients – steak and ale pie – and three bedrooms. *Closed Mon.*

along the B4371 between Much Wenlock and Easthope, where you can begin short walks. One is a 6-mile walk to **Ippkins Rock** near Hilltop, haunted by the ghost of robber Ippkins. Another is the Jack Mytton Way between Wenlock Edge and Church Stretton. The 14-mile ridge walk is disappointing, as it is too wooded to see the views.

The Church Stretton Hills

From the Shropshire Plain, the Church Stretton hills stand out against the horizon. You can spot whale-backed **Lawley** and the ragged, conical outline of **Caer Caradoc,** site of the Roman defeat of British resistance leader Caractacus, son of Cunobelin, king of the *Catuvellauni*. He was taken to Rome where, according to Tacitus, he was pardoned as a worthy opponent. To the southwest is hog-backed **Ragleth Hill**.

Church Stretton

Church Stretton inhabits the narrow gap through which the old Roman road and the railway pass. On one side are the Caer Caradoc hills and on the other the **Long Mynd**, a bleak, sandstone plateau stretching 6 miles to the west. The Church Stretton side of the Long Mynd is cut by a series of deep valleys or batches which provide routes to the top for walkers. The **Carding Mill Valley** is the most popular ascent (6 miles round trip). Caer Caradoc is more friendly (3½ miles up and down again).

Stiperstones

West of the Long Mynd and 100ft higher at 1,759ft is another ridge, 6 miles end to end. Along its crest are a dozen jagged tors, carved into sharks' fins by the last Ice Age. The biggest tor is the **Devil's Chair**, and all the loose boulders fell from the devil's apron when he stood up to fill in the gap between Stiperstones and the Long Mynd. From his seat there are grandstand views. To reach it from Bishop's Castle take the

Getting Around

Regular **bus** service from Shrewsbury to Ludlow, and **trains** on Manchester–Cardiff line.

Tourist Information

Church Stretton: Church Street, **t** (01694) 723 133. *Open Easter–Sept Mon–Sat 10–1 and 2–5.*
Bishop's Castle: Old Time, 29 High Street, **t** (01588) 638 467.

Local **beer festival** Fri and Sat of second weekend in July.

Where to Stay and Eat

Church Stretton t (01694) –

Belvedere, Burway Road, **t** 722 232, *www.belvedereguesthouse.btinternet.co.uk* (*moderate*). Tall creeper-clad Victorian house on the Carding Mill Valley road with 12 clean, simple bedrooms and terrific views.

Brookfield's, Watling Street North, **t** 722 314 (*moderate*). Red-brick Edwardian house looking out towards Long Mynd, set back from A49 behind large garden; four pretty bedrooms and one single with private bathroom. Evening meals available.

Juniper Cottage, All Stretton (near Church Stretton), **t** 723 427 (*moderate*). Pretty little cottage, tucked away behind conifers; neatly-folded towels and plump pillows.

Jinlye Guest House, Castle Hill, All Stretton (near Church Stretton), **t** 723 243, *www.jinlye.co.uk* (*moderate*). Former crofters' cottage a mile out of the village on the open moor; terrific large garden; bedrooms sumptuous bordering on cheesy with splendid Gothic bedsteads and a '1940s Italian boudoir suite'. Ideal for walkers who like a bit of pampering in the evening.

The Studio Restaurant, 59 High Street, **t** 722 672 (*moderate*). Upmarket Continental cooking in friendly, informal environment. *Closed Sun eve and Mon; advisable to book.*

The Bucks Head, High Street, **t** 722 898 (*cheap*). Quiet at lunchtime for pub lunch.

Acorn Wholefood Café, 26 Sandford Avenue, **t** 722 495 (*cheap*). Friendly café with tea garden at back, where you can get a decent tea or coffee and cake or light vegetarian meal including home-made soup, nut roast, flan, pizza or pitta sandwich. *Closed Wed and Thurs except school holidays.*

The Yew Tree Inn, All Stretton (near Church Stretton), **t** 722 228 (*cheap*). Friendly old-fashioned pub offering hearty portions of home-made grub. *Closed Mon.*

Bishop's Castle t (01588) –

The Castle Hotel, The Square, **t** 638 403 (*moderate*). Austere 17th-century coaching inn with several small bars, one with dark wood panelling, leather arm chairs and hunting scenes on the walls; another with 40 malt whiskeys. Excellent pub grub with especially good desserts; six top-floor bedrooms with views of valley or garden.

The Poppy House, 20 Market Square, **t** 638 443, *www.poppyhouse.co.uk* (*moderate*). Elegant, friendly café and gallery overlooking market square, with solid wooden furniture and a sunny courtyard at the back. Three comfy rooms. Home-cooked lunches.

Lower Broughton Farm, Lower Broughton, Montgomery, Powys, **t** 638 393 (*moderate*). Two miles out of town, beautiful, homely farmhouse with polished oak floorboards and oak furniture; bright. Cottage-style bedrooms. Breakfast room stocked with maps and books.

Bank House, High Street, **t** 638 146, *ann@bankhousebc.co.uk* (*cheap*). Sturdy-looking house at top of town with impressive double flight of wooden stairs.

Three Tons, Salop Street, **t** 638 797 (*cheap*). Large woody pub attracting younger drinking crowd, with brewery and bar rooms around courtyard; you are invited to sample home-brewed beer before ordering.

The Six Bells Inn, Church Street, **t** 630 144 (*cheap*). At bottom of hill beside church, best real-ale pub in town, with old-fashioned furniture, large stone fireplace and microbrewery. Pub grub available.

A488, turn off to the Bog and Shelve and walk. From Church Stretton drive west through Ratlinghope and Bridges to the Bog and Shelve.

Bishop's Castle

Bishop's Castle, on the edge of the lonely Clun Hills, is an appealing small border town and an excellent walking base. The bishop was the Bishop of Hereford, who in 1127 built himself a castle, a church and road running between the two. The **castle** stood where the Castle Hotel is now. The pubs serve real ale and the colourful, painted old buildings house second-hand bookshops. The High Street leads to a dainty 18th-century **town hall** at the top of the hill. Beyond, a cobbled path leads under the **'house on crutches'**, an Elizabethan building with its gable end supported on wooden posts, which houses a small local history **museum**.

Clun

Clunton and Clunbury, Clungunford and Clun
Are the quietest places under the sun.
An old jingle, quoted by A.E. Housman

The gaunt stone ruins of the 13th-century castle of the Fitzalans (later Earls of Arundel) stand above the River Clun in a lonely sheep-grazed spot. It is at its most picturesque from a distance, outlined against the sky, with the Clun Hills as a backdrop. The square beneath the castle belongs to the Norman 'new town', which proved too remote to flourish. Lunch in the Buffalo Inn or in the tearoom by the bridge.

Ludlow

It had balls at the assembly rooms. Miss Burney's and Miss Austen's heroines might perfectly well have had their first love affair there; a journey to Ludlow would certainly have been a great event to Fanny Price or Emma Woodhouse.
Henry James, 1877

The beautiful old country town stands in the loop of the rivers Teme and Corve, surrounded by magnificent countryside and crumbling Marcher castles. Ludlow is a gourmet capital too, with no fewer than three Michelin-starred restaurants. The town was founded by the de Lacy family in the 12th century and became a thriving wool centre. The area was the heartland of the Mortimers, powerful Earls of March, whose stronghold was Wigmore Castle. One of the most decisive battles of the Wars of the Roses took place beneath the castle at Mortimer's Cross in 1461. A month later, Edward of March, head of the Yorkist army, became Edward IV, and Ludlow Castle fell into royal hands, along with all the other Mortimer properties. Edward brought prestige to Ludlow by sending his two sons to the castle, which became the seat of the Council of the Marches, governing the region until 1688. In the 18th and 19th centuries Ludlow became the fashionable resort of the county gentry, boasting Georgian townhouses, walks around the castle, assembly rooms and a museum, founded by the Natural History Society in 1833. At the core of its collections were the rocks and fossils that formed the basis of Roderick Murchison's classification of *The Silurian System* in 1839.

Getting There and Around

You can join the A49 to Ludlow 20 minutes south of Shrewsbury, off M5 junction 3.

Ludlow **railway station** is a short walk from the town centre. Direct trains run from Hereford, Shrewsbury and Newport, where connections can be picked up for the rest of the country. There are **coaches** from Birmingham and Kidderminster. **Traveline**, **t** 0870 608 2608, for local transport.

Tourist Information

Ludlow: Castle Street, **t** (01584) 875 053. *Open Mon–Sat 10–5, April–Sept also Sun 10.30–5.*

Festivals

Ludlow Festival takes place late June–early July, **t** (01584) 872 150, *www.ludlowfestival.co.uk*. Shakespeare plays performed every evening (except Sun) in the inner bailey of castle, plus talks by writers, and concerts in the church and Assembly Rooms. A 'fringe' **Jazz Festival** takes place one weekend mid-festival in the courtyard of the Bull Hotel, **t** (01584) 873 611.

Where to Stay

Ludlow t (01584) –

The Feathers Hotel, Bull Ring, **t** 875 261 (*expensive*). England's most magnificent timber-framed building, its overhanging storeys enriched with decorative timberwork; comfortable if pricey rooms. Drop in for a drink in the snazzy bar.

Dinham Hall Hotel, **t** 876 464 (*expensive*). Elegant Georgian townhouse next to castle; 15 charming, understated rooms, each with a complimentary decanter of sherry; two small guest lounges and enclosed garden. Excellent modern French restaurant offers lobster, crab, foie gras and vegetarian dishes.

Number Twenty Eight, 28 Lower Broad Street, **t** 876 996, *www.no28.co.uk* (*expensive*). Six bedrooms, immaculately decorated. Neat and professional.

Eight Dinham, 8 Dinham Street, **t** 875 661 (*moderate*). Gorgeous place to stay, offering treats such as bread hot from the oven, fresh fruit, umbrellas, binoculars and maps.

Hen and Chickens, 103 Old Street, **t** 874 318 (*moderate*). Impersonal but not cold; small, clean, bright rooms; good poached eggs.

The Wheatsheaf Inn, Lower Broad Street, **t** 872 980 (*cheap*). Old-world pub on quiet street near Broad Gate, has five pleasant bedrooms with sloping floors and exposed beams.

Eating Out

Merchant House, 62 Lower Corve Street, **t** 875 438 (*expensive*). Black-and-white building next to the Unicorn Inn housing unaffected and informal restaurant whose chef patron Shaun Hill put Ludlow on the gastronomic map. Superb modern English food. *Open Tues–Sat dinner, Fri and Sat also lunch.*

Hibiscus, 17 Corve Street, **t** 872 325 (*expensive*). Exciting French cooking in restrained oak-and-stone restaurant including all the gourmet gluttonies: foie gras, suckling pig, spring lamb and veal. The atmosphere is gracious and attentive, the clientele suave and well-dressed. *Open Mon–Sat dinner, Wed–Sat also lunch.*

Mr Underhill's, Dinham Weir, **t** 874 431, *www.daisy.co.uk/sites* (*expensive*). Named after the owner's cat; top-quality modern European food made from fresh local ingredients in bright, relaxed restaurant. *Open Wed–Mon dinner.* Six beautiful rooms with king-size beds and river views.

The Unicorn Inn, Lower Corve Street, **t** 873 555 (*moderate*). Wobbly timber-framed pub which attracts lively mix of people for quality beer and top-notch food, including interesting vegetarian options.

The Courtyard, Quality Square, **t** 878 080 (*moderate*). Informal restaurant with farmhouse kitchen tables decorated with posies in earthenware vases. Menu includes stuffed chicken breast, seafood casserole and spinach, herb and stilton risotto cakes.

The Olive Branch, Old Street (*cheap*). Delicious wholefood lunches washed down with beer and cider. Good selection of coffees.

Ego Café-Bar, Quality Square, **t** 878 000 (*cheap*). Vaguely hip café-restaurant down cobbled alley, offers strong coffee and good-value light lunches and suppers.

The Charlton Arms Hotel, Ludford Bridge, **t** 872 813 (*cheap*). Ludlow's only riverside pub.

To geologists, Ludlow is the shrine of the Upper Silurian period: in its limestone hills, Murchison identified a 40-million-year slab of geological time between the Cambrian and Devonian, in which primitive forms of animal life were abundant in tropical seas.

Climb the church tower for a view of the town. The market place and hub of the old town is **Castle Square**. In the Middle Ages a street as broad as Castle Square led all the way to the Bull Ring, 300 yards away; since then, the old market stalls that lined it have become a jumble of narrow lanes. Down an alley near the grand 18th-century neo-classical Butter Cross is the **church of St Laurence**. Deprived of the long view, you have no idea of its size until you are at the door. In the soaring Perpendicular style of the 15th century, everything leads your eyes upwards. The chancel and its chapels are the climax of the interior with its dark wooden choir stalls, miserichords, medieval stained glass, and 17th-century monuments to Marcher lords.

Ludlow Museum on Castle Street (*__t__ (01584) 813 666; open Easter–Oct Mon–Sat, June–Aug daily 10.30–5; adm*) not only houses Murchison's geological specimens, but can give you the lowdown on Ludlow's role in the Wars of the Roses and so on.

Ludlow Castle

Open Jan weekends 10–4, Feb–Mar, Oct and Dec daily 10–4, April–July and Sept 10–5, Aug 10–7; adm.

Enter the large outer bailey through the gatehouse or walk around the castle walls on the 18th-century paths to get a sense of the castle's strong defensive position. It grew over six centuries, from the border fortress of the de Lacys to the palace of the Grenvilles and Mortimers and base of the Council of the Marches. The architectural gems are in the inner bailey: the round chapel of St Mary mimics the Holy Sepulchre in Jerusalem. The great hall was the castle's hub, the private apartments flanking it the home of royals including the tragic young princes of Edward IV, bumped off by Richard III in the Tower of London, and Prince Arthur, whose death paved the way for his younger brother to become Henry VIII. From **Whitcliffe Common**, across the Teme, you can see the view of the castle painted by Turner.

Castles Around Ludlow

Stokesay Castle

I have rarely had, for a couple of hours, the sensation of dropping back personally into the past so straight as while I lay on the grass beside the well in the sunny court of this small castle and lazily appreciated the still definite details of medieval life.

Henry James, 1877

Five miles north of Ludlow on the A49 to Church Stretton, Stokesay Castle (*__t__ (01588) 672 544, www.english-heritage.org.uk; open April–Sept daily 10–6, Oct 10–5, Nov–Mar Wed–Sun 10–4; adm*) stands alone in the middle of the Onny Valley. Its charm lies in the domesticity of the place: a cluster of buildings around a courtyard, with one crenellated tower to show the castle meant business; a range of private stone rooms; and the reassuring old church. Stokesay was built in the late 13th century by wool merchant Lawrence of Ludlow, a few years after Edward I had annexed Wales. Lawrence was able to design his new castle for comfort, as well as defence. Enter through the anachronistic 17th-century timber-framed gatehouse. The curtain wall was reduced to the height of a garden wall in the Civil War, opening up the 'sunny court' to the meadows and hills. Inside, the highlight is the great hall, with a roof like the upturned hull of a ship. Swallows fly in and out of the arrow slits, nesting in the rafters. The first floor of the solar is encased in Jacobean panelling, elaborately carved above the fireplace.

Mortimer's Trail

The rolling hills southwest of Ludlow between the rivers Lugg and Teme are peppered with fortifications dating back as far as the Iron Age; this was always the most militarized stretch of the frontier. The most powerful of the Marcher lords, the Mortimers, were based at **Wigmore Castle**. The ruins of their castle stand on the end of a ridge north of Mortimer's Cross, where Yorkist Edward, 7th Earl of March, defeated the Lancastrians under Jasper Tudor to become Edward IV. Walk up to the ruins.

The Battle of Mortimer's Cross took place on the estate of Sir Richard Croft, a staunch Yorkist and one of Edward's commanders on the day. His family has been at

The Battle of Mortimer's Cross

Ludlow and Wigmore castles were the medieval strongholds of the Mortimers, Earls of March, who in the 15th century produced three successive Yorkist kings of England – Edward IV, Edward V and Richard III – by marriage and war. Edmund Mortimer, 3rd Earl of March, married Philippa, granddaughter of Edward III, in the mid-14th century. It was a matter of time and a marriage of cousins before Richard of York, descended from both the second and fourth sons of Edward III, had a solid claim to the throne. Richard was killed fighting the Lancastrians at Wakefield in 1460 but his son Edward of York, the 7th Earl of March, became Edward IV after an impressive victory at the Battle of Mortimer's Cross in 1461.

The battle was one of the decisive clashes of the Wars of the Roses. Henry VI was ill and out of the picture. His queen, Margaret, was marching south at the head of a Scottish army. The Welsh pillar of the Lancastrians, Jasper Tudor, half-brother of Henry, was on his way from Pembroke to join Margaret when Edward set out to cut him off. Eighteen years old, tall and strong, Edward was a story-book king in waiting. The battle was on home ground and his army loyal men from the southern Marches. On the morning of the battle, both armies awoke to the atmospheric illusion of three suns in the sky. Edward declared it a good omen and adopted the Sun in Splendour as his personal badge. The Lancastrian army was overwhelmed. Jasper's father, Owen Tudor, was captured and 'the head that was wont to lie in Queen Katherine's lap' was chopped off at Hereford. A mysterious woman placed it on the steps of Hereford market cross surrounded by candles. Jasper lived to fight another day.

A month later Edward of March was crowned King Edward IV. He ruled well for 20 years, but we know little about him, as *Richard III* starts only at his deathbed.

Croft Castle (*t (01568) 780 246; house open Mar–Sept Wed–Sun, gardens 11.30–5; adm*) since Domesday. You can find Sir Richard's tomb in the parish church. The castle was rebuilt in the late 16th century, embellished in the 18th with Gothic additions, and is now furnished in Georgian style. Good walks include one to Croft Ambrey Iron Age hill fort and another down Chestnut Avenue.

Herefordshire

Herefordshire is a quiet rural backwater of orchards, meandering rivers and rolling hills, shielded from the Midlands by the Malverns, the Forest of Dean on its doorstep. Its valleys are more rewarding than its hills, in particular the **Wye Valley**. The eccentric book town of **Hay-on-Wye** is an excellent base for the **Golden Valley**, once a defensive corridor into Wales. The old Cistercian church of **Abbey Dore**, in the valley, is one of half a dozen churches in Herefordshire worth a special trip. The best feature is the playful carvings of a group of 12th-century sculptors known as the Herefordshire School. **Kilpeck** is the finest example. The county town of **Hereford** is disappointing, spoiled by post-war town planning, but the cathedral's treasures include the 13th-century *Mappa Mundi* and a chained library. Around Ledbury, you're into cider and vineyard country. South of Ledbury, around **Much Marcle**, is a low-lying countryside of orchards and lanes. Here you have Weston's, the county's second largest cider and perry producer, after Bulmer's of Hereford. Before the First World War this area was adopted by a group of poets, rising young stars known as the Dymock poets; several (including Rupert Brooke and Edward Thomas) enlisted and died in the trenches. Their nostalgic poems have cast a spell over the woods, hedges and lanes around **Dymock**.

Base yourself in **Ross-on-Wye** for the lower **Wye Valley** and Forest of Dean. There are impressive medieval castles at the river crossing, and terrific scenery along the Wye. The **Symonds Yat Gorge**, where peregrine falcons nest in the wooded cliffs, has been attracting tourists since the 18th century. The woods thicken as you enter the **Forest of Dean**, a royal hunting forest and industrial centre in the Middle Ages, producing oak for the royal fleet and iron ore for armour. It's a magical place to explore on foot.

To the north, in the valleys of the Lugg and Arrow, are the **Black and White Villages**, sagging but pristinely painted. The gentle countryside of Weobley and Eardisland is ideal for driving, cycling or walking between churches, gardens and country houses.

Hereford

Hereford is the county's only large town, more prosaic than Ludlow or Shrewsbury, but more charming than most Midlands towns. The town's biggest industry is cider, produced by **H.P. Bulmer's Limited** since 1887; another bastion is the **cattle market**. You'll have no trouble finding good coffee and lunch here.

Hereford is an ancient cathedral city with a long history of Welsh skirmishes. It was founded as a Mercian stronghold, only 6 miles east of the frontier with Wales, marked in no uncertain terms by Offa's Dyke at the end of the 8th century. King Offa secured

Getting There and Around

Hereford is west of the Worcester to Bristol section of the M5, reached via M50 junction 8, then the Ledbury road. **Trains** connect from Shrewsbury and Worcester, and National Express **coaches** from London via Birmingham.

Tourist Information

Hereford: 1 King's Street, **t** (01432) 268 430. *Open Mon–Sat 9–5, summer also Sun 10–4.*

Festivals

The **Three Choirs Festival** takes place in Hereford Cathedral for one week in mid-Aug every third year, in rotation with Worcester and Gloucester, and comprises choristers from the 'three choirs' counties of Herefordshire, Worcestershire and Gloucestershire. It is the oldest musical festival in Europe, going back some 250 years. Elgar headlined in the 1920s and '30s. For information call **t** (01432) 274 455 or go to *www.3choirs.org*.

The ***Broad Sheep*** events guide covers the Welsh borders (free from tourist information centre or 50p from newsagents), and lists live music nights including **The Volunteer**, Harold Street, **t** (01432) 276 189 (Irish music Wed), **The Victory**, St Owen's Street, **t** (01432) 274 998 (bands Sun) and **Doodies Restaurant**, 48–50 St Owen's Street, **t** (01432) 269 974 (live Jazz occasional Tues).

The Courtyard Arts Centre, t (01432) 359 252. Snazzy modern building of glass, stone and wood; two auditoriums for plays, shows, films and concerts, and café-bar-restaurant.

Where to Stay

Hereford t (01432) –

Castle House, Castle Street **t** 356 321, *www.castlehse.co.uk* (*luxury*). Lovely, sunny Georgian townhouse in the nicest part of Hereford, with uniformed staff, colourful décor, flower displays and smart furnishings. The garden drops down to the old castle moat, beyond which is the site of Hereford Castle. Stop off for high tea on the lawn or cocktails in the bar, or splash out on dinner at the excellent restaurant (*expensive*) or one of the 15 suites of rooms.

Aylestone Court Hotel, Aylestone Hill, **t** 341 891 (*expensive*). Red-brick Georgian townhouse set back from busy Commercial Road, 5 minutes' walk into town. Nine rooms.

The Somerville, 12 Bodenham Road, **t** 273 991 (*moderate*). Grand Victorian yellow-brick guesthouse with nine decent rooms; 15 minutes' walk down Commercial Road.

Charades, 34 Southbank Road, **t** 269 444 (*moderate*). Pleasant Victorian guesthouse on quiet road off Commercial Road.

Holly Tree Guest House, 19–21 Barton Road, **t** 357 845 (*cheap*). Friendly place to stay in red-brick semi-detached house on main road, 5 minutes' walk from cathedral.

Eating Out

Castle House, La Rive, Castle Street, **t** 356 321 (*moderate*). Dimly lit restaurant overlooking the old castle moat; offers contemporary-style English/French lunch and dinner.

Floodgates Brasserie, Bridge Street, **t** 349 009 (*cheap*). Bright bar and brasserie overlooking the Wye, where you can get coffee and pastries, meat and fish dishes, or tapas in the cocktail bar upstairs.

Doodies Restaurant and Café-Bar, 48–50 St Owen's Street, **t** 269 974 (*cheap*). Glass-fronted corner restaurant with rugs on bare floorboards and cheerful walls. Tapas with a drink, or Mediterranean-style dishes such as vegetable kebabs, steak and fish. *Closed Sun.*

Mirpur Palace Restaurant, 60 St Owen's Street, **t** 343 464 (*cheap*). Balti with enormous naan breads. No credit cards; BYO.

Spread Eagle, King Street, **t** 272 205 (*cheap*). Smooth walls, solid, uniform furniture and soulful early evening music; somewhere to have a quiet week-night drink.

Café@All Saints, High Street (*cheap*). Wholesome vegetarian meals (ploughman's and hotpot) served by friendly staff in the nave and gallery of an old Gothic chapel.

his kingdom by murdering his rivals, including King Ethelbert of East Anglia, who was beheaded at Offa's orders at his own wedding feast in Marden, just north of Hereford.

To assuage his guilt, Offa built a shrine to the martyred king in Hereford cathedral, which remained popular into the early Middle Ages. After the Norman Conquest, Hereford became the seat of a powerful Marcher earldom and the springboard for several more centuries of war against the Welsh. All that is left of the rough-and-tough border period is a plaque commemorating Owen Tudor, the Lancastrian leader and father of the Tudor monarchy, who was executed in High Town after the Battle of Mortimer's Cross in 1461 (*see* box). Famous residents of Hereford include David Garrick (1717–79), the actor and stage manager, born in Widemarsh Street; Nell Gwynne, the actress and mistress of Charles II, born in Pipewell Lane, now Gwynne Street; and the composer Edward Elgar, who moved to Hereford in 1904, composed *Symphonies*, *Violin Concerto* and *The Kingdom* there, and headlined the Three Choirs Festivals.

Hereford Cathedral

Mappa Mundi *and chained library open summer Mon–Sat 10–4.15, Sun 11–3.15; winter Mon–Sat only 11–3.15; adm.*

First impressions of the west front are forbidding. Inside lurks something from just about every period: a Norman nave, with drum columns and round arches, and south transept; an Early English north transept and Lady Chapel; Victorian reconstruction (the west front); and a new library housing the cathedral's treasures, the *Mappa Mundi* – a unique 13th-century map of the world – and chained library.

The cathedral was always run by canons not monks, which may be why so many treasures survived the Reformation. The 12th-century **font** features carvings of the apostles by the Herefordshire School of sculptors. In the north transept is the **shrine of Thomas Cantilupe**, Bishop of Hereford in the cathedral's 13th-century heyday, with weeping knights. An early medieval **statue of King Ethelbert** stands on the right of the Victorian high altar; Ethelbert's shrine, founded by the rival who killed him, King Offa, was destroyed in 1055 by Welsh raiders who burned down the Saxon cathedral.

The new library building is reached through the Bishop's Cloister. Here you can see the ***Mappa Mundi***, which has been in the cathedral's possession for 700 years. Its creation has been dated to 1289, when it was drawn in Lincolnshire (the cartographer signed his name, 'Richard of Haldringham of Lafford'). The 5ft by 4ft sheet of vellum doesn't tally with modern conceptions of the world, which is drawn in a large circle dotted with seas, rivers, churches, castles, animals and people. Jerusalem is at the centre of three continents, Asia, Africa and Europe. The Red Sea stands out – painted red. The British Isles are at the bottom left of the map, on the edge of the world. England, Ireland, Scotland and Cornwall each appear as a separate island.

A heavy door leads into the **chained library**, containing about 1,500 books. The system was common from the Middle Ages until the 18th century: in the two rows of 17th-century bookcases, each book is fastened by a metal chain to the shelf. The 8th-century **Hereford Gospels** are one of 229 manuscripts given to the cathedral by Athelstan, 11th-century Bishop of Hereford. There are more than 200 manuscripts on theological subjects and the law, but most of the books are printed, many acquired by the cathedral library from dissolved monasteries after the Reformation.

The Museum, River and High Town

Back in town, the **City Museum and Library** (*open Tues–Sat 10–5, April–Sept also Sun 10–5*) was founded by the Woolhope Naturalists Field Club in 1874. Pause to look at its Broad Street façade: the columns on the front support carved animals representing the four continents of Africa, Asia, Europe (squirrels) and America. Inside is an eclectic collection of geology and folklore. From there, wander down **Gwynne Street**, named after Charles II's mistress, who was born here. Continue over the 15th-century **Wye Bridge**, turn left through playing fields to a Victorian footbridge and recross the river into **Castle Green**, now a bowling green.

Broad Street leads into **High Town** and the old market square, rather desolate apart from a plaque to Owen Tudor and the black-and-white-painted Jacobean **Old House** (*open Tues–Sat 10–5, April–Sept also Sun 10–5*). Down Eign Street, past **All Saints' Church**, where Garrick was baptized, is the **Cider Museum** (***t*** *(01432) 354 207; open April–Oct daily 10–5.30; Nov and Dec daily 11–5, Jan–Mar Tues–Sun 11–3; adm*).

Between the Lugg and the Wye

Thoughts of cattle rustling and invasion have been replaced by ones of fishing and picnics.

Clive Aslet, editor of *Country Life*

The River Lugg flows down off the Welsh hills through Mortimer country into the patchwork fields and hedgerows of the Herefordshire lowlands. The River Arrow winds through its flood plain past picturesque villages and farms, joining the Lugg below Leominster. Base yourself in Weobley to explore the wedge of countryside between Leominster, Kington and Eardisley (ideal cycling country). Highlights are Leominster Priory, Shobdon church, Hergest Croft Garden and Arrow Cottage Garden.

Leominster

This market centre (pronounced 'Lemster') comes alive on market day, when it is pleasant to wander the medieval streets, squares and alleys like Drapers' Lane. At the **museum** on Etnam Street (***t*** *(01568) 615 186; open April–Oct Mon–Fri 10.30–4, Sat 10.30–1; adm*) you can find out about cider-making. But the **Priory Church** is the reason to come here. At the Reformation, the monastic buildings of the old Benedictine priory were pulled down, leaving the church, without its chancel and high altar. The west end of the Norman monastic nave incorporates an arched window and elaborately carved doorway, attributed to the Herefordshire School of sculptors. The 12th-century stone carvings of animals, beasts and monsters, Celtic, Saxon and Norman imagery, compare with the best. Next to the Norman nave end is the Perpendicular west window of the 13th-century nave, added on to fit the wealthy wool-trade parishioners. In the 14th century a Decorated south aisle was added, as wide as another nave, its windows decorated with ballflowers and geometric tracery. A fire in 1699 gutted the interior, but two bouts of restoration – one just after the fire, the other in the 19th century by George Gilbert Scott – have preserved the contrasting

Tourist Information

The Black and White Villages Visitor Centre: East Street, Pembridge, **t** (01544) 388 761.

Leominster: 1 Corn Square, **t** (01568) 616 460. *Open summer Mon–Sat 9.30–5, winter Mon–Sat 9.30–4.*

Where to Stay and Eat

Leominster t (01568) –

A good place to stock up on local specialities.

Orchard, Hive and Vine, High Street. Frome Valley and Dunkerton's cider and perry, and other delicious local produce.

Barber and Manuel's Delicatessen and Grocers, just off Corn Square. Wholesome goodies and locally made cider and perry.

The Old Merchants' House Tea Room, 10 Corn Square, **t** 616 141 (*cheap*). Much-restored timber-framed house combining antique shop and olde-worlde tea rooms. *Closed Sun.*

Weobley and Around t (01544) –

The Salutation Inn, Market Pitch, Weobley, **t** 318 443 (*expensive*). Lovely old pub with cosy bar and highly praised restaurant, with crisp tablecloths; four frilly rooms upstairs.

Mellington House, Weobley, **t** 318 537, *www.mellingtonhouse.co.uk* (*moderate*). Behind handsome 1920s Queen Anne-style façade, a long timber-framed building with four comfortable bedrooms and a self-contained hayloft conversion.

Manor House, Bell Square, Weobley, **t** 318 425 (*moderate*). Charming 14th-century house with sturdy oak front door and inglenook fireplace in lounge; two bedrooms.

Jules Restaurant, Weobley, **t** 318 206 (*moderate*). Excellent small restaurant serving imaginative food; dominated by large and friendly personality of proprietor.

Lowe Farm, Pembridge, **t** 388 395, *www.lowe-farm.co.uk* (*moderate*). Picturesque white-painted 14th-century farmhouse, 1½ miles west of Pembridge on A44 (turn right for Marston, then follow signs), with four clean, cheerful bedrooms.

Bedford House, Dilwyn (north of Weobley, signposted off the A4112), **t** 388 260 (*moderate*). Tucked away down narrow lanes, a pretty old brick house with a lovely garden; friendly and relaxed atmosphere; rooms simple and comfortable.

Manor House, Eardisland, **t** 388 138, *www.manorhousebandb.co.uk* (*moderate*). Beautiful 17th-century timber-framed house with terraced garden and dovecote, stylishly decorated, with grand dining room.

Hill Top Farm, Wormsley (¾ mile off Weobley–Hereford road), **t** (01981) 590 246, *www.farmmanagement.co.uk* (*cheap*). Friendly farmhouse up long track, with two sheep dogs, 200 acres of arable and sheep farmland, and amazing views.

architectural splendours of the three interior spaces, including a view down the Norman nave flanked on one side by tiers of stout Romanesque pillars and on the other by slender Victorian-Gothic arcading. Note the ducking stool in the north aisle.

Berrington Hall

t (01568) 615 721; open April–Oct Sat–Wed 12.30–6 or dusk if earlier; adm.

On a wooded ridge above the Lugg Valley is the elegant 18th-century country house of Thomas Harley, a wealthy London banker and politician. Harley commissioned Capability Brown to landscape the grounds, and Brown's son-in-law, the suave French neo-classicist Henry Holland, to build the house. Its elegant rooms contain decorative allusions to Admiral Rodney, hero of the 1782 Battle of Saints, whose son married Harley's daughter Anne, bringing the Rodneys to Berrington. In the smallest rooms, domed ceilings and scagliola columns create an illusion of space. The lavender and herbaceous borders of the walled garden are pleasant.

Pembridge

The busy Leominster–Kington road cuts through pretty old black-and-white Pembridge. The **Black and White Visitor Centre** can tell you all about it. Wander up the main road to the market place and church. The New Inn, facing the market place, is more than 600 years old. This is where the future Edward IV is said to have signed the treaty after the Battle of Mortimer's Cross in 1461. The modest 16th-century market hall is open about its age, with disintegrating wooden piers and mossy tiled roof. A kissing gate leads up to **St Mary's church**, known for its unusual detached belfry.

There is a lovely 2-mile walk from Pembridge along the south bank of the Arrow to **Eardisland**, a picture-postcard village of half-timbered cottages and river banks.

Cider- and perry-maker **Dunkerton's** (***t*** *(01544) 388 653; open summer Mon–Sat 10–6, winter 10–5*) is 2 miles south of the village near Lower Bearwood.

Shobdon Church and Arches

From Pembridge, the Shobdon road crosses the Arrow to the church (*closed for restoration*). It stands in parkland next to the 18th-century country house of antiquary Richard, Lord Bateman, who demolished the old Norman church in the 1750s and replaced it with a miniature rococo Gothic masterpiece. The curlicues of the ogee arches around the windows prepare you for the interior, painted white and decorated like a wedding cake. In the south transept, the Bateman pews have a fireplace and armchair. The Norman stone font with lions prowling around its base is a reminder of what was lost: the old church was in all likelihood the first masterpiece of the Herefordshire School of sculptors, who moved on to Kilpeck, Hereford cathedral and Leominster priory. Some of the best sculptural fragments were incorporated into a Gothic folly on the hill above the church, up an oak avenue, sadly eroded.

Above the village, Shobdon Hill Wood is dissected by footpaths including Mortimer's Trail, and drops down on the north side to the Lugg.

Kington

The old London–Aberystwyth coaching road (the modern A44) crosses the Arrow at Kington, a small border market town between Hergest Ridge and Bradnor Hill. The town was founded in the 11th century by King Harold, during a military campaign against the King of Powys. Kington is a pretty stop-off *en route* to **Hergest Croft Garden** (***t*** *(01544) 230 160; open April–Oct 12.30–5.30; adm*). Drive up Church Street to reach the Banks family garden. The Edwardian garden is one of a handful associated with the expeditions of plant hunters in northern Vietnam, western China and Japan. Exotic trees and shrubs flourish in the Maple Grove. W.H. Banks developed the garden around his swanky Arts and Crafts house in the early 1900s. Azalea gardens, maple groves and ornamental woodland are enhanced by the location. The garden flows naturally into the park and a 30-acre beech and oak woodland.

Weobley

The tidy black-and-white village of Weobley (pronounced 'Web-bly') sits beneath wooded Burton Hill. It's a pleasing place, with the view of its church spire rising out of flat meadows. Stay over in one of the timber-framed old houses and visit **Arrow Cottage Garden** (*t (01544) 318 468; open April–Sept Wed 10–5; adm*), 1½ miles south of the village towards Ledgemoor. It's a young (15 years old) cottage garden, laid out according to fashion in a series of 'rooms' divided by yew and beech hedges.

Eardisley

Driving into Eardisley from Kington, the road plunges 200 yards down into the Wye Valley. The **church of St Mary** on the edge of the village contains a 12th-century font carved by the Herefordshire School of sculptors. The bowl incorporate motifs and imagery from Celtic, Norman and Saxon art. One scene represents the *Harrowing of Hell*: Christ leads Man out of the forest towards God. The dove and the lion are symbolic of the forces of good and evil. An unusual scene, depicting two combatant knights, portrays the 12th-century duel between local lord Ralph de Baskerville and his father-in-law, who perished in the contest. The creeper and owl are medieval symbols of ignorance. The font was commissioned by Sir Ralph as part of his penance.

Hay-on-Wye and Around

Lord Host of Host, asleep on High
Awake and cast a kindly eye
On independent Hay-on-Wye.

First verse of the Hay-on-Wye 'national' anthem

From Hereford, the A438 follows the River Wye through the Herefordshire plain into the ravishing hill country around the old border town of Hay-on-Wye. Hay was the prototype for around 20 'book towns' in the world; its local economy revolves around the second-hand book trade. The Hay book trade was founded by the entrepreneurial and eccentric Richard Booth in 1961. There are 29 bookshops in this small, grey stone

The King of Hay

Richard Booth, a tall, shambolic, outspoken Oxford man whose family has lived in the area for a century, opened the first of a string of Booth bookshops in Hay in 1961. Over the next decade he gained a reputation championing his own brand of anti-government, anti-big-business values at every opportunity. On April Fool's day in 1977, he crowned himself King of Hay, which he declared an independent country. Press coverage gave the ludicrous campaign for Home Rule a degree of plausibility, although it was refuted by local councillors. Since then Hay has developed its own peerage system, a 'national' anthem written by Hay's poet laureate, and a house of lords, which meets annually in the state room of the castle.

Booth's Bookshop in Lion Street is the largest in Hay. In the mid-1980s, he opened a second bookshop on the ground floor of the semi-derelict Hay Castle. You are most likely to catch the King in his castle on 1 April making his annual speech to his loyal subjects wearing a copper crown and holding a sceptre made of a plumber's ballcock.

Tourist Information

Hay on Wye: Oxford Road, **t** (01497) 820 144. *Open summer 10–1 and 2–5, winter 11–1 and 2–4.*

Hay is a good place to pick up the **Wye Valley Walk**. You can also join the **Offa's Dyke path** here; follow the white acorns!

Celtic Canoes, Celtic Lodge, Newport Street, Hay-on-Wye, **t** (01497) 847 422. Explore the River Wye aboard a large Canadian canoe. Day hire or guided day trips.

Festivals

Hay Literary Festival takes place annually over Whitsun for 10 days, attracting around 50,000 visitors, and big-name speakers. Tickets sold separately for each event, **t** (01497) 821 299, *www.hayfestival.co.uk*. For a small fee the organizers of the festival can arrange accommodation, **t** (01497) 821 217, *www.hayfestival.co.uk/Site/accom.*

Where to Stay

Hay-on-Wye t (01497) –

The Felin Fach Griffin, Felin Fach, **t** (01874) 620 111, *www.eatdrinksleep.ltd.uk* (*expensive*). Excellent gastro hotel in lovely valley 10–15 minutes' drive south of Hay, with stone-flagged restaurant and friendly atmosphere.

Swan at Hay Hotel, Church Street, **t** 821 188, *www.swanathay.co.uk* (*expensive*). Attractive white-shuttered town-centre hotel with pleasant bedrooms and pretty garden at back. Restaurant (*moderate*) strong on *noisettes*, *medallions* and *tornados* of meat.

Kilvert's Hotel, The Bullring, **t** 821 042, *www.hay-on-wye.co.uk/kilverts* (*expensive*). Creeper-clad hotel in own grounds with 11 comfortable, clean bedrooms, good bar and restaurant, but somehow lacks charisma you desire from a traditional old country inn.

Tinto House, Broad Street, **t** 820 590 (*moderate*). Attractive with pine furniture, rugs on boards and sunny yellow walls.

Clifton House, Belmont Road, **t** 821 618, *www.cliftonhousehay.co.uk* (*moderate*). Welcoming Georgian townhouse opposite the clock tower, with two spacious and bright bedrooms, a lounge with wood-burning stove and lots of board games.

The Bear, Bear Street, **t** 821 302 (*moderate*). Gorgeous 16th-century low-roofed house with wide stairway and corridor, exposed stone and beamwork; four rooms.

The Firs Guesthouse, Church Street, **t** 820 275, *www.thefirshayonwye.com* (*cheap*). Warm, friendly, comfortable accommodation behind Hay Cinema Bookshop.

Eating Out

The Pear Tree, 6 Church Street, **t** 820 777 (*moderate*). Snug restaurant in Georgian townhouse with beams and wood burner. French-trained chef does all kinds of wonderful things with fresh local produce. *Open eves only, closed Sun and Mon.*

Shepherd's Ice Cream Parlour, 9 High Town, **t** 821 898 (*cheap*). Friendly café selling home-made ice cream and sorbet.

The Granary, Broad Street, **t** 820 790 (*cheap*). Popular, long-established, rustic-style restaurant offering a wide range of food including pasta, vegetarian flans and snacks, three choices of home-made soup and rolls. *Open eves too during festival.*

Oscar's Bistro, High Town, **t** 821 193 (*cheap*). Pleasant little café with rough floorboards, old furniture and cappuccino machine frothing over classical music; baguettes, quiches and hot pots. *Winter closed Tues.*

Of the many pubs in town, the most friendly are **The Blue Boar**, Castle Street, **t** 820 884 and **The Old Black Lion**, Lion Street, **t** 820 841.

border town, including the Dickens specialist Boz Books, in Booth's original bookshop, and B&K Books, where you will find only books on bees, bee-keeping and honey. Books are sold in the old cinema, the ruined castle and even a passage between two buildings, known as Passage Books. Hay also has a number of art and craft galleries, good shops and pubs, catering for browsers at the town's annual literary festival.

Into the Black Mountains

Hay Bluff, the dark shoulder of the Black Mountains, looms 2,227ft above the town, over the gentle scenery of the Wye and Dore valleys. To reach the bluff on foot, follow Offa's Dyke Path from the main Hay car park. Otherwise drive up on the Capel-y-ffin pass road, park beneath the bluff, and make the final ascent from there. The road continues through Llanthony Valley to the ruins of Llanthony Priory, an Augustinian foundation evacuated in the 12th century after frequent attacks by Welsh raiders.

Golden Valley

If you are staying in Hay-on-Wye, set aside a day to follow the Golden Valley of the River Dore, which passes through villages of bright red sandstone and brick. The valley wasn't always such a gentle spot: it is dotted with the remains of Iron Age hill forts and Norman motte and bailey castles. The monks of Abbey Dore transformed the wild, fortified valley into an Arcadia, clearing the oak woods to plant wheat fields and orchards. Stop at the Neolithic longbarrow known as **Arthur's Stone** at the north end of the valley, a mile north of **Dorstone**, near Bredwardine. The earth mound, once 85ft long and 10ft high, has been washed away to reveal a collapsed burial chamber of pink sandstone. At the south end of the valley are Charis Ward's lovely **Abbey Dore Gardens** (***t*** *(01981) 240 419; open April–Sept Tues, Thurs and weekends 11–5.30; adm*).

Abbey Dore Church

The Abbey Dore was founded in the 12th century by 12 Cistercian monks from Morimond Abbey in the Champagne region of France. All that survives is the dark red sandstone church in a green meadow. The 'odd-looking church' (Pevsner) is missing its

Offa's Dyke

> ***There was in Mercia in recent times a certain valiant king called Offa, who was feared by all the kings and kingdoms around, who ordered a great dyke to be built from sea to sea between Britain and Mercia.***
>
> Asser, King Alfred's biographer, at the end of the 9th century

Offa's Dyke is the longest earthwork in Europe, constructed in the 780s by Offa, King of Mercia, as a frontier between England and Wales. The border has not moved much since. The dyke originally comprised an earth bank rising 7 yards from the bottom of a deep ditch, and stretched 150 miles between the rivers Dee and Severn, borrowing natural features in the landscape like the Wye. The dyke served as a defensible boundary in a disputed area, annexing prosperous lowland farms into Mercia and leaving the Welsh Britons with the poorer upland pastures.

The **Offa's Dyke Path** runs between Chepstow, at the mouth of the Severn, and Prestatyn on the north Wales coast. It more or less follows the course of the 8th-century dyke, about 80 miles of which survive intact, between the Wye and the Severn. One of the most impressive sections crosses the empty hills of Clun Forest, over Llanfair Hill, south of Clun, and above Mainstone, west of Bishop's Castle.

nave, so that the surviving east end is absurdly tall. The tower was added in the 17th century by John Scudamore, whose family had acquired the monastic lands at the Dissolution. He filled the high vaulted interior with ornate wood, including an oak musicians' gallery.

Ledbury and Around

Ledbury is tucked under the southwest slope of the Malvern Hills, over the ridge from the Worcestershire plain. On a clear day, take the Jubilee Drive (follow the A438 out of town and turn off past the Malvern Hotel) through the Wych Cutting for the views. Around the town, the apple and pear orchards of the **Frome Valley** support a cider and perry industry. The **Leadon Valley** was the stomping ground of the Dymock poets. Robert Frost's poem *Iris by Night* describes a 'moon-made prismatic bow' – a rare moon rainbow – seen on a walk with Edward Thomas from Leddington to British Camp on the Malverns. There are three walks, each about 10 miles long, along the paths trodden by the Dymock poets. They all start at Dymock church.

Ledbury

Another poet, Elizabeth Barrett Browning (1806–61), was born in Ledbury. A precociously gifted child, she published *Poems* in 1844, defied her father to marry Robert Browning in 1846, and spent the rest of her life dying in Italy. She was commemorated in 1896 in the Elizabeth Barrett Browning Institute (now a library) with its clock tower. The whole town centre, with its handsome Georgian and Victorian architecture, is under a preservation order. The black-and-white 17th-century **market hall** at the bottom stands on oak pillars. From there, cobbled Church Lane leads between timber-framed townhouses towards the needle spire of the church and the oldest part of town. The old **grammar school** (now a Heritage Centre*; t (01531) 635 680; open Easter–Oct daily 10.30–4.30*) was built in the mid-16th century out of the endowments of three pre-Reformation chantries. **Butcher's Row House**, once part of a row of market buildings in the middle of the High Street, exhibits clay pipes and lace.

The 18th-century spire of the sandstone **church** rises from a detached bell tower, built around 1230. The main body of the church is 13th century, from the west front with its zigzag carvings around the doorway to the chancel with its porthole clerestory windows above round arches; the wide Gothic side aisles were added later. The square chapel is thought to have been built as a chapter house in 1330, part of a failed attempt by the Benedictine monks of Hereford to turn Ledbury into a collegiate church (look for the eroded effigy of a Benedictine monk under a stone canopy). The Decorated windows are studded with ballflower decoration, like Leominster church.

Eastnor Castle

t (01531) 633 160; open Easter–Oct Sun 11–5, July–Aug Sun–Fri 11–5; adm.

Three miles east of Ledbury, the sham baronial castle of the Hervey-Bathurst family thrusts its dreamy round towers above ornamental woodland and casts its reflection

Getting There

By **car**, turn off M5 at junction 8 onto M50 towards Ross-on-Wye, then at junction 2 follow A417 north to Ledbury.

Ledbury is on the Worcester–Hereford railway line.

Tourist Information

Ledbury: 3 The Homend, **t** (01531) 636 147. *Open Mar–Nov Mon–Sat 10–5, mid-July–mid-Sept also Sun 10–5, rest of year Mon–Sat 10–4.*

Guided Walks begin at Market House, May–Sept Mon and Thurs 11am.

Ledbury Poetry Festival lasts 10 days in early July. It's one of the biggest in the country, with poetry readings, workshops and discussions in various venues around town including the Burgage Hall. Information, **t** (01531) 634 156.

Where to Stay

Around Ledbury t (01531) –

Moor Court Farm, Stretton Grandison (on Worcester–Hereford road), **t** 670 408 (*moderate*). Set among orchards, an idyllic low timber-framed farmhouse with loads of little windows, covered in climbing plants and wisteria.

Pridewood, Ashperton (7 miles from Ledbury), **t** 670 416 (*moderate*). The setting on a hop farm is everything. Bay-window views over lake; large walled garden; farm built around courtyard at end of long private road; rooms large and bright, not flashy.

Hopton Arms, Ashperton (short drive north of Ledbury), **t** 670 520 (*moderate*). A popular country inn recently refurbished in rich Victorian style with nine bedrooms in an old coach house and a large beer garden.

Hill Farm, Eastnor (a mile from Ledbury), **t** (632 827 (*cheap*). Beautiful, secluded L-shaped cottage with jasmine-covered porch and sunny dining room; three bedrooms with green views; evening meals by arrangement.

Eating Out

Ledbury and Around t (01531) –

The Malthouse Restaurant, Church Lane, **t** 634 443 (*moderate*). Ledbury's best restaurant, with sunny courtyard enlivened by plants and fairy lights; rural-chic décor with exposed wood and stonework. Modern European cooking using local produce. *Open daily eves, Fri and Sat also lunch.*

The Talbot Hotel, New Street, **t** 632 963 (*moderate*). Pop in for a drink, or a traditional English dinner in the oak-panelled restaurant of this appealing 16th-century inn with its black-and-white timber-framed exterior; six modest bedrooms off narrow corridors.

Malvern Hotel Inn, by the British Camp hill fort, reached by foot or car (*moderate*). On sunny days you see hot, sticky walkers sitting at the tables outside .

The Scrumpy House Restaurant and Bar, The Bounds, Much Marcle, **t** (01531) 660 626 (*moderate*). Bustling stone-walled restaurant overlooking Weston's cider-making farm buildings; lunch or dinner menu might include milk-poached haddock with rosemary mash and poached free-range egg, fresh Grimsby fish, sausages and mash, or you could have a baguette and salad.

Mrs Muffins, Church Lane (*cheap*). For delicious home-made cakes (gooseberry and elder, raspberry and white chocolate, pear and ginger) and cream teas.

Ceci Paulo Delicatessen, 21 High Street (*cheap*). Takeaway panini and salads. *Closed Sun.*

into the lake. Despite the illusion of medieval grandeur, Eastnor Castle was built by the first Earl Somers between 1811 and 1824 with inherited wealth (his unmarried uncles owned a London bank) and fierce aristocratic aspirations stemming from his great-grandfather, who was Lord Chancellor of England. Twenty-one of the castle's 90 rooms are open to the public, decorated with typical Victorian exuberance by the 3rd, 'collector', Earl with patterned wallpaper, tapestries and suits of armour. The 3rd Earl was one of the social in-crowd of his day, travelling around Europe, mixing with celebrities such as Tennyson, and marrying the most beautiful of the seven renowned

Dymock Poets

'Twas in July
Of nineteen-fourteen that we sat and talked:
Then August brought the war, and scattered us.

Wilfred Gibson, 'The Golden Room'

There were six of the so-called Dymock poets: Lascalles Abercrombie, Wilfrid Gibson, Rupert Brooke, Robert Frost, John Drinkwater and Edward Thomas. Three of them – Abercrombie, Frost and Gibson – lived near the village of Dymock in the Leadon Valley just before the First World War. Abercrombie led the way, moving into The Gallows in Ryton, 2 miles east of Dymock, in 1911. The Gibsons honeymooned in Abercrombie's cottage, fell in love with the area and moved into a cottage called The Old Nailshop, 2 miles west of Ryton on the Ledbury road. The Frosts spent 11 months at Little Iddens, on the other side of the River Leadon. The three of them published a quarterly magazine, *New Numbers*, featuring their poems. The others visited, joining them on rambling walks in the daffodil woods and cornfields, and spending evenings around the table drinking cider and talking poetry. Edward Thomas, encouraged to start writing by his closest friend, Robert Frost, rented rooms in Oldfields farmhouse, north of Little Iddens. The two of them walked around Leddington, the Malverns and Dymock. Thomas wrote his most famous poem, 'Adlestrop' ('Yes, I remember Adlestrop – The name, because one afternoon of heat the express-train drew up there Unwontedly') on his way to see the Frosts. John Drinkwater frequently visited The Gallows ('A little land of mellowed ease I find beyond my broken gate') after receiving a glowing review of one of his poems by Abercrombie. Rupert Brooke, the best known of them all, for his social charm and early death in the war, as well as his poetry, met the Dymock poets in London, visiting The Gallows only to discuss *New Numbers* ('Abercrombie's cottage is the most beautiful you can imagine [with] a porch where one drinks great mugs of cider, and looks at fields of poppies in the corn. A life that makes London a very foolish affair.').

The war split the group up, and bathed Dymock in the perpetual golden sunshine of nostalgia. The sense of loss became the common subject of their poetry ('And yet, Was it for nothing that the little room...thrilled with golden Laughter from hearts of friends that summer night?' wrote Gibson in 'Golden Room'). Abercrombie worked as an inspector of shells in a munitions factory in Liverpool. Gibson worked as a clerk in the Army Service Corps, having been turned down as a soldier for bad eyesight. Brooke died of blood poisoning on 23 April 1915 on a troop ship to the Dardanelles. His most famous poem, 'The Soldier' ('If I should die, think only this of me...'), was written at Blandford camp in Dorset for *New Numbers* and edited by Gibson, who changed its name from 'The Recruit'. Thomas enlisted in July 1915, and was killed fighting in France on 9 April 1917. Frost, who had returned to America in 1915, was devastated at the news of his friend's death ('I had meant to talk endlessly with him still, either here in our mountains as we had said or, as I found my longing was more and more, there at Leddington where first we talked of war.').

Pattle sisters (society darlings, one of whom was the portrait photographer Julia Cameron). He collected the medieval armour in the Great Hall and portraits by G.F. Watts in the Octagon Saloon (including Shakespearean actress Ellen Terry, his wife Virginia Pattle, and Tennyson) and planted the 40-acre arboretum around the lake. The most lavish room, however, is the **Gothic Drawing Room**, designed by Pugin for the 2nd Earl in 1849; even the furniture and carpets were made to Pugin's designs.

The Frome Valley

It's easy to spend a day touring the pink stone villages of the Frome Valley, stopping off at vineyards and pubs; the best bit is between Ledbury and Bromyard.

Coddington Vineyard (***t*** *(01531) 640 668; open April–Oct Thurs–Sun 2–5*), the small vineyard of the Savage family, is buried in lush countryside three miles north of Ledbury along winding lanes (signposted from the village of Coddington). The old red-brick farmhouse, rambling gardens around the pond and the vineyard on its sunny hillside are idyllic. You may get a free wine tasting.

Just off the B4214 halfway between Ledbury and Bromyard a track leads to the 12th-century **Castle Frome Church** (the castle is long gone). Pevsner called the font 'one of the masterworks of Romanesque sculpture in England.' It stands on three crouching figures; exuberant carvings around the basin include more figures with moustaches and flowing robes, a lion and rope patterns. The baptism of Christ could belong on a Viking shield. This lively mix of Norman, Scandinavian and pagan Saxon imagery is the masterpiece of the Herefordshire School (*see* Eardisley church, p.557, Leominster priory, p.554, and Kilpeck church, p.564). Don't miss the 17th-century Unnet family tomb, with lifelike alabaster figures of a cavalier and his wife.

From Castle Frome, the main B-road crosses the river to Bishop's Frome, where a minor road runs along the bottom of the valley to **Frome Valley Vineyard** (***t*** *(01885) 490 735; open April–Oct Wed–Sun 11–5; call in advance for tours; adm*). David and Clare Longman have been growing vines at Paunton Court since 1992, and now produce around 5–6,000 bottles a year of white and rosé wines, which you can taste.

Much Marcle and Around

South of Ledbury, amid narrow lanes, small cider mills and daffodil woods, is the village of Much Marcle, which has a superb church, the country house of Hellens and Weston's Cider Mill. It was to a cottage in Much Marcle that the poet Lascalles Abercrombie came in April 1910, encouraged by his sister Ursula, who was renting Hellens from Lord Beauchamp. A year later, he moved to The Gallows, just outside the village of Dymock (Ursula had seen it empty while out hunting), which became the office of the quarterly magazine *New Numbers*, publishing the poetry of a group of friends known as the Dymock poets (*see* box). 'I have lived in a cottage in daffodil country,' wrote Abercrombie in 1932, 'and I have, for a time, done what I wanted to do... and I have known what it is to have Wilfrid Gibson and Robert Frost for my neighbours; and John Drinkwater, Rupert Brooke, Edward Thomas...have drunk my cider, and talkt in my garden.'

Much Marcle's **church of St Bartholomew** is a treasure-house of funerary monuments. Against the north wall of the chancel is the stone effigy of Blanche Mortimer, daughter of Roger Mortimer, 1st Earl of March, the most powerful man in England in the early 14th century. She looks about 30 years old, her age when she died childless in 1347, three years before the death of her husband, Sir Peter Grandison. Her hands rest unclasped on her stomach, fingering a rosary, as she lies beneath a stone canopy featuring the coat of arms of her father. The effigies in the locked **Kyrle Chapel** have nothing on Blanche's beauty. There is an unknown 14th-century lady, next to a knight, her hands stiffly clasped in prayer while two puppies nibble at the hem of her dress. The mid-17th-century effigies are Sir John Kyrle, High Sheriff of Herefordshire, and his wife, Sybil. His feet rest on a hedgehog, hers on a paw in a coronet. Most striking of all is the wooden effigy of a mid-14th-century man in the nave, carved out of a single block of oak. He stands 6ft 4in high, dressed in a close-fitting red tunic buttoned down the middle and gathered at the waist, with a purse and short sword attached to a low-slung belt.

A track opposite the church leads to **Hellens** (***t** (01531) 660 504; open Easter–Sept, Wed, Sat and Sun; tours 2, 3 and 4; adm*), the Tudor brick manor house of the Walwyns. You have to stoop as you enter the arched doorway into the 'stone hall' with its carved stone fireplace, stone table and flagstone floor. You can visit the 17th-century apartments of the Walwyns, with paintings by Van Dyck, Hogarth and Reynolds.

Down the road, **Weston's Cider Mill** (***t** (01531) 660 233; tours of mill Mon–Fri 2.30; adm*) is one of the oldest producers of cider and perry in Herefordshire, dating back to 1878. It's a good place for lunch or a sandwich.

Ross-on-Wye and Around

The market town of Ross-on-Wye is on a loop in the River Wye where the old road crosses into South Wales. It's a wholesome, handsome place, but its real attraction is the countryside of the lower Wye Valley with its wooded gorges and Norman castles.

Ross's main street climbs to the handsome 17th-century market house, a rough-hewn red sandstone building on pillars with a clock on top, surrounded by pleasant streets. At the top of town is an elegant spired church. The riverside is ruined by big roads: waste no time in heading south to Goodrich Castle and Symonds Yat.

Hoarwithy and Kilpeck Churches

Northwest of Ross-on-Wye are these two extraordinary churches, buried deep in the countryside. The Italian Romanesque church at **Hoarwithy**, built in the 1870s by the vicar William Poole, commands the hillside above the River Wye as if it were Tuscany. A long flight of steps climbs up to it from the road, creating a dramatic vista of the tower, rising out of a loggia, against the sky. The vision of Italy continues inside with a mosaic tiled floor and marble columns supporting a golden dome in the chancel.

The red sandstone church at **Kilpeck** is a perfect Norman church, nothing having been added or taken away since it was built in the 12th century. Around the outside of

Tourist Information

Ross on Wye: The Swan House, Eddecross Street, **t** (01989) 562 768. *Open winter Mon–Sat 9.30–4.30, summer Mon–Sat 9.30–5.15, high summer also Sun 10–4.*

Ross Market is held on Thurs and Sat.

The **Wye Valley Walk** runs for 75 miles between Chepstow and Hay-on-Wye including the stunning Lower Wye Valley.

Ross Festival runs for 10 days of music, dance, comedy and theatre in Aug; **t** (01989) 565 760, or go to *www.festival.com*.

Where to Stay

Ross-on-Wye t (01989) –

The Royal Hotel, Palace Pound, **t** 565 105 (*moderate*). Large white-painted Victorian hotel with sham Gothic tower, above town next to church with Wye Valley views; 40 bedrooms and pleasant hotel ambience; reasonable country-inn-style food.

The Rosswyn Hotel, The Market Place, **t** 562 733 (*moderate*). In the middle of Ross, this pleasant hotel has eight bedrooms, decorated with William Morris fabrics and pine.

Radcliffe Guest House, Wye Street, **t** 563 895, *radcliffegh@btinternet.com* (*moderate*). Old coaching inn, now friendly guesthouse with six pleasant bedrooms.

Vaga House, Wye Street, **t** 563 024, *www.vagahouse.co.uk* (*moderate*). Attractive white-painted 18th-century merchant's house, now relaxed, informal place to stay with seven comfortable bedrooms; dinner available.

Lindon House, 14 Church Street, **t** 565 373, *www.lindenhouseguesthouse.com* (*moderate*). Brick-fronted 17th-century guesthouse in centre of town with six bright bedrooms and a cosy dining room.

Around Ross-on-Wye

The Royal Hotel, Symonds Yat East (5 miles from Ross), **t** (01600) 890 238 (*moderate*). On the east bank of the Wye directly beneath Yat Rock, this friendly hotel, once visited by Charles Dickens, has 21 pleasant rooms.

Ye Hostelrie Hotel, Goodrich, **t** (01600) 890 241, *www.ye-hostelrie.co.uk* (*moderate*). About 3 miles from Ross and a stone's throw from Goodrich Castle, imposing Victorian-Gothic building with grey stone towers and pinnacles; bedrooms well furnished.

Broom Farm, Peterstowe (2 miles north of Ross towards Hereford), **t** (01989) 562 825 (*moderate*). Pretty cider farm among orchards. B&B, cream teas and rural charm.

Eating Out

There are Italian, French, Nepalese and Hungarian restaurants, and lots of pubs.

Pheasant, Edde Cross Street, **t** 565 751 (*moderate*). English 'fine dining' with local produce and old recipes like mock goose (stuffed and braised venison heart) and duck pie, married with top-quality wines. Really exciting food. *Open Thurs–Sat eves.*

Meader's Hungarian Restaurant, 1 Copse Cross Street, **t** 562 803 (*moderate*). Friendly, pleasant place to eat, with stained-glass partitions. Polite waitresses serve goulash (spicy meat soup), smoked sausage, creamy potatoes layered with sliced hard boiled eggs and cheese sauce, with gherkin and spicy red cabbage. *Closed Sun and Mon.*

The King's Head, 8 High Street **t** 0800 801 098 (*cheap*). Comfortable Georgian-fronted medieval coaching inn. Good place for coffee, with well-padded leather armchairs.

Antique Tea Shop, 40 High Street **t** 566 123 (*cheap*). Small, quaint tea shop overlooking market place with delicate china tea things and plates piled high with scones and cakes.

Oat Cuisine, 47 Broad Street, **t** 566 271 (*cheap*). Wholesome snacks and light lunches – salads, quiches, sandwiches, pasties, pizza and nut roast – which you eat elbow to elbow at long tables among shelves of seeds, essential oils and vitamins. *Open late Fri and Sat.*

Canio's Italian Restaurant and Pizzeria, Cantilupe Road, **t** 567 155 (*cheap*). Italian restaurant that comes into its own when the chef's home-made pizza and pasta are on offer.

Yaks 'n' Yetis Restaurant, 1 Brookend Street **t** 564 963 (*cheap*). Relaxed restaurant offering Sherpa soup, Kathmandu curry and Himalayan Stew among other exotic Nepalese and Tibetan dishes. *Open eves only, closed Sun and Mon.*

the building, and decorating the chancel arch, are stone carvings of the Herefordshire School sculptors, whose work compares well with the French Romanesque churches. Widely travelled, they seem to have drawn inspiration from the Romanesque, Saxon and Viking traditions. Examine the carvings of snakes, birds and fish, and two 'Welsh warriors' walking through foliage. Grotesques include a dog, a ram, a sheela-na-gig of a woman opening her vagina to the world, and lots of sticking-out tongues.

Goodrich Castle

t (01600) 890 538; open Mar–Sept 10–6, Oct–Nov 10–5, Dec–Feb 10–4; adm.

A few miles downriver from Ross, the pink sandstone ruins of Goodrich Castle stand above the Wye. A remote spot today, it was once a major river crossing. Goodrich, Chepstow, Monmouth and Hereford formed a chain of Norman castles along the Wye, which to the south is still the Welsh border. The powerful medieval earls of Shrewsbury and Pembroke held Goodrich from the 13th to 15th centuries. They built three separate halls with private rooms. The unusual D-shaped barbican, reached over a drawbridge, defended the apparently impregnable main gatehouse, with its double set of portcullises, murder holes and arrow slits. You can walk around the walls, admire the views from the keep, visit the dungeons and examine the engineering of the impressive drum towers on the corners.

Just south of Goodrich castle, the **Coppett Hill walk** (5 miles) takes you along a ridge in a loop of the river to Symonds Yat Rocks – a nesting ground for peregrine falcons.

If you don't want to walk, from Goodrich Castle it is about four miles on minor lanes to the riverside hamlet of **Symonds Yat East**, tucked into the bottom of the Yat gorge, whose wooded slopes, protruding rocks and white-painted cottages were made famous in the 18th century by travel writers, poets and painters in search of the picturesque. It's still a beauty spot, good for a picnic or a boat ride. From the Royal Hotel, a steep path leads up to a falcon-watching lookout (the birds are best observed in nesting season, from April to September).

Forest of Dean

The Forest of Dean is a remote wooded upland between the Wye and Severn rivers. The forest roads take you up and down, in and out of conifer- and broadleaf-wooded hills. Although it's an ancient forest, managed for more than a thousand years, the oldest trees in it are only 200 years old. The Normans made Dean a royal hunting forest, imposing all sorts of rules on the foresters to preserve it for royal fun. Nonetheless, the woodland had almost gone by the mid-17th century, felled for charcoal to smelt iron. Around 30 million acorns were planted after the Napoleonic wars to ensure future supplies of timber for the Navy, but as things turned out iron and steel soon superseded timber in shipbuilding. The Second World War ate up a quarter of the oak; post-war the emphasis shifted to fast-growing conifers. The Cannop Valley is now the heartland of the 19th-century oak plantations – the best of the forest. Since

Getting There and Around

If you're arriving **by car**, Gloucester, Ross-on-Wye, Monmouth and Chepstow define the corners of the forest, so head towards any one of them; from Bristol you can cross the Severn and head north into the forest up the A466 Monmouth road, following the River Wye, or you can approach from Gloucester on the A48 or A40.

By train, you will have to change at either Gloucester or Newport and catch a local train to Lydney.

National Express runs **coaches** to Gloucester, where you can pick up **local buses** to Coleford, Lydney and Cinderford. **Traveline, t** 0870 608 2608, for local transport information.

There is a large network of **cycleways** around the forest, around 200 miles, on the former mineral railways. The 11-mile **Family Trail** heads south from the Pedalabikeaway Cycle Centre along the Severn and Wye Railway line, skirting the edge of the Nagshead Reserve to New Fancy View, where it loops back via the old Lightmoor Colliery around the north side of the Beechenshurst woods.

Pedalabikeaway Cycle Centre, Cannop Valley, **t** (01594) 860 065. *Open April–Oct Tues–Sun, Nov–Mar weekends, school holidays daily*. Rents bikes for the day or longer.

Tourist Information

Forest of Dean: High Street, Coleford, **t** (01594) 812 388. *Open summer Mon–Sat 10–5, July–Aug also Sun 10–2; winter Mon–Fri 10–4 and Sat 10–2.*

Where to Stay and Eat

Coleford t (01594) –

Lambsquay House Hotel, t 833 127 (*expensive*). Pretty and friendly stuccoed Georgian hotel near Clearwell Caves; rooms are generally tidy and cheerful.

Forest House, Cinderhill, **t** 832 424, *www.forest-house-hotel.co.uk* (*expensive*). Recently restored pink forest-stone town-house of the 'Forester' Mushets, 19th-century father and son industrialists of steel and iron. They rented it from 1803 to 1850, doing many of their experiments in what used to be large grounds. There are seven bedrooms with period furniture, and a high-quality restaurant (*moderate*).

The Speech House, t 822 607, *www.thespeechhouse.co.uk* (*expensive*). Formerly the foresters' parliament building on the road between Cinderford and Coleford, now owned by Best Western, with 35 bedrooms.

St Briavels t (01594) –

Briavels Youth Hostel, The Castle, **t** 530 272 (*cheap*). Most atmospheric place to stay in the forest, in a romantic medieval castle on the edge of the village near the church. Dormitories called Hanging Room and Guard's Room in gatehouse; can get booked up well in advance.

the 1970s, broadleafs have again been planted and are once more beginning to dominate the woodland.

From the Middle Ages until the 18th century the forest was one of England's industrial heartlands, more so than the Weald, which lacked coal. Underneath it all is an exhausted coalfield and around the margins are abandoned iron workings dating back to pre-Roman times. The medieval forest produced timber for warships, cathedrals and castles, and cast iron for armour and weapons (crossbow bolts were a speciality of the forest forges). The rights of the king, foresters and miners were upheld by the constables of St Briavel's Castle until 1680, when special courts at Speech House (now a hotel, on the main Cinderford to Coleford road) assumed this responsibility. The last coal mine closed down in the 1960s and today only a handful of Free Miners manage to make a living in small private collieries, exercising ancient mineral rights. But it remains a working forest, producing wood and pink stone.

Just over the border in Wales are the ruins of romantic **Tintern Abbey**, painted by Turner and the subject of a poem by Wordsworth, the pretty old town of **Chepstow** with its magnificent castle above the river, and **Monmouth Castle**, the sturdy stone birthplace of Henry V.

Around the Forest

Try to avoid the forest towns of Coleford and Cinderford and follow one of the forest footpaths instead. The **Dean Heritage Centre** (***t*** *(01594) 822 170; open April–Sept 10–5.30, winter 10–4; adm*) is a good place to start exploring, with a small museum telling the history of the forest and plenty of information about walks. **Beechenhurst Lodge** (***t*** *(01594) 827 357; open summer 10–6, winter 10–dusk*) is the start of a 3½-mile woodland Sculpture Trail. The 6-mile **Cannop Valley Trail** takes you through the oldest oak woods. **Hopewell Colliery Museum** on Cannop Hill (***t*** *(01594) 810 706; open Easter–Oct 10–4.30; adm*), near Beechenhurst, takes you underground down still-working mine shafts.

Clearwell Caves (***t*** *(01594) 832 535; open Mar–Oct daily 10–5; adm*) on the western edge of the forest, about a mile and a half south of Coleford on the B4228, take you into a vast system of limestone caves, excavated by water thousands of years ago. Since the Iron Age, 3,000 years ago, the caves have been mined for iron ore and coloured oxides.

The moated castle of **St Briavels** (pronounced 'Brevels') (***t*** *(01594) 530 272 for opening times*) was the headquarters of the constable of the forest and the hunting lodge of kings of England, including King John (who must have done a lot of hunting, judging by the number of hunting lodges associated with him). The gatehouse was built by Edward I, doubling up as a keep. Within the curtain walls are 13th-century buildings including the great hall, chapel and courtroom, and apartments to accommodate the king on hunting trips. It's now a youth hostel.

Opposite the castle is the **church**: short round Norman arches and deeply recessed windows on one side of the nave, and large, pointed Gothic arches and windows on the other. Look for the effigies of William Warren and his wife Mariana.

East Midlands

Derbyshire, Nottinghamshire, Leicestershire, Rutland, Lincolnshire and Northamptonshire

15

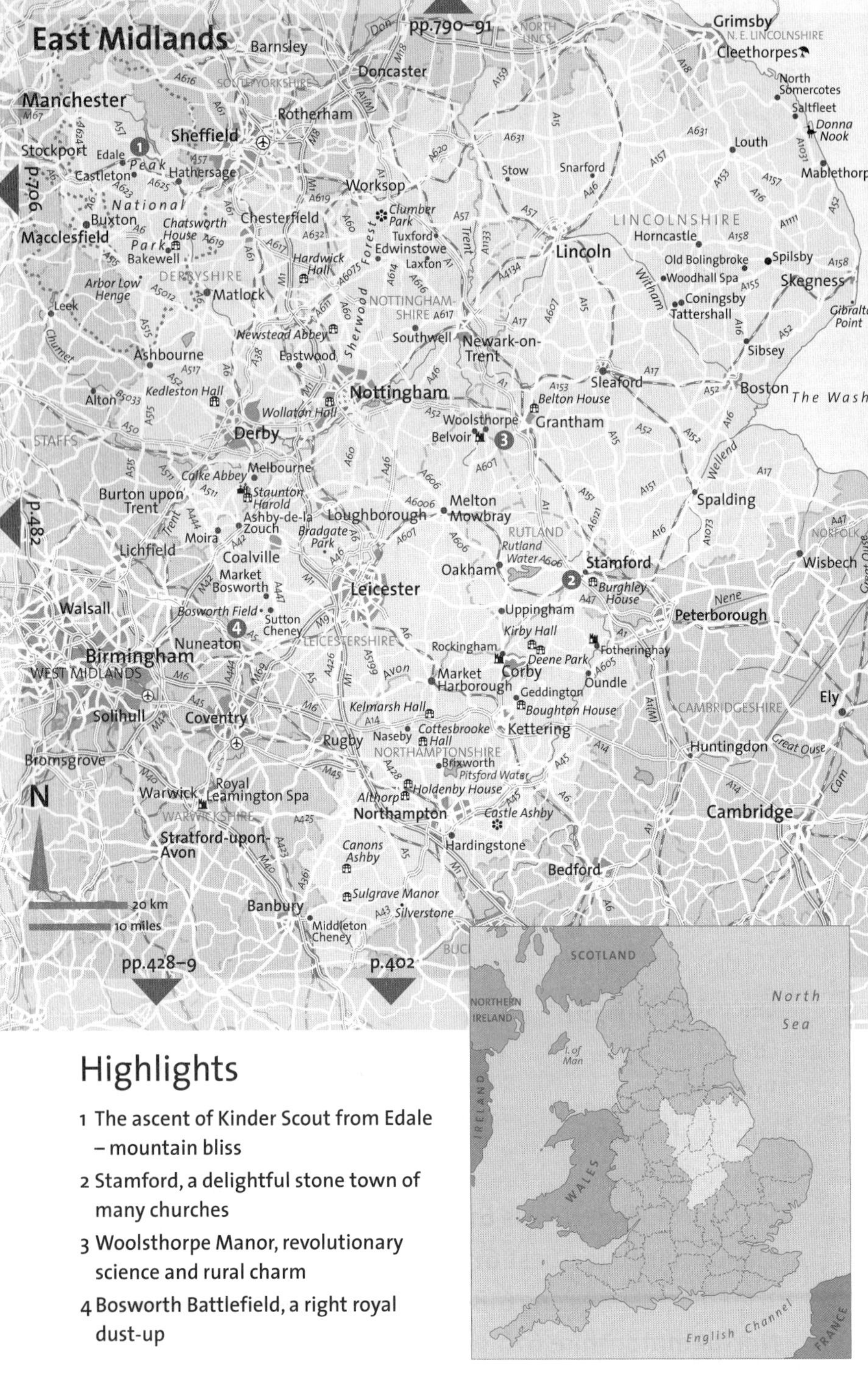

Highlights

1. The ascent of Kinder Scout from Edale – mountain bliss
2. Stamford, a delightful stone town of many churches
3. Woolsthorpe Manor, revolutionary science and rural charm
4. Bosworth Battlefield, a right royal dust-up

The East Midlands – Derbyshire, Nottinghamshire, Leicestershire, Rutland, Lincolnshire and Northamptonshire – are a mixed bag of scenery. There is mild arable countryside and upland moor in the magnificent **Derbyshire Peak District**, where the tail end of the Pennines protrudes into the English lowlands. **Charnwood Forest** grows on some of the oldest rocks in existence – Precambrian. The vast, empty **Lincolnshire Fens**, on the other hand, were drained only a few centuries ago.

Rutland Water and **Sherwood Forest** are delightful natural habitats too.

The East Midlands region boasts some interesting towns too. For charm, the handsome old stone towns of **Stamford, Oundle, Buxton and Oakham** stand out. The county towns are of mixed appeal, but all packed with history. **Lincoln**: Roman town of *Lindis Colonia*, medieval cloth-making town with castle and magnificent cathedral, modern tourist centre off the beaten track. **Nottingham**: Saxon 'cave-dwelling town', stronghold of medieval kings and Robin Hood legend, Victorian industrial centre of lace-making and hosiery, modern university town of clubs and bars. **Leicester**: insignificant Roman town of *Ratae*, medieval town of Simon de Montfort and John of Gaunt, Victorian town of hosiery and shoe manufacturing, modern multicultural town with first division football and rugby teams, and a National Space Centre. **Northampton**: a long history of shoe manufacturing. **Derby**: old manufacturing town and headquarters of the Midland Railway Company, in the shadow of Nottingham. Follow the Derwent back towards its source in the Peak District from here and things get much more interesting.

The **Belper and Cromford Mills** on the lower Derwent between Derby and Matlock Bath were the first successful attempts at large-scale, water-powered cotton yarn manufacturing by pioneering 18th-century industrialists Richard Arkwright and Jedediah Strutt. You can visit their mills and industrial villages. Later, the steam-powered machines of the 19th century enabled industrialists to locate their factories in the middle of a ready-made urban workforce. Meanwhile, the coalfields on the Derbyshire-Leicestershire-Nottinghamshire border turned great swathes of countryside into industrialized regions.

D.H. Lawrence, a miner's son from Eastwood, blamed the Victorian businessmen and industrialists for what he called 'the tragedy of ugliness' in England. Lawrence is one of many large personalities that give character to the mixed East Midlands: Byron lived at Newstead Abbey in Nottinghamshire; William Stukeley, Sir Isaac Newton and Alfred, Lord Tennyson were all Lincolnshire men; Thomas Cook began his travel company in Leicester; King Richard III crops up all over the place – born in Fotheringhay in Northamptonshire, died at Bosworth in Leicestershire, and knocked off Sir William Hastings and Lord Richard Grey (cream of the Leicestershire aristocracy) in between. The female figurehead of the East Midlands is the much-married Bess of Hardwick: she lived with her fourth husband, the Earl of Shrewsbury, at Chatsworth House in Derbyshire, but left him for Hardwick Hall, 15 miles east on the Nottinghamshire border. Bess set up her sons in houses in the area too, including Bolsover Castle, and was buried in Derby.

The East Midlands have a wealth of magnificent properties open to visitors, including **Burghley House**, near Stamford in Lincolnshire, one of the greatest of the

Elizabethan 'prodigy houses' built at bank-breaking expense in case the Queen should ever decide to visit. Northamptonshire has a concentration of privately owned great old houses, several of which are open to the public, including Althorp, the Spencer family home, and Broughton Hall. Paradoxically, the trail east leads you west: hundreds of Lincolnshire families emigrated to America in the 17th and 18th centuries, including Captain John Smith of Pocahontas fame. The mass emigrations started with a group of non-Conformists who came to the old port of Boston in 1617 to escape to Holland; they failed to get away that time, but many of them numbered among the Pilgrim Fathers some 13 years later.

Derbyshire Peak District

The Peak District National Park is the southern tail of the Pennines, a wedge of upland scenery between the sprawling industrial cities of the north Midlands. It is said to be within an hour's drive of half the population of England. The 17th-century philosopher Thomas Hobbes identified seven natural wonders of the Peaks, including two limestone caves, a shivering mountain, a thermal spring and an enormous hole in the ground, which has since disappeared into itself; new wonders have taken its place in the core of the district, known as the White Peak or Low Peak with its lovely rolling hills and deep, wooded valleys such as Miller's Dale and Dovedale. The boggy gritstone moorland in the north of the district – known as the Dark Peak or High Peak – is less accessible. Alfred Wainwright, in his *Pennine Way Companion*, drily warns walkers: 'make no mistake you are going to suffer and wish you had never heard of the Pennine Way.' From these sombre northern moors two gritstone fingers stretch south around White Peak, creating dramatic rock escarpments and tors, popular with climbers. On the eastern edge near Hathersage the prehistoric fortress Carl Wark is exceptional for being built in stone not earth. Gritstone – coarse sandstone – is an excellent building material (Chatsworth House). Cromford Mill is one of several mills built by inventor-industrialist Richard Arkwright (1732–92) in the lower Derwent Valley. The Victorians celebrated Arkwright as an archetypal self-made man on a par with Wellington and Nelson; he had a go at wig-making, hairdressing and pub management before turning his hand to cotton spinning.

Buxton

Buxton whose fame the milk-warm waters tell,
whom I perhaps shall see no more, farewell.

Latin verse scratched by Mary Queen of Scots on her bedroom window at Buxton

The handsome Georgian spa town of the High Peak, more than a thousand feet above sea level, is a major nodal centre. To the west are the dark gritstone moors, crossed by the lonely 'cat and fiddle' pass road (A537). To the east is some of the loveliest limestone scenery in the district, including Miller's Dale. Today, residents of

Huddersfield
Derbyshire
WEST YORKSHIRE
Barnsley
Manchester
SOUTH YORKSHIRE
Peak District
Rotherham
Stockport
High Peak
Derwent Res.
Sheffield
Kinder Scout
Hayfield
Edale
Peak
Castleton
Hope
Hathersage
Chapel-en-le-Frith
National
CHESHIRE
Eyam
Buxton
Tideswell
Park
Macclesfield
Chesterfield
Chatsworth House
Bakewell
Haddon Hall
The Roaches
DERBYSHIRE
Arbor Low Henge
Hardwick Hall
Matlock
Matlock Bath
Leek
Churnet
NOTTS
Ashbourne
STAFFORDSHIRE
Eastwood
Alton Towers
Cheadle
Alton
Kedleston Hall
Derby
N
10 km
5 miles
LEICESTERSHIRE
A640
A616
A638
A628
M1
A635
A6024
A629
A616
A628
M67
A6102
A61
A629
A560
A626
A57
A624
M8
A57
A6
A625
A6135
M1
B5470
A623
A5002
A6
A61
A537
A6
A619
A54
A515
A617
A632
A61
M1
A523
A53
A5012
A6
A515
A523
A520
A608
A52
A38
A517
A6
B5417
A52
B5032
B5033
M1
A522
A515
A50
A50
A511
A38

Getting There and Around

From Manchester Piccadilly a branch-line **rail** service runs via Stockport to Buxton. From London or the north change at Manchester or Stockport. For all train information call **National Rail Enquiries, t** 08457 484950, *www.thetrainline.com.*

Daily **Transpeak bus** services run every 2 hours from Manchester to Nottingham via Buxton. Contact **Trent Buses, t** (01773) 712 265. Bus service **X18** runs every 2 hours between Stoke and Sheffield via Buxton, operated by **Potteries Motor Traction, t** (01782) 207 999.

National Express coaches run from London Victoria to Manchester once a day via Buxton. For all coach travel enquiries call **t** 08705 808080, *www.gobycoach.com.*

Tourist Information

Buxton: The Crescent, **t** (01298) 25106. *Open summer daily 9.30–5, winter daily 10–4.*

Festivals

Buxton Opera Festival runs for two weeks in July at the Opera House. **Festival Office**, 5 The Square, **t** (01298) 70395; **Buxton Opera House, t** 0845 1272190.

The **Gilbert and Sullivan Festival** follows on. **International Festival of Musical Theatre**, The Old Vicarage, Haley Hill, Halifax, **t** (01422) 323 252, or **Buxton Opera House, t** (01298) 72190.

Where to Stay

Buxton t (01298) –

The Palace Hotel, Palace Road, **t** 22001, *www.paramount-hotels.co.uk* (*very expensive*). A stone Victorian hotel with iron balconies built by London architect Henry Currey in 1868, set amid lawns and trees, 2 minutes walk from town centre; 94 en-suite bedrooms, gym, indoor pool and sumptuous public rooms including restaurant and bar.

The Old Hall Hotel, The Square, **t** 22841, *www.oldhallhotelbuxton.co.uk* (*expensive*). Atmospheric 16th-century townhouse opposite opera house, built by the Earl of Shrewsbury and briefly home to Mary Queen of Scots in 1573; 38 comfortable rooms. Popular wine bar open for coffee, pre- and post-theatre meals too (*moderate*).

Victorian Guesthouse, 3/a Broad Walk, **t** 78759, *www.buxtonvictorian.co.uk* (*expensive*). In a handsome stone terrace overlooking the park with themed bedrooms (including an Egyptian Room). Three nights minimum during festivals.

Roseleigh Hotel, 19 Broad Walk, **t** 24904, *www.roseleighthotel.co.uk* (*moderate*). Attractive stone townhouse overlooking the lake.

Sevenways Guest House, 1 College Road, **t** 77809 (*moderate*). Friendly, grand, stone Victorian house on fringes of Buxton, cheerful bedrooms and real fire in lounge.

Eating Out

Columbine, Hall Bank, **t** 78752 (*moderate*). Popular restaurant in old brick cellars. Honey-roasted Gressingham duck or fillet of halibut with brown shrimps, lemon and parsley sauce. *Open eves only; closed Sun, and Tues out of season.*

Flamenco, 7–9 Concert Place, **t** 27392 (*cheap*). Lively tapas restaurant. *Closed Mon.*

The Club House, t 70117. Old-fashioned pub with dark wood and shiny brass opposite the Opera House.

Buxton regularly fill their plastic bottles at the old thermal spring which brought Buxton to the attention of the Romans, Mary Queen of Scots – who came for her rheumatism – and Thomas Hobbes, who calls it St Ann's Well in his *Wonders of the Peak*. Then came the development of the spa in the 18th century by William Cavendish, the 5th Duke of Devonshire.

From the Victorian **town hall** and market place at the top of town – the site of the Roman fort *Aquae Arnemetiae* – a grassy slope drops down to the old spa buildings at the bottom of town. These 18th–19th-century gritstone buildings form an outstanding architectural cluster: the 1818 Natural Baths, the Pump Room, Frank

Matcham's Opera House and The Crescent, a three-storied pillared building that once housed three hotels, private lodging houses, an assembly room with a Robert Adam ceiling, a card room, billiard room, post office and shops under the colonnade. The architect was John Carr of York, who was employed by Cavendish in 1780 to build something to rival Bath's Royal Crescent. The spectacular unsupported slate dome of Carr's Great Stables (154ft across) was added by the Victorians.

Founded by Buxton worthies and antiquarians in 1891, the **museum** (***t*** *(01298) 24658; open Tues–Fri 9.30–5.30, Sat 9.30–5, Sun 10–5; winter closed Sun; adm minimal*) on Terrace Road is worth a visit for its geological and archaeological displays.

It takes about 10 minutes to walk to **Poole's Cavern** (***t*** *(01298) 26978; open June–Sept daily, April, May and Oct Thurs–Tues 10–5 for 45-minute tours; adm*) from the Pavilion Gardens. This deep natural limestone cavern with its spectacular mineral formations and long history of human settlement (including notorious 15th-century robber

The *Wonders of the Peak*

A country so deformed, the traveller
Would swear those parts nature's pudenda were.
Like warts and wens, hills on the one side swell,
To all but natives inaccessible.
The other a blue scrofulous scum defiles,
Flowing from the earth's impostumated boils.

Charles Cotton's *Wonders of the Peak* (1681)

There are two versions of the *Wonders of the Peak*, written at either end of the 17th century. The first was written in Latin verse by philosopher Thomas Hobbes, who was tutor to the 2nd and 3rd Earls of Devonshire at Chatsworth House. Hobbes went to Chatsworth after graduating from Oxford, and spent 20 years there gallivanting around with the 2nd Earl, hunting and hawking, until his interest in philosophy was stimulated on Grand Tours with the young earls in the 1620s and 1630s. The second *Wonders of the Peak* was written in imitation of Hobbes' *De Mirabilibus Pecci* by Charles Cotton, a Derbyshire poet/soldier/gentleman and friend of Izaak Walton (author of *The Compleat Angler*).

Both poems take the form of a journey around the Peaks. Hobbes begins with a eulogy to his home at **Chatsworth**, his first wonder of the Peak, then heads down the **Hope Valley** to a great cave commonly known as the **Devil's Arse** (around which the mountains bulge like buttocks 'when we bend our bodies to the ground'). The third wonder, towering over Hope Valley, is **Mam Tor** – the shivering mountain – so-named because it is in a state of permanent landslide but never seems to gets any smaller. After that he visits a huge **hole** whose 'form obscene' reminds him of a woman's parts and, after a dip in **Buxton's warm spring waters**, ends up in **Poole's Cave**, named after 'the famous thief' who used it as his hideaway. Charles Cotton did the same trip the other way around, describing the High and the Low Peak as 'twin provinces of nature's shame' with its 'black heaths, wild rocks, bleak crags and naked hills'.

Poole), has been visited by all serious Peakland tourists since Hobbes named it the seventh wonder. Daniel Defoe, Ben Jonson, Mary Queen of Scots and John Betjeman have all been here. Evidence of Romano-British metalwork (brooches, coins and tools) has been found in the cave. Tours take you about 1,050 feet into the cave to the source of the River Wye, past fantastic stalagmites and stalactites, named after animals by the Victorians. The cavern is renowned for its yellow-tipped white fluorite pillars known as 'poached eggs'. A 20-minute walk up a track through Grinlow Woods takes you to **Solomon's Temple**, a Victorian folly built in 1896 to provide work for quarrymen on the site of a Bronze Age burial mound, with a panoramic view.

For a good walk, stop on the road to Bakewell by the Monsal Head Hotel, and walk up **Miller's Dale**, passing **Tideswell** with its glorious church (known as the 'cathedral of the peaks'), an 8½-mile round trip.

Bakewell

The old market town of Bakewell is at the junction of main roads across the Peak between Derby, Manchester and Sheffield. When the traffic stops it is a lovely town with its old church and walks along the River Wye. Shops sell pottery, woollen jumpers and traditional **Bakewell puddings**, a jam and almond puff on a pastry base – not to be confused with Bakewell tarts (said by locals to be inferior). The pudding was first made in 1860 by a Bakewell cook who muddled the ingredients for a strawberry tart, adding them all in the wrong order – or so the story goes. The **Original Bakewell Pudding Shop** claims to have the secret recipe. An annual Agricultural Show is held on the edge of town in August.

A mile south of Bakewell on the A6, **Haddon Hall** (***t*** *(01629) 812 855; open May–Sept daily 10.30–5, Oct Thurs–Sun 10.30–4.30; adm exp*) stands hidden behind trees above the River Wye. 'As I descried the grey walls among the rock-haunted elms I felt not like a dusty tourist, but like a successful adventurer... and if there had been a ghost on the premises I certainly ought to have seen it,' wrote Henry James, visiting in 1872. Dark archways and enticing stairways lead off the walled courtyard, with its worn paving stones, and the rose-covered stone terraces of the gardens drop down to the river in a charming ensemble. In the 18th century, however, the dukes of Rutland abandoned the old manor house and moved into Belvoir Castle in Leicestershire. The feasting hall remained fireless and feastless for 300 years. Now Haddon – not the hall, but a farm-house on the estate – is the Derbyshire home of the younger brother of the 11th duke.

Chatsworth House

t *(01246) 582 204; open Easter–Christmas daily 11–4.30; adm.*

The classic approach to Chatsworth House, home of the dukes of Devonshire, is from Bakewell, through Capability Brown parkland to the great house at the bottom of the Derwent Valley. Charles Cotton, in his *Wonders of the Peak,* called it a 'bright diamond' in the midst of 'nature's shame and ills'. Certainly it is a national treasure. Chatsworth is one of the greatest country houses in England, bigger and more

Getting There and Around

The nearest **railway** station is Buxton.

National Express London–Manchester **coach** services stop off once a day in Bakewell. Local **buses** run from Manchester, Nottingham, Derby and Sheffield, call **Traveline, t** 0870 608 2608.

Tourist Information

Bakewell: National Park and Tourist Information centre, The Old Market Hall, Bridge Street **t** (01629) 813 227. *Open daily summer 9.30–5.30, winter 10–5.*

Bakewell Agricultural Show takes place in the town's showgrounds over two days in the first week of August, **t** (01629) 812 736.

Where to Stay and Eat

Bakewell t (01629) –

The Rutland Arms Hotel, The Square, **t** 812 812, *www.bakewell.demon.co.uk* (*expensive*). Handsome 1804-built hotel where the Bakewell pudding was invented; 35 period-style rooms and good restaurant (*moderate*) offering traditional English cooking.

Easthorpe, Buxton Road, **t** 814 929 (*moderate*). Homely rooms 200 yards from centre.

Haddon Park Farm, **t** 814 854 (*moderate*). Handsome hill-top farmhouse in unbeatable countryside a mile or two out of Bakewell on Matlock road, then half a mile up a country track; easy walk to Chatsworth House. *Open Easter–Sept.*

The Castle Inn, Castle Street near the River Wye bridge, **t** 812 103 (*moderate*). Good old-fashioned pub with flagstones and rustic pews, serving bangers and mash; four comfortable rooms in detached block.

Avenue House, Haddon Road, **t** 812 467 (*moderate*). Elegantly furnished Victorian house on Matlock road with four rooms.

The Old Original Bakewell Pudding Shop, The Square, **t** 812 193, *www.bakewell-pudding-shop.co.uk*. Bakewell puddings have been sold here for more than a century. You can still get one from the shop on the ground floor, or hot with custard upstairs in the restaurant, to top off a meal of lamb and apricot cobbler, or with a pot of tea or coffee.

Renaissance, Bath Street, **t** 812 687 (*moderate*). Upmarket French restaurant in converted barn with 10–12 tables. Blue cheese soufflé followed by shank of lamb in Bordelaise sauce. *Closed Mon.*

Aitch's Wine Bar and Bistro, 4 Buxton Road, **t** 813 895 (*moderate*). Buzzing bistro in former gritstone factory. Soup or fishcakes for lunch, sweet and sour duck, fish risotto or monkfish for dinner. *Closed Sun.*

2 Lunford Cottages, off Holme Lane, **t** 813 273 (*cheap*). Lovely riverside spot, a short, pleasant walk across meadows into town.

splendid than all the others, and associated with Thomas Hobbes and Joseph Paxton, engineer of the Great Exhibition building in 1851, who was head gardener for many years – and these were merely the staff. Mary Queen of Scots, spent seven months at Chatsworth under house arrest. The family fortune rests on the marriage of William Cavendish, 5th Duke of Devonshire, to the redoubtable Bess of Hardwick, whose personal empire was based in Derbyshire, but also included large parts of Yorkshire, Nottinghamshire, Sussex, Ireland and more. Generations of Cavendishes – almost all Williams – expanded the Devonshire estates through lucky inheritances and clever marriages. The ones to watch for are the 1st, 4th and 6th dukes who did most of the work on the house and garden. It was the 4th duke who demolished the neighbouring village of Edensor simply to improve his view to the west. There's too much for a single visit; ceilings by Laguerre, furniture by Kent, the bed in which George III died, and the throne of George IV are among the highlights, while for many people the 105 acres of gardens landscaped by Capability Brown are the real highlight.

Hope Valley

Thomas Hobbes, in his *Wonders of the Peaks*, travelled west from Chatsworth House down the Hope Valley into the heart of the peaks, finding three of his seven wonders – a hole on top of Eldon Hill, Peak Cavern and Mam Tor, 'the shivering mountain'. Thirty years ago, Mam Tor did a big shiver and dumped half the hillside on the main valley road to Chapel-en-le-Frith. Now the dead-end green valley is peaceful and undisturbed, but two centuries ago Hope Valley was the heart of the mining industry in the Peaks, with more than 200 mines within five miles of Castleton in 1750. Miners exploited the natural caves in the hills to reach the mineral veins to the south; some of them have now been opened as tourist attractions.

There's an excellent 6-mile walk from Castleton to the top of Mam Tor and back.

Castleton

The Hope Valley stream flows out of the mouth of Peak Cavern in Castleton, a tourist hub with steep lanes and little shops selling trinkets made from the local blue john stone (in the 18th century a blue-john clock on your mantelpiece was the height of good taste). High above the old stone village is the ruined Norman keep of Peveril Castle (***t** (01433) 620 613; open daily 10–6 or dusk if earlier; adm*), built by William Peveril to protect his lead mines. A zigzag path leads to the top, and the romantic Limestone Way leads down the south side of castle hill.

Hope Valley Cave Tours

A wooded limestone gorge leads to **Peak Cavern or the 'Devil's Arse'** (***t** (01433) 620 285; open Mar–Oct 10–4.30, Nov–Feb weekends 10–4; adm*), the largest natural cave mouth in Britain, 102 feet wide and 60 feet high, at the foot of Peveril Castle. About

The Pennine Way

You do it because you want to prove yourself that you are man enough to do it. You do it to get it off your conscience.

Alfred Wainwright, *Pennine Way Companion*

The Pennine Way is a long-distance upland walking trail about 250 miles long, following the moorland spine of the Pennines down half the country, including the whole of Yorkshire and Northumberland. Most people start at Edale in the Peak District and finish in Kirk Yetholm, just over the Scottish border. The walking is not much up and down, but strenuous because of the boggy terrain. The highest points (and possibly the highlights) are Kinderscout, Crossfell and The Cheviot. It takes about three weeks to do in one go, or you can do it in chunks like Wainwright, who spent 18 months 'floundering in glutinous peat bogs'. But he was unlucky with the weather and was going through a divorce almost as mucky as the peat bogs at the time. He ends his guide mischievously, 'I shall feel a bit sorry for you', with a cartoon drawing of himself walking through pouring rain.

The Battle of Kinder Scout

Before the National Parks Act of 1949, great areas of moorland and mountain, including the northern grouse moors of the Peak District, were completely closed off to the public. Most of the countryside of the 11 national parks of England and Wales remains in private ownership. But the Kinder Scout mass trespass of 1932 heralded the opening up of the countryside. It began with a notice in the *Manchester Chronicle* inviting people to trespass on Kinder Scout – one of the largest areas of prohibited land at the time – on 24 April. Police and gamekeepers positioned themselves around the mountain, while ramblers from Manchester met at the Bowden Bridge quarry in Hayfield and ascended from the west, planning to meet Sheffield ramblers, who were making their assault from the east, in the middle. It was class struggle of a very English sort. Five of the ring leaders were imprisoned for six months for riotous assembly – moral victory to the trespassers. The Peak District was the first of the national parks, created in 1951, almost 20 years after the trespass.

half a mile west of Castleton, at the foot of the Winnats Pass, **Speedwell Cavern** (***t** (01433) 620 512; open summer daily 9.30–5, winter 10–3.30, for 30–40-minute boat trip*) follows the underground canal of an old lead mine, dug out in 1774. Steps descend to a landing stage, where you catch a boat for a 30–40 minute boat trip deep into the hill. At the end of the abandoned A625, the **Treak Cliff** (***t** (01433) 620 571; open Mar–Oct 10–5, Nov–Feb 10–4; adm*) and **Blue John Caverns** (***t** (01433) 620 638; open 9.30–5.30 or dusk if earlier; adm*) are natural limestone caves with blue john stone.

Edale

West from Hope, the Sheffield–Manchester railway follows road and river down Edale Vale, stopping at the village of Edale. On the border of the Dark and White Peaks, it is the true heart of the district, and the start of the ascent up gritstone monster Kinder Scout, 'the most desolate, wild and abandoned country in all England,' according to Daniel Defoe. It is also the start of the Pennine Way. Indefatigable Alfred Wainwright spent four days in Edale, battling in sheet rain to do the legwork for his *Pennine Way Companion*. At one point he had to be rescued from a peat bog on Blackhill. But when it is sunny in Edale, the ritual trek up **Kinder Scout** is as festive and memorable as Helvellyn in the Lake District.

The traditional **Edale Ascent** of the Scout starts from the National Trust car park in Edale, while the historic mass trespass **Hayfield Ascent** starts at the Bowden Brook quarry car park in Hayfield (where a plaque commemorates the trespass).

Hathersage and Eyam

East of Castleton, the village of **Hathersage** is the gateway to the Peak District from Sheffield and a popular base for rock climbers on Stannage Edge. From here, it is only about 10 minutes by train to Edale and Kinder Scout. To the northwest, the Snake Pass moorland road crosses the Pennine Way just south of Bleaklow Head – 'the toughest

Getting There and Around

There is a direct link to Edale on the **Hope Valley Railway** Manchester–Sheffield line, or you can get off at Hope and link up with the Sheffield bus to Castleton. At weekends, a shuttle bus runs from Edale station to Castleton via the show caves.

Otherwise you can catch **bus** no. 272, which runs regularly all the way from Sheffield to Castleton, or bus no. 173 from Bakewell. Contact **Traveline**, **t** 0870 608 2608.

You can hire a bicycle in Ashbourne at **Cycle Hire**, Mappleton Lane, about half a mile out of town, **t** (01335) 343 156. *Open Jan–Feb weekends, Mar–Oct daily, Nov Sat–Wed, Dec closed.*

Tourist Information

Castleton: **t** (01433) 620 679. *Open summer 9.30–5.30, winter 10–5.*

Edale: Peak District National Park Information Centre, Fieldhead, Edale, Hope Valley **t** (01433) 816 200. *Open daily 9–1 and 2–5, summer until 5.30.*

Where to Stay and Eat

Castleton t (01433) –

Bargate Cottage, Market Place, **t** 620 201, *www.peakland.com/bargate* (*moderate*). Small, friendly cottage overlooking little green with pretty bedrooms.

Dunscar Farm, Hope Valley, **t** 620 483, *www.hopenet.co.uk/dunscarfarm* (*moderate*). Charming stone farm at end of long track in middle of valley, about a mile from village, overlooking Mam Tor and Winetts Pass; five bedrooms.

Castleton Youth Hostel, Castle Street, **t** 620 235, *www.YHA.org.uk* (*cheap*). Dormitory accommodation in magnificent stone building behind courtyard. *Closed Jan, book well in advance.*

Edale t (01433) –

The Rambler Country House Hotel, at top of Edale village near railway station, **t** 670 268 (*expensive*). Stone Victorian real-ale pub offering hearty pub meals; nine rooms.

Edale House, Edale, **t** 670 399, *edale.house@btinternet.com* (*moderate*). Big, comfortable old stone house about a mile from the village; views of the valley and sound of rushing water. Big breakfasts. Very helpful and relaxed owners.

Stonecroft Guest House, Edale village, Hope Valley, **t** 670 262, *www.stonecroftguesthouse.co.uk* (*moderate*). Warm, helpful, friendly welcome at this perfect Edale base, near both village pubs.

Old Nags Head, at end of village road, on small square next to school, **t** 670 291 (*cheap*). Another atmospheric Victorian pub, offering a traditional bar menu including rabbit stew, as well as real ales and log fires.

Cheshire Cheese, Hope, **t** 620 381 (*cheap*). Four miles down the valley road in the direction of Hope; small, cosy pub with a low, beamy bar and good food including grilled cod.

Hathersage t (01433) –

The George Hotel, Main Road, **t** 650 436, *www.george-hotel.net* (*expensive*). Ancient stone-built country inn in the centre of Hathersage with Brontë associations and 19 simple, stylish rooms; elegant restaurant.

Moor View Cottage, Cannonfields, off Jaggers Lane, just outside Hathersage, **t** 650 110

part of the Pennine Way' according to Wainwright, 'frightening in the mist'. Robin Hood legend tells that Little John was born and died in the village, where he worked as a nailor most of his life. You can find his unusually long grave (containing a three-foot long thigh bone) in the churchyard. Charlotte Brontë stayed at the vicarage in 1845 and based elements of *Jane Eyre* on the village.

It takes about half an hour to walk north from Hathersage to **Stannage Edge**, from where you can continue south along the gritstone ridge to the Iron Age fortress of **Carl Wark**, on Hathersage Moor. Otherwise drive from Hathersage to one of the car parks on the A6187, Surprise View or Longshaw NT car park by the Fox House Inn.

(*moderate*). Beautiful quiet spot with three rooms; very friendly and comfortable.

Millstone Country Inn, Sheffield Road, **t** 650 258, *www.millstoneinn.co.uk* (*moderate*). Friendly gastro pub with comfortable rooms in a glorious spot above the valley, 5 minutes walk from Hathersage; good food served in restaurant with big windows or outside.

Sladen Cottage, Jaggers Lane, **t** 650 706 (*moderate*). Large three-bedroom stone Victorian house in its own grounds.

Moorgate, Castleton Road, **t** 650 293 (*cheap*). Stone house behind conifers with two loft rooms and a shared bathroom, 5 minutes' walk from Hathersage.

Hathersage Youth Hostel, Castleton Road, **t** 650 493 (*cheap*). Small, friendly Victorian house with shared bunk rooms. *Open April–Oct.*

Scotsmans Pack, School Lane, **t** 650 253 (*cheap*). Hathersage's best pub for real ale and food, near the church.

Ashbourne t (01335) –

Callow Hall Hotel, Mappleton (2 minutes' drive from Ashbourne on A515), **t** 300 900, *www.callowhall.co.uk* (*very expensive*). Large Victorian country house set in 44 acres with 16 period-style double bedrooms; antlers and tapestries in the hall and an excellent restaurant (*expensive*). Modern English menu includes breast of Barbary duck with caramelized apple and redcurrant tart.

Omnia Somnia, The Coach House, The Firs, **t** 300 145, *www.omniasomnia.co.uk* (*expensive*). Beautiful gabled Victorian coach house full of imagination and care with William Morris wallpaper, paintings, lovely furniture and gorgeous bedrooms, one with a huge bath, another with a huge bed, and one with a cosy sitting room and its own little flight of stairs leading up to the bedroom.

The Green Man Royal Hotel, St John Street, **t** 345 783 (*moderate*). Nine rooms above two bars. Noisy at weekends.

Hurtswood, Sandybrook, **t** 342 031, *www.hurtswood.co.uk* (*moderate*). Large cream house up long drive, half a mile from Ashbourne; seven comfortable rooms and friendly, relaxed atmosphere.

Tan Mill Farm, Mappleton Road, **t** 342 387 (*moderate*). Cattle farm with neat, tidy rooms, 10 minutes' walk from town centre.

Bent Farm, Tissingston (4 miles from Ashbourne on Buxton road), **t** 390 214 (*moderate*). A 17th-century farmhouse with small windows in thick stone walls; rooms stocked with lots of blankets; log fire in snug on chilly evenings. *Open Easter–Oct.*

Taste, St John Street, **t** 300 305 (*moderate*). Set in vaulted former beer cellars serving a good range of English/French food including home-made game pie in port wine sauce. *Closed Mon.*

Lamplight Restaurant, 4 Victoria Square, **t** 342 279 (*moderate*). Old-fashioned restaurant on lower market square offering traditional English/French menu including fillet steak with green peppercorn sauce or stuffed beef tomato. *Closed Sun eve and Mon and winter lunch.*

Coach and Horses, Fenny Bentley (near Ashbourne), **t** 350 246 (*cheap*). Pleasant, quiet gastro pub run by husband and wife, with horse brasses on the walls; good fish and vegetarian dishes, roast chicken or game casserole with crunchy vegetables.

South of Hathersage in the direction of Bakewell, the village of **Eyam** sits prettily in limestone hills. It looks fabulous in the sunshine – old stone houses stacked above each other at the crossroads, pretty cottage gardens and grass verges – but it's known as the plague village. In 1665 a parcel of flea-infested clothes arrived in the village from a London tailor, carrying the plague. After the first deaths, the young rector William Mompesson persuaded the panic-stricken villages to stay put and contain the infection. While 259 lives were lost in 14 months and there were only 50 survivors, the outbreak was contained. The **church** has plague relics including Mompesson's pulpit and chair. In the churchyard is the grave of his wife Katherine, one of the last to succumb. There are regular tours around **Eyam Hall** (**t** *(01433) 631 976; open July–Aug Wed, Thurs and Sun 11–4; adm*), a Jacobean manor house set back from the main street behind a wrought-iron gateway. At the top of the village, the **Plague Museum** (**t** *(01433) 631 371; open Easter–Oct Tues–Sun 10–4.30; adm minimal*) details gory symptoms such as 'pustules striking inward from the skin to the heart'.

Dovedale

The deep wooded limestone gorge of the River Dove, with its rock pinnacles and caves, is one of the most famous 'wonders' of the Peak District, although it didn't appear on Cotton's or Hobbes' list. It was, however, popularized by Cotton, who wrote a fly fishing supplement to Walton's *The Compleat Angler* in 1676. The path between Milldale and the Izaak Walton Hotel is an easy stroll.

Signposted off the A515 Ashbourne–Buxton road, with a short walk through a farm to the top of a small hill, is **Arbor Low Henge**, a flattened circle of rough limestone slabs surrounded by a ditch and a bank. It is an early religious site, with a round burial mound set into the henge bank, a long barrow linked by a bank-and-ditch avenue and panoramic views of the moors to the northeast. The circular earthworks are 4,500 years old, the stone megaliths 500 years more recent.

The old market town of **Ashbourne**, just outside the southern edge of the National Park, is a good base for exploring the deep dales of the rivers Manifold and Dove.

Matlock Bath and the Lower Derwent Valley

Happening to be at Matlock in the summer of 1784, the conversation turned on Arkwright's spinning machinery. One of the company observed that as soon as Arkwright's patent expired so many mills would be erected and so much cotton spun that hands would never be found to weave it.

Edmund Cartwright

Travelling south of the town of Matlock on the A6 – leaving the national park along the Derwent – you find yourself in a limestone gorge with a cliff on one side and the wooded slopes of Abraham Heights on the other.

Halfway down, the faded Victorian spa town of **Matlock Bath** flattens itself against the rock wall, its painted bay windows protruding towards the river. On sunny weekends, bikers congregate along the Promenade and riverside gardens *en route* to the open roads of the northern moors. In the old Victorian **baths** (*open April–Oct 10–5.30, Nov–Mar weekends 10–5; adm*), the old thermal water pipe has been turned into a petrifying well: a fine drizzle of mineral-rich water sprinkles old shoes, teapots and other random debris, which become encrusted with limescale and 'turn to stone'.

Towering over the spa, **Abraham Heights** was an industrial wasteland landscaped and redeveloped in the early 19th century. It's a short, steep walk up the zigzag path, or you can take a **cable car** (**t** *(01629) 582 365; Mar–Oct daily 10–5; adm*) to the top, where there are woodland paths and tours down two 18th-century lead mines. The Rutland Cavern (Nestors Lead Mine) includes three natural limestone caves.

Tourist Information

Matlock Bath: The Pavilion, **t** (01629) 55082. *Open summer daily 9.30–5, winter weekends 10–4.*

The **Matlock Bath Illuminations** run from the Late August Bank Holiday to the end of October, with illuminated tableaux strung up over the river and through the village, and entertainments in Lovers' Walk and Derwent Gardens (*Sat and Sun eves*), including clowns, dancers and illuminated boats on the river, and fireworks. Contact the Tourist Information centre or go to *www.derbyshiredales.gov.uk*.

Derby: Assembly Rooms, Market Place, **t** (01332) 255 802. *Open Mon–Fri 9.30–5.30, Sat 9.30–5, Sun 10.30–2.30.*

Where to Stay and Eat

Matlock Bath t (01629) –

Temple Hotel, Temple Walk, **t** 583 911, *www.templehotel.co.uk* (*expensive*). Set high up on hill (follow 'Gulliver's Kingdom' signs off main road), attractive white-painted family hotel with 14 rooms, good clean air and great views from sun-trap patio.

Hodgkinson's Hotel, South Parade, **t** 582 170, *www.hodgkinsons-hotel.co.uk* (*expensive*). Bell tinkles as you open door into friendly Victorian atmosphere with dark wooden bar and elegant dining room where dinner (*moderate*) might include roast duck with orange sauce; six comfortable double rooms (and one single) with William Morris wallpaper and original cast-iron fireplaces.

Sunny Bank, Clifton Road **t** 584 621 *www.cressbrook.co.uk/matlock/sunnybank* (*moderate*). Elegant, friendly Victorian house on hillside with five excellent rooms.

Fountain Villa, 86 North Parade, **t** 56195, *www.fountainvilla.co.uk* (*moderate*). Large 1840s house set back from main road opposite Jubilee footbridge, very tasteful; delightful small double at top with sundeck.

Princess Victoria, South Parade, **t** 57462. Small, friendly locals' bar with twinkly fairy lights on ceiling and hearty pub grub (*cheap*) including spaghetti bolognese.

Derby t (01332) –

Stelianas and Sapphos Greek Taverna, 7 Old Blacksmith's Yard, Saddler Gate, **t** 385 200 (*moderate*). Long-established family restaurant, popular for meze. *Open Mon–Sat.*

Darleys, Darley Abbey Mill, Darley Abbey, **t** (01332) 364 987 (*moderate*). Two miles north of city centre off A6, excellent modern English cooking in stylish converted mill on the weir, offering scallops on creamy leeks with crab risotto cakes, slow-roast belly of pork, home-made sausage or black pudding and mustard mash.

The **Lower Derwent Valley** was Arkwright country, a forerunner to the Lancashire cotton industry in the same way that Coalbrookdale anticipated the Black Country. Now it is a shrine to 'the father of the factory system'. With the help of clock-maker Joseph Kay, Sir Richard Arkwright (1732–92) designed a power-driven spinning machine that needed no skill to operate. His first factory in Nottingham was powered by horses. His second factory at Cromford (in partnership with Jedediah Strutt of Derby) used water power. Arkwright's yarn was much stronger than that produced on the spinning jenny. He patented his mechanism and made a fortune, was knighted and became sheriff of Derbyshire, buying the manor of Cromford, where he built himself a grand home overlooking his first factory. He died in 1792 before moving in.

The valley was not only the hub of Arkwright's cotton empire, but the site of the first mass production of 100-percent cotton cloth and the first industrial village. Half a mile south of Matlock Bath (buses every 20 mins), **Masson Mills Museum** (*open Mon–Sat 10–4, Sun 11–4; adm*) was once Arkwright's flagship cotton factory, built in 1783, 12 years after Cromford Mill. It closed in 1991 after more than 200 years of spinning cotton thread. The mills are now a factory shopping village and working museum. Note the floorboards worn down by workers' clogs. A mile or two south of Masson Mills down the A6 gorge road is **Cromford Mill** (***t** (01629) 824 297; open daily 9–5; regular guided tours; adm minimal*), the first water-powered cotton spinning mill in the world, designed by Arkwright. The original 1771 factory building is flanked by the fast-flowing Bonsall Brook and Cromford Sough, turning wheels. Arkwright went on to build factories in Derbyshire, Lancashire, Staffordshire and Scotland but he never lost interest in Cromford. Just above the road opposite Cromford Mill is **Rock House**, where he lived between 1782 and 1792. He also developed Cromford village on the far side of the A6, one of the first industrial villages. The one-storey shops around the market place were part of the original development. Arkwright's last contribution to the valley was Willesley Castle, where he planned to retire.

Belper Mill was built in 1776 by Arkwright's business partner Jedediah Strutt. Around it sprung up a dense industrial town, anticipating the 19th-century cotton towns of the East Lancashire Valleys. All that is left is North Mill; Round Mill, West Mill and Reeling Mill were demolished before the revival of interest in industrial heritage.

Derby

From the Peak District, the Derwent flows south through Cromford and Belper to the county town of Derby, where it's worth stopping to see the **cathedral**, formerly the church of All Hallows, with its monument to Bess of Hardwick, designed by Robert Smythson, the architect of Hardwick Hall. The technologies of mass production developed by Arkwright were first pioneered by Thomas Lombe on the site of the **Industrial Museum** (*open Mon 11–5, Tues–Sat 10–5, Sun 2–5*) in Derby earlier in the century. In 1722 Lombe took over his cousin John Lombe's silk-throwing business on the banks of the Derwent, refining the water-powered machines invented by John, and soon had a workforce of 300 people.

Considered by many to be the finest Robert Adam house in England, **Kedleston Hall**, 4½ miles northwest of Derby (***t** (01332) 842 191; house open Sat–Wed 12–4.30, gardens and park daily 10–6; adm*), has been the Derbyshire home of the Curzon family for 850 years. It was built for the first Lord Scarsdale like a Roman temple in Derbyshire stone, complete with decorated urns, capitals, columns, festoons and a double flight of steps curving up to the first-floor entrance. Scarsdale wanted his house to reflect Roman grandeur through its austerity and purity, like a temple of virtue. The highlight is a double-height room with marble columns around it and statues in niches.

Nottinghamshire

'The country is so lovely. The man-made England is so vile,' wrote D.H. Lawrence in 1930 of the area around his home town of Eastwood, five miles west of Nottingham. That was 70 years ago; now the M1 motorway runs like a scar down the west of the county. East of it, Nottinghamshire is mostly rural: scattered villages, the River Trent meandering through its wide flood plain, cornfields stretching as far as Lincolnshire.

Danelaw

...it is my will that secular rights be in force among the Danes according to as good laws as they can best decide on.

The law code of King Edgar (959–75)

On the face of it, the East Midlands is not a coherent region: the Lincolnshire Fens have little in common with the Peak District or the Leicestershire–Derbyshire coalfield, for instance. The reason for lumping them together goes back to the Danish conquest of Mercia in the 9th century and the creation of the Five Boroughs of Derby, Nottingham, Lincoln, Leicester and Stamford. The Danish hold was consolidated in 886 in the Treaty of Wedmore between King Alfred and Guthrum, leader of the Danes. The country was cut in half: everything east of a diagonal line running from London to the top of Northumbria was controlled by the Danes. Everything west of the line was controlled by the dominant West Saxon kings. The line followed the natural boundary of the Pennines in the north. In the Midlands it followed the line of Watling Street (the modern A5), establishing the future border of the counties of Leicestershire and Warwickshire. The Danelaw was colonized by Norse-speaking Danes, who established villages with Danish names (-bys, -thorps and -holmes). Although the 10th-century king of the Anglo-Saxons, Edward the Elder (reigned 899–924), conquered everything south of the Humber (the East Midlands), you can see from King Edgar's law code that the Scandinavian influence was not eradicated.

Here you have **Sherwood Forest** and the dukeries. The forest is not quite the wild woodland of Robin Hood – the Forestry Commission has planted most of it with conifers – but you can still walk among centuries-old oak trees near Edwinstowe. Large sections of the royal forest were sold off to a handful of Midlands aristocrats in the centuries after the Reformation; the dukes of Portland, Newcastle and Norfolk built great houses here, although few stayed. You can visit **Clumber Park**, former seat of the Newcastles. Several of the dukes, including Newcastle, were descendants of the Elizabethan dynast Bess of Hardwick. Her son owned **Bolsover Castle**, borrowing Bess's architect Robert Smythson, whose other outstanding work is **Wollaton Hall**.

Only university students really warm to the county town of **Nottingham**, although its redundant industrial buildings are being converted into bars and nightclubs. The Lace Market, however, is one of the great architectural monuments of the Industrial Revolution in England, and the market place and castle have some charm.

Nottingham

Among provincial towns it has always passed for the most frivolous... There were goings-on in Nottingham.

J.B. Priestley's *English Journey*, 1933

The leafy Nottingham admired by Daniel Defoe as 'one of the most beautiful and pleasant towns in England' soon after turned into one of the most dense industrial

Getting There and Around

By **car**, the M1 shoots from London to Nottingham, the M42 whizzes in from Birmingham, the A50 from Stoke on Trent, and from Manchester the A6 runs via Buxton and Matlock Bath across the Peak to Derby, just west of Nottingham.

There are direct **train** services from London, Manchester and Birmingham, or via Derby or Sheffield from Leeds.

National Express runs regular **coach** services from London and major airports. Local **buses** run from Derby and Sheffield. Call Traveline, **t** 0870 6082608.

Tourist Information

Nottingham: 1–4 Smithy Row, **t** (0115) 915 5330. *Open Mon–Fri 9–5.30, Sat 9–5, July–Aug also Sun 1–3.*

Where to Stay

Nottingham t (0115) –

Lace Market Hotel, 29–31 High Pavement, The Lace Market, **t** 852 3232, *www.lacemarkethotel.co.uk* (*luxury*). Stylish Georgian townhouse with 29 understated bedrooms, all with CD players; restaurant and bar equally cool in chrome and gleaming glass.

Nottingham Hilton, Milton Street, **t** 934 9700, *www.hilton.com* (*expensive*). Huge 19th-century hotel near Victoria Centre with 177 bedrooms, restaurant and bar, and leisure facilities including pool and gym.

Royal Moat House Hotel, Mansfield Road, **t** 936 9988, *www.moathousehotels.co.uk* (*expensive*). Huge, modern hotel with 200 rooms, heated pool and gym; two restaurants – à la carte and carvery.

The Rutland Square Hotel, St James Street, **t** 941 1114, *www.forestdalehotels.com* (*expensive*). Six-storey, brick former warehouse, a minute's walk from the castle, with more than 100 en-suite bedrooms, formal restaurant and relaxed Terrace Bar.

Eating Out

Nottingham comes alive in the evening – in fact nightlife is Nottingham's strong point. The city centre buzzes around Hockley and the Lace Market, with countless trendy and/or grungy bars and clubs; Market Square with its downmarket chain pubs; the castle area, which has a couple of good restaurants and the Trip pub; and the canalside, just south of the city centre, with several large café-bars in converted warehouses, lots of outside tables and chairs, and walks along the towpath. Eating out is the new going out here.

Hart's Restaurant, 1 Standard Court, Park Row, **t** 911 0666 (*moderate*). Stylish modern English restaurant in part of old Victorian Nottingham General Hospital (now smart flats) near castle. Fillet of brill and asparagus or haloumi cheese and vegetable fritters; two-course theatre menu.

areas in the country. 'Nowhere else shall we find so large a mass of inhabitants crowded into courts, alleys and lanes as in Nottingham,' said the official Health Report in 1845. The workers packed into these slums were the first to riot, letting rip with Luddite machine-breaking. You won't find much that is pre-industrial now. The river is hidden and the scale of modern building has flattened the hillsides that gave the original Saxon town its defensive advantage. But the old hosiery and lace-making factories give the town a particular red-brick Victorian atmosphere; the Lace Market is one of the most impressive monuments of the industrial era. 'The city has always had a name for enjoying itself,' wrote Priestley in 1930; in the last decade proliferating bars and clubs in the old industrial areas of Hockley, the canalside and Lace Market have revived this reputation.

World Service Restaurant, Newdigate House, Castle Gate, **t** 847 5587 (*moderate*). Beautiful Georgian townhouse through Japanese patio garden, formerly a club for ex-servicemen. Modern English cuisine.

Punchinello, 35 Foreman Street, **t** 941 1965 (*cheap*). An old-fashioned restaurant ideal for pre- or post-theatre suppers, which might include chargrilled calf's liver; on two floors with crisp white table cloths and brick walls. *Closed Sun.*

Mogal-E-Azam, Royal Centre, 7–9 Goldsmith Street, **t** 947 3820 (*cheap*). Friendly, airy Tandoori restaurant opposite Theatre Royal, much frequented by visiting theatrical celebrities.

Merchant's Bar, 29–31 High Pavement, Lace Market Hotel, **t** 852 3232 (*cheap*). Civilized and pleasant with windows overlooking St Mary's Church and Shire Hall.

Ye Olde Trip to Jerusalem, Brewhouse Yard, **t** 947 3171, *www.triptojerusalem.com* (*cheap*). Quaint old inn with outside tables backing onto castle rock. Its small, dark flagstone interior incorporates lamp-lit caves hewn out of sandstone, dating back to 1189, when Crusaders stopped off at the brewhouse on site before leaving for the Holy Land.

Pitcher and Piano, Weekday Cross, The Lace Market, **t** 958 6081 (*cheap*). Redundant Unitarian church turned fashionable watering hole; gets noisy and crowded in the evenings, but nice in daytime.

Fashion, Middle Pavement, **t** 950 5850 (*cheap*). The name's off-putting, but it's an excellent place for lunch, coffee or a glass of wine, halfway between the Lace Market and castle; outdoor seating and funky music.

Broadway Cinema, 14–18 Broad Street (*cheap*). Unpretentious place for lunch or coffee, with movie stills projected onto the walls.

Canal House Bar and Restaurant, 48–52 Canal Street, **t** 955 5011 (*cheap*). Smartest of canal-side café-bars, in old 1890s warehouse; a short branch of the canal divides the bar into two sections, linked by a metal foot-bridge. All-day bar menu, or modern English restaurant upstairs.

Entertainment

Theatre Royal, Royal Centre, Theatre Square, **t** 989 5555. Georgian theatre with proscenium stage and 1,500 seats; touring musicals and drama.

The Royal Concert Hall, Royal Centre, Theatre Square, **t** 989 5555, *www.royalcentre-nottingham.co.uk*. Huge 1983 glass-fronted concert venue seating 2,600; range of musical and non-musical events: classical, opera, ballet, pop, and big-name comedians.

The Nottingham Playhouse, Wellington Circus, **t** 941 9419. In-house and touring productions of drama; panto at Christmas. The **Playhouse Café-Bar**, **t** 941 8467, has outside seating overlooking Wellington Circus and does bistro-style food in the evenings (*Mon–Sat*); *bar open 11–11.*

Broadway Cinema, 14–18 Broad Street, **t** 952 6611, *www.broadway.org.uk*. Two-screen independent and world cinema with lively café-bar. *Open from 9.30am for breakfast.*

Around Town

The pedestrianized core of the town is bordered by Upper Parliament Street in the north, and High, Middle and Low Pavement in the south, beyond which you drop down the hill to busy roads and the canal. Off the main streets are a number of boutiques. Shops radiate in all directions off Old Market Square, an attractive public space bordered with handsome 19th- and 20th-century buildings, busy with pigeons, flower baskets, and the constant crisscrossing of shoppers. A classic meeting place is 'under the lions' outside the Council House, built in grand classical style in 1927–9 with a domed clock tower on top, and a peal of bells like Big Ben. It is now a designer shopping arcade and the tourist information centre. Head east into Hockley and the Lace Market to wander. If it is raining, go in the other direction to the Castle Museum and Art Gallery and Tales of Robin Hood attraction.

Hockley and the Lace Market

Hockley and the Lace Market are the hub of Nottingham's nightlife. In **Hockley**, the Art Nouveau building on the corner of Long Row and High Street was the flagship store of Jessy Boot's (the Chemists), founded in 1888; note the cherubs holding a shield with the initial 'B'. The author of *Peter Pan*, J.M. Barrie (1860–1937), worked for the *Nottingham Journal* in Journal Chambers, a multicoloured brick building on Pelham Street. Down George Street are the flamboyant old offices of Victorian Gothic Revival architect Watson Fothergill. Note the statue of a medieval architect with a cathedral at his feet. Fothergill preferred to use all the Gothic architectural devices – timber-framing, patterns of coloured bricks, oriel windows, dormers and towers – at once. He also built the Nottingham and Notts Bank on Thurland Street; note the chained monkey, a reference to the burden of a mortgage, at the base of a chimney.

The Victorian factories of the **Lace Market** are where manufactured lace was finished, displayed and sold. The red-brick industrial buildings are being converted into bars and 'luxury loft-style apartments'. Pick up an audio wand from the **Lace Market Visitor Centre** on High Pavement (***t** (0115) 988 1849; open summer Mon–Sat daily 10–5, Sun 10.30–4*) to guide yourself around. The main trading street was Stoney Street, where you pass the Adams Building, with a grand flight of steps leading up to the first-floor entrance. It was built in 1855 by T.C. Hine, the other major Nottingham Victorian architect, who also built Broadway, a canyon-like street between warehouses, for lace manufacturer Richard Birkin.

In *Robin Hood and the Monk*, Robin Hood is ambushed in old **St Mary's Church** by the sheriff's men. It's hard to imagine now, as nothing survives of the medieval town. The new Victorian church sits in a red-brick Victorian square next to another of T.C. Hine's buildings, the Victorian **Shire Hall**.

Nottingham Castle

Approach the castle up Castlegate. On the way, look out for W.H. Smith's; it stands on the site of the surgical goods factory where the young D.H. Lawrence spent three months as a junior clerk – described in his novel *Sons and Lovers*. Beneath the castle walls, it gets prettier, with cobblestones and Georgian townhouses. The sheer castle walls rise out of a sandstone outcrop, pierced with secret tunnels. Bring your imagination: the curtain walls and 13th-century gatehouse, both much restored, are all that is left of the medieval castle. The Italianate ducal mansion of William Cavendish sits on the highest point, the inner bailey of the old castle. T.C. Hine converted it into the **Nottingham Museum and Gallery** (***t** (0115) 915 3700; open 10–5; adm*), whose highlight is the Ballantyne Collection of 20th-century studio ceramics and a small collection of Wedgwood jasperware. The Story of Nottingham takes you through the town's history, and hourly tours go down **Mortimer's Hole** (***t** (0115) 952 0555; open 10.30–4.30; adm*), the longest of the old tunnels under the castle, coming out in Brewhouse Yard, the route taken by the henchmen of Edward III to arrest Roger Mortimer and Queen Isabella in 1330. Near the castle, on Maid Marion Way, in a converted 1970s supermarket, is the **Tales of Robin Hood** (***t** (0115) 948 3284; open daily 10–5.30; adm exp*), a fabulous story-telling experience for children.

The Usurping, Suspect and Unfortunate Kings of Nottingham Castle

Once upon a time, Nottingham Castle was the major royal stronghold in the Midlands, frequented by unpopular kings. The action of *Robin Hood* takes place in the reigns of absentee **Richard I Cœur de Lion** and his usurping brother **John**, the Earl of Nottingham. The castle is the symbol of John's authority, embodied in the sheriff. One of Richard's first acts on returning from the Third Crusade in 1194 was to storm the castle, which was holding out for John. He stayed on for a few days to go hunting in Sherwood Forest. A century later, in 1330, the usurper **Roger Mortimer** – who had murdered Edward II with a red-hot spitting iron – barricaded himself into the castle until he was flushed out by the men of young King Edward III; they entered through an underground tunnel, one of the few features of the medieval castle that you can still see today. **Richard III** – the worst king of all – made the castle his stronghold, building a new tower and refurbishing the royal suite. On hearing the news of Henry Tudor's planned invasion in 1485, Richard rushed straight to his 'castle of care' to raise an army. In August 1642, **Charles I** responded to impending war in the same way, rushing to the castle to muster an army. He raised the royal standard outside the gatehouse to the cry of 'God save King Charles and hang up the Roundheads'. After the Civil War and a surfeit of bad kings, the old castle was demolished. William Cavendish, Duke of Newcastle (and grandson of Bess of Hardwick), built himself a baroque mansion on the inner bailey.

Wollaton Hall

t *(0115) 915 3915; open Mar–Oct daily 11–5, Nov–Feb 11–4; adm minimal.*

Three miles west of Nottingham, the Tudor mansion of Sir Francis Willoughby stands with its decorative chimneys and gables at the end of an avenue of beech trees. The architect was Robert Smythson, who went on to build Hardwick Hall. The best views of the hall are from the lake; the Prospect Room, originally a ballroom and dining room, rises semi-derelict out of the middle of the building like a castle keep. When the Willoughbys left in 1925, the city corporation moved in with dull natural history collections and messed up the interiors.

Eastwood

If you are in those parts again, go to Eastwood where I was born, go to Walker Street and stand in front of the third house and look across at Crich on the left, Underwood in front, Highbury Woods and Annesley on the right. I know that view better than any in the world. That's the country of my heart.

D.H. Lawrence, in a letter he wrote in 1926

Eastwood, birthplace of industrial Midlands novelist D.H. Lawrence, is eight miles west of Nottingham, following the A610 out of the city, on the far side of the M1. Lawrence, the son of a coal miner and a school teacher, spent 23 years in this red-brick mining town with its views over the countryside. Several of his novels, including his most popular and autobiographical, *Sons and Lovers*, are based in the area.

D.H. Lawrence's Houses

D.H. Lawrence (1885–1930) was born in the house in Victoria Street (now the Birthplace Museum). Soon afterwards, the family moved to 28 Garden Road, which appeared in *Sons and Lovers* as 'The Bottoms'. You can peer in through the downstairs window. Next they moved to Walker Street, the 'third house', according to Lawrence, but a plaque on the block points out that 'it is not known from which end they were then numbered.' They stayed there for 11 years from 1891 to 1902; Lawrence cherished and remembered the view out across the countryside. The family lived in one more house in Eastwood (97 Lynncroft), after which Lawrence (aged 23) moved to Croydon to teach, later travelling through Europe, America and Australia. He died of tuberculosis in France aged 44.

Head first to **Durban House Heritage Centre and Museum** (**t** *(01773) 717 353; open April–Oct daily 10–5, Nov–Mar daily 10–4; adm*) in Durban House, a grand building set back from the road, which was once the offices of local mining company Barber Walker & Co, employers of D.H. Lawrence's father. Lawrence dramatized the excruciation of collecting his father's wages from here in *Sons and Lovers*. In 1998 the tables were turned: the building now houses an exhibition on Lawrence's books and life in Eastwood. From here it's a short walk to the **Birthplace Museum** (***t** (01773) 763 312; same hours as Durban House; adm*). Lawrence was born in this two-up-two-down house in a red-brick terrace, built by Barber Walker & Co in the 1820s. Today, visitors are shown into the old kitchen, with its black-leaded range, the parlour, used only for special occasions, and the main bedroom, where Lawrence was born. From the attic window you still have the views over the countryside that Lawrence described.

North Nottinghamshire

This is Sherwood Forest, stretching from Nottingham to Worksop, and including the dukeries – areas of the old royal forest of Sherwood that passed into the hands of a group of Nottinghamshire aristocrats with the fall of Charles I. Their main seats were at Welbeck Abbey and Clumber Park (dukes of Newcastle), Worksop Manor (dukes of Norfolk) and Thoresby Hall (dukes of Kingston). Only Clumber Park is open to visitors. All these powerful dukes were descendants of the great Elizabethan dynast Bess of Hardwick. The Byrons of Newstead Abbey were Bess's neighbours, with a family tree going back to the Norman Conquest, but not quite dukes.

Newstead Abbey

Through thy battlements, Newstead, the hollow winds whistle.

Byron, On Leaving Newstead Abbey, 1803 (to go back to school, aged 15)

Newstead Abbey (***t** (01623) 455 900; house open April–Sept 12–4, abbey and gardens all year 9–dusk; adm*), 5 miles north of Nottingham off the A60, is known as the home of the Romantic poet George Gordon, sixth Lord Byron.

The bachelor-poet's reputation for hedonism and profanity is borne out and embellished here by stories of forest animals kept as pets, the young lord cavorting with servant girls, pistol-shooting in the Great Hall, fencing in the salon and drinking claret from a skull. The Byron family came into possession of the abbey at the Dissolution, retaining the ruined west front of the Augustinian priory church and building new apartments around the old cloisters. The poet Byron moved to Newstead aged 21, after graduating from Cambridge, and stayed for six years before emigrating to Italy. He sold up in 1817 to an old school friend called Thomas Wildman, who restored the place in splendid style. Byron built a monument to his dog Boatswain (whose painting hangs in the West Gallery) inscribed with a poem on the site of High Altar of the church. On a sunny day, bring a picnic and make the most of the grounds.

On the Ridge

A limestone ridge runs north–south along the Nottinghamshire-Derbyshire border, with rolling scenery and views over the Vale of Scarsdale. **Creswell Crags** is its most dramatic feature, full of dank caves containing evidence of prehistoric hunters and animals. Bess of Hardwick established herself and her family in a string of fabulous homes along its crest. The most magnificent, **Hardwick Hall**, is one of the finest Elizabethan country houses in the country. She also built **Owlcotes** for her eldest son, William Cavendish. Her third son, Charles, bought **Bolsover Castle** and **Welbeck Abbey** (*closed to the public*) from his brother-in-law George Talbot, and hired his mother's architect Robert Smythson to recreate an elegant medieval-style castle.

Hardwick Hall

***t** (01246) 850 430, www.english-heritage.org.uk; open Easter–Oct, house Wed, Thurs, Sat and Sun 12.30–5, gardens Wed–Sun 11–5.30; park all year 8–6; adm exp.*

Down a lane off junction 29 of the M1 is the lasting monument of Elizabeth, Countess of Shrewsbury, a Derbyshire squire's daughter who founded a dynasty that outlasted her by 500 years. Hardwick Hall was her own, independent of any of her four husbands, built when she was in her 70s. She bought the old hall (where she was born) from her brother and commissioned the new hall next door, at the same time cutting herself off from her fourth husband, the 6th Earl of Shrewsbury, whom she accused of having an affair with Mary Queen of Scots. From then on she was known as 'Bess of Hardwick'. Fashionable architect Robert Smythson built a symmetrical, flat-roofed house with six projecting towers; at the top of each tower are her initials, E.S., in stone. The servants' rooms were on the ground floor, the living rooms on the middle floor and the state rooms on the top floor, up grand flights of stairs. Most of the furnishings are original to the house: the tapestries and needlework are famous, especially those in the **Green Velvet Room** and the *Gideon* hangings in the **Long Gallery**, which Bess bought in London when she was settling the disputed will of her late husband, the 6th Earl. The house is surrounded by beautiful gardens and acres of parkland. The ruined **Old Hall** (***t** (01246) 850 431; open April–Sept Wed, Thurs, Sat and Sun 11–6; adm*) frames the view over the valley.

Bess of Hardwick (1520–1608)

By the end of the 19th century, most of the aristocratic families in England could claim Bess as their common ancestor: the current Duke of Devonshire is a direct descendant of her son William Cavendish; the dukes of Portland descend from her other son Charles; from her daughter Frances came the dukes of Kingston; and her granddaughter Arabella married the great-nephew of Henry VIII. Bess built houses at Hardwick, Chatsworth and Owlcotes. From her fourth and last husband, George Talbot, 6th Earl of Shrewsbury, she took the name Countess of Shrewsbury. He was the wealthiest man in the land, Lord Lieutenant of Yorkshire, Derbyshire and Nottinghamshire – quite a catch. He was also the keeper of Mary Queen of Scots, whom he moved frequently (46 times in all) between his eight houses to keep her out of trouble. To secure their power and wealth, Bess and the 6th Earl married off two sets of sons and daughters on the same day – then fell out, as Bess bought land in the name of her sons to keep it out of her husband's grasp, while the Earl's nerves and finances were drained by his royal prisoner. The feud reached a peak when the Earl's men attacked Chatsworth House and intimidated Bess's employees. It was then that Bess left Chatsworth for good, setting herself up at Hardwick Hall, where she had been born 70 years earlier, the daughter of a modest Derbyshire squire.

Bolsover Castle

***t** (01246) 823 349, www.english-heritage.org.uk; open Easter–Sept daily 10–6; winter Wed–Sun 10–4, adm.*

Despite their parents' falling out, Charles Cavendish, third son of Bess of Hardwick, and Gilbert Talbot, second son of the 6th Earl of Shrewsbury, got on well. Cavendish bought Welbeck Abbey and Bolsover Castle off his brother-in-law, in need of cash. He moved his family into Welbeck, and hired Robert Smythson to rebuild Bolsover. It may seem whimsical, but it saw Civil War action. The Terrace Range and Riding School off the Great Court were added by Charles's son, William Cavendish, 1st Duke of Newcastle, Royalist military commander of the north of England during the Civil War and author of a book on horsemanship. It's a ruin now, but the old fireplaces, Riding School with its hammer-beam roof, and views of the Vale of Scarsdale are marvellous.

Creswell Crags

***t** (01909) 720 378; visitor centre open Feb–Oct daily 10.30–4.30, Nov–Jan Sun 10.30–4.30; cave tours at 11.30, 1.30 and 3; adm.*

Halfway between Worksop and Bolsover are Creswell Crags, where 24 caves have thrown up England's most interesting Palaeolithic finds – thousands of fragments of animal bone, and stone and bone tools from Neanderthal hunters about 45,000 years ago to the end of the last Ice Age, about 12,000 years ago. The oldest remains are the bones of hippos and rhinos which roamed the area 100,000 years ago. Fragments of Ice Age art on bone, the earliest painted images in Britain (similar in style to the cave paintings at Lascaux in France) were found too – most famously an engraving on a rib bone of a horse's head in profile, showing details of the mane, eye and nostrils.

Sherwood Forest

Sherwood Forest stretches north from Nottingham to Worksop. The A614 from Nottingham takes you through it, past heaths and woodland. In fact the medieval royal hunting park contained more heath than oak and beech woods. The carving up of the forest into private estates, followed by the exploitation of the Nottinghamshire coalfields, has encroached on the medieval landscape. The best woodland enclosures

The Legend of Robin Hood

Robin Hood, legendary hero of 12th-century England who robbed the rich to help the poor, was the hero of at least 30 Middle English ballads, and many later stories and plays. The oldest recorded ballad, *Robin Hood and the Monk*, written in 1450, tells the story of Robin's ambush in a church by the evil sheriff's men, and his rescue by Little John (Robin's chief archer). Stock characters include Friar Tuck, Will Scarlet, Much the Miller's son and of course Maid Marion; their adventures range from comic to downright nasty. In the gruesome *Robin Hood and Guy of Gisborne*, Robin kills Guy the bounty hunter and disfigures his face so he won't be recognized. Stock heroics recur: the archery tournament at the castle, which Robin wins incognito in front of a huge crowd; the fight in the forest, in which Robin gets knocked into the stream and invites the champion to join his outlaw band; and the death scene in which Robin fires an arrow through the window of Kirklees Abbey to mark his own grave. The best authentic source of Robin Hood stories is the late medieval poem *A Gest of Robyn Hode* (gest meaning story), a compilation of traditional ballads and stories. The earliest reference to Robin Hood is in William Langland's *Piers Plowman* (1377); the character Sloth confesses that he can't quote from the Bible, but knows all the rhymes of Robin Hood – an oral tradition long before they were written down.

As you wander Sherwood Forest you may wonder if any of it is true. The name Hood crops up often in 13th-century criminal records, but there's no way of tracing its links with the legendary outlaw. *Gest* is set during the reign of King Edward I or II in Barnsdale, Yorkshire, about 40 miles north of Sherwood Forest; the action was not moved to Sherwood until later, when it also shifted in time to the troubled reign of bad King John (who attempted to supplant his brother Richard I while he was off fighting a Crusade, then misruled to such a degree that the barons imposed the *Magna Carta*), giving Robin a justification for his anti-social heroics. The common outlaw of the early tales had metamorphosed into an upper-class hero by the 16th century. Henry VIII's antiquarian Leland calls him '*nobilis*' and the Elizabethan playwright Anthony Mundy makes him heir to an earldom in *The Downfall of Robert, Earl of Huntington*; Richard I returns at the end of Mundy's play to restore order – a favourite ending of later tellings. It was at this time that Robin took on the trait of stealing from the rich to give to the poor, and the forest gained its connotations of freedom. In Shakespeare's *As you Like It*, the banished duke is said to be 'already in the Forest of Arden, and a many merry men with him; and there they live like the old Robin Hood of England.'

are in the great parks of the dukeries. North of Ollerton off the A614, **Clumber Park** (***t** (01909) 476 592, www.nationaltrust.org.uk; open daily dawn–dusk; adm*) is the former seat of the dukes of Newcastle; 4,000 acres of landscaped woodland park survive, with a Victorian Gothic chapel (*open daily 10–4*) by the lake.

Sherwood Forest Country Park

***t** (01623) 823 202; visitor centre open April–Oct 10–5, Nov–Mar 10–4.*

Just north of Edwinstowe, the 450-acre park includes Birklands, one of the largest tracts of ancient oak woodland and the hub of Robin Hood legend. Six-hundred oak trees older than 500 years grow in it; the dead or dying are known as stag-headed oaks because of their antler-like branches. The girth of the oldest tree in the forest, the **Major Oak**, is 30 feet around its hollow trunk; 800 years old, it could have witnessed the exploits of Robin Hood. Walks include the **Greenwood Walk** (1¾ miles) and the **Birklands Ramble** (3½ miles).

Southwell Minster

Southwell is a mellow 18th-century brick town dominated by its Minster. Charles I surrendered to the Scottish Parliamentarian army here in the Saracen's Arms, ending the Civil War. The most striking features of the Minster's exterior are its stout central tower and pinnacles on the west front, Victorian embellishments carried out shortly before the Norman church became cathedral of the new diocese of Southwell in 1884. The highlight, however, is the Norman nave with its short, stocky pillars and three storeys of round arches. The clerestory is a misnomer; it is so deeply recessed that it lets in hardly any light. Southwell has been run since the 13th century by a 'chapter' of priests; the carvings in the octagonal chapterhouse are another gem, with carved oak leaves and little green men around the door and the pointed arches of the seats.

A couple of miles beyond Southwell Minster in the direction of Newark stands the grand Georgian façade of the **Thurgaton Hundred Incorporated Workhouse** (***t** (01636) 817 250; open April–Oct Thurs–Mon 12–5, Aug 11–5; adm*), the prototype for more than 600 similar infamous institutions built after the New Poor Law Act of 1824. It was set up by the Reverend J.T. Becher and housed up to 158 paupers from 49 parishes around Southwell. Men, women and children were segregated and worked to the bone. Adults were further divided into the 'old and infirm' (or blameless poor) and the 'idle, profligate, immoral and improvident' (the destitute and disenfranchised of England's population explosion). Becher's philosophy was that 'an empty workhouse is a successful one.' Workhouses were finally scrapped by the modern welfare system in 1948. This one has been restored to give you an idea of the harsh regime.

Newark-on-Trent

Approaching by car from Southwell, you glimpse first the spire of St Mary's Church, then Newark Castle rising out of the waters of the Trent, as it did in the Middle Ages. Newark has an old market place with regular market days, green riverbanks, lots of places to eat and drink and a good number of impressive old buildings.

The Civil War in the East Midlands

The East Midlands in many respects had its own Civil War. The strategic value of the region was as a corridor for communications and men between the Royalist north-east, which was controlled by William Cavendish, Earl of Newcastle, and the King's headquarters in Oxford.

However, for the most part the war in the East Midlands was conducted as a private, tit-for-tat war between two big Leicestershire families, the Hastings and the Greys, who had been at each other's throats since the Wars of the Roses. Leicestershire was the first English county to militarize for the impending war. The Greys of Groby and Bradgate wasted no time in mustering Parliamentarian troops. Henry Hastings of Ashby-de-la-Zouch castle did the same thing for the King. A few months later, Charles I chose Nottingham as a rallying point for his army, raising his standard on 22 August 1642. Meanwhile the Parliamentarian army under the Earl of Essex garrisoned Northampton. Four days later, Lord Hastings stormed Bradgate House, striking an immediate blow against his old enemy. For the duration of the war, the Royalists garrisoned the splendid East Midlands country houses (including the Cavendish houses Welbeck, Bolsover and Wingfield) and the Parliamentarians held the cities of Leicester, Derby and Nottingham.

Hastings had a particularly bad reputation for dirty tactics. One of his favourite underhand ploys was to ambush dispatch riders passing through the county, for which he was nicknamed 'the Grand Rob Carrier'.

The major flashpoint of the East Midlands Civil War was Newark, standing strategically at the junction of major roads and the Trent crossing, which was held by the Royalists. It suffered three Parliamentarian sieges, the first of which featured a young Oliver Cromwell, attacking from Lincolnshire. The second siege was relieved by a combined force under Hastings and Prince Rupert, who charged down Beacon Hill shouting 'For God and the King'. The last siege was waged by a Scottish army, which had come into the war on the side of Parliament. It ended with the surrender of the King, who had escaped from Oxford dressed as a servant, hoping to get better terms from the Scots. There were some minor skirmishes afterwards, but effectively the Civil War ended with Newark's surrender.

Newark Castle (*t (01636) 655 765; guided tours of towers, undercroft and dungeons in summer, call to book; minimal*) turns out to be an illusion, a theatrical backdrop to the river – a long curtain wall backed by a public park. What survives, including the gate-house, was built in the 12th century to control the Trent bridge and the crossing of major roads (the old Great North Road and Fosse Way). King John died ignominiously of dysentery in the castle. During the Civil War, it was subjected to three major Parliamentarian sieges (*see* 'The Civil War in the East Midlands', above). A short walk takes you along a branch of the river that was turned into a canal at the end of the 18th century to boost trade. The riverbank is lined with brick warehouses, and the Georgian buildings dotted around town show the wealth it generated.

The **Market Place** is the hub of town, with produce stalls and interesting shops in the streets and alleyways around it – Chain Lane, Boar Lane and the -gates (from Old

Norse for street). Note the old coaching inn, the **Clinton Arms**, where Byron stayed waiting for a book of poems to be printed. His printers occupied the Queen Anne building in the corner of the square nearest **St Mary's Church**. An early 16th-century Dance of Death wall painting depicts a smiling skeleton dancing while a merchant hangs onto his purse. Just off the A46 southwest of the town, a Civil War earthwork known as the **Queen's Sconce** survives.

Laxton

Northwest of Newark, taking the Tuxford exit off the A1 and following the signs, Laxton is the only village in England still farming by the medieval open field system. It's the perfect English village: the narrow village lanes meet at a crossroads by a church, a pub and a tiny green. Park outside the Dovecote Inn, get a drink and go to

Tourist Information

Newark: The Gilstrap Centre, Castlegate, **t** (01636) 655 765. *Open winter 9–5, summer 9–6.*

Market takes place in the Market Place on Wed, Fri and Sat, with fruit, veg, and flower stalls. Bric-a-brac market on Mon and Thurs.

A huge **antiques fair** takes place at the Newark and Nottinghamshire Showground every two months. Ask at the tourist information centre for dates.

Newark Line River Cruises, **t** (01636) 525 246, run two boats from Town Wharf and Cuckstool Wharf, below the castle, to Farndon, from Easter to Sept; trips last 1½ hours.

Where to Stay and Eat

Newark t (01636) –

The Grange Hotel, 73 London Road,703 399, *www.grangenewark.co.uk* (*expensive*). Superb family-owned hotel with 16 rooms, restaurant and large bar, and garden.

Millgate House Hotel, Millgate, **t** 704 445. Rustic-style hotel opposite Millgate Museum, 2 minutes' walk from town centre; some bedrooms in warehouse-style block.

Deincourt Hotel, 40 London Road, **t** 602 100 (*expensive*). Newish hotel in converted nurses' home opposite old hospital; 39 modern bedrooms.

Gannets, Castlegate, **t** 702 066. Lovely, calm place with big windows. Good coffee, loose-leaf tea, home-made lemonade, light lunches and toasted tea cakes.

Café Bleu, Castlegate, **t** 610 141 (*moderate*). Stylish, popular French-style brasserie with jazzy piano music. On warm days you can eat out on the terrace. *Closed Sun eve; book for summer weekends.*

Il Castello, Castlegate, **t** 674 000 (*cheap*). Simply furnished and pleasant Italian restaurant, strong on meat and fish. *Open Mon–Sat eves, Wed–Sat lunch.*

Navigation Waterfront, Millgate, **t** 704 763 (*cheap*). Shares cobbled yard, where you can sit, with Millgate Museum. Converted warehouse with big windows overlooking the river, serves lasagne and salad.

Trumps Bistro and Restaurant, 25 Castlegate, **t** 610 661 (*cheap*). Small modern English-style restaurant; roasted crispy duck or spinach, feta and olive filo pastry with chardonnay sauce. *Open Tues–Sat.*

Laxton t (01777) –

Dovecote Inn, Moorhouse Road, **t** 871 586 (*moderate*). Friendly traditional village pub serving good home-cooked lunches and dinners such as steak and kidney pie; two bedrooms in converted wheat store.

Crosshill House, **t** 871 953, *www.crosshillhouse.com* (*moderate*). Old brick house up steep steps behind village green, opposite pub; cosy and friendly with three pretty bedrooms and various health and beauty treatments on offer.

Manor Farm, **t** 870 417 (*cheap*). Lovely old farmhouse with barns and rambling garden; low doors, twisting stone spiral staircase; three modest bedrooms, a couple of dogs and wholesome farming smells.

the **visitor centre** (*t (01777) 871 586; open daily dawn–dusk*) to find out about open field farming. The farmers of Laxton work narrow strips of three common fields – Mill Field, West Field and South Field – all of which existed already in the 12th century. Every year each field is devoted to a single crop, in rotation, and one of the three remains fallow. The farmers all live next door to each other in the village.

Leicestershire

The mild countryside of south and east Leicestershire is lovely, with canal towpaths, rolling fields, and historic links with the Belvoir and Pytcherly Hunts. Leicester, the county town, grows on you slowly. To the northwest are relics of the county's coal-mines. But it is historical associations that bring the region to life: a visit to Ashby Castle, Bradgate Hall and Bosworth Battlefield fleshes out the dynastic struggles of the Wars of the Roses; the Greys of Bradgate and the Hastings of Ashby opposed each other for three centuries until the Civil War, when their terror tactics were reported in the new press. Hastings' descendants exploited the Leicestershire coalfield in the 19th century. Pioneering travel agent Thomas Cook conducted early tours of Leicester, Market Harborough, Melbourne and Belvoir Castle.

Leicester

Leicester has lost its charm. There is no shortage of history here: Simon de Montfort, John of Gaunt and Richard III all make appearances, and the Royalist Leicester Siege was one of the Civil War's most infamous – 'in the ruins of Leicester you may behold a large map of misery' – bringing Charles I to trial. When Thomas Cook moved here in 1841, the whole city was employed in shoe manufacturing. Now Leicester's claims to fame are football and rugby teams, two universities and a National Space Centre. It is also predicted that it will be England's first black majority city.

The centre of town is marked by the Victorian-Gothic **clock tower**, built in 1868 to commemorate four city founders, including De Montfort, father of parliamentary democracy and scourge of Leicester Jews. On the High Street is the old headquarters of **Thomas Cook & Son** with a frieze of pyramids and steam trains. Nearby is the jostling **market place**, with 300 stalls selling old clothes and West Indian fruit and vegetables. Beside the Venetian stairway of the **Corn Exchange** is a statue of the 5th Duke of Rutland, who turned Belvoir into a mock-medieval castle, looking drunk. There are fish, meat and fabric stalls in the 1970s market centre. Around **St Martin's Square** are medieval lanes, where few old buildings survive other than the **Guildhall** (*t (0116) 253 2569; open April–Sept Mon–Sat 10–5, Sun 1–5; adm*), half-timbered hall of the guild of Corpus Christi. Next door is old **St Martin's**, elevated to cathedral status in 1927, with its richly decorated interior and 16ft bishop's throne. Down by the River Soar is the oldest part of town, with Victorian townhouses around Millstone and Friar Lane.

The High Street leads into St Nicholas' Circle, a horrific roundabout on the ring road. Here, of all places, are the sunken remains of a **Roman bath complex** and the 40ft

Getting There and Around

By **car**, Leicester is in the heart of England, just off the M1, south of Nottingham and east of Birmingham.

Trains run direct to Leicester from London St Pancras (1½ hours) and Birmingham New Street (1 hour), Nottingham and Sheffield.

Regular **buses** run from the city centre to the Space Centre and Abbey Pump Rooms.

Tourist Information

Leicester: 7–9 Every Street, Town Hall Square, **t** 0906 294 1113. *Open Mon–Wed and Fri 9–5.30, Thurs 10–5.30 and Sat 9–5.*

Indoor market Tues–Sun, **outdoor market** Mon–Sat, both in the Market Place.

Where to Stay

Leicester t (0116) –

Ramada Jarvis Hotel, Granby Street, **t** 255 5599, *www.ramadajarvis.co.uk* (*very expensive*). City-centre hotel, behind elaborate Dutch-gabled, stone-dressed Victorian façade; 100 bedrooms including 12 modern studio rooms; carvery, café and two bars.

The Belmont House Hotel, De Montfort Street, **t** 254 4773, *www.belmonthotel.co.uk* (*expensive*). Handsome porticoed building on corner of leafy New Walk; 78 pleasant bedrooms, conservatory restaurant and brasserie bar.

Spindle Lodge Hotel, 2 West Walk, **t** 233 8801 (*moderate*). Attractive Victorian townhouse in quiet conservation street off New Walk, with friendly atmosphere and period-style décor; 13 plain bedrooms, some with private showers.

Burlington Hotel, Elmfield Avenue, Stoneygate, **t** 270 5112, *www.burlingtonhotel.co.uk* (*moderate*). Pleasant family-run Victorian townhouse hotel near Victoria Park with six clean, comfortable bedrooms and courteous, helpful service.

Regency Hotel, 360 London Road, **t** 270 9634, *www.the-regency-hotel.com* (*moderate*). Friendly, business-like Victorian townhouse hotel with a conservatory porch full of plants and period décor; 32 bedrooms and two dining rooms: a formal restaurant with crisp linen tablecloths and a brasserie-style conservatory.

Eating Out

Opera House Restaurant, Guildhall Lane, **t** 223 6666 (*moderate*). Hushed no-smoking dining room upstairs, brick-vaulted cellar

arched Jewry Wall. Roman *Ratae*, on the Fosse Way, was a *civitas* capital of non-Roman citizens. The **Jewry Wall Museum** (***t** (0116) 225 4971; open April–Sept Mon–Sat 10–5, Sun 1–5; adm*) displays Roman mosaic pavements and wall paintings.

Up Welles Street is a **Sikh Temple** in an old stocking factory (*open Thurs 1–4*).

Castle Gardens and Newark

A pedestrian bridge takes you over busy roads to the Norman motte. Little survives of the medieval **castle** of the Beaumonts and De Montforts, favourite residence of John of Gaunt, earl of Leicester from 1362. When Gaunt's son succeeded to the throne as Henry IV Leicester's earldom and its castle faded away. Richard III stayed at an inn when he came to Leicester in 1485 to raise an army; a statue here shows the armour-clad king holding his crown aloft, inscribed 'Killed at Bosworth...buried at Leicester'. A plaque on Bow Bridge commemorates the place where the corpse of 'the last of the Plantagenets' was dumped in the river.

Newark, or 'new work', to the south of the walled town abutting the castle walls, was *the* sought-after address in the 17th–19th centuries. A turreted gateway from the castle and the magazine gateway, used as an ammo dump in the Civil War, are all that downstairs. Modern English menu might include parmesan and truffle salad followed by seared Cornish sea bass or venison casserole. *Closed Sun.*

Stones, Millstone Lane, **t** 291 0004 (*moderate*). Highly recommended restaurant in converted hosiery factory with art on the walls and attentive service; grilled monkfish and tiger prawn kebab.

The Case, Hotel Street, **t** 251 7675 (*moderate*). Stylish modern European restaurant above wine bar with courtyard seating; salmon with poached egg, parmesan and hollandaise. *Closed Sun.*

Liquid, Loseby Lane (off Every Street), **t** 253 1771 (*cheap*). Friendly, stylish café with cool music and art on the walls. Seasonal fruit juices, dairy-free coffees, chocolate croissants, toasted crumpets with peanut butter, chocolate milk and elderflower ice cream.

Royal Chef, 202–3 Narborough Road, **t** 224 4228 (*cheap*). Modern, fast-service Chinese restaurant with English desserts. *Open eves only, until midnight.*

Café Bruxelles, 90–2 High Street, **t** 224 3013 (*cheap*). Stop here for a baguette or ciabatta and Belgian beer (or coffee), choose from the 'business lunch' menu (Cajun chicken breast or vegetable pancake) or go à la carte with salmon in Parma ham.

Friends Tandoori, 41–3 Belgrave Road, **t** 266 8809 (*cheap*). Smartish, air-conditioned Punjabi restaurant on outskirts of the city beyond the ring road and flyover (follow signs to Melton Mowbray). *Closed Sun.*

Thali Restaurant, 49 Belgrave Road, **t** 266 5888 (*cheap*). Tiny Indian restaurant where food is served on metal trays; authentic dishes of vegetables and pulses.

Entertainment

Phoenix Arts Centre, 21 Upper Brown Street (off Newark Street), **t** 255 4854. Drama, films, comedy and dance. Also café.

Jongleurs, Granby Street, **t** 0870 7870707. National chain of stand-up comedy stores. *Open Thurs–Sat.*

The Fan Club, 40 Abbey Street, **t** 242 5765. Leicester's stalwart club.

The Haymarket Theatre, Belgrave Gate, **t** 253 9797. In-house and touring productions in 752-seater old-fashioned auditorium.

De Montfort Hall, Granville Road (at end of New Walk), **t** 233 3111. Large 1913 venue with musical emphasis from soul divas to the Philharmonia Orchestra.

City Gallery, 90 Granby Street, **t** 254 0595, *www.leicester.gov.uk/citygallery*. Three gallery spaces showing contemporary art.

survive of old Newark. The **Newark Houses Museum**, in two 16th-century houses (***t** (0116) 225 4980; open April–Sept Mon–Sat 10–5, Sun 1–5*) tells the story of Leicester. For a glimpse of multicultural Leicester, turn right down Oxford Street to see the white marble façade of the **Jain Centre** (*open Mon–Fri 2–5*), in an old Congregational chapel. Quiet **New Walk** cuts across town; half-way down, behind a grand portico, is the **New Walk Museum and Art Gallery** (***t** (0116) 255 4100; open April–Sept Mon–Sat 10–5, Sun 1–5; adm*). Opened in 1859,its highlight is the collection of 18th- and 19th-century coffee cans (straight-sided cups) and studio pottery (Bernard Leach *et al*).

National Space Centre

The brand new **National Space Centre** (***t** 0870 607 7223; open Mon 12.30–4.30, Tues–Sun 10–4.30; adm exp*) is 1½ miles north of the city (take bus no. 54 from Charles Street, a shuttle bus from the station, or walk through Abbey Park; by car follow signs from the city centre or M1 junctions 21a and 22.) A millennium project, the £52-million space centre is based on Leicester University's physics and astronomy department and was designed by Nicholas Grimshaw. It is dominated by the Rocket Tower, a 138ft inflated plastic pod holding two 1950s satellite launchers that never made it into space, the American Thor Able and British Blue Streak. Space miscellanea include the hairbrush that went up to the Mia space station in 1991 with British astronaut Helen Sharman, and a Soyuz capsule. The Victorian **Abbey Pumping Station** (*t (0116) 299 5111; open April–Sept Mon–Sat 10–5, Sun 1–5; adm*) next door brings you down to earth; it pumped sewage until 1964, and is now a hygiene museum.

Around Leicester

The wedge between Derby, Leicester and Burton-upon-Trent incorporates Charnwood Forest – once a royal hunting ground, now a deer park bissected by the M1 – and the new National Forest, a scheme to transform the old coal-mining belt by planting 30 million trees. Here you can visit the country houses of 19th-century mineral lords.

The ruins of the Grey family's Tudor mansion are in **Bradgate Park** (*open dawn–dusk*), 840 windswept acres of heathery hills a few miles northwest of Leicester. At the park visitor centre along the River Lyn you can mug up on Grey family history Bradgate was the childhood home of Lady Jane Grey (1537–54), queen for nine days between Edward VI and Bloody Mary. Brick **Bradgate House** (*open April–Oct Wed, Thurs and Sat 2–5, Sun 10–12.30 and 2–5*) is a romantic ruin amid hills.

Noble Walk-Ons in Shakespeare's *Richard III*

The king's the thing in Shakespeare's history plays, and no one pays much attention to the noble walk-ons. But Dorset, Grey, Rivers and Hastings of *Richard III* are all on the family tree at Bradgate Hall. **Dorset** is Thomas Grey, Marquis of Dorset, builder of Bradgate Hall and eldest son of Sir John Grey of Groby and Elizabeth Woodville. **Grey** is Lord Richard Grey, second son of Sir John and Elizabeth (executed in Act III, Scene 3). **Rivers** is Anthony, Earl Rivers, brother of Elizabeth (executed along with Grey, with the words 'as for my sister and her princely sons, be satisfied, dear God, with our true blood, which, as thou know'st, unjustly must be spilt'). **Hastings** is Sir William Hastings of Ashby-de-la-Zouch, most trusted councillor of Edward IV (bumped off in Act III, Scene 4: 'Hastings can die, I hope.').

The Greys and Woodvilles were sworn enemies of Richard III. It all started when Sir John of Groby died and his widow, Elizabeth Woodville, secretly married Edward IV and had two sons, Edward and Richard ('those bastards in the Tower'). Elizabeth showered her family, including Dorset, Grey and Rivers, with titles and power. Shakespeare's *Richard III* is taken up with the feud between the Queen's family and the King's (Richard, Clarence and their supporters, Hastings and Buckingham). When Edward IV died, the factions drew their swords. The Woodvilles and Greys seized the princes and royal treasure. Richard, the protector, initiated a bloodbath by executing the princes, Hastings (who at the 11th hour sided with the Greys), Grey, Rivers and even his old friend Buckingham. A few survived to carry on the dynastic drama: Elizabeth took sanctuary; Dorset fled to Brittany, allying himself with the future king, Henry Tudor. As Henry VII his first act was to marry Elizabeth Woodville's daughter, Elizabeth of York, half-sister of Thomas Grey of Bradgate Hall. But that's another play.

Thomas Cook (1808–92)

My constant aim has been to render excursion and tourist travelling as cheap, as easy, as safe and as pleasant as circumstances would allow.

The pioneer of popular tourism, Thomas Cook was born in Melbourne, south Derbyshire, set himself up as a cabinet-maker and teetotaller in Market Harborough and moved to Leicester. Always entrepreneurial, he worked as a printer, bookseller, hotel owner and travel agent. Cook's travel business grew out of a trip he organized to a temperance meeting in Loughborough in 1841, 'the first publicly advertised excursion known in the country'. It was followed by trips around the East Midlands in the spirit of 'enthusiastic philanthropy'. His first commercial railway excursion was to Liverpool in the summer of 1845, when he arranged a cheap return ticket for 1,200 people from Leicester, Derby and Nottingham and printed a 60-page guide book. Cook carried on with 350 tourists on a steamer to Caernarvon and climbed Snowdon. He firmly believed that the new railways should provide 'rational recreation' for the masses, whose main diversion at the time was drink. In the 1850s he took 100,000 tourists to the Scottish Highlands; in the 1860s he chaperoned groups of tourists to the Continent and the Middle East, negotiating cheap rates and accommodation, making sure everyone caught their train, boat or mule and advising on money and language. He camped outside Jerusalem and nearly drowned in the Nile. Soon *The Times* was complaining that railway excursionists like Cook 'spoil the pleasures of the regular traveller'. In 1862 he sold the first package holiday (from Leicester to London). He introduced the Circular Note or travellers' cheque soon after. Before his 64th birthday, he accompanied eight travellers on the first ever Round the World Tour, for £283 per person. In a letter from America, he wrote approvingly that 'the Americans do not provide drinks on the table, and only the English and Scotch people call for them. Iced water is the beverage on the tables'. By the time of his retirement the company had 28 offices in Europe and the Middle East, six in America and one in Australia. It has continued to grow and organize getaways from places like Leicester.

The market town of **Ashby-de-la-Zouch** is famous for its castle. The ruins inspired Sir Walter Scott, in the early 1800s, to set the jousting tournament in *Ivanhoe* here. The Zouch family built the first manor house at Ashby in 1160. Sir William Hastings, royal chamberlain, committed Yorkist and Edward IV's most powerful courtier, took over the house and most of north Leicestershire in 1464, adding defensive towers and crenellated walls. As devoted to child-king Edward V as to his father, Hastings was executed by Richard III (*see* box). The Hastings family, however, maintained its position until the Civil War, when **Ashby Castle** (***t*** *(01530) 413 343, www.english-heritage.org.uk; open April–Sept daily 10–6, Oct daily 10–5, Nov–Mar Wed–Sun 10–4; adm*) became HQ of Henry Hastings, notorious Royalist commander of the East Midlands. Henry caused havoc, plundered the countryside and roused the Greys – Leicestershire Parliamentarians – by ambushing their convoys and despatch riders. He offered to surrender if he could keep his estates and have the freedom to travel abroad. 'Too good conditions indeed,'

Where to Stay and Eat

Ashby-de-la-Zouch

Dolce, Market Street, **t** (01530) 563 385 (*cheap*). Italian-style café down alley, where you can get ice cream, tiramisù and panini with basil and mozzarella, or just a coffee. *Closed Sun.*

Crewe and Harpur Arms, Swarkestone Causeway (north of Ashby between Melbourne and Derby), **t** (01332) 700 641. Popular sunny-day pub with riverside garden below magnificent stone causeway.

Bosworth t (01455) –

Bosworth Hall Hotel, The Park, Market Bosworth, **t** 291 919, *www.brittania-hotels.com* (*expensive*). Beautiful red-brick Georgian country house with bedrooms in outbuildings; two restaurants, including self-service carvery and formal à la carte; tennis courts and leisure facilities.

Royal Arms, Sutton Cheney, **t** 290 263 (*moderate*). Handsome old pub on quiet country road with bland restaurant and stables converted into motel-style rooms.

Dixie Arms Hotel, 6 Main Street, **t** 290 218, *www.dixiearmshotel.co.uk* (*moderate*). Friendly old hotel with four plain rooms; pool table and music in bar.

Black Horse, Market Place, **t** 290 278. Friendly gastro pub with pavement seating and black beams; small bar and restaurant (*moderate*) with an excellent reputation.

Softleys, Market Place, **t** 290 464, *www.softleys.com* (*moderate*). Eighteenth-century townhouse restaurant; menu might include seafood risotto followed by grilled steak with roasted vegetables. Bedrooms on top floor include a family room with armchairs.

Market Harborough t (01858) –

Angel Hotel, 37 High Street, **t** 462 702, *www.bookmenzies.com* (*moderate*). It's hard not to notice the white-painted 18th-century façade of this hotel as you come into town; 37 bedrooms on three floors, restaurant and lounge bar with open fire.

Three Swans Hotel, 21 High Street, **t** 466 644, *www.threeswans.co.uk* (*moderate*). Striking old coaching inn with carriage arch and bay windows; reputedly where Charles I stayed before the Battle of Naseby in 1645; 60 bedrooms, some in modern extension at the back; good restaurant.

Black Horse Inn, Main Street, Foxton (near Market Harborough, at the top of the village beside the church), **t** 545 250 (*moderate*). Serves good food in homely main bar or restaurant; excellent views from the garden.

Bewicke Arms, Eastgate, Hallaton, **t** 555 217. Traditional thatched pub on village green overlooking the Harepie Bank where bottle-kicking takes place on Easter Monday (although the pub removes to a tent in the car park). The **Bewicke Tea Room** next door in the converted stables serves light lunches, home-made cakes and soft-whipped ice cream, and offers the same glorious views.

according to a parliamentary reporter, 'for such a desperate and wicked Rob-Carrier as Hastings was, but that the kingdom might be glad to be rid of such wretches'.

Wealthy landowners like the 2nd Earl of Moira developed Leicestershire's coal industry in the early 19th century aided by the arrival of the Leicester–Swannington Railway in 1832. The Moira collieries were mined by the Earl after a failed attempt at iron smelting: the **Moira Blast Furnace and Foundry** (***t*** *(01283) 224 667; open Wed–Sun 11–4; adm*) was built in 1804 next to Ashby Canal; the venture closed in 1811, the year that Moira mining village was built. James Stephenson, brother of the famous railway engineer, opened Snibston Colliery in 1832; it closed in 1983 after 151 years. The site at Coalville is now **Snibston Discovery Park** (***t*** *(01530) 278 444; open 10–4; adm*), a technology museum with tours of the old mine buildings (conducted by an ex-miner).

North of Ashby the scenery changes. You could tour the gracious country houses of this area by bicycle. Tourism entrepreneur Thomas Cook was born in the pretty yellow stone town of **Melbourne** in 1808. An early tour was to **Melbourne Hall** (***t*** *(01332) 862*

The Wars of Roses

The trouble began in the mid-14th century with Edward III, who had five strong, healthy sons – four too many – who all produced strapping sons of their own, including the dukes of York (whose emblem was the white rose) and the dukes of Lancaster (the red rose). Over the next hundred years, the houses of York and Lancaster each put three kings on the throne: the Lancastrians – Henrys IV, V and VI; the Yorkists – Edwards IV and V, and Richard III. The dynastic struggle known as the Wars of the Roses flared up when Henry V died, leaving the nine-month-old Henry VI, King of England and France, at the mercy of his protectors. Into the power vacuum stepped Richard of York, who claimed descent from Edward III on both sides through the marriage of cousins. Richard and Henry both died in the ensuing conflict, but Richard's son, Edward IV, ended up on the throne. Edward died in his 40s, leaving two sons, Edward V and Richard, aged 12 and nine, again at the mercy of protectors. The chief protector was Edward IV's brother, Richard of Gloucester; within three months the young princes were dead and Richard had crowned himself Richard III. Henry Tudor, Richard's opponent at Bosworth, was the grandson of Henry V's widowed French queen, Catherine de Valois, mother of Henry VI. She had two more sons by a Welsh courtier called Owen Tudor, hence the name Tudor and the future Henry VII's invasion from France. More important to Henry's claims to the royal succession was his link to the house of Lancaster on his mother's side. To secure the legitimacy of the new Tudor dynasty, Henry VII married Elizabeth of York (Edward V's sister) and adopted the emblem of the red and white rose. The defining histories of the Wars of the Roses were written in Tudor times; Shakespeare's *Richard III* established the characters of Richard and Henry, villains and heroes.

163; gardens open April–Sept Wed, Sat and Sun 1.30–5.30; hall Aug Tues–Sun 2–5; adm), next to the church; '109 respectably attired, and apparently happy individuals, mostly ladies' travelled in nine horse-drawn carriages. The town turned out to greet them with a brass band. The hall was the home of Victorian prime ministers Melbourne and Palmerston. Cook paid for the almshouses on the High Street. Stop by the grand 18th-century house of **Staunton Harold** to visit the Gothic church (*open April–Sept Wed–Sun 1–5, Oct weekends 1–5*). An inscription over the door tells that the church was built 'in the yeare 1653 when all things sacred were throughout ye nation Either demollisht or profaned.' Sir Robert Shirley built it in defiance of the Cromwellian regime, and died in the Tower of London for this act of defiance three years later.

Calke Abbey (***t*** *(01332) 863 822, www.nationaltrust.org.uk; house open April–Oct Sat–Wed; adm*) has been preserved as an 18th-century neo-classical 'country house in decline', complete with cracked ceilings, peeling wallpaper, chipped paint, scuffed furniture and junk. Its treasure is the state bed of George I. The grounds are glorious.

Bosworth Field

Bosworth Field, at Sutton Cheney, Market Bosworth (***t*** *(01455) 290 429; battlefield open dawn–dusk; visitor centre open April–Oct daily 11–5, Nov–Dec Sun 11–4, Mar weekends 11–5; adm*) is in the heart of the Midland shires, a few miles west of Leicester.

Here medieval kings confronted each other with horses, trumpets and banners in the culmination of the Wars of the Roses. The fighting contingents of 1485 came from all over England: from Leicester (Richard III), London (Brackenbury, the constable of the Tower of London who murdered the princes), East Anglia (Norfolk, a title bestowed on the Howards by Richard III), the northeast (Northumberland), the northwest (the Stanleys) and North Wales (Henry Tudor, sailing from France). Watling Street and the Fosse Way cross at Bosworth, although the fighting took place on Ambion Hill. The Italian historian Polydore Vergil recorded the details of the battle 18 years later. Invited by Henry VII to write the first *Historia Anglica*, the not impartial Vergil was unenthusiastic about Richard III. Subsequent writers all borrowed from him, including Edward Hall (who had Richard skulking out of his mother's womb three years late with teeth and long hair), Raphael Holinshed and Shakespeare – who immortalized the battle with Richard's words – 'my kingdom for a horse' – and turned it into a rip-roaring yarn: the treachery of the Stanleys, Richard's soldierly death and the crown plucked from the thorn bush and placed on the new Tudor king Henry VII's head on the battlefield.

There were three forces at Bosworth. Richard III occupied the summit of the hill; Norfolk and Brackenbury commanded the vanguard, Richard the main body of troops, and Northumberland the rearguard (he never saw action). Henry Tudor was at the bottom of the hill, near Shenton, with a smaller army. The Stanleys came in with Henry at the last moment. Around 15,000 men fought for two hours, until Richard was vanquished and Henry Tudor crowned king. The battle trail follows Richard's cavalry charge ('the swan song of medieval English chivalry') downhill into the thick of the battle, where he died fighting. Nearby **Sutton Cheney** church is central to the legend of Richard III; he took Mass there before the battle (22 August 1485).

A few miles north, stop at **Foxton Locks**, where 10 locks carry the canal up the hill. Built in 1812, the locks connected the canals of the north Midlands with London and the south. In 1900, the Foxton Incline Plain, a boat lift that bypassed the locks, was added. It was closed 11 years later and the locks declined. The **Foxton Canal Museum** (***t*** *(01162) 792 657; open Easter–Oct daily 10–5, winter Sat–Wed 11–4; adm*) tells the tale.

Belvoir Castle

t (01476) 870 262; open Mar and Oct Sun 11–5, April–June and Sept Tues–Thurs and Sat 11–5, July and Aug daily 11–5; adm.

The flamboyant Victorian castle of the dukes of Rutland overlooks the Vale of Belvoir (pronounced 'beaver'), traditional fox-hunting country. The castle with its towers is the fourth Belvoir Castle. The first was destroyed in the Wars of the Roses, the second in the Civil War and the third by fire. The ornate Picture Gallery displays paintings by Gainsborough, Holbein, Poussin and Teniers – portraits and hunting scenes.

Rutland

Rutland is the smallest county in England, 16 miles by 16 miles. The name comes from the old Norse for 'red land'. Rutland was in fact the dower land of Mercian

Getting There and Around

By **car**, Oakham is on the A606 from Nottingham, which joins the A1 at Stamford. From the M1, turn off at Leicester, junction 21. Uppingham is 22 miles from Peterborough, on the A1, 17 miles from Leicester, on the M1, M9 and A47, and 4 miles south of Oakham, which can be reached by local bus.

By **train**, you will have to change at Leicester or Peterborough from London Liverpool Street and King's Cross or the north. A direct train runs between Oakham and London Stansted.

There is a good **local bus** service. The Rutland Flier runs north–south from Melton Mowbray to Corby stopping at Oakham, Uppingham and Rockingham Castle; the 2A runs east–west between Nottingham and Oakham stopping at Stamford and Rutland Water.

Rutland Water Cruises, **t** (01572) 787 630, *www.rutlandwatercruises.com*, runs 40-minute cruises on the *Rutland Belle*. Embark at the Whitwell landing stage, just off the A606 on the north shore, and disembark at Normanton on the opposite shore. *April and Oct weekends only, May–Sept daily*.

You can hire a **bicycle** at the **Whitwell Centre**, **t** (01780) 460 705 (north shore) and **Normanton Centre**, **t** (01780) 720 888 (south shore). *Open April–Oct daily 9–6, Nov–Mar weather permitting 9–5*.

Tourist Information

Oakham: Flores House, 34 High Street, **t** (01572) 724 329. *Open Tues–Sat 11–3*.

Rutland Water: Sykes Lane, Empingham, **t** (01572) 653 026. *Open daily 10–4*.

Where to Stay and Eat

Oakham t (01572) –

Flores House Café and Deli, High Street, **t** 755 601. Smashing little place serving strong coffee, *pain au chocolat*, cakes and light lunches.

Lord Nelson's House Hotel, 11 Market Place, **t** 723 199, *www.nelsons-house.com* (*moderate*). Medieval timber-framed building on corner of square with four stylish bedrooms named after Nelson, his wife, mistress and captain; classic French-style restaurant offers pork with creamy cider potatoes and lots of fish. *Hotel and restaurant closed Sun night and Mon*.

The Admiral Hornblower, High Street, **t** 723 004, *www.hornblowerhotel.co.uk* (*moderate*). Former 17th-century farmhouse with flagstone and wood floors, solid wooden benches in the bar, pleasant dining rooms and bedrooms with big pine beds.

The Whipper-In Hotel, Market Place, **t** 756 971, *www.brook-hotels.co.uk* (*moderate*). Stone-built low-slung former 17th-century coaching inn, with 24 comfortable, attractive bedrooms, brasserie and bar.

The Old Wisteria Hotel, 4 Catmose Street, **t** 722 844, *www.wisteriahotel.co.uk* (*moderate*). It looks like a pub from the street, with flower baskets and an old sign; inside 25 bedrooms with a pleasant hotel atmosphere.

Uppingham t (01572) –

Falcon Hotel, Market Place, High Street East, **t** 823 535, *www.thefalconhotel.com* (*moderate*). Beautiful 16th-century gabled sandstone coaching inn in the centre of town; 25 rooms, restaurant and brasserie.

The Lake Isle, High Street East, **t** 822 951, *www.lakeislehotel.com* (*moderate*). Attractive 18th-century townhouse with 12 pretty bedrooms and cottage suites in the walled garden; scrubbed country-kitchen-style restaurant serves hearty meals which might include roulade of duck on a bed of red onion marmalade or lemon sole stuffed with fresh crab.

The Garden Hotel, 16 High Street, **t** 822 352 (*moderate*). Tall townhouse opposite the public school. Archway off East High Street leads into garden courtyard; sweet little bedrooms and courteous to a fault.

The Vaults, Market Square, **t** 823 259 (*cheap*). Four bedrooms in cottage on courtyard behind a friendly pub with outside seating.

Paddy Sanchez, Market Place, **t** 822 255. Newish tapas restaurant serving a selection of chorizo, seafood, *patatas bravas* and so on, all washed down with Spanish reds.

queens. This anachronism survived the 10th-century mapping of the English shires, a relic of the old estate system, only to be abolished in 1974 and reinstated again in 1996. Rutland has a certain cachet, with two posh old public schools, stone villages, sailing clubs and a landscape of patchwork fields and narrow lanes.

Oakham

Oakham is the county town of Rutland, a stone's throw from Rutland Water. Stone houses flank the old streets – Mill Street, Church Street and High Street. A pump and butter cross stand in the stone-flagged Market Square, abutted by the grey-gabled public school and church. A cobbled lane leads off the square to medieval **Oakham Castle** (*open Mon–Sat 10.30–5, Sun 2–4*). All that remains of the Ferrers family manor house is the 12th-century great hall. Inside is a display of more than 200 horseshoes, left as tokens by members of the aristocracy and monarchs passing through the town (according to a tradition connected to the Ferrers family emblem of a horseshoe).

Rutland Water

Rutland Water is a horseshoe-shaped reservoir created 30 years ago, with paths around its 25-mile perimeter, water sports and nature reserves. **Normanton Church Museum** (*open April–Sept daily 11–4, Oct weekends 11–4*) in a Georgian church tells you all about the lake. **Egleton Reserve** (***t*** *(01572) 770 651; visitor centre open summer 9–5, closes earlier in winter; adm*) at the western end is the best of the nature reserves.Its lagoons and tussocky islets are a breeding ground for ospreys.

Uppingham

Rutland's second market town, 4 miles south of Rutland Water, is quieter than Oakham, but as pleasant, with handsome old buildings and second-hand bookshops. On High Street West, you find yourself beneath the high stone walls of **Uppingham School** (***t*** *(01572) 822 211; tours Easter and summer holidays Sat 2.15 from the Market Square; adm, tickets from Uppingham Sports and Bookshop*), founded in 1584 by Archdeacon Robert Johnson, who founded Oakham School in the same year. Nowadays, this is the grander of the two schools, with its Victorian-Gothic gate.

Lincolnshire

It's hard to sum up Lincolnshire – the Edge, the Fens, the Wolds and the Marsh. The **Edge** is an escarpment surmounted by Lincoln Cathedral. **Stamford**, **Grantham** and **Lincoln** all flourished on the medieval wool trade, with links east by river to the Wash and up and down the country on the Great North Road. The M1 bypasses Lincolnshire now, leaving the county unspoilt. Around Stamford is a cluster of stately mansions. The flat expanse of drained marshland that is the **Fens** extends into Cambridgeshire. The rolling chalk **Wolds** are hilly and much more the thing. The **Marsh** has an atmosphere of its own, with bracing North Sea air. The resorts of **Skegness**, **Mablethorpe** and **Cleethorpes** are the blowy eastern edge of the country lined with picnic rugs.

Famous Men and Women of Lincolnshire

Lincolnshire adventurers have cut quite a dash in the New World. Arctic explorer **Sir John Franklin** was born in the market town of Spilsby in 1786, served in the Royal Navy at the battles of Copenhagen and Trafalgar, led voyages of exploration to the Arctic, was lieutenant governor of Tasmania, and died in 1847, trapped in the ice of Victoria Strait. The botanist **Joseph Banks** (1744–1820) travelled with James Cook to Australia, New Zealand and New Guinea, later inherited the Revesby Abbey estate between Horncastle and Spilsby on the southern slopes of the Wolds, and bought a townhouse in Horncastle. Thousands of east coasters left for the New World in the 17th and 18th centuries, some in governing roles. **Captain John Smith** was born at Willoughby, south of Alford, in 1580, and educated at Lough Grammar School. He emigrated to Virginia in 1607 and became governor of the colony at Chesapeake Bay. There he got into trouble with the native Americans, and was rescued from certain death by the chieftain's daughter, Pocahontas, whom he brought back to England (she died at Gravesend, *see* p.162). **John Cotton** was vicar of Boston on both sides of the Atlantic (Lincs. and Massachussets). The antiquarian **William Stukeley**, born in Holbeach in 1687, later vicar of All Saints in Stamford, travelled the country on horseback speculating about ancient monuments, saving the stones at Stonehenge and Avebury. The scientist and mathematician **Sir Isaac Newton** was born on Christmas Day 1642 at Woolsthorpe Manor and educated at Grantham. And the poet **Alfred, Lord Tennyson** was born at Somersby Rectory in 1809 and educated in Louth at the same grammar school as Captain John Smith.

But perhaps the most notorious person to come out of Lincolnshire is **Margaret Thatcher**, prime minister from 1979 to 1990, who was born in Grantham in 1925 and did away with British society during her time in office.

Lincoln

Two old Roman roads (now the A15 and A46) run ruler-straight into Lincoln, but Lincoln has been off the beaten track for centuries. From miles in all directions, the only landmark is the double tower of Lincoln cathedral. The playwright J.B. Priestley, visiting in winter 1933, called the cathedral view 'one of the Pisgah sights of England', and compared the medieval city to the 'twisted, dark, and icy old Paris of Villon'. Nathaniel Hawthorne, visiting in 1857, wrote that the main street leading up to the cathedral and castle was 'the steepest I ever saw'. Once up on Lincoln Hill, you can gratefully ignore the modern part of the city down in the plain.

There are two parts of Lincoln: uptown, handsome and old; downtown, drab and modern. The long High Street leads up from the railway station and over the River Witham, becoming **Steep Hill** near the top. Brayford Pool was the shipping centre from Roman to medieval times and the name Lincoln comes from *Lindis Colonia* – a colony for retired soldiers by the pool. At the foot of Steep Hill you come to **Jews House**, a handsome Norman house which marks the beginning of the old city. It gives you some idea of the wealth coming into early medieval Lincoln, from wool and cloth-making. ('Lincoln Green' was Robin Hood's robe of choice.) By the 14th century it was

Getting There and Around

By **car**, Lincoln is east of the A1 at Newark, and on the A15 from Peterborough.

There are direct **train** services from Leicester, Nottingham, Boston and Newark; change at Newark from London King's Cross.

National Express runs one **coach** a day from London Victoria.

Tourist Information

Lincoln: 21 Cornhill, **t** (01522) 873 256. *Open Mon–Thurs 9.30–5.30, Fri 9.30–5, Sat 10–5.*

Lincoln's **Christmas market** attracts tens of thousands of visitors every year. It takes place over a long weekend in early December, around the cathedral, castle and lawns, with stalls selling cheeses and wooden toys, people wandering around in Victorian costume, carol singers and Dickensian ambience.

Where to Stay

Lincoln t (01522) –

The White Hart Hotel, Bailgate, **t** 526 222, *www.macdonaldhotels.co.uk* (*expensive*). Grand old building near the cathedral with 48 rooms; grand ballroom-style dining room, domed orangerie and bar.

D'Isney Place Hotel, Eastgate, **t** 538 881, *www.disneyplacehotel.co.uk* (*expensive*). Handsome old house with 17 rooms (three with Jacuzzis), diaphanous lime-green curtains and pastel walls. Breakfast in bed.

The Courtyard by Marriott, Brayford Wharf, **t** 544 244, *www.courtyard.co.uk/lcndt* (*expensive*). Swish, modern hotel overlooking Brayford Pool; 97 comfortable rooms.

The Castle Hotel, Westgate, **t** 538 801, *www.castlehotel.net* (*moderate*). Old-fashioned hotel in large Victorian house, with variable bathrooms.

Minster Lodge Hotel, 3 Church Lane, **t** 513 220 (*moderate*). Fifty yards from Newport Arch, huge house with large rooms; guests' lounge with piano and views of cathedral through bay windows.

30 Bailgate, 30 Bailgate, **t** 521 417 (*cheap*). Pretty, airy and bright Georgian house, just north of cathedral, with two pleasant rooms at top of tall house.

The Old Rectory Guesthouse, 19 Newport Road, **t** 514 774 (*cheap*). Three-storeyed Victorian townhouse near cathedral, with

all over: the Witham had silted up, diverting maritime trade to Boston, and the new bridge across the Trent at Newark diverted the Great North Road too. Now, Steep Hill is lined with art galleries and cafés. At the top of the hill are two stone gates – one into the cathedral and the other into the castle – and handsome timber-framed buildings. The west towers of the cathedral rise above the three-storey **Exchequer Gate**. Castle and cathedral stand on the site of the Roman legionary fortress and *colonia*. A short walk along Bailgate brings you to **Newport Arch**, the northern exit of *Lindis Colonia*, which still spans the road, and marks the northern extent of old Lincoln.

Lincoln Cathedral

> *...it does not seem like an inanimate object, but something that has a vast quiet life of its own... I only talk nonsense by trying to give my sense of this and other cathedrals.*
>
> Nathaniel Hawthorne, 1857

Entering the cathedral close through Exchequer Gate you are confronted by the spectacular **West Front**, a cliff of carved yellow stone. There are three tall arches; every other bit of space is covered in niches and decoration. Look out for the Romanesque frieze, illustrating Old Testament scenes to the right of the west door and New Testament scenes to the left. Inside, you get a theatrical experience of architecture broad staircase, slightly Spartan bedrooms and friendly atmosphere.

Eating Out

You may want to avoid the loud bars along the High Street and stay up town; the nicest restaurants are on Steep Hill.

Jews House, Steep Hill, **t** 524 851 (*moderate*). The city's most chic restaurant in its most ancient stone building, with two small dining rooms upstairs and another downstairs; chicken liver and foie gras pâté with mango chutney and melba toast, pan-fried John Dory with squid stir fry and saffron butter sauce. *Closed Sun and Mon.*

Black Horse Chambers, 6 Eastgate, **t** 544 404 (*moderate*). Lincoln's most welcoming pub, with intimate bistro serving such delicacies as grilled Lincolnshire sausages or cured salmon with mustard dressing. *Closed Sun and Mon.*

Le Papillon, St Paul's Lane, **t** 511 284 (*moderate*). Red-brick building tucked away beneath northeast tower of castle with flickering candles and partitions between tables creating intimate atmosphere; salmon in puff pastry. *Open Mon–Sat eves.*

Gino's, 7 Gordon Road (off Bailgate), **t** 513 770 (*moderate*). Brisk, bright, lively Italian restaurant with tiled floors, bare stone walls and orderly rows of tables.

Brown's Pie Shop, 33 Steep Hill, **t** 527 330 (*cheap*). Friendly restaurant near castle with pies including fish, game and rabbit.

Café Zoot, 5 Bailgate (opposite the White Hart Hotel), **t** 536 663 (*cheap*). Modern-style blue floor tiles and blue walls. Coffees and snacks all day, modern European cooking at night.

Pimento's, 26–27 Steep Hill, **t** 569 333 (*cheap*). Friendly hotchpotch tea room entered through clothes shop.

Bombay Restaurant, 6 The Strait (at bottom of Steep Hill), **t** 523 264 (*cheap*). Long-established, cosy restaurant with drawing-room atmosphere. *Open eves only.*

Entertainment

Theatre Royal, Clasketgate, **t** 525 555. Traditional theatre with prestigious touring productions.

There are occasional candle-lit **concerts in the cathedral**, **t** 544 544.

Lincoln Castle hosts summer productions of Shakespeare, **t** (01522) 511 068.

caused by variations of light and space and the shifting geometric perspectives of pointed Gothic arches and high vaulted ceilings. The star pattern of ribs down the nave is one of the earliest of its kind in England. The so-called crazy vault in **St Hugh's Choir** has an asymmetrical pattern of ribs that never quite resolve into shapes, no matter how hard you look. At either end of the transept crossing are the **Dean's Eye** and **Bishop's Eye**; these round windows are on the look out for good on the south side of the cathedral, where it is warm and bright, and evil lurking on the dark northern side. Standing under the central tower with your back to the nave is the **choir**, blocked off by the magnificent stone **choir screen**, carved in Decorated Gothic style. Every inch of it is carved in embroidered detail. The decoration continues around the archway into the south aisle of the choir with the tale of dragon-slayer St George. On your left is the ruined **shrine of Little St Hugh**, a boy allegedly executed by the Lincoln Jews in 1255 – resulting in their persecution and rapid departure from the city. Further east, you come to the **tomb of Catherine Swynford**, Duchess of Lancaster and third wife of John of Gaunt, one of whose many titles was Earl of Lincoln. From this marriage came the Beaufort line, from which Henry VII descended. Other tombs in the **Angel Choir** include the **visceral tomb of Eleanor of Castile**, Edward I's queen, who died in Harby, west of Lincoln; her internal organs were buried here, a cross was placed at each stop along the processional route back to London, and her body buried in Westminster

Abbey. Look out for the famous **Lincoln Imp**, a tiny carved devil with horns, cloven feat and a relaxed cross-legged posture.

From the north choir aisle, you enter the **cloisters**, which lead to the **old libraries**. Lincoln was never a monastic cathedral; these cloisters were for the canons. Cloisters and libraries suffered badly in a medieval fire; medieval manuscripts are displayed upstairs. Beyond is the pale, bright **Wren Library**, built in 1664 in place of the ruined north range. It stands on pillars so that the cloister walk can run all the way round.

On one side of the cathedral close are red-brick Georgian buildings. The other side drops down through a stone archway to the old (12th–17th-century) **Bishop's Palace** (*open April–Sept daily 10–5; adm*), an impressive ruin next to the 19th-century bishop's palace, now the diocesan offices. (The bishop now lives on East Gate.)

Lincoln Castle

***t** (01522) 511 068; open Mar–Oct Mon–Sat 9.30–4.30, Sun 11–4.30, Nov–Feb closes 3.30; adm*

Opposite Exchequer Gate at the top of Steep Hill, flanked by battlemented walls, is the main gateway into the castle. The walls *are* the castle really; within them are 18th- and 19th-century buildings – a red-brick prison and the Victorian Gothic Crown Court, on the site of the old great hall. The prison builders also restored Cob Tower, a 13th-century stone vaulted tower. In the Georgian prison is the Lincoln copy of the *Magna Carta* (one of four surviving copies).

North of Lincoln

The limestone ridge to the north of Lincoln is crisscrossed by quiet winding lanes with views over the patchwork fields of the Trent Valley. Take the B1398 north out of Lincoln in the direction of Kirton in Lindsey and turn off left to the village of **Stow**, with its interesting Saxon-Norman church next to the pub. Hidden behind a chestnut tree off a lane in the hamlet of **Snarford**, northeast of Lincoln up the A46, the church of St Lawrence holds the magnificent St Pauls family tombs. The St Pauls were successful Tudor lawyers and members of parliament, who acquired monastic lands after the Dissolution and built themselves Snarford Hall, an H-shaped Renaissance palace (now long gone). Sir Thomas (who died in 1582) and his wife, Faith, lie clutching prayer books on a six-poster bed. Sir Thomas's son George (who died in 1613) and his wife lie on their sides next door, propped up on their elbows.

Grantham and Around

Grantham is a spoiled old town in the Witham Valley, which developed as a major coaching centre on the Great North Road (the modern A1). Before the M1 motorway was built, travellers from London to Edinburgh passed through Grantham, stopping at one of the inns. In 1483, Richard III signed Buckingham's death warrant in the Angel

Where to Stay and Eat

Grantham t (01476) –

Archway Guest House, 15 Swinegate, **t** 561 807 (*moderate*). Attractive Georgian façade behind hedge; inside older with narrow flagstone hallway; cosy walled garden at back full of climbing plants and a jungle of pot plants.

Church View, 12 North Parade, **t** 560 815, *churchview@excite.com* (*cheap*). View of the neo-classical Roman Catholic church over the road; several pretty and comfortable bedrooms, almost next door to Maggie Thatcher's birthplace.

The Red House, 74 North Parade, **t** 579 869, *www.theredhouse.com* (*cheap*). Five-bedroom guesthouse at end of pretty Georgian terrace with bright red front door and lovely tiled hallway; very friendly.

Blue Pig, 9 Vine Street, **t** 563 704. Stone pub with black-and-white upper storey; inside heavy beamed ceilings and dark cosy rooms; home-made curry and sausages.

and Royal Hotel. The travel writers Celia Fiennes and Daniel Defoe both thought Grantham was a 'well-built town', oddly enough using exactly the same phrase. Charles Dickens had a soft spot for the old town, describing the George as 'the very best inn I have ever put up at' in a letter to his wife and 'one of the best inns in England' in *Nicholas Nickleby*. There is just enough of old Grantham – the church, some handsome Georgian buildings and the old timber-framed inns – to give an impression of the well-built town with the best inn. Famous Granthamians include the mathematician and natural philosopher Sir Isaac Newton (1642–1727), who was educated at King's School opposite St Wulfram's Church, and Margaret Thatcher, prime minister from 1979 to 1990, born here in 1925. Belton to the north, Woolsthorpe to the south and Belvoir Castle just over the Leicestershire border are all in easy reach.

Head for **St Wulfram's Church**, whose slender Gothic spire embellished with pinnacles is the glory of the town, rising out of a lovely close off Church Street. The sight of it made Ruskin faint. The aisles are as wide as the nave, the piers and arches between them so tall and thin as to be practically invisible. The shrine of St Wulfram is in the crypt chapel. Have a look at the tiny 16th-century chained library, up a narrow flight of stone stairs. On the south side of the church is the old **King's School**, which Sir Isaac Newton attended, lodging down the road. Back down High Street, past the façade of the old **George Inn**, are the civic buildings on St Peter's Hill. The **museum** (*t (01476) 568 783; open Mon–Sat 10–5*) has display cases on Newton (whose statue stands outside the Guildhall), and Maggie kitsch. The Iron Lady's birthplace is on the corner of Broad Street and North Parade.

Belton House (*t (01476) 566 116; open April–Oct Wed–Sun 12.30– 5.30; adm*), the magnificent Restoration house of the Brownlows, is 3 miles north of Grantham in beautiful countryside, just off the A607. It was built between 1685 and 1688 in Dutch style for Sir John Brownlow, who had inherited the Belton estate and a vast sum of money from his great-uncle, a London lawyer. It remained in the Brownlow family until 1984. The house – H-shaped with symmetrical honey façades crowned with a cupola – stands within formal gardens surrounded by parkland. There are more than 200 pictures, Regency furniture, ornate plaster ceilings, wood carvings, tapestries and some rooms by James Wyatt, who altered the house in the 1770s. Belton appeared as Rosings in the 1995 BBC *Pride and Prejudice* starring Colin Firth as Darcy.

Woolsthorpe Manor (**t** *(01476) 860 338; open April–Sept Wed–Sun 1–5, Mar and Oct weekends 1–5; adm*) was the home of Sir Isaac Newton. Turn off the A1 south of Grantham onto the B767, and follow signs to the old stone farmhouse. The family of the mathematician were yeomen farmers, modestly prosperous to judge by the sturdy look of the place, all Ancaster stone walls and oak. Isaac would have been a fifth generation farmer. Instead he went to Trinity College, Cambridge. He returned home after graduating to avoid the plague, and developed his ground-breaking ideas about optics, the motion of falling and rotating bodies and calculus. All that remains of Newton here is a lock of hair and his death mask.

Stamford

The handsome old stone town of Stamford, astride the River Welland, grew rich on wool and cloth in the Middle Ages, developed as a coaching town in the 18th and 19th centuries and went into decline in the late 19th century when the Marquis of Exeter forced the new northern railway route through Peterborough instead – preserving old Stamford. The old stone buildings are crammed together and the old churches appear in *Nicholas Nickleby*, rising 'frowning and dark from the whitened ground' when Nicholas's coach passes through on its way to Yorkshire. There are five churches in cobbled squares framed by Georgian townhouses. The charm of Stamford's tangle of narrow streets, shops selling country produce and antiques, and decent old-fashioned pubs is compounded by the proximity of Rutland Water and magnificent stately piles.

The River Welland divides Stamford into two unequal sections, each with its own High Street. The heart of town is north of the river. **All Saints**, one of two spired churches, is in its own cobbled enclave at the top of town, surrounded on two sides by Georgian townhouses (and an excellent pub). The antiquarian William Stukeley (1687–1765) was vicar from 1729 to 1747. On the other side of the road is **Red Lion Square** (the market square), sealed off by the tower of St John's.

Broad Street, leading off All Saints Place, also has stalls running up and down on market days. The chapel of **Brown's Hospital** (*open summer weekends 10–5*) was consecrated in 1494, five years after the death of benefactor William Brown, a wealthy Stamford wool merchant. The almshouses frame a pretty grass courtyard behind the chapel. At the end of Broad Street is **Stamford Museum** (**t** *(01780) 766 317; open all year Mon–Sat 10–5, April–Sept also Sun 2–5*),with a life-sized replica of Daniel Lambert, a famous 52-stone fat man, who died in 1809 at the Stamford races. Tom Thumb, on tour in Britain, used to entertain a crowd by standing in the armhole of his waistcoat. Scenes of a 1993 TV adaptation of *Middlemarch* were filmed in St George's Square, south of Broad Street, with the church at one end, theatre at the other and Georgian stone houses in between.

The beautiful spired church of **St Mary's** commands a prominent position at the top of St Mary's Hill leading down to the bridge. Across the river, the road becomes High Street St Martin's, flanked by several old inns as it heads towards Burghley House. From the George Hotel a wooden gallows beam reaches across the street. **St Martin's**

Getting There

By **car**, Stamford is just off the A1. There is cheap all-day **parking** in the Cattle Market car park on the St Martin's side of Town Bridge. Walk over the footbridge into town.

By **train** from north or south change at Peterborough. From the southwest change at Birmingham for the cross-country service.

National Express runs one **coach** a day from London Victoria.

Tourist Information

Stamford: 27 St Mary's Street, **t** (01780) 755 611. *Open Mon–Sat 9.30–5, Sun 11–4.*

Friday is **market day**, with stalls running down Broad Street and spilling down Iron Mongers' Lane. There is a small **farmers' market** on Red Lion Square on Saturday, and a larger one every other Friday in Red Lion Square, selling local produce such as cheese, honey and ostrich burgers.

Stamford Festival takes place late June–early July, opening with a parade and riverside music festival. Ask at tourist information centre for details.

Burghley Horse Trials, a four-day event, takes place late Aug–early Sept, at Burghley Park, **t** (01780) 752 131, one of the top cross-country courses in the country, set up by the 5th Marquis of Burghley, the Olympic hurdler David Cecil, in 1961.

Where to Stay and Eat

Stamford t (01780) –

The George Hotel, St Martin's, **t** 750 750, *www.georgehotelofstamford.com* (*very expensive*). Stamford's largest, oldest coaching inn, projecting an old gallows beam over the High Street, has put up the rich and famous for centuries. It is a place of big fireplaces, oak panelling and several bars and restaurants; on one side of the entrance hall is the York Room and on the other the London Room, once departure lounges for north- and south-bound travellers along the Great North Road. If you can't afford to stay in one of the 47 rooms, at least come for (*expensive*) dinner of Woodbridge duck or roast pork, lunch in the florid cobbled courtyard, a drink or morning coffee.

The Garden House Hotel, High Street St Martins, **t** 763 359, *www.garden-house-*

houses the Cecil family monuments, including that of Sir William Cecil, right-hand man to Elizabeth I and builder of Burghley House, whose effigy is stretched out on a coloured marble six-poster bed, peering up at a golden canopy. The 5th Earl, who furnished Burghley, is commemorated with spears and togas to show off his cultural affinity with Italy. In the churchyard is the grave of Daniel Lambert (*see* above). His sturdy walking stick is pinned up underneath his portrait in the George Hotel.

Burghley House

t *(01780) 752 451; open Easter–Oct daily 11–5; adm exp.*

It would be endless to give a detail of the fine pieces his lordship bought from Italy, all originals, and by the best masters; 'tis enough to say, they infinitely exceed all that can be seen in England, and are of more value than the house itself, and all the park belonging to it.

Daniel Defoe, 1724

Burghley House is 1½ miles east of Stamford; you can reach it on the B1443 (Barnack Road) or on foot through Burghley Park. The 1st Lord Burghley, Sir William Cecil, was lord treasurer and adviser to Elizabeth I. The Queen liked to travel around the country *hotel.com* (*expensive*). An 18th-century townhouse in a quiet area with flagstone hall and Belgian tapestries in the dining room; dinner (*moderate*) might be monkfish kebab; conservatory bar full of plants; 20 bedrooms with handsome beds.

The Crown Hotel, All Saints Place, **t** 763 136, *www.thecrownhotelstamford.co.uk* (*moderate*). Handsome, gabled stone-built inn overlooking Red Lion Square and All Saints Church with 19 bedrooms and an excellent bar with high-backed wooden settles and daylight flooding in through its bay window. Eat in the bar or civilized restaurant.

Candlesticks Hotel and Restaurant, 1 Church Lane, **t** 764 033 (*moderate*). Attractive corner building just off High Street St Martins, with eight tiny, crowded bedrooms; cosy, candle-lit restaurant in the old cellars serves hearty French, English and Portuguese food. *Closed Mon.*

Fratelli Ristorante, 13 St Mary's Hill, **t** 754 333 (*cheap*). Lively Italian restaurant with three dining rooms including cellar and conservatory; welcoming; jaunty music.

Rush Internet Café, 5 St Mary's Street, **t** 767 874 (*cheap*). Newspapers, sofas, all sorts of tea and coffee, ciabatta rolls and bagels.

Central Restaurant and Tea Shop, Red Lion Square (*cheap*). Beautiful old building with upstairs seating overlooking the square, gentle old-world atmosphere and décor and quietly diligent uniformed staff. Serves hearty lunches of steak and ale pie, fish and chips, Lincolnshire sausages.

8 South View Terrace, Newcross Road (up Scotgate from town centre), **t** 755 987 (*cheap*). Comfortable, friendly house with cosy rooms; short walk into town.

Entertainment

Stamford Arts Centre, 27 St Mary's Street, **t** 480 846. Beautiful old Georgian theatre with one auditorium doubling as theatre and cinema. Resident Shoestring Company puts on four productions a year, plus touring productions and children's puppet theatre. Café and bar.

Rutland Open Air Theatre at Tolethorpe Hall (3 miles north of Stamford), **t** 756 133, *www.stamfordshakespeare.co.uk*. Stamford Shakespeare Company puts on outdoor productions of Shakespeare plays here every summer; the audience sits under a canopy.

in summer and be entertained at the expense of her courtiers; many were bankrupted trying to meet her needs. Lord Burghley built his prodigy house, as these royal lodgings were known, around a quadrangle. The elaborate Renaissance roof, with its onion-domed turrets, arches, obelisks and chimneys disguised as Ionic columns, doubled up as a promenade. But the Queen never made it to Burghley. The interiors were rebuilt and furnished in the 17th century by the 5th Earl, who married Anne Cavendish, daughter of the 3rd Earl of Devonshire. They toured Europe, buying more than 400 paintings, furniture, tapestries and ceramics, and brought in the leading decorative artists and craftsmen of the day (Antonio Verrio, Louis Laguerre and Grinling Gibbons) to work on the place in their absence. Long galleries were done away with in favour of a series of apartments with more walls for hanging paintings and corners for furniture and large decorative pots. The 7th Earl continued to transform Burghley, bringing in Capability Brown to remodel the park and expanding the collection of paintings.

The highlight of the decorative artwork is the ceiling and wall-paintings by Verrio in the **Heaven Room** and **Hell Staircase**. On the walls are portraits, Romantic Italian landscapes and religious paintings. The 19th-century poet John Clare worked as gardener here for a time, when he was living just down the road in Helpston.

The Lincolnshire Wolds

The chalk scenery of the Wolds stretches from Louth to Old Bolingbroke. The rolling Wolds roads are just the thing for gentle touring through the countryside. On summer weekends you are guaranteed to be overtaken by bikers from the Cadwell Park race track. The market towns of **Spilsby**, **Horncastle** and **Alford** are pleasant stop-offs, their town squares appealingly shabby. Each has produced a famous adventurer: Joseph Banks (Horncastle), Sir John Franklin (Spilsby) and 17th-century Massachusetts Nonconformist leader Ann Hutchinson (Alford). Alford is the most charming, with its manor-house folk museum, a 17th-century thatched building with brick-clad mud and straw walls (on the verge of collapse).

Louth

Louth, on the eastern edge of the Wolds, is the best base for the area. Its Georgian townhouses, market square and magnificent church steeple – the tallest in England – are a pleasure to behold. Off Market Place are shopping streets, as well as the old Market Hall – now selling everything from socks to garden tools. The Ancaster stone church steeple is 295 feet high, 23 feet higher than Grantham's (but two hundred years younger) and decorated with ballflowers and pinnacles. In October 1536, shortly after it was finished, the vicar was executed at Tyburn for his part in the Lincolnshire Rising, a rebellion against the Reformation, which started in Louth. In summer, you can climb to the base of the spire for the views over the marshes to the coast.

For pleasant chalk scenery walk or drive to **Hubbard's Hills**, a steep wooded valley a mile south of Louth (turn off Upgate into Gospelgate, then Crowtree Lane).

Woodhall Spa

Woodhall Spa, south of Horncastle on the B1191, developed in the 1830s around mineral-rich spring waters discovered by prospectors for coal. It feels like a cross between a German spa of the 1920s and an Edwardian garden suburb. At the end of the Broadway is a memorial to the 617 'Dambusters' squadron. Petwood House Hotel, a Victorian confection smothered in black-and-white beamwork, and surrounded by sweeping lawns and clipped hedges, was used as the officers' mess of 617 squadron in the Second World War. The bar is a shrine, full of Dambusters memorabilia.

Tattershall and Coningsby

Half way along the Sleaford–Bolingbroke road, Tattershall and the RAF town of Coningsby run into one another. In 1434, Ralph Cromwell, one of Henry VI's councillors, pulled down the old castle of Robert de Tattershall, and built himself a new **Tattershall Castle** (***t*** *(01526) 342 543, www.nationaltrust.org.uk; open Mar and Nov–Christmas weekends 12–4, April–Oct Sat–Wed 11–5.30, Oct 11–4; adm*) out of the profits of a career in royal service. Sea-going boats, sailing up the Witham into the Bain, had direct access into the double moat. Later it was the home of the Countess of Lincoln, who financed the transatlantic expedition in 1630 that led to the creation of the American Boston. In 1911 Lord Curzon (of Derbyshire) restored the castle at huge

Getting There and Around

By **car** along the A1 to Newark-on-Trent, then cross-country via Lincoln.

It's a hard area to reach by train: the nearest stations are Market Rasen (10 miles) and Grimsby (14 miles); from London King's Cross you have to change at Newark.

A National Express **coach** runs daily from London Victoria to Louth.

The **Viking Way** long-distance footpath and Hull–Harwich **cycle route** run though Woodhall Spa.

Tourist Information

Louth: Newmarket Hall (off Cornmarket), **t** (01507) 609 289. *Open Mon–Sat 9–5*. Wed, Fri, Sat **market** in Cornmarket

Where to Stay and Eat

Louth t (01507) –

Beaumont Hotel, Victoria Road (1½ miles from the town centre), **t** 605 005, *www.thebeaumonthotel.co.uk* (*moderate*). Pretty white-painted building with creeper climbing up wall and shutters; 16 bedrooms. Italian-style restaurant.

The Priory, Eastgate, **t** 602 930, *www.theprioryhotel.com* (*moderate*). Homely Victorian-Gothic country house, 10 minutes' walk along Eastgate from town centre; 12 en-suite bedrooms with leafy William Morris quilt covers; beautiful lounge and tiny restaurant and garden.

Kennington House, 5 Kennington Road, **t** 603 973, *www.kenningtonhouse.co.uk* (*moderate*). Informal and relaxed, rambling, richly wallpapered Victorian house with friendly hosts; short walk into town.

Beverley's Café, Eastgate, **t** 354 193 (*cheap*). Small, stalwart café beside town hall for cakes, teas and dinners.

Mason's Arms, Cornmarket, **t** 609 525 (*cheap*). Best pub for grub, serving fresh Grimsby haddock, still tasting of the sea, with rocket salad and mushy peas.

Thai Silk, Mercer Row, **t** 354 193 (*cheap*). Good Thai classics.

Via Italia, Upgate, **t** 608 464 (*cheap*). Lively Italian place serving a good range of pasta, meat and fish.

Woodhall Spa t (01526) –

The Petwood Hotel, Stixwould Road (on edge of Woodhall Spa), **t** 352 411, *www.petwood.co.uk* (*expensive*). Huge black-and-white timber-clad oak-panelled building in 30 acres of gardens – all clipped hedges, rhododendrons and woods – home of the 617 'Dambuster' Squadron in the Second World War. There are 50 bedrooms, a restaurant (*moderate*) and bars including the squadron bar, full of memorabilia. Nice place to have lunch or drink on terrace.

Dower House Hotel, Manor Estate, **t** 352 588, *www.dowerhousehotel.co.uk* (*moderate*). Secluded family-run Victorian hotel, surrounded by pretty wooded garden; grand hunting-lodge-style stairway, stained glass and seven comfortable bedrooms. English restaurant (*moderate*).

expense in solid Edwardian style, with magnificent details such as fireplaces and brick ribbing in the passages. From the roof: you can see the Boston Stump to the south, Lincoln Cathedral to the west, and the Wolds to the north.

On the other side of the moat, the vast Perpendicular church of Ancaster stone, almost transparent with its massive windows, was also commissioned by Cromwell though not built in his lifetime. It has a tea shop and cake stall at one end.

The RAF flies tornados out of **Coningsby**, one of two RAF airbases remaining in Lincolnshire. It is also the base of the **Battle of Britain Memorial Flight Museum** (**t** *(01526) 344 041;open summer Mon–Fri 10–3.30 (last tour), winter 10–3 (last tour); adm*), a collection of Second World War planes including the Hurricane, Lancaster and Spitfire (sometimes the Decoter as well) which perform fly-pasts at air shows around the country in summer.

Of the 7,377 Lancaster bombers built in the Second World War, only three remain in airworthy condition, one at RAF Coningsby, another in Canada and the third 5 miles from Coningsby at the **Lincolnshire Aviation Heritage Museum** (***t*** *(01790) 763 207; open Easter–Oct Mon–Sat 9.30–5, Nov–Feb 9.30–4; adm*), on the site of the old East Kirkby airfield, home to two bomber squadrons, 57 and 630. This one, the Lancaster NX 611, was built in 1945, too late for the war. Now, sitting on the original Tarmac in a restored hangar, it looks off-the-assembly-line good – 37,330 pounds of gleaming black, its Merlin engines roaring to join the Dambusters. Next to it is one of the 4½-ton practice bouncing bombs, recovered from Reculver Bay off the east Kent coast.

From the A155 Coningsby road, a narrow lane leads off to **Old Bolingbroke**, a tiny village of pretty cottages. Here are the low stone ruins of **Bolingbroke Castle** (*open daily dawn–dusk*), one of John of Gaunt's – D-shaped towers and the remains of a moat. This is where Henry Bolingbroke, the future Henry IV, was born on 3 April 1367.

The Lincolnshire Coast

There are no bays, coves, headlands, cliffs, rock pools or coastal roads with sea views on the Lincolnshire coast. Just sand, lots of sand and the starry skies above, extending in an unbroken line from Gibraltar Point to Cleethorpes behind tussocky dunes. The Lincolnshire seaside is backed by fields of cows and wheat, and covered by endless skies. It is a place of great wide views. The faded resort towns of the East Midlands holiday coast – Skegness, Maplethorpe, Cleethorpes – are tacky and ordinary, like Blackpool without the Tower, but between them, even during school holidays, the beaches are empty but for the odd dog walker. That's where to go – walking, kite-flying, filling your lungs with North Sea air, picnicking behind windbreaks, plunging into the cold, getting tired out so that you can drink hot tea and eat cakes for the rest of the day. For a half day's walk, head to Huttoft Bank car park and walk south down the beach to Anderby Creek, a cheerful little chalet-and-caravan resort with a little café and shop selling ice creams, buckets and spades, Frisbees and so on.

A mile or two south of Skegness, **Gibraltar Point National Nature Reserve** (***t*** *(01754) 762 677; visitor centre open May–Oct daily 10.30–5, Nov–April weekends 11–4; adm minimal*) inhabits the 'ness' at the northern tip of the Wash. The marshes and l agoons behind the sand dunes attract flocks of birds – thrushes, starlings, geese and ducks in winter, and migrating waders including cranes in the spring and summer.

One of the best stretches of coast road runs between Mablethorpe and North Somercotes. The **Donna Nook Nature Reserve** includes six miles of coastline between North Somercotes and Saltfleet Haven (parts of it are used by the military to test weapons, so watch out for red flags). Follow the RAF signs to the Stonebridge car park, north of North Somercote, down the long the straight marsh road to the sea. The big attraction is the colony of grey seals, which every year in November and December come in on the high tide and pup on the dunes behind the beach. At other times the beach, wide and wet at low tide, is deserted. Watch out for the rapidly incoming tide, and RAF signs warning not to touch any debris, which 'may explode and kill you'.

The Lincolnshire Fens

The A16 and A17 Fenland roads give a good feel for the Lincolnshire Fens, the flat region of arable farmland around the Wash, extending inland to Market Deeping and south into Cambridgeshire. They have not always been so monotonous. When the antiquarian William Camden travelled through Lincolnshire in the 16th century, he found 'foule and flabby quaremires, yea, and the most troublesome Fennes, which the very inhabitants for all their stilts cannot stalke through.' Within a generation, the Dutch engineer Cornelius Vermuyden had begun draining the Bedford Levels, for which he got a parcel of reclaimed farmland about the size of Rutland. Now much of the fenland is several feet below sea level and falling. If the pumps stopped pumping water out, some of the best wheat fields in the country would revert to quagmires.

Spalding and Crowland

From Stamford, the River Welland flows north over the levels to **Spalding**. It has been navigable from Spalding to the Wash since the 1600s. There has always been produce to export; it was wool before the Earl of Bedford drained the Fens. It has been bulbs since the 19th century, daffodils and tulips which you see grown in colourful strips in spring. If you can, come for the flower festival at the beginning of May; the floral parades originated in 1959 to use up the waste product (flowers) of the bulb-growing industry. Pop into **Ayscoughfey Hall** (***t** (01775) 725 468; closed until 2005*), the grand 15th-century home of a wool merchant. The **church of St Mary and St Nicholas** has an impressive 15th-century hammer-beam roof carved with angels.

The A16 Spalding–Crowland road is a good Fenland road, raised above the level of the fields. **Crowland** grew up around an island monastery, founded by Saxon hermit St Guthlac. It feels like the setting for an M.R. James ghost story. At the crossroads is a 14th-century stone bridge, **Trinity Bridge**, which once spanned the confluence of three rivers. They have dried up, but there the bridge still stands, bridging the ghost of a river. On one side is the stone statue of either King Ethelbald or Jesus Christ, taken from the old abbey church. East Street leads to the old Benedictine abbey. The Abbot of Crowland founded Magdalene College in Cambridge in 1439 for his monks to study. After the Dissolution, the north aisle was converted into the parish church. Next to it is the west front, covered in statues and magnificent St Guthlac carving.

Boston

The whole scene made an odd impression of bustle, and sluggishness and decay, and a little remnant of wholesome life; and I could not but contrast it with the mighty activity of our own Boston, which was once the feeble infant of this old English town.

Nathaniel Hawthorne, 1857

The old Hanseatic seaport stands just inland of the Wash, connected to the sea by a tidal channel known as the Haven. However you get there, your landmark is the tower of St Botolph's church, known as the **Boston Stump** (*open daily 8.30–5*), which shoots nearly 300 feet above the surrounding flatness. Hawthorne envied the jackdaws 'who

Getting There and Around

By **car**, take the A1 to Stamford, then the A16, or continue on the A1 to Newark-on-Trent where you can pick up the A17 via Sleaford.

Trains run from London King's Cross to Peterborough, then a branch line to Boston.

National Express **coaches** from London Victoria run daily.

Tourist Information

Boston: Market Place, **t** (01205) 356 656. *Open Mon–Sat 9–5.*

Where to Stay and Eat

Boston t (01205) –

New England Hotel, Wide Bargate, **t** 365 255, *www.thenewengland.co.uk* (*moderate*). The only decent hotel in town, a handsome Georgian building with low plaster ceilings, panelled walls and a wide staircase; 28 bedrooms with slightly tired décor and a (*moderate*) restaurant.

Otherwise, your best bet is to try one or two modest guesthouses on the main roads into Boston. Try **Fairfield Guest House**, London Road, **t** 362 869 (*cheap*), an Edwardian house with 15 bedrooms, a big garden and modern extension at back, or **Bramley House**, Sleaford Road, **t** 354 538 (*cheap*) with nine bedrooms, 1½ miles from town centre.

Boston isn't much fun at night: its pubs cater for a rowdy crowd, while the restaurants all specialize in mixed grills.

The Italian Connection, 8–10 West Street, **t** 350 287 (*moderate*). Low-ceilinged restaurant with shiny tiled floor and marble tables; sunny Mediterranean atmosphere, good pizzas and courteous, uniformed Italian waiters.

Maud Foster Windmill, Willoughby Road, **t** 352 188 (*cheap*). Working flour mill with café-restaurant. Home-cooked lunches make use of local produce like Lincolnshire poacher cheese, Boston sausage and Bateman's beer marinades. *Open Wed, Sat and Sun pm, July–Aug also Thurs and Fri.*

Eagles Fish and Chip Shop, 50 Main Bridge (*cheap*). *Closed Sun and Mon.*

Good Barns Yard, Wormgate. Friendly family pub behind church with riverside beer garden through coaching arch. Popular in the afternoon for a drink and chips.

Entertainment

If you're here overnight, **Black Friar's Art Centre**, Spain Lane (near Customs House Quay), **t** (01205) 363 108, is the best place to while away an evening, watching a film and having a drink at the upstairs bar.

live a delightful life up there'. It was built in the Middle Ages, when Boston was one of the richest towns in the country, exporting raw wool to Flanders, Belgium and northern France. Inevitable decline, due to the silting of the river, was arrested in the 18th century. The draining of Holland Fen on the west side of the Witham, followed by East Fen and West Fen north of Boston, placed the old seaport at the centre of some of the best arable farming in England. New docks opened downriver in 1884, which continue in a modest way today. As Hawthorne pointed out, Massachusetts was founded by Nonconformist settlers from this little Fenland port. Various high-powered old Bostonians assumed key government positions when they got there. There is another New World connection. It was from Boston in 1607 that a group of Nonconformists (from Scrooby in north Nottinghamshire), made their first attempt to escape to Holland. They were betrayed and ended up in Boston prison, but some of them were among the Pilgrim Fathers on the *Mayflower* 13 years later.

Come on market day if you can, when the large main square in front of the church is filled with covered stalls, and the impression of 'sluggishness and decay' is alleviated to some extent by 'bustle'.

The Haven flows through the middle of town, at low tide revealing mildewy river walls and a great deal of mud. On the east bank, the tower of **St Botolph's** rises out of the shabby Market Square. Tall and elegant, its nickname – the Boston Stump – refers to the lack of a point in a county remarkable for church spires. Instead it has a regal-looking lantern tower encased in pinnacles, which would not look out of place in the Netherlands. The medieval wool trade produced a glorious, cathedral-sized interior, with light pouring in through windows and clerestory. One of the windows in the north aisle commemorates the departure of the new Bostonians in 1630. The vicar of St Botolph's, John Cotton, followed the first wave of around 250 families three years later. In the chancel are some good examples of 14th-century miserichords, one of a school master birching a boy who protects himself with a book. You can climb the tower (*open 10–4; adm*), up a narrow stone staircase, for the views.

From the Market Place, narrow lanes and alleys lead off in all directions. Follow the Haven south to the old **Customs House Quay**, which used to be the main Boston dock (until the Victorians built a new one in 1884). You get an impression of its former importance from the old customs house and medieval guildhall on its banks. The 15th-century **Guildhall of St Mary** (***t*** *(01205) 365 954; closed until 2006*) was converted into the town hall and court after the Reformation (when all the old religious guilds were suppressed); prison cells were added later. You can see the cells downstairs in which the Scooby Nonconformists were imprisoned, before being sent back home. Next to the Guildhall is **Fydell House**, the handsome Georgian house of William Fydell, three times mayor of Boston. Go inside and left into the American Room, which was opened in 1938 by US ambassador Joseph Kennedy, father of JFK.

The Pilgrim Fathers' Memorial at Fishtoft

You will need a car to get from Boston to Fishtoft. Aim for the docks and turn down Skirbeck Road, through the back end of Boston for a few miles, until you see the sign for the Pilgrim Fathers' Memorial. The memorial marks the spot where the Scooby Puritans (the nucleus of the Pilgrim Fathers' expedition in 1620) were betrayed by the Dutch captain of the ship supposed to take them to Holland, and thrown into Boston prison. It's an atmospheric spot with tugs going up and down, views of the Stump, and dockyard cranes. From here, there is a 2½-mile walk down the Haven to the Cut End bird hide on the edge of the Wash.

Northamptonshire

The limestone belt is always lovely, from Rutland through Northamptonshire to the Cotswolds. It used to be the countryside of fox hunts, like the old Pytchely Hunt in north Northamptonshire. The villages are unusually pretty, built in the local stone, warm brown to creamy-white. The number of great houses in Northamptonshire, many still privately owned, can be explained by the scenery, building materials, hunting, farmland and links to London down the old north road – the modern M1/A5. However, many of the towns in Northamptonshire, excluding Oundle, developed as industrial centres, and are best avoided. If you can, base yourself in the countryside outside the towns, or in neighbouring towns like Stamford, Oakham and Uppingham.

Northampton

Northampton is disappointing, except for the area around Market Place and Giles Street, with its Gothic town hall and old banks. The market bustles, surrounded by handsome townhouses built after the great fire of 1675, but the glory of the town is the Wren-style **All Saints' Church**, built by Henry Bell of King's Lynn. Northamptonshire poet John Clare, as an inmate of Northampton General Asylum, used to sit on the steps of the portico between the Ionic columns and watch the world go by. The old Gothic medieval tower rises above the neo-classical portico as if it were its natural

Getting There and Around

By **car**, follow the A45 from the M1.

There are regular, direct **trains** from London Euston.

Direct National Express **coaches** from London Victoria.

Tourist Information

Northampton: Museum and Art Gallery, Guildhall Road, **t** (01604) 622 677. *Open Mon–Fri 10–5, Sun 2–5.*

A **hot-air balloon festival** is held annually over the second weekend of August on the Northampton race course.

Where to Stay

Northampton t (01604) –

You are unlikely to want to stay overnight in Northampton, but the countryside around is full of cosy pubs and good places to stay.

Broom Hill Hotel, Holdenby Road, Spratton, **t** 845 959, *www.broomhillhotel.co.uk* (*moderate*). Gabled red-brick Victorian hotel set on hill amid rolling countryside, 8 miles north of Northampton. Large, well-tended gardens feature swimming pool and tennis court. Traditional English cooking in the restaurant.

Red Lion Hotel, East Haddon, **t** 770 223, *www.redlionhoteleasthaddon.co.uk* (*moderate*). Seven miles from Northampton, off the A428 to Rugby, a thatched ironstone building with neat bedrooms and Victorian décor in restaurant and bar.

Nobottle Grange, near Brington villages, on edge of Althorp estate, **t** 759 494 (*moderate*). Nicely furnished red-brick farmhouse with sweeping views and four comfortable bedrooms

Eating Out

Fox and Hounds, Great Brington, **t** 770 651 (*cheap*). Outstanding village pub with flagstone floors, open fireplace, fresh flowers and 10 real ales. Serves hearty, home-cooked English country-inn-style food including steak and kidney pie, beef and Guinness casserole, pheasant and partridge in season.

Spencer Arms, Chapel Brampton (on Northampton road), **t** 842 237 (*cheap*). Large, popular old pub with friendly young staff; roast lamb or gammon, egg and chips.

For a quick boost, get a takeaway coffee and roll to eat on the steps of All Saints' church, as John Clare used to on his trips out from the asylum, or try one of the following:

The Corner House, St Giles' Square, **t** 636 943. You can sit outside with a coffee looking towards the tower of All Saints' Church.

Rat and Parrot, St Giles' Square, **t** 239 534. Another place to sit outside, with an appealing courtyard.

Lawrence's Bakery, St Giles' Street, **t** 637 939. Pleasantly old-fashioned, with small coffee shop and sandwiches to take away.

foundation. Daylight streams through the dome into the peach-and-white plastered interior. In the entrance lobby is a **bust of John Clare** (1793–1864). To get an idea of the great man, go to **Abington Street Library** and look up 'Journey out of Essex' in *Autobiographical Writings*, which describes his escape back to Northampton-shire on foot from Epping Forest Hospital. In the town **museum** *(**t** (01604) 837 837; open Mon–Sat 10–5, Sun 2–5)* you can find out about shoe-making, Northampton's main industry since the Middle Ages, when shoe-makers were known as cordwainers. The shoes on display range from court shoes worn by royalty to a 19th-century post boy's boots, as big as moon boots.

Both the Leicester and Rugby roads out of Northampton head into a countryside of golden summer fields, pretty ironstone villages (the Bringtons and Bramptons and Holdenby) and leafy minor lanes.

Althorp Park

t (01604) 770 006; open July–Sept daily 10–5; adm exp.

Since the death of Diana, Princess of Wales in 1997, the Spencer family home near Northampton has been receiving about 2,000 visitors a day during its short opening season. The Spencers have been at Althorp since the 1500s. They came from Warwickshire, having already established themselves as major-league sheep farmers. Over the next few hundred years they notched up titles (including the earldom of Sunderland), political careers and married into the Marlborough family in the 18th century. The 3rd Earl married Lady Anne, daughter of the Blenheim war hero the Duke of Marlborough. The Duke's wife, Sarah Jennings, was lady-in-waiting to Queen Anne and reputedly ruled for her. When the Marlboroughs produced no male heir, the title went with their daughter to Althorp, returning to Blenheim with the next generation, Charles Spencer, 5th Earl of Sunderland, who became the 3rd Duke of Marlborough. The youngest son, John Spencer, in place of titles, inherited his grandmother Sarah Jennings' entire worldly fortune: houses, paintings, furniture and cash. John's son, another John, became the 1st Earl Spencer in 1765. The house was remodelled by Henry Holland in a restrained French neo-classical style, which seems rather plain compared with Blenheim. Althorp is known for its collection of portraits, including a wall of Peter Lely portraits of the ladies of Charles II's court. One of the most famous paintings in the collection is the double portrait by Van Dyck at the end of the Picture Gallery of the Earl of Bristol and the Duke of Bedford, both of whom are related to the Spencers. There are family portraits of sporting types on horses on the walls of every room, complimented by photographs of faces you have seen in *Hello!* magazine.

Princess Diana is buried on a wooded island in the middle of an oval lake, a short walk from the house. At the far end is the **Diana Temple**. The **Diana Exhibition**, on one side of the stables courtyard, includes all sorts of memorabilia such as her outfits and the books of condolence signed by thousands of the people for the 'queen of hearts' after her tragic death. Video montages feature a young Diana jumping around at birthday parties, a grown-up Diana with her boys and, of course, the funeral.

Walk down to **St Mary's Church**, where you can see the family monuments of 20 generations of Spencers. You have to peer through the screen into the Spencer chapel, built in 1514, to see their richly canopied and carved tombs.

Great Houses of Northamptonshire

Holdenby House (*t (01604) 770 074; open Easter–Sept, gardens and falconry centre Sun 1–5, July–Aug Sun–Fri 11–5; house by appointment only; adm*), a few miles from Althorp, was home of Christopher Hatton, a prominent figure in Northamptonshire and one of Elizabeth I's favourites, who rose to Lord Chancellor in 1587. He refused to move into Holdenby until the Queen's first visit, for which it was built in 1583. Only one wing – an eighth of the original building – survives of his mansion, which in its time was the largest house in England, with 123 glass windows. The cost of building both Holdenby and Kirby Hall, up the road, bankrupted Hatton, who died in 1591. Holdenby went to James I, in lieu of debts, then the Marlboroughs, and finally the Lowthers, who still own it. The house is rarely open, so you may have to make do with the gardens and falconry centre.

Brixworth church forms the visual focus of a vista over the park from **Cottesbrooke Hall** (*t (01604) 505 808; open May–Sept Wed and Thurs 2–5.30; adm*), whose precise Queen Anne geometry and elaborate formal gardens suggest an absolute degree of composure, rather than a statement of power, within the countryside. In spite of its acres of farmland and priceless art and furniture collections, this is a comfortable country house. The highlight is the renowned **Woolavington Collection** of sporting paintings, the largest in Europe. It was assembled in the late 19th and early 20th centuries by Lord Woolavington, down in Sussex (his house, Lavington Park, is now Seaford College, but the family still owns the Lavington stud) and came to Cottesbrook with his descendants between the wars. The paintings, many by George Stubbs and Ben Marshall, with their horsy titles – *Gimcrack on Newmarket Heath* and *Thomas Oldaker on Pickle* – hang on every wall. The formal terraced gardens, laid out by Sir Geoffrey Jelicoe with statuary and cone-shaped yews, are worth coming to see even if the house is closed.

Further north on the Market Harborough road, you come to the Palladian mansion of **Kelmarsh Hall** (*t (01604) 686 485; house and gardens open Easter–Sept Sun 2–5, July and Aug also Thurs 2–5; adm*), built by James Gibbs between 1728 and 1732. Nancy Lancaster, one of the 20th century's most influential interior decorators, lived here twice, first as the wife of Ronald Tree, a wealthy American, then as Nancy Lancaster, having divorced Tree and remarried her former landlord, Colonel Lancaster. Here she developed her trademark brand of shabby chic, a combination of chintzy fabrics and antiques suggesting taste without fastidiousness, informal grandeur and unstuffy glamour. When she and the colonel separated, Nancy bought the interior design firm Colefax and Fowler and established her reputation. The best example of her work here is the Chinese Room, which takes its name from the mid-18th-century Chinese wallpapers and oriental vases. Nancy collaborated on the gardens too, with Norah

Lindsey (who had worked on the gardens of her aunt, Lady Astor of Cliveden). Lindsey was queen of the shabby-chic garden, planting, within a rigid classical framework, mixed-up, self-seeding, billowing borders, regardless of colour and size. Sir Geoffrey Jelicoe laid out the West Terrace, having also worked for Nancy at Ditchley.

Naseby Battlefield

The battle of Naseby, on 14 June 1645, a Saturday morning, was the first full-scale run-out for the New Model Army under Fairfax and Oliver Cromwell, crippling King Charles I's only experienced field army. Everything that took place after Naseby in the Civil War was minor. Most of the action took place in front of the monument, just off the Sibertoft road, north of the village. The king was *en route* to Leicestershire to get reinforcements from Henry Hastings. The New Model Army set off in hot pursuit from Oxford, catching up on the Northamptonshire and Leicestershire border. The king held a council of war at Market Harborough and decided to attack, even though his army was smaller and held the weaker strategic position. The New Model Army drew up on the ridge north of Naseby, looking down at the Royalists, who attacked first. Prince Rupert did exactly as Cromwell had predicted, crashing straight through the left wing and getting stuck into the baggage train. One of Cromwell's divisions turned on him, keeping him out of the action until it was too late. The King attempted a counter-attack, failed and fled, followed by Rupert, all the way to Ashby Castle. The Royalist army lost in the region of 1,000 men, while Cromwell's lost only a few hundred.

Oundle and Around

Oundle, on the edge of Rockingham Forest, is Northamptonshire's most attractive town, with its handsome ironstone **church** and **old school**. Narrow roads converge on the **Market Place**, where a few stalls appear around the Victorian town hall once a week. The school buildings are grouped around the church, whose magnificent needle spire soars above them. To north and south, the valley of the River Nene is lush and dotted with tiny villages.

Fotheringhay

The village of Fotheringhay, north of Oundle along the River Nene, was once a Yorkist stronghold. Two Yorkists are buried in the church, and one of them – the future Richard III – was born in the castle. A rough track beside Castle Farmhouse leads to the Nene, and, raised above it, the motte, all that remains of the powerful 15th-century **castle** of the dukes of York. (It became a royal castle under the Yorkist kings, Edward IV and Richard III.) This is where Richard III was born in 1452, with hair and nails (so they say) and, a hundred or so years later, where Mary Queen of Scots was executed.

The **church** was founded as a collegiate church by Edward, 2nd Duke of York, around 1411, four years before his death at Agincourt, and 40 years before his great-nephew Richard was born. The college buildings on the south side have been demolished, as well as the choir in which Edward was buried. His body, and that of his nephew

Tourist Information

Oundle: 14 West Street, **t** (01832) 274 333. *Open Mon–Sat 9–5, Easter to August Bank Holiday also Sun 1–4.*

Getting There and Around

By **car** along the A1/M and down the A605.

Trains run from London King's Cross to Peterborough or London St Pancras to Kettering, from where you may be able to catch a local bus or hire a taxi. National Express **coaches** also go to Peterborough.

Where to Stay and Eat

Oundle t (01832) –

Talbot Hotel, New Street, **t** 273 621, *www.oldenglish.co.uk* (*expensive*). Grand 17th-century coaching inn with a carriage arch and medieval back range; 35 very ordinary bedrooms on either side of narrow yard.

China Town, 6 New Street, **t** 272 347 (*moderate*). Popular Chinese restaurant opposite the Talbot Hotel. *Closed Mon.*

San Giorgio's, 74 West Street, **t** 272 720 (*cheap*). Popular Italian restaurant serving good hearty dishes. *Closed Mon.*

Rose and Crown, Market Place, **t** 273 284. Where 19th-century poet John Clare was billeted for a while.

Around Oundle t (01832) –

Castle Farm Guest House, Fotheringay, **t** 226 200 (*moderate*). Beautiful stone farm buildings around yard with bedrooms in converted store houses and farmhouse; friendly family atmosphere.

The Falcon, Fotheringhay, **t** 226 254. Serves good food, or bring a picnic and sit on the banks of the River Nene.

Shuckleborough Arms, Stoke Doyle, **t** 272 339. Beautifully positioned pub in Nene Valley.

King's Head, Wodenhoe, **t** 720 024. Delightful place to stay or eat, surrounded by open countryside, with terrace overlooking river.

The Chequered Skipper, Ashton (2 miles from Oundle), **t** 273 494. Traditional pub on Rothschild estate, named after a rare butterfly, where the World Conker Championships are held on the second Sunday in October.

Richard, 3rd Duke of York, killed at the battle of Wakefield in 1460, were reinterred in the church at the orders of Elizabeth I. Richard III was killed at Bosworth, and chucked into the river at Leicester, but there is a chapel dedicated to him.

Rockingham Forest

Between Kettering, Corby and the A1 is what is left of the old royal hunting forest that once stretched from Northampton to Stamford, bordered by the River Welland on one side and the River Nene on the other. The forest was gradually turned over to the private parks of Rockingham Castle, Deene Park and Boughton House, all of which are open to visitors. Between them, you pass through pretty ironstone villages like Apethorpe with its thatched cottages, spotless Kingscliff and Bulwick. The forest was long exploited for its natural resources, woodcutting and ironworking. The latter intensified in the 19th century around Corby, whose steel works closed in the 1970s.

West of the A43 is **Deene Park** (*t (01780) 450 278; open Easter and June–Aug Sun 2–5; adm*), the mansion of the Brudenells, seven of whom were earls of Cardigan. The house has developed over six centuries, retaining the look of a fortified Tudor manor with its elaborate crenellated roof and Great Hall. The 7th Earl, James Brudenell, bought his way into the 8th Hussars and achieved immortality during the Crimean

The Rehabilitation of Richard III

The reputation of Richard III suffered at the hands of Tudor historians, who vilified Richard in order to redeem their own monarchs. Shakespeare, of course, did more damage than anybody else. Since 1924, however, the Richard III Society has dedicated itself to 'reclaiming' the Yorkist king. Their Richard, far from the Shakespearean monster, was a great guy. Loyal (to Edward IV), generous (handing out lots of honours), soldierly (never in question) and Christian. In an act of redemption worthy of Oprah Winfrey, they say that Richard was only cruel at the end because he had been falsely accused of murdering the two princes in the tower, and had suffered the trauma of losing his son and wife.

So here's how the Tudor revisionists turned Richard into a monster. First the battle of Tewkesbury in 1471. This was when Edward IV defeated Margaret of Anjou, the queen of Henry VI (who was locked up in the Tower), and where the only son of Margaret and Henry VI, prince Edward of Lancaster, was killed on the battlefield; Tudor historians claimed that the Yorkist brothers murdered the young prince after he had surrendered. (In Shakespeare's *Richard III* Queen Margaret cries for her 'sweet son'.) The Richard III Society dismisses this as nonsense. Second, the assassination of Henry VI shortly afterwards, which according to Thomas More, was personally carried out by Richard. Shakespeare even shows Richard wooing Prince Edward's widow, Anne Neville, over the Henry's corpse. In fact Richard married Anne a year after Tewkesbury, and no one saw anything wrong with it at the time. The pair lived in Yorkshire, where Richard controlled the Scottish borders for the King, to whom – point out the pro-Ricardians – he stayed loyal when his other brother George, Duke of Clarence, rebelled in 1470. But loyal to his brother too, Richard pleaded for Clarence's life eight years later when Edward had finally had enough of him.

Make up your own mind.

War for leading the Charge of Light Brigade into Russian artillery fire at Balaclava in 1854, and for giving his name to a knitted jacket. His memorial is in the church.

The magnificent ruined shell of Sir Christopher Hatton's second Northamptonshire home, **Kirby Hall** (***t*** *(01536) 203 230; open April–Sept daily 10–6, Oct daily 10–4, Nov–Mar weekends 10–4; adm*), is a mile down the lane from Deene Park. Its ornamental stone features and sheer scale give a better impression of former grandeur than the surviving wing of Holdenby Hall. Hatton bought an existing house at Kirby in 1575, and transformed it over 15 years, rounding off improvements in 1590 by demolishing the medieval village around it. The plan is typically Elizabethan, with ranges of buildings around a courtyard – long galleries, a great hall and renowned gardens. The Queen's glamorous chancellor died childless and in debt. Holdenby was forfeited to the Crown, and Kirby passed to his godson, Christopher Hatton II, who entertained James I three times.

Rockingham Castle (***t*** *(01536) 770 240; open Easter–Sept Sun, July–Aug also Tues and Thurs, house 1–5, grounds 12–4.30; adm*) stands high on a hill just outside Corby, above the Welland, with tremendous views in all directions. Medieval kings, particularly John and Edward III, used Rockingham for rest and relaxation – hunting in the forest. In

1530 it passed out of royal hands into those of the Watsons, local landowners who converted it into a comfortable Tudor manor house within the old castle walls, and turned the motte into a rose garden. The Long Gallery has paintings by Zoffany and Reynolds, and some Dickens memorabilia. Dickens was a friend of the Watsons, often visiting the castle, which became the model for gloomy Chesney Wold in *Bleak House* (although he called Rockingham 'that bright house'). After one visit, Mrs Watson wrote in her diary: 'Nov. 30. Dickens and Family left. Last night he and Miss Boyle acted a scene out of *Nicholas Nickleby* and from the *School for Scandal* in the Hall most admirably. He afterwards performed some conjuring tricks.'

Just north of Kettering, near Geddington, is **Boughton House** (*t (01536) 515 731; house open Aug Sat–Thurs 2–4.30; grounds open May–Aug Sat–Thurs 1–5.30; adm*), the stately home of the Duke of Buccleuch (pronounced 'Bukloo') and Queensberry, and his Montagu ancestors. The Montagues got the old Boughton monastery at the Dissolution. Successive family members added a wing here and a court there. The events that transformed the family's fortunes came in the 17th and 18th centuries. First Queen Anne gave Ralph Montagu, ambassador to Louis XIV for nine years, his own dukedom. Then Ralph married the widowed heiress of the Northumberland fortune and transformed Boughton into a grand French-style house, befitting his rank. He added the north front and state rooms, and landscaped the park. His son John married one of the heiresses of the Duke of Marlborough of Blenheim (the other one having married into the Spencer family of Althorp). Two generations later, the Montagu dukedom died out with the last male heir. Boughton remained with a daughter who married the 3rd Duke of Buccleuch, later also Duke of Queensberry. The rooms are full of 17th–18th-century French and English furniture, Mortlake tapestries, Sèvres porcelain and Old Master paintings, including 40 Van Dyck sketches. The lawns, lakes and woodland were landscaped for the 1st Duke by a Dutchman.

In the middle of ironstone **Geddington** is a 39ft 13th-century monument to love, the **Geddington Eleanor Cross**. Edward I's queen, Eleanor, died at Harby in Nottinghamshire in 1290. Her internal organs were buried in Lincoln Cathedral and her body in Westminster Abbey. The grief-stricken king erected 12 crosses along the route taken by the funeral procession from Lincoln to London, at Lincoln, Grantham, Stamford, Geddington, Hardingstone, Stony Stratford, Woburn, Dunstable, St Albans, Waltham and London Charing Cross. Three survive, two – Geddington and Hardingstone – in Northamptonshire, the other at Waltham on the outskirts of London. The one outside Charing Cross station is a Victorian replica.

North of the village is a roadside **memorial to the men of the 384th bomber group** who flew B-17s from the American airbase at Grafton Underwood in the Second World War. In all, the 384th lost more than 1,600 flyers in two years of operations against Germany. They had the distinction of dropping the first US Air Force bombs on Germany in 1942 and the last in 1945. Nothing is left of the 500-acre site, which had its own cinema and hospital. It was one of many 8th Air Force bases in Northamptonshire, including one at Harrington, about five miles west of Kettering, where black Liberators flew Carpetbagger operations – night missions over France and Germany to drop radio-equipped spies and munitions to Resistance groups. There is a memorial there too.

Southwest Northamptonshire

Between the M1 and M40 motorways, south of Northampton, is a chunk of beautiful limestone countryside, rolling towards the Cotswolds to the southwest. Here you are edging close to the heart of the Midlands, in the thick of Civil War battle sites and canal junctions, and in shooting distance of Stratford-upon-Avon and Oxford. Two relatively modest houses stand out: delightful Canons Ashby and Sulgrave Manor.

Buried in the countryside, with views down the terraced gardens towards Oxfordshire, **Canons Ashby** (***t*** *(01327) 860 044, www.nationaltrust.org.uk; open Easter–Oct Sat–Wed 1–5.30 grounds and church 11–5.30, house 1–5.30; adm*) is the atmospheric manor house of the Dryden family, built in the mid-16th century and more or less unchanged since. The poet laureate John Dryden, son of a Northamptonshire clergyman, never lived here, but he visited his cousin, who did. The Drydens lived modestly, without honours or titles (except a baronetcy, which they bought in 1621). The low, creaking long gallery overlooks the old cobbled courtyard.

South of Canons Ashby, **Sulgrave Manor** (***t*** *(01295) 760 205; open Easter–Oct Tues–Thurs and weekends 2–5.30; adm*) was the home of George Washington's ancestors between 1539, when it was built by Lawrence Washington, and 1656, when it was sold out of the family. The Washingtons of Northamptonshire were wealthy sheep farmers, connected by marriage to the Spencers of Althorp, who were even bigger sheep farmers. Their family coat of arms, featuring two stripes and three stars, was the template of the American flag. The Northamptonshire Washingtons were only a few generations removed from the first American president, selling wool across the Atlantic in exchange for American tobacco before emigrating in the mid-17th century. Sulgrave Manor is the only George Washington memorial in England. It was bought by an Anglo-American Peace Committee in 1913, restored by Sir Reginald Bloomfield and Sir Hugh Clifford Smith (two prestigious architects), and opened to the public in 1921. American tourists were much more interested in Sulgrave then than they are now, travelling up by steam train from Marylebone Station. Ford Motor Cars provided the curator with a special charabanc-style car to pick them up from Helmdon station. In the museum room is George Washington memorabilia donated over the years, including letters, his coat and saddlebags, and the presidential seal.

The rector of All Saints' church in **Middleton Cheney** was a friend of Burne-Jones, hence the fabulous display of Morris and Co. stained glass in his church, on the outskirts of Banbury. All the Pre-Raphaelites contributed, including panels of typically vivid colour and physicality by Morris, Webb, Madox Brown and Burne-Jones, whose west window, depicting the *Fiery Furnace*, is the highlight.

East Anglia
Essex, Suffolk, Norfolk and Cambridgeshire

16

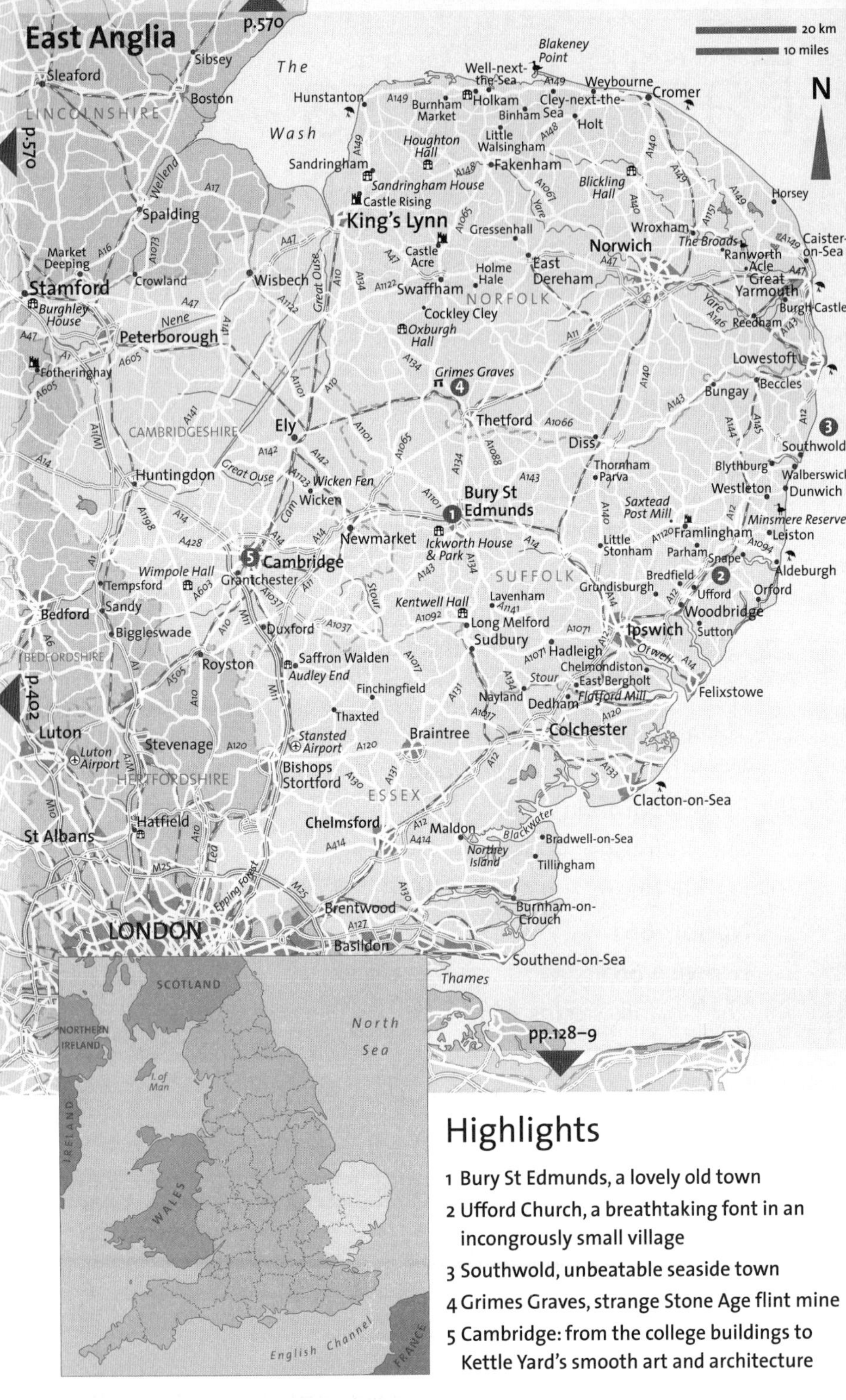

Highlights

1. Bury St Edmunds, a lovely old town
2. Ufford Church, a breathtaking font in an incongrously small village
3. Southwold, unbeatable seaside town
4. Grimes Graves, strange Stone Age flint mine
5. Cambridge: from the college buildings to Kettle Yard's smooth art and architecture

East Anglia, comprising **Essex**, **Suffolk**, **Norfolk** and **Cambridgeshire**, is an intensely atmospheric part of England under wide liquid skies. The best bits are at its edges, where the lovely seaside towns and villages of **Woodbridge**, **Aldeburgh**, **Southwold**, **Blakeney** and **Cley** are bases for walks around the coastal marshes and reed-fringed creeks of the rivers Deben, Orwell, Stour, Colne, Alde, Ore or Blyth, abuzz with insects and bird life. The East Anglian stories of M.R. and P.D. James revel in the region's mysterious past, dwelling on the wealth of ancient remains; the protagonists find either refuge or horrors in its churches, where the daylight streams through the clear expanses of Perpendicular windows. The region's other distinguishing features are **Grimes Graves** Stone Age flint mines and **Sutton Hoo**, the most prestigious Saxon burial site in the country. On the **Denghie Peninsula** stands St Peter's Church, built in the 7th century by St Cedd, who took the sea road from Northumbria to evangelize the heathen southerners. Two of the largest Roman hoards have been found in the Breckland; East Anglian treasures are not only metaphoric.

When Boudicca led the Iceni to revolt against the Romans, she burned Colchester, the 'City of Victory', to the ground; in retaliation the Romans incinerated the Iceni capital at Thetford. Boudicca started an East Anglian tradition of heroic, doomed last stands: 9th-century King Edmund, ritually shot to pieces by Viking arrows, became the heart of a medieval cult at **Bury St Edmunds**. Alderman Bryhtnoth of Essex was finished off by the Vikings too, and achieved immortality in a 10th-century poem, *The Battle of Maldon*. Hereward the Wake fought the Norman invaders in the Fens until 1071, a legend even in his own lifetime.

In the Middle Ages East Anglia was one of the most populous regions in the country. Now the wealthy medieval port of **Dunwich** has fallen off its cliff into the sea. The wool towns of **Lavenham**, **Long Melford**, **Saffron Walden** and **Dedham** were some of the wealthiest in the country in the late Middle Ages. They look like picture-postcard villages today, but the churches at **Ufford**, **Grundisburgh**, **Blythburgh**, **Lavenham**, **Long Melford**, **Southwold**, **Earl Stonham**, **Eye** and **Salle** are fine examples of woollen ostentation. Oversized, they were built by cash-splashing cloth merchants, with hammer-beam roofs like upturned boats, more glass than flint, fonts the size of spires, carved angels, clock smiters, painted screens and countless other show-off details. **Framlingham**'s church contains the Renaissance tomb of Thomas Howard, 3rd Duke of Norfolk, one of the greatest noblemen in Tudor England. He controlled East Anglia like a small kingdom, answerable to no one, although his Tudor palace at Kenninghall in Norfolk has long gone.

Essex

Despite its reputation as home of the Essex boy (white socks), Essex girl (white stilettos) and Sierra man, who brought Margaret Thatcher to power, Essex has some charming historic towns and landscapes. Bypass the semi-industrial sprawl of southern Essex along the northern banks of the Thames estuary and head straight for Roman Colchester and Constable's Dedham Vale, on the Suffolk borders.

Colchester

Colchester lies on the River Coln, a few miles inland from its estuary, on the London road. It is a garrison and university town but, despite a long history, its charm is confined to the High Street. Cunobelin, king of the *Catuvellauni* from 5 BC to AD 40, came from Colchester. His reputation as *Rex Britannorum* travelled to Rome before the Roman Conquest and when the imperial army landed on British shores in AD 43 it marched straight to *Camulodunum* and secured the southeast by defeating the tribe. The XXth legion fort was south of the High Street until AD 49, when it became a *colonia* for retired soldiers, named after the imperial victory – *Colonia Claudia*

Getting There and Around

By **car**, follow signs to Colchester off the A12.

Direct, frequent, regular **trains** run from London Liverpool Street to Colchester. For all train information call **National Rail Enquiries**, **t** 08457 484950, *www.thetrainline.com.*

National Express **coaches** from London Victoria go to most major towns in East Anglia. For coach travel information call **t** 08705 808080 or go to *www.gobycoach.com.*

Tourist Information

Colchester: 1 Queen Street, **t** (01206) 282 920. *Open summer daily 10–5, winter closed Sun.*

Where to Stay

Colchester t (01206) –

The Red Lion Hotel, High Street, **t** 577 986, *www.brook-hotels.co.uk* (*expensive*). One of Colchester's oldest buildings, with a jettied, timber-framed front and carriage arch; 24 bedrooms. Restaurant (*moderate*).

The George Hotel, High Street, **t** 578 494, *www.bestwestern.co.uk* (*moderate*). Beautifully converted 16th-century coaching inn with 45 lovely bedrooms and a wealth of floorboards, rugs, lamps, lilies, ancient beams, pale yellow walls and designer sofas; leafy courtyard with wrought-iron garden furniture. Brasserie-style restaurant (*cheap*).

The Old Manse, 15 Roman Road, **t** 545 154, *www.doveuk.com/oldmanse* (*moderate*). Comfortable accommodation in quiet cul-de-sac with antique pine farmhouse kitchen table and dresser in breakfast room; pleasant 5-minutes walk into town through Castle Park.

Athelstan House, 201 Maldon Road, **t** 548 652, *enquires@athelstanhouse.com* (*moderate*). Comfortable Victorian house, 20-minute walk from centre.

Eating Out

North Hill Exchange Brasserie, North Hill, **t** 769 988 (*moderate*). Large open-plan restaurant with art on the walls. Typical menu includes grilled fillet of Scottish beef, pan-fried calf's liver with bubble and squeak or lots of fish. *Closed Sun and Mon.*

Thai Dragon, 35 East Hill, **t** 862 785 (*moderate*). Selection of Thai dishes.

Ruan Thai, 82/a East Hill, **t** 870 770 (*moderate*). Another large selection of Thai dishes.

Garden Café at Minories Art Gallery, High Street, **t** 500 169 (*cheap*). Cakes, toasted bagels and light vegetarian lunches such as mushroom and tarragon risotto. Unusual 18th-century folly in garden. *Closed Sun.*

The Lemon Tree, 48 St John's Street, **t** 767 337 (*cheap*). Open-plan converted warehouse. Offers traditional English, Mediterranean and Swiss fare. Informal.

Entertainment

Mercury Theatre, Balkerne Gate, **t** 573 948, *www.mercurytheatre.co.uk*. Colchester's main theatre. Resident repertory company performs classic drama.

Colchester Arts Centre, St Mary-at-the-Wall, Church Street, **t** 500 900. In converted church; strong on jazz, folk and comedy.

Victricensis. There are a few vestigesof this era: defensive earthworks, the site of Britain's largest Roman theatre, a temple dedicated to Claudius (who died in AD 53 and became a god, like all dead Roman emperors) with a Norman castle on top (the keep and St Botolph's Priory were built with recycled Roman bricks), an archway and walls. Colchester resurfaced more than 1,000 years later as the leading maker of bays and says (high quality woollen cloth), when Dutch Protestant refugees from the Spanish Netherlands settled here after the Reformation.

All the good stuff is within the old Roman walls. The town hall and Georgian town-houses of the High Street are flanked by Castle Park and the old Dutch quarter, which drops down to the river. **Hollytrees**, the best Georgian house, is now a toy museum (*open daily 10–5, Sun 11–5*). The **Minories Art Gallery**, which inhabits two 18th-century houses, hosts good exhibitions. The Roman **walls**, built after the Boudiccan revolt in AD 60, extend from the ruined Roman arch of the old Balkerne Gate. The superb Norman ruin of **St Botolph's Priory**, the first English Augustinian house, has retained its drum columns and rounded arches.

The **Castle Museum** (*open Mon–Sat 10–5, Sun 11–5; 45-minute tour; adm minimal*) on Museum Street is in the old Norman keep, bigger than any but that of Rochester Castle and the White Tower of London, but certainly pinker than either. Its highlight is the collection of Roman belt buckles, sword handles, figurines of gods, pots and urns. An armless bronze statue of Mercury stands at the door. Inside, Longinus Sdapeze, a cavalryman from Bulgaria, tramples a Celt on his tombstone. There are good mosaics too. The Roman vaults served as the foundation of the Roman temple of Claudius.

At the back of the castle is an **obelisk**, on the spot where Royalist leaders Sir Charles Lucas and Sir George Lisle were shot after the 1648 Siege of Colchester. The staunchly Parliamentarian town of Colchester was bullied into submission by a diehard Royalist faction just before Charles I's execution. Besieged by the Parliamentarians, the half-dead city was then fined for its Royalist sympathies.

In Maidenburgh Street you can see traces of the **Roman theatre**. On Trinity Street, half-timbered **Tymperleys Clock Museum** (*open Tues–Sat 10–5, Sun 11–5*) is home to a collection of 17th–19th-century clocks, many turret clocks from Suffolk churches.

Dedham Vale

> *I associate my careless boyhood with all that lies on the banks of the Stour. Those scenes made me a painter.*
>
> John Constable, in a letter to a friend, 1821

Dedham Vale is the lush, unspoiled valley of the River Stour around Dedham, East Bergholt and Flatford where landscape painter John Constable was born on 11 June 1776. It later became the subject of his most famous paintings. You can identify Constable's birthplace, his father's flour mills, his school in Dedham, and the Stour Valley views of *Boat Building at Flatford* (1815), *Flatford Mill* (1817) and *The Cornfield* (1826), among others. Constable painted in the open air – revolutionary at the time – and depicted a bucolic English landscape. 'Painting is with me but another word for

Tourist Information

Dedham: Flatford Lane, Flatford, East Bergholt, **t** (01206) 299 460. *Open summer daily 10–5, winter weekends only 10–4.*

Guided Constable Walks from Bridge Cottage between Easter and Sept.

Take out a rowing boat from **Flatford Boat Hire** on the Stour, perhaps to Dedham. Contact Mr Tripp, **t** (01206) 298 111.

Where to Stay and Eat

Dedham Vale t (01206) –

Maison Talbooth, Stratford Road, Dedham, **t** 322 367 (*luxury*). Victorian country house in lovely gardens overlooking Dedham Vale; 10 double suites. Breakfast in rooms, courtesy car to restaurant a few minutes away.

Le Talbooth, Gun Hill, Dedham, **t** 323 150, *www.talbooth.com* (*expensive*). Sixteenth-century timbered house beside river beneath road bridge, with terrace. Serves steamed fillet of sea bass, roasted fillet of cod, lamb or beef.

Dedham Hall, Brook Street, Dedham, **t** 323 027, *www.dedhamhall.demon.co.uk* (*moderate*). Snug group of cream-painted buildings surrounded by gardens at end of long gravel drive, a quiet place of wood pigeons and watercolour painters (on painting holidays, *Feb–Nov*) wearing straw hats at easels in the garden. Also houses the English-style **Fountain House Restaurant** (*moderate*) offering dinners of sirloin steak, peppered salmon fillet or mushroom and cream-cheese pancakes. *Closed Sun and Mon.*

The Sun Hotel, High Street, Dedham, **t** 323 351 (*moderate*). Sixteenth-century coaching inn with rare external covered staircase, just opposite Dedham church. Bar meals, restaurant and a handful of rooms.

The Rookery, Stratford Road, Dedham, **t** 323 118 (*cheap*). Sixteenth-century glowing terra-cotta-painted house at end of wooded track, just outside Dedham, with two beautiful bedrooms with fireplaces, rugs and period furniture; 300-year-old tulip tree in gardens.

Rosemary's, Rectory Hill, East Bergholt, **t** 298 241 (*cheap*). Flourishing garden with weeping silver birches and rose garden. Three bright and airy bedrooms. Well-stocked book shelves, no TV.

Bridge Cottage Shop and Restaurant, Flatford, **t** 298 260 (*cheap*). You can get a cheese scone and soup and a glass of wine, and sit outdoors among the ducks. *Winter closed Mon and Tues.*

feeling,' he said. You can feel his spirit here among the willows by the meandering river where cows drink from the muddy banks. Dedham church tower is constantly in view. Park in Flatford, East Bergholt or Dedham, and walk.

Flatford

In the cottage beside Flatford Bridge is a small exhibition about Constable. Copies of his paintings are displayed alongside letters describing his feelings for the Essex and Suffolk countryside. An hour-long guided walk (***t** (01206) 298 260 for times*) takes you on a tour of Constable views.Just downriver is the subject of *Boat Building at Flatford* (1815). White weatherboard **Flatford Mill**, painted by Constable in 1816–17, is the last of the old Stour Valley mills. 'When I look at a mill painted by John,' said his brother, 'I see that it will go round.' His father, Golding, inherited it in 1765, and had his first three children here, before moving to a grander house in East Bergholt, where John was born. Just beyond is **Willy Lott's house** on the mill pool. Lott, a local farmer, was a friend of the Constables, and lived here all his long life. The *Hay Wain* (1821), which decorates many a biscuit tin, was painted here – where there was once a shingle ford.

Dedham

Pevsner was right when he said that 'there is nothing to hurt the eye in Dedham', a small, prosperous medieval cloth-manufacturing village. The wide, curving High Street is lined by houses half-timbered and askew, trim and colour-washed. On the main square is the 15th-century wool merchant's **Marlborough Head**; **Constable's old school**; and the imposing **church** with its 130ft pinnacled tower – a striking feature of the Stour Valley which appears in many of Constable's paintings. In the south aisle of the church is a monument to Judith Eyre who died '... in consequence of having accidentally swallow'd a Pin.' About 200 yards down a track is **Southfields**, a medieval cloth factory with leaning timber-framed ranges around a lovely little courtyard.

On the corner of Castle Hill and East Lane is the home and studio of equestrian painter Alfred Munnings from 1919 until his death in 1959. Like Constable, he was the son of a Suffolk miller and Royal Academician. It is now a **gallery** (***t*** *(01206) 322 127; open May–Sept Sun and Wed 2–5, Aug also Thurs and Sat 2–5; adm*) of his paintings.

Blackwater Estuary

Maldon

At the head of the Blackwater Estuary is Maldon, a small boating town amid the sprawl. Its quayside bustles with black-stained wooden sheds, pubs, boatyards and sailing clubs. Along the sea wall is the Promenade, an Edwardian marine lake and ice-cream booths. Reclaimed marshland, mud and salt marshes line the river. A causeway, flooded at high tide, leads to **Northey Island** – the site of the Battle of Maldon in 991 and the first recorded instance of English fair-play. An Anglo-Saxon ballad tells how the Vikings, encamped on Northey, faced a Saxon army led by the Essex alderman Byrhtnoth across the river. Taunts were exchanged as the causeway was left exposed by the ebbing tide. Byrhtnoth let the Vikings cross to regroup on the other bank. Forfeiting their advantage, the Saxons lost disastrously, beginning a long period of Danish rule. It is a desolate spot. The town was the setting for the recent film *Lawless Heart*, which made the most of the muted coastal light and busy skies.

There are two interesting churches in town. **All Saints'** has the only triangular tower in England, and Victorian statues of Essex worthies St Cedd of Bradwell, Byrhtnoth and the 15th-century patron of the church, Sir Robert D'Arcy. **St Peter's** flint tower is attached to a brick building – the old **library** built to house the books of Maldon astronomer-clergyman-scientist Thomas Plume (1630–1704). Here you can see the 42ft-long **Millennium Embroidery**, stitched 1,000 years after the Battle of Maldon, in 1991. The tower stairs lead up to Plume's wood-panelled library, where you can leaf through one of the 8,000 books.

East of Maldon, the estuary is marshy and unspoiled. Follow the B1026 to the yachting village of **Tollesbury** for a walk around the creeks.

Getting There and Around

By **car**, Maldon is signposted off the A414, which connects with the A12.

There is no railway station, but you can catch a **train** from London to Chelmsford, or from elsewhere in East Anglia to Whitham, and then a **bus** to Maldon.

Tourist Information

Maldon: Coach Lane, **t** (01621) 856 503, *www.maldon.co.uk*. *Open Mon–Sat 10–4*.

Where to Stay and Eat

Maldon t (01621) –

The Blue Boar Hotel, Silver Street, **t** 855 888, *www.blueboarmaldon.co.uk* (*moderate*). Large, blackened London-brick hotel with coaching arch, cream-painted windows and pillared porch; 25 bedrooms, comfortable old bar and relaxed restaurant serving typical English food: steak, lamb and salmon.

The Limes, 21 Market Hill, **t** 850 350, *www.maldonlimes@ukonline.co.uk* (*moderate*). Terracotta-painted house in town centre with brick fireplace, some bedrooms with four-poster bed, others in attic with rooftop views.

Greg's, 122 High Street, **t** 852 009 (*moderate*). Newish family-run restaurant serving modern English food with emphasis on fish. *Closed Mon*.

Saffron Kitchen Tea Rooms, 9 High Street, **t** 856 111 (*cheap*). Pleasant old-fashioned tea rooms and garden where staff wear period costume. Light lunches, scones and cakes. *Closed Sun*.

Burnham-on-Crouch t (01621) –

Ye Olde White Hart Hotel, The Quay, **t** 782 106 (*moderate*). Handsome red-brick quayside building; 11 bedrooms, eight with shared bathrooms. Large upbeat bar, with (*cheap*) restaurant serving standard fare.

Contented Sole, High Street, **t** 782 139 (*moderate*) Traditional French/English restaurant, in business since 1965, serving fresh fish. Try the *crêpes fruits de mer* – pancakes filled with prawns, scampi and monk fish – followed by *sol brulé*, caramelized ice cream. *Open Tues–Sat dinner and Sun lunch*.

Clouds, High Street, **t** 782 965 (*moderate*). Bistro-style restaurant cheerfully decorated in lemon yellow, white and cream with exposed timbers and brick. Modern English food such as chargrilled beef with new potatoes, steamed salmon or baked goats' cheese in filo pastry. *Open Tues–Fri lunch and dinner, Sat dinner only, Sun lunch only*.

The Star Inn, 31 High Street, **t** 782 010 (*cheap*). Pleasant old-fashioned pub with functional bedrooms facing quay. Plain pub grub such as ploughman's or scampi and chips (*cheap*).

Denghie Peninsula

Almost an island between the Blackwater and Crouch estuaries, Denghie is empty and windswept, with its own nuclear power station amid the salt marshes and cabbage fields. The cheerful yachting town of **Burnham-on-Crouch** has Georgian buildings on the quayside, walks along the sea wall and river views. The village green of **Tillingham** is surrounded by weatherboard houses; the church and shop have local walks information.

The best place for walks is **Bradwell-on-Sea**. From here the old Roman East End Road leads to the Saxon church of **St-Peter-on-the-Wall**. Its foundation goes back to St Cedd, a missionary from Lindisfarne who arrived on the Essex coast in AD 653 to convert the pagan southerners (St Augustine had already tried from Canterbury fifty years earlier in AD 597). It stands on the site of the Saxon shore fort *Othona*, and you can see Roman stones and red tiles in the building.

Bradwell Nuclear Power Station has finally closed after years of protest, leaving the peninsula a fraction less grimly desolate than it used to be.

Saffron Walden and Around

Saffron Walden is a delightfully complete town. Its small square boasts handsome Victorian buildings and a Great Exhibition fountain. Old townhouses display their skewed timber frames. It has both an unusual turf maze and a Victorian hedge maze, a ruined Norman castle, a Perpendicular church and the Natural History Society's museum, founded in 1832. All the best elements of an English town are brought together in a charming ensemble. The prosperous medieval market town grew up around the castle, manufactured cloth and bone-handled cutlery, and made a name growing saffron as a dye and medicine. It has never looked back.

The **church** is the largest in the county, rebuilt in the 15th century in lofty style by John Wastell, the master mason of King's College chapel in Cambridge. Inside is an Italian-style black Tournai marble **monument to Thomas Audley** (d. 1544) of Audley End, Henry VIII's lord chancellor. His reputation was as black as his tomb: he had a

Tourist Information

Saffron Waldon: 1 Market Place, **t** (01799) 510 445, *www.uttlesford.gov.uk*. *Open summer 9.30–5.30, winter 10–5.*

Where to Stay

Saffron Walden t (01799) –

Archway Guest House, Church Street, **t** 501 500, *archwayguesthouse@ntlworld.com* (*moderate*). Charming modern house in among the old ones by the parish church. Crammed with miniature trains, racing cars, toys and paintings. Delightful breakfast room on first floor.

Red Gates Farmhouse, Red Gates Lane, Sewards End, **t** 516 166 (*moderate*). You are sure to be made welcome in this 15th-century farmhouse in a beautiful setting 1½ miles east of town.

Rowley Hill Lodge, Little Waldon, **t** 525 975 (*moderate*). Set in large secluded gardens between Saffron and Little Waldon; 1830s farm lodge enlarged into house with five bedrooms, two of them available for B&B, with good power showers. Own hens produce breakfast eggs.

Pudding House, 9/a Museum Lane, **t** 522 089 (*cheap*). Modern house in quiet conservation area opposite church.

Bell House, Castle Street, **t** 527 857 (*cheap*). Former 15th-century inn in beautiful setting next to church. Attractive with wealth of exposed beams.

Eating Out

The Cricketers, Wicken Road, Clavering, **t** 550 442 (*expensive*). Delightful free house with 14 bedrooms in old 16th-century coaching inn 5 miles southwest of town towards Buntingford. The food is the big attraction, with an excellent restaurant (*moderate*).

Tylers Wine, Tapas and Jazz, 9 Market Hill, **t** 524 532 (*cheap*). Fun, lively bistro-style restaurant offering hot lemon chicken salad, griddled sword fish and popular tapas platter with seven dishes. Cheerful décor, walls decorated with jazz posters, old 78 records and brass instruments. Live jazz Thurs eve. *Open Mon–Sat morning coffee and lunch, Thurs–Sat also dinner.*

The Eight Bells, Bridge Street, **t** 522 790 (*cheap*). Traditional 16th-century inn with dark wooden furniture and black beams. Good hot and cold pub grub.

hand in the deaths of St Thomas More (the chancellor who refused to recognize Henry's spiritual power), Thomas Cromwell (another chancellor who fell out of favour with the king), Anne Boleyn and Catherine Howard (two of Henry's eight wives, both executed), as well as in the Dissolution of the monasteries.

The grand red-brick **museum** on Museum Street (***t*** *(01799) 510 333; open Mar–Oct Mon–Sat 10–5, Sun 2.30–4.30; Nov–Feb Mon–Sat 11–4, Sun 2.30–4.30; adm minimal*) is like a metropolitan museum in miniature. It has prehistory, natural history, social history, geology and ethnology displays. You can pick up a key to the **hedge maze** in the Victorian Bridge End Gardens from the tourist information centre. The **turf maze** on the Common is a labyrinth of unknown antiquity, re-laid with bricks in the 20th century; although you can't get lost in it, it's a mile from start to finish.

Audley End

t *(01799) 522 842; open April–Sept Wed–Sun 11–6; Oct Wed–Fri 11–4, weekends 11–5; adm.*

Just outside Saffron Walden, Audley End is one of the great Jacobean houses. Like Hatfield in Herts it was built to impress the king. With a range of Jacobean, 18th- and 19th-century rooms – an interesting mishmash – it stands in Capability Brown parkland strewn with monuments. Its history begins with the Machiavellian Tudor Thomas Audley, who in 1538 acquired the lands of an abbey he had dissolved. Some time later Thomas Howard, son of the 4th Duke of Norfolk, turned it into a palace three times the size of the present house. The **Great Hall** is the only room that survives from this period. John Griffin, a retired soldier-politician, inherited the house from his aunt in 1762 and did some home improvement. He employed the young Robert Adam for the interiors, Capability for the grounds, and was made 1st Lord Braybrooke, as befitted the neo-classical splendour. **Adam's interiors** have been reconstructed on the ground floor. Upstairs, neo-Jacobean apartments were installed by the 3rd Lord Braybrooke and are hung with **Old Master paintings**. Lady Braybrooke's sitting room brings a touch of humanity to the place – a snug, informal little room with chintzy furnishings, portraits on the walls, comfy armchairs and tea tables. The ornate beds of the walled Victorian vegetable garden and *parterre* were designed by William Sawrey Gilpin in 1832.

Thaxted

The rolling Essex countryside north of the Dunmows and upper Coln is home to the charming villages of Finchingfield, the Bardfields and Thaxted – none more charming than Thaxted, 5 miles south of Saffron Walden on the B184. The needle-sharp spire of the **church** towers over colour-washed Georgian and medieval buildings. Composer Gustav Holst (1873–1934) lived on Town Street for a while and played the church organ. From the churchyard a track leads south between medieval, thatched almshouses to **John Webb's Windmill** (*open May–Sept weekends 2–6*) in a field, with its brick tower and wooden sails.

Suffolk

It's tempting to race straight for the Suffolk coast, to the North-Sea-wind-blown fishing towns of Southwold, Walberswick, Orford and Aldeburgh. But the wealthy medieval wool towns of inland Suffolk have plenty to delay you – oversized churches in picture-postcard villages, pubs serving real ale and good food, the Saxon burial site at Sutton Hoo and some pleasantly rolling countryside, not as flat as Norfolk.

Ipswich

Anything more than 300 years old (including its 12 medieval churches) looks lost in Suffolk's busy modern county town. Ipswich docks boomed in the Victorian period and statues of justice, commerce, law, learning and agriculture on the town hall embody the ethos of the era. Victorian industrialist Joseph Chevalier Cobbold (1797–1882) is the embodiment of them all: he sponsored the wet dock, became MP and mayor of Ipswich, introduced the railway and endowed the gallery. The docks are now a place of shed warehouses, lorries and forklift trucks. Elsewhere handsome Georgian-Victorian streets are ruined by the roar of traffic and modern life. The town centre is a wasteland of brick paving dotted with medieval churches, from which escape is offered by mobile phone and cheap holiday shops. An interesting cluster of buildings around Cromwell Square includes the shiny black kidney-shaped **Willis Corroon building**, designed by Norman Foster in 1975. The **Unitarian Meeting House**, built in 1699, is all polished woodwork inside, with old box pews you can't see over the top of; the carved wooden pulpit may be the work of Grinling Gibbons. But it is the Museum and Christchurch Mansion that redeem Ipswich.

Red-brick **Ipswich Museum** on the High Street (***t*** *(01473) 433 550; open Tues–Sat 10–5*) is decorated with statues of Newton and Hogarth, terracotta fruit, flowers and fossils. Its highlight is the natural history gallery, where exhibits include a 17ft-high stuffed African giraffe and a diorama of jungle animals. Sixth-century archaeological finds in the Saxon gallery suggest that Ipswich was one of the earliest Anglo-Saxon towns.

Christchurch Mansion in Christchurch Park (***t*** *(01473) 213 761; open April–Oct Tues–Sat 10–5, Nov–Mar 10–4, Sun all year 2–4.30*) was presented to the town in 1895 by brewer Felix Thornley Cobbold (1841–1909), who became mayor of Ipswich a year later and bequeathed £20,000 to purchase art. The Elizabethan mansion is set amid bowling greens and fish ponds. Its 30 rooms reflect 18th-century modifications: deal and pine panelling, rococo plasterwork, flock wallpaper. The furnishings include carved panelling from the Ipswich home of Sir Humphrey Wingfield.

The highlight of the collection is the work of **East Anglian artists** Constable, Gainsborough, Alfred Munnings and Frederick George Cotman. The Constables include his painting of William Lock's house and the mill stream in Flatford, and some of his early, precise drawings from the attic of his father's house in East Bergholt. Gainsborough's portraits and landscapes include one of Holywell Park under a big sky, and atmospheric paintings of Walberswick, Minismere and Dunwich.

Getting There and Around

By **car**, from the Midlands you come into Ipswich on the A14; from London follow the A12 all the way.

There's an hourly **train** service from London Liverpool Street.

Tourist Information

Ipswich: St Stephen's Church, St Stephen's Lane, **t** (01473) 258 070. *Open Mon–Sat 9–5*.

Guided Walking Tours start here May–Sept Tues and Thurs at 2.15pm.

Where to Stay

Ipswich t (01473) –

Salthouse Harbour Hotel, 82 Fore Street, **t** 257 677, *www.salthouse.co.uk* (*very expensive*). Brand-new seven-storey hotel in a converted Victorian warehouse near the Customs House; 43 large 'executive' bedrooms, all overlooking the water, with DVD players and private bathrooms with bath and separate shower. Ground-floor brasserie (*moderate*).

The Great White Horse Hotel, Tavern Street, **t** 256 558 (*moderate*). Old city-centre coaching inn whose former guests include George II and Charles Dickens; 62 cheerful bedrooms, with William Morris quilt covers. The old courtyard is now a tiled bar. Restaurant serves traditional, hearty English food (mainly meat).

Redholme, 52 Ivry Street, **t** 250 018, *www.redholmeipswich.co.uk* (*moderate*). Victorian house in quiet spot above town with pretty garden, outdoor pool and four large bedrooms with own sofas and dressing tables.

Eating Out

The Galley, 22 St Nicholas Street, **t** 281 131 (*moderate*). Friendly, well-established Ipswich restaurant where you might find Cajun salmon, Mediterranean and North African food on the menu, as well as Bungay pork. Home-marinated olives and home-made ice cream. *Closed Sun*.

Mortimer's, 1 Duke Street, **t** 230 225 (*moderate*). Candle-lit seafood restaurant with pictures of the Suffolk coast on the walls. Fish soup, grilled sardines or oysters, followed by salmon fillet, halibut, swordfish or Thai-style red snapper on noodles and stir-fried vegetables. *Open dinner only, closed Sun*.

Pickwicks, 1 Dial Lane, **t** 254 241 (*cheap*). Behind Art Nouveau façade, you can drink coffee from every coffee region of the world, and unblended 'single estate' teas. In summer you can sit out at tables in the old churchyard of St Lawrence's next door.

Vagabonds, 13 Queen Street, **t** 254 666, *www.vagabondsonline.com* (*cheap*). Lively contemporary-style café where you can have coffee and bagels or sandwiches listening to chill-out jazz. *Open Mon–Sat 9–5*. New restaurant promises fresh local produce. *Open Thurs–Sat eves*.

The Brewery Tap, Cliff Road, **t** 281 508 (*cheap*). Pink-painted Victorian house next to the old Tolly Cobbold brewery on the other side of harbour, serves real ales including Tolly Cobbold Cobnut and Original Bitter. Standard pub grub.

Cobbled on the Quay, Neptune Quay (*cheap*). Lively, crowded night-time drinking hole in bottle-shaped former malt kiln. Choice of around 80 flavours of vodka as well as German, Polish and Czech beers.

Pin Mill

From Ipswich, the B1456 wiggles under Orwell Bridge along the south side of the Orwell towards Chelmondiston, where you turn left at the Foresters' Arms to Pin Mill. Despite serving the major ports at Ipswich, Felixstowe and Harwich, the Orwell is a delightful river – mud flats flanked by rolling green hills, container ships gliding up and down, the cranes of Ipswich and big Suffolk skies. Pin Mill is a picturesque quay-side popular with the boating crowd. Have lunch in the Butt and Oyster pub, washed down with Tolly Cobbold beers. River walks take you to remote beaches.

Felixstowe

Oh wind and water, this is Felixstowe
John Betjeman

Heading down the A14 between the Orwell and Deben takes you to Felixstowe, an Edwardian resort developed by Ipswich brewers Cobbold and Tollemache. Felixstowe docks, founded in 1846, are now Britain's busiest container port. It was here that Mrs Wallis Simpson of Baltimore spent six weeks in 1936, enjoying flying visits from her suitor, Edward VIII, to qualify for divorce from her husband. 'Not a hint of distant concern penetrated Felixstowe,' she said, referring to the abdication crisis. Felixstowe's pride is its **seafront gardens**, climbing in colourful terraces up to the old neo-Jacobean **Felix Hotel,** built in 1903 by T.W. Cotman for a Tollemache, with 250 bedrooms, 20 grass tennis courts and an 18-hole putting green. The Empress of Germany spent a month at the Italianate **South Beach Mansion** in 1891, the resort's heyday. There is another side of Felixstowe too; it is the 'Burnstow' of M.R. James's ghost story *O Whistle and I'll Come, My Lad*, with its Martello towers, shingle beach and liminal east-coast air – an atmosphere best evoked on **Landguard Point**, a lonely shingle spit extending into the mouth of the River Orwell. From the spit you get good views of container ships being piloted in and out of port.

Tourist Information

Felixstowe: The Seafront, **t** (01394) 276 770. *Open daily 9–5.30.*

Where to Stay and Eat

Felixstowe t (01394) –

The Alex, 123 Undercliff Road West, **t** 282 958 (*moderate*). Contemporary-style bar and bistro occupying the old Cordy's tea rooms. Plain restaurant upstairs with sea views and relaxed tempo. At night it's the busiest bar in Felixstowe, but Sunday lunches are a family affair. Fish and chips, Spanish omelette or sausage and mash for lunch, moules marinières for dinner. *Restaurant closed Sun eve.*

The Castle Lodge Hotel, Chevalier Road, **t** 282 149 (*moderate*). Pretty Edwardian cream-painted building with bay windows in quiet residential area. Fresh and airy inside.

The Elizabeth Orwell Hotel, Hamilton Road, **t** 285 511, *www.elizabethhotels.co.uk* (*moderate*). Late Victorian Dutch-style hotel, now caters for conferences and coach parties, but its 58 bedrooms are comfortable and standards remain high. Restaurant serves traditional English-style food including roast beef and Yorkshire pudding or poached salmon and dill.

Cliff Top Tea Rooms, Cliff House, Cobbold Road, **t** 277 929 (*cheap*). A striking building, built by the Cobbold brewers as a private seaside home. Now you can get tea, coffee and cakes, as well as light lunches and roast dinners on Sunday. Open Tues–Sun.

Mrs Simpson's Tea Rooms, Undercliff Road East, **t** 670 396 (*cheap*). Attractive Dutch-gabled hall, built in 1904 and for a time used as a function room by Thomas Cotman's Fludyer Hotel. It is named after the infamous Mrs Simpson, who stayed two doors down (the house has long gone) while her divorce papers were going through in Ipswich. You can get a decent pot of tea, cakes and light lunches. *Winter closed Thurs.*

Entertainment

The Spa Pavilion, The Seafront, **t** 282 126. Concerts including tribute bands, classical orchestras, touring popular musicals, drama, stand-up comedy and occasional films.

The Suffolk Wool Towns

Suffolk is full of wool towns that grew rich on the manufacture of woollen cloth in the late medieval and Tudor periods and have changed little since, characterized by timber-framed buildings, painted pink, cream and yellow, and late Perpendicular churches with flushwork towers and large windows. The best are clustered around the rivers Stour, Box and Brett: **Lavenham**, **Sudbury**, **Long Melford**, **Hadleigh**, **Bildeston**, **Lindsey**, **Kersey** and **Boxton**. These picturesque confections of pargetting (decorative bands of plasterwork grapes, flowers and hanging fruit) and timber were the thriving industrial centres of the 15th and 16th centuries, turning wool into fine cloth long before the cotton towns of the north took up their looms. Clothiers, like the Cloptons of Long Melford and Springs of Lavenham, were the first capitalists. They invested in raw materials and equipment, supervised the manufacturing and exported the finished cloth to domestic and foreign markets. They grew rich, particularly in the boom years between 1400 and 1555, and built grandiose guildhalls and churches.

Lavenham

Lavenham is the queen of the wool towns, perfect in every detail. Narrow streets lead off the old market place and the edges of town fade into the Suffolk countryside. Every building boasts a unique pattern of exposed timbers. Now a village, in the 15th century Lavenham was wealthier than York or Lincoln, its wealth based on quality broadcloth. This is when the long lime-washed **guildhall** was built on the market place. It now houses a **museum** (*open Easter–Oct daily 11–5; adm*) of the cloth industry, and has a walled garden of plants used for dying wool in the Middle Ages – yellow chamomile, lily of the valley, rue, purple roses and woad. Opposite, the **Little Hall** (*open Easter–Oct Wed, Thurs and weekends 2–5.30; adm minimal*), once the home of a wealthy clothier, was restored in the 1920s by the Gayer-Andersons, twin brothers, who moved in with their widowed mother. Both ex-army, 'the colonel' and 'the major' collected art and antiques, specializing in Egyptian antiquities and Indian water-colours. There are no treasures left here, but you can look around the house.

The **church** stands on the hill, its 141-foot-high tower of knapped flint broadcasting the wealth of its benefactors in glorious late Perpendicular style. The big names behind it are John de Vere, Earl of Oxford, and the Thomas Springs, father and son. Lord of the manor De Vere returned to England in 1485 at the head of Henry VII's army. To celebrate the victory at Bosworth and the restoration of his estates, he made the wealthy merchants fund a new church. Thomas Spring was the biggest donor; you can see his merchant mark and coat of arms in the fan-vaulted south porch, around the base of the tower and above the windows of the lady chapel. In the north aisle, behind an elaborately carved oak screen, is the old chantry of Thomas Spring the younger. You can see the Spring coat of arms in among the naturalistic tracery. St Blaise, the patron saint of wool merchants, carries a wool comb on one of the corner posts.

Long Melford

From Sudbury you approach up a broad main street of handsome colour-washed buildings, which opens out into a green, framed by the red-brick wall and pepper-pot turrets of Melford Hall, a group of painted Georgian houses and the great flushwork church – the superlative attractions of Long Melford, along with Kentwell Hall. The **church**, completed in 1484, embodies to perfection the late-Perpendicular ideal of semi-transparency with its huge windows in the aisles and clerestory. Its chief benefactors were the Cloptons of Kentwell and the Cordells of Melford Hall. The other donors are remembered in the stained-glass windows of the north aisle: one shows three rabbits sharing three ears of corn, symbolizing the Trinity; another, of Elizabeth Talbot, Duchess of Norfolk, inspired John Tenniel's drawings of the duchess in *Alice in Wonderland*. In the **Kentwell Chapel** is the tomb of William Clopton (d. 1446), father of John, the largest purse behind the church. Duck through an archway, and a tiny vaulted passageway leads into the **Clopton Chantry**, from which you emerge into the warmth of the red-brick almshouses and pink roses.

Behind a brick wall, topiary hedge, dry moat and grounds, the Tudor mansion of **Melford Hall** turns a shoulder to the road; you have to go round the back to reach its two-storey Caen stone porch. The house was built by Sir William Cordell, advisor to queens Mary and Elizabeth, whose tomb stands beside the high altar in the church. The Parker family of admirals later commissioned fashionable architect Thomas Hopper to liven it up with florid Regency door cases and a neo-Greek staircase – quite a surprise, leading up from the Tudor hall between colonnades of smooth Ionic columns and Chinese vases. Upstairs is an exhibition of sketches by Beatrix Potter, a cousin and frequent visitor of the Hyde Parkers.

At the end of an avenue of lime trees, and encircled by a carp-infested moat, stands **Kentwell Hall** (***t*** *(01787) 310 207, www.kentwell.co.uk; open Easter–June Sun and Tues–Thurs 12–5, July–Aug daily 12–5, Sept Sun, Wed and Thurs 12–5, Oct Sun 12–5; call or check website for dates and times of Tudor recreations; adm exp*), the magnificent Tudor mansion of the Cloptons, a vision of red brick and glass around a patterned Tudor Rose courtyard, featuring gables, chimneys and every kind of fiendish architectural protuberance known to man. It has been heavily restored in the last thirty years. The interior, gutted by fire in 1826, still has some wood-simulated plasterwork by Thomas Hopper, but Kentwell's real charm is its Tudor recreations in summer.

Sudbury

A bronze statue of Thomas Gainsborough (1727–88) stands on top of Market Hill, in front of one of Sudbury's three churches. His birthplace, an 18th-century townhouse at the bottom of the hill, holds a remarkable collection of his paintings. Sudbury is a busy old town, which reinvented itself after the wool boom as a centre of silk weaving. From it you can walk along the Stour Valley to Long Melford, starting off across the Commons, 115 acres of flood plain grazed by cows.

Gainsborough's House (***t*** *(01787) 376 991; open Tues–Sat 10–5, Sun 2–5; Nov–Mar closes at 4*) is the handsome Georgian house where Gainsborough grew up. His father

Tourist Information

Lavenham: Lady Street, **t** (01787) 248 207. *Open Easter–Oct daily 10–4.45, Nov–Dec and Mar weekends 11–4.*

Sudbury: The Town Hall, Market Hill, **t** (01787) 881 320. *Open Mon–Fri 9–5, Sat 10–2.25.*

Sudbury has a general **market**, selling fruit, clothes and cat baskets, on Thurs and Sat on Market Hill and in front of the Town Hall.

Hadleigh: Hadleigh Library, 29 High Street, **t** (01473) 823 778. *Open 9.30–5.*

A big **agricultural show** takes place annually on the third Saturday in May at Holbecks Park, a large field on the outskirts of Hadleigh, featuring terrier-racing, sheep-shearing, trade stands, arts and craft stalls, fun fair and bike stunts. Contact Barbara Jones, **t** (01473) 827 920, *www.hfaa.agripro.co.uk.*

Where to Stay and Eat

Lavenham t (01787) –

Lavenham Priory, Water Street, **t** 247 404, *www.lavenhampriory.co.uk* (*expensive*). At the heart of this grand, ancient house is a large medieval hall, reached down a cobbled passage. All bedrooms have crown posts, individually decorated, and four-poster beds; some have late-medieval wall paintings and sloping floors.

The Great House Hotel, Market Place, **t** 247 431, *www.lavenham.demon.co.uk/restaurants/greathouse* (*moderate*). Creaky medieval building behind Georgian façade. Massive oak fireplace in restaurant which serves big helpings of hearty French/English food – halibut with hollandaise or pan-fried sea bass. Otherwise you can sit outside in a leafy courtyard with umbrellas, gas heaters and dripping candles. Charming bedrooms with pretty fabrics and antique furniture.

The Angel Hotel, Market Place, **t** 247 388, *www.lavenham.co.uk/angel* (*moderate*). One of the few buildings in Lavenham without beams all over it, but inside the age of the building shows with the 17th-century moulded ceilings, massive brick fireplace and scraps of painting on the old timbers. Eight understated bedrooms and a sitting room whose window opens onto the market place. The restaurant serves dinners of steak and ale pie, red snapper fillet with crab and ginger sauce, sirloin steak, leek and sweet potato crumble.

Sparling and Faiers Bakery, Market Place, **t** 247 296 (*cheap*). Delicious baguettes to fill with smoked Orford seafood or cheese.

Long Melford t (01787) –

The Countrymen Hotel and Wine Bar, The Green, **t** 312 356, *www.blacklionhotel.net* (*expensive*). A 17th-century restaurant with rooms overlooking the green. The bedrooms have painted walls, patchwork quilts, checked cushion covers and bookshelves. Mediterranean-style cooking includes cured ham, spinach and walnut pastry tartlet or leek and sun-dried tomato pie in the **wine bar** (*moderate*), where old French wine posters line the walls. Suave candle-lit **restaurant** (*expensive*) serves sirloin steak, chargrilled tuna, giant prawns wrapped in bacon or ricotta cheese, spinach and parmesan pudding.

The Bull Hotel, Hall Street, **t** 378 494, *www.oldenglish.co.uk* (*expensive*). Creaky, timber-framed 15th-century wool merchant's house with sloping corridors; 23 bedrooms decorated with tapestry-style quilt covers and comfy armchairs. Restaurant (*moderate*) with good fireplace and beams serves good old English specialities including steak, venison and beef.

Sudbury t (01787) –

The Mill Hotel, Walnut Tree Lane, **t** 375 544, *www.millhotelsuffolk.co.uk* (*moderate*). White weatherboard old mill building on the River Stour, which still turns the old 16ft waterwheel in the lounge bar. The **Riverside Restaurant** looks like it belongs on a cruise ship. Lunch might include tiger prawns or Mediterranean salad followed by poached salmon or 'a tower of aubergine

was a Sudbury cloth dealer and his uncle ran the grammar school, where young Thomas's attendance record was marred by unauthorized sketching trips to the Suffolk countryside. At 13 he left for London to study art, earning money as an and courgette'. There are 56 comfortable bedrooms overlooking meadows.

Red Onion Bistro, Ballingdon Street, **t** 376 777 (*moderate*). From the centre of town it's a reasonable walk along an attractive but busy road to this charming restaurant (formerly a Quaker meeting house) with pine box pews and gingham table cloths. *Closed Sun and Mon.*

Brasserie 47, 47 Gainsborough Street, **t** 374 298 (*cheap*). Informal brasserie with pine wooden pews and tables serving morning coffee, lunch and dinner. Warm, buttery baguettes or stuffed chicken breast, pan-fried salmon and vegetable stir fry. *Closed Sun and Mon.*

Waggon and Horse, Acton Square, **t** 312 147 (*cheap*). Excellent, atmospheric little pub near the town centre, with murals of the town decorating the patio. Decent pub grub and three functional bedrooms.

Hadleigh and Around

Edge Hall Hotel, 2 High Street, **t** (01473) 822 458, *www.edgehall-hotel.co.uk* (*moderate*). Grand Georgian-fronted hotel at top of High Street with flagstone hall and Zoffany print wallpaper; eight comfortable bedrooms.

Odds and Ends, 131 High Street, **t** (01473) 822 032, *www.oddsandends.org.uk* (*moderate*). Three bedrooms, plus another three in the converted stable block.

College Farm, Hintlesham (4 miles east of Hadleigh on the Ipswich road), **t** (01473) 652 253, *www.smoothhound.co.uk/hotels/collegefarm* (*moderate*). Ancient, low-ceilinged farmhouse on edge of 600 acres of arable farmland with winding wooden staircase, sloping floors and four bedrooms including large double overlooking garden.

Weavers Restaurant, 25 High Street, **t** (01473) 827 247, *www.weaversrestaurant.co.uk* (*cheap*). Behind the old shop window you find a restaurant and bar with patio garden. Formerly part of a row of weavers' cottages, the old building features beams and wonky floors, but the atmosphere is not at all creaky. Dishes include Thai chicken curry, baked salmon, pasta or whitebait. Three attractive white-painted bedrooms with beams (*moderate*).

Fair View, Priory Hill, **t** (01473) 828 606 (*cheap*). Attractive 17th-century cottage with pine and wicker furniture, exposed timber and brickwork, cosy carpets and two bedrooms with views across valley to church.

The Fleece Inn, Broad Street, Boxford, **t** (01787) 210 796 (*cheap*). Georgian-fronted timber-framed inn with Friday jazz evenings.

The Fox and Hound, Groton (near Boxford), **t** (01787) 210 474 (*cheap*). Small pink pebble-dashed pub on hill top surrounded by open fields, serves Green King and Adnams, fresh pies and fish.

Nayland t (01206) –

The White Hart Inn, High Street, **t** 263 382, *www.whitehart-nayland.co.uk* (*moderate*). Fifteenth-century coaching inn just north of the River Stour. Six tasteful bedrooms. The restaurant is French fusion, and produces elaborate dishes such as salad of quail stuffed with foie gras on mango chutney followed by roast loin of suckling pig and strawberry charlotte. *Closed Mon.*

The Angel Inn, Stoke By Nayland, **t** 263 245, *www.horizoninns.co.uk* (*moderate*). People travel miles to eat in the **Well Room**, with its rough brick walls, raftered ceiling and 52ft well, on a remote crossroads near St Mary's Church. A meal might include grilled liver and bacon on bubble and squeak, or locally smoked trout fillet followed by steamed apple pudding. Sunday lunch includes roast pork with crackling. Six beautifully decorated bedrooms and a cosy bar with beams. In summer you can sit on patio.

Entertainment

The Quay Theatre, Quay Lane, Sudbury, **t** (01787) 374 745. Former granary on the Quay basin with small 125-seater brick-walled auditorium hosting amateur dramatics and touring professional theatre.

engraver and illustrator. The artist returned briefly to Sudbury with his wife, Margaret, en route to Ipswich, Bath and London again. His reputation was made by setting portrait figures in landscapes, and providing unwelcome insights into the characters of the society figures who were his subjects. In Sudbury, Gainsborough painted Mr and Mrs Andrews of Ballington Hall, set among Suffolk wheat fields beneath thunder clouds, and an intriguing portrait of a boy and a girl, of which only the boy and the girl's hand and dress edge remain. The portrait of a mother and daughter 'in a landscape with a lamb and ewe' once hung on a wall of Holywell Park, home of Ipswich brewers the Cobbolds.

Hadleigh

Halfway between Ipswich and Sudbury, Hadleigh's handsome pargetted and colour-washed High Street is full of shops selling power tools – but the main attraction is the **church**. The steeple – often painted by Gainsborough – is unusual in a county of pinnacled towers; it rises above the turreted tower of the deanery and the rust-red medieval guildhall. The interior is the largest in Suffolk.

Nayland

The church here is as cheerful as the village, with its creeping roses, wisteria and herbaceous borders. Above the altar is Constable's only religious painting, *Christ Blessing the Elements*, painted for church in 1809, stolen in the 1990s and now so well secured behind reflecting glass that you can barely see it.

Woodbridge and Around

Woodbridge is a good stop-off on the A12 from London to the Suffolk coast. The town prospered on shipbuilding and trade into the first decades of the 20th century, with its flat-bottomed Thames sailing barges. The Deben is a classic Suffolk river and the Sutton Hoo Saxon boat burial on the north bank has recently come of age.

Market Hill

Market Hill is all old world charm: the King's Head pub, painted houses and Shire Hall with its Dutch gables and double flight of external stairs. The church tower peeps over the roofs, and two parallel streets slope down to the quay. In the hall is the **Shire Horse Museum** (*open Easter–Sept daily 2–5; adm minimal*), run by the Suffolk Horse Society. The Suffolk Punch was a short-legged heavy horse that was the tractor of pre-industrial Suffolk; today there are only about 80 breeding mares left.

On one side of the square is the **town museum** (***t*** *(01394) 383 984; open Easter–Oct Thurs–Sat 10–4, Sun 2.30–4.40; adm minimal*), with an introduction to Sutton Hoo (*see* below), Woodbridge painter Thomas Churchyard and the poet Edward Fitzgerald, who is buried in Boulge churchyard. The porch of **St Mary's Church** proclaims the Suffolk wool money of 16th-century cloth merchant Thomas Seckford, buried inside.

The **quay** is pretty and workmanlike. You can walk along the river to Kyson Point. Across it is Sutton Hoo. The 18th-century white weatherboard **Tide Mill** (*open May–Sept daily 11–5, Oct weekends 11–5; adm minimal*) is said to be the last of its kind.

Tourist Information

Woodbridge: Station Buildings, **t** (01394) 382 240. *Open summer daily 9.30–5, winter Mon–Fri 9.30–5, Sat 10–4 and Sun 10–1*. Good selection of walking guides and maps.

Until a couple of years ago the small Thursday **market** took place in front of the Town Hall, around the town pump. Now, to spare Woodbridge residents the climb up Market Hill, it's held in the car park at the top of Brook Street.

Where to Stay and Eat

Woodbridge t (01394) –

The tourist information centre has a number of guesthouses and B&Bs on its lists, also at *www.suffolkcoastal.gov.uk/leisure/wheretostay*. Mrs Schlee of Deben Lodge, **t** (01394) 382 740, organizes the **Oxfam B&B scheme**, with about 12 places to stay in town, and more in neighbouring villages. One-third of your tariff goes to the charity. Since the scheme began in 1984 it has raised almost a quarter of a million pounds.

The Crown Hotel, Thoroughfare, **t** 384 242, *www.oldenglish.co.uk* (*expensive*). Pleasant place to stay on corner of Quay Street with 20 bedrooms. Refurbished in 2003.

The Captain's Table, 3 Quay Street, **t** 383 145 (*moderate*). Popular, classy cottage restaurant. Slow-roasted duck, roasted vegetable risotto and lots of good seafood. *Closed Sun eve and Mon.*

The Bull Hotel, Market Hill, **t** 382 089 (*moderate*). Former coaching inn with striking yellow-and-white painted façade, offers 14 basic rooms with showers somehow squeezed in.

Deben Lodge, Melton Road, **t** 382 740 (*cheap*). Victorian house in large gardens with tennis court and stream on edge of town. You can walk down to river from house and along sea wall into town.

Mrs Coates' B&B, 99 New Street, **t** 382 521 (*cheap*). Victorian townhouse with sweet little bedroom; neat, clean and quiet. Close to centre and The Bell and Steelyard pubs.

Around Woodbridge

The Ramsholt Arms, Dock Road, Ramsholt, **t** (01394) 411 229 (*moderate*). Old-fashioned pub in delightfully remote location on the other side of the River Deben from Woodbridge, 20 minutes' drive in the direction of Bawdsey. Ramsholt was once a busy quay, and now consists of a few rusty trawlers, a handful of yachts, nodding reeds and smells of river mud, salt and pine trees. Grandstand views of sun setting over Deben from patio, and meals of freshly caught Dover sole and new potatoes or roast partridge followed by sticky toffee pudding.

The Old Rectory, Campsea Ashe, **t** (01728) 746 524, *www.theoldrectorysuffolk.com* (*moderate*). Treat yourself to a night or two in one of eight lovely bedrooms (one with Victorian washstand and cast-iron bath) in this classy Georgian rectory beside the church. Tea and cake are offered to guests in the afternoon. In the evenings you can relax in the elegant drawing room before sitting down to dinner, served in the dining room or conservatory.

Sutton Hoo

t (01394) 389 700; visitor centre open Mar–April and Oct Wed–Sun 10–5, May–Sept daily 10–5, Nov–Feb weekends 10–5; adm.

The famous Anglo-Saxon barrow cemetery of Sutton Hoo above the estuary of the Deben, near the village of Sutton, yielded the remains of a 90-foot-long clinker-built long ship containing the coffin of an East Anglian king. The grave treasures included a magnificent crested helmet and shield, Byzantine silver, gold ornaments and jewels and musical instruments. In another of the 18 barrows, a young warrior was found next to the grave of his horse. Combine your visit with lunch at the Ramsholt Arms and a walk to Ramsholt church.

Suffolk Churches

Suffolk is crammed with beautiful little churches built on the back of the wool trade. Even the most unassuming villages have hidden gems. These are just a few.

The Church of the Assumption, Ufford

A few miles north of Woodbridge, obscure Ufford has a world-class treasure hidden away in its church of the Assumption – the hanging font cover. It is 18 feet high, encrusted with pinnacles and niches and topped by a pelican.

The Church of St Mary, Grundisburgh

Down minor lanes west of Woodbridge, Grundisburgh is not short of charm, with its village green and duck splash. R.F.J. Williams' general shop is a Suffolk institution, an Aladdin's Cave for adults, where Wellington boots, socks and bags of seeds acquire a patina of desirability. If the church is locked, the shop has a key. The church's glory is the magnificent 15th-century double hammer-beam roof with more than 50 winged angels leaning out from the posts and beams. On the north wall is a faint painting of a headless St Christopher carrying the boy Jesus on his shoulders over the water.

Boulge Church

The church visitors' book is full of a mixture of sentiment and practicality: 'E.F.'s rose tree needs pruning.' E.F. is the poet Edward Fitzgerald (1809–83), best known for his 1859 translation of *The Rubaiyat of Omar Khayyam* from the Persian. To find the church, aim for Bredfield off the A12, north of Woodbridge; about 650 yards after the pump is a rough track to the church. You can identify Fitzgerald's grave in the overgrown churchyard by the large rose bush at its foot.

Bury St Edmunds

Halfway between Ipswich and Cambridge on the A14, Suffolk's cathedral town is the epitome of old English charm: quiet, wide streets and bright, neat Georgian buildings; excellent pubs, restaurants and hotels; and considerable architectural interest, both secular and religious. Bury grew up around the abbey, a popular pilgrimage site and one of the most powerful in the country by the time of the Reformation. It was founded in 1020 to house the tomb of King Edmund (841–70), the last of the East Anglian kings, defeated and killed by the Viking 'great army', led by Ivor the Boneless, at Hoxne near Diss. The pathos of his doomed stand and his execution by multiple arrows in a ritual sacrifice to Scandinavian gods turned Edmund into a legendary good king.

The town has two centres: the old market place and Angel Hill, a street of religious buildings and Georgian architecture. On one side of **Angel Hill** is the battlemented abbey gate, the west front of the cathedral, the magnificent Norman tower and the hidden marvels of St Mary's Church. To the rear, public gardens are dotted with the flint ruins of the abbey. Across the street is the Angel Hotel, its Georgian front

Getting There

By train, change at Stow Market from London Liverpool Street, Cambridge from King's Cross, or Peterborough from the north.

There are two National Express **coaches** a day from London, and one from Liverpool.

Tourist Information

Bury St Edmunds: Angel Hill, **t** (01284) 764 667. *Open Easter–Oct Mon–Sat 9.30–5.30, Sun 11–4; winter Mon–Fri 10–4, Sat 10–1.*

Wed and Sat **markets** in Butter Market, spreading into Cornhill.

Walking Tours with Blue Badge Guides run all summer, starting here at 2.30 and taking you into the abbey ruins, gardens and around town. Contact the tourist information centre for these and **Cathedral Tours**.

Where to Stay

Bury St Edmunds t (01284) –

The Angel Hotel, Angel Hill, **t** 753 926, *www.theangel.co.uk* (*expensive*). Ideally located opposite the Abbey Gardens, a striking building with a portico protruding from the foliage of thick Virginia creeper. Good place for a cup of coffee and sandwiches, two restaurants ('fine dining' and brasserie) and 65 comfortable bedrooms.

Ounce House B&B, Northgate Street, **t** 761 779, *www.ouncehouse.co.uk* (*expensive*). Beautiful, detached Victorian house with large bay window, elaborate carved fire surround, large oval mahogany breakfast table, sitting room with chunky sofas and a snug with honesty bar and bookshelves.

83 Whiting Street B&B, **t** 704 153 (*moderate*). A minute away from the town centre, behind the pink Georgian stuccoed façade is a medieval hall house full of treasures, including a 16th-century mural, beams, beautifully painted Georgian panelling and rooms furnished in pine. Lovely bedspreads.

Ash Cottage B&B, 59 Whiting Street, **t** 755 098, *www.ash-cottage.com* (*moderate*). Homely town-centre cottage. Old brick fireplace with wooden lintel, lots of family photographs and flourishing rear garden.

The Old Cannon Brewery, Cannon Street, **t** 768 769 (*moderate*). Old Victorian pub and brewery in back streets of Bury. Five modest, clean bedrooms. The pub has its own micro brewery in the bar, which produces Old Cannon Best Bitter or the stronger Gunner's ale, in winter Black Pig and in summer Blond Bombshell. Also a 60-seater restaurant.

South Hill House, 43 Southgate Street, **t** 755 650, *www.southill.freeserve.co.uk* (*moderate*).

smothered in creeper, and the elegant, porticoed Athenaeum, the social nexus of the Georgian town. The **Abbey Visitor Centre** (***t*** *(01284) 763 110; open April–Oct daily, Nov–Mar Wed, Sat and Sun pm*) has a reconstruction of the abbey – very useful as what remains has very little in common with the painted stonework of the old abbey. It is housed in **Samson's Tower**, itself worth a look. The **Norman Tower** was once the grand entrance into the abbey church, doubling up as the bell tower of St James's Church (now the cathedral) next door. The decorative carving around the arches is sharply defined. At the high altar, a plaque commemorates an oath made here on 20 November 1214 by the English barons 'that they would obtain from King John the ratification of *Magna Carta*'.

St James's was elevated into a **cathedral** in 1914, ending an age-old grudge against the East Anglian cathedral towns of Thetford and Norwich. The nave of the original church was replaced in 1503 by John Wastell, architect of King's College chapel in Cambridge. The colourful, high-pitched roof was added by George Gilbert Scott in 1862–4. Around the walls of the choir are the coats of arms of the barons of *Magna Carta*, who are supposed to have met at the abbey before Runnymede. The cathedra

Georgian façade and Victorian bell tower. It was once an Academy for Young Ladies where Charles Dickens used to visit to read to the girls. Extraordinary interior with Tudor fireplace.

Regency Hotel, 3 Looms Lane, **t** 764 676 (*moderate*). A short stroll from the centre, a beautiful cream-painted 18th-century town-house hotel with shutters, covered colonnade, elegant conservatory bar and restaurant and 16 bedrooms including six in old stable block.

Eating Out

Bury is so charming that it redeems the chain café-bars and restaurants – Pizza Express, Café Rouge and Café Uno – all on Abbeygate Street.

Maison Bleu Seafood Restaurant, 30–31 Churchgate Street, **t** 760 623 (*moderate*). Charming seafood restaurant with pine floors, a brick fireplace and sea-blue walls featuring a mural of the White Cliffs. *Closed Sun, Mon and Jan.*

The Angel Hotel, Angel Hill, **t** 753 926 (*moderate*). Two high-quality dining rooms: Abbeygate for formal lunches and dinners and The Vaults brasserie. *Open dinner only.*

Bangkok City, Angel Hill, **t** 704 870 (*cheap*). Thai restaurant in an old Tudor building. Special lunches (three starters, four main dishes and rice). *Open eves only, closed Sun.*

Harriet's Café, 57 Cornhill Buildings, **t** 756 256 (*cheap*). Stylish 1940s traditional English tearooms. Period-style waitresses in black with white aprons. Real coffee, no tea bags. Afternoon tea served on a silver platter. Pianist at weekends and alternate Tues and Wed. Breakfasts and home-made lunches such as chicken pie.

The Nutshell, The Traverse, **t** 764 867 (*cheap*). This curious museum-like drinking hole in the centre of town calls itself the smallest pub in Britain; 200 years ago it was a pawn-brokers, which might explain the unusual collection of bits and pieces on display. The walls are papered with yellowing old bank notes, postcards and coins, and the shelves are stacked with old pint bottles of Green King, hats and stuffed animal heads. One glass case contains a mummified frog. On another wall, a copy of a 19th-century execution list includes the name William Corder for the date 11 August 1828 (for crimes unknown). In 1982, 102 people and a dog called Blob were packed in.

Scandinavia Coffee House, Angel Hill **t** 700 853 (*cheap*). Unassuming coffee shop located across from the abbey gardens with outside seating overlooking the abbey gatehouse and friendly service.

(bishop's throne) incorporates a carving of St Edmund's severed head at the feet of a protective wolf. The refectory serves wholesome lunches.

Step into **St Mary's Church**, further up Angel Hill, and you step back into the Middle Ages. Its double hammer-beam roof was carved in 1433; below the beams are 11 pairs of winged angels in a procession at the Coronation of the Virgin Mary.

Churchgate Street leads off Angel Hill to the **Unitarian Meeting House**, built in 1711 in elegant baroque style. It is a classic Nonconformist meeting house, the central space surrounded by galleries on three sides and still containing the original box pews, although it is now a concert and exhibition venue.

The **Green King Brewery** (*Westgate Street, **t** (01284) 714 382; museum open Mon–Sat 11–5; tours Mon–Fri 11am, 2pm and 7pm; adm; best to book ahead*) has been a feature of Bury for 200 years. Tours of the red-brick buildings include the brewhouse, milling room, malt store and mash tun floor. The **Theatre Royal** on Westgate Street (***t** (01284) 769 505; box office open Mon–Sat 10–8; tours once a month on Sat*) is another Bury architectural gem. Built by the architect of London's National Gallery, William Wilkins, it opened in 1818, hosting a short season between October and November every year.

The **Art Gallery** on Cornhill (*open Tues–Sat 10.30–4.30; adm minimal*) is in the middle of the commercial part of town, next to the Victorian corn exchange. It is housed on the first floor of the old Market Cross, built in fine neo-classical style by Robert Adam in 1780. The gallery used to be a theatre, while the open market was on the ground floor. Adam's building became the town hall when Wilkins' theatre was built.

The dark, flint gables of **Moyse's Hall Museum** (*adm minimal*), in a late 12th-century townhouse, loom over the market place. The identity of Moyse remains a mystery, but the vaulted stone undercroft with its stocky pillars might have been a merchant's stores. It was turned into a museum in 1899 and filled with tools, coins, weapons and jewellery from every era: a 4th-century Romano-British coffin, a 15th-century decorated corner post from an old Bury inn, a collection of 18th-century rapiers and truncheons and a 19th-century horse-skull fiddle. For many the highlight is relics of the 19th-century 'Murder in the Red Barn' – a celebrated case which became the subject of a popular play; gruesome trophies include the murderer William Corder's scalp and ear 'tanned by George Creed' ('still visible is the stubble') and a book bound in his skin, as well as the lantern by whose light Maria Marten's body was found in the Red Barn – a search prompted by her mother's prophetic dream.

Ickworth House

Open 20 Mar–31 Oct, house Tues–Wed and Fri–Sun 1–5, gardens daily 10-5; adm.

Two miles south of Bury on the A143, Ickworth is as impractical as it is beautiful, an Italian oddity in the Suffolk countryside. Its creator was Frederick Augustus Hervey, Bishop of Derry and 4th Earl of Bristol, known as the bishop-earl. He owned large estates in Ireland and East Anglia, and built treasure houses to exhibit the collections he bought on European Grand Tours – but the French invaded Italy in 1798 and occupied Rome, imprisoning the bishop-earl and confiscating his collections. He was released after nine months but never returned to England; he died on travels south of Rome in 1803.

The bishop-earl's son, the 5th Earl, arranged the muted interiors, which allow the paintings by Gainsborough, Hogarth, Titian and Poussin, and sculptures by Flaxman, to shine. The entrance hall is more flashy: shiny marble and family portraits (including one of the bishop-earl) beneath the skylit dome of the rotunda. The centrepiece is Flaxman's marble *Fury of Athamas*, commissioned by the bishop-earl in Italy in 1790, showing the scene from Ovid's *Metamorphosis* in which Athamas swings his child by the foot, about to dash out his brains on a rock. Most of the Hervey family portraits hang in the drawing room, including Gainsborough's full-length portrait of Vice Admiral Augustus John Hervey, the 3rd Earl, casually leaning against a ship's anchor. The best likeness of the bishop-earl is said to be the portrait by Madame Vigée Lebrun. The Pompeian Room was designed by J.D. Crace in 1879, based on Roman frescoes acquired by the 4th Earl on his Italian travels. The house is surrounded by early 19th-century Italianate gardens studded with conifers.

The Suffolk Coast

Aldeburgh

'The place on the east coast which the reader is asked to consider is Seaburgh,' wrote M.R. James at the start of his ghost story *Warning to the Curious*. Seaburgh was Victorian Aldeburgh. James describes the long higgledy-piggledy seafront of painted, Dutch-gabled, bay-windowed houses, the marshes around the River Alde and the Martello tower where his hapless antiquarian gets his brains bashed in by a barefoot ghost. That scene is pretty much unchanged: fishing boats, early-morning swimmers, the pebble beach cluttered with boats and fishing tackle, and black wooden huts

Getting There and Around

Aldeburgh is a 15-minute drive from the A12. It's not an easy place to reach by public transport: you can catch a **train** or **coach** to Ipswich, then Anglia Railways runs a service to Saxmundham (just under an hour), or a local bus goes all the way to Aldeburgh. There is a shuttle bus between Aldeburgh and Snape during the festivals.

Tourist Information

Aldeburgh: 152 High Street, **t** (01728) 453 637, *www.aldeburgh.co.uk. Open summer 9–5.30, winter 9.30-5.*

Festivals

Music

The Aldeburgh Festival of Music and Arts is run by Aldeburgh Productions, who are based at Snape Maltings Concert Hall. It lasts two weeks in June in and around the town, including Aldeburgh church and Jubilee Hall, the purpose-built concert hall at Snape and occasionally Blythburgh and Orford churches. It was started by Benjamin Britten in 1948, and has grown and grown, attracting international celebrity performances as well as unknowns. Some events are sold out months in advance, others you can just turn up for. If you plan to stay and eat in town you must book early.

Aldeburgh Productions founded the **Snape Proms** in the mid 1980s. They now last the whole of August. The venue is the Snape Maltings Concert Hall, and the programme features light classical, folk, jazz and cabaret.

The **Britten Festival** takes place over the last weekend in October. Works by Britten and a guest composer are played in the concert hall.

For all three festivals contact the box office, **t** (01728) 687 110, *enquiries@aldeburgh.co.uk*.

The Britten emporium also holds **Snape Master Classes** at Snape Maltings Concert Hall; contact the Britten-Piers Young Artists Program, **t** (01728) 688 671. The classes take place between Easter and October. It's a chance to listen in on the very best young musicians (mainly singers) learning their craft. Each class lasts 45 minutes, but you can come and go as you please, as long as you do it quietly so as not to disturb the proceedings.

Poetry

The **Poetry Festival** takes place over the first weekend in November. It was founded about 15 years ago, and now claims to be the country's leading poetry festival (they all do). The main venue for this weekend of poetry readings, workshops, master classes and lectures is Jubilee Hall. Some years are completely sold out, so book early. The full programme is available in August and the box office opens in early September, **t** (01728) 687 110, *www.aldeburghpoetryfestival.org*, *info@aldeburghpoetryfestival.org*.

Theatre

The actress and director Jill Freud has been running a summer season of theatre in Southwold since 1984, when her company took over the repertory theatre for the whole summer season. It has since expanded into a mini Southwold Festival with lunchtime shows, jazz, poetry and celebrity evenings. In 1994 the Jubilee Hall Trust invited the where you can buy the morning's catch of rock eel, sole and flounder. The Alde and a long shingle bank cut Aldeburgh off from the south, and half of the lower town and the old harbour have been eroded away by the sea: the Tudor moot hall, once in the middle of town, now stands only a few yards back from the shore, and the birthplace of the poet George Crabbe (1754–1832) has vanished underwater.

The hero of Crabbe's poem *The Borough* inspired Suffolk composer Benjamin Britten's first opera, *Peter Grimes*, which put Aldeburgh on the map. The annual Aldeburgh arts festival, now an international event, was started in 1948 by Britten. Cheerful and crowded in summer, Aldeburgh puts on a special show of wind-lashed desolation in winter.

company of 21 actors (including Jill), 10 students and about 10 technicians down to Aldeburgh to do the same. The hall now hosts a two-week festival in conjunction with Southwold (*see* p.658).

Jill Freud and Company Summer Theatre, 152 High Street, Aldeburgh **t** (01728) 453 007 (advance booking); Jubilee Hall, **t** (01728) 454 002 (during festival).

Carnival

At the carnival grand finale of the Aldeburgh Festival in mid-August, people process through the town carrying Chinese lanterns and there is a huge display of fireworks over the sea. Worth attending even if you miss the music, poetry and theatre.

Where to Stay

Aldeburgh t (01728) –

Wentworth Hotel, Wentworth Road, **t** 452 312, *www.wentworth-aldeburgh.com* (*very expensive*). This large 1900s gabled hotel overlooks the fishing beach. There are two sitting rooms with log fires, a sunken garden for eating outside and 37 bedrooms, many with sea views. The delightful white-shuttered Darfield House just behind offers stylish bedrooms with window seats and glinting new bathrooms.

The Brudenell Hotel, The Parade, **t** 452 071, *www.brudenellhotel.co.uk* (*expensive*). Large, informal sea-facing hotel with bright and breezy entrance hall and 42 comfortable, recently refurbished bedrooms. Sea-facing restaurant serves mainly English food (*moderate*).

Uplands Hotel, Victoria Road, **t** 452 420 (*moderate*). Four-square, white-painted Georgian former family home of the Newson Garretts, where the pioneering female physician Elizabeth Garrett spent her childhood. Appealing, with its beautiful conservatory, checked floor tiles and 10 comfortable bedrooms.

Ocean House, 25 Crag Path, **t** 452 094 (*moderate*). Victorian seaside house with big bay windows overlooking sea, decorated with old rocking horses, Turkish rugs and a grand piano in the top room, which is occasionally used by visiting Snape Master Class musicians. The breakfast room is a chatty sort of place where you might be served delicious home-made scones and jams. Gets booked up very quickly as it is easily the best place to stay in Aldeburgh. There are bicycles you can borrow.

The White Lion Hotel, Market Cross Place, **t** 452 720, *www.whitelion.co.uk* (*moderate*). Friendly and comfortable Best Western Hotel with glorious sea views. Tends to attract an older crowd; 38 bedrooms, bar and restaurant (*moderate*), which specializes in seafood, including deep-fried cod and chips and crab salad.

Snape, Thorpness and Aldringham t (01728) –

The Crown Inn, Bridge Road, Snape, **t** 688 324 (*moderate*). Cosy, attractive old pub on main road a few miles out of Aldeburgh. Menu includes Thai curry, rack of lamb and local fish. In the beamed interior are two enormous wooden settles around the fire. Also has three bedrooms, one of which has a four-poster.

Crag Path, the seafront promenade, passes the Victorian Jubilee Hall and the 16th-century **moot hall** (*open April–May weekends 2.30–5, June, Sept and Oct daily 2.30–5, July and Aug daily 10.30–12.30 and 2.30–5; adm minimal*), which features in the prologue of *Peter Grimes* as the scene of the trial. Britten lived in **Crag House** from 1947 to 1957. A pleasant walk takes you along the sea wall towards **Slaughdon Quay**, once a busy port guarded by the Martello tower, now a marsh of wooden huts and sailing boats. Ten miles downriver the shingle is the mouth of the Ore and Alde; upriver, you can walk along the river wall, past clinking masts and fields. The church commands the hill above the town, its northeast window commemorating Britten designed by John Piper. There is a Victorian bust of Crabbe, who was curate of the

The Dolphin, Thorpness, **t** 454 994 (*moderate*). Replica of earlier pub in village centre with bright and cheerful dining room where you can eat seafood or perhaps a courgette tart with Dijon mustard and tarragon. Three elegant bedrooms with William Morris-patterned bedspreads.

House in the Clouds, Thorpness, **t** (020) 7224 3615 (*cheap*). One of the unlikeliest places to stay that you are ever likely to find. It was originally the Thorpness village water tower, built in 1920 and cunningly disguised to look like a tree house. Now the tank has been removed and it is a five-bedroom house, standing 70 feet above the Meare. Sleeps 12; winter two days minimum stay, summer a week at a time.

Fern House, 6 The Follies, Aldringham, **t** 830 759, *gallowaymd@aol.com* (*cheap*). Tucked away in a little row of houses down a long fern-banked track on Aldringham Common, beside golf course. Extremely friendly, clean and fresh with pine furniture, blue-and-white checked duvet covers and lovely garden with big old apple tree and pond. You can walk to the sea in 30 minutes, or to the cliffs at Sizewell in 45 minutes.

Eating Out

The Lighthouse, 77 High Street, **t** 453 377 (*moderate*). Informal, crowded, buzzing bistro-style restaurant with stripped wooden floorboards, wooden tables and the sort of eager conversation that always accompanies good simple food and an earnest music-loving clientele. Book ahead (a week or two if possible), particularly on summer weekends and during the festivals. *Closed two weeks in Jan and one week in Oct.*

Regatta, 171 High Street, **t** 452 011 (*moderate*). Another lively eating spot with stripped wooden floorboards, and paintings on the walls. The menu might include crab, lobster, oysters, Dover sole and other local fish. *Winter closed Wed.*

The Mill Inn, Crabbe Street, **t** 452 563 (*cheap*). Friendly locals' pub on the corner of Market Cross Place, opposite the Moot Hall, serving Adnams beer and good bar meals, including fresh fish. *No dinner Thurs and Sun.*

Lawson's at 152, 152 High Street, **t** 454 052 (*cheap*). Good old-fashioned delicatessen, ideal for picnic shopping. Sells cold meat, salami and Suffolk roast ham, and an excellent selection of cheeses including Orford smoked cheddar and stilton, and Suffolk chutneys. Fresh bread, quiches and pork pies on Thurs. *Half-day Mon and Wed, closed Sun.*

The Golden Galleon, 137 High Street, **t** 454 685 (*cheap*). Aldeburgh's best fish and chip shop, with takeaway shop and restaurant.

Entertainment

If all that music, poetry and theatre is not enough to keep you entertained, there are two good cinemas.

Aldeburgh Cinema, 51 High Street, **t** 452 996. Unassuming arthouse cinema with excellent programming.

Leiston Film Theatre, High Street, Leiston, **t** 830 549. Nothing exceptional about the films, but behind its mock-Tudor front, it is the oldest purpose-built cinema in Suffolk.

church. At the back of the churchyard are the graves of Britten (d. 1976), his lover and tenor Peter Pears (d. 1986) and Imogen Holst (d. 1984), daughter of Gustav Holst.

Around Aldeburgh

Follow signs to **Snape Maltings**, a Victorian red-brick brewery taken over by Britten in 1965 as a venue for the Aldeburgh festival. It's a great place to browse and wander in the salt marshes, even if you're not here for a concert.

Four miles north of Aldeburgh, the small town of **Leisten** is home to the fascinating **Long Shop Steam Museum** (***t*** *(01728) 832 189; open April–Oct Mon–Sat 10–5, Sun 11–5; adm*). The old Victorian factory of Richard Garrett & Sons on Main Street is a Grade II listed factory building housing threshing machines, traction engines, steam rollers and electric trolleybuses, manufactured here until 1932 using the new-fangled American-style assembly line. The third Richard Garrett developed the town on the proceeds of his steam engines, installing gas, water, fire engines, a school and sports club, and bringing in the branch line from Saxmundham – which came up the drive in front of the head office. His brother Newson founded the Snape Maltings, and built the Jubilee Hall in Aldeburgh and the family home – now the Uplands Hotel – opposite Aldeburgh church. His daughter, Elizabeth Garrett Anderson, was exceptional: she became the first female doctor in 1865, founding the Elizabeth Garrett Anderson Hospital in London, and became the first female mayor (of Aldeburgh) in 1908.

Orford

By the 16th century Aldeburgh's shingle bar had blocked off the harbour at Orford. The fortified port, with its 12th-century Angevin castle, resumed life as a fishing town, its speciality oysters. It remains a fossilized medieval town between castle and church. Quay Street leads between red-brick walls and pretty cottages to the quay, which looks out across the river to the low shingle ridge of Orford Ness, where secret weapons were tested in the 1960s. The river is the Alde, which here becomes the Ore. There are boat trips to the Ness (sworn to be safe) and around **Havergate Island** (***t*** *(01394) 450 844*), a bird sanctuary a mile downriver. The river wall is good for walks.

The 90-foot-high polygonal keep of the **castle** (*open daily April–Sept 10–6, Oct 10–6 or dusk; Nov–Mar Wed–Sun 10–4; adm*), built by Henry II in 1165, dominates Orford. Just off Market Hill, on Front Street, the Orford Craft Centre hosts an **exhibition of underwater Suffolk** (*open daily 11–5*). The submerged medieval port of Dunwich, explored by 70 divers working in complete darkness in the 1970s and '80s, is the highlight.

Orford Ness

This bleak shingle spit, stretching for 10 miles between Aldeburgh and Shingle Street, was acquired by the Government in 1913 for research into ballistics and aerial warfare, and later for testing atomic weapons. From the quay you see six concrete test cells on pillars, built in the 1960s to test the components of the nuclear bomb under the extreme conditions that it would experience on its journey from storage to impact. In the case of an accidental explosion, the pillars were supposed to blow out and the lid collapse downwards, sealing it in. The spit is now a nature reserve.

Where to Stay and Eat

Orford t (01394) –

The Crown and Castle, Orford, **t** 450 205, *www.crownandcastlehotel.co.uk* (*expensive*). Handsome old inn opposite the Norman keep with 18 attractive bedrooms (10 in garden where dogs are welcome). It prefers to call itself a 'restaurant with rooms' to draw attention to the high standard of cooking that has attracted a flurry of Michelin, AA, Routier and Good Food Guide awards. The style is French/English/Italian with an emphasis on seafood. The shrimps are home-potted, the fish comes from Orford Quay and the asparagus from the next village (in season). Filling breakfasts include French toast with crispy bacon and maple syrup.

Butley-Orford Oysterage, Market Hill, **t** 450 277 (*moderate*). The specialities of this small restaurant with its formica tables and fish counter are fresh oysters from Butley Creek and smoked fish, served with horseradish sauce. You can order a side portion of local samphire (a succulent marsh plant) or brown bread and butter. *Open lunch all year daily; dinner winter Wed–Sat, summer daily.*

There are two good old-fashioned pubs in Orford, both serving decent pub food and Adnams beer, plus basic accommodation: The **Jolly Sailor**, Quay Street, **t** 450 243 (*moderate*) and **King's Head**, Front Street, **t** 450 271 (*moderate*), which does a mean fish pie.

The Little Tern, Quay Street, **t** (01206) 262 087, *www.cccottages.com* (*cheap*). Quaint self-catering cottage with pretty garden and wood-burning stove. *Available weekends in winter, by the week in summer.*

Richardson's Smokehouse, Baker's Lane, off Market Hill, **t** 450 103 (*cheap*). Here you can buy all kinds of Suffolk oak-smoked produce, including wild duck, pheasant, kippers and fish from Scotland and Iceland. The smoked Alaskan wild salmon fishcakes are very popular. *Open 10–4.*

Dunwich t (01728) –

The Ship Inn, **t** 648 219 (*moderate*). Hearty pub food – pies, soup, ploughman's and fish and chips – in the cosy, old-fashioned bar or sunny conservatory; four cheerily furnished bedrooms.

The Barn Cottage, Mill Street, Westleton, **t** 648 437 (*moderate*). Although Mrs Allen is winding down her B&B, she is not yet stopping altogether. Her pretty cream-painted cottage with its rose garden, brick floor-tiles and low beams has three comfortable bedrooms and two bathrooms.

The Pond House, The Hill, Westleton, **t** 648 773 (*moderate*). Pretty white-painted 17th-century cottage with heaps of geraniums overlooking the village green. Three cheerful twin bedrooms, one en-suite.

The White Horse Inn, Darsham Road, Westleton, **t** 648 222 (*cheap*). Busy, popular Adnams pub with crowded walls, good fish and chips and a sign warning that 'any tourists left on the premises will be sold to the circus', so make sure to put this book well away in your bag before entering.

Dunwich

Dunwich is an out-of-the-way hamlet of five marsh-facing houses at the end of a long straight road through the Suffolk heaths. Its long straight beach is backed by low sandy cliffs, held together by tree roots. Every so often a medieval coffin handle or human bone drops out of the cliff. 'Dunwich is not even the ghost of its dead self,' wrote Henry James after visiting on his bicycle in 1879, 'almost all you can say of it is that is consists of the mere letters of its old name.' What remains of the old town – a medieval port similar in size to Ipswich, with a population of 4,000, 12 churches, two hospitals and two priories – is buried under sand and mud hundreds of yards out to sea. A yard of land has been lost to erosion every year for the last 400 years. The excellent **museum** (*open April–Sept daily 11.30–4.30; Oct daily 12–4; Mar weekends 2–4.30*) contains finds from underwater archaeology of the old town. It lost its market place in the 17th century and the last medieval church of All Saints' in the early 20th century. Just up the road are the only remains of the medieval town, the ruins of Greyfriars monastery; they have about 70 years before they join the rest of the town. Read P.D. James' *Unnatural Causes* to get in the mood.

Dunwich Heath

Driving south beyond Greyfriars wood through a purple sea of heather, you come to a lonely group of Victorian coastguard cottages. The heath around them was used for sheep-grazing and a source of thatching and bedding material in the Middle Ages, when Dunwich was a thriving town. It's a good place for walks, with 214 acres of sandy heath bounded by cliffs to the east and Minismere bird reserve to the south.

Near **Westleton**, a mile west of Dunwich, **Minismere RSPB Nature Reserve** (*car park open Wed–Mon 9–9 or dusk if earlier; visitor centre open Wed–Mon 9–5, closes at 4 in winter; adm*) incorporates 930 acres of heathland, woodland, coastal lagoons, unspoilt sand dunes and several hides. Avocets returned to Minismere in 1947 after 100 years absence from Britain. You can hire binoculars and follow one of the trails.

Southwold

Southwold tops them all for class and charm; by comparison the big resorts up the coast appear bereft. There it sits on a hill above the River Blyth, looking north and south over delightfully empty marshland and heath, with 'hardly a building that is a visual nuisance', according to Pevsner. One of its most charming features are the numerous little triangular greens introduced as firebreaks in 1659 after a blaze fanned by North Sea winds destroyed the old town; they have become so many village centres. Landmarks include the white lighthouse, Adnams brewery, the church tower (the only medieval building to have survived the fire), a long row of colourful beach huts and Southwold Pier, a private enterprise backed by individual sponsors.

At the hub of town is the market place, dominated by the white bays of the Swan Hotel, one of two well known gastronomic hotels in town. The other one, the Crown, is just up the High Street. From here, East Street leads to the cliff top up above the beach huts. Here, the **Sailors' Reading Room** is one of the delights of Southwold, with its threadbare chairs, photographs of long-dead fishermen, figure heads, clocks and models of boats. It stands as a Victorian memorial to a sea captain by his widow. North from the market place up Church Street you come to **East Green**, one of Southwold's trademark green triangles, surrounded by spic-and-span houses, the Sole Bay Inn and the brick and weatherboard mass of Adnams Brewery. Since the Adnams brothers took over the Sole Bay Brewery in 1872, the brewery has grown to own the Swan and Crown hotels, the Harbour Inn and a wine merchant.

Look into the **museum** (*open Easter–Oct 2.30–4.30, Aug also 11–12.30*) a few steps up Victoria Street, housed in a tiny 17th-century cottage with a Dutch gable on the end. It recounts how the Dutch and English fought an inconclusive sea battle off Southwold in 1672, and that the town was briefly England's leading herring port in the 18th century. There are marine specimens, figure heads from ships and relics of the old Southwold railway.

Getting There and Around

By **car**, Southwold is north of Blythburgh, signposted off the A12

The nearest **railway** station is Halesworth, west of Southwold on the Ipswich to Lowestoft line.

National Express **coaches** run to Bungay and Lowestoft, where you can pick up local buses.

Tourist Information

Southwold: 69 High Street, **t** (01502) 724 729. *Open summer Mon–Fri 10–5, Sat 10–5.30, Sun 11–4; winter Mon–Fri 10.30–3.30, Sat 10–4.30.*

Jill Freud's summer theatre began in Southwold in 1983, only moving to Aldeburgh in the mid-1990s. From mid-July to mid-Sept the company of 21 actors, 10 students and 10 technicians puts on five plays. From early June you can book at the tourist information centre or from early July you can book directly at the theatre box office.

Jill Freud and Company Summer Theatre, St Edmund's Hall, Cumberland Road, **t** (01502) 722 389.

Where to Stay

Southwold t (01502) –

Accommodation fills up quickly in season, so book well ahead.

The Swan Hotel, Market Place, **t** 722 186, *www.adnams.co.uk* (*expensive*). A glorious-looking Adnams hotel dating back to the Middle Ages. There are 42 bedrooms, 17 of which are grouped around the old bowling green at the back of the building. Full range of Adnams beers in the bar. For details of the **restaurant** *see* below.

The Crown Hotel, High Street, **t** 722 275, *www.adnams.co.uk* (*expensive*). Handsome 18th-century inn with 12 cosy, attractive bedrooms. Adnams in the bar. For details of the **restaurant** *see* below.

Sutherland House, 56 High Street, **t** 722 260, *www.sutherlandhouse.co.uk* (*expensive*). Delightful townhouse dating back to the 15th century, which served as the head-quarters of James II, then the Duke of York, during the Battle of Sole Bay against the Dutch in 1672 (both sides claimed victory). Both bedrooms and restaurant are super. Guests have breakfast overlooking the garden, which is dominated by an ancient weeping ash and mature shrubs.

Victoria House, 9 Dunwich Road, **t** 722 317, *www.victoria.southwold.info* (*moderate*). Distinguished-looking guesthouse in Georgian terrace with a white-painted iron balcony. The balconied double room has a cloud-painted ceiling. Come down from the clouds to the breakfast room with its linen tablecloths, fruit bowl and shelves of blue and white china.

Dunburgh Guest House, 28 North Parade, **t** 723 253, *www.southwold.ws/dunburgh* (*moderate*). The best place to stay on the seafront, with its Victorian front porch, four lovely bedrooms with William Morris print fabrics, glinting bathrooms, soft sofas and antique furniture in the sitting room.

Amber House, 24 North Parade, **t** 723 303, *www.blytheweb.co.uk* (*moderate*). Homely, welcoming Victorian townhouse with a long, tiled hallway, large bay-windowed sitting room/breakfast room and five comfortable bedrooms.

Northcliffe Guesthouse, 20 North Parade, **t** 724 074, *www.northcliffe-southwold.co.uk* (*moderate*). Friendly, bright and airy Victorian sea-facing house with a pretty

The museum overlooks Bartholomew Green, which is dominated by the **church of St Edmund** (*guided tours Mon at 5, Thurs at 3*), a Perpendicular giant of flushwork and glass. Its superb hammer-beam roof is decorated with winged angels. The Southwold Jack, a bleary-eyed, stubbly-chinned Yorkist soldier, is one of few surviving medieval clock-smiters to bash out the hours with their hatchets. The armrests of the choir stalls are beautifully carved, and painted angels and saints in faded red, gold and green cover the chancel screen.

patio garden and six homely bedrooms, including four doubles with sea views. You can have a drink in the elegant candle-lit guest lounge.

Prospect Place, 33 Station Road, **t** 722 757, *www.prospect-place-demon.co.uk* (*moderate*). Elegant detached Victorian house on road into town, 5 minutes' walk from the sea, with five bedrooms; kippers and local sausages for breakfast. *Open Mar–Oct only.*

Walberswick t (01502) –

The Bell Inn, Walberswick, **t** 723 109 (*moderate*). There are six comfortable bedrooms above this friendly village pub with its flagstone floors and high-backed wooden settles.

Eating Out

Southwold

Sutherland House, 56 High Street, **t** 722 260 (*moderate*). A classy restaurant in one of Southwold's oldest buildings, with royal connections (*see* below). The restaurant, with its oak beams and a huge log fire, opens at 9am for breakfast and stays open until 10pm. The lunch and dinner menu is mainly seafood. Three-course roast on Sun.

The Crown Hotel, High Street, **t** 722 275 (*moderate*). Book ahead if you want to eat in the restaurant, but the front bar is more informal, with a mix of eating, drinking and newspaper reading. Good range of Adnams beers in the bar, where the restaurant-standard bar menu might include Caesar salad, smoked chicken leg or seared fillets of trout. The restaurant is one of the best in town.

The Swan Hotel, Market Place, **t** 722 186 (*moderate*). The atmosphere is more rarefied than at the Crown, with a smart-casual dress code and signs warning 'no shorts after 6pm'. You can eat in the bar, with a full range of Adnams beers or in the restaurant (book). Sunday roasts in the bar are popular.

Drifter's Bistro, 36 East Street, **t** 724 806 (*cheap*). Modest little place with plastic tablecloths, on corner of East Street and Trinity Street. You can get coffee and toasted tea cake in the morning, but the emphasis is on bistro lunches and dinners including fish and dishes such as slow-cooked lamb shank or stuffed red peppers. Fresh produce and home-made desserts. *Closed Mon; book Fri and Sat eves.*

Lord Nelson, East Street, **t** 722 079 (*cheap*). One of Southwold's best pubs, with pine settles and nautical pictures on the walls. You can drink Adnams and eat good gammon or fish with chips. Enclosed garden at the back.

Christina Cara Fish Shop, Blackshore Quay, Southwold Harbour, **t** 724 709 (*cheap*). Delicious seafood snacks including smoked salmon tartlets, lobster mousse and dressed lobsters, but the most popular offering is freshly made fish and chips, which may well be the best you will eat in all of East Anglia. *Closed Mon.*

The Harbour Inn, Southwold Harbour, **t** 722 381 (*cheap*). A pub beside the harbour (look for the 1953 flood mark on the wall above the ground-floor windows) serving standard pub grub. You can sit out the back overlooking the marshes. Live music at weekends.

Walberswick t (01502) –

The Bell Inn, Ferry Road, Walberswick, **t** 723 109 (*cheap*). Lively pub in centre of village with undulating brick-tiled floor around front bar, flagstones and Victorian checked floor tiles. Big plates of pub grub.

South from the market place, down Queen Street, you come to the triangle of **South Green**, surrounded by the elegant marine villas of the early 19th-century gentry. From it, you can take in the sea, the marsh and the Regency architecture in slow rotation.

Southwold to Walberswick

It is a pleasant walk down Constitution Hill, taking Ferry Path over the marsh, to Southwold harbour. In the blue and white boatshed the old Southwold clinker-built,

44-foot lifeboat, the *Alfred Corry*, is under restoration. A rough track leads on along Blackshore quay past rickety wooden jetties to the Harbour Inn. You can cross the Blyth on the old railway bridge, or catch the Walberswick ferry – a rowing boat (*9–12.30 and 2–5.30*) – for a small fee. On the other side, the footpath leads into pretty **Walberswick** and back to the marshy, Dickensian banks of the river.

Blythburgh Church

You can catch a glimpse of Blythburgh church from the A12, all glass and tracery. Guarding the Blyth estuary, it is the sole survivor of Blythburgh's days as a commercial port. Its eccentric tiled floor, the bright space and the magnificent tie-beamed roof make it well worth a visit. Look out for the wood-carvings: pairs of winged angels peering down from the roof; bench ends depicting the seven deadly sins, with Sloth sitting upright in bed; the Jack o' the Clock, dressed in armour. A narrow spiral stairway leads to a little stone cell above the porch; here the priest was paid to say Mass for the souls of the benefactors – the Hoptons, Uffords and Swillingtons – whose shields are up there on the angel roof. Have a look around the back of the church at the north door: the scorch marks are said to be the devil's fingerprints, left when the church was struck by lightning during morning service in 1577, knocking two parishioners stone dead.

The church of neighbouring **Wenhaston** possesses a rare 'doom' painting of the last judgement. It has been hung on the north wall, but once would have hung menacingly above the chancel arch. A demon is shown dragging the condemned souls into the gaping jaws of Hell.

Framlingham and Around

The A1120 meanders around the Suffolk countryside between the A12 and A14, between rolling fields and big skies. In the middle is the old town of Framlingham, once the stronghold of the most powerful East Anglian families.

Framlingham

Framlingham is not prettified, but the feudal attractions are complemented by one or two restaurants and a handful of shops around the market square. The church contains the splendid mortuary chapels of the Howards, dukes of Norfolk, the richest and most powerful family in England in the mid 16th century. With nothing left of Kenninghall, their Tudor palace in Norfolk, the group of Renaissance tombs is their memorial. Thomas Howard, 3rd Duke of Norfolk, rebuilt the chancel and flanking chapels, and transferred the remains of the 1st and 2nd Dukes from Thetford Priory. The 3rd Duke survived the Reformation by the skin of his teeth, only spared from execution by the death of Henry VIII, to die in 1554, aged 80, after being released from prison on the accession of Mary I. He had all his estates and titles restored to him and gloried in the restoration of the old faith and his rank, and in the persecution of his enemies. His magnificent tomb is decorated in defiant Catholic motifs.

Tourist Information

There is a small Saturday **market** in the old Market Place with a few stalls selling fruit and veg, fish, nuts, hardware and bric-a-brac.

Where to Stay and Eat

Framlingham t (01728) –

The Crown Hotel, Market Hill, **t** 723 521, *www.framlingham-crown.com* (*expensive*). Impressive-looking 16th-century coaching inn with huge beams, worn stone steps and the old coaching yard; 14 bedrooms, overlooking the market square or courtyard. Coffee, lunch or dinner.

Colston Hall, Badingham, **t** 638 375 (*moderate*). Well-to-do Suffolk-pink farmhouse 3 miles north of Framlingham, with brick-tiled floors. Three bedrooms in the farmhouse and another three in the converted stable.

Castle Inn, Castle Street, **t** 724 033 (*cheap*). Great spot for refreshment on a sunny day, when you can sit out front overlooking the pond and the castle. Food includes tasty local sausages. Real ales pulled here are Adnams, IPA and Courage.

Eye t (01379) –

Beards, 39 Church Street, **t** 870 383 (*moderate*). Lovely, beamy old house in the middle of Eye with three pleasantly furnished rooms, each with its own wash basin and writing table for guests. From some windows you can see the old castle and, if you really twist your neck, Eye church.

Entertainment

Eye Theatre, Broad Street, **t** 870 519. Perhaps the smallest professional theatre in the country. It occupies the assembly room of the old White Lion, a former 18th-century coaching inn. An evening well spent in this delightful little town.

Framlingham Castle

Up from the market square stands the ancestral castle of the Bigods, Mowbrays and Howards, the powerful earls and dukes of Norfolk, warmongers and courtiers who never ran shy of forfeiting lands and heads in the pursuit of power and wealth. The Bigods received the castle from Henry I, had it confiscated by Henry II, returned by Richard I and confiscated again by John. The 16th-century Howards owned most of south Norfolk, and east Suffolk from the Broads to the Stour, augmented by monastery lands after the Reformation, and maintained large houses in Kenninghall, Tendring and Castle Rising as well as Framlingham. What survives here is a complete circuit of high stone walls, punctuated by 13 square towers and some elaborate Tudor chimneys. In one corner are the modified ruins of the Tudor great hall, which became a poorhouse in 1635. You can take a walk around the walls, and see the decorated chimneys in close-up. The meer, on the other side of the moat, is a good picnic spot.

Around Framlingham

The Suffolk hinterland is full of surprising little villages and bucolic attractions. **Bruisyard Vineyard** (**t** *(01728) 638 281; open 10.30–5; adm*), a few miles north of Framlingham above the Alde Valley, has 10 acres of vines, an old red-brick winery around a pan-tiled courtyard and sells wine. **Saxtead Post Mill**, built in the 18th century, remains in full working order.

Just south of Framlingham on the Parham Airfield is the **390th Bomb Group Memorial Museum** (*open Mar–Oct Sun 11–6 and June–Aug Wed 11–4*). From here American B17 bombers flew raids on Berlin, Kiel and the Ruhr Valley, guiding themselves home by the castle ruins. The old control tower is packed with uniforms, documents and weapons, and an exhibition about the British resistance network, 'specialists in bomb-making, sabotage and silent killing' who were 'trained for dirty tricks' (very *Dad's Army*).

The elaborate 15th-century hammer-beam roof of **Mary the Virgin Church** in **Little Stonham**, just off the A1120-A140 crossing, is carved in chestnut wood and adorned with a double row of winged angels and pendant bosses.

Shoot up the A140 in the direction of Diss, and you come to **St Mary's** in **Thornham Parva**, one of the most dinky of the Suffolk churches, a single cell with a thatched roof and tower. Inside are faded early 14th-century wall-paintings telling the story of King Edmund's martyrdom (*see* p.648), and the 14th-century painted retable that once belonged to Thetford Priory – lost at the Dissolution and found in the stable loft of Thornham Hall in 1927. In the churchyard is the grave of the architect Sir Basil Spence. A few miles east is the little village of **Eye**, with a ruined hilltop castle, a theatre in a beamed old coaching inn and the most remarkable church tower in the county. It soars above the town, 101 feet of flint flushwork panelling with pinnacles on top. Inside the large nave is the church's other glory, a 15th-century screen. Pevsner wrote off the painted saints on the dado as 'all bad', missing the charm of the stories they tell. Look for the dagger sticking into the throat of St Agnes and the 11 virgins under the cloak of St Ursula.

Norfolk

Without the wool wealth, and that much further from the capital than Suffolk, Norfok is slightly less picture perfect. But it too has some magnificent churches, a fine cathedral, a couple of good stately homes, charming fishing villages and stretches of bleak sand-and-shingle coastline.

Norwich

The county and cathedral town of Norwich has not been immune to the 20th-century spoilers, who have demolished old buildings and built some charmless modern developments. But its powers to please are intact. For J.B. Priestley, visiting in 1933, it had the atmosphere of an ancient metropolis amid solid East Anglian farming country; he dreamed of a time when the good burghers of Norwich would wrest their region back from Westminster. Norwich had a Dickensian atmosphere, he found: 'It was difficult to believe that behind those bowed and twisted fronts there did not exist an assortment of misers, mad spinsters, saintly clergymen, eccentric comic clerks and lunatic sextons,' he wrote. He stayed in Maids Head Hotel, wandered around Tombland at night, saw pre-Restoration am dram at the Maddermarket Theatre, sat in a snug pub – and did pretty much what you'd do today in Norwich.

Getting There and Around

By **car**, Norwich is all the way up the A11 from Cambridge, or cross-country on the A47.

There are regular direct **train** services from London Liverpool Street to Norwich.

A couple of **coaches** a day run from London Victoria to Norwich.

Tourist Information

Norwich: The Forum, Millennium Plain, **t** (01603) 727 927. *Open summer Mon–Sat 10–6, Sun 10.30–4.30pm; winter Mon–Sat 10–5.30.*

A general **market** takes place in the old market square Mon–Sat, with stalls selling army surplus, second-hand clothes, CDs and some fresh produce.

The **Norwich Festival**, Norwich's summer music and arts festival, takes place over two weeks between May and June in various venues around town including the Norwich Playhouse. The repertoire is mostly classical, with some jazz and contemporary music. Contact the **festival office**, **t** (01603) 614 921 or *www.n-joy.org.uk* for programme details.

Where to Stay

Norwich t (01603) –

There is a concentration of B&Bs in the Victorian townhouses on Earlham Road, leading to the university. Otherwise, the city centre provides some good, basic, standard places to stay.

Maids Head Hotel, Tombland, **t** 209 955 (*expensive*). One of Norwich's oldest inns, with a handsome façade of Georgian brickwork. It has had the corporate treatment and a modern extension, but the 84 old and new bedrooms are furnished in wood, with trouser presses and matching fabrics.

By Appointment, 25–9 St Georges Street, **t** 630 730 (*moderate*). This theatrical restaurant (*see* below) has four rooms up a narrow flight of stairs, full of antique furniture, scatter cushions, old hat boxes and even the odd old corset on a hanger. Full of charm and atmosphere.

The Beeches Hotel and Victorian Gardens, 2–6 Earlham Road, **t** 621 167, *www.beeches.co.uk* (*moderate*). Behind the RC cathedral, really three separate Victorian hotels: The Beeches, Plantation House and The Governor's House (formerly the home of the governor of the old city gaol, which stood on the site of the cathedral). Creeper-clad, porticoed Plantation House was built in 1865 by a wealthy furniture-maker and has a patio overlooking an extraordinary Victorian-Gothic garden.

The Georgian House Hotel, 32–4 Unthank Road, **t** 615 655, *www.georgian-hotel.co.uk* (moderate). Two townhouses set back behind a large gravel drive off the main road; 28 cheerful bedrooms.

Eating Out

Adlard's Restaurant, 79 Upper St Giles Street, **t** 633 522 (*moderate*). Norwich's swankiest restaurant, and the only one boasting a

Around Town

Beneath the Scandinavian neo-classicism of the city hall, with its tall clock tower, Norwich has a permanent market in its old **market place**, providing the instant factor of a bustling commercial hub. At the top of the market place is Edwin Lutyens' sober stone **war memorial**. From there, with your back to the city hall, on one side you have the flint medieval **guildhall**. On the other is **St Peter Mancroft Church**, the merchants' church of the medieval city, a wonder of Perpendicular Gothic architecture. On the next hill stands the **castle keep**, a skyscraper of the Middle Ages. Beside the city hall is Norwich's £63.5-million millennium building, a hi-tech glass-fronted library designed by Sir Michael Hopkins.

Michelin star, offers modern English/French cooking in a classic-style dining room. Popular starters are scallops with garlic potatoes and rocket salad followed by roast halibut or tomato and aubergine tart with herb salad. *Closed Mon lunch and Sun.*

By Appointment, 25–9 St Georges Street, **t** 630 730 (*moderate*). You enter around the back through the kitchen into a world of wonderfully over-the-top rich furnishings, draped curtains and low roof beams. Two small drawing rooms for smoking and coffee, and four dining rooms furnished with antique furniture and ornaments. The individual English-style menu is chalked up on gilt-framed boards. Look out for themed dinners linked to performances at the Theatre Royal, with Rolls Royces chauffeuring guests between the two. *Open Tues–Sat eves. Book.*

Logan's, Swan Street (*cheap*). Deli serving delicious take-away baguette sandwiches.

Take 5, St Andrew's Street (*cheap*). Informal café-bar attached to cinema. Serves decent vegetarian food in medieval hall house with pretty cobbled courtyard. *Closed Sun.*

Britons Arms, 9 Elm Hill, **t** 623 367 (*cheap*). Thatched 15th-century house and former pub on quaint conservation street. Serves tea, coffee, scones, cakes, and soup and quiches for lunch.The atmosphere is wholesome and friendly. On warm days you can sit in the leafy roof garden. *Closed Sun.*

The Adam and Eve, Bishopgate, **t** 667 423 (*cheap*). Atmospheric Dutch-gabled pub north of the cathedral, with small rooms containing high-backed settles and a small pewter-topped bar. The pub traces its history back to 1249, when it was a brewhouse for the workmen building the cathedral. Serves Adnams and Green King beers and pub grub.

The Fat Cat, 49 West End Street, **t** 624 364 (*cheap*). Follow the Dereham road a mile out of the centre to Norwich's best drinking pub. Vast range of beers which might include Tanglefoot, Black Sheep and Oyster Stout which you can have from the barrel ('gravity') or the hand pump ('pump'). The décor is matchboard, high-backed pews and old pub signs and the atmosphere as thick and smoky. Rolls and pork pies for ballast.

Entertainment

Maddermarket Theatre, St John's Alley, **t** 620 917. North of the market, this charming little theatre is reached through the dark arch of St John Maddermarket church tower. This was the site of a medieval market where madder (a vegetable dye essential to the wool trade) was sold. The theatre was built as a RC chapel in 1794, and taken over by the Guild of Norwich Players, an amateur repertory company, in 1921. The guild has evolved into the Maddermarket Theatre Company of amateur actors directed by professionals.

Playhouse Theatre, St George's Street, **t** 612 580, *www.norwichplayhouse.org.uk*. Beside river, with bar and garden; shows comedy.

Cinema City, St. Andrews Street, **t** 622 047, *www.cinemacity.co.uk*. Arthouse cinema attached to ancient medieval hall house.

Theatre Royal, Theatre Street, box office **t** 630 000, *www.theatreroyalnorwich.co.uk*. The theatre that hosts big touring musicals, opera, ballet, drama and pantomime.

The city's main shopping streets radiate out from the market place. Most of the town is down **London Street** or through the **Royal Arcade**, a Victorian Art Nouveau gallery with painted wooden shop fronts and stained glass. **Colman's Mustard Shop** is here, with a museum about Jeremiah Colman's mustard factory (est. 1814).

Have a look at the knapped-flint wall of **St Andrew's Church** before you go inside **Bridewell Museum** in Bridewell Alley (***t** (01603) 667 228; open Feb–Oct Mon–Sat 10–5; adm*), Until it became a Bridewell (or prison) in 1583, the building was a medieval merchant's house. Now it's devoted to old Norwich's industrial, commercial and agricultural life. Exhibits include an old cattle-market gate, a wrought-iron sunflower made by a Norwich firm for the Philadelphia International Exhibition in 1876, a

Jacquard loom, and Start-rite children's shoes. From the museum, it is a short walk to Elm Hill, an assortment of flint-faced old houses, now selling art, crafts and pottery.

From the market place, Upper St Giles Street is lined with old-fashioned shops. The **Roman Catholic cathedral** stands at the end of the street like a marooned liner. It was built at the turn of the 20th century by George Gilbert Scott and his brother John Oldrid Scott under the patronage of Henry Fitzalan Howard, the 15th Duke of Norfolk – his second cathedral after St Philip's in Arundel. Vespers is the best time to visit, when the Romanesque interior is thrown into chiaroscuro.

Norwich Castle Museum and Art Gallery

***t** (01603) 493 625; open 10.30–5 Mon–Sat and Sun 2–5; adm.*

The curtain walls are gone, the defensive ditch has been landscaped, but the mighty Norman keep still towers above the city. It is the rock around which the town has grown. The royal castle, where Henry I spent Christmas in 1121, became the county gaol in the 13th century and the museum in 1887. The keep is a shell of flint walls and arrow slits. Inside are tableaux of Henry's Yuletide celebrations. Archaeology, Norwich School watercolours, the Egyptians and natural history are all exhibited in galleries around a central rotunda, recently renewed with lottery lolly. The **archaeology gallery** covers the Icenis (including a Boudicca chariot simulation), Vikings and Saxons. But the highlight is the **Norwich School paintings** and drawings, bequeathed to the museum in 1946 by a Colman's mustard heir. The school flourished around artists John Crome (1768–1821), John Sell Cotman (1782–1842) and Robert Ladbrooke (1769–1842) between 1803 and 1833. They earned a reputation for closely observed depictions of the East Anglian landscape using rainbows, sunsets and moonlight to emphasize the strangeness of it. Cotman's *Croyland Abbey* comes with a story of boys pestering him while he drew: 'I am sorry to say I was obliged to give one of the ring-leaders a sound flogging'. The **regimental museum** is housed in the old Shire Hall.

Norwich Cathedral

The cathedral (***t** (01603) 764 385; donation requested*) inhabits a corner of the city between Tombland and the river, where the Dickensian tilt and sag of the buildings convinced J.B. Priestley that he was going to bump into Edwin Drood any moment. It looks of another world than the solid domestic buildings of the close around it. From Tombland, go through the **Erpingham Gate**, endowed by Sir Thomas Erpingham, one of the knights who fought for Henry V at Agincourt. You approach the west front down a lane of assorted houses (now owned by Edward VI school), a straight line to test the lean of the 315-foot-high spire. The cathedral was built between 1096 and 1145 and, although it has gone through several style changes, the layout is Norman: long and narrow with a rounded ambulatory around the east end. This, with its solid drum columns, is the wonder of Norwich cathedral, not the 15th-century Decorated spire, nor the close. In the middle of the sanctuary, in a commanding position, stands the ancient **bishop's throne**, two of the original stones under a modern wooden chair. All around the cathedral are stone carvings, which have a fairy-tale air of petrification.

The cream ranges of the **cloisters** took more than a century to build, from 1297 to 1430. You can see the old washing place in the west walk, the outlines of book shelves on the walls, a worn step leading to the old dormitory door. The old infirmary is now the choir school; if you are lucky your visit will be accompanied by singing. Outside, at the east end, is the grave of First World War heroine Edith Cavel, who was executed by the Germans in 1915 for helping Allied soldiers to escape from Belgium.

From the lower close, Ferry Road drops down to **Pull's Ferry**, the old medieval water-gate on the banks of the river, named after the last ferryman. You can walk along the river through the playing fields of Edward VI school for views of the cathedral.

North of Norwich

North of Norwich you find one of Norfolk's most charming stately homes, Blicking Hall, and a magnificent wool church – the county's finest – at Salle.

Blickling Hall

Open April–Oct Wed–Sun 1–4.30; adm.

North of Norwich, straight up the A140, is Blickling Hall, a Jacobean mansion with frills: clover-leaf gables, long chimneys, dark windows, neat little bricks. The architect was Robert Lyminge, whose most famous work is Hatfield House, the corporate head-quarters of the Cecils. Blickling is lighter, more domestic. The symmetrical wings, which frame the south front picturesquely, look like almshouses with twin cottage-style gables and plants climbing up them. The founder was London lawyer Sir Henry Hobart, who bought and rebuilt the Tudor house of the Boleyns as a retirement gift to himself, planting his crest and initials on the walls to mark the beginning of a great dynasty. His descendents, the earls of Buckingham and marquises of Lothian, improved the house and gardens until June 1940, when they handed it over to the nation. Highlights include the oak and flagstone **great hall**, the Jacobean **long gallery** – 123-foot-long, with bookcases all along one wall and a ceiling dripping plasterwork pendants and heraldic decorations – and the Victorian *parterre* and **Temple Walk**, created by Lady Lothian and remodelled by Norah Lindsay with herbaceous beds in a framework of yew pillars, sharp-edged gravel paths and yew hedges.

Salle

Eight miles west of Blickling Hall, the pinnacles of Norfolk's finest wool church – ostentatious in size – can be seen for miles. The donors were local cloth magnates: the Fountaines, the Briggs and Thomas Boleyn of Blickling Hall. You go in through the west door, guarded by two angels in the spandrels wielding censers like clubs. The Perpendicular space, brushed and clean, smells of brick dust and Norfolk air, every surface and stick of furniture beautifully faded. The treasures are the 15th-century **font cover**, suspended from a wooden crane in the bell-ringer's gallery, and the carved heads, animals and flowers on the **choir stalls**.

The Norfolk Broads

Between Norwich and the east coast is the area of low-lying wetland known as the Norfolk Broads – six rivers and around 40 'broads' or lakes fringed with reed beds, fens, grazing marsh and tangled woodland. The rivers are navigable for most of their length and numerous cuts or dykes feed into the broads, about half of which are accessible to boats. Boating is big business in the holiday season: you can charter a boat at **Wroxham**, which is shockingly over-commercialized, Hunter's Yard or **Brudall**, and spend a week or two exploring either the northern rivers (Bur, Ant and Thurn) or

Getting There

The Norfolk Broads are scattered along the rivers east of Norwich. Your **car** will get you to the main boating centres including Wroxham-Hoveton, Potter Heigham, Great Yarmouth and Horning.

You could also change **trains** at Norwich to get to one of the boating centres, such as Wroxham, Great Yarmouth or Lowestoft.

Getting Around

The only way to get around the Broads is by **boat**. The Broads are full of boat yards, which in turn are full of boat companies hiring out boats. At Wroxham the river is jam-packed with white motor cruisers belonging to competing companies. To hire a boat for a few hours or the day, get yourself down to Wroxham, Potter Heigham, Brundall, Great Yarmouth or Lowestoft and look around for a good deal.

If you are planning a longer trip to the Broads, you will need to book a boat in advance. You can go through one of the two main booking agents, **Blakes**, **t** (01603) 739 400 or **Hoseasons**, **t** (01502) 500 505.

Here are two unassuming, smaller boat yards to try:

Hunter's Yard, Womack Water (off River Thurne), **t** (01692) 678 263. Just outside Ludham village. Sailing boats for hire by the week (in season) or the day.

Whispering Reeds Boatyard, Hickling Broad, **t** (01692) 598 314. Hires out sailing boats and cruisers by the day on one of the most unspoiled stretches of water in the Norfolk Broads, north of Potter Heigham.

Tourist Information

Wroxham-Hoveton: Station Road (just over the bridge from Wroxham), **t** (01603) 782 281. *Open Easter–Oct 9–1 and 1.30–5.*

Ranworth: The Staithe, **t** (01603) 270 453. *Open Easter–Sept 9–5.*

Beccles: **t** (01502) 713 196.

Great Yarmouth: **t** (01493) 332 095.

The Broads Authority, Norwich, **t** (01603) 610 734. Can give you information about navigation, mooring, conservation and so on; has eight information centres dotted around the region.

There is a huge **antiques fair** in the first week of July on Earsham Street in Bungay, and a Thursday weekly **market** at Butter Cross.

Where to Stay and Eat

Bungay

Kings Head Hotel, Market Place, **t** (01986) 893 583 (*moderate*). Friendly old-fashioned inn with 12 cheerful bedrooms and a bistro-style restaurant serving home-made curry, chilli, pasta, liver and bacon with Yorkshire pudding, Lowestoft fish.

Castles, 35 Earsham Street, **t** (01986) 892 283, *castles@lineone.net* (*moderate*). Unassuming restaurant serving traditional English food including steak and kidney pudding and roast dinners, with four clean-smelling rooms furnished with nice pine furniture, one handsome four-poster bed and one or two interesting fireplaces.

Buttercross Tea Rooms, Cross Street (*cheap*). Small, long-established tea room in town centre where you can get a cup of strong tea, greasy breakfast, omelette and chips or a full roast lunch.

the southern ones (Waveney, Yare and Chet), mooring outside the riverside pubs. Environmentalists and bird-watchers get very het up about the motorboats (or hullaballoos, as any Arthur Ransome fan calls them). If you can't get on a boat, one or two nature reserves provide a taste of the watery landscape, but do get onto the water if you can. The sight of a sail gliding silently across the landscape is an integral part of the Broads scene: single-sail wherries, traditional trading craft, used to ply the rivers from the coastal towns to Norwich for centuries before the Victorian tourist boom.

The landscape is man-made, created by the drainage of the wetlands since the Norman Conquest. The broads themselves are the result of peat-cutting in the Middle Ages, flooded when the sea level rose. If the Wildlife Trust stopped managing the broads – harvesting the marsh hay and shoring up the riverbanks – they would be lost to global warming; much of the area is already below sea level.

The Northern Rivers

For a taste of the Norfolk Broads, head to the village of **Ranworth**, north of the A47. Park at **Malthouse Staith**, where there is an information centre overlooking Malthouse Broad. There are guided trips (*Mon–Sat 10.15am,* **t** *(01603) 270 453*) around the broad and up the River Bure to **Cockshoot Broad**. A 400-yard stroll on duckboard brings you to the wildlife reserve at **Ranworth Broad**. The Wildlife Centre (*open April–Oct daily 10–5*) has bird-watching binoculars.

Back in Ranworth, pop into the **church**, which holds a rare treasure: a complete medieval screen runs the width of the church, painted with expressive apostles and saints holding books, staffs and swords. There are good views from the tower.

To the north, the grassy hillside of **How Hill** overlooks Turf Fen and the reed-fringed bend of the River Ant. Hidden in the woods on the far side is **Toad Cottage** (1780–1820), a thatched marshman's cottage furnished in Victorian style. From **How Hill Staith** there are boat trips (*hourly Easter–May and Oct 11–3, June–Sept 10–5, lasting 50 mins; adm*) through the dykes of the How Hill Nature Reserve. Otherwise a pleasant walk takes you north along the Ant to the old **Clayrack Mill**.

Horsey Mere, just off the B1159 coast road on the remote eastern fringes of the broads, is home of Horsey wind pump, which you can climb for views of the reed beds, marshes and dunes (*open Easter–Oct; adm; buy your ticket in the Staith shop*). You can walk around the mere too. A mile west is Hickling Broad, one of the wilder reserves.

The Southern Rivers

The landscape of the southern rivers is less intimate than that of the northern rivers. **Reedham**, halfway between Norwich and Lowestoft on the River Yare, is a remote riverside spot under an immense fenland sky, with a pleasant pub, the Ferry, just by the chain bridge over the river. Off the A143 Great Yarmouth road just before the town you come to the imposing remains of **Burgh Castle**, a late Roman Saxon Shore fort on the banks of the Waveney. The strong flint walls of the rounded bastions stand in a windswept spot. It is thought to have guarded the south side of a wide sea inlet (where Yarmouth is now). Today there are good views over the marshes, a stump of a windmill and white sails gliding through the fields. A footpath drops down along Breydon Water to the Castle pub.

Bungay

The small town of Bungay, in a loop of the River Waveney, takes its name from the Norwegian 'bunga', meaning 'a little heap'. Beside its two army surplus shops and a wet fish shop, it has a ruined Bigod castle, a slippery Tudor well, a reeve instead of a mayor, a town crier, an ostentatious 17th-century domed buttercross surmounted by the figure of Justice – and a legend. 'A strange and terrible wonder wrought very late in the parish church of Bungay,' begins an account of the strange events. During a great storm in 1577 the devil appeared in the form of a big black dog, tore through the congregation of **St Mary's Church** and 'many people slew'. The small **museum** on Broad Street has a copy of the descriptive manuscript, memorabilia of Norfolk-born writer Rider Haggard, and an edition of *Bungay Castle*, an 18th-century romantic novel by Mrs Bonhote, who lived in a cottage in the castle ruins. To see the overgrown remains of the castle fetch the key from the tea shop on the Buttercross. What you see are the two gatehouse towers of the 13th-century castle of Roger Bigod and the flint foundations of the earlier Norman keep, built by Hugh Bigod.

Breckland

Breckland is the backwoods of East Anglia, a large, lonely area of pine plantations and arable fields centred on the ancient town of Thetford. It is more productive than attractive, with convoys of military vehicles trundling to and from the military airbases of Mildenhall and Lakenheath (home to the US Air Force) and army training grounds at West Toft. Breckland, however, has a long history of human habitation, starting in the New Stone Age. **Grimes Graves** is the largest group of Neolithic flint mines in Britain, calculated to have produced between 2.5 and 5 million axes and knives. **Thetford** developed at the river-crossing of the Icknield Way, a prehistoric main road; it was a royal settlement of the Iceni tribe, incinerated by the Romans after Boudicca's revolt. Two of the greatest Roman treasure hoards have been dug up in Breckland, one at Mildenhall, the other at Thetford. In 869 the Viking 'great army', garrisoned in Thetford, killed King Edmund at Hoxne near Diss, conquering the kingdom of East Anglia. By Domesday, Breckland had lost much of its woodland and population, but Thetford acquired a Norman cathedral (the diocese moved to Norwich soon after) and the priory of Roger Bigod, which became the mausoleum of the dukes of Norfolk. Later, rabbits were farmed as a source of game, multiplying so rapidly in the sandy ground that they stripped it of vegetation. The name Breckland was minted by a Victorian historian, adapting the old word 'breck', used to describe the shifting patterns of cultivation traditional to the region. The introduction of conifer plantations by the Forestry Commission in the early 20th century boosted a dwindling national resource and stalled the process of desertification.

Thetford

Like all good market towns, Thetford in some way embodies the countryside around it, being dour and solidly wholesome-looking around its flint and yellow brick market square and along its main shopping street. Its only grand statement is the gilded statue of Thetford-born **Thomas Paine** outside the Georgian council offices, presented by the Thomas Paine Society of New York in 1964. The town's former glories include the Iceni hill fort, ruined priory and memories of a Norman cathedral. The **Ancient House Museum** (*open Mon–Sat 10–5, Sun 2–5*) on White Hart Street (where the author of *The Rights of Man* was born in 1737) is packed with local interest: the flora and fauna of Breckland and replicas of Roman treasures. Down Minstergate is the **Charles Burrell Museum** of traction engines (*open April–Oct Sat 10–5, Sun 2–5; adm*), housed in the old Victorian finishing shop of the Burrell steam-engine factory. At the end of the street, an underpass ducks under the A11 into the low flint ruins of **Thetford Priory**, sadly engulfed by modern housing estates. The great twisted claw of the Lady Chapel is the heart of the site. The Cluniac foundation was established by Roger Bigod in 1104 in the former cathedral, later becoming the mausoleum of the Howard family, the dukes of Norfolk, until the Dissolution.

You can walk along the river from the town bridge, near the Anchor Hotel, to the picturesque hump-backed **Nuns' Bridges** over the Thet and The Little Ouse, where willow and horse chestnut trees trail in the water. Across the river is **Castle Hill**, an 81-foot-high Norman motte within Iron Age ramparts.

Thetford Forest's **High Lodge Forest Centre** (**t** *(01842) 815 434; open Easter–Oct 10–5*) is a few miles west of Thetford on the B1107 Brandon road. It's a good base for walks, as is the Lynford Arboretum, near Mundford, with its ornamental woodlands, lakes and magnificent Victorian hall for refreshments.

Grimes Graves

***t** (01842) 810 656; open 9–1 and 2–5, winter until 4; adm minimal.*

Grimes Graves is reached down a minor forest road off the A134, north of Thetford. Set among conifers, the extraordinary pockmarked site is a prehistoric industrial zone, a vast Neolithic flint mine. Only 17 of around 350 known shafts have been excavated; they range from 20 to 65 feet in diameter at the surface and are up to 40 feet deep, with galleries radiating out along the jet-black seam of flint. The miners used red deer antlers as picks and the flint was manufactured on site into axe and knife blades.

About 12 miles south, on a low hill in the Lark Valley, off the A1101, is the site of an **Anglo-Saxon village**, now reconstructed for visitors (*open daily 10–5; adm*). It was part of the kingdom of the East Angles, whose most powerful leader, Raedowald, is thought to have been buried at Sutton Hoo (*see* p.647). An excellent exhibition describes the Anglo-Saxon colonization of East Anglia. The village itself is an authentic-looking cluster of thatched wooden huts, fenced allotments and free-ranging chickens, sometimes populated by grubby re-enactors making pots and wooden implements, dying wool and throwing spears.

Where to Stay and Eat

Thetford and Around t (01842) –

Lynford Hall (about 15 minutes' drive north of Thetford on the A134, turning right at the Mundford roundabout towards Swaffham), **t** 878 351, *www.lynfordhallhotel.co.uk* (*expensive*). Magnificent Victorian country house with Dutch gables, tall chimneys and deep archways between the courtyards. The odd royal and John F Kennedy have visited in the past for the hunt balls. Now it is owned by the Organic Group and has a restaurant and 21 good bedrooms.

The Old Red Lion, Icklingham (just outside West Stow), **t** (01638) 717 802 (*moderate*). A stylish old-world country inn with an enormous fireplace and polished floorboards, furnished with beautiful rugs, wooden pews and substantial old wooden furniture and flickering candles; à la carte menu features local and seasonal produce including game, fresh fish and vegetarian options. Real ales, country wines and cheaper bar meals. **The Bell Hotel**, King Street, **t** 754 455, *www.oldenglish.co.uk* (*moderate*). The hotel is bigger than its Tudor jettied front suggests, with 46 bright, pleasant bedrooms down long corridors. The **King James Restaurant** provides good, solid English cooking, or you can get full meals in the subdued bar.

The Wereham House Hotel, 24 White Hart Street, **t** 761 956, *www.werehamhouse.co.uk* (*moderate*). One of four town-centre hotels virtually next door to each other. Small, functional and friendly, with reasonable bedrooms.

The Dolphin, Market Street, **t** 752 271 (*cheap*). Homely old pub with pictures on walls, carpeted floors and alcoves of bookshelves and ornaments. Basic bar food, including vegetarian dishes.

The Old Rectory, 30 Raymond Street, **t** 765 419 (*cheap*). This large Georgian townhouse belonged to the Raymond Street brewery before it was sold off to the church. Now it is an unassuming, bright, friendly private home with three rooms to let.

The White House, 4 Raymond Street, **t** 754 546 (*cheap*). Large house in town centre with clean, functional bedrooms.

Oxburgh Hall

t (01366) 328 258, www.nationaltrust.org; open April–Oct Sat–Wed, house 1–5, garden 11–5.30; Aug daily 11–5; Mar Sat–Wed 11–4; adm.

Oxburgh Hall, right off the A134 north of Thetford at Stoke Ferry, provides welcome glamour in the Breckland wilds: mellowed 15th-century brickwork and battlemented towers reflected in a moat of lilies, bright formal gardens and memories of royal visitors. It was built by Sir Edmund Bedingfield, a pro-Yorkist knight of solid Norman stock who became sheriff of Suffolk and Norfolk. His descendants have not budged: 18 generations of Bedingfields, staunch Catholics at the Reformation and Royalists in the Civil War, have hung on to their ancestral seat against all the odds. Dutiful, principled and unthreatening, they were always on hand to take the bum jobs at the top – taking care of royal divorcée Catherine of Aragon, welcoming Anne 'face like a Flanders mare' of Cleves at Deal, acting as gaolers of Princess Elizabeth in the Tower of London. They were granted a baronetcy at the Restoration of Charles II, but gained rank and fortune by marrying the daughters of dukes, earls and viscounts. The greatest treasure of Oxburgh, the naturalistic tapestry of Mary Queen of Scots and Bess of Hardwick, came into the family with the daughter of Viscount Montague of Cowdray Park. The main rooms – dining room, drawing room and library – were remodelled in the 19th century with the addition of heraldic ceilings, panelling and sumptuous flock wallpapers. When Henry VII and his queen, Elizabeth of York, visited

Oxburgh soon after Bosworth, they stayed in the gatehouse. The Queen's Room contains a Sheldon tapestry map of Oxfordshire and Berkshire, one of a handful of county maps made by the great West Midlands firm in the 17th century.

Outside the estate wall, the old church stands a ruin, crushed in 1948 by the falling spire. The **Bedingfield Chapel**, however, escaped undamaged. It was first endowed by Sir Edmund (d. 1496), the builder of Oxburgh Hall, and his wife Margaret (d. 1514) to house their tombs. These are the finest early Tudor Renaissance-style monuments in terracotta anywhere, their classical features and relief decoration as smooth and detailed as if they had been carved out of soap.

Swaffham

On the northern edge of Breckland, Swaffham is the careless younger sibling of staid Thetford. The town thrived in the 18th century, when there was cockfighting, horse and greyhound racing, and the assembly rooms were lively. The market place is vastly out of proportion to the rest of town. Standing on the steps of the domed buttercross, a panorama of Georgian buildings and plane trees is backed by two towering landmarks – the giant white sails of a turbine designed by Norman Foster, and the parish church. Step into the austere **church** to see the chestnut-wood double-hammer-beam roof, adorned with a flying formation of 88 angels. The furniture is all Victorian, except the carved bench ends, which are medieval. These include the figure of John Chapman, the legendary peddler of Swaffham, with his backpack and muzzled dog. The story goes that Chapman, a real-life businessman and benefactor of the church, travelled to London in search of his pot of gold. A shopkeeper on London bridge told him to go home and dig in his garden. You can guess the rest. Another Swaffham boy was the Egyptian treasure-hunter Howard Carter, who discovered the tomb of Tutankhamen in 1922. The **museum** (***t*** *(01760) 721 230; open April–Oct Tues–Sat 11–1 and 2–4; adm minimal*), in the town hall on London Street, has all the stories about Carter and the peddler of Swaffham, as well as a collection of 66 handmade figures based on characters from Dickens, Tolkien and Shakespeare made by a Swaffham craftsman.

Ghostly Happenings and Wall Paintings

The old church of St Mary, Houghton-on-the-Hill (*open Sun afternoon or call Robert Davey, t (01760) 440 470, for an appointment*) will appeal to fans of ghost stories in the M.R. James tradition. Out of Swaffham on the B1107, follow signs to South Pickenham, Houghton and Holme Hale. The church stands alone up a bridleway. Recently unearthed from under ivy and trees, its early medieval wall paintings are now under restoration, including a Holy Trinity and two Resurrections featuring angels blowing trumpets to awaken the dead. The ghost is a 14th-century Carmelite friar in a cape and wide-brimmed hat, who haunts the south porch. A visitor has photographed him next to her husband. Two such monks were installed in the church in 1304 to say Mass for the soul of Sir Robert Neville, whose execution for treason brought his body to this far-flung corner of the Warwick estates for burial.

Tourist Information

Swaffham: **t** (01760) 722 255, *www.aroundswaffham.co.uk*.

Where to Stay and Eat

Swaffham **t** (01760) –

Strattons, Stratton House, 4 Ash Close, **t** 723 845, *www.strattons-hotel.co.uk* (*expensive*). Delightful Palladian villa tucked away behind market place with oval lawn and free-ranging chickens, cats and rabbits. You can stay in one of eight individually themed bedrooms, including the Venetian Room, which has Botticelli's Venus painted on the bathroom wall, or the Red Room, which has an enormous cast-iron bath, wine-red walls and ceilings and a four-poster bed with baroque-style drapes. The guest lounge is full of lived-in charm with patchwork sofa covers, porcelain cats, lamps and figurines on the mantlepiece and family photos on the walls. In the restaurant (*expensive*) you are served delicious seasonal East Anglian produce including organic vegetables, marsh samphire and Stewkey Blue cockles.

The Lydney House Hotel, Norwich Road, **t** 723 355 (*expensive*). Square Georgian townhouse with comfortable bedrooms, a few hundred yards from the market place.

Romford House Restaurant, 5 London Street, **t** 722 552 (*moderate*). Cosy two-room restaurant on market place with large open fire and sunny yellow walls. Stuffed chicken breast, nut roast with spinach sauce and lots of seafood (swordfish, turbot, lobster). *Closed Sun, and Mon lunch.*

The Teapot, Plowright Place, **t** 722 301 (*cheap*). Opposite market place down arcade of shops. Lace tablecloths and teapots arranged around the room on a high shelf. Teas, cakes and light lunches include jacket potatoes and excellent toasted sandwiches. *Closed Sun.*

Pickenham **t** (01760) –

Riverside House, Meadow Lane, North Pickenham, **t** 440 219, *jeannorris@discali.co.uk* (*cheap*). An 18th-century former pub made of flint and stone with sloping ceilings, low door frames and a narrow stairway. The River Wissey flows through the back garden under a bridge. Three cottage bedrooms.

Sporle **t** (01760) –

Cambridge Cottage, Love Lane, Sporle, **t** 723 718 (*cheap*). Cheerful, no-frills place to stay in pink bungalow a few miles northeast of Swaffham. Near the excellent Squirrel's Drey pub.

The Squirrel's Drey, Sporle, **t** 724 842 (*cheap*). Lovely, cosy old pub just outside Swaffham with inglenook fireplace, real ales and a long wine list. The **restaurant** is another big draw with its traditional country-inn cooking: pot-roasted haunch of venison, rabbit casserole, poached fish or vegetable bourguignon with dumplings. *Closed Mon, no food Sun eve.*

Castle Acre **t** (01760) –

The Old Stores, 9 Bailey Street, **t** 755 165 (*moderate*). Beautiful flint-faced cottages with large living room, sweeping staircase, four bedrooms and hearty vegan breakfast.

Willow Cottage, Stocks Green, **t** 755 551, *willowcottage@webwise.fm* (*moderate*). Four neat, cheerful bedrooms with showers and hand basins in characterful old building above tearooms.

Ostrich Inn, **t** 755 398 (*cheap*). Big coaching arch, ancient walls and brick fireplaces. Delicious food and Green King ales.

Ecotricity Turbine

The huge white blades of architect Norman Foster's 'ecotricity' wind turbine provide electricity for 3,000 homes. Up 3,000 steps, 65 feet up, is a viewing platform (*adm*). The Ecotech Centre, made of sustainable resources (Norwegian spruce timber, renewable lino and organic paint) gives you a whistlestop environmental education.

Castle Acre

This picture-postcard village in the Nar Valley has the ruins of a Cluniac priory and Norman castle, founded in the heart of the Norfolk estates of the powerful Sussex magnate William de Warrenne. The **castle** (***t*** *(01760) 755 394; open April–Sept daily 10–6, Oct daily 10–5, Nov–Mar Wed–Sun 10–4; adm*) is reached down a footpath just before the Bailey Gate into the village. Most of the castle buildings have gone; what is left is an impressive configuration of humps and bumps like the stumps of old teeth, and the grey stone keep.

The **priory** is on the other side of the village, past the bulky Tudor gatehouse, where the land drops down to the river. The remains date from the 11th and 12th centuries, built of flint and chalk faced with local red-brown sandstone and cream-grey limestone. The decorated west front is virtually intact, and the prior's house still habitable; after the Dissolution it became a private house, and a large oriel window and fireplace were added. Look out for the corbel by the door, an angel playing a stringed instrument. The flushwork porch, added in the 16th century, has a picturesque tilt. At the bottom of the hill, a narrow ditch flows under the monks' latrine block – the finest surviving medieval loo anywhere.

Gressenhall

Gressenhall, just north of East Dereham, is home to the **Norfolk Rural Life Museum and Union Farm** (*open Easter–Oct Mon–Sat 10–5, Sun 12–5.30; adm*) – a nostalgic mix of reconstructed shops and cottages, farming history, farm animals and home-made snacks, located in an elegant Georgian brick workhouse and its outbuildings: tiny Cherry Tree Cottage, built in 1853 for elderly married couples, and Union Farm, incorporated into the workhouse in 1776. Below the farm, a footpath runs along the river through meadows past chickens and red cows. But it was never such a wholesome place as it seems today: the Poor Law Amendment Act of 1834 introduced new, deliberate harshness into the workhouse system, breaking up families and subjecting inmates to gruelling work.

King's Lynn and Around

King's Lynn

King's Lynn is at the end of the old London road, on the corner of the Wash. Neighbouring Boston, over the border in Lincolnshire (*see* p.618), has the stump, but Lynn has greater charm. In the ladder of streets between High Street and the Ouse you can imagine yourself back to the time of the religious guilds and Hanse. The medieval port of Lynn traded with Germany, the Baltic and Iceland, competing successfully with the Hanseatic merchants of northern Germany. Its major exports were corn, Wash salt, Derbyshire lead, and cloth from Lincoln and Stamford; its biggest imports were Gascony wine, dried cod from Iceland, timber and pitch from the Baltic, Prussian beer, Norwegian hawks, Flemish cloth and swords from Cologne. Between them, Boston and Lynn did a bigger trade than London. The Hanse had a

Getting There and Around

By **car**, King's Lynn is straight up the A10 from Cambridge and London, or on the A47 cross-country from Peterborough.

Direct **trains** run from London Liverpool Street via Cambridge and Ely.

National Express **coaches** go most days from London Victoria.

Tourist Information

King's Lynn: The Customs House, Purfleet Quay, **t** (01553) 763 044. *Open April–Oct Mon–Sat 9.15–5, Sun 10–5; Nov–Mar daily 10.30–4.*

Guided Walks start at Gaol House, Saturday Market Place. *May–Oct Tues and Wed 10.30am, Sat 2pm and Sun 11.30am; Aug–Sept Mon and Fri 10.30am.* They last around 1½ hours.

There are two general **markets** in Lynn. The biggest is the Tuesday market, with a reduced version in the Saturday Market Place.

The **King's Lynn Festival** takes place late July for two weeks, and incorporates classical music, literature, dance and drama. There is a closely-packed programme of events in the Corn Exchange and Arts Centre, St Margaret's Church and the Town Hall. Classical music is the main focus, with past performances by the Royal Philharmonic and English Symphony orchestras, and literary, political and media speakers. Contact the **festival office**, **t** (01553) 767 557 or *www.kl-festival.freeserve.co.uk.*

Where to Stay

King's Lynn t (01533) –

The Duke's Head Hotel, Tuesday Market Place, **t** 774 996, *www.regalhotels.co.uk/dukeshead* (*moderate*). Behind pink-painted 17th-century façade you find an ancient wooden staircase with worn banisters, a handful of lovely bedrooms and 50 more in modern extension. Two restaurants: brasserie and main dining room.

The Old Rectory, 33 Goodwins Road, **t** 768 544, *clive@theoldrectory.kingslynn.com* (*moderate*). Handsome period-style Victorian house 10-minute walk from town centre across a park. Attractive bedrooms with mood-lifting colours, old pine furniture and big windows.

The Stuart House Hotel, 35 Goodwins Road, **t** 772 169, *www.stuart-house-hotel.co.uk* (*moderate*). Pleasant, comfortable, slightly

permanent trading post in Lynn, opposite St Margaret's Church. It is still there today, the only Hanseatic building to survive in the eastern ports (Newcastle, Hull, York, Boston, Lynn, Yarmouth, Norwich, Colchester and London). Trade has long since shifted north to the modern docks, and the 20th-century improvements are grim, but the narrow strip between Saturday Market Place and Tuesday Market Place, and the wide views across the river are more than a match for Boston.

The **Saturday Market Place** is the oldest part of Lynn, established by the Bishop of Norwich around the church of St Margaret in the 1100s. Its miscellany of old town-houses is packed around the Caen stone church and the flushwork gable-end of the town hall, formerly the Trinity guildhall. Next to the town hall, the **Tales of the Old Gaol House** (*open Easter–Oct daily 10–5, Nov–Easter Fri–Tues 10–5; adm*) is housed in the old police station. Its gruesome exhibits on crime, witchcraft and punishment are good for children. In the undercroft of the town hall municipal charters are displayed alongside a medieval chalice known as the King John Cup – although it missed his reign by a hundred years. The **Town House Museum**, on the other side of the town hall, takes you through Lynn's social history.

Nelson Street, Queen Street and King Street take you into **Tuesday Market Place** past beautiful old buildings (few are open to the public, but you may be able to talk pretentious place to stay with restaurant, bar and garden at end of long gravel drive, 10 minutes' walk across park into town. The 18 bedrooms include a honeymoon suite with Jacuzzi and a four-poster bed.

Russet House Hotel, 53 Goodwins Road, **t** 773 098 (*moderate*). Big Victorian red-brick family-run hotel behind large gravel drive with cosy bar, smoking and non-smoking lounges well stocked with books and newspapers; 13 fresh, clean bedrooms.

Fairlight Lodge, 79 Goodwins Road, **t** 762 234, *www.fairlightlodge-online.co.uk* (*cheap*). Friendly private house in quiet residential area with eight comfortable bedrooms, piles of china on the shelves in the breakfast room and home-made biscuits. Short walk into town across the park.

Eating Out

The Riverside Restaurant, 27 Kings Street, **t** 773 134 (*moderate*). Well-established Lynn restaurant on the courtyard behind the Guildhall, with windows and a terrace overlooking the Great Ouse. The traditional English menu includes roasts, meat pies, local fresh fish and vegetarian dishes followed by apple pie or banoffee tart. *Closed Sun.*

Crofters Coffee House, 27 King Street, **t** 773 134 (*cheap*). Run by the Riverside Restaurant in a brick tunnel below the Guildhall, that used to be a navigable water channel all the way to the river, for loading and unloading. Coffee, tea, sandwiches, salads, quiches and cakes. *Closed Sun.*

Entertainment

The Corn Exchange, Tuesday Market Place, **t** 764 864. The old Victorian corn exchange hosts touring shows, and is the main stage of the summer arts festival.

King's Lynn Art Centre, 27–9 King Street, **t** 764 864. A complex of theatre, arthouse cinema and three gallery spaces, as well as a coffee shop and restaurant. Beneath the ancient timber truss roof of the old guildhall is the 349-seater auditorium. Grouped around the old yard at the back are the white-painted Fermoy Gallery, the beamy Red Barn and the Old Warehouse. The biggest exhibition is the Eastern Open, a longstanding annual competition between artists from East Anglia; it runs from March to April.

your way into some). The narrow brick fronts of the old merchants' houses give no real indication of their size: they were built at right angles to the street, and their full length runs about 200 feet back to the quayside. A good one is the 15th-century **Hanseatic warehouse**, now the offices of the county council, whose wobbly half-timbered range extends down St Margaret's Lane. It is one side of a quadrangle of buildings around a courtyard occupied by a colony of north German merchants 500 years ago. The Hanseatic League originated in the 13th century; a group of merchants from the cities of Lubeck, Bremen and Hamburg banded together to protect themselves against the extortionate demands of foreign princes and barons, and eventually became strong enough to dictate terms and go to war if need be. They were thrown out of England in 1598 by Elizabeth I. One block down, **Thoresby College**, built in the early 1500s to accommodate the chantry priests of the old Trinity guild, inhabits another large site. The old **Purfleet quay** has been rescued from neglect by a millennium tidy-up. Architect Henry Bell and merchant John Turner collaborated on the delightful 17th-century **Custom House** (*open Easter–Oct Mon–Sat 9.15–5, Sun 10–4; Nov–Easter daily 10–4; adm minimal*), originally the merchants' exchange. Pale stone, its Dutch roof rising to a clock tower, it is as perfect as a doll's house. An exhibition on maritime Lynn features Turner's office and stories of Lynn mariners. From the Custom

House, a brand new footbridge crosses the Purfleet. A statue of the Lynn-born New World explorer **George Vancouver** (1757–98), who sailed with Cook and charted the west coast of North America, stands in front of it. Further down King Street, just before Tuesday Market Place, is the old **St George's Guildhall**, one of the most complete medieval guild complexes in England (most, if not pulled down at the Reformation, have since been destroyed by Second World War bombs or post-war town planners). This one is now Lynn's arts centre, based around the old courtyard.

The **Tuesday Market Place** is a windswept space surrounded by imposing 17th-, 18th- and 19th-century buildings, including the grand **Duke's Head Hotel**, built by Bell and Turner for foreign merchants, and the neo-classical Victorian corn exchange.

True's Yard (*open daily 9.30–3.45; adm*) is a short walk north in the direction of the modern docks. The area has been a no-man's land since the slum clearances of the 1930s, with nothing to recommend it but the museum, which tells the tale of the old port – once a thriving fishing port with pubs, school and chapel, and loads of people crammed into tiny two-room cottages like those around the lobster-pot-filled yard. It was King's Lynn's bustling, seamy fishing community, known as the North End.

Castle Rising

Just off the A149 north of King's Lynn stands the 12th-century square keep of William d'Albini, Earl of Arundel. It is a lovely, quiet spot of no apparent strategic value, but in the Middle Ages it was a port, connected to the Wash by the Babingley River. The church, market square (now the village green) and market cross are the remains of the planned medieval town, laid out beside d'Albini's castle.

Sandringham

Open April–20 July and 5 Aug–3 Oct daily 11–5; adm.

A few miles north of Castle Rising, the Norfolk home of the present Queen Elizabeth inhabits a Nordic countryside of Scots pines and sandy heaths. The estate was bought in 1861 for the wayward 21-year-old Prince of Wales (later Edward VII) in preference to Houghton Hall (*see* below). The house, rebuilt in neo-Jacobean style, resembles a golf hotel at St Andrews; it consists of a multitude of gables, dormers and bay windows,

King John's Treasure

King John spent most of his 17-year reign fending off rebel armies. At the end, he faced an invasion from the son of the French king, backed by disgruntled English barons, and the raiding Scottish king, Alexander II. John marched north to deal with the Scots, then south again, plundering his way through Lincolnshire and East Anglia. In Lynn he fell ill, but struggled on to Newark (where he died) via Wisbech and Sleaford. His treasure, buoyed up with fines collected from disloyal northern towns, took another route, around the Wash. The chronicler, Roger of Wendover, describes how 'the ground opened in the midst of the waters and whirlpools and sucked in everything, men and horses.' No traces have ever been found.

and great phalanxes of chimneys. In 1902, *Country Life* described its panelled and patterned interior as 'full of corridors with a decorative scheme consisting entirely of mementos from imperial tours'. The Royal family spends Christmas at Sandringham; crowds gather to watch them all go to church.

Houghton Hall

***t** (01485) 528 569; open Easter–Sept Wed, Thurs and Sun; adm.*

Houghton Hall is the most palatial East Anglian stately pile, its columns and domes a monument to the great man of the 18th century, Sir Robert Walpole. In 1721, Walpole became First Lord of the Treasury and Chancellor of the Exchequer, prime minister in all but name. He lived, however, like a king, knocking down an entire village to provide a parkland setting for his palace, employing William Kent for the interiors and amassing one of the finest art collections in the country. His Palladian-style house is a commanding presence, the grey Whitby stone walls enlivened by four baroque domes at the corners, a portico of four huge columns and numerous statues and urns on the roof balustrade. Not one but two service wings flank the main building, connected by curving colonnades.

Sir Robert's grandson and heir ruined it all for the Walpoles by flogging off hundreds of masterpieces to meet his debts. The house passed to the 4th Earl of Cholmondeley who leased it out; it hasn't changed much since. The main reception rooms are on the first floor, reached by a magnificent mahogany staircase, its walls lined with *trompe l'oeil* by William Kent. In the stairwell stands a bronze statue of a nude gladiator wielding his sword and shield in the direction of the stone **hall**. This is the best room in the house, a perfect cube of 40-foot dimensions, with a stone-painted wooden gallery half way up. The hall is full of allegorical neo-classical carvings and sculpture by Kent and Rysbrack, including a bust of Sir Robert in a Roman toga on the chimney piece. The saloon, next door, is a superb contrast in gilt and crimson, with a riot of allegorical paintings and furniture by Kent.

In the stables is the model soldier collection of the 6th Marquis of Cholmondeley.

Wisbech

Wisbech (pronounced Wisbeach) is a memorable old river port, 10 miles south of the Wash. The River Nene cleaves through the middle of town; boats moored to the high mildewy walls bob up and down on the tide. The handsome Georgian townhouses of wealthy Wisbech businessmen stand on either bank, the grandest on the North Brink (bank). It is the picture of a wealthy Georgian inland port. Peckover House, the North Brink home of a Quaker banking family; the birthplace museum of Octavia Hill, one of the founders of the National Trust, on the South Brink; and the Wisbech and Fenland Museum are all worth a visit.

The **Wisbech and Fenland Museum** (***t** (01945) 583 817; open Tues–Sat April–Sept 10–5, Oct–Mar 10–4; adm*) is just south of the market place. It stands on the far side of a pretty double Georgian crescent, which forms an O around a Regency villa, now the council offices. Its wrought-iron magnificence is down to the prosperity of the early

Victorian town. Among its benefactors were William (1790–1877) and Algernon (1803–93) Peckover, the sons of the founder of the Wisbech and Lincolnshire Bank, both of whom donated specimens from their own fossil collections. The main gallery is devoted to geology, and includes an ichthyosaur skull from Lyme Regis in Dorset. A handsome double flight of stairs leads to the upper gallery, where there is a display on slave trade abolitionist John Clarkson (1764–1828), who campaigned alongside William Wilberforce. Private collections include the Townsend collection of figurines.

Two hundred yards from the town bridge is **Peckover House** (*open Easter–Oct Wed, Sat and Sun 12.30–5.30; gardens also Mon, Tues and Thurs 12.30–5.30; adm*), a highly desirable residence. The front is elegantly proportioned, the garden façade more elaborate. The house was bought in 1795 by Quaker banker Jonathon Peckover, just married and flush from forging a lucrative partnership with Norwich bank Gurney & Co. His sons Algernon and William took over the business, endowing the museum, hospital and public park with its profits. The magnificent interiors are more or less intact, with wood and plaster around the doors and fireplaces, and up the stairs. The interiors have been embellished by the gift of paintings and furniture such as the collection of Norwich School watercolours in the breakfast room.

The **Octavia Hill Birthplace Museum** on South Brink (***t** (01945) 476 358; open Easter–Oct Wed, Sat and Sun; adm*) is the birthplace of one National Trust co-founder, Octavia Hill. Three floors of the Grade II listed Georgian building are devoted to her life and work; the Trust was merely the culmination of her housing reforms. She was born in 1838 to social-reforming parents, who founded Wisbech's first newspaper, *The Star in the East*, to promote their ideas, and built and endowed the Wisbech Infant School on humane principles. Her mother, Caroline, moved to London to manage the Ladies' Guild, a Ruskinesque cooperative of independent craftswomen. Ruskin visited the guild in 1854, and employed Octavia as a copyist for the illustration of his books. Together they began a new housing venture, buying a miserable group of cottages in Marylebone and renting them out under Octavia's benevolent management. She carried on campaigning to save open spaces in the crowded inner city until, in 1895, she co-founded the National Trust to preserve historic buildings.

The North Norfolk Coast

North Norfolk between Cromer and Hunstanton is a place where sublime coastal scenery (big skies, long sandy beaches, *David Copperfield* creeks and salt marshes), unspoiled flint villages and magnificent stately homes meet the modern world of inflated house prices, celebrity sightings, the yacht crowd and swanky restaurants serving local seafood. The sea channels that once supported fleets of fishing boats have silted up behind Blakeney Point, a long shingle bank extending west from Salthouse. It is hard to image the sleepy villages of Salthouse, Cley next the Sea and Wiverton as ports wealthy enough to build handsome Perpendicular churches.

Getting There

The main route to this delightful, unspoiled section of the East Anglian coast is along the A11, which links up with the A1 and M11 motorways.

By **train**, you will have to change at King's Lynn, which can be reached from London King's Cross and Liverpool Street, or change at Norwich from London Liverpool Street, then local train or bus.

Walsingham can be reached from Wells-next-the-Sea on the **Wells and Walsingham Light Railway**, a narrow-gauge steam railway. Seasonal service (*Easter–Oct*) with four or five trains a day. It takes about half an hour each way. Talking timetable, **t** (01328) 710 631.

Depending on the tide and weather, 1 or 2-hour **boat trips** run most days, and sometimes more than once a day, from Morston Quay (signposted just off the coast road) to see the seals basking on **Blakeney Point**. Bring a thermos of tea with you. You can book the trips at the Anchor pub in Morston, **t** (01263) 740 791.

Tourist Information

Wells-next-the-Sea: Staithe Street, **t** (01328) 710 885. *Open Easter–Oct Mon–Sat 10–5 and Sun 10–4.*

Little Walsingham: The Common Place, **t** (01328) 820 510. *Open Easter–Oct daily 10–4.30, winter weekends and snowdrop season 10–4.*

Where to Stay and Eat

Cromer t (01263) –

Hotel de Paris, High Street, **t** 511 828 (*moderate*). Vast 56-bedroomed Victorian-Gothic pile giving the sea what for. Pop in for morning coffee, light lunches or meat-and-gravy dinners in the bar, with sea views.

Mary James, 27–9 Garden Street, **t** 511 208 (*cheap*). Top-notch fish and chip shop and restaurant, where you can get your battered fish with mushy peas. *Closed Sun.*

Cley next the Sea t (01263) –

Cley Mill, **t** 740 209, *www.cleymill.co.uk* (*expensive*). Beautiful 18th-century flour mill with six delightful bedrooms and superb breakfasts and dinners on the edge of marshes and River Glaven. The ground-floor sitting room is stocked with antique furniture and paintings. From the beamed dining room delicious foody smells pervade the marshes on warm evenings.

Dochu La, Coast Road, **t** 740 862 (*moderate*). The spirit of travel is strong in this charming little B&B, named after the Tibetan word for 'mountain path'. There are two bedrooms, leaning walls and heavy floor tiles with rugs. Organic produce and eggs from the owner's hens for breakfast.

King's Head Cottage, **t** 740 322, *www.northnorfolkcoast.co.uk* (*moderate*). Large flint-stone former stables originally belonging to the old King's Head pub (now a guesthouse), behind the High Street down a track. Two bedrooms and two very sweet Lhasa Apso Tibetan mountain dogs.

Cromer

The Edwardian resort of Cromer has a moribund, theatrical air, as if it were the backdrop of a West End musical, its pier a piece of set dressing. It is overshadowed by Gothic Victorian and Edwardian turrets and gables, set dramatically against the cliffs. The Hotel de Paris is the queen of the oversized sea-piles. It's a good town to explore, especially to buy fresh fish and crab (try J. Lee & Son on the High Street) and to browse dark interiors (try Bookworms for cheap hardback literature). East of the pier, where fishing boats are launched off the beach, is the old lifeboat station, now the **Henry Blogg Lifeboat Museum** – named after a famous local coxswain who served 53 years (1894–1947), saving 873 lives; the prize exhibit in the old boatshed is his boat, H.F. Bailey. A narrow flight of stone steps leads from here back up the cliff towards the **museum**, housed in a row of old fishermen's cottages beside the medieval church. Its

Blakeney t (01263) –

The Blakeney Hotel, **t** 740 797, *www.blakeney-hotel.co.uk* (*luxury*). Large 1920s hotel down by the quay with 60 bedrooms, bar, restaurant and leisure facilities including sauna and pool.

Morston Hall, Morston (near Blakeney), **t** 741 041, *www.morstonhall.com* (*expensive*). Beautifully converted 17th-century cobblestone house on A149 coastal road between Blakeney and Wells-next-the-Sea, with flagstone floors and perfect lawns. Dinner every evening in the Michelin-starred restaurant and lunch on Sun (*expensive*). If you book ahead, you can stop for afternoon cream tea in the garden or conservatory.

The White Horse Hotel, 4 High Street, **t** 740 574, *www.blakeneywhitehorse.co.uk* (*moderate*). Upmarket old coaching inn with 10 comfortable bedrooms and a highly-regarded restaurant in the old stables, where you might be offered roast lamb, sea bass or Thai green chicken and prawn curry. Local seasonal produce on the specials board. Bar menu might include fisherman's pie or sausage, red cabbage and mash.

Wells-next-the-Sea t (01328) –

The Corner House, Staithe Street, **t** 710 701 (*moderate*). At the junction of Station Road, newish and gathering steam with jazz evenings. *Open Mon–Sat eves and Wed–Sun lunch*. Also B&B.

The Crown Hotel, The Butlands, **t** 710 209, *www.thecrownhotelwells.co.uk* (*moderate*). Set back from a green, this attractive white-painted former coaching inn has 11 pleasing bedrooms, a high-quality restaurant and brasserie. Nice little sun trap out the back.

The Old Customs House, East Quay, **t** 711 463, *www.eastquay.co.uk* (*moderate*). The white-painted former customs house faces the water with the old crest of Queen Victoria in painted cast iron on the front. It functioned as the Wells customs house from 1560 until the early 20th century. There are three rooms to let including a self-contained apartment on the ground floor.

The Artist's House, Wingate, 2 Furlong Hill, **t** 711 814 (*moderate*). The house is named after local wildlife artist Frank Southgate, for whom it was built as a wedding present in 1903. The new owners have reintroduced some period style to Frank's old house with its elegant hallway and conservatory off the dining room. Three bedrooms and a big garden, well off the road.

East House, East Quay, **t** 710 408, *scottseasthousewells@talk21.com* (*cheap*). Homely white house with three bedrooms.

Nelsons, 21 Staithe Street, **t** 711 650 (*cheap*). Good old-fashioned English tea and coffee shop, crammed with stout tables with big cooking pots bubbling away in the kitchen. Lunch menu of home-made square meals: beef stew and dumplings, steak and kidney pie, roast beef and Yorkshire pudding and cheesy pasta bakes.

The Three Horse Shoes, Warham, **t** 710 547 (*cheap*). Delightful cobblestone pub with open fire and flagstones in village about 3 miles out of Wells. The bar meals are home cooked and high quality, and the desserts to

tiny rooms tell Cromer's story, from remote fishing village to popular Victorian resort, the subject of Romantic paintings by the Norwich school and popular stories by Victorian writer Clement Scott. The church rises to a 160ft tower, Norfolk's tallest.

Inland from Cromer, the **Muckleburgh Collection**, at Weybourne Military Camp, near Holt (***t*** *(01263) 588 210*) is a vast private collection of military vehicles, tanks and guns in a Second World War anti-aircraft artillery range at the foot of Muckleburgh Hill. The main hangar is crammed with fully restored tanks from all over the world, and various ex-military buildings house planes, guns and dioramas. The tour may be accompanied by the roar of fighter planes from RAF Weybourne.

Travelling westwards along the A149, the wide expanse of the **Salthouse Marshes** opens out between the coast road and the sea, grazed by cattle and horses. In the Middle Ages a navigable sea channel swept through the undrained marshes to die for; choices may include spotted dick, crumble, trifle, jam pudding or banoffee pie.

The Red Lion, 44 Wells Road, Stiffkey, **t** 830 552. Another lovely old pub, this one with wooden pews and an open fire, next to the river and meadows. Excellent reputation for food, with meat pies, Stiffkey mussels and fresh fish from Coles of King's Lynn.

Holkham t (01328) –

The Victoria Hotel, Park Road, **t** 711 008, *www.victoriaatholkham.co.uk* (*very expensive*). A 19th-century flint stone pub on the edge of the Holkham estate, 5 minutes' walk from Holkham beach; 11 beautifully furnished bedrooms and a superb restaurant with dark wood colonial furniture, piles of Indian cushions and church candles flickering away at night. Makes good use of local produce including venison from Holkham estate, Cromer crab, Brancaster mussels and fresh eels from Holkham lake.

Burnham Market t (01328) –

The Hoste Arms, The Green, **t** 738 777, *www.hostearms.co.uk* (*expensive*). Attractive cream-painted pub with well furnished, top-notch bedrooms, and an excellent informal restaurant with wooden tables and art on the walls. The bar is open all day, but does not serve food. You can get a sandwich or home-made burger for lunch in the restaurant. Fish is the big seller with Burnham Creek oysters and Brancaster mussels regularly appearing on the menu. Seven of the 43 bedrooms are down the road at the Railway Inn, a former pub, with en-suite showers and guest lounge.

The Lifeboat Inn, Ship Lane (near Thornham), **t** (01485) 512 236 (*moderate*). An atmospheric pub off the road out of Thornham with log fires and rough chalk walls, overlooking salt marshes and sea. Good walking countryside all around. Views from 10 of the 14 bedrooms over the harbour to the sea. Hearty bar meals. Dogs welcomed.

Gurney's Fish Shop, Market Place, **t** 738 967 (*cheap*). Good local fish shop selling locally caught oak-smoked fish, pâtés and pies. Also fishy nibbles like shrimps and dressed crabs that you can take away to eat on the square outside. *Open summer daily 9–5, winter Mon–Sat 9–1 only.*

Walsingham t (01328) –

The Old Bakehouse Restaurant, High Street, **t** 820 454 (*moderate*). Good wholesome restaurant serving traditional English food, hearty but delicious. *Open Fri and Sat eves only; book ahead.*

The Black Lion, Friday Market Place, **t** 820 235 (*cheap*). Good old-fashioned pub serving light bar meals and desserts at lunchtime, a more substantial menu for dinner.

Walsingham Tea Rooms, High Street, **t** 820 686 (*cheap*). Old-fashioned café serving home-baked cakes, cream teas, crumpets and tea cakes, as well as substantial and filling hot lunches including macaroni cheese or ham, eggs and chips. *Closed Mon and mid-Nov–Christmas.*

Blakeney Haven, and the fishermen of Salthouse did big business. Stop in the layby beside the duck pond and wander up Cross Street to the handsome Perpendicular church, dedicated to St Nicholas, the patron saint of fishermen. People clamour to be buried in its glorious churchyard overlooking the salt marshes.

Cley next the Sea is a higgledy-piggledy village of cobblestone cottages and Dutch gables, nestled in a bend of the coast road. As you approach from Salthouse, you may spot twitching binoculars poking out of the grass of the **Cley Marshes**. This is Norfolk's oldest nature reserve, famous for bitterns, bearded tits and marsh harriers. There is a two-hour loop walk, taking in a stretch of shingle beach, or you can pick up a pass to the bird-watching hides in the visitor centre. Just beyond the marshes, a narrow lane follows the River Glaven to the beach. From here the long shingle arm of **Blakeney Point** shoots westwards, wrapping around a vast area of marshes, creeks and sand. Don't think about walking to the point; it is a long and thankless tramp. The Glaven is what remains of the old harbour – wooden jetties and tall whispering reeds – that funded the large, elegant Custom House in Cley. The village has a smart 'Made in Cley, pottery, smokehouse, bookshop and deli.

The harbour used to reach the **church**, about a mile west of the present village on the coast road. As the harbour contracted in the 17th century, the village migrated eastwards, leaving the church – one of the glories of Norfolk – high and dry. Its elaborate decorative features include the ruined south transept with its magnificent windows and the grandiose two-storey south porch. The lofty interior contains canopied niches, carved corbels featuring a lion chewing a bone and a font depicting the seven sacraments.

From Cley, get yourself down to **Blakeney quayside**, following the attractive old High Street with its cobblestone houses and painted doors and window frames. The quay sits on a long, muddy tidal channel that runs through the salt marshes and is often too low even at high tide for boats to get in and out. There is a wonderful walk out into the marshes along an embankment, which veers east to Cley after about half a mile. The vast expanse of oozing mud, long spiky grasses and sea lavender is clamorous with feeding birds at low tide, and you can always hear the dull roar of the North Sea behind Blakeney Point.

Wells-next-the-Sea is the main tourist hub of the north Norfolk coast, a delightful colour-washed town on the edge of salt marshes, about a mile from the sea. Sloping down to the Victorian stone quay, Staith Street is full of tiny shops with windows at knee level to the street. There is a lot of activity in the harbour on the tides; here is the biggest working quay on the north coast. If you walk east along the harbour, you come to the old Victorian custom house, a large white building with an impressive painted crest, looking out over the salt marshes, which stretch for miles. In the other direction, a footpath leads north for a mile along the sea wall to the beach. On one side is the sea channel winding around sand banks, on the other acres of reclaimed farmland screened from the sea winds by pine woods. Beyond the pines are dunes, and beyond them is the beach, at low tide a desert of wet sand.

Holkham Hall

t *(01328) 710 227; open June–Sept Sun–Thurs 1.30–5; adm.*

From Wells along the coast road towards Burnham, the long drive of Holkham Hall winds through acres of Capability Brown parkland to the rear of the house. It is a grand Palladian affair built by William Kent and inhabited by seven generations of Leicesters. The house was rebuilt in 1734 by the 1st Earl of Leicester on his return from a Grand Tour, armed with a collection of paintings to rival the 4th Earl of Pembroke at Wilton House and the 3rd Earl of Egremont at Petworth. Sumptuous state rooms include the galleried marble hall, packed with paintings, sculpture, tapestries and elaborate coffered ceilings. The grounds boast a lake (with boat rides), stone monuments, woods and a museum of bygones.

Opposite the main entrance, an estate road leads north to sandy **Holkham beach**. Not only is it an attractive wilderness, but the last scene of *Shakespeare in Love* was filmed here, as was an All Saints' video for *The Beach*.

Back on the Coast Road

From Holkham heading east you come to **the Burnhams**, about five or six villages including Burnham Overy Staith, Burnham Market and Burnham Thorpe, where Horatio Nelson was born in 1758, the son of a clergyman. It is supposed that the future naval commander and hero of Trafalgar learned to sail down at the Staith, among the reeds and creeks. Further on you come to **Titchwell Marsh**, an RSPB reserve with lagoons, freshwater reed beds, salt marshes and a shingle beach. It is a breeding ground for avocets and marsh harriers in spring.

Little Walsingham

England does well for market towns, cathedral towns and old industrial towns, but religious towns are thin on the ground. Little Walsingham, just south of Wells-next-the-Sea, is the real thing, a medieval time-warp with two shrines – one Anglican, the other Roman Catholic – shops selling icons and badges, hostels for pilgrims (who arrive by the coach load), and the odd raving, bare-footed zealot yelling at passers-by. There are six or seven major pilgrimages each year, but every day is a religious day in Little Walsingham, making it feel more like Loreto or Lourdes than a small town in Norfolk. The walls are of flint, the pavements narrow, the overhanging jetties two or three storeys high and the standing ruins of the medieval priory still a pilgrimage site. The priory gatehouse fronts onto Common Place, a delightful square in the centre of town around the medieval pump. Behind it are the **priory grounds** (*open Easter–Sept, Wed and Thurs 11–5, June–Aug also Sat 2–5*), a peaceful garden dominated by the tall east window, standing alone, untroubled by lesser ruins. This is the end of the Walsingham pilgrimage, revived early last century. The original shrine of Our Lady stood on the north side of the priory church, housed in a replica of the Holy House of Nazareth – the holy house, that is, of Mary's Annunciation. The founder of the shrine was the widow Richeldis de Favarches, who was carrying out instructions that came to her in a visionary dream. About a hundred years later the Augustinian priory was tacked on, growing into a centre of pilgrimage visited by most kings of England up to and including Henry VIII. A Georgian mansion incorporates the low-vaulted refectory. The grounds are accessed through the **Shirehall Museum** abutting the priory gatehouse, which narrates the history of the place, but is also worth a look in its own right: an 18th-century shire hall with its original wooden pews, cubicles and gallery.

A short walk from Common Place on Knight Street is the modern Anglican church containing the **shrine of Our Lady of Walsingham**, housed in another replica of the Holy House. A mile south of Little Walsingham you find the national **Roman Catholic shrine of Our Lady**, based around the small and exquisite medieval **Slipper Chapel** (***t** (01328) 820 217*). The chapel was the last pit stop for pilgrims *en route* to Our Lady of Walsingham, so-called because the pilgrims removed their shoes and walked the final stage barefoot.

Binham Priory Church

A few miles northeast of Little Walsingham, you get another blast of pre-Reformation Catholic England: the nave of the old Benedictine priory church, preserved for the use of the parishioners after the Dissolution. The west window is bricked up, but still magnificent, with its unusual decorative stone shafts. The interior, however, is as much about atmosphere as architecture. Three tiers of arcading run around the walls. At the back of the church is the remains of the ancient rood screen that originally separated the nave and the chancel. It was painted over after the Reformation with Biblical text, but if you look closely you can see the ghostly images of the old saints behind the heavy black lettering.

Cambridgeshire

The county of Cambridgeshire disappears into a flat expanse from the famous university town of Cambridge, oddly located in the middle of this characterless fenland. Cambridge will be any visitor's first stop here, but there are one or two other highlights, best of all the fabulous cathedral at Ely, with its octagonal lantern tower.

Cambridge

...of all the pictoral accidents of a great English university, Cambridge is delightfully and inexhaustibly rich. I looked at the colleges one by one and said to myself always that the last was the best...

Henry James, 1879

On the edge of the Fens, Cambridge seems rather less snug-in-the-shires, less metropolitan, less self-consciously historic than Oxford. Like its arch-rival, it is dominated by its university: 30 colleges federated to form the university. Architecturally, those in the centre are sublime; all are interesting, with their classic arrangement of hall, chapel, library and private rooms around a central court or quadrangle, reinterpreted in different styles over several hundred years. Star attractions include King's College chapel and the Wren Library in Trinity College. Like Oxford, it has bicycles; punts; town-versus-gown antagonism; archaic rules; out-of-bounds areas; famous men (and women) – Newton, Darwin, Milton, Wordsworth, Coleridge, Tennyson, Marlowe; Victorian-style college porters. But in Cambridge you are never far from open green space – the Backs, Jesus Green or Midsummer Common – creating an illusion of constant summer picnics; the past seems ever-present.

The university's origins go back to the early 1200s, when a wandering 'mob of clerks' arrived from Oxford, which they had been thrown out of for uncertain reasons. No one knows why they picked Cambridge, although it was between Stamford and Northampton, which they also tried, and on the edge of the wealthy East Anglian wool country. The first university was an ecclesiastical body under the Bishop of Ely. The early college founders founded their colleges to ensure a supply of parish priests,

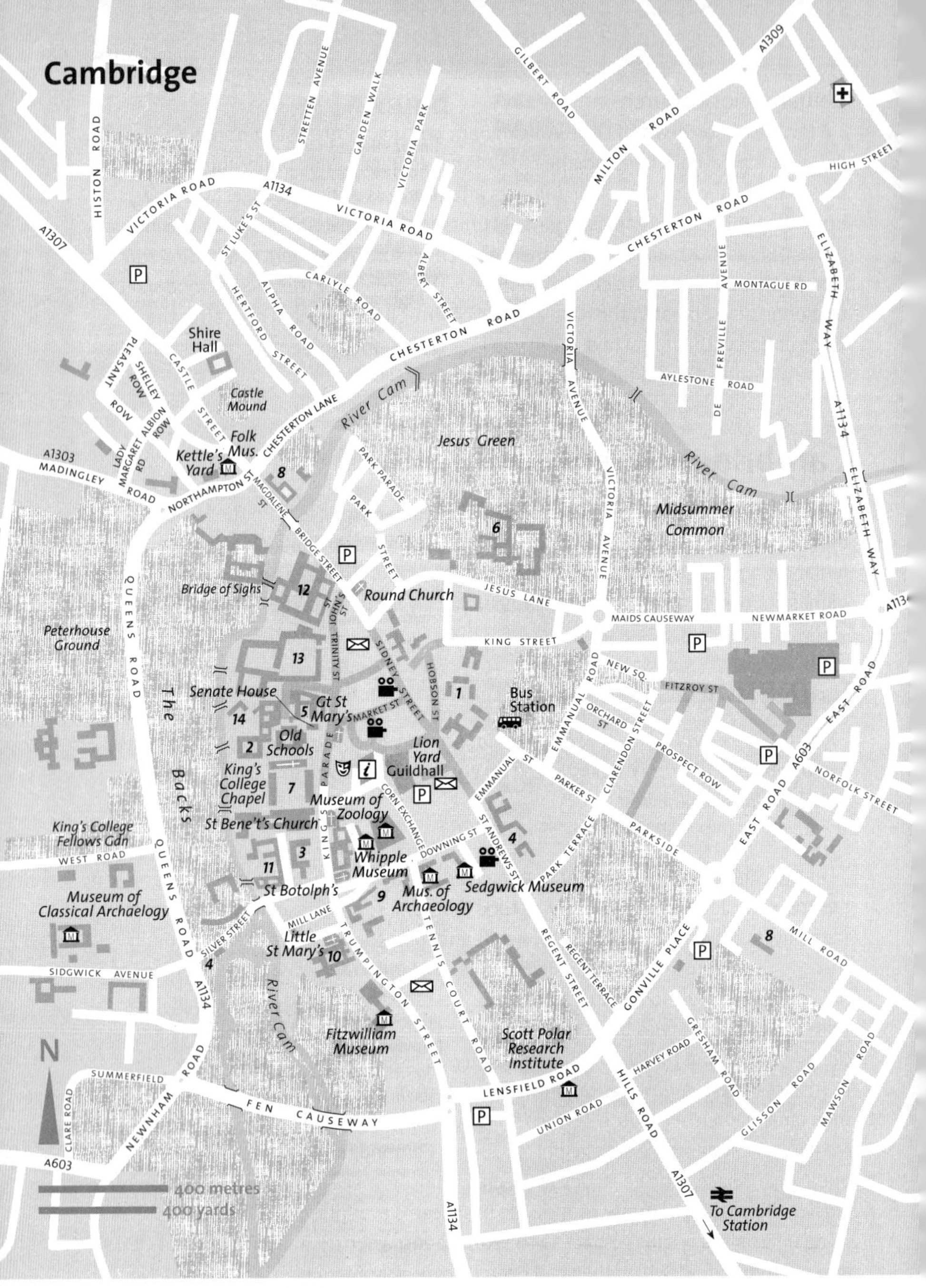

clerks and educated monks. Medieval students began studying in their teens and spent seven years getting their degree, another 10 for a masters in law or theology. Tudor founders glammed up the place, building palatial colleges fit for the governing classes, who came to fine-tune their education, which was gradually becoming less

Key to Cambridge Colleges

1 Christ's
2 Clare
3 Corpus Christi
4 Emmanuel
5 Gonville and Caius
6 Jesus
7 King's
8 Magdalene
9 Pembroke
10 Peterhouse
11 Queen's
12 St John's
13 Trinity
14 Trinity Hall

theological and more humanistic. The next centuries brought the age of science, with new courses created in chemistry, astronomy, anatomy, botany, geology and medicine, and the foundation of the great Cambridge museums – the Fitzwilliam and Sedgewick. Today Cambridge is Britain's forerunner in institutionalized science and technology, with the Cavendish Laboratory, Cambridge Instrument Company and numerous computer technology companies in west Cambridge's own Silicon Valley.

Central Cambridge is more-or-less contained within the triangle of King's Parade, Sidney Street – the main high street – and Pembroke Street.

Trumpington Street, King's Parade, Trinity Street and St John's Street

Trumpington Street, King's Parade, Trinity Street and St John's Street are all the same thoroughfare, running parallel to the river past the main colleges, eight of which stand in a row, fronting onto the road. King's is the grandest, but not everyone's favourite. The colleges back onto the river and what follows, wrote Henry James in 1879, 'is the loveliest confusion of Gothic windows and ancient trees, of grassy banks and mossy balustrades, of sun-chequered avenues and groves, of lawns and gardens and terraces, of single-arched bridges spanning the little stream'. The Backs, as they are known, are the glory of Cambridge. Back on the main drag, past King's, you reach the market place, a bustling hub where gown meets town. From the 114-foot-high tower of **Great St Mary's Church** you can get the whole town in your sights. Beyond the market is Sidney Street, Cambridge's main shopping street. Turn around with your back to the market, and you face the central university buildings: the ducal palace standing end-on to the road facing its own green baize lawn is James Gibbs' **Senate House**, which took over the administration of the university from Great St Mary's in 1730. On the other side of the lawn, looking like a handsome market building, is the **Old Schools**, the oldest part of the university headquarters, separated by a railing from King's College chapel. The scale of the chapel is impressive: long, slim and tall, its roof a forest of decorated pinnacles and pierced crenellations, sitting there on its own as if conscious of its own special virtues.

Queens' College

Queen's Lane, **t** *(01223) 335 511; open daily 11–3, July–Oct 10–4.30; adm.*

Backtracking a little, Queens' has a medieval feel about it, with painted half-timbering, warm brickwork, pink-flowering rose bushes, a jaunty 18th-century sundial

Getting There

By **car**, leave the M11 motorway at junction 11 and follow city-centre signs for 2 miles. There is very little parking in town, and what there is is expensive, so either make sure your hotel or guesthouse has off-road parking, or park-and-ride outside the city centre.

Rail is the ideal way to arrive: there are direct **trains** from London Liverpool Street and King's Cross (express trains take 50 minutes), and you can take a bicycle on the train.

National Express **coaches** run regular services to Cambridge from London Victoria.

Getting Around

By Bicycle

Bicycle is the ideal way to get around this compact, flat town (it's what the locals and students do).

The Bike Man, Market Square, **t** 07850 814 186. *Bikes for hire Mon–Thurs 8–6; good daily and weekly rates.*

H. Drake, Hills Road, **t** (01223) 363 468. *Open Mon–Thurs 8.30–5.30, Fri 8.30–6; by the day or week.*

Mike's Bikes, Mill Road (next to Parker's Piece), **t** (01223) 312 591. *Open Mon–Sat 9–6, Sun 10–4; good rates.*

By Punt

Punts are generally available Mar–Oct, weather permitting.

Scudamore's Boat Yard, Granta Place, The Mill Pond, **t** (01223) 359 750. At the corner of Granta Place and Mill Lane, the biggest punt company, with a range of different boats including rowing boats. You can get all the way to Grantchester without having to drag your boat up the weir. Also hire punts for exploring the Backs outside the Anchor pub by the Silver Street bridge and down at Quayside on Bridge Street.

Tyrell's Marina, Quayside, Bridge Street, **t** (01480) 413 517. Chauffeured and self-punt punts for exploring the Backs (it's more fun, though less dignified, to do it yourself).

Cambridge Chauffer Punts, Silver Street bridge, **t** (01223) 354 164. Chauffeured and self-punt punts along the Backs.

Tourist Information

Cambridge: Wheeler Street, **t** 0906 586 2526, *www.tourismcambridge.com. Open Oct–Easter Mon–Fri 10–5.30, Sat 10–5; Easter–Sept Mon–Fri 10–6 and Sat 10–5, Sun 11–4.*

The daily **market**, on Market Hill, is excellent, with stalls selling fruit and vegetables, bread, cakes and cheeses, tea, hats, second-hand books and clothes; also bicycle hire and repair.

Craft market, Fri and Sat,in All Saints' Gardens, opposite Trinity College gates.

Festivals, Fairs and Bumps

Shakespeare Festival: The Cambridge Shakespeare Company puts on six open-air productions in college quads and gardens in July and Aug. For enquiries call **t** (01223) 511 139, go to *www.cambridgeshakespeare.com*, or visit the city-centre box office, Wheeler Street, **t** (01223) 357 851.

Midsummer Fair, **t** (01223) 457 521. Third Saturday in June on Midsummer Common, following the smaller **Strawberry Fair** (*www.strawberry-fair.org.uk*), with lots of music and stalls.

The **Bumps Races** are peculiar to Cambridge and Oxford (very peculiar). They involve college rowing teams lining up in their boats on the River Cam and at the starter gun trying to 'bump' the boat in front. The boat that gets bumped loses a position in the starting line-up at the next race. The Lent Bumps take place in February, and the May Bumps, bizarrely, in June. For enquiries, call **t** (01223) 467 304. In July, the townspeople have a go.

Where to Stay

Cambridge t (01223) –

Splash out on a hotel with parking if you can afford it. Guesthouses are concentrated on the charmless main roads in and out of town, such as Chesterton Road/Milton Road, and around Hills Road.

The Crowne Plaza, Downing Street, **t** 464 466, *www.cambridge.crowneplaza.com* (*very expensive*). Big, modern, upmarket city-centre hotel with 198 bedrooms. The hotel was purpose-built in the 1990s and recently refurbished. Businesslike but comfortable, with a hair salon and 'traditional' Irish bar built with materials imported from Ireland.

Royal Cambridge Hotel, Trumpington Street, **t** 351 631, *www.forestdale.com* (*very expensive*). Huge hotel with long stuccoed front set back behind plane trees; 57 bedrooms, period décor and a nice bar for evening drinks; free parking.

University Arms Hotel, Regent Street, **t** 351 241, *www.devereonline.co.uk* (*very expensive*). Hotel built in 1834 as a post house on the edge of Parker's Piece, a large green space which was formerly farmland belonging to Trinity College and farmed by the college cook, Edward Parker. It was the first hotel to possess electric lighting in Cambridge; 120 bedrooms, period-style décor, uniformed staff, red leather armchairs, twinkly lights and a hushed, serious atmosphere. Restaurant overlooking the park, or light meals in the bar. Ample car parking for a fee.

Lensfield Hotel, 53 Lensfield Road, **t** 355 017, *www.lensfieldhotel.co.uk* (*expensive*). Cheerful-looking cream-painted Victorian building with patio seating outside; 2 minutes' walk from Scott Polar Museum. Cosily cramped, with 32 bedrooms and conservatory dining room in summer.

The Regent Hotel, 41 Regent Street, **t** 351 470, *www.regenthotel.co.uk* (*moderate*). Comfortable, recently refurbished Georgian-fronted hotel on shopping street, overlooking Parker's Piece at the back.

The Centennial Hotel, 67–71 Hills Road, **t** 314 652, *www.centennialhotel.co.uk* (*moderate*). Courteous and pleasant hotel on busy road near station, 15 minutes' walk from town centre. Some quieter 'de luxe' bedrooms at the back; bar and pleasant little restaurant.

Victoria Guest House, 57 Arbury Road, **t** 350 086 (*moderate*). You are guaranteed a warm welcome at this friendly, clean, comfortable family-run guesthouse on a nondescript street off busy Milton Road, just over a mile from the town centre.

Cambridge Guest House, 201/a Milton Road, **t** 423 239 (*moderate*) Hospitable place to stay 15–20 minutes' walk from the town centre. Newish, enthusiastic and recently redecorated.

Newnham t (01223) –

There are some smashing guesthouses in Newnham, halfway to Grantchester, in big, handsome houses on broad, tree-lined roads. Book well ahead.

77 Grantchester Meadows, **t** 316 363 (*moderate*). Pretty, cottagey Victorian terraced house on a quiet back street with a rose climbing over the front bay window.

Upton House, 11/b Grange Road, **t** 323 201 (*moderate*). Grand 1912 Arts and Crafts-style house in handsome, quiet street. Big garden and friendly dog; only one, sought-after double bedroom.

Hobson's House, 96 Barton Road,, **t** 304 906 (*moderate*). Two rooms available in this pretty green cottage in a quiet, tree-lined road, a pleasant mile or so's walk from town centre. Plant pots outside front door and sweet peas growing up fence. Tasteful and bright inside.

Segovia Lodge, 2 Barton Road, **t** 354 105 (*moderate*). Homely, pretty cottage with sweet little front garden and two immaculately tiled bathrooms, one a striking shade of blue. Ten minutes' walk into town centre.

Eating Out

Cambridge is full of chain bars and restaurants including Café Uno, Café Rouge, Pizza Express, The Dome, All Bar One and no fewer than three Starbucks. **Bella Pasta**, The Watermill, Newnham Road, **t** 367 507, occupies a delightful spot with a balcony overlooking the mill pond.

Midsummer House, Midsummer Common, **t** 369 299 (*expensive*). Upmarket but informal French restaurant in a Victorian house in the middle of the common, where the poshest students are taken by their parents after graduation. *Closed Sun.*

Restaurant Twenty-Two, 22 Chesterton Road, **t** 351 880 (*moderate*). A highly regarded restaurant with green shutters and cream-painted brickwork on busy road, about 2 miles out of centre. *Closed Sun and Mon.*

Loch Fyne, The Little Rose, 37 Trumpington Street, **t** 362 433 (*moderate*). One of a small chain of seafood restaurants (incorporating a fishmonger's). Breakfast of kedgeree, smoked kippers or croissant and smoked salmon, light lunch or dinner of lobster mayonnaise, Loch Fyne oysters served on ice, mussel stew or smoked fish.

Rainbow Vegetarian Bistro, 9/a King's Parade, **t** 321 551 (*cheap*). Friendly, informal basement bistro down King's Parade, with wooden tables, terracotta-painted walls, and vegetarian food like Thai green curry, mushroom crumble and Mexican enchiladas.

Bangkok City, 24 Green Street, **t** 354 382 (*cheap*). Splendid old building on cobbled street which houses Cambridge's most popular Thai restaurant.

Browns, 23 Trumpington Street, **t** 461 655 (*cheap*). Popular, large, open-plan restaurant in old VD clinic opposite Fitzwilliam Museum. Colonial-style décor, with stripped floorboards, high ceiling fans and Lloyd Loom chairs. Brasserie-style menu of ale pie and Caesar salad.

Dojo Noodle Bar, 1–2 Millers Yard, Mill Lane, **t** 363 471 (*cheap*). Down Mill Lane towards the river, a busy little restaurant where big bowls of fresh noodles are brought to diners sitting elbow-to-elbow at long tables.

Sala Thong, 35 Newnham Road, **t** 323 178 (*cheap*). Small, airy and charming Thai restaurant with blue-painted wooden tables, stripped floorboards and tons of daylight. The service is friendly, attentive and quick and the food delicious. Book for dinner. *Closed Mon.*

Cafés and Tea Rooms

Cambridge is disappointingly, and surprisingly, low on café culture. On a sunny day, you're better off buying provisions in the market or baguettes from Nadia's Patisserie on Silver Street and picnicking on the Backs.

Indigo Coffee House, 8 St Edward's Passage, **t** 368 753. Stripped floorboards, windows thrown open onto the street, and a tiny second-hand bookshop next door. Salads, filled baguettes and lots of coffees and herbal teas. *Open Mon 10–7, Tues–Sat 10am–11pm and Sun 11–6.*

Clowns Café, 54 King Street, **t** 355 711. Popular, colourful Italian-run café with tiny roof terrace, cosy interior. Good cakes, cooked breakfasts and hot meals. Well positioned near Jesus College. *Open 8am–11pm.*

Trockel, Ulmann and Freunde, 13 Pembroke Street, **t** 460 923. German café on Victorian street where you can get good croissants in the morning, baguettes and German küchen. *Open Mon–Sat 10–5.*

The Orchard, Mill Way, Grantchester, **t** 845 788, *www.orchard-grantchester.com*. Delightful and famous 1900s tea gardens with deckchairs under apple trees and Rupert Brooke nostalgia, serving teas, cakes and light lunches. *Open 9.30–6, later in summer.*

Pubs and Bars

The **Quayside** has become a busy social hub with the arrival of a number of chain café-bars including Starbucks, Henrys, Quay Bar, Café Galleria and Bar Med, all with patio seating.

Ha Ha!, 17 Trinity Street, **t** 305 089. Stylish bar-restaurant. Brunch until midday, then salads, fish and chips or pasta dishes until about 10pm. Coffee and cold beer all day.

The Castle Inn, 38 Castle Street, **t** 353 194. Civilized Adnams pub away from the student crowds with nooks and alcoves for private conversation and a beer garden.

The Anchor, Silver Street, **t** 353 554. A Cambridge institution with its solid pine pews, low beams and rustic-style beer barrels. Grab a table on the riverside terrace and watch punting incidents under the Mathematical Bridge.

The Eagle, 8 Bene't Street **t** 505 020. A classic old Cambridge pub with bars around a pretty courtyard, including the Air Force bar where you can see the squadron numbers and nicknames of American and RAF pilots stationed nearby scratched onto the ceiling during the Second World War. A blue plaque on the front commemorates the work of Watson and Crick, who discussed their theories here and announced the discovery of DNA to the assembled drinkers in the early 1950s. Pub grub available.

The Mill, 14 Mill Lane, **t** 357 026. Another Cambridge institution, on the corner of Granta Place. A cosy bar and ample grassy riverbanks outside.

The Free Press, 7 Prospect Row, **t** 368 337. This non-smoking pub set in a delightful villagey part of Cambridge behind Parker's Piece is somewhere to chat, drink real ale or good whisky and play old pub games. No music or mobile phones. Home-cooked bar meals including game pie, fresh fish, and ploughman's with proper pâtés. Does special Thanksgiving dinners.

The Granta Inn, Mill Pond, Newnham Road, **t** 505 016. Old-fashioned Victorian pub with garden and deck overlooking the mill pond, willow trees, punts and ducks, and meadows beyond. Buzzing atmosphere, pub grub and its very own fleet of punts to let out to punters.

Entertainment

Clubs and Discos

There are lots of night clubs with student nights, including **Fifth Avenue**, Heidelberg Gardens, **t** 364 222, with 1970s and '80s nights, or **Life**, 22 Sidney Street, **t** 324 600, which does 'Chart Cheese' nights. It's a constantly changing (like anywhere) though minuscule scene so ask around.

Theatre and Film

Arts Picture House, St Andrews Street, **t** 504 444. Three screens showing new films, sub-titled foreign-language films and late-night shows. Good café-bar and poetry readings.

ADC Theatre, Park Street, **t** 359 547, *www.adc-theatre.cam.ac.uk*. The university theatre puts on a mix of student plays including Footlights revue (the launch pad for Peter Cook and other comedians), professional touring shows, and fringe shows during Camfest.

Cambridge Arts Theatre, Peas Hill (off Market Hill), **t** 503 333, *www.cambridgeartstheatre.com*. Cambridge's main theatre, with bars and Roof Garden Restaurant, **t** 578 930. Lively and interesting repertoire of new plays, touring shows and all kinds of music.

Music

Many Cambridge pubs host live music, comedy and DJs. Ask around.

The Boat Race, 170 East Road, **t** 508 533, *www.boat-rac.co.uk*. Live music including jazz, indie, rock, blues, folk and reggae every night of week; comedy once a month on Fri.

Kettle's Yard, Castle Street, **t** 352 124. Regular classical music concerts including free concert given by students every Fri lunch during term at 1.10pm.

The University Concert Hall, West Road, **t** 335 184. Ask at the tourist Information centre for a programme of concerts.

Most university colleges have sung evensong during term, open to the public and free of charge. **King's College Chapel**, **t** 331 447, is the most famous (you'll have seen the Christmas Carols concert service on TV unless you've spent your life on another planet). The following also have regular services: **Clare College Chapel**, **t** 333 200; **Jesus College Chapel**, **t** 339 339 and **St John's College Chapel**, **t** 339 339.

and a pretty little court named after a walnut tree. It is the foundation of two queens, Margaret of Anjou and Elizabeth Woodville, one a Lancastrian, the other a Yorkist. Although their reigns were separated by the Wars of the Roses, and the murder of Margaret's husband, Henry VI, their money and prestige produced something of exceptional beauty. Above the southeast corner of the **Cloister Court**, a sensational half-timbered quadrangle standing on dusky redbrick pillars, you see the tower in which the Dutch humanist **Erasmus** (1469–1536) stayed on his extended trip to England in 1510–14. Beyond is the **Wooden Bridge**; stand on it long enough and you'll hear a punter telling the yarn that it was built by Sir Isaac Newton on mathematical principles without using any screws.

As you leave Queens', there is a pleasant walk down Silver Street over the road bridge, turning left at Darwin College and back over the meadows to **Mill Lane**. You can hire punts from the Granta pub, on Newnham Road, or sit on the wall outside the Mill pub. If you go straight across the junction at the end of Silver Street onto Sidgwick Avenue, a tree-lined road of Victorian red-brick family houses, you come to the **Museum of Classical Archaeology** (*open Mon–Fri 10–5, Sat 10–1*), which houses more than 600 plaster casts of all the major Greek and Roman statues.

King's College

King's Parade, entered from Trinity Lane, **t** *(01223) 331 100; open term Mon–Sat 9.30–3.30, Sun 1.15–2.15; vacations Mon–Sat 9.30–4.30, Sun 10–5; exam term (May–mid-June) grounds closed, but chapel open; adm.*

You can get a good look at King's from the Backs, over the Great Lawn (a much-painted view), or through the screen walls on King's Parade. It was founded in 1441 by the 18-year-old Henry VI for the boys of Eton School, his other educational foundation. A block of the old town centre was cleared for it, including shops, warehouses, riverside quays and a church. The outbreak of the Wars of the Roses in 1455 and the king's overthrow in 1461 put an end to the building work, which continued in fits and starts under Edward IV, Richard III, Henry VII and Henry VIII, whose patronage finally turned Cambridge into the sort of place an ambitious young aristocrat would want to go before applying for a top job at a Renaissance court. The kingly appearance of King's today is largely the work of the grand Victorian-Gothic gatehouse and screen walls, and the south range, built by William Wilkins in the 1820s. **King's College chapel** choir is internationally renowned, especially for its Christmas Eve concert. The setting provided by the Tudor kings couldn't be better. As Henry James put it, the chapel is only 'saved from being the prettiest church in England by the accident of its being one of the noblest'. The proportions belong to Henry VI; the fan-vaulted ceiling – the longest anywhere – with its central bosses of alternating Tudor roses and portcullises to Henry VII; and the dark oak screen to Henry VIII, carved with his initials and those of Anne Boleyn. You step out of the chapel into the exposed **Front Court**, which sends you around the back into the **Great Lawn**, another open space sloping down to the river. It is a magnificent college, but it has no secluded corners. Old boys include the poet **Rupert Brooke** (1887–1915), who later moved out to Grantchester, and the novelist **E.M. Forster** (1879–1970), who became a member of the Apostles, the forerunner to the Bloomsbury Group.

Clare College

Clare College, Trinity Lane, ***t*** *(01223) 333 200; open Easter–Sept daily 10–4.30; adm; Oct–Easter unrestricted entry.*

Clare is next door to King's but quite different: smaller and more secluded, like a Florentine palace on the banks of the Arno. It is more than a hundred years older for starters, founded by the chancellor of the university in 1326, then refounded in 1338 with another injection of funds by Elizabeth de Clare, the granddaughter of Edward I. The Old Court was rebuilt from 1638 in magnificent neo-classical style – reputedly by Inigo Jones. From it you walk out onto Clare Bridge, the prettiest of the Cam footbridges – identified by its cannonball decorations – built at the same time as the Old Court, to link land on the west bank bought from King's. Over the river you can go into the charming Fellows' Gardens and stretch out on the riverbank. Famous alumni include Hugh Latimer (1485–1555) who became a Fellow in 1510, later assumed the position of royal chaplain to Henry VIII, and was martyred in Oxford for his beliefs.

Trinity Hall

Trinity Lane, ***t*** *(01223) 332 500; open 9–12 and 2–5.30 except Easter term when closed to visitors.*

Trinity Hall is overshadowed by its more renowned neighbours, but is still delightful, all climbing roses and wisteria. It was founded in 1350 by the Bishop of Norwich to restock the clergy after the Black Death. Old boys include J.B. Priestley (1894–1984), who wrote for the *Cambridge Review* and went on to write more than 50 plays, including *An Inspector Calls*, novels and travelogues, including *An English Journey* (1934), in which he confessed 'I was always faintly uncomfortable, being compelled to feel – and quite rightly too – a bit of a lout and a bit of a mountebank'.

Gonville and Caius College

Trinity Street, ***t*** *(01223) 332 400; open term 9–2, vacations also afternoons; closed exam term (May–mid-June).*

Gonville and Caius (pronounced 'keys') was founded twice, first in 1348 by Edmund Gonville, a priest from Norfolk, and then again in 1557 by John Caius, the Tudor royal physician to Henry VIII's children. Its three courtyards take you through at least one of the allegorical gates of humility, virtue and honour, symbolizing the academic path of the ideal Gonville and Caius student to graduation in Senate House.

Trinity College

*Trinity Street, **t** (01223) 338 400; quads, backs and chapel open daily 10–5, hall open 3–5, Wren Library open Mon–Fri 12–2, Sat 10.30–12.30; adm.*

'What institution is more magnificent than Trinity?' asked Henry James. It was founded in 1546 by Henry VIII, allegedly to out-do Cardinal Wolsey's Christchurch in Oxford, and endowed with the wealth of 24 recently Dissolved monasteries. Henry died the next year, so the building was left to its masters over the following 300 years. You enter the Tudor brick **Great Gate**, set back off Trinity Street behind cobblestones and bicycles, and guarded by a statue of Henry VIII holding a chair leg instead of a sceptre. The gatehouse belonged to the former college of King's Hall, founded by Edward III and absorbed into Henry's new super-college. Through the gatehouse you are in the **Great Court**, a quarter of a mile of magnificent Tudor-Gothic architecture, enclosing two acres of lawns, in the midst of which rises a crown-shaped fountain. The architect was Thomas Neville, the master of Trinity appointed by Elizabeth I in 1593. This was the court in which Harold Abrahams and Lord Burghley raced at noon between the first and last gongs of the clock in *Chariots of Fire*. The mathematician **Sir Isaac Newton** (1642–1727) lived here as an undergraduate, in the ground floor rooms between the Great Gate and the chapel. He came up in 1661, was elected a Fellow of Trinity in 1667, and Lucasian Professor of Mathematics in 1669, publishing *Principia* in 1687. Beyond Newton's rooms, you can usually walk up a flight of steps and straight through the screens passage into cloistered **Neville's Court**, handsomely framed on the far side by **Christopher Wren's library**. With its open arcade on the ground floor, tall arched windows and stone columns, it looks magnificent. The long bright room is flooded with daylight, lined with oak bookcases and decorated with lime-wood carvings by Grinling Gibbons. Treasures on show include a hand-written manuscript of Milton's poems; a first edition *Principia* (1687); letters by Byron, who, according to college legend, kept a tame bear in Neville's Court; and, possibly the most prized of them all, a manuscript of *House at Pooh Corner* by A.A. Milne.

St John's College

*St John's Street, **t** (01223) 338 600; open Mon–Fri 10–5.30, weekends 9.30–5.30; adm.*

Massive St John's extends a mighty Victorian range onto the west bank of the river, with grand battlemented Tudor gatehouses, pinnacles and corner towers and hundreds of dormer windows. You can get a sneak preview into the **First Court** (where Wordsworth lived from 1787 to 1791) through a gap between the front range and Gilbert Scott's chapel, which backs onto St John's Street. The **gate tower** carries the elaborate coat of arms of the founder, Margaret Beaufort, mother of Henry VII, featuring a pair of mythical goats and a pot pourri of Tudor emblems. The highlight is the **Second Court**, built around 1600 in austere Tudor style; you can't help thinking that a climbing plant or two would cheer the place up a bit. From the bridge over the Cam, neat lawns sweep away to a wrought-iron gate. On the far side of the river is the

Victorian New Court, a neo-Gothic building with battlements, turrets and a large central tower known as the wedding cake. It is linked to the old college buildings by the handsome covered **Bridge of Sighs**.

Corpus Christi

Trumpington Street, ***t*** *(01223) 338 000; open 2–4 except exam term (May–mid-June).*

Founded in 1352 by the Guild of Corpus Christi for training priests after the Black Death, its **Old Court** is the real thing after the splendid Victorian neo-Gothic of the gatehouse and New Court. It is smaller, lower and darker than some of the riverbank colleges. Old Court was the prototype Cambridge court (influenced by New College in Oxford) with dining hall, library and private rooms around the sides, while the ancient church of St Benet's served as the chapel. Illustrious Corpus old boys include the Elizabethan dramatist **Christopher Marlowe** (1564–93), who left in 1584, having already written *Tamburlaine* and got involved in espionage for Francis Walsingham.

From Bridge Street up Castle Hill

St John's Street emerges onto Bridge Street, which heads north over Magdalene Bridge – a lively place of bustling café-bars – towards Castle Mound, the strategic nexus of Cambridge from the Iron Age to the Civil War. The view from the top is not particularly rewarding, but on the way you pass a ragbag of Cambridge attractions.

The Round Church

Bridge Street, ***t*** *(01223) 306 693; open 9–5.*

Across Bridge Street you see a grey stone round church resembling a medieval buttercross. It is one of a handful of Norman crusaders' churches in the country, built in the round in imitation of the Church of the Holy Sepulchre in Jerusalem, which stood on the site of Jesus's tomb. The chancel with its angel roof and the north aisle were added in the later Middle Ages, and the south aisle in 1841. It is now the Christian Heritage Centre.

Magdalene College and the Pepys Library

Magdalene Street, ***t*** *(01223) 332 100; open 8–6.30 except exam term (May–mid-June); Pepys Library open term only, mid-April–July Mon–Sat 11.30–12.30, Oct to early Dec and mid-Jan–mid-Mar 2.30–3.30.*

As you pass through the screen walls out of the First Court of Magdalene College you glimpse the Pepys Library, a beautiful late 17th-century building resembling a shire hall with its cloister arches, gables and classical motifs. Pepys died on 26 May 1703, donating his whole library of 3,000 books to his old college. He specified the building, then known simply as 'new building', which was subsequently renamed Pepys Library. He also specified that his library should be kept in its present form 'without addition or subtraction' and that the books be arranged according to height, the smallest in the bottom corner, gradually getting bigger around the room. It is a small library, full of the personality of the man: there are special collections of naval history, medieval manuscripts plus the six small volumes of his short-hand diary, housed in his own bookcases and bound in his own binding.

Folk Museum

2–3 Castle Street, ***t*** *(01223) 355 159; open Mon–Sat 10.30–5, Sun 2–5; Oct–Mar closed Mon; adm.*

The Folk Museum was established in 1934 in a former pub on Castle Hill, Cambridge's old red-light district. There are seven rooms, including the old hatch bar and grand dining hall of the pub, full of 19th- and early 20th-century domestic items and trade tools. Some of the most interesting relate to the working life of college domestics, including old jelly moulds from Magdalene kitchen and a wicker bed-bug trap. There are curiosities too, such as a pair of nutcrackers that belonged to a local woman, Elizabeth Woodcock, who survived nine days buried in snow, and a medal dug up in Chesterton inscribed 'The Noted Liar'.

Kettle's Yard

Castle Street; ***t*** *(01223) 352 124; house open Tues–Sun 2–4, summer 1.30–4.30; gallery open Tues–Sun 11.30–5.*

The home of modern art collector Jim Ede has been immaculately preserved with everything in it, a time-capsule of understated whitewashed and cream-linen chic. Ede was the curator of the Tate Gallery from 1921 to 1936, and started the change in its collecting policy from British art to modern international art. He bought the four old cottages of Kettle's Yard in 1956, extending them in the 1970s to provide more hanging space for his growing collection of work by his many painter friends. Paintings hang on every wall, including in the loo. You can sit on the chairs, pull a book from the shelves and flick through a folder of letters and articles about Alfred Wallis, the Cornish fisherman-artist and real star of the place. Ede was his biggest fan, although they never met. But they exchanged letters and occasionally Ede would receive a parcel of paintings, mostly on thick cardboard. Wallis, a retired fisherman, began painting aged 70 after the death of his wife. He was never taught, and observed no conventions. 'I do most what used To Be what we shall never see no more every Thing altered,' he explained in a letter to Ede. He painted all day, six days a week until his death in 1942 aged 87, on matchboxes, bits of wood, whatever came to hand. He was brought to the attention of the art world in 1928 by artists Ben Nicholson and Chris Wood who, on a visit to St Ives, 'passed an open door in Back Road West and through it saw some paintings of ships and houses on odd pieces of paper and card-board nailed up all over the wall, with particularly large nails through the smallest ones.' The adjoining gallery shows contemporary art exhibitions.

Sidney Street and Around

Head back down Bridge Street past St John's Street and you come to Sidney Street, the town's shopping street. The colleges on either side are sublime self-contained architectural worlds, including a cloistered Wren chapel in Emmanuel College. Market Street takes you back to King's Parade, via Market Hill (the flat-as-a-pancake market place) and boutiquey Rose Street.

Jesus College

*Jesus Lane, **t** (01223) 339 339; unrestricted access in daylight hours except exam term (May–mid-June).*

A little out of the way of the other colleges, it is worth the walk to see Jesus's **Cloister Court**. In one corner of the court rises the tower of the old nuns' church turned college chapel, which features a roof by Pugin, nave and tower ceilings by William Morris. Jesus was founded in 1496 on the site of a defunct Benedictine nunnery. Some of its buildings were incorporated into the Tudor foundation, called 'The College of the Blessed Virgin Mary, St John the Evangelist and the Glorious Virgin St Radegund' – or Jesus for short. This was the college of archbishop **Thomas Cranmer** (1489–1556), who gave up his college fellowship and shelved his career in the church to marry a local girl, but was ordained and welcomed back after she died in childbirth. He was burned at the stake in Oxford along with Hugh Latimer (of Clare) and Nicholas Ridley (of Pembroke) for his part in the Reformation.

Carry on walking up Jesus Lane, and you come to **Jesus Green**, an open green space adjoining Midsummer Common where you sometimes see fairs. Return to Sidney Street via King's Street and Sussex Street, a narrow, arcaded shopping street.

Christ's College

*St Andrew's Street, **t** (01223) 334 900; open term 9.30–12 noon, vacations 9–dusk, closed exam term (May–mid-June).*

The small college of God's-house was turfed out of its riverside location by Henry VI, to build King's College, and refounded as Christ's by Margaret Beaufort, Henry VII's mother, in 1505. You can see her goats rampant on the gate tower. The bell-towered hall in the leafy First Court looks like a chapel, and the chapel looks like a hall. Inside the hall are portraits of **John Milton** (1608–74), who came up in 1625 and was suspended for a term for getting into a fist-fight with his tutor, and **Charles Darwin** (1809–82), who was sent here to study theology in 1827 but confessed in his *Autobiography* that he spent most of time shooting, riding and hunting. 'But no pursuit in Cambridge was followed with nearly so much eagerness or gave me so much pleasure as collecting beetles,' he added. He lived for a while at 22 Fitzwilliam Street, today marked with a plaque. An archway through the Fellows' Building takes you into the landscaped, wooded Fellows' Garden.

The Scientific Museums of the New Museum Site and Downing Site

Running between St Andrew's Street and Trumpington Street, is the university's purpose-built 19th-century science area. The New Museum Site grew up around the Victorian zoology museum and developed an international reputation in the 20th century as the home of the prestigious department of physics (which moved to west Cambridge in 1974). Almost everything of consequence in physics over the last hundred years happened in its Cavendish Laboratory: the discovery of the electron (1897), the proton (1920), the neutron (1932), the splitting of the atom (1932), the determination of the structure of DNA (1953). Since the foundation of the awards in 1901, more than 20 Cavendish physicists have won the Nobel prize for physics and chemistry, including Watson and Crick in 1962 (for DNA research). Across the road, the Downing Site specializes in general sciences. It developed around the geology museum, founded in 1904, and the anthropology museum, founded in 1910.

Start at the **Whipple Museum of the History of Science** (*New Museums Site, Free School Lane; open Mon–Fri 1.30–4.30 in term*). Robert Stewart Whipple (1871–1953), collected more than a thousand scientific instruments – mainly to do with optics, navigation, surveying and mathematics – and just as many rare books.

Enter the University Museum of Zoology (*New Museum Site, Downing Street,* ***t*** *(01223) 336 650; open Mon–Fri 10–1 and 2–4.45 in holidays, 2–4.45 only in term*) via the old gateway on Free School Lane, passing the old Cavendish Laboratory and the first calculation of the EDSAC computer. The 19th-century collections include the huge skeleton of a Fin Whale, hundreds of stuffed birds and the mounted skeletons of the elephant seal, polar bear, giraffe, rhino, and a whole line of monkeys.

The **Sedgewick Museum of Earth Sciences** (*Downing Street,* ***t*** *(01223) 333 456; open Mon–Fri 9–1 and 2–5, Sat 10–1*) is a classic Victorian museum. The collection was founded by a London physician, John Woodward (1665–1728), and expanded by Adam Sedgwick (1785–1873), who became the sixth Woodwardian Professor of Geology in 1818. As well as the portable writing table that went with the geologist to Devon, Cornwall and North Wales to probe the Devonian, Silurian and Cambrian systems, there are exhibits on everything from Jurassic to Tertiary, and Triassic to Precambrian – the specimens displayed in the original oak cabinets and drawers. Peer into the Woodwardian Room, housing Woodward's collection of fossils and minerals, set up as the study of a late 17th-century gentleman collector.

The collections of the **Museum of Archaeology and Anthropology** (*Downing Street,* ***t*** *(01223) 333 516; open Tues–Sat 2–4.30*) include a 45-foot-high totem pole from British Columbia, canoes, carved Ambrym gongs and painted wooden objects.

Back on Trumpington Street

Heading out of town, Trumpington Street is flanked by two of the oldest Cambridge colleges and the Fitzwilliam Museum. **Pembroke College** (*Trumpington Street,* ***t*** *(01223) 338 100; open daily 9–5pm except exam term*) was founded in 1347 by the widowed French Countess of Pembroke. Under the 18th-century facing, its gatehouse is the oldest in Cambridge. You can walk through its honey-coloured courts, with their lawns, borders and trees. The brick **chapel** in the First Court is said to have been

Christopher Wren's first completed work, in 1665. The extension in yellow stone was added in 1880 by George Gilbert Scott. Beside the Victorian library is a statue of **William Pitt the Younger**, who came up in 1773, aged 14, and graduated in 1776.

Across the road, **Peterhouse** (*Trumpington Street*, **t** *(01223) 338 200; open daily 9–5 except exam term*) is the oldest and smallest Cambridge college, founded in 1284 by the Bishop of Ely. Its **Old Court** is on the medieval scale, but with classical facing. Have a look inside the hall if you can, for the Pre-Raphaelite windows and tiles by Morris & Co. in the Tudor fireplace. **Thomas Gray** (*Elegy Written in a Country Churchyard*) studied law at Peterhouse in 1742.

The Fitzwilliam Museum

Trumpington Street, **t** *(01223) 332 900; open Tues–Sat 10–5, Sun 2–5.*

In 1816, Richard, 7th Viscount Fitzwilliam, bequeathed his collection of books, prints and manuscripts to the university, along with a large endowment which paid for the magnificent neo-classical building by George Basevi and C.R. Cockerell. Pick up a map as you go in to locate the treasures. The **Lower Floor** is devoted to antiquities and ceramics, drily displayed: 'Pyxis. Both sides: Neirids bringing news to Nereus of Peleus' wooing of Thetis. Attic red-figure *ca* 470 BC'; 'Wine-Mixing Krater. Biochrome II ware. Cypro-archaic 8 BC'. On the Upper Floor are paintings and drawings by Titian, Rubens, Poussin, Rembrandt, Leonardo, Picasso, Reynolds, Hogarth, Gainsborough, Turner, the Pre-Raphaelites, Constable and Blake (among others).

Scott Polar Museum

Lensfield Road, **t** *(01223) 336 540; open Mon–Fri 2.30–4.*

This small museum, part of the Polar Research Institute set up in 1920 in memory of Captain Scott's doomed expedition, contains maps, journals, clothing and photographs illustrating polar exploration.

Botanic Garden

Bateman Street, **t** *(01223) 336 271; open daily, winter 10–4, summer 10–6; adm Mar–Oct and weekends.*

The Botanic Garden was founded in 1846 by John Stevens Henslow, the professor of botany who put forward his pupil Charles Darwin for the Beagle exploration of the southern hemisphere. It covers more than 40 acres and includes a lake, glasshouses and winter garden.

The Orchard, Grantchester

Open daily 10–7.

You can walk or take a chauffeured punt upstream to Grantchester, two miles south of Cambridge, if you've got all day; otherwise drive. The Orchard is a popular but nonetheless memorable spot, with groups of people reading and chatting in deckchairs under the apple trees. Tea and cakes here was a Cambridge tradition even before the poet Rupert Brooke left Cambridge in 1909 to lodge in Grantchester (first at Orchard House, then The Old Vicarage) after graduating from King's. His gifted friends E.M. Forster, Virginia Woolf, Bertrand Russell, Maynard Keynes, Augustus John and Ludwig Wittgenstein were all Grantchester regulars. Philosopher Russell spent 10 years at the Mill House, next to the Old Vicarage, writing about mathematics. Painter Augustus John camped in a gypsy caravan in Grantchester meadows with two wives and seven children. But it was Brooke who immortalized afternoon tea in the orchard in his nostalgia-laden poem written in a Berlin café: 'The Old Vicarage, Grantchester' – 'Yet/Stands the church clock at ten-to-three?/And is there honey still for tea?'

Cambridge American War Cemetery

Down the Madingley Road, west out of town, the 3,810 white crosses of the cemetery are arranged in perfect curves on the hillside. The only US Second World War cemetery in Britain, it commemorates American men and women who served in British-based aircraft. The names of the missing are inscribed on a wall leading to the memorial chapel, a monumental building of funereal white Portland stone with a huge relief map of the Battle of the Atlantic inside.

South of Cambridge

Duxford Imperial War Museum

t (01223) 835 000; open daily, summer 10–6, winter 10–4; adm exp.

South of Cambridge, just off junction 10 of the M11, there is no missing the huge green hangars of the old Duxford aerodrome. Three of them are original Second World War hangars, with memories of Spitfires, Hurricanes, Flying Officer Douglas Bader, the Battle of Britain, and the Mustangs and Thunderbolts of the American 8th Air Force, who took over the RAF station in 1943. Now a branch of the Imperial War Museum, its displays include Concorde, as well as tanks, trucks and artillery. The American collection is displayed in a new Norman Foster building, shaped like an aeroplane's wing. In the Restoration Hangar you can see battered wings and machine parts, and sawn-off sections of aeroplanes, being restored on long work benches.

Wimpole Hall

t (01223) 207 257; open mid-Mar–Oct, Tues–Thurs and weekends, hall 1–5, home farm 10.30–5; adm.

Southwest of Cambridge off the A603, this elegant red-brick Georgian house with its long balustraded wings was refurnished by Elsie Bambridge, the daughter of Rudyard Kipling, after she and her husband George bought it in 1938. Whenever possible they bought paintings and furniture associated with its illustrious previous owners: Thomas Chicheley, who built the original Stuart mansion; Edward Harley, 2nd Earl of Oxford, who owned much of central London (Harley Street), and transformed Wimpole Hall into a baroque treasure house, employing the Scottish architect James

Gibbs and the gardener Charles Bridgeman; and finally the earls of Hardwicke, powerful Whigites who hired the likes of Henry Flitcroft, Capability Brown, John Soane and Humphrey Repton to modernize their house and park, adding shades of Greece and Rome.

What you get, after all that, is an architectural hotchpotch. Interiors range from Gibbs' splendid baroque chapel and library, built to house Lord Harley's collection of 50,000 books, to Soane's yellow drawing room, and a small bath house to the grannyish Bambridge bedrooms, full of ornaments and the colour pink. In fact, the cosy, fussy, grannyish style of Elsie and George prevails.

The gardens and parkland are equally mixed-and-matched with Charles Bridgeman's magnificent south avenue, running for over two miles, Capability Brown's landscaped parkland, with its Gothic tower and Chinese bridge, and the Victorian parterre on the north side between the wings. The Victorian stables, built around a quadrangle with a bell tower, now house a shop and café. A short walk northeast of the house brings you to Soane's farm buildings, now a centre for breeding rare breeds.

North of Cambridge

Peterborough

Whiz up the motorway from Cambridge, battle your way through Peterborough's hideous road system, dump your car in the first city-centre car park you find, and head straight for the **cathedral**. The west front is made up of three floor-to-roof Gothic arches big enough to fly an aeroplane through, topped with three pointed gables and finished off with pinnacles and flanking Gothic towers. It has been described as 'like a good deed in a naughty world', standing in the middle of such a drab town. The present building was completed in 120 years between 1118 and 1238 (the third abbey church on the site, 500 years after the first). The old Norman drum columns and three levels of round-headed arches march all the way down the nave to the Norman apse. In the north presbytery aisle is the **burial place of Catherine of Aragon**, the hapless first wife of Henry VIII whom he divorced to marry Anne Boleyn, bringing about the English Reformation. For 25 years the tomb of another queen, Mary Queen of Scots, stood next to her in the south presbytery aisle. It was transplanted to Westminster Abbey by the Scottish King of England, James I. The dismembered right arm of another monarch, King Oswald of Northumbria, was housed in a chapel in the south transept. His generosity was legendary, and only gave out when his **Uncorrupted Arm** was thrown out at the Reformation. You can still see the unusual 12th-century watch tower, from where one of the monks guarded the precious relic. The last addition to the church was the fan-vaulted **New Building** (1496–1508), built onto the end of the apse by John Wastell, the architect of King's College chapel in Cambridge and Canterbury cathedral's Tom Tower.

The cathedral close is worth exploring. The bishops' palace stands on one side of the west front, incorporating part of the old abbots' lodging; elsewhere are fragments of the old monastic buildings.

Ely

The small cathedral town is 10 miles north of Cambridge on the King's Lynn road, on a hillock above the Great Ouse looking out to wide horizons. The wide Fenland horizons were not always so mild and monotonous. Looking out from Crowland, near Peterborough, the Saxon hermit Guthlac saw 'swamps and bogs, and an occasional black pool, exuding dark mists, sprinkled with islands of marshy heaths and criss-crossed by winding waterways.' Ely means 'island of eels' in Saxon English: 50,000 of them were caught a year at the time of the Domesday book. After Ely fell to the Normans in 1071, five years after the official date of the conquest, the East Anglian leader of the Saxon resistance, Hereward, escaped into the Fens, disappearing out of history and into yellow-haired and strong-limbed legend. Today Ely is all about the cathedral. On your way there, stop at **Oliver Cromwell's House** (*adm*), which stands on St Mary's Street next to the church, black-and-white half-timbered. Here the future Lord Protector of England, then a farmer, collector of tithes and MP for Cambridge, lived from 1636 to 1646 with his mother, his wife, two sisters and six children. The Cromwell trail continues to Huntington, where he was born in 1599 and attended the grammar school. Here the **Cromwell Museum** (*open April–Oct Tues–Fri 11–1 and 2–5, weekends 11–1 and 2–4; Nov–Mar Tues–Fri 1–4, Sat 11–1 and 2–4, Sun 2–4*) displays memorabilia, including his old medicine chest and swords.

Ely Cathedral

Ely's splendour is in the detail of blind arcading, columns and profuse Gothic decoration. Above it all floats the octagonal lantern, an absurdly complex piece of medieval engineering, unique in the architectural repertoire of British cathedrals.

Inside, you are treated to the long view down the Norman three-decker nave. Around the chancel, reclining effigies of bishops crowd the walls. At the crossing, you look up into the lantern, supported at the corners by eight massive Gothic piers. It was built in the 14th century after the old tower collapsed, destroying most of the east end of the cathedral. Extraordinary wood and stone carvings and vaulted roofs were added too.

At the northeast corner of the north transept is the **Lady Chapel**, populated by numerous tiny figures whose heads have been lopped off, probably by the reformers of local boy Cromwell. The southwest transept is all Romanesque pizzazz. The south triforium (the middle arcade) houses the **Stained Glass Museum** (***t** (01353) 660 347; open Easter–Oct Mon–Fri 10.30–5, Sat 10.30–5.30, Sun 12–6; rest of year Mon–Fri 10.30–4.30, Sat 10.30–5, Sun 12–4.30; adm*), with a collection of stained glass rescued from churches around England.

The south door leads out to the remains of the cloisters and former monastic buildings including the old infirmary buildings. Firmary Lane was the central hall of the

Getting There and Around

Ely is a short drive up the A10, or a 15-minute train journey, from Cambridge, which is well connected by road and rail to London.

Tourist Information

Ely: Oliver Cromwell's House, 29 St Mary's Street, **t** (01353) 662 062. *Open April–Oct daily 10–5.30; Nov–Mar Mon–Fri 11–4, Sat 10–5 and Sun 11.15–4.*

There's a general **market** every Thurs, craft and bric-a-brac every Sat and a farmers' market on the second and the last Sat of each month.

Where to Stay

Ely t (01353) –

The Lamb Hotel, 2 Lynn Road, **t** (01353) 663 574, *www.oldenglish.co.uk* (*moderate*). Large, civilized old coaching inn on corner of Lynn Road and St Mary's Street, a few steps from cathedral; 32 comfortable bedrooms, bar and French-style restaurant (*moderate*).

Old Egremont House, 31 Egremont Street, **t** 663 118 (*moderate*). Beautiful 16th-century house with early 18th-century makeover. Elegant dining room with polished dark mahogany table; two bedrooms overlooking garden with glimpses of the cathedral.

Cathedral House, 17 St Mary's Street, **t** 662 124, *www.cathedralhouse.co.uk* (*moderate*). Lovely Georgian house just a few steps from the cathedral and Old Fire Engine House. Fairy-tale garden which used to be part of cathedral precinct. All guests eat breakfast together around one big kitchen table; three bedrooms to let.

Eating Out

The Old Fire Engine House, 25 St Mary's Street, **t** 662 582 (*expensive*). Ely's best restaurant inhabits an 18th-century house that was used by the fire brigade for a while. It has been functioning as a restaurant (and gallery) since 1968, and uses local recipes and Fens produce where possible. Gamey menu. The dining room features old brick floor tiles, wooden floorboards and table candles. You can have afternoon tea in the walled garden on a fine day. *Closed Sun eve.*

The Almonry Restaurant, High Street, **t** 666 360 (*moderate*). You can enter the old medieval undercroft from the north end of the cathedral grounds or from the High Street. Hot lunches of steak and kidney pie, lemon sole, chops and gravy *served 12–2. Open daily 10-5.*

The Stagecoach Restaurant, 39–41 Market Street, **t** 669 930 (*moderate*). Friendly place with a popular carvery. *Closed Sun eve.*

The Cutter Inn, Annesdale, **t** 662 713. (*cheap*) Traditional pub on towpath with half a rowing boat as its bar. On a sunny day you can jostle for a seat out front overlooking the river. Real ales including Green King. Bar meals served.

The Old Boat House, Annesdale, **t** 664 388 (*cheap*). Almost next door to the Cutter, a traditional restaurant serving home-made steak and kidney, game and vegetable pies. *Open Wed–Sun 10–5, also Wed–Sat eves by advance booking only.*

BKK, 8 St Mary's Street, **t** 665 011 (*cheap*). Newish Thai restaurant.

infirmary; the arches and columns on either side were incorporated into the post-Reformation houses. The Dean's Meadow brings you back to the fortified gatehouse of the cathedral precincts, the *Porta*.

The Cambridgeshire Fens

There are two Fens: one of endless perspectives and skies that exists largely in the imagination; the other of long, straight roads racing on embankments past huge, dreary fields, every so often crossing a ditch or passing a garish new housing estate. Its lovers tend to be natural historians. Fenland has been shaped by market forces: its lime-rich peat, an ever-dwindling resource formed thousands of years ago in the choked, oxygen-starved depths of reed swamps and vegetated marshes, has been exploited almost to extinction.

Today, four Fenland reserves preserve something of the old habitat and support much of the traditional Fenland wildlife. Wicken Fen (established in 1899), Walton Fen (1952), Holme Fen (1952) and Chippenham Fen (1953).

Wicken Fen National Nature Reserve (*Lode Lane, Wicken, Ely;* **t** *(01353) 720 274; open dawn–dusk, visitor centre Tues–Sun 10–5*) began life as a private hunting ground for Victorian entomologists. It is the only piece of undrained fen left, with wetland, bird habitats, including high whispering reed beds, wet 'carr' woodland, meadows and bird hides. Follow the tourist signs off the main Wicken road (A142 south from Ely, then right onto the A1123).

The Northwest
Cheshire, Manchester, Liverpool and Lancashire

17

Highlights

1 Chester's Rows and cathedral carvings

2 Liverpool's docks, graced by magnificent port buildings

3 The Lowry art centre on Manchester's Salford Quays

4 An autumn evening of Shakespeare at Lancaster Castle

Between the ridge of the West Pennines and the Irish Sea are the great industrial and cultural powerhouses of **Manchester** and **Liverpool**, the bleak old factories of **Lancashire**, and the county of **Cheshire**, the Surrey of the Northwest.

The industrial heritage of sprawling metropolitan Manchester, Liverpool and the East Lancashire mill towns offers mixed rewards to visitors. In the mid-19th century, manufactured cotton cloth counted for nearly half of all England's export earnings, and this densely packed urban region was the centre of wealth creation: Manchester was nicknamed 'Cottonopolis'; Liverpool was the greatest cotton- (and slave-) trading port of the age. The region is packed with monumental Victorian structures that bear the symbolism of their era – icons of manufacture, trade, distribution, civic rule and cultural provision – by great architects and engineers such as George Stephenson, James Brindley, Alfred Waterhouse and Peter Ellis. Notable are the LMR buildings in Manchester and the Albert Docks in Liverpool, which, after years of decline, have arisen phoenix-like from the ashes of their past as new-fangled cultural attractions, while landmark projects such as the Lowry on Salford Quays have revived interest in industrial landscapes, buildings and art. It's not all new, though: philanthropic benefactors having been giving their names to museums and art galleries founded on industrial wealth for nearly two centuries: the Lady Lever Art Gallery, Walker Art Gallery, Whitworth Gallery and Howarth Gallery are renowned for their collections, including some of the finest Victorian and Edwardian art in the country.

To the south of this densely packed urban conglomeration is Cheshire, semi-rural bolthole of the Northwest's 'captains of industry' and soccer stars.

Cheshire and the Wirral

Players in the Liverpool and Manchester United football squads all seem to have a Cheshire home; their red-brick piles with turrets and sweeping gravel drives appear in *Hello!* or *OK* magazine when the celebrity strikers marry or divorce. The county capital of **Chester** is by far the most interesting place to visit, in a mixed bag of countryside. The **Wirral Peninsula** with its estuary views is home to the prestigious Lady Lever Art Gallery and Ness Gardens. East of Chester, the **Plain** may reveal hidden pleasures at a snail's pace on minor roads. **Knutsford** is a pleasant town amid a few attractions.

Chester

Chester, with its **city walls**, medieval **Rows**, boat trips on the Dee and picturesquely crumbling **cathedral**, has been attracting visitors since the 18th century, when its medieval gates were demolished and replaced by ornamental stone bridges to create a promenade around the walls. Chester was a favourite of visiting Americans in the 19th century, first stop after Liverpool. In November 1856, Herman Melville was taken around the walls by fellow-novelist Nathaniel Hawthorne, who describes their walk in his *English Notebooks* in over-enthusiastic detail. Henry James visited in 1872, and was delighted by the 'perfect feast of crookedness' of the medieval town. Today most

Getting There and Around

By **car**, take the M56, which links up with the M6 and M1 from London, into Chester. Park-and-ride at Chester Racecourse.

It takes 5–6 hours by **coach** from London Victoria on **National Express**, **t** 08705 808080, *www.gobycoach.com*. Three **buses** a day from Manchester Coach Station, taking 1 hour.

Frequent open-top **bus tours** depart from the visitor centre and major attractions.

Frequent **trains** from London Euston take 3 hours. Hourly service from Manchester Airport and regular trains from Manchester in just over 1 hour. Around 40 mins from Liverpool. For information call **National Rail Enquiries**, **t** 08457 484950, or go to *www.thetrainline.com*.

There are regular 30-minute **boat** trips on the River Dee in summer, or you can take a 2-hour cruise (departs summer daily 11am, July–Aug Wed and Sat 8pm) to Ironbridge.

Tourist Information

Chester: Vicar's Lane (opposite the Roman Amphitheatre), **t** (01244) 402 111. *Open Nov–April Mon–Sat 10–5, Sun 10–4; May–Oct Mon–Sat 10–5.30, Sun 10–4.*

Knutsford: Council Office, Toft Road (A50), **t** (01565) 632 611. Good on the region.

Where to Stay

Chester t (01244) –

Chester Grosvenor, **t** 324 024, *chesgrove@chestergrosvenor.co.uk* (*very expensive*). Chester's 5-star hotel. It has been owned for more than a hundred years by the dukes of Westminster, and popular with assorted VIPs. Beautiful 17th-century building with marble reception; 85 luxurious bedrooms.

Blossoms Hotel, St John Street, **t** 323 186 (*expensive*). Five-storey hotel dating back to the 17th century, around the corner from the cathedral. Popular with fashionable locals since the 19th century. Sweeping staircase, and elegant furnishings in its 64 bedrooms.

The Queen Hotel, City Road, **t** 305 000 (*expensive*). Opposite the Victorian railway station, with an imposing neo-classical façade of columns, red brick and stucco. Named after Queen Victoria, whose statue adorns the portico, it's an elegant hotel. Reception in William Morris style with a grand staircase; 128 bedrooms; cocktail bar and restaurant; cream tea in Albert Lounge.

Hotel Romano, 51 Lower Bridge Street, **t** 325 091 (*moderate*). A Grade II listed building within the old city walls, close to the Rows. Italian-run with two restaurants, Dino's Pizzeria in the basement and La Fontana. Welcomes families in its 28 rooms.

Mill Hotel, Milton Street, **t** 350 035 (*moderate*). Converted Victorian corn mill beside the Shropshire Canal with 76 rooms. Restaurant, bar and dinner dances Fri and Sat.

The Cavendish Hotel, 42–4 Hough Green, **t** 675 100 (*moderate*). A short stroll from the centre, it feels like a country hotel with its welcoming entrance hall and 19 individually furnished bedrooms. Candlelit dining room overlooks gardens; French meals.

Redland Hotel, 64 Hough Green, **t** 671 024 (*moderate*). Traditional red-brick Victorian outside, inside full of curiosities including suits of armour, a Jacobean four-poster and immaculately furnished bedrooms.

Castle House, 23 Castle Street, **t** 350 354 (*cheap*). Charming, family-run guesthouse in the heart of the city. Looks like a Georgian townhouse, but conspicuous beams shows it is much older. Friendly and comfortable with fire in lounge and shiny new showers.

Carmaletta, 18 Hough Green, **t** 677 876 (*cheap*). Handsome Victorian house, 10 minutes' walk over Grosvenor Bridge. Very pleasant rooms.

Cheshire Plain t (01829) –

The Wild Boar Hotel, Whitchurch Road, Beeston, Tarporley, **t** (01829) 260 309 (*expensive*). A striking black-and-white Victorian house with 37 bedrooms. Quiet atmosphere and lovely views. Good restaurant.

Cholmondeley Arms, Cholmondeley, **t** (01829) 720 300 (*moderate*). Converted village schoolhouse with atmospheric high ceiling. Six bedrooms across the playground in old headmaster's house. Excellent food, real ale.

Manor Farm, Egerton, Cholmondeley (north of Whitchurch), **t** (01829) 720 261 (*cheap*). Converted sandstone barn and old farmhouse, with views of Bickerton hills. Homely, with fire blazing. Meals by arrangement.

Knutsford t (01565) –

Long View Hotel, Manchester Road, **t** 632 119 (*expensive*). Victorian townhouse with views over old racecourse and bags of character. Open fire in reception hall; 23 rooms. Award-winning restaurant and snug bar.

Angel Hotel, King Street, **t** 651 165 (*moderate*). Fresh, clean 18th-century pub with eight rooms. Friendly, large bar with pub grub.

Cross Keys Hotel, King Street, **t** 750 404 (*moderate*). A family-owned 18th-century coaching inn, one of the town's oldest buildings. All 12 rooms have original features. Cellar restaurant and bar.

Rose and Crown, King Street, **t** 652 366 (*moderate*). Black-and-white-fronted hotel with nine en-suite rooms. Comfortable but basic with Italian restaurant and wine bar.

Eating Out

Chester

The Chester Grosvenor, Eastgate, **t** 324 024 (*expensive*). Subdued, formal atmosphere with leather-bound menus, black-uniformed staff, and long wine list.

Brasserie 10–16, Brookdale Place, **t** 322 288 (*moderate*). Modern European cuisine: filo pacels filled with wild mushrooms.

Brookes Restaurant, Blossoms Hotel, St John's Street, **t** 323 186 (*moderate*). Classy, serving modern English and European food, plus a Mongolian barbecue stir-fry.

Pasta Razzi, Grosvenor roundabout, **t** 400 029 (*cheap*). Behind imposing Victorian façade, an informal and bustling restaurant.

Shere Khan Restaurant, Pepper Row, **t** 342 349 (*cheap*). Indian food, trendy décor.

Fat Cat Bar and Restaurant, Watergate Street, **t** 316 100 (*cheap*). One of small northern chain, buzzing in evenings, good old-fashioned nosh and modern style. Serves breakfast, snacks, lunch and dinner.

Boulevard de la Bastille, Bridge Street Row (*cheap*). Hint of old-fashioned charm with chessboard floor, big mirrors, fake-marble tables and waitresses in waistcoats. Piano playing on second floor in afternoons.

The Falcon, Bridge Street (*cheap*). Pub grub includes fish and chips with mushy peas in black-and-white building near riverside.

The Cheese Shop, Northgate Street. Cheshire's famous cheeses and freshly baked bread.

Four Square, Watergate Street. Excellent take-away sandwich shop; polite and generous.

Cheshire Plain

Peppers, Mill Street, Nantwich, **t** (01270) 629 100 (*cheap*). Coffee or afternoon tea, snacks or meals; set Sunday lunch. All local produce. Wine bar, restaurant and garden terrace.

Hiltons Tea Rooms, 27 Beam Street, Nantwich, **t** (01270) 611 488 (*cheap*). Family-run and friendly. Scones and cakes, all-day breakfasts and lunches such as liver and onions; even the chips are home-made.

Cholmondeley Arms, Cholmondeley, **t** (01829) 720 300 (*cheap*). Used to be village school until 1982, still has school desks and massive radiators; highly recommended for food. Home-made puddings. Children welcome

For a picnic in the sleepy countryside, stock up at one of the following.

Shady Oak, Tiverton (turn right out of Beeston Castle and take second right, down country lanes), **t** (01829) 733 279 (*cheap*). Views of Beeston Hill from canalside garden.

Tatton Park, Knutsford, **t** (01625) 534 400. Local farm cheeses, apple juice, pickles and cakes.

Ravens Oak Dairy, Burland Farm, Burland (west of Nantwich on Wrexham road), **t** (01270) 524 624. Hand-made cheeses include organic Burland Green and Brindley.

Knutsford

Belle Epoque Brasserie and Hotel, 60 King Street, **t** 633 060, *info@thebelleepoque.com*, (*moderate*). Stalwart Knutsford restaurant for more than 30 years; bar and informal dining room where you can eat home-made fish and chips. Restaurant serves English fusion food: Gressingham duck with lemon-grass relish and noodles; long wine list; six homely rooms. *Closed Sun eve and Sat lunch.*

Knutsford Wine Bar, 41/a King Street, **t** 750 459. Airy with wood, brick and tiled floors.

Bells of Peover, Lower Peover (from B5081 take cobbled lane signposted to the church, south of Knutsford), **t** 722 269 (*cheap*). Shares a gateway with the church; wonderful old-fashioned pub. Snug at the bar with two tables, bench seating and shelf full of Toby jugs. Good real ales, soup or full meals.

of the town's visitors come from North Wales, northwest England and southern Scotland – the region that the Roman legionary fort *Deva* controlled at the end of the 1st century AD, when *Deva* was the biggest permanent legion of them all. The estuary of the Dee lapped the fort, so troops could be moved fast by sea, and Roman roads shot out south to London, north to York and west to the Wirral. In the Middle Ages, much of the Roman fort and town remained intact. All that is left now are four streets and one or two impressive chunks of masonry in the walls.

The old city centre consists of four main streets – **Northgate**, **Eastgate**, **Watergate** and **Bridge Street** – with two storeys known as the **Rows**. An upper level of shops sits behind a covered walkway propped up on pillars. Henry James declared that 'these shop fronts have always seemed to me the most elegant things in England'. They make the streets doubly exciting, with two levels of shop signs, two levels of bustle and twice as many shops for your money. 'I have quite lost my heart to this charming creation,' said Henry James, 'and there are so many things to be said about it that I hardly know where to begin.'

Around the centre, the **city walls** are there to be walked. Although Chester has long since expanded beyond the medieval walls, they will frame your visit. For much of their length, the walls follow the outer wall of Chester's **Roman fort**. From Northgate you can see an excellent section of the original Roman masonry *in situ*. The old fort walls were dismantled on the south and west side so that the medieval city could expand to the waterfront (which has since retreated west). Where once the west wall overlooked the Roman harbour, it now looks over the **Roodee**, an extremely short (a mile long) racecourse squeezed in between wall and Dee. The south wall still drops dramatically down to the waterfront, reached via Bridge Street. Look back up at the sandstone outcrop and you can understand why the fort was built here. Hire a rowing boat, go on a cruise, or wander beneath the lime trees by the bridge.

Not much remains of the medieval **castle**, the seat of one of the three great Norman earldoms of the Marches, from where Henry III and Edward I launched Welsh campaigns in the 13th century. Imposing 18th-century law courts have replaced it. Just outside Newgate you can see the foundations of a Roman amphitheatre.

St Werburgh's Cathedral

Between Northgate and Eastgate is Chester's cathedral of St Werburgh, with its dusky interior. Monks rebuilt the original Norman church in sinuous, medieval-Gothic style with elaborate oak and stone carvings. You can see traces of the old church: a round arch, some floor tiles and the base of a column in the north aisle of the choir. Allow time for your eyes to pick out the detail of the miserichords and bench-ends in the choir: look for the man being swallowed by a dragon, the elephant with horses' hooves, and the Chester pilgrim, as well as countless human faces and allegorical images. Nathaniel Hawthorne viewed them by gas lamp; he admired them but, all American rationality, found they were 'lavished most wastefully, where nobody would think of looking'. Have a look at the mouldering stone cloisters and the 17th-century ecclesiastical courtroom at the west end of the church, said to be the most complete in the country.

Grosvenor Museum and Dewa Roman Experience

The **museum** (***t*** *(01244) 321 616; open Mon–Sat 10.30–5, Sun 2–5)* houses an important collection of 150 early 3rd-century **Roman tombstones** (40 of which are on display), many with sculpted panels. Found in the infill of the city wall, hidden from the elements, their inscriptions have survived intact, telling all sorts about the movement of soldiers around the empire. A piece of lead piping whose inscription dates back to AD 79 is rare evidence of the governorship of Agricola.

Tucked away down Pierpoint Lane, a cobbled alley off Bridge Street, Dewa (***t*** *(01244) 343 407; open Dec–Jan 10–4, Feb–Nov 9–5; adm*) is how the Roman name *Deva* was pronounced (or so they say). An archaeological excavation in 1991, which took place when a motorbike dealer applied for planning permission to extend his showroom, revealed four layers of occupancy, from Roman to Tudor. The 'experience' now takes you from a creaking audio-visual Roman galley – 'Row you dogs!' – through the city gates into the dirty, straw-scattered streets of the fort, and on into the real dig. The thickness of the Roman walls suggests the building may have been an officer's residence or military hospital (conveniently close to the bath house).

Chester Zoo

t *0870 066 4242; open April–Oct 10–6, Nov and Feb–Mar 10–5, Dec–Jan 10–4.30; adm exp.*

If you like zoos, this 'zoo without bars', where water or natural barriers are used to fence the animals, is a good one to visit. It's 2½ miles out of the city centre and you'll need half a day to get around the 50 acres and see it all. Highlights include the monkey house, with a 'test-your-strength' handle inside it. If you're strong, your strength may be 50kg, compared with the male orang-utan's 190kg.

The Wirral Peninsula

The Wirral Peninsula juts out between the Mersey and Dee estuaries northwest of Chester. A ridge down the middle carries the **Wirral Way**. To the north, **Merseyside**, facing Liverpool across the water, is built-up and dotted with oil refineries. **South Wirral** is quiet and rural, with views over the Dee marshes towards Wales (best seen from the clay cliffs of Wirral Country Park at Thustaston). The sleepy Victorian resort of **Parkgate**, with its black-and-white seafront Parade, is a good stop for fish and chips. Until 1815 it was a passenger port for Ireland; ships anchored in the channel, 50 yards from the shore, until the river was diverted to the Welsh shore.

Ellesmere Port Boat Museum

t *(0151) 355 5017; open Mar–Oct daily 10–5, Nov–Feb Sat–Wed 11–4; adm.*

North of Chester, travelling through Ellesmere Port (take junction 9 off M53), you emerge at the widening estuary of the River Mersey where it turns north towards the chemical factories of Warrington. The Boat Museum occupies the enormous dock complex that developed at the junction of the Shropshire Union Canal and

Manchester Ship Canal (constructed by Manchester merchants to avoid Liverpool dock tolls) and the River Mersey. Here the cargoes of the industrial Midlands were transferred from the narrow boats of the inland waterways to coastal craft via brick warehouses straddling the water. Enough of the warehouses and canal workers' cottages are still standing to show the scale of the place. Exhibitions in the old dock-side buildings include a display of traditional canal boats. In August costumed guide Ted the Toll Clerk gives you a guided tour followed by a half-hour trip on a canal boat.

Ness Botanic Gardens

t (0151) 353 0123; open summer 9.30–5, winter 9.30–4; adm.

Retired Liverpool cotton broker A.K. Bulley established his 64-acre botanical gardens on a sandstone hill above the Dee at the close of the 19th century. Bulley is known as the first of the great 20th-century plant-collecting patrons, who sponsored plant hunters George Forrest and Kingdom Ward on expeditions to Yunnan, southeast China, in 1904 and 1911, and made the seeds of Himalayan mountain plants sent back to him widely available, selling them in penny packets at Woolworth stores. Bulley had the common touch: the rock and heather garden, azalea walk, rhododendron and pine woods of Ness Gardens have always been open to the public. Since 1948, shortly after Bulley's death, they have been in the hands of the University of Liverpool.

Port Sunlight

Approaching Port Sunlight from the sprawling mass of Merseyside, you enter a leafy Victorian village of red-brick cottages set back from chestnut-tree-lined boulevards. It may look pretty ordinary, but this model village 'neat and cheerful' is one of Victorian England's most enlightened examples of social housing. Its creator, William Hesketh Lever, built the Lever Brothers soap factory next door in 1889 along with 28 workers' cottages, to the design of William Owen of Warrington. Adopting a liberal philosophy of social reform, Lever set out to improve the working and living conditions of his workers, creating a content, healthy and efficient workforce – and increasing his own profits. The first cottages were soon followed by more until in 1909 there were 700 houses, mainly in the 'Old English' style (two of them reproductions of Shakespeare's birthplace at Stratford-upon-Avon), all with bathrooms. Far exceeding the average for contemporary working-class house design, they were let at fair rents to Lever's workers, who also benefited from a school, shop, theatre and concert hall (which later hosted Ringo Starr's first outing with the Beatles in 1962), a library, gymnasium, swimming pool, bowling green and improving literary, music and art societies. The experiment was deemed a success, as demonstrated by high standards of health, morality and a strong sense of community, as well as the quality and quantity of factory output, although critics viewed the scheme as a despotic means to control the workers lives, which were dominated by 'the spirit of soap'.

Nowadays more than half the 850 houses have been sold off and only a fraction of the factory's 10,000 employees live and work in the village, but the factory continues to churn out soap in the name of Unilever – no longer Sunlight soap, on which the

Lever empire was founded, but liquid Persil, Radon and Surf. **Port Sunlight Heritage Centre** (**t** *(0151) 644 6466; open Mar–Sept daily 10–4, Oct–Feb Mon–Fri 10–4*) on Greendale Road has a model of the village and factory.

Residents have one of the largest private collections of Victorian and Edwardian art in England on their doorsteps, in the **Lady Lever Art Gallery** (**t** *(0151) 207 0001; open Mon–Sat 10–5, Sun 12–5*). It is a monument to Lady Lever, but also to industry. 'All the beauty of Venice,' said the widowed husband, 'all the art of Venice was the result of the foresight and energy of her merchants; it was not the result of an idle wealthy class.' The gallery, with its neo-classical portico, pediments and columns, opened in 1922. Lever collected a range of art, from landscape paintings of the British golden age to 18th-century furniture, Wedgwood pottery, enamelled Chinese porcelain and classical sculpture. From his own collection, which constituted 16 percent of his total wealth in 1912, he selected the contents of the new public gallery. Highlights include Reynolds' *Portrait of Lady Peter Beckford* and works by Turner, Constable, Zoffany, Romney, Gainsborough, Stubbs and the Pre-Raphaelites. Give yourself a few hours to see it all in its setting of domed skylights, classical columns, coloured glass and mosaic-patterned floors.

The Cheshire Plain

You can trace the outline of the Plain on a road map, denoted by a thinning out of villages and a thickening of the blue squiggles of rivers and canals. The waterways, in particular the Weaver and Trent rivers and the Mersey Canal, were the highways of the salt industry for which the Cheshire '-wiches' – Northwich, Middlewich and Nantwich – have been renowned since Saxon times ('wich' is Old English for a trading centre). Nantwich went into decline in the 18th century, leading to the preservation of its old character, but Northwich, Middlewich and Winsford have expanded into grim centres of modern salt mining and industry. The **Northwich Salt Museum** on London Road (**t** *(01606) 41331; open Tues–Fri 10–5, weekends 2–5; adm*) explores salt technology and the role of the River Weaver. (There's also a café.) Then visit the **Anderton Boat Lift** (**t** *(01606) 77699*), a mile north. This recently restored Victorian 'wonder of the waterways' formed a link between canal and river, lifting boats from one to the other.

Running north–south down the the Plain, from Frodsham to the Shropshire border, is a sandstone ridge, with its own walking trail – the **Sandstone Trail** – and superb views. The rest of the Plain is dull and featureless, but the wooded ridge is beautiful, particularly around Beeston Castle. Between Chester and Nantwich as the crow flies, **Beeston Hill** rises 500ft above the Plain. From the inner bailey of the castle that crowns it, on a clear day you can make out the Wrekin in Shropshire and, poking out of the trees on neighbouring Peckforton Hill, the sham battlements of Peckforton Castle, home of the first Lord Tollmarch, who bought the picturesque ruin in 1840. **Beeston Castle** (*Torporley;* **t** *(01829) 260 464; www.english-heritage.org.uk; open April–Sept 10–6, Oct 10–5, Nov–Mar 10–4; adm*) was built in 1220 by the 6th Earl of Chester, Randolph de Blunderville, as part of a defensive chain of castles on the Welsh border. Over the centuries it passed in and out of royal hands, playing second fiddle to Chester Castle – which enabled Randolph to try out one or two design innovations, ditching the keep in favour of an inner and outer bailey, each with a high curtain wall and a snarling gatehouse. Around the curtain wall of the inner bailey runs a deep rock-cut ditch; with the woods around its rocky outcrop, it's still rather wild.

Nantwich

The old Chester–London road travelled past the market town of Nantwich on the edge of the Plain. Stop off for lunch and a quick leg-stretch around the old, narrow streets of this town with their evocative medieval names – Wall Lane, Pillory Street and Monks Lane. Pop into the grand old **church** with its soaring Gothic arches and carved miserichords in the choir stalls. Nantwich has always been well-to-do: in the 18th century it had more clock-makers per head than any other provincial town in the country, and in the 19th century a third of its working males were shoemakers – both signs of prosperity according to the town **museum** (***t*** *(01270) 627 104; open summer Mon–Sat 10.30–4.30, winter Tues–Sat 10.30–4.30*), which is well stocked with clocks and shoes. Welches deli and tearoom on Hospital Street stocks Cheshire cheeses.

Knutsford and Around

Trapped between the M6 and M56 motorways and a little too close to the suburbs of Manchester for comfort, the otherwise pleasant small town of Knutsford with its antiques shops and restaurants is a good base for northeast Cheshire. The writer Elizabeth Gaskell (1810–65) moved to Knutsford to live with her aunt after her mother died, and based her 1850 novel *Cranford* on the town and its residents. **Mrs Gaskell's grave** is in the old Unitarian graveyard near the station. The town is worth a visit for this literary association and the elevating presence of **Tatton Park** (*adm minimal*) on its doorstep; a mile-long footpath through the grounds to the old neo-classical mansion of the Wyatts begins from the end of King Street.

Jodrell Bank

Five miles southeast of Knutsford, **t** *(01477) 571 339; open Nov–mid-Mar Mon–Fri 10.30–3, Sat–Sun 11–4.30; mid-Mar–Oct daily 10.30–5.30; adm.*

In 1945, when Bernard Lovell, an assistant physics lecturer at Manchester University, needed an electrically quiet environment to continue his research into radio waves, he came to the university's botanical gardens at Jodrell Bank. Sixty years on, you can't miss the **Lovell Telescope**, the world's third largest fully steerable radio telescope, with a solid steel bowl 250ft across which can be aimed at any point in the sky. The Lovell receives radio waves from matter in space, rather than images, perfectly suiting it to the murky English climate. In the mid-1960s it was joined by the **Mark II Telescope**, which has since become the centre of a network of seven MERLIN telescopes. Together these pick up high-resolution radio waves comparable to one huge single telescope. The **Astronomy Centre** deals with all aspects of space and radio astronomy, with gadgets, blinking lights and demonstrations of scientific principles. Best of all, however, is the **Planetarium** with its twinkling 39ft dome.

Macclesfield

Macclesfield, below the western ridge of the Peak District, deserves a visit for its **silk museums**. Paradise Mill dates back to the 19th century, when Macclesfield was the most important silk-weaving town in the country. At first the weaving was done by hand in garret houses with large windows. When the weavers were brought under one factory roof, they still worked on the old hand looms, because the highest quality silk could not be mass produced on power looms. Three firms continued hand weaving until after the Second World War. One of them – Cartwright and Sheldon – kept its hand-loom department until 1981.

Park beside the **Heritage Centre** (*t (01625) 613 210; open Mon–Sat 11–5, Sun 1–5; adm*), in a Georgian Sunday School, which traces the history of the silk industry from 1st-century China along the Silk Road to the mills of the Industrial Revolution. (The shop stocks locally made silk scarves and handkerchiefs.) It's a short walk to **Paradise Mill** in Park Lane (*t (01625) 618 228; open Mon–Sat 11–5; adm*). The top floor of the brick factory is preserved as an industrial museum, with rows of work-worn rickety wooden Jacquard looms, the shimmer of coloured silk threads still strung across them. To complete the picture, pop into the **Silk Museum** next door (*t (01625) 612 045; open Mon–Sat 11–5; adm*).

Quarry Bank Mill

t (01625) 527 468; open Mar–Sept daily 10.30–5.30, Oct–Mar Tues–Sun 10.30–5; adm.

The River Bollin rises in the hills above Macclesfield, cutting through a steep valley at Styal, where it drives the waterwheel of the Quarry Bank Mill (1½ miles north of Wilmslow off B5166, 2½ miles from M56 junction 5). Here you can become an expert on cotton manufacture, with special knowledge of innovations like the flying shuttle, spinning jenny and parallel motion. The Georgian cotton mill was built in 1784 by Samuel Greg, adopted son of a Manchester textile merchant, and extended to house the new power loomsin 1834–75. The manager and 100 apprentices lived next to the mill; married couples were housed in a purpose-built community across the fields. It stopped work in 1959, and the mill is now a museum, with demonstrations of the processes involved in turning the downy fibres of the cotton plant into cloth – all of which lent themselves to mechanization, giving birth to the factory system.

Liverpool

We will leave this city not less but greater, better and more beautiful than it was left to us.

Oath of the ancient Athenians

Liverpool is an imploded dark star of a city. A city gone supernova...

Will Self

In the 19th century, the patrons and architects of Liverpool set about turning Britain's gateway to the Empire into a modern version of ancient Athens. They built

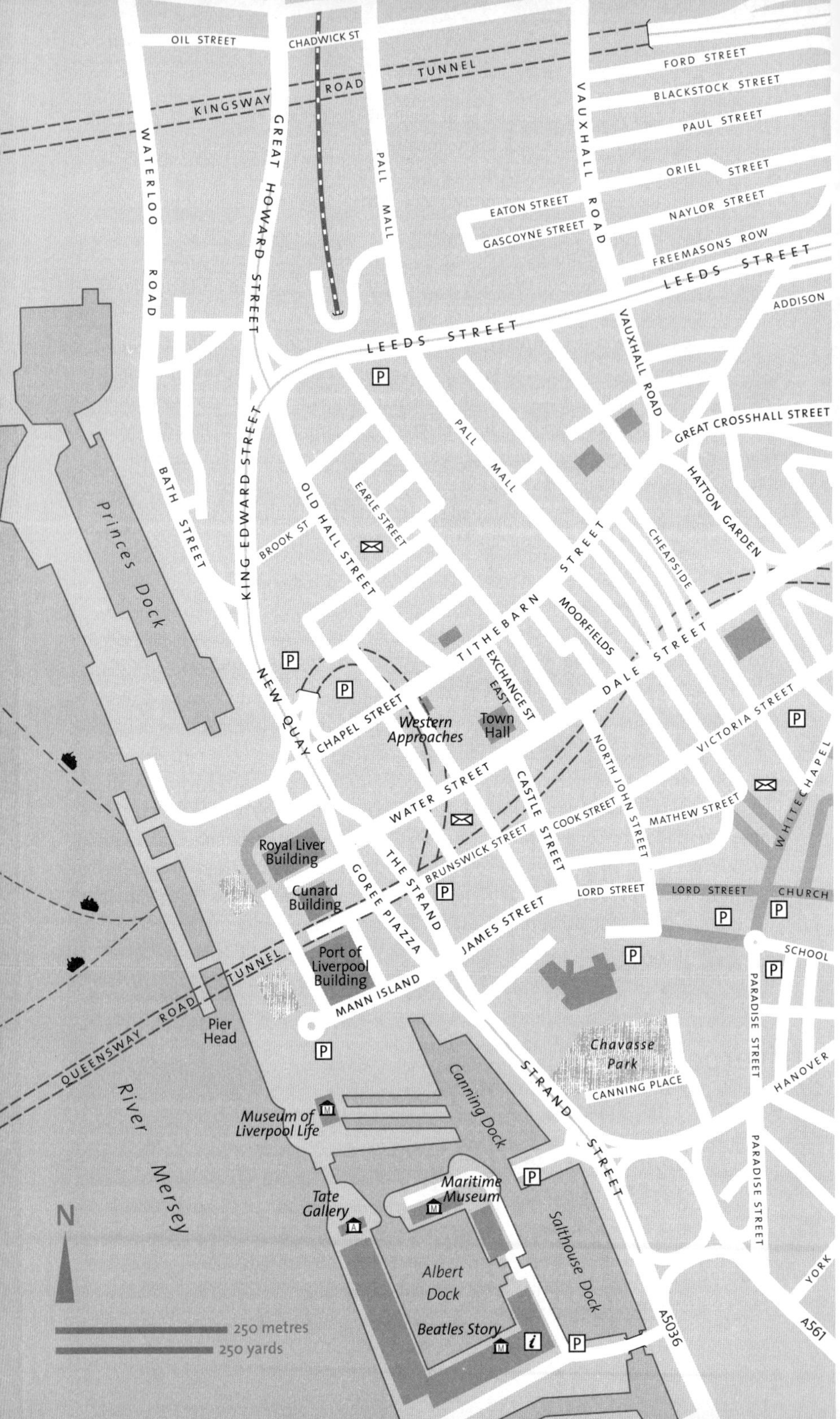
OIL STREET
CHADWICK ST
KINGSWAY ROAD TUNNEL
FORD STREET
BLACKSTOCK STREET
PAUL STREET
ORIEL STREET
EATON STREET
GASCOYNE STREET
NAYLOR STREET
FREEMASONS ROW
LEEDS STREET
VAUXHALL ROAD
WATERLOO ROAD
GREAT HOWARD STREET
PALL MALL
ADDISON
GREAT CROSSHALL STREET
HATTON GARDEN
KING EDWARD STREET
BATH STREET
Princes Dock
BROOK ST
OLD HALL STREET
EARLE STREET
CHEAPSIDE
TITHEBARN STREET
MOORFIELDS
EXCHANGE ST EAST
DALE STREET
NEW QUAY
CHAPEL STREET
Western Approaches
Town Hall
VICTORIA STREET
WATER STREET
CASTLE STREET
NORTH JOHN STREET
WHITECHAPEL
COOK STREET
MATHEW STREET
BRUNSWICK STREET
Royal Liver Building
Cunard Building
THE STRAND
GOREE PIAZZA
LORD STREET
CHURCH
JAMES STREET
SCHOOL
Port of Liverpool Building
MANN ISLAND
QUEENSWAY ROAD TUNNEL
Pier Head
PARADISE STREET
Chavasse Park
CANNING PLACE
STRAND STREET
HANOVER
River Mersey
Museum of Liverpool Life
Canning Dock
Maritime Museum
Tate Gallery
Salthouse Dock
Albert Dock
Beatles Story
YORK
A5036
A561
N
250 metres
250 yards

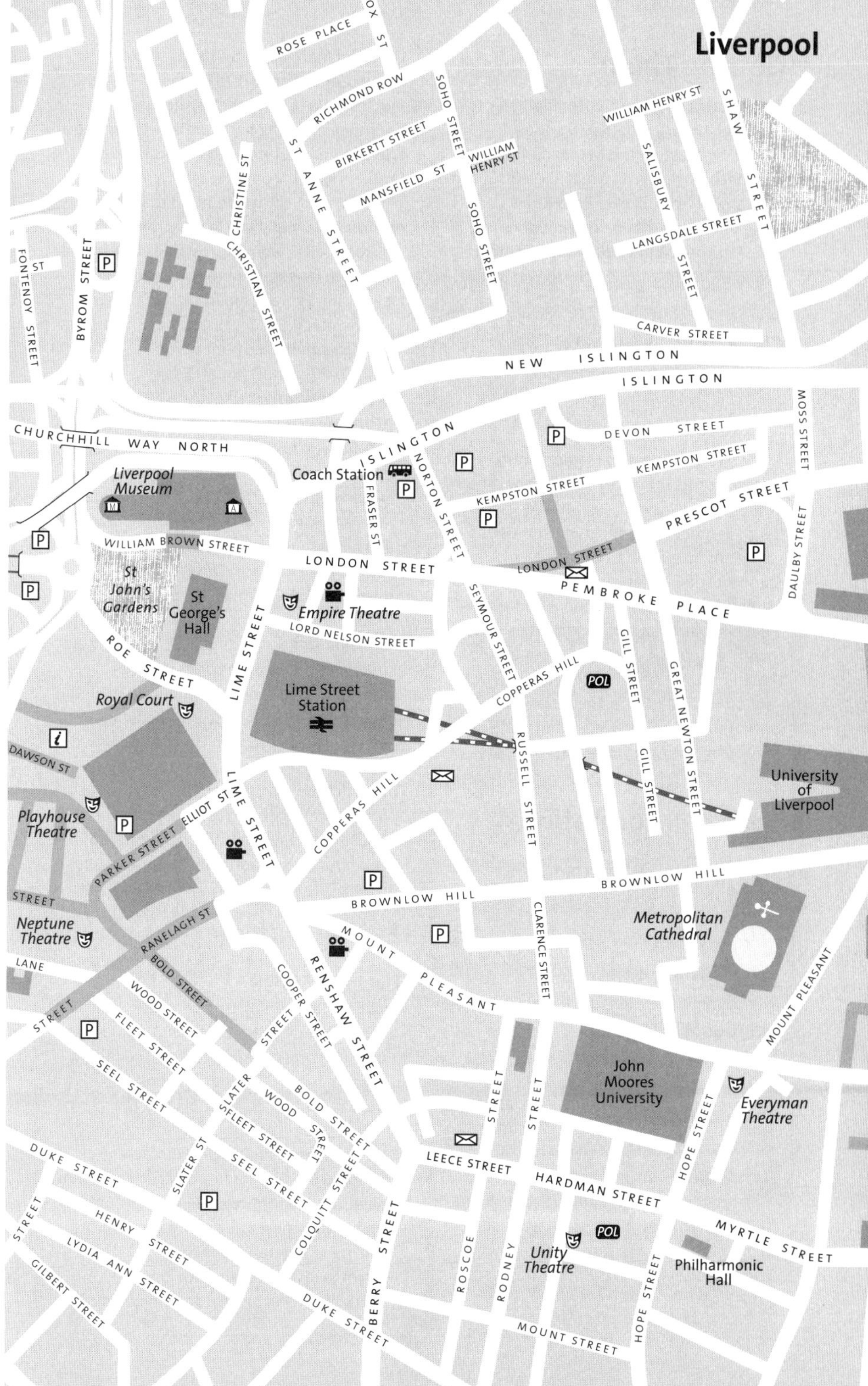

Liverpool
Liverpool Museum
Coach Station
St John's Gardens
St George's Hall
Empire Theatre
Lime Street Station
Royal Court
Playhouse Theatre
Neptune Theatre
University of Liverpool
Metropolitan Cathedral
John Moores University
Everyman Theatre
Unity Theatre
Philharmonic Hall
CHURCHHILL WAY NORTH
NEW ISLINGTON
ISLINGTON
LONDON STREET
PEMBROKE PLACE
WILLIAM BROWN STREET
LIME STREET
ROE STREET
COPPERAS HILL
BROWNLOW HILL
MOUNT PLEASANT
RENSHAW STREET
BOLD STREET
SEEL STREET
DUKE STREET
HARDMAN STREET
MYRTLE STREET
HOPE STREET
LEECE STREET
BERRY STREET
MOUNT STREET

Getting There

Domestic and a few charter **flights** fly to Liverpool Airport, **t** (0151) 288 4000.

The city is just off the M57 and M62 by **car**. The **coach station** is on Norton Street. Coaches to Liverpool from all over Britain.

The main **train** station is Liverpool Lime Street, at the top of William Brown Street, served by Virgin and First North Western.

Getting Around

For bus and train travel around Merseyside contact Local Transport Mersey Travel (LTMT), **t** (0151) 236 7676.

The two-hour **Beatles Magical Mystery Tour** (*t (0151) 709 3285*) takes you to Penny Lane, Strawberry Fields and the birthplaces of the band members. One trip midweek, two at weekends; midweek pick-ups in Queen Square (2.10pm) and Beatles Museum, Albert Docks (2.30pm); weekends additional tour leaves Queen Square (11.40am) and Beatles Museum (noon), dropping you off at Cavern Club.

Minibus tours of childhood homes of John Lennon and Paul McCartney leave from Albert Docks (am, **t** (0151) 708 8574) and Speke Hall (pm, **t** (0151) 427 7231); 2 hours.

Tourist Information

Liverpool: Queen's Square Centre, Roe Street or Atlantic Pavilion, Albert Docks, **t** 0906 680 6886.

Where to Stay

Liverpool t (0151) –

The Britannia Adelphi, Ranelagh Place, **t** 709 7200 (*very expensive*). In the city centre and once Liverpool's grandest, most exclusive hotel, the Adelphi is a large period hotel with marble floors and crystal chandeliers, in its heyday used by first-class passengers from the Atlantic ocean liners in transit from New York. J.B. Priestley stayed, commenting that a musical comedy producer could use its lavish interiors for the big finale number.

Liverpool Marriott Hotel South, Speke Aerodrome, **t** 494 5000 (*expensive*). A few miles from the city centre, the 1930s art deco terminal building has been converted into a 164-room hotel with bar and restaurant.

Feathers Hotel, Mount Pleasant, **t** 709 9655 (*moderate*). Fully modernized tourist and commercial hotel in a long Victorian terrace; 73 rooms; has won awards for its quality, eat-as-much-as-you-like breakfast buffet.

Holiday Inn Express, Albert Dock, **t** 709 1133, (*moderate*). A Grade II listed warehouse in a good location; 100 rooms.

Sefton Park t (0151) –

Three miles from the centre, **Sefton Park** has some homely hotels in the Victorian villas of rich city merchants and shipping magnates.

Solna Hotel, Croxteth Drive, **t** 734 3398 (*expensive*). In a large Victorian house; 20 rooms. Bar snacks or restaurant overlooking park.

Alicia Hotel, 3 Aigburth Drive, **t** 727 4411 (*expensive*). A villa that was once a cotton trader's home; 40 rooms, restaurant and bar.

Blenheim Lodge, 37 Aigburth Drive, **t** 727 7380 (*moderate*). One of the original villas, overlooking the boating lake, family home in the early '60s of Stuart Sutcliffe, the Beatle who died tragically young in Hamburg. Bar and evening meals for guests; 17 rooms.

The Park Lane, 23 Aigburth Drive, **t** 727 4754 (*moderate*). Tastefully refurbished Georgian house with an excellent Italian restaurant; 17 bedrooms, including three four-posters.

Eating Out

Liverpool t (0151) –

Tate Café Restaurant, Liverpool Tate Gallery, Albert Dock, **t** 702 7400 (*cheap*). Modern and airy with orange leather sofas. Good salad Niçoise and interesting filled breads.

Bluecoat Centre Café, School Lane, **t** 709 5297 (*cheap*). Come here for the setting.

Café Number 7, Faulkner Street, **t** 709 9633 (*cheap*). Windows onto a quiet street in most salubrious part of town. Pine, bright colours and pavement seating. Coffee, fruit juices and good vegetarian lunches.

Everyman Bistro Restaurant, Hope Street, **t** 708 9545 (*cheap*). An established Liverpool institution for nearly 50 years. Queue for food at this lively, informal diner. Sturdy wooden furniture and old brick walls. Coffee and cake or beef stew and vegetarian dishes. *Open Mon–Sat noon until early hours*.

60 Hope Street, **t** 707 6060 (*expensive*). Attractive Georgian end-of-terrace at the Anglican cathedral end of Hope Street, with large ground-floor restaurant (wood, cream and blue, with comfy settles) and basement café-bar. Popular modern European food.

Simply Heathcotes, Beetham Plaza, 25 The Strand, **t** 236 3536 (*expensive*). Small chain which specializes in modern-style northern English food – Cumberland sausages and mash – in stylish setting; good wine list.

Café Renouf, 16 Rodney Street, **t** 708 8698 (*cheap*). Friendly, wintry place on quiet Georgian street, with small candle-lit tables and sophisticated music. Good French food.

Tai Pan, Great Howard Street, **t** 207 3888 (*moderate*). Always buzzing with diners, a Liverpool institution above a Chinese supermarket in docks. Strong on seafood. Queue at Sun lunchtime for dim sum.

Blue Bar and Grill, Albert Dock, **t** 709 7097 (*cheap*). Trendy place with dock views. Décor is warehouse-chic. Local football heroes have been spotted here. Soup and sammies or English staples (steak and kidney pie).

Pumphouse, Albert Dock, **t** 709 236 (*cheap*). Old pumphouse with red-brick chimney. Serves decent, filling pub grub.

Pig and Whistle, Covent Garden, **t** 236 4760. Opposite Western Approaches, on edge of car park. Setting uninviting, but snug inside.

Philharmonic, 36 Hope Street (corner of Hardman Street), **t** 709 1163 (*cheap*). A sumptous gin palace with lavish Art Nouveau interior: mosaic-tiled serving counter, mahogany-panelled rooms and cubicles, stained glass and bronze panels and the best gents lavatory anywhere. Good bar food includes filled baguettes, mixed grills and fish pie, also Sunday roast lunches.

Entertainment

Theatre, Film, Music and Dance

Philharmonic Hall, Hope Street, **t** 709 3789. Built by Herbert J. Rowse in 1939, after the Victorian hall burned down. Comfortable art deco auditorium is home to illustrious Royal Liverpool Philharmonic Orchestra.

Empire Theatre, Lime Street (opposite St George's Hall), **t** 0870 606 3536. Grandiose theatre, hosts touring theatre and opera.

The Playhouse Theatre, Williamson Square, **t** 709 4776. Next to Radio City Tower in the city centre, this magnificent baroque theatre (1865) housed Liverpool's repertory theatre until 1998. Revamped, shows popular drama.

Everyman Theatre, 5–9 Hope Street, **t** 709 4776. Located between two cathedrals, this modern theatre shows lots of school-syllabus Shakespeare. A reliable and lively venue with excellent basement bistro.

The Royal Court, Roe Street (off Lime Street), **t** 709 4321. Long-established theatre, rebuilt in art deco syle after 1937 fire. Now does musicals, tribute bands, drama and opera.

Unity Theatre, 1 Hope Place (off Hope Street), **t** 709 4988. Attractive modern theatre in former synagogue, with two small modern auditoriums for new writing and dance.

Neptune Theatre, Hanover Street (beside Liverpool Central Station), **t** 709 7844. Intimate Edwardian theatre (445 seats), with stand-up comedians, folk and blues bands.

Bars and Clubs

The **Cavern Quarter** is a rowdy, cheap and cheerful area of Irish bars and chain café-bars, heavily revamped in the early 1980s with a Wall of Fame, listing all the bands who have played at the Cavern Club, including the Beatles, Rolling Stones and Oasis.

Cavern Club, Matthew Street, **t** 0871 222 1957. A brick arcaded basement with a small stage reconstructed in the 1980s to resemble the Cavern Club of early Beatles performances; lively venue with DJs and contemporary live bands Thurs–Sat and Sun afternoons. *Open Thurs–Sat noon–2am, Mon–Wed noon–6pm, Sun 12noon–12.30am*.

Liverpool is a magnet for clubbers, with a plethora of nightclubs in crumbling old 19th-century warehouses around Concert Square, Bold Street, Berry Street and Slater Street. Details of club nights appear in *Itchy Liverpool*, an insiders' guide to Liverpool available from bookshops and newsagents, or *What's On*, the monthly listings magazine for Merseyside.

banks, concert halls and office buildings to look like Greek temples, culminating in the neo-classicism of St George's Hall, which Queen Victoria called 'worthy of ancient Athens'. Now, after years of morbid economic decline, followed by lavish European Union and lottery subsidies, the optimism of the new Athenians is in the air again; crumbling old buildings and lifeless spaces are being restored and put to new uses. Liverpool is abuzz again, with businesses and residents returning to the city centre at last. The air of nostalgia that has lingered over Liverpool and the sad demise of a great maritime city is finally in retreat.

Liverpool has long been the site of myths: the romance of the River Mersey; football legends (from the city's two teams, Liverpool and Everton); the music of the Beatles; the cheeky Scouser type and the quasi-mythical Liver birds on the Pierhead. Visitors once compared views of the Mersey docks with the skylines of Shanghai and Manhattan. 'Liverpool is simply Liverpool,' wrote the playwright J.B. Priestley, visiting in 1933. Liverpool sounded different to the rest of England too. 'Its people have an accent of their own; a thick, adenoidy, cold-in-the-head sort of accent,' added Priestley.

Liverpool was among the west-coast ports to profit from the American trade in the 18th century. Before industrialization, profits came from the import of luxury goods like tobacco and sugar and, more lucratively, the trade of West African slaves to the colonial plantations; much of Liverpool's personal and civic wealth is based on the infamous slave triangle between Europe, Africa and America. The mid-19th-century boom was based on cotton, brought into the city's docks raw from plantations in the West Indies and the southern states of America, manufactured into finished cotton goods in Manchester and the Lancashire mill towns, and exported from Liverpool around the world. The port thrived and the city grew at an alarming rate. Liverpool became the headquarters of powerful shipping and insurance companies which built the first high-rise office buildings to demonstrate their importance, while the Corporation adopted the neo-classical style to show its noble aspirations.

Liverpool became the chief port of embarkation for emigrants to the New World in the 19th century: five million Europeans left Liverpool for New York during Queen Victoria's reign. Some never made it onto the boats and set down roots in the dark streets of the dockside slums, alongside the earliest and largest Chinese and Irish immigrant communities. Priestley was guided round the slums by the local vicar, and could not get over the appearance of mixed-race children: 'The woolly curls of the negro, the smooth brown skin of the Malay, the diagonal eye of the Chinese, they were all there, combined with features that had arrived in Lancashire by way of half a dozen different European countries, from Scandinavia to Italy.'

The mass emigrations gave way to the leisured Edwardian era of transatlantic travel on cruise liners. The Liverpool Cunard Steamship Company and White Star dominated the cruise market from magnificent offices in the South Docks. These early skyscrapers were some of the first in the world to use new engineering techniques – pioneered in New York and Chicago – of stacking additional storeys on top of each other. 'Here emphatically was the seaport second only to London,' wrote Priestley.

Orientation

Even if you arrive by train at Lime Street Station at the top of town, head straight for the docks. Here Liverpool's historic role as England's chief Atlantic seaport becomes evident. You can also get a bite to eat and take a ferry across the Mersey. Then head into the city's business district with its Victorian-Edwardian offices and banks packed in close. From there, carry on uphill through the grid of commercial streets to the museum and art gallery, among an extraordinary group of neo-classical buildings on William Brown Street, dominated by St George's Hall. Beyond are the magnificent neo-Gothic Anglican and modern Roman Catholic cathedrals, back at the top of town.

Liverpool Docks

The docks are at the heart of the city's return to form, with the redevelopment of redundant warehouses and empty spaces. There are plans to add a fourth grace to the famous Pierhead group of buildings – known as the 'three graces' – and to build a football stadium on the old King's Dock. It's a far cry from 1933, when J.B. Priestley wandered glumly around and found 'a vast amount of gloom and emptiness and decay', the Mersey 'a misty nothingness, hooting dismally'. The old industries have since moved upriver, and the greyness has resolved into brightness and cheer. The docks extend into the Mersey on reclaimed flat land (the dock road marks the old water's edge). The original dock (covered over) was on the site of Canning Place. **Salthouse** and **Canning Docks** were built next, followed by the great **Albert Docks**, now the nexus of activity. At the heart of the docks, standing on the Pierhead like proud ambassadors of the city greeting port arrivals, is an impressive group of buildings. The first to be completed, in 1907, was the creamy Portland stone **Mersey Docks and Harbour Board Building**, resembling a domed neo-classical church atop a ducal palace. In 1911 the grey granite-clad **Royal Liver Friendly Society Building** was built next door, its reinforced concrete frame supporting one of the earliest skyscrapers. Perched on its twin art-nouveau towers are the **Liver Birds**, one of Liverpool's most evocative symbols, designed by German sculptor Carl Bernard Bartels (1866–1955). In the middle of the group is the more restrained **Cunard Building** (completed in 1914).

From the Pierhead, you can take the 50-minute **ferry across the Mersey** and back to get the best view of Liverpool. Herman Melville, sailing into the port in 1837, compared the 4-mile dock wall with the Great Wall of China. Looking back from the ferry you can see the red-and-white stripes of the **White Star Offices**, designed by Norman Shaw in 1897, and the bulky, brick fortress of the **Albert Dock Warehouses**. As you get further away from the shore, the city hoves into view, with Gilbert Scott's cathedral floating above it. Across the Mersey is the skyline of **Birkenhead** – the red-brick railway station tower, green-domed town hall and ventilation shaft of the Mersey Tunnel. The town's main claim to fame is its public park, which was the first in the country (opened in 1847) and influenced the naturalistic design of Central Park in Manhattan.

The Albert Docks

Fireproof, built of stone, brick and iron, five storeys high on cast-iron columns around the docking basin, the Albert Dock Warehouses (built 1839–45) enabled cargoes to be loaded and unloaded directly to and from ships, and to be stored duty free until the goods were sold or re-exported. When the docks were abandoned by modern shipping, they were converted into cafés, bars and museums. The **Merseyside Maritime Museum** (*t (0151) 478 4499, www.merseysidemaritimemuseum.org.uk; open 10–5*) has exhibitions devoted to Liverpool's maritime history, including the *Titanic* and the *Lusitania*, sunk in mid-Atlantic by an iceberg and a German U-boat. The basement examines Liverpool's role in the transatlantic slave trade: the port of Liverpool dominated the trade in the late 18th century; it is reckoned that three-quarters of all European slave ships left from Liverpool, transporting half of the three million Africans carried by British slavers before abolition in 1807. **HM Customs and Excise Museum** on the ground floor shows security procedures on boats and aeroplanes.

The **Liverpool Tate** (*t (0151) 702 7400, www.tate.org.uk; open Tues–Sun 10–6*) backs onto the river, with fabulous views from the top. It is the northern home of the Tate collection of modern art (also exhibited at Tate Britain and Tate Modern in London and Tate St Ives in Cornwall), founded on a sugar-trading fortune, and the largest gallery of modern and contemporary art outside London. Its collections are extensive.

Finally, the **Beatles Story** (*t (0151) 709 1963; open daily 10–5.30; adm exp*) offers a nostalgic walk-through history of the band up to its final split, with reconstructions of the Cavern Club, Brian Epstein's record shop and the Abbey Road Studio.

Museum of Liverpool Life

t (0151) 478 4080, www.museumofliverpoollife.org.uk; open daily 10–5.

Over a footbridge from the Albert Docks, in a cluster of old port buildings, the Museum of Liverpool Life focuses on the cultural history and identity of Liverpool. 'The town is full of Germans, Jews, Welsh, Irish and Dutch...and the Docks are wondrous,' the painter Augustus John wrote in 1900. Not only did thousands of migrants pass through Liverpool *en route* to new lives across the Atlantic, many settled down here, into Britain's first black African and Chinese communities, alongside Irish, Welsh, Scottish and other Europeans. With them, new tastes in fashion and music drifted back across the Atlantic from America, influencing the cultural life of the city and re-emerging in numerous bands, of which the Beatles is only the most famous.

The City

Between the docks and the dismal commercial centre is the small financial district: office buildings, sandwich bars, barber shops, newsagents and banks. Walk through it on a weekday. This is the financial clout (as expressed in imposing architecture) behind the docks. Charles Reilly (1874–1949), head of Liverpool's school of architecture, described **Water Street** as 'more like a ravine than a street' with its tall buildings on either side. One of the tallest is the **India Building**, built in 1923 as head office of the

Ocean Steamship Company. Reilly commented: 'it would not disgrace Fifth Avenue; indeed it would sit there very happily and those who know most of modern architecture will known that this is very high praise'. Its architect was Herbert J. Rowse, whose masterpiece was the wedding-cake **Bank Building**; on its balcony the Beatles received the Freedom of Liverpool. Next door is the **Town Hall**, built in 1749 by John Wood the Younger of Bath. **Oriel Chambers**, opposite the India Building, looks like a modern glass-fronted office block, but was built in 1864 by Peter Ellis. It has been called one of the most important buildings in the world for its use of prefabricated structural units in cast iron and its large oriel windows, flooding the offices with daylight. Tucked away down Rumford Street is the underground HQ of the Battle of the Atlantic, now the **Western Approaches Museum** (***t*** *(0151) 227 2008; open Sat and Mon–Thurs 10.30–4.30; adm*). In the Main Operation Room strategies to evade U-boats were devised.

The Commercial Centre

The shops around the city centre (Queen's Square, Williamson Square and Church Street) have none of the affluence or glamour of the shopping scene in Birmingham, Manchester or Leeds. If you walk up **Church Street**, however, don't miss the comic statues outside Littlewoods of its founders, the Moores brothers, looking like Dickens' Cheeryble brothers. John Moores was one of Liverpool's great philanthropists. Matthew Street is the centre of the so-called **Cavern Quarter** of pubs and clubs, with the Cavern Club (on the original site) and Beatles street sculptures. The area has some kitsch appeal in the daytime, but feels cheap and seedy at night. Root out the **Old Bluecoat School**, just off Church Street. The idea for the school was mooted 'to teach poor children to read, write and cast accounts' at the beginning of the 18th century, when Liverpool was already Britain's third largest port, but still small in population. The beautiful Queen Anne building (1717–25) stands on three sides of a courtyard, its deep red brickwork sharply contrasting with cream-painted stone quoins around the windows. You can get a cup of tea, browse in the bookshop and enjoy the garden.

The narrow grid of streets around Concert Square is reinventing itself as a 'quarter' of graphic designers, photo-galleries, independent record and clothing shops, and night clubs – including the celebrated **Cream** – although many of the Victorian warehouses and terraces are still crumbling away, their doors and windows boarded up.

William Brown Street and the Cultural Quarter

When you step out of Lyme Street Station you are confronted with a spectacular collection of columns, great flights of stone steps leading up to handsome porticoes, and the bronze statuary of the civic buildings. You won't find a more handsome group of neo-classical buildings, nor a more striking example of Victorian philanthropy in the provision of culture and education. The street was named after William Brown, a wealthy businessman and MP for South Lancashire. He donated the plot of land opposite **St George's Hall** (opened 1854), whose classical revivalist style of architecture set the tone for the complex. Richard Norman Shaw described the hall, delicate and airy in its cage of monumental pillars, as 'one of the great edifices of the world'. The American novelist Nathaniel Hawthorne took part in a banquet in the hall. 'I can't think of anything finer than this hall,' he wrote in his notebook. Opposite stands the **Walker Art Gallery** and drum-shaped **Picton Reading Rooms**, designed by architect Cornelius Sherlock. Mayor of Liverpool Andrew Walker put up most of the money. At the far end, the ornate County Sessions House is the last neo-classical building.

Liverpool Museum

t (0151) 478 4399, www.liverpoolmuseum.org.uk; open Mon–Sat 10–5, Sun 12–5.

In 1941 an incendiary bomb landed on the museum, leaving only the façade; the interiors were rebuilt in functional style. Recent lottery-funded improvements have included the restoration of galleries in the Mountford Building, an elaborate horse-shoe-shaped extension built in 1906. Here you will find the natural history collections of the 13th Earl of Derby around which the museum was based. The **Derby Bequest** was bolstered in 1867 by the collection of medieval and ancient artefacts (metalwork, jewellery and pottery) of Joseph Meyer, a wealthy Liverpool goldsmith. You will find the **Meyer Collection** in the Upper Horseshoe Gallery, along with the **Ince Blundell Collection** of classical sculpture – more than 400 pieces collected in the late 18th century by Henry Blundell of Ince Blundell Hall in Lancashire.

Walker Art Gallery

t (0151) 478 4199, www.thewalker.org.uk; open Mon–Sat 10–5, Sun 12–5.

The Walker Art Gallery was built as a venue for the once-famous Liverpool Autumn Exhibitions; the bequests came later, notably a collection of late-medieval and early-Renaissance paintings left by William Roscoe, an outstanding 19th-century citizen of Liverpool (a banker, botanist, historian and anti-slavery campaigner, who campaigned for abolition at a time when most Liverpool notables were still backing the slave trade). The Victorian High Art Room displays the small but renowned collection of **Pre-Raphaelites**, enthusiastically collected and exhibited in Liverpool, inspiring the **Liverpool School**. The European sculpture gallery includes about 40 pieces of the Ince Blundell Collection, 17th-century paintings hung on red damask, including one of Rembrandt's earliest self portraits and a brand new **Craft and Design gallery**. The Walker also hosts the prestigious John Moores contemporary painting exhibition every autumn (part of the lively Liverpool Biennial of visual arts).

The Cathedrals

The two contrasting cathedrals – Anglican and Roman Catholic – face each other down Hope Street in an area of handsome Victorian streets. The **Philharmonic Hall** and **Everyman Theatre** are here. Paul McCartney and George Harrison went to the boys' grammar school down Mount Street, now McCartney's **Liverpool Institute of Performing Arts**. The site of Liverpool's **Anglican cathedral** was found in 1902 on a hill overlooking the city and the docks, and the design competition won by the 23-year-old Gilbert Scott. His massive, dark-red sandstone, neo-Gothic cathedral rises out of a rocky outcrop dotted with Victorian funerary monuments. Inside, its cruciform vastness is unimpeded; terrific views soar through the great arch at the transept crossing.

The **Roman Catholic cathedral** stands on the site of the largest workhouse in Victorian England, with a peak capacity of 4,000 inmates. The cathedral building did not get under way until 1962. The exterior is tractor engine, the interior space ship. Original architect Edwin Lutyens planned an immense neo-classical structure that would have overshadowed Scott's effort, but attitudes changed and he was replaced.

The Suburbs

South of the city centre on Aigburth Road is **Sefton Park**, one of Liverpool's largest green spaces. It was donated to the city in 1896 by millionaire Henry Yates Thomson and is ringed by a tree-lined avenue and large Victorian townhouses. Head on to **Sudely House** (***t*** *(0151) 724 3245, www.sudleyhouse.org.uk; open Mon–Sat 10–5, Sun 12 –5*), on Mosely Hill Road. In 1884, when retired Liverpool shipping merchant George Holt, bought the house, it was surrounded by countryside with river views. He added a wing, bay windows and panelling, and collected contemporary paintings, including Pre-Raphaelites, small narrative paintings and seascapes including Turner's *Wreck Buoy*. The works are hung against flock wallpapers and elaborate chimney pieces. (It was the setting for the recent television version of *The Forsyte Saga*.)

Prepare for a culture clash at **Speke Hall** (*8 miles southeast of central Liverpool;* ***t*** *(0151) 427 7231, www.nationaltrust.org.uk; open April–Oct Wed–Sun 1–5, Nov weekends 1–4.30;adm*)between the elaborate patterned timberwork, cobbled courtyard and dark corridors, and the international airport. Ignore the planes and you are in a Tudor manor house on the banks of the Mersey, built one wing at a time until the central yard was enclosed. The striking black-and-white exterior, heavy interior oak panelling, elaborate door frames and the William Morris wallpaper were all added by the Victorians, who loved their creaking ancient piles with as much exposed wood as possible. A novel feature is the corridor facing onto the courtyard all the way round.

Manchester

Hovering like a small space ship above Manchester's ring road is the sales office of Urban Splash, the pioneering property development company that has led the regeneration of the city's old wharves. The futuristic glass pod, in among the metal railway bridges, dirty brick arches and congested roads, is a symbol of modern Manchester. Twenty years ago the dilapidated warehouses and high-rise blocks that dominated post-industrial city centres were valued only by architects; now a tower-block studio or loft-style apartment in the city centre is the ultimate in city-slicker chic. Developers have reinvented urban life in Manchester: bright new shops, clubs, galleries, cafés, bars and restaurants inhabit the old structures of the 19th-century cotton capital. The speed of change was given an unlikely boost in 1996 when an IRA bomb smashed the commercial hub to smithereens. Out of the damage has emerged a shiny new public space flanked by world-class architecture. Manchester is booming, hyped by countless magazine articles and books. New Manchester is the cultural legacy of the late

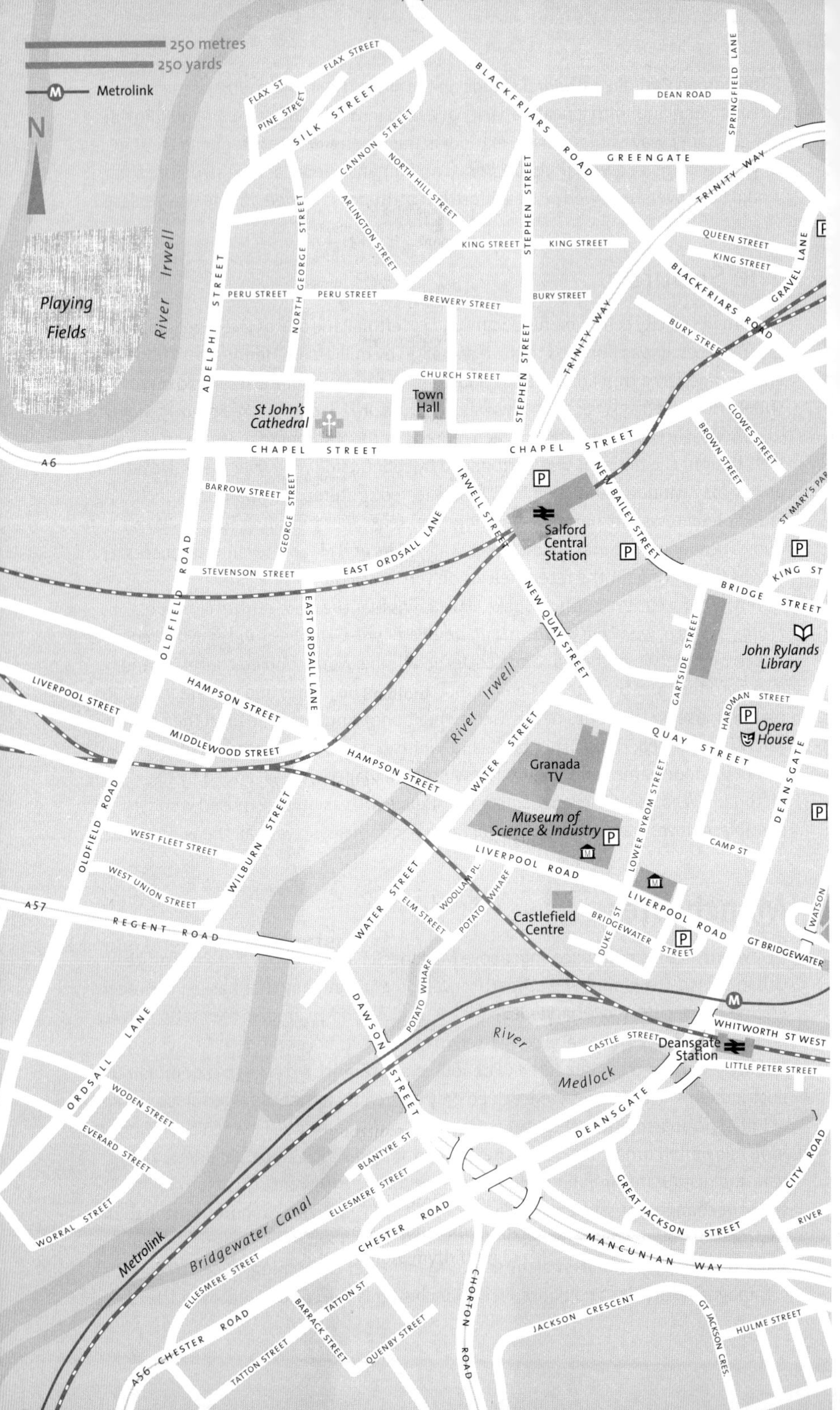

250 metres
250 yards
Metrolink
N
Playing Fields
River Irwell
St John's Cathedral
Town Hall
Salford Central Station
Granada TV
Museum of Science & Industry
Castlefield Centre
John Rylands Library
Opera House
Deansgate Station
River Medlock
Bridgewater Canal
Metrolink
A6
A57
A56
CHAPEL STREET
BLACKFRIARS ROAD
GREENGATE
DEAN ROAD
SPRINGFIELD LANE
TRINITY WAY
QUEEN STREET
KING STREET
GRAVEL LANE
BURY STREET
FLAX STREET
FLAX ST
PINE STREET
SILK STREET
CANNON STREET
NORTH HILL STREET
ARLINGTON STREET
NORTH GEORGE STREET
STEPHEN STREET
ADELPHI STREET
PERU STREET
BREWERY STREET
CHURCH STREET
BARROW STREET
GEORGE STREET
STEVENSON STREET
EAST ORDSALL LANE
OLDFIELD ROAD
IRWELL STREET
NEW BAILEY STREET
CLOWES STREET
BROWN STREET
ST MARY'S PA
KING ST
BRIDGE STREET
NEW QUAY STREET
GARTSIDE STREET
HARDMAN STREET
QUAY STREET
DEANSGATE
LIVERPOOL STREET
HAMPSON STREET
MIDDLEWOOD STREET
WATER STREET
LOWER BYROM STREET
CAMP ST
WEST FLEET STREET
WEST UNION STREET
WILBURN STREET
LIVERPOOL ROAD
WOOLLAM PL.
POTATO WHARF
ELM STREET
BRIDGEWATER STREET
DUKE ST
WATSON
GT BRIDGEWATER
REGENT ROAD
DAWSON STREET
WHITWORTH ST WEST
CASTLE STREET
LITTLE PETER STREET
ORDSALL LANE
WODEN STREET
EVERARD STREET
WORRAL STREET
BLANTYRE ST
ELLESMERE STREET
CHESTER ROAD
GREAT JACKSON STREET
CITY ROAD
RIVER
MANCUNIAN WAY
CHORLTON ROAD
JACKSON CRESCENT
GT JACKSON CRES.
HULME STREET
TATTON ST
TATTON STREET
BARRACK STREET
QUENBY STREET

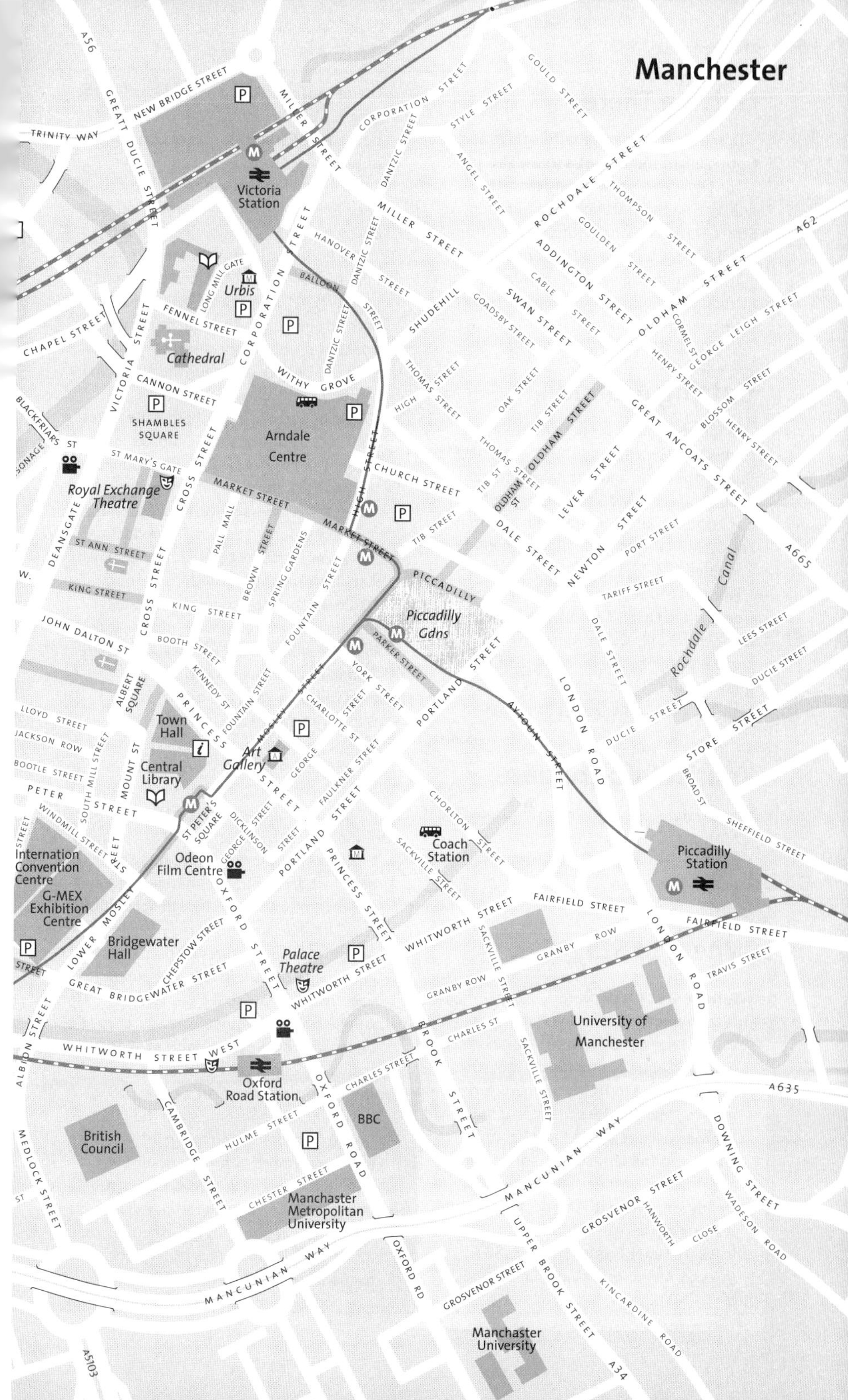
Manchester
Victoria Station
Urbis
Cathedral
Arndale Centre
Shambles Square
Royal Exchange Theatre
Piccadilly Gdns
Town Hall
Central Library
Art Gallery
St Peter's Square
Odeon Film Centre
Coach Station
Piccadilly Station
Internation Convention Centre
G-MEX Exhibition Centre
Bridgewater Hall
Palace Theatre
Oxford Road Station
University of Manchester
British Council
BBC
Manchester Metropolitan University
Manchester University
Rochdale Canal
Deansgate
Market Street
Piccadilly
Oxford Road
Portland Street
Princess Street
Mosley Street
Whitworth Street
Whitworth Street West
Mancunian Way
Oldham Street
Rochdale Street
Great Ancoats Street
London Road
Upper Brook Street
A56
A62
A665
A635
A34
A5103

Getting There

Domestic **flights** and charters fly to and from Manchester Airport, **t** (0161) 489 3000.

The city is easily reached by **car** on the M6 and M1. The **coach** station is on Chorlton Street; National Express runs services from all over England, twice an hour from London.

The mainline **railway** station is Manchester Piccadilly. Virgin Trains runs regular services from London Euston.

Getting Around

Manchester has a modern **Metrolink** tramway system around the city, reaching Bury to the north and Altrincham to the south, and Eccles via Salford Quays, **t** (0161) 205 2000. For local **bus** and **train** information call Greater Manchester Public Transport Enquiries, GMPTE, **t** (0161) 228 7811.

From May to Sept you can go on a **boat trip** from Salford Quays, **t** (0161) 440 0277, on the Manchester Ship Canal. Allow an hour.

The Blue Badge Guides organize all kinds of **guided walks** and **coach tours** of both the city centre and the wider area, **t** (0161) 234 3157.

Tourist Information

Manchester: Town Hall Extension, Lloyd Street, **t** (0161) 234 3157, **f** (0161) 236 9900, *manchester_visitor_centre@notes.manchester.gov.uk*

Where to Stay

Manchester t (0161) –

The Lowry Hotel, Dearmans Place, Chapel Wharf, **t** 827 4000, *www.thelowryhotel.com* (*luxury*). Centrally situated on the banks of the Irwell next to Trinity Bridge. Big, new and modern, Manchester's first 5-star hotel, with the **Marco Pierre White River Room** for 126 diners and **The Terrace** for informal dining and drinks in summer. Suites and rooms in trendy loft style, with Lowry prints. Within walking distance of centre.

The Palace Hotel, Oxford Street, **t** 288 1111 (*luxury*). An imposing Victorian red-brick Grade II listed building which looks like the Kremlin. Built by Alfred Waterhouse, it housed the Refuge Assurance Company until 1930. Peep inside and admire the circular domed foyer, even if you don't stay. The banking hall is now the main lounge; beyond is the **Waterhouse Restaurant**.

Crowne Plaza Midland, Peter Street, **t** 236 3333 (*luxury*). Used to be Manchester's main railway hotel, an elegant Edwardian hotel with 303 bedrooms that can be completely booked up when Manchester United plays at home. Despite grandeur, the atmosphere is friendly and relaxed.

Le Meridien Victoria and Albert, Water Street, **t** 832 1188 (*luxury*). Behind Granada TV studios, and much used by them. Converted Victorian warehouse, made homely with flowers. Attentive service; two restaurants; 156 rooms themed around TV productions.

Malmaison, Piccadilly, **t** 278 1000 (*expensive*). A stylish, central hotel with 112 rooms and a traditional brasserie opposite Piccadilly Station. Cool contemporary interior; jazzy bar; French brasseries; CD players, satellite TV and room service in 110 rooms.

Eleven Didsbury Park, 11 Didsbury Park, Didsbury Village, **t** 448 7711, *www.elevendidsburypark.com* (*expensive*). Victorian townhouse in conservation area, 20 minutes by bus from centre, modern décor, walled garden and rooftop terrace; 14 bedrooms.

Britannia Sacha's House, Tib Street, Piccadilly, **t** 228 1234 (*moderate*). Corner building with grand art deco entrance, marble steps and bell tower. Exotic interior décor (cascading water, chandeliers and mirrored ceilings, ornately framed pictures on purple and red patterned wallpapers); 223 modern rooms. Carvery restaurant and pizzeria.

Castlefield Hotel, Liverpool Road, **t** 832 7073 (*moderate*). By the canal, with 48 modern rooms. Functional and central.

Mitre Hotel, Cathedral Gates, **t** 834 4128 (*moderate*). A handsome stone-built hotel beside cathedral in shopping district. Clean and comfortable with 32 bedrooms.

Rembrandt, 33 Sackville Street, **t** 236 1311 (*moderate*). Gay hotel in the Gay Village; 20 bedrooms, thoughtfully furnished. Six rooms above the bar can be noisy. First-floor bistro overlooks canal. Close to station.

Eating Out

Manchester t (0161) –

The once-dilapidated quaysides, railway arches and warehouses are buzzing with café-bars, restaurants and clubs. At night try Castlefields, the Gay Village, Deansgate Quay, Printworks, Chinatown or Indian Rusholme. For daytime coffee, try **Café Revive**, in the flagship Marks & Spencers on Millennium Square.

Marco Pierre White River Room, Lowry Hotel, 50 Dearmans Place, Chapel Wharf, Salford, **t** 827 4041 (*very expensive*). As impeccable as you would expect.

Crowne Plaza Midland French Restaurant, Peter Street, **t** 236 3333 (*expensive*). Setting formal, but trad menu given contemporary treatment; delicious sauces and puddings.

Mash and Air, 40 Chorlton Street, **t** 661 1111 (Air), **t** 661 6161 (Mash). Dinner on the top floor (Air; *expensive*), smart tables and view of cityscape, good wines, vegetarian meals; all day menu downstairs (Mash; *moderate*), pizza from wood-fired oven, grilled fish.

Pan Asia, Faulkner Street, **t** 236 6868 (*moderate*). Stylish, behind a cascade of water, with open stainless-steel kitchen.

Simply Heathcotes, Jackson Row, 151 Deansgate, **t** 835 3536 (*moderate*). Spacious first-floor dining room. Traditional northern fare given modern makeover: corned beef terrine with brown sauce, baked cod with black olive mash and pesto, red wine risotto, bread and butter pudding; good wine list.

Livebait, 22 Lloyd Street, Albert Square, **t** 817 4110 (*moderate*). Buzzy seafood restaurant (one of a chain) in hip, relaxed setting.

Le Petit Blanc, 55 King Street, **t** 832 100 (*moderate*). Superior chain. Separate menus cater for vegetarians and vegans. Simple ingredients delightfully prepared.

Sarasota, Canal Street, **t** 236 2667 (*moderate*). Above Manto Café-Bar, conservatory with an overhanging roof terrace. The soft top rolls back in summer.

Stock, Norfolk Street, **t** 839 6644 (*moderate*). A great Southern Italian restaurant run by a father, the chef, and son, front of house. In the grandiose Stock Exchange building with its high, domed ceiling. Antipasti and fish.

Market Restaurant, High Street, Northern Quarter, **t** 834 3743 (*moderate*). Long-established, serves top-quality modern English food in a homely setting – a refreshing change from all the stark, trendy new restaurants. *Open Wed–Sat*.

Cornerhouse Café, Oxford Street, **t** 200 1508 (*cheap*). Pasta, hot pots, soups and salads. Relaxed and informal, one of the first of the new breed of café-bars in Manchester.

Tampopo, Albert Square, **t** 819 1966 (*cheap*). An inviting basement restaurant. Thai and Indonesian influences, good for vegetarians.

Dimitris, Campfield Arcade (off Liverpool Road), **t** 839 3319 (*cheap*). Lively Greek restaurant, with red gingham tablecloths and murals of gladiators. Meze is a popular choice. In summer ask for a table under the arcade.

Yang Sing, 34 Princess Street, **t** 236 2200 (*cheap*). Chinatown stalwart. Superb Cantonese cuisine, dim sum lunches a speciality. Let the waiter choose your meal.

China City, Faulkner Street, **t** 236 2427 (*cheap*). Perfect balance: understated good quality.

Pacific, 58–60 George Street, **t** 228 6668 (*cheap*). Two in one: upper floor Thai, lower floor Chinese with dim sum and vegetarian dishes. Light, bright and contemporary.

The Rusholme 'Curry Mile' (Wilmslow Road) boasts a mile of Indian restaurants, from 250-seat monsters like **Sangam** (**t** 257 3922; *cheap*) to upmarket eateries like **Hanaan** (**t** 256 4786; *cheap*) and tiny unlicensed cafés. Open all night, Rusholme serves families both Asian and Western, clubbers and students. Cheap and cheerful. Food is northern Indian, mainly Punjabi. Try the **New Tabak** (**t** 248 7812; *cheap*) for a taste of Nepal, especially good choice for vegetarians.

Entertainment

Film, Theatre, Music and Dance

Palace Theatre, Oxford Street, **t** 0870 401 6000. Art deco building which hosts touring productions of big West End musicals such as *Lion King* and *Chitty Chitty Bang Bang*.

Opera House, Quay Street, **t** 0870 4016 000. Neo-classical façade with fluted columns and glittering porch, hosts shows including comedians and tribute bands (not opera!).

The Bridgewater Hall, Lower Moseley Street, **t** 907 9000. Part of a swish complex of glass and sandstone buildings, including the GMEX exhibition centre. Its concert hall, built in 1996 for Manchester's world-famous Halle Orchestra, has excellent acoustics. Pre-concert restaurant, café and bar in spacious atrium; *open Mon–Sat 10–8, Sun noon–6.*

Royal Exchange Theatre, St Anne's Square, **t** 833 9833. The main theatre-in-the-round, suspended in a space-age pod in the old Exchange Hall, stages in-house productions; the small studio theatre hosts touring plays too. Interesting repertoire includes serious drama (new and old) and comedy. Bar, café and bookshop. Look out for matinée standby.

The Lowry, Pier 8, Salford Quays, **t** 876 2000. Beside the Manchester Ship Canal, a bustling venue with two cafés and a smart restaurant. Its Lyric theatre is known for high-brow touring opera and dance. The Quays hosts Shakespeare, newer drama and smaller musical performances.

The Printworks, t 0870 010 2030. Film entertainment emporium with IMAX cinema.

The Cornerhouse, corner of Oxford Street, **t** 200 1500. Art gallery, arthouse cinema, bar and café in arty venue.

Manchester Cathedral, t 833 2220. Concerts including Cantata choral performances and Choral Evensong Tues–Thurs at 5.30.

The Comedy Store, Whitworth Street West, Deansgate Locks, **t** 08705 932 932. A reliable source of laughs.

Clubs

The fast-changing club scene is bewildering, with around 150 clubs at any one time. Only locals can hope to keep up with latest trends. Check *City Life* magazine, *www.citylife.co.uk*, available from any Manchester newsagent, for complete listings.

Café-Bars and Pubs

Gay Village

Manchester has a much-hyped gay scene. Most café-bars in this area are open until 2am, when clubs take over until 6am. Straight people are welcome, although on Saturday nights some bars become exclusive.

Manto Café-Bar, Canal Street, **t** 236 2667. Kick-started the whole gay scene in Manchester. Pop art hangs on bright walls; balcony overlooking the canal; club fliers to lead you on.

Velvet, Canal Street, **t** 236 9003. Probably the trendiest café-bar of the lot, overlooking the canal. Chunky purple and pink seats on scrubbed pine floors, and chunky portions of pan-fried fish, sausages and savoury pancakes too.

New Union, 111 Princess Street, **t** 228 1492. A drinker's pub with cabaret, always packed. Very gay on Friday and Saturday nights.

Around Town

Rain Bar, 80 Great Bridgewater Street, **t** 235 6500. Former umbrella factory. Café-bar upstairs, where snacks include toasted panini, meals pasta and grills. Traditional pub downstairs, with terraces overlooking Rochdale Canal. Draught J.W. Lees beer.

Night and Day, Oldham Street, **t** 236 4597. Local bands every night except Sun. Indie, rock and pop, and the odd poetry reading. Sometimes small door charge. Sit, drink, dance as you like. Well scuffed.

Dry Bar, Oldham Street, **t** 236 9840. Near Night and Day, but you might walk straight past it – it looks like a vacant shop. Long bar and sofas contribute to rough-edged cool.

Temple of Convenience, Great Bridgewater Street. Tiny Victorian pub that was once a gents loo. Good, friendly place to meet up at the start of an evening out.

Sand Bar, Grosvenor Street, **t** 273 3141. In an 18th-century townhouse with bags of character. Popular with students. Good range of draught beers.

Peverel of the Peak, Chepstow Street. Cosy old-world Victorian feel. Exterior green-tiled with period decoration around windows. Interior woody with small rooms.

Loaf, Deansgate Locks, **t** 819 5858. Enormous café-bar with pre-club atmopshere, on two levels with a boardwalk over the canal. Good food and a dance floor. One of a number of newly converted bars in old railway arches by the canal at the southern end of the city centre. Long queues even when not busy.

The Didsbury, Wilmslow Road, Didsbury, **t** 819 5858. A short drive out of the city along Oldham Road. Heavy oak beams, partitions, brick walls, stout wooden tables and a big specials board. Next to it is the attractive Fletcher Moss Park with a rock garden dropping colourfully down to the River Mersey.

1980s, the Hacienda night club, rave culture, The Smiths, New Order, M-People and Happy Mondays – when Manchester was crowned 'Madchester'. Until recently the city was most associated with industrial decay and the bleak paintings of L.S. Lowry, who worked across the River Irwell in Salford, 'unarguably the most grim place in the North of England,' wrote one traveller. Now Manchester is turning those associations on their head. The **Lowry**, built to show off the painter's works, is the dazzling centre of a massive redevelopment of the Salford Quays, also including the **Imperial War Museum North**. Major projects like the new **City Art Gallery** and city centre coincided with the 2002 Commonwealth Games in the new **City of Manchester Stadium**.

The 19th-century city, nicknamed 'Cottonopolis', the cotton capital of the world, became the symbol of a modern industrial city when nobody knew what that meant. 'It is the philosopher alone who can conceive the grandeur of Manchester and the immensity of its future,' wrote Benjamin Disraeli, while Thomas Carlyle compared it to a 'prophetic city' built upon 'infinite abysses'. Charles Dickens and Elizabeth Gaskell both wrote grim Manchester novels. Its meteoric growth and polarization into rich businessmen and poor factory workers seemed to foreshadow a new social order.

The two major political movements of 19th-century Britain – the Anti-Corn Law League and Chartism – came from Manchester. The Leaguers preached free trade and the Chartists agitated for universal suffrage, equal electoral privileges and modern democracy. The violent charge of mounted soldiers waving cavalry swords into a mass protest in the city in 1816 (the Peterloo Massacre) inspired Shelley's revolution-inciting poem, *The Mask of Anarchy*. Friedrich Engels, co-author of the *Communist Manifesto*, came to Manchester in 1843 and prophesied revolution too. Revolution didn't come, but the Corn Laws were repealed, to celebrate which the Free Trade Hall was built, and the city got a handful of new cultural institutions, including a free library, the famous Halle Orchestra and the university.

Orientation

You can get around the city centre on foot, with the odd tram or bus ride. Although Greater Manchester is massive, the centre is confined to a grid of streets between the Rochdale Canal and the River Irwell. In the middle is the Civic Quarter: prestigious public buildings dominated by the Town Hall. To the south is the Convention Quarter, around the G-MEX centre. The shopping area occupies a strip bounded by King's Street, Deansgate, Fennel Street and Corporation Street/Cross Street. To the south, the pioneering redevelopment of the old industrial area of Castlefields (the terminus for early trains and canals) has acted as a catalyst for the conversion of derelict warehouses. Here the main attraction is the Museum of Science and Industry, in the buildings of the old Liverpool and Manchester Railway. North of Piccadilly Gardens are the old factories of the Northern Quarter, another industrial area in the throes of renewal. East of the Civic Quarter is China Town, around Faulkner Street, and the Gay Village, around Canal Street (more restaurants and bars). A bus ride down Oxford Road in the direction of Didsbury takes you past the main buildings of Manchester University, including the brilliant Manchester Museum and Whitworth Art Gallery.

The Civic Quarter

The prestigious public buildings that constitute Manchester's Civic Quarter were forced to squeeze into some awkward shapes. The **Town Hall** (1877; ***t*** *(0161) 234 5000; open Mon–Fri 9–4.30*) is triangular; the Central Reference Library (1934) circular; and the Town Hall Extension (1938), squashed in between. Walk down canyon-like Lloyd Street or Library Walk to Lutyens' sombre, white Portland stone **Cenotaph**. The **City Art Gallery** buildings, built by Charles Barry in the 1830s, are solidly metropolitan neo-classicism. Beyond Peter Street is the conference quarter of St Peter's Field.

The idiom of most 19th-century civic buildings is classical – nobility by association. Manchester chose Gothic instead, to show its links with medieval merchant cities. Alfred Waterhouse's neo-Gothic **Town Hall** (*open Mon–Sat 9–5, tours Wed and Sat 2pm*), was completed in 1877, a belated statement of pride in local government, long after the Exchange and Free Trade Hall had stated the power of the city's merchants. Go upstairs into the Great Hall to see the famous murals by Ford Madox Brown depicting 12 episodes in the city's history from the Roman fortress to the Bridgewater Canal.

Manchester Art Gallery

t *(0161) 235 8888, www.manchestergalleries.org.uk; open Tues–Sun 10–5.*

The Manchester Art Gallery on Mosley Street has recently reopened after a £35-million redevelopment incorporating the adjacent Athenaeum building and a new wing by architect Sir Michael Hopkins. The gallery boasts a fine collection of British and Continental fine and decorative arts, imaginatively displayed. Pre-Raphaelite paintings of the 19th century are the collection's pride: Rossetti, Holman Hunt, Millais and Burne-Jones are all here, and Madox Brown's masterpiece, *Work*, an icon of the Victorian age. The 18th century is represented by Gainsborough, Reynolds, Stubbs, Constable and Turner, including 37 Turner watercolours. Henry Moore, Paul Nash and Ben Nicholson are among the 20th-century British painters. The brand new **Gallery of Craft and Design** displays ceramics, glass, metal, furniture, textiles, toys and armour from 1000 BC to the present. The **Manchester Gallery** shows how art and design is woven into the fabric of Manchester.

John Rylands Library

t *(0161) 275 3751; call for post-renovation opening times.*

When cotton millionaire John Rylands died in 1888 his wife commissioned Basil Champneys to design a public library dedicated to him. The neo-Gothic building stands on Deansgate, its reddish Penrith sandstone blackened. The acquisition of the private library of Lord Spencer in 1892 and the manuscripts of the earls of Crawford in 1901 transformed the new foundation into an important research library.

St Peter's Fields

The site of the Peterloo Massacre of 16 August 1819 has been commemorated in the name of the convention quarter, around the G-MEX centre. The massacre took place on St Peter's Fields, used for mass meetings in the absence of a large enough public hall. Around 50,000 people gathered to listen to radical orator Henry Hunt calling for an extension of the vote to all adults. In an attempt to arrest Hunt, the local Yeomanry marched in with their swords, leaving 11 dead and 600 wounded. It was the worst clash to come out of social and political tension in the new industrial towns. The gulf between rich owners and poor workers was widening; hard living conditions united the workers into a powerful force, which made the politicians fear revolution.

The ornate, Italianate **Free Trade Hall** on Peter Street was rebuilt in grand style to celebrate the repeal of the Corn Laws in 1846.

Northern Quarter

The old red-brick factories and warehouses north of Piccadilly Gardens are slowly being converted into trendy bars and shops such as the award-winning **Smithfield Buildings** on the corner of Oldham Street and Tib Street, but many are still boarded up. The Northern Quarter was once the manufacturing centre of the city. Now the mix of crumbling industrial buildings and narrow back streets have taken on a bohemian edge. On Oldham Street there are independent record shops and bars. On Church Street is **Affleck's Palace** (*open Mon–Fri 10–5.30, Sat 10–6*), a venerable alternative shopping institution – four storeys of stalls selling second-hand clothes, toys and psychic counselling galore. The Victorian fish market is now a **Crafts Centre**.

Castlefields

Castlefields, in the southeast of the city centre, was the site of the original Roman fortress, and the hub of the city's 19th-century transport links. An uninviting area of old wharf buildings and railway bridges, it is an Urban Heritage Park. The **Bridgewater Canal**, constructed in the 1760s by engineers James Brindley and John Gilbert to bring coal from the Duke of Bridgewater's collieries at Worsley, 7 miles away, into town, runs through it. The **Liverpool and Manchester Railway** operated the first passenger rail service out of Castlefields. The canalside is another bar zone, while the rail sheds are now the superb Museum of Science and Industry.

It's a good walk along the canal towpath to the Gay Village.

Museum of Science and Industry

t (0161) 832 2244, www.msim.org.uk; open daily 10–5.

The **Fibres, Fabrics and Fashion** exhibition is the obvious place to start, in the middle of 19th-century cotton manufacturing. Working looms demonstrate how cotton fibres are turned into cloth. In an old freight shed, the **Power Hall** displays mill engines from coal and steam to internal combustion. In the **Old Station** you can find out enough about the LMR to satisfy any trainspotter, and even to excite the interest of ordinary travellers.

The New Commercial Centre

The upmarket bit of the city centre runs from King's Street to Victoria Station, bounded by Deansgate/Victoria Street and Cross/Corporation Street. Big changes have been made here in the wake of the IRA bomb that exploded in a van outside the Arndale Centre in 1996. The terrorists ironically gave the centre, which epitomised the worst of 1960s urban planning, a second chance. Public spaces have been created in **Exchange Square**, opposite the new **Printworks** complex of pubs, cinemas, shops and restaurants. The two timber-framed buildings are sole survivors of the old medieval city below. The **Corn Exchange**, revamped Cinderella-style from flea market to pricey boutique-land, faces the square and cathedral.

Manchester Cathedral started life in 1421 as the collegiate church of St Mary, St Denys and St George, and was elevated to cathedral status in 1847, when it was treated to a Victorian-Gothic makeover. On the north side of New Cathedral Street, Chetham's School of Music, the medieval dormitory of the collegiate church, has been transformed by the dazzling plate-glass pyramid of **Urbis** (***t*** *(0161) 605 8200; open 10–6; adm exp*), an interactive multimedia experience.

South of Exchange Square the **Royal Exchange** has stood here since 1729, a symbol of the power and wealth of the city's cotton traders. The neo-classical structure (1929) houses the hi-tech **Exchange Theatre**, suspended like a space station beneath the coloured glass domes of the old trading hall. Trade closed on 31 December 1968. South of the exchange is **St Anne's Square**, one of the prettiest squares in the city, and the narrow Victorian **Barton Arcade**.

China Town and the Gay Village

They have little in common, but these two communities are separated only by Portland Street. Faulkner Street, the main axis of **China Town**, buzzes with Chinese restaurants and shops selling torch ear-picks. The **Gay Village** leads down to Canal Street where cafés, bars and clubs are open every night until dawn. The late licences, buzz and all-round good atmosphere draw huge crowds, both gay and straight.

The University Quarter

Around the university, a few miles down Oxford Road, are the Manchester Museum and Whitworth Art Gallery. Buses ferry students up and down all day so you will have no trouble getting there. Hop off after the university bridge.

Manchester Museum

t (0161) 275 2634, www.museum.man.ac.uk; open Mon–Sat 10–5, Sun 11–4.

Three generations of Waterhouse architects, starting with Alfred, collaborated on the three *museum* buildings in the Victorian Gothic style. A new fourth building takes visitors into the museum. All the fun bits of the traditional museum repertoire are here – Archaeology, Egyptology, Ethnology and Zoology – in a department of the university, representing the obscure research enthusiasms of academics. A small collection of reconstructed ancient faces, including the King of Macedonia and prehistoric Lindow Man, came out of pioneering work conducted by Dr Richard Neave in the school of biological sciences in the last 15 years; his reconstructive techniques are now used in police detective work. One of Britain's top collections of ancient Egyptian objects was secured by textile merchant Jesse Haworth, who funded the expeditions of Egyptologist Sir Flinders Petrie in the 1890s. The Ethnology collection includes Peruvian pottery donated by a Manchester solicitor, South Pacific weapons given by a Rochdale businessman, and Japanese swords left by a director of Christies.

Whitworth Art Gallery

***t** (0161) 275 7450, www.whitworth.man.ac.uk; open Mon–Sat 10–5, Sun 2–5.*

Ten minutes' walk further up Oxford Road is the **Whitworth Art Gallery** renowned for its collections of textiles, wallpapers and fine art. Founder Joseph Whitworth's engineering firm developed the international standard for screw threads and left more than a million pounds in trust to found a new museum of industrial art and design to improve the city's textile industry. The collection of historic textiles was acquired in 1891 in line with this mission. A bequest of 154 English watercolours, including Blakes and Turners, traces the genre. In 1958 the university took over the gallery, and acquired modern art by Henry Moore, Barbara Hepworth *et al*.

Salford

The Lowry

*Pier 8, Salford Quays, Salford, **t** (0161) 876 2020; open daily 10am–11.30pm; galleries open Mon–Sat 11–5, until 7 in summer; artworks on view in summer daily 10–5, winter until 4; adm for galleries.*

A lottery-funded millennium project aimed at regenerating an area of urban decay, the Lowry art centre is devoted to the works of Lawrence Stephen Lowry (1887–1976), who worked as a rent collector in Manchester and Salford and painted the industrial landscape around him – panoramas of mills, smoking chimneys, terraced housing and churches, all peopled with his trademark stick people. Architect Michael Wilford has designed a great big fun building to house the 330 Lowry paintings. Composed of awkward curved and angular shapes stuck together like a sophisticated child's building blocks, the complex also houses two theatres, the **Deck** (upstairs) for contemporary art and the **Promenade** (downstairs) for photography exhibitions.

The Imperial War Museum North

***t** (0161) 836 4000, www.iwm.org.uk/north; open 10–6.*

The northern branch of the Imperial War Museum, in a dazzling new building on the south bank of the Ship Canal, opened in summer 2002. Its three interlocking halls or 'shards', designed to show a world fragmented by war and reassembled in pieces, are the concept of architect Daniel Libeskind, a Polish-born American living and working in Germany. The shards explore conflicts on land, in the air and on the water from 1914 to the present day with aircraft (including a Harrier jump jet), armoured vehicles, weapons, equipment, uniforms and medals. The air shard is a giant lattice of steelwork 180ft high with views over Manchester from a 95ft-high platform. The earth shard has a domed floor to recreate the experience of walking on the planet; the lights are dimmed hourly for an impressionistic multimedia show. The water shard extends over the Ship Canal by the Lowry, with restaurants and views.

Lancashire

Lancashire has been a small, rural county since it lost great chunks to Cumbria, Greater Manchester and Merseyside when county borders were moved in 1974. New Lancashire retains urban slithers along the Fylde coast of **Blackpool**, and between Preston (the new county town) and Colne, along the **East Lancashire Valleys**. Here the attractions are swamped by urban sprawl, but you are never far from a core of rugged open countryside; the **Forest of Bowland** and **Pendle Hill** define the towns, and even from the heart of Burnley but you have views of green fells.

Explore Lancashire from **Blackpool**, isolated on the Fylde Peninsula but fun if you're in the mood; **Lancaster**, with its looming castle, close to delightful Morecambe Bay and the marshes of the River Lune; or the old market town of **Clitheroe** in the Ribble Valley, a good base for walks around the Bowland Fells and Pendle Hill.

East Lancashire Valleys

Bonnie Colne, Bonnie Colne
Bonnie Colne let come what will
Tha'lt ever be most dear to me
Bonnie Colne upon the hill

Colne's Song, 1873

The grim old cotton towns of Blackburn, Burnley, Accrington and Colne inhabit the low-lying valleys of southern Lancashire, framed by the bulky gritstone Pendle Hill massif and the south Pennine moors. 'Towns meant to work in and not really to live in,' wrote J.B. Priestley in 1933. Now there's not much work either.

Burnley was still the world's main cotton-weaving centre in 1900. A photograph of its industrial heart then shows the Leeds and Liverpool Canal twisting past smog-blackened factories, with around 30 chimneys puffing smoke; now only five are left, but the wharfside of **Burnley Weavers' Triangle** is a well-preserved mill setting. Pick up the Weavers' Triangle Trail at the canal bridge, stopping at the old Wharfmaster's House visitor centre (***t*** *(01282) 452 403; open Easter–Sept, Sat–Tues 2–4; Oct Sun 2–4*) for maps and information. You can get a drink and pie at the Inn on the Wharf, or a sandwich from Montague's sandwich shop by the Mechanics Institute.

Where to Stay

East Lancashire Valleys t (01282) – There are two farmhouse B&Bs in East Lancashire from which you can walk the Pendle Way in stages.

Higher Wanless Farm, Red Lane, Colne (near Barrowford), **t** 865 301, *www.stayinlancs.co.uk* (*moderate*). A white-painted old farmhouse with Virginia creeper covering its gable end in an ideal setting, overlooking Liverpool–Leeds Canal and shire horses. Comfortable, flowery and clean, helpful and welcoming.

Parson Lee Farm, Wycoller Country Park (near Colne), **t** 864 747 (*moderate*). Lovely place to stay at head of Wycoller Valley. Superb Georgian stone farmhouse with thick walls. Friendly hosts. In the evening, borrow a torch, and walk up the hillside to the Herders Inn for dinner.

At the end of the railway line from Preston, the old Cloth Hall in **Colne** bears the motto 'We Will Endure'. **Accrington**'s Italianate Town Hall has its own slogan, 'Industry and Prudence Conquer', inscribed in mosaic floor tiles. These tough, proud towns are now strongholds of urban poverty, racial segregation and the British National Party.

South of Accrington, towards the Rossendale hills, you come to the recently refurbished **Howarth Art Gallery** (*t (01254) 233 782; open Wed–Fri 2–5, weekends 12–4.30*), in the handsome Edwardian mansion of cotton magnate William Howarth. The prize exhibit is a display of handmade art nouveau Tiffany glassware – the gift of an émigré Accrington engraver who became art director to Louis Tiffany in New York. He came home in 1933 with a then unfashionable collection of the glass and donated it to the town. The gallery has a good shop selling contemporary Tiffany glass.

Up the B6250 from Colne to Trawden, **Wycoller Country Park** (*t (01282) 870 253*) is 350 acres of rough Brontë-esque farmland around the Wycoller beck. The atmospheric ruins of Wycoller Hall are thought to have been Charlotte Brontë's inspiration for Ferndean Manor in *Jane Eyre*; the Brontë family home is only 9 miles away in Haworth (*see* p.857) along the Brontë Way, a superb walk.

Blackpool

Blackpool is the queen of British seaside resorts, but the queen has had more than one '*annus horribilis*', sold off her jewels and daubed herself in cheap make-up. Either you will see Blackpool as a great British institution, or an ugly sprawl of brick terraces and arcades built on the flat, dreary landscape of the Fylde Peninsula. More than 17 million visitors don't come every year for nothing, but lashings of irony may help.

Victorian Blackpool was as glossy and new-fangled as they came, with three piers, the tallest building in the UK, and the first electric tram system in Britain (installed in 1885). In the 1930s you could dance all night in the ballroom of the Winter Gardens, see a new Noël Coward play at the Grand Theatre, and fall in love at an afternoon tea dance in the Tower. In the 1950s it was a family resort, where the children of those romances came to see variety acts like Morecambe and Wise on the North Pier, and Charlie Cairoli in the Tower Circus. The demise of the industrial north and the advent of cheap flights to Benidorm did it for Blackpool, but there is life in the old place yet: Blackpool plans to become a wet and windy Las Vegas, if it gets a casino licence.

Getting There and Around

To reach Blackpool by **car** take the M55 into town from the M6 north of Preston. National Express runs **coaches** to Blackpool from all over England. From Manchester, Stagecoach Ribble (**t** (0161) 228 7811) runs services from Chorlton Street Coach Station (2¾ hours), via Preston. Blackpool **local buses** (**t** (01253) 473 000) include hop-on-hop-off tourist buses.

Virgin Trains run a direct daily **rail** service from London to Blackpool. Frequent Intercity trains from London Euston via Preston (3½–4 hours). Several trains daily from Manchester airport and stations (1¼ hours).

Tourist Information

Blackpool: 1 Clifton Street, **t** (01253) 478 222. *Open Mon–Sat 9–4.30, daily during Illuminations.*

The Blackpool season builds up from June on, reaching a peak during the Illuminations, from the end of August to Hallowe'en.

Where to Stay

Blackpool t (01253) –

There are 168 large hotels, 1,002 small hotels and 874 guest houses listed by the Tourist Office, and probably the same number again that aren't. The streets behind the Promenade are packed with B&Bs, mostly dives. A handful are smart, catering for conference delegates.

De Vere Heron's Reach Hotel, East Park Drive, **t** 08706 063 606, *www.devereonline.co.uk* (*expensive*). One of swankiest hotels in town, super-modern and set behind a golf course at the end of a long drive. Friendly staff, pool, golf and all mod cons; 166 bedrooms.

The Savoy Hotel, Queen's Promenade, **t** 352 561, *www.savoyhotelblackpool.com* (*expensive*). Handsome traditional building, good stop for sandwiches and strong tea; 123 rooms, all furnished to a good standard.

Imperial Hotel, North Promenade, **t** 623 971, *imperialblackpool@paramount-hotels.co.uk* (*expensive*). Magnificent shiny columns and polished woodwork. Courteous, uniformed staff. Popular venue for political conferences; 180 comfortable rooms, pool, gym and spa. **Palm Restaurant** (à la carte and carvery).

Old Coach House, 50 Dean Street, **t** 349 195, *www.TheOldCoachHouse.freeserve.co.uk.* (*moderate*). Best small hotel in town, in welcoming Victorian house in heart of brash South Shore; 11 bedrooms, sparkling bathrooms and nice furniture. No-smoking dining room serves four-course menu.

The Grand Hotel, South Parade, Lytham St Anne's, **t** 721 288, *www.the-grand.co.uk* (*moderate*). Buses every 7–8 mins along the Promenade to this large Victorian building with a period feel and piano in lounge.

Cartford Country Inn, Cartford Lane, Little Eccleston, **t** (01995) 670 166 (*moderate*). Pleasant location beside toll bridge over River Wyre, 15 mins north of Blackpool. Own brewery and restaurant.

Eating Out

Blackpool t (01253) –

There are hundreds of places for all-day breakfasts or fish and chips. Good restaurants are scarcer. Try hotels or the following.

September Brasserie, 15–17 Queen Street, **t** 623 282 (*cheap*). No-nonsense, scruffy, but tasty food. Walls lined with restaurant reviews. *Closed Sun and Mon.*

La Fontana, 17 Clifton Street, **t** 622 231. Just off Talbot Square. Lively, friendly Italian with good enough food. Often very busy.

The Stocks German Restaurant, 33 Market Place, Poulton-le-Fylde, 3 miles inland from Blackpool, **t** 882 294. Filling dishes with creamy potatoes.

Entertainment

Grand Theatre, 33 Church Street, **t** 290 190. Matcham's finest. Family shows and panto.

Winter Gardens, Church Street, **t** 292 029. Three main venues: the **Pavilion Theatre** (nostalgic music nights); the **Opera House** (touring musicals, pop concerts, comedy); the **Empress Ball Room** (conferences and dance championships).

North Pier Theatre, **t** 292 029. Popular shows.

Central Pier Theatre, **t** 292 029. Celebrity look-alike shows and the like.

Casting a brighter light on it all from summer to autumn are about £12-million worth of illuminated tableaux and coloured lights stretching 6 miles along the Promenade – the Blackpool Illuminations – which make you feel that it is Christmas.

For visitors, Blackpool is the 7-mile coastal **Promenade**, carrying trams, cars, people and the odd horse and cart. On one side is the sea and on the other the Golden Mile of amusement arcades, tat stalls, burger bars, rock shops, fortune tellers and hotels, punctuated by the great iron finger of the Blackpool Tower. Three piers – North, Central and South – calibrate the uneventful distances. The **North Pier** is the most old-fashioned, with decking and Victorian lamps, cast-iron benches and an electric tram rattling up and down. The **Central Pier** was built to cater for the crowds with a Ferris wheel, dancing and skating; now it is a fairground with more arcades. You can go bungee jumping off the **South Pier** in summer. At low tide the wide, sandy beach is exposed – the venue for one of Blackpool's most charming institutions: **donkey rides.**

Talbot Square is the civic centre of town, with the Town Hall, Winter Gardens and Grand Theatre clustered nearby. Join a guided tour of the **Grand Theatre** (***t*** *(01253) 290 111*) to admire the sumptuous Frank Matcham interiors. Noël Coward premièred and appeared in his plays *Present Laughter* and *This Happy Breed* at the Grand in 1942.

Back on the Promenade, the unvarying mix of seaside tat continues all the way to the Pleasure Beach, getting tackier – if possible – along the way.

Blackpool Tower

t *(01253) 292 029, www.blackpooltower.co.uk; open Easter–Oct 10–dusk; adm exp.*

The Tower opened on 14 May 1894, a red-brick fortress which once housed an aquarium, zoo, ballroom and circus. The five floors of entertainment are mainly fruit machines now, but it's worth a peek for the ballroom and circus. Tea dances still start at 2pm in the red velvet plush and gilded **ballroom**. Go early to get a good ringside seat. Excellent dancers dress in silver heels, swirling skirts and bright coloured shirts. When the tempo changes everyone locks in step, dipping their knees and turning all at once. On the hour a Wurlitzer organ rises majestically centre stage with the sound of a dozen instruments. If you go to the **circus** only once in your life, go to this one. Then go up the lift to the top for the views.

Pleasure Beach

t *0870 444 5566; open Mar–Nov daily 10–dusk; unlimited day ticket available, otherwise you pay for each ride; adm exp.*

The Pleasure Beach, at the southern end of the Promenade, doesn't have much to do with pleasure or beaches; it's a high-octane fairground. The **Pepsi Max Big One** was the world's fastest and tallest rollercoaster when it was built in 1994, at a cost of £12 million. In 1997 the £2-million **Playstation** ride opened, shooting passengers hundreds of feet into the air. **Valhalla** is the most recent attraction, a 'high-speed water coaster in the dark'. Most of the rest of the white-knuckle rides date from the 1970s, including the **Revolution Rollercoaster** with its 360-degree loop.

Forest of Bowland and the Ribble Valley

East of the Lancashire Plain, beyond the M6, rise the sombre **Bowland Fells**. To the east are the Yorkshire Dales (*see* pp.794–816). To the south is **Pendle Hill**, where the Pendle Witches were rounded up in 1612, and marched over the Trough of Bowland to be tried and executed in Lancaster Prison. At dusk, you can see the glittering urban lightshow of the old cotton towns stretched out along the East Lancashire valleys.

Travelling from Lancaster to **Clitheroe**, beneath Pendle Hill, much of the upland plateau is in private hands, but there is public access to some remote fells. Park at the Jubilee Tower, not far from Lancaster, for **Clougha Pike** (1,355ft) and walk east over the **Ward's Stone** (1,837ft) to Brown Syke. Take a picnic to eat on the mossy banks of a stream in the **Trough of Bowland**; leave the heathery upland at Dunsop Bridge, following the River Hodder through a wooded gorge to the Inn at Whitewell; or head to **Chipping**, a tiny, stone market town at a crossroads on the moors with three pubs. To the north of the town are three fells to climb: **Fairsnape** (1,706ft), **Saddle Fell** (1,575ft) and **Wolf Fell**. Park just below Fell Foot and take the well-beaten path.

Tourist Information

Clitheroe: 12–14 Market Place, **t** (01200) 425 566. *Open Mon–Sat 9–5*.
Market days Tues, Thurs and Sat.

Where to Stay

Clitheroe and Around t (01200) –

The Inn at Whitewell (near Dunsop Bridge on banks of River Hodder), **t** 448 222 (*moderate*). Beautiful stone-gabled 1818 country-house hotel beside church. Flagstone floors, rugs, antique settles and sporting prints. Rooms full of antiques, some with peat fires, along corridors lined with old saddle bags and battered leather suitcases. River fishing in season for residents. Book for lunch or dinner in **restaurant**: roast loin of Bowland lamb, roast breast of Goosnargh duckling, market fish – or have posh nosh (fish and chips, bangers and chips, fish chowder) in crowded bar.

The Calf's Head, near Clitheroe off A59, **t** 441 218, *www.calfshead.co.uk* (*moderate*). Victorian stone-built country pub in quiet spot 2 miles from Clitheroe with lovely garden, non-smoking à la carte restaurant and bar meals. Eight comfortable bedrooms with views over Pendle Hill (it is a good base for walks).

Brooklyn Guest House, 32 Pimlico Road, **t** 428 268 (*cheap*). Five minutes' walk from town centre in a Victorian terrace. Homely, comfortable and warm inside.

Brooklands, 9 Pendle Road, **t** 422 797 (*cheap*). On edge of town, cluttered but appealing.

Wood End Farm, Dunsop Bridge, **t** 448 223 (*cheap*). Friendly working farm with proper furniture, on edge of delightful little village in heart of Bowland.

Eating Out

Clitheroe and Around t (01200) –

Exchange Coffee Shop, 24 Wellgate, **t** 442 270 (*cheap*). Short walk from Market Place, sacks of coffee on floor, shelves packed with tea caddies and a small café behind infused with coffee, serving ciabatta and salad.

Brown's Bistro, 10 York Street, **t** (01299) 426 928 (*cheap*). Quaint little restaurant with gingham tablecloths and wooden floor-boards. Fishcakes, tiger prawns in filo pastry, beef stroganoff, meat and potato pie. *Closed Sun, no lunch at weekends, no dinner Fri.*

Sun Inn, Talbot Road, Chipping (*cheap*). A superb old pub in attractive stone village in Forest of Bowland, some tables in cobbled yard at back. Serves pies and peas with gravy; vegetarians can have a butter potato pie with mushy peas, delicious crusty pastry.

The River Ribble flows off the Yorkshire Dales to Clitheroe and south into the Irish Sea at Preston. North of Clitheroe, **Ribblesdale** carries the famous Settle–Carlisle railway into the Pennines. South of Bowland, pastoral limestone valleys contrast with dark fells. There is no getting away from **Pendle Hill**; on its summit Quaker George Fox saw his vision of a 'great people to be gathered'. Many valley villages are lovely. From **Bolton-by-Bowland** walk down Skirden Beck to the ruined Cistercian abbey at **Sawley** and the pretty stone town of **Ribchester** with remains of its 1st-century Roman fort, *Bremetennacum veteranorum*; the **Roman Museum** (*open Mon–Fri 9–5, Sat–Sun 12–5; adm minimal*) has a good collection of excavated objects including a Roman helmet.

Clitheroe

Clitheroe is a busy little market town on the Ribble, with narrow streets and cheerful painted houses. From Bowland, you see its church steeples and Pendle Hill, then the castle ruins. Lakeland walking guru Alfred Wainwright's early adventures took place in Clitheroe with the Pendle Club, a group of ramblers from the Borough Treasurer's office in Blackburn Town Hall. 'Hence our practice to date,' he wrote to a friend, 'has been to clear off to a strange town (Clitheroe, usually), have tea, and then do a bit of groping on the back row of the local picturedrome.' The **'drome** is still there, and there is a little **museum** (***t*** *(01200) 424 635; open Feb and Nov–Dec weekends 11–4.30, Mar Sat–Wed 11–4.30, April–Oct daily 11–5; adm*) in the castle, with prints including Turner's view of the town from Edisford Bridge.

Pendle Hill

> *As we travelled we came near a very great hill, called Pendle Hill, and I was moved of the Lord to go up to the top of it; which I did with great difficulty, it was so very steep and high... and there, on the top, the Lord let me see in what places He had a great people to be gathered.*
>
> George Fox, Quaker founder, *Journal*, 1652

The summit of Pendle Hill is no neat peak, but a plateau 7 miles long. **Barley** is the most popular start for the ascent (a mile), but there is a gentler approach from the pretty village of **Downham** (also an excellent pub). From the top you can see the Lakeland Fells, Yorkshire Dales and Blackpool Tower. The village of **Newchurch** is the heart of Pendle Witch country, the home of Alice Nutter, hanged in 1612; there are Nutter family graves in the churchyard, and an oval window on the tower beneath the clock known as the 'Eye of God'. Below Barley, on Noggarth Road, stop at Noggarth Top café, an old tollhouse with just enough room for a table with two stools.

Lancaster

Early autumn is the time to visit this fortress town on the River Lune, when you can catch a Shakespeare performance in the castle. The castle, looming over the city like Kafka's castle, next to the old priory church, is a prison. Richard Owen, the Victorian anatomist who coined the word dinosaur and founded the Natural History Museum

Tourist Information

Lancaster: 29 Castle Hill, **t** 32878. *Open Mon–Sat summer 10–5, winter 10–4.*

Lancaster Literary Festival takes place in autumn. One of England's first, it has been a Lancaster fixture since 1978. Top-flight writers and poets. Contact Dukes Theatre (**t** 598 500) or Lancaster Litfest (**t** 62166, *www.litfest.org*).

Where to Stay

Lancaster t (01524) –

The Royal Kings Arms, Market Street, **t** 32451 (*expensive*). Large Victorian hotel at castle end of town, where Charles Dickens stayed twice; now rather corporate. Restaurant and bar upstairs, with Muzak.

Edenbreck House, Sunnyside Lane, **t** 32464 (*moderate*). Five minutes' walk from station in leafy area. Built 20 years ago in old style with stone walls and gables. Red velvet and dark mahogany décor. Sumptuous rooms.

The Shakespeare Hotel, 96 St Leonardgate, **t** 841 041 (*moderate*). Opposite the Grand Theatre, one of a terrace of tall Victorian townhouses. Good, clean, straightforward rooms, popular with actors.

Castle Hill, Castle Hill, 27 St Mary's Parade, **t** 849 137 (*cheap*). Small B&B opposite castle and priory church. Décor simple and modern.

Old Station House, 25 Meeting House Lane, **t** 381 060 (*cheap*). Old stationmaster's house opposite railway, now a comfortable B&B.

Eating Out

Il Bistro Morini, 26 Sun Street, **t** 846 252 (*expensive*). Small Italian restaurant with marble tables. Sicilian chef and English wife prepare upmarket nosh, strong on fish.

Etna Pizza Pasta, New Street, **t** 69551 (*moderate*). Bigger Sicilian restaurant. Lots of small tables with gingham tablecloths and pan-tiled bar feature. *Closed Mon.*

Sultan, 18 Brook Street (*cheap*). Excellent Indian restaurant in old Victorian chapel, with waiters in ethnic costume.

The Gatehouse, White Cross Industrial Estate, South Road, **t** 849 111 (*cheap*). Don't be put off by the address. A stylish, informal Mediterranean restaurant in a handsome old building by the canal.

Folly Cafe, 26 Castle Park, **t** 388 540 (*cheap*). Small café beneath contemporary photography gallery, a few steps from castle.

John of Gaunt, Market Street (*cheap*). Snug, lively drinking hole. Live music three eves a week and Sun lunchtime.

George and Dragon (*cheap*). Friendly family pub on St George's Quay serving hearty pub grub (bangers and mash, Sunday roasts). You can sit on meadow with dogs and children.

Whale Tail Vegetarian Café, 78/a Penny Street, **t** 845 133 (*cheap*). Behind courtyard, above 'green' general store, frequented by mothers in homespun jumpers. Cooked breakfasts, mid-morning snacks, cakes, coffee, herbal teas and hearty lunches.

Simply French, 27/a St George's Quay, **t** 843 199 (*cheap*). Décor haphazard and service erratic, but cheerful French food in nice location.

Entertainment

Lancaster has a lively theatrical life; amateur and professional, outdoors and in the castle.

Dukes Theatre and Cinema, Moor Lane, **t** 598 500. Converted Victorian chapel on cobbled lane. Popular classics to contemporary drama and comedy. Also arthouse cinema. Puts on 'promenade' theatre in Williamson Park – from Shakespeare to Grimms' Tales. *Shows July–early Aug Mon–Sat 7.15pm.*

The Grand Theatre, St Leonardsgate, **t** 64695. Handsome theatre with amateur dramatics in beautiful Edwardian auditorium. *Theatre tours July–Aug Sat 11am and 2pm.*

Shakespeare in Lancaster Castle, **t** 64998. Atmospheric, it will be the highlight of your stay. Also medieval music, Christmas poetry readings and other events in castle year-round. *Shakespeare Oct Mon–Sat.*

St John's Church, Chapel Street. Lunchtime concerts. *May–Sept, alternate Thurs, 12.45pm.*

The Gregson Arts Centre, 33 Moorgate, **t** 849 959, *www.gregson.co.uk*. Live jazz and blues at weekends, rough-and-ready bar.

Lancaster University, **t** 0800 028 3042. Classical music concerts in Great Hall. International artists, orchestra, chamber and solo. *Mid-Oct–mid-Mar Thurs eve.*

in London, first conducted post-mortems in the prison infirmary, but like many Lancastrians his fortune was linked to slavery. His father was a draper who became rich exporting woollen cloth to the West Indies at the height of the Atlantic slave trade. The cabinet-making firm founded by Robert Gillow in 1728 made use of Caribbean mahogany also imported on slave ships. The riches coming down the Lune Navigation into St George's Quay paid for a new town hall, customs house and the town's grand private houses – such as the Owens' house off Dalton Square.

Lancaster Castle and Priory Church of St Mary

Dominating the town, **Lancaster Castle** (*t (01524) 64998; tours daily 10.30–4; adm*) is now one of Her Majesty's training prisons with 240 low-security inmates learning welding or painting and decorating. A Roman fort stood on this site above the Lune, a good defensive position for the harbour. Shakespeare's 'time honoured' John of Gaunt, who fathered a line of kings starting with Henry IV, is honoured by a statue outside the castle. The medieval castle plays a part in Gaunt's story, as dramatized in Shakespeare's *Richard II*. After the death of Gaunt, the most powerful baron in England, Richard II seized his Lancashire estates. Gaunt's rightful heir, exiled son Bolingbroke, returned to England with an army, killed Richard and crowned himself Henry IV. From then on the Duchy of Lancaster was in royal hands. The castle walls, county courts and cells were built at the end of the 18th century. Until 1835 it was

the only criminal court in old Lancashire, handing out more death sentences than any other in Britain; Lancaster became known as the hanging town. Famous cases included the Pendle Witches in 1612, Quaker George Fox, and the Birmingham Six in the 1970s (suspected IRA terrorists whose convictions were later quashed). The main court moved to Preston in 1975, but jurors still convene for lesser trials in the old Drop Room, from where condemned prisoners stepped out onto the scaffold. To the left of the visitors' entrance you can see the hanging corner. Crowds of up to 7,000 gathered to watch the hangings, the dramatic finale to trials staged in the round in the Crown Court with its dark wooden stalls and red velvet seats.

Down the cobbled road stands the **priory church of St Mary** (*t (01524) 65338; open 10–4.30*), founded for the Benedictines in 1094 by Roger Pitou, who acquired vast estates in the Northwest after the Norman Conquest. Look at the elaborate choir stalls carved with monsters' heads and foliage, and take in the views down the estuary over a dreary wilderness of warehouses and estates to Morecambe Bay.

Judges' Lodgings

Below the castle and priory church are the classically proportioned Judges' Lodgings, in an early 17th-century building occupied from the start by influential men like Thomas Covell (1561–1639), six times mayor and justice of the peace. It became the residence of visiting judges to the Assize Courts in the 19th century. Now it's a **museum** (*t (01524) 32808; open Easter–June and Oct Mon–Fri 1–4, weekends 12–4; July–Sept Mon–Fri 10–4, weekends 12–4; adm*), with a display of Gillow furniture; cabinet-makers to Queen Victoria, three generations of Gillows furnished Westminster Palace as well as many of the great Cunard Liners.

Around Town

From Castle Hill, Market Street heads down into town. Have a look up Meeting House Lane. On the corner is the neo-Gothic **Storey Institute**. Thomas Storey turned his father's oil-cloth company into a small business empire, and ran against rival lino king Lord Ashton as Lancaster MP. His gifted the town a free library, gallery and school of art, technology and science. Further up the lane is the **Friends Meeting House**, built in 1708 on the site of a 1677 building (*call* ***t*** *(01524) 62971 for tours*), a plain building with black-rimmed windows. In its porch you can see the tomb of John Lawson, the first Lancastrian Quaker, converted by founder George Fox in 1652. Fox preached several times in Lancaster and was imprisoned in the castle in 1660 and 1664.

Down town, you can find out about Lancaster in the **City Museum** (***t*** *(01524) 64637; open Mon–Sat 10–5*) in the old Town Hall (1781–3) on the Market Place. Its handsome main room is enlivened by historical tableaux for children. Exhibits include a group of Roman heads representing the four seasons and portraits by James Lonsdale and George Romney. East of Market Place is **Dalton Square**, inhabited by council departments thanks to the city's main benefactor, Lord Ashton, the Lancaster lino king who turned his father's oil-cloth business into the city's biggest employer in the 1850s. He gifted the city the **new Town Hall** (1909–16) on one side of the square, its neo-classical portico facing a bronze **statue of Queen Victoria** (1907, by Sir Herbert Hampton), another of Ashton's gifts; around its base is a frieze in raised relief of the great and the good of the Victorian world – about 35 men including Prince Albert, Disraeli, the patron's father, and just two women, George Eliot and Florence Nightingale.

New Street is lovely with its old shop fronts and hanging signs. Carry on down China Street to **St George's Quay**, stopping off at Atkinson's Coffee Shop (***t*** *(01524) 65470*) for a special blend of Lancaster Tea. The Quay was built on the Lune in the 1750s; it was Britain's fourth largest port until trade shifted to Glasson Docks at the estuary mouth. Now it's a lonely place, with the old Customs House, built in 1764 by Richard Gillow, elder son of Robert. It houses a **Maritime Museum** (***t*** *(01524) 382 264; open April–Oct 11–5, Nov–Mar 12.30–4; adm minimal*) about the port, trade and fishing.

The **Ashton Memorial**, Lord Ashton's memorial to his second wife Jessy (who died in 1904), is an elaborate folly of columns and domes rising 220ft from its hilltop above the city. Pevsner called it 'the grandest monument in England'.

Morecambe Bay

Four rivers – the Leven, Kent, Lune and Wyre – flow into Morecambe Bay. At low tide, it is possible to hop over the sea wall at Arnside on the Lancashire shore of the Kent estuary and stroll across the wet sand to Grange-over-Sands, continuing over the Leven Sands to Ulverston in Cumbria. This Morecambe Sands crossing is the ancient route into southern Lakeland; an official guide is appointed by the Duchy of Lancaster to this day. Wordsworth, in his *Guide to the Lakes*, recommends visitors approach the Lake District in this way (*see* pp.752–83). **Silverdale** and **Arnside** developed into genteel holiday resorts in the poet's time, with sea bathing and walks. The railway

Tourist Information

Morecambe: Old Station Buildings, Marine Road Central, **t** (01524) 582 808. Runs **Art Deco Walking Tours** over Easter, May Bank Holidays and June–Oct on last Sat of month.

Morecambe Summer Festival takes place June–Oct weekends; events include world music, street theatre, comedy and fireworks.

Where to Stay

Morecambe t (01524) –

Unless the **Midland Hotel** is revamped (plans to save this modernist classic have been abandoned due to the cost of removing asbestos), there is nowhere of note to stay in Morecambe. Ask at the tourist information centre for a list of B&Bs.

Eating Out

Brucciani's Ice Cream Parlour, 217 Marine Road, **t** 421 386 (*cheap*). Original 1930s interior with wooden panelling and alcoves, engraved mirrors and frosted glass. Specialities are rum coffee and knickerbocker glory (ice cream, fruit and umbrella).

Harts Restaurant, 271 Marine Road, **t** 410 307 (*cheap*). Cheap-and-cheerful first-floor restaurant, with traces of plusher era: wooden panelling, big windows, piano music and uniformed staff. Serves steak and kidney pie, chips, peas and gravy.

boosted their popularity, along with that of Morecambe, which became the resort of West Yorkshire factory workers. The coast north of the Lune is fascinating: acres of salt marshes around Sunderland Point; rock-cut Saxon graves on Heysham Cliffs; and even Morecambe turns out to be a treasure-house of art deco architecture.

Morecambe

The seaside resort of Morecambe is 6 miles west of Lancaster past interminable roundabouts and derelict buildings. The resort that invented the Helter-skelter and sent Eric Morecambe and Thora Hurd into the world is in trouble. Two things stand between Morecambe and meltdown: the Lakeland views and preservation orders. Head for the Promenade, join an art deco walk, enjoy a trademark Knickerbocker Glory at Brucciani's Ice Cream Parlour, and you'll be ready for Morecambe's art nouveau façades with stained glass windows and decorative ironwork. Most prominent are the palatial red-brick **Winter Gardens** (*closed to the public*), all minarets and terracotta roundels, and the crenellated **Promenade Railway Station** with its decorative carving and tiles in the foyer. The **Royalty Theatre** is remembered for launching the career of Thora Hurd. The opening of the art deco **Midland Hotel** on the seafront on 12 July 1933 – as elegant as an ocean liner against the Victorian brick and bay windows – brought an international edge to the town. London, Midland and Scottish (LMS) Railways commissioned architect Oliver Hill and the top decorative artists of the day to work on it (at vast expense): Eric Gill designed the two seahorses, Eric Ravilious the mural in the café, Marion Dorn the rugs, and Duncan Grant the curtains and fabrics. Some feared that such a modern building would scare off the resort's traditional clientele, but people came especially to stay in the Midland. It spawned striking modern buildings on the Promenade, including Woolworths and Littlewoods stores, Brucciani's and Harts Crescent Café. Now it stands sadly close to derelicition. Once you've read the catch-phrases inscribed in concentric circles around the statue of Eric Morecambe ('Tell Peter Cushin the cheque's in the post') you've done Morecambe.

South of Morecambe

South of Morecambe in the sprawl is **Old Heysham**, the pretty, old core of the town around the harbour. Head to **St Peter's Church**, among trees on the edge of the bay, its churchyard sloping down to the beach. Inside is a hog's back stone carved with Viking figures, animals and patterns. Carry on up the steps to the ruins of **St Patrick's Chapel**, a single-cell Saxon chapel, and next to it six graves cut into the solid rock, each with a socket that once held a wooden cross. They date back to the 8th or 9th century.

From Heysham to **Sunderland Point** on the west of the Lune the scenery is flat and empty, dominated by a power station. At low tide beyond **Overton** a muddy causeway crosses the salt marsh to the point (at high tide skirt round). At the end of the road you come to a muddy shingle beach. In the 18th century this was a commercial harbour engaged in the West Indian slave trade. All that remains is a Georgian pillar and the grave of Sambo, a black slave boy abandoned by his shipping master.

North of Lancaster

North of Lancaster, a gentle peninsula of hills, woodland and salt marshes extends to the mouth of the Kent estuary. Victorian novelist Elizabeth Gaskell spent a summer with her daughters in the remote, marsh-fringed village of **Silverdale**, which she fictionalized as Abermouth in *Ruth*. It's an excellent base for walking in the silver birch woods. Walk down the road past Lindeth Tower (where Mrs Gaskell stayed in 1850) to Jenny Brown Point on the shore. You can also walk north to **Arnside**, a quiet Victorian resort beneath Arnside Knott. It is best known as the start of the Morecambe Sands walk, across shifting sands into Cumbria – only to be attempted with the Queen's Official Guide (*Cedric Robinson,* ***t*** *(01539) 532 165; guided walks Sat mornings*).

In 1822 Lancaster cabinet-maker Richard Gillow bought **Leighton Hall** (***t*** *(01524) 734 474; open May–Sept Tues–Fri and Sun 2–5, Aug 12.30–5; adm*), tucked away in the hills behind Silverdale. His descendants still live in the house with the slim Gothic towers and crenellations that he tacked on, and let you sit on the Gillow chairs.

Cumbria and the Lake District

18

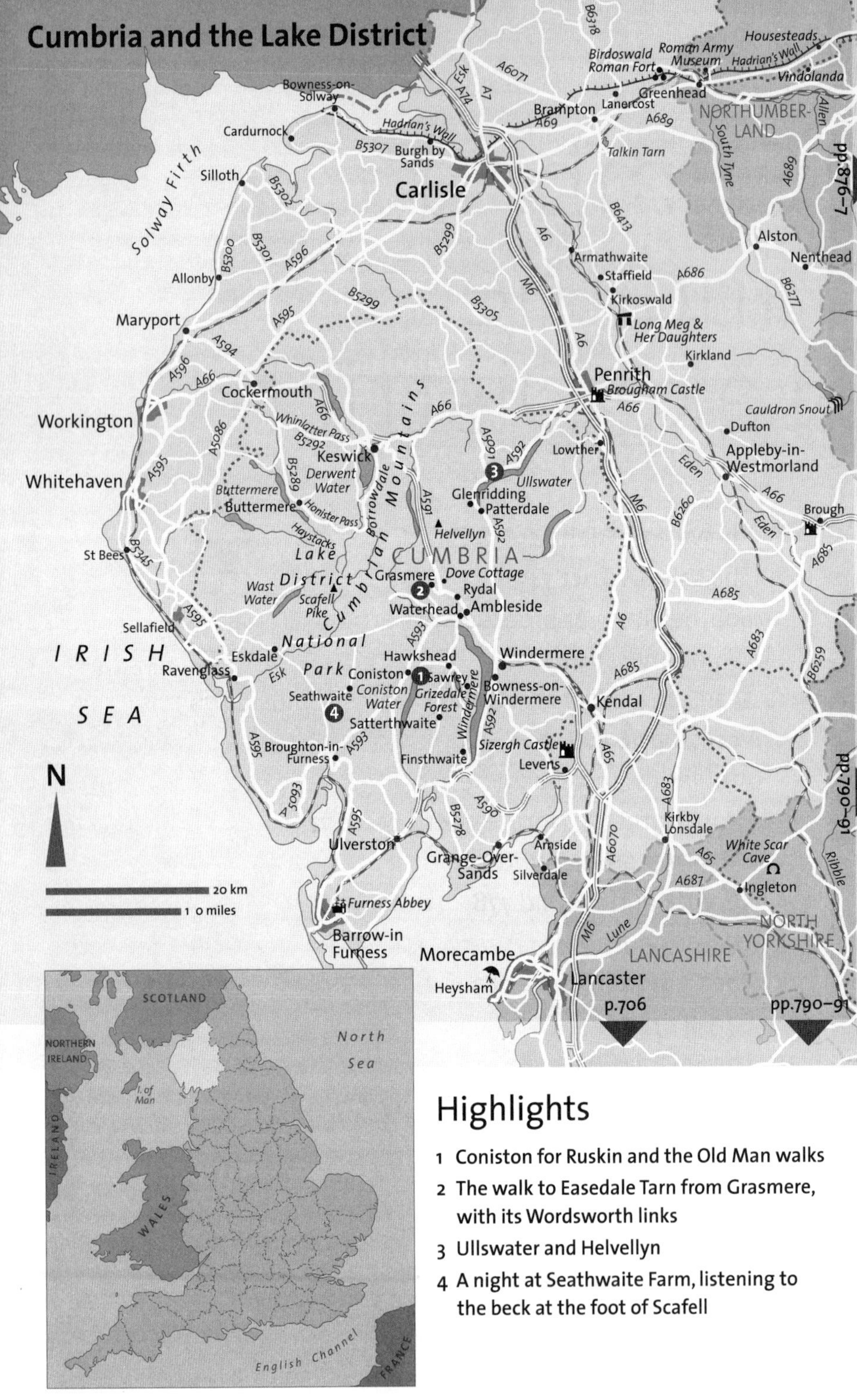

Highlights

1 Coniston for Ruskin and the Old Man walks
2 The walk to Easedale Tarn from Grasmere, with its Wordsworth links
3 Ullswater and Helvellyn
4 A night at Seathwaite Farm, listening to the beck at the foot of Scafell

The Lake District is at the heart of modern Cumbria, carved out of the historic northwestern counties of Cumberland, Westmorland and the Furness region of Lancashire in 1974 (the first county border changes since Domesday). Here, ancient rocks gouged out by Ice Age glaciers have created England's own mini-Alps. The mountain and lake scenery that inspired the Romantic poets and continues to inspire countless romantic spirits rises to Scafell Pike, the highest peak in England; the Lakes radiate out from the hub of Scafell like the spokes of a wheel, as Lakeland poet William Wordsworth famously put it.

While the 900 square miles of the Lake District National Park are one of England's most visited regions, the Lakes have not always appealed to outsiders. The Romans built vertiginous pass roads High Street and Hardknott Pass to bypass them, and the Normans stopped at the peripheral market towns of Kendal and Cockermouth, building castles in the Vale of Eden to guard the strategic north–south route. Only the Celts and Vikings bothered with the mountains. Many of the words describing the region's topography come from Old Norse: tarn (mountain lake), dale (valley), fell (hill), gill (cleft or ravine), ness (promontory), force (waterfall) and beck (stream). The Herdwick sheep came with the Norse settlers in the 10th century too, creating the close-cropped look of Lakeland that, along with the dry-stone walls, quaint villages and of course the lakes, inspired the 18th-century craze for picturesque tourism.

At the north of the county is the hard-won Scottish border. A string of Roman forts – Ravenglass, Maryport and Bowness-on-Solway – runs around the Cumbrian coast to Carlisle, linking up with the great northern frontier of Hadrian's Wall. The Roman wall cuts across from Bowness-on-Solway to Birdoswald, and through Northumbria to the east coast. The fortress city of Carlisle was long at the centre of a war zone between the kings of Scotland and England, frequently changing hands as the border was won and lost (the Scottish border at times extended as far south as the Mersey).

If you are visiting Cumbria for the first time head straight for Lakeland, heading on to Ravenglass and St Bees on the coast. Carlisle is the best base for Hadrian's Wall and the Solway Coast. You can return south via the delightful villages of the Vale of Eden, from where there are fabulous walks up the Pennine escarpment.

The Vale of Eden

At the east of Cumbria the **River Eden**, running north to the Solway Firth, forms a lush green corridor of fields and pretty market towns and villages. It has always been the main north–south route, guarded by Norman castles at **Pendragon**, **Appleby-in-Westmorland**, **Brougham** (*see* p.775) and **Brough**. The dramatic eastern valley side is the scarp (steep) slope of the **Pennines** – not a single cliff face but a series of crags and pikes, which have been carved out by streams flowing down to the Eden, creating monster feet sticking into the vale. Every so often the powerful helm wind rushes down off the Pennines into the scarp-foot villages, which turn their backs on the ridge with small windows to keep the wind out. The loveliest section of the Vale of Eden is between Appleby and Armathwaite. Base yourself at Penrith or Appleby and

Getting There and Around

Appleby is halfway along the 72-mile scenic route of the **Settle–Carlisle Railway**. You can go south towards Settle through the Yorkshire Dales (*see* p.800), or north through the Vale of Eden, 31 miles to Carlisle. A 'Freedom of the Settle–Carlisle Line' ticket gives you three days of unlimited travel; there are seven or eight trains a day, fewer on Sundays.

For information call **National Rail Enquiries**, **t** 08457 484950, *www.thetrainline.com*.

Tourist Information

Appleby: The Moot Hall, Boroughgate, **t** (017683) 51177, *www.applebytown.org.uk*. *Open summer Mon–Sat 9.30–5, Sun 12–4, winter Mon–Thurs 10–12, Fri–Sat 10–3.*

Appleby Horse Fair takes place for a week in June on Fair Hill, just north of town. The gypsy horse-trading often spills down into town.

Alston: Town Hall, Front Street, Alston, *www.visiteden.co.uk*

Where to Stay and Eat

Appleby t (017683) –

Wemyss House, 48 Boroughgate, **t** 51494, *nickhirst@aol.com* (*expensive*). Handsome stone house with pretty yellow front door and garden behind railings; three bedrooms.

Tufton Arms Hotel, Market Place, **t** 51593 (*expensive*). Old-world country inn with rich Victorian-style furnishings. Friendly and civilized; 21 rooms; conservatory restaurant.

Courtfield Hotel, Bongate, **t** 51394 (*moderate*). Former Georgian vicarage set in 3 acres of lawned gardens. Friendly and pretty inside with wide corridors and creaky stairs, patterned carpets and attractively painted walls; 11 simple rooms. Restaurant serves beef and Yorkshire pudding, or trout.

Bongate House, Bongate, **t** 51245, *mdayson@aol.com* (*moderate*). Georgian farmhouse with eight rooms on top floor; slightly jaded, but friendly. Pretty garden at back, with box hedges and gravel, lawns and paddock.

Old Hall Farmhouse, Bongate, **t** 51773, *www.oldhallfarmhouse.co.uk* (*moderate*). Delightful long-house farm, modernized inside with three bedrooms, sash windows and window seats. Open fire and panelling in breakfast room, and a cosy lounge.

Hoagies Bistro, just off Boroughgate, **t** 52368 (*moderate*). Fish, meat and poultry.

The Royal Oak Inn, Bongate, **t** 51463, *royaloakinn@mortalmaninns.fastnet.co.uk* (*moderate*). Old-fashioned country inn in a low, whitewashed stone building. Cosy wood-panelled bar with comfy chairs around a fire. Restaurant-style presentation of dishes such as baked salmon and red cabbage, and excellent service. Nine bedrooms including garden rooms with French windows.

Lady Anne's Pantry, Bridge Street, **t** 53550 (*cheap*). Tea and cakes. Upstairs good hearty home-cooked food in restaurant.

The Bread Shop, Market Square (*cheap*). Good deli for walkers' sandwiches.

Brough t (017683) –

Augill Castle, Brough, **t** 41937, *augill@aol.com* (*expensive*). Picture-book Victorian castle with views towards the Pennines and Cumbrian fells. Period furniture, walk-in wardrobes in the turrets, home-made biscuits and freshly ground coffee in the rooms; excellent food served in sumptuous dining room on Fri and Sat (*moderate*).

Up the Vale of Eden t (01768) –

Fox and Pheasant, Armathwaite (through village and over Eden Bridge, then a few hundred yards and you can't miss it), **t** 898 435 (*moderate*). Small friendly bar with flagstone floor. Pub grub (bangers and mash) and excellent restaurant (lots of fish). Book at weekends, but they can usually squeeze you into the bar.

Crown Inn, Kirkoswald, **t** 898 435 (*cheap*). Best of two pubs on tiny market square, real ales including Cumberland and a guest ale. *Closed Wed lunch.*

The Village Bakery Restaurant, Melmerby (on A686 between Penrith and Alston), **t** 881 811 (*cheap*). Bakery shop and restaurant established in 1976, where you can buy organic bread and cakes to take away, or sit down for breakfast, coffee, light snacks or home-cooked lunch.

explore the country lanes, stopping off at castles and villages along the way. The best walks start in villages like **Dufton** and **Kirkland**, tracing streams up onto the Pennine ridge, from where you get views back towards the Lakeland fells. Or drive up **Hartside Pass** and onto the ridge, continuing to the tiny, upland market town of Alston.

North of the A686 the rolling valley floor looks like parkland and the lanes dip and weave. Near Little Salkeld is a prehistoric stone circle known as **Long Meg and Her Daughters**. Further north, **Kirkoswald** and **Armathwaite** are both interesting little villages with good pubs. Between them, near **Staffield**, are the **Nunnery Walks**, a series of paths created in the 18th century following the Croglin Beck down to the Eden where it flows through a dramatic limestone gorge. The walks are named after the nuns of the Benedictine priory that once owned this section of the riverside. Wordsworth once stopped here and wrote Sonnet XLI of his 1833 *Itinerary Poems*:

The floods are roused and will not soon be weary
Down from the Pennine Alps how fiercely sweeps
Croglin, the stately Eden's tributary.

Appleby-in-Westmorland

Try to catch Appleby early in the morning. This Norman planned town in a defensive loop of the Eden was once the county town of Westmorland. It still has a famous horse fair in June, when gypsy travellers come in jeeps and caravans to buy and sell horses, washing them in the river. The main street, **Boroughgate**, leads uphill from the church to the castle. At the bottom, around the market place, are old-fashioned shops selling meat and vegetables, and some large 18th-century buildings. **St Lawrence's Church** is set back behind the arcades of the old **Buttermarket**; the tomb of Lady Anne Clifford, 'the great lady of Westmoreland', is in the church's north aisle. The 3rd Countess of Dorset, her family came to the area in the 14th century. While married to Richard Sackville, Duke of Dorset, she was wrongly deprived of the Clifford estates, but when he died she inherited the lot and transformed herself into a feudal-style magnate, processing regally between her castles, endowing hospitals and churches, dressing roughly and smoking a pipe. She died aged 85, almost 40 years after her husband. The poet Thomas Gray, on visiting her tomb in 1761, wrote an epitaph:

Now clean, now hideous, mellow now, now gruff,
She swept, she Hiss'd, she ripen'd, and grew rough
At Brougham, Pedragon, Appleby, and Brough.

Further up, Boroughgate is lined with pretty cottages with little cottage gardens and rambling roses around the doors. An avenue continues through the iron gates of the castle, while the road carries on around the wall. It makes a nice walk down to the Eden, across the footbridge and back down Bongate into town. **Appleby Castle** was Lady Anne's headquarters in the 17th century. The great lady used to travel between her four Vale of Eden castles with her own mobile court like a medieval monarch. She restored and extended the old castle, and her grandson, the Earl of Thanet, added the east range, turning the 11th-century castle into a palatial family house, which it remains. Lady Anne Clifford also restored the church, and built the almshouses on Boroughgate (knock at no. 8 to be let into the chapel).

Vale of Eden Walks

One of the best Eden Vale walks is up **High Cup Nick** (7–8 miles). From Appleby follow signs to Dufton, where the Pennine Way heads east along High Cupgill Beck between Dufton Pike (1,543ft) and Murton Pike (1,949ft), up the horseshoe-shaped valley known as High Cup Nick. The Stag Inn in Dufton serves hearty lunches and there's a deli in Appleby where you can get sandwiches.

Another challenging walks is up **Cross Fell** (10 miles), best approached from Kirkland (8 miles north of Appleby along narrow lanes). From the summit there are panoramic views of Lakeland fells Skiddaw and Helvellyn, and east towards Alston.

Over the Hartside Pass to Alston

From Penrith (*see* p.775), the A686 heads northeast over the River Eden up to **Hartside Height** (1,904ft) on the scarp, where the Hartside Café (which claims to be the highest café in England) has a fabulous view. From there, the dramatic pass road to Alston is popular with cyclists and bikers in red leather. High up in the Pennines, the old-fashioned market town of **Alston** grew up at the junction of major trans-Pennine roads and the three counties of Cumbria, Northumbria and Yorkshire. Its market place is said to be the highest in England. In the 19th century Alston became a centre for the distribution of lead from the Nenthead mines by road or rail. With its steep cobbled streets, it was the perfect set for a recent TV dramatisation of *Oliver Twist*. You can visit the mines and take a short steam train ride to Kirkhaugh. For something to eat, try the quaint Blueberries tea shop on the market square, or the Angel Pub.

Following the River Nent east of Alston to its source on Alston Moor, you come to the purpose-built Quaker mining village of **Nenthead**, the highest inhabited village in England. With its bleak rows of pebble-dash and stone buildings, it is an early prototype of the 19th-century model villages of Port Sunlight, Bournville and Saltaire; in its heyday it had a market hall, school and one of the first free libraries. Above the village in the Upper Nent Valley are the old Nenthead **lead mines** (***t*** *(01434) 382 037; open Easter–Oct daily 10.30–5; adm*). An exhibition tells you about the site and village, while tours take you 55 feet down a horizontal drift-mine. A leaflet guides you around the crumbling old mine buildings, spoil heaps and sectioned-off mine shafts.

The Lake District

I am not afraid of asserting that in many points of view our lakes are much more interesting than those of the Alps.

Guide to the Lakes, William Wordsworth

The term Lake District was not coined until the late 18th century, when the Romantic cult of the picturesque brought a new interest in scenery to this rugged corner of Cumbria. The area became a fashionable tourist centre from the 1750s on,

Getting There

By Air

Manchester International Airport, **t** (0161) 489 3000, *www.manairport.co.uk*, has a busy domestic and international flight schedule.

By Car

The M6 runs from Manchester to Carlisle, along the east side of the Lake District, branching off at Kendal to Windermere and Ambleside on the A591, and at Penrith to Keswick and Cockermouth on the A66.

By Train

Virgin trains, **t** 0845 722 2333, run to Oxenholme, from where you can connect for Windermere and Kendal (20 minutes). From Manchester Airport and Lancaster trains run to Barrow, from where the Cumbrian Coast Line continues to Whitehaven, Workington and Carlisle. There is a direct link to Carlisle and Whitehaven from Newcastle. For all train information, contact **National Rail Enquiries**, **t** 08457 484950, *www.thetrainline.com*.

By Coach

Coaches run from London to Kendal, Windermere, Ambleside and Keswick in about 7½ hours. There are also services via Milton Keynes, Birmingham, Wigan, Preston, Lancaster and Morecambe. For all National Express coach information contact **t** 08705 808080, *www.gobycoach.com*.

Getting Around

For public transport information call **Traveline**, **t** 0870 608 2608.

A one-day **Explorer** ticket (buy on the bus), gives you unlimited travel on Stagecoach buses around Cumbria; a four-day Explorer is also available (buy in advance from tourist information centres).

Lakeland Safari Tours, 23 Fisherbeck Park, Ambleside, **t** (015394) 33904, *www.lake-safari.co.uk*. Tours from Windermere, Bowness, Ambleside and Grasmere. The Photo Romance takes you to 'seek the beauty spots that inspired the literary giants in central lakeland'.

Tourist Information

In July, August and September almost every valley has its sports and/or agricultural show, in which prize bulls and sheep compete for rosettes, and traditional Lakeland sports and skills are shown off: hound-trailing, fell-running, drystone walling, Cumberland–Westmorland wrestling, shepherd's crook-making. Local tourist information centres can give you all the details.

publicized by landscape paintings, prints and coffee-table books, early guidebooks and the raptures of the Lakeland poets – all of which illuminated the sublime beauty of what had been just a poor farming area with a few mines. Writers from Wordsworth to Beatrix Potter have enshrined the mountains and lakes of the region in our collective imagination. They have also helped to give nature its value as a commodity. Today you will find the Lake District overrun with walkers and literary pilgrims, but you can still find tranquil corners of this 'sweetest scene' (Thomas Gray).

The Lake District National Park was created in 1951 to protect the Cumbrian Mountains, almost 900 square miles of England's most dramatic and beautiful uplands. The scenery is the product of four Ice Ages which left glaciers that deepened and widened the valleys until they melted to leave the lakes. For the last thousand years, sheep have been the main landscape designers, roaming freely on unfenced fells – to the extent that recent outbreaks of foot and mouth disease threatened to wipe out not only the sheep but the picture-postcard Lakeland views; without them the fells would revert to scrub. The ten lake valleys radiate from the hub of Scafell, the highest peak in England, like a wheel – in Wordsworth's famous analogy.

Lakeland Highlights

- Ascent of Scafell Pike (3,210ft), the highest peak in England, from Seathwaite. In his *Pictoral Guides* Wainwright paid Scafell the ultimate compliment of a double-page drawing.
- Ascent of Bowfell from Dungeon Ghyll.
- Ascent of Harter Fell from Boot in Eskdale.
- High-level walk known as the Coniston Round.
- Profile of the Langdale Pikes and the steep climb up Harrison Stickle (the highest of the pikes) via Stickle Tarn.
- Exploring Loughrigg Fell from Ambleside or Rydal on a sunny day.
- Helvellyn from Striding Edge – the most nerve-wracking of the Lakeland fells.
- Up Haystacks from Buttermere, one of Wainwright's favourites and where his ashes are sprinkled.
- The valleys: you'll not find any more beautiful than the Duddon Valley, Eskdale and Borrowdale.
- The lakes: the most enchanting are Ullswater, Buttermere, Derwent Water, Wasdale and Grasmere.
- For gentler scenery, explore the low, green hills and woods of southern Lakeland, particularly west of Windermere.
- The walk across Morecambe Sands is legendary (*see* p.765).
- If you have a week in Lakeland, you could follow Wainwright's proposed walkers' itinerary – Fairfield Horseshoe, Coniston Fells (ridge walk, Wetherlam to Old Man), Bowfell and the Crinkle Crags, Harrison Stickle, Sergeant Man and the Silver How Ridge, the Easedale Fells (circuit of Far Easedale) and Hellvellyn; and separate ascents of Red Screes and Wansfell Pike (which 'can't possibly be omitted').

The Discovery (or Invention) of the Lake District

Until the mid-18th century the lakes and mountains of Cumberland, Westmorland and Lancashire were a place to avoid – dark, forbidding and dangerous. Even **Daniel Defoe**, travelling in the 1720s, saw the region as 'barren and wild, of no use or advantage either to man or beast'. But just one generation later, a new fashion emerged for seeing the landscape as a picture. **William Beller**'s *Six Select Views of the North of England*, published in 1752 for one guinea, included the first published images of Windermere, Derwent Water and Ullswater. **Thomas Smith of Derby** and **Joseph Farington** were quick to cash in on the new trend with their own Lakeland view prints and books. Cumberland-born **Reverend William Gilpin** (1724–1804), formalized the whole thing with his two-volume *Observations, relative chiefly to picturesque beauty made in the year 1772... particularly the mountains and lakes of Cumberland and Westmorland*. He not only coined the word picturesque for landscape, but came up with a ready-made descriptive language – sublime, horrid, precipitous, grand and so on. **Thomas West** (1717–79), a Catholic priest from Furness, took it a stage further in his *Guide to the Lakes of Cumberland, Westmorland and Lancashire* (first published in 1778 and reissued seven times before 1800): he told tourists what route to take and even what places, or 'stations', to stop at and see the best view. He also advised using a

Claude glass (named after the French painter), a convex mirror which framed the scene; ironically it required the viewer to turn his back on the real thing. However this did not stop the traveller and poet **Thomas Gray** (1716–71) from adopting the device. He wrote of the view of Derwent Water: 'I saw in my glass a picture, that if I could transmit it to you, and fix it in all the softness of its living colours, would fairly sell for a thousand pounds,' signalling the onslaught of nature's commodification. Retired naval officer Peter Crosthwaite opened a museum and shop in Keswick soon after, selling West's guide, Claude glasses and local maps; he recorded 1,540 visitors in 1793.

More and more, however, the view was being ruined by other tourists looking at the same view from a different angle on the other side of the lake. Then along came William Wordsworth (1770–1850) with his sister Dorothy to break down the picture-frame in his passionate brand of poetry. In November 1799 they moved back to the area where he had grown up (he was 29 years old) spending one night in Hawkshead, then settling permanently in Grasmere. They were closely followed by an influential group of poets including Coleridge, Southey and De Quincey. Soon the literary pilgrims were pouring in too, on trains to Ambleside, Kendal and Windermere.

The Lake Poets

By such accidents of personal or family connection as I have mentioned, was the Lake colony gathered; and the critics of the day, unaware of the real facts, supposed them to have assembled under common views in literature – particularly with regard to the true functions of poetry, and the true theory of poetic diction.

Thomas De Quincey

The true Lake poets were **William Wordsworth**, **Samuel Taylor Coleridge** and **Robert Southey**, although **Thomas De Quincey** gets his name on the list too for following his heroes to the Lakes – he just never wrote any poems. Southey and Coleridge were university friends, hatching idealistic plans together and writing radical pamphlets. They married sisters and lived in the West Country, where coincidentally Wordsworth was living at the time too. Coleridge wangled an introduction to his hero Wordsworth and they became bosom friends, co-writing *Lyrical Ballads*, which (as it turned out) changed the face of poetry. They expressed Wordsworth's yearning for the lost Eden of pre-industrial Britain and his loathing for the 'cities where the human heart is sick'. De Quincey called the *Ballads* 'the greatest event in the unfolding of my own mind' and, while an undergraduate at Oxford, wrote Wordsworth a fan letter which ended 'you will never find any one more zealously attached to you – more full of admiration for your mental excellence and of reverential love for your moral character – more ready to sacrifice even his life – when ever it could have a chance of promoting your interest and happiness.' Wordsworth had by then moved back to the Lake District and was living in Grasmere with his sister, Dorothy. Coleridge had followed his new best friend, and was living in Keswick with Southey, who had come at his invitation. Southey and Wordsworth had little in common and didn't much care for each other, although gradually, through familiarity, they warmed. Wordsworth married Mary Hutchinson, from Penrith, who joined him and Dorothy in Dove Cottage, bringing

Alfred Wainwright and his *Seven Pictoral Guides to the Lakeland Fells*

Alfred Wainwright's *Seven Pictoral Guides to the Lakeland Fells* are the classic walking guides to the Lake District. Each book was hand-written and illustrated in pen and ink with monkish devotion by the author, including 214 fells, with various routes up and down and over the ridges between them – all done on foot and public transport. The first editions are worth a small fortune. To 'fellwanderers' in Lakeland, the man – who died on 20 January 1991 at 84 – was a god. His ashes were scattered beside Innominate Tarn on Haystacks and a commemorative window and tablet installed in Buttermere church. Wainwright was born and bred in Blackburn, down the road in Lancashire, and became a municipal accountant. At the age of 23, he made the first of many visits to Lakeland with his cousin Eric. It was a life-changing experience. He wrote in *Ex-Fellwanderer* of his first impressions at Orrest Head: 'It was a moment of magic, a revelation so unexpected that I stood transfixed, unable to believe my eyes. I saw mountain ranges, one after another, the nearer starkly etched, those beyond fading into the blue distance... God was in his heaven that day and I was a humble worshipper.' Wainwright's marriage to Ruth Holden, a Blackburn cotton weaver, in 1931, was a failure. His escape and obsession was walking. In 1938 he walked the length of the Pennines and wrote his first book about it, *Pennine Campaign* (although it was not published until 1986). He moved to Kendal as an accounting assistant in 1941, writing: 'Kendal is delightful. So is life in Kendal. So is work in Kendal.' He ran Kendal Museum and was promoted to borough treasurer in August 1948, aged 41. He spent all his free time walking the fells, and between 1952 and 1966 wrote the *Seven Pictoral Guides*: *The Eastern Fells*; *The Far Eastern Fells*; *Central Fells* (including the Langdale Pikes); *Southern Fells* (including Scafell Pike); *Northern Fells* (Blencathra); *North Western Fells*; and *The Western Fells*.

along her sister Sarah. Coleridge developed a crush on Sarah, and spent most of his time at Dove Cottage too. The three poets were different in almost every way (although De Quincey and Coleridge shared a similar unorthodox brilliance as well as an inferiority complex towards Wordsworth). Wordsworth read chiefly travel books and wrote while out on long walks. Coleridge was an intellectual who, according to Southey, had the greatest mind on the planet, but lacked moral strength, suffering various addictions and periods of total inactivity. In his day, Southey was as big a literary figure as Wordsworth, writing heavyweight histories of Brazil, Portugal, the Peninsular War and a biography of Nelson (he also wrote the children's story *The Three Bears*). Surprisingly, he beat Wordsworth to the job of Poet Laureate, although Wordsworth took it over after his death. Coleridge went on daring walks up mountains like Scafell and Helvellyn, which he once climbed by moonlight, Wordsworth liked gentler walks around the lower hills, while Southey managed only the odd stroll around Derwent Water with a book in his hand. For a while the Lake District was a literary power-house, centred on Keswick and Grasmere, to which a stream of eminent visitors came, including Walter Scott, William Wilberforce, Thomas Telford and William Hazlitt, as well as a stream of wannabe poets. In 1807 one of the wannabes, De Quincey, finally met Wordsworth, five years after his fan letter, and moved into Dove Cottage when the Wordsworths moved out. Wordsworth helped him get the job as editor of the *Westmorland Gazette* (published in Kendal), but he didn't last long as he filled it with poetry and philosophy instead of farm news. He eventually became famous as a periodicals writer, writing for the *London Magazine* what later became his *Confessions of an English Opium-Eater*. It turned him into an instant literary sensation. In 1830, having fallen out with Wordsworth, he moved to Edinburgh, writing the less-than flattering *Recollections of the Lakes and the Lake Poets* for *Tait's Magazine* after the death of Coleridge in 1834. Wordsworth refused to read it, while Southey implored Coleridge's son Hartley to go straight up to Edinburgh and beat up De Quincey.

From Wordsworth to the National Trust

In 1822, Wordsworth wrote his bestselling *Guide to the Lakes*, with 'minute directions for tourists' and the famous wheel analogy. He also set down his Lakeland bugbears: the demise of the traditional Lakeland environment and cottage industries, the intrusion of gaudy new houses, the planting of larches and the whitewashing of old stone buildings. He describes the Lakes as 'a sort of national property, in which every man has a right and interest, who has an eye to perceive and a heart to enjoy,' anticipating the National Trust by about 70 years. In 1872 **John Ruskin** moved to Coniston. A Wordsworthian, he believed mountains to be the 'link between heaven and earth', preaching in books and lectures about the moral development of working people through manual work, clean air and an appreciation of art and literature. He promoted the revival of traditional weaving skills in the **Langdale Linen Industry** and

Fell-walking

I incline to the view, never before expressed, that a rucksack is not at all necessary on a walking tour. How some hikers can enjoy themselves beneath the weight of their huge, fifty-pound burdens completely passes my comprehension...The clothes I wear when I set off must suffice: if they get wet, it is unfortunate.

Alfred Wainwright, *Pennine Campaign*

Alfred Wainwright encourages fell-walkers to go it alone in order to get the most out of the landscape. Wordsworth didn't rely on hi-tech gear to get him up the fells either. All Coleridge took with him on his long, solo walking expeditions was a spare pair of socks, a flask of tea and plenty of paper and pens. Fell-walking is the best way to get close to the scenery, but it need not be a complicated business.

On the other hand, it is worth going prepared. Wear stout walking boots or shoes, take a waterproof and fleece or jumper and some food, and be prepared for rapid changes in the weather at any time of year (check the forecast before you set out).

There are countless walking guides on sale, none of which really compares with Wainwright's, and tourist information centres are piled high with walks leaflets. For serious walkers the Ordnance Survey maps are your best guide, either the 1:50,000 Landranger series, or the 1:25,000 Outdoor Leisure series. A good general map of the area is the OS inch-to-the-mile Touring Map and Guide 3.

furniture making in the **Coniston Institute**. Inspired by Ruskin, **Canon Hardwicke Rawnsley**, the vicar of Crosthwaite, set up the **Keswick School of Industrial Arts**, producing trays, vases, jugs, tea caddies and altar crosses. The inscription over the factory door reads: 'The Makers are the poets! Ply your skill! Beat rhythmic hammers! Work, harmonious will! Coleridge and Southey watch from yonder hill!' In 1895 Rawnsley co-founded 'a Land Company' called the **National Trust** to safeguard the public interest in open spaces in the Lakes. Its first success was an appeal for land after Ruskin's death around Friar's Crag on Derwent Water. **Beatrix Potter**, a dumpy woman in tweeds and clogs, with a hessian apron around her waist, vigorously supported Rawnsley's crusade to protect traditional forms of land management. She bred Herdwick sheep and won awards at Lakeland shows but is best known as the author of *Peter Rabbit*. With the royalties of 23 children's books she bought 18 farms around Hawkshead, Sawrey and Coniston which she bequeathed to the Trust.

Southeastern Approaches

Approaching from the south, you reach the Lake District at Kirkby Lonsdale and Kendal. Seven miles west of Kendal you reach Windermere, the biggest lake of them all and the first in a series of attractions including Tarn Hows, Ruskin's Brantwood, Beatrix Potter's Hill Top and the showcase village of Hawkshead with its Wordsworth and Potter associations.

Orientation

The Lake District attracts almost 20 million visitors a year. On a sunny day in high season on the popular summits you can expect to meet a group of cub scouts, five white-haired men with unusually thick calves, a spaniel, a couple in unsuitable sandals with blisters and a baby in a papoose. But don't be put off if it is the solitude of the fells you are after: even at the busiest of the busy period, you can still get away from the crowds with relative ease. Most tourists come in either from the south on the M6-A591, or from the north on the A66, and stick to the Windermere–Keswick touring route (A591), staying a night or two in the small towns and villages in the valleys – **Windermere**, **Ambleside**, **Keswick** and **Coniston** – and taking in the literary shrines and famous fells. The east side of the district is busier than the west, with most of the main roads and major tourist attractions, while the remotest part of all is the western wedge between Scafell, Eskdale and Buttermere. Wordsworth recommends this region to travellers 'who are not afraid of fatigue; no part of the country is more distinguished by sublimity'. The most dramatic and popular walking country is from Keswick to Ambleside – the southern and central fells in Alfred Wainwright's classic walking guides to the region. 'All Lakeland is exquisitely beautiful; the southern fells just happen to be a bit of heaven fallen upon the earth,' he writes. Wordsworth advises visitors to avoid the summer holiday season, and instead come in spring or autumn when the colours make everything looks fantastic; it is still the best advice. Avoid school holidays and Bank Holidays if you can.

Kirkby Lonsdale

The quiet market town of Kirkby Lonsdale sits on the gentle western side of the Lune Valley, looking across to the dramatic, brown-topped Pennines. It's a place that may inspire you to take up watercolour painting. Its quiet lanes are pleasant to wander in. **Market Street** nose-dives at a crazy, photogenic angle down to the river, past the old market cross, while the old churchyard deserves a rosette for all-round loveliness. Beyond the church, there's a nice little river walk, starting at **Ruskin's View**. (Ruskin mentioned the view to Turner, who came to this very spot, painting the wide valley in front of him, with the river looping extravagantly from one side to the other, and called his painting *Ruskin's View*.) From there, **Radical Steps** (86 of them) go down to the river, and the path continues along the bank to **Devil's Bridge**, a handsome double-arched stone bridge. Another path takes you back into the market square.

Tourist Information

Kirkby Lonsdale: 24 Main Street, **t** (015242) 71437. *Open summer Mon–Fri 9.30–5, weekends 10.30–4; winter Mon–Fri 10–3, weekends 10.30–3.*

Kendal: Town Hall, Highgate, **t** (01539) 725 758. *Open Mar–June Mon–Sat 9–5, Sun 10–4; July–Aug Mon–Sat 9–6, Sun 10–5; Sept–Dec Mon–Sat, Sun 10–4.*

K-Village Outlet Centre, Lound Road (follow signs from Kendal), **t** (01539) 721 892. A large range of shops, including K Shoes, at discount prices. *Open Mon–Fri 9.30–6, Sat 9–6, Sun 11–5.*

Festivals

Kendal Mountain Film Festival, main venue **Brewery Arts Centre**, **t** (01539) 725 133, is held every November. The festival features three days of films about mountains, with lectures and seminars and photo, painting and sculpture exhibitions. The **Penrith Rheged Centre**, **t** (01768) 860 077, half an hour's drive from Kendal, shows a programme of related Imax films. The best films of the festival are shown in March at the **Theatre by the Lake** in Keswick, **t** (017687) 74411.

Where to Stay

Kirkby Lonsdale t (015242) –

Royal Hotel, Market Place, **t** 71217, (*moderate*). Handsome stuccoed old hotel in centre of town with 23 very ordinary bedrooms, 17 of them en-suite.

Wyck House, 4 Main Street, **t** 71953, *www.studioarts.co.uk/wyckhouse.htm* (*moderate*). Five bedrooms including two small cottage-style single rooms with patchwork quilts.

Weavers Cottage, 37 Mitchelgate, **t** 72002 (*cheap*). Cared-for little place on long, narrow, steep lane into town centre. Climbing plants and pots outside front doors; twin and double room.

Mill Brow Guest House, Mill Brow, **t** 71615 (*cheap*). On a gorgeous lane leading down to the river off Market Street.

Kendal t (01539) –

Only 8 miles from Windermere, with its glamorous lakeside hotels, Kendal lacks great places to stay. There are a few semi-detached B&Bs on Windermere Road, just out of town, or try the following.

Riverside Hotel, Stramongate Bridge, **t** 734 861, *www.macdonaldhotels.co.uk* (*expensive*). Converted 17th-century tannery beside the River Kent; 47 rooms on five floors, all with river view, and restaurant.

Highgate Hotel, 128 Highgate, **t** 724 229, *www.highgatehotel.co.uk* (*moderate*). Handsome Georgian house on busy road, which once belonged to a wealthy 18th-century chemist. Original staircase and fireplaces inside. Nice homely feeling.

Hillside Guesthouse, 4 Beast Banks, **t** 722 836 (*moderate*). Bog-standard B&B in greystone Victorian terrace a short walk from town centre, on the road to Scout Scar.

Kendal

On the southeastern edge of big fell country, Kendal developed as a fortified medieval market town and became a magnet for local industries. Even before the Industrial Revolution, wool and leather manufacturing flourished on the banks of the River Kent, and by the end of the 19th century products 'made in Kendal' included bicycles, carpets and turbines. Nowadays, Kendal is best known for mint cake – a famous high-energy snack first sold in 1839 and popular with adventurers including Sir Edmund Hillary and Ernest Shackleton – and K Shoes. The main axis of the town is north–south along the river. On its west side, the congested main road and shopping street climbs through the town in the direction of Windermere, changing its name three times. At the bottom – where it is called **Kirkland** – are the handsome church and **Abbot's Hall** (***t*** *(01539) 722 464; open summer 10.30–5, winter 10.30–4; adm*). At the

Eating Out

Kirkby Lonsdale

Snooty Fox, Main Street, **t** 71308, *www.mortal-man-inns.co.uk*. Excellent old-fashioned pub; superb country-inn comfort food (*moderate*), including roast pheasant, steamed huss, pan-fried sea bass, tomato and aubergine gâteau; and nine cosy bedrooms (*moderate*).

Avanti Restaurant and Bar, 57 Main Street (down alley beside deli), **t** 73500. Restaurant above bar serves salmon, pan-fried calf's liver, sea bass, king prawns and bean sprouts (*moderate*).

The Courtyard Restaurant and Wine Bar, 2 Mill Brow, **t** 71779. Modern, lively, stone-floored wine bar with Mediterranean-style menu (*cheap*) and restaurant (*moderate*) with live jazz and acoustic nights. Serves modern English cuisine with lots of olives, balsamic vinegar and basil, and interesting chutneys. *Wine bar open daily, restaurant closed Mon.*

Artisan Café, 48–50 Main Street, **t** 73324. Up outside stairs in pretty little yard to first-floor converted barn with roof timbers. Café (delicious strong coffee, Provençal tartlet, soup, salads, home-made ice cream), organic wine bar and restaurant: modern English and world food, local and organic produce, set lunch and *à la carte* dinner (*cheap–moderate*). Jazz pianist Wed eve in season. *Closed Sun eve and Mon.*

Bay Tree, 44 Main Street, **t** 72160 (*cheap*). Good morning fry-ups to set you up for a hard day's walking.

Mews Coffee Shop, Main Street, **t** 71007 (*cheap*). In courtyard through archway. Traditional tea shop with jam for sale.

Kendal

Déja-Vu, 124 Stricklandgate, **t** 724 843 (*moderate*). Cosy French/Spanish corner restaurant with scuffed wooden floor-boards, old French posters on wall, French music, candles on tables and a cheerful plastic daffodil in a jar. Excellent value. *Open Mon–Sat lunch, Fri–Sat also dinner.*

1657 Chocolate House, Branthwaite Brow, **t** 740 702 (*cheap*). Beamy old-world café above chocolate shop. Bonneted waitresses serve 38 varieties of chocolate drink and 22 varieties of scrumptious gateaux. (1657 is the year that chocolate arrived in England.)

Farrers Coffee House, 13 Stricklandgate, **t** 731 707 (*cheap*). Established in 1819, its shelves are stacked with antique coffee and tea caddies, its atmosphere dense with the delicious smells of freshly ground coffee, home-baked cakes and scones.

Entertainment

Brewery Arts Centre, Highgate, Kendal, **t** (01539) 725 133. The social hub of Kendal, with exhibitions, two cinemas, theatre, concert hall for regular live jazz and acoustic music, two bars and the **Green Room Restaurant** (*cheap*), serving pizza, pasta and salads in a relaxed, airy setting where classical music plays. **Vats Bar** has ingenious seating made out of old beer vats.

top – **Stricklandgate** – is the old market place, with narrow passageways or yards, such as the quaint Victorian shambles (now selling essential oils instead of butcher's meat) leading down to the river. In between – **Highgate** – are interesting old buildings reflecting the town's former prosperity, such as the town hall. On the other side of the main road, residential streets climb steeply up the valley side. Abbot's Hall is now the **Museum of Lakeland Life and Industry** (*t (01539) 722 464; open daily April–Oct 10.30–5, Nov–Dec and Feb–Mar 10.30–4; adm*), with a small arts and crafts room showing work by the Keswick School of Industrial Arts and Langdale Linen Industry. In the gallery are portraits by George Romney, often ranked third after Gainsborough and Reynolds in the pecking order of English portraitists. You can see lively exhibitions of contemporary art and photography in the **Brewery Arts Centre** (*Highgate, t (01539) 725 133; open Mon–Sat 9am–11pm, box office 10–8; adm to events*). **Kendal Museum** (*Station Road, t (01539) 721 374; open summer Mon–Sat 10.30–5, winter 10.30–4; adm*) has a collection of Wainwright memorabilia, including a pair of darned socks and his old knapsack. Upstairs, the natural history gallery elucidates Lakeland's 500-million-year geology.

On a wet day (and there are many in Lakeland), you may be glad to take refuge at **Sizergh Castle** (*t (01539) 60070; open April–Oct Sun–Thurs, castle 1.30–5.30, gardens 12.30–5.30; adm*). It started as a 14th-century pele tower and grew into a splendid Tudor country house with two wings and some beautifully panelled and plastered rooms. The gardens are lovely too. The castle has been home to the Strickland family for 700 years; the ancestors are well represented in portraits.

Levens Hall (*5 minutes from M6 junction 36, t (01539) 560 321; open April–Oct Sun–Thurs, gardens 10–5, house 12–5; adm*) is another Tudor house built around a pele tower, with more unusual gardens. They were developed by Guillaume Beaumont at the end of the 17th century and are famous for the topiary-filled parterre and the incorporation of a gorge in the River Kent. William Gilpin called it 'a happy combination of everything that is lovely and great in landscape'.

Windermere

Most visitors' first encounter with Lakeland, Windermere is both the longest, lushest lake in Lakeland – dotted with islands and fringed with low wooded hills – and a charmless Victorian railway town. Between lake and town, on the lakeshore, is Bowness, all higgledy-piggledy streets and wooden piers, from where boat trips leave.

Windermere has always been the most popular of the lakes; it was a favourite of wealthy Victorian industrialists from Leeds and Manchester, who built luxurious villas around the edges (many of them now hotels). Even now, with the sun glinting off masts, it has a faintly glitzy air. Wordsworth in his *Guide* suggests that the first thing you do in the Lakes is take a trip on the **Bowness ferry**; still today no trip to the Lake District would be complete without a cruise (45 minutes) around the lake. Above the gentle wooded slopes at the north end there are glimpses of the towering bare fells,

Getting Around

By Bus

Mountain Goat Minibus Tours, Victorian Street, Windermere, **t** (015394) 45161, *www.mountain-goat.com*. Day-long sightseeing tours all year, with pickup at local hotels. Commentary, photo ops and not much walking.

By Boat

The Windermere **car ferry** runs from Ferry Nab, south of Bowness Bay, to the Hawkshead side every 20 minutes from 6.30am to 8.45pm, for a small fee. Windermere Lake Cruises run a **foot/bike ferry** (every 20 minutes 10am–5pm) from Bowness Bay to Hawkshead side, which links up with a mini-bus service (with bike racks) to take you further afield, including Hawkshead and Coniston. **Self-drive motor boats** and **row boats** are for hire at Bowness and Waterhead (Ambleside).

Windermere Lake Cruises, **t** (015394) 43360, *www.windermere-lakecruises.co.uk*. Offers four options: the full lake cruise takes three hours, stopping at Bowness, Ambleside and Lakeside (you can get off and on when you like); return to Ambleside takes 70 minutes; return to Lakeside takes 90 minutes; or you can opt for a 40-minute circular tour. A 'Freedom of the Lake' ticket gives you 24 hours unlimited cruising. In summer, you can combine the lake cruise with a trip to the pretty village of Newby Bridge via the **Lakeside and Haverthwaite Railway**.

By Bike

Bicycles can be hired at:

Hartley Hire, New Road, Windermere, **t** (015394) 45406.

The Cranleigh Hotel, Kendal Road, Bowness, **t** (015394) 43293.

Country Lanes, The Station, off High Street, Windermere, **t** (015394) 44544. *Open summer only*.

Tourist Information

Windermere: The Station, off High Street, **t** (015394) 46499. *Open winter daily 9–5, summer daily 9–6*.

Bowness on Windermere: Glebe Road, **t** (015394) 42895, *bownesstic@lakedistrict.gov.uk. Open summer 9.30–5.30, high summer 9–6, winter 10–4*.

Hawkshead: main car park, **t** (015394) 36525, *hawksheadtic@lakedistrict.gov.uk. Open summer 9.30–5.30, high summer 9.30–6, winter 10–3.30*.

Where to Stay

Windermere and Around t (015394) –

The Samling, Ambleside Road, **t** 31922, *www.thesamling.com* (*luxury*). Price for the night includes four-course meal and full breakfast (B&B rates also available). Glamorous country-house hotel on north-eastern lakeshore, in 67 acres of grounds; 10 rooms, with open fires, two-person baths and posh toiletries. Excellent dining room.

Gilpin Lodge, Crook Road, **t** 88818, *www.gilpin-lodge.co.uk* (*luxury*). Two miles southeast of Windermere, white-painted Victorian country-house hotel in its own 20-acre hilltop gardens and woodland above the lake; beautifully furnished with period furniture; 14 bedrooms with bathrobes and home-made biscuits, real fires and fresh flowers; four dining rooms (*expensive*) offer superb modern European food, including five-course set menu of terrines, soups, local meats and designer desserts. Modern annexe with private terraces and Jacuzzis.

Miller Howe, Rayrigg Road (on A592 between Windermere and Bowness), **t** 42536, *www.millerhowe.com* (*luxury*). Set back from town in 5½ acres of gardens overlooking the lake; 15 extremely comfortable rooms, including four with spa baths; its airy restaurant (*expensive*) has a strong reputation for English country-house style food.

Holbeck Ghyll Country House Hotel, Holbeck Lane (3 miles north of Windermere, follow Troutbeck signs from A591), **t** 32375, *www.slh.com/holbeck* (*luxury*). Beautiful gabled Victorian hunting lodge in its own large grounds, overlooking fells and Lake Windermere, with Michelin-starred French restaurant (*expensive*). Management more than a little off-hand, sadly letting the place down.

Crag Brow Cottage Hotel, Helm Road, Bowness, **t** 44080, *www.cragbrow.com* (*expensive*). Modestly glamorous hotel superbly positioned above Bowness, two minutes' walk to ferries; use of nearby leisure-club facilities; 12 rooms, some overlooking lake. Dinner available.

Alice Howe Guesthouse, 3 The Terrace, **t** 43325, *info@alicehowe.co.uk* (*moderate*). Pretty little stone cottage with garden.

The Coach House, Lake Road (between Windermere and Bowness), **t** 44494, *www.lakedistrictbandb.com* (*moderate*). Small, extremely friendly, modern and cheerful with uncluttered, brightly painted rooms and excellent breakfast.

Hawkshead and Around t (015394) –

Borwick Lodge, Outgate (a mile north of Hawkshead, east of Tarn Hows) **t** 36332, *www.borwicklodge.com* (*expensive*). Delightful 17th-century house with elegant period-style rooms. Its 3-acre gardens fall away to green fields, sheep and trees, and the dim shapes of the eastern fells beyond.

Waterside House, Hannakin, Esthwaite Water, **t** 36045 (*moderate*). Farmhouse on outskirts of Hawkshead, about half a mile from centre; two bedrooms, each with separate front door.

Ann Tyson's Guest House, Wordsworth Street, Hawkshead, **t** 36405, *www.anntysons.co.uk* (*moderate*). Six doubles – five en suite – and one single, down cobbled lane in centre of Hawkshead; flower baskets and low ceilings; part of a block owned by Ann Tyson, Wordsworth's landlady during his time at Hawkshead Grammar School.

The Old School House, Hawkshead, **t** 36403 (*cheap*). Friendly, comfortable place to stay in centre of Hawkshead, numbered keys and 'granny's spare room' décor.

Eating Out

Windermere and Around

The high-standard restaurants belong to the country-house hotels, including Gilpin Lodge, The Samling and Miller Howe, while the restaurants in town tend to be more lively and fun.

Jerichos, Birch Street (off High Street), **t** 42522 (*moderate*). Much-praised brasserie style of food with emphasis on local produce, set up by former head chef of Miller Howe Hotel. *Closed Mon, last two weeks of Nov and first week of Dec.*

The Porthole, Ash Street, **t** 42793 (*moderate*). Extremely popular French/Italian restaurant in converted cottage; numerous small dining rooms upstairs and downstairs, some with alcoves and patio seating, decorated with souvenirs and wine bottles. No pizzas, lots of pasta, local fish and meat. *Book ahead. Closed Tues and most of Dec, Jan and Feb except for Christmas holidays.*

Villa Positano, Ash Street, **t** 45663 (*moderate*). Large, lively and friendly Italian place. Pizza, pasta, steak or fish. *Book ahead. Closed Wed.*

Lamplighter Bar, Oakthorpe Hotel, High Street, **t** 43547 (*cheap*). An unpromising building, where real ale, battered cod and Thai food are served. Popular with locals.

Jackson's Bistro, West End (near the church), Bowness, **t** 46264 (*cheap*). Charming, cosy, old-fashioned restaurant on two floors, established for more than 20 years. Roast lamb shank and red wine sauces, sea bass or good vegetarian dishes.

Hawkshead and Around

Queen's Head Hotel, Main Street, **t** 36271, *www.queensheadhotel.co.uk* (*expensive*). Charming old pub with oak panelling and log fires in a low beamy interior. Old-English-style menu – venison, mallard duck, fish – in bar or brighter restaurant.

Drunken Duck (2 miles north of Hawkshead), **t** 36347, *www.drunkenduckinn.co.uk*. Picturesque, ever-popular Lakeland pub in the middle of nowhere, with its own brewery, fantastic views of north end of Windermere, 16 bedrooms (*expensive*), some in pub, others across courtyard. Excellent upmarket restaurant (*moderate*), where you might get lemon sole, venison, grilled pasta, aubergine, sautéed spinach, or monkfish, cooked to order.

Sun Cottage, Main Street, **t** 36488 (*cheap*). Small five-table family-run café serving hearty home-cooked meals, with a reputation for tasty omelettes. *Closed Mon.*

and on a bright autumn day you get the benefit of the colour on the wooded banks. It was at **Orrest Head**, just north of Windermere town, that walks writer Wainwright had his Lakeland 'revelation'.

The Western Shore of Lake Windermere

Avoid the eastern shore of Windermere, where the main road goes, and take the ferry to the unspoilt western shore. From the jetty, several paths head north into hilly, wooded **Claife Heights** or south along the lakeside. The countryside between Windermere and Coniston Water is the gentlest in Lakeland, and easily walkable.

Hill Top

Another option is to follow the Hawkshead lane beside Esthwaite Water – a puddle next to Windermere – to **Hill Top** (***t*** *(01539) 436 269, www.nationaltrust.org.uk; open Easter–Oct Sat–Wed 10.30–4.30; gardens also Thurs–Fri 10.30–4.30; adm*) in the tiny village of Sawrey. Beatrix Potter bought her delightful 'old house, full of cupboards' with views across to the Coniston and Langdale Fells in 1905, with royalties from *Peter Rabbit*, and within two years owned 30 Herdwick sheep, 10 cows, 14 pigs, ducks and hens and a collie called Kep. The house is just as she left it: flagstone floor in the parlour, rag rug in front of the range, horse brasses, little windows. You can play at locating corners of her house and garden that pop up as drawings in *Tom Kitten* or *Samuel Whiskers*. Expect long queues.

Hawkshead

The hilly area west of Windermere and south to the Leven and Crake estuaries is **High Furness**, while the low-lying peninsula as far as Barrow-in-Furness is **Low Furness** (Furness means far headland). It was all owned by Furness Abbey (*see* p.767) in the Middle Ages, and Hawkshead was the monks' administrative centre. Wool – big business at the time – built the large church above grey slate roofs and white walls. From here the village appears snug in the midst of smooth, green hills under the dark shadow of the central fells further north. Better still, you can't see the gargantuan car park and visitor centre built to cope with the thousands of tourists who pour into the tiny village to worship a the shrines of William Wordsworth and Beatrix Potter.

In 1779 William and his three brothers were sent to live in Hawkshead with Ann Tyson, a joiner's widow, after their mother died. Their father died too in 1783. The boys attended the grammar school and, encouraged by his headmaster, William started reading and writing poetry. From the age of 10 he would disappear on his famous rambles into the hills at all hours of the day and night. You can see **Ann Tyson's house** on Rag, Putty and Leather Street (now Wordsworth Street) and inspect the graffiti on the wooden desks of the tiny **grammar school** (*open Easter–Sept Mon–Sat 10–5, Sun 1–5; Oct until 4.30 only; adm minimal*), looking for the initials WW.

More than a hundred years later, in 1913, Beatrix Potter married the Hawkshead solicitor William Heelis, who had helped her buy the house at Sawrey. His offices are now the **Beatrix Potter Gallery** (*open Easter–Oct Sat–Wed 10.30–4.30; adm*), where you can see exhibitions of watercolours and drawings from her books.

South of Hawkshead is Grizedale Forest, which was planted as coppice woodland by the Furness monks as a resource for tanning, iron smelting and basket making. It is now managed by the Forestry Commission, which has recently planted some broadleaf trees to break the monotony of conifer plantations. A quiet lane off the Hawkshead–Coniston road leads to **Tarn Hows**, a popular lake with wooded banks in the shadow of the big Furness Fells. Surprisingly, in a region not short of natural beauty, Tarn Hows is man-made, created in the 19th century by damming a stream and planting pretty swathes of Scots pines and larch. It gets very crowded.

From Bowness to **Stott Park Bobbin Mill** (***t*** *(01539) 531 087, www.english-heritage.org.uk; open April–Sept 10–6, Oct 10–5; adm*), you can either catch the ferry (*summer only*) to Lakeside, at the bottom of Windermere, or walk or cycle (3½ miles) from the Hawkshead jetty. When the Lancashire cotton industry was crying out for bobbins and reels in the 19th century there were 45 mills like this in High Furness (due to all the Grizedale trees). Now Stott Park is the only one left. A guided tour shows you the bobbins being cut from the wood like pastry shapes. The sawing and lathing machines around the edges of the factory floor, all powered by one central drive shaft, once produced 150,000 bobbins a week. A short walk through the woods takes you to High Dam, created to power the machines before the steam engine took over.

Morecambe Sands and the Furness Peninsula

The quickest way into southern Lakeland was traditionally at low tide across the shifting sands of Morecambe Bay (*see* p.744). The earliest guides were the monks of Cartmel Priory and Furness Abbey. At the Reformation an official royal guide was appointed, a position which still exists. The 8-mile Saturday morning walk across the **Morecambe Sands**, from Arnside to Grange-over-Sands, is one of the most popular pilgrimages in Lakeland (*contact the Queen's Official Guide, Cedric Robinson,* ***t*** *(01539) 32165 for details*), returning by train. Prince Philip tried it once, but starting from Silverdale as the River Kent had changed its course. The guide plots a route the day before, planting laurel boughs to mark a safe passage around the river. Walkers are asked to spread out to distribute their weight, and lie down if they start to sink.

Ulverston

Ulverston is the hub of the Furness Peninsula, at the cliff foot of high Lakeland, skirted by the fast-traffic A590 Kendal road. Its brief heyday in the 17th and 18th centuries (exporting locally mined iron ore) followed by rapid decline in the 19th century (failing to compete with Barrow-in-Furness) has left a small market centre with some neat Georgian buildings and modest civic buildings. Visit early in the morning on market day (Thurs and Sat) when the town is waking up and stalls are set up in the handsome **Market Place** and along Market Street, where every shop seems to be charmingly old fashioned anyway. King's Street and Queen Street are pleasant to wander in too, stocking up on walking provisions like boiled sweets and new socks

Tourist Information

Ulverston: Coronation Hall, County Square, **t** (01229) 587 120. *Open Mon–Sat 9–5*.

Where to Stay

Ulverston t (01229) –

Lonsdale House Hotel, 11 Daltongate, **t** 582 598 (*expensive*). Stuccoed 18th-century town-house with William Morris wallpaper and wood-panelled reception; back garden with curious castle folly and *trompe l'œil* décor in basement dining room; lovely large rooms.

Virginia House Hotel, 24 Queen Street, **t** 584 844, *www.ulverstonhotels.com* (*moderate*). Attractive, cream-painted house in centre of town with seven modest no-smoking rooms; friendly atmosphere.

Church Walk House, Church Walk, **t** 582 211, *churchwalk@mchadderton.freeserve.co.uk* (*moderate*). Beautiful 18th-century cream house with red door, bold wallpaper, lovely bathrooms; friendly and helpful; lounge well-stocked with Lakeland guide books.

Around Ulverston t (01229) –

Force Mill Farm, a mile south of the village of Satterthwaite (15 minutes' drive from Ulverston), **t** 860 205, *www.forcemillfarm.co.uk* (*moderate*). Stone-built 17th-century farmhouse beside waterfall. Sit on terrace and listen to sounds of wood and water. Simple rooms, perfect for walkers or people who like peace and quiet.

White Hart Inn, Bouth, **t** 861 229 (*cheap*). Cosy, low and beamy, packed with stuffed animals, crockery and brass, two log fires, tasty pub grub including pizza; real ales and pub games.

Eating Out

Ulverston

Cinnamon Room, 33 King Street, **t** 480 668 (*moderate*). Brasserie-style smallish restaurant with spice-coloured walls, wooden tables and a Mediterranean menu including lots of olive oil, herbs and flaked parmesan.

Farmers Arms, Market Place, **t** 584 469 (*cheap*). Of Ulverston's 30 pubs, this is the most popular with its patio seating overlooking Market Street, and menu of hot garlic prawns on toast or gammon and pineapple.

Rose and Crown, King Street, **t** 583 094 (*cheap*). Striking building with worn flagstone floor and cosy corners; pleasant shaded back garden with sturdy wooden furniture. Lunch and dinner most days – filled baguettes, Cumberland sausage and chilli con carne.

Jade Fountain, 5 Fountain Street, **t** 585 047 (*cheap*). Large, family-run Cantonese restaurant; friendly atmosphere, very accommodating to vegetarians and special diets. *Open eves only, closed Mon.*

Laurel's International Bistro, 13 Queen Street, **t** 583 961 (*cheap*). Range of 'international' food – peppered steak, chicken fajitas, sea bass – in lively 52-seater bistro-style restaurant. *Closed Sun, and Mon lunch.*

from the old **Market Hall** (*open Mon–Tues and Thurs–Sat*). Down Upper Brook Street is the **Laurel and Hardy Museum** (***t** (01229) 582 292; open Feb–Dec daily 10–4.30; adm*), created by a self-proclaimed 'out-of-hand hobbiest' in homage to Stan Laurel, who was born in Ulverston. Priceless memorabilia includes stage props such as Stan's bowler hat. In the old Kendal Bank on Theatre Street, **Furness Gallery** sells excellent handmade toys, wooden wind chimes and dolls houses. There is also the popular **Lakes Glass Centre**, selling ornamental and table glassware.

High above Ulverston, on the 400ft crest of Hoad Hill, is a **replica of the Eddystone Lighthouse**, built as a memorial to Sir John Barrow, admiralty secretary and founder of the Royal Geographical Society. In summer when the flag is flying you can walk or drive up and climb the tower for the views.

Furness Abbey

***t** (01229) 823 420, www.english-heritage.org.uk; open April–Sept 10–6, Oct 10–5, Nov–Mar 10–4; adm.*

Take the A590 from Ulverston, following signs to Furness Abbey, just before the outskirts of Barrow-in-Furness. The railway turned the abbey into such a popular Victorian tourist attraction that a hotel was built next door. It also made Barrow-in-Furness the industrial centre of the Furness Peninsula, with its imperial dockyards and imposing buildings. Wordsworth visited the abbey in 1845, noting that even the 'simple hearted men' working on the railway were 'moved' by the spirit of the imposing dusty red ruin in the valley of Bekaner Ghyll. At the time of the Dissolution, the abbey was the second richest Cistercian monastery in England, with money coming in from sheep pastures, mineral rights, tanneries and fulling mills not only on the peninsula and the Furness Fells, but all over Lancashire and the Isle of Man. Much survives, including the great east window, the church tower, elaborately carved sedilia in the presbytery and five recessed and beautifully decorated arches of the cloisters, one leading to the Chapter House. You can still see the abbey orchards beneath the steep grassy slopes within the walls. Gargoyles, pieces of statues, corbels and an effigy of a knight are on display in the little museum.

Coniston

Coming to it, we used to run down to the lake, dip our hands in and wish, as if we had just seen a new moon. Going away from it, we were half drowned in tears.

Arthur Ransome, remembering childhood holidays

The old mining town of Coniston is tucked away on the northwest side of Coniston Water, at the foot of a huge, battered fell known as the Old Man – the southern bastion of the high fells. It is more subdued than the other Lakeland resort towns. In his guides, Wainwright describes the Old Man as a benevolent giant bathing his feet in the lake while shedding quiet tears into his two tarns because of all the disfigurement he suffered through mining and quarrying in the 19th century. At the height of mining activity, 500 miners worked 1,500ft underground digging green slate and copper, and the village got its school, a church restoration and many new buildings. John Ruskin, who lived across the water at Brantwood and is buried in the churchyard under a carved Celtic cross, was involved in local life, promoting traditional craft skills under threat from industrialisation at the **Coniston Mechanics Institute** and **Langdale Linen Industry**. In the 20th century, Coniston Water became internationally famous through the water-speed record breaking attempts of Sir Malcolm Campbell (141mph) and his son, Donald Campbell, who died in January 1967 on his second attempt to break the 300mph. Donald's body and the ***Bluebird*** were recovered from Coniston Water in 2001 by his nephew, another Campbell water-speed-racer. There is plenty of *Bluebird* memorabilia around town, including a Bluebird beer made in the brewery of the Bull pub.

Tourist Information

Coniston: Ruskin Avenue, **t** (015394) 41533, *conistontic@lakedistrict.gov.uk. Open summer 9.30–5.30; winter 10–3.30.*

Broughton-in-Furness: Old Town Hall, The Square, **t** (01229) 716115, *www.lakelandgateway.info. Open April–Oct 10–12.30 and 1.30–4; winter Tues–Sat 11–1.*

Where to Stay and Eat

Coniston t (015394) –

Sun Hotel, t 41248, *www.smoothhound.co.uk/hotels/sun.html* (*expensive*). At foot of the Old Man, superb old-fashioned country house and beamy old bar hung with photos of Donald Campbell, who stayed here in 1967 before his final world water-speed record attempt, and Anthony Hopkins, who starred in the film about it all. Can provide packed lunches, mapped walks and odd bits of equipment. Conservatory restaurant (*moderate*) serves hearty meals including Cumberland sausage or venison pie.

Coniston Lodge Hotel, Sunny Brow, **t** 41201, *www.coniston-lodge.com* (*expensive*). Twinkly alpine chalet; inside cosy and warm, all dark wood and colourful patterned fabrics; six bedrooms named after Lakeland tarns. *Dinner available Tues–Sat* (*moderate*).

Yew Tree Farm (north of Coniston village on Ambleside road), **t** 41433, *www.yewtreefarm.com* (*moderate*). Lovely 16th-century white-painted farmhouse, one of 15 Lakeland farms owned by Beatrix Potter; upstairs extraordinary oak-wood panelling between the bedrooms.

Bank Ground Farm (on northeast side of Coniston lake on Brantwood road), **t** 41264, *www.bankground.co.uk* (*moderate*). Wonderful Lakeland farmhouse, the setting for *Swallows and Amazons*.

Bull Inn, Yew Dale Road, **t** 41335 (*cheap*). Friendly country pub with micro-brewery producing Bluebird and Old Man Ale, and pub grub.

Broughton-in-Furness t (01229) –

Middlesyke, Church Street, **t** 716 549 (*moderate*). Friendly Victorian house with two handsome bedrooms and huge bathrooms, 50 yards from town centre.

Broom Hill, **t** 716 358 (*moderate*). Delightful, homely 18th-century townhouse, with two storeys of flagged floors and 1½ acres of garden.

The Manor Arms, The Square, **t** 716 286 (*moderate*). Pleasant, modest, real-ale pub with comfortable rooms.

Beswick Restaurant, Langholme House, The Square, **t** 716 285 (*moderate*). Reception and bar on ground floor, downstairs to main restaurant, which serves traditional seasonal English food. *Three-course special served Tues–Thurs. Closed Sun and Mon.*

Blacksmith's Arms (a mile north at Broughton Mills, in the knotty landscape of the Duddon Fells), **t** 716 824 (*cheap*). Cosy, slate-flagged pub with chickens pecking around outside; serves delicious roast ham open sandwiches, Herdwick lamb and Cumberland sausage.

Arthur Ransome's classic children's adventure book *Swallows and Amazons* is based on Coniston Water; Peel Island is Wild Cat Island – 'It was not just an island. It was the island, waiting for them. It was their island. With an island like that within sight, who could be content to live on the mainland and sleep in a bed at night?' You can hire small motor boats from Coniston Pier and there are two motor launches, *Ransome* and *Ruskin*, run by the **Coniston Launch Company** (*t (015394) 36216*), which tour the lake. The restored Victorian steam yacht *Gondola* does a round trip, stopping at Peel Island and Brantwood. Much of the shoreline is privately owned, but a footpath follows a good stretch of the western shore, and a narrow lane hugs the entire length of the eastern shore.

Ruskin is one of those eminent Victorians whose achievements are hard to pin down. Tolstoy called him 'one of those rare men who think with their hearts'. He is said to have influenced Ghandi and Marx. His classic book *Modern Painters* (1843), which he wrote at the age of 24, helped to launch the career of Turner. His art criticism boosted the Pre-Raphaelites in a similar way; his patronage even extended to buying their paintings when they weren't selling. The **Ruskin Museum** *(**t** (01539) 441 164; open April–mid-Nov daily 10–5.30, mid-Nov–Mar Wed–Sun 10.30–3.30; adm)*, was set up in 1901, a year after Ruskin's death, by his secretary W.G. Collingwood. Displays include carved wooden products of the Mechanics Institute, Langdale Linen samples, watercolours and architectural sketches from Ruskin's European tours, and Campbell memorabilia.

Ruskin bought **Brantwood** (*t* *(01539) 441 396; open Mar–Oct daily 11–5.30, Nov–Mar Wed–Sun 11–4.30; adm*) on the northeastern shore of Coniston Water in 1871. He moved in with his cousin Joan Severn at the age of 52, having never seen the place, but been assured of the magnificent views of the lake and the Coniston Fells. At first he found it dreary and dilapidated, and made some large-scale improvements, including the addition of a wooden bedroom tower and as much land as he could lay his hands on. Already past his prime and increasingly prone to periods of instability bordering on madness, he continued nonetheless to write books, patronise the arts and champion his good causes. It's hard now to imagine the clutter and life of Brantwood in its heyday, when 'every table, chair, and most of the floor would be littered with a wonderful profusion of sketches, photographs, missals, Greek coins, and uncut gems'.

Southwest of Coniston Water is the old market town of **Broughton-in-Furness**, with its beautiful Georgian square, good pubs and easy access to **Duddon Valley** or

The Coniston Fells

Why does a man climb mountains? Why has he forced his tired and sweating body up here when he might instead have been sitting at his ease in a deckchair at the seaside, looking at girls in bikinis, or fast asleep, or sucking ice cream... It is a question every man must answer for himself.

Alfred Wainwright

The Coniston tourist information centre has leaflets about walks up the Old Man and Coppermines Valley. The trek up the **Old Man** (2,633ft) is one of the most popular sunny-day Lakeland pilgrimages. Head west up the Walna Scar packhorse road past the Sun Hotel, following the path to the summit via Low Water. On a clear day you can see across Morecambe Bay to Blackpool Tower. Another route is from the Ruskin Museum via quiet Church Beck. This **Coppermines Valley** walk is atmospheric in greyness and spectacular in the blue. The path passes miners' cottages, slag heaps and old copper workings. It is worth enduring the short, aching climb round Kennel Cragg to Levers Water, where strange mists hover. Another good walk is the **Coniston Round**: Wainwright recommends you go along the Walna Scar path to Goats Water and climb Dow Crag (2,555ft and 'the grandest spot on the walk'), continue to the summit of the Old Man over Brim Fell to Swirl How, crossing to Wetherlam and returning to Coniston by the ridge known as the Lad Stones.

Dunnerdale. The valley drives a corridor into the heart of Lakeland mountain country, one of the spokes on Wordsworth's metaphoric wheel. It was the poet who brought Duddon Valley to the public's attention with *The Excursion*, a story about a parson who lived in the valley for 66 years and did charitable works, although he was as poor as anybody. Now, hump-backed **Birk's Bridge** is one of the most photographed and painted in Lakeland. The Newfield Inn (***t** (01229) 716 208*) at **Seathwaite** in the heart of the valley is a good place to begin a walk (admire its striated slate floor tiles). The inn sells a booklet of walks which includes the **Wallowbarrow Walk**, a perfect loop neither too easy nor too strenuous, crossing the footbridge over the River Duddon and climbing around Wallowbarrow Crag (a popular climbing crag). The path passes a stepping-stone bridge over the river, long views of the Coniston Fells from the crag, scree slopes and boulders to picnic on by the rushing river. Beyond Seathwaite the scenery changes, with dramatic bare fells turning the flat, green valley floor into an amphitheatre before the road climbs up to the vertiginous mountain passes of **Wrynose** and **Hardknott**, dropping down into the valleys of **Little Langdale** and **Eskdale** respectively.

Ambleside and Grasmere

From Windermere, the A591 tourist route leads north to Ambleside and Grasmere, where at last you are in striking distance of the big fells at the heart of the Lake District: Scafell Pike, Bow Fell and the Langdale Pikes.

Ambleside

With its narrow streets of dark slate houses and the impressive surrounding fells, Ambleside is the most exciting of the resort towns. There are good shops, including Stewardson Country Clothing on Main Street (where you can get a good pair of leather walking boots), restaurants and plenty of places to stay. In the small **Armitt Museum** (***t** (01539) 431 212; open daily 10–5; adm*) you can find out about Lakeland writer Harriet Martineau, and Beatrix Potter's interest in natural science, Herdwick sheep and fungi (with excellent drawings). From Ambleside, the mountainous **Kirkstone Pass** climbs north to Ullswater. De Quincey once galloped down the pass at full speed in complete darkness, except for the occasional flash of lightning revealing the horrifying gradient of the road.

Down the Langdales and into the High Fells

From Ambleside, the A593 heads west along the River Brathay to Skelwith Bridge, where it veers south to Coniston, while two smaller roads continue west along separate, more or less parallel valleys known as Great Langdale and Little Langdale. If you are arriving in the Lake District from the south, this will be your first taste of true mountain country. Great Langdale is the busiest of the two, with a couple of big pubs, coach parks and campsites along the roadside. The flat valley floor carries the road between bare, steep fells. On the north side of the road are the five summits of the

Langdale Pikes: Pike o' Stickle, Loft Crag, Thorn Crag, Harrison Stickle and Pavey Ark. One of the most important Neolithic stone-axe manufacturing sites in Britain was discovered in the scree slopes of Pike o' Stickle and around the upper slopes of the other pikes. You can walk up from Ambleside or park in the Old Dungeon Ghyll Hotel car park and walk directly up the well trodden National Trust stone staircase to Dungeon Ghyll Force waterfall and Stickle Tarn. The strong-legged carry on up the jagged grey south side of Harrison Stickle (736ft), the tallest of the pikes. This is one of the most popular routes in the Lakes, so avoid it at peak times if you are looking for solitude. But the higher it goes, the quieter it becomes. A more interesting route up to the Stickle Tarn starts from Elterwater village, crossing the main road up to Huntingstile Crag. From there, head westwards along the ridge path for about four

Getting Around

Biketreks, Compston Road, **t** (015394) 31245. Bike hire, route information and maps. *Open summer daily 10.30–5.30, winter Fri–Tues.*

Ghyllside Cycles, The Slack (opposite Zeffirelli's), **t** (015394) 33592. Bike hire. *Open summer daily 9.30–5.30, winter closed Wed.*

Tourist Information

Ambleside: Central Buildings, Market Cross, **t** (015394) 32582, *www.amblesidetic@southlakeland.gov.uk. Open 9–5.*

Waterhead: main car park, **t** (015394) 32729, *waterheadtic@lakedistrict.gov.uk. Open summer 9.30–5.30; closed winter.*

Grasmere: Red Bank Road, **t** (015394) 35245, *grasmeretic@lakedistrict.gov.uk. Open summer 9.30–5.30; winter Sun–Fri 10–3.30.*

Where to Stay

Ambleside t (015394) –

The Old Vicarage, Vicarage Road, **t** 33364, *www.oldvicarageambleside.co.uk* (*expensive*). Gorgeous slate-brick Victorian vicarage with pointed gables and church-style windows, tucked away near St Mary's Church, elegant and spacious inside with 10 rooms.

Queen's Hotel, Market Place, **t** 32206 (*expensive*). Popular town-centre Victorian coaching inn with 26 pleasant rooms, and the odd clash of flowery wallpaper.

Swiss Villas, Vicarage Road, **t** 32691, *www.amblesideonline.co.uk* (*moderate*). Off the main drag in attractive Alpine-style Victorian terrace, reached up stone steps; two rooms with shared bathroom.

Compston House Hotel, Compston Road, **t** 32305, *www.compstonhouse.co.uk* (*moderate*). Cheerful American-run small hotel with amusing themed rooms.

Around Ambleside t (015394) –

Old Dungeon Ghyll Hotel, Great Landgale, **t** 37272, *www.odg.co.uk* (*expensive*). Ideal spot for fell-walkers, with a Walkers' Bar; 14 rooms, four en suite; can organize horse-riding, canoeing, climbing and ballooning; nice home-cooked evening meals available.

The Britannia Inn, Elterwater, **t** 37210 (*expensive*). Real-ale country pub with 12 rooms, nine en suite, overlooking village green; lunches, afternoon teas and evening meals.

The Three Shires Inn, Little Langdale, **t** 37215, *info@threeshiresinn.co.uk*. Friendly family-run pub with restaurant; pub grub or set menu including meat, fish and vegetarian (*moderate*) and accommodation (*expensive*); lovely views and magnificent countryside.

Grasmere t (015394) –

Michael's Nook, **t** 35496, *www.grasmere-hotels.co.uk* (*luxury*). Named after Wordsworth's shepherd. Beautiful Victorian country-house hotel above lake, full of antiques; 14 bedrooms, one with private patio, another on two floors.

The Wordsworth Hotel, **t** 35592, *www.grasmere-hotels.co.uk* (*very expensive*). Victorian country-house hotel in large gardens; 35 cosy, country-house-style bedrooms; large lounge and conservatory; indoor pool; trad restaurant, pub next door.

miles via Silver How, Lang How, Little and Great Castle How and Blea Rigg, and you will come to the tarn from above. From there you can carry on up the pikes, or drop down to the climber's bar in the Old Dungeon Ghyll Hotel. Wainwright recommends the 6-mile ridge walk along all of the pikes, setting off west from the hotel along the side of Mickleden stream beneath Gimmer Crag, and taking the steep zig-zag path up Troughton Beck on to Martcrag Moor. From there, you go east, first to Pike o' Stickle, then Loft Crag, Thorn Crag, Harrison Stickle, north to Pavy Ark and down to Stickle Tarn, picking up the path down to the hotel and the valley road.

Little Langdale is gentler, without any real summits, just mountains stacked on mountains, a single track road and paths climbing away among tumbled boulders. The views are astonishing back down the valley as the road climbs up to Wrynose

Lancrigg Vegetarian Country House Hotel, Easedale Road, **t** 35317 (*very expensive*). Rambling bohemian house in magical 30-acre gardens, once the haunt of Lake poets (Wordsworth is said to have advised on the extension); flagstone terrace overlooking Easedale; inside gorgeous with 13 elegantly furnished rooms. Georgian dining room is the loveliest restaurant setting in Grasmere; reasonably priced four-course meal, catering for special diets including vegans and allergics.

Silver Lea, Easedale Road, **t** 35657, *www.silverlea.com* (*expensive*). Delightful cottage 3 minutes' walk from Grasmere village; five large rooms; tables and chairs in sun trap beneath climbing plants; book months in advance for busy period in May and June. *Open Feb–Nov.*

The Grasmere Hotel, Broadgate, **t** 35277, *www.grasmerehotel.co.uk* (*expensive*). Dour grey stone country house on the edge of the village; inside Victorian décor with dark wood, rich furnishings and courteous, uniformed staff.

Beck Allans (just north of churchyard), **t** 35563, *www.beckallans.com* (*moderate*). Only modern guesthouse in Grasmere, purpose-built in 1992 beside the fast-flowing Rothay, cheerful and homely with five rooms.

Eating Out

Ambleside

Lucy's on a Plate, Church Street, **t** 32288 (*moderate*). Wholesome food on wooden candlelit tables. *Book in advance.*

The Glass House, Rydal Road, **t** 32137 (*moderate*). Contemporary restaurant in former woollen mill; open-plan split-level floors with old working machinery turning wheels and belts. Modern English-style food, including cheaper 'early doors' menu before 7.30pm; main meal might include grilled red snapper with herb butter sauce, roast duck breast, or wild rice pilau, rosemary rice with chick peas and cannelloni. *Closed Tues.*

Zeffirelli's Cinema and Pizzeria, Compston Road, **t** 33845 (*cheap*). Four-screen cinema and pizzeria, also serves vegetarian food in snazzy cinema atmosphere: pizza, salads, two-course meal and cinema package.

Grasmere

If you don't eat at one of the top-class country-house hotel restaurants (see above), try this one for the setting at least.

Dove Cottage Restaurant, Town End, **t** 35268 (*moderate*). Not what the Wordsworths would have eaten: imaginative Mediterranean-style dishes featuring goats' cheese, mozzarella, balsamic vinegar, Puy lentils and olive oil served in a setting to match. *Tea rooms closed Jan; restaurant open summer daily, winter Wed–Sat.*

Rydal Water t (015394) –

White Moss House, Rydal Water (between Ambleside and Grasmere), **t** 35295, *www.whitemoss.com* (*very expensive*). Five bedrooms in hotel, and hillside cottage with two bedrooms, kitchen and sitting room, formerly home of Wordsworth's son. Good roast dinners.

Ambleside Fell Walks

Even another few steps can alter a view, change the perspective, move mountains, bring lakes out of the hat, makes houses disappear, alter the shape of valleys.

Hunter Davies

The Ambleside tourist information centre has good walking leaflets. Fell-walking highlights here are the Langdale Valleys, Loughrigg Fell and the Fairfield Horseshoe.

The **Fairfield Horseshoe** (11 miles) is one of the best known high-level walks in Lakeland, tracing an arc formed by Fairfield and its two southern ridges around the deep valley of Rydal Beck. Wainwright recommends a full day for this walk with lots of stops, and suggests you go about it anti-clockwise, starting off along the steep Kirkstone road and turning off at Sweden Bridge Lane to a gate at the end of the Tarmac road. The path goes off parallel to Scandale Beck towards High Sweden Bridge, crosses the bridge then continues north over Low Pike, High Pike, Dove Crag and Hart Crag to the flat top of Fairfield. From here, you turn due south for the second leg of the Horseshoe to Great Rigg and Heron Pike, dropping down to Nab Scar overlooking Rydal Water and the main road back into Ambleside.

'Everybody likes **Loughrigg**,' says Wainwright: it's an easy climb and varied, with four lakes, a broad tarn, crags and a cave. From Ambleside, go west along the road beside St Mary's Church over Miller Bridge via Brownhead Farm to the foot of Loughrigg Fell, picking up a path northwest to the top. From the summit, you can drop down to Grasmere via Deerbolts Wood.

Pass, leading into Hardnott Pass – a white-knuckle, one-in-three gradient road with hairpin bends between crags and sheer drops. This was the Roman road between Ambleside and the important Roman seaport at Ravenglass, passing the 2nd-century Hardnott Fort on the southwest slope of Hard Knott overlooking the River Esk. It is a spectacular, naturally defensive site, once manned by a Roman garrison (the walls have been restored to a formidable height by English Heritage). From the fort, you drop down into the beautiful Eskdale Valley (*see* p 784), which stretches 12 miles into the flat, wooded coastal plain. This is 'walkers territory *par excellence*.' (Wainwright).

Grasmere

All the morning I was busy copying poems. Gathered peas, and in the afternoon Coleridge came, very hot; he brought the 2nd volume of the Anthology. The men went to bathe, and we afterwards sailed down to Loughrigg. Read poems on the water, and let the boat take its own course. We walked a long time upon Loughrigg. I returned in the gray twilight. The moon was just setting as we reached home.

Dorothy Wordsworth, *Diary*

Grasmere is a few miles north of Ambleside along the A591, where the valley opens up behind Loughrigg Fell into a lovely, flat-bottomed bowl in the midst of high, encircling fells. There is a wonderful sense of space and the hills are inviting. Wordsworth fell in love with Grasmere during a walking tour with his brother, and moved into an old pub south of the village with his sister Dorothy in December 1799. When his family grew too big, and his long-staying guests too frequent, they moved briefly into one or two other houses in Grasmere, before settling into much roomier Rydal Mount, south of Grasmere nearer Ambleside overlooking Rydal Water. He died there on 23 April 1850 at the grand old age of 80 and was buried in Grasmere churchyard. Their Grasmere home got its name, Dove Cottage, much later on, but was a place of pilgrimage even when Wordsworth was living in it. Now coachloads of whistle-stop tourists knock each other off the narrow pavements. It feels oddly desolate once the Wordsworth feeding frenzy ends at teatime.

Dove Cottage and Rydal Mount

> *While we were at breakfast ... he wrote the poem to a butterfly! He ate not a morsel, nor put on his stockings, but sate with his shirt neck unbuttoned and his waistcoat open while he did it.*
>
> Dorothy Wordsworth, *Diary*

The Wordsworths lived at **Dove Cottage** (***t*** *(01539) 435 544; open Feb–Dec 9.30–5.30, tours 10–4.50; adm*) for just eight and a half years, but it is everyone's favourite Wordsworth shrine – small, creaky and cottage-like, and altogether less bourgeois than the poet's other Lakeland homes. William Wordsworth was 29 when he moved in, hard up, idealistic and with a growing literary reputation due to the success of his *Lyrical Ballads*. He grew runner beans and peas in the little garden at the back and wrote some of his most memorable poetry here, including *The Prelude* and *Daffodils*. He married Mary Hutchinson, who moved in with her sister Sarah, and had three children here (John, Dora and Thomas) and two more later; two (Thomas and Catherine) died young.

De Quincey took over Dove Cottage when the Wordsworths moved out in 1808 and kept it for 28 years, although he was increasingly absent towards the end, moving to Edinburgh for good in 1830 and turning on his Lakeland heroes. The guided tours are excellent and anecdotal, pointing out all sorts of memorabilia such as William's ice skates and where they kept the cheese.

While you wait for your tour, look around the **museum** (*same hours*) next door. Here Wordsworth's poetry is set in the context of Lakeland myths created by earlier 18th-

Easedale Tarn Walk

The walk up to Easedale Tarn is one of the gentlest, with farmyard smells, small fields, dry-stone walls and sheep. De Quincey called the little valley of Easedale 'one of the most impressive solitudes of the Lake District' and Wordsworth called the tarn 'one of the finest in the country'. From Grasmere, the path climbs up the rushing Sour Milk Gill into a bulging green ring of open hills, in the midst of which the tarn gurgles placid and lovely. From there, either you can do as Wordsworth suggests, continue southwest to Stickle Tarn and the Langdale Pikes, or return to Grasmere through the next valley of Far Easedale, stopping for a drink on the terrace of the Lancrigg Hotel.

century travellers like Thomas West and the poet Thomas Gray, who turned Borrowdale into the Vale of Elysium and inspired idealised paintings by fashionable painters Philippe Jacques de Loutherbourg, Paul Sandby and Thomas Hearne of boats, wandering figures and strange, wind-tossed trees. Wordsworth didn't create the myths, but came to live among them.

Since the Wordsworth Trust opened the cottage to the public in 1981, the collection has grown to include some 50,000 letters, manuscripts and paintings by the Romantic poets and artists, more than half of which are the manuscripts, letters and diaries of William and Dorothy.

Rydal Mount (***t*** *(01539) 433 002; open Mar–Oct 9.30–5, Nov–Feb Wed–Mon 10–4, closed last 3 weeks in Jan; adm)*, a few miles down the road in the direction of Ambleside, shows you Wordsworth in a more comfortable stage of his life, entertaining in his smart dining room and lounging on his sofa. He lived here for the last 37 years of his life (1813–50), although at first he felt the need to reassure friends that despite the conspicuous luxury they were not 'setting up for fine fellows'. There are more letters and cuttings in Wordsworth's old study as well as bits and pieces of around the house. The poet put a lot of work into the garden, which climbs up the hillside to the house on terraces with trees and winding paths.

Penrith and the Northeastern Lakes

All the main roads – the M6/A6 from the north and the A686 trans-Pennine road – converge at the old market town of **Penrith**, half way along the Vale of Eden on the northeastern fringe of the National Park. This is Lowther country, with old Lowther Castle and the present Lowther family home to the south, while the A66 shoots west to the source of Lowther wealth – the coal mines and ports of Whitehaven and Maryport. Penrith, at the foot of its own hill, is a great base for northeast Lakeland, the Vale of Eden and the Pennines.

Beacon Hill may not be the Coniston Old Man, but it is somewhere for rich Penrithians to plant big houses with an eyeful of the eastern fells from the summit. Wordsworth's mother came from Penrith and for a while William and Dorothy went to the local school. They went for picnics on Beacon Hill together, but when their mother died of pneumonia William was sent to Ann Tyson's at Hawkshead and Dorothy was packed off to relations in Yorkshire.

Penrith is quieter than Keswick or Windermere. Have a look at the **church** and the Wordsworths' old **school** in the close. Opposite the station is the ruin of **Penrith Castle**. There's not much to see, but it was the most important link in the chain of medieval command on the Scottish border, built by Richard Neville, the 'kingmaker' and given to the Duke of Gloucester, Edward IV's brother. There is a deli on the market square that has been selling cheese and bread for years, and lots of 'father and sons' shops, selling leather goods and clothes modelled on 1950s mannequins.

About a mile and a half south of Penrith, on the A66, you come to the ruins of **Brougham Castle** (pronounced 'broom') at the confluence of the Eamont and Lowther

Where to Stay

Penrith t (01768) –

Portland Place, by the town hall, and Victoria Road are both lined with B&Bs.

Roundthorn Country House, Beacon Edge, **t** 863 952, *www.roundthorn.co.uk* (*expensive*). Handsome white-painted Georgian mansion in large gardens at end of long drive, just out of Penrith; views over Eden Valley and Lakeland Fells; 10 rooms.

The George Hotel, Devonshire Street, **t** 862 696, *www.georgehotel.penrith.co.uk* (*expensive*). Handsome red sandstone town-centre hotel with lamp-lit, polished-wood interiors; atmosphere of old-fashioned country inn; bar, restaurant and 34 bedrooms, some very comfortable.

Norcroft Guesthouse, Graham Street, **t** 862 365, *www.norcroft-guesthouse.co.uk* (*moderate*). Large red sandstone Victorian building, spacious and homely; simple flowery rooms on three floors.

Beacon Bank Hotel, Beacon Edge, **t** 862 633, *beaconbank.hotel@virgin.net* (*moderate*). Among larger detached Victorian properties with splendid views over roofs of town and across vale to mountains of northern Lakeland; set back behind gravel drive, covered in creeper; inside sturdy dark wooden furniture suited to style of house, lovely bedrooms with handsome beds and soft furnishings; friendly and grand.

Eating Out

Bit on the Side, Brunswick Square, **t** 892 526 (*moderate*). Penrith's only upmarket restaurant, offers canapés with drinks downstairs, dinner served upstairs. Pan-fried chicken breast with wild mushrooms, fillet of bream with prawns and scallops. *Open Fri and Sat.*

Café Ruhm, 15 Victoria Street, **t** 867 453 (*cheap*). Hip, relaxed, airy café with art for sale on walls, range of coffees, pavement seating, bagels and nice soups. *Closed Mon.*

Lowther Arms, Queen Street, **t** 862 792 (*cheap*). Cosy, beamy pub with stone walls, bench seating and log fire; huge plates of Cumberland sausage and chips, or mushroom bake with mashed potato; friendly crowd.

Costa's Tapas Bar, Queen Street, **t** 895 550 (*cheap*). Fun and informal; fairy lights and flags outside; tapas bar inside, and restaurant with gingham tablecloths and candles.

Bewick Coffee House and Bistro, Princes Court, **t** 864 764 (*cheap*). Bistro-style menu, roasted aubergine and feta fritters, roasted vegetable and goats' cheese salad. *Café open Mon–Sat, restaurant Fri and Sat eves.*

rivers and the crossing of historic roads. The naturally strategic site was first fortified by the Romans whose fort survives as an outline next to the castle. The whole place is picturesque, with sheep munching the grass around the castle and a handsome 17th-century arched bridge over the Eamont, close to the site of the old Roman bridge. In the 14th century the Norman castle was enlarged into a fortified palace by Robert Clifford, right-hand man to Edward I and Warden of the Western Marches. Lady Anne Clifford added many of the civilizing features such as fireplaces and plastered walls to the keep before she died here in 1676. Sadly, several serious fires have gutted the rooms, leaving only traces of their former grandeur. The spiral stairs of the keep lead to the chapel, with great views of the mountains.

Further south down narrow lanes is Lowther HQ: the fairy-tale façade of **Lowther Castle** and the Lowthers' present family home in the village of **Askham**, one of several pretty villages in the area.

Ullswater and Around

Thou hast clomb aloft, and gazed from the watch-towers of Helvellyn;
awed, delighted, and amazed!

Wordsworth, *To –, on her first ascent to the summit of Helvellyn, 1816*

Ullswater is the second largest lake in the district, curling from the eastern fells to within a stone's throw of Penrith. Gentle green slopes run down to the lake; behind them are big crags. Its accessibility from the northeast makes Ullswater popular, but without a lakeside town it has kept its romance. Wordsworth called its scenery 'the happiest combination of beauty and grandeur', and devoted six pages of his *Guide* to it. 'Daffodils' ('I wandered lonely as a cloud') was inspired by the host of golden flowers in **Gowbarrow Park** near the lakeshore. The poet spotted them on a walk with his sister Dorothy on 15 April 1802, in spite of the 'furious wind' and 'heavy rain'.

Base yourself in **Glenridding**, a walker's village on the southern tip of the lake. Just beyond it is a small National Trust car park and a footpath leading to the 65ft-high **Aira Force** waterfall, a famous beauty spot, and the daffodil woods. In summer, you can catch a boat from Glenridding pier to Howtown on the eastern shore, and walk back (7 miles) along the lakeshore path. Best of all, climb **Helvellyn**, the highest peak between Ullswater and Thirlmere, which has two razor-sharp buttresses, known as Striding and Swirral Edge. It was one of Coleridge's favourite climbs, and Wordsworth made it to the top in his 70s. Start from Glenridding, following the path up the side of a hidden valley. In peak season, you often find a queue to get onto Striding Edge, which from afar looks dangerously vertiginous, poised above the Red Tarn. You can get down to it via Swirral Edge, which takes you off the windy mountain top, and from there simply follow the beck back to Glenridding.

Tourist Information

Glenridding: Beckside car park, **t** (017684) 82414, *glenriddingtic@lakedistrict.gov.uk*. *Open summer 9–6, winter 9.30–3.30.*

Where to Stay and Eat

Ullswater t (017684) –

Sharrow Bay Country House Hotel, Ullswater, **t** 86301 (*luxury*). Victorian private-house-turned-hotel set in lovely 12-acre gardens and woodland, beneath Barton Fell overlooking Ullswater; antiques and fresh flowers, private jetty and boathouse, so you can go out on the lake in a boat, swim or fish without leaving the grounds; 26 bedrooms, six in grounds. Outstanding French/English restaurant.

Glenridding and Around t (017684) –

Inn on the Lake, Glenridding, **t** 82444, *www.innonthelakeullswater.com* (*expensive*). Forbidding greystone Victorian lakeside hotel set in 15 acres; 46 bedrooms; good restaurant; Rambler's Bar; comfortable lounge with lovely lake views. Come for tea on the patio on a mild day.

Mosscrag, Glenridding, **t** 82500 (*moderate*). One of most popular and comfortable low-budget Ullswater guesthouses, with six bedrooms; dinner also available.

Beech House, Glenridding, **t** 82037 (*moderate*). Pleasant family-run guesthouse.

Greystones Café, Glenridding, **t** 82392 (*cheap*). Home-made lunches and cakes.

White Lion Inn, Patterdale, **t** 82214 (*moderate*). Tall, narrow building at the narrowest part of the valley; comfortable, straightforward and popular with coast-to-coast walkers.

Keswick and Around

I walked with my brother at my side from Kendal to Grasmere, 18 miles and afterwards from Grasmere to Keswick, 15 miles through the most delightful country that was ever seen.

Dorothy Wordsworth, *Diary*

Keswick, in the shadow of **Skiddaw** and **Blencathra**, is the resort town of the north – touristy, pubby and with its own lake, **Derwent Water**, a short walk from the town. Visitors arrive on the A66 from Penrith and the M6, which cuts off the northern fells from all the good stuff to the south. Wainwright, however, devotes a whole book to the northern fells on the grounds that although they are lower, greener and less dramatic than those in the south, they are quiet and delightful nonetheless. In the Middle Ages, Keswick was known for its cheeses (the name means cheese town), but things changed in the 1500s, when the world's purest deposit of graphite was discovered in **Borrowdale**, the valley to the south of Derwent Water. Borrowdale graphite was so valuable that expert German miners were brought over to dig it out of the ground and an armed stage coach carried it to London where it was turned into cannon-ball moulds. It was good for pencils too, although the government discouraged this frivolous use. In the 19th century, the Cumberland Pencil Company exhausted the supply of pure graphite in a few decades of mass production and has since had to import its pencil leads.

Thomas Gray visited Borrowdale in the 1780s and, oblivious to the mining, called it the Vale of Elysium. Coleridge and his wife Sarah moved into **Greta Hall** in 1800 to be near Wordsworth in Grasmere, and Southey joined him there in 1801, bringing his own wife (Sarah's sister) as well as a third Fricker sister, the widowed Mrs Lovell. The Coleridges had three children (Hartley, Derwent and Sarah), and the Southeys had eight (although two died young) making the house a crowded place at times. Shelley visited Greta Hall in the winter of 1811–12, and was astounded by the number of books stashed in every conceivable space; other visitors included Ruskin and Walter Scott. After that, everyone wanted to see Borrowdale and the Keswick poets. Thanks to Canon Rawnsley's National Trust, however, Keswick was not allowed to expand down to the lakeshore; Derwent Water and Borrowdale are still beautiful.

Around Town

Keswick is part old market town, part Victorian resort (museum and public gardens) and part northern holiday town. At the top of a broad, busy street of hotels, pubs and shops is the 17th-century **Moot Hall** (largely rebuilt in 1813) with its Bavarian hat roof and one-handed clock, and behind it is the **Market Square**. The town is full of outdoor clothing shops. The largest, George Fisher's, was the photographic studio of the Abraham brothers, pioneering mountain and landscape photographers and rock climbers. The **Museum and Art Gallery** (***t*** *(017687) 73263*), on the edge of Fitz Park, has a 20ft Skiddaw-stone Glockenspiel with a seven octave range, a relief model of the Lake District, work from the Keswick School of Industrial Art, letters and manuscripts

Getting Around

Stagecoach, **t** 0870 608 2608, run regular buses from Keswick into Borrowdale.

Derwent Launch Service, **t** (017687) 72263. Ferries around the lake, stopping at Ashness, Lodore and Hawesend. *Services summer daily, winter weekends only.*

Keswick Mountain Bike Hire, Southey Hill Industrial Estate, near Greta Bridge, **t** (017687) 75202, *www.keswickbikes.co.uk*. Bike hire by the day. *Open daily 9–5.30.*

Tourist Information

Keswick: Moot Hall, **t** (017687) 72645, *keswicktic@lakedistrict.gov.uk. Open summer daily 9.30–5.30, winter 9.30–4.30.*

Seatoller: Borrowdale, **t** (017687) 77294, *seatollertic@lakedistrict.gov.uk. Open summer daily 10–5.*

Where to Stay

Keswick **t** (017687) –

The Keswick Country House Hotel, Station Road, **t** 72020 (*expensive*). Splendid Victorian hotel with turrets at foot of Skiddaw.

Queens Hotel, Main Street, **t** 73333, *www.queenshotel.co.uk* (*expensive*). Old-fashioned hotel on busy thoroughfare, with 35 bedrooms, mix of modern and fusty.

The Ravensworth Hotel, 29 Station Street, **t** 72476 (*moderate*). Cheerful, peaceful hotel with sweet-smelling rooms.

Portland House, 19 Leonard Street, **t** 74230, *www.portlandhouse.net* (*moderate*). Edwardian townhouse with five rooms; popular with walkers; stands out among the Victorian guesthouses behind town.

Derwent Water **t** (017687) –

Highfield Hotel, The Heads, **t** 72508 (*expensive*). Attractive spot beside Derwent Water, with 18 rooms, turret views; restaurant serves beef and Yorkshire pudding, trout on risotto, and stuffed roast pepper.

Borrowdale **t** (017687) –

Langstrath Country Inn, Stonethwaite, **t** 77239, *www.info@thelangstrath.com* (*expensive*). Superb place to stay, looking down Langstrath Valley; excellent *après*-walk atmosphere; restaurant serves traditional Cumbrian sausages and wild boar pies.

Royal Oak Hotel, Rosthwaite, **t** 77214, *www.royaloakhotel.co.uk* (*expensive*). Welcoming former farmhouse, popular with walkers; friendly; 12 bedrooms and snug bar with green slate serving counter.

Yew Tree Farm, Rosthwaite, **t** 77675 (*moderate*). Rough-cast 18th-century farmhouse in wide amphitheatre of crags, with cobbled yard and stone barns, beautiful rooms with stout furniture and three chintzy guest rooms (the Prince of Wales stayed here in 2001, writing in the visitors' book: 'It's a marvellously cosy place – very special'); hearty breakfasts.

Seathwaite Farm, Seathwaite, **t** 77394 (*moderate*). Wonderful farmhouse at head of Borrowdale where the sound of Sour Milk Ghyll sends you to sleep.

High Lodore Farm, **t** 77221 (*cheap*). Delightful 15th-century whitewashed farmhouse with charming café next door.

Eating Out

Keswick

Luca's Ristorante, Greta Bridge, High Hill, **t** 74621 (*moderate*). Upmarket restaurant in the Keswick School of Industrial Arts building; lots of pasta and fish dishes, as well as home-made stone-baked pizzas. *Book at weekends and in summer.*

Lakeland Pedlar, Hendersons Yard, **t** 75752 (*cheap*). Tasty vegetarian snacks including full breakfast, falafel, humus and pita bread, soups, sandwiches and bike hire.

Sweeney's Bar-Restaurant, 18–20 Lake Road, **t** 72990 (*cheap*). Sausage and mash and mushy peas, lamb and mustard mash, fresh fish specials. Large beer garden at back with sturdy wooden tables.

Dog and Gun, Lake Road, **t** 73463 (*cheap*). Atmospheric town-centre pub for quieter drinking crowd.

Borrowdale

Farmhouse Café, Borrowdale, **t** 77221 (*cheap*). Idyllic for coffee and pastries, with garden overlooking Derwent Water and Cat Bells.

of Southey and the other lake poets. The school and Greta Hall are at the far end of town (both closed to the public). The **Cumberland Pencil Museum** (***t*** *(01768) 773 626; open daily 9.30–4; adm*) in the old pencil factory is aimed at children; you can also buy pencils, from a child's set to a top-quality Derwent Artist wooden box of 120 pencils.

Just off the A66, east of Keswick, have a look at **Castlerigg Stone Circle**, a squat ring of Neolithic standing stones surrounded by Lakeland monsters including saddle-backed Blencathra, Skiddaw and Helvellyn. Wordsworth and Coleridge climbed up here only to find the stones daubed with white paint. The climb up Skiddaw over the back of Latrigg from Keswick is a hard tramp, redeemed by the views from the top. Wainwright recommends an alternative route from the Ravenstone Hotel on the A591 north of Keswick, over the Ullcock Pike ridge above Bassenthwaite Lake.

Keswick's highlight is **Derwent Water**, whose shores become a beach in summer. Wordsworth devoted a whole section of his *Guide* to the best views of the lake; Ruskin's first memory was the view of Derwent Water from Friar's Crag and Canon Rawnsley founded the National Trust to preserve it from developers. It's powerful stuff, with its wooded islands and mountains. Most visitors stick to the quayside with its wooden jetties and Friar's Crag, a little further down the lakeside, but you can catch ferries to landing stages all around the lake, where you can take short walks. (The road runs along the eastern shore, so the western side is best for walking.)

Derwent Water is guarded from Borrowdale by the tightly clenched rock gnashers known as the **Jaws of Borrowdale** – a product of the Ice Age, when two major glaciers came down the Seathwaite and Langstrath valleys, combining forces in the wide middle section around Rosthwaite and forcing their way through the hard, volcanic jaws, before expanding into the softer, older sedimentary rocks that later became Derwent Water.

'No Keswick holiday is consummated without a visit to Cat Bells,' wrote the inescapable Wainwright. From the Hawse End landing stage it is a 1½-mile walk, 'rewarding out of all proportion to the small effort needed'. From the top of **Cat Bells**, you can continue along the ridge which runs along the entire length of Borrowdale, dropping down to Rosthwaite where you can catch the bus back to Keswick.

From Borrowdale into the High Fells

The place reminds me of those passes in the Alps, where the guides tell you to move with speed and say nothing, less the agitation of air should loosen the snows above.

Thomas Gray

The valley road on the east side of Derwent Water and the River Derwent is scenic, with several beauty spots along the way and access to some of the most dramatic fell country. **Ashness Bridge** is a popular place to stop and take a photograph, and the **Lodore Falls**, reached from High Lodore Farm at the southern tip of Derwent Water, are a good picnic site. Southey wrote a pleasantly un-Romantic poem about the falls 'thumping and plumping and bumping and jumping and hissing and whizzing'. Following Watendlath Beck on foot from the falls you enter the lovely, hanging Watendlath Valley, which culminates in a lonely tarn and a path over High Tove to the

Ascent of Scafell Pike from Seathwaite (10 miles)

Scafell Pike (3,205ft) is the highest mountain in England. Wainwright wrote that its ascent from Borrowdale was the best fell walk in the Lake District. Head up the path to Stockley Bridge from Seathwaite, where you can carry on up via Sty Head or through Grain's Gill (Wainwright's choice). Don't miss Sprinkling Tarn on the far side of Grain's Gill. The path carries on around the Great End, which blocks the direct route to Scafell Pike, and cuts west before Ill Crag, eventually picking up the path up to Scafell Pike again. Return to Seathwaite via the Corridor Route to Sty Head.

Coleridge made a reckless descent of Scafell down the channel of a dry waterfall and wrote to all his friends about it, describing how he dropped from ledge to ledge, shaking all over, knowing it was impossible to return, and sure he was going to kill himself: 'I lay upon my back to rest myself, and was beginning according to my custom to laugh at myself for a madman.'

lake of Thirlmere. Back on the Borrowdale route, the road is squeezed up against the river through the Jaws of Borrowdale. Above Rosthwaite, the valley divides into the steep-sided **Langstrath** or **Stonethwaite Valley** (explored from the Langstrath Country Inn) and the **Seathwaite Valley**, whose reputation as the wettest place in England vies with that as the main corridor to **Great Gable** (2,949ft), **Bowfell** (2,959ft) and **Scafell Pike** (3,205ft). Walkers ceaselessly trudge though the cobbled courtyard of Seathwaite Farm into mountain country. The main valley road, however, turns west through Seatoller and climbs out of Borrowdale over the steep **Honister Pass** past old slate quarries and mines and down to Buttermere (*see* p.782). Wainwright lists the ascent of Great Gable among his 18 favourite walks: from the small car park at Seatoller Fell walk west along the old tramway to ruined Drum House, then head south to the summit plateau of Great Gable, with breathtaking views down into Wasdale Head and Wast Water; return north via Windy Gap over Green Gable and Grey Knotts.

Cockermouth

Cockermouth is tucked away in the northwest corner of the Lake District, reached via the A595 from Carlisle or the A66 from Keswick and Penrith. It is a pleasant market town, crammed with colourful picture-book houses and surrounded by rolling green countryside, with the grey shapes of the big fells to the south. Two mountain rivers meet in the middle of town, the Cocker rising above Buttermere and the Derwent coming off the peaks around Scafell. Most visitors probably wouldn't stray this far from the central lakes if it weren't that Wordsworth was born here in 1770, and mentioned it in the *Prelude*. There are plenty of pubs, one or two nice restaurants and a surprising number of attractions in the town, including a brewery, a printers' museum, a collection of famous cars and, of course, the **Wordsworth Birthplace** (***t*** *(01900) 824 805, www.nationaltrust.org.uk; open April–Oct Mon–Fri, June–Aug also Sat; adm*). This grand Georgian house on the main street is often a bit of a shock to Wordsworth lovers, who expect a humbler home. Wordsworth's father, John, was a

Tourist Information

Cockermouth: Town Hall, Market Street, **t** (01900) 822634. *Open summer daily 9.30–5, winter Mon–Sat 9.30–4.*

Where to Stay

Cockermouth t (01900) –

The Manor House Hotel, Crown Street, **t** 828 663 (*expensive*). Almost-elegant with spiral staircase, mouldings and alcoves. Highly-regarded restaurant (*moderate*) serves chicken breast stuffed with black pudding and smoked bacon, fresh Fleetwood fish or roast lamb with Mediterranean vegetables.

The Rook Guesthouse, 9 Castlegate, **t** 828 496 (*expensive*). Charming with extraordinary spiral stone stairway and massive beams.

The Globe Hotel, Main Street, **t** 822 126 (*moderate*). Endless corridors and plush Victorian décor with 30 comfortable rooms. Robert Louis Stevenson stayed in 1871.

The Castle Gate Guesthouse, Castlegate, **t** 828 496 (*moderate*). Large and characterful; popular with coast-to-coast cyclists.

Rose Cottage, Lorton Road, **t** 822 189 (*moderate*). Cheerful and friendly, bright and clean, on outskirts of Cockermouth.

Riverside, 12 Market Street, **t** 827 504 (*cheap*). Attractive, friendly Georgian townhouse with three modest bedrooms, one en-suite.

Eating Out

Quince and Medlar, 13 Castlegate, **t** 823 579 (*moderate*). Excellent vegetarian restaurant in elegant, intimate 18th-century drawing-room setting with cosy pre/post-dinner snug. *Closed Sun and Mon.*

Over the Top Café, 38 Kirkgate, **t** 827 016 (*cheap*). Largely vegetarian food served in a pleasantly ramshackle and informal setting, with *National Geographic* magazines littered around and great soup.

The Bitter End, Kirk Gate, off Market Place (*cheap*). Friendly locals' pub with micro-brewery behind glass at back.

You can get lunch at either of the two hotels at the north end of Buttermere; the Walkers' Bar in the **Bridge Hotel** is nicest.

lawyer who worked as a steward for the Lowther family, later the Earls of Lonsdale – some of the richest landowners in the north of England – and the Wordsworths lived in the tied house rent-free. In the house are one or two pieces of memorabilia and some interesting early prints of the Lakes, including etchings by William Green from *Forty Views of Ambleside and Keswick* and a Turner landscape. At the back of the garden with its fountain and box-edged lawn is the Terrace Walk, which appears in the *Prelude*, overlooking the River Derwent.

Buttermere

South of Cockermouth along the River Cocker valley road you reach **Crummock Water** and Buttermere. Beyond, the road climbs over Honister Pass into Borrowdale. Buttermere is lucky enough to sit in one of the most picturesque valleys in the district. **Haystacks** makes a fabulous walk with thrilling scenery up top (where Wainwright's ashes were scattered beside Innominate Tarn), cliff top views down to Buttermere and glimpses of Pillar and the dim form of Great Gable to the south. 'For a man trying to forget a persistent worry,' says Wainwright, 'the top of Haystacks is a complete cure.' The easiest ascent is from a car park on the Honister Pass road, saving you the steep climb, but most walkers start either from Buttermere village or Gatesgarth Farm car park at the southern end of lake, climbing up the deeply scored, loose track towards Scarth Gap. On the west side of the lake are the shoulders of

Red Pike, **High Stile** and **High Crag**. A superb high-level ridge walk known as the **Buttermere Trio** or High Stile Range links them together, starting up the well-worn path above the village to the summit of Red Pike, then following the ridge over High Stile and High Crag down to Scarth Gap, which brings you back to the lake.

The Cumbrian Coast

The A595-A596 runs along the coast from Furness to Maryport, initially through fabulous National Park countryside, but not for long. The discovery of coal and iron on the coastal plain in the 18th century led to the rapid industrialisation of the coast, transforming Whitehaven, Workington and Maryport into ports of national importance, before their equally dramatic decline in the 20th century. **Maryport** is the only one that won't completely deter you, with its harbour and museums. The Romans built a series of fortifications along the Cumbrian coast, linking up with Hadrian's Wall to the north; Maryport is likely to have been the command headquarters for these coastal defences as well as the chief supply depot for the Hadrian's Wall forts. **The Senhouse Roman Museum** (*The Battery, Sea Brows,* **t** *(01900) 816 168; open April–June Tues–Sun 10–5, July–Oct daily 10–5, Nov–Mar Fri–Sun 10.30–4; adm*), housed in an old Victorian battery on a headland overlooking the harbour, is well worth a visit. It has a collection of inscribed altar stones belonging to the First Cohort of Spaniards, who were garrisoned here between AD 132 and AD 138, and one of the oldest private archaeological collections in the country – collected by the Senhouse family and first mentioned in the 1695 edition of *Campden's Britannia*. A new altar was dedicated annually on the emperor's birthday – usually to Jupiter, the god of war – and the old altar disposed of. The inscriptions give potted biographies of the auxiliary commanders (name, birthplace, rank, previous postings and time spent at Maryport). One commander, Marcus Maenius Agrippa, was known to be a personal friend of Emperor Hadrian; Maryport was a prestigious posting.

Tourist Information

St Bees: 122 Main Street, **t** (01946) 822 343. *Open Mon–Sat 9.30–5, Sun 10–1.*

Where to Stay and Eat

St Bees t (01946) –

Fleatham House, High House Road, **t** (01946) 822 341, *www.fleathamhouse.com* (*expensive*). Beautiful, secluded and extremely friendly; popular with holidaying politicians, including Tony Blair and family in summer 2002; moderately priced menu offers pan-fried duck breast, fillet steak Rossini and Dover sole.

Manor House Hotel, 12 Main Street **t** 822 425 (*moderate*). Eight extremely comfortable, tasteful bedrooms. Slightly brash Coast to Coast Bar.

Stonehouse Farm, 133 Main Street, **t** 822 224, *www.stonehousefarm.net* (*moderate*). Sheep in garden and Jack Russell dog; wide stone staircase leads up two floors; simple, friendly place; six bedrooms, one in cottage outside.

Queens Hotel, Main Street, **t** 822 287, *www.queenshotel-stbees.com* (*moderate*). Attractive, white-painted hotel; cosy bar with velvet settles around the edge and red lamp shades; 14 simple bedrooms; cheap pub grub in conservatory restaurant.

Ravenglass was the Roman port of *Glannaventa*, supplying the Lakeland forts and much of the north via Eskdale and the mountain passes over Hardknott and High Street. **Eskdale** is one of the most remote, unspoilt valleys in Lakeland, one of Wainwright's favourites. From Ravenglass, you can take the **Ravenglass and Eskdale Railway**, a 7-mile Victorian narrow-gauge track to Eskdale *(**t** (01229) 717 171, www.ravenglass-railway.co.uk)* and return on foot from Irton Road station over Muncaster Fell. Wainwright's *Walks from L'aal Ratty*, sold at the station, describes ten walks from the Ravenglass–Eskdale miniature railway. The A595 is also the only route into **Wasdale**, where **Wast Water** is the most secretive of the lakes, exerting a grail-like attraction through its inaccessibility. It is popular with walkers heading for Great Gable and Scafell Pike, who stay at Wasdale Head Hotel. **Sellafield** nuclear reprocessing plant is just off the main road near the coast. Surprisingly – given its links to weapons production – its visitor centre is one of Cumbria's most visited tourist attractions. The prettiest coastal village is **St Bees**. The red sandstone cliffs of its headland are the start of Wainwright's coast-to-coast walk, which ends at Robin Hood Bay.

Carlisle

Cumbria's fortress city is an excellent base for exploring Hadrian's Wall and the Solway Coast, and a launch pad for Scotland; in fact Carlisle has always been a natural base for military advances north of the border. It was the site of a Roman fort called *Luguvalium* long before Hadrian built his wall. After the Romans, Carlisle constantly switched sides of the border as the border moved north and south. At the time of Domesday, Cumberland was Scottish. Anglo-Norman kings William II, Henry I, Edward I and Henry VIII built castles, burned towns and villages, imposed draconian laws and did everything in the conqueror's handbook to stabilise the border and wrest control of everything south of it back to Westminster. Scottish kings (and Pretenders) played a similar game. But at least half of the inhabitants of the border region refused to recognise the laws at any given time, whether they came from Scotland or England. The backup forces of the Norman Conquest did not secure Carlisle until 1603, when James VI of Scotland became James I of England too.

The atmospheric old part of the city is small enough to see in a day or less. It is defined by the limits of the old city walls, guarded in the north by the castle and in the south by the drum towers of Henry VIII's citadel, which was converted into law courts in the early 1800s, but remains one of the most powerful symbols of Carlisle's turbulent past.

Start in the fan-shaped **Market Place** in the middle of town; there are no markets today, but note the market cross in the middle and attractive old buildings around the edge, including the 17th-century **Old Town Hall** and 15th-century **Guild Hall**. A narrow lane between the two leads to the covered market (now selling cheap clothes). All the good stuff is up **Castle Street** – the cathedral, museum and castle – passing **Bullough's** (est. 1910), Carlisle's department store, with a tea shop at the top.

Tourist Information

Carlisle: Old Town Hall, **t** (01228) 625 600. *Open Nov–Feb Mon–Sat 10–4; Mar–June and Sept–Oct Mon–Sat 9.30–5; July Mon–Sat 9.30–5.30; Aug Mon–Sat 9.30–6; May–Aug also Sun 10.30–4.*

Getting There and Around

Frequent **trains** run between Newcastle and Carlisle, stopping at Hexham and Haltwhistle, and along the Cumbrian coast to Barrow-in-Furness via Cockermouth. Mainline West Coast trains go to London and Edinburgh. The scenic **Settle–Carlisle Railway** (*see* p.800) takes you through the Pennines and Vale of Eden. For all train information contact **National Rail Enquiries**, **t** 08457 484950, *www.thetrainline.com.*

Hadrian's Wall Bus runs summer and less frequently in winter. A **day ticket** gives unlimited travel for one day; bus departs Carlisle from outside County Courts on English Street, stopping at Lanercost Priory and all the Roman wall forts.

Other **local bus services** also run along Hadrian's Wall. Contact the tourist information centre or call **Traveline**, **t** 0870 608 2608 for details. All services infrequent in winter.

Where to Stay

Carlisle t (01228) –

Central Plaza, Victoria Viaduct, **t** 520 256 (*expensive*). Old-fashioned Victorian-style central hotel with 84 bedrooms, restaurant, bar and lounge.

The Lakes Court Hotel, Court Square, **t** 531 951 (*expensive*). Handsome, large Victorian neo-classical hotel with Dutch-style roof next to the railway station by the Citadel; 70 rooms.

Number 31, Howard Place, **t** 597 080 (*expensive*). Victorian townhouse, civilized and homely, with delicious cooking smells. Host greets you in striped apron. Best place to stay in town, but only three rooms. Dinner available (*moderate*).

Howard House, 27 Howard Place, **t** 529 159, *howardhouse@bigfoot.com* (*moderate*). Civilized, quiet Victorian townhouse with two bedrooms.

Abberley, 33 Victoria Place, **t** 521 645 (*moderate*). Large Victorian house with tiled porch; bedrooms with pine furniture.

Warwick Lodge Guesthouse, 112 Warwick Road, **t** 523 796 (*cheap*). Comfortable, homely feel.

Courtfield Guesthouse, 169 Warwick Road, **t** 522 767 (*cheap*). Warm, homely, chintzy.

Eating Out

Most bars and restaurants are around the Citadel. At the top of town, near the cathedral, Fisher Street off Market Place has several delis and sandwich bars.

Vivaldi, 30 Lowther Street, **t** 818 333 (*moderate*). Popular, style-conscious Italian.

DaVids, 62 Warwick Road, **t** 523 578 (*moderate*). Georgian-style restaurant with high-backed chairs, fire in winter and plates of steak, roast Gressingham duck and other English delicacies. *Closed Sun.*

Prior's Kitchen Restaurant (undercroft of Carlisle Cathedral), **t** 543 251 (*cheap*). Morning and afternoon coffee, hot and cold lunches including Cumberland Tattie Pot.

John Watts and Son, Bank Street, **t** 521 545 (*cheap*). Attractive Victorian shopfront with coffee smell wafting out. Loose-leaf teas, Horlicks and honeyed crumpets as well as coffee to drink or buy by the packet.

Howard Arms, Lowther Street, **t** 532 926 (*cheap*). Traditional 19th-century pub with green-ceramic-tiled façade, hanging lanterns and pub sign; small rooms inside with dark wooden walls and settles, rough and ready with lively music, mixed crowd.

Le Gall, Devonshire Street, **t** 818 388 (*cheap*). Glass-fronted café-bar on a handsome old street. Perfect for a leisurely morning or at the end of the day for a coffee or cold beer. If you get settled in you might want to order chilli, burritos, an omelette or beef burger.

Café Solo, corner of Botcher Street and The Crescent, **t** 631 600 (*cheap*). Young and hip.

Gianni's Pizzeria, 3 Cecil Street (off Warwick Street), **t** 21093 (*cheap*). Cheerful Italian with walls covered in bunting and fairy lights – the sort of place where there's often a birthday party at a large table. *Closed Sun.*

The red sandstone **cathedral** stands in a beautiful 17th-century brick close. It dates back to 1122, when Henry I established an Augustinian priory in the city. A decade later it became the cathedral at the centre of the new diocese of Carlisle. Parliamentarian soldiers destroyed the nave in the Civil War, using the stone to build guardhouses on each of the city gates and in the market place. The proportions are all messed up: the truncated Norman nave with its thick columns and rounded arches looks like a chapel, while the Gothic presbytery with its famous east window looks more like the nave. But it is small and charming, with striking details like the 14th-century stone carved miserichords and dark, spiky stalls in the choir. Walter Scott got married in the Norman west end on Christmas Eve 1797. Outside, not much of the monastery escaped the stone-grabbing Parliamentarians – just a few cloister arches and the 13th-century fratery (now the cathedral restaurant).

Leave the cathedral close via Paternoster Row and Abbey Street to get to **Tullie House Museum and Gallery** (*main entrance on Castle Street, **t** (01228) 534 781; open Nov–Mar Mon–Sat 10–4, Sun 12–4; April–June and Sept–Oct Mon–Sat 10–5, Sun 12–5; July–Aug Mon–Sat 10–5, Sun 11–5; adm*). The pretty Jacobean house in the middle of it was built by Thomas Tullie in 1689. Its displays include a series of Pre-Raphaelite drawings with full-lipped Rossetti women and chalk cartoons by Burne-Jones for the east window of Brampton church. Most of the museum is given over to Carlisle's history, notably Roman Carlisle, with tools, ornaments, jewellery, weapons and so forth from the western sector of Hadrian's Wall, and finds from excavations of Agricola's timber fort under the city centre. Miscellaneous masonry includes the so-called **Conquest Tomb** (found in 1787), depicting a cavalry man riding over the body of a native Briton, and a moustachioed Roman head found in Appleby-in-Westmorland. Readings from the diary of 18-year-old Isaac Tullie, who later became mayor, bring the city during the 1644–5 siege alive, and people come for miles to see the audio-visual telling of the story of the Reivers and the Debatable Lands.

Carlisle Castle

***t** (01228) 591 922; open April–Sept 9.30–6, Oct 10–5, Nov–Mar 10–4; adm.*

Sadly, a busy ring road cuts **Carlisle Castle** off from the city centre. This tremendous red sandstone fortress was at the centre of one of the most contested military zones in the country for hundreds of years. In its lifetime, there have been three major sieges, first by Robert the Bruce (1315), then the Parliamentarians (1644–5), who took a year to starve the city into submission, and finally Bonny Prince Charlie (1745) – the last time an English city was besieged. William II chose the strategic site on high ground in the crook of the River Eden and its tributaries. His motte and bailey fortress survives with improvements by Henry I and Scottish King David I, who controlled Carlisle from 1135 to 1153. The inner and outer bailey each have their own defensive wall, dry moat and powerful gatehouse, protecting the great stone keep in the middle. The Victorian barrack blocks date from the period when the castle was used as a regimental depot for the King's Own Border Regiment, between 1703 and 1959.

From the castle, a footbridge leads back over the main road into West Walls, a narrow street along the old west walls; from here you can easily cut back down alleys into the city centre.

The Solway Coast

The main road runs from Maryport to Carlisle, leaving a wedge of marshy countryside along the Solway Coast with views west over the estuary to the Scottish mountains – silhouetted at sunset. Heading west on the B5307 out of Carlisle, turn off onto the coast road which continues around the **Cardurnock Peninsula**, one big bird sanctuary; the Solway mud is a crucial stop for migrating birds on major flight paths. From **Burgh by Sands** you come to a monument on the marsh, marking where Edward I died campaigning against the Scots in 1307. **Bowness-on-Solway** was the western end of Hadrian's Wall with forts at Drumburgh and Burgh by Sands.

The Victorian resort of **Silloth** was developed to raise money for the building of its docks, where Carr's flour originally incorporated a reading room, school room, library and hot baths for the workers. The resort is unspoilt and shabby, its esplanade set back from the sea behind a green planted with Scots pines.

The pretty little village of **Allonby** was visited by Charles Dickens and Wilkie Collins in September 1857. You can watch the sunset over Allonby Bay from the grassed-over ruins of the small Roman fort known as Milefortlet 21 on the cliff top – a small link in the chain of coastal defence stretching from Hadrian's Wall to Ravenglass.

East into Hadrian's Wall Country

From Carlisle, heading east up the A69, you come to the market town of **Brampton**, on the edge of the most exciting section of Hadrian's Wall. You can smell wood smoke in the air, and everything looks charmingly decrepit. In the centre of the cobbled market place is the old **Butter Cross,** shaped like a wedding cake with a clock tower on top. The cobbled streets are crammed on market day (Wednesday). The highlight of this unassuming place is **St Martin's Church**. It's the only church designed and built by Philip Webb, with stained-glass windows designed by Burne-Jones and manufactured by William Morris.

From Brampton, if it's a nice day, and you're not itching with impatience to see the wall, head south up the B6413 to **Talkin Tarn**, a beautiful upland lake in a bowl of rough countryside. You can walk all the way around, and there's a good pub in Talkin where you can have lunch. Brampton is also the start of a wonderful scenic drive on the A689 across the Pennines, following the River South Tyne for much of the way, to the lonely market town of **Alston** (17 miles) right in the middle of the moors.

However, it's far more likely you'll be heading northeast, following signs to Hadrian's Wall leading you off the A69, up and then down a narrow county lane into the beautiful **Irthing Valley** and **Lanercost Priory** (*near Brampton*, **t** *(01697) 73030; open Easter–Sept 10–6, Oct 10–5; adm*). The old Augustinian monastery was built using

Where to Stay and Eat

Along Hadrian's Wall t (016977) –

Farlam Hall Hotel, Brampton, **t** 46234, *www.farlamhall.co.uk* (*luxury*). Beautiful country-house hotel off A689 near Brampton; by the time you have parked the car next to its beautiful gardens you are under its spell; walk into a world of splendid wallpapers and old-fashioned charms. A rare treat if you can afford it. Dinner is included in the price for a night's stay.

The Blacksmiths Arms, Talkin (near Brampton), **t** 3452, *www.blacksmithsarmstalkin.co.uk* (*moderate*). Excellent lunches in friendly and popular pub with high culinary standards – fisherman's pie, lots of vegetarian dishes, Cumberland sausage, chicken casserole; bedrooms all cared-for and comfortable.

The Hill on the Wall, Gilsland, **t** 47214 (*moderate*). Gorgeous 16th-century house, once a castle, with yard-thick walls and deeply recessed window and doorways, loudly ticking clocks, solid, chunky antique pine furniture, sturdy white-panelled doors and lovely bedrooms with views of Hadrian's Wall where it crosses River Irthing.

Huntington's Wine Bar and Restaurant, Brampton, **t** 5481 (*cheap*). Busy little place, with very friendly management and simple décor. Food off the specials board is delicious.

pilfered stone from the wall, but its proximity to the border put it in the firing line during the Anglo-Scottish wars and it was ransacked by William Wallace, Robert the Bruce and King David II of Scotland. Edward I 'Hammer of the Scots' stayed here for six months. After the Dissolution, the monastic buildings were turned into a private house for Sir Thomas Dacre of Naworth Castle, and the nave, with its extraordinary west front, was made into the parish church. Of the rest of the ruins, only the undercroft of the refectory survives in a recognisable way.

The road climbs out of the Irthing Valley from Lanercost, and before long you pass a turret, and a good section of the wall leading up to **Birdoswald Fort**, the first permanent barracks on the line of the wall. The main stretch of Hadrian's Wall, with all the forts, is about 12 miles between Birdoswald and Housesteads Fort (*see* p.899).

Yorkshire

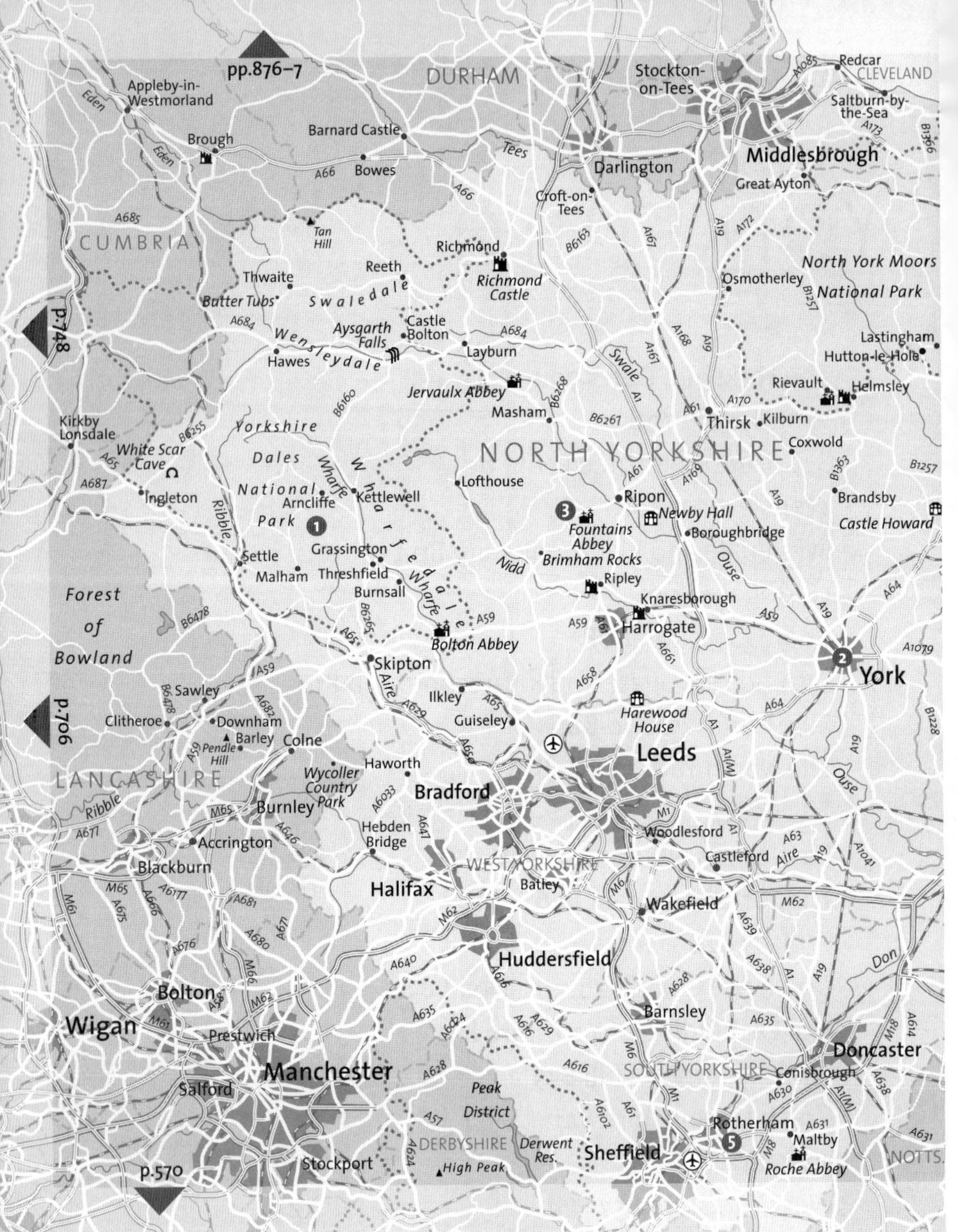

They are hard to lead, and impossible to drive.

Charlotte Brontë on Yorkshiremen

Ask anyone in England and they will proffer one 'fact' about Yorkshire: its people have a reputation for being terse, stubborn and tight-fisted. But be warned: most of what you hear about Yorkshire is more myth than fact.

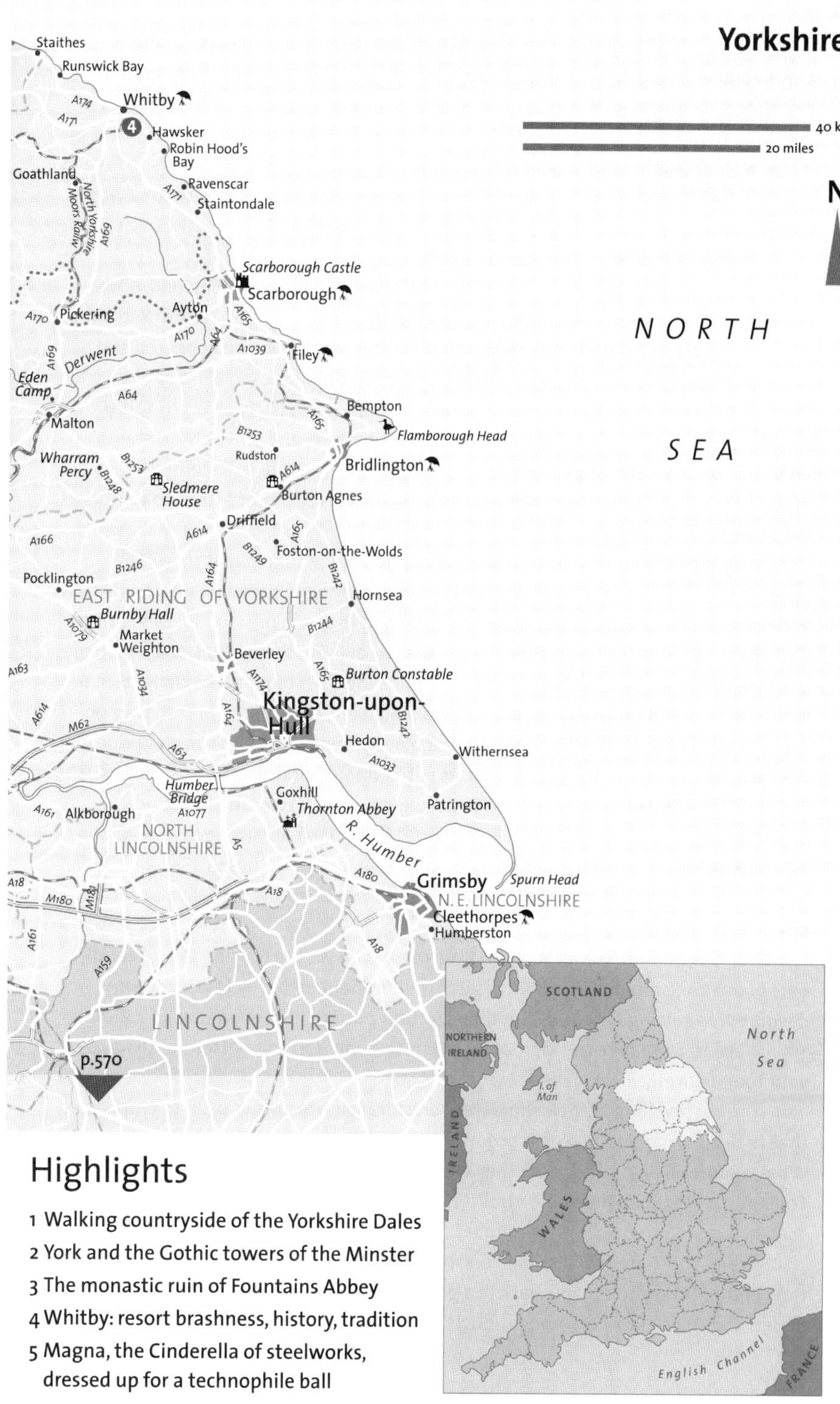

Highlights

1 Walking countryside of the Yorkshire Dales
2 York and the Gothic towers of the Minster
3 The monastic ruin of Fountains Abbey
4 Whitby: resort brashness, history, tradition
5 Magna, the Cinderella of steelworks, dressed up for a technophile ball

For a start, Yorkshire is not a county but a spiritual homeland. Precisely where it begins and ends is a matter of tradition, emotion and the state of cartographic reshuffles. Historically – until radical local government reorganization in the 1970s – Yorkshire covered everything from the Humber to the Tees, stretching to Sheffield in its deep south, with its western border meandering along the Pennine hills to take in the Forest of Bowland and Sedbergh. This unmanageable administrative area was split into three sub-counties called 'ridings': North, West and East – with South Riding existing only as the title of a work of fiction.

Modern Yorkshire, after much tinkering with the political map of England, now comprises four different parts, still named after the compass points: North Yorkshire, West Yorkshire, South Yorkshire and East Riding (the last having disappeared and reappeared in the blink of an eye). But it is not quite the same Yorkshire of old: 'Teesside' has been cut adrift from its Yorkshire roots; some parts of South Yorkshire have been filched from Nottinghamshire and Derbyshire; and parts of Yorkshire's arch-rival county, Lancashire, have been added to West Yorkshire. To complicate the map further, the area known as North Lincolnshire likes to present itself to visitors as if it were part of Yorkshire.

The only way you can be sure whether or not you are in Yorkshire is to ask the locals: if they say they are from Yorkshire, you are. For them, Yorkshire is the only sane and respectable part of the world to hale from and they will pity you for being born elsewhere. The strange thing about this is that by owning themselves as 'tykes' (true born Yorkshire men and women) they are embracing a list of personal characteristics which you wouldn't have thought anyone would want to admit to. In fact, they go even further and make their meanness and bloody-mindedness a source of pride. They will be the first to sell you beer mats with famous Yorkshire mottos such as: 'Tha can allus tell a Yorkshireman but tha can't tell him much' (You can always tell a Yorkshireman but you can't tell him much) or 'See all, hear all, say nowt; eat all, sup all, pay nowt and if ivver tha does owt fer nowt allus do it fer thysen' (See all, hear all but don't say anything; eat all, drink all, but don't pay anything; and if you ever do anything for free, do it for yourself).

The Yorkshire 'national' anthem, *On Ilkla' Moor Baht 'At*, is a rousing tale of cannibalism of a Yorkshireman, sung with gusto but without empathy for the person devoured, as getting eaten was his own fault for putting himself in that situation. You'll have to ask a tyke the logic of this. Or is the only Yorkshire essential to have your tongue firmly in your cheek?

Apart from revelling in their character, Yorkshire folk are always keen to emphasize that theirs is not only the biggest county but also the one with the most variety. What features haven't they got? they will demand: Yorkshire is a microcosm of England, so why visit anywhere else? It has even given Britain half its national dish: Yorkshire pudding to go with roast beef.

Scenically, there are two distinct Yorkshires. **South and West Yorkshire** seems at time like one enormous conurbation, a great, grey sprawl of industry based on the underlying coalfield where two products made the fortunes of generations of entrepreneurs: wool in Bradford, Leeds, Halifax and Huddersfield; and steel in Sheffield and Rotherham. As the old heavy industries have declined these cities have sought to reinvent themselves with tourist attractions drawing on their economic history, and there is no doubt that Yorkshire's old industrial heartland is thick with interesting places to visit.

North Yorkshire and the East Riding, on the other hand, are predominantly rural with barely a factory in sight. Good quality farmland rolls in all directions, punctuated only by villages, market towns, ruined abbeys, the odd castle and the stately homes that aristocratic landowners built themselves in the 17th and 18th centuries. The countryside is fringed by a long coastline of cliffs, coves and sandy beaches.

If anything unites these two extremes it is hills and rivers. The entire west wall of Yorkshire is formed by the **Pennines** which are often bleak but in the north become the pretty **Yorkshire Dales**. More hills, the **North York Moors**, rise above the coast behind Whitby, and the **Yorkshire Wolds** spring in a wide arc between York and Hull. Numerous rivers flow out of or through these hills, most of them travelling roughly northwest to southeast and merging to pour out into the North Sea as the Humber Estuary. Rivers there are aplenty, but natural lakes are about the only geographical feature that Yorkshire doesn't do well.

On the banks of one of the north of England's longest rivers, the Ouse, stands **York**, a walled city around an immense cathedral, where layers of history seem to have been painted thickly over each other: the spiritual capital of Yorkshire.

Getting There and Around

By Air

The region's main airport is **Leeds-Bradford International Airport**, at Yeadon, **t** (0113) 250 9696, *www.lbia.co.uk*. **Manchester Airport** is also convenient for Yorkshire. **Humberside** and **Sheffield** have small airports too.

By Train

GNER operates 124 trains per day to stations in Yorkshire and the Northeast on the east coast mainline railway between London King's Cross and Scotland. GNER telesales and enquiries, **t** 08457 225 225, *www.gner.co.uk*.

Other mainline train operators serving Yorkshire stations are:

Hull Trains, *www.hulltrains.co.uk*.

Virgin Trains, *www.virgintrains.co.uk*.

Contact **National Rail Enquiries, t** 08457 484950, *www.thetrainline.com*, for all sevices.

By Coach

National Express coaches go to and from the major cities of Yorkshire, **t** 08705 808080 (within the UK) or **t** (+44) 121 625 1122 (from abroad), *www.gobycoach.com*.

By Sea

P&O North Sea Ferries operate from Hull, **t** 0870 129 6002, *www.ponsf.com*.

By Bicycle

The **White Rose Cycle Route** forms part of the National Cycle Network. For details, call Sustrans, **t** (0117) 929 0888 or visit the website *www.nationalcyclenetwork.org.uk*.

By Bus and Other Public Transport

For bus and other public transport information for Yorkshire, contact **Traveline, t** 0870 608 2608, *www.yorkshiretravel.net* or *www.pti.org.uk*.

Tourist Information

Yorkshire Tourist Board, t (01904) 707 070, *www.yorkshirevisitor.com*; *www.yorkshirenet.co.uk* is useful for accommodation.

Walking in Yorkshire

Yorkshire has plenty of good walking country. You'll enjoy the outdoors better if you take sensible precautions: wear good footwear, take warm and waterproof clothing (the weather can change suddenly), carry a good map and let someone know where you are going if you are heading for remote country.

For general information on walking in Yorkshire, call **t** (01904) 707 070, or go to *www.walkyorkshire.com*.

The following are the best-known long-distance footpaths:

The **Pennine Way National Trail** (268 miles), which takes an average of 16 days to complete. Its highlights are Kinder Scout, Stoodley Pike, Malham Cove, Pen-y-Ghent, Hadrian's Wall and the Cheviot Hills. For more information contact the National Trail Officer, The Countryside Agency, Leeds, **t** (0113) 246 9222, *www.nationaltrail.co.uk*.

The **Coast-to-Coast Walk** (191 miles), devised by the famous walker/writer Alfred Wainwright; 14 days; the Lake District, Pennines, Swaledale and North York Moors; tourist information centre, Richmond, **t** (01748) 850 252, *www.coast2coast.co.uk*.

The **Cleveland Way National Trail** (110 miles); 9 days; Helmsley Castle, Rievaulx Abbey, Robin Hood's Bay, Whitby Abbey and Staithes Harbour; National Trail Officer, North York Moors National Park, **t** (01439) 770 657, *www.nationaltrail.co.uk*.

The **Wolds Way National Trail** (79 miles); 5 days; Humber Bridge, Wharram Percy and Fridaythorpe; National Trail Officer, North York Moors National Park, **t** (01439) 770 657, *www.nationaltrail.co.uk*.

The **Pennine Bridleway National Trail** (206 miles), the region's most recently completed trail, a circular route around Halifax; 12 days; views across Calderdale, Rochdale and Lancashire; the Rochdale Canal and Watergrove Reservoir; National Trail Officer, Countryside Agency, Manchester, **t** (0161) 237 1061, *www.nationaltrail.co.uk*.

The Yorkshire Dales

The Dales are the pride of Yorkshire's countryside, a part of the Pennine chain in which hills and valleys form a pleasing harmony of forms and vistas. The 'dales' themselves are the broad valleys which were initially carved by rivers but largely scooped out by glaciers in the Ice Age. At their heart, the Dales are composed of limestone, a rock which is easily eroded and gives rise to dramatic landscape features: gorges, dry valleys, crags, caves, potholes, waterfalls and limestone pavements.

Half the area of the **Yorkshire Dales National Park** is wild, bleak upland moors, but the Dales are far from being mountain wilderness. This is a living landscape whose appearance reflects traditional lifestyles with some controlled modernization to keep the local economy afloat and cater for tourism. Most of the land – even the moorland – is actively farmed. A typical sight is the shaggy, black-faced, curly-horned sheep that scratch a living in even the most inhospitable terrain. Everywhere, fields are separated by the ingeniously assembled dry-stone walls that are so characteristic of the Dales – about 5,500 miles of them in all.

The two most accessible and hence most visited dales are **Wharfedale** and **Wensleydale** and a good trip is to drive (or walk) up one and down the other, crossing the moors between the two from Buckden to Hawes. The extraordinary limestone formations around Malham also attract large numbers of visitors and should not be missed. The other dales are more remote. **Swaledale** and **Ribblesdale** (known as 'the Three Peaks' area) in particular are worth exploring if you have time. One of the most beautiful railway lines in Britain, the **Settle–Carlisle line**, runs up Ribblesdale (*see* box). Westwards, the Dales area continues into Cumbria with **Dentdale** and **Garsdale** (*see* p.800) and northwards into County Durham as **Teesdale** (*see* p.886).

It is possible to drive through the Dales in a day, enjoy the landscapes and have afternoon tea in one of the many well-preserved stone villages, but better by far is to take your time and do some walking. tourist information centres are replete with leaflets detailing walks both easy and strenuous. More than 1,250 miles of footpaths and bridleways crisscross the Dales, most of them well marked. A stroll along the banks of one of the rivers is a good way to spend a few hours, but to get to know the Dales you'll need to put on walking boots and sweat to the top of one of the peaks (none of them is very high). Only then will you really appreciate the variety of the

Getting Around

By Train

The **Settle–Carlisle railway** is a good way to get into the Dales or to spend a day sightseeing through a train window (*see* p.800).

By Bus

For bus information check *www.dalesbus.org*

Useful services for the Dales include:

York or Harrogate to Grassington: service 26 operated by Stephenson's of Easingwold, **t** (01347) 838 990.

Skipton to Grassington and Buckden: service 72 operated by Arriva Northeast, **t** (0191) 281 1313.

Northallerton to Hawes: service 156/7 operated by Dales and District, **t** (01677) 425 203.

Leeds to Ingleton and Morecambe: service 200 operated by Keighley and District, **t** (01535) 603 284.

Skipton to Malham: service 210 operated by Pennine Motor Services, **t** (01756) 749 215.

Ingleton to Kendal: service 567 operated by Stagecoach Cumberland, **t** (01539) 722 143.

Leeds to Grassington and Hawes: service 800/804 operated by Arriva Yorkshire, **t** (01757) 708 177.

Skipton to Hawes service 807 operated by Keighley and District, **t** (01535) 603 284.

Tourist Information

Yorkshire Dales: *www.yorkshiredales.org*.

Some tourist information centres in the park close in winter.

National Park Visitor Information: *www.destinationdales.org*.

Where to Stay

The Yorkshire Dales have many small hotels and B&Bs. There are also **Youth Hostels** at Keld, Grinton Lodge, Ellingstring, Aysgarth, Kettlewell, Linton, Malham, Stainforth, Kirby Stephen and Dentdale. For information contact the YHA, **t** 0870 870 8808, *www.yha.org.uk*.

Bunkbarns are inexpensive, self-catering places designed for individual walkers and groups. As their name suggests, most have been converted from stone barns, although one was a stables and coach house and another a chapel. All have bedrooms, kitchen/dining room with lounge/recreation area, toilets and showers, drying room, hot water and heating, and parking space. For locations and more details see *www.yorkshirenet.co.uk/ydales/bunkbarns/*.

landscapes, as you pass from grassy pastures and wooded dells to squelchy moors with great gritstone boulders strewn about them like some giant's bowling alley.

The weather in the Dales can be as changeable as the landscape, but this can add to their charm. Sunshine and blue skies may show the dinkiest Dales villages at their best, but there is a magnificence in the ever-changing light and colours on the hills and moors that is really more typical of Yorkshire. On a stormy day in summer or a sharp winter's day of broody skies, when there is a dusting of new-fallen snow and any sane person is safely indoors, the Dales acquire an extra grandeur for anyone with the valour to step out in them and the eyes to see.

Wharfedale

Perhaps the best introduction to the Dales is Wharfedale, easily reached via the A59 from Harrogate. Its starting point is **Bolton Abbey** (***t*** *(01756) 718 009, www.bolton-abbey.com, open dawn-dusk, car park locked at 9 in summer and 6 in winter*), the Yorkshire country estate of the Duke and Duchess of Devonshire, centred on the romantic ruins of a 12th-century Augustinian priory. One of the classic easy Dales walks, to **Simon's Seat**, starts from the Cavendish Pavilion, a short way beyond Bolton Abbey. The distance covered by the footpath is 7½ miles, which takes about 3–4 hours (stops included) for an average walker. The beauty of this walk is that you get a sense of the variety of the Dales in a morning or an afternoon, ranging from the wooded **Valley of Desolation** to the moors of **Barden Fell**. The summit, named after a shepherd called Simon, is an outcrop of gritstone. On a clear day it is possible to see west into Lancashire and as far east as the White Horse at Kilburn from the shepherd's seat.

A much easier stroll from Cavendish Pavilion (or from the car park up the road) is to the **Strid**, where the Wharfe, which elsewhere looks like a pacific enough river, is funnelled down a crevice between sandstone rocks. The old saying about Yorkshire's rivers sums up the Strid's reputation: 'Wharfe is clear, and the Aire is lithe./ Where the Aire drowns one, Wharfe drowns five.' To the casual eye, the Strid is just an attractive natural rock formation but the two banks of the river come so close that many people have been tempted to make the short stride (hence Strid) across. Most of them made

Walking in the Yorkshire Dales

The Yorkshire Dales are walking country par excellence. Most footpaths are well marked and well trodden. Leaflets describing classic walking routes are available at all tourist information centres in the Dales. Even if you have a good description of the walk it is wise to carry an Ordnance Survey 1:50,000 map of the area. While some walks are along the flat valley bottoms, most will involve at least some stiff uphill walking and appropriate footwear, preferably walking boots, can make the difference between an enjoyable excursion and an uncomfortable slog. The weather in the Dales (indeed the whole of the north of England) can turn from warm and sunny to cold and rainy unexpectedly fast and it is wise to pack a pullover and a waterproof jacket, not to mention water and food.

Tourist Information

Grassington: Colvend, Hebden Road, **t** (01756) 752 774. *Summer open daily 9.30–7.15. Nov–Mar limited hours.*

Kettlewell: *www.kettlewell.info.*

Skipton: 35 Coach Street, **t** (01756) 792 809, *www.skiptononline.co.uk.*

Malham: *www.malhamdale.org.uk* and *www.malhamdale.com.*

Malham village: **t** (01729) 830 363. *Open April–Oct daily 9.30–5, Nov–Mar limited hours.*

Where to Stay and Eat

Bucken and Around t (01756) –

Devonshire Arms, Bolton Abbey, **t** 710 441, *www.thedevonshirearms.co.uk* (*very expensive*). The sort of place you could arrive in a private helicopter without raising eyebrows. Burlington restaurant for elegant dining; brasserie and bar for more informality.

Yockenthwaite Farm (near Buckden), **t** 760 835, *www.yockenthwaitefarm.co.uk* (*moderate*). Traditional, family-run sheep hill farm offering B&B. As a souvenir you can always take home a leg of Dales-reared lamb.

Redmire Farm (near Bucken), **t** 760 253, *www.redmirefarm.co.uk* (*moderate*). Farmhouse B&B 10 minutes' walk from Buckden village, close to excellent Dales walking country.

West Deepdale Farm, Langstrothdale (near Buckden), **t** 760 204 (*moderate*). Old farmhouse near the banks of the River Wharfe offering B&B and a vital extra service: 'courtesy lift to/from pub'.

The Buck Inn, Buckden, **t** 760 228, *www.thebuckinn.com* (*moderate*). Georgian pub with restaurant and bar menu (including vegetarian choices). Home-made bread, cakes, biscuits and packed lunches also available; 14 rooms.

Bridge End Farm, Threshfield, Grassington, **t** 752 463, *www.bridge-end-farm.co.uk* (*moderate*). A 17th-century riverside cottage offering rooms to sleep in and home-cooking along with log fires, a large garden and private fishing.

Church Farm, Hubberholme, **t** 760 240 (*moderate*). B&B in working hill farm and 16th-century farmhouse at the top of Wharfedale on the banks of the river.

Skipton t (01756) –

Low Skibeden Farm House, **t** (01756) 793 849, *www.yorkshirenet.co.uk/accgde/lowskibeden* (*moderate*). A working farm raising pedigree cattle and sheep, close to town but in open country. Hearty farmhouse breakfasts. No smoking, no pets and no small children.

Bizzie Lizzies, 36 Swadford Street, **t** (01756) 793 189, *www.skiptononline.co.uk* (*cheap*). Claims to sell 'the UK's finest fish and chips'.

Hemingway's Tea Shop, 10–11/a Craven Court, **t** (01756) 798 035 (*cheap*). Well-known place not only for tea but also for hot dishes, sandwiches, salads and home-made cakes. Live pianist on Saturday afternoon. *Closed Sun.*

Malham t (01729) –

Lister Arms Hotel, **t** 830 330, *www.listerarms.co.uk* (*moderate*). A 17th-century coaching inn, owned by the Lord of Ribblesdale in 1797. The bar has several interesting features including an inglenook fireplace. Weather permitting, you can drink or dine in the garden. There is an attractive garden behind the hotel where you can drink and eat.

Holgate Head, Kirkby Malham, **t** 830 376 (*moderate*). An old house, altered in the course of its history but with some 17th-century oak panelling left. It stands in a large garden. The owners are a wine importer and trained caterer.

it, but those who slipped were sucked into a malicious series of slippery overhangs, underwater potholes and sucking currents. The first victim, according to legend, was the noble-born Boy of Egremond, the only son of Alice de Romilly, who lived during the 12th century. He used to jump over the Strid on his pony with a greyhound beside him on a lead. One day the dog pulled back and all three were drowned.

Calendar Girls

The ladies of Rylstone and District Women's Institute (W.I.), based in the Wharfedale village of Cracoe, made headlines in 1999 when they decided to produce their own pin-up calendar, a pastiche of the famous Pirelli calendar, instead of the usual W.I. style of calendar picturing flowers and village greens. Eleven of the members, aged between 44 and 65 and all from a small rural community in which everyone knows each other, posed tastefully in the nude, engaged in familiar domestic activities: painting, making jam, playing the piano.

The idea for the calendar grew out of a joke but turned into a homage to the husband of one of their number, John Baker, former Assistant National Park Officer for the Yorkshire Dales, who died of cancer in 1998 at the age of 54.

Each photograph was very carefully set up so as not to be in any way revealing or titillating and the photographer, husband of one of the lady models, was warned not to show any 'hairy bits or bottoms'. The poses mask anything risqué behind table-cloths and kitchenware, and the resulting photographs are reminiscent if anything of the innocence of early naturist photography. The captions did go for some saucy *double entendre*, however, and the calendar's coverline cheekily claimed that 'When the ladies of Rylstone and District W.I. drop everything for their traditional crafts, Jam and Jerusalem will never be the same again.'

The calendar was done for fun and a good cause but was rapidly picked up by the national media. As Lesley Gillian wrote in the *Guardian*, it also dealt with some unfinished business of the feminist revolution. Showing 'middle-aged, post-menopausal and even pensionable bodies' broke a taboo against anything other than young (or artificially rejuvenated) female flesh. 'Women have such a hang-up about age,' explained Tricia Stewart, one of the W.I. women behind the calendar 'and too many of us hit 50 and think, oh my God, I might as well go and lie down for the rest of my life. This is not about looks or age, it's about spirit. I like to think of it as a celebration of women in full bloom.'

The British press was delighted with the story and a local stunt turned into a national phenomenon. The calendar sold an unexpected 80,000 copies, and the following May a 19-month edition was issued. Altogether, worldwide, 200,000 copies were sold. The story even got onto the front page of the *New York Times*. All sales were in aid of leukaemia research, for which the women raised £350,000 in Britain and a further £150,000 when the calendar appeared in America.

Two years after the calendar was made, Tricia Stewart published a book, *Calendar Girl*, about it and sold the film rights to the story. The Disney-backed film *Calendar Girls*, starring British actresses Helen Mirren and Julie Walters, was released in 2003 to wide critical acclaim.

Continuing past Barden Tower, a hunting lodge turned into a mini-castle in the 15th century by Henry Clifford, nicknamed the 'Shepherd Lord', the road climbs and falls down to **Burnsall**, a pretty village with a handsome arched bridge. A little further on is **Grassington**, the *de facto* capital of Wharfedale, where the shops and cafés grouped around the pretty square do a roaring trade with walkers and day-trippers.

The road up the valley now passes beneath **Kilnsey Crag**, an overhanging cliff of limestone, and crosses the river into **Kettlewell**, a more demure service centre for walkers. The valley continues to **Buckden** and then splits into two, **Langstrothdale** and **Bishopdale**, both leading to Wensleydale.

Instead of going to Kettlewell, a less trodden variation is to take the road up **Littondale** to **Arncliffe**, which Charles Kingsley visited from Malham when he was writing *The Water Babies*; he immortalized the river as the one into which the hero of the book, Tom the chimney sweep, slips at the start of his adventures. Wordsworth also found inspiration here for his poem 'White Doe of Rylestone'.

Skipton

Skipton, near the start of Wharfedale, is the largest town in the Dales and stands at a crossroads easily reached from the Leeds/Bradford or Manchester conurbations. The Leeds–Liverpool canal also flows conveniently past it. It is a popular place to shop, especially on market days (*Mon, Wed, Fri and Sat*). Its **castle** (***t*** *(01756) 792 442, www.skiptoncastle.co.uk; open Mon–Sat 10–6, Sun 12–6, Oct–Feb closes at 4; adm*) has to be one of the best-preserved medieval castles in England, despite a three-year siege during the Civil War. After the defeat of the king's army at the Battle of Marston Moor in 1644 Skipton Castle was the only Royalist stronghold to survive in northern England. A surrender was negotiated the following year by the governor, Sir John Mallory, but Oliver Cromwell ordered the castle's roofs to be removed to prevent further resistance – they were replaced 10 years later on the proviso that they would not bear the weight of a cannon.

The A65 eastwards from Skipton is your route to the western Dales, to Malham, Settle and the Three Peaks.

Malham

The chief natural wonder of the Yorkshire Dales is **Malham Cove**, a 265ft-high arc of sheer limestone wall that looks like a sea bay stranded far inland. Meltwater is

The Leeds and Liverpool Canal

At 127 miles long, the Leeds and Liverpool is Britain's longest canal. Authorized by Parliament in 1770, the first length (between Bingley and Skipton) was completed three years later but it took more than 40 years to build the 91 locks necessary to get it all the way over the Pennines. The canal was finally opened in 1816. During the Industrial Revolution, the Leeds and Liverpool acted as an aqueous artery between centres of production on the east and west of northern England. In the 20th century, as railways and then roads gained importance, waterborne freight traffic declined. The canal is now used for recreation by boaters, walkers and cyclists making use of its straight, flat towpaths.

Supplied by reservoirs high up in the hills and maintained by British Waterways, the canal flows past the **Bingley Five Rise Locks** and **Saltaire**. At several points along its length you can take a boat trip or hire your own boat and chug along at 4mph admiring the Pennine scenery.

The Settle–Carlisle Railway

This is England's most scenic line, the one that 'should never have been built' over the Pennines from Settle to Carlisle. Only the entrepreneurial Victorian tenacity of the Midland Railway company pushed through the remarkable feat of engineering needed to succeed across the inhospitable terrain. The 72 miles of track had to be carried over 20 viaducts and through 14 tunnels. These were built by the sheer muscle power of an army of navvies housed in a wild upland shanty town. Around 200 men died from accidents and smallpox during the building of the line. At an exorbitant cost of £3.5 million, the line opened on 1 May 1876.

In the 1980s, the Thatcher Government passed the death sentence on a line whose dwindling passenger numbers did not justify the expense of keeping it open. Ironically passenger numbers picked up again when the line was granted a reprieve in 1989. Now there are several passenger services a day up and down the line, as well as freight trains and the occasional steam-pulled excursion. Reopened stations have attracted day trippers and hikers for whom the line is an easy way from populous West Yorkshire to the heart of some of the best walking country in the Dales. From Ribblehead station it is only a two-hour climb to the top of Whernside.

The line's regular services are operated by Arriva between **Leeds** and **Carlisle**. Trains call at **Saltaire**, **Keighley** (connecting with the **Keighley and Worth Valley line** for **Haworth**) and **Skipton** before reaching **Settle**. From here the train runs up Ribblesdale – in the days of steam the fireman would be continuously shovelling coal to beat the prolonged gradient. The highlight of the trip comes after **Horton-in-Ribblesdale** (heading north) when the train crosses the 24 arches of **Ribblehead viaduct**, 105ft above Batty Moss. **Dent** is the highest mainline station in England (1,150ft), four miles from the village it serves. Garsdale was a junction; there are plans to reopen the Wensleydale line (closed in 1959) and make it one again. Over **Ais Gill Summit** (1,169ft) the line drops into the **Eden Valley** in Cumbria, passing through Kirkby Stephen and Appleby before reaching Carlisle. From Carlisle it is possible to connect with the Hadrian's Wall bus service.

For information call National Rail Enquiries, **t** 08457 484950, or see *www.settle-carlisle.co.uk*. Trains are operated by Arriva, *www.arrivatrainsnorthern.co.uk*.

thought to have flowed over the lip of the cove at the end of the last Ice Age – a sight to rival Niagara Falls, if you'd been there at the time. Malham always draws a crowd: even when it is not heaving with tourists there is a bus-load of children on a field trip.

You can walk to the cove from the village of Malham, but a much more satisfying expedition is to go up **Gordale Scar**, a dry limestone valley which, it is speculated, is a collapsed cavern (allow around 3 hours for the round trip back to Malham). This much-transited route takes you past **Janet's Foss** waterfall and brings you eventually to **Malham Tarn**, a frosty highland lake in the middle of moors. Drop down from here to the limestone pavements above the cove. These consist of flattish blocks of rock called clints divided up by cracks (grikes) where natural joints in the rock have been widened by chemical weathering. Peer into these cracks and you can see how shade-loving plants such as harts-tongue fern, wood sorrel, anemone and enchanter's nightshade thrive in the sheltered microclimates.

Settle and the Three Peaks

Settle, now bypassed by the main road, has always been a commercial place. It used to be a trading town full of the warehouses of wool and cotton merchants – as witnessed by numerous hoists on walls above shops. It is now a busy market town (market day is Tuesday) and centre for visitors to the Dales. One curiosity to look out for is the **Naked Man Café**, which has the figure of a naked man on the wall. It was originally an inn with its counterpart, the Naked Woman at Langcliffe. The naked man is said to have been covered up during the reign of Queen Victoria so that she would not be shocked.

The area around **Ribblesdale**, north of Settle, is best-known for the three most famous Yorkshire mountains, the **Three Peaks**: **Pen-y-Ghent** (2,277ft), **Ingleborough** (2,372ft) and **Whernside** (2,415ft). A very fit walker can climb them all in a day and win

The Pennine Way

The Pennine Way was the vision of writer and walker Tom Stephenson, who wrote an article in the *Daily Herald* in 1935 headlined 'Wanted: A Long Green Trail'. It wasn't until 1965, however, that Britain's most famous footpath was officially designated.

The 268-mile trail, from **Edale** in the Derbyshire Peak District to **Kirk Yetholm** in Northumberland, covers some of the finest upland landscape Britain has to offer, including **Malham Cove**, **High Force** and **High Cup Nick**. Well-signposted and well-maintained by the Countryside Agency and local authorities, it runs through three national parks, across motorways and Hadrian's Wall, using old miners' tracks, packhorse routes and drove roads.

The official guide to the route is in two parts, *Pennine Way South* and *Pennine Way North*, both by Tony Hopkins and published by Aurum Press in partnership with the Countryside Agency. For further information contact **The Pennine Way National Trail Officer** at the Countryside Agency in Leeds, **t** (0113) 246 9222, *www.nationaltrail.co.uk* or **The Pennine Way Association**, John Needham, 23 Woodland Crescent, Hilton Park, Prestwich, Manchester.

Walking the Three Peaks

For information on walking the Three Peaks see *www.3-peaks.co.uk* or ask in the Pen-y-Ghent Café in Horton in Ribblesdale (*t (01729) 860 333*) which is not only a café and information centre but also the official start point for undertaking the ascent of the Three Peaks. They will log you out and send out the emergency services if you are not back before nightfall. Don't even think about it unless you are fit and an experienced hill walker as the whole circuit is approximately 23 miles long and includes, of course, three tough ascents to 3,000 feet. If you make it, you will be eligible to join the Three Peaks of Yorkshire Club.

Tourist Information

Settle: **t** (01729) 825 192, *www.settle.org.uk*.
Horton-in-Ribblesdale: **t** (01729) 860 333.
Clapham: **t** (01524) 251 419. *Open April–Oct daily 10–5, Nov–Mar weekends 10–4.*
Ingleton: *Seasonal office.*

Where to Stay and Eat

Settle and the Three Peaks t (01729) –

Whitefriars Country Guest House, Church Street, Settle, **t** 823 753, *www.smoothhound.co.uk/hotels/whitefri.html* (*moderate*). A 17th-century family house in the middle of Settle with its own gardens and courtyard. Nine guest rooms, most en-suite.

Ye Olde Naked Man Café, Settle, **t** 823 230 (*cheap*). Apart from its curiosity value, you can also get sandwiches, bread, pies and other snacks here.

The Golden Lion Hotel, Horton-in-Ribblesdale, Settle, North Yorkshire, **t** 860 206, *www.goldenlionhotel.co.uk* (*cheap*). Real ales and a varied menu from beefburgers to vegetarian dishes, all served with 'real' chips. Free camping in the grounds.

membership of the Three Peaks of Yorkshire Club, but for most hikers one a day is sufficient. Pen-y-Ghent and Ingleborough share a similar appearance: flat gritstone summits raised above crags and pavements of limestone. Whernside looks rounded and less distinctive from a distance. Horton-in-Ribblesdale makes the best base.

The limestone beneath the mountains is riddled with caves and potholes. One route up Ingleborough takes in the yawning **Gaping Gill**. A mile long, **White Scar Cave** (***t** (01524) 241 244, www.wscave.co.uk; open daily, weather permitting, 10–5.30; adm*), on the B6255 from Ingleton to Hawes, claims to be the longest cave in Britain open to visitors. On the 80-minute guided tour visitors are shown prehistoric mud pools, two waterfalls and the gigantic Battlefield Cavern, which is 100ft high and has clusters of stalactites on its ceiling.

Wensleydale

Wensleydale is a big, fat, friendly dale, full of green fields, waterfalls, brass bands and cows.

Mike Harding

While most of the other dales run roughly north–south and are named after rivers, Wensleydale runs west–east and takes its name from one of the villages along its course rather than from its river, the River Ure.

Its principal village-cum-town is **Hawes**, its centre usually packed with cars and people. Hawes' main attractions, however, are at the top and bottom of town, where it's easier to park. At the bottom is the old station, which has been converted into the tourist information centre and the **Dales Countryside Museum** (*Station Yard, **t** (01969) 667 450; open daily 10–5; adm*), an excellent account of life in the Dales over the last 10,000 years. Part of the museum is housed in the red and cream carriages of a train permanently parked at the station platform (the line doesn't go anywhere any more). Back in the station building, the second half of the museum is a reconstructed lead mine and village craft shops.

Opposite the station is the thriving workshop of **The Hawes Ropemaker** (*t (01969) 667 487, www.ropemakers.co.uk; open Mon–Fri 9–5.30*). The visit begins with an area where you can practise tying knots, and ends with a gift shop selling skipping ropes and dog leads. In between you can slip into a trance to the gentle clatter of twine being spun into colourful chords and ropes.

Above all, Hawes is the cheese capital of Wensleydale and at the **Wensleydale Cheese Visitor Centre at the Wensleydale Creamery** (*Gayle Lane,* ***t*** *(01969) 667 664; open Mon–Sat 9.30–5, Sun 10–4.30; cheese-making tours 10.30–3.30; adm*) you can see the stuff being made before buying some to take home or with which to make a sandwich. Wensleydale cheese, the favourite snack of cartoon characters Wallace and Gromit (The Wrong Trousers), is creamy, pale, soft and crumbly in texture and mild in taste. It was originally made from ewes' milk by the Cistercian monks of Jervaulx Abbey but is now made from cows' milk. Purists (like Wallace and Gromit) would say the original, unadulterated cheese is best, but there are now endless exotic varieties to choose from, with cranberries, cumin and other ingredients added.

Not far beyond Hawes is the waterfall of **Hardraw Force**, a short walk from the Green Dragon Inn (*adm*). The local name for a waterfall, 'force', seems to evoke the power of the water bursting off the moors, but it is actually an Anglicization of the Norse word for waterfall, 'fuss'.

Downstream from Hawes, in the middle of Wensleydale, the River Ure cascades over a series of low waterfalls. To see **Aysgarth Falls**, park at the National Park Visitor Centre (across the river, on the Castle Bolton road). Two of the waterfalls, Middle and Lower Falls, are reached by walking through Freeholders Wood from the visitor centre. The other falls, Upper Falls, can be seen from the bridge, much closer to the car park.

Tourist Information

www.wensleydale.co.uk.

Hawes: Station Yard, **t** (01969) 667 450. *Open April–Oct daily 10–5. Nov–Mar limited hours.*

Leyburn: **t** (01969) 623 069. *Open all year.*

Aysgarth Falls: **t** (01969) 663 121. *Open April–Oct daily 10-5, Nov–Mar weekends only 10–4.*

Where to Stay and Eat

Wensleydale

Simonstone Hall Country House Hotel, Hawes, **t** (01969) 667 255, *www.simonstonehall.co.uk* (*expensive*). A former hunting lodge built in the 1700s, now a hotel with views over Wensleydale; 20 bedrooms, individually furnished. Two rooms have four-poster beds, two have king-size 'sleigh beds' and two rooms have their own lounges.

The Hall, Newton-le-Willows, Bedale, **t** (01677) 450 210 (*expensive*). Georgian house on the edge of Wensleydale, not far off the A1. Paddocks and gardens to wander around. The main suite has a giant square bed covered with a duvet containing the down from 226 ducks.

Braithwaite Hall, East Witton, Leyburn, **t** (01969) 640 287, *www.braithwaitehall.co.uk* (*moderate*). B&B in a 17th-century manor house on a working farm in Coverdale. Horse-riding available.

The Buttery, Wensleydale Creamery, Gayle Lane, **t** (01969) 667 664 (*moderate*). Licensed restaurant serving home-cooked meals. The dining room has picture windows looking onto Wensleydale.

The Wheatsheaf, Caperby, **t** (01969) 663 216, *www.wheatsheafinwensleydale.co.uk* (*moderate*). Eight bedrooms. Bar and restaurant. Lounge with original 17th-century fireplace.

Lower Wensleydale widens out around **Castle Bolton** (*t (01969) 623 332, www.boltoncastle.co.uk; open Mar–Nov daily 10–5; adm*), built in the 14th century by Lord Scrope, Chancellor of England. In 1568 Mary Queen of Scots and her retinue were imprisoned here for six months.

The castle stands on a rise near the market town of **Leyburn**, near which are three attractions. One is **The Teapottery** (*t (01768) 773 983, www.teapottery.co.uk; open daily 9–5*) located on a small industrial estate just outside the town, where novelty teapots are made. Near Coverham is the provocatively named **Forbidden Corner** (*Tupgill Park Estate, t (01969) 640 638; open by prior appointment only; adm*), a walled garden with underground chambers, passages and follies to explore.

Heading from Leyburn towards Masham and Ripon are the ruins of the Cistercian **Jervaulx Abbey** (*t (01677) 460 226; open daily dawn-dusk; adm*). Apart from the historical interest, the ruins are a riot of wildflowers; youcan get a leaflet to identify them.

Swaledale and Richmondshire

Like Wensleydale, Swaledale runs west–east but it is much less visited or developed. The most spectacular way to approach it is from Hawes (continuing along the Hardraw road) which takes you over the bleak **Butter Tubs Pass**. The Butter Tubs, yawning limestone potholes, are impressive close up, but imperceptible from the road unless you know what you are looking for. On the way down from the pass, look out for a parking space on the left-hand side of the road flanked by a curvy stone wall. Park here and peer warily over the fences on either side of the road to see the fluted potholes down which moorland streams crash headlong and at the top of which sheep graze precariously but nonchalantly.

Tourist Information

Reeth: Literary Institute, **t** (01748) 884 059. *Open April–Oct daily 10–5, Nov–Mar weekends 10–5.*

Richmond: Friary Gardens, Victoria Road, **t** (01748) 850 252, *www.richmondshire.gov.uk* and *www.richmond.org.uk*. *Open all year.*

Where to Stay and Eat

Swaledale and Richmondshire

The King's Arms, Reeth, **t** (01748) 884 259, *www.thekingsarms.com* (*moderate*). Independent free-house in the centre of Reeth selling a range of beers; 10 rooms. Bar and restaurant menus.

Tan Hill Inn, Keld, **t** (01833) 628 246, *www.tanhillinn.co.uk*. Lonely inn high on the moors with seven rooms all with panoramic views (*moderate*). Both restaurant or bar meals available. Meals include Yorkshire Pudding and the spicy Tan Hill sausage (*cheap–moderate*).

The Old Rectory, Barningham, **t** (01833) 621 122 (*moderate*). Spectacular views and good walks from the door. Between them the owners are authorities on thoroughbred racehorses, salmon fly-casting and Cordon Bleu cookery.

Brook House, Middleton Tyas, **t** (01325) 377 713 (*moderate*). Georgian farmhouse B&B with some elegant furniture and log fires. French and British country cooking.

The Frenchgate Café, 29 Frenchgate, Richmond, **t** (01748) 824 949 (*cheap*). A café and licensed restaurant a short walk from the market square. A simple place with bright yellow walls, blue chairs, blue and yellow curtains. Sandwiches also available.

The Butter Tubs road brings you to the villages of **Thwaite** and **Muker** from where you can follow the river down to **Reeth**, Swaledale's largest town, which prospered on lead mining in the 19th century and is today a pleasant place to have tea, walk around or simply get your breath back. If you are in the mood for exploration, a long lonely road sets off from here north up **Argengarthdale** through Langthwaite and Whaw to reach **Tan Hill Inn** on the border with Durham, the highest pub in England (1,732ft).

Downstream of Swaledale stands the old town of **Richmond**, built around a large sloping market square with a block of buildings in the middle of it. The town grew up around ancient **Richmond Castle** (***t*** *(01748) 822 493, www.english-heritage.org.uk; open daily mid-July–Aug 9.30–7, April–mid-July and Sept 10–6, Oct 10–5, Nov–Mar 10–4; adm*), only a few steps away from the square, a survivor from Norman times with 11th-century walls and a 12th-century rectangular keep. The castle's newly laid-out Cockpit garden is a memorial to the 'Richmond Sixteen', conscientious objectors who were held prisoners in the castle during the First World War. The decision to honour these prisoners was controversial, since Richmond's livelihood is bound up with Catterick Garrison, an army camp just down the road from it.

Down one of the town's side streets is the real star turn, the **Georgian Theatre Royal and Museum** (*Victoria Road,* **t** *(01748) 823 021; museum open April–Oct 10–5; theatre by guided tour only open Mar–Dec; adm*). It hardly looks big enough to contain the egos of a company of actors, let alone an audience. It was built in 1788 by the actor-manager Samuel Butler and is the oldest theatre in Britain still in its original state.

Harrogate

Between the arable plains of central Yorkshire and the dramatic scenery of the Dales stands the genteel spa town of **Harrogate**, whose fortunes have risen, fallen and risen again in the few centuries of its existence.

Until the 16th century, the ancient town of Knaresborough stood in the middle of the royal Forest of Knaresborough which was (like most English forests) not an area of unbroken tree cover but a wild and lonely expanse of woodland, scrub and heath dedicated to royal hunting expeditions. But then, in 1571, William Slingsby discovered a well near his home of Bilton Hall which he believed to have similar healing properties to the spas of Belgium. The reputation of these waters spread and the town of **Harrogate Spa** was established around a couple of poor hamlets in the forest. By the year 1700 some 88 springs had been found and 20 public bathing houses were in operation. Harrogate became a fashionable place for the leisured rich to visit and while away their time. The **Promenade Inn** (now the Mercer Art Gallery) was opened in 1806 as a place for visitors to make 'polite conversation' after 'taking the waters'. The inn also acted as a theatre: in 1884 Edward VII's mistress Lillie Langtry performed Sheridan's *School for Scandal* here, and on another occasion Oscar Wilde gave a lecture on how to dress. Other famous visitors to Harrogate in its lengthy heyday included Lord Byron, Sir Edward Elgar and Agatha Christie, who was found in the Old Swan Hotel after going missing for 11 days.

Getting There and Around

Harrogate and Knaresborough are on the **railway** line between Leeds and York. Trains are run by Metro, **t** (0113) 245 7676, *www.wymetro.com.*

Buses run from Harrogate to the main towns in the district as well as to Leeds, Bradford and York. For information call **t** (01423) 566 061 or go to the website *www.harrogate.gov.uk/tourism.*

Tourist Information

Harrogate: Royal Baths, Crescent Road, **t** (01423) 537 300, *www.harrogate.gov.uk/tourism.*

Where to Stay

Harrogate t (01423) –

Old Swan Hotel, Swan Road, **t** 500 055, *www.oldswanhotel.com* (*expensive*). One of Harrogate's two top hotels but with far more character than its modern rival, the Moat House. Close to the town centre.

Grants, Swan Road, **t** 560 666, *www.grantshotel-harrogate.com* (*expensive*). Lovely intimate hotel in a listed building.

Boar's Head, Ripley (near Harrogate), **t** 771 888, *www.boarsheadripley.co.uk* (*expensive*). Sir William Ingilby (1829–1918) closed Ripley's three pubs by forbidding them to open on Sundays. The present Boar's Head opened in 1990 as a four-star hotel with a bar in the middle of Harrogate district's most delightful village.

Hob Green, Markington, **t** 770 031, *www.hobgreen.com* (*expensive*). Country hotel and restaurant between Harrogate and Ripon with garden views over valley.

Cedar Court, Queen Building, Park Parade, **t** 858 585, *www.cedarcourthotels.co.uk* (*expensive*). 'Harrogate's first hotel', dating back to 1671, reopened in 1999.

Ashbrooke House, 140 Valley Drive, **t** 564 478, *www.harrogate.com/ashbrooke* (*moderate*). Victorian townhouse B&B beside the Valley Gardens. Guests have use of a health and leisure club.

Mrs Murray's Guesthouse, 67 Franklin Road, **t** 505 857, *www.harrogate.com/mrsmurrays* (*moderate*). One of a number of guesthouses on road near the Conference Centre.

Franklin View, 19 Grove Road, **t** 541 388, *www.franklinview.com* (*moderate*). A restored Edwardian home, now a no-smoking hotel. Private car park.

The Alexander, 88 Franklin Road, **t** 503 348 (*moderate*). Small family-run hotel in a Victorian house. Double glazed and heated.

Eating Out

Harrogate Brasserie, 28–30 Cheltenham Parade, **t** 505 041, *www.brasserie.co.uk/brasserie* (*expensive*). Informal place with swing jazz playing three nights a week.

After the First World War, demand for spa treatment declined and once-fashionable Harrogate sank into economic doldrums until, after the next war had been fought, the town was recreated as a conference and trade-fair centre. In 1969 the last vestiges of the spa disappeared and in 1981 a monstrous new conference centre confirmed the town's new identity. The coming of the **Harrogate International Centre** may have safeguarded the local economy but it was also the catalyst for Harrogate to turn itself into a themed leisure complex aimed at shoppers, drinkers and business visitors. It is as if the city fathers wished to shake off the harmonious Victorian and Edwardian spa atmosphere that gave Harrogate its very charm. But there is just enough of the dignified old Harrogate left if you look for it. Fortunately, a large tract of the Forest of Knaresborough was put permanently out of the hands of developers by an act of parliament in 1770. This was declared **The Stray** and is today a vast green swathe of public land to the south of the town centre where you can stroll.

Town-centre location with its own off-street parking.

Drum and Monkey, 5 Montpellier Gardens, **t** 502 650 (*expensive*). Famous Harrogate seafood restaurant, long established. *Book months ahead.*

Biscaya Bay, 11/13 Mount Parade, **t** 500 089 (*moderate*). Basque French cuisine. *Closed Sun.*

Chez la Vie, 94 Station Parade, **t** 568 018 (*moderate*). French bistro.

Court's, 1 Crown Place, **t** 536 336 (*moderate*). Wine bar and restaurant in Crown Hotel. Live music Sun eve.

Hedley's, 5 Montpellier Parade, **t** 562 468 (*moderate*). Home cooking with some vegetarian dishes.

Lords, 8 Montpellier St, **t** 508 762, *www.lordsrestaurant.co.uk* (*moderate*). English/French food against a background of county cricket memorabilia.

Sous la Table, 31 Cheltenham Crescent, **t** 565 806 (*moderate*). French bistro.

William and Victoria, 6 Cold Bath Road, **t** 506 883 (*moderate*). Two wine-bar restaurants in one.

Damn Yankee, 4 Station Parade, **t** 561 424, *www.damnyankee.co.uk* (*moderate*). If you don't want too much ceremony, this long-established Tex-Mex restaurant serves 'beer by the pitcher and the best margaritas in town'. As well as burgers and burritos there are also vegetarian dishes. A change from the Yorkshire scene and its fare.

Brio, 44 Commercial Street, **t** 529 933 (*cheap*). Modern, fun place for pizza/pasta. Good for kids and teenagers.

Pinocchio's, Empire Buildings, Cheltenham Parade, **t** 563 900, *www.pinocchios.co.uk* (*cheap*). Pasta and pizza restaurant which children love.

Thai Elephant, 15 Cheltenham Parade, **t** 530 099 (*cheap*). Thai restaurant.

Cafés and Tea Rooms

Bettys, 1 Parliament Street, **t** 502 747 (*cheap*). The archetypal English tea room, immaculately kept. A place to take your time over tea, coffee, snacks (including specialities such as hot buttered pikelets and Yorkshire fat rascal – a 'large plump fruity scone made with citrus peels, almonds and cherries'), English breakfast or a full meal (try Yorkshire rarebit made with beer, for instance). Speciality teas and coffees, breads and cakes are sold in the shop.

Pubs

Old Bell, 6 Royal Parade, Harrogate, **t** 507 930, *www.markettowntaverns.co.uk* (*moderate*). An unpubby pub – no games machines; no music and a no-smoking room – in the dignified part of Harrogate. Range of beers including foreign ones. Food served upstairs.

Gardeners Arms, Bilton Lane, **t** 506 051 (*cheap*). A pub in a remarkably little-altered 18th-century building on the suburban fringe of Harrogate. An unpretentious place to have a pint or two.

The **Royal Baths Assembly Rooms** used to be the centre of Harrogate Spa but have recently become a gentrified drinking den. If you want to get a sense of what the spa must have been like, book yourself in for a session in the **Turkish Baths** (*Crescent Road, **t** (01423) 556 746, www.harrogate.co.uk/turkishbaths; open all year: women Mon and Fri 9–12.30, Tues and Thurs 1–9, Fri 9–12.30, Sun 9–11.30, 11.45–2.15 and 2.30–5; men Mon and Wed 1–9, Fri 1–5, Sat 9–5; mixed sessions (couples only) Tues 9–12, Fri and Sun 5.30–9; adm*) in the basement, which still has its original 1897 mock-oriental tiled hot chambers and plunge pool.

Another gem which has survived the modernizers is **Harrogate Theatre** (***t** (01423) 502 116*), with its rich 1900s interior. On the main square of Harrogate (the Cenotaph) stands another old institution, **Bettys Café** (*see* p.808).

Follow Montpellier Gardens down from Betty's and you reach **Low Harrogate**, the prettiest corner of the town. Just off the roundabout at the bottom of the hill is the

Bettys

Jonathan Wild, Chairman of the Bettys & Taylors Group is in no doubt: Harrogate is the tea-drinking capital of Britain. In 1907 his great-uncle, Frederick Belmont, a baker, confectioner and *chocolatier* who had been orphaned early in life, travelled from Switzerland to England in search of his fortune. Unable to communicate with the porters at a London railway station, he found himself unintentionally on a train bound for Yorkshire. He got off at Wakefield where he stayed and worked in whatever jobs he was able to find for the next three years.

In Harrogate he discovered a place where the air reminded him of his native Alps and in 1917 he married his landlady's daughter, Clare. The couple opened Bettys tea rooms and patisserie in 1919 in the centre of town, opposite the established Café Imperial; soon they counted princesses and admirals among their genteel clientele. The business grew in the 1920s and '30s and continued to thrive in the post-war world, when other great English tea rooms were in decline.

In 1962 Bettys bought Taylors, a tea importers founded in 1886. The purchase brought with it the old rival Café Imperial, which became Bettys' flagship shop and café, at Harrogate's most prestigious address, 1 Parliament Street. The Taylors side of the business was expanded with a new Yorkshire Tea blended to suit the local water.

Bettys & Taylors is still run as a family business and is deliberately kept small – just five tea rooms in prime Yorkshire locations 'so that we can keep a watchful eye on every detail', the company claims.

Royal Pump Room Museum (*Crown Place,* **t** *(01423) 556 188, www.harrogate.gov.uk/museums; open April–Oct Mon–Sat 10–5, Sun 2–5; Nov–Mar Mon–Sat 10–4, Sun 2–4; adm*), built over a stinky well of Harrogate's once-famous sulphur water, where you can find out about the history of Harrogate. It is essential to take a draught of the water, which tastes as bad as its name suggests. In 1926, 1,500 glasses of sulphur water were served here within the same morning.

It is only a short step from here across the road into the **Valley Gardens**, where Harrogate's pride in its floral displays is maintained. Keep going all the way up the garden and through the coniferous woods at the top and eventually you will come to **Harlow Carr Gardens** (*Crag Lane,* **t** *(01423) 565 418, www.rhs.org.uk; open all year daily 9.30–6 or dusk if earlier; adm*), the 'Wisley of the North' where the Royal Horticultural Society demonstrates what it is possible to grow in the northern climes of Yorkshire.

There are flowers everywhere you look in Harrogate and the civic floral display reaches a peak in late February–early March, when the crocuses bloom on the Stray.

Knaresborough

Harrogate and Knaresborough practically run into each other, and they complement each other nicely. Upstart Harrogate may be a once-grand spa with gardens, shops and a thriving leisure life, but Knaresborough has a scenic site and is smug in the knowledge that it is much older and riddled with history and legend.

The town grew up after the Norman Conquest beside its castle on the side of a gorge of the River Nidd and, as if in defiance of geography, or just to emphasize the drama of the site, a great railway viaduct was thrust from one lip of the gorge to the other in 1851. When it was built it must have seemed like all the horrors of the modern world had arrived at once; now it is hard to imagine what Knaresborough would look like without it.

Beneath the bridge the shadows fall early but you can walk all the way along the bank of the river beneath cliffs and town from the **High Bridge** to beyond **Low Bridge**, where there are three interesting features in the rock: the **Chapel of Our Lady of the Crag**, a 15th-century wayside shrine; the **House in the Rock**, constructed in the 18th century; and **St Robert's Cave**, where the hermit Robert Flower lived until his death in 1218, when his cave became a pilgrimage site for princes, bishops and commoners. Parts of the river are navigable; punts and rowing boats are for hire near High Bridge.

The main part of town is uphill from the river: a steep climb by ancient, twisting stone stairways. Ruined **Knaresborough Castle** (*Castle Yard,* **t** *(01423) 556 188, www.harrogate.gov.uk/museums; open April–Sept daily 10.30–5; adm*) is perhaps the obvious place to begin exploring, a good viewpoint as well as the heart of the original settlement. There is a legend that the four murderers of St Thomas à Becket fled to Knaresborough after committing their crime and shut themselves for a year in the castle. Here they were eaten by remorse and visited by signs of Divine wrath: no animal would come near them and dogs refused the crumbs which dropped from their table. From Knaresborough they departed for Rome to confess their crimes and were sent to the Holy Land where three of them died; the fourth died at sea.

The **market place** still hums with life. On it stands what is supposedly the oldest chemist's shop in England (est. 1720), although it no longer serves its original purpose. In this age of heritage exploitation, **Ye Oldest Chymist Shoppe** now serves as an outlet for 'Farrahs' Famous Harrogate Toffee', and as a tea room.

Knaresborough's most famous tourist attraction – claimed as the first tourist attraction in England – is across the river from the town. The first visitors to **Mother**

Tourist Information

Knaresborough: 9 Castle Courtyard Market Place, **t** (01423) 866 886. *Open summer only.*

Where to Stay and Eat

Knaresborough t (01423) –

Dower House, Bond End, **t** 863 302, *www.bwdowerhouse.co.uk* (*expensive*). Well-known restaurant and hotel with 31 bedrooms, an indoor pool and a gym.

Carriages, 89 High Street, **t** 867 041, *www.carriageswinebar.co.uk* (*moderate*). Wine bar with a delightful garden looking over the picturesque railway station. Eclectic snacks and meals cooked under the supervision of Australian chef and proprietor, Bruce Gray.

Dil Tandoori, 44 Market Place, **t** 869 556 (*moderate*). BYO Indian restaurant.

Off The Rails, Knaresborough Station, **t** 866 587 (*moderate*). Bistro housed in the railway station.

Mario's Ristorante & Pizzeria, 15 Waterside, **t** 863 117, *www.harrogate.com/marios* (*moderate*). Italian restaurant right by the riverside.

Lavender Tea Rooms, Market Place, **t** 860 555 (*cheap*). In the oldest chemist's shop in England. Lavender and lemon scones are the house speciality.

The End of the World is (Not) Nigh

The prophetess who became known as Mother Shipton is believed to have been born as the illegitimate Ursula Sontheil one night in July 1488, 15 years before Nostrodamus. Her life story owes more to legend than fact; the first accounts of her were not written until the 17th century. According to her biography, she was ugly and deformed. In 1512, when she was 24, she married a carpenter called Toby Shipton, acquiring the name she was better known by.

There are various versions of the tale telling how she first demonstrated an ability to predict the future. She is, for instance, supposed to have prophesied that Cardinal Wolsey, who had been appointed archbishop of York by Henry VIII, would see York but not reach it. Hearing this, the cardinal swore to have her burnt as a witch when he arrived in the city. He was unable to make good his threat, however, because he was arrested for high treason in Cawood, a stone's throw south of York. Returning to London he fell ill from dysentery and died in Leicester before he could be tried.

Some of the prophecies still popularly attributed to her – of railways (Carriages without horses shall go/ And accidents fill the world with woe), the telephone or internet (Around the world thoughts shall fly/ In the twinkling of an eye) and steam ships (Iron in the water shall float/ As easy as a wooden boat) – are known to be 19th-century forgeries but are nevertheless delightful snippets of cod poetry.

Mother Shipton is said to have ended her career by prophesying the hour of her death in 1561 at the age of 73. She left one last prophecy for posterity to chew over:

The world shall end when the High Bridge is thrice fallen.

Knaresborough's High Bridge, next to the entrance to Mother Shipton's Cave, has already fallen down twice. Check it for cracks before you cross.

Shipton's Cave and the Petrifying Well (*Prophesy House, High Bridge,* **t** *(01423) 864 600, www.mothershipton.co.uk; open Mar–Nov 9.30–5.30; Nov–Feb weekends 10–4.30; adm*) are said to have come in the year 1630, although they weren't here to gawp but to hear the news before it happened from the prophetess Mother Shipton (*see* above). The Petrifying Well, formerly known as the Dropping Well, is a waterfall which turns any object hung beneath it to stone. Both cave and well are contained within a remnant of the Forest of Knaresborough on the banks of the Nidd, which makes a pleasant walk in itself.

Come to Knaresborough in June and you can see the annual **Bed Race** in which teams compete to push decorated 'beds' through the town and across the river.

Around Harrogate and Knaresborough

The Harrogate District extends northwest to meet the Dales; several interesting sights can be linked in a circuit starting off northwards on the A61 towards Ripon, taking in Ripley and Nidderdale.

Ripley

Not far out of Harrogate is the pretty little village of Ripley, which has been the property of the Ingilby family since 1308. The family has had an interesting history and sedate **Ripley Castle** (***t*** *(01423) 770 152, www.ripleycastle.co.uk; open 10.30–3, June–Aug daily, Sept–May Tues, Thurs, Sat and Sun; adm*) with its armour, furniture, chandeliers and priest hole gives only a hint of it. The Capability Brown grounds of the castle have a lake and deer, and are home to the national hyacinth collection.

Blind Jack the Road Builder

The achievements of the Harrogate area's favourite local hero, John Metcalf (1717–1810), would be enough for any man, but his was truly a tale of triumph over adversity. Born the son of a labourer, he was blinded by smallpox at the age of six. Not to be deterred by this, 'Blind Jack' became a competent horseman, swimmer and violinist. As a young man he fought at the Battle of Culloden (1746) and returned to Harrogate to start the town's first public transport service, a four-wheeled chaise. He also established the first stagecoach service between York and Knaresborough and a system of delivering fish from Whitby to Harrogate by packhorse. A gambler and sometime contrabandist, his life was never dull: when the parents of the woman he loved forbade her to marry the 'blind fiddler' he eloped with her.

But Blind Jack is best remembered as a road builder, laying routes through Yorkshire, Lancashire, Cheshire and Derbyshire using innovative construction techniques. He is estimated to have built 180 miles of road and is remembered as one of the most successful of England's early road builders. When he was 86 he dictated his life story, which was published as the *Life of John Metcalf*. He died aged 93 and is buried in Spofforth near Harrogate.

The anonymous inscription his tombstone at Spofforth reads:

Here lies John Metcalf one whose infant sight
Felt the dark pressure of an endless night:
Yet such the fervour of his dauntless mind,
His limbs full strung, his spirit unconfin'd,
That long ere yet life's bolder years began,
His sightless efforts mark'd th'aspiring man.
Nor mark'd in vain High deeds his manhood dar'd,
And commerce, travel both his ardour shar'd:
Twas his a guide's unerring aid to lend;
O'er trackless wastes to bid new roads extend;
And when Rebellion rear'd her giant size,
Twas his to burn with patriot enterprize,
For parting wife and babes one pang to feel,
Then welcome danger for his country's weal.
Reader! like him exert thy utmost talent giv'n;
Reader! like him adore the bounteous hand of Heav'n.

The appearance of Ripley village is mostly due to Sir William Amcotts Ingilby (1783–1854), a wastrel in his youth and eccentric in later life. One horrified lady wrote to her friend about him: 'this eccentric baronet walks about Ripley and Ripon too, in his dressing gown, without smalls or loincloth on...' He clearly had a sense of humour: shortly before his death he signed one of his letters as 'Le Corpse'. He became hooked on Continental travel and liked people to call him 'the Graf' and his castle 'the Schloss'. This love of all things European led him to rebuild Ripley's dilapidated thatched houses in the model of an estate village he had seen in Alsace Lorraine. Each house was solidly built as part of a harmonious whole, including market square, village shop, butcher's, tailor's, blacksmith's, three pubs, a cricket pitch and a town hall marked 'Hotel de Ville'. The colour of the stone, cobbled square, village stocks and

The Ingilbys of Ripley

The family name means 'Tribe of Angels' but the present Sir Thomas writes frankly in his official guidebook to the castle: 'it has been quite impossible to see any semblance of that description in the Ingilby family for some generations.' When a previous Sir Thomas Ingilby (1310–69) saved Edward III's life while they were hunting wild boar, the king allowed him to add a boar's head to his family crest, hence the boar-drinking fountain in Ripley market square and the name of the village pub, the Boar's Head. The family has had a colourful history since then but has managed to survive with its possessions intact and unspoilt.

After the Reformation the Ingilbys continued to profess the Catholic faith against the new Establishment norm. Francis Ingilby (1550–86) was a Catholic priest who was hanged, drawn and quartered for his faith but is now on the road to canonization and sainthood. King James I stayed at Ripley in 1603 on his way south from Scotland to take up the English throne, apparently showing thereby that he felt no ill will towards Catholic households. If it was a PR exercise, his hosts obviously did not buy it: two years later nine of the 11 main conspirators who tried to kill James, his family and his parliament in the Gunpowder Plot were connected to the Ingilbys. (One of the other two was Guy Fawkes, the most famous to be remembered on 5 November.) Sir William Ingilby (1546–1618) was tried for conspiracy, but the trial collapsed.

When the Civil War broke out, however, the Ingilby family threw in its lot with the Royalist cause. Another Sir William Ingilby (1594–1652) rode into the Battle of Marston Moor accompanied by his 43-year-old sister, 'Trooper' Jane. The King's army was routed. William and Jane fled back to Ripley Castle, the former hiding in the priest hole in the Knights' Chamber. When the victor of the battle, Oliver Cromwell, arrived at Ripley and asked for lodgings for him and his men, he was met at the gatehouse by Trooper Jane brandishing two loaded pistols. She reluctantly allowed Cromwell to lodge in the castle and his men in the church, but insisted on keeping an eye on him all night across the table in the library, pistols on her lap, lest he should search the castle and find her brother. Cromwell's Roundhead troops shot some of their prisoners against the wall of the church and the gatehouse; the marks of musket balls can still be seen.

market cross are more typically Yorkshire, but the inspiration is clearly imported. It was a bold endeavour by a man who could afford it and also had the necessary aplomb to put it into practice. 'Such projects as these that Sir William dreamed up would be speedily stamped upon today as being politically, aesthetically and architecturally incorrect,' writes the current Sir Thomas Ingilby.

Nidderdale

From Ripley, a small main road sets off up Nidderdale, one of the least explored of the Yorkshire Dales. The main points of interest in Nidderdale are two geological formations before and after you get to the dale's main town of Pately Bridge.

It is easy to believe that some Victorians suspected the unearthly rock formations of **Brimham Rocks** (*t (01423) 780 688; open daily 8–dusk; car park fee*) to be man-made – the work of the Druids – but the truth is more prosaic: they are the work of 320 million years of geological movements, glaciation and weathering. Children love the rocks: you couldn't create a better place for hide and seek. Adults may also enjoy scrambling around, crawling through natural tunnels, jumping from rock to rock or following the paths that wind among the trees. There is some shelter but the rocks are slippery when it rains and Brimham is not recommended for a wet day.

At the top of Nidderdale is **How Stean Gorge** (*Lofthouse, **t** (01423) 755 666; open daily 10–6; adm*), a mini limestone canyon which is explored by narrow footpaths and bridges. If you are feeling bold, you can walk through Tom Taylor's Cave, a pitch-black passage which comes out in a field.

Masham

A small road runs over the moors from upper Nidderdale towards Masham. After passing through Ilton an unmarked road to the left leads into a plantation of conifers which conceals Yorkshire's most intriguing folly: the **Druid's Temple** looks prehistoric and is vaguely reminiscent of Stonehenge but dates from only 1820 when William Danby, squire of Swinton Hall, devised it as a way to create some local employment.

Tourist Information

Nidderdale: 18 High Street, Pately Bridge, **t** (01423) 711 147, *www.nidderdale.co.uk. Open summer only.*

Where to Stay and Eat

Nidderdale t (01423) –

Low Hall, Dacre, **t** 780 230 (*moderate*). A stone-built Dales farmhouse (dating from 1635) in a beautiful garden. A conservatory allows you to take advantage of the sparse Yorkshire sunshine for breakfast.

Yorke Arms, Ramsgill, *www.yorke-arms.co.uk* (*moderate*). Pub on village green with restaurant and guest rooms. Good food; exquisite beer.

Station Fisheries, Station Square, King Street, Pately Bridge, **t** 711 215 (*cheap*). Traditional fish and chips to eat in the restaurant or take away.

Masham t (01765) –

Swinton Park, **t** (01765) 680 900, *www.swintonpark.com* (*expensive*). Castle hotel in large area of parkland. Snooker room and private cinema.

Black Sheep Brewery and Visitor Centre, **t** (01765) 680 101 (*moderate*). Who could resist the allure of a 'bistro and baa...r'? Irresistible after a brewery tour, anyway.

Getting There and Around

There are several useful **bus** services running to Ripon from around Yorkshire:

Ripon to Harrogate and Leeds: service no. 36 every 20 minutes

Knaresborough: service no. 56, every 2 hours

Boroughbridge: service no. 142 or 143, every 2 hours

Masham: service no. 159, every 2 hours.

Tourist Information

Ripon: Minster Road, **t** (01765) 604 625, *www.riponcity.info.*

Where to Stay and Eat

Ripon and Around t (01765) –

The Ripon Spa Hotel, Park Street, **t** 602 172, *www.stemsys.co.uk/spa* (*expensive*). A plush, place to stay, in its own extensive grounds.

Unicorn, Market Place, **t** 602 202, *www.unicorn-hotel.co.uk* (*expensive*). Former coaching inn dating back 500 years right in the centre of Ripon.

Lawrence House, Studley Roger, **t** 600 947 (*moderate*). Listed Georgian house in a village not far from Ripon. The garden adjoins Studley Royal Deer Park and Fountains Abbey. Log fires in winter.

Masham itself is known for its two breweries, which are both open for tours. **Theakstons' Brewery and Visitor Centre** (***t*** *(01765) 684 333, www.theakstons.co.uk; tours Mar–Oct Mon–Fri and weekends during North Yorkshire School holidays; closed Nov–Feb; adm*) has been there longest and is home to one of only eight working coopers in Britain. When the Theakston Brewery was taken over by Scottish and Newcastle in 1989 one of the family, Paul Theakston, set up the **Black Sheep Brewery and Visitor Centre** (*Welgarth,* ***t*** *(01765) 689 227, www.blacksheep.co.uk; open Jan–Feb Wed–Sat 11–11, Sun 11–5.30; Mar–Dec Wed–Sat 11–11, Sun and Tues 11–5.30; July–Aug Sun–Tues 11–5.30, Wed–Sat 11–11; adm for tours*). The tour here shows the traditional methods by which Black Sheep produces five variety of ales.

Ripon and Around

From Masham it is an easy run to Ripon, a small town clustered around a large **cathedral** (***t*** *(01765) 602 609, www.ripon-cathedral.org.uk; open April–Oct Mon–Sat 8.30–6.30, Sun'til 7.30; Nov–Mar daily 8–5.30*). Saint Wilfrid built one of the first stone churches in En gland on this site in 672 and the crypt is as he left it 1,300 years ago. The building above, however, is an accumulation of the subsequent centuries, beginning with a complete rebuilding in Norman Transitional style in around 1180. The Early English front was added in 1220, the east end is a 1300 Decorated-style addition and the nave Perpendicular. The bestiary depicted in the miserichords includes one of a rabbit hiding down its hole, which is said to have inspired Lewis Carroll to write *Alice in Wonderland*. His father was a canon of Ripon between 1852 and 1868.

Maybe it is the influence of a large cathedral over a small town but Ripon has a disciplinarian bent, with no fewer than three museums of law and order: the **House of Correction Prison and Police Museum** (*27 St Marygate,* ***t*** *(01765) 690 799, www.ripon.co.uk/museums; open April–Jun and Sept–Oct daily 1–4; July–Aug daily 11–4; adm*), where you can see what it was like to be in the village stocks or to spend time in a Victorian police cell; the **Workhouse Museum** (*Allhallowgate; same hours*); and the

Courthouse Museum (*Minster Road; same hours*). The citizens of Ripon are still keen on an orderly life: every night at nine o'clock the Ripon Hornblower blows the curfew at the corners of the main square.

Fountains Abbey

t (01765) 608 888, www.fountainsabbey.org.uk; open daily Oct–Mar 10–4, April–Sept 10–6 or dusk if earlier; guided tours April–Oct; adm.

Outside Ripon are two places worth spending a day at. Fountains Abbey is an outstanding ancient monument and if you see only one monastery in England make it this one, the largest monastic ruin in the country and a World Heritage Site.

The abbey began life humbly in 1132 with 13 monks from York seeking a simpler way of life. Under the Cistercian rule, their life was austerely religious: they endured long hours of silence, lived on a diet only just above subsistence level and wore habits of coarse undyed wool. Soon, however, the abbey prospered and grew rich, largely thanks to the labour of lay brothers who took on routine jobs as masons, tanners, cobblers, blacksmiths and so on, and also looked after the abbey's ever-expanding flock of sheep, which grazed land as far away as the Lake District and Teesside.

By the time of the Dissolution of the Monasteries in 1539, Fountains Abbey had become exemplary of the kind of wealth and power that Henry VIII so resented. Along with his monastery, the last abbot, Marmaduke Bradley, surrendered to the crown 2,356 head of cattle and 1,326 sheep. The precious glass and lead from the empty abbey were pilfered and the building left to fall into ruins.

The land and ruins were sold at the end of the 16th century and some of the stone from the monastery was used to build the Elizabethan mansion of **Fountains Hall**. Almost 200 years later Fountains Abbey was bought by William Aislabie, who lived next door on the Studley Royal Estate. It was the height of fashion among the land-owning classes in the 18th century to have one's own set of crumbling ruins as a prefabricated folly, and William Aislabie had the valley they stood in landscaped to join up with the **water gardens** laid out by his father. In 1983 the estate passed into the hands of the National Trust.

Somehow the ensemble of ruined 12th-century abbey, Elizabethan manor house and 18th-century water gardens with their accompanying statues and faux temples

Tourist Information

Boroughbridge: Fishergate, **t** (01423) 323 373. *Open April–Oct only.*

Where to Stay and Eat

Boroughbridge t (01423) –

Three Horse Shoes, Bridge Street, Boroughbridge, **t** 322 314 (*cheap*). Pub owned by the Porter family since 1900 and remarkably little altered within. Several en-suite guest rooms.

Ferrensby t (01423) –

General Tarleton, Boroughbridge Road, Ferrensby, **t** 340 284 (*moderate*). An 18th-century coaching inn well-known for its food but with some accommodation also available. Choose between the restaurant or pub dining, both with hand-pumped ales and a good wine list. Friday night is fish night at the General Tarleton.

seems to work perfectly: there is – for once the cliché is true – something for everyone. But be prepared to do a lot of walking if you want to see it all. From the visitor centre and car park it is a short hike to Fountains Hall and the abbey. From here, follow the water gardens through the valley and you will eventually reach Studley Royal with its lake and medieval park, which is home to 500 semi-wild deer.

Newby Hall and Gardens

***t** (01423) 322 583, www.newbyhall.com; open April–Sept Tues–Sun, house 12–5, gardens 11–5.30; adm.*

The other day out from Ripon is to Newby Hall and Gardens. The house was designed under Christopher Wren's guidance and its interior is considered one of Robert Adam's masterpieces. Fine Chippendale furniture, classical statuary, tapestries and a collection of chamber pots from Europe and the Far East all add interest. The gardens, created in the 1920s, are designed to have something to see from spring to autumn, but are best in April and May, when rhododendrons and cherry trees are in flower. Newby Hall has an adventure playground and miniature railway for children.

Boroughbridge and Around

Downriver from Newby Hall is Boroughbridge, which has two ancient sites just outside it. Take Roecliffe Lane from the centre of the town and look out for three prehistoric standing stones, the **Devil's Arrows**, aligned along a north–south axis. The tallest of the three, beside the road, is taller than any of the stones erected at Stonehenge. It is thought that there used to be a fourth stone but at some point it disappeared. Why the stones were erected here and in this way, no one can be sure. Local tradition has it that they were hurled at Aldborough by the devil but missed. **Aldborough Roman Site** (*Front Street, Aldborough, **t** (01423) 322 768; open April–Sept daily 10–1 and 2–6; Oct 10–1 and 2–5; adm*) is the other ancient site, but it is positively youthful in comparison. It was here, at a fording point of the River Ure, that the Roman 9th legion in Britain established its HQ, *Isurium Brigantium*. The site as it is today reflects Victorian landscaping. Two Roman mosaic pavements are still *in situ*.

The North York Moors

This block of upland between the Tees Estuary, the Vale of York and the Vale of Pickering, which joins the coast near Whitby, is more than just bleak, lonely moorland. It is the moorland, however, that gave rise to the creation of the North York Moors National Park. This is the largest expanse of heather moorland in England, and such moorland is an endangered habitat: there is far less of it remaining in the world than tropical rainforest. If you like open space, you'll like the bleak beauty of the moors, which are at their best when the heather flowers in late summer. The North York Moors also have woods filled with bluebells in spring, a few small rivers, valleys, market towns, pretty villages, ruined abbeys, ancient stone crosses, packhorse bridges, prehistoric monuments and a picturesque steam train that refused to die.

Getting There and Around

For North York Moors public transport information see *www.countrygoer.org/nymoors.*

By Train

Two railways, the North Yorkshire Moors Railway and the Esk Valley railway, give access to large areas of the park.

North Yorkshire Moors Railway, Pickering Station, Park Street, **t** (01751) 472 508, *www.northyorkshiremoorsrailway.com. Services 23 Mar–3 Nov daily, 9 Nov–29 Dec weekends only*. In summer there are eight steam-hauled services a day in each direction from Pickering to Grosmont. Stations along the way include Levisham, Newton Dale (request stop) and Goathland.

Esk Valley Railway, National Rail Enquiries, **t** 08457 48 4950, *www.arrivatrainsnorthern.co.uk*. From Middlesborough to Whitby via Great Ayton, Danby and Grosmont. Connections from Newcastle and Darlington. Every station between Castleton Moor and Whitby has waymarked walks from it.

By Bus

Moorsbus, t 0870 608 2608, *www.moorsbus.net. Daily services late July–Sept, rest of the year Sun only*. Network of bus services to and around the North York Moors. Buses are marked by a yellow and green triangle. They stop at bus stops in villages and can be hailed on any road wherever it is safe to stop. A **Moorslink ticket** allows you to use the two railway lines (*see* above) as well as the buses. Cheap go-as-you-please day tickets if you board in Easingwold, East Ayton, Guisborough or Malton. Higher fare, but still reasonable for a day out, if you board the bus further afield, in Darlington Middlesborough, Thirsk, Northallerton, Pickering or York.

Tourist Information

North Yorkshire County Communities: *www.nycc.org.uk, or northyorkmoors-npa.gov.uk.*

The two main **national park** centres are at Sutton Bank and Danby

An excellent directory of places to buy arts and crafts made in the North York Moors, the Yorkshire Wolds and on the coast can be found at *www.brigantia.co.uk.*

Where to Stay

Youth Hostels, *www.yha.org.uk*. There are youth hostels at Osmotherley, Helmsley, Lockton and on the coast at Boggle Hole, Whitby and Scarborough.

Thirsk

The main roads encircle the North York Moors and only a few B-roads strike out north to south across country. The best way to approach the North York Moors is to begin at the market town of Thirsk, beneath the Hambleton Hills, and go either north or east. You can always make a circular tour of the moors with forays into the interior to see the main sights.

Thirsk, the pivotal point, is a pleasant market town which trades unashamedly on its fame as the capital of 'Herriot Country'. James Herriot was the pseudonym of vet Alf Wight, who was born in Sunderland but moved to Thirsk in 1940. Thirty years later, in 1970, he published his first story based on his experiences as a north-country vet, *If Only they could Talk*. His books, including *All Creatures Great and Small*, found almost instant appeal for their humour, sentimentality and nostalgia for simpler times and places – and were turned into an even more popular TV series. The **World of James Herriot** (*23 Kirkgate, **t** (01845) 524 234, www.worldofjamesherriot.org; open all year, April–Oct daily 10–6; Nov–Mar daily 10–5; adm*), a recreation of a 1940s veterinary surgery filled with Herriot memorabilia, is a celebration of the author and his work.

Getting Around

Teesside International Airport, Darlington, **t** (01325) 332 811, *www.teesside airport.com*, serves this area.

Middlesborough is the start of the **Esk Valley railway** (*see* p.819).

Tourist Information

Thirsk: 49 Market Place, **t** (01845) 522 755, *www.hambleton.gov.uk* or *www.herriot country.com. Open all year.*

Market day in Thirsk is Mon and Sat.

Northallerton: Applegarth car park, Northallerton, **t** (01609) 776 864, *www.northallerton-online.co.uk.*

Esk Valley: *www.eskvalley.com.*

Tees Valley: *www.visitteesvalley.co.uk.*

Middlesborough: The Get It Centre, Information and Learning Shop, 99–101 Albert Road, **t** (01642) 243 425, *www.middlesborough.gov.uk.*

National Park: The Moors Centre, Danby, **t** (01287) 660 654.

Great Ayton: High Green car park, **t** (01642) 722 835. *Open summer only.*

Guisborough: Priory Grounds, Church Street, Guisborough, **t** (01287) 633 801. *Open summer only.*

Where to Stay and Eat

Thirsk and Around t (01845) –

Three Tuns Hotel, Market Place, **t** 523 124, *www.three-tuns-thirsk.com* (*moderate*). In the centre of town; 10 rooms.

Spital Hill, **t** 522 273 (*moderate*). A Georgian house with Victorian additions. Not far off the A1 but peaceful enough to break a journey or to use as a base for the North York Moors. Home-baked bread and meals making use of garden produce. No-smoking house.

Around Thirsk

McCoys, The Cleveland Tontine, Staddlebridge, **t** (01609) 882 671, *mccoysatthetontine.co.uk* (*moderate*). A bistro run by three brothers which has become an institution for its eccentric jumble of furniture and varied blackboard menu. Rooms (*expensive*).

Crab and Lobster, Asenby, **t** (01845) 577 286, *www.crabandlobster.co.uk* (*moderate*). The thatched crab and lobster on the roof prepare you for the interior stuffed with tables and objects and odd chairs (you may end up sitting in an old dentist's chair). A cosy, cluttered place where you could get by with a couple of starters and a glass of wine, or have a full set menu.

Middlesborough and Stokesley t (01642) –

The Purple Onion, 80 Corporation Road, Middlesbrough, **t** 222 250, *www.thepurple onion.co.uk* (*moderate*). Informal brasserie-style atmosphere with an eclectic menu. Cocktails and live music most nights in the cellar bar.

Busby House, Stokesley, **t** 710 425 (*moderate*). Old farmhouse with cobbled courtyard and guestrooms looking onto the garden and out over fields.

A 10-minute walk from the market place (take the footpath from St Mary's Walk) is **Millennium Green**, where there is a mosaic depicting a tree of life, local wildlife and buildings of the town.

Osmotherley and Mount Grace Priory

The eastern route out of Thirsk, the A170, is the fastest route into the national park but there is plenty to see, too, if you start your tour northwards on the A19. At the end of the Cleveland Hills, near Osmotherley, is **Mount Grace Priory** (*Staddlebridge, Near Northallerton, **t** (01609) 883 494, www.english-heritage.org.uk; open April–Sept daily 10–6; Oct 10–5; Nov–April Wed–Sun 10–1 and 2–4; adm*). Although in ruins, this is considered the best of Britain's surviving Carthusian monasteries, or charter houses.

(one of only nine in the country). It was founded in 1398 and its monks lived solitary, silent lives, meeting their fellow inmates only at church services. One of the two-storey individual cells with its own herb garden has been recreated.

Osmotherley itself is a pretty village and the starting point for the Lyke Wake Walk long-distance footpath (*see* below).

Middlesborough and Cleveland

The A19 continues into the industrial conurbation of Middlesborough, but the only reason to go into the city is to see the **Transporter Bridge** (*Ferry Road,* **t** *(01642) 247 563; open Mon–Sat 5am–11.05pm, Sun 2–11.05pm; small toll for the crossing*) across the River Tees. Whereas cars and pedestrians normally move across a bridge, here a suspended section of the bridge itself moves, carrying the people and traffic. There is a visitor centre near the southern approach.

Captain James Cook was born at Marton on the outskirts of Middlesborough, at a site marked by the **Captain Cook Birthplace Museum** (*Stewart Park,* **t** *(01642) 311 211, www.middlesborough.gov.uk*). The **Esk Valley Railway** follows Cook's progress from his birthplace to his point of departure from land at Whitby. On Easby Moor above Great Ayton station stands the 1,063ft-tall **Captain Cook Monument**.

There aren't many good hills to climb in the North York Moors but the best of them is **Roseberry Topping** (1,000ft), which can be ascended from **Great Ayton**. If you are in a car, the A171 takes a less interesting route than the railway to reach Whitby.

Walking in the North York Moors

There are 1,400 miles of paths and tracks in the North York Moors suitable for walking, cycling and horse-riding. Ordnance Survey Explorer maps are recommended for general walking. Sheet OL26 covers the western half of the national park and Sheet OL27 the eastern half. Keep to marked footpaths to avoid trespassing on private land or trampling on the vegetation. The usual precautions for walking in upland Britain are advised: wear appropriate footwear and clothing; take a map and let someone know where you are going. Visit *www.walkyorkshire.com* for walks.

The Lyke Wake Walk

The Lyke Wake Walk long-distance footpath was devised in 1955 by the late Bill Cowley. Since then, more than 160,000 people have completed the walk and the paths have become worn-out from overuse.

The 40-mile route across the heather moors from Osmotherley to the coast at Ravenscar (between Whitby and Scarborough), from Bronze Age burial mound to Bronze Age burial mound, has to be completed in less than 24 hours to gain membership of the Lyke Wake Club, although the average time for doing it is now 13 hours (runners do it in less than five). For details on the path see *The Lyke Wake Walk – The Official Guide*, published by Dalesman, or contact **The Lyke Wake Club**, P.O. Box 24, Northallerton, North Yorkshire; *www.lykewakewalk.co.uk*. The Club is also responsible for two other moorland walks within the North York Moors National Park, both circular routes: **Shepherd's Round** (40 miles) and the **Hambleton Hobble** (32 miles).

East from Thirsk

Sutton Bank

The other route out of Thirsk is the A170, which has to climb the escarpment of Sutton Bank to get into the national park. A popular place for gliding, the crest of the bank is also one of the best places for a view of Yorkshire: on a clear day you can see across the Vale of Mowbray and the Vale of York to the Yorkshire Dales.

If the hillside is a good place from which to see, it is also a place to be seen and since the 19th century it has been engraved with one of the most visible and best-loved landmarks of Yorkshire: the **White Horse** on Roulston Scar above **Kilburn** looks ancient, but it is not. In 1857 the local schoolmaster, Thomas Hodgson, was inspired by a trip to the stylized white horse carved at Uffington on the Berkshire Downs to make

Tourist Information

Sutton Bank National Park Centre: **t** (01845) 597 426.

Helmsley: The Old Town Hall, Market Place, **t** (01439) 770 173.

Where to Stay and Eat

Coxwold and Crayke t (01347) –

Oldstead Grange, Oldstead, Coxwold, **t** 868 634, *www.oldsteadgrange.free-online.co.uk* (*expensive*). The grange was founded by monks from Byland Abbey but the present house is 17th century with thick walls and what is believed to be a priest hole. Varied and plentiful breakfast. A good base for walks in the area.

Durham Ox, Westway, Crayke, **t** 821 506, *www.thedurhamox.com* (*expensive*). Acclaimed restaurant with stone floors, log fires, beamed ceilings and wooden panelling situated on the hill made famous by the nursery rhyme, 'The Grand Old Duke of York'. Accommodation also available.

Helmsley t (01439) –

Black Swan Hotel, Market Place, Helmsley, **t** (01439) 770 466 (*expensive*). A modernized combination of Tudor rectory, Elizabethan coaching inn and Georgian house on the main square of the town. There are 45 bedrooms and several pleasant lounges.

The Hawnby Hotel, Hilltop, Hawnby (near Helmsley), **t** (01439) 798 202, *www.hawnbyhotel.co.uk* (*moderate*). The hotel's hilltop location gives great views of the national park countryside.

Lastingham and Around

Lastingham Grange, Country House Hotel, Lastingham, **t** (01751) 417 345, *www.lastinghamgrange.com* (*very expensive*). This converted farmhouse on the edge of the moors has been called 'the most peaceful hotel in Britain' where 'the only sound is the sound of morning birdsong'. It stands in 10 acres of gardens and fields.

Inn on the Moor, Goathland, **t** (01947) 896 296 (*expensive*). A hotel in its own grounds looking out over the North York Moors National Park. The 24 en-suite rooms include two family suites.

The Orange Tree, Rosedale East, Rosedale Abbey, **t** (01751) 417 219, *www.theorangetree.com* (*cheap*). Peaceful location. Good walking. Sociable meals and generous portions.

Rosedale Bakery and Tea Rooms, **t** (01751) 417 468 (*cheap*). Fresh bread, pies, teacakes, scones, sandwiches to order.

Birch Hall Inn, Beck Hole (near Goathland), **t** (01947) 896 245, *www.beckhole.com* (*cheap*). Diminutive pub (two bars and a sweet shop) in a peaceful location which has been little altered by modernity. Hand-pulled cask ales and a simple bar menu including home-baked scones, beer cake and Beck Hole butty sandwiches all contribute to the unspoiled atmosphere of the place.

Captain James Cook (1728–79)

James Cook was born the son of an agricultural labourer in a humble cottage in **Marton** (now on the edge of the Middlesborough conurbation) on 17 October 1728. The family later moved to the village of **Great Ayton**, where he went to Postgate's School. He worked in a haberdasher's shop in **Staithes** before being apprenticed to a **Whitby** shipowner. In 1755 he joined the navy as an ordinary seaman. As well as serving in the Seven Years War, his voyages over the next few years included trips to survey the **St Lawrence River** in Canada and the coasts of **Newfoundland**.

In 1768 the British Admiralty put Cook in command of the *Endeavour*, built in Whitby, which was to take a Royal Society expedition to the Pacific to study the transit of Venus across the sun (a rare event that would help measure the distance to the sun). This mission complete, Cook was also to look for the Southern Continent, *Terra Australis Incognita*, which had been supposed to exist since Greek times. He set sail on 26 August 1768 and was away for three years, making his reputation both as an explorer and a humane captain. No one on board died of scurvy, although Cook did not realize that this was due to his insistence on the crew eating fresh vegetables. On the return trip he sailed round **New Zealand**, visited the coasts of **Australia** (which had already been discovered by the Dutch but which nobody accepted as the fabled Southern Continent) and discovered 40 islands before heading for home.

A year after returning to England he set sail again on his second voyage, this time on the *Resolution*, also built in Whitby, which also lasted three years. He was the first sailor to cross the **Antarctic Circle**, reaching latitude 71 degrees before further progress was prevented by ice. He also visited **Tahiti** and the **New Hebrides**, and discovered New Caledonia and other island groups.

He set sail on his last voyage in 1776 to look for a passage to the north of America around Canada and Alaska (we now know that such a passage does not exist). Cook was forced to turn back from the Bering Straits in 1779, putting in to **Hawaii** to repair his ship and rest his crew. The manner of his death is ironic since Cook had a reputation as a fair man and a natural diplomat. At first the Hawaiians treated their visitors with great respect but the mood changed and one of the landing craft was stolen. When Cook went ashore on St Valentine's day, 14 February, he intended to take the local king hostage. The crowd of natives on the beach around him turned hostile and Cook was clubbed and repeatedly stabbed to death in the back before he had time to retreat off the beach.

For more on Cook see *www.captaincook.org.uk* or *www.captaincooksociety.com*.

one of his own. On returning home, he got his pupils to carve a horse to a design based on his own sketches of horses. The horse measures 314ft by 228ft and its eye is big enough for 12 people to picnic on. The horse may not be ancient but the hilltop above it is Yorkshire's largest prehistoric hill fort, dating from 400BC.

Kilburn village has another location to be proud of. You need look no further for the perfect souvenir of Yorkshire than the **Mouseman Visitor Centre** (**t** *(01347) 869 102; open June–Sept daily 10–5; April, May and Oct Tues–Sun 10–5*), the workshop of furniture-maker Robert Thompson, nicknamed 'the Mouseman' because he carved a small

The Life and Opinions of Laurence Sterne

I live in a constant endeavour to fence against the infirmities of ill health, and other evils of life, by mirth; being firmly persuaded that every time a man smiles, – but much more so, when he laughs, it adds something to this Fragment of Life.

Laurence Sterne, Dedication of *Tristram Shandy*

Laurence Sterne (1713–68) was born in Tipperary, the son of an army subaltern, and spent his early years travelling before the family settled in Halifax. After his father died he studied at Cambridge, then took orders and became the vicar of Sutton-on-the-Forest and later prebendary of York Minster, although a biographer has described him as 'temperamentally unsuited to the church, then one of the few refuges for the ingenious poor man.' Nonetheless he obtained the curacy of Coxwold and moved to Shandy Hall, where he lived on and off until 1767.

His novel, *The Life and Opinions of Tristram Shandy, Gentleman* (published in nine instalments from 1759 to '67) was written at Shandy Hall, with pauses to go out into the garden 'to weed, hack up old roots or wheel away rubbish.' It was and is extremely modern in its approach: its deliberately chaotic treatment of time, its misuse of learning, and its digressions and free association of ideas. 'Writing,' he says in the novel, 'when properly managed (as you may be sure I think mine is), is but a different name for conversation.' The book brought him almost instant fame and he was lionized by the fashionable society of London on his visits there. It is regarded as the first English novel. In his last years, Sterne travelled often on the Continent in search of a cure for TB. He died, still at the height of his fame, the year following the last instalment of *Tristram Shandy*, of pleurisy in his lodgings in London, while attending to the publication of his second major work, *A Sentimental Journey* (1768).

mouse on each piece that he produced. Thompson (1876–1955) began his working life as a wheelwright before teaching himself the arts of wood-carving and joinery. He would work only in naturally seasoned oak and made particular use of an old craftsman's tool, the adze, to give a wavy surface to each object he made. How he came to carve a mouse as a trademark he could never say but he may have been inspired by a fellow carver who remarked that they and other craftsmen were 'as poor as church mice.' The business is still carried on by the Mouseman's family.

Coxwold and Further South

If you have come down off Sutton Bank to visit Kilburn you may as well follow the road to Coxwold, a village that consists of a single inclined road with two perfectly preserved lines of houses facing each other across it. Outside the village is **Shandy Hall** (***t*** *(01347) 868 465, www.shandy-hall.org.uk; house open May–Sept Wed 2–4.30, Sun 2.30–4.30; gardens open May–Sept Sun–Fri; adm*) which was the home of the novelist and humourist Laurence Sterne (*see* above).

Ruined **Byland Abbey** (***t*** *(01347) 868 614; open April–Sept daily 10–6, Oct 10–5; adm minimal*), also outside Coxwold, is not one of the most interesting abbeys; you can get a good feel of it over the wall beside the Wass-Coxwold road without paying to get in.

Having strayed this far from the North York Moors onto the plains you may want to go a little further and see a little-visited sight, the **City of Troy Turf Maze** near **Brandsby** (on the north side of the little road between Dalby and Brandsby). This is the smallest and most northerly of the few remaining turf mazes in Britain, and like most of the others, it is not a maze at all but an intricate design that guides you to its centre without any chance of your choosing your own route let alone of getting lost. Although the age of the Brandsby maze is unknown, this same pattern is extremely ancient in origin and may have been used for ritualistic purposes.

Helmsley

From Coxwold or Brandsby you can pick up the main A170 to the north again without much problem and this will bring you to the pleasant town of **Helmsley**, built around a castle and a market square (*market day Friday*). Helmsley is the start of the Cleveland Way, a 110-mile footpath right around the edge of the Moors and down the coast to Filey. Beside the castle is **Helmsley Walled Garden** (*t (01439) 771 427, www.helmsleywalledgarden.co.uk; open daily April–Oct 10.30–5, Nov–Mar 12–4; adm*), a working kitchen garden which was built in 1756 as part of the Duncombe Estate but fell into disrepair in the 1980s. It has been renovated by a team of volunteers and is now run as a charitable place offering 'horticultural therapy for those in need'.

Beyond the castle is **Duncombe Park** (*t (01439) 770 213, www.duncombepark.com; open May–Oct Sun–Thurs; grounds 11–5.30; house by guided tour 12.30–3.30; adm*), the 18th-century home of the Fevershams, a stately home within Arcadian parkland.

Better Never than Early

The photogenic 'golf balls' – radar dishes housed in gigantic white globes – may have disappeared but RAF Fylingdales is still performing the same vital service for democracy: keeping an eye on the Reds. During the Cold War the British public was reassured to know that Fylingdales would give them a 'four-minute warning' of impending attack. Actually it would have been more like three minutes, but that was deemed long enough – long enough for Britain and allies to launch a retaliatory strike against the Soviets so they wouldn't get away with it: the principle of MAD (Mutually Assured Destruction) had to be adhered to. The United States, patron of Fylingdales and its sister bases at Thule in Greenland and Clear in Alaska, would have got slightly longer to prepare themselves.

The Cold War was won, but the paranoia continues, and Fylingdales now forms an integral part of the National Missile Defence system, NMD, better known as 'Son of Star Wars'. It is operated as a franchise by the RAF.

In 1992 the golf balls were replaced by the monolith that stands on the moors today, a truncated pyramid containing a solid-state phased-array radar (SSPAR) which can track 800 objects as small as 0.5sqm at any one time. Its range is 3,000 miles. The information is relayed to US Space Command at Cheyenne Mountain, Colorado.

For a very detailed, unofficial explanation of how Fylingdales helps to make the free world safe, see *www.yorkshirecnd.org.uk/ycndintro.htm*.

Rievaulx

From Helmsley you can walk the 3 miles to Rievaulx along the wooded valley of the River Rye to visit the 13th-century Cistercian **Rievaulx Abbey** (*off the B1257*, **t** *(01439) 798 228; open daily April–Sept 10–6, Oct 10–5, Nov–Mar 10–4; adm*) 'Everywhere peace, everywhere serenity, and a marvellous freedom from the tumult of the world,' the monastery's third abbot St Aelred wrote of his home. You can get good views of the abbey from the nearby **Rievaulx Terrace and Temples** (**t** *(01439) 798 340; open daily Mar–Nov 10.30–6, Oct–Nov 10.30–5; adm*), an 18th-century landscape with two neo-classical temples (but note that there is no access between the two sites).

Eight miles further up the B1257, north of Rievaulx at Bilsdale is **Spout House** (*open Easter–Oct Fri–Wed 10–4; adm*), a 16th-century thatched cruck-framed house.

Lastingham and Hutton-le-Hole

Continuing to the coast from Helmsley leads you towards Pickering but there is a nice little detour to be made to **Lastingham**. A pretty village sited at the foot of the Tabular Hills, it has important connections with early Christianity in Britain. St Cedd, 7th-century bishop, founded the church in 654 and is buried in the church beneath the Norman crypt. More prosaically, an early 18th-century curate of Lastingham, Jeremiah Carter, supplemented his stipend by running the local ale-house.

Hutton-le-Hole, near Lastingham, has an interesting museum, the **Ryedale Folk Museum** (**t** *(01751) 417 367; open Mar–Oct daily 10–5.30, Nov 10–4.30; adm*), a village of rescued and restored buildings enshrining the traditional North York Moors life.

Pickering and the Eastern Moors

Pickering has a **castle** and a **church**, St Peter and St Paul's, with medieval murals, but above all it is a staging post for travellers about to trek north across desolate country

Getting There and Around

Pickering is the start of the **North Yorkshire Moors Railway**.

The nearest mainline station is **Malton**, on the line between York and Scarborough.

Tourist Information

Pickering: The Ropery, **t** (01751) 473 791.
Malton: 58 Market Place, **t** (01653) 600 048.

Where to Stay and Eat

Pickering t (01751) –

White Swan Hotel, Market Place, **t** 472 288, *www.white-swan.co.uk* (*expensive*). Built in 1532 as a four-room cottage, the White Swan was extended as a coaching inn and used as a transit point for smugglers between Whitby and York. Today it has 12 bedrooms on two floors, each themed. One has a 6ft-long bath. Some rooms have antique beds and cashmere throws.

Allerston Manor House, near Thornton-le-Dale, **t** 850 112, *www.allerston-manor.com* (*expensive*). A 300-year-old house on the site of an old castle. Medieval dining room.

Black Swan, 18 Birdgate, **t** 472 286, *www.blackswanpickering.co.uk* (*moderate*). An 18th-century building with spacious B&B bedrooms. The restaurant on the ground floor serves home cooking. In the basement is Whistler's Bistro, where Continental dishes are accompanied by New World wines.

to Whitby. There are few points of interest on the route, especially since the powers that be converted the eerie giant 'golf balls' of Fylingdales into an even more sinister but less spectacular pyramidal monolith (*see* p.823).

A far more pleasant way of getting to Whitby is to take the **North Yorkshire Moors Railway**, one of the world's oldest railway lines. Both Pickering and Goathland stations have been restored to period condition. The station in picturesque Goathland is Hogwarts station in the *Harry Potter* films.

Otherwise, as a contrast to the moors, try **Dalby Forest Drive** (***t*** *(01751) 474 503, www.forestry.gov.uk/dalbyforest; open daily dawn–dusk; adm*) a 9-mile drive through woodlands which starts just outside Pickering.

Castle Howard and the Vale of Pickering

When you are finished with the Moors, turn south and you are in the gentle Vale of Pickering, the bed of a long-vanished lake, which can boast both England's most famous stately home and its smallest.

Don't bother with the latter (Ebberston Hall) but don't miss the former. **Castle Howard** (***t*** *(01653) 648 444, www.castlehoward.co.uk; open mid-Mar–Oct daily; grounds, garden, exhibition wing and plant centre from 10–5, house from 11–5; adm*), 4 miles southwest of Malton, is one of the finest stately homes in England, and one of the most adroitly managed. Since the 1980s it has been synonymous with the fictional 'Brideshead' after a TV adaptation of Evelyn Waugh's book, *Brideshead Revisited*, was filmed here. The Howard family still lives in the 18th-century house designed by Vanburgh as it has done for the last 300 years, surrounded by a collection of period furniture and paintings (including Canaletto, Reynolds, Holbein and Gainsborough). Just think of the upkeep: the house has 100 rooms and 500 windows under 1½ acres of roof. The family needs a staff of 100 to keep the place running and the housekeeper has the daunting task of turning on 83 light switches each morning.

The treasures inside the house include 300 items of rare china on the China Landing, Holbein's portrait of Henry VIII, an oak and silver wine cooler given to Lord Morpeth in 1841 'as a consolation prize for his defeat in a Parliamentary election', three embroidered panels by William Morris in the chapel, and a piano made in 1796.

The grounds provide plenty of lighter entertainment. On one side of the house are formal gardens around an Atlas fountain; on the other the lawns slope down to the shore of a boating lake. Paths lead through Ray Wood to the Temple of the Four Winds, where you can often lose the crowds that mill about the house and cafés.

Outside Malton, not far from Castle Howard, is **Eden Camp** (***t*** *(01653) 697 777, www.edencamp.co.uk; open daily 10–5; advisable to arrive before 2*) an unusual and educational museum which is housed in the huts of Prisoner of War camp No. 83, built in 1942. Each of the 32 huts presents a display on a different theme of the Second World War, the emphasis on the effects of wartime on ordinary people.

The Yorkshire Coast

The hard cliffs of the northern Yorkshire coast are holding their own against the North Sea, while the soft southern cliffs are being rapidly eroded by the waves, taking villages and all else with them – making the coast below Flamborough Head look as if a giant had taken a bite out of Yorkshire.

All the way along the coast are seaside resorts, most small and not all charming. Many of the larger coastal towns have a touch of the tackily appealing seaside atmosphere – amusement arcades, burger bars, theme pubs, sweet and souvenir shops – that England excels at: Scarborough, Filey and Bridlington are fine examples; Whitby stands apart from them as an interesting place to visit on or off season. In between the resorts are some charming villages and beauty spots.

If you're an optimist or a masochist bring your swimming togs for a day at the coast: with courage you may be able to paddle or even swim in the chilly waters of the North Sea, but if the sun doesn't shine you may just as easily end up huddling behind rocks to keep out of sleet and biting wind. The hardy Yorkshire folk are not easily deterred by the temperature of water and air, however, and descend *en masse* on their coastline during the summer holidays and at weekends throughout the year. If you want to get the atmosphere of the coast at its best, avoid these busy times.

The Cleveland Coast

The name for the northernmost stretch of the Yorkshire coast, Cleveland, comes from the Viking for 'Cliffland' and that sums up the character of the coastline from the Tees Estuary to Flamborough Head. The cliffs are often brittle and packed with fossils, and the coast has been dubbed the 'Dinosaur Coast'. They also yield jet, a black stone that has spawned its very own jewellery industry in Whitby.

Redcar, nearest the mouth of the Tees, is a resort distinguished only by its horse-racing track. More interesting is **Saltburn-by-the-Sea**, a short way south, which has Victorian character. The brightly painted carriages of its **cliff lift** (*Lower Promenade,* ***t*** *(01287) 622 528; operates daily Easter–Whitsun 10–1 and 2–5, Whitsun–mid-Sept 10–1 and 2–7; adm*) shuttle up and down the cliff behind the beach. The oldest water-balanced lift in Britain, it began operating in 1884. Saltburn also has a Victorian **pier**, which once stretched 1,400ft into the sea but had to be pruned to 600ft in 1974 after damage by freak tides. You are now on the designated 'Heritage Coast'; these days even lawbreakers are dear to the hearts of the peddlers of all things heritage, as you can see at the **Saltburn Smugglers Heritage Centre** (*next to the Ship Inn,* ***t*** *(01287) 625 252; open April–Sept 10–6; adm*).

The cliffs of England's east coast are highest around **Staithes**, the most unspoilt of Yorkshire's fishing village. It is divided into two parts, Staithes proper and Cowbar, by the gorge of Staithes Beck. Its cobbled streets include Dog Loup, one of the narrowest streets in England. Cobles, traditional fishing boats built to be launched and landed on the beach, are still used by local fishermen to catch cod, lobsters and crabs.

Getting There and Around

Trains from Whitby to Middlesborough are operated by **Arriva Trains Northern**.

Buses to Middlesborough. Leeds to Whitby 840 **Yorkshire Coastliner**, **t** (01653) 692 556, *www.yorkshirecoastliner.co.uk*.

Tourist Information

Redcar: West Terrace, Esplanade, **t** (01642) 471 921, *www.redcar-cleveland.gov.uk*.

Saltburn by the Sea: 4 Station Buildings, Station Square, **t** (01287) 622 422.

Ravenscar: National Trust Coastal Centre, **t** (01723) 870 138. *Open summer only*.

Whitby: Langborne Road, **t** (01947) 602 674, *www.whitbytourism.com*.

Robin Hood's Bay: The Old Coastguard Station, **t** (01947) 885 900.

Where to Stay and Eat

The Cleveland Coast

The Rose Garden, 20 Hilda Place, Saltburn by the Sea, **t** (01287) 622 947, *www.therosegarden.co.uk* (*moderate*). Victorian terraced house with three guest rooms. Full organic English breakfast.

Claxton Hotel, 194–8 High Street, Redcar, **t** (01642) 486 745, *www.claxtonhotel.co.uk* (*moderate*). Most bedrooms (including some family rooms) look onto the sea. Beamed dining room with inglenook fireplace.

Whitby t (01947) –

Ashford Guest House, 8 Royal Crescent, **t** 602 138, *www.ashfordguesthouse.co.uk* (*moderate*). Family-run guesthouse in Royal Crescent, looking out onto Crescent Gardens and over the sea.

The Queensland Hotel, 2 Crescent Avenue, West Cliff, **t** 604 262, *www.queensland.co.uk* (*moderate*). Close to the Spa Theatre, the Royal Gardens; children's paddling pool, boating lake, golf course and other key entertainments and amenities. Rooms with four-poster beds.

Magpie Café, 14 Pier Road, **t** 602 058, *www.magpiecafe.co.uk* (*cheap*). Truly a legend in its own lunchtime, this glorified café and fish and chips restaurant is the most famous place to eat in, as indicated by the queue up the steps. The cosy, slightly old-fashioned dining rooms have views of the harbour and the abbey. The menu includes up to 10 varieties of fish but also vegetarian options. Surprisingly inexpensive considering its fame.

Trenchers, New Quay Road, **t** 603 212, *www.trenchersrestaurant.co.uk* (*cheap*). Fish and chips restaurant: a bright, modern alternative to the Magpie Café, all stainless steel, marble and *faux* leather. Child-friendly and without pretension: the bread comes pre-buttered.

Elizabeth Botham and Sons, 35/39 Skinner Street, **t** 602 823, *www.botham.co.uk* (*cheap*). Old-fashioned English tea rooms and craft bakery. Ploughman's lunches and hot dishes also available.

Around Whitby t (01947) –

Stakesby Manor, Manor Close, Stakesby, **t** 602 773, *www.stakesby-manor.co.uk* (*expensive*). Family-run Georgian manor house in its own grounds. Open fires blaze.

Bottom House Farm, Robin's Hood Bay, **t** 880 754 (*moderate*). B&B in a working farm with fabulous views of the countryside and sea.

An extremely steep hill leads down into **Runswick Bay**, where a village looks out over a long sandy beach from the cliff-foot. If it looks a little nervous, it has reason to: the original village was sited further to the north, but one night in the 17th century the entire place, except one cottage, slid into the sea. Luckily some of the villagers were returning home from a wake when they saw their homes about to drift away, and were able to raise the alarm and evacuate the rest of the populace.

Whitby

If you have time to see only one place on the coast make it Whitby, picturesquely squeezed into a cleft between cliffs at the mouth of the River Esk. It manages to combine the brashness of the Yorkshire coast with the sort of history and tradition that other towns would kill for.

Whitby developed as an all-purpose port: a centre for fishing and whaling, for shipbuilding, sail-making, rope-making and other maritime crafts. In 1706 it was the sixth most important port in Britain, building 130 ships in that year and bustling with merchants, ship owners, drunken sailors and press gangs. Captain James Cook was the most famous of many men who went to sea from here.

The town is built on both sides of the estuary and West Side (or Cliff) and East Side could not form more of a contrast. The town centre and the holiday resort are on the west side. One of the streets has the delightfully incongruous name of Khyber Pass. The various amusement arcades along the top of West Cliff have that seedy English seaside atmosphere, but you can easily escape them by walking or taking the lift down to the beach below, **Whitby Sands**. Lewis Carroll was inspired to write his poem 'The Walrus and the Carpenter' by walks along this beach, with its 'quantities of sand' inhabited by ingenuous and ill-fated oysters. He visited the resort several times between 1854 and 1871 and his first published work, a poem entitled 'The Lady of the Ladle', appeared in the *Whitby Gazette*.

Whitby is also famously associated with Dracula. From the **Bram Stoker Memorial Seat** (south end of Spion Kip on West Cliff) you can see where the Whitby scenes of the novel are played out. For more commercialized thrills you can visit the **Dracula Experience** (*9 Marine Parade,* ***t*** *(01947) 601 923; usually open winter weekends only 11–5, Mar–June and Sept–Oct daily 10–6, July and Aug daily 10–9, but check before visiting; adm*), which recreates Count Dracula's links with the Yorkshire seaside with 'live actors'; dead actors might be more fitting!

You're better off simply crossing the bridge to the other side of the harbour to the oldest and more atmospheric part of town, where you can easily get a flavour of the Gothic Victorian Whitby that inspired Stoker.

Turn right at the end of the bridge and you reach the **Captain Cook Memorial Museum** (*Grape Lane,* ***t*** *(01947) 601 900, www.cookmuseumwhitby.co.uk; open Mar weekends 11–3, April–Oct daily 9.45–5; adm*), housed in the former home of ship owner John Walker, who gave the 17-year-old Cook his first sea-going job.

Most of the crowds flow left off the bridge into a couple of busy streets in which jewellery shops trade Whitby's trademark gemstone, jet. Jet is a highly compressed remnant of prehistoric monkey-puzzle trees. Cut and polished, it becomes a deep black stone, which has been ascribed magical properties such as protection against the Evil Eye. Queen Victoria made jet popular by wearing it in mourning after the death of her beloved Albert, and in the 19th century jet manufacturing was one of Whitby's main sources of livelihood. The **Victorian Jet Works** (*123/b Church Street,* ***t*** *(01947) 821 530, www.whitbyjet.net*) employed 1,700 people. W. Hamond, across the

Dracula in Whitby

Three chapters (6,7 and 8) of Bram Stoker's *Dracula* (1897) are set in Whitby. Stoker never visited his most famous location, Transylvania, but his observations of Whitby were clearly made at first hand, and as well as being a gripping Gothic fantasy the book is a good evocation of a Victorian seaside resort. One of the book's heroines, Mina Murray, describes it in her journal:

'This is a lovely place. The little river, the Esk, runs through a deep valley, which broadens out as it comes near the harbour. A great viaduct runs across, with high piers, through which the view seems somehow further away than it really is. The valley is beautifully green, and it is so steep that when you are on the high land on either side you look right across it, unless you are near enough to see down. The houses of the old town – the side away from us – are all red-roofed, and seem piled up one over the other anyhow, like the pictures we see of Nuremberg.'

The peace of Whitby, however, is shattered by the dramatic arrival of Count Dracula. He has chartered the Russian schooner Demeter to carry his mysterious cargo of 'fifty cases of common earth' to England. As the ship is seen off Whitby a storm blows up and a Gothic night descends:

'...masses of sea-fog came drifting inland. White, wet clouds, which swept by in ghostly fashion, so dank and damp and cold that it needed but little effort of imagination to think that the spirits of those lost at sea were touching their living brethren with the clammy hands of death..'

The ship, with all its sails set, inexplicably rushes towards the shore so that 'she must fetch up somewhere, if it was only in hell'. Instead it crashes into the harbour pier and:

'...a shudder ran through all who saw her, for lashed to the helm was a corpse, with drooping head, which swung horribly to and fro at each motion of the ship. No other form could be seen on the deck at all.

'But, strangest of all, the very instant the shore was touched, an immense dog sprang up on deck from below, as if shot up by the concussion, and running forward, jumped from the bow on the sand.'

Upon investigation it is found that all the crew have gone missing – they were shipboard provisions for Dracula, a stowaway, to eat on the voyage.

Dracula, metamorphosed into the dog, runs down what is now Henrietta Street which, legend says, used to be haunted by a 'thost-dog' or spectral hound, and climbs the 199 steps towards the abbey. When he gets to St Mary's Church he makes himself

road at the foot of the steps to the abbey, claims to be the Original Whitby Jet Shop (est. 1860), but there are several other jewellery shops in these streets, which all look as authentic as each other.

Sandgate or Church Street will lead you to the Market Place, beyond which you have a choice between a staircase of 199 steps or the steep Church Lane to get up the headland where stands the abbey.

at home in the unhallowed grave of a suicide. By chance or misfortune Mina has settled on this as her favourite vantage point:

'This is to my mind the nicest spot in Whitby, for it lies right over the town, and has a full view of the harbour and all up the bay to where the headland called Kettleness stretches out into the sea. It descends so steeply over the harbour that part of the bank has fallen away, and some of the graves have been destroyed.

'In one place part of the stonework of the graves stretches out over the sandy pathway far below. There are walks, with seats beside them, through the churchyard, and people go and sit there all day long looking at the beautiful view and enjoying the breeze.'

One night, Mina rescues her friend Lucy from a close encounter with the count. Mina wakes to find Lucy has gone sleepwalking in her nightdress:

'At the edge of the West Cliff above the pier I looked across the harbour to the East Cliff, in the hope or fear, I don't know which, of seeing Lucy in our favourite seat.

'There was a bright full moon, with heavy black, driving clouds, which threw the whole scene into a fleeting diorama of light and shade as they sailed across. For a moment or two I could see nothing, as the shadow of a cloud obscured St. Mary's Church and all around it. Then as the cloud passed I could see the ruins of the abbey coming into view, and as the edge of a narrow band of light as sharp as a sword-cut moved along, the church and churchyard became gradually visible. Whatever my expectation was, it was not disappointed, for there, on our favourite seat, the silver light of the moon struck a half-reclining figure, snowy white. The coming of the cloud was too quick for me to see much, for shadow shut down on light almost immediately, but it seemed to me as though something dark stood behind the seat where the white figure shone, and bent over it. What it was, whether man or beast, I could not tell.'

She rushes across the harbour and up the steps towards the abbey:

'When I got almost to the top I could see the seat and the white figure, for I was now close enough to distinguish it even through the spells of shadow. There was undoubtedly something, long and black, bending over the half-reclining white figure. I called in fright, 'Lucy! Lucy!' and something raised a head, and from where I was I could see a white face and red, gleaming eyes.'

Lucy makes a lucky escape and, after a 10-day seaside break, Dracula departs on the 9.30 goods train to King's Cross, inside one of his boxes. Lucy, sadly, will not be so lucky when they next meet...

St Mary's parish church greets you at the top of the steps. Bram Stoker was inspired by the graveyard overlooking the sea with its blackened tombstones. Inside, all the pews are boxed in and hearing trumpets adorn an unusual three-storey pulpit.

Whitby Abbey (*Cliff Top, East Side,* **t** *(01947) 603 568, www.english-heritage.org.uk; open April–Sept daily 10–6, Oct 10–5, Nov–Mar 10–4; adm*) looks sinister even on a summer's day, but you get the full blast of its atmosphere on a misty day in winter with no one else around. The site was first used in prehistoric times. In AD 657 the pioneering Saint Hilda (614–80) founded a monastery here. In 664 the Synod of Celtic and Roman Christians (better known as the Synod of Whitby) was convened at the abbey by Abbess Hilda to thrash out a date for England to celebrate Easter: the Celtic Christians agreed to adopt the Roman system. Among the population of the monastery was the lay brother (St) Caedmon (died around 680), who is considered the first English poet. He was an illiterate cowherd for the abbey whose poetry came to him in a vision and was written down at Hilda's orders.

After the Dissolution the abbey fell into decay and became a romantic ruin owned by the Chomley family, which built a house beside it (where the Visitor Centre is now housed). An interesting feature is the 17th-century cobbled garden.

South of Whitby: Robin Hood's Bay

No one knows how Robin Hood's Bay got its name, but it has a long tradition of law-breaking. For centuries the bay took advantage of its inaccessible location to land contraband goods. In around 1800 the entire population was living off smuggling. The cottage cellars were connected by tunnels so that a bale of contraband silk could pass from the seashore to the top of the village without attracting attention.

Now connected to the outside world and gentrified, Robin Hood's Bay is one of the prettiest places on this coast of England and a favourite subject for painters. The **Old Coastguard Station** (*The Dock, **t** (01947) 885 900, www.nationaltrust.org.uk; open April–May and Oct weekends 10–5, Whitsun–Sept daily 10–5, Nov–Mar weekends 11–4*) forms the centrepiece of several National Trust holdings on this stretch of coast.

Down the Coast to Spurn Head

Scarborough

The mood of the coast changes when you reach Scarborough, 'Britain's first holiday resort', a spa which had its heyday in Victorian and Edwardian times, then fell from grace. Now it is a family holiday centre. It's divided into North Bay and South Bay, with the castle in the middle. The **South Bay** has the harbour, the town centre, and the once classy Spa Complex and Esplanade along the waterfront. Behind **North Bay** is popular **Peasholme Park**. At the far end from town is a **Sealife and Marine Sanctuary** (*Scalby Mills, **t** (01723) 376 125, www.sealife.co.uk; open daily 10–6; adm*), an aquarium which includes tanks of seals, otters, octopuses and seahorses, and runs a Sea Turtle Convalescence Centre. From Sealife, a **miniature railway** (*Northstead Manor Gardens, **t** (01723) 373 333; open Easter–Oct 10.30–5.30; adm*) runs to the other large attraction, **Atlantis** (***t** (01723) 372 744; open summer 10–6; adm*), a water park (with heated water).

It's not all for the kids, however. Playwright Alan Ayckbourne is artistic director of the **Stephen Joseph Theatre** in Westborough (***t** (01723) 370 541*), one of England's best regional theatres, which regularly premières his new plays and reprises the old.

Filey to Flamborough Head

Continuing down the coast, **Filey** is another holiday resort – a place of fish and chips, amusement arcades, paddling pools and playgrounds – standing on a great

Getting There and Around

Scarborough is linked to York, Leeds and Hull on the **railway** by Arriva Trains Northern.

Bus connections to Filey, Bridlington and Hull. To Leeds and York, **Yorkshire Coastliner**, **t** (01653) 692 556, *www.yorkshirecoastliner.co.uk*.

Tourist Information

Scarborough: Unit 3, Pavilion House, Valley Bridge Road, **t** (01723) 373 333, *www.e-sbc.co.uk*.

Filey: Evron Centre, John Street, **t** (01723) 518 000.

Bridlington: 25 Prince Street, **t** (01262) 673 474, *www.bridlington.net*.

Hornsea: 120 Newbegin, **t** (01964) 536 404, *www.hornsea.net* and *www.hornsea.com*.

Withernsea: 131 Queen Street, **t** (01964) 615 683; seasonal opening hours.

Where to Stay and Eat

Scarborough t (01723) –

Scarborough Hotels Association: *www.s-h-a.co.uk*

Ox Pasture Hall Country Hotel, Lady Edith's Drive, Throxenby, **t** 365 295 (*expensive*). Set in forests and meadows three miles from the centre of Scarborough. Most of the rooms look onto the courtyard garden.

Lanterna Restaurant, 33 Queen Street, **t** 363 616, *www.lanterna-ristorante.co.uk* (*expensive*). Fish and pasta restaurant with the emphasis on local fish. From September to February try white truffle shaved onto pasta. Home-made desserts.

Lyncris Manor, 45 Northstead Manor Drive, **t** 361 052, *www.manorhotel.fsnet.co.uk* (*moderate*). Detached house looking onto Peasholme Park and the attractions of North Bay. Four of the six bedrooms are en suite.

Outlook Hotel,18 Ryndleside, **t** 364 900, *www.outlookhotel.co.uk* (*moderate*). Guesthouse in quiet location looking on to Peasholme Glen. En-suite rooms, residents' lounge and garden and own parking.

Golden Grid, 4 Sandside, **t** 360 922, *www.goldengrid.co.uk* (*moderate*). Famous fish restaurant which has been going for more than a hundred years. Spacious dining rooms on three floors overlooking Scarborough harbour. Breakfast too.

Filey t (01723) –

White Lodge Hotel, The Crescent, **t** 514 771 (*expensive*). Many of the bedrooms have panoramic sea views. A la carte restaurant and bistro.

Gables Guest House, Rutland Street, **t** 514 750 (*moderate*). Edwardian guesthouse. Reductions for three nights or more.

Bramwells Tea Room, 33 Belle Vue Street, **t** 513 344 (*cheap*). Old-fashioned place for tea or a meal. Try the crab sandwiches.

Bridlington t (01262) –

The Manor House, Flamborough, **t** 850 943, *www.flamboroughmanor.co.uk* (*moderate*). An 18th-century manor house owned by an author and a 'gansey' knitter (ganseys are traditional fishermen's sweaters). Dinner makes use of local seafood but bring your own wine.

Sixties Coffee Bar, 2 Marlborough Terrace, **t** 608 400, *www.sixtiescoffeebar.co.uk* (*cheap*). The name says it all.

Skipsea t (01262) –

Skipsea Grange, Hornsea Road, **t** 468 745 *www.skipseagrange.activehotels.com* (*moderate*). Guesthouse, restaurant and tea room in a listed building which has been in the owner's family for five generations. The child-friendly restaurant serves cream cakes, snacks, main meals and special dishes such as roasts, Lancashire hotpot, fish pie or vegetarian bake. Seven guest rooms including two equipped for disabled guests. Two suites have their own dining area and Jacuzzis – and one a private sauna.

sweep of sand which is safe for children to romp around on. There is a good walk to be made to Filey Brigg. You can keep going up the coast from here on the Cleveland Way or head off in the other direction on the Wold's Way.

Bridlington is another scaled-down version of Scarborough with good beaches and a range of family visitor attractions. For a very English experience, you can watch cliff-top cricket matches at Sewerby, just outside Bridlington, on summer weekends. Here **Flamborough Head**, a rocky headland, protrudes defiantly into the North Sea. On it are two lighthouses, one of them the oldest standing in Britain.

To the north of Flamborough Head are **Bempton Cliffs** (*Cliff Lane*, **t** *(01262) 851 179, www.rspb.org.uk; open Mar–Nov daily 10–5; Dec–Feb weekends 9.30–4; car park adm*), where the Royal Society for the Protection of Birds protects up to 200,000 seabirds. The birds take refuge on the vertical chalk cliffs, which rise to 400ft above the sea. The RSPB has built five shelters from which you can see kittiwakes, guillemots, razorbills and fulmars between April and mid-August. Occasionally seals and porpoises can be seen in the water below. The only colony of gannets in England is at Bempton. But everyone comes to see the puffins. The best time to see them is in May, on a puffin cruise (*see www.rspb.org.uk/East Yorkshire/ Seabird Cruises*).

Hornsea and Spurn Head

South from Bridlington on the coast there are a few smaller resorts. **Hornsea** is distinguished by a lake; **Hornsea Mere**, on the inland side of the town, is Yorkshire's largest freshwater lake, home to 250 species of bird, 65 of which breed here. To get the best view of the lake, approach Hornsea on the road from Hull.

The coast of this low-lying corner of Yorkshire is vulnerable to erosion from the sea, and at least 22 villages are known to have been sucked into the North Sea or into the Humber Estuary. Eventually the Yorkshire coast peters out around the sand and shingle **Spurn Peninsula**, a spit held together by marram grass and sea buckthorn. Whether it provides shelter and a point of interest or a navigational hindrance depends on your point of view. For birdwatchers it is a paradise in the winter months, when vast numbers of wildfowl and waders congregate on the mudflats.

The peninsula is now a nature reserve to protect its bird life. You can walk or drive along the little road that gets ever narrower and rougher as it approaches **Spurn Head**. A lighthouse was built here in 1427, perhaps even earlier, but the 19th-century black and white lighthouse which stands there today was switched off at dawn on 31 October 1986 and left as an empty shell. Far from being deserted, Spurn Head is home to a maritime community of pilots waiting to guide ships up the estuary, and Britain's only full-time lifeboat crew standing by in case of accidents at sea.

The East Riding of Yorkshire

My living in Yorkshire was so far out of the way, that it was actually twelve miles from a lemon.

Sidney Smith

In the ever-shifting geography of Yorkshire only one region has managed to reassert itself under its traditional name. The East Riding is a flat region of rich agricultural land stretching from the Vale of Pickering to the Humber Estuary and the borders of

Yorkshire on the Screen

Yorkshire likes nothing better than to see itself on the screen. It specializes in two types of location, for both small and silver screen: gritty realism, in which no-nonsense northerners expose taboos; and timeless, untouched towns, villages and stately homes, in which there is nothing to detract from pure sentiment.

While there was still heavy industry (cut to belching chimneys, slums and kids with dirty faces in the streets), Yorkshire's cities were used as a definition of working-class life. The classic ***Room at the Top*** (1958), one of the first films to treat sex (between the classes) seriously, and ***Billy Liar*** (1963), the story of a young man who escapes the drabness of everyday life through his fantasies, were both filmed in Bradford. ***Spend, Spend, Spend*** (a BBC2 TV 'Play for Today', 1977) is a true cautionary tale about a Castleford woman whose life was changed by winning the pools. In ***Kes*** (1969) a boy from a dysfunctional Barnsley family forms a close relationship (his only one) with a kestrel he has found.

Although (or because) the traditional industries have declined, the Yorkshire working-class genre has continued to be exploited, but with added humour. ***Rita, Sue and Bob Too*** (1986), also shot in Bradford, is a story of a middle-aged man having a sexual fling with two teenage girls, who feel they have nothing to lose. ***Brassed Off*** (1996) follows the fate of a colliery band in the era of Yorkshire's pit closures (1992–3). Most famous is ***The Full Monty*** (1997), in which six unemployed Sheffield steel-workers face up to their hopeless poverty by staging a strip show. In art-imitates-life-imitates-art ***Calendar Girls***, a group of women strips off for a calendar (*see* p.798).

At the other extreme, Yorkshire is still the perfect place for film-makers to find rural nostalgia: the kind of place we all wish had really once existed. The comic books of country vet James Herriot were filmed in 1974 as ***All Creatures Great and Small***, using Wensleydale and Swaledale as the backdrop. ***Last of the Summer Wine***, the country's longest-running TV comedy series, about a group of old men misbehaving their way through a second childhood is shot in the Holme Valley of West Yorkshire.

Harrogate in its heyday is recreated in the film ***Agatha*** (1978), based on the true story of the 11-day disappearance of author Agatha Christie. The spa was also used in two scenes of ***Chariots of Fire*** (1981). Castle Howard famously became Brideshead for the TV adaptation of Evelyn Waugh's 1945 novel ***Brideshead Revisited***, another story of upper-class life. Even the 1960s have now become the stuff of nostalgia and ***Heartbeat***, a police series set then, is shot in the North York Moors and Whitby.

Several children's films have also found the locations they needed in Yorkshire: ***The Secret Garden*** (1993) used Fountains Abbey and Allerton Park near Knaresborough; ***The Railway Children*** (1970) is built around the Keighley and Worth Valley Railway; and Goathland on the North York Moors Railway doubles as Hogwart's station in ***Harry Potter and the Philosopher's Stone*** (2000).

The more TV and film you watch, the more you will feel at home in Yorkshire – which seems unconcerned that it is selling itself to the world as a caricature of itself: a place of cute villages and rolling hills inhabited by straight-talking, salt-of-the-earth mill-workers. But don't mistake the screen reality for the real thing.

York to Bridlington Bay. An arc of low hills, the **Yorkshire Wolds**, extends from the Humber to Bridlington across these flatlands, giving the landscape some relief. This rural area is sprinkled with market towns such as **Heden**, **Howden** and **Driffield**, and picturesque villages centred around pond, pub and parish church. Only the port city of **Hull**, in the south, breaks the rural idyll.

Plain but prosperous, the East Riding is the hardest area of Yorkshire to pin an identity to – until you tot up the number of odd stories originating here. A meteorite landing site, England's tallest monolithic monument (standing incongruously in a churchyard), the outsize chair of the tallest Englishman ever to have lived, a street called the Land of Green Ginger, a lawn mower archived for its literary associations, a scold's bridle to silence a gossip, and a trawler hijacked to the Caribbean could all be assembled as proof that this is one of the most eccentric corners of England.

The broad **Humber Estuary** puts an end to Yorkshire proper, but across the Humber Bridge is the area known as **North Lincolnshire**, which has managed to attach itself to the East Riding as an honorary part of Yorkshire for the sake of promoting itself to tourists. It has just enough points of interest to make it worth crossing the river.

Kingston-upon-Hull

From Hull, from Halifax, from Hell, 'tis thus,
From all these three, good Lord, deliver us.

'The Thief's Litany' (traditional)

The first settlement at the confluence of the Hull and Humber rivers was founded in the 12th century by the Cistercian monks of Meaux Abbey to export the wool they produced. In 1293 the town passed into the ownership of Edward I and was hence-

Getting There and Around

Domestic flights go to **Humberside International Airport**, **t** (01652) 688 456, *www.humberside-airport.co.uk*.

Hull Trains run four services daily to London King's Cross, **t** (01482) 606 388. Hull is also connected to Leeds and York, Beverley, Filey and Scarborough.

On the **sea**, you can get from Hull to Rotterdam and Zeebrugge by **P&O Ferries**, **t** 0870 129 6002, *www.ponsf.com*.

Tourist Information

East Riding: *www.eastriding.gov.uk*.

Hull: 1 Paragon Street, **t** (01482) 223 5599, *www.hullcc.gov.uk/visithull*.

Humber Bridge: **t** (01482) 640 852.

Holderness: 100–102 Queen Street, Withernsea, *www.holderness-online.com*.

Where to Stay and Eat

Around Hull t (01482) –

Ask at the tourist information centre for a free leaflet to guide you on the **Hull Ale Trail**. Includes details of pubs welcoming children.

Ramada Jarvis Hotel, Grange Park Lane, Willerby, **t** 656 488, *www.ramadajarvis.co.uk* (*expensive*). Hotel in its own grounds convenient for both Hull and Beverley. Own leisure club. Cheaper rates at weekends.

Little Weghill Farm, Weghill Road, Preston (near Hull), **t** 897 650 (*moderate*). Georgian farmhouse near Hull offering bed and Aga-cooked breakfast using fresh local produce.

forth known as Kingston-upon-Hull. Over the next few centuries Hull, as it is usually known, grew to be Britain's third most important seaport, after London and Liverpool, and the country's largest deep-sea fishing port. That made it a prime target for German bombers in the Second World War, and the docks and city centre were badly damaged. The reconstruction left the city with just a scattering of old monuments.

Famous sons of Hull include three poets: **Andrew Marvell** (1621–78, educated at Hull Grammar School and sometime MP for the town), **Stevie Smith** (born here as Florence Margaret Smith, 1902–71, and author of the poem 'Not Waving but Drowning') and **Philip Larkin** (1922–85, *see* 'Larkin's Law Mower', below) who was born in the Midlands but became librarian of the University of Hull in 1955. Another pupil of the grammar school was **William Wilberforce** (1759–1833), MP and slavery abolitionist. The determined female aviator **Amy Johnson** (1903–41), who made a record-breaking solo flight to Australia but died in a flying accident while still young, was also born in Hull.

Hull has always been a singular place, out on a rural limb from the rest of Yorkshire. For a long time it set itself apart from the rest of the United Kingdom by having its own telephone company, established in 1904. The M62 motorway and the Humber Bridge put Hull in much better contact with the world, which is just as well because as its traditional fishing industry declines, it is trying to attract tourists instead.

The Deep

t (01482) 381 000, www.thedeep.co.uk; open daily 10–5; adm.

Many if not most visitors to Hull bypass the city centre and go straight to its latest attraction, The Deep, advertised as the world's only '*submarium*.' If you don't know what the word means, this is the place to find its definition. The Deep presents the history of the earth's oceans from their conception sometime after the Big Bang to the present day. The building is futuristic and built around the deepest aquarium tank in Europe, which includes the world's deepest viewing tunnel (30ft below the surface)

Larkin's Lawn Mower

The University of Hull's Philip Larkin archive includes the poet's blue rotary lawn mower, value £20 without its literary connections, but worth a lot more since it was immortalized in Larkin's 1979 poem, 'The Mower', about a tragic (and gory) domestic accident: 'The mower stalled, twice; kneeling, I found/ A hedgehog jammed up against the blades,/ Killed.' Being the scene of such a famous accident is thought to have added to the value of Larkin's home in Newlands Park, Hull, when it was put up for sale. The lawnmower is probably the only one in a literary archive.

Larkin's reputation is still being assessed and reassessed. From his seat in Hull he projected an image of himself as a 'xenophobic, reactionary old fogey, downcast and ill at ease in the modern world' (*Chambers Biographical Dictionary*), but his defenders claim that his tongue was in his cheek all the while. He was more interested as a poet in the mundane than the sublime; he 'made us aware of the holiness of the drab, of the quiet passion and persistence of submerged lives, of the heroism of compromise with frustration' (G. S. Fraser).

and the world's only underwater lift. The visit takes you from the shallows to the depths, starting at the top of the building and descending. Next to the entrance turnstiles is a café with an observatory over the brown waters of the Humber Estuary. The view takes in the docks and the Humber Bridge, and you may be lucky enough to see a seal poking its head out of the waters beneath you.

City Centre

Having come this far, take a look at Hull city centre, which has a medieval cobbled heart; one lane is charmingly named **The Land of Green Ginger** – probably because a conserve of ginger and lemon was once made here. There are seven free museums to visit in Hull, of which the most interesting are perhaps the **Streetlife Transport Museum** (*26 High Street,* **t** *(01482) 613 956; open 13 April Mon–Sat 10–5, Sun 1.30–4.30*), which covers 200 years of transport history by horse-drawn carriage, bicycle, car and tram, the **Maritime Museum** (*Queen Victoria Square,* **t** *(01482) 613 902; open Mon–Sat 10–5, Sun 1.30–4.30*) and the **Town Docks Museum** (**t** *(01482) 613 902; open Mon–Sat 10–5, Sun 1.30–4.30*).

Also of interest are two moored ships, the ***Spurn Lightship*** (*Marina, Castle Street,* **t** *(01482) 613 902; open Easter–Oct Mon–Sat 10–5, Sun 1.30–4.30; closed rest of year; adm*), which stood guard over the entrance to the Humber Estuary from 1927 until 1959, and the ***Arctic Corsair*** (*on the River Hull between Drypool Bridge and Myton Bridge,* **t** *(01482) 351 445; open Easter–Oct Mon–Sat 10–5, Sun 1.30–4.30; closed rest of year; adm*), the last sidewinder trawler, moored behind the transport museum. The 18th-century merchant's residence, **Maister House** (*160 High Street,* **t** *(01482) 324 114, www.nationaltrust.org.uk; staircase and entrance hall open Mon–Fri 10–4; adm minimal*), gives a glimpse of Hull when it was at its peak as a trading centre.

Holderness

Between Hull and the North Sea is Holderness, an intensively farmed area of rich soils fringed by a line of cliffs made of clay so soft that it is being eroded at a rate of nearly 6ft a year. It is estimated that, since the Middle Ages, between 20 and 30 villages here have slipped into the sea. But while some places fall, others rise: the bulge of flat arable land in the lower Humber Estuary known as **Sunk Island** appeared out of the waters in 1560. At first it was nothing more than a sandbar revealed only at low tide. Now it is no longer an island, let alone sunken, but the name has stuck.

It may be hard to believe but **Hedon**, incontrovertibly sited inland, was the first port on the Humber until the rise of Hull. Nearby **Fort Paull** is a Napoleonic fortress, a labyrinth of tunnels and underground vaults (*Battery Road, Paull,* **t** *(01482) 882 655, www.fortpaull.com; open summer 10–6, winter 11–4; adm*) which has been turned into a military theme park.

Hedon's large parish church is known as the 'king' of Holderness. The 'queen' is that of **Patrington**, which John Timpson and other writers have called 'the most beautiful parish church in England'. Another admirer of it was the poet John Betjeman who wrote 'it sails like a galleon over the wide, flat expanse of Holderness'.

Holderness peters out in the Spurn Peninsula beyond Patrington (*see* p.837). The only other site to see on its flat expanses is the stately home of **Burton Constable** (**t** *(01964) 562 400, www.burtonconstable.com; open Easter–Oct Sat–Thurs 1–5; adm*), an Elizabethan manor house with gardens landscaped by Capability Brown in the 18th century.

Beverley

Between Holderness and the Yorkshire Wolds, a short way to the north of Hull, stands the delightful minster town of Beverley, which has a core of narrow medieval streets lined with antique and craft shops. The best approach is from the north, as you enter the town through the only gateway remaining from its medieval walls, North Bar. A short way down the street of North Bar Within, you come to one of two churches for which Beverley is renowned.

St Mary's' Church (*www.stmarysbeverley.org.uk*) was originally built as a chapel of the minster but is a triumph of architecture and detail in its own right. Built over a long period between 1120 and 1525, it is a celebration of English Gothic. In the graceful west front you can see the precursor of the famous King's College Chapel in Cambridge, built 80 years after St Mary's was completed.

Before going inside, note the memorial plaque to two Danish soldiers in the employ of William of Orange, which is pinned to one of the south aisle buttresses. One soldier killed the other during a quarrel in December 1689 and the survivor was duly beheaded. This tragic drama is pithily told: 'Here two young Danish soldiers lye./ The one in quarrell chanc'd to die./ The other's Head by their own Law./ With sword was severed at one Blow.'

Inside the church there are exceptional wood and stone carvings. In particular there are 34 carvings of musicians around the building, indicating the importance of music in medieval worship. The best of them are the five figures facing the pulpit from the capital of the **Minstrel's Pillar**, a pillar given to the church by the Guild of Musicians in the 16th century. Animals are another important theme. The **War Memorial Door** was carved by Robert Thompson, the 'Mouseman' of Kilburn (*see* p.821) and if you look

Tourist Information

Beverley: 34 Butcher Row, **t** (01482) 391 672, *www.inbeverley.co.uk*.

Where to Stay and Eat

Beverley and Around

Beverley Arms Hotel, North Bar Within, Beverley, **t** (01482) 869 241, *www.regalhotels.co.uk/beverleyarms* (*expensive*). Historic coaching inn.

The Manor House, Northlands, Walkington, **t** (01482) 881 645, *www.the-manor-house.co.uk* (*expensive*). Country-house hotel with seven of the East Riding's most luxurious bedrooms.

Eastgate Guest House, 7 Eastgate, Beverley, **t** (01482) 868 464 (*moderate*). Comfortable family-run B&B in a Victorian house in the centre of Beverley.

Bishop Burton College, Bishop Burton (near Beverley), **t** (01964) 553 017 (*moderate*). Residential college offering B&B.

carefully you will find his trademark rodent carving. On the right of the Sacristy door is a rabbit holding a pilgrim's scrip, which was carved around 1330 and is accepted as the inspiration for the White Rabbit in Lewis Carroll's *Alice in Wonderland*.

The pride of the church is **St Michael's Chapel**, which has fine tracery. An imp, meanwhile, presides over the doorway to the **Priest's Rooms** (ask the verger to let you in), where several unusual items from parish history are displayed, including stocks, the parish bier and a scold's bridle or branks, which was used to punish gossips by screwing down the offender's tongue.

The carved 15th-century misericords in the choir stalls show something of the life, including sport and costume, of the era when they were carved. The ceiling of the chancel has painted representations of 40 English kings from the 7th century to Henry VI, in whose reign the ceiling was made. The Latin scrolls record each king's name, dates and place of burial. To make up a round number, a few mythical monarchs had to be added – Brutus, Ebraucus and Lud – but from Egbert (802–39) the history is accurate. When the ceiling was restored in the 20th century one of the legendary characters, Lochrine, was replaced with the reigning sovereign, George VI.

Continue through town down Saturday Market (in which stands the old market cross) and Wednesday Market, and you come to the **Minster** (***t*** *(01482) 868 540, www.beverleyminster.co.uk; open Feb–April Mon–Sat 9–5, Sun 12–4.30; May–Sept Mon–Sat 9–6; Oct–Jan Mon–Sat 9–4*). The first church on the site was founded in the 8th century by St John of Beverley, who is buried beneath the nave. The present church is the result of much rebuilding and altering, beginning in 1220. As an indication of Beverley Minster's importance, Henry V came here to give thanks after winning the Battle of Agincourt in 1415. Two items survive from the earlier buildings: the Saxon sanctuary chair and the Norman font. The 68 miserichords carved in oak in the 16th century make up the largest such collection in England. The building's best known feature is the **Percy Tomb**, with a canopy in Decorated Gothic style intricately ornamented with angels, fruit, foliage and beasts. As in St Mary's, the minster has its musical carvings, indeed there are more carvings of medieval musicians in this church than in any other church in Europe, and tradition is kept up by using the Minster as a venue for Beverley's **Early Music Festival** in May.

The Yorkshire Wolds

This crescent of low hills from the north end of the Humber Bridge to Flamborough Head makes for variety in the otherwise flat landscapes of East Yorkshire. The hills are rounded and never high but offer pleasing views. A long-distance walking route, the **Wolds Way**, leads from one end to the other. **Driffield** is the only town of any size, and most of the settlements of the Wolds are villages built in valleys and hollows, grouped around village greens, market crosses and ponds.

The infamous highwayman Dick Turpin was arrested in the Green Dragon Inn at **Welton**, at the southern end of the Wolds, before being taken to York for execution. **Market Weighton**, to the north, was the home of England's tallest man, William

Tourist Information

Yorkshire Wolds: **t** (01845) 597 426.
Driffield: *www.driffield.net.*
Market Weighton: *www.wicstun.com.*
Pocklington: *www.pocklington.gov.uk* .
Middleton: *www.middletononthewolds.org.uk.*
Thixendale: *www.thixendale.org.uk/links.htm* (good links).
Wolds Way: *www.woldsway.gov.uk.*

Where to Stay and Eat

Driffield t (01377) –

The Bell Hotel, Market Place, **t** 256 661 (*expensive*). Modernized Georgian house with swimming pool and more than 350 malt whiskies to choose from in the bar.

Kelleythorpe Farm, **t** 252 297 (*moderate*). Georgian farmhouse at the foot of the Wolds. Home cooking. Children welcome.

Clematis House, 1 Eastgate Lund (near Driffield), **t** 217 204, *www.clematisfarm.co.uk* (*moderate*). Family-run arable and livestock farm with en-suite rooms and a log fire. The owners recommend the village pub for hearty dinners.

Around the Wolds

Londesborough Arms Hotel, High Street, Market Weighton, **t** (01430) 872 214 (*expensive*). Georgian building with 18 rooms, a restaurant and a bistro. A good base for the Wolds, Beverley and even York.

The Wold Cottage, Wold Newton, **t** (01262) 470 696, *www.woldcottage.com* (*moderate*). Georgian farmhouse overlooking woodlands in its own peaceful grounds away from busy roads. Home cooking. No smoking.

Ramblers Rest Tea Rooms, Main Street, Millington, **t** (01759) 305 220 (*cheap*). Home-cooked food. *Open weekends all year, at other times on request.*

Bradley, who died in 1820 at the age of 33 and is buried in All Saints' Church. Bradley was born in 1787 as one of 13 children, all the others of average height. A cast of his footprint can be seen on the wall of his house. He measured 7ft 9in and weighed 27 stone (a foot shorter than the world's tallest ever man, the American Robert Wadlow, who was 8ft 11in). Market Weighton also claims to be the home of the oldest horse race in the world, the **Kiplingcotes Derby**, which is run in late March.

Three stately homes to either side of the Wolds offer various attractions. Just south of Pocklington is **Burnby Hall** (***t** (01759) 302 068, www.burnbyhallgardens.co.uk; open April–Sept 10–6; adm*), which has the largest collection of waterlilies in Europe. They bloom from May to October but are at their best from mid-June to mid-September. **Burton Agnes Hall** (*between Driffield and Bridlington, **t** (01262) 490 324, www.burton-agnes.com; open April–Oct 11–5; adm*) is an Elizabethan country house, completed in 1603, with magnificent period wood carving around the staircase. **Sledmere House** (*between Driffield and Malton, **t** (01377) 236 637, www.sledmerehouse.freeserve.co.uk; open Sun and Tues–Fri 11.30–4.30; adm*) has parkland laid out by Capability Brown.

Foston on the Wolds was the home of the journalist, parson and wit Sidney Smith (1771–1845) who lived in the Old Rectory between 1809 and 1829. Although he wrote prolifically, he is best remembered today for his many apt remarks delivered in letters, speeches and conversation ('I have no relish for the country; it is a kind of healthy grave'). He was particularly good at put-downs that it would be hard to be offended by ('He has occasional flashes of silence that make his conversation particularly delightful'), pithy definitions (heaven as a place for 'eating pâté de foie gras to the sound of trumpets') and earthy philosophical observations ('There is not the least use in preaching to anyone unless you chance to catch them ill').

Sidney Smith might have sympathized with the vicars of **Rudston** in their efforts to preach in the shadow of England's largest standing stone, which looms out of its churchyard. Legend says that the stone was thrown at the church by the devil but he missed. However, the 25ft-high monolith was placed here long before the Norman church by hands unknown, sometime between 1600 and 1000BC. Early Christian missionaries tended to build their churches on pre-existing sites of religious worship in order to attract the superstitious populace, and only as Christianity established itself, and ever grander churches were built, could dolmens and holy wells be covered over or simply left to disappear. But at Rudston, the Church was competing with a giant phallic symbol that even today would be hard to shift.

Another lump of stone actually dropped out of the sky, at **Wold Newton**. In the mid-afternoon of 13 December 1795 a meteorite landed in a field southeast of the village, narrowly missing a labourer. It was taken to the Natural History Museum in London, where it is still on display as the museum's oldest meteorite. A monument marks the point of impact.

The Wolds have one last curiosity to reveal, the deserted medieval village of **Wharram Percy** (*Wharram le Street, Malton, www.english-heritage.org.uk; open all year*). This is not the only such village in the Wolds or in Britain – there are estimated to be 3,000 similar villages in the country – but it is the best-preserved and most researched. Excavations began here in 1950 and transformed scholarship on the Middle Ages. Hitherto, our understanding of medieval life had been based on documents written by the privileged and wealthy few, while the bulk of the medieval population was made up of the rural peasantry, who left no records of their lives. Assumptions about medieval life at ground level – that it was unremittingly grim and always at subsistence level – were disproved. Rural Yorkshire at least was a monetary not a subsistence economy, cleanliness was a virtue and there was sophistication in the adornment of dress.

It used to be thought that such villages were deserted in the wake of the Black Death in the 14th century, but recent research has shown that they were depopulated because of economic pressures a century later. The last house in Wharram Percy was abandoned in 1500. Three centuries on, the arrival of the railway and the exploitation of the chalk quarries in the age of steel manufacture would have revitalized the village – although both railway and chalk quarry have also since closed down.

North Lincolnshire

When the **Humber Bridge** was opened in 1981 it was the world's longest single-span suspension bridge. You can walk, drive or cycle across it for views of the river and its two banks: North Lincolnshire and East Yorkshire.

The land on the other side of the river is still in search of an identity for itself. In local government reorganizations of the 1970s, North Lincolnshire became half of the short-lived county of Humberside, and nowadays likes to identify itself more with Yorkshire than with Lincolnshire.

Getting There and Around

The **Barton Line** runs between Barton, Grimsby and Cleethorpes.

Tourist Information

North Lincolnshire: *www.nelincs.gov.uk* and *www.northlincs.gov.uk*.
Barton on Humber: *www.barton-net.org*.

Where to Stay and Eat

North Lincolnshire

Winteringham Fields, Winteringham, **t** (01724) 733 096 (*expensive*). According to one of the most prestigious food guides this is 'Britain's best restaurant'. It is a place where you can expect technical excellence in the kitchen and impeccable service in an elegant setting. Accommodation also available.

The Cottage, Melton Road, North Ferriby, **t** (01482) 631 162 (*moderate*). Comfortable family home with walled garden and swimming pool. Close to the Humber Bridge – a good base for day-trips into Hull. No-smoking house.

Brantingham Hall, Brough, **t** (01482) 667 497 (*moderate*). Listed building in an attractive village with its own garden and swimming pool, open for guests' use. Large, nicely decorated rooms and a calm, friendly, relaxed atmosphere.

Grimsby, the main town of North Lincolnshire, was the largest fishing port in the world until the 1970s, landing a fifth of Britain's fish. The **National Fishing Heritage Centre** (*Alexandra Dock*, **t** *(01472) 323 345, www.welcome.to/NFHCentre/; open April–Oct Mon–Fri 10–4, Sat and Sun 10.30–5.30; adm*) keeps alive the memory of those times. From Grimsby you can take a trip on the trawler *Impulsive* around the Humber Estuary. **Cleethorpes** is the respectable face of Grimsby, a holiday resort which can think of little to boast of except being on the Greenwich meridian.

There are two places to make a detour for in North Lincolnshire: **Thornton Abbey** (*grounds open 10–6; gatehouse open April–Sept 1st and 3rd Sun of month 10–6, Oct–Mar 3rd Sun of month 10–6*), an Augustinian abbey founded in 1139 with a crenellated fortified gate house and octagonal chapter house; and the village of **Alkborough**, at the confluence of the Ouse and Trent rivers, where there is a medieval Christian turf maze, **Julian's Bower** (*Back Street, open all year*) of uncertain origin, although it dates back to at least 1671.

York

The history of York is the history of England.

George VI

Medieval travellers would have had almost the same view of York ahead as they approached it as you get today: the great Gothic towers of the Minster (cathedral) rising above a city cowed as if in reverence beneath it. Do not doubt, however, that York is a modern city: it may appear to have changed little in the last half millennium, but if it seems more rooted in its past than most places in Britain, it's because that past is its prime economic asset. Here, everything is history.

The traditional capital of Yorkshire – at the meeting point of the three ancient ridings but belonging to none – and the ecclesiastical heart of the north of England (the only archdiocese outside Canterbury, in fact), York stands on the banks of the River Ouse almost exactly midway between London and Edinburgh. A small city built on a plain, it is easy to get to and easy to get around. Forget buses and taxis: it is quicker to walk. There's plenty to fill a couple of days' visit: the Minster, of course, the famous circuit of medieval walls and a couple of world-class museums. You'll spend most of your time in centuries past, but can return easily to the present for lunch.

The **Romans** were here first. Quintus Pestilius Cerealis, military governor of Britain, established a fortress, *Eboracum*, on the banks of the Ouse in AD 71 to act as his northern headquarters. Centuries later, in 306, Constantine the Great was declared emperor while on a visit to York, about as far as he could be from the city that he gave his name to, Constantinople. A statue of him sits languidly outside the Minster.

When the Romans withdrew in 400 the **Saxons** moved in. There had been a small Christian community here since the 2nd century and now its tenacity was rewarded: in 625 the first archbishop of York, Paulinus, was appointed, and two years later the Saxon King Edwin was baptized in an early Minster building.

The **Danes** (aka the dreaded Vikings) took the city in 867 and used it as their capital. Their rule did not last long, but their name for the city, Jorvik, stuck, and so did their word for street: 'gate'.

After the **Norman Conquest** the city was all but destroyed, and the land around it flooded, as the conquerors struggled to subdue the unruly north of England. When they had got the upper hand, the Normans rebuilt the city five times bigger than it had been and protected by two castles, one on either side of the river.

The city began to grow again as a commercial centre, now specializing in the wool trade. From about 1100 to 1500 York was England's second city. Its fortunes waned thereafter but revived in the 18th century – as can be seen from its many fine Georgian houses. The **Industrial Revolution**, which transformed the other urban centres of Yorkshire, left the medieval core of York unscathed, but gave the city a new role in life as a route centre for Britain's expanding railway network.

Modern York is obsessed with its past, warts and all, and seems to be on a mission to rescue reputations. There was a time when no one could find a good word to say about the raiding, raping and pillaging Vikings, but then the archaeologists of York proved that they were civilized people who worked hard and loved their children after all. If you thought the last word on Richard III was had by Shakespeare, who portrayed him as the archetypal villain, for the people of York the jury is still out (*see* also p.626). And even if railway capitalist and mayor George Hudson ended his career in disgrace over his financial affairs, York forgave him and put his name on a street sign. Sinner or saint, famous or infamous – anyone historical is good for York's tourist industry.

York Minster

Deangate, **t** *(01904) 557 200, www.yorkminster.org; open daily April–May 9–6.30, June–Sept 9–8.30, Oct–Mar 9-6; donation requested.*

The obvious place to begin to get to know York is inside the giant that towers over all else – the **Minster**, the largest Gothic cathedral in northern Europe. Ignore the rest

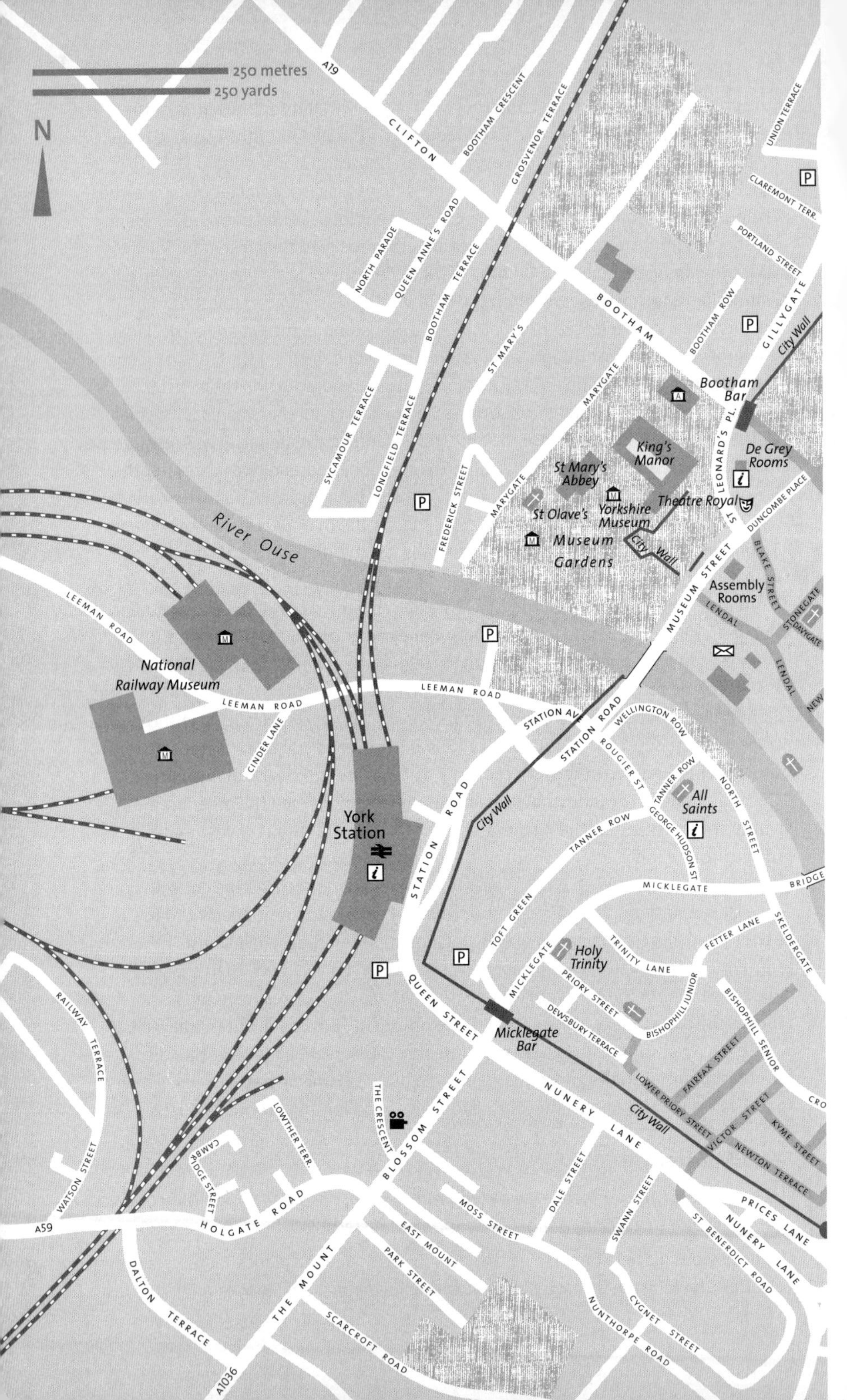

250 metres
250 yards
N
A19
CLIFTON
BOOTHAM CRESCENT
GROSVENOR TERRACE
UNION TERRACE
CLAREMONT TERR.
PORTLAND STREET
NORTH PARADE
QUEEN ANNE'S ROAD
BOOTHAM TERRACE
BOOTHAM
BOOTHAM ROW
GILLYGATE
City Wall
ST MARY'S
MARYGATE
Bootham Bar
SYCAMOUR TERRACE
LONGFIELD TERRACE
King's Manor
St Mary's Abbey
De Grey Rooms
ST LEONARD'S PL.
FREDERICK STREET
MARYGATE
Yorkshire Museum
Theatre Royal
St Olave's
DUNCOMBE PLACE
River Ouse
Museum Gardens
City Wall
BLAKE STREET
MUSEUM STREET
Assembly Rooms
LENDAL
STONEGATE
DAVYGATE
LEEMAN ROAD
National Railway Museum
LEEMAN ROAD
LEEMAN ROAD
STATION AV
STATION ROAD
WELLINGTON ROW
CINDER LANE
ROUGIER ST
TANNER ROW
All Saints
NORTH STREET
City Wall
York Station
STATION ROAD
TANNER ROW
GEORGE HUDSON ST
MICKLEGATE
BRIDGE
TOFT GREEN
FETTER LANE
SKELDERGATE
Holy Trinity
TRINITY LANE
MICKLEGATE
PRIORY STREET
BISHOPHILL JUNIOR
BISHOPHILL SENIOR
QUEEN STREET
Micklegate Bar
DEWSBURY TERRACE
FAIRFAX STREET
RAILWAY TERRACE
LOWER PRIORY STREET
VICTOR STREET
KYME STREET
NUNERY LANE
City Wall
NEWTON TERRACE
THE CRESCENT
BLOSSOM STREET
LOWTHER TERR.
CAMBRIDGE STREET
WATSON STREET
DALE STREET
SWANN STREET
PRICES LANE
A59
HOLGATE ROAD
MOSS STREET
ST BENEDICT ROAD
NUNERY LANE
EAST MOUNT
PARK STREET
DALTON TERRACE
THE MOUNT
SCARCROFT ROAD
NUNTHORPE ROAD
CYGNET STREET
A1036

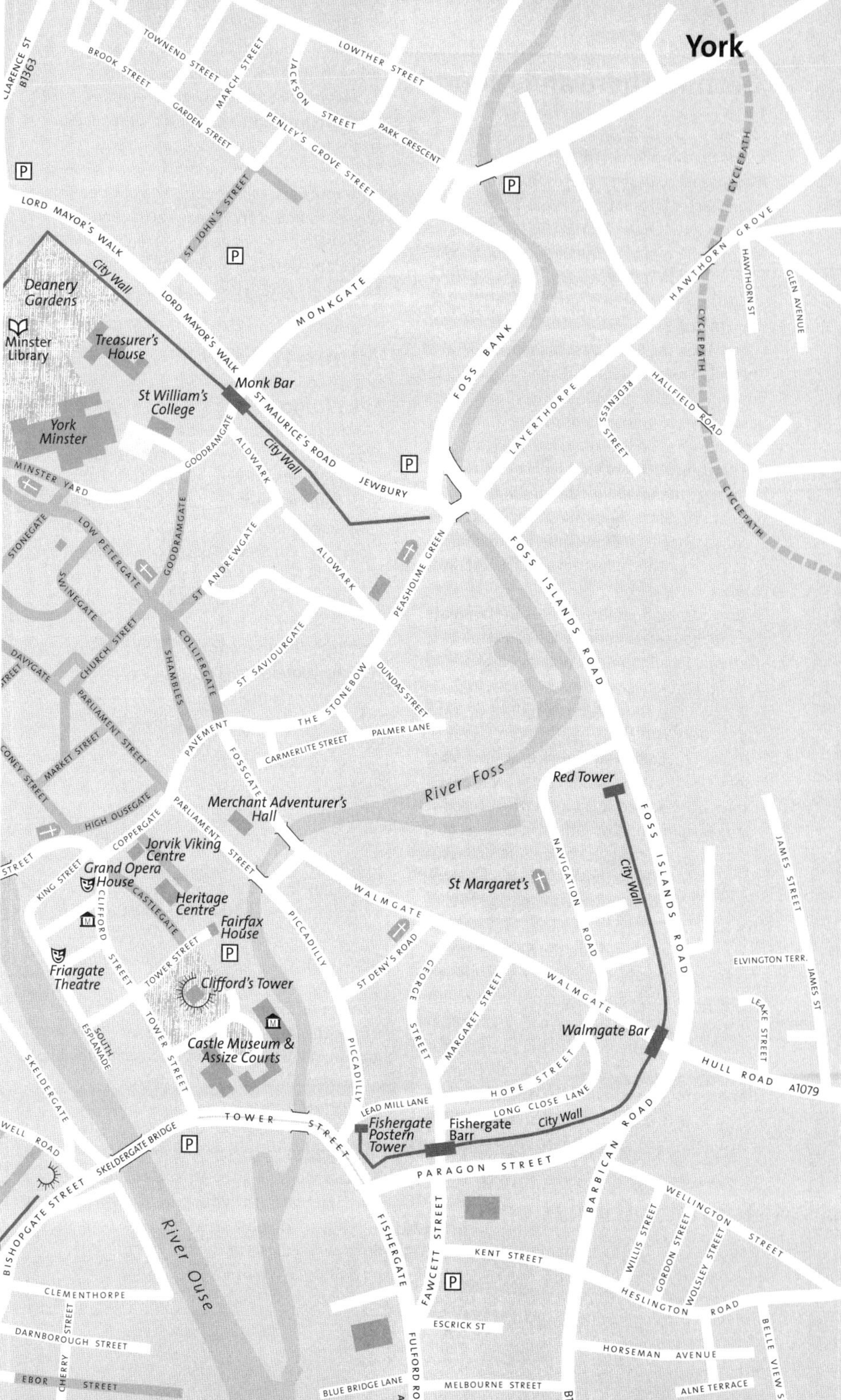
York
Deanery Gardens
Minster Library
Treasurer's House
St William's College
York Minster
Monk Bar
City Wall
Merchant Adventurer's Hall
Red Tower
Jorvik Viking Centre
Grand Opera House
Heritage Centre
Fairfax House
Friargate Theatre
Clifford's Tower
Castle Museum & Assize Courts
St Margaret's
Walmgate Bar
Fishergate Postern Tower
Fishergate Barr
River Foss
River Ouse
Lord Mayor's Walk
Monkgate
Foss Bank
Layerthorpe
Jewbury
St Maurice's Road
Goodramgate
Aldwark
Peasholme Green
Foss Islands Road
Hawthorn Grove
Cyclepath
Hallfield Road
Walmgate
Piccadilly
Tower Street
Paragon Street
Barbican Road
Hull Road A1079
Fishergate
Fulford Road A19
Fawcett Street
Kent Street
Heslington Road
Wellington Street
Bishopgate Street
Skeldergate Bridge
Clementhorpe
Darnborough Street
Ebor Street
Melbourne Street
Blue Bridge Lane
Horseman Avenue
Alne Terrace
Belle Vue St
B127

Getting There and Around

By Air

Leeds Bradford Airport, **t** (0113) 250 9696, *www.lbia.co.uk*; 45 minutes from York by car.

Manchester International Airport, **t** (0161) 489 3000, *www.manairport.co.uk*; two hours from York by car. Frequent direct rail services to and from York.

By Train

York is on the **East Coast mainline** (operated by GNER) between London and Edinburgh. The journey to or from London King's Cross takes less than two hours. Trains go every half hour at peak times on weekdays.

There are also direct rail services from York to many other mainline stations in the UK. Edinburgh, Glasgow, Birmingham, Bristol, Leeds, Manchester, Newcastle, Nottingham and Liverpool are all within a half day's travel of York.

Arriva Trains operates services to **Harrogate**.

For all rail travel information contact **National Rail Enquiries**, **t** 08457 484 950, *www.thetrainline.com.*

By Coach and Bus

There are direct coach services to York from many UK cities. For details contact **National Express**, **t** 08705 808080, *www.gobycoach.com.*

The **Bus Information Office** on George Hudson Street can give you details of local bus services. Main bus stops are on Rougier Street.

By Car

York is 20 minutes from the M1/A1 main north–south route. A park-and-ride scheme is in operation to keep cars out of the city centre. Park at one of the following car parks and take a bus to the centre: **Askham Bar** (coming from Leeds; White Line, **t** (01904) 707 726), **Grimston Bar** (from the coast and A64; Yellow Line, **t** (01904) 431 388), **Rawcliffe Bar** (from Harrogate; Green Line, **t** (01904) 541 333).

Tourist Information

York: De Gray Rooms, Exhibition Square and Railway Station, **t** (01904) 621 756.

York websites: *www.york-tourism.co.uk* or *www.visityork.org* (tourist information); *www.york.gov.uk* (city council). Other useful websites include *www.welcometoyork.co.uk* and *www.thisisyork.com.*

The **York Pass**, valid for one, two or three days, gives free entry to many attractions. It comes with an 80-page trilingual (English, French and German) guidebook with maps (**t** 0870 242 9988, *www.yorkpass.com*).

Where to Stay

York t (01904) –

For further information on places to stay in and around York see: *www.ydha.org* and *www.bedandbreakfastyork.co.uk.*

Dean Court Hotel, Duncombe Place, **t** 625 082, *www.deancourt-york.co.uk* (*luxury*). Finest location in the centre of the city almost in the shadow of the Minster. Individually designed rooms, some with Minster views. Full meals in the restaurant or lighter meals in the café conservatory.

Monkbar Hotel, Monkbar, **t** 638 086, *www.monkbarhotel.co.uk* (*luxury*). Close to the Minster and the city walls.

Jorvik Hotel, 50–52 Marygate, Bootham, **t** 653 511, *www.jorvikhotel.co.uk* (*very expensive*). Centrally located, with bar and restaurant.

Middlethorpe Hall, Bishopthorpe Road, Middlethorpe, **t** 641 241, *www.middlethorpe.com* (*very expensive*). A grand house standing in parkland five minutes from the city centre. Part of the Relais and Chateaux network of grand hotels.

The Grange, 1 Clifton, **t** 644 744, *www.grangehotel.co.uk* (*very expensive*). Regency town-house with three restaurants. A short walk from the Minster. Private car park.

Alhambra Court, 31 St Mary's Bootham, **t** 628 474, *www.alhambracourthotel.co.uk* (*expensive*). Family-run hotel in quiet cul-de-sac a short walk from the city centre. Two lounges and a no-smoking restaurant.

Ambassador, 123–5 The Mount, **t** 641 316, *www.ambassadorhotel.co.uk* (*expensive*). Georgian townhouse with private parking.

Beechwood Close, 19 Shipton Road, Clifton, **t** 658 378, *www.beechwood-close.co.uk*

(*expensive*). Small hotel with garden and car park. Bar meals served.

Judges Lodging Hotel, 9 Lendal, **t** 638 733, *www.judges-lodging.co.uk* (*expensive*). Centrally located. Many rooms have four-poster beds and spa baths. Family rooms available. Restaurant. Private parking.

Kilima Hotel, 129 Holgate Road, **t** 625 787, *www.kilima.co.uk* (*expensive*). Modernized 19th-century rectory with indoor swimming pool and Turkish steam room.

The Mount Royale, The Mount, York, **t** 628 856, *www.mountroyale.co.uk* (*expensive*). Hotel with great personal character; a labyrinth of lounges packed with decorations. Many rooms look out onto the garden. French-inspired food served in Oxo restaurant.

23 St Mary's, Bootham, **t** 622 738, *www.23stmarys.co.uk* (*moderate*). Across the Museum Gardens from the city centre. En-suite bedrooms.

Abbeyfields Guest House, 19 Bootham Terrace, **t** 636 471, *www.abbeyfields.co.uk* (*moderate*). Victorian house within walking distance of the centre. No smoking. Private parking.

Brontë Guest House, 22 Grosvenor Terrace, Bootham, **t** 621 066, *www.bronte-guest-house.com* (*moderate*). Family-run Victorian guesthouse.

Crook Lodge, 26 St Mary's Bootham, **t** 655 614, *www.crooklodge.co.uk* (*moderate*). Walk across the Museum Gardens or along the river to the centre. Private car park.

Curzon Lodge, 23 Tadcaster Road, Dringhouses, *www.smoothhound.co.uk/hotels/curzon.html* (*moderate*). A 17th-century former farmhouse and stables looking out onto the racecourse. No smoking. One minute's walk to nearest restaurant.

Elliots Hotel, 2 Sycamore Place, Bootham, **t** 623 333, *www.elliotshotel.co.uk* (*moderate*). In a quiet cul-de-sac across the Museum Gardens – or along the riverside – from the city centre.

Novotel, Fishergate, **t** 611 660, *www.accor-hotels.com* (*moderate*). Family-friendly hotel on the River Foss. Indoor swimming pool, play areas indoors and out for children, and its own car park. Late breakfasts served. Children can share their parents' room for no extra charge.

Nunmill House, 85 Bishopthorpe Road, **t** 634 047, *www.nunmill.co.uk* (*moderate*). B&B in restored Victorian house.

Riverside Walk, 8–9 Earlsborough Terrace, Marygate, **t** 620 769 (*moderate*). On the banks of the River Ouse. En-suite rooms with four-poster beds.

The Bar Convent ,17 Blossom St, **t** 464 901, *www.bar-convent.org.uk* (*moderate*). Working convent with 15 rooms as well as a café serving snacks and meals. Two-course evening meal also available.

Alcuin Lodge, 15 Sycamore Place, Bootham, **t** 632 222 (*cheap*). Five-minutes' walk across Museum Gardens from the centre. En-suite double and twin rooms. Big breakfast served. No children.

Farthings, 9 Nunthorpe Avenue, **t** 653 545, *www.farthings.york.co.uk* (*cheap*). In a quiet cul-de-sac.

Wheatlands Lodge Hotel, 75-85 Scarcroft Road, **t** 654 318 (*cheap*). Large family-run hotel of en-suite rooms. Two lounges and a bar. Breakfast and evening meal served.

Eating Out

Blue Bicycle, 34 Fossgate, **t** 673 990, *www.bluebicyclerestaurant.com* (*moderate*). Stylish restaurant with a sense of humour, specializing in fish and seafood.

19 Grape Lane, **t** 636 366, *www.19grapelane.com* (*moderate*). The name is the address (and vice versa). One of the city's most celebrated restaurants. English food prepared with flair, fresh local produce used as much as possible. No smoking. Reservation advised.

Maxis, Ings Lane, Nether Poppleton, **t** 783 898, *www.maxi-s.co.uk* (*moderate*). One of a small chain of Chinese restaurants doing Cantonese and Pekingese cuisine. Special lunch menu. 'Wok and Roll dinner dance' on Thurs and Fri eves.

Melton's, GFG, 7 Scarcroft Road, **t** 634 341, *www.meltonsrestaurant.co.uk* (*moderate*). Small, much-commended restaurant a short way outside the centre. Drawing on local produce, the menu changes with the market. Booking advised.

St William's Restaurant, 5 College Street, **t** 634 830 (*moderate*). The Minster's own restaurant in medieval St William's College. Coffee and light lunches during the day; dinner from 6pm.

Ask, The Grand Assembly Rooms, Blake Street, **t** 637 254 (*cheap*). Chain pizzeria in the incomparable setting of one of York's historic buildings.

Oscar's Wine Bar, 8 Little Stonegate, **t** 652 002 (*cheap*). Bar bistro with a beautiful courtyard. Children are welcome.

Pizza Express, 17 Museum Street, **t** 672 904, *www.pizzaexpress.co.uk* (*cheap*). Centrally located in old gentleman's club near Lendal Bridge. Outdoor dining by the river.

Rubicon, 5 Little Stonegate, **t** 676 076, *www.rubiconrestaurant.co.uk* (*cheap*). Vegetarian café and bar with an all-day menu of sandwiches, salads, tapas and light lunches. Organic wines.

The Blake Head, 104 Micklegate, **t** 623 767 (*cheap*). Bookshop with vegetarian restaurant.

Villa Italia, 69 Micklegate, **t** 670 501, *www.villaitalia.co.uk* (*cheap*). Italian food served in family-run restaurant.

Wetherby Whaler, Ings Lane, York Business Park, Nether Poppleton, **t** 784 500, *www.wetherbywhaler.co.uk* (*cheap*). Purpose-built out-of-town fish and chip shop. There can be queues but the service is usually fast. Stick to the basics: haddock and chips with mushy peas, washed down with tea. No smoking.

Cafés

Bettys, 6–8 Helen's Square, **t** 659 142 (*cheap*). Branch of the renowned Yorkshire tearoom chain (*see* Harrogate, p.807 and 808). *Open 9–9*, with a pianist playing every evening. The **Belmont Room** (*open 11–4*) is a replica of one of the staterooms of the cruise liner *Queen Mary*.

Little Bettys, 46 Stonegate, **t** 622 865 (*cheap*). Mini branch of the Bettys chain with a shop downstairs and café and tea room upstairs.

Earl Grey Tea Room, 13–14 The Shambles, **t** 654 353 (*cheap*). Tea room which also serves light meals. Walled garden outside. Gift shop attached.

Pubs

For full details of pubs in York check *www.yorkpubguide.com.*

Blue Bell, 53 Fossgate, **t** 654 904, *www.bluebellyork.co.uk*. One of York's smallest pubs and one of very few pubs to have Grade II listed status for its Edwardian interior.

Kings Arms, Kings Staith, **t** 659 435. A small whitewashed pub on the quay beside the River Ouse. Menu includes Yorkshire puddings and gravy. Outdoor seating in good weather.

Maltings, Tanners Moat, **t** 655 387, *www.maltings.co.uk*. Real-ale pub at the end of Lendal Bridge. Traditional pub food.

Old White Swan, 80 Goodramgate, **t** 540 911. A 16th-century pub with three bars around a courtyard. Live music on four nights of the week. Home cooking served.

Punchbowl, 7 Stonegate, **t** 615 491. A 450-year-old pub supposedly haunted by two ghosts. Food served, but can get very crowded at lunchtime.

The Three Legged Mare, 15 High Petergate, **t** 638 246, *www.thethreeleggedmare.co.uk*. Modern pub run by the Mildly Mad Company (partly owned by York Brewery) according to the rules: 'no jukebox, pool table or games machines, and no children'.

The Last Drop Inn, 27 Colliergate (off Kings Square), **t** 621 951, *www.thelastdropinn.co.uk*. Another Mildly Mad Company pub.

Ye Olde Starre, 40 Stonegate, **t** 623 063. The oldest still-functioning pub in the city.

Entertainment

York Theatre Royal, St Leonard's Place, **t** 623 568, *www.yorktheatreroyal.co.uk*. Big productions. Interesting, serious drama as well as pantos, musicals and the like.

Grand Opera House, Cumberland St, **t** 671 818, *www.york-operahouse.co.uk*. Pop concerts, musicals, mainstream comedy and the odd all-singing all-dancing opera production.

Friargate Theatre, Lower Friargate, **t** 0845 961 3000, *www.ridinglights.org*. Studio theatre. York's highbrow venue, staging events from Passion plays to poetry readings.

of the building for the moment and head for the south transept where the gruelling ascent of the **tower** (*adm*) begins. There are 275 steps up the steep, narrow spiral staircase that climbs to the top of the Minster's central tower with barely a resting place – not for claustrophobics. But when you get to top, you have the city at your feet. The Minster is not only the tallest building in the city, but also in the Vale of York: from here you can survey half of Yorkshire. On the southern horizon, beyond Terry's chocolate factory, plumes of steam rise from the cooling towers of power stations near Pontefract, Goole and Doncaster, like an apocalyptic vision. To the north you can see past another chocolate factory (Rowntree) to the North York Moors and the White Horse on Sutton Bank. Westwards the view is to Harrogate and the Yorkshire Dales.

Back at the bottom of the tower steps, keep going down into the **Undercroft** (*adm*), where (with the aid of an audio guide) you can get a clear idea of the many layers of building that typify York and the Minster. Every structural building fault has a silver lining: in 1967 the tower was found to be dangerously weak and, when work began to shore up its foundations, a wealth of archaeology was revealed. It's all now displayed between the concrete and steel underpinnings that keep the 16,000 tonnes of masonry above your head from falling down.

The present Minster is probably the fourth church to have stood on this site. At the bottom of the archaeological heap, however, is a pagan building, a Roman fort, of which little remains except some stretches of wall (one bearing a painting) and a still-working Roman culvert (drain). It is assumed that the earliest church in York, a Saxon oratory built of wood in 627, was erected on this site; this was later rebuilt of stone but nothing remains of these two churches except the name, Minster, which derives from the Saxon for a large church. The Normans erected a cathedral here between 1080 and 1100; in its day it was the largest church in England. Construction of the present Minster started around 1220 and continued for 250 years, the last major work being completed by 1474. A detour from the Undercroft leads into the **Treasury** and the **Crypt** where the bases of massive Norman pillars decorated with geometric designs – now holding up nothing but air – can be seen.

Back up the stairs, look up at the bosses on the **south transept** ceiling (where you emerge from the Undercroft). Six of them were designed by children, the winners of a competition by BBC TV's *Blue Peter* programme: two show astronauts, one a diver and a whale, and another a famine victim. The original bosses here were destroyed in a fire caused by a lightning strike in 1984. Some people at the time attributed this 'act of God' to the Almighty's displeasure at the views of the new Bishop of Durham, the controversial David Jenkins, whose consecration had taken place three days earlier.

The glory of York Minster is its **stained glass**. The Minster has the largest collection of medieval stained glass in Britain, more than a hundred windows made with two million pieces of glass. The earliest dates from the 12th century, but every century since then is represented as well. The **Great East Window** is the largest area of medieval stained glass in the world, roughly the size of a tennis court. It is the work of John Thornton of Coventry, in 1405–8.

The second most famous window is also the least impressive. The **Five Sisters' Window** was installed in the north transept around 1260 and is the Minster's oldest complete window. It is made up of grey and greenish 'grisaille' glass assembled in geometric patterns. Two interesting windows in the nave to look out for are the **Monkey's Funeral Window** (1320), fifth on the left from the door and, next to it on the right, the **Bellfounder's Window**, made in the early 1300s. The heart-shaped tracery of the **Great West Window**, over the door end of the nave, has been nicknamed the Heart of Yorkshire.

The City Walls

Streets are gates, gates are bars and bars are pubs.

York saying

The centre of the city is neatly enclosed within just over two miles of medieval walls, which originally had four main ways through them, the 'bars'. These checkpoints-cum-tollbooths controlled the roads into the city and were locked at night between 9pm and 4am. The oldest gateway, **Bootham Bar**, was built on the site of a Roman gateway and commanded the road in from the north. In 1501 a door knocker was fitted to the gateway and Scottish people coming to York had first to knock and ask permission to come in. **Monk Bar** is the tallest and most elaborate of the gates, and guarded the road from the nearest port, Scarborough. Its portcullis was regularly raised and dropped until 1970. The road from Hull was policed by **Walmgate**, which still has its barbican (fortified outer defence tower). This gateway is the setting for a scene in Shakespeare's *King Henry VI, Part III*. Several of the gateways were inhabited, and people lived above Walmgate until 1957. **Micklegate Bar** faces south, ultimately towards London. This is the way that the monarch traditionally enters York. In the past, to greet him or her, the symbols of his displeasure – the severed heads of traitors – would be placed over the gateway. More pleasantly, for Henry VI's visit to York in 1448, a 'representation of heaven' was built at Micklegate Bar: as his subjects looked on, a crown placed on red and white roses (representing the two sides in the Wars of the Roses) descended from this heaven to a world where trees bowed in obeisance.

The Wars of the Roses

The White Rose is the emblem of Yorkshire and the Red Rose that of Lancashire. While the rivalry between the two counties today is mainly friendly, it was not always so. Between 1455 and 1485, nobles and royal pretenders of the houses of York and Lancaster fought the Wars of the Roses – effectively a first English civil war – over which of them would be heir to the crown after the death of Edward III. The battles that raged barely affected Yorkshire and Lancashire – these just happened to be the names under which the two sides battled it out.

In an ending that could almost have been written for Hollywood – and which Shakespeare made good use of – Henry Tudor defeated and killed Richard III at Bosworth Field on 22 August 1485 to become Henry VII. He then married Edward IV's daughter Elizabeth of York in 1486, thus uniting the claims to the throne of both the Yorkists and Lancastrians (*see* also p.603).

The Heads of Micklegate

'Off with his head and set it on York gates; So York may overlook the town of York,' says Queen Margaret in *Henry VI, Part 3*. She is referring to Richard, Duke of York, whose head was stuck up above Micklegate Bar in 1461. He joined a distinguished company of aristocrats among whom were: 1403, Sir Henry Percy (Hotspur); 1405, Sir William Plumpton; 1415, Lord Scrope; 1461, Earl of Devon; 1572, Earl of Northumberland; 1663, Four of the Farnley Wood Conspirators; 1746, William Conolly and James Mayne

Each severed head was skewered on a pike-staff and put on public display on the roof of the bar to be pecked at by crows as an indignity worthy of a traitor. Some heads were left there for up to nine years. Richard, Duke of York, was on the bar for only three months, however. In 1461 his son Edward IV took revenge by replacing his father's head with those of the Lancastrian leaders taken prisoner at the Battle of Towton, the most prominent of whom was the Earl of Devon.

If you just want a feel of the walls, you can walk from Bootham Bar (not far from the door of the Minster) to Monk Bar in less than half an hour. Or you can walk the entire circuit in two to three hours. The walls are not continuous and you have to link up the various stretches by crossing roads at traffic level. The walk will take longer if you stop to visit the museums that have been installed in two of the bars. **Micklegate Bar Museum** (*t (01904) 634 436, www.micklegate.co.uk; open Feb–Oct 9–5, Nov–Jan 9–dusk; adm*) tells the gory story of the decapitated heads (*see* box). The **Richard III Museum** (*t (01904) 634 191; www.richardiiimuseum.co.uk; open daily Nov–Feb 9.30–4; Mar–Oct 9–5; adm*) in Monk Bar is a reappraisal of England's most notorious king. The last ruling monarch (1483–85) from the House of York has little to do with York except his family name, but any excuse to re-examine his reputation is good. The museum is in the form of a retrospective trial: was he a scheming murderer only interested in his own ambition, or a progressive ruler turned into a scapegoat by historians? After your visit, you are invited to pass judgement.

Medieval Streets

Within the area enclosed by the walls there are only two high points, both man-made. One of these is the Minster; the other is the castle, Clifford's Tower. Between the two is a maze of medieval streets, mainly pedestrianized, which are delightful to wander through. The most lively old street is **Stonegate**, near the Minster end of the warren, the only street in York to be mentioned in the *Domesday Book*. It has several interesting details above shop-window level, including the **Red Devil** under the eaves of a former printer's shop ('printers' devils' were printers' errand boys). Off Stonegate are the **Twelfth Century House** and **Ye Olde Starre Inn**, which claims to be the city's oldest pub, opened in 1644.

Equally picturesque is the **Shambles**, off King's Square, a narrow street of overhanging buildings. One of the houses was the residence of Margaret Clitherow, wife of a butcher. She was a Roman Catholic who harboured fugitive priests after the Reformation, but was arrested and crushed to death under the weight of a door in 1586. The house is now a shrine to her 'martyrdom'.

Near the Pavement end of the Shambles is the city's shortest street, which also has one of the longest and certainly the most curious name, **Whip-ma-whop-ma-gate**. Accounts of the derivation vary so much that you soon suspect no one has a clue. One version is that on the day before a fair the inhabitants would whip all the dogs out of the street; another is that convicted felons were whipped along it; yet another, highly misogynous, explanation is that the name used to be 'Whit-nour-what-nour-gate' and meant that here husbands whipped their drunken wives until they sobered up. The least contentious version is that the name is a mangled Saxon rendering of 'neither one thing nor the other'.

Medieval York is riddled with odd little streets, as well as semi-secret 'ginnels' or alleyways and courtyards. **Lund's Court**, **Pope's Head Lane**, **Coffee Yard**, **Straker's Passage**, **Lady Peckett's Yard** and other enticing little paths between the buildings mark the tracks trodden by people between home, work, church and market. The term 'snickelways' has been invented for these byways, which are agreeably quiet after the bustle of tourist York. Pick up a guide at the tourist information centre.

The medieval area of the city ends in the south with **Fossgate**. Just before this crosses the River Foss, a doorway on the right leads to the **Merchant Adventurers' Hall** (*Fossgate*, **t** *(01904) 654 818, www.theyorkcompany.sagenet.co.uk; open Easter–Sept Mon–Thurs 9–5, Sat 9–3, Sun 12–4 30; Oct–Dec Mon–Sat 9–3; adm*), probably the finest example of a medieval guildhall produced by mercantile Europe.

Jorvik, the Viking City

Coppergate, **t** *(01904) 643 211, www.vikingjorvik.com; open daily April–Oct 9–5.30, Nov–Mar 10–4.30; adm.*

Coppergate, the heart of Viking York, is also at the southern end of the medieval labyrinth. Not much was known about the Viking era in York until the 1970s, when three timber buildings were found preserved in peaty soil out of which a bank vault was being dug. The York Archaeological Trust moved in and began excavations.

The result of this work was the creation of **Jorvik**, a recreation of Viking York in the 10th century. Although it is, in essence, a theme park, to describe it as such would be to insult the laborious archaeological research that underpins everything you see. As you wait in a mock archaeologist's site shed for your 'time machine', a commentary tells you that even 'the very contents of toilets' were studied to garner evidence of what life in the city was like. You are taken back in time to one peaceful afternoon in 975 as you board a six-seater buggy for a ride through a mock-Viking town peopled by static tableaux. Women gossip over a wall in Vikingese, a wood turner works over a pole lathe and the whole place reeks pleasantly of the time and place (as imagined by historians). At the end you are brought back to the present and reminded of the serious archaeology.

The creators of Jorvik also run the **Archaeological Resource Centre** (*St Saviourgate,* **t** *(01904) 643 211, www.vikingjorvik.com; open school holidays Mon–Sat 11–3; adm*), housed in a medieval church. It sounds dry and scientific, but its purpose is to make archaeology exciting. Visitors (it mainly appeals to children) are asked to become 'archaeological detectives': they follow clues, explore a Viking rubbish tip and handle genuine archaeological finds as they piece together a picture of life in Viking York.

The value of Jorvik and the ARC is that they present an alternative view of Viking civilization. The Vikings certainly dispatched bloodthirsty warriors overseas in long-ships, but the tough guys were followed by craftsmen, merchants, farmers and their families. For the first time since the Romans, houses of planked sides and thatched roofs were built end on to planned streets. Even though one Viking ruler was known by the name of Eric Bloodaxe, York as the Viking capital enjoyed a period of relative peace, prosperity and artistic production – until it was recaptured by the Saxons.

The Castle Area

Keep going away from the Minster, past Jorvik, and you emerge out of the medieval streets at **Fairfax House** (*Castlegate,* **t** *(01904) 655 543, www.fairfaxhouse.co.uk; open 16 Feb–6 Jan Mon–Thurs and Sat 11–5, Sun 1.30–5, Fri guided tours only at 11 and 2; adm*). This Georgian town house was built by Viscount Fairfax in the 1760s but was later used as a gentlemen's club, cinema and dancehall until it was saved by York Civic Trust and restored to its original state. It now contains period furniture and clocks.

Just beyond is the little that's left of York's castle, **Clifford's Tower** (*www.english-heritage.org.uk; open April–Sept 10–6 daily, Oct 10–5, Nov–Mar 10–4; adm*), sitting on a perfect mound of grass. The mound was built by the Normans to hold a wooden castle with a corresponding hillock, Baile Hill, and castle across the River Ouse.

The Norman castle was destroyed during anti-Jewish rioting in 1190, a sorry event which is commemorated by a plaque at the foot of the steep, straight staircase that leads to the entrance to the tower. Pursued by rioters, a large part of the Jewish population crowded into the castle seeking sanctuary. When the mob began to assault the tower, the Jews within feared the worst and took pre-emptive action; the men cut the throats of their wives and children, then killed themselves.

The tower is a stone structure which looks as if its walls are bursting outwards. It was built by Henry III and is named after Roger de Clifford, who rebelled against Edward II, was captured at the Battle of Boroughbridge and brought back to York to be hanged in chains from the top of the tower in 1322. Inside it is an empty shell, but there are good views from the battlements.

York Castle Museum (*The Eye of York,* **t** *(01904) 653 611, www.york.castle.museum; open April–Oct daily 9.30–5; Nov–Mar 9.30–4.30; adm*) at the foot of Clifford's Tower is one of the greatest folk museums in England and gives a perspective of life in the past. The museum was created by John Kirk, a doctor in the rural North Riding, who began by acquiring simple everyday objects but did not stop until he had added fire engines and shop fronts to his collection. In 1935 he gave the whole lot to the city of York and it was put on display in two former prisons, the Women's Prison and, next door, the Debtors' Prison, built by Sir John Vanburgh. The most famous feature of the museum is **Kirkgate**, a recreated Victorian cobbled street. One of the shops on it is a sweetshop owned by Joseph Terry, precursor of one of York's two chocolate factories. In the middle of the street, frozen in time, is a Hansom cab, invented by York architect Joseph Hansom (1803–82). More macabre is the cell of the Debtors' Prison where

City of Ghosts

It's harder to find somewhere that isn't haunted in York than somewhere that is. Not for nothing did the Ghost Research Foundation International call York the most haunted place in Europe; it says the world title will almost certainly be a formality.

The **Theatre Royal** is said to be haunted by a ghost called the Grey Lady. The building stands on the site of St. Leonard's Hospital, which was run by an order of nuns. When one of the nuns was found to be having a love affair with a nobleman, she was bricked up in a windowless cell. The cell was later incorporated into a coffee lounge for the theatre's dress circle. The ghost's appearance is seen as a good sign for the evening's performance.

In 1953 an apprentice plumber was installing a new central heating system in the **Treasurer's House** when a carthorse mounted by a Roman soldier plunged out of a brick wall. He was followed by more Roman soldiers, visible from their knees up. The plumber was able to describe the Roman uniforms in great detail to an expert. It was later revealed that the Roman *Via Decumana* runs 15 inches beneath the house.

Lund's Court (between Swinegate and Low Petergate) used to be known as Mad Alice Lane, after Alice Smith, who lived there until 1825, when she was hanged at York Castle for the crime of insanity. Her spirit is still believed to loiter about the alleyway.

Catherine Howard, fourth wife of Henry VIII, is another woman who won't go away. She walks through walls at the **King's Manor**, where she entertained her lover shortly before she was executed.

Old churches are obvious places for spectres to lurk. Funeral-goers at **All Saints' Church** on Pavement are sometimes welcomed by an elegant, long-haired lady who may herself have been denied a Christian burial. Thomas Percy, luckless earl of Northumberland, hunts in vain through the churchyard of **Holy Trinity** for his head, which was spiked on Micklegate Bar for many years before being buried here.

And don't think you can escape the phantasms in pubs: they are the most haunted places of all. **The Olde Starre** on Stonegate has a pair of spectral black cats and an old lady who climbs the stairs; the pub rings to the cries of wounded soldiers in agony.

highwayman Dick Turpin was kept on the night before he was hanged (on the site of what is now York racecourse) in 1739. Other exhibits in the museum include jewellery, costumes, armour and early 20th-century household items.

Yorkshire Museum

Museum Gardens, **t** *(01904) 551 800, www.york.yorkshire.museum; open daily 10–5; adm.*

From the Minster it is a short walk to another interesting museum, the **Yorkshire Museum**, which has one of the most important provincial archaeological collections in Europe. Among its Roman, Anglo-Saxon, Viking and medieval treasures is an outstanding piece of medieval gold jewellery, the Middleham Jewel. The museum stands in gardens that run down to the riverbank, taking in two ancient monuments: the **Multi-angular Tower**, part of the Roman defences of York, and ruined **St Mary's**

A young woman wearing a long white dress stares into the fireplace of the **Black Swan** in Peasholme Green. Another regular is a Victorian man who seems to be waiting for someone but eventually gives up and fades away into another realm. George Villiers, Duke of Buckingham, who scandalized the court of Charles II with his affairs, sometimes fondles women in the **Cock and Bottle** in Skeldergate. The **Snickleway Inn** on Goodramgate has ghosts on all floors: on the top floor is one whose presence can only ever be detected by a smell of lavender; an amiable Victorian child sits on the stairs; while in the cellar is an imp who sometimes turns the beer taps off. In the **York Arms** on Low Petergate, over the road from the Minster, objects are moved by an unseen hand, and doors open and close by themselves.

Another pub ghost apparently decamped with a customer. **The Golden Fleece** was said to be haunted by the ghost of a US bomber pilot who had been shot down during the Second World War but he followed a tourist back home to Quincy in California where he now pulls at her hair at night.

York would rather hang on to its ghosts, however, for the tourist trade. No fewer than five companies run regular guided walks around haunted sites:

The Ghost Trail, **t** (01904) 633 276, *www.ghostrail.co.uk*; meets nightly at 7.30pm at the Minister's entrance (at the west end).

The Ghost Hunt, **t** (01904) 608 700, *www.ghosthunt.co.uk*; 7.30pm in the Shambles.

The Original Ghost Walk, **t** (01904) 764 222; 8pm in the King's Arms by Ouse Bridge.

The Haunted Walk of York, **t** (01904) 621 003; 8pm in Exhibition Square.

Mad Alice Ghost Walk, **t** (01904) 425 071; Tues–Sun 7.30pm from Clifford's Tower.

Each charges a small fee; there is no need to book – just turn up.

Finally, how about a real 'ghost' story? On 27 March 1643, John Bartendale, a York piper was hanged as a felon. After swinging from the gibbet for almost an hour he was cut down and buried on the spot. Shortly after, one Mr. Vavasour came riding past. When he saw the ground moving he ordered a servant to get a spade and dig. The resurrected Bartendale sat up in his freshly dug grave. He was as amazed at his good fortune as the crowd of onlookers that had gathered.

Abbey, which has been used many times as a setting for performances of the *York Mystery Plays*, a cycle of religious plays which formed part of the traditional Corpus Christi celebrations between the 14th and 16th centuries, and which were successfully revived in the 20th century (*see www.yorkmysteryplays.org*).

South of the River

The National Railway Museum

Leeman Road, **t** *(01904) 621 261, www.nrm.org.uk; open 10–6.*

Across the river, behind the railway station (a handsome arc of roof) is York's finest museum, winner of the best museum in Europe accolade. If you have children with you, or like railways, you'll need to allow the best part of a day for this museum alone. The **National Railway Museum** houses one of the greatest railway collections in the world. The three enormous galleries are a *Who's Who* of famous trains, from a repro-

Guy Fawkes

Guy Fawkes (1570–1606), proto-terrorist, was born in York and baptized a Protestant (in St Michael le Belfrey Church) but later converted to Catholicism and became a religious zealot. He was recruited by the conspirators who intended to blow up the houses of Parliament with King James I and his ministers inside in protest of their repression of Roman Catholics in England. The plot was discovered and Fawkes was arrested on 4 November 1605 after planting 20 barrels of gunpowder in a cellar beneath parliament. He was tortured and interrogated in the Tower of London and executed for treason two months later, on 31 January 1606. On 5 November (the day the plot would have been put into practice) people all over England burn an effigy of Guy Fawkes on a bonfire and celebrate with fireworks. Everywhere except St Peter's School in York, which Fawkes attended: it would be bad form to burn an old boy.

duction of Stephenson's Rocket to the only Japanese Bullet Train outside of Japan. The latter has a reputation not only for speed but also for punctuality: Bullet Trains arrive, on average, within 24 seconds of scheduled time (compare this to British trains). At first glimpse, the similarly aerodynamic Mallard doesn't look all that different, although it belongs to a different age: it set the world record for steam in 1938.

The earliest authentic locomotives in the museum are *Agenoria* and *Sans Pareil*, both built in 1829. Another interesting historical specimen is the biggest engine ever built in Britain (15ft high and 93ft long), which goes by the unromantic name of *Class KF7 No. 607*. Most visitors are fascinated by the luxurious décor of the royal trains. The museum is an unending resource of railway information – steam engines are still built occasionally in China and Switzerland – and trivia: here is documented the first level crossing keeper (Widow Howbourne of Gateshead, 1640); the Victorians' fear that vibrating railway carriages might awaken latent lust in their passengers; and the answer to whether or not train toilets flush directly onto the track. Lesser exhibits include a lock of Stephenson's hair, models, tickets, uniforms, cutlery, buttons, thousands of posters, thousands of engineering drawings and 200 original works of art.

All Saints' Church and the Bar Convent

There are two little-known York sights on the same side of the river as the railway station and railway museum. The **Bar Convent** (*17 Blossom St*, **t** *(01904) 464 901, www.bar-convent.org.uk; guided tours only Mon–Fri 10.30 and 2.30; adm*) is the oldest active convent in the UK and now also a museum explaining the development of Christianity in northern England. It also offers food and accommodation.

Of York's 18 surviving medieval churches the best is judged to be **All Saints** in North Street (*www.allsaints-northstreet.org*), for its stained glass. One famous window shows the last 15 days of the world, based on a Middle English poem called the 'Pricke of Conscience'. This call to repentance makes depressing 'reading'. The first nine panels depict the destruction of the earth, with the seas roaring and spewing out monsters; earthquakes and fires make short work of buildings. Then it is mankind's turn: hiding in holes cannot save him. Everyone on earth dies, the stars fall out of the sky, the bones of the dead rise up and 'the world burns on every side'.

You can cheer yourself up by brushing up on your angel lore. One window in the church shows the nine medieval orders of angels: Seraphim, Cherubim, Thrones, Dominions, Virtues, Powers, Principalities, Archangels and common-or-garden Angels. There is another intriguing feature: a medieval man holding a pair of spectacles.

West Yorkshire

West Yorkshire is inseparable from its now almost extinct textile industry. Long before the Industrial Revolution, Pennine Yorkshire had large flocks of sheep – many owned by monastic houses – grazing on its infertile uplands. Woollen cloth was made in many homes in the hills and was even being exported as early as 796. This cottage textile industry made use of Yorkshire's abundant water: the soft water filtered through moorland peat was ideal for washing wool, and faster-flowing streams were used to drive simple machines to speed up the manufacturing processes.

This rural, low-tech economy was transformed by the invention of the steam engine. The valleys of West Riding (as it then was) were ripe for the textile trade revolution: they still had the sheep and water but above all they also had the coal needed to raise steam in the great engines that were appearing everywhere.

Roads, railways and canals were crammed into the valleys to ferry in raw materials and carry finished products to market. Fortunes were made, and once-minor towns – Leeds, Bradford, Halifax – prospered and merged in a mass of frenzied activity.

Textile manufacturing was always subject to the vicissitudes of the market but, after the Second Word War, the introduction of synthetic fabrics and a flood of cheap imports made it hard for the ageing mills and unionized workforces, with rising expectations, to compete. Proud industrial buildings – some in exotic architectural styles – were shut down, put to other uses or demolished. Economies that once gave no thought to their dependence on textiles suddenly had to diversify, and as the cities slid into decline they had to find new identities. Mass immigration, mainly from the Indian subcontinent, created the multiethnic communities now typical of West Yorkshire, where it's as easy to find a good curry as an authentic Yorkshire pudding or a plate of fish and chips.

You might well expect there not to be much to attract you to this region and the sad remains of the powerhouse of the northern economy. Even in its prime, life here was built around the utilitarian needs of wool-processing, which, with exceptions, put hard labour and productivity before aesthetics. And it is true that West Yorkshire is a place built entirely of stone, brick and steel, best characterized by redundant mill chimneys and endless dark gritstone walls begrimed by decades of pollution; you can

Getting There and Around

Being so densely populated, and with an industrial infrastructure, West Yorkshire is an easy place to get around making the most of **public transport**.

For information contact **MetroLine, t** (0113) 245 7676, *www.wymetro.com*. A **Metrocard** is available for travel on buses and trains. The **West Yorkshire Day Rover** ticket gives unlimited travel on buses and trains after 9.30am on weekdays.

drive for miles and the only greenery you will see will be in threadbare parks and the discarded wastelands of industry.

But, approached with an open mind, this is one of the most rewarding parts of Yorkshire to visit. West Yorkshire is making great strides to clean itself up and exploit its post-industrial charm, and there is something compelling about the visuals of hard economics set against the austere natural grandeur of Pennine landscapes. Graceful chimneys, once hated for the smoke and lung-clogging pollution they poured out, are now valued as ingenious architectural structures; the old mills have gripping stories to tell about life in hard times. And it was not all hard grind: art and beauty were produced here too. Nowhere is West Yorkshire's oxymoronic nature better illustrated than in Haworth, a grim, smoke-blackened village in which the short-lived Brontë sisters wrote romantic novels of lasting fascination.

Leeds

You must like it very much or not at all.

Charles Dickens, on Leeds

Whether by luck or design, Leeds has become one of Britain's fastest-growing cities. Shamelessly on the make, these days it barely speaks of its past as a weaving and cloth-making centre, when it was the capital of 'ready-to-wear'. Now it has only two things on its mind: shopping and clubbing.

The central axis of the city is the **Headrow** and its extensions **West Gate** and **East Gate**. The latter slopes downhill to where the city centre peters out around the bus station, and you come to the **West Yorkshire Playhouse** theatre, which describes itself as 'the UK's leading regional theatre' – not without some justification: it is associated with such northern talents of the theatre world as Alan Bennett, who was born in Leeds and premieres his new plays at the theatre (***t** (0113) 213 7700, www.wyplay house.com*). From Quarry Hill, behind the theatre, the monolithic **DSS** (Department of Social Services) **Headquarters** looks up the Headrow. One of the most prominent of Leeds' many new buildings, it has earned the local nickname of 'the Kremlin'. Oddly enough, local tradition also insists that Hitler had planned to use the flats which stood on the site as his northern headquarters had he won the war.

At the other end of the Headrow is the **Town Hall**, a classical revival building of the 1850s, opened by Queen Victoria, which looks as grand as all town halls should. Beside it is the **City Art Gallery** (***t** (0113) 247 8248; open Mon–Sat 10–5, Sun 1–5*) and the **Henry Moore Institute** (***t** (0113) 246 7467, www.henry-moore-fdn.co.uk; open daily 10–5.30; adm*) the two joined by a glass bridge. Henry Moore said that one of his major influences was seeing a huge outcrop of stone on the Yorkshire moors.

The Headrow slices through a city centre almost devoid of historical monuments, and dedicated to shopping. It's like walking through a purpose-built retail park containing all the famous high-street brand names of Britain. To the north of the Headrow is **The Light** and **St John's Centre**, behind which is the first big shopping

Getting There and Around

Leeds-Bradford airport, **t** (0113) 250 9696. Domestic and charter flights.

Leeds is served by three main **train** companies: **Arriva**, **GNER** and **Virgin**. GNER runs an hourly service to London King's Cross. **National Rail Enquiries**, **t** 08457 484950, *www.thetrainline.com*.

National Express **coaches** also travel to the town, **t** 08705 808080, *www.gobycoach.com*.

Bus information can be picked up from **Leeds Bus Station**, **t** (0113) 242 0922, *www.firstgroup.com*. A **Dayrider** ticket enables you to travel all day on buses within Leeds.

Tourist Information

Leeds: Gateway Yorkshire Regional Travel and Tourist Information Centre, Leeds City Station, **t** (0113) 242 5242, *www.leeds.gov.uk*. Visit *www.vrleeds.co.uk* for a virtual tour.

Where to Stay

Leeds t (0113) –

Malmaison, Sovereign Quay, **t** 398 1000 (*very expensive*). Striking hotel in a restored red-brick bus depot. Rooms come as 'standard' – each with its own ironing board, CD player and two phone lines – or 'superior' should you need more than this.

42 The Calls, **t** 244 0099, *www.42thecalls.co.uk* (*very expensive*). Converted corn mill looking onto the canal. Some rooms overlook the water but the view is not all that desirable.

Avalon Guest House, 132 Woodsley Road, **t** 243 2545 (*moderate*). Family-run hotel near the university and a short hike from the city centre.

Eating Out

Rascasse, Canal Wharf, Water Lane, **t** 244 6611, *www.rascasse-leeds.co.uk* (*expensive*). Anglo-French restaurant by the waterside with an interesting wine list.

Brasserie Forty Four, 44 The Calls, **t** 234 3232 (*moderate*). Judged the city's best brasserie in a recent edition of the *Good Food Guide*.

Darbar, 16–17 Kirkgate, **t** 246 0381, *www.darbar.co.uk* (*moderate*). Highly regarded Indian restaurant.

Hansa's Gujarati Restaurant, 72–4 North Street, **t** 244 4408, *www.hansarestaurant.co.uk* (*moderate*). Indian vegetarian restaurant popular with students.

Harvey Nichols Fourth Floor Café and Bar, 107–11 Briggate, **t** 204 8000 (*moderate*). Starkly modern surroundings of the trendy

centre to be built in the city, **The Merrion Centre**. To the north is more interesting: it is made up of the **Headrow Centre**, **Victoria Quarter** (built around a roofed-in street and proud home of the first branch outside London of trendy department store Harvey Nichols) and **Trinity Quarter**.

Parallel with the glamour of Leeds as retail therapy there is, however, a less visible old Leeds. On the Headrow itself is the **City Varieties**, the best preserved music hall in Britain and home to the TV variety show *The Good Old Days*. Behind it, between Briggate and Lands Lane, are two handsome arcades: **County Arcade** and **Thornton's Arcade**, where there is a mechanical clock.

By far the most interesting place to shop or stroll around is in and around **Kirkgate Market**. The old part is all handsome dressed stone; inside it is a delightful flight of commercial fancy: green columns with burgundy and gold decorations, a light glass ceiling and red dragons holding up the balconies. There are 437 stalls inside the market and a further 201 outside.

Leeds' best building stands beside the market, the **Corn Exchange**, built by the same architect as the town hall. This Zeppelin-like trading hall has been given over to more department store. Views over the Leeds rooftops to be enjoyed day or night.

Leodis Brasserie, Victoria Mill, Sovereign Street, **t** 242 1010, *www.leodis.co.uk* (*moderate*). Brasserie in a converted warehouse.

Sous le Nez, The Basement, Quebec House, Quebec Street, **t** 244 0108 (*moderate*). Popular basement restaurant serving either a light lunch or a hearty meal.

Bretts Fish Restaurant, 12 North Lane, **t** 289 9322 (*cheap*). Long-established fish and chip restaurant in an ivy-clad cottage with garden near Headingley cricket ground.

The Italian Job, 9–11 Bridge End, **t** 242 0185 (*cheap*). Booking is recommended for this informal family-run Italian restaurant.

Roots and Fruits, 10–11 Grand Arcade, **t** 242 8313 (*cheap*). Licensed vegetarian restaurant.

Pubs, Bars and Cafés

Whitelocks, Turk's Head Yard, **t** 245 3950 (*cheap*). This famous Leeds pub runs all the way down an alleyway that is connected to the busy shopping streets by covered passageways at either end. Inside it has low ceilings, mirrors, dark wood and stained glass. Tables and benches outside. There is a quieter bar at the top end of the alley. Sandwiches and other pub food available lunch and dinner.

Arts Café, 42 Call Lane, **t** 243 8243 (*cheap*). Young, informal, light with bright yellow walls and tasteful music playing gently in the background.

Norman, 36 Call Lane, **t** 343 988 (*cheap*). A shockingly modern place with a great arched red sofa behind its plate glass window. One description of it would be 'beer and noodles' another is 'one of the best 100 bars in the world'. As far from average as you can get.

Observatory, 40 Boar Lane, **t** 242 8641 (*cheap*). Domed interior and balcony for observing the city nightlife.

The Conservatory, Albion Place, **t** 205 1911 (*cheap*). Cellar bar in the shopping area, with a fish pond in it. *Breakfast served from 8am; full menu available from 12–8.*

Entertainment

In the 1990s Leeds developed a thriving club scene which even attracted people up from London for a night or a weekend on the town. It is still going, and 'serious party lovers' can buy a **North Nights Leeds Weekender** card which gives admission to a selection of the city's best clubs. Call **t** 0800 5872872 or go to *www.northnights.co.uk/weekender* to find out more about clubs and card.

shopping, this time in the form of youth culture. Downhill from it you come to the riverside, which is being gentrified, but does not yet have much charm.

It is a bit of a walk from the city centre to what is supposed to be the main tourist attraction of modern Leeds, the **Royal Armouries Museum** (*Armouries Drive, **t** (0113) 220 1999, www.armouries.org.uk; open Mon–Fri 10–5*), a collection of arms and armour which protests that it is 'about preserving life as well as taking it'. The five galleries deal with War, Tournament, The Orient, Self-Defence and Hunting.

Around Leeds

Leventhorpe Vineyard and Harewood House

Within Leeds' boundaries are several places worth seeing. One surprise is **Leventhorpe Vineyard** (*Bullerthorpe Lane, Woodlesford, **t** (0113) 288 9088; open Mon–Fri 11–5, weekends 12–5*), the most northerly commercial vineyard in Britain.

Harewood House (***t** (0113) 218 1010, www.harewood.org; open Mar–Oct daily, house and terrace gallery 11–5, grounds and bird garden 10–5; Nov–New Year weekends, same* *hours; adm*), on the road from Leeds to Harrogate, is one of the country's most magnificent stately homes. It is now run by its owners, the Earl and Countess of Harewood, as an attraction for family days out. The house was completed in 1772, with interiors by Robert Adam, pelmets and furniture by Thomas Chippendale. Fine art from the Renaissance to the present hangs on the walls. The grounds of the house were laid out by Capability Brown and include fountains, a Lakeside Walk, Victorian Terrace, rhododendron collection (April–June) and the Walled Garden with its Spiral Meadow. The Bird Garden and Adventure Playground entertain children.

Ilkely

Ilkley is a spa town in the Wharfe Valley, more a place to stroll and shop than to see any particular sights. Above the town is formidable Rombalds Moor, the nearest part of which is **Ilkely Moor**, immortalized in the anthem of Yorkshire, 'On Ilkla' Moor Baht 'At' ('On Ilkley Moor Without a Hat'). The moor was inhabited in prehistoric times, when it was above flood and swamp levels, and 'primitive' humans left three hundred enigmatic rock carvings. Most of these are 'cup and ring' markings – circular hollows in the rock surrounded by concentric circles – of a type found elsewhere in Britain and also in America, Australia and other parts of the world; but some have a feature unique to Ilkley: a ladder motif. All these carvings are believed to have been made in the late-Neolithic or Bronze Age, between 2800 and 500BC, but their meaning remains as elusive as ever. The most famous petroglyph in Yorkshire is the Swastika stone on Woodhouse Crag (the emblem had a long life before its adoption by the Nazis). To see the carvings takes patience, a map and imagination: the tourist information centre in Ilkley publishes a series of leaflets to help you locate them.

Heading from Ilkely towards Bradford you pass through **Guiseley**, where, on a roundabout, stands Harry Ramsden's, 'the most famous fish and chip shop in the world'. The business that the 'uncrowned king of fish and chips', started in a green-and-white wooden hut in 1928 has now become a brand name, with branches all over Britain, in Disneyworld and in Jeddah. Eat in or take away: it's up to you.

Tourist Information

Ilkley: Station Road, **t** (01943) 602 319, *www.visitilkley.com*.

Where to Stay and Eat

Around Leeds t (01943) –

Rombalds Hotel and Restaurant, West View, Wells Road, Ilkley, **t** 603 201 (*expensive*). On the edge of Ilkely Moor. Renowned for its restaurant.

Bettys, 32 The Grove, Ilkley, **t** 608 029, (*cheap*). Although its windows overlook the town-centre car park, this is still a pleasant tea room with stained-glass windows and a fine collection of teapots. A piano player sometimes tinkles away in the background. Snacks, cakes and hot meals are available. For more on Bettys, *see* Harrogate, p.807–8.

Harry Ramsden's, White Cross, Guiseley (near Leeds), **t** 874 641, *www.harryramsden.co.uk* (*cheap*). The elegant white dining room with pot plants, white plaster decorations, stained glass, red curtains and crystal chandeliers are slightly over the top but 'the most famous fish and chip shop in the world' has to live up to its name. For all the extra trappings, however, this is still just a glorified fish-and-chip shop.

On Ilkla' Moor Baht 'At (On Ilkley Moor Without A Hat)

It is thought that this mordantly humorous song was invented after a ramble and picnic on Ilkley Moor by a chapel choir from a West Riding town. The words, in dialect, are a leg-pulling caution to one of their number who wandered away from the group with his sweetheart. The tune comes from a Methodist hymn. No one quite knows how it has come to be the 'national' anthem of Yorkshire.

Wheear 'as tha binn since ah saw thee?
On Ilkla' Moor baht 'at
Wheear 'as tha bin since ah saw thee?
Wheear 'as tha bin since ah saw thee?
On Ilkla' Moor baht 'at
On Ilkla' Moor baht 'at
On Ilkla' Moor baht 'at
(Where have you been since I saw you last?
On Ilkely Moor without a hat)

Tha's bin a coortin' Mary Jane
On Ilkla' Moor baht 'at
Tha's bin a coortin' Mary Jane
Tha's bin a coortin' Mary Jane
On Ilkla' Moor baht 'at
On Ilkla' Moor baht 'at
On Ilkla' Moor baht 'at
(You've been courting Mary Jane
On Ilkely Moor without a hat)

Tha's bahn t' catch thi death o' cowd
On Ilkla' Moor baht 'at
Tha's bahn t' catch thi death o' cowd
Tha's bahn t' catch thi death o' cowd
On Ilkla' Moor baht 'at
On Ilkla' Moor baht 'at
On Ilkla' Moor baht 'at
(You're going to catch your death of cold
On Ilkely Moor without a hat)

Then we shall ha' to bury thee
On Ilkla' Moor baht 'at
Then we shall ha' to bury thee
Then we shall ha' to bury thee
On Ilkla' Moor baht 'at
On Ilkla' Moor baht 'at

On Ilkla' Moor baht 'at
(Then we'll have to bury you
On Ilkely Moor without a hat)

Then t' worms 'll cum an' eat thee up
On Ilkla' Moor baht 'at
Then t' worms 'll cum an' eat thee up
Then t' worms 'll cum an' eat thee up
On Ilkla' Moor baht 'at
On Ilkla' Moor baht 'at
On Ilkla' Moor baht 'at
(Then the worms will come and eat you up
On Ilkely Moor without a hat)

Then t' ducks 'll come an' eat up t' worms
On Ilkla' Moor baht 'at
Then t' ducks 'll come an' eat up t' worms
Then t' ducks 'll come an' eat up t' worms
On Ilkla' Moor baht 'at
On Ilkla' Moor baht 'at
On Ilkla' Moor baht 'at
(Then some ducks will come and eat the worms
On Ilkely Moor without a hat)

Then we shall come an' eat them ducks
On Ilkla' Moor baht 'at
Then we shall come an' eat them ducks
Then we shall come an' eat them ducks
On Ilkla' Moor baht 'at
On Ilkla' Moor baht 'at
On Ilkla' Moor baht 'at
(Then we shall come and eat the ducks
On Ilkely Moor without a hat)

Then we shall all 'av etten thee
On Ilkla' Moor baht 'at
Then we shall all 'av etten thee
Then we shall all 'av etten thee
On Ilkla' Moor baht 'at
On Ilkla' Moor baht 'at
On Ilkla' Moor baht 'at
(Then we will have eaten you |
because you were walking around on Ilkley Moor without a hat)

Bradford

For centuries Bradford was a nondescript backwater, but when it was discovered that steam power could do the work of manpower in manufacturing, its fortunes took off. It was sited on coal and iron-ore deposits and raring to go. In the early 19th century Bradford's population soared as people left the countryside for the cities, where mills and factories promised steady employment. Canals and, later, railways linked Bradford with the outside world, and it became the world's undisputed wool capital. This triumph was earned at some social cost, as 19th-century Bradford was plagued by typhoid, cholera and anthrax – also known as 'wool sorters' disease'. Later in the century Bradford put some of its wealth into cleaning itself up, and built itself buildings to suit its growing stature. After the Second World War, however, synthetic fibres and cheap imports of wool dealt harshly with Bradford, and its fortunes declined again. From the 1950s on, waves of immigrants poured into the city, altering its ethnic composition and breathing new life. Bradford was less quick to regenerate itself than Leeds but the city now has several good museums to pull the punters in.

If you want to see what life was like at the height of Bradford's economic success try the **Bradford Industrial Museum and Horses at Work** (*Moorside Mills, Moorside Road,* ***t*** *(01274) 631 756; open Tues–Sat 10–5, Sun 12–5*), a 19th-century worsted spinning-mill complex, including the mill owner's house and back-to-back houses.

Bradford's baroque art gallery, **Cartwright Hall** (*Lister Park,* ***t*** *(01274) 751 212; open Tues–Sat 10–5, Sun 1–5*) proudly wears its multiethnicity: its permanent collection of British art is hung beside a 'trans-cultural' collection of art from around the Indian subcontinent and South Asia.

Bradford's biggest draw, however, is the **National Museum of Photography, Film and Television** (***t*** *(01274) 202 030, www.nmpft.org.uk; open Tues–Sun 10–6, also Mon during school holidays*). Here, in eight galleries on five floors, you can sate yourself on interactive technology and make yourself giddy in the IMAX cinema. Founded in 1983, the NMPFT is the most visited national museum outside London, attracting 750,000 visitors each year. The museum was located in Bradford because of the city's historic links with film-making in the UK: its collection includes the world's first moving picture – Louis Le Prince's 1888 film of Leeds Bridge – and the first ever camera with panning

Tourist Information

Bradford: City Hall, **t** (01274) 753 678, *www.visitbradford.com or www.bradford.gov.uk.*

Where to Stay and Eat

Bradford t (01274) –

Carnoustie, 8 Park Grove, Frizinghall (on Keighley–Bradford road), **t** 490 561 (*moderate*). Detached Victorian guesthouse outside the city centre. En-suite rooms.

Castle Hotel, 20 Grattan Road, **t** 393 166 (*moderate*). City-centre hotel.

The Kashmir Restaurant, 27 Morley St (on corner of Wilton Street), **t** 726 513, *www.thekashmirrestaurant.co.uk* (*cheap*). Oldest Indian restaurant in West Yorkshire and the best Indian restaurant in the city; some people rate it as the best Indian restaurant in the UK or even the world in its price bracket. The atmosphere is informal. You can consult the menu on the web before you visit.

Fairy Tale

The five photographs of fairies taken by two girls in Cottingley in West Yorkshire were called the hoax of their century. The first two pictures were taken in 1917 by Elsie Wright and her cousin Frances Griffiths, using Elsie's father's box-plate camera. The first, Frances with a group of fairies flying in front of her, is one of the most reproduced photographs of all time. When the girls took a second picture, of Elsie playing with a gnome, Elsie's father banned her from borrowing the camera again and the matter was forgotten. Three years later, however, Elsie's mother mentioned the photographs to a friend at a meeting on folklore in Bradford. Her remark was overheard by Edward Gardner, a leading Theosophist who was anxious to find proof of the existence of spiritual beings. The plates were sent to Gardner and word of them reached Sir Arthur Conan Doyle. The famous detective-story writer asked the two girls, now aged 18 and 13, to take some more fairy pictures. They obliged.

When asked if the photos were real, the two girls had agreed to answer only: 'They are pictures of figments of our imagination' – which they were; it was a truthful reply which would not disappoint the believers. Debate about the authenticity of the photos continued to generate press coverage. Only in 1972, when Elsie sold the camera to buy an electric lawn mower, did she admit that the pictures were faked by rigging up cut-out model fairies using hatpins and knicker elastic.

'Of course there are fairies,' Geoffrey Crawley wrote in the *British Journal of Photography* at the end of a long article examing the affair, 'just as there is Father Christmas. The trouble comes when you try to make them corporeal. They are fine poetic concepts taking us out of this at times too ugly real world.'

device, used by Robert W. Paul to film Queen Victoria's Diamond Jubilee procession in 1897. Alongside these you will find the *Playschool* toys and the 'Clapometer' used on *Opportunity Knocks* (it is a national museum, after all), as well as a digital media gallery, the IMAX cinema, a Cinerama cinema and historical collection of photographic and film-making equipment. The museum explores not only how photos, film and TV are made, but also the impact of the image – still or moving – on society. As you leave, you can ponder the truth of Isaac Shoenberg's words upon the success of the first electronic television camera in 1934: 'Well, gentlemen, you have now invented the biggest time-waster of all time.'

If your interests are in things visual you should also look at the unusual **Colour Museum** (*Perkin House, Providence Street,* **t** *(01274) 390 955, www.sdc.org.uk; open Tues–Sat 10–4; adm*), created by the Society of Dyers and Colourists. The displays play tricks with your eye as the museum grapples with what colour is, how we recognize it, how it affects us and how colours can be reproduced on a commercial scale. Many of the exhibits are interactive.

One other museum deserves a visit, to offset the Royal Armouries in Leeds. The **Peace Museum** (*10 Piece Hall Yard,* **t** *(01274) 754 009, www.peacemuseum.org.uk; open Wed and Fri 11–3 or by appointment*) is the only one of its kind in Britain. If your instinct is that most conflicts in the world can and should be solved without violence, here you will find evidence to back up your case.

Getting There and Around

There are regular **train** services to Bradford, Leeds, Skipton and Keighley. Saltaire is linked to Shipley by **minibus**.

Tourist Information

Saltaire Gift and Visitor Centre: 2 Victoria Road, Saltaire, **t** (01274) 774 993.

Saltaire websites: *www.visitsaltaire.com* or *www.saltaire.yorks.com*.

Where to Stay and Eat

The Boathouse Inn, Victoria Road, Saltaire, **t** (01274) 590 408 (*moderate*). Sir Titus's former boathouse, with a terrace on the River Aire for afternoon tea in summer. Bar meals or *à la carte* menu.

Saltaire Industrial Museum

Saltaire, just north of Bradford near Shipley, destroys the image of the 19th-century West Riding as a place of dark satanic mills where unscrupulous entrepreneurs kept their workforces in semi-slavery. This model Victorian industrial village was built by mill owner Sir Titus Salt out of paternalism, philanthropy and, of course, the quest for profit. It was intended to be 'a paradise on the sylvan banks of the Aire, far from the stench and vice of the industrial city.'

The mill was opened on Sir Titus's 50th birthday in 1853, but the grid of 22 streets (many named after members of the Salt family) and 850 neat little workers' houses took another 20 years to complete. The self-contained community had its own hospital, school, fire station, Methodist and Congregational churches, park, wash-house and railway station. The abstemious Sir Titus would not allow a pub to tempt his workers but he did build an institute for their moral welfare. The village is still more or less as Sir Titus left it on his death in 1876. In 2001 Saltaire was declared a World Heritage Site for its visionary planning, which had a direct influence on the 'garden city' movement (*see* also Bournville and Letchworth).

The community revolved around Salts Mill beside the Leeds–Liverpool canal, where 3,000 men were employed at 1,200 looms to produce mohair and alpaca. When it was working, it was Europe's largest factory. It now houses the **1853 Gallery** (*Victoria Road, **t** (01274) 531 163, www.saltsmill.org.uk; open daily 10–6*), where the world's largest collection of works by Bradford-born artist David Hockney is on display. (Hockney has long left Bradford for California.)

Haworth

The hillside village of Haworth, outside Keighley on the edge of Pennine moorland, has become, improbably, one of England's two most famous literary shrines. The other, Stratford-upon-Avon, is more convincing: it is pretty enough to serve as the contrived hometown of the nation's greatest playwright. But where Stratford peddles a myth of faraway Tudor-Stuart England, Haworth pretends to preserve the character of a much nearer time; it tries to encapsulate a 19th-century industrial Yorkshire spiced with a whiff of tragic romanticism. Had it not once been the home of English literature's first family, the Brontës, it would not get a passing glance from anyone.

As in Stratford, here too fact and fiction are often difficult to disentangle. Most people who visit 'Brontë Country' come looking for the fictional *Wuthering Heights* – the bleak, blustery trysting place of doomed lovers Catherine Earnshaw and Heathcliffe – as portrayed on the big and little screens.

Whether you find the famous moors which surround Haworth and inspired the Brontës either 'hauntingly beautiful' or plain depressing depends on your temperament. If you're of a melancholic or consumptive disposition, you'll fit right in; but if you are not, Haworth is best visited on a sunny day when its depressive atmosphere isn't quite so bleak. On a drab day in winter, today's prettified village of cafés and souvenir shops begins to evoke the village as found by the Brontës on their arrival in 1820, when the 'rapid expansion of the weaving industry in the 18th century had left Haworth a legacy of congested dwellings, polluted water and inadequate sanitation; pigs roamed the streets, there was a dunghill before each door and typhus, cholera, dysentery and smallpox were rife' (Patrick and Biddy Nuttgens).

Like so many films about the Brontës, Haworth comes in black and white. You either buy into the myth of the Brontës as geniuses, or you don't. The Brontë Society, which has documented every last detail of the family and converted it all into hagiography, maintains that the literature is the thing: 'Charlotte and Emily are ranked among the world's greatest novelists; Anne is a powerful underrated author, and both their father, the Revd. Patrick Brontë, and brother Branwell also saw their own works in print.' A detractor would say that the public image of the family is out of proportion to the size or merit of its literary output. The Brontës' combined efforts resulted in only two memorable books, *Jane Eyre* and *Wuthering Heights*. The sisters' other works are read today only because of these two books.

All the fuss surrounds one small building near the top of the village, off the main street, the **Brontë Parsonage Museum** (*Church Street, Haworth,* **t** *(01535) 642 323,*

Getting There and Around

The **Keighley and Worth Valley Railway** is the most appropriate way to get to Haworth. For general information on the line call **t** (01535) 645 214, for talking timetable call **t** (01535) 647 777, or visit *www.kwvr.co.uk*. *Services run mid-June–Sept daily 9–6, the rest of the year weekends only.*

Haworth can also be reached easily by car, a beautiful drive over the moors.

Tourist Information

Haworth: **t** (01535) 642 329, *www.visithaworth.com*, *www.Brontëcountry.co.uk* or *www.visitBrontëcountry.com*, which includes a 360-degree picture viewer.

Where to Stay and Eat

Haworth t (01535) –

Weavers, West Lane, **t** 643 822 (*moderate*). Haworth's best restaurant.

Hilltop, Haworth Moor, **t** 643 524 (*moderate*). Comfortable farmhouse which does B&B and evening meal.

Three Sisters Hotel, Brow Top Road, **t** 643 458, *www.threesisters-hotel.co.uk* (*moderate*). Hotel with nine en-suite bedrooms and decent restaurant.

Haworth Tea Rooms and Guesthouse, 68 Main Street, **t** 644 278 (*moderate*). Family-run in a listed building with views over Haworth Main Street and beyond. Meals, snacks and en-suite bedrooms.

Black Bull, 119 Main Street, **t** 642 249 (*cheap*). Branwell Brontë's old local.

The Brontës: a Real-life (Romantic) Tragedy

You only have to hear the barest details of the lives of the Brontë sisters to know that as in literature, so in life, there is no happy ending. In 1820 Patrick Brontë, an Irish clergyman and poet who had changed his surname from 'Brunty' to sound more impressive, moved to the curacy of Haworth with his Cornish-born wife Maria and their six children (born in Thornton, near Bradford). Maria was appalled by the grimness of the village and died of cancer only nine months after the family's arrival.

Illness would carry off almost all the family members before their time. Three years later, in 1824, two sisters, Maria (aged 11) and Elizabeth (10), died of tuberculosis. The other children were brought up by their father and a reclusive aunt, Elizabeth Branwell, learning to rely on each other for moral support and entertaining each other with stories from their imagination.

Charlotte worked for a while as a teacher and Anne as a governess. The only son, Branwell, tried a series of professions and was dismissed from one for 'proceedings bad beyond expression' – presumed to be a love affair with the wife of his employer. His greatest talent seems to have been as a conversationalist at the bar of the Black Bull. Charlotte and Emily both studied in Brussels for a time with the aim of opening their own school in Yorkshire but not a single pupil could be found to enrol.

Charlotte, Emily and Anne's first attempt at writing was also a failure. They compiled their own collection of poetry but only sold two copies.

However Charlotte's second novel, *Jane Eyre* (published in October 1847) was an instant success. *Wuthering Heights* by Emily appeared two months later. But just as the sisters gained literary fame disaster struck. Weakened by his dependence on alcohol and opium, Branwell succumbed to tuberculosis and died on 24 September 1848 aged 31. Three months later Emily died too, aged 30. By this time Anne was also ill and she too died, while seeking a sea-cure in Scarborough, on 28 May 1849. She had written two novels: *Agnes Grey* and *The Tenant of Wildfell Hall*.

That just left Charlotte, successful and mildly famous, to live on with her father. Having refused three proposals of marriage she eventually married the Reverend Arthur Bell Nicholls, curate to her father, in 1854 – but died during pregnancy the following year, three weeks before her 39th birthday.

Patrick survived all his children and lived on at the parsonage until 1861, when he died without direct descendants at the age of 84.

www.Brontë.info; open April–Sept daily 10–5, Oct–Mar daily 11–4.30; adm). It's described as the 'lifelong' home of the sisters, but their lives were far from long. The old Brontë home opened as a museum in 1928 and uses the family's furniture and belongings to recreate the rooms as they would have been when the precociously talented Brontë children were pushing their imaginations into overdrive to escape from the reality of living next door to a graveyard in industrial Victorian Yorkshire.

At the bottom of the village is Haworth station, on the **Keighley and Worth Valley Railway**, a preserved branch line, five miles long, between Keighley and Oxenhope, served by steam engines pulling period rolling stock (*see* box for details). One of the other stations, Oakworth, was used in the classic 1972 film of *The Railway Children* starring Jenny Agutter. Near the Ingrow West station is a small railway museum.

Calderdale and Kirklees

At the height of the Industrial Revolution, raw materials and finished products were shunted across northern England between Manchester and Leeds-Bradford to keep the production lines going. To cross the Pennines, everything had to be funnelled into the few east–west valleys that could carry rail, road and canal. These were guarded by Halifax and Huddersfield, capitals of the modern-day districts of Calderdale and Kirklees. The monumental blackened ruins of industry have largely been preserved and restored,while the steep-sided valleys climb onto bleak moorland, in agreeable contrast to the more cosy scenery of the Yorkshire Dales to the north.

Halifax

If you are travelling around Yorkshire with children, set aside time for **Eureka! The Museum for Children** (*Discovery Road, Halifax,* **t** *(01422) 330 069, www.eureka.org.uk; open daily 10–5; adm*), the first museum designed for children where almost everything is both entertaining and unobtrusively educational, beginning with a working model of Archimedes taking a bath over the entrance. Once inside, with or without adult help, children can deposit and withdraw money in a bank, learn to change the wheel of a car, read the news on TV and deliver the post.

Halifax itself has a few historic monuments, notably the 18th-century Piece Hall (**t** *(01422) 358 087*), which contains shops, markets, a café and art gallery, and the octagonal **Wainhouse Tower** (*open 10 days a year; ask at tourist information centre; adm*), which was built as a chimney in the 1870s by dye-works owner John Edward Wainhouse but never used for its original purpose. Instead of smoke, a spiral staircase of 400 steps leads to a viewing balcony.

Tourist Information

Halifax: Piece Hall, **t** (01422) 368 725.
Hebden Bridge: 1 Bridge Gate, **t** (01422) 843 831, *www.pennineyorkshire.co.uk* or *www.calderdale.gov.uk.*
Huddersfield: 3–5 Albion Street, **t** (01484) 223 200, *www.kirklees.gov.uk.*

Where to Stay and Eat

Hebden Bridge t (01422) –

Laughing Gravy, The Birchcliffe Centre, Birchcliffe Road, **t** 844 425, *www.laughinggravy.co.uk* (*moderate*). Licensed vegetarian restaurant with delicious food.

Robin Hood Inn, Keighley Road, Pecket Well, **t** 842 593, *www.robinhoodinn.com* (*moderate*). Pub serving home-made food made with fresh vegetables. Rooms too.

Sowerby Bridge t (01422) –

Thurst House Farm, Ripponden, **t** 822 820 (*moderate*). A 17th-century farmhouse surrounded by open Pennine country. Owner Judith Marriott specializes in English dishes.

The Hobbit Hotel, Hob Lane, Norland, **t** 832 202, *www.hobbit-hotel.co.uk* (*moderate*). Not many hobbits visit Sowerby Bridge these days (they're all in New Zealand working as film extras), but if they do they will find a welcome here.

Heptonstall and Hebden Bridge

Further into the Pennines from Halifax is the old weaving town of **Heptonstall**, where the poet Sylvia Plath is buried. In 1963, 30 years old and recently separated from her husband, Ted Hughes, she put out milk and bread for her two young children in her London flat and gassed herself to death, earning almost instant immortality.

Below Heptonstall, in the valley, is **Hebden Bridge**, a packhorse stop which flourished as a mill town when the Rochdale canal was built. By the 1960s it seemed to have gone into terminal decline, but over the next two decades was rescued by an influx of writers, artists, musicians, and practitioners of all things alternative, green and nonconformist. As a result, Hebden Bridge has become a desirable halfway house between urban living and the moors.

North of Hebden Bridge and Heptonstall are **Hardcastle Crags** (***t** (01422) 844 518; always open*), in a pretty wooded valley managed by The National Trust.

Standedge Tunnel

Over the other side of the M62, the principal east–west road between Yorkshire and Lancashire, is a singular piece of industrial archaeology. In 2001 Standedge Tunnel, the longest, highest and deepest canal tunnel in Britain, reopened after 57 years of closure and almost 30 years of dedicated restoration work. The canal was dug in the early 19th century. Fifty navvies died in explosions and rock falls before the tunnel was ready for the first barge to sail through it between Huddersfield and Ashton-under-Lyme in 1811. Construction gangs had worked from either end but reached the middle 16ft apart from each other, a difference which had to be corrected by a bend in the canal. The tunnel is 3¼ miles long and 645ft above sea level. At its deepest it reaches 638ft below the sheep grazing on the Pennine slopes. The canal towpaths end at the mouth of the tunnel and, in the heady days of industry, 'leggers' would use their feet to walk barges through the tunnel, taking about four hours each way – although in 1914 a record 85 minutes for a man-powered journey was set. Today passenger boats are propelled through the tunnel by electric tug from the **Standedge Visitor Centre** (*Tunnel End, Waters Road, Marsden, Huddersfield, **t** (01484) 844 298, www.standedge.co.uk; open daily Easter–May and Sept–Oct 11–5, June–Aug 10–6; adm*), a rehabilitated transhipment warehouse.

Huddersfield

There's not much inducement to stop in Huddersfield, but things have improved since John Wesley wrote in his journal for 1757: 'I rode over the mountains to Huddersfield. A wilder people I never saw in England, the men, women and children filled the streets as we rode along and appeared just ready to devour us. They were, however, tolerably quiet while I preached; only a few pieces of dirt were thrown.'

Batley and Wakefield

The otherwise undistinguished town of Batley, on the edge of the Leeds-Bradford conurbation, has a delightfully eccentric museum, the **Bagshaw Museum** (*Wilton Park, Batley, **t** (01924) 326 155, www.kirkleesmc.gov.uk; open Mon–Fri 11–5, weekends*

12–5) is a Victorian-Gothic mansion packed with weird and wonderful objects from around the world.

South of Wakefield is another artistic treasure. The **Yorkshire Sculpture Park** (*West Bretton, Wakefield,* **t** *(01924) 830 302; park open daily summer 10–6, winter 10–4; café, galleries and shops open daily summer 11–5, winter 11–4*), the country's first ever permanent sculpture park, occupies the grounds of the 18th-century Bretton Hall Estate. The foliage makes an interesting setting for the sculptures. There are also two indoor galleries.

Much of West Yorkshire seems bent on a break with the past. The **National Coal Mining Museum for England** (*NCM, Caphouse Colliery, New Road, Overton, Wakefield (on A642 halfway between Wakefield and Huddersfield),* **t** *(01924) 848 806, www.ncm.org.uk; open 10–5; arrive at 10am to get a place on underground tour in school holidays*), however, exists to keep it alive. Here you can descend 460ft into one of the oldest working mines in Britain, guided by local miners, to learn about coal mining from the beginning of the 19th century to the present day (warm practical clothing and walking shoes are advised).

If you have seen enough grime for a lifetime by now, on the eastern edge of this great industrial area, beside the A1 north–south trunk road, and in the shadow of the cooling towers of Ferrybridge power station, is a place of peace, quiet and wildlife. **Fairburn Ings** (**t** *(01977) 603 796, www.rspb.org.uk*) near Castleford is managed by the Royal Society for the Protection of Birds. The brilliant blue flashes of kingfishers are often seen here.

South Yorkshire

South Yorkshire is dominated by four urban centres, **Sheffield**, **Rotherham**, **Barnsley** and **Doncaster**, which owe their character to the reason for their existence: the underlying coalfield and the steel industry. These places have a post-industrial appeal if you are interested in them as the working cities that they are. In the gaps left between mines and factories there is the odd glimpse of countryside and there are a couple of historic monuments worth visiting, notably **Roche Abbey**.

Above all, the interest of South Yorkshire lies in the imaginative projects that have been dreamt up to regenerate communities whose main sources of employment are in decline. Some of these contrived tourist attractions work, others don't. The fate of Sheffield's National Centre for Popular Music, brought to life with big ideas, even bigger ambitions and buckets of public money, but which closed for lack of visitors after little more than a year, is a cautionary tale whose message has not been lost. If you see only one place in South Yorkshire, make it **Magna**, the Cinderella of steel-works, which has somehow found the right formula to exploit the region's recent past for a sophisticated, technophile modern audience.

Sheffield

Sheffield has always been steel. The first cutlers set up shop here in the Middle Ages and the Miller in Chaucer's *Canterbury Tales* (*c*.1387) carries 'a Sheffield thwytel' or case-knife in his hose. The steel industry took off during the Industrial Revolution because of a local abundance of iron ore, oak wood (to make charcoal) and water-power, and Sheffield grew into the world's steel centre. Thomas Boulsover invented Sheffield Plate, a process whereby cheap metal could be coated with a layer of silver, and Harry Brearley revolutionized the cutlery business with his invention of stainless steel, first used commercially in 1913. Sheffield still produces steel, but these days it's in modern factories that produce more with less pollution and less manpower.

The consolidation of the British steel industry that began in the 1960s and is still going on has left Sheffield looking for a new identity. Hopes for the National Centre for Popular Music were dashed by its closure 15 months after opening. Meanwhile Sheffield gained renown in another medium, as the location for *The Full Monty*, a runaway success of a film about unemployed steelworkers becoming male strippers.

The modern city centre is an uncomfortable marriage between the old and the new, centred around a large grimy late-Victorian town hall. It prides itself on its cultural and sports facilities and its universities, but has few sights to tempt tourists. The

Getting There and Around

Domestic and some charter flights fly in and out of **Sheffield City Airport**, **t** (0114) 201 1998, *www.sheffieldcityairport.com*.

The **Hope Valley railway line** runs from Sheffield to New Mills and Manchester via scenic Edale. There are also trains to Leeds, York and Manchester. Enquiries about local **buses** and **trams (Supertrams)** and long-distance coaches can be made at **Sheffield Interchange**. Otherwise call **t** (01709) 515 151. National Express **coaches** go to London. There are also buses into the Peak District.

For local **bicycle** route advice in this hilly town go to *www.pedalpushers.org.uk*.

Tourist Information

Sheffield: 1 Tudor Square, **t** (0114) 221 1900, *www.sheffieldcity.co.uk*.

Where to Stay

Sheffield t (0114) –

Cutlers, George Street, **t** 273 9939, *www.cutlershotel.co.uk* (*expensive*). Centrally located 'boutique' hotel popular with theatrical types, comedians, snooker stars and other visiting entertainers.

Bristol, Blonk Street, **t** 220 4000, *www.hotel-bristol.co.uk* (*expensive*), Modern hotel with individually styled rooms, each with its own video player.

Quarry House, Rivelin Glen Quarry, Rivelin Valley Road, **t** 234 0382, *www.quarryhouse.org.uk* (*moderate*). The former quarry master's house at Rivelin Glen Quarry, a traditional stonemasonry business in a wooded valley 10 minutes by car from the city centre. Rates include not only breakfast but laundry too. Evening meal available: home-cooking using local organic produce with excellent vegetarian options.

Eating Out

Nonna, 539–41 Ecclesall Road, **t** 268 6166. Italian restaurant offering plenty of choice for vegetarians.

UK Mama, 275 Fulwood Road, **t** 268 7807 (*moderate*). Yorkshire's first African restaurant, still one of few and generally considered the best.

newest attraction is the **Winter Gardens**, just off the main square, a temperate plant house composed of wooden and glass neo-Gothic arches.

The **Millennium Galleries** (*Arundel Gate,* ***t*** *(0114) 278 2600, www.sheffieldgalleries.org.uk or www.millenniumgalleries.co.uk; open Mon–Sat 10–5, Sun 11–5*) is well designed, with four interesting galleries (one for temporary exhibitions). The best of the four is the Ruskin Gallery, 'about the way we look at things; about patterns of nature'. It holds a small part of an important collection of drawings, paintings, prints, minerals, manuscripts, books and plastercasts of architectural detail assembled by the writer, artist and critic John Ruskin (1819–1900). He has been described as 'the greatest Victorian bar Victoria'. In 1875 Ruskin's Guild of St George, an organization that he set up to promote his ideas about art and social justice, started a small museum for the artisans of Sheffield. As on every subject, Ruskin had a strong opinion on museums:

'In all museums intended for popular teaching, there are two great evils to be avoided. The first is superabundance; the second, disorder. The first is having too much of everything. You will find in your own work that the less you have to look at, the better you attend. You can no more see twenty things worth seeing in an hour, than you can read twenty books worth reading in a day. Give little, but that little good and beautiful, and explain it thoroughly.'

Ruskin hoped that his Sheffield museum would be the first of many in industrial centres around the country, but the others never materialized (*see* Coniston, p.767).

Outside the Ruskin Gallery, next to the bookshop, is a moving sculpture apposite to Sheffield. Called *Barking up the Right Tree*, it is made of knives, forks and spoons.

Around South Yorkshire

Rotherham and Magna

To the northeast, Sheffield blends into another steel town, Rotherham, whose only interest to the outsider used to be **Bridge Chapel** – until the inauguration of **Magna** (*Sheffield Road, Templeborough; to get there take junction 33 northbound or junction 34 southbound off the M1;* ***t*** *(01709) 720 002, www.magnatrust.org.uk; open Mar–Oct daily 10–5, Nov–Feb Mon 10–2; adm*). Ostensibly a 'science adventure centre' in the former Templeborough steelworks, its backdrop makes more of an impact than the techno toys. Phantasmagoric lighting partially illuminates parts of the immense shed which, at a third of a mile long, was once the largest electric steel melting shop in the world. Where the lights don't reach, the building is left in permanent penumbra. The understatement leaves room for the imagination. A walkway runs the length of the building, leading to an electric arc furnace which has lain dormant since it was last used in 1993. Here a show, *The Big Melt*, is put on at regular intervals to explain the process of steel-making. The interactive exhibits are arranged in four 'pavilions' built around the elements: earth is in the bowels of the steel shed, air is an airship on the fourth floor, fire a black box, and water a stainless-steel wave incorporating a wet play area. In the fire pavilion is one of only three fire tornado machines in the world. There is usually a queue to try operating a JCB digger in the earth pavilion.

Doncaster and the Earth Centre

Outside Doncaster is another regenerative project: a coal mine has been turned into an ecology park that hopes to teach the virtues of sustainable development and recycling. The **Earth Centre** (*t (01709) 513 933, www.earthcentre.org.uk; open daily 10–5; adm*) is a worthy idea. At times more like a glorified adventure playground, where it does fulfil its eco-education brief in entertaining ways it starts to get interesting: you can take off your shoes and hang out in a yurt, and build your own green food chain from algae, microbugs and sticklebacks, then recycle the whole lot. If you go to the toilet your waste goes into a Living Machine; you can see this machine, where a biofilter feeds a greenhouse of tropical plants without noxious chemicals.

Just down the road from the Earth Centre is **Conisborough Castle** (*t (01709) 863 329, www.conisboroughcastle.org.uk; open daily summer 10–5, winter 10–4; adm*), a circular castle keep that was the northern stronghold of the earls of Surrey until they left it to fall into ruins in the 1400s.

Roche Abbey

South Yorkshire doesn't have much virgin countryside although Sheffield abuts the Peak District of Derbyshire. But beyond the M1 from Sheffield and Rotherham the built-up area at last gives way to the rural and here is to be found one of Yorkshire's most pleasing monastic ruins, **Roche Abbey** (*Maltby, t (01709) 812 739, www.english-heritage.org.uk; open April–Sept daily 10–6, Oct 10–5; adm*). This Cistercian abbey was founded in 1147 and, although there is not much left of it, the land it stands in was handsomely landscaped in the 18th century by Capability Brown. After exploring the coal and steel towns, you can hear the birdsongs at last and smell the flowers.

The Renaissance of 'Barnsili'

The fourth city of South Yorkshire, Barnsley, does not have many charms to offer visitors – yet. But come back in a few years, by when it is hoped that Barnsley will have undergone a regenerative project to put all the others to shame. Plans to turn humble, flat-cap-and-fish-and-chips Barnsley into the Yorkshire equivalent of a Tuscan hill town were treated as a joke by the British press when announced in 2002 (on April Fool's Day). But the architects and town councillors who are promoting the idea are serious about their plans and believe that it will result not only in a better place to live but one which will attract economic development. Why not Barnsley? they argue: it has the hill; it has a higgledy-piggledy medieval street plan; and it even has a campanile in the shape of a 1930s tower rising above the Civic Hall. If the scheme goes ahead, the town centre will be encircled by a wall; derelict and under-used buildings will be swept away to be replaced by houses, workshops and restaurants in harmony with their surroundings; and there will be plenty of 'public realm' spaces provided for the hill-town dwellers. When you remember that in its industrial heyday the mill owners and burghers of West and South Yorkshire often drew on imported architectural styles for mills and public buildings, applying the idea to a whole town doesn't seem quite as odd.

Durham and Northumbria

20

Durham and Northumbria

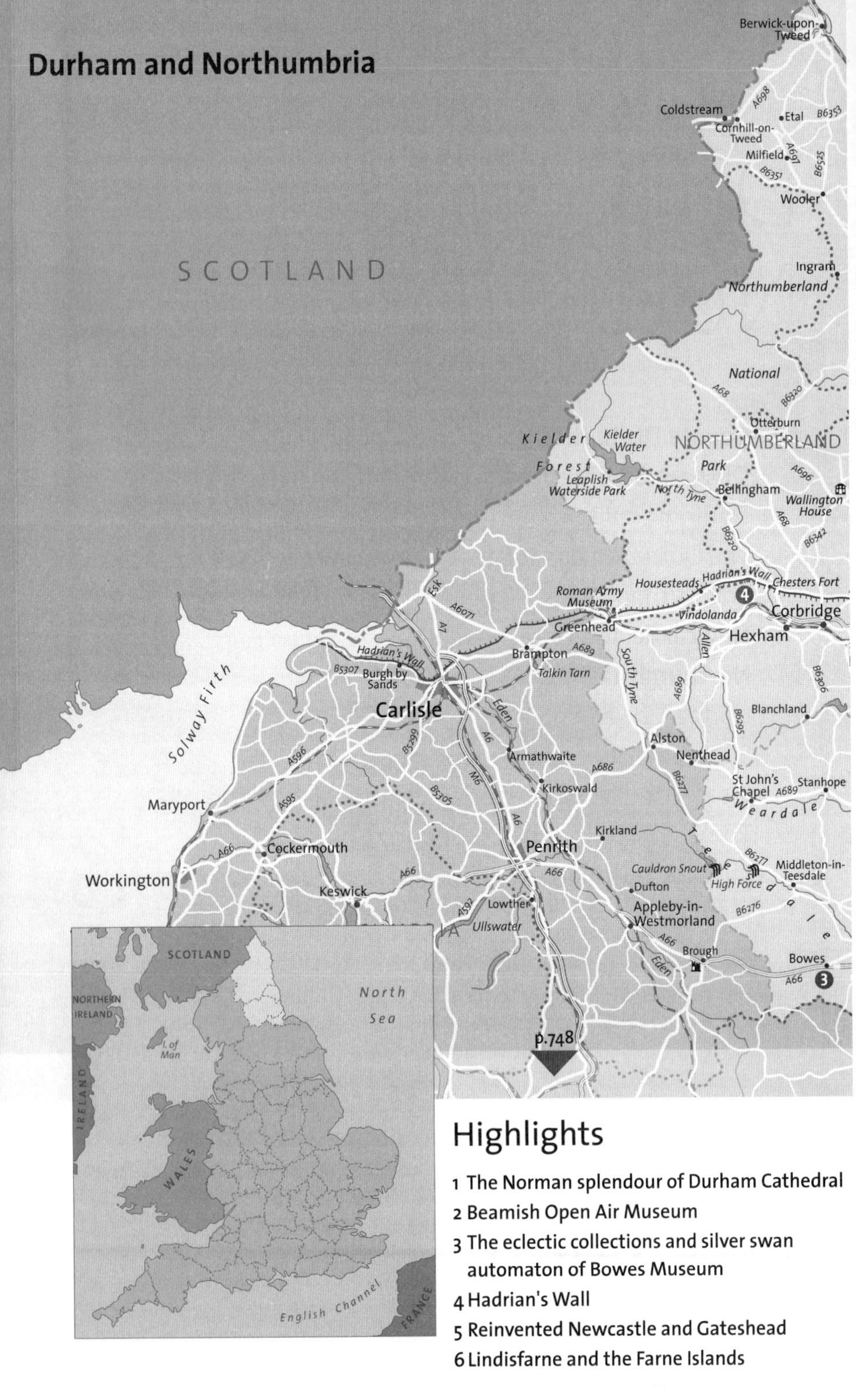

Highlights

1 The Norman splendour of Durham Cathedral
2 Beamish Open Air Museum
3 The eclectic collections and silver swan automaton of Bowes Museum
4 Hadrian's Wall
5 Reinvented Newcastle and Gateshead
6 Lindisfarne and the Farne Islands

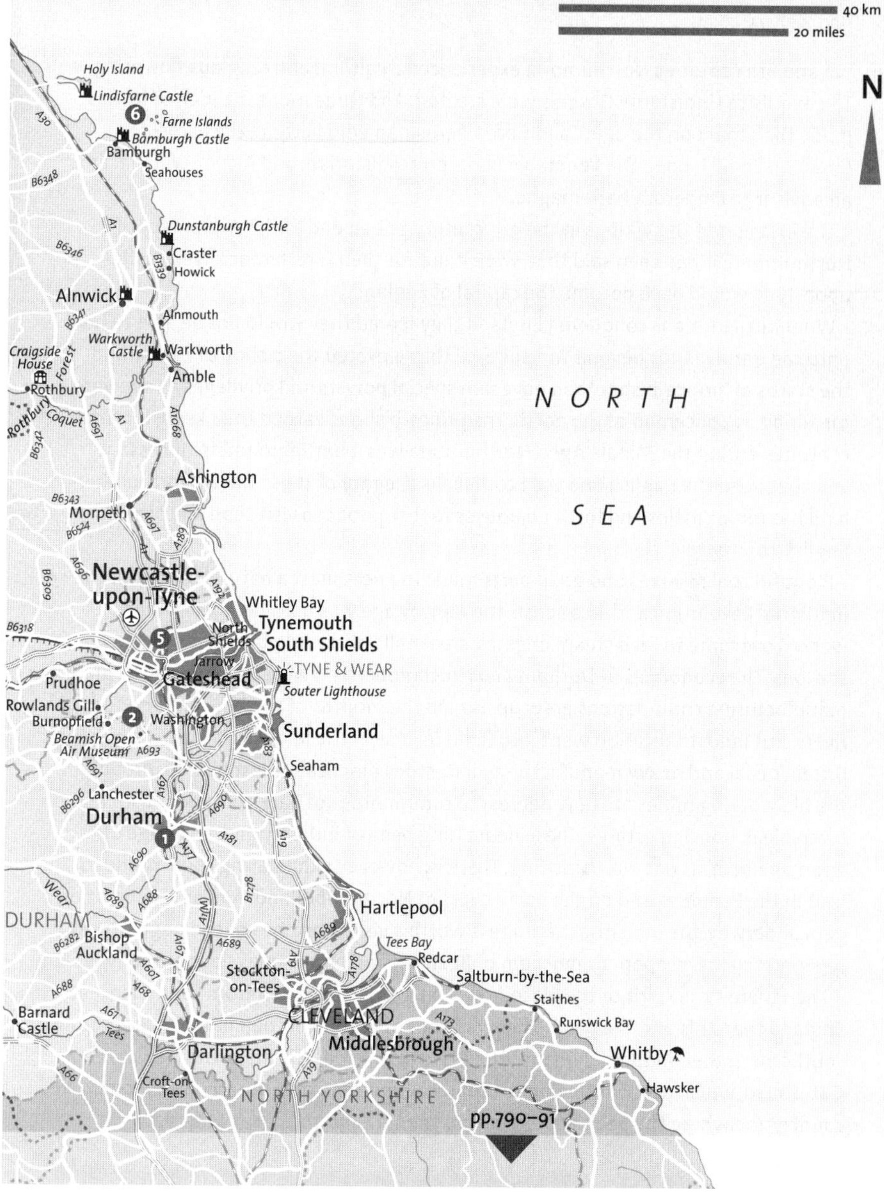

The Scottish would disagree, but to historians the counties of Durham and Northumberland once marked the edge of the civilized world. Why else would Emperor Hadrian have built his famous wall across the north of England, a northern frontier to the Roman Empire, beyond which there was nothing worth conquering?

Two hundred years after the Roman legions pulled out – leaving the stone of the wall for locals to plunder – the Anglo-Saxon Kingdom of Northumbria arose to guard the edge of Christendom. At its height, this kingdom stretched from the River Forth in Scotland to the River Humber; its influence, however, reached much further. In the

7th and 8th centuries Northumbria experienced a cultural and religious flowering. The exquisite Lindisfarne Gospels were created. And three monastic men of letters made their mark on the age: Caedmon, a herdsman who became the earliest Christian English poet; the Venerable Bede, proto-historian; and Alcuin, who became an advisor to Emperor Charlemagne.

The invasion of the Vikings in the 9th century put an end to the supremacy of Northumbria; it has been said that, were it not for their interference, Newcastle-upon-Tyne would have become the capital of England.

When the Normans conquered England they feared they would not be able to hold onto the unruly lands beyond Yorkshire, so they elevated the bishop of Durham to the status of 'prince-bishop' and gave him special powers and privileges as a reward for acting as policeman of the north. The prince-bishops earned their keep: for three centuries during the Middle Ages, Northumbria was a battleground for incessant wars between the English and the Scottish. As a legacy of these times, Northumberland has more castles and fortified houses for the public to visit than any other English county.

Plentiful coal reserves and good ports made the northeast a natural centre for the Industrial Revolution and, in a sense, the railway age was born here. Coal mines worked overtime to feed steam engines, steel mills, shipyards, factories and power stations. The economies of Durham and Northumberland were transformed as great manufacturing conurbations grew up around the mouths of the Tyne and the Tees rivers. But industrialization went into rapid reverse in the late 20th century, when Britain's coal and heavy manufacturing industries practically disappeared. Around the old working mines are now depressed communities of back-to-back houses and often bleak housing estates. These depressing belts of industry give an image of 'grim up north' as not worth visiting. There is, however, exhilarating countryside to visit in the Pennines and on the north coast of Northumberland. And as regeneration gets underway, the industrial heritage is worth a visit too; it has been imaginatively regenerated in the open-air museum of Beamish and on the quaysides of the Tyne.

Then there's the spirit of the place. You can't get further away from London in England than this and the people know it. They are proud of their independence from southerners, their industrial history, their two main cities (Durham and Newcastle Gateshead, which could not be more different from each other), and of their big, wild countryside where the people are terse but friendly and the pace of life slow.

County Durham

The city of Durham is the emblem of its county, with the cathedral and castle of the Prince Bishops standing proudly over it. But beyond the old city lie a bleak stretch of coast, Dales dotted with stately old piles and some interesting industrial relics. Durham was the inspiration for Lewis Carroll's 'Jabberwocky' and, more gloomily, Charles Dickens' Dotheboys Hall (*Nicholas Nickleby*).

Durham

I paused upon the bridge, and admired and wondered at the beauty and glory of this scene... it was grand, venerable, and sweet, all at once; I never saw so lovely and magnificent a scene, nor (being content with this) do I care to see a better.

Nathaniel Hawthorne

Durham's fame rests squarely on the architecture of its great Norman cathedral, but the whole city is the cultural oasis of the north, its grandeur heightened by its location between the industrial conurbations of Teesside and Tyneside. With mines and mills never far away, it's a hard-working town without pretensions. Arguably the third most important university city in Britain, it also has a top-security Victorian prison (which has held its share of mass murderers) a stone's throw from the city centre.

Getting There and Around

Durham is roughly equidistant between Newcastle and Teesside **airports**.

By **car** it's around 5 hours' drive up the M1 from London.

Coaches from London Victoria take roughly the same time. For coach travel information contact **National Express**, **t** 08705 808080 *www.gobycoach.com*.

The city is on the London–Edinburgh east coast mainline **railway**. For all train travel information contact **National Rail Enquiries**, **t** 08457 484950, *www.thetrainline.com*.

Tourist Information

www.visitnorthumbria.com, *www.holidaynorthumbria.com*.

Durham: Millennium Place, **t** (0191) 384 3720, *www.durhamcity.gov.uk*

Darlington: 13 Horsemarket, **t** (01325) 388 666, *www.visitdarlington.net*.

Where to Stay

Durham t (0191) –

University of Durham colleges (*cheap*). Student rooms, some en-suite, are let out to visitors during the holidays (*July–Sept*). Book through the tourist information centre, colleges or the university's tourism office, **t** 374 7360, *www.dur.ac.uk/conference-tourism*. Choice among halls of residence is **University College**, in the castle, **t** 374 3863.

Durham Marriott Hotel Royal County, Old Elvet, **t** 386 6821, *www.marriotthotels.com* (*very expensive*). A plush hotel near the cathedral and castle, with two restaurants: the **Bowes** is more relaxed while the **County** is formal. Hotel facilities include swimming pool, sauna and gym. Good views of Durham's annual Miners' Gala (in July) from the windows.

Three Tuns Hotel, New Elvet, **t** 386 4326, *www.swallowhotels.com* (*expensive*). Sixteenth-century coaching inn across the river from the castle and cathedral with original beams, panelling and other decorative features.

Eating Out

Bistro 21, Aykley Heads House, Aykley Heads, **t** 384 4354 (*moderate*). Restaurant in a renovated 17th-century building. One of a small local chain.

Brocks, off Silver Street (*cheap*). The oldest tea rooms in Durham, which serve a range of light food.

Pubs

Shakespeare, 63 Saddler Street, **t** 386 9709. Old, narrow pub serving real ale, in the street leading up to the cathedral.

Victoria, 86 Hallgarth Street, **t** 386 5269. Historic Durham pub with a great atmosphere and plenty of beers to choose from. Guest bedrooms upstairs.

Court Inn, Court Lane, **t** 384 7350. Near the prison. Bar meals served.

The old part of Durham stands on high ground within a tight loop of the River Wear, a peninsula which is almost a *presqu'île*. The famous cathedral and adjacent castle look down on the city from on high, the twin paternalistic powers, spiritual and temporal, which were historically combined in the hands of the prince bishops. The market place and town are below, and four bridges lead off the peninsula to more modern streets, houses and shopping centres.

Durham Cathedral

t (0191) 386 4266, www.durhamcathedral.co.uk; open mid-June–early Sept daily 9.30–8; rest of year Mon-Sat 7.30–6.15, Sun 7.45–5. Tower open early April–late Sept Mon–Sat 9.30–4; rest of year Mon–Sat 10–3. Access may be restricted by church services; donation requested.

Most people take the shortest route from town to castle and cathedral, Saddler Street, but a more quiet and pleasant route is to walk along the wooded riverbank to pedestrian Prebends Bridge, which leads you gently on to the peninsula. However you get there, the cathedral has to be your first stop in Durham. It is widely considered to be the most perfect surviving example of Norman architecture (British Romanesque). It was built in the 11th and 12th centuries to house the itinerant, uncorrupted remains

The Prince Bishops of Durham

After his subjugation of southern Britain, William the Conqueror realized that the north would not be as easy to bring and keep under his sway. If his authority ever faltered, rebellious Anglo-Saxons or invading Scots would soon fill the power gap. So he appointed Bishop Walcher of Durham (1071–81) as Earl Bishop of Northumbria, concentrating spiritual and secular power in a single pair of semi-autonomous hands. Walcher was killed by a mob in Gateshead in 1081 but the king stuck to his policy and Bishop Carileph (1081–96) became Prince Bishop with vice-regal powers over the Palatinate of Durham, which covered Durham and parts of present-day Northumberland. A steward working for a later prince bishop, Bishop Bek (1284–1310) proudly boasted of his master: 'There are two kings in England namely the Lord King of England wearing a crown in sign of his regality and the Lord Bishop of Durham wearing a mitre in place of a crown in sign of his regality in the diocese of Durham.'

Within their dominion, the prince bishops of Durham enjoyed similar powers to those of the king. They had their own parliament – Durham did not have to send representatives to London – and law courts; they could impose taxes and mint coins; they could grant charters for fairs and markets; they had the 'right of wreck' for whales and ships washed up on their shores; they could create barons and grant permission to crenellate castles; and they even had the authority to negotiate with the kings of Scotland and, if necessary, raise armies to fight wars.

The last of the prince bishops, Bishop Van Mildert (1826–36) was active in founding the University of Durham in 1832 and handed over his palace, Durham Castle, to be the home of the new institution. Only on the death of Van Mildert did the secular powers of the Bishops of Durham finally revert to the monarch.

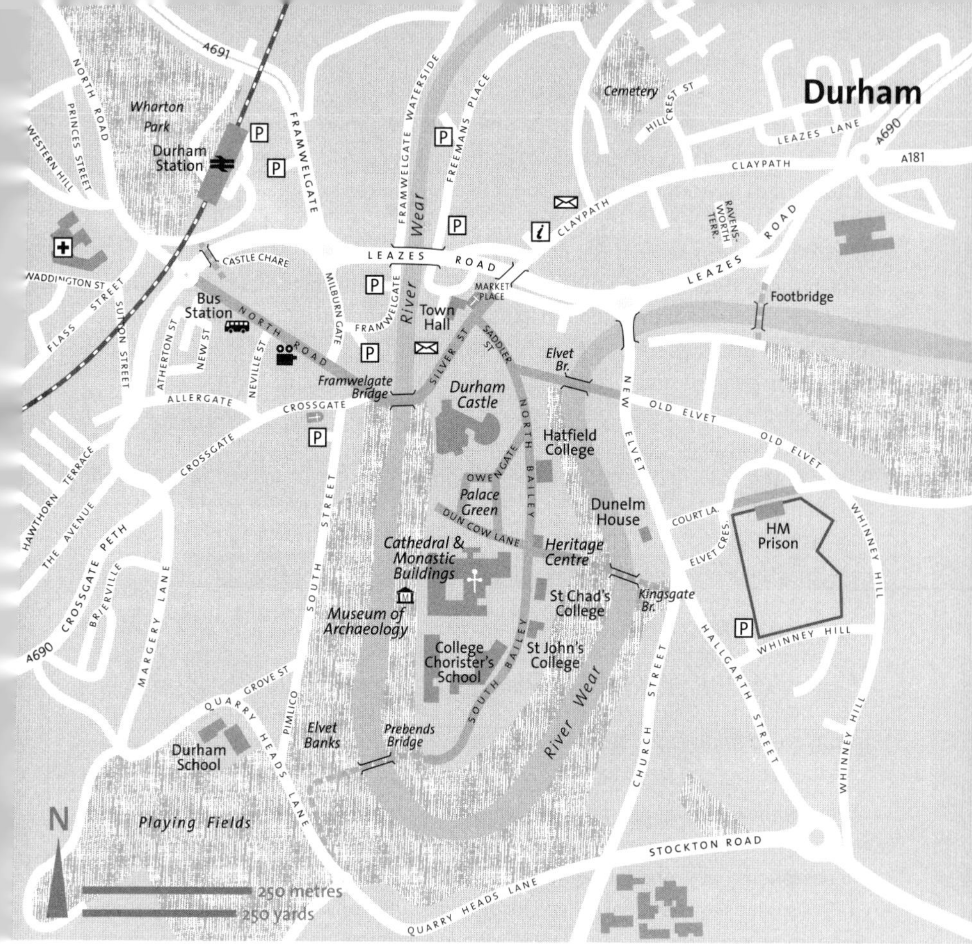

of St Cuthbert, patron of Northumberland. He had been buried on the holy islands of Lindisfarne, but when the isles were overrun by the Vikings the monks removed his body and moved it around with them for almost a century – until the new cathedral was built on a scale fitting to serve as a mausoleum.

St Cuthbert was one of the most famous saints of medieval England and his shrine one of the country's most visited places – long before St Thomas of Canterbury had earned his sainthood. From time to time in the Middle Ages, St Cuthbert's body was examined and found to be still incorrupt, but by 1899, when the shrine was opened for the last time, he was mere bones. The coffin in which he lay, his pectoral cross and some embroidered stoles were removed and are on display inside the building.

You enter the cathedral by the northwest door from Palace Green. On this door is a replica of the **sanctuary knocker** (the original is on display inside) which an accused criminal could use to summon the watchman. The church would grant the fugitive sanctuary for 37 days at its expense; in return he had to confess the details of his crime and was obliged to wear a black robe marked with a yellow cross on the shoulder. When the 37 days were up, the fugitive had to choose between standing trial or leaving the country by the nearest port, Hartlepool. Failure to comply with this rule was punished with execution by the civil authorities.

This door takes you into the **nave**. Down its sides two rows of stout columns march towards the altar. Every other one is cylindrical and decorated with bold geometric patterns; the chevrons show a Moorish influence and the lozenge shapes derive from prehistoric stone carvings. The roof is supported by stone ribbed vaulting; this was the first building in which this innovative technique was successfully applied.

The **bishop's throne**, facing the high altar, is said to be the highest in Christendom. Also at the east end of the church, behind the high altar in the **Chapel of the Nine Altars**, is St Cuthbert's shrine. Beside him is buried the head of St Oswald (604–42), King of Northumbria and martyr, 'slain in battle by the heathen whom he so long defied'. He aimed to evangelize the whole of Britain but was killed in battle against Penda of Mercia, who championed paganism. In this chapel is also the tomb of Bishop Anthony Bek (1284–1310), one of the prince bishops, King of the Isle of Man and Patriarch of Jerusalem, and the first person after St Cuthbert buried in the cathedral.

At the far end of the nave is the **Galilee Chapel**, housing the tomb of the Venerable Bede, the 8th-century monk who wrote the first history of England.

The Castle

***t** (0191) 374 3863, www.durhamcastle.com; guided tours 2–17 Jan daily 10–12 and 2–4; 20 Jan–21 Mar Mon, Wed, Sat and Sun 2–4; 24 Mar–25 April daily 10–12 and 2–4; 28 April–27 June daily 2–4; 5 July–3 Oct daily 10–12 and 2–4; 6 Oct–20 Dec Mon, Wed, Sat and Sun 2–4; adm*

William the Conqueror first ordered the construction of a fortification on this site, across Palace Green from the cathedral. The castle became the seat of the powerful prince bishops but in the 19th century was handed over to the University of Durham, which uses it as a residential college for students and dons. The tour takes you to the dining room, still-functioning Jacobean kitchens, and the tall Black Staircase ,which is supposed to be haunted by the ghosts of a woman, the Grey Lady, and a monk.

The Oriental Museum and Crook Hall

The city's best museum is the **Oriental Museum** (*Elvet Hill, off South Road, **t** (0191) 374 7911, www.dur.ac.uk/oriental.museum; open Mon–Fri 10–5, weekends 12–5; adm*), one of only two specialized collections of oriental art and antiquities in England. The other main sight is **Crook Hall** (*Sidegate, **t** (0191) 384 8028, www.crookhallgardens.co.uk; open Easter, 4, 5, 25 and 26 May–3 Aug, 26 Oct Sun–Fri 1-5; adm*), a medieval manor house on the banks of the river, surrounded by gardens that include a maze, orchard and wildflower meadow. The house's Jacobean Room is supposed to be haunted by the White Lady (no relation of the castle's Grey Lady).

Darlington

Darlington, in the south of County Durham, has been a railway town since the world's first steam-powered public railway ran along the line built by engineer George Stephenson between Darlington and Stockton-on-Tees in 1825. North Road station is now the **Darlington Railway Centre and Museum** (*t (01325) 460 532; open daily 10–5; adm*). The ticket includes admission to Darlington Locomotive Works, where the first mainline steam locomotive to be built in Britain since 1960 is taking shape. If you're whizzing past, you can get a glimpse of the town's railwayphilia in the life-size brick sculpture of a steam engine by David Mach, beside the A66.

The author of *Alice in Wonderland*, Lewis Carroll, came to live in **Croft-on-Tees**, outside Darlington, aged 11, when his father was made rector of the church. His grinning Cheshire cat is said to have been inspired by a carving on the sedilia (seat for the clergy) in **St Peter's Church**. Another unusual carving in the church, next to the main door, is of a Sheela Na Gig, an erotic female figure found in Norman churches although no one knows why. Carroll began writing his sublimely nonsense poem, 'Jabberwocky', while in Croft, and a local historian has suggested that it was inspired by the local legend of the Sockburn Worm, a dragon killed by Sir John Conyers.

The Durham Coast

Upon this dreary coast, we have nothing but county meetings and shipwrecks.

Lord Byron

The Durham coast between the two conurbations of Newcastle Gateshead and Middlesborough was, until recently, a chill, polluted strip of shore. Its sober lack of charm can be seen in the last scene of the cult 1971 film *Get Carter*, in which the eponymous anti-hero (Michael Caine) takes brutal revenge on a fellow gangster on top of a conveyor belt drearily tipping mining waste into the sea. There never was much cheer here: the poor used to scavenge for coal by hand on the 'black sands' and drowned seamen were dragged from shipwrecks on Deadman's Bank. But the Turning the Tide project has been cleaning up this bleak coast since 1993 and you can now walk the 11-mile **Durham Coastal Footpath** from Trimdon (north of Hartlepool) to Seaham (outside Sunderland). It is still a deprived area and not an obvious tourist attraction but may appeal if you want to see another side of England.

Sunderland, the largest place on the coast, is an industrial town busy reinventing itself, partly by celebrating one of its traditional industries, glass-making. In 680, the abbot of the monastery at Monkwearmouth, on the north bank of the River Wear, invited French craftsmen to make stained glass for his church. This was the first time stained glass was manufactured in Britain, although little of it survives. **St Peter's Church**, rebuilt in the late 19th century, incorporates part of the old abbey. The **National Glass Centre** (*open daily 10–5; Liberty Way,* ***t*** *(0191) 515 5555, www.nationalglasscentre.com*) tells the story of glass and the technology of modern glassmaking.

The Durham Dales

Inland County Durham is a world away from the industrial cities near the coast. Two dales, **Teesdale** and **Weardale**, steer their way into the high Pennines. Of them, the former is the most attractive, but you can drive up one and down the other, linking the two across the moors and even continuing to Hadrian's Wall.

Barnard Castle

The entry point for Teesdale is the well-to-do market town of Barnard Castle. There is not much to do in the town centre except visit the **castle** (***t*** *(01833) 638 212; open April–Sept daily 10–1 and 2–6, Oct daily 10–1 and 2–5, Nov–Mar Wed–Sun 10–1 and 2–4; adm*) and take a stroll up the main street. This is interrupted by a structure officially called the Market Cross but universally referred to as the Butter Market, because on market day farmers' wives would set up their dairy stalls here. Down the road from the Butter Market (on the left) is an ancient house housing **Blagraves** restaurant, which has four carved stone figures on its façade, three of them playing musical instruments. Oliver Cromwell was entertained in this house (then an inn) in 1648. There is rumoured to be a secret tunnel from the house to the castle.

The Bowes Museum

t *(01833) 690 606, www.bowesmuseum.org.uk; open daily 11–5; adm.*

All else in Barnard Castle bows to the extraordinary Bowes Museum. Looking like some great French rationalist institution erroneously erected in a backwater of Britain, the Bowes is a place to restore your belief in philanthropy (after Dotheboys Hall). Take time to watch the video on its origins before you explore the collections.

John Bowes was born illegitimately into an established mine-owning family and, despite being Eton and Cambridge educated, he was never accepted into aristocratic

Dickens in County Durham

In 1838 Charles Dickens came to Barnard Castle accompanied by the illustrator, Hablot Knight Browne (Phiz), to research his third novel, *Nicholas Nickleby*. He found what he was looking for in the neighbouring village of Bowes: **Shaw's Academy**, which he used as a model for Dotheboys Hall, to draw attention to the degrading nature of the north of England's boarding schools. Such schools routinely neglected and ill-treated their charges in return for 20 guineas a year from ignorant or unfeeling parents. Children were kept on a starvation diet, poorly clothed and subjected to various cruel punishments; there were no holidays and no visits home, so they couldn't complain to their parents even if they would listen.

William Shaw, the owner of the school, had been prosecuted five years before Dickens' visit for allowing two of his pupils to go blind because of beatings and poor nutrition. Even after the prosecution – when things had supposedly improved – an average of one pupil a year died at the school. Dickens condemned the perpetrators of such education as: 'Traders in the avarice, indifference, or imbecility of parents, and the helplessness of children; ignorant, sordid, brutal men, to whom few considerate persons would have entrusted the board and lodging of a horse or a dog; they formed the worthy cornerstone of a structure, which, for absurdity and a magnificent high-minded *laissez-aller* neglect, has rarely been exceeded in the world.'

Tourist Information

Tees Valley: *www.visitteesvalley.co.uk.*
Barnard Castle: 'Woodleigh', Flatts Road, **t** (01833) 690 909, *www.barnard-castle.com.*
Middleton-in-Teesdale: 10 Market Place, **t** (01833) 641 001.
Stanhope, Durham Dales Centre, Castle Gardens, **t** (01388) 527 650.

Where to Stay and Eat

Barnard Castle t (01833) –

Jersey Farm Hotel, Darlington Road, **t** 638 223, *www.jerseyfarm.co.uk* (*expensive*). The only hotel of any size in Barnard Castle, a town well served by its B&Bs (ask at the tourist information office for a full list).
The Old Well Inn, Bank, **t** 690 130, *www.oldwellinn.co.uk* (*expensive*). Celebrated small hotel with comfortable rooms, a restaurant and two bars.
Spring Lodge, Newgate, **t** 638 110 (*moderate*). An elegant B&B in a prettily decorated house, which echoes to the sounds of children and dogs. Spacious bedrooms with fine white duvet covers. All guests eat a splendid home-made breakfast together. Private parking. Both the main street and the Bowes Museum are within an easy stroll.
Marwood House, 98 Galgate, **t** 637 493, *www.kilgarriff.demon.co.uk* (*moderate*). Victorian terraced house set back from the road to Bishop Auckland.
Blagraves House, Bank, **t** 637 668 (*moderate*). The best restaurant in Barnard Castle, in a historic house with low ceilings and open fires. Surprisingly reasonable.
Valentines, 11 Galgate, **t** 637 146 (*moderate*). A restaurant with a light Mediterranean feel. Dishes well-presented, including some vegetarian options.

Around Teesdale

The Rose and Crown, Romaldkirk, **t** (01833) 650 213, *www.rose-and-crown.co.uk* (*expensive*). A coaching inn built on the village green in 1733 which retains much of its original character, including an oak-panelled restaurant and an enormous fireplace to keep off the winter chill.
Headlam Hall, Gainford, **t** (01325) 730 238, *www.headlamhall.co.uk* (*expensive*). A Jacobean mansion standing in a large walled garden and its own farmland.
The Teesdale Hotel, Market Square, Middleton-in-Teesdale, **t** (01833) 640 264, *www.teesdalehotel.com* (*moderate*). Decent place to stay or to eat. The excellent bar menu includes a vegetable gratin and venison sausages.

circles. This snub by the snobs drove him to an unconventional but successful career. Having bought himself a Paris theatre, he fell in love with and married an actress, Josephine. The couple were unable to have children; instead Josephine conceived the idea of pouring their love into a public museum. Tragically, both the Bowes died before the museum opened. Their portraits hang in the first-floor gallery.

So well designed for its purpose is the building that you sometimes don't notice it, but the windows were purposely made large to let the light in and even the radiators are beautiful. The collection is nothing if not eclectic. It concentrates on European art, with a slight bias towards France. Paintings include works by Canaletto, El Greco, Boudin and Turner. Josephine herself was a brilliant painter, influenced by Courbet, and many of her landscapes hang in the museum, although without the emphasis they deserve. There is a costume gallery, much expanded since the Bowes' death. There is an example of every type of thing of beauty: altarpieces, 15th-century alabaster reliefs, pottery and porcelain, harps, cabinets, a sedan chair and a Japanese palanquin, clocks, cutlery, tapestries, glass, a gilt bronze mask of a river god from France, Tarot cards, sugar sculptures (made with carved moulds) and even a series of rooms assembled and furnished in the style of different periods of English history.

The most famous exhibit is a **silver swan automaton**, which has a swivelling neck and appears to catch a fish. For the perplexed, a sign on the case explains: 'Please note that real swans do not eat fish. This is the only fish-eating swan in the world.' The swan plays daily at 12.30 and 3.30; try to fit your visit around these times.

Teesdale and Weardale

From Barnard Castle the B6277 ascends Teesdale, passing through the pretty villages of **Cotherstone** and **Romaldkirk**. **Middleton-in-Teesdale** is a larger place: chosen as the northern HQ of the London Lead Company, it enjoyed an economic boom in the early 19th century which left it with a handful of handsome buildings. After Middleton, Pennine scenery sets in and moors start to appear above you.

In the midst of gentle-looking woods are some of the most impressive waterfalls in northern England, **High Force** (*Forest-in-Teesdale,* ***t*** *(01833) 640 209, www.rabycastle.com; open all year, supervised mid-April–Oct daily 10–5; adm minimal*). There is a lovely walk through the woods alongside the tea-coloured foaming River Tees to a viewing balcony from which you can see the broad torrent of white water falling into a round basin of rock. When the river is in spate there are two waterfalls. The path continues to the top of the waterfall, where you can clamber on the rocks.

Beyond High Force you come out onto the moors proper. There is another good waterfall, **Cauldron Snout**, at the end of Cow Green Reservoir (an easy 3-mile walk). Much of this upland area is protected as the Moor House–Upper Teesdale National Nature Reserve, stretching to the highest point in the Pennines, **Cross Fell** (2,930 feet).

You can extend the tour by carrying straight on into the Pennines to Alston, before doubling back along **Weardale**, but if you don't want to go any further, from Langdon Beck you can cut across the bleak moorland road to **St John's Chapel**.

The only town worth a pause in Weardale is **Stanhope**. Here, on the edge of the churchyard, is a tree stump fossilized 250 million years ago. If you are heading back to Barnard Castle to complete the tour, make a detour to the outskirts of Bishop Auckland to see **Escomb Church** (***t*** *(01388) 662 265; open daily 9–4, until 8 in summer*), one of the best of the few remaining Saxon churches in Britain.

Beamish, The North of England Open Air Museum

t *(0191) 370 4000, www.beamish.org.uk; open 2 Jan–4 April and 27 Oct–2 April, weekends and Tues–Thurs, 10–4; 5 April–26 Oct daily 10–5; town and tramway only open in winter; adm.*

North of Durham City, Beamish is one of a rash of 'living museums' that have opened around Britain in the last thirty years, with the aim of bringing history alive, especially popular social history. Established in 1970, Beamish is one that has the perfect balance of entertainment and education. It's a family attraction, but with plenty to stimulate adults too. It's worth a full day's visit in good weather.

The focus of Beamish is the recent past and everyday life in the northeast of England. More particularly, it recreates the atmosphere of two precise dates: 1825 (when the area was still rural and sparsely populated) and 1913 (the height of the industrial age). Costumed people take the place of glass cases, labels and hi-tech virtual-reality gizmos.

The museum is laid out around a circular tramway in the middle of the Durham countryside. The tram is the easiest to get around, but you can also walk between the four principal stops or take an old-fashioned bus which follows the same circuit.

The core of Beamish is an assembly of old buildings, mostly salvaged from elsewhere, reconstructed here and brought back to life. A few of the buildings you see were already on the site, however, including **Pockerley Manor**, the first stop on the tram going clockwise round the loop. Next to this yeoman's farmstead is a short rail track, **Pockerley Waggonway** (1825), along which an open carriage is hauled achingly slowly by an early locomotive, the Steam Elephant. The grimy, sweating engineers are proof that the olden days were hard work, and recreating them almost equally so.

Most of the activity is around the next tram stop, **Beamish Town**, the highlight of the visit. This glimpse of well-to-do urban Britain, frozen in time the year before the First World War broke out, appears idyllic. The single street has everything you could need on it; you are free to wander in and out of each building as if you were an invisible time traveller. There is a bank, solicitor's office, music teacher's house, garage, newspaper office with a print shop upstairs (note the highly ornamented Victorian press), cooperative hardware and draper's shop, and a grocer's. The counter of the confectionery shop is obscured by a permanent scrum of children buying old-fashioned sweets made in the adjacent factory. The Sun Inn is a period pub and museum exhibit which still functions as a pub (selling beer at 2003 prices). At one end of the street is a park with a bandstand and, just outside the mini urban area, a railway station – although the lines don't go anywhere. The last two stops on the tram route are at **Home Farm**, a working farm with traditional livestock breeds, and the **Colliery Village** (1913), which has a pithead and drift mine.

Not far from Beamish is **Causey Arch**, a wonder of pre-industrial engineering. The oldest surviving railway bridge in the world, it was built in 1725–6 to carry coal along a wagonway which crosses a small wooded gorge.

Newcastle and Gateshead

Newcastle (to the north, largely well-to-do) and Gateshead (to the south, more down-at-heel) once looked at each other from their respective banks of the Tyne as two cities sharing nothing more than the five bridges between them. But in this era of rebranded cities, they would now like us to think of them as one city – the reborn Newcastle-Gateshead conurbation. Hard-nosed no-nonsense commerce and industry built both, but Newcastle-Gateshead wants to be something else: a city of art in which even new bridges – there are now seven of them – make creative statements.

Time was when Geordie creativity went into useful inventions: Joseph Swan of Gateshead – not Edison – invented the light bulb in 1878, and thanks to him Mosley Street was the first street in the world to be illuminated by electricity. George Stephenson's Rocket, the world's first successful steam locomotive, was built in

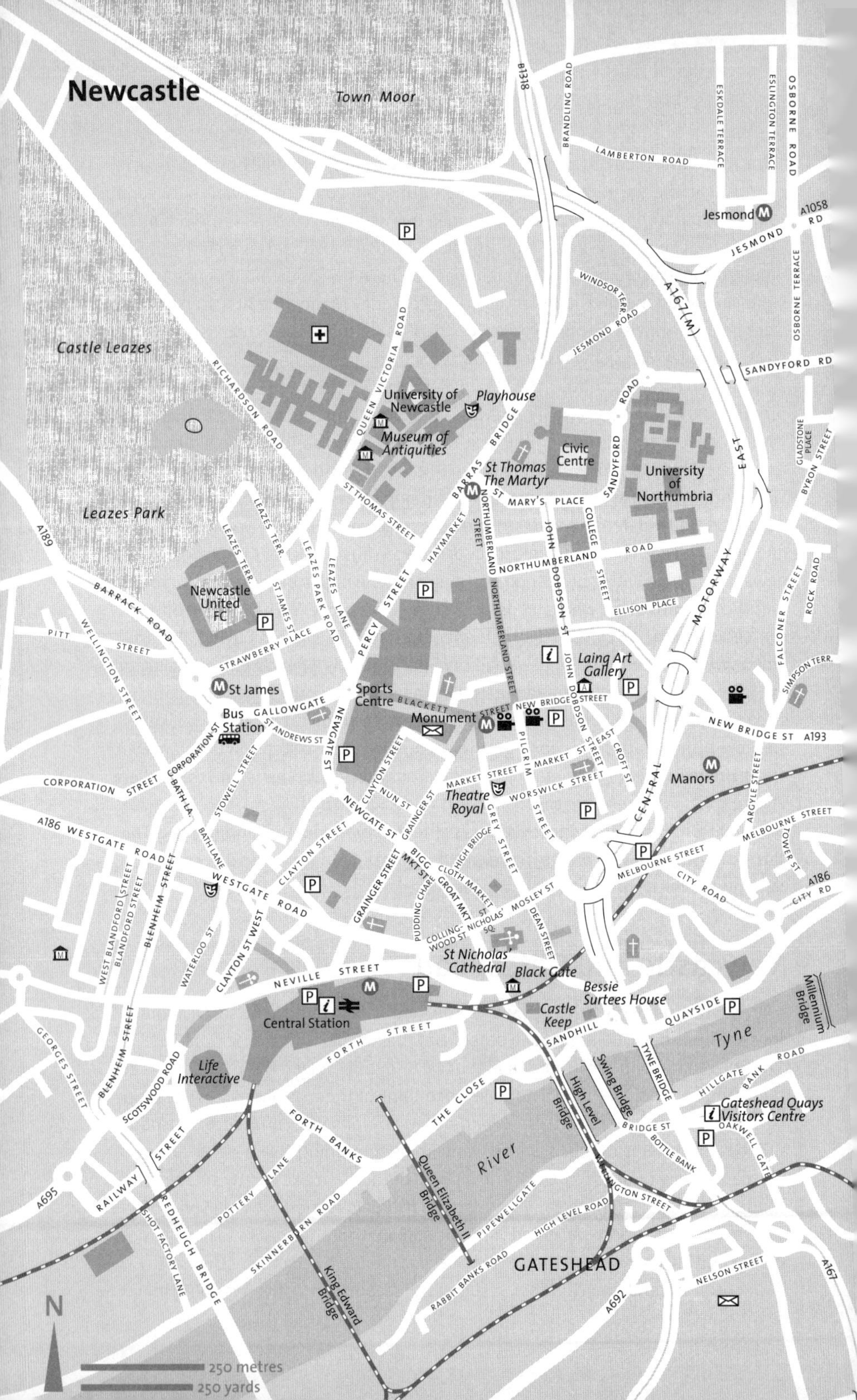
Newcastle
Town Moor
Castle Leazes
Leazes Park
University of Newcastle
Playhouse
Museum of Antiquities
St Thomas The Martyr
Civic Centre
University of Northumbria
Jesmond
Newcastle United FC
St James
Bus Station
Sports Centre
Monument
Laing Art Gallery
Manors
Theatre Royal
St Nicholas' Cathedral
Black Gate
Bessie Surtees House
Castle Keep
Central Station
Life Interactive
Tyne
River
Millennium Bridge
Swing Bridge
High Level Bridge
Tyne Bridge
Queen Elizabeth II Bridge
King Edward Bridge
Gateshead Quays Visitors Centre
GATESHEAD
250 metres
250 yards
N

Getting There and Around

By Air

Newcastle International Airport, near Ponteland, handles UK and European flights. There are 13 flights a day from London airports (Stansted, Gatwick and Heathrow), less than an hour's flying time away. Scheduled flights come from Holland, Germany, Belgium Norway and France; *t (0191) 214 4444, www.newcastleairport.com.*

By Sea

International Ferry Terminal, Royal Quays, North Shields. **DFDS Seaways, t** (0191) 293 6283, *www.dfdsseaways.co.uk*, sail daily for Amsterdam (Ijmuiden) and bi-weekly to Norway and Sweden. **Fjord Line, t** (0191) 296 1313, also operates out of North Shields.

By Train

GNER trains between London King's Cross, Edinburgh and Aberdeen call at Newcastle Central Station roughly every half hour. **Virgin Cross Country** trains between Edinburgh and Penzance call at Newcastle. For all train information contact **National Rail Enquiries, t** 08457 484950, *www.thetrainline.com.*

By Coach

National Express operates daily services between Newcastle and Edinburgh and twice-daily services from London Victoria. There are also coaches from Newcastle to Nottingham, Manchester, Leeds and Birmingham. For times and prices contact **National Express,** *t 08705 808080 www.gobycoach.com.*

By Bus and Metro

The **Tyne and Wear Metro** has a reputation for cleanliness and efficiency. **Buses** are usually plentiful and frequent. For information call **Traveline, t** 0870 608 2608.

Tourist Information

Newcastle-Gateshead: *www.visitnewcastle gateshead.com* and *www.newcastle.gov.uk.*

Grainger Town (central): 132 Grainger Street.

Railway Station, Central Station Concourse, Neville Street. For both offices, **t** (0191) 277 8000.

Newcastle International Airport, **t** (0191) 214 4422.

Gateshead: *www.gateshead.gov.uk* and *www.gateshead-quays.com.*

MetroCentre, 7 The Arcade, MetroCentre, **t** (0191) 460 6345.

Gateshead Quays, St Mary's Church, **t** (0191) 477 5380. Seasonal opening hours.

Central Library, Prince Consort Road, **t** (0191) 477 3478.

South Tyneside: *www.s-tyneside-mbc.gov.uk.*

Where to Stay

Newcastle-Gateshead t (0191) –

Copthorne, The Close, Quayside, **t** 222 0333, *www.millenium-hotels.com* (*luxury*). Hotel overlooking the river. Bars, restaurants and leisure club.

Seaham Hall, t 516 1400, *www.seaham-hall.com* (*luxury*). On the Durham coast, 25 minutes by car southeast of the city centre. Old-fashioned looking on outside but modern inside. Byron was married here in 1815. Swimming pool and spa.

Newcastle Marriott, Gosforth Park, **t** 236 4111, *www.marriott.com* (*expensive*). Next to the race course, 10 minutes by car from the city centre. Gym, pool and beauty salon.

Malmaison, Quayside, **t** 245 5000, *www.malmaison.com* (*expensive*). Part of the group that turns unusual buildings into innovative hotels. This one overlooks the Tyne and has a spa and bistro.

Royal Station Hotel, Neville St, **t** 232 0781, *www.royalstationhotel.com* (*expensive*). Modernized Victorian building. Central and with good transport links.

New Northumbria, 61–9 Osborne Road, **t** 281 4961, *www.newnorthumbriahotel.com* (*moderate*). In Jesmond. Rooms have satellite TV, mini-bar, hair dryer, and tea and coffee facilities. Internet café.

Newcastle, and the town's Central Station was the world's first purpose-built railway station anywhere. Charles Parsons developed the steam turbine, which would

Premier Lodge, The Exchange, The Quayside, **t** 0870 7001504, *www.premierlodge.com* (*moderate*). Hotel with 136 rooms all at the same fixed and reasonable price.

Eating Out

The Valley (*see* Hadrian's Wall, p.897, for details). Out-of-town Indian restaurant: the train fare is included in the price of a four-course meal and you order from the menu on the journey.

Fisherman's Lodge, Jesmond Dene, **t** 281 3281, *www.fishermanslodge.co.uk* (*expensive*). The best seafood restaurant in the city. Situated in a wooded valley, Jesmond Dene, about five minutes' drive from the centre.

Café Royal, Nelson Street, **t** 261 4298 (*moderate*). Downstairs is for drinks and snacks with newspapers and magazines to help you while away the time. Upstairs is a highly rated restaurant.

Paradiso, 1 Market Lane, **t** 221 1240, *www.paradiso.co.uk*. Italian-style brasserie in old printing works. Sandwiches salads and pasta in the daytime (*cheap*). Evening menu (*moderate*) includes handmade pasta.

Pani's Café, 61 High Bridge, **t** 232 4366, *www.pani.net* (*cheap*). Italian restaurant on a quiet street doing everything but pizzas. Ciabatta sandwiches available at lunchtime.

Harry Ramsden's, Metro Park West, Gibside Way, **t** 460 2625 (*cheap*). Gateshead Branch of Yorkshire's famous fish and chip shop

Pubs, Bars and Cafés

Crown Posada, 31–33 Side, **t** 232 1269. An 1880s pub not far from the riverside, with a neo-classical façade. Full of character inside, with large mirrors, woodwork and stained-glass windows.

Cooperage, 32 The Close, **t** 233 2940. Large 14th-century timber-framed building (one of the oldest buildings in the city) near the Tyne Bridge, Swing Bridge and Quayside. Formerly a cooper's workshop.

Pitcher and Piano, 108 The Quayside, **t** 223 4110. Modern pub on the waterfront (one of a good chain) serving bar meals. Also a restaurant (*moderate*).

Blake's Coffee House, 53 Grey Street, **t** 261 5463. An arty, studenty place with low ceilings, bare wooden floorboards and lots of excited chatter. Speciality coffees served, also sandwiches, snacks and light meals. Busy at lunchtimes.

Bob Trollop, Sand Hill, **t** 261 1037. Winner of the 'best vegetarian pub' award – if that is not a contradiction in terms. Relaxed atmosphere. Near the base of the Tyne Bridge.

Centurion, Neville St, **t** 261 6611, *www.centurion-newcastle.com*. The former first-class waiting room of the railway station, now a bar with a Continental atmosphere.

Entertainment

Nightlife

There are three main areas of nightlife in Newcastle. The first, the **Bigg Market**, is the most established, with an entrenched clientèle bent on serious drinking. The second, the new places popping up along the **Quayside**, is where you will want to go to mingle with football players and other celebrities. The third, **Osborne Road** in Jesmond, is lined with new middle-class 'gastro-pubs'.

Cinema and Theatre

Theatre Royal, Grey Street, **t** 232 2061. Early Victorian theatre. Royal Shakespeare Company season each autumn.

The Cluny, 36 Lime Street, **t** 230 4475, box office **t** 230 4474. Café-bar-cum-gallery-cum-performance space.

Newcastle Playhouse and Gulbenkian Studio, Haymarket, **t** 230 5151, *www.northernstage.com*. Home to the Northern Stage Ensemble.

Sport

Newcastle United Football Club, St James' Park, **t** 201 8400, *www.nufc.co.uk*. The city's football team.

Newcastle Racecourse, High Gosforth Park, **t** 236 2020, *www.newcastleracecourse.co.uk*. There are 29 racing fixtures a year.

revolutionize the maritime world and later be used for generating electricity. Some other local inventions were more hedonistic: Earl Grey gave his name to an afternoon tea, and the dark strong brew of Newcastle Brown, first brewed in 1927, is the biggest-selling premium bottled ale in Britain.

But now is the era of art. It begins, even before you arrive in the city, with the ***Angel of the North***, a gigantic statue by Antony Gormley which looms over the A1 and the east coast mainline railway just to the south of the city. Made of steel and copper, it is 66ft high, with a wing-span of 177ft, making it the largest sculpture in Britain. It is almost certainly also the country's most viewed work of art, if not the most admired. In Britain's car society it has a captive audience: an estimated 90,000 motorists see it as they drive by each day (unless they are looking at the road). The initial scepticism that greets a lot of public art in Britain seems now to have given way to respect.

The River and the Quayside

The best art is concentrated in the centre of the city, specifically on the quaysides of the Tyne and leaping across the river itself. If you see nothing else or do nothing else, at least walk across the stunning **Millennium Bridge**. Nominated as his Wonder of the World by (bagless-vacuum-cleaner) inventor James Dyson, and the first bridge to be named Building of the Year, it is not only beautiful but clever, being the first pivoting bridge of its kind in the world. It consists of two elegant white arcs, one carrying a pedestrian walkway and a cycle track. When a ship approaches, these two arcs swivel out of its way, opening the bridge like a blinking eye. Even more ingeniously, it is self cleaning: any litter dropped on the bridge simply rolls to the nearest end.

The drawback of this slick new bridge is that there is no longer an incentive to cross the emblematic **Tyne Bridge**, which is windy, noisy and has unattractive approaches. It is, however, higher up and you get a good view of the quayside and the old town from 85ft above the high water mark. The Tyne Bridge was opened by George V and Queen Mary on 9 October 1928. Until the similar Sydney Harbour Bridge opened in 1932, this was the world's largest single-span bridge. Upstream are two more fine bridges. Next to, but far below, the Tyne Bridge is the cute red, white and blue **Swing Bridge**, built in 1876 on the site of the Roman bridge over the river. Hydraulically powered, it pivots around its mid point. Beyond this is the **High Level Bridge** designed by Robert Stephenson, George's son and also an engineer, and opened in 1849 by Queen Victoria. It was the first bridge to combine road (below) and railway (upper deck).

Earl Grey

Charles Grey, the second Earl Grey (1764–1845) was Whig Prime Minister under William IV from 1830 to 1834 and responsible for the Reform Act, which extended the parliamentary franchise and did away with some corrupt 'rotten boroughs'. But his name lives on mostly in a blend of black tea flavoured with oil of bergamot (a citrus fruit). There are several stories of how the tea became associated with the man. It is probable that the first caddy-full was a gift from a Chinese mandarin in gratitude for a successful bit of diplomacy. When his supply ran out, Earl Grey requested his tea merchants, Twinings (who still have a factory in Newcastle), to blend it anew. How else could society people who wanted to emulate the prime minister ask for the blend but as 'the Earl Grey's tea'?

The main reason to cross the river is to see the lonely, monolithic building at the end of the Millennium Bridge, the **Baltic** (***t*** *(0191) 478 1810, www.balticmill.com; open Mon–Wed and Fri–Sat 10–7, Thurs 10–10, Sun 10–5; Quayside South, Shore Road, Gateshead*). Once a flour mill, it has been converted into a centre for contemporary art whose doors are intended to welcome the masses, not just the *cognoscenti*. Whether or not you fancy any of the current exhibitions, take one of the glass lifts on the side of the building for a view of the Quayside and the Tyne Bridge. The best views are from the fourth floor 'viewing box' or the restaurant next to it.

Gateshead's **Quayside** is to be developed around the Baltic and this side of the river is likely to get more and more agreeable as the years pass. The next project to be completed will be the **Music Centre**, a 1,650-seater concert hall covered by a curved glass and steel roof which it is hoped will rival the Sydney Opera House.

There is little incentive to wonder further into Gateshead unless you are tempted to take an off-beat guided tour of the unfinished 1960s **Gateshead Multi-Storey Car Park**, to see where Michael Caine throws a fellow villain off a flight of steps in the cult 1971 film *Get Carter* (*tour times erratic; ask at tourist information centre*).

Grainger Town

Central Newcastle, Grainger Town, was effectively replanned and rebuilt in the 1820s and '30s by Richard Grainger, a property developer and speculator who was able to acquire large amounts of land through his civic connections. The Georgian city centre he laid out is only comparable in grandeur to Bath (to which it comes second in the density of Grade 1 listed buildings). Grainger Town is currently undergoing a regeneration programme that should leave it looking almost as good as new.

The backbone of Grainger Town and all Newcastle is the inclined **Grey Street**, which has been called 'probably the most magnificent classical Georgian street in England'. At the head of it stands **Earl Grey's Monument** (there's a good view from the top when it's open – which is rare) erected in honour of a reforming 19th-century prime minister more famous for his tea connections.

Near the top of Grey Street, but easy to miss, is **Central Arcade**, handsomely decorated in brown and cream tiles. A step or two away is **Grainger Market** where the last of the four early Marks and Spencer stalls is still operating. Dated 1895, it has a lovely original frontage with brass lamps.

Downhill, Grey Street continues more steeply but not as elegantly as **Dean Street**, which takes you to the foot of the Tyne Bridge. There are some nice architectural decorations on the right as you go down, but otherwise the walk is not that interesting. Veer right from the bottom of Grey Street, however, onto **Mosely Street**, and you'll find what's left of medieval Newcastle.

The 14th–15th-century **St Nicholas' Cathedral** (*St Nicholas Street,* ***t*** *(0191) 232 1939, www.newcastle-ang-cathedral-stnicholas.org.uk; open Mon–Fri 7.30–6, Sat 8–4, Sun 8–12 and 4–7.30*) is notable for its lantern tower.

The **Castle Keep** (*St Nicholas Street,* ***t*** *(0191) 232 7938, www.castlekeep-newcastle.org.uk; open April–Sept daily 9.30–5.30; Oct–Mar daily 9.30–4.30; adm*), further down the same street, is one of the country's finest surviving Norman keeps – although

Hunter Davies, who passed this way in 1973, wrote: 'it looks like a shipwreck, a stranded piece of masonry, fallen off the back of some passing century.' It was built between 1168 and 1178 on the site of the 'New Castle' (1080) from which the city gets its name. This is also thought to be the eastern point of origin of Hadrian's Wall. Beside the keep stands the Black Gate, built around 1247.

Museums and the Centre for Life

As a regional capital, Newcastle has several fine museums. Because of the proximity of Hadrian's Wall, the most interesting of these is the **University of Newcastle's Museum of Antiquities** (*through the arches at the top of Kings Walk,* **t** *(0191) 222 7849, www.ncl.ac.uk/antiquities; open Mon–Sat 10–5*), which is big on the Romans but also includes medieval jewellery and finds up to the time of the Stuarts. Its prize exhibit is the three altars to Mithras found at Carrawburgh (*see* p.897).

The best permanent art collection is the **Laing Art Gallery** (*New Bridge Street,* **t** *(0191) 232 7734, www.twmuseums.org.uk; open Mon–Sat 10–5, Sun 2–5*) which contains silver, glass and costume as well as paintings from the Pre-Raphaelites to Ben Nicholson and Henry Moore, and works by local engraver Thomas Bewick.

If you have children in tow, the only place to go is **Life** (*Times Square, Scottwood Road,* **t** *(0191) 243 8210, www.centre-for-life.co.uk; open Mon–Sat 10–6, Sun 11–6; adm*) next to the railway station. It's an indoor theme park which aims to teach a little science. Life's subject is, of course, life on earth in all its diversity, from DNA to dinosaurs. It is divided into nine zones: River of Life, Cell City, Tunnel of Love, Big Brain Show, Life Arcade, Life's Amazing Journey, Sensory Zoo and the Crazy Motion Ride – 'the longest motion simulator in the world' – which takes you dinosaur-hunting, bobsleighing or bungee-jumping off the Tyne Bridge.

Satellite Sights

There are further sights to see outside the city, unexpected survivors of history amidst the industrial and residential sprawl. Follow the north bank of the Tyne and you come to **Tynemouth**, which has the ruins of an 11th-century priory and castle attractively scattered over a headland. Between Newcastle and Tynemouth is the only fragment of Hadrian's Wall left in the urban area: ***Segedunum* fort** (*Buddle Street, Wallsend,* **t** *(0191) 295 5757, www.twmuseums.org.uk; open April–Oct Mon–Sun 10–5, Nov–Mar Mon–Sat 10–3.30*), where an airport control tower has been erected to give visitors a view over the remains.

On the other side of the river is **Jarrow**. The monk and early English writer known as the Venerable Bede spent his entire life in a monastery here, but only the chancel from that building survives, as part of a church. In these heritage-obsessed times, it was inevitable that something like **Bede's World** (*Church Bank, off the A185, Jarrow,* **t** *(0191) 489 2106, www.bedesworld.co.uk; open Jan–Mar and Nov–Dec Mon–Sat 10–4.30, Sun 12–4.30; Mar–Oct Mon–Sat 10–5.30, Sun 12–5.30; adm*) would open beside it, with the aim of bringing alive the age in which Bede lived and wrote.

Just north of Tynemouth is **Whitley Bay**, Newcastle-Gateshead's seaside resort, popular with locals needing a shot of ozone in summer.

The Venerable Bede

Study, teaching, and writing have always been my delight.

The Venerable Bede

Bede was born in 673 at Wearmouth (north of Sunderland) and as a child entered the double monastery of Wearmouth-Jarrow. Revered as the greatest Anglo-Saxon scholar and an exemplary Benedictine monk, he spent his whole life 'always writing, always praying, always reading, always teaching'. After the Bible, his principle subject of study was history. He wrote around 40 books, but is best remembered for the *Ecclesiastical History of the English Nation,* which chronicles events from the Roman occupation until the date it was composed, 731. The accuracy of his account is sometimes disputed – he probably never travelled further than York to the south and Lindisfarne to the north – but so little is known about the Dark Ages that his testimony is invaluable to historians. Bede died in 735; in 836 the church declared him 'venerable' and canonized him in 1899.

A short way down the coast towards Sunderland is **Souter Lighthouse** (*Coast Road, Whitburn, South Shields,* **t** *(0191) 529 3161, www.ntnorth.demon.co.uk; open Feb–Mar daily 11–5.30, Mar–Oct Sat–Thurs 11–5; adm*), now in the care of the National Trust. It was built in 1871 and was the first lighthouse to be powered by electricity.

Northumbria

Heading north into Northumbria you enter historian G.M. Trevelyan's 'land of far horizons, where the piled or drifted shapes of gathered vapour are for ever moving along the farthest ridge of hills.' The industrial north is left behind for the history of the Border country, long-contested and now beautifully bleak and empty.

Hadrian's Wall

Building such a stone wall as Hadrian's all the way across northern England would be hard enough in the age of the JCB, mechanical crane, angle grinder and articulated lorry, but doing it with the technology of the 1st century AD, relying on the muscle and ingenuity of the Roman Army, was a far more remarkable feat.

What the Roman emperor wanted, the Roman emperor got. In AD 122 Hadrian came to Britain and it was probably during this tour that he ordered the construction of a wall along the northern limit of his empire. It was never meant to be a manned defence or an impenetrable barrier, it is not even certain that it had a walkway and crenellations along the top, as seen in most reconstructions. Rather it was a frontier to separate Roman Britain from the Barbarians beyond: something more definite to concentrate the mind than a fence or a dotted line on a map. They may have been a warrior race, but the Romans often relied on treaties to secure their frontiers rather than military force.

Northumberland's most famous monument begins in Newcastle but there is barely a trace of it left in the urban area. These days the wall is no longer any kind of frontier. It is sometimes assumed to divide England from Scotland, but this is incorrect: only at its extreme western end does it come anywhere near the present-day border; most of Northumberland – including the city of Newcastle – lies north of it.

Hadrian obviously intended his empire to end with a bang not a whimper: rather than expand his domains indefinitely northwards, where his troops would become thinly spread in return for dubious gains, he preferred to consolidate. He already had enough territory to administer: the wall was to be the northern edge of an empire which stretched southwards as far as Iraq and the Sahara Desert.

The wall links two bodies of water, the River Tyne on the east coast and the Solway Firth near Carlisle in the west. Three legions took at least six years to build the wall, although they were still making modifications at Hadrian's death in AD 138. Halfway through the building process, the wall was reduced from 10 to eight Roman feet. It is thought to have been about 15 feet high. When finished, it was 80 Roman miles long (73 modern miles) from Wallsend (now lost in the Newcastle conurbation) to Bowness-on-Solway (*see* p.787). Every mile was placed a **mile castle** and, between these, two **turrets**. Outside the wall there was a parallel ditch and mound, except where the wall ran over crags, which offered their own natural defences.

The plan was modified while in progress and 16 forts were built astride the wall, a day's march apart so that reinforcements could quickly deal with any incursion. A road, the **Military Way**, linked these forts.

A more curious addition was the ***Vallum***, a ditch protected by mounds to either side of it, which runs south of the wall. This could be crossed only at the forts or on the main roads through the wall. Its purpose has been much discussed by archaeologists (why place a line of defence to the south when the enemy was to the north?), but it is now thought to have been a civil boundary behind the military one, or the Roman equivalent of barbed wire, to keep people out of the military zone near the wall.

The wall continued to perform its function until the early 5th century when the legions withdrew from Britain. Many of its stones were reused in local buildings over the next 14 centuries, but a few remained *in situ*. In 1987 the wall was declared a UNESCO World Heritage Site, 'an example of the organization of a military zone, which illustrates the techniques and strategic and geopolitical views of the Romans'.

The history and statistics can lead visitors to expect more than they get. Hadrian's Wall is a ruin – there are only around 10 miles of it visible – and you need to bring some imagination with you. The excavated sites are little more than neat piles of rubble and you have to take the archaeologists' word for it that they are significant. Most of the treasures found are behind glass in museums. But since the 1970s there has been a move to present the wall in a more stimulating way: the **Roman Army Museum** perhaps best exemplifies this tendency.

It is advisable to select a few key places to visit, or fort fatigue will quickly set in. Although the wall begins at Wallsend on the maps, the most visited stretch is between **Corbridge** and **Walltown**. This is also the most scenic: the bleak north-country landscapes set off the wall, and even on a grim winter's day it has definite

Getting Around

Arriva Trains Northern operate **trains** on the Newcastle–Hexham–Carlisle line. The trains stop at Corbridge, Bardon Mill and Haltwhistle.

Hadrian's Chariot, bus service AD 122, from Carlisle to Hexham (May–Sept) with guides on board, **t** (01434) 344 777. Stops at Haltwhistle, Brampton and the main Roman sites. There is a reduced service, without guide, in winter between Carlisle and Housesteads.

The **'Military Road'** (not to be confused with the Romans' Military Way), the B6318, follows the best bits of the wall from Heddon-on-the-Wall to beyond Haltwhistle. This was built by General Wade after the Jacobite Rebellion to facilitate troop movements east to west.

Hadrian's Cycleway is not a surprising archaeological discovery but route 72 of the National Cycle Network, which runs from Wallsend to Ravenglass Roman Bath House. The Tyne Valley railway line takes bikes for free, but to a maximum of two per train (first come first served). The AD 122 bus service also carries bikes, but check first.

Hadrian's Wall Path National Trail (84 miles) takes seven days on average to walk. You are asked to walk beside the wall, not on it, in order to preserve it.

Tourist Information

Local tourist information offices are the best source of information, but for enquiries about the wall in general call **t** (01434) 322 002, or see *www.hadrians-wall.org*.

Haltwhistle: The Railway Station, Station Road, **t** (01434) 322 002, *www.haltwhistle.org*.

Once Brewed: National Park Visitor Centre, Military Road, Bardon Mill, **t** (01434) 344 396 (*seasonal opening*).

Hexham: Wentworth car park, **t** (01434) 652 220, *www.tynedale-online.co.uk/hexhamhistory*.

Corbridge: Hill Street, **t** (01434) 632 815. *Seasonal opening*.

Tynedale: *www.hadrianswallcountry.org*.

Parts of the wall are maintained by the **National Trust**, *www.nationaltrust.org.uk*, and **English Heritage**, *www.english-heritage.org*.

Where to Stay and Eat

Corbridge t (01434) –

The Angel of Corbridge, Main Street, **t** 632 119, *www.theangelofcorbridge.co.uk* (*expensive*). A 17th-century inn which is good for both food and accommodation. The Angel has a set menu early evening and then you have to eat *à la carte*.

atmosphere. The view across the plain towards the Cheviots has changed little since the Romans decamped – a few fewer trees, certainly, but you still get the idea of what it must have been like to be garrisoned here.

If you are a serious walker you can follow the course of the wall from one end to the other. Where there are no stones exposed you can still follow the wall in place names: one village is even helpfully called 'Wall'.

Corbridge and Hexham

Perhaps the first place to head for is **Corbridge**, the Roman settlement of *Corstopitum*, which was the main garrison and supply town for the central stretch of the wall. It was built at the lowest point of the Tyne that could be forded, a short way downstream of the confluence of the Tyne's north and south streams. Roman Dere Street crossed the river here on its way between York (*Eboracum*) and *Barbaricum*. Modern Corbridge is a useful place to stay or eat, but is also a pretty place in itself.

Nearby **Hexham** is a larger but also agreeable town. Its **abbey** (***t** (01434) 602 031, www.hexhamabbey.org.uk*), on the market place, was founded in 674 by St Wilfrid.

The Valley, The Old Station House, Station Road, **t** 633 434 (*moderate*). Indian restaurant which gets very busy; also does takeaways. The Passage to India train brings customers direct from Newcastle Central Station.

Riverside Guest House, Main Street, **t** 632 942, *www.theriversideguesthouse.co.uk* (*moderate*). A modernized 18th-century house, now a clean and efficiently run guest-house with a small garden and a view of the river. The 10 bedrooms have TVs and phones. Small private parking area.

Blanchland t (01434) –

Lord Crewe Arms, Blanchland, **t** (01434) 675 251, *www.crewearms.freeserve.co.uk* (*expensive*). One of the historic buildings of Blanchland village. Restaurant and bar meals served.

Hexham and Around t (01434) –

Langley Castle, Langley on Tyne, **t** 688 888, *www.langleycastle.com* (*expensive*). A castle built in the 14th century now equipped with luxury guest accommodation.

Hexham Royal Hotel, Priestpopple, **t** (01434) 602 270, *www.hexham-royal-hotel.co.uk* (*moderate*). Worth staying in just to be able to say the street name. Food served in the Café Royal or Mr Ant's Bar.

West Close House, Hextol Terrace, **t** 603 307 (*moderate*). A 1920s house in a private cul-de-sac. Victorian-style revolving summerhouse in the garden. Choice of wholefood, Continental or English breakfast.

De Vere Slaley Hall, Slaley (near Hexham), **t** 673 350, *www.devereonline.co.uk* (*luxury*). In extensive lands of forest and moorland, and with not one but two championship golf courses. Restaurant and bars.

Allerwash Farmhouse, Allerwash, Newborough (near Hexham), **t** 674 574 (*moderate*). Stone Georgian farmhouse with two guest bedrooms. No smoking. Within walking distance (4 miles) of Hadrian's Wall.

The Garden Station, Langley (near Hexham), **t** 684 391 (*cheap*). Restored Victorian railway station now doing teas and coffees as well as peddling artworks and books.

Haltwhistle t (01434) –

Centre of Britain Hotel, **t** 322 422, *www.centre-of-britain.org.uk* (*moderate*). Hotel built around a 15th-century Pele Tower which became in turn manor house, excise office and coaching inn.

Ashcroft House, Lanty's Lonnen, **t** 320 213, *www.ashcroftguesthouse.co.uk* (*moderate*). Former vicarage in terraced gardens on the edge of town. No smoking.

Along the Wall

Holmhead Guest House, Thirlwall Castle Farm, Greenhead, **t** (01697) 747 402 (*moderate*). B&B convenient for the wall and walking.

There are two other venerable buildings in the town centre which merit strolling past: the **Old Gaol** and the **Moothall**, the tower of a gatehouse dating from the medieval Border wars. There is an agreeable strip of deciduous woodland to walk along at **Allen Banks** (*Bardon Mill, **t** (01434) 344 218; open daily dawn to dusk; adm*), between Hexham and Bellingham.

Chesters and Carrawburgh

North of Hexham, the first sight to see on the wall is **Chesters fort and museum** (***t** (01434) 681 379; open daily April–Sept 9.30–6, Oct 10–5, Nov–Mar 10–4; adm*) in a part of the north Tyne Valley which was landscaped in the 19th century. This was home to a cavalry unit originally raised in Asturias in northern Spain. Three of its four main gates open to the north of the wall. The bath house outside the fort is one of the best preserved Roman monuments in Britain – although that still doesn't mean much of it is left standing. A museum on the site has a collection of Roman sculpture.

On the site of nearby **Carrawburgh** (which the Romans knew as *Brocolitia*) was found a *mithraeum*, a temple to the Eastern deity of Mithras. Christians disliked

Mithraism because they saw it as a caricature of their own form of worship and it may have been they who destroyed the temple in the 4th century. Whoever it was left three altars still standing; replicas of these are on the site and the originals are in the Museum of Antiquities in Newcastle. North of the Mithras temple is **Coventina's Well**, a sacred spring where 13,490 coins (as well as brooches, sculptures and pottery) were found in 1876.

Vindolanda

Bardon Mill, Hexham; **t** *(01434) 344 277, www.vindolanda.com; open daily 15–28 Feb and 1–16 Nov 10–4; Mar and Oct 10–5; April and Sept 10–5.30; May–June 10–6; July–Aug 10–6.30; adm.*

Much of the credit for transforming the wall from esoteric archaeological speciality to history at its most accessible must go to the Vindolanda Trust, which was founded in 1970 to do high-quality research but also to educate and display its excavations to the public in the most attractive way.

Vindolanda fort is not actually on the wall because it predates it, having being constructed 40 years earlier as part of the Stanegate Frontier. The first part of the visit is around the ruins of an extensive Roman settlement, which are bleak and shelterless on a wet day. To the untutored modern eye, these don't look more interesting than any other foundation stones, but ground conditions here caused finds to be much better preserved than elsewhere. *Vindolanda*'s **museum** (Chesterholm), in a leafy dell, gives an excellent idea of everyday life in northern Britain almost 2,000 years ago. There are letters, bone tent pegs and counters, hair used for a helmet crest, daggers, arrowheads, javelin heads, lead slingshot, locks and keys, writing tablets and styluses, shoes, carpentry and knives, ladles, spoons, lamps, a wig and horse equipment. A set of

The *Vindolanda* Tablets

Archaeology doesn't come sexier than *Vindolanda*. The site's most important find, a collection of Roman writing tablets, was voted number one by a panel of specialists in the British Museum's survey of the Top Ten Treasures from Britain's past, a sort of Oscar for the luckiest excavation.

The first tablets, two slivers of wood covered in spidery writing, showed up in 1973, in a deep trench on the southern edge of the settlement. The writing faded in a few hours before it could be read but the text was analyzed by infra-red photography. The inscription was revealed to be a fragment of a letter written to a soldier at *Vindolanda*, informing him that a package of shoes, socks and underpants was on its way. This underwear delivery note was the first of approximately 1,900 tablets that would get the archaeologists' juices going. The *Vindolanda* tablets are the earliest written records to be found in Britain, and the earliest documents of the everyday life of ordinary people – whose comings and goings history tends not to record.

Another first is the birthday invitation from Claudia Severa to Sulpicia Lepidina, wife of the prefect of Vindolanda, dated to AD 100/104, which has on it the earliest surviving writing by a female hand.

Further Reading on Hadrian's Wall

The best non-technical background reading is Hunter Davies' *A Walk Along the Wall*, the royalties from which go to help the archaeology of the *Vindolanda* Trust. Davies takes as his inspiration *The History of the Roman Wall*, written in 1801 by William Hutton, a 78-year-old shopkeeper who set off from Birmingham and walked the length of the wall twice, which is enough to leave anyone breathless. *The Handbook to the Roman Wall* by J. Collingwood Bruce, first published in 1863 but periodically edited and updated, is the amateur archaeologist's classic.

crockery from Millau in France, broken in transit and not used, still has the manufacturers' marks clearly visible on it. It all gives the impression of real people living real lives at *Vindolanda*, in ways not that different from our own. In his classic book, *A Walk Along the Wall*, Hunter Davies observes how little life has changed as he looks at a display of Roman instruments and tools: 'all of them I swear, not the remotest bit different in design from their modern counterparts. Today's versions are sometimes lighter, using alloys or steel, but as far as looks go they're identical.'

Housesteads

Haydon Bridge, **t** *(01434) 344 363; open April–Sept daily 10–6; Oct daily 10–5; Nov–Mar daily 10–4; adm.*

For a true Hadrian's Wall fort you need to look at Housesteads (*Vercovicium*), the best-preserved Roman fort in Britain. It was occupied by the delightfully named First Cohort of Tungrians, an infantry regiment. Settlements of houses, shops and inns were built in the lee of such forts to service the military communities, and there is evidence – too late to be used in court – that a murder was committed in one of the houses outside Housesteads as the bones of a man (with a sword stuck in his ribs) and a woman were found buried beneath the floor.

The car park and visitors' centre for Housesteads is a couple of fields back from the wall and the fort. Leave your car here for the most popular wall walk to Steel Rigg over Cuddy's Crags (three miles each way).

If you don't want to get out of your car (more than likely with Northumberland's erratic weather) drive on past Housesteads to **Steel Rigg**, where there is a car park from which the scenic stretch of wall is visible.

Walltown and the Roman Army Museum

There is another well-preserved bit of wall at Walltown (although there is no town). **Walltown Quarry** has a spacious car park and picnic area and there is a more makeshift car park up a pretty little lane at **Walltown Crags** – both are free (Housesteads and Steel Rigg are pay-and-display). Aim for the highest point of the wall you can see. On a clear day there is a view all the way to the Solway Firth.

The **Roman Army Museum** (*Carvoran,* **t** *(01697) 747 485, www.vindolanda.com; open daily April–Oct 10–5.30, Feb, Mar and Nov 10–4; adm*), run by the Vindolanda Trust, is also up the Walltown road. Save this for a rainy day. Whereas *Vindolanda* is almost all authentic pieces, this museum is stronger on reproduction *romana* than original finds. Its aim is to give an idea of what life was like for the squaddies stationed on the empire's northern border. There is a great video: a recruitment film purportedly made by Roman troops talking about their armour, weaponry and camp life, acted out by a cast of computer programmers and middle managers who like to dress up as Roman soldiers at weekends.

Southeast Northumberland

When you can't look another Roman in the eye, there is a national park spread out to the north before you (*see* below). On the other side of the wall, the southeast of Northumberland is a neglected corner of Britain whose inhabitants and tourist sights are both sparsely distributed.

Cherryburn, between Stocksfield and Prudhoe, was the birthplace of the naturalist and prolific wood engraver, Thomas Bewick. His old workshop can be visited (*Station Bank, Mickley, Stocksfield,* **t** *(01661) 843 276; open April–Oct Thurs–Mon 1–5.30; adm*).

A long way to the south of the wall, in remote country reached only by dedicated travellers, is **Blanchland**, which was founded by Premonstratensian monks in the 12th century – the name derives from the white habits that they wore – but abandoned at the Dissolution. In the 18th century the village was rebuilt to house a community of lead miners and it has been little altered since then. The church incorporates some elements of the medieval abbey. Blanchland's hotel and restaurant, the **Lord Crewe Arms**, is said to be haunted by the ghost of Dorothy Forster, sister of one of the plotters of the 1715 Jacobite Rebellion. If you want to see her haunts you will have to ask to be let through the large door (the original inn sign) at the top of the stairs.

Kielder and Northumberland National Park

The Northumberland landscape is already getting wild at Hadrian's Wall, but further north it gets bleaker. From the wall to the Scottish border stretches the Northumberland National Park, two thirds owned by the Forestry Commission and one fifth by the Ministry of Defence. Varying from lush woodland to lonely moors grazed by black-faced sheep, the park is for the most part sparsely populated. Land use has changed little on the moors since they were cleared of trees around 4,000 years ago, and many prehistoric remains have survived intact.

Bellingham

Bellingham marks the transition from woods and pastures to the wilder moors beyond. This is also the start of one of the easiest and most pleasant walks in the park, the 3-mile round trip to the **waterfall of Hareshaw Linn**. To start the walk, go through the kissing gate from the car park across Hareshaw Burn from the town.

Tourist Information

Northumberland National Park: *www.nnpa.org.uk*

There are National Park visitor centres at:

Ingram: Powburn, Alnwick, **t** (01665) 578 248. *Open daily Easter–Oct, closed in winter.*

Rothbury: Church House, Church Street, **t** (01669) 620 887. *Open daily Easter–Oct, weekends only in winter.*

Once Brewed: Military Road, Bardon Mill, **t** (01434) 344 396. *Open daily Easter–Oct, weekends only in winter, 10–3.*

There is one other tourist information centre in the area:

Bellingham: t (01434) 220 616.

Where to Stay and Eat

Bellingham t (01434) –

Westfield House, t 220 340 (*moderate*). Decent, clean accommodation.

Riverdale Hall, t 220 254 (*moderate*). Accommodation, food and bar.

Lyndale Guest House, t 220 361, *www.s-h-systems.co.uk/hotels/lyndalehtm* (*moderate*). House with sun lounge, good views and walled garden.

Kielder Forest t (01434) –

Kielder Forest, self-catering forest cabins and bunkbarn, contact Leaplish Waterside Park, **t** 250 312 (*moderate*).

Kielder Forest and Kielder Water

Kielder Castle Forest Park Visitor Centre, ***t*** *(01434) 250 209, www.kielder.org; Tower Knowe Visitor Centre,* ***t*** *(01434) 240 398; open April–Oct 10–4, June–Sept 10–5.*

Kielder Water is Europe's largest man-made lake and Kielder Forest one of the continent's largest areas of planted woodland. There are 150 million trees in the forest, which are harvested to produce timber. The main species is Sitka spruce because of its suitability to inhospitable inland, upland Northumberland, but the monotony is relieved by lesser numbers of Norway spruce, lodgepole pine, Scots pine and larch. The proportion of broadleaf trees (one percent) is being expanded through a planting programme. Red squirrels and otters are the most interesting animals to be seen.

Kielder is run not only as a timber factory but also as a 'nature resort' – a managed wildlife park where people come to walk, cycle, fish, picnic and water-ski. **Leaplish Waterside Park** (***t*** *(01434) 250 312; open daily April–Oct; log cabins and pool open Feb–Dec*) has various entertainments to offer the family: a heated swimming pool and sauna, cruises on Kielder Water, an adventure playground, birds of prey centre and waymarked walking routes.

A collection of 13 contemporary works of art raises Kielder above the level of processed wilderness. Particularly worth seeing is the **Kielder Skyspace** at Cat Cairn by the American sky and space artist James Turrell.

Otterburn

The upland country around the English-Scottish border has been in perpetual warfare, it seems, since the Middle Ages. At least now the fighting is only in rehearsal for wars to be fought elsewhere; a huge chunk of the national park is owned by the Ministry of Defence and used as one of the eight Army Field Training centres in Britain, the largest one in which live ammunition is fired. Much of Otterburn Training Area is farmed or wooded and there are access roads and footpaths open all year, whatever exercises are taking place. But don't go beyond any gate marked by a red flag or lamp, and you are asked not to 'pick up, kick or remove any object...it could kill'.

Heading down from the hills towards Morpeth, off the A696, is **Wallington House** (*Cambo,* **t** *(01670) 773 600; open Wed–Mon 1–5.30; grounds open daily dawn–dusk; adm*) a 17th-century palace with rococo plasterwork inside and magnificent gardens.

Rothbury, Simonside and Crag Side

There is a theory that the flat-topped hill of **Simonside** (1,411ft), near Rotherbury, was a sacred mountain to prehistoric people. The evidence for this is speculative: mainly that the lower slopes were farmed but upper Simonside was left untouched. In the woods below are dozens of cairns (burial mounds) and legends recount that sinister little people inhabit the crags. Between Simonside and Rothbury is **Lordenshaws**, an Iron Age hill fort, which also has the best cup and ring markings in Northumberland. Although they have never been dated precisely, and their purpose is obscure, it is believed that they may be 5,000 years old.

Cragside House (**t** *(01669) 620 150; open April–Oct Tues–Sun, gardens 10.30–7, house 1–5.30*), outside Rothbury, was built by the 1st Lord Armstrong, owner of Bamburgh Castle, and was the first house to be lit by hydro-electricity. The extensive gardens are best known for their rhododendrons, which flower in May and June.

The Cheviots and the Border

Only one road crosses the rounded but bleak Cheviot Hills: the A68 over the pass of **Carter Bar**, which is certainly the most scenic way to enter or leave Scotland. The Cheviot population is thinly spread, and farms often remote. For the most part, the hills are given over to grass and heather moorlands, which support grouse, sheep and even a herd of wild goat. Only dedicated and experienced walkers venture up here.

Northumberland's far northern border, however, runs along the River Tweed. For centuries people living along the border had to live with shifting or reiving – large scale cattle rustling and general thievery. As defence, the inhabitants built themselves fortified farmhouse mini-castles with thick walls, strong doors and small windows. Set back from the border is a group of villages around Ford and Etal that have clubbed together to promote their attractions.

Knights of the Garter

A mound on the bank of the River Tweed beside the village of Wark is all that remains of a motte and bailey castle of Wark where, it is claimed, the highest order of chivalry in England was created. Edward III (1327–77) was at a court ball in the castle when he noticed his mistress, Lady Salisbury, drop her garter. The king replaced it himself, to the giggles and sniggers of his courtiers. He rounded on them with the words, 'honi soit qui mal y pense' ('evil to him that thinks evil'). Hence the Most Noble Order of the Garter was established as a reward for honour. But this is just one version of its founding; *see* Windsor, p.437, for another.

Tourist Information

Ford and Etal: *www.ford-and-etal.co.uk*
The Cheviot Centre:12 Padgepool Place, Wooler, **t** (01668) 282 406.

Where to Stay and Eat

The Cheviots

The Coach House, Crookhill, Cornhill-on-Tweed, **t** (01890) 820 293, *www.coachhousecrookham.com* (*moderate*). B&B in complex of old farm buildings, part dating from the 1680s, around a sunny courtyard. Four-course evening meals.

Winton House, 39 Glendale Road, Wooler, **t** (01668) 281 362, *www.wintonhouse.ntb.org.uk* (*moderate*). Edwardian house in quiet location. Walkers and cyclists always made welcome.

The Bull, Etal, **t** (01890) 820 200 (*cheap*). Thatched pub serving real ales, lunch and dinner including vegetarian options and children's meals.

Etal Village Post Office, Etal, **t** (01890) 820 220 (*cheap*). Post office, shop and tea room combined in one.

Etal has a 14th-century castle (***t*** *(01890) 820 332; open daily May–Sept 10–6, Oct 10–5; adm*) with an exhibition on border warfare, and **Ford** has a village hall (***t*** *(01890) 820 503; open 23 Mar–3 Nov 10.30–12.30 and 1.30–5.30*) with murals of Biblical scenes painted by Lady Waterford, an amateur Victorian artist who used local people as her models. The **Heatherslaw Light Railway** (***t*** *(01890) 820 244; open daily Easter–Sept; hourly service Mar–June 11–3, July–Aug 10.30–4.30, Sept 11–3; adm*) runs between Etal and the 19th-century water-powered **corn mill** at Heatherslaw (***t*** *(01890) 820 338; open daily Easter–Sept 10–6, Oct 10–5; Nov–Mar Mon, Fri and other days when milling; adm*). At Milfield, meanwhile, is the **Maelmin Heritage Trail** (*open daily dawn to dusk*) with a life-sized reproduction of a Stone Age wooden henge monument.

The Northumberland Coast

Heading north from Newcastle, when you have finally shaken off the conurbation and its satellites, you find yourself on one of the most beautiful, moody stretches of British coast, with shimmering islands close to land, vast sprawling skies and miles of empty sand to walk along between fishing villages and castles. Parallel to the coast and useful for access, are the A1 and England's east coast mainline railway.

Alnwick

Alnwick (pronounced 'Annick') makes the most strategic base for exploring the coast and its hinterland. You'd be forgiven for getting the impression that the town is synonymous with **Alnwick Castle** (***t*** *(01665) 510 777, www.alnwickcastle.com; open April–Oct daily 11–5; adm*), owned by the Duke of Northumberland, one of the largest landowners in Britain. Marcel Proust thought this aristocratic title possessed a 'sort of thunderous quality'. It has been owned by the Percy family since 1309 when Henry de Percy bought it along with the castle from Anthony Bek, prince bishop of Durham. Idle tongues among historians say that the deal was not entirely above board and that an illegitimate heir, William de Vescy of Kildare, was denied his rightful title and

Getting There and Around

The main GNER intercity **rail** service between Newcastle and Edinburgh stops at Alnmouth, five miles from Alnwick.

Regular **buses** run from Newcastle to Alnwick.

Tourist Information

Alnwick: The Shambles, **t** (01665) 510 665, *www.alnwick.gov.uk.*

Where to Stay and Eat

Alnwick t (01665) –

White Swan Hotel, Bondgate Within, **t** 602 109 (*moderate*), Alnwick. As novelty value, this hotel possesses the oak-panelled dining room and some of the stained glass from the *Olympic*, sister ship to the *Titanic*.

Tower Restaurant and Guest Rooms, Bondgate Within, **t** 603 888, *www.hotspur-tower.com* (*moderate*). Small guesthouse in middle of Alnwick run by a former policeman. Full English breakfast served. Licensed restaurant serves both snacks and full meals.

property. Since then the Percy family has never been out of the news, as Jonathan Sumption sums it up: 'Over the past eight centuries, two earls and one duke have been killed in battle, most recently in 1940; one has been lynched by a mob; one beheaded for treason, one shot by government assassins, five incarcerated in the Tower for more or less prolonged periods, and one beatified by the church of Rome. It is a striking record of public service or disservice, depending on your point of view.'

Aside from the historical interest of the place, Alnwick puts on a good display of aristocratic life interrupted: a drinks trolley has been left in the Library, and the silver-framed Percy family photos are all on show; in the Drawing Room a brandy glass sits half-drunk on a table, and old cigar stubs rest in ashtrays.

There are, of course, all the trappings of nobility you would expect to see in such a palatial home: ornate ceilings, marble fireplaces, mirrors, pieces of furniture in exotic woods, porcelain, an antique roulette wheel and the 3rd Duke's dress sword. In the last few years a Rembrandt has been identified among the dusty Old Masters on the walls. One room contains an exhibition of the Percy family's relations with the monarchy, as if to prove that the Percys are not just superior to the rest of us but linked to the highest in the land.

Outside, you can take a stroll around the grounds laid out by Capability Brown, which were painted by Canaletto – you can do this without going into the castle – and see the location for the quidditch pitch in the first two *Harry Potter* films.

The Duchy of Northumberland's latest project is the **Alnwick Garden** (***t*** *(01665) 511 133, www.alnwickgarden.com; open Jan–April daily 10–5; May–Sept daily 10–8; Oct–Dec daily 10–5; adm*), a scheme to transform an 18th–19th-century walled garden into something more contemporary. The design is by Belgians Jacques and Peter Wirtz. Its main feature, a grand curving cascade (controlled by computer) sloping down hill towards the entrance, has already been built and the rest of the garden, although now open to the public, is a work in progress.

Alnwick town comes as a refreshing breath of normality, although you can't help feeling that the Duke's influence extends over the locals too (try asking and you'll be met with guarded looks and silence). Drop in to **Barter Books** in Alnwick's former station (**t** *(01665) 604 888, www.barterbooks.co.uk; open daily 9–5, in summer 9–7*). It claims to have a stock of a quarter of a million books. It is a browser's paradise, with red sofas to slump in, a coffee corner and an informal children's book room. There are plenty of features to keep you amused: a mural of famous authors, literary quotations peppered around and an electric train running around a track above the stacks.

In the middle of town is **Ye Olde Cross Inn** (on Narrowgate). Its bow window is full of dirty bottles and always will be. They were put here 150 years ago by a man who then collapsed and died. Anyone touching them, it is said, will suffer the same fate, so there they remain to demonstrate how much dust gathers over a century and a half if you give up cleaning.

Amble to Dunstanburgh

The scenic part of the Northumberland coast starts around **Amble**, a dozy little seaside place which used to ship out vast quantities of Northumberland coal and now styles itself, almost pleadingly, as 'the friendliest port'. Just offshore here is a pancake of rock, **Coquet Island**, an RSPB nature reserve. You can take a boat around it to see the puffins and eider ducks but you cannot land.

A short way down the muddy estuary of the Coquet from Amble you come to the ruined but well-maintained **Warkworth Castle** (**t** *(01665) 711 423; open April–Sept daily 10–6; Oct daily 10–5; Nov–Mar daily 10–1 and 2–4; adm*) which surveys the coast from the top of a rise a few fields back from the sea. This pile of masonry would not be so impressive were it still intact and still inhabited, but it is atmospheric as ruins and manicured turf. Warkworth is actually two castles in one: a typical medieval castle built in the 12th century and a mighty 14th-century keep placed inside it. Its most famous resident was Harry Hotspur, son of the first Earl of Northumberland. Shakespeare's play Henry IV opens here at Hotspur's home, which is later described as 'this worm-eaten hold of ragged stone'. From the Percy family's private chamber there is a good view over Amble and Coquet Island.

An attractive walk along the River Coquet from the castle takes you to **Warkworth Hermitage** (*open Wed and Sun; check at castle before setting out*), a medieval chapel cut into solid rock in the 14th century with living quarters for the hermit on two levels. It was inhabited by a hermit until the 16th century. Enchantingly, you have to be ferried across to it by boat. Warkworth village is a pretty place in its own right, with an old parish church and bridge.

The next settlement you reach along the coast is **Alnmouth**, a quaint little seaside town with one street and several inviting pubs. It is now so quiet the local tourist brochure feels compelled to assure visitors: 'In 1895 Alnmouth even had its own riot'. It is claimed that Charles Dickens proposed to his cousin in Alnmouth, not knowing that she was already pregnant by a sailor. She rejected him and on the very same night her seafaring lover went down with his ship.

After Alnmouth, you have to turn inland and take little roads to get to **Craster**, a fishing village renowned for its kippers (smoked herrings). From the village a footpath

Getting There and Around

The closest **railway** station is Chathill, 4 miles from Seahouses. By **bus**, take the Alnwick–Belford route and get off at Seahouses.

Bird Cruises and Boat Trips

For **bird cruises to Coquet Island** contact Dave Gray, **t** (01665) 711 975, *www.rspb.org.uk*. Departures throughout the summer from New Quayside steps in Amble Harbour.

Trips to the Farnes last from 1½ hours (no landing) to 6 hours (all day; landing on both islands). Unless you are an ornithologist, the 3-hour trip to Inner Farne and back will be enough. The boat companies have booths beside Seahouses Harbour, where there is a car park. Bad weather can prevent sailings.

Mr Billy Shiel, 4 Southfield Avenue, Seahouses, **t** (01665) 720 308, *www.farne-islands.com*; *open April–Oct daily from 10am; Nov–Easter by appointment only*; offers a variety of tours on the MV *Glad Tidings* fleet. The largest boat-tour operator.

Hanvey's, 29 King Street, Seahouses, **t** (01665) 720 388, *www.farneislands.co.uk*; trips from 10am daily on MV *St Cuthbert*. Trips to Staple, Inner Farne and Longstone Island.

Jack Shiel Boat Trips, MV *Golden Gate*, 3 James Street, Seahouses, **t** (01665) 721 819. Two-hour trip with a landing on Longstone Island (*lighthouse adm*).

Once on **Lindisfarne**, leave your car behind. Everything is in walking distance.

Tourist Information

Amble: Queen Street, **t** (01665) 712 313.

Craster: car park, **t** (01665) 576 007.

Seahouses: 16 Main Street, **t** (01665) 721 099, *www.seahouses.org*.

For information on landing on the islands contact the **Property Manager**, The Sheiling, 8 St Aidan's, Seahouses, **t** (01665) 720 651.

Inner Farne and Staple Island open April–Sept daily 10.30–6. Staple Island open May–July daily 10.30–1.30. Inner Farne open May–July daily 1.30–5.

Lindisfarne Heritage Centre, Marygate, **t** (01289) 389 004, *www.lindisfarne-heritage-centre.org. Open April–Oct daily 10–5 (or later depending on tides); Nov–Mar daily 10–4; adm.*

Where to Stay and Eat

Amble to Craster t (01665) –

Tuggal Hall, Chathill, **t** 589 229 (*expensive*). Peaceful place from which it is possible to walk along the coast. Walled garden and horse paddocks. Home produce served up for dinner. No smoking.

Bilton Barns, Alnmouth, **t** 830 427, *www.bilton barns.co.uk* (*moderate*). B&B in the 1715 house of a working beef, sheep and arable farm. Self-catering cottages also available to let for minimum one week in summer, weekends in winter.

Charlie's Fish and Chips, Albert Street, Amble, **t** 710 206, *www.charlieschips.com* (*cheap*). Licensed restaurant and takeaway. Vegetarian and healthy eating options also on offer. **The Jolly Fisherman**, Craster, **t** 576 218 (*cheap*). Pub serving bar snacks.

Bamburgh and Around t (01668) –

Waren House, Waren Mill, Belford, **t** 214 581, *www.warenhousehotel.co.uk* (*expensive*). On the edge of Budle Bay not far from Bamburgh, looking out to Lindisfarne. Choice of more than 250 wines. No children under 14.

Greengates, 34 Front Street, **t** 214 535 (*cheap*). A B&B in the village near the castle which has been running since 1925. Every room has castle views.

Blacketts of Bamburgh, **t** 214 714, *www.blackettsofbamburgh.co.uk* (*cheap*). Restaurant and tea shop serving food from breakfast to dinner.

Lindisfarne t (01289) –

The Ship, Marygate, **t** 389 311, *www.lindisfarne accommodate.com* (*moderate*). Three rooms with central heating, TV and hair dryer. No smoking.

Britannia House, **t** 389 218 (*moderate*). Guesthouse in the village near the Priory. Also tea rooms.

Rose Villa, Fiddlers Green, **t** 389 268 (*moderate*). B&B. Comfortable rooms with TV, tea- and coffee-making facilities.

leads to another ruined fortification, **Dunstanburgh Castle** (*t (01665) 576 231, www.english-heritage.org.uk; open April–Sept daily 10–6; Oct daily 10–5; Nov–Mar Wed–Sun 10–4; adm*), reputedly haunted by Sir Guy the Seeker.

Near **Howick** archaeologists have found the remains of what they believe to be the oldest house in Britain, dating back to the Mesolithic period, 10,000 years ago.

Farne Islands

Now you see them; now you don't – the Farne Islands vary in number from 16 to 28, depending on the tide – but visit them you must to see their seabird and seal colonies. The flat black rocks are divided into two groups (separated by a sound) and lie 2–5 nautical miles off the coast near Bamburgh. The best time to visit is during the bird-breeding season in May, June and July, but in the months before and after at least you'll see seals and get a feel for the place.

Choose your cruise: some boats land; others don't. The trip is shorter (and cheaper) if you don't set foot on land, but a walk onshore will make your visit more interesting. Landings are restricted by the National Trust, guardians of the Farne Islands. In good weather you can land on Staple Island and Inner Farne (*adm*).

After a sprint across open water, your boat will heave close to the seal colonies on and around the volcanic rocks. There are estimated to be 4,000 Atlantic (or Grey) seals in the Farne Islands and each autumn their numbers are boosted by around 1,000 new pups. Basking on the rocks or bobbing in the chilly waters, they don't seem to mind the boat loads of visitors.

In the breeding season, eider ducks, guillemots, razorbills and terns will be pointed out. But it is the puffins that everyone comes to see. An estimated 70,000 of them nest in the soft sand in a good year but they leave once their young have fledged. The most popular cruise is punctuated by a visit to **Inner Farne**. One hour is just enough time onshore to eat a picnic and walk around the waymarked footpaths. In a couple of places you can look over the low cliffs to see the birds nesting.

Apart from the ornithological interest, the island forms part of England's early Christian history. **St Cuthbert** built a cell for himself and lived here from 676 to 684, quenching his thirst with rainwater. He spent the next two years away as bishop of Lindisfarne but returned to Inner Farne to die in 687. He is said to have been the first protector of wildlife in Britain, permitting the eider ducks to nest on the steps of his makeshift altar. The chapel in his honour was built in the 14th century and repaired in the 1840s.

Bamburgh

Bamburgh Castle (*t (01668) 214 515, www.bamburghcastle.com; open April–Oct daily 11–5; adm*) is one of the finest in England, perfectly sited on a basalt outcrop above a sandy beach, with views of the Farne Islands and Lindisfarne. Bamburgh was the capital of the Anglo-Saxon Kingdom of Northumberland and a wooden castle stood on this defensible rock until the Normans replaced it with one of stone. That castle lasted until the end of the Wars of the Roses, surviving numerous sieges without being taken but, like most castles, becoming obsolete upon the invention of the

Grace Darling

On the outermost island of the Farne Islands stands the Longstone Lighthouse (*www.lighthouse-visits.co.uk*), famous for the events of the early morning hours of 7 September 1838. A storm was blowing and the *Forfarshire*, a paddle steamer, ran aground on the island of Big Harcar when its boilers failed. Grace Darling, aged 23, and her father the lighthouse keeper rescued nine people at the risk of their own lives in a cobble (a heavy wooden rowing boat). Another nine people were rescued, but 43 died. The rescue turned Grace Darling into a Victorian heroine: feminine, yet tough of spirit and ever ready to do her duty. Sadly, three years after her heroic deed, she died, like all Victorian heroines, of TB. The lighthouse was automated in 1990.

cannon. It owes its present appearance to the 1st Baron Armstrong, an industrialist, shipbuilder and engineer, who restored his family home in the 1890s. The visit includes the King's Hall, the Cross Hall, bakehouse and Victorian scullery, armoury and dungeon, with paintings, furniture, tapestries, porcelain, glass, arms and armour along the way. The old laundry contains two museums: the **Armstrong Museum**, explaining the achievements of the 1st Baron, and the **Bamburgh Castle Aviation Artefacts Museum**, containing relics from the history of flight.

In the village of Bamburgh there is a **Grace Darling museum** (***t*** *(01668) 214 465; open Mon–Sat 10–5 and Sun 12–5; adm*). The monument to her in the churchyard is sited so as to be seen by passing ships.

Lindisfarne

From a distance, it is easy to see what first attracted the early Christians of Northumbria to Lindisfarne, also known as Holy Island. A cone of rock seems to rise abruptly out of the flat, shallow sea like the foundations of the Tower of Babel. This cone, topped off by a castle, stands on a slice of land which struggles to rise above sea level. It looks like an island, but is not always one; tantalisingly close to shore and joined to it by a causeway half the time, Lindisfarne is cut off by each high tide and reconnected when the tide ebbs.

In the year 635 a monk called **Aidan** from another holy island, Iona, was invited to spread the Gospel in northern England by Northumbrian King Oswald. Aidan (later canonized) chose the tidal island of Lindisfarne as his base and founded a monastery. He was succeeded by **St Cuthbert**, who became abbot of Lindisfarne in 685. In around 700 the monks of Lindisfarne produced the famous illuminated **Lindisfarne Gospels**. On 8 June 793 the Vikings began their spree of violence with a raid on the defenceless monastic community, as recorded in *The Anglo-Saxon Chronicle*: 'Terrible portents appeared over Northumbria, and miserably frightened the inhabitants: these were exceptional flashes of lightning, and fiery dragons were seen flying in the air'.

The Vikings returned in 875 and this time it was too much for the monks. They took St Cuthbert's incorrupt body and fled. **Lindisfarne Priory** was refounded, however, in 1082, and a small community of monks continued to live on the island until Henry VIII dissolved the monasteries in 1536. Shortly after, in 1549, a castle was built on the island as a stronghold in the wars between England and Scotland.

Give yourself time to soak up the atmosphere of Lindisfarne. The first thing to do before visiting is to get a tide table, so that you get stranded only if you want to. Lindisfarne is a different place when the day-trippers have fled to the mainland and the seas have closed in over the mud flats and salt marsh. To experience the place as the monks would have known it you'll either have to hang about for four to six hours waiting for the next low tide or put yourself up in one of the island's guest houses. Most people drive on and off within one low tide, which gives you six to seven hours on the island if you time it right.

The settlement on Lindisfarne is small – mainly cafés and Celtic souvenir shops. The **Lindisfarne Heritage Centre** (***t** (01289) 389 004, www.lindisfarne-heritage-centre.org; open daily 10–5.30; adm*) is worth looking into. It has exhibitions on Lindisfarne's landscapes and history, and the islanders' lives. Here you can thumb through some of the pages of the Lindisfarne Gospels, created by the monk Eadfrid in 698, in an electronic version produced by the British Library (the keeper of the original manuscript).

The other two places to visit are the romantic pink ruins of the **priory** (***t** (01289) 389 200; open daily April–Sept 10–6; Oct 10–5; Nov–Mar 10–4; adm*) and the **castle,** less than a mile's walk around the harbour from the settlement (***t** (01289) 389 244; open April–Oct Sat–Thurs 12–3; adm*) which was restored by Edwin Lutyens in 1902. After that, walk around and enjoy the countryside and seascapes.

Lindisfarne Gospels

It is believed that the illustrated manuscript of the Lindisfarne Gospels, now kept in the British Library, was the work of the hand and creative brain of Eadfrith, a monk and scribe of Lindisfarne. It used to be thought that he undertook the work while awaiting the elevation (or translation) of his master, St Cuthbert (that is, the disinterment and reburying of his bones) which took place 11 years after his death, in 698. But recently the Gospels have been redated to around the year 720. During his two years in the *scriptorium* Eadfrith produced page after page, most bearing the calligraphic text in Latin, but a few dedicated to exquisite artwork. The major divisions of the book are marked by 15 wholly decorative pages. A sequence of three such pages precedes each Gospel: title page, 'carpet' page (an intricate design without text) and initial page, on which the Evangelist's name and the opening words of his Gospel are superbly illuminated. Eadfrith used 45 colours for these pages, including the expensive pigment of ultramarine from a precious stone found in the Himalayas. His illustrations fall into four groups: dogs and birds, straight line patterns, curved line patterns and interlace patterns or knotwork. After creating his Gospels, Eadfrith was made bishop of Lindisfarne.

When the monks left Lindisfarne in 875 to escape Viking attacks they took the book with them for safe keeping. For a time it was kept at Chester-le-Street and here a 'gloss' was added: an English translation written in a fine hand above the Latin text. The elaborate original cover to the Lindisfarne Gospels, made of leather inset with jewels and precious metals, was lost at the time of the Dissolution.

St Cuthbert's Way

This 62-mile waymarked footpath leads from Melrose in the Scottish borders, where St Cuthbert is believed to have first preached, to Lindisfarne, where he died. It takes five to six days on average to complete (*www.scot-borders.co.uk*).

Berwick-upon-Tweed

Northumberland and England end at Berwick-upon-Tweed, or at least a short way north of it. If you can hear a Scottish twang creeping into the local accent it may be that Berwick is the main town of the border country; it changed hands 14 times between 1147 and 1482, but is now firmly part of England.

Three great bridges stride across the Tweed here. Side by side are the sandstone **Old Bridge** of 1634 and the more humble 1920s **Royal Tweed Bridge**. Most impressive of the three by far is the **Royal Border Railway Viaduct** built by Robert Stephenson and opened by Queen Victoria in 1849: more than a mile long, it rises 120 feet above the water below. The town centre on the north bank of the Tweed is agreeable to stroll around, but particularly recommended is a walk along the walls and bastions, which were completed in 1565 and, unlike earlier fortifications, were intended to withstand cannon-fire. The other point of historical interest is **Berwick Barracks** (*The Parade, off Church Street,* **t** *(01289) 304 493; open April–Sept daily 10–6, Oct 10–5, Nov–Mar Wed–Sun 10–4; adm*), a military museum in an 18th-century building.

Tourist Information

Berwick-upon-Tweed: 106 Marygate, **t** (01289) 330 733, *www.berwickonline.org.uk*.

Where to Stay and Eat

Berwick-upon-Tweed t (01289) –

No. 1 Sallyport, off Bridge St, **t** 308 827, *www.1sallyport-bedandbreakfast.com* (*expensive*). A 17th-century listed house right in the middle of Berwick, a place to relax and be pampered. There are several restaurants adjacent or you can try the 'orgasmic home baking'.

Middle Ord Manor House, Middle Ord Farm, **t** 306 323, *www.middleord.ntb.org.uk* (*expensive*). Georgian manor house.

Marshall Meadows Country House Hotel, **t** 331 133, *www.marshallmeadows.co.uk* (*expensive*). 'England's most northerly hotel' is a Georgian mansion in woodlands and gardens. English and Continental cuisine.

Garden Cottage, West Kyloe, **t** 381 279 (*moderate*). Peaceful place with views of the coast. Large sitting room and pretty garden.

High Letham Farmhouse, **t** 306 585 (*moderate*). South-facing Georgian farmhouse standing in its own land, two miles from Berwick. Three bedrooms plus drying room, rod room and gun room. Cordon Bleu dinners with good wine list.

Index

Main page references are in **bold**. Page References to maps are in *italics*.

England touring atlas

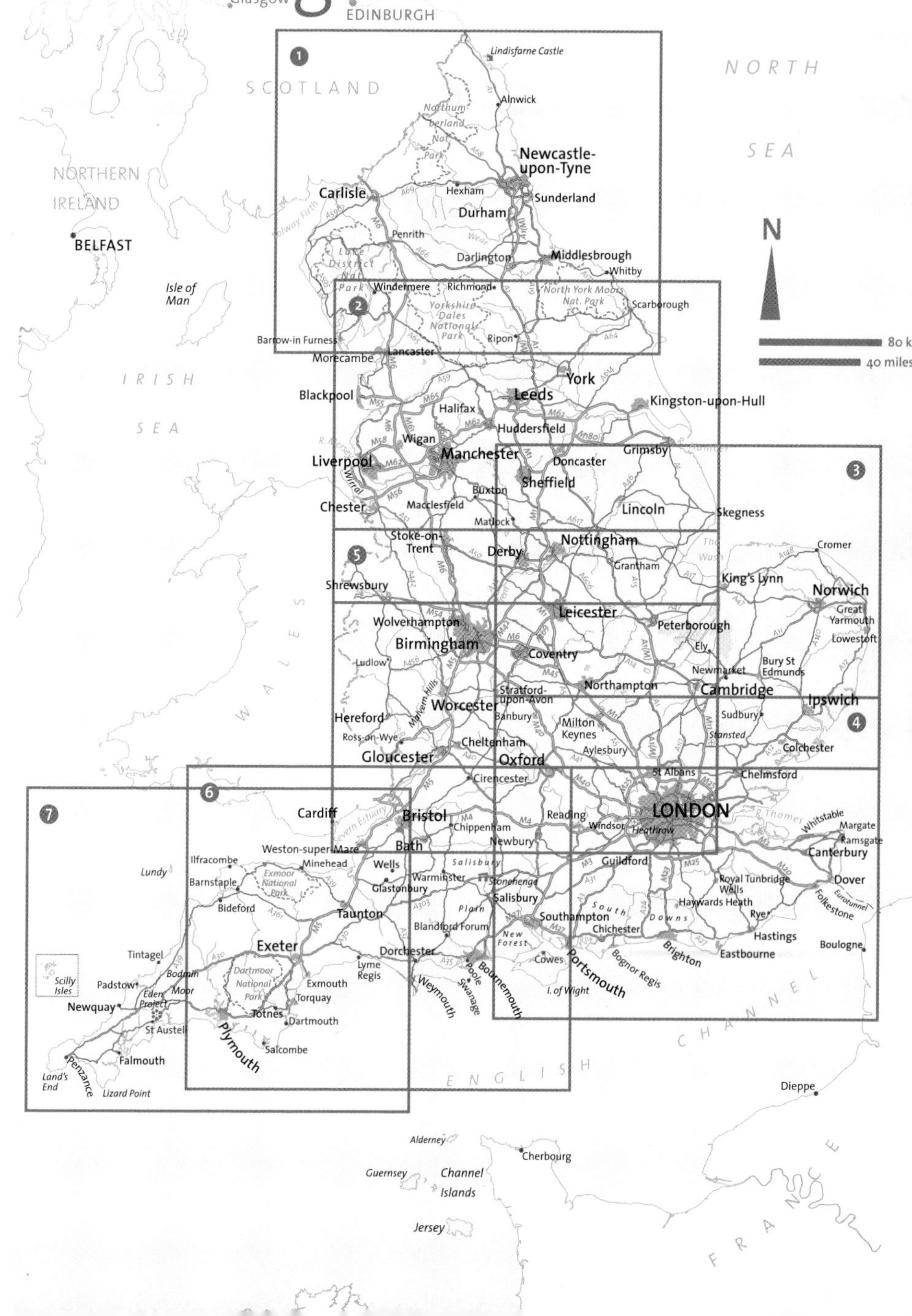

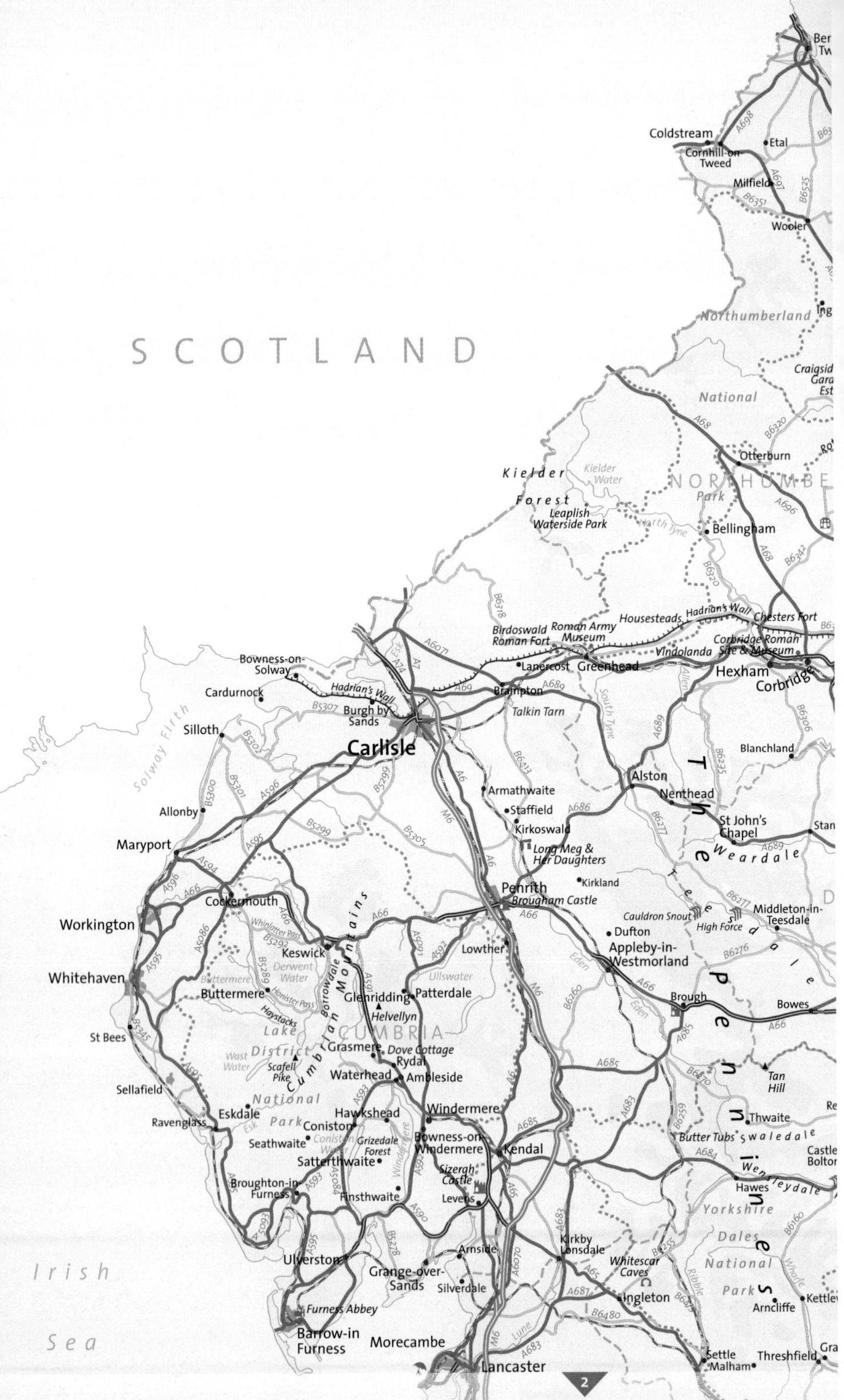

SCOTLAND
Coldstream
Cornhill-on-Tweed
Etal
Milfield
Wooler
Northumberland
National
Park
NORTHUMBE
Otterburn
Kielder
Forest
Kielder Water
Leaplish Waterside Park
North Tyne
Bellingham
Birdoswald Roman Fort
Roman Army Museum
Housesteads
Hadrian's Wall
Chesters Fort
Corbridge Roman Site & Museum
Vindolanda
Lanercost
Greenhead
Hexham
Corbridge
Bowness-on-Solway
Cardurnock
Burgh by Sands
Brampton
Talkin Tarn
South Tyne
Solway Firth
Silloth
Carlisle
Blanchland
Alston
Nenthead
St John's Chapel
Weardale
Armathwaite
Staffield
Kirkoswald
Long Meg & Her Daughters
Allonby
Maryport
Penrith
Brougham Castle
Kirkland
Cockermouth
Workington
Whinlatter Pass
Cumbrian Mountains
Keswick
Derwent Water
Borrowdale
Lowther
Ullswater
Cauldron Snout
High Force
Dufton
Middleton-in-Teesdale
Teesdale
Appleby-in-Westmorland
Eden
Whitehaven
Buttermere
Honister Pass
Haystacks
Glenridding
Patterdale
Helvellyn
Brough
Bowes
St Bees
Lake District
National Park
CUMBRIA
Grasmere
Dove Cottage
Rydal
Wast Water
Scafell Pike
Waterhead
Ambleside
The Pennines
Tan Hill
Sellafield
Eskdale
Ravenglass
Hawkshead
Coniston
Coniston Water
Windermere
Thwaite
Swaledale
Butter Tubs
Seathwaite
Grizedale Forest
Bowness-on-Windermere
Kendal
Satterthwaite
Sizergh Castle
Wensleydale
Hawes
Broughton-in-Furness
Finsthwaite
Levens
Yorkshire
Dales
National
Park
Arnside
Kirkby Lonsdale
Whitescar Caves
Ulverston
Grange-over-Sands
Silverdale
Ingleton
Irish Sea
Furness Abbey
Arncliffe
Barrow-in-Furness
Morecambe
Lancaster
Settle
Malham
Threshfield
2

40 km
20 miles
N
North Sea
Holy Island
Lindisfarne Castle
Farne Islands
Bamburgh Castle
Bamburgh
Seahouses
Dunstanburgh Castle
Craster
Howick
Alnwick
Alnmouth
Warkworth Castle
Warkworth
Amble
Rothbury
Ashington
Wallington House
Morpeth
Newcastle-upon-Tyne
Whitley Bay
Tynemouth
South Shields
North Shields
Jarrow
Gateshead
TYNE & WEAR
Souter Lighthouse
Prudhoe
Tyne Riverside Country Park
Rowlands Gill
Washington
Sunderland
Beamish Open Air Museum
Seaham
Lanchester
Durham
Hartlepool
Tees Bay
Redcar
Bishop Auckland
Stockton-on-Tees
Saltburn-by-the-Sea
Staithes
Runswick Bay
Barnard Castle
Darlington
Middlesbrough
Whitby
Great Ayton
Croft-on-Tees
Hawsker
Robin Hood's Bay
Richmond
Goathland
North York Moors National Park
North Yorkshire Moors Railway
Ravenscar
Staintondale
Osmotherley
Layburn
Lastingham
Hutton-le-Hole
Scarborough Castle
Scarborough
Aysgarth Falls
Jervaulx Abbey
Rievault
Helmsley
Pickering
Ayton
Masham
Thirsk
Kilburn
Filey
Coxwold
NORTH YORKSHIRE
Lofthouse
Eden Camp
Bempton
Ripon
Brandsby
Castle Howard
Malton
Bridlington
Fountains Abbey
Newby Hall
Boroughbridge
Rudston
Brimham Rocks
Wharram Percy
Sledmere House
Burton Agnes
2

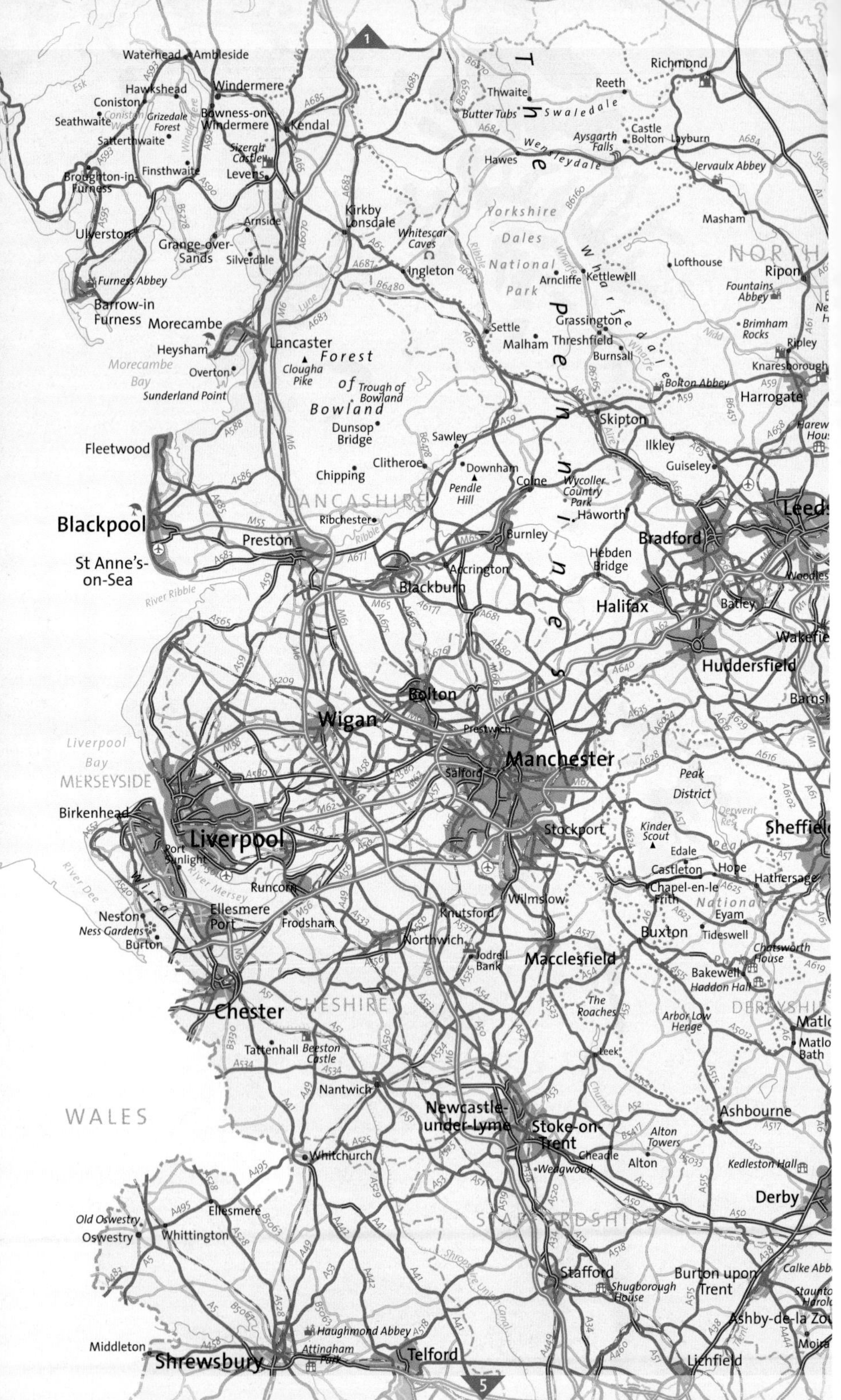

1
Waterhead
Ambleside
Hawkshead
Windermere
Coniston
Seathwaite
Grizedale Forest
Bowness-on-Windermere
Kendal
Satterthwaite
Sizergh Castle
Broughton-in-Furness
Finsthwaite
Levens
Ulverston
Arnside
Grange-over-Sands
Silverdale
Furness Abbey
Barrow-in Furness
Morecambe
Heysham
Lancaster
Morecambe Bay
Overton
Sunderland Point
Kirkby Lonsdale
Whitescar Caves
Ingleton
Forest of Bowland
Clougha Pike
Trough of Bowland
Dunsop Bridge
Fleetwood
Chipping
Clitheroe
Sawley
Downham
Pendle Hill
LANCASHIRE
Ribchester
Blackpool
Preston
St Anne's-on-Sea
River Ribble
Blackburn
Accrington
Burnley
Colne
Wycoller Country Park
Haworth
Hebden Bridge
Halifax
Bradford
Leeds
Batley
Huddersfield
Richmond
Reeth
Thwaite
Butter Tubs
Swaledale
Castle Bolton
Layburn
Aysgarth Falls
Hawes
Wensleydale
Jervaulx Abbey
Masham
Yorkshire Dales National Park
The Pennines
Wharfedale
Arncliffe
Kettlewell
Lofthouse
Ripon
Fountains Abbey
Brimham Rocks
Ripley
Knaresborough
Harrogate
Settle
Malham
Grassington
Threshfield
Burnsall
Bolton Abbey
Skipton
Ilkley
Guiseley
Bolton
Wigan
Prestwich
Manchester
Salford
Liverpool Bay
MERSEYSIDE
Birkenhead
Liverpool
Port Sunlight
Wirral
River Dee
River Mersey
Runcorn
Neston
Ness Gardens
Burton
Ellesmere Port
Frodsham
Knutsford
Northwich
Jodrell Bank
Wilmslow
Stockport
Macclesfield
Peak District
Kinder Scout
Edale
Castleton
Hope
Hathersage
Chapel-en-le-Frith
Eyam
Buxton
Tideswell
Chatsworth House
Bakewell
Haddon Hall
Sheffield
Derwent Res
The Roaches
Arbor Low Henge
DERBYSHIRE
Matlock
Matlock Bath
Chester
CHESHIRE
Tattenhall
Beeston Castle
Nantwich
Leek
WALES
Newcastle-under-Lyme
Stoke-on-Trent
Alton Towers
Cheadle
Alton
Wedgwood
Ashbourne
Kedleston Hall
Derby
Whitchurch
Old Oswestry
Oswestry
Whittington
Ellesmere
STAFFORDSHIRE
Stafford
Shugborough House
Burton upon Trent
Calke Abbey
Ashby-de-la Zouch
Middleton
Shrewsbury
Haughmond Abbey
Attingham Park
Telford
Lichfield
Shropshire Union Canal
5

2
1
40 km
20 miles
N
North York Moors
National Park
Goathland
North Yorkshire Moors Railway
Ravenscar
Staintondale
Osmotherley
Lastingham
Hutton-le-Hole
Scarborough Castle
Scarborough
Rievault
Helmsley
Pickering
Ayton
Thirsk
Kilburn
Filey
Coxwold
YORKSHIRE
Eden Camp
Malton
Bempton
Flamborough Head
Brandsby
Castle Howard
Boroughbridge
Wharram Percy
Rudston
Bridlington
Sledmere House
Burton Agnes
North
Sea
Driffield
Foston-on-the-Wolds
York
Pocklington
EAST RIDING OF YORKSHIRE
Hornsea
Burnby Hall
Market Weighton
Beverley
Burton Constable
Kingston-upon-Hull
Hedon
Withernsea
Castleford
Humber Bridge
Goxhill
Alkborough
Patrington
Thornton Abbey
NORTH LINCOLNSHIRE
R. Humber
Grimsby
Spurn Head
N. E. LINCOLNSHIRE
Cleethorpes
Humberston
Doncaster
SOUTH YORKSHIRE
Conisbrough
North Somercotes
Saltfleet
Rotherham
Donna Nook
Maltby
Roche Abbey
Louth
Stow
Snarford
Mablethorpe
Worksop
Chesterfield
Clumber Park
LINCOLNSHIRE
Tuxford
Lincoln
Hardwick Hall
Edwinstowe
Laxton
Horncastle
Old Bolingbroke
Spilsby
Woodhall Spa
Skegness
Sherwood Forest
NOTTINGHAMSHIRE
Coningsby
Tattershall
Gibraltar Point
Newstead Abbey
Southwell
Newark-on-Trent
Sibsey
3
Eastwood
Sleaford
Boston
Nottingham
Belton House
Wollaton Hall
The Wash
Woolsthorpe
Grantham
Belvoir
Melbourne
Spalding
Loughborough
Melton Mowbray
Bradgate Park
Coalville
RUTLAND
Market Deeping
Crowland
Wisbech
5

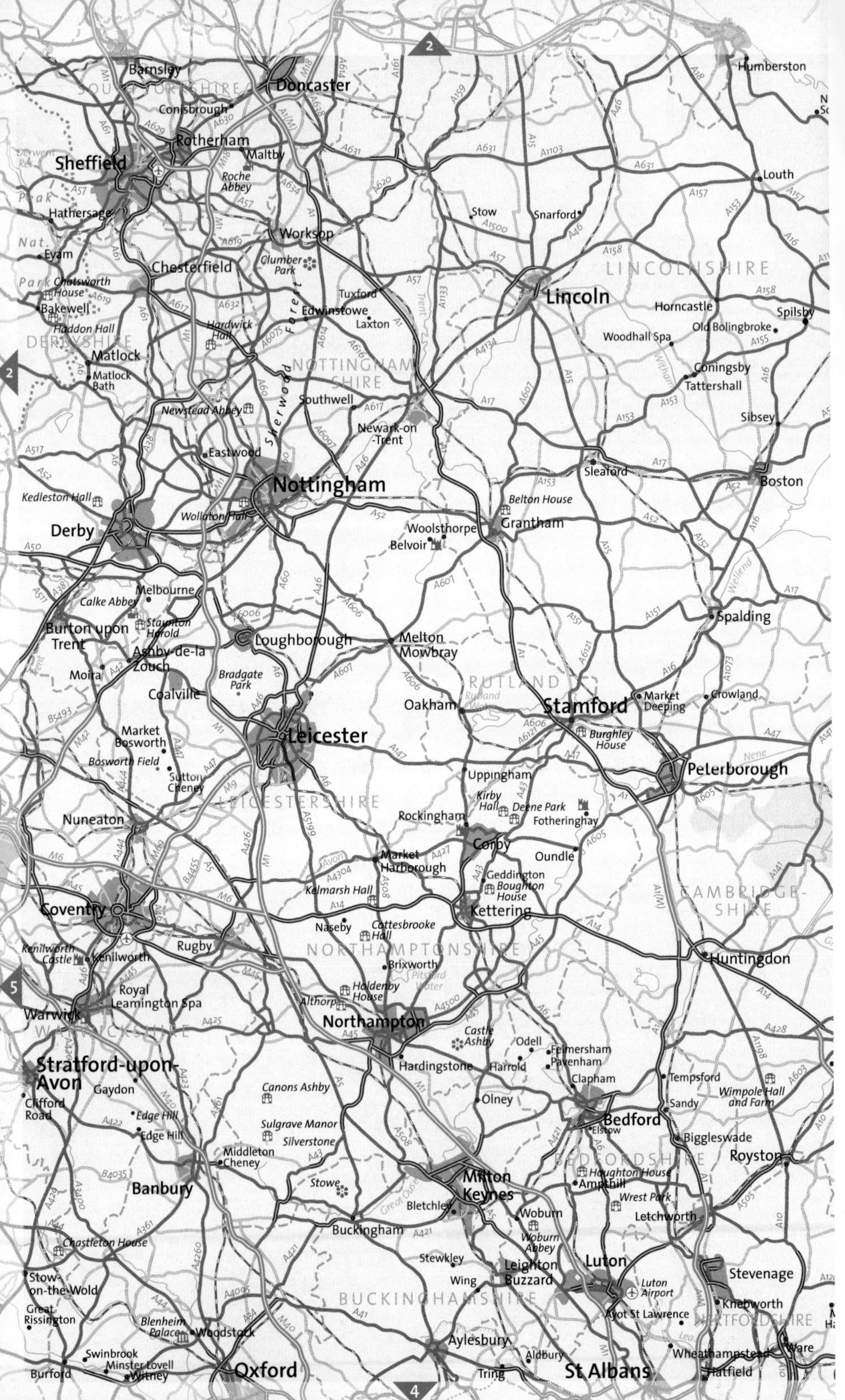
2
Barnsley
Doncaster
Humberston
SOUTH YORKSHIRE
Conisbrough
Rotherham
Maltby
Sheffield
Roche
Abbey
Hathersage
Eyam
Worksop
Clumber
Park
Chesterfield
Chatsworth
House
Bakewell
Haddon Hall
DERBYSHIRE
Matlock
Matlock
Bath
Hardwick
Hall
Tuxford
Edwinstowe
Laxton
Sherwood Forest
NOTTINGHAMSHIRE
Southwell
Newstead Abbey
Newark-on
-Trent
Eastwood
Nottingham
Kedleston Hall
Wollaton Hall
Derby
Louth
Stow
Snarford
LINCOLNSHIRE
Lincoln
Horncastle
Spilsby
Old Bolingbroke
Woodhall Spa
Coningsby
Tattershall
Sibsey
Sleaford
Boston
Belton House
Grantham
Woolsthorpe
Belvoir
Melbourne
Calke Abbey
Staunton
Harold
Burton upon
Trent
Ashby-de-la
Zouch
Loughborough
Melton
Mowbray
Moira
Coalville
Bradgate
Park
Spalding
RUTLAND
Rutland
Water
Oakham
Stamford
Market
Deeping
Crowland
Burghley
House
Leicester
Market
Bosworth
Bosworth Field
Sutton
Cheney
LEICESTERSHIRE
Uppingham
Peterborough
Nene
Kirby
Hall
Deene Park
Fotheringhay
Rockingham
Corby
Oundle
Nuneaton
Market
Harborough
Avon
Geddington
Boughton
House
Kelmarsh Hall
Kettering
CAMBRIDGESHIRE
Coventry
Naseby
Cottesbrooke
Hall
NORTHAMPTONSHIRE
Kenilworth
Castle
Kenilworth
Rugby
Brixworth
Pitsford
Water
Huntingdon
5
Royal
Leamington Spa
Holdenby
House
Althorp
Warwick
WARWICKSHIRE
Northampton
Castle
Ashby
Odell
Felmersham
Pavenham
Stratford-upon-
Avon
Hardingstone
Harrold
Gaydon
Clifford
Road
Canons Ashby
Clapham
Tempsford
Wimpole Hall
and Farm
Olney
Sandy
Edge Hill
Edge Hill
Sulgrave Manor
Silverstone
Bedford
Elstow
Biggleswade
Middleton
Cheney
BEDFORDSHIRE
Royston
Banbury
Stowe
Milton
Keynes
Houghton House
Ampthill
Wrest Park
Great Ouse
Bletchley
Woburn
Woburn
Abbey
Letchworth
Buckingham
Chastleton House
Stewkley
Leighton
Buzzard
Luton
Stevenage
Wing
Luton
Airport
Stow-
on-the-Wold
BUCKINGHAMSHIRE
Knebworth
Great
Rissington
Ayot St Lawrence
HERTFORDSHIRE
Blenheim
Palace
Woodstock
Aylesbury
Wheathampstead
Ware
Swinbrook
Minster Lovell
Aldbury
Burford
Witney
Oxford
Tring
St Albans
Hatfield
4
M1
M18
A1(M)
A614
A161
A159
A18
A46
A630
A629
A61
A57
A631
A15
A1103
A620
A634
A619
A1500
A157
A153
A16
A158
A632
A617
A6075
A616
A1133
A4134
A6
A60
A38
A607
A17
A6097
A517
A52
A50
A511
A6006
A606
A151
A6121
A1073
B5493
M42
A447
A47
A147
M69
M6
A444
A4304
A5199
A427
A43
A605
A14
A508
A45
A4500
A1(M)
A141
A425
A422
M40
A361
A423
B4035
A429
A3400
A4260
A4095
A44
A34
A41
A421
A5
A603
A1198
A428
A505
A10

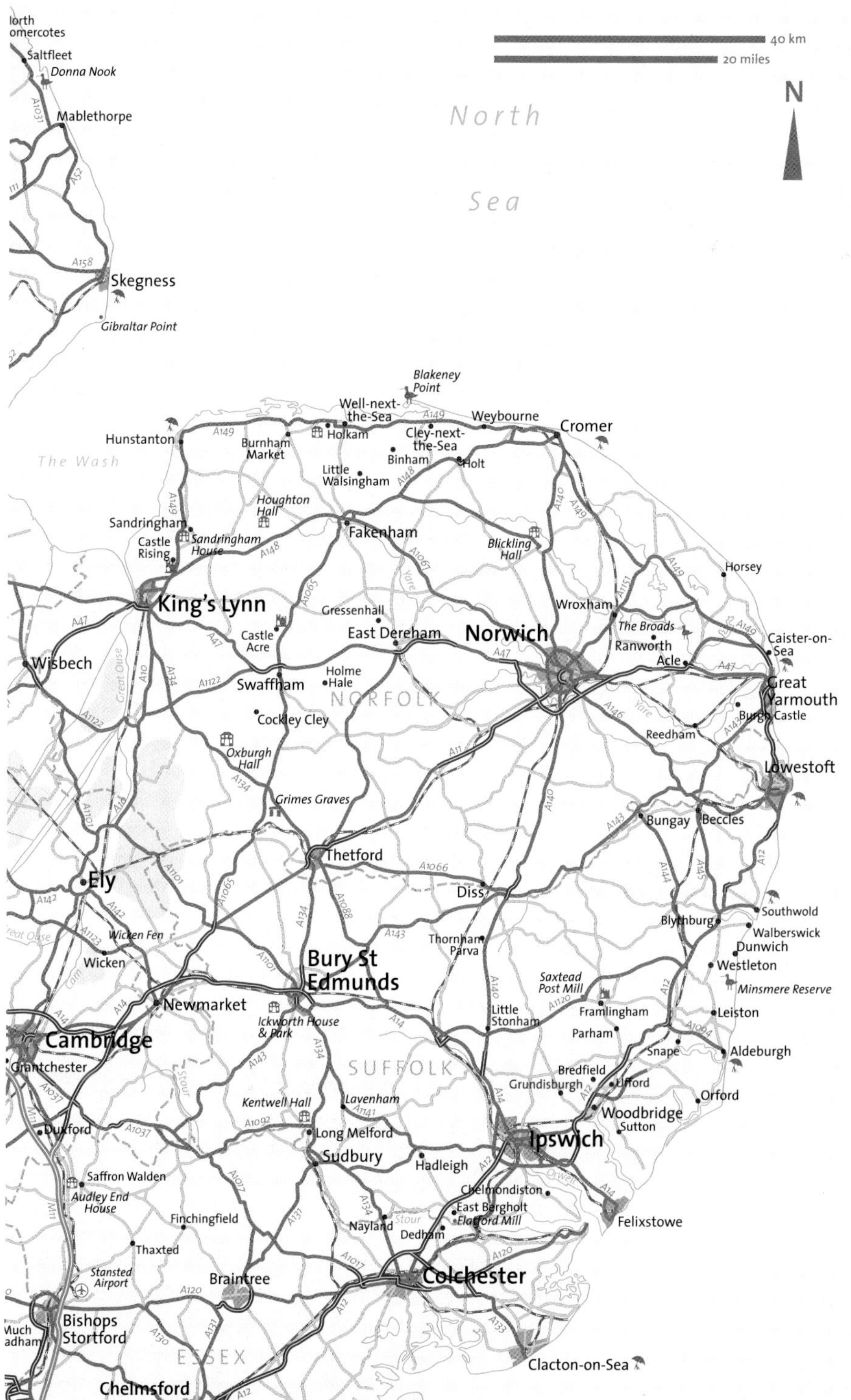

40 km
20 miles
N
North Sea
Saltfleet
Donna Nook
Mablethorpe
Skegness
Gibraltar Point
Blakeney Point
Well-next-the-Sea
Weybourne
Cromer
Hunstanton
Burnham Market
Holkam
Cley-next-the-Sea
Binham
Holt
Little Walsingham
The Wash
Houghton Hall
Sandringham
Sandringham House
Castle Rising
Fakenham
Blickling Hall
Horsey
King's Lynn
Gressenhall
Wroxham
Castle Acre
East Dereham
Norwich
The Broads
Ranworth
Caister-on-Sea
Acle
Wisbech
Swaffham
Holme Hale
NORFOLK
Great Yarmouth
Burgh Castle
Cockley Cley
Reedham
Oxburgh Hall
Lowestoft
Grimes Graves
Bungay
Beccles
Thetford
Ely
Diss
Southwold
Blythburg
Walberswick
Wicken Fen
Thornham Parva
Dunwich
Wicken
Bury St Edmunds
Westleton
Saxtead Post Mill
Minsmere Reserve
Newmarket
Little Stonham
Framlingham
Leiston
Ickworth House & Park
Parham
Cambridge
Snape
Aldeburgh
Grantchester
SUFFOLK
Bredfield
Grundisburgh
Ufford
Orford
Kentwell Hall
Lavenham
Woodbridge
Sutton
Duxford
Long Melford
Ipswich
Sudbury
Hadleigh
Saffron Walden
Chelmondiston
Audley End House
East Bergholt
Flatford Mill
Felixstowe
Finchingfield
Nayland
Dedham
Thaxted
Stansted Airport
Braintree
Colchester
Bishops Stortford
ESSEX
Clacton-on-Sea
Chelmsford
A149
A148
A47
A10
A134
A1122
A11
A140
A143
A1066
A12
A14
A1101
A1065
A1088
A142
A1123
A1120
A1094
A1141
A1092
A1017
A131
A120
A133
A130
A1307
M11
A1151
A146
A144
A145
A1067
A158
A52
A1031
Great Ouse
Cam
Stour
Yare
Orwell

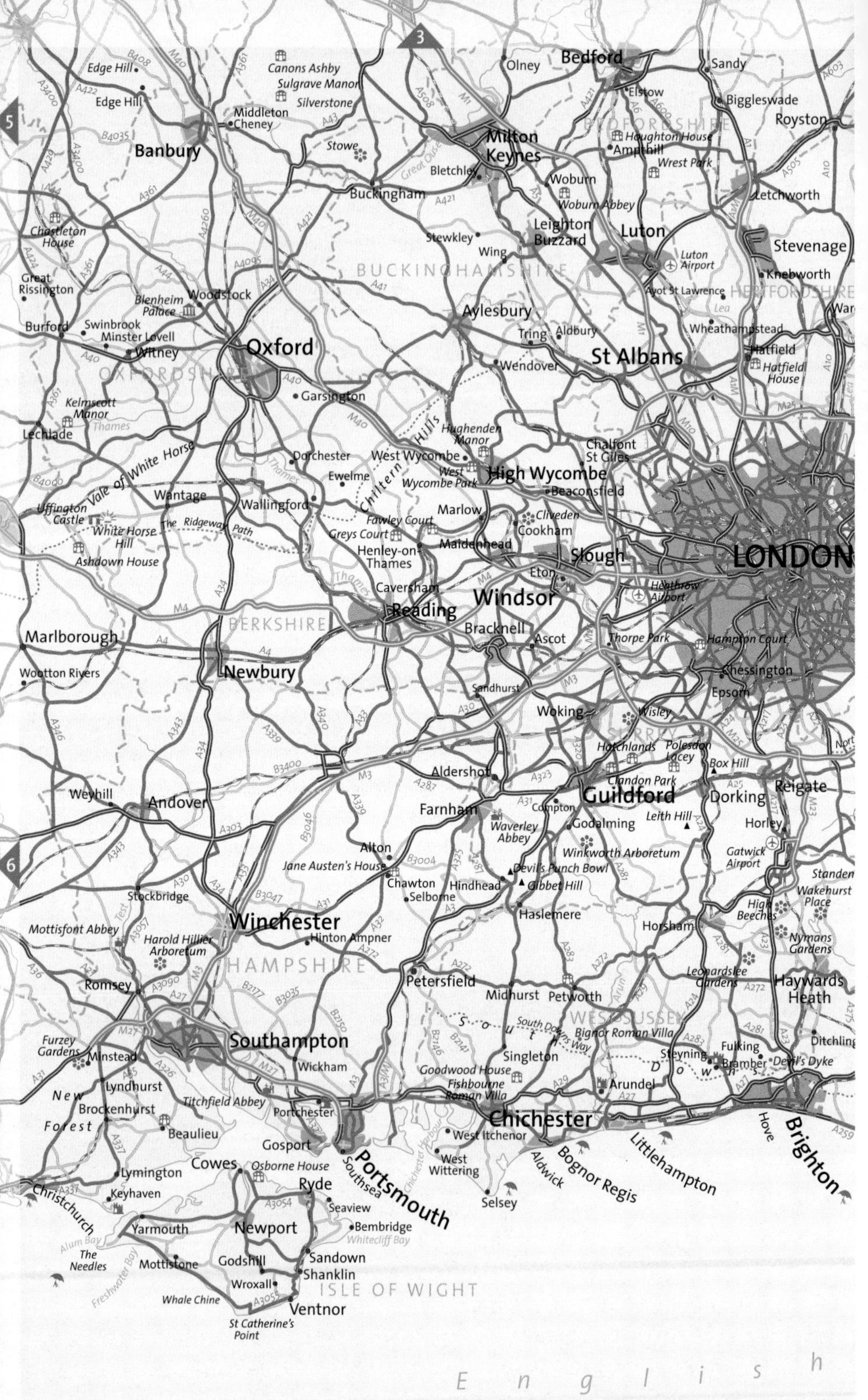

3
5
6
Edge Hill
Canons Ashby
Sulgrave Manor
Silverstone
Olney
Bedford
Sandy
Elstow
Biggleswade
Royston
BEDFORDSHIRE
Middleton Cheney
Banbury
Stowe
Milton Keynes
Houghton House
Ampthill
Wrest Park
Bletchley
Buckingham
Woburn
Woburn Abbey
Letchworth
Chastleton House
Stewkley
Leighton Buzzard
Luton
Stevenage
Wing
Luton Airport
Knebworth
BUCKINGHAMSHIRE
Great Rissington
Blenheim Palace
Woodstock
Ayot St Lawrence
HERTFORDSHIRE
Burford
Swinbrook
Minster Lovell
Witney
Oxford
Aylesbury
Tring
Aldbury
Wheathampstead
Hatfield
Hatfield House
OXFORDSHIRE
Wendover
St Albans
Garsington
Kelmscott Manor
Lechlade
Thames
Hughenden Manor
Chalfont St Giles
Vale of White Horse
Dorchester
West Wycombe
Chiltern Hills
Ewelme
West Wycombe Park
High Wycombe
Beaconsfield
Wantage
Wallingford
Uffington Castle
White Horse Hill
The Ridgeway Path
Ashdown House
Marlow
Fawley Court
Greys Court
Cliveden
Cookham
Henley-on-Thames
Maidenhead
Slough
LONDON
Eton
Caversham
Windsor
Heathrow Airport
Reading
BERKSHIRE
Marlborough
Bracknell
Ascot
Thorpe Park
Hampton Court
Wootton Rivers
Newbury
Chessington
Epsom
Sandhurst
Woking
Wisley
SURREY
Hatchlands
Polesden Lacey
Box Hill
Aldershot
Clandon Park
Guildford
Dorking
Reigate
Weyhill
Andover
Farnham
Compton
Leith Hill
Horley
Waverley Abbey
Godalming
Gatwick Airport
Alton
Winkworth Arboretum
Jane Austen's House
Chawton
Selborne
Hindhead
Devil's Punch Bowl
Gibbet Hill
Stockbridge
Wakehurst Place
High Beeches
Haslemere
Winchester
Horsham
Mottisfont Abbey
Hinton Ampner
Nymans Gardens
Harold Hillier Arboretum
HAMPSHIRE
Leonardslee Gardens
Haywards Heath
Romsey
Petersfield
Midhurst
Petworth
WEST SUSSEX
South Downs Way
Bignor Roman Villa
Furzey Gardens
Minstead
Southampton
Singleton
Steyning
Fulking
Bramber
Devil's Dyke
Ditchling
Wickham
Goodwood House
Fishbourne Roman Villa
Arundel
Lyndhurst
New Forest
Titchfield Abbey
Brockenhurst
Portchester
Chichester
Beaulieu
West Itchenor
Gosport
Portsmouth
Southsea
West Wittering
Aldwick
Bognor Regis
Littlehampton
Hove
Brighton
Chichester Harbour
Lymington
Cowes
Osborne House
Ryde
Christchurch
Keyhaven
Seaview
Selsey
Yarmouth
Newport
Bembridge
Whitecliff Bay
Alum Bay
The Needles
Mottistone
Godshill
Sandown
Shanklin
Freshwater Bay
Wroxall
ISLE OF WIGHT
Whale Chine
Ventnor
St Catherine's Point
E n g l i s h

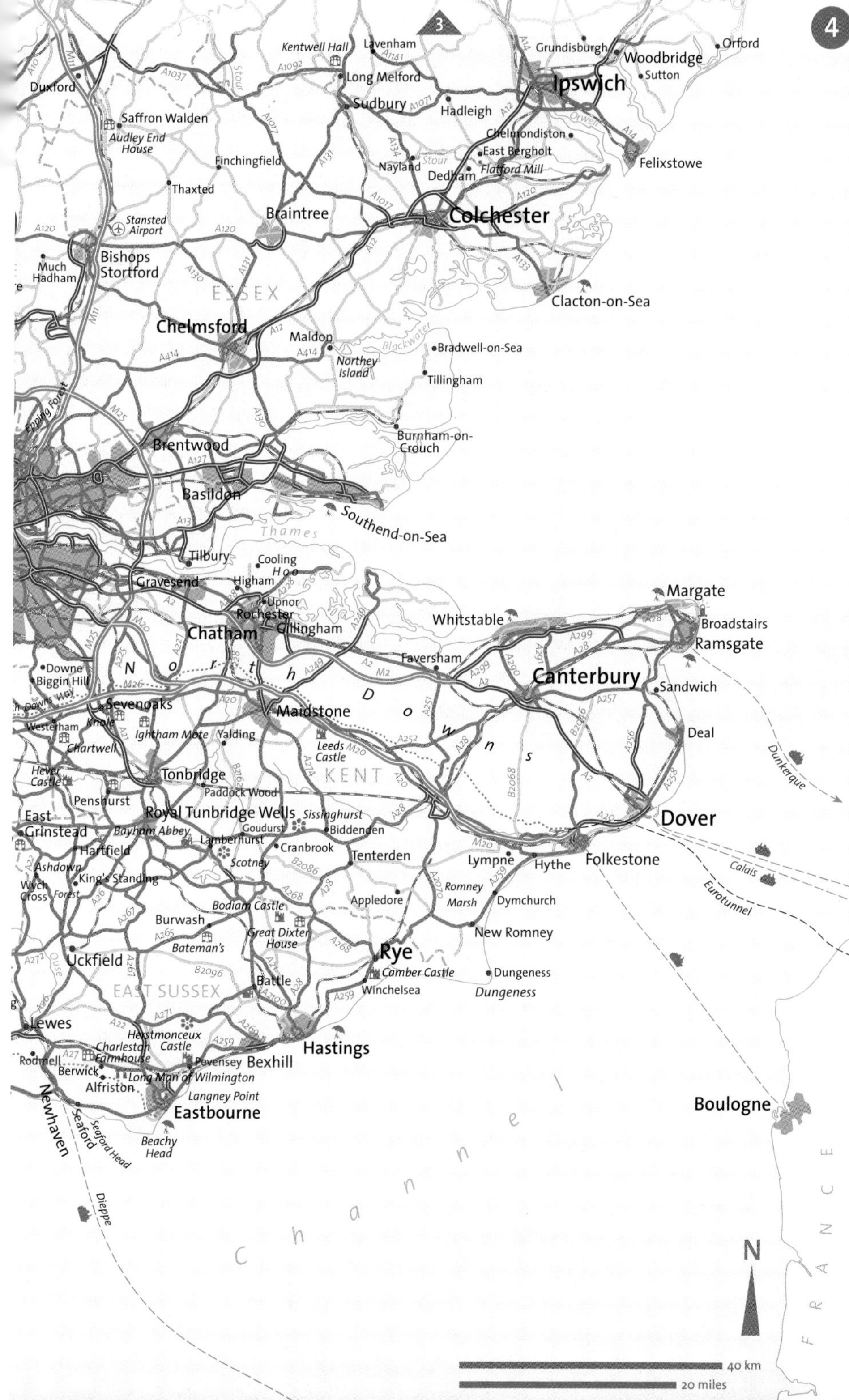
3
Kentwell Hall
Lavenham
Grundisburgh
Woodbridge
Orford
Sutton
Duxford
Long Melford
Ipswich
Sudbury
Hadleigh
Saffron Walden
Audley End House
Chelmondiston
Felixstowe
East Bergholt
Finchingfield
Nayland
Dedham
Flatford Mill
Thaxted
Braintree
Colchester
Stansted Airport
Bishops Stortford
Much Hadham
ESSEX
Clacton-on-Sea
Chelmsford
Maldon
Bradwell-on-Sea
Northey Island
Tillingham
Blackwater
Epping Forest
Brentwood
Burnham-on-Crouch
Basildon
Southend-on-Sea
Thames
Tilbury
Cooling
Hoo
Gravesend
Higham
Upnor
Rochester
Margate
Whitstable
Broadstairs
Chatham
Gillingham
Ramsgate
Faversham
Downe
Biggin Hill
North Downs
Canterbury
Sandwich
Sevenoaks
Maidstone
Westerham
Knole
Ightham Mote
Yalding
Deal
Chartwell
Leeds Castle
Dunkerque
Hever Castle
Tonbridge
KENT
Penshurst
Paddock Wood
East Grinstead
Royal Tunbridge Wells
Sissinghurst
Dover
Bayham Abbey
Goudurst
Biddenden
Lamberhurst
Hartfield
Cranbrook
Folkestone
Lympne
Hythe
Scotney
Tenterden
Ashdown Forest
Calais
Wych Cross
King's Standing
Romney Marsh
Eurotunnel
Dymchurch
Appledore
Bodiam Castle
Burwash
Great Dixter House
New Romney
Bateman's
Rye
Uckfield
Camber Castle
Dungeness
Battle
EAST SUSSEX
Winchelsea
Lewes
Herstmonceux Castle
Hastings
Charleston Farmhouse
Rodmell
Pevensey
Bexhill
Berwick
Long Man of Wilmington
Alfriston
Langney Point
Newhaven
Seaford
Eastbourne
Boulogne
Seaford Head
Beachy Head
Channel
Dieppe
FRANCE
N
40 km
20 miles

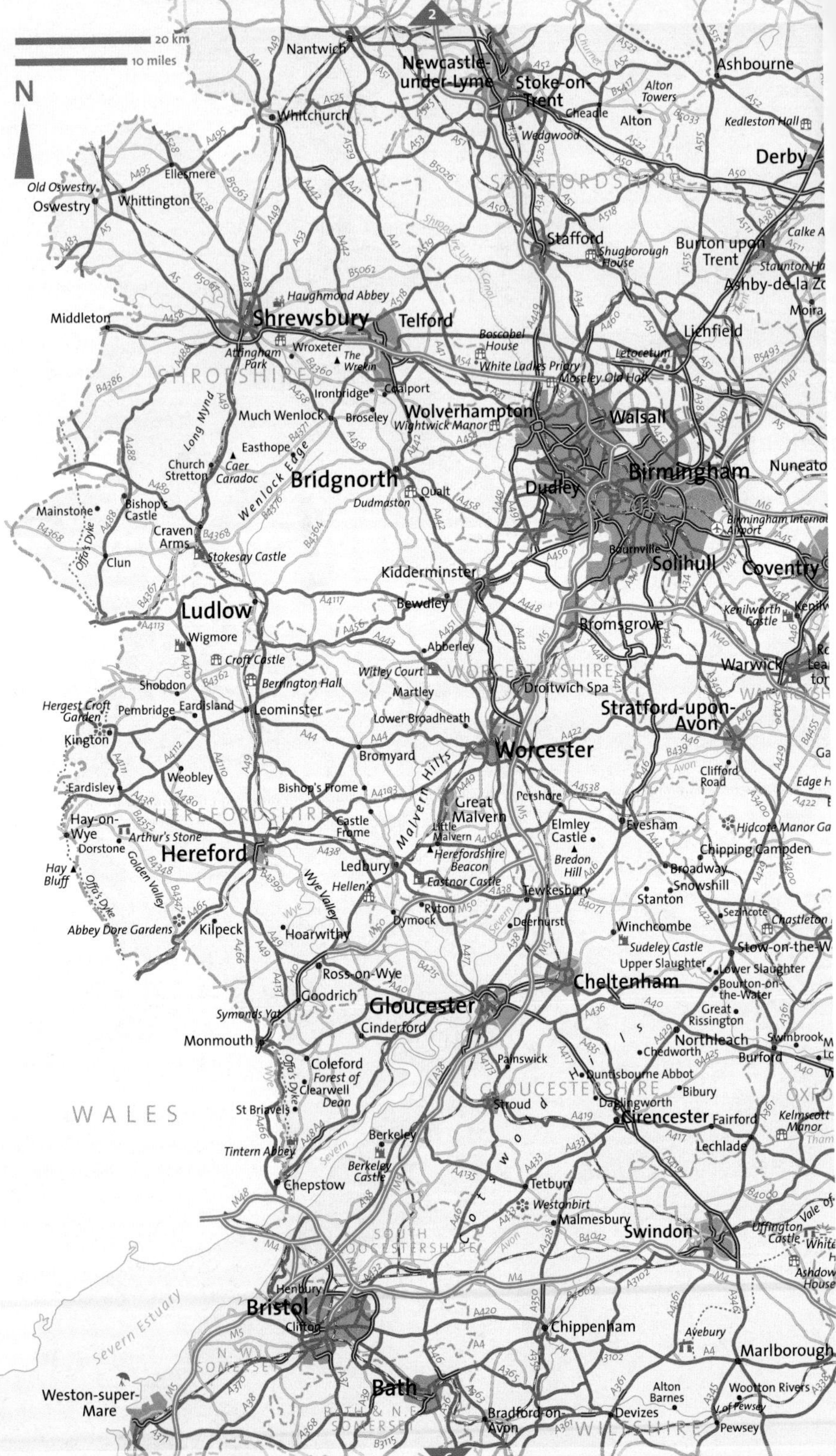

20 km
10 miles
N
2
Nantwich
Newcastle-under-Lyme
Stoke-on-Trent
Ashbourne
Alton Towers
Cheadle
Alton
Kedleston Hall
Whitchurch
Wedgwood
Derby
Ellesmere
Old Oswestry
Oswestry
Whittington
STAFFORDSHIRE
Stafford
Shugborough House
Burton upon Trent
Calke A
Staunton Ha
Ashby-de-la Zo
Moira
Haughmond Abbey
Middleton
Shrewsbury
Telford
Boscobel House
Lichfield
Attingham Park
Wroxeter
The Wrekin
White Ladies Priory
Letocetum
SHROPSHIRE
Moseley Old Hall
Ironbridge
Coalport
Long Mynd
Much Wenlock
Broseley
Wolverhampton
Wightwick Manor
Walsall
Easthope
Church Stretton
Caer Caradoc
Wenlock Edge
Bridgnorth
Dudley
Birmingham
Nuneato
Quatt
Dudmaston
Mainstone
Bishop's Castle
Offa's Dyke
Craven Arms
Clun
Stokesay Castle
Birmingham Internat Airport
Bournville
Solihull
Coventry
Kidderminster
Ludlow
Bewdley
Kenilworth Castle
Kenilw
Wigmore
Bromsgrove
Abberley
Croft Castle
Warwick
Ro Lea to
Witley Court
WORCESTERSHIRE
Shobdon
Berrington Hall
Martley
Droitwich Spa
Hergest Croft Garden
Pembridge
Eardisland
Leominster
Stratford-upon-Avon
Kington
Lower Broadheath
Worcester
Bromyard
Malvern Hills
Weobley
Clifford Road
Edge H
Eardisley
Bishop's Frome
Pershore
HEREFORDSHIRE
Great Malvern
Hay-on-Wye
Arthur's Stone
Castle Frome
Little Malvern
Elmley Castle
Evesham
Hidcote Manor Ga
Dorstone
Hereford
Herefordshire Beacon
Chipping Campden
Hay Bluff
Golden Valley
Ledbury
Bredon Hill
Broadway
Wye Valley
Hellen's
Eastnor Castle
Snowshill
Tewkesbury
Stanton
Ryton
Sezincote
Chastleton
Abbey Dore Gardens
Kilpeck
Dymock
Deerhurst
Winchcombe
Hoarwithy
Sudeley Castle
Stow-on-the-W
Upper Slaughter
Lower Slaughter
Ross-on-Wye
Cheltenham
Bourton-on-the-Water
Goodrich
Symonds Yat
Gloucester
Great Rissington
Cinderford
Monmouth
Northleach
Swinbrook
Chedworth
Burford
Coleford
Painswick
Duntisbourne Abbot
Forest of Dean
Clearwell
Cotswold Hills
GLOUCESTERSHIRE
Bibury
WALES
St Briavels
Stroud
Daglingworth
Cirencester
Fairford
Kelmscott Manor
Berkeley
Lechlade
Tintern Abbey
Berkeley Castle
Chepstow
Tetbury
Westonbirt
Malmesbury
Vale of
Uffington Castle
SOUTH GLOUCESTERSHIRE
Swindon
White H
Ashdown House
Henbury
Severn Estuary
Bristol
Clifton
Chippenham
Avebury
N. W. SOMERSET
Marlborough
Weston-super-Mare
Bath
Alton Barnes
Wootton Rivers
V. of Pewsey
BATH & N.E. SOMERSET
Bradford-on-Avon
Devizes
Pewsey
WILTSHIRE
6

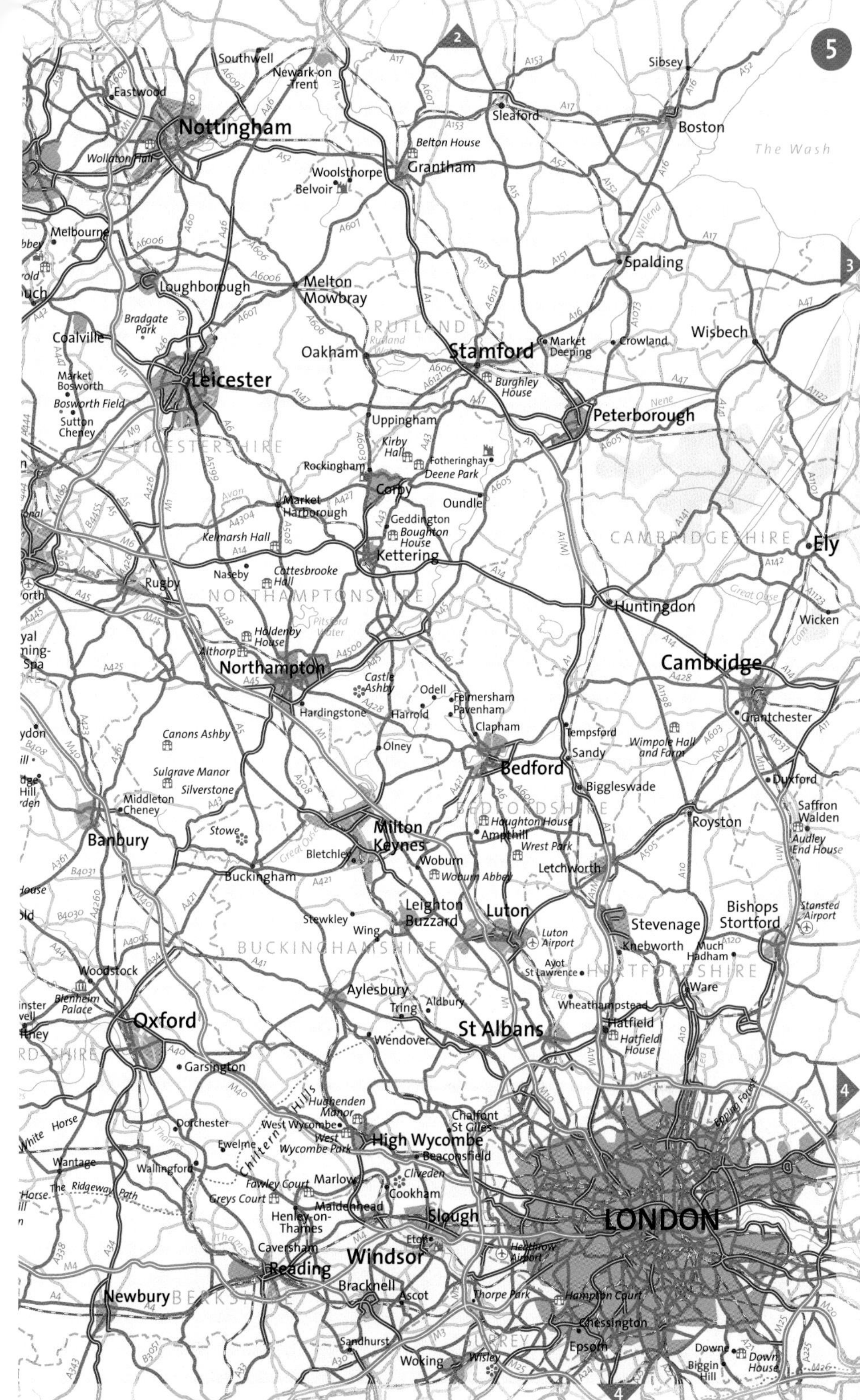

5
Southwell
Newark-on-Trent
Sibsey
Eastwood
Nottingham
Sleaford
Boston
Wollaton Hall
Belton House
The Wash
Woolsthorpe
Grantham
Belvoir
Melbourne
Spalding
Loughborough
Melton Mowbray
Bradgate Park
RUTLAND
Rutland Water
Coalville
Oakham
Stamford
Market Deeping
Crowland
Wisbech
Market Bosworth
Leicester
Burghley House
Bosworth Field
Sutton Cheney
Peterborough
Uppingham
LEICESTERSHIRE
Kirby Hall
Rockingham
Fotheringhay
Deene Park
Corby
Oundle
Market Harborough
Geddington
Boughton House
Kelmarsh Hall
CAMBRIDGESHIRE
Ely
Kettering
Naseby
Cottesbrooke Hall
Rugby
NORTHAMPTONSHIRE
Huntingdon
Wicken
Pitsford Water
Holdenby House
Althorp
Northampton
Cambridge
Castle Ashby
Odell
Felmersham
Pavenham
Hardingstone
Harrold
Grantchester
Clapham
Canons Ashby
Tempsford
Wimpole Hall and Farm
Olney
Sandy
Bedford
Sulgrave Manor
Silverstone
Duxford
Middleton Cheney
Biggleswade
BEDFORDSHIRE
Saffron Walden
Houghton House
Ampthill
Royston
Audley End House
Banbury
Stowe
Milton Keynes
Wrest Park
Bletchley
Woburn
Woburn Abbey
Letchworth
Buckingham
Leighton Buzzard
Luton
Bishops Stortford
Stewkley
Stevenage
Stansted Airport
Wing
Luton Airport
BUCKINGHAMSHIRE
Knebworth
Much Hadham
Ayot St Lawrence
HERTFORDSHIRE
Woodstock
Blenheim Palace
Aylesbury
Ware
Tring
Aldbury
Wheathampstead
Oxford
Hatfield
St Albans
Hatfield House
Wendover
Garsington
Hughenden Manor
Chiltern Hills
Chalfont St Giles
West Wycombe
West Wycombe Park
Dorchester
Epping Forest
High Wycombe
Ewelme
Beaconsfield
Wantage
Wallingford
Cliveden
Fawley Court
Marlow
The Ridgeway Path
Cookham
Greys Court
Maidenhead
Henley-on-Thames
Slough
LONDON
Eton
Caversham
Heathrow Airport
Windsor
Reading
Bracknell
Newbury
BERKSHIRE
Ascot
Thorpe Park
Hampton Court
Chessington
Sandhurst
SURREY
Epsom
Downe
Down House
Woking
Wisley
Biggin Hill

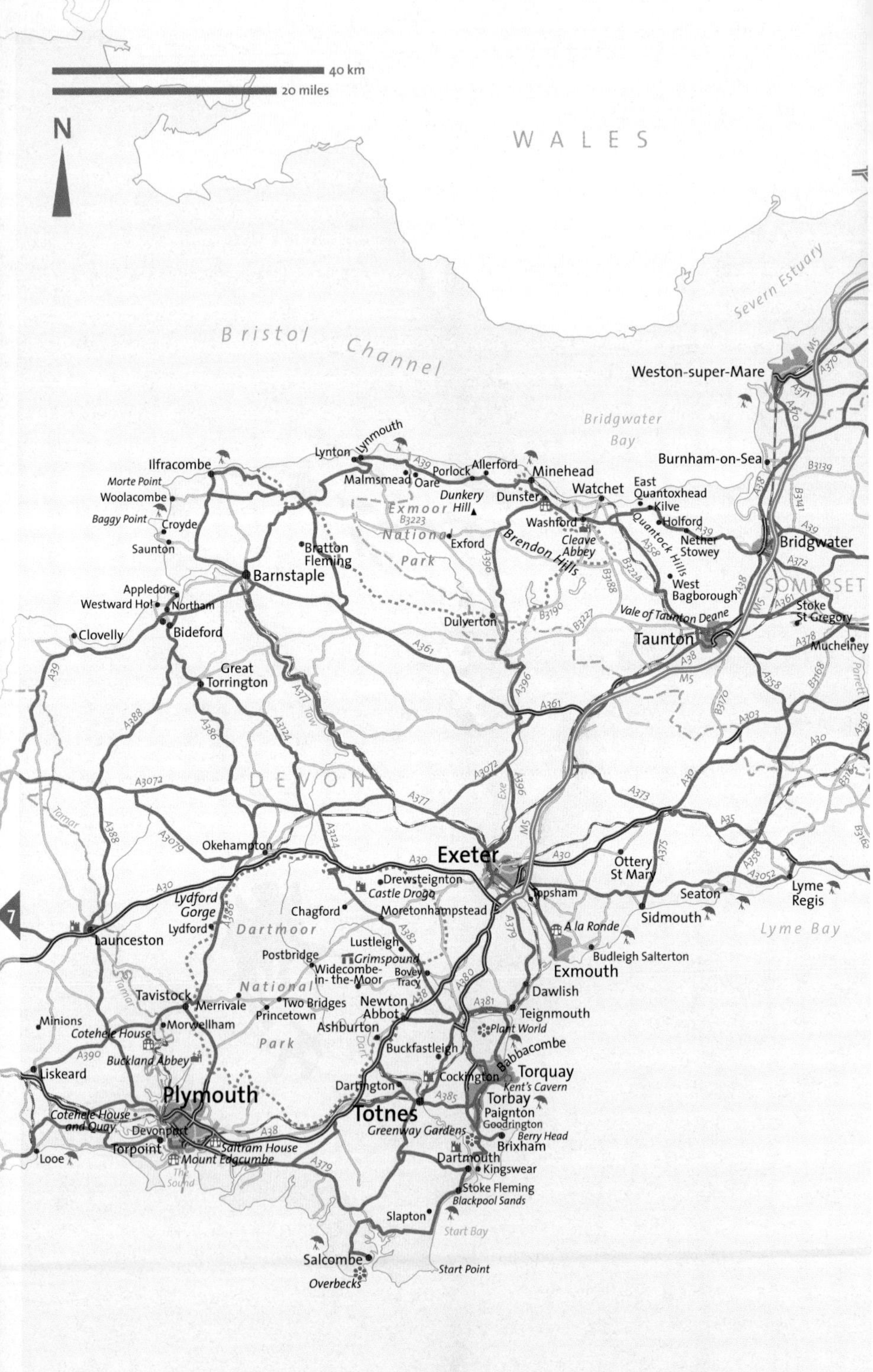
40 km
20 miles
N
WALES
Bristol Channel
Severn Estuary
Bridgwater Bay
Weston-super-Mare
Burnham-on-Sea
Ilfracombe
Morte Point
Woolacombe
Baggy Point
Croyde
Saunton
Lynton
Lynmouth
Malmsmead
Oare
Porlock
Allerford
Minehead
Dunster
Dunkery Hill
Watchet
East Quantoxhead
Kilve
Holford
Nether Stowey
Bridgwater
Exmoor National Park
Exford
Washford
Cleave Abbey
Brendon Hills
Quantock Hills
West Bagborough
SOMERSET
Stoke St Gregory
Muchelney
Bratton Fleming
Barnstaple
Appledore
Westward Ho!
Northam
Bideford
Clovelly
Dulverton
Vale of Taunton Deane
Taunton
Great Torrington
DEVON
Okehampton
Exeter
Ottery St Mary
Drewsteignton
Castle Drogo
Topsham
Seaton
Lyme Regis
Sidmouth
Lyme Bay
A la Ronde
Budleigh Salterton
Exmouth
Lydford Gorge
Lydford
Chagford
Moretonhampstead
Dartmoor National Park
Launceston
Lustleigh
Postbridge
Grimspound
Widecombe-in-the-Moor
Bovey Tracy
Dawlish
Tavistock
Merrivale
Two Bridges
Princetown
Newton Abbot
Teignmouth
Minions
Cotehele House
Morwellham
Ashburton
Plant World
Babbacombe
Buckland Abbey
Buckfastleigh
Torquay
Liskeard
Cockington
Kent's Cavern
Plymouth
Dartington
Torbay
Paignton
Goodrington
Totnes
Cotehele House and Quay
Devonport
Torpoint
Saltram House
Greenway Gardens
Berry Head
Brixham
Looe
Mount Edgcumbe
The Sound
Dartmouth
Kingswear
Stoke Fleming
Blackpool Sands
Slapton
Start Bay
Salcombe
Start Point
Overbecks
7

6
5
4
GLOUCESTERSHIRE
OXFORDSHIRE
SOUTH GLOUCESTERSHIRE
BERKSHIRE
WILTSHIRE
BATH & N.E. SOMERSET
HAMPSHIRE
DORSET
ISLE OF WIGHT
Oxford
Bristol
Bath
Swindon
Salisbury
Winchester
Southampton
Dorchester
Bournemouth
Poole
Newbury
Andover
Chippenham
Cirencester
Marlborough
Devizes
Warminster
Shaftesbury
Blandford Forum
Weymouth
Yeovil
Glastonbury
Salisbury Plain
New Forest
Isle of Purbeck
English Channel

40 km
20 miles
N

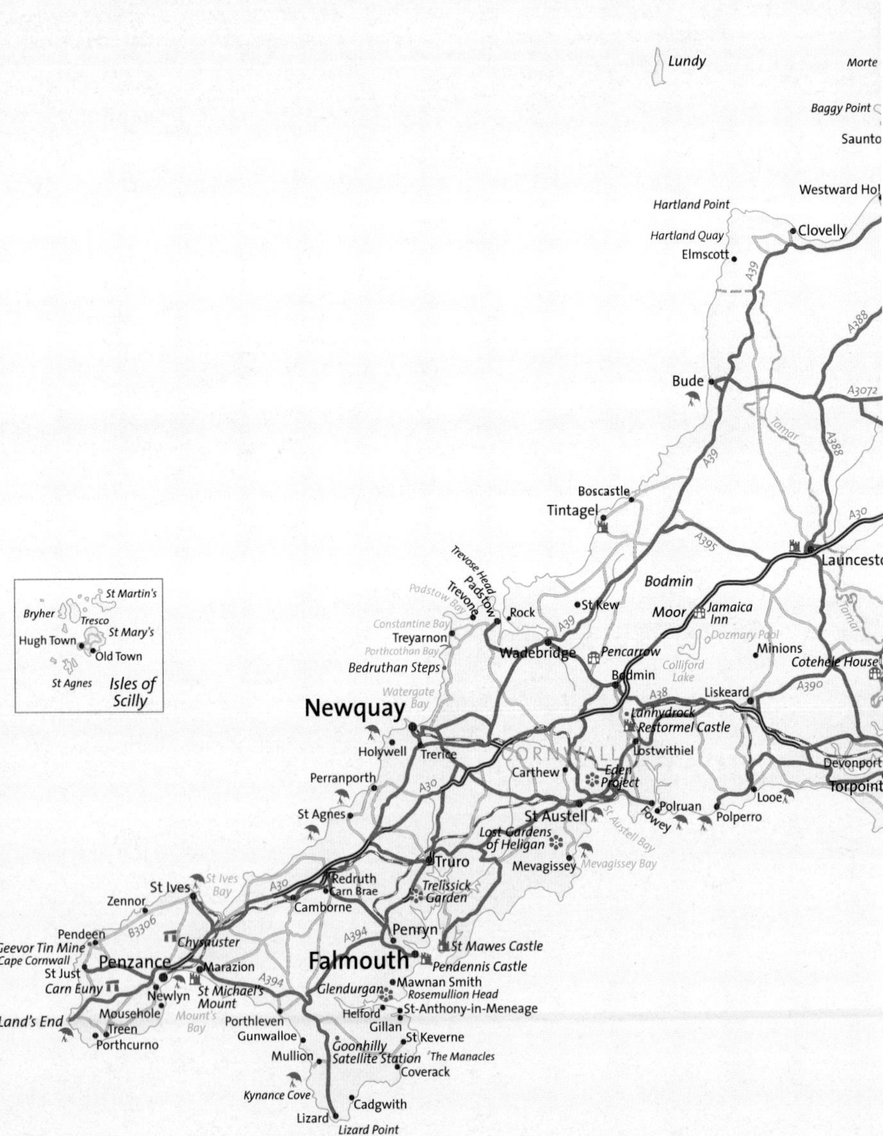

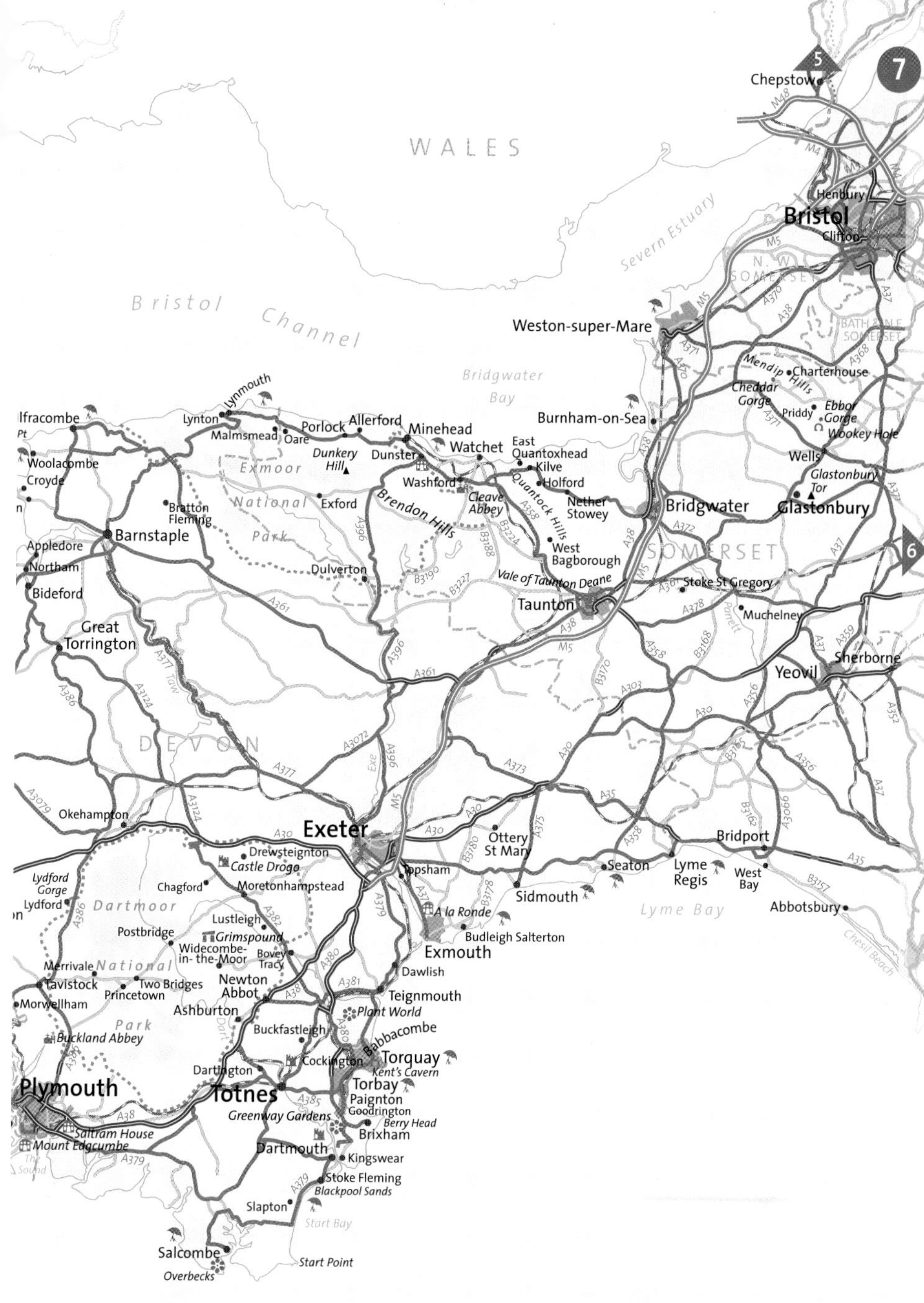

7
5
6
WALES
Chepstow
Bristol
Henbury
Clifton
Severn Estuary
N. W. SOMERSET
BATH & N.E. SOMERSET
Bristol Channel
Weston-super-Mare
Bridgwater Bay
Mendip Hills
Charterhouse
Cheddar Gorge
Priddy
Ebbor Gorge
Wookey Hole
Wells
Glastonbury Tor
Glastonbury
Burnham-on-Sea
Ilfracombe
Lynmouth
Lynton
Malmsmead
Oare
Porlock
Allerford
Minehead
Watchet
East Quantoxhead
Kilve
Holford
Nether Stowey
Quantock Hills
Dunkery Hill
Dunster
Washford
Cleave Abbey
Exmoor National Park
Exford
Brendon Hills
Woolacombe
Croyde
Bratton Fleming
Barnstaple
Appledore
Northam
Bideford
Dulverton
Bridgwater
SOMERSET
West Bagborough
Vale of Taunton Deane
Taunton
Stoke St Gregory
Muchelney
Great Torrington
Yeovil
Sherborne
DEVON
Okehampton
Exeter
Drewsteignton
Castle Drogo
Ottery St Mary
Topsham
Bridport
Seaton
Lyme Regis
West Bay
Abbotsbury
Lyme Bay
Chesil Beach
Lydford Gorge
Lydford
Chagford
Moretonhampstead
Dartmoor National Park
Sidmouth
A la Ronde
Budleigh Salterton
Exmouth
Lustleigh
Postbridge
Grimspound
Widecombe-in-the-Moor
Bovey Tracy
Dawlish
Merrivale
Tavistock
Two Bridges
Princetown
Newton Abbot
Teignmouth
Morwellham
Ashburton
Plant World
Buckland Abbey
Buckfastleigh
Babbacombe
Cockington
Torquay
Kent's Cavern
Dartington
Torbay
Plymouth
Totnes
Paignton
Goodrington
Greenway Gardens
Berry Head
Saltram House
Brixham
Mount Edgcumbe
The Sound
Dartmouth
Kingswear
Stoke Fleming
Blackpool Sands
Slapton
Start Bay
Salcombe
Overbecks
Start Point
English Channel